Mobil
Travel Guide®

California
2002

ExxonMobil Travel Publications

ACKNOWLEDGMENTS

We gratefully acknowledge the help of our representatives for their efficient and perceptive inspection of the lodging and dining establishments listed; the establishments' proprietors for their cooperation in showing their facilities and providing information about them; the many users of previous editions of the Mobil Travel Guides who have taken the time to share their experiences; and for their time and information, the thousands of chambers of commerce, convention and visitors bureaus, city, state, and provincial tourism offices, and government agencies who assisted in our research.

PHOTO CREDITS

Nancy Hoyt Belcher: 168; **California Stock Photo:** Larry Brownstein: 71; Richard Carroll: 278, 414; Christopher Talbot Frank: 165; Thomas Hallstein: 86, 163, 228; Andrew McKinney: 394; Richard Pasley: 1; **Scott Campbell/International Stock:** 283; **Maxine Cass Photography:** 438; **Ed Cooper Photography:** 94; **Gerald L. French/The PhotoFile:** 44; **Thomas Hallstein/Outsight:** 89; **Robert Holmes Photography:** 105, 115, 116, 143, 160, 225, 351, 373, 378, 405, 425, 451, 477; **Andre Jenny/Unicorn Stock Photos:** 358; **Kelly/Mooney Photography:** 346; **Legoland, California:** 61; **Oz Mallan/Travelfools:** 458; **Mark Newman/Photo Network:** 48; **Richard Price/FPG International:** 497; **Larry Prosor Photography:** 111; **David Sanger Photography:** 314, 387; **SuperStock:** 21, 36, 127, 171, 181, 191, 216, 255, 301, 357; **Andrea Wells Photography:** 133, 178, 243; **Randy Wells Photography:** 342, 366; **Nik Wheeler Photography:** 185, 268, 325, 335.

Published by Publications International, Ltd.
7373 North Cicero Avenue
Lincolnwood, Illinois 60712

info@exxonmobiltravel.com

ISBN 0-7853-5811-0

Manufactured in China.

10 9 8 7 6 5 4 3 2 1

Contents

Welcome A-19
A Word to Our Readers A-20
How to Use This Book A-23
Making the Most of Your Trip A-31
Important Toll-Free Numbers and Online Information A-35
Four- and Five-Star Establishments in California A-37

California

Mileage Chart A-6
California 1
Appendix A: Attraction List 505
Appendix B: Lodging List 526
Appendix C: Restaurant List 549
City Index 563

Maps

Interstate Highway Map of the United States A-4
Distance and Driving Times A-8
Northern California A-10
Southern California A-12
Anaheim 16
Fresno 110
Lake Tahoe 161
Los Angeles 174
Monterey Bay 212
Palm Springs 264
San Diego 323
San Francisco 349

A-4 INTERSTATE HIGHWAY MAP OF THE UNITED STATES

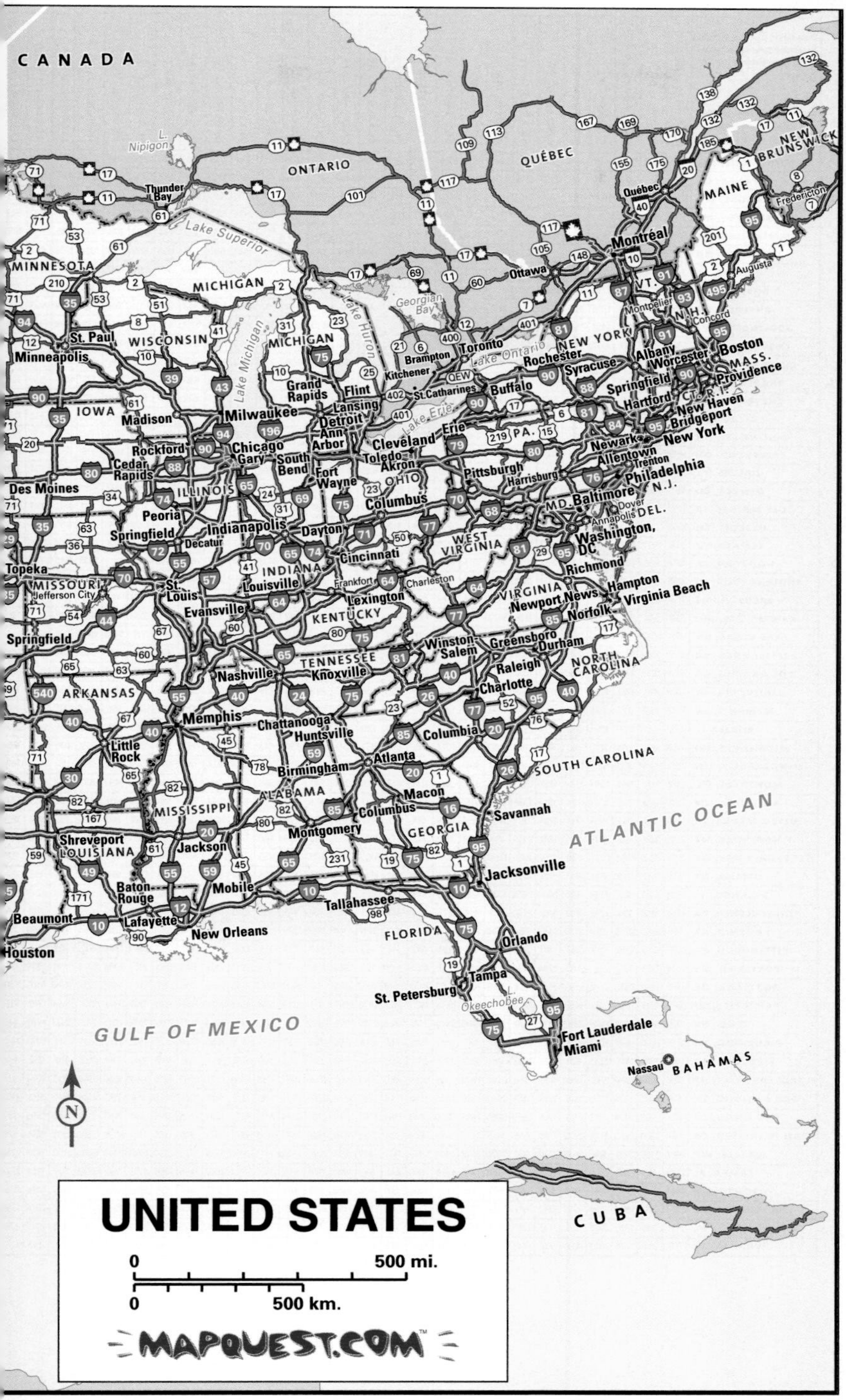
CANADA
ONTARIO
QUÉBEC
NEW BRUNSWICK
MAINE
Fredericton
Augusta
L. Nipigon
Thunder Bay
Lake Superior
MINNESOTA
MICHIGAN
WISCONSIN
Lake Michigan
Lake Huron
Georgian Bay
Lake Ontario
Lake Erie
Ottawa
Montréal
Québec
Toronto
Brampton
Kitchener
St. Catharines
St. Paul
Minneapolis
IOWA
Madison
Milwaukee
Grand Rapids
Flint
Lansing
Detroit
Ann Arbor
Rockford
Chicago
Gary
South Bend
Cedar Rapids
Des Moines
ILLINOIS
Fort Wayne
Toledo
Cleveland
Akron
Erie
Buffalo
Rochester
Syracuse
NEW YORK
VT.
N.H.
Montpelier
Concord
Albany
Worcester
Boston
MASS.
Springfield
Hartford
Providence
R.I.
New Haven
Bridgeport
New York
Newark
Allentown
Trenton
Philadelphia
N.J.
PA.
Pittsburgh
Harrisburg
OHIO
Columbus
Peoria
Springfield
Decatur
Indianapolis
Dayton
INDIANA
Cincinnati
WEST VIRGINIA
MD.
Baltimore
Dover
Annapolis
DEL.
Washington, DC
Topeka
MISSOURI
Jefferson City
St. Louis
Evansville
Louisville
Frankfort
Lexington
Charleston
KENTUCKY
VIRGINIA
Richmond
Newport News
Hampton
Norfolk
Virginia Beach
Springfield
TENNESSEE
Nashville
Knoxville
Winston-Salem
Greensboro
Durham
Raleigh
NORTH CAROLINA
Charlotte
ARKANSAS
Memphis
Chattanooga
Huntsville
Little Rock
Columbia
SOUTH CAROLINA
Atlanta
Birmingham
ALABAMA
MISSISSIPPI
Macon
Columbus
GEORGIA
Savannah
ATLANTIC OCEAN
Shreveport
LOUISIANA
Jackson
Montgomery
Jacksonville
Baton Rouge
Mobile
Tallahassee
Beaumont
Lafayette
New Orleans
Houston
FLORIDA
Orlando
Tampa
St. Petersburg
L. Okeechobee
Fort Lauderdale
Miami
GULF OF MEXICO
Nassau
BAHAMAS
CUBA
N
UNITED STATES
0
500 mi.
0
500 km.
MAPQUEST.COM

A-6 Mileage Chart

Distances in chart are in miles. To convert miles to kilometers, multiply the distance in miles by 1.609

Example:
New York, NY to Boston, MA = 215 miles or 346 kilometers (215 x 1.609)

	ALBUQUERQUE, NM	ATLANTA, GA	BALTIMORE, MD	BILLINGS, MT	BIRMINGHAM, AL	BISMARCK, ND	BOISE, ID	BOSTON, MA	BUFFALO, NY	BURLINGTON, VT	CHARLESTON, SC	CHARLESTON, WV	CHARLOTTE, NC	CHEYENNE, WY	CHICAGO, IL	CINCINNATI, OH	CLEVELAND, OH	DALLAS, TX	DENVER, CO	DES MOINES, IA	DETROIT, MI	EL PASO, TX	HOUSTON, TX	INDIANAPOLIS, IN	JACKSON, MS	KANSAS CITY, MO	LAS VEGAS, NV
ALBUQUERQUE, NM		1490	1902	991	1274	1333	966	2240	1808	2178	1793	1568	1649	538	1352	1409	1619	754	438	1091	1608	263	994	1298	1157	894	578
ATLANTA, GA	1490		679	1889	150	1559	2218	1100	910	1158	317	503	238	1482	717	476	726	792	1403	967	735	1437	800	531	386	801	206
BALTIMORE, MD	1902	679		1959	795	1551	2401	422	370	481	583	352	441	1665	708	521	377	1399	1690	1031	532	2045	1470	600	1032	1087	244
BILLINGS, MT	991	1889	1959		1839	413	626	2254	1796	2181	2157	1755	2012	455	1246	1552	1597	1433	554	1007	1534	1255	1673	1432	1836	1088	965
BIRMINGHAM, AL	1274	150	795	1839		1509	2170	1215	909	1241	466	578	389	1434	667	475	725	647	1356	919	734	1292	678	481	241	753	185
BISMARCK, ND	1333	1559	1551	413	1509		1039	1846	1388	1773	1749	1347	1604	594	838	1144	1189	1342	693	675	1126	1597	1582	1024	1548	801	1378
BOISE, ID	966	2218	2401	626	2170	1039		2697	2239	2624	2520	2182	2375	737	1708	1969	2040	1711	833	1369	1977	1206	1952	1852	2115	1376	760
BOSTON, MA	2240	1100	422	2254	1215	1846	2697		462	214	1003	741	861	1961	1003	862	654	1819	2004	1326	741	2465	1890	940	1453	1427	275
BUFFALO, NY	1808	910	370	1796	909	1388	2239	462		375	899	431	695	1502	545	442	197	1393	1546	868	277	2039	1513	508	1134	995	229
BURLINGTON, VT	2178	1158	481	2181	1241	1773	2624	214	375		1061	782	919	1887	930	817	567	1763	1931	1253	652	2409	1916	878	1479	1366	268
CHARLESTON, SC	1793	317	583	2157	466	1749	2520	1003	899	1061		468	204	1783	907	622	724	1109	1705	1204	879	1754	1110	721	703	1102	237
CHARLESTON, WV	1568	503	352	1755	578	1347	2182	741	431	782	468		265	1445	506	209	255	1072	1367	802	410	1718	1192	320	816	764	2122
CHARLOTTE, NC	1649	238	441	2012	389	1604	2375	861	695	919	204	265		1637	761	476	520	1031	1559	1057	675	1677	1041	575	625	956	222
CHEYENNE, WY	538	1482	1665	455	1434	594	737	1961	1502	1887	1783	1445	1637		972	1233	1304	979	100	633	1241	801	1220	1115	1382	640	843
CHICAGO, IL	1352	717	708	1246	667	838	1708	1003	545	930	907	506	761	972		302	346	936	1015	337	283	1543	1108	184	750	532	176
CINCINNATI, OH	1409	476	521	1552	475	1144	1969	862	442	817	622	209	476	1233	302		253	958	1200	599	261	1605	1079	116	700	597	1955
CLEVELAND, OH	1619	726	377	1597	725	1189	2040	654	197	567	724	255	520	1304	346	253		1208	1347	669	171	1854	1328	319	950	806	210
DALLAS, TX	754	792	1399	1433	647	1342	1711	1819	1393	1763	1109	1072	1031	979	936	958	1208		887	752	1218	647	241	913	406	554	133
DENVER, CO	438	1403	1690	554	1356	693	833	2004	1546	1931	1705	1367	1559	100	1015	1200	1347	887		676	1284	701	1127	1088	1290	603	756
DES MOINES, IA	1091	967	1031	1007	919	675	1369	1326	868	1253	1204	802	1057	633	337	599	669	752	676		606	1283	992	481	931	194	142
DETROIT, MI	1608	735	532	1534	734	1126	1977	741	277	652	879	410	675	1241	283	261	171	1218	1284	606		1799	1338	318	960	795	203
EL PASO, TX	263	1437	2045	1255	1292	1597	1206	2465	2039	2409	1754	1718	1677	801	1543	1605	1854	647	701	1283	1799		758	1489	1051	1085	717
HOUSTON, TX	994	800	1470	1673	678	1582	1952	1890	1513	1916	1110	1192	1041	1220	1108	1079	1328	241	1127	992	1338	758		1033	445	795	147
INDIANAPOLIS, IN	1298	531	600	1432	481	1024	1852	940	508	878	721	320	575	1115	184	116	319	913	1088	481	318	1489	1033		675	485	184
JACKSON, MS	1157	386	1032	1836	241	1548	2115	1453	1134	1479	703	816	625	1382	750	700	950	406	1290	931	960	1051	445	675		747	1735
KANSAS CITY, MO	894	801	1087	1088	753	801	1376	1427	995	1366	1102	764	956	640	532	597	806	554	603	194	795	1085	795	485	747		1358
LAS VEGAS, NV	578	2067	2445	965	1852	1378	760	2757	2299	2684	2371	2122	2225	843	1768	1955	2100	1331	756	1429	2037	717	1474	1843	1735	1358	
LITTLE ROCK, AR	900	528	1072	1530	381	1183	1808	1493	1066	1437	900	745	754	1076	662	632	882	327	984	567	891	974	447	587	269	382	147
LOS ANGELES, CA	806	2237	2705	1239	2092	1702	1033	3046	2572	2957	2554	2374	2453	1116	2042	2215	2374	1446	1029	1703	2310	801	1558	2104	1851	1632	274
LOUISVILLE, KY	1320	419	602	1547	369	1139	1933	964	545	915	610	251	464	1197	299	106	356	852	1118	595	366	1499	972	112	594	516	1874
MEMPHIS, TN	1033	389	933	1625	241	1337	1954	1353	927	1297	760	606	614	1217	539	493	742	466	1116	720	752	1112	586	464	211	536	161
MIAMI, FL	2155	661	1109	2554	812	2224	2883	1529	1425	1587	583	994	730	2147	1382	1141	1250	1367	2069	1632	1401	1959	1201	1196	915	1466	273
MILWAUKEE, WI	1426	813	805	1175	763	767	1748	1100	642	1027	1003	601	857	1012	89	398	443	1010	1055	378	380	1617	1193	279	835	573	180
MINNEAPOLIS, MN	1339	1129	1121	839	1079	431	1465	1417	958	1343	1319	918	1173	881	409	714	760	999	924	246	697	1530	1240	596	1151	441	167
MONTRÉAL, QC	2172	1241	564	2093	1289	1685	2535	313	397	92	1145	822	1003	1799	841	815	588	1772	1843	1165	564	2363	1892	872	1514	1359	259
NASHVILLE, TN	1248	242	716	1648	194	1315	1976	1136	716	1086	543	395	397	1240	474	281	531	681	1162	725	541	1328	801	287	423	559	182
NEW ORLEANS, LA	1276	473	1142	1955	351	1734	2234	1563	1254	1588	783	926	713	1502	935	820	1070	525	1409	1117	1079	1118	360	826	185	932	185
NEW YORK, NY	2015	869	192	2049	985	1641	2491	215	400	299	773	515	631	1755	797	636	466	1589	1799	1121	622	2235	1660	715	1223	1202	2552
OKLAHOMA CITY, OK	546	944	1354	1227	729	1136	1506	1694	1262	1632	1248	1022	1102	773	807	863	1073	209	681	546	1062	737	449	752	612	348	1124
OMAHA, NE	973	989	1168	904	941	616	1234	1463	1005	1390	1290	952	1144	497	474	736	806	669	541	136	743	1236	910	618	935	188	129
ORLANDO, FL	1934	440	904	2333	591	2003	2662	1324	1221	1383	379	790	525	1926	1161	920	1045	1146	1847	1411	1180	1738	980	975	694	1245	251
PHILADELPHIA, PA	1954	782	104	2019	897	1611	2462	321	414	371	685	454	543	1725	768	576	437	1501	1744	1091	592	2147	1572	655	1135	1141	250
PHOENIX, AZ	466	1868	2366	1199	1723	1662	993	2706	2274	2644	2184	2035	2107	1004	1819	1876	2085	1077	904	1558	2074	432	1188	1764	1482	1360	285
PITTSBURGH, PA	1670	676	246	1719	763	1311	2161	592	217	587	642	217	438	1425	467	292	136	1246	1460	791	292	1893	1366	370	988	857	2215
PORTLAND, ME	2338	1197	520	2352	1313	1944	2795	107	560	233	1101	839	959	2059	1101	960	751	1917	2102	1424	838	2563	1988	1038	1550	1525	285
PORTLAND, OR	1395	2647	2830	889	2599	1301	432	3126	2667	3052	2948	2610	2802	1166	2137	2398	2469	2140	1261	1798	2405	1767	2381	2280	2544	1805	1188
RAPID CITY, SD	841	1511	1626	379	1463	320	930	1921	1463	1848	1824	1422	1678	305	913	1219	1264	1077	404	629	1201	1105	1318	1101	1458	710	1035
RENO, NV	1020	2440	2623	960	2392	1372	430	2919	2460	2845	2741	2403	2595	959	1930	2191	2262	1933	1054	1591	2198	1315	2072	2073	2337	1598	442
RICHMOND, VA	1876	527	152	2053	678	1645	2496	572	485	630	428	322	289	1760	802	530	471	1309	1688	1126	627	1955	1330	641	914	1085	244
ST. LOUIS, MO	1051	549	841	1341	501	1053	1628	1181	749	1119	850	512	704	892	294	350	560	635	855	436	549	1242	863	239	505	252	1610
SALT LAKE CITY, UT	624	1916	2100	548	1868	960	342	2395	1936	2322	2218	1880	2072	436	1406	1667	1738	1410	531	1067	1675	864	1650	1549	1813	1074	417
SAN ANTONIO, TX	818	1000	1671	1500	878	1599	1761	2092	1665	2036	1310	1344	1241	1046	1270	1231	1481	271	946	1009	1490	556	200	1186	644	812	1272
SAN DIEGO, CA	825	2166	2724	1302	2021	1765	1096	3065	2632	3020	2483	2393	2405	1179	2105	2234	2437	1375	1092	1766	2373	730	1487	2122	1780	1695	337
SAN FRANCISCO, CA	1111	2618	2840	1176	2472	1749	646	3135	2677	3062	2934	2620	2759	1176	2146	2407	2478	1827	1271	1807	2415	1181	1938	2290	2232	1814	575
SEATTLE, WA	1463	2705	2775	816	2657	1229	500	3070	2612	2997	2973	2571	2827	1234	2062	2368	2413	2208	1329	1822	2350	1944	2449	2249	2612	1872	1256
TAMPA, FL	1949	455	960	2348	606	2018	2677	1380	1276	1438	434	845	581	1941	1176	935	1101	1161	1862	1426	1194	1753	995	990	709	1259	2526
TORONTO, ON	1841	958	565	1762	958	1354	2204	570	106	419	1006	537	802	1468	510	484	303	1441	1512	834	233	2032	1561	541	1183	1028	226
VANCOUVER, BC	1597	2838	2908	949	2791	1362	633	3204	2745	3130	3106	2705	2960	1368	2196	2501	2547	2342	1463	1956	2483	2087	2583	2383	2746	2007	1390
WASHINGTON, DC	1896	636	38	1953	758	1545	2395	458	384	517	539	346	397	1659	701	517	370	1362	1686	1025	526	2008	1433	596	996	1083	244
WICHITA, KS	707	989	1276	1067	838	934	1346	1616	1184	1554	1291	953	1145	613	728	785	995	367	521	390	984	898	608	674	771	192	1276

LITTLE ROCK, AR	LOS ANGELES, CA	LOUISVILLE, KY	MEMPHIS, TN	MIAMI, FL	MILWAUKEE, WI	MINNEAPOLIS, MN	MONTRÉAL, QC	NASHVILLE, TN	NEW ORLEANS, LA	NEW YORK, NY	OKLAHOMA CITY, OK	OMAHA, NE	ORLANDO, FL	PHILADELPHIA, PA	PHOENIX, AZ	PITTSBURGH, PA	PORTLAND, ME	PORTLAND, OR	RAPID CITY, SD	RENO, NV	RICHMOND, VA	ST. LOUIS, MO	SALT LAKE CITY, UT	SAN ANTONIO, TX	SAN DIEGO, CA	SAN FRANCISCO, CA	SEATTLE, WA	TAMPA, FL	TORONTO, ON	VANCOUVER, BC	WASHINGTON,DC	WICHITA, KS
900	806	1320	1033	2155	1426	1339	2172	1248	1276	2015	546	973	1934	1954	466	1670	2338	1395	841	1020	1876	1051	624	818	825	1111	1463	1949	1841	1597	1896	707
528	2237	419	389	661	813	1129	1241	242	473	869	944	989	440	782	1868	676	1197	2647	1511	2440	527	549	1916	1000	2166	2618	2705	455	958	2838	636	989
1072	2705	602	933	1109	805	1121	564	716	1142	192	1354	1168	904	104	2366	246	520	2830	1626	2623	152	841	2100	1671	2724	2840	2775	960	565	2908	38	1276
1530	1239	1547	1625	2554	1175	839	2093	1648	1955	2049	1227	904	2333	2019	1199	1719	2352	889	379	960	2053	1341	548	1500	1302	1176	816	2348	1762	949	1953	1067
381	2092	369	241	812	763	1079	1289	194	351	985	729	941	591	897	1723	763	1313	2599	1463	2392	678	501	1868	878	2021	2472	2657	606	958	2791	758	838
1183	1702	1139	1337	2224	767	431	1685	1315	1734	1641	1136	616	2003	1611	1662	1311	1944	1301	320	1372	1645	1053	960	1599	1765	1749	1229	2018	1354	1362	1545	934
1808	1033	1933	1954	2883	1748	1465	2535	1976	2234	2491	1506	1234	2662	2462	993	2161	2795	432	930	430	2496	1628	342	1761	1096	646	500	2677	2204	633	2395	1346
1493	3046	964	1353	1529	1100	1417	313	1136	1563	215	1694	1463	1324	321	2706	592	107	3126	1921	2919	572	1181	2395	2092	3065	3135	3070	1380	570	3204	458	1616
1066	2572	545	927	1425	642	958	397	716	1254	400	1262	1005	1221	414	2274	217	560	2667	1463	2460	485	749	1936	1665	2632	2677	2612	1276	106	2745	384	1184
1437	2957	915	1297	1587	1027	1343	92	1086	1588	299	1632	1390	1383	371	2644	587	233	3052	1848	2845	630	1119	2322	2036	3020	3062	2997	1438	419	3130	517	1554
900	2554	610	760	583	1003	1319	1145	543	783	773	1248	1290	379	685	2184	642	1101	2948	1824	2741	428	850	2218	1310	2483	2934	2973	434	1006	3106	539	1291
745	2374	251	606	994	601	918	822	395	926	515	1022	952	790	454	2035	217	839	2610	1422	2403	322	512	1880	1344	2393	2620	2571	845	537	2705	346	953
754	2453	464	614	730	857	1173	1003	397	713	631	1102	1144	525	543	2107	438	959	2802	1678	2595	289	704	2072	1241	2405	2759	2827	581	802	2960	397	1145
1076	1116	1197	1217	2147	1012	881	1799	1240	1502	1755	773	497	1926	1725	1004	1425	2059	1166	305	959	1760	892	436	1046	1179	1176	1234	1941	1468	1368	1659	613
662	2042	299	539	1382	89	409	841	474	935	797	807	474	1161	768	1819	467	1101	2137	913	1930	802	294	1406	1270	2105	2146	2062	1176	510	2196	701	728
632	2215	106	493	1141	398	714	815	281	820	636	863	736	920	576	1876	292	960	2398	1219	2191	530	350	1667	1231	2234	2407	2368	935	484	2501	517	785
882	2374	356	742	1250	443	760	588	531	1070	466	1073	806	1045	437	2085	136	751	2469	1264	2262	471	560	1738	1481	2437	2478	2413	1101	303	2547	370	995
327	1446	852	466	1367	1010	999	1772	681	525	1589	209	669	1146	1501	1077	1246	1917	2140	1077	1933	1309	635	1410	271	1375	1827	2208	1161	1441	2342	1362	367
984	1029	1118	1116	2069	1055	924	1843	1162	1409	1799	681	541	1847	1744	904	1460	2102	1261	404	1054	1688	855	531	946	1092	1271	1329	1862	1512	1463	1686	521
567	1703	595	720	1632	378	246	1165	725	1117	1121	546	136	1411	1091	1558	791	1424	1798	629	1591	1126	436	1067	1009	1766	1807	1822	1426	834	1956	1025	390
891	2310	366	752	1401	380	697	564	541	1079	622	1062	743	1180	592	2074	292	838	2405	1201	2198	627	549	1675	1490	2373	2415	2350	1194	233	2483	526	984
974	801	1499	1112	1959	1617	1530	2363	1328	1118	2235	737	1236	1738	2147	432	1893	2563	1767	1105	1315	1955	1242	864	556	730	1181	1944	1753	2032	2087	2008	898
447	1558	972	586	1201	1193	1240	1892	801	360	1660	449	910	980	1572	1188	1366	1988	2381	1318	2072	1330	863	1650	200	1487	1938	2449	995	1561	2583	1433	608
587	2104	112	464	1196	279	596	872	287	826	715	752	618	975	655	1764	370	1038	2280	1101	2073	641	239	1549	1186	2122	2290	2249	990	541	2383	596	674
269	1851	594	211	915	835	1151	1514	423	185	1223	612	935	694	1135	1482	988	1550	2544	1458	2337	914	505	1813	644	1780	2232	2612	709	1183	2746	996	771
382	1632	516	536	1466	573	441	1359	559	932	1202	348	188	1245	1141	1360	857	1525	1805	710	1598	1085	252	1074	812	1695	1814	1872	1259	1028	2007	1083	192
1478	274	1874	1611	2733	1808	1677	2596	1826	1854	2552	1124	1294	2512	2500	285	2215	2855	1188	1035	442	2444	1610	417	1272	337	575	1256	2526	2265	1390	2441	1276
	1706	526	140	1190	747	814	1446	355	455	1262	355	570	969	1175	1367	920	1590	2237	1093	2030	983	416	1507	600	1703	2012	2305	984	1115	2439	1036	464
1706		2126	1839	2759	2082	1951	2869	2054	1917	2820	1352	1567	2538	2760	369	2476	3144	971	1309	519	2682	1856	691	1356	124	385	1148	2553	2538	1291	2702	1513
526	2126		386	1084	394	711	920	175	714	739	774	704	863	678	1786	394	1062	2362	1215	2155	572	264	1631	1125	2144	2372	2364	878	589	2497	596	705
140	1839	386		1051	624	940	1306	215	396	1123	487	724	830	1035	1500	780	1451	2382	1247	2175	843	294	1652	739	1841	2144	2440	845	975	2574	896	597
1190	2759	1084	1051		1478	1794	1671	907	874	1299	1609	1654	232	1211	2390	1167	1627	3312	2176	3105	954	1214	2581	1401	2688	3140	3370	274	1532	3504	1065	1655
747	2082	394	624	1478		337	939	569	1020	894	880	514	1257	865	1892	564	1198	2063	842	1970	899	367	1446	1343	2145	2186	1991	1272	607	2124	799	769
814	1951	711	940	1794	337		1255	886	1337	1211	793	383	1573	1181	1805	881	1515	1727	606	1839	1216	621	1315	1257	2014	2055	1654	1588	924	1788	1115	637
1446	2869	920	1306	1671	939	1255		1094	1632	383	1625	1300	1466	454	2637	607	282	2963	1758	2756	714	1112	2232	2043	2931	2972	2907	1522	330	3041	600	1547
355	2054	175	215	907	569	886	1094		539	906	703	747	686	818	1715	569	1234	2405	1269	2198	626	307	1675	954	2056	2360	2463	701	764	2597	679	748
455	1917	714	396	874	1020	1337	1632	539		1332	731	1121	653	1245	1548	1108	1660	2663	1643	2431	1002	690	1932	560	1846	2298	2731	668	1302	2865	1106	890
1262	2820	739	1123	1299	894	1211	383	906	1332		1469	1258	1094	91	2481	367	313	2920	1716	2713	342	956	2189	1861	2839	2929	2864	1150	507	2998	228	1391
355	1352	774	487	1609	880	793	1625	703	731	1469		463	1388	1408	1012	1124	1792	1934	871	1727	1331	505	1204	466	1370	1657	2002	1403	1295	2136	1350	161
570	1567	704	724	1654	514	383	1300	747	1121	1258	463		1433	1228	1440	928	1561	1662	525	1455	1263	440	932	927	1630	1672	1719	1448	971	1853	1162	307
969	2538	863	830	232	1257	1573	1466	686	653	1094	1388	1433		1006	2169	963	1422	3091	1955	2884	750	993	2360	1180	2467	2918	3149	82	1327	3283	860	1434
1175	2760	678	1035	1211	865	1181	454	818	1245	91	1408	1228	1006		2420	306	419	2890	1686	2683	254	895	2160	1774	2779	2900	2835	1062	522	2968	140	1330
1367	369	1786	1500	2390	1892	1805	2637	1715	1548	2481	1012	1440	2169	2420		2136	2804	1335	1308	883	2343	1517	651	987	358	750	1513	2184	2307	1655	2362	1173
920	2476	394	780	1167	564	881	607	569	1108	367	1124	928	963	306	2136		690	2590	1386	2383	341	611	1859	1519	2494	2599	2534	1019	321	2668	240	1046
1590	3144	1062	1451	1627	1198	1515	282	1234	1660	313	1792	1561	1422	419	2804	690		3223	2019	3016	670	1279	2493	2189	3162	3233	3168	1478	668	3301	556	1714
2237	971	2362	2382	3312	2063	1727	2963	2405	2663	2920	1934	1662	3091	2890	1335	2590	3223		1268	578	2925	2057	771	2322	1093	638	170	3106	2633	313	2824	1775
093	1309	1215	1247	2176	842	606	1758	1269	1643	1716	871	525	1955	1686	1308	1386	2019	1268		1151	1720	963	628	1335	1372	1368	1195	1970	1429	1328	1620	712
2030	519	2155	2175	3105	1970	1839	2756	2198	2431	2713	1727	1455	2884	2683	883	2383	3016	578	1151		2718	1850	524	1870	642	217	755	2899	2426	898	2617	1568
983	2682	572	843	954	899	1216	714	626	1002	342	1331	1263	750	254	2343	341	670	2925	1720	2718		834	2194	1530	2684	2934	2869	805	660	3003	108	1274
416	1856	264	294	1214	367	621	1112	307	690	956	505	440	993	895	1517	611	1279	2057	963	1850	834		1326	968	1875	2066	2125	1008	782	2259	837	441
1507	691	1631	1652	2581	1446	1315	2232	1675	1932	2189	1204	932	2360	2160	651	1859	2493	771	628	524	2194	1326		1419	754	740	839	2375	1902	973	2094	1044
600	1356	1125	739	1401	1343	1257	2043	954	560	1861	466	927	1180	1774	987	1519	2189	2322	1335	1870	1530	968	1419		1285	1737	2275	1195	1714	2410	1635	624
1703	124	2144	1841	2688	2145	2014	2931	2056	1846	2839	1370	1630	2467	2779	358	2494	3162	1093	1372	642	2684	1875	754	1285		508	1271	2481	2601	1414	2720	1531
2012	385	2372	2144	3140	2186	2055	2972	2360	2298	2929	1657	1672	2918	2900	750	2599	3233	638	1368	217	2934	2066	740	1737	508		816	2933	2643	958	2834	1784
2305	1148	2364	2440	3370	1991	1654	2907	2463	2731	2864	2002	1719	3149	2835	1513	2534	3168	170	1195	755	2869	2125	839	2275	1271	816		3164	2577	140	2769	1843
984	2553	878	845	274	1272	1588	1522	701	668	1150	1403	1448	82	1062	2184	1019	1478	3106	1970	2899	805	1008	2375	1195	2481	2933	3164		1383	3297	916	1448
1115	2538	589	975	1532	607	924	330	764	1302	507	1295	971	1327	522	2307	321	668	2633	1429	2426	660	782	1902	1714	2601	2643	2577	1383		2711	563	1217
2439	1291	2497	2574	3504	2124	1788	3041	2597	2865	2998	2136	1853	3283	2968	1655	2668	3301	313	1328	898	3003	2259	973	2410	1414	958	140	3297	2711		2902	1977
036	2702	596	896	1065	799	1115	600	679	1106	228	1350	1162	860	140	2362	240	556	2824	1620	2617	108	837	2094	1635	2720	2834	2769	916	563	2902		1272
464	1513	705	597	1655	769	637	1547	748	890	1391	161	307	1434	1330	1173	1046	1714	1775	712	1568	1274	441	1044	624	1531	1784	1843	1448	1217	1977	1272	

MAPQUEST.COM™

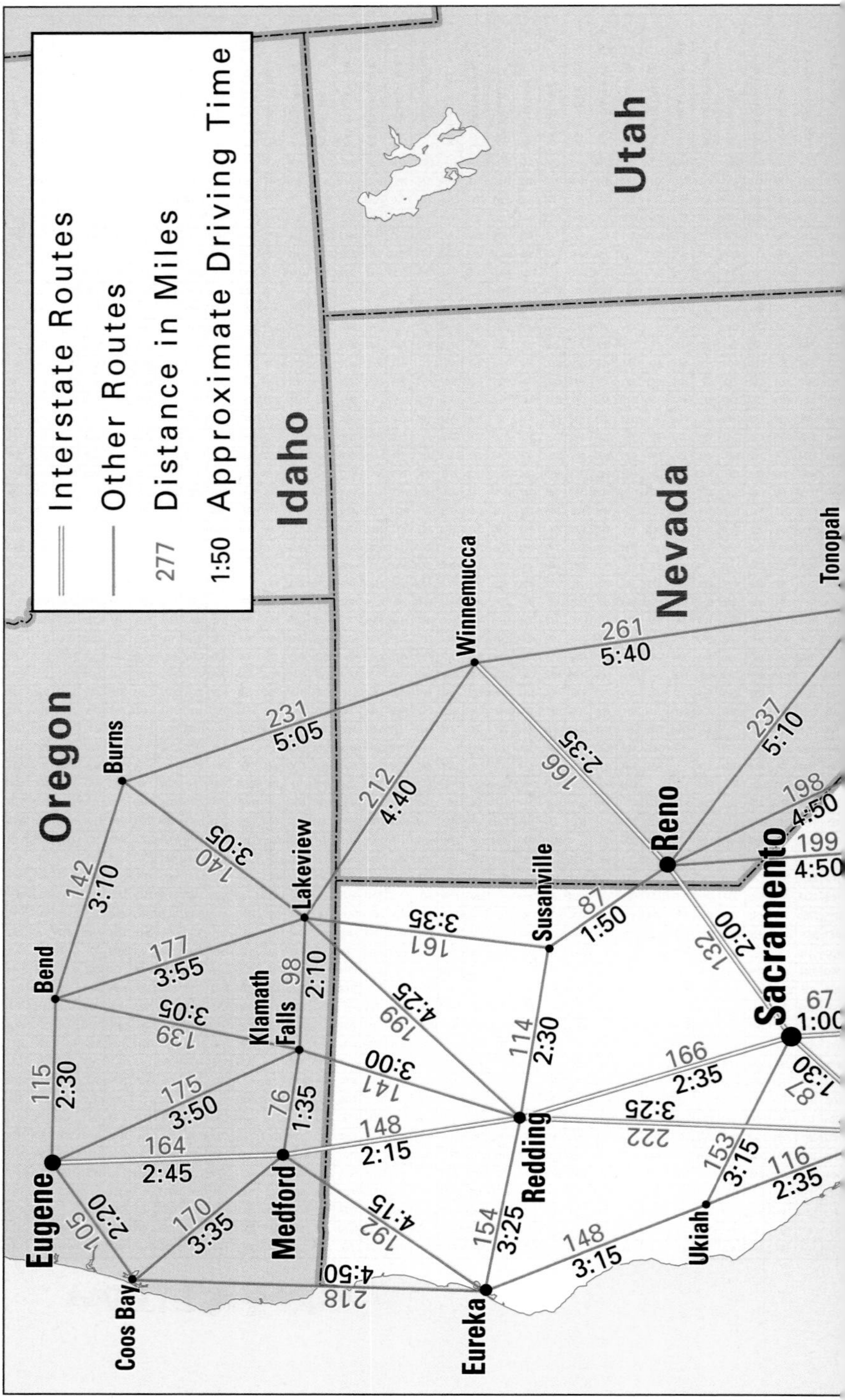
Interstate Routes
Other Routes
277 Distance in Miles
1:50 Approximate Driving Time
Oregon
Idaho
Utah
Nevada
Eugene
Coos Bay
Medford
Eureka
Bend
Burns
Lakeview
Klamath Falls
Winnemucca
Susanville
Redding
Reno
Sacramento
Ukiah
Tonopah
115 2:30
105 2:20
164 2:45
175 3:50
170 3:35
142 3:10
177 3:55
139 3:05
140 3:05
231 5:05
212 4:40
261 5:40
98 2:10
76 1:35
218 4:50
192 4:15
148 2:15
141 3:00
199 4:25
161 3:35
166 2:35
87 1:50
114 2:30
154 3:25
148 3:15
166 2:35
222 3:25
132 2:00
237 5:10
198 4:50
199 4:50
67 1:00
87 1:30
153 3:15
116 2:35

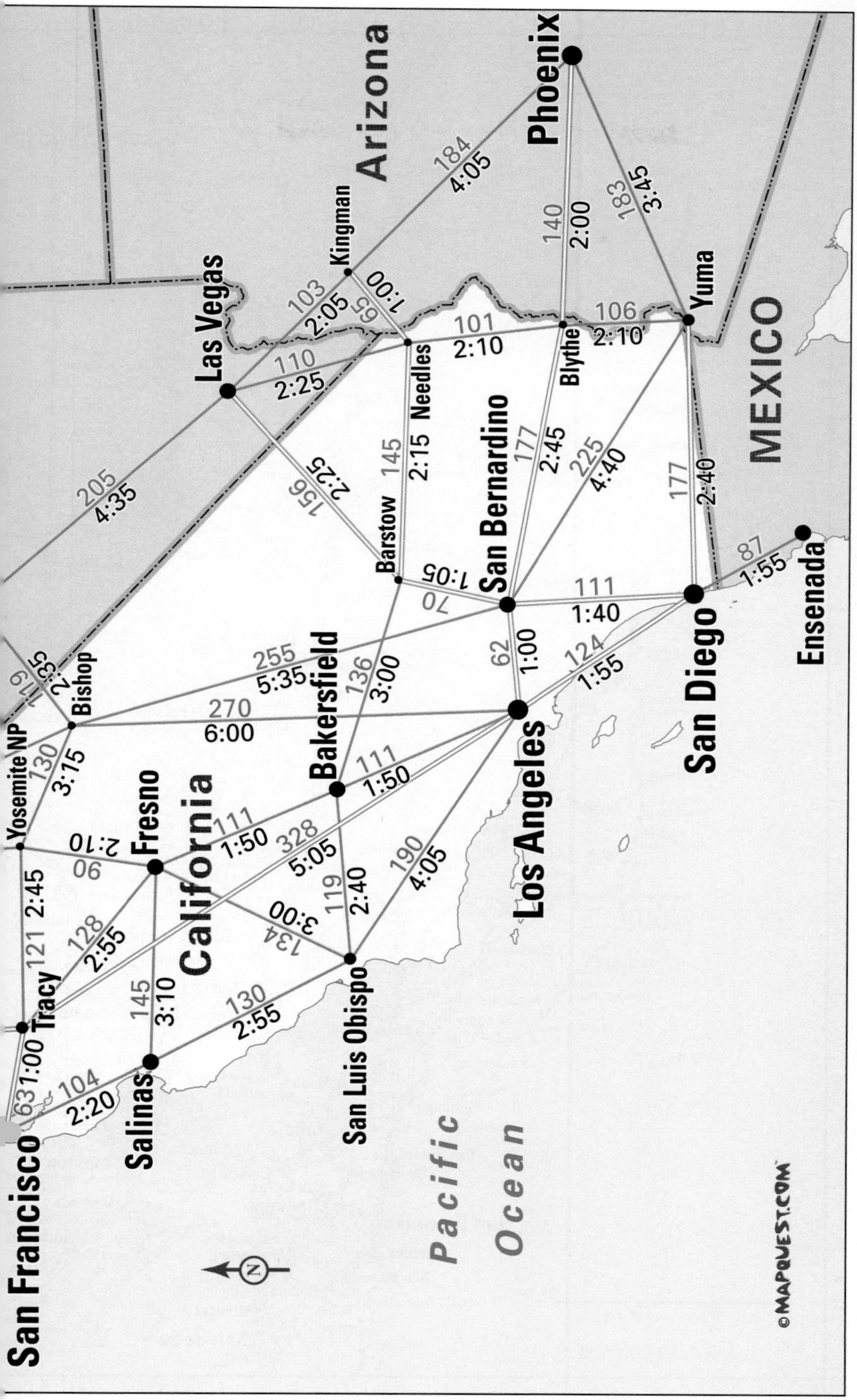
Arizona
Phoenix
Kingman
Las Vegas
Needles
Blythe
Yuma
MEXICO
San Bernardino
Barstow
Bishop
Yosemite NP
Fresno
California
Bakersfield
Los Angeles
San Diego
Ensenada
Tracy
Salinas
San Luis Obispo
San Francisco
Pacific
Ocean
184
4:05
183
3:45
140
2:00
103
2:05
65
1:00
110
2:25
101
2:10
106
2:10
205
4:35
156
2:25
145
2:15
177
2:45
225
4:40
177
2:40
87
1:55
70
1:05
111
1:40
62
1:00
124
1:55
255
5:35
270
6:00
136
3:00
111
1:50
130
3:15
90
2:10
111
1:50
328
5:05
119
2:40
190
4:05
134
3:00
121
2:45
128
2:55
145
3:10
130
2:55
104
2:20
63
1:00
©MAPQUEST.COM

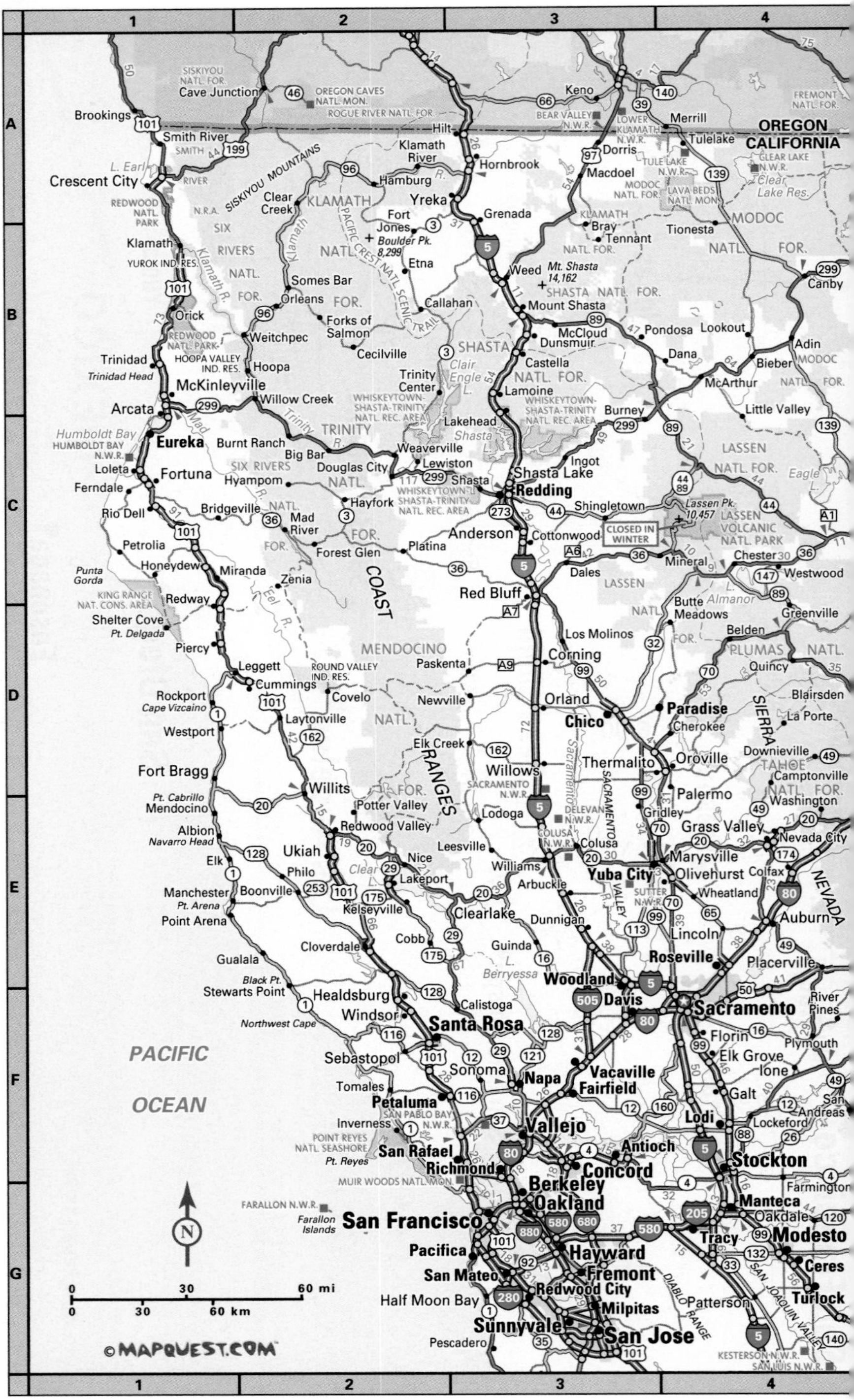
1
2
3
4
A
B
C
D
E
F
G
SISKIYOU NATL. FOR.
Cave Junction
OREGON CAVES NATL. MON.
ROGUE RIVER NATL. FOR.
Keno
BEAR VALLEY N.W.R.
LOWER KLAMATH N.W.R.
Merrill
FREMONT NATL. FOR.
OREGON
CALIFORNIA
Brookings
Smith River
Hilt
Klamath River
Hornbrook
Dorris
Tulelake
Macdoel
TULE LAKE N.W.R.
CLEAR LAKE N.W.R.
Clear Lake Res.
MODOC NATL. FOR.
LAVA BEDS NATL. MON.
L. Earl
Crescent City
SMITH RIVER N.R.A.
SISKIYOU MOUNTAINS
Hamburg
Yreka
REDWOOD NATL. PARK
Clear Creek
KLAMATH
Fort Jones
Boulder Pk. 8,299
Grenada
KLAMATH NATL. FOR.
Bray
Tennant
Tionesta
MODOC NATL. FOR.
SIX RIVERS NATL. FOR.
Klamath
YUROK IND. RES.
PACIFIC CREST NATL. SCENIC TRAIL
Etna
Weed
Mt. Shasta 14,162
SHASTA NATL. FOR.
Canby
Somes Bar
Orleans
Callahan
Mount Shasta
Orick
Forks of Salmon
McCloud
Pondosa
Lookout
REDWOOD NATL. PARK
Weitchpec
Dunsmuir
Dana
Adin
HOOPA VALLEY IND. RES.
Cecilville
SHASTA
Castella
MODOC
Trinidad
Trinidad Head
Hoopa
Trinity Center
Clair Engle L.
NATL. FOR.
Bieber
McArthur
McKinleyville
Willow Creek
WHISKEYTOWN-SHASTA-TRINITY NATL. REC. AREA
Lamoine
Arcata
Burney
Little Valley
Humboldt Bay
HUMBOLDT BAY N.W.R.
Eureka
Burnt Ranch
TRINITY
Lakehead
Shasta L.
LASSEN NATL. FOR.
Eagle L.
Big Bar
Weaverville
Ingot
Loleta
Fortuna
SIX RIVERS NATL.
Hyampom
Douglas City
Lewiston
Shasta
Shasta Lake
Ferndale
Redding
Hayfork
Shingletown
Lassen Pk. 10,457
LASSEN VOLCANIC NATL. PARK
Rio Dell
Bridgeville
Mad River
CLOSED IN WINTER
Anderson
Cottonwood
Chester
Petrolia
FOR.
Forest Glen
Platina
Mineral
Westwood
Honeydew
Miranda
Dales
LASSEN
Punta Gorda
Zenia
COAST
Red Bluff
Almanor
Butte Meadows
Greenville
KING RANGE NAT. CONS. AREA
Redway
Shelter Cove
Pt. Delgada
Eel R.
Los Molinos
Belden
Piercy
MENDOCINO
Corning
PLUMAS NATL.
Quincy
Leggett
ROUND VALLEY IND. RES.
Paskenta
Cummings
Rockport
Cape Vizcaino
Covelo
Newville
Orland
Blairsden
Paradise
La Porte
Westport
Laytonville
NATL.
Chico
Cherokee
SIERRA
Elk Creek
Downieville
Fort Bragg
RANGES
Willows
Thermalito
Oroville
TAHOE NATL. FOR.
Camptonville
Pt. Cabrillo
Mendocino
Willits
SACRAMENTO N.W.R.
Sacramento R.
Palermo
Washington
Potter Valley
Lodoga
DELEVAN N.W.R.
Gridley
Albion
Navarro Head
Redwood Valley
Leesville
COLUSA N.W.R.
Colusa
Grass Valley
Nevada City
Elk
Ukiah
Nice
Marysville
Clear L.
Williams
Yuba City
Olivehurst
Colfax
Philo
Lakeport
Arbuckle
NEVADA
Manchester
Boonville
Kelseyville
SUTTER N.W.R.
Wheatland
Pt. Arena
Point Arena
Clearlake
Dunnigan
Auburn
Cobb
Lincoln
Cloverdale
Guinda
Gualala
Roseville
Placerville
L. Berryessa
Black Pt.
Stewarts Point
Healdsburg
Calistoga
Woodland
Davis
Sacramento
River Pines
Windsor
Northwest Cape
Santa Rosa
PACIFIC
Sebastopol
Florin
Plymouth
Sonoma
Elk Grove
Vacaville
Ione
Napa
Fairfield
OCEAN
Tomales
Petaluma
Galt
SAN PABLO BAY N.W.R.
San Andreas
Inverness
Vallejo
Lodi
Lockeford
POINT REYES NATL. SEASHORE
Pt. Reyes
San Rafael
Antioch
Stockton
Richmond
Concord
MUIR WOODS NATL. MON.
Berkeley
Farmington
FARALLON N.W.R.
Oakland
Manteca
Farallon Islands
San Francisco
Oakdale
Tracy
Modesto
Pacifica
Hayward
Ceres
San Mateo
Fremont
SAN JOAQUIN VALLEY
Redwood City
DIABLO RANGE
Turlock
Half Moon Bay
Milpitas
Patterson
Sunnyvale
San Jose
Pescadero
KESTERSON N.W.R.
SAN LUIS N.W.R.
N
0
30
60 mi
0
30
60 km
©MAPQUEST.COM

PARTIAL INDEX TO CITIES AND TOWNS

Antioch F3
Berkeley G3
Carson City E5
Ceres G4
Chico D3
Concord F3
Davis F3
Eureka C1
Fairfield F3
Fremont G3
Hayward G3
Lodi F4
Manteca G4
Merced G5
Milpitas G3
Modesto G4
Napa F3
Oakland G3
Pacifica G3
Paradise D4
Petaluma F2
Redding C3
Redwood City G3
Reno D5
Richmond F3
Roseville E4
Sacramento F4
San Francisco G3
San Jose G3
San Mateo G3
San Rafael F3
Santa Rosa F2
Sparks D5
Stockton F4
Sunnyvale G3
Tracy G4
Turlock G4
Vacaville F3
Vallejo F3
Woodland E3
Yuba City E3

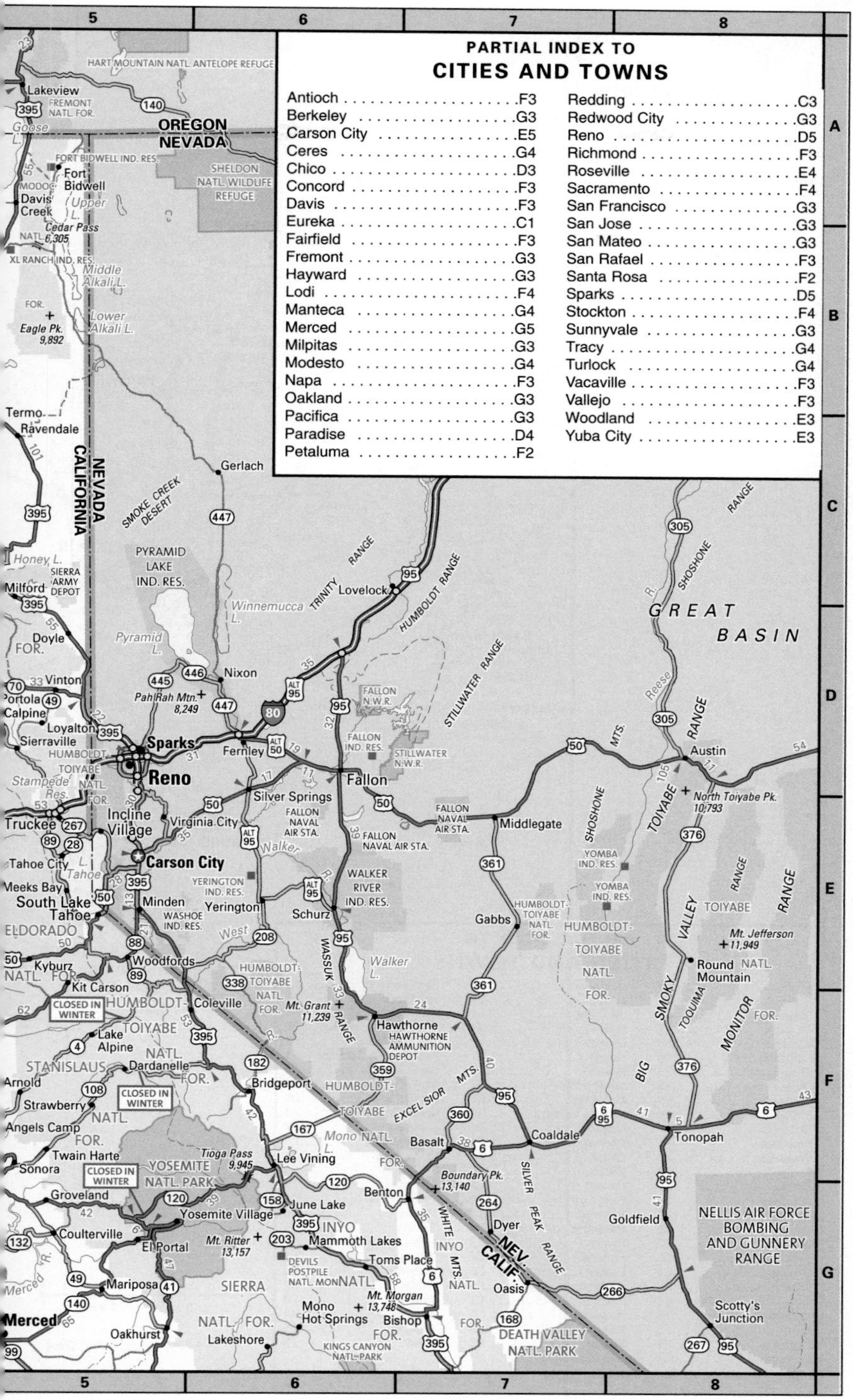

Southern California

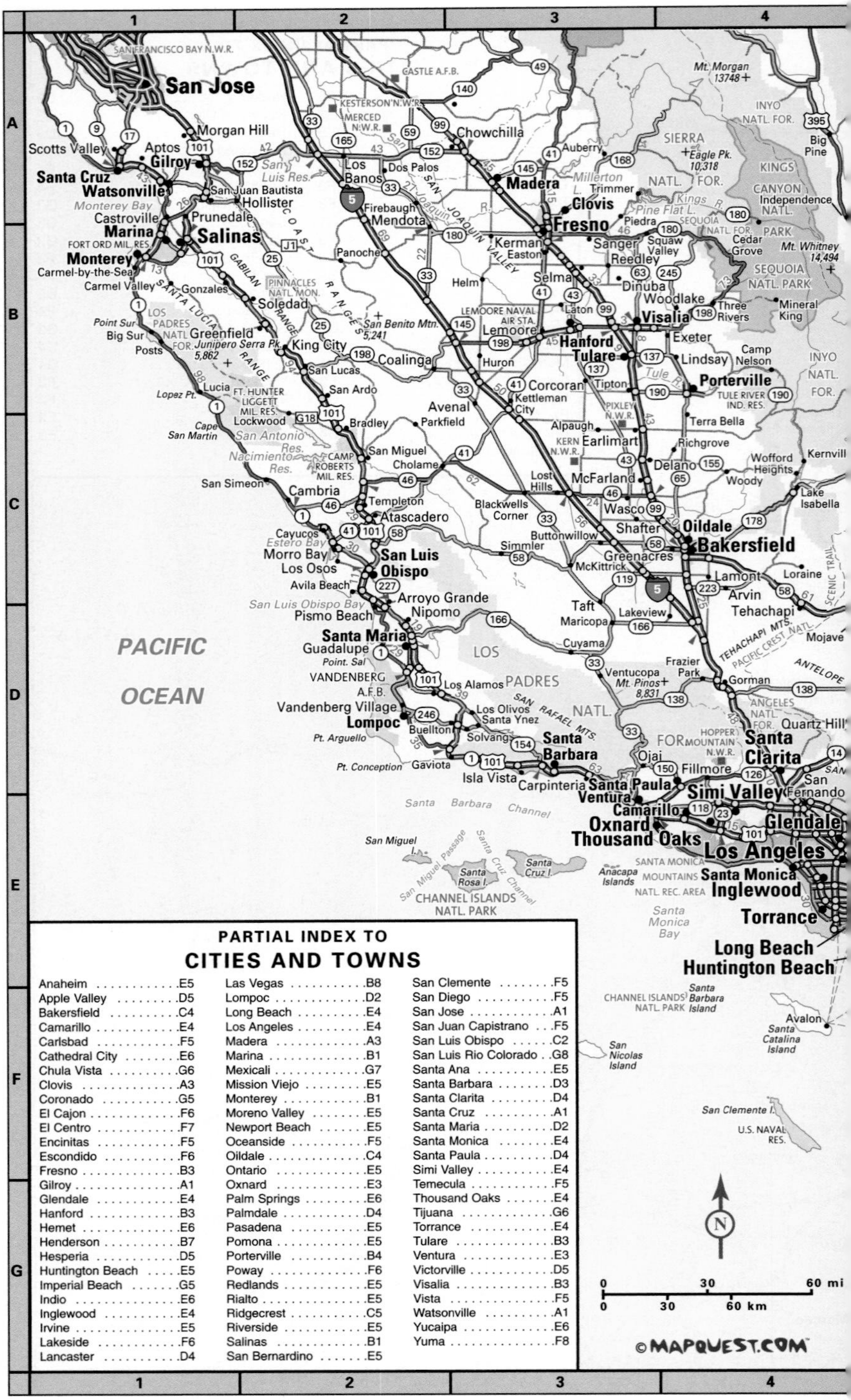

PARTIAL INDEX TO CITIES AND TOWNS

Anaheim	E5	Las Vegas	B8	San Clemente	F5
Apple Valley	D5	Lompoc	D2	San Diego	F5
Bakersfield	C4	Long Beach	E4	San Jose	A1
Camarillo	E4	Los Angeles	E4	San Juan Capistrano	F5
Carlsbad	F5	Madera	A3	San Luis Obispo	C2
Cathedral City	E6	Marina	B1	San Luis Rio Colorado	G8
Chula Vista	G6	Mexicali	G7	Santa Ana	E5
Clovis	A3	Mission Viejo	E5	Santa Barbara	D3
Coronado	G5	Monterey	B1	Santa Clarita	D4
El Cajon	F6	Moreno Valley	E5	Santa Cruz	A1
El Centro	F7	Newport Beach	E5	Santa Maria	D2
Encinitas	F5	Oceanside	F5	Santa Monica	E4
Escondido	F6	Oildale	C4	Santa Paula	D4
Fresno	B3	Ontario	E5	Simi Valley	E4
Gilroy	A1	Oxnard	E3	Temecula	F5
Glendale	E4	Palm Springs	E6	Thousand Oaks	E4
Hanford	B3	Palmdale	D4	Tijuana	G6
Hemet	E6	Pasadena	E5	Torrance	E4
Henderson	B7	Pomona	E5	Tulare	B3
Hesperia	D5	Porterville	B4	Ventura	E3
Huntington Beach	E5	Poway	F6	Victorville	D5
Imperial Beach	G5	Redlands	E5	Visalia	B3
Indio	E6	Rialto	E5	Vista	F5
Inglewood	E4	Ridgecrest	C5	Watsonville	A1
Irvine	E5	Riverside	E5	Yucaipa	E6
Lakeside	F6	Salinas	B1	Yuma	F8
Lancaster	D4	San Bernardino	E5		

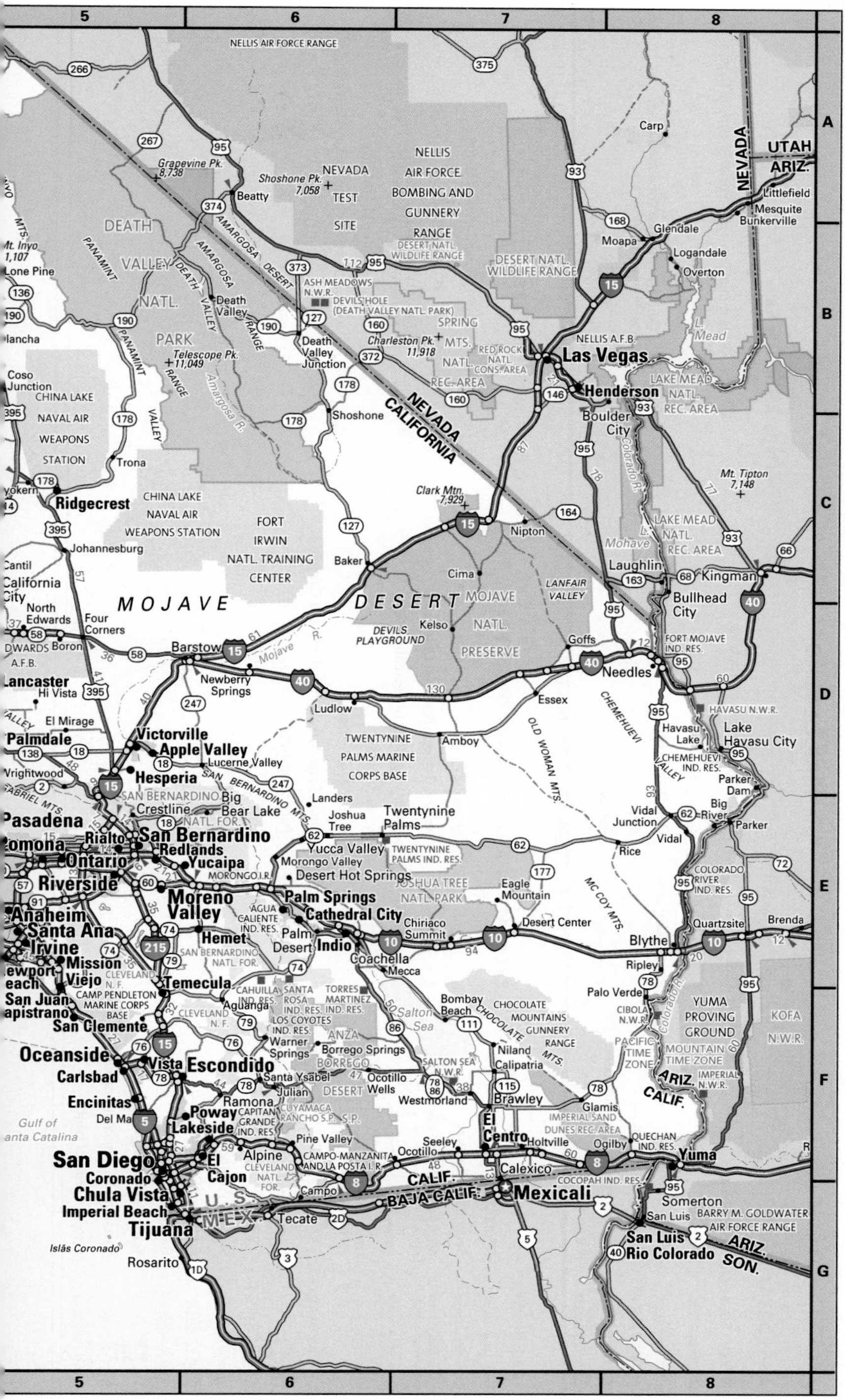
NELLIS AIR FORCE RANGE
NELLIS AIR FORCE BOMBING AND GUNNERY RANGE
NEVADA TEST SITE
DESERT NATL. WILDLIFE RANGE
Grapevine Pk. 8,738
Shoshone Pk. 7,058
Beatty
Carp
UTAH
ARIZ.
NEVADA
Littlefield
Mesquite
Bunkerville
Glendale
Moapa
Logandale
Overton
DEATH VALLEY NATL. PARK
PANAMINT
AMARGOSA DESERT
AMARGOSA RANGE
Mt. Inyo 11,107
Lone Pine
Death Valley
ASH MEADOWS N.W.R.
DEVILS HOLE (DEATH VALLEY NATL. PARK)
SPRING MTS. NATL. REC. AREA
RED ROCK NATL. CONS. AREA
Charleston Pk. 11,918
NELLIS A.F.B.
Las Vegas
Henderson
Boulder City
L. Mead
LAKE MEAD NATL. REC. AREA
Death Valley Junction
Telescope Pk. 11,049
Coso Junction
CHINA LAKE NAVAL AIR WEAPONS STATION
Shoshone
Amargosa R.
NEVADA CALIFORNIA
Colorado R.
Mt. Tipton 7,148
Trona
Ridgecrest
Clark Mtn. 7,929
Nipton
FORT IRWIN NATL. TRAINING CENTER
Johannesburg
Baker
Cima
Mohave
Laughlin
Kingman
Bullhead City
Cantil
California City
MOJAVE DESERT
LANFAIR VALLEY
MOJAVE NATL. PRESERVE
North Edwards
Four Corners
Boron
EDWARDS A.F.B.
DEVILS PLAYGROUND
Kelso
Goffs
FORT MOJAVE IND. RES.
Barstow
Mojave R.
Needles
Lancaster
Hi Vista
Newberry Springs
Essex
CHEMEHUEVI VALLEY
HAVASU N.W.R.
Ludlow
El Mirage
Palmdale
Victorville
Apple Valley
Amboy
OLD WOMAN MTS.
TWENTYNINE PALMS MARINE CORPS BASE
Havasu Lake
Lake Havasu City
Hesperia
Lucerne Valley
SAN BERNARDINO MTS.
CHEMEHUEVI IND. RES.
Parker Dam
Wrightwood
SAN GABRIEL MTS.
SAN BERNARDINO NATL. FOR.
Landers
Crestline
Big Bear Lake
Joshua Tree
Twentynine Palms
Vidal Junction
Big River
Parker
Pasadena
Rialto
San Bernardino
Redlands
Yucca Valley
TWENTYNINE PALMS IND. RES.
Vidal
Rice
Pomona
Ontario
Yucaipa
Morongo Valley
MORONGO I.R.
Desert Hot Springs
COLORADO RIVER IND. RES.
Riverside
JOSHUA TREE NATL. PARK
Eagle Mountain
MC COY MTS.
Moreno Valley
Palm Springs
Anaheim
AGUA CALIENTE IND. RES.
Cathedral City
Chiriaco Summit
Desert Center
Quartzsite
Brenda
Santa Ana
Hemet
Palm Desert
Indio
Blythe
Irvine
SAN BERNARDINO NATL. FOR.
Coachella
Mecca
Ripley
Newport Beach
Mission Viejo
CLEVELAND N.F.
Temecula
CAHUILLA IND. RES.
SANTA ROSA IND. RES.
TORRES MARTINEZ IND. RES.
Palo Verde
San Juan Capistrano
CAMP PENDLETON MARINE CORPS BASE
Aguanga
CLEVELAND N.F.
LOS COYOTES IND. RES.
Salton Sea
Bombay Beach
CHOCOLATE MOUNTAINS GUNNERY RANGE
CHOCOLATE MTS.
CIBOLA N.W.R.
YUMA PROVING GROUND
KOFA N.W.R.
San Clemente
Warner Springs
ANZA BORREGO DESERT
Borrego Springs
Niland
Calipatria
PACIFIC TIME ZONE
MOUNTAIN TIME ZONE
Oceanside
Vista
Escondido
SALTON SEA N.W.R.
ARIZ.
CALIF.
IMPERIAL N.W.R.
Carlsbad
Santa Ysabel
Julian
Ocotillo Wells
Westmorland
Brawley
Glamis
Encinitas
Ramona
CUYAMACA RANCHO S.P.
IMPERIAL SAND DUNES REC. AREA
Gulf of Santa Catalina
Del Mar
Poway
CAPITAN GRANDE IND. RES.
Lakeside
El Centro
Holtville
Ogilby
QUECHAN IND. RES.
Pine Valley
Seeley
San Diego
El Cajon
Alpine
CLEVELAND NATL. FOR.
CAMPO-MANZANITA AND LA POSTA I.R.
Ocotillo
Calexico
Yuma
Coronado
COCOPAH IND. RES.
Chula Vista
Campo
CALIF.
BAJA CALIF.
Mexicali
Somerton
Imperial Beach
U.S.
MEX.
Tecate
San Luis
BARRY M. GOLDWATER AIR FORCE RANGE
Tijuana
San Luis Rio Colorado
ARIZ.
SON.
Islās Coronado
Rosarito

Map Legend

TRANSPORTATION

CONTROLLED-ACCESS HIGHWAYS

- Free
- Toll; Toll Booth
- Under Construction
- Interchange and Exit Number
- Ramp
  Downtown maps only

OTHER HIGHWAYS

- Primary Highway
- Secondary Highway
- Multilane Divided Highway
  Primary and secondary highways only
- Other Paved Road
- Unpaved Road
  Check conditions locally

HIGHWAY MARKERS

- Interstate Route
- US Route
- State or Provincial Route
- County or Other Route
- Business Route
- Trans-Canada Highway
- Canadian Provincial Autoroute
- Mexican Federal Route

OTHER SYMBOLS

- Distances Along Major Highways
  Miles in US; kilometers in Canada and Mexico
- Tunnel; Pass
- One-Way Street
- Airport
- Railroad
  Downtown maps only
- Auto Ferry; Passenger Ferry

RECREATION AND FEATURES OF INTEREST

- National Park
- National Forest; National Grassland
- Other Large Park or Recreation Area
- Military Lands
- Indian Reservation
- Small State Park with and without Camping
- Public Campsite
- Trail
- Point of Interest
- Golf Course
  Professional tournament location
- Hospital
  City maps only
- Ski Area

CITIES AND TOWNS

- National Capital; State or Provincial Capital
- County Seat
  State maps only
- Cities, Towns, and Populated Places
  Type size indicates relative importance
- Urban Area
  State and province maps only
- Large Incorporated Cities

OTHER MAP FEATURES

- JEFFERSON — County Boundary and Name
- Time Zone Boundary
- + Mt. Olympus 7,965 — Mountain Peak; Elevation
  Feet in US; meters in Canada and Mexico
- Perennial; Intermittent River
- Perennial; Intermittent or Dry Water Body
- Dam
- Swamp

WHETHER YOU'RE IN A...

...TRACK RACE

...TRUCK RACE

...DRAG RACE

...OR THE RAT RACE,

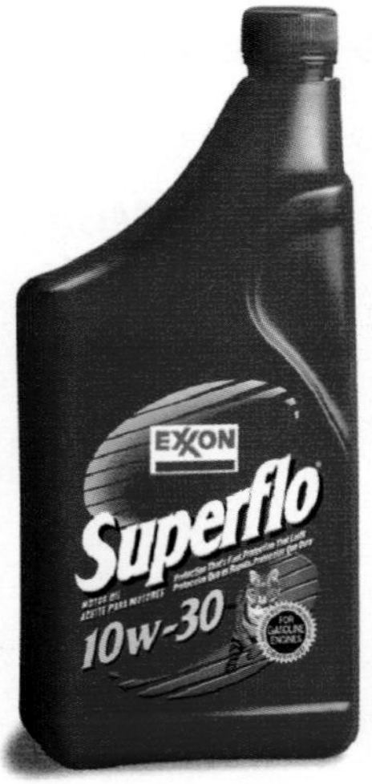

...SUPERFLO® GIVES PROTECTION THAT'S FAST, PROTECTION THAT LASTS.

High-speed straightaways of the Busch Series. Treacherous mud pits of CORR (Championship Off Road Racing). Earth-shaking quarter miles of NHRA. They're all brutal on a car and its engine. Yet the drivers of these Exxon Superflo® racing vehicles can tell you firsthand, Exxon Superflo motor oil goes the distance. And if it can protect their engines, imagine what it can do for yours.

Superflo races its protection to your engine's vital parts at the start and keeps protecting mile after mile after mile. So protect your car's engine with Exxon Superflo motor oil. Protection That's Fast, Protection That Lasts!™

EXXON

Welcome

Dear Traveler,

Since 1958, *Mobil Travel Guides,* an ExxonMobil Travel Publication, has provided North American travelers with reliable advice on finding good value, special getaways, and entertaining attractions. Today, our Mobil, Exxon, and Esso brands provide a full array of products and services to accommodate your travel needs.

We appreciate the opportunity to assist you with your leisure and business travels. Our nationwide network of independent, professional evaluators offers their expertise on thousands of lodging, dining, and attraction options, allowing you to plan an economical family vacation, a scenic business retreat, or a memorable 5-Star experience.

Your feedback is important to us as we strive to improve our product offerings and better meet the needs of the modern traveler. Whether you dine out only occasionally or travel extensively, please take the time to complete the customer feedback form at the back of this book. Or, contact us at www.exxonmobiltravel.com. We hope to hear from you soon.

Best wishes for safe and enjoyable travels.

Lee R Raymond

Lee R. Raymond
Chairman
Exxon Mobil Corporation

A WORD TO OUR READERS

The exciting and complex development of the US interstate highway system was formally—and finally—established in 1956, allowing Americans to take to the roads in enormous numbers. They have been going on day trips, long weekends, extended family vacations, and business trips ever since. Traveling across the country—stopping at National Parks, major cities, small towns, monuments, and landmarks—remains a fantasy trip for many.

Airline travel, too, is on the increase. Whether for business or pleasure, we can take flights between relatively close cities and from coast to coast.

You, the traveler, deserve the best food and accommodations available in every city, town, or village you visit. But finding suitable accommodations can be problematic. You could try to meet and ask local residents about appropriate places to stay and eat, but that time-consuming option comes with no guarantee of getting the best advice.

That's where the *Mobil Travel Guides* come in. This trusted, well-established tool can direct you to satisfying places to eat and stay, as well as to interesting events and attractions in thousands of locations across North America. Prior to the merger with Exxon Corporation, Mobil Corporation had sponsored the *Mobil Travel Guides* since 1958. Now ExxonMobil presents the latest edition of our annual Travel Guide series in partnership with Consumer Guide publications.

In 2001, we introduced driving tours and walking tours to the *Mobil Travel Guides.* This year we've taken that idea a bit further by adding additional walking and driving tours that are more detailed and more colorful. With more specific directions, the driving tours will help you navigate off the beaten path, so you can spend the day (or two if you choose) getting a taste of local history and culture by exploring the sites around your destination city. Walking tours let you stretch your legs and explore your destination more thoroughly, pointing you in the direction of historic points of interest, must-see attractions, and even a great place to grab a bite.

Last year's inclusion of full-color photos was a great success. This year we've filled the guides with even more new pictures to help you envision your trip and perhaps encourage you to stop and take your own pictures. The photos aren't the only color in the guides, though. MapQuest's maps are also in full-color.

The hi-tech information database that is the foundation of every title in the *Mobil Travel Guide* series is an astonishing resource: It is enormous, detailed, and continually updated, making it as accurate and useful as it can be. Highly trained field representatives, spread out across the country, generate exhaustive, computerized inspection reports. Senior staff members then evaluate these reports, along with the comments of more than 100,000 readers. All of this information is used to arrive at fair, accurate, and useful assessments of hotels, motels, and restaurants. Mobil's respected and world-famous one- to five-star rating system highlights valuable capsulized descriptions of each site. All of this dependable information, plus details about thousands of attractions and things to do, is in the dynamic Mobil database!

Although the ten-book set allows us to include many more hotels, restaurants, and attractions than in past years, space limitations still make it impossible for us to include every hotel, motel, and restaurant in America. Instead, our database consists of a generous, representative sampling, with information about places that are above-average in their type. In essence, you can confidently patronize any of the restaurants, places of lodging, and attractions contained in the *Mobil Travel Guide* series.

What do we mean by "representative sampling"? You'll find that the *Mobil Travel Guide* books include information about a great variety of establishments. Perhaps you favor rustic lodgings and restaurants, or perhaps you're most comfortable with elegance and high style. Money may be no object or, like most of us, you may be on a budget. Some travelers place a high premium on 24-hour room service or special menu items. Others look for quiet seclusion. Whatever your travel needs and desires, they will be reflected in the *Mobil Travel Guide* listings.

Allow us to emphasize that we have charged no establishment for inclusion in our guides. We have no relationship with any of the businesses and attractions we list and act only as a consumer advocate. In essence, we do the investigative legwork so you won't have to.

Look over the "How to Use This Book" section that follows. You'll discover just how simple it is to quickly and easily gather all the information you need—before your trip or while on the road. For terrific tips on saving money, travel safety, and other ways to get the most out of your travels, be sure to read our special section, "Making the Most of Your Trip."

Keep in mind that the hospitality business is ever-changing. Restaurants and places of lodging—particularly small chains or stand-alone establishments—can change management or even go out of business with surprising quickness. Although we have made every effort to double-check information during our annual updates, we nevertheless recommend that you call ahead to be sure a place you have selected is open and still offers all the features you want. Phone numbers are provided, and, when available, we also list fax and Web site information.

We hope that all your travel experiences are easy and relaxing. If any aspects of your accommodations or dining motivate you to comment, please drop us a line. We depend a great deal on our readers' remarks, so you can be assured that we will read and assimilate your comments into our research. General comments about our books are also welcome. You can write us at Mobil Travel Guides,

7373 N Cicero Ave, Lincolnwood, IL 60712, or send email to info@exxonmobiltravel.com.

Take your *Mobil Travel Guide* books along on every trip. You'll be pleased by their convenience, ease of use, and breadth of dependable coverage.

Happy travels in the new millennium!

EDITORIAL CONTRIBUTOR AND CONSULTANT FOR DRIVING TOURS, WALKING TOURS, ATTRACTIONS, EVENTS, AND PHOTOGRAPHY:

Clark Norton is a freelance travel writer and a longtime San Francisco resident who now splits his time between California and New York. He is the author of *Where Should We Take the Kids?: California* and *Around San Francisco with Kids* and has contributed to several other California guides, including *California's Best Bed and Breakfasts*. Clark has also written about traveling in California for *San Francisco Magazine, Los Angeles,* and *West.*

How to Use This Book

The *Mobil Travel Guides* are designed for ease of use. Each state has its own chapter. The chapter begins with a general introduction, which provides both a general geographical and historical orientation to the state; it also covers basic statewide tourist information, from state recreation areas to seatbelt laws. The remainder of each chapter is devoted to the travel destinations within the state—cities and towns, state and national parks, and tourist areas—which, like the states, are arranged alphabetically.

The following is an explanation of the wealth of information you'll find regarding those travel destinations—information on the area, on things to see and do there, and on where to stay and eat.

Maps and Map Coordinates

Next to each destination is a set of map coordinates. These are referenced to the appropriate state map in the front of this book. In addition, we have provided maps of selected larger cities and of key neighborhoods within the city sections.

Destination Information

Because many travel destinations are close to other cities and towns where visitors might find additional attractions, accommodations, and restaurants, cross-references to those places are included whenever possible. Also listed are addresses and phone numbers for travel information resources—usually the local chamber of commerce or office of tourism—as well as pertinent vital statistics and a brief introduction to the area.

What to See and Do

Almost 20,000 museums, art galleries, amusement parks, universities, historic sites and houses, plantations, churches, state parks, ski areas, and other attractions are described in the *Mobil Travel Guides*. A white star on a black background ★ signals that the attraction is one of the best in the state. Because municipal parks, public tennis courts, swimming pools, and small educational institutions are common to most towns, they are generally not represented with the white star on the black background.

Following the attraction's description, you'll find the months and days it's open, address/location and phone number, and admission costs (see the inside front cover for an explanation of the cost symbols). Note that directions are given from the center of the town under which the attraction is listed, which may not necessarily be the town in which the attraction is located. Zip codes are listed only if they differ from those given for the town.

Driving and Walking Tours

The driving tours are usually day trips—though they can be longer—that make for interesting side trips. This is a way to get off the beaten track and visit an area often overlooked. These trips frequently cover areas of natural beauty or historical significance. The walking tours focus on a particularly interesting area of a city or town. Again, these can be a break from more everyday tourist attractions. The tours often include places to stop for a meal or snack.

Special Events

Special events can either be annual events that last only a short time, such as festivals and fairs, or longer, seasonal events such as horse racing, summer theater and concerts, and professional sports. Special event listings might also include an infrequently occurring occasion that marks a certain date or event, such as a centennial or other commemorative celebration.

Major Cities

Additional information on airports and ground transportation, suburbs, and neighborhoods may be included for large cities.

Lodging and Restaurant Listings

ORGANIZATION

For both lodgings and restaurants, when a property is in a town that does not have its own heading, the listing appears under the town nearest its location with the address and town immediately after the establishment name. In large cities, lodgings located within five miles of major commercial airports are listed under a separate "Airport" heading, following the city listings.

LODGING CLASSIFICATIONS

Each property is classified by type according to the characteristics below. Because the following features and services are found at most motels and hotels, they are not shown in those listings:

- Year-round operation with a single rate structure unless otherwise quoted
- European plan (meals not included in room rate)
- Bathroom with tub and/or shower in each room
- Air-conditioned/heated, often with individual room control
- Cots
- Daily maid service
- In-room phones
- Elevators

Motels/Motor Lodges. Accommodations are in low-rise structures with rooms easily accessible to parking (which is usually free). Properties have outdoor room entry and small, functional lobbies. Service is often limited, and dining may not be offered in lower-rated motels and lodges. Shops and businesses are found only in higher-rated properties, as are bellhops, room service, and restaurants serving three meals daily.

Hotels. To be categorized as a hotel, an establishment must have most of the following facilities and services: multiple floors, a restaurant and/or coffee shop, elevators, room service, bellhops, a spacious lobby, and recreational facilities. In addition, the following features and services not shown in listings are also found:

- Valet service (one-day laundry/cleaning service)
- Room service during hours restaurant is open
- Bellhops
- Some oversize beds

Resorts. These specialize in stays of three days or more and usually offer American plan and/or housekeeping accommodations. Their emphasis is on recreational facilities, and a social director is often available. Food services are of primary importance, and guests must be able to eat three meals a day on the premises, either in restaurants or by having access to an on-site grocery store and preparing their own meals.

All Suites. All Suites' guest rooms consist of two rooms, one bedroom and one living room. Higher rated properties offer facilities and services comparable to regular hotels.

B&Bs/Small Inns. Frequently thought of as a small hotel, a bed-and-breakfast or an inn is a place of homelike comfort and warm hospitality. It is often a structure of historic significance, with an equally interesting setting. Meals are a special occasion, and refreshments are frequently served in late afternoon. Rooms are usually individually decorated, often with antiques or furnishings representative of the locale. Phones, bathrooms, or TVs may not be available in every room.

Guest Ranches. Like resorts, guest ranches specialize in stays of three days or more. Guest ranches also offer meal plans and extensive outdoor activities. Horseback riding is usually a feature; there are stables and trails on the ranch property, and trail rides and daily instruction are part of the program. Many guest ranches are working ranches, ranging from casual to rustic, and guests are encouraged to participate in ranch life. Eating is often family style and may also include cookouts. Western saddles are assumed; phone ahead to inquire about English saddle availability.

Extended Stay. These hotels specialize in stays of three days or more and usually offer weekly room rates. Service is often limited and dining might not be offered at lower-rated extended-stay hotels.

Villas/Condos. Similar to Cottage Colonies, these establishments are usually found in recreational areas. They are often separate houses, often luxuriously furnished, and rarely offer restaurants and only a small variety of services on the premises.

Conference Centers. Conference Centers are hotels with extended meeting space facilities designed to house multiday conferences and seminars. Amenities are often geared toward groups staying for longer than one night and often include restaurants and fitness facilities. Larger Conference Center Hotels are often referred to as Convention Center Hotels.

Casinos. Casino Hotels incorporate areas that offer games of chance like Blackjack, Poker, Slot machines, etc. and are only found in states that legalize gambling. Casino Hotels offer a wide range of services and amenities, comparable to regular hotels.

Cottage Colonies. These are housekeeping cottages and cabins that are usually found in recreational areas. Any dining or recreational facilities are noted in our listing.

DINING CLASSIFICATIONS

Restaurants. Most dining establishments fall into this category. All have a full kitchen and offer table service and a complete menu. Parking on or near the premises, in a lot or garage, is assumed. When a property offers valet or other special parking features, or when only street parking is available, it is noted in the listing.

Unrated Dining Spots. These places, listed after Restaurants in many cities, are chosen for their unique atmosphere, specialized menu, or local flavor. They include delis, ice-cream parlors, cafeterias, tearooms, and pizzerias. Because they may not have a full kitchen or table service, they are not given a *Mobil Travel Guides* rating. Often they offer extraordinary value and quick service.

QUALITY RATINGS

The *Mobil Travel Guides* have been rating lodgings and restaurants on a national basis since the first edition was published in 1958. For years the guide was the only source of such ratings, and it remains among the few guidebooks to rate restaurants across the country.

All listed establishments were inspected by experienced field representatives or evaluated by a senior staff member. Ratings are based upon their detailed inspection reports of the individual properties, on written evaluations of staff members who stay and dine anonymously, and on an extensive review of comments from our readers.

You'll find a key to the rating categories, ★ through ★★★★★, on the inside front cover. All establishments in the book are recommended. Even a ★ place is above average, usually providing a basic, informal experience. Rating categories reflect both the features the property offers and its quality in relation to similar establishments.

For example, lodging ratings take into account the number and quality of facilities and services, the luxury of appointments, and the attitude and professionalism of staff and management. A ★ establishment provides a comfortable night's lodging. A ★★ property offers more than a facility that rates one star, and the decor is well planned and integrated. Establishments that rate ★★★ are professionally managed and staffed and often beautifully appointed; the lodging experience is truly excellent, and the range of facilities is extensive. Properties that have been given ★★★★ not only offer many services but also have their own style and personality; they are luxurious, creatively decorated, and superbly maintained. The ★★★★★ properties are among the best in North America, superb in every respect and entirely memorable, year in and year out.

Restaurant evaluations reflect the quality of the food and the ingredients, preparation, presentation, service levels, as well as the property's decor and ambience. A restaurant that has fairly simple goals for menu and decor but that achieves those goals superbly might receive the same number of stars as a restaurant with somewhat loftier ambitions, but the execution of which falls short of the mark. In general, ★ indicates a restaurant that's a good choice in its area, usually fairly simple and perhaps catering to a clientele of locals and families; ★★ denotes restaurants that are more highly recommended in their area; ★★★ restaurants are of national caliber, with professional and attentive service and a skilled chef in the kitchen; ★★★★ reflect superb dining choices, where remarkable food is served in equally remarkable surroundings; and ★★★★★ represent that rare group of the best restaurants in the country, where in addition to near perfection in every detail, there's that special something extra that makes for an unforgettable dining experience.

A list of the four-star and five-star establishments in each region is located just before the state listings.

Each rating is reviewed annually and each establishment must work to maintain its rating (or improve it). Every effort is made to assure that ratings are fair and accurate; the designated ratings are published purely as an aid to travelers. In general, properties that are very new or have recently undergone major management changes are considered difficult to assess fairly and are often listed without ratings.

LODGINGS

Each listing gives the name, address, directions (when there is no street address), neighborhood and/or directions from downtown (in major cities), phone number (local and 800), fax number, number and type of rooms available, room rates, and seasons open (if not year-round). Also included are details on recreational and dining facilities on the property or nearby, the presence of a luxury level, and credit card information. A key to the symbols at the end of each listing is on the inside front cover. (Note that Exxon or Mobil Corporation credit cards cannot be used for payment of meals and room charges.)

All prices quoted in the *Mobil Travel Guide* publications are expected to be in effect at the time of publication and during the entire year; however, prices cannot be guaranteed. In some localities there may be short-term price variations because of special events or holidays. Whenever possible, these price charges are noted. Certain resorts have complicated rate structures that vary with the time of year; always confirm listed rates when you make your plans.

RESTAURANTS

Each listing gives the name, address, directions (when there is no street address), neighborhood and/or directions from downtown (in major cities), phone number, hours and days of operation (if not open daily year-round), reservation policy, cuisine (if other than American), price range for each meal served, children's menu (if offered), specialties, and credit card information. In addition, special features such as chef ownership, ambience, and entertainment are noted. By carefully reading the detailed restaurant information and comparing prices, you can easily determine whether the restaurant is formal and elegant or informal and comfortable for families.

TERMS AND ABBREVIATIONS IN LISTINGS

The following terms and abbreviations are used throughout the listings:

A la carte entrees With a price, refers to the cost of entrees/main dishes that are not accompanied by side dishes.

AP American plan (lodging plus all meals).

Bar Liquor, wine, and beer are served in a bar or cocktail lounge and usually with meals unless otherwise indicated (e.g., "wine, beer").

Business center The property has a designated area accessible to all guests with business services.

Business servs avail The property can perform/arrange at least two of the following services for a guest: audiovisual equipment rental, binding, computer rental, faxing, messenger services, modem availability, notary service, obtaining office supplies, photocopying, shipping, and typing.

Cable Standard cable service; "premium" indicates that HBO, Disney, Showtime, or similar cable services are available.

Ck-in, ck-out Check-in time, check-out time.

Coin lndry Self-service laundry.

Complete meal Soup and/or salad, entree, and dessert, plus nonalcoholic beverage.

Continental bkfst Usually coffee and a roll or doughnut.

Cr cds: A, American Express; C, Carte Blanche; D, Diners Club; DS, Discover; ER, enRoute; JCB, Japanese Credit Bureau; MC, MasterCard; V, Visa.

D Followed by a price, indicates room rate for a "double"—two people in one room in one or two beds (the charge may be higher for two double beds).

Downhill/X-country ski Downhill and/or cross-country skiing within 20 miles of property.

Each addl Extra charge for each additional person beyond the stated number of persons at a reduced price.

Early-bird dinner A meal served at specified hours, typically around 4:30-6:30 pm.

Exc Except.

Exercise equipt Two or more pieces of exercise equipment on the premises.

Exercise rm Both exercise equipment and room, with an instructor on the premises.

Fax Facsimile machines available to all guests.

Golf privileges Privileges at a course within ten miles.

Hols Holidays.

In-rm modem link Every guest room has a connection for a modem that's separate from the phone line.

Kit. or **Kits**. A kitchen or kitchenette that contains stove or microwave, sink, and refrigerator and that is either part of the room or a separate room. If the kitchen is not fully equipped, the listing will indicate "no equipt" or "some equipt."

Luxury level A special section of a lodging, covering at least an entire floor, that offers increased luxury accommodations. Management must provide no less than three of these four services: separate check-in and check-out, concierge, private lounge, and private elevator service (key access). Complimentary breakfast and snacks are commonly offered.

MAP Modified American plan (lodging plus two meals).

Movies Prerecorded videos are available for rental.

No cr cds accepted No credit cards are accepted.

No elvtr In hotels with more than two stories, it's assumed there are elevators; only their absence is noted.

No phones Phones, too, are assumed; only their absence is noted.

Parking There is a parking lot on the premises.

Private club A cocktail lounge or bar available to members and their guests. In motels and hotels where these clubs exist, registered guests can usually use the club as guests of the management; the same is frequently true of restaurants.

Prix fixe A full meal for a stated price; usually one price is quoted.

Res Reservations.

S Followed by a price, indicates room rate for a "single," i.e., one person.

Serv bar A service bar, where drinks are prepared for dining patrons only.

Serv charge Service charge is the amount added to the restaurant check in lieu of a tip.

Table d'hôte A full meal for a stated price, dependent upon entree selection; no a la carte options are available.

Tennis privileges Privileges at tennis courts within five miles.

TV Indicates color television.

Under certain age free Children under that age are not charged if staying in room with a parent.

Valet parking An attendant is available to park and retrieve a car.

VCR VCRs in all guest rooms.

VCR avail VCRs are available for hookup in guest rooms.

Special Information for Travelers with Disabilities

The *Mobil Travel Guides* D symbol shown in accommodation and restaurant listings indicates establishments that are at least partially accessible to people with mobility problems.

The *Mobil Travel Guides* criteria for accessibility are unique to our publication. Please do not confuse them with the universal symbol for wheelchair accessibility. When the D symbol appears following a listing, the establishment is equipped with facilities to accommodate people using wheelchairs or crutches or otherwise needing easy access to doorways and rest rooms. Travelers with severe mobility problems or with hearing or visual impairments may or may not find facilities they need. Always phone ahead to make sure that an establishment can meet your needs.

All lodgings bearing our D symbol have the following facilities:

- ISA-designated parking near access ramps
- Level or ramped entryways to building
- Swinging building entryway doors minimum 39"
- Public rest rooms on main level with space to operate a wheelchair; handrails at commode areas
- Elevators equipped with grab bars and lowered control buttons
- Restaurants with accessible doorways; rest rooms with space to operate wheelchair; handrails at commode areas
- Minimum 39" width entryway to guest rooms
- Low-pile carpet in rooms
- Telephone at bedside and in bathroom
- Bed placed at wheelchair height
- Minimum 39" width doorway to bathroom
- Bath with open sink—no cabinet; room to operate wheelchair
- Handrails at commode areas; tub handrails
- Wheelchair-accessible peephole in room entry door
- Wheelchair-accessible closet rods and shelves

All restaurants bearing our D symbol offer the following facilities:

- ISA-designated parking beside access ramps
- Level or ramped front entryways to building
- Tables to accommodate wheelchairs
- Main-floor rest rooms; minimum 39" width entryway
- Rest rooms with space to operate wheelchair; handrails at commode areas

In general, the newest properties are apt to impose the fewest barriers.

To get the kind of service you need and have a right to expect, do not hesitate when making a reservation to question the management in detail about the availability of accessible rooms, parking, entrances, restaurants, lounges, or any other facilities that are important to you, and confirm what is meant by "accessible." Some guests with mobility impairments report that lodging establishments' housekeeping and maintenance departments are most helpful in describing barriers. Also inquire about any special equipment, transportation, or services you may need.

Making the Most of Your Trip

A few hardy souls might look with fondness upon the trip where the car broke down and they were stranded for a week. Or maybe even the vacation that cost twice what it was supposed to. For most travelers, though, the best trips are those that are safe, smooth, and within their budget. To help you make your trip the best it can be, we've assembled a few tips and resources.

Saving Money

ON LODGING

After you've seen the published rates, it's time to look for discounts. Many hotels and motels offer them—for senior citizens, business travelers, families, you name it. It never hurts to ask—politely, that is. Sometimes, especially in late afternoon, desk clerks are instructed to fill beds, and you might be offered a lower rate, or a nicer room, to entice you to stay. Look for bargains on stays over multiple nights, in the off-season, and on weekdays or weekends (depending on location). Many hotels in major metropolitan areas, for example, have special weekend package plans that offer considerable savings on rooms; they may include breakfast, cocktails, and meal discounts. Prices can change frequently throughout the year, so phone ahead.

Another way to save money is to choose accommodations that give you more than just a standard room. Rooms with kitchen facilities enable you to cook some meals for yourself, reducing restaurant costs. A suite might save money for two couples traveling together. Even hotel luxury levels can provide good value, as many include breakfast or cocktails in the price of the room.

State and city sales taxes, as well as special room taxes, can increase your room rates as much as 25 percent per day. We are unable to include this specific information in the listings, but we strongly urge that you ask about these taxes when placing reservations to understand the total cost of your lodgings.

Watch out for telephone-usage charges that hotels frequently impose on long-distance calls, credit-card calls, and other phone calls—even those that go unanswered. Before phoning from your room, read the information given to you at check-in, and then be sure to read your bill carefully before checking out. You won't be expected to pay for charges that they did not spell out. (On the other hand, it's not unusual for a hotel to bill you for your calls after you return home.) Consider using your cell phone; or, if public telephones are available in the hotel lobby, your cost savings may outweigh the inconvenience.

ON DINING

There are several ways to get a less expensive meal at a more expensive restaurant. Early-bird dinners are popular in many parts of the country and offer considerable savings. If you're interested in sampling a 4- or 5-star establishment, consider going at lunchtime. While the prices then are probably relatively high, they may be half of those at dinner and come with the same ambience, service, and cuisine.

ON PARK PASSES

Although many national parks, monuments, seashores, historic sites, and recreation areas may be used free of charge, others charge an entrance fee (ranging from $1 to $6 per person to $5 to $15 per carload) and/or a "use fee" for special services and facilities. If you plan to make several visits to federal recreation areas, consider one of the following National Park Service money-saving programs:

Park Pass. This is an annual entrance permit to a specific unit in the National Park Service system that normally charges an entrance fee. The pass admits the permit holder and any accompanying passengers in a private noncommercial vehicle or, in the case of walk-in facilities, the holder's spouse, children, and parents. It is valid for entrance fees only. A Park Pass may be purchased in person or by mail from the National Park Service unit at which the pass will be honored. The cost is $15 to $20, depending upon the area.

Golden Eagle Passport. This pass, available to people who are between 17 and 61, entitles the purchaser and accompanying passengers in a private noncommercial vehicle to enter any outdoor National Park Service unit that charges an entrance fee and admits the purchaser and family to most walk-in fee-charging areas. Like the Park Pass, it is good for one year and does not cover use fees. It may be purchased from the National Park Service, Office of Public Inquiries, Room 1013, US Department of the Interior, 18th and C sts NW, Washington, D.C. 20240, phone 202/208-4747; at any of the ten regional offices throughout the country; and at any National Park Service area that charges a fee. The cost is $50.

Golden Age Passport. Available to citizens and permanent residents of the United States 62 years or older, this is a lifetime entrance permit to fee-charging recreation areas. The fee exemption extends to those accompanying the permit holder in a private noncommercial vehicle or, in the case of walk-in facilities, to the holder's spouse and children. The passport also entitles the holder to a 50 percent discount on use fees charged in park areas but not to fees charged by concessionaires. Golden Age Passports must be obtained in person. The applicant must show proof of age, i.e., a driver's license, birth certificate, or signed affidavit attesting to age (Medicare cards are not acceptable proof). These passports are available at most park service units where they're used, at National Park Service headquarters (see above), at park system regional offices, at National Forest Supervisors' offices, and at most Ranger Station offices. The cost is $10.

Golden Access Passport. Issued to citizens and permanent residents of the United States who are physically disabled or visually impaired, this passport is a free lifetime entrance permit to fee-charging recreation areas. The fee exemption extends to those accompanying the permit holder in a private noncommercial vehicle or, in the case of walk-in facilities, to the holder's spouse and children. The passport also entitles the holder to a 50 percent discount on use fees charged in park areas but not to fees charged by concessionaires. Golden Access Passports must be obtained in person. Proof of eligibility to receive federal benefits is required (under programs such as Disability Retirement, Compensation for Military Service-Connected Disability, Coal Mine

Safety and Health Act, etc.), or an affidavit must be signed attesting to eligibility. These passports are available at the same outlets as Golden Age Passports.

FOR SENIOR CITIZENS

Look for the senior-citizen discount symbol in the lodging and restaurant listings. Always call ahead to confirm that the discount is being offered, and be sure to carry proof of age. At places not listed in the book, it never hurts to ask if a senior-citizen discount is offered. Additional information for mature travelers is available from the American Association of Retired Persons (AARP), 601 E St NW, Washington, D.C. 20049, phone 202/434-2277.

Tipping

Tipping is an expression of appreciation for good service, and often service workers rely on tips as a significant part of their income. However, you never need to tip if service is poor.

IN HOTELS

Door attendants in major city hotels are usually given $1 for getting you a cab. Bellhops expect $1 per bag, usually $2 if you have only one bag. Concierges are tipped according to the service they perform. It's not mandatory to tip when you've asked for suggestions on sightseeing or restaurants or help in making reservations for dining. However, when a concierge books you a table at a restaurant known to be difficult to get into, a gratuity of $5 is appropriate. For obtaining theater or sporting event tickets, $5-$10 is expected. Maids, often overlooked by guests, may be tipped $1-$2 per days of stay.

AT RESTAURANTS

Coffee shop and counter service waitstaff are usually given 8 percent–10 percent of the bill. In full-service restaurants, tip 15 percent of the bill, before sales tax. In fine restaurants, where the staff is large and shares the gratuity, 18 percent–20 percent for the waiter is appropriate. In most cases, tip the maitre d' only if service has been extraordinary and only on the way out; $20 is the minimum in upscale properties in major metropolitan areas. If there is a wine steward, tip him or her at least $6 a bottle, more if the wine was decanted or if the bottle was very expensive. If your bus person has been unusually attentive, $2 pressed into his hand on departure is a nice gesture. An increasing number of restaurants automatically add a service charge to the bill instead of a gratuity. Before tipping, carefully review your check. If you are in doubt, ask your server.

AT AIRPORTS

Curbside luggage handlers expect $1 per bag. Car-rental shuttle drivers who help with your luggage appreciate a $1 or $2 tip.

Staying Safe

The best way to deal with emergencies is to be prepared enough to avoid them. However, unforeseen situations do happen, and you can prepare for them.

IN YOUR CAR

Before your trip, make sure your car has been serviced and is in good working order. Change the oil, check the battery and belts, and make sure tires are inflated properly (this can also improve gas mileage). Other inspections recommended by the car's manufacturer should be made, too.

Next, be sure you have the tools and equipment to deal with a routine breakdown: jack, spare tire, lug wrench, repair kit, emergency tools, jumper cables, spare fan belt, auto fuses, flares and/or reflectors, flashlights, first-aid kit, and, in winter, windshield wiper fluid, a windshield scraper, and snow shovel.

Bring all appropriate and up-to-date documentation—licenses, registration, and insurance cards—and know what's covered by your insurance. Also bring an extra set of keys, just in case.

En route, always buckle up! In most states it is required by law.

If your car does break down, get out of traffic as soon as possible—pull well off the road. Raise the hood and turn on your emergency flashers or tie a white cloth to the roadside door handle or antenna. Stay near your car. Use flares or reflectors to keep your car from being hit.

IN YOUR LODGING

Chances are slim that you will encounter a hotel or motel fire. The in a listing indicates that there were smoke detectors and/or sprinkler systems in the rooms we inspected. Once you've checked in, make sure that any smoke detector in your room is working properly. Ascertain the locations of fire extinguishers and at least two fire exits. Never use an elevator in a fire.

For personal security, use the peephole in your room's door.

PROTECTING AGAINST THEFT

To guard against theft wherever you go, don't bring anything of more value than you need. If you do bring valuables, leave them at your hotel rather than in your car, and if you have something very expensive, lock it in a safe. Many hotels have one in each room; others will store your valuables in the hotel's safe. And of course, don't carry more money than you need; use traveler's checks and credit cards, or visit cash machines.

For Travelers with Disabilities

A number of publications can provide assistance. The most complete listing of published material for travelers with disabilities is available from The Disability Bookshop, Twin Peaks Press, Box 129, Vancouver, WA 98666, phone 360/694-2462.

The Reference Section of the National Library Service for the Blind and Physically Handicapped (Library of Congress, Washington, D.C. 20542, phone 202/707-9276 or 202/707-5100) provides information and resources for persons with mobility problems and hearing and vision impairments, as well as information about the NILS talking program (or visit your local library).

IMPORTANT TOLL-FREE NUMBERS AND ONLINE INFORMATION

Hotels and Motels

Adams Mark *800 444-2326*
www.adamsmark.com
Amerisuites *800 833-1516*
www.amerisuites.com
AMFA Parks & Resorts *800 236-7916*
www.amfac.com
Baymont Inns *800 229-6668*
www.baymontinns.com
Best Western *800 780-7234*
www.bestwestern.com
Budget Host Inn *800 283-4678*
www.budgethost.com
Canadian Pacific *800 441-1414*
www.fairmont.com
Candlewood Suites *888 226-3539*
www.candlewoodsuites.com
Clarion Hotels *800 252-7466*
www.choicehotels.com
Clubhouse Inns *800 258-2466*
www.clubhouseinn.com
Coast Hotels & Resorts *800 663-1144*
www.coasthotels.com
Comfort Inns *800 252-7466*
www.choicehotels.com
Concorde Hotels *800 888-4747*
www.concorde-hotel.com
Country Hearth Inns *800 848-5767*
www.countryhearth.com
County Inns *800 456-4000*
www.countryinns.com
Courtyard by Marriott *888 236-2437*
www.courtyard.com
Crown Plaza Hotels *800 227-6963*
www.crowneplaza.com
Days Inn *800 544-8313*
www.daysinn.com
Delta Hotels *800 268-1133*
www.deltahotels.com
Destination Hotels & Resorts
800 434-7347
www.destinationhotels.com
Doubletree *800 222-8733*
www.doubletree.com
Drury Inns *800 378-7946*
www.druryinn.com
Econolodge *800 553-2666*
www.econolodge.com
Embassy Suites *800 362-2779*
www.embassysuites.com
Fairfield Inns *800 228-2800*
www.fairfieldinn.com
Fairmont Hotels *800 441-1414*
www.fairmont.com
Family Inns of America *800 251-9752*
www.familyinnsofamerica.com
Forte Hotels *800 300-9147*
www.fortehotels.com
Four Points by Sheraton
888 625-5144 *www.starwood.com*
Four Seasons *800 545-4000*
www.fourseasons.com
Hampton Inns *800 426-7866*
www.hamptoninn.com
Hilton *800 774-1500*
www.hilton.com
Holiday Inn *800 465-4329*
www.holiday-inn.com
Homestead Village *888 782-9473*
www.stayhsd.com
Homewood Suites *800 225-5466*
www.homewoodsuites.com
Howard Johnson *800 406-1411*
www.hojo.com
Hyatt *800 633-7313*
www.hyatt.com
Inn Suites Hotels & Suites
800 842-4242 *www.innsuites.com*
Inter-Continental *888 567-8725*
www.interconti.com
Jameson Inns *800 526-3766*
www.jamesoninns.com
Kempinski Hotels *800-426-3135*
www.kempinski.com
Kimpton Hotels *888-546-7866*
www.kimptongroup.com
La Quinta 800-531-5900
www.laquinta.com
Leading Hotels of the World
800-223-6800 *www.lhw.com*
Loews Hotels *800-235-6397*
www.loewshotels.com
Mainstay Suites *800-660-6246*
www.choicehotels.com
Mandarin Oriental *800-526-6566*
www.mandarin-oriental.com
Marriott *888-236-2427*
www.marriott.com
Nikko Hotels *800-645-5687*
www.nikkohotels.com
Omni Hotels *800-843-6664*
www.omnihotels.com
Preferred Hotels & Resorts Worldwide
www.preferredhotels.com
800-323-7500

Quality Inn *800-228-5151*
www.qualityinn.com
Radisson Hotels *800-333-3333*
www.radisson.com
Ramada *888-298-2054*
www.ramada.com
Red Lion Inns *800-733-5466*
www.redlion.com
Red Roof Inns *800-733-7663*
www.redroof.com
Regal Hotels *800-222-8888*
www.regal-hotels.com
Regent International *800-545-4000*
www.regenthotels.com
Renaissance Hotels *888-236-2427*
www.renaissancehotels.com
Residence Inns *888-236-2427*
www.residenceinn.com
Ritz Carlton *800-241-3333*
www.ritzcarlton.com
Rodeway Inns *800-228-2000*
www.rodeway.com
Rosewood Hotels & Resorts
888-767-3966
www.rosewood-hotels.com
Sheraton *888-625-5144*
www.sheraton.com
Shilo Inns *800-222-2244*
www.shiloinns.com
Shoney's Inns *800-552-4667*
www.shoneysinn.com
Sierra Suites *800-474-3772*
www.sierrasuites.com
Sleep Inns *800-453-3746*
www.sleepinn.com
Small Luxury Hotels *800-525-4800*
www.slh.com
Sofitel *800-763-4835*
www.sofitel.com
Sonesta Hotels & Resorts
800-766-3782 *www.sonesta.com*
SRS Worldhotels *800-223-5652*
www.srs-worldhotels.com
Summerfield Suites *800-833-4353*
www.summerfieldsuites.com
Summit International *800-457-4000*
www.summithotels.com
Swissotel *800-637-9477*
www.swissotel.com
The Peninsula Group
www.peninsula.com
Travelodge *800-578-7878*
www.travelodge.com
Westin Hotels & Resorts
800-937-8461 *www.westin.com*
Wingate Inns *800-228-1000*
www.wingateinns.com
Woodfin Suite Hotels
www.woodfinsuitehotels.com
800-966-3346
Wyndham Hotels & Resorts
800-996-3426 *www.wyndham*

Airlines

Air Canada *888-247-2262*
www.aircanada.ca
Alaska *800-252-7522*
www.alaska-air.com
American *800-433-7300*
www.aa.com
America West *800-235-9292*
www.americawest.com
British Airways *800-247-9297*
www.british-airways.com
Continental *800-523-3273*
www.flycontinental.com
Delta *800-221-1212*
www.delta-air.com
Island Air *800-323-3345*
www.islandair.com
Mesa *800-637-2247*
www.mesa-air.com
Northwest *800-225-2525*
www.nwa.com
SkyWest *800-453-9417*
www.skywest.com
Southwest *800-435-9792*
www.southwest.com
TWA *800-221-2000*
www.twa.com
United *800-241-6522*
www.ual.com
US Air *800-428-4322*
www.usair.com

Car Rentals

Advantage *800-777-5500*
www.arac.com
Alamo *800-327-9633*
www.goalamo.com
Allstate *800-634-6186*
www.bnm.com/as.htm
Avis *800-831-2847*
www.avis.com
Budget *800-527-0700*
www.budgetrentacar.com
Dollar *800-800-3665*
www.dollarcar.com
Enterprise *800-325-8007*
www.pickenterprise.com
Hertz *800-654-3131*
www.hertz.com
National *800-227-7368*
www.nationalcar.com
Payless *800-729-5377*
www.800-payless.com
Rent-A-Wreck.com *800-535-1391*
www.rent-a-wreck.com
Sears *800-527-0770*
www.budget.com
Thrifty *800-847-4389*
www.thrifty.com

FOUR-STAR AND FIVE-STAR ESTABLISHMENTS IN CALIFORNIA

★★★★★ Lodgings

The Beverly Hills Hotel, *Beverly Hills*

Chateau du Sureau, *Oakhurst*

Mandarin Oriental, San Francisco, *San Francisco*

The Peninsula Beverly Hills, *Beverly Hills*

Raffles L'Ermitage Beverly Hills, *Beverly Hills*

★★★★★ Restaurants

The French Laundry, *Yountville*

Gary Danko, *San Francisco*

Ginza Sushiko, *Beverly Hills*

★★★★ Lodgings

Auberge du Soleil, *St. Helena*

Bacara Resort & Spa, *Santa Barbara*

Bernardus Lodge, *Carmel Valley*

Campton Place Hotel, *San Francisco*

Carmel Valley Ranch, *Carmel Valley*

Casa Del Mar, *Santa Monica*

Casa Palmero, Pebble Beach, *Pebble Beach*

The Century Plaza Hotel and Spa, *Los Angeles*

Desert Springs Marriott Resort and Spa, *Palm Desert*

The Fairmont San Jose, *San Jose*

The Fairmont San Francisco, *San Francisco*

Four Seasons Hotel, *Los Angeles*

Four Seasons Hotel, *Newport Beach*

Four Seasons Resort Aviara, *Carlsbad*

Four Seasons Resort Santa Barbara, *Santa Barbara*

Gaige House Inn, *Sonoma*

Hilton La Jolla Torrey Pines, *La Jolla (San Diego)*

Hotel BelAir, *Los Angeles*

Hotel Palomar, *San Francisco*

Hyatt Regency La Jolla at Aventine, *La Jolla (San Diego)*

Inn at Depot Hill, *Santa Cruz*

The Inn at Spanish Bay, *Pebble Beach*

Inn on Mount Ada, *Avalon (Catalina Island)*

L'Auberge Del Mar Resort and Spa, *Del Mar*

La Residence, *Napa*

Le Meridien at Beverly Hills, *Los Angeles*

Le Merigot Beach Hotel & Spa Santa Monica, *Santa Monica*

The Lodge at Pebble Beach, *Pebble Beach*

Mark Hopkins Inter-Continental San Francisco, *San Francisco*

Meadowood Resort Hotel, *St. Helena*

The Pan Pacific, *San Francisco*

Park Hyatt, *San Francisco*

Post Ranch Inn, *Big Sur*

Quail Lodge and Resort and Golf Club, *Carmel*

Rancho Valencia Resort, *Rancho Santa Fe*

Regent Beverly Wilshire, *Beverly Hills*

The Ritz-Carlton, Huntington Hotel & Spa, *Pasadena*

The Ritz-Carlton, Laguna Niguel, *Laguna Beach*

The Ritz-Carlton, San Francisco, *San Francisco*

The Ritz-Carlton Marina del Rey, *Marina del Rey*

The Ritz-Carlton Palm Springs, *Palm Springs*

The St. Regis, Los Angeles, *Los Angeles*

Sheraton San Diego Hotel & Marina, *San Diego*

The Sherman House, *San Francisco*

Simpson House Inn, *Santa Barbara*

Sonoma Mission Inn & Spa, *Sonoma*

The Westin St. Francis, *San Francisco*

W Hotel San Francisco, *San Francisco*

The Willows Historic Palm Springs Inn, *Palm Springs*

★★★★ Restaurants

Aqua, *San Francisco*
Auberge du Soleil, *St. Helena*
The Belvedere, *Beverly Hills*
Boulevard, *San Francisco*
Campton Place Dining Room, *San Francisco*
Cielo Big Sur, *Big Sur*
Club XIX, *Pebble Beach*
Diaghilev, *Los Angeles*
The Dining Room, *Palm Springs*
The Dining Room, *Laguna Beach*
The Dining Room, *San Francisco*
Downey's, *Santa Barbara*
Elisabeth Daniel, *San Francisco*
Erna's Elderberry House, *Oakhurst*
Fifth Floor, *San Francisco*
Five Feet Restaurant, *Laguna Beach*
Fleur De Lys, *San Francisco*
Gustaf Anders, *Santa Ana*
Hawthorne Lane, *San Francisco*
Jardiniere, *San Francisco*
La Folie, *San Francisco*
Laurel, *San Diego*
L'Orangerie, *Hollywood (L.A.)*
Marinus, *Carmel Valley*
Masa's, *San Francisco*
Melisse, *Santa Monica*
Ocean Front, *Santa Monica*
Patina, *Hollywood (L.A.)*
Pavilion, *Newport Beach*
Pisces, *San Francisco Airport Area*
Postrio, *San Francisco*
Sierra Mar Restaurant, *Big Sur*
Spago Beverly Hills, *Beverly Hills*
Terra, *St. Helena*
Wally's Desert Turtle, *Palm Springs*
Water Grill, *Los Angeles*

CALIFORNIA

California has the largest population of any state in the United States. Within it, only 80 miles apart, are the lowest and highest points in the contiguous United States—Death Valley and Mount Whitney. California has ski areas and blistering deserts, mountains and beaches, giant redwoods and giant missiles, Spanish missions and skyscrapers. The oldest living things on earth grow here—a stand of bristlecone pine said to be 4,600 years old. San Francisco, key city of northern California, is cosmopolitan, beautiful, proud, old-worldly. Los Angeles, in southern California, is bright and brazen, growing, modern. California, with 1,264 miles of coastline and a width of up to 350 miles, does things in a big way.

Population: 33,145,000
Area: 158,693 square miles
Elevation: 282 feet below sea level— 4,494 feet
Peak: Mount Whitney (Between Inyo, Tulare Counties)
Entered Union: September 9, 1850 (31st state)
Capital: Sacramento
Motto: *Eureka* (I have found it)
Nickname: Golden State
Flower: Golden Poppy
Bird: California Valley Quail
Tree: California Redwood
Fair: August 16-September 2, 2002, in Sacramento
Time Zone: Pacific
Website: www.gocalif.ca.gov

Almost every crop in the United States grows here. Prunes, huge oranges, bales of cotton, and tons of vegetables roll out from the factory farms in the fertile valleys. California leads the nation in the production of 75 crop and livestock commodities including grapes, peaches, apricots, olives, figs, lemons, avocados, walnuts, almonds, rice, plums, prunes, dates, and nectarines. It also leads in the production of dried, canned, and frozen fruits and vegetables; wine; eggs; turkeys; safflower; beeswax; and honey. Homegrown industries include Hollywood movies, television, electronics, aircraft, and missiles.

Golden Gate Bridge, San Francisco

Spaniards, Mexicans, English, Russians, and others helped write the history of the state. The first explorer to venture into the waters of California was Portuguese—Juan Rodriguez Cabrillo, in 1542. In 1579, Sir Francis Drake explored the coastal waters and is believed to have landed just northwest of what is now San Francisco. Beginning in 1769, Spanish colonial policy sprinkled a trail of missions around which the first towns developed. The Mexican flag flew over California after Mexico won independence from Spain in 1821. American settlers later wrenched the colony from Mexico and organized the short-lived Bear Flag Republic. On July 7, 1846, Commodore John D. Sloat raised the US flag at Monterey. Under the Treaty of Guadalupe Hidalgo, California became part of what was to be the coastal boundary of the United States in 1848.

Perhaps the most important event in its history was the discovery of gold in January of 1848, which set off a sudden mass migration that transformed the drowsy, placid countryside and accelerated the opening of the Far West by several decades. The 49ers who came for gold found greater riches in the fertile soil of the valleys and the markets of the young cities.

During and after World War II, California grew at an astounding pace in both industry and population. Jet travel across the Pacific makes the state a gateway to the Orient.

When to Go/Climate

We recommend visiting California in the mid- to late spring or early to mid-fall, when the fog generally lifts and the heavy tourist traffic is over. Winter is rainy; summers are dry and hot in much of the state.

AVERAGE HIGH/LOW TEMPERATURES (°F)

LOS ANGELES		
Jan 68/49	**May** 74/58	**Sept** 83/65
Feb 69/51	**June** 78/61	**Oct** 79/60
Mar 70/52	**July** 84/65	**Nov** 72/54
Apr 72/54	**Aug** 85/66	**Dec** 68/49
SAN FRANCISCO		
Jan 56/46	**May** 63/51	**Sept** 69/56
Feb 60/49	**June** 64/53	**Oct** 69/55
Mar 61/49	**July** 65/54	**Nov** 63/52
Apr 62/50	**Aug** 66/55	**Dec** 56/47

Parks and Recreation Finder

Directions to and information about the parks and recreation areas below are given under their respective town/city sections. Please refer to those sections for details.

NATIONAL PARK AND RECREATION AREAS

Key to abbreviations. I.H.S. = International Historic Site; I.P.M. = International Peace Memorial; N.B. = National Battlefield; N.B.P. = National Battlefield Park; N.B.C. = National Battlefield and Cemetery; N.C.A. = National Conservation Area; N.E.M. = National Expansion Memorial; N.F. = National Forest; N.G. = National Grassland; N.H.P. = National Historical Park; N.H.C. = National Heritage Corridor; N.H.S. = National Historic Site; N.L. = National Lakeshore; N.M. = National Monument; N.M.P. = National Military Park; N.Mem. = National Memorial; N.P. = National Park; N.Pres. = National Preserve; N.R.A. = National Recreational Area; N.R.R. = National Recreational River; N.Riv. = National River; N.S. = National Seashore; N.S.R. = National Scenic Riverway; N.S.T. = National Scenic Trail; N.Sc. = National Scientific Reserve; N.V.M. = National Volcanic Monument.

Place Name	Listed Under
Angeles N.F.	PASADENA
Cabrillo N.M.	SAN DIEGO
Channel Islands N.P.	same
Cleveland N.F.	PINE VALLEY

Death Valley N.P.	same
Devils Postpile N.M.	same
El Dorado N.F.	PLACERVILLE
Eugene O'Neill N.H.S.	PLEASANTON
Fort Point N.H.S.	SAN FRANCISCO
Golden Gate N.R.	SAN FRANCISCO
Inyo N.F.	same
John Muir N.H.S.	MARTINEZ
Joshua Tree N.P.	same
King's Canyon N.P.	SEQUOIA & KINGS CANYON N.P.
Klamath N.F.	YREKA
Lassen N.F.	SUSANVILLE
Lassen Volcanic N.P.	same
Lava Beds N.M.	same
Los Padres N.F.	KING CITY
Mendocino N.F.	WILLOWS
Modoc N.F.	ALTURAS
Muir Woods N.M.	same
Pinnacles N.M.	same
Plumas N.F.	QUINCY
Point Reyes N.S.	INVERNESS
Redwood N.P.	CRESCENT CITY
San Bernardino N.F.	SAN BERNARDINO
Santa Monica Mountains N.R.A.	SANTA MONICA
Sequoia N.P.	SEQUOIA & KINGS CANYON N.P.
Sequoia N.F.	PORTERVILLE
Shasta-Trinity N.F.	REDDING
Sierra N.F.	FRESNO
Six Rivers N.F.	EUREKA
Stanislaus N.F.	SONORA
Whiskeytown-Shasta-Trinity N.R.	REDDING
Yosemite N.P.	same

For general information about national forests within California, contact USDA, Forest Service, 1323 Club Dr, Vallejo 94592. Phone 707/562-8737. For camping reservations only, phone 800/280-CAMP or phone the supervisor of any particular forest directly.

STATE PARK AND RECREATION AREAS

Key to abbreviations. I.P. = Interstate Park; S.A.P. = State Archaeological Park; S.B. = State Beach; S.C.A. = State Conservation Area; S.C.P. = State Conservation Park; S.Cp. = State Campground; S.F. = State Forest; S.G. = State Garden; S.H.A. = State Historic Area; S.H.P. = State Historic Park; S.H.S. = State Historic Site; S.M.P. = State Marine Park; S.N.A. = State Natural Area; S.P. = State Park; S.P.C. = State Public Campground; S.R. = State Reserve; S.R.A. = State Recreation Area; S.Res. = State Reservoir; S.Res.P. = State Resort Park; S.R.P. = State Rustic Park.

Place Name	Listed Under
Andrew Molera S.P.	BIG SUR
Angel Island S.P.	SAN FRANCISCO
Año Nuevo S.R.	SANTA CRUZ
Anza-Borrego Desert S.P.	same
Armstrong Redwoods S.R.	GUERNEVILLE

Big Basin Redwoods S.P.	same
Calveras Big Trees S.P.	SONORA
Carmel River S.B.	CARMEL
Carpinteria S.B.	SANTA BARBARA
Castle Crags S.P.	DUNSMUIR
Caswell Memorial S.P.	MODESTO
Clear Lake S.P.	CLEAR LAKE AREA
Colonel Allensworth S.H.P.	BAKERSFIELD
Columbia S.H.P.	SONORA
Del Norte Coast Redwoods S.P.	CRESCENT CITY
D. L. Bliss S.P.	LAKE TAHOE AREA
Donner Memorial S.P.	TRUCKEE
Emerald Bay S.P.	LAKE TAHOE AREA
Emma Wood S.B.	VENTURA
Folsom Lake S.R.A.	AUBURN
Forest of Nisene Marks S.P.	SANTA CRUZ
Fort Ross S.H.P.	same
Garrapata S.P.	BIG SUR
Grizzly Creek Redwoods S.P.	REDWOOD HWY
Grover Hot Springs S.P.	LAKE TAHOE AREA
Henry Cowell Redwoods S.P.	SANTA CRUZ
Henry W. Coe S.P.	GILROY
Humboldt Redwoods S.P.	same
Indian Grinding Rock S.H.P.	JACKSON
Jedediah Smith Redwoods S.P.	CRESCENT CITY
Julia Pfeiffer Burns S.P.	BIG SUR
Lake Oroville S.R.A.	OROVILLE
MacKerricher S.P.	FORT BRAGG
Malakoff Diggins S.H.P.	NEVADA CITY
Marshall Gold Discovery S.H.P.	PLACERVILLE
McArthur-Burney Falls Memorial S.P.	BURNEY
Mendocino Headlands S.P.	MENDOCINO
Millerton Lake S.R.A.	FRESNO
Montana de Oro S.P.	MORRO BAY
Morro Bay S.P.	MORRO BAY
Mount Diablo S.P.	same
Mount San Jacinto S.P.	IDYLLWILD
Mount Tamalpais S.P.	MILL VALLEY
Natural Bridges S.B.	SANTA CRUZ
Patrick's Point S.P.	TRINIDAD
Pfeiffer-Big Sur S.P.	BIG SUR
Prairie Creek Redwoods S.P.	CRESCENT CITY
Providence Mountains S.R.A.	NEEDLES
Railtown 1897 S.H.P.	SONORA
Richardson Grove S.P.	same
Russian Gulch S.P.	MENDOCINO
Salton Sea S.R.A.	same
Samuel P. Taylor S.P.	INVERNESS
Salt Point S.P.	FORT ROSS STATE HISTORIC PARK
San Buenaventura S.B.	VENTURA
San Clemente S.B.	SAN CLEMENTE

Seacliff S.B.	SANTA CRUZ
Silverwood Lake S.R.A.	CRESTLINE
Sonoma Coast S.B.	FORT ROSS STATE HISTORIC PARK
South Carlsbad S.B.	CARLSBAD
Sugar Pine Point S.P.	LAKE TAHOE AREA
Tahoe S.R.A.	LAKE TAHOE AREA
Tomales Bay S.P.	INVERNESS
Torrey Pines S.R.	LA JOLLA
Turlock Lake S.R.A.	MODESTO
Van Damme S.P.	MENDOCINO
Will Rogers S.H.P.	LOS ANGELES

Water-related activities, hiking, riding, various other sports, picnicking, nature trails, and visitor centers, as well as camping, are available in many of these areas. Some parks limit camping to a maximum consecutive period of 7-30 days, depending on season and popularity of area. Campsite charges are $10-$29/night/vehicle; trailer hookups $9-$25. For campsite reservations phone 800/444-7275 from anywhere in the continental United States; out of country phone customer service at 800/695-2269. Day-use fee is $2-$6/vehicle; vehicle with sailboat over eight feet and all motor vessels, $3-$5 additional; all other boats, $1 additional; annual pass for $75 unlimited day use, $125 with boat; boat launching $3-$5. Fees may vary in some areas. There are also small fees for some activities at some areas. Pets on leash only, permitted in campground and day-use areas only, $1/night (camping), $1 (day use). Reservations for Hearst-San Simeon State Historical Monument (Hearst Castle) (see) can be made by phoning 800/444-4445. For map folder listing and describing state parks ($2), contact the California State Parks Store, PO Box 942896, Sacramento 94296-0001; 916/653-4000. For general park information, phone 916/653-6995.

SKI AREAS

Place Name	**Listed Under**
Alpine Meadows	LAKE TAHOE AREA
Bear Valley	SONORA
Big Bear Mountain	BIG BEAR LAKE
Boreal Ski Area	TRUCKEE
Dodge Ridge Ski Area	SONORA
Donner Ski Ranch	TRUCKEE
Heavenly Ski Resort	LAKE TAHOE AREA
June Mountain Ski Area	JUNE LAKE
Kirkwood Ski Area	LAKE TAHOE AREA
Mammoth Mountain	MAMMOTH LAKES
Mountain High Ski Area	SAN BERNARDINO
Mount Shasta Ski Park	MOUNT SHASTA
Northstar-at-Tahoe Ski Area	TRUCKEE
Royal Gorge Cross-Country Ski Resort	TRUCKEE
Sierra At Tahoe	LAKE TAHOE AREA
Sierra Summit	FRESNO
Snow Summit	BIG BEAR LAKE
Snow Valley Ski Resort	LAKE ARROWHEAD
Squaw Valley USA	LAKE TAHOE AREA
Sugar Bowl Ski Area	TRUCKEE
Tahoe Donner Ski Area	TRUCKEE

For skiing information, contact the California Ski Industry Association, 74 New Montgomery St, Suite 750, San Francisco 94105; 415/543-7036.

CALENDAR HIGHLIGHTS

JANUARY

Tournament of Roses Parade (Pasadena). Spectacular floral parade on Colorado Blvd attracts more than a million people. Culminates with the Rose Bowl in the afternoon. Phone 626/449-4100.

Bob Hope Chrysler Classic (Palm Desert). Golf pros and celebrities play at four country clubs at Bermuda Dunes, La Quinta, Palm Desert, and Indian Wells. Phone 760/346-8184.

FEBRUARY

Chinese New Year (San Francisco). Chinatown. Largest and most colorful celebration of this occasion held in US. Week-long activities include Golden Dragon Parade, lion dancing, carnival, cultural exhibits. Contact Chinese Chamber of Commerce. Phone 415/982-3000.

MARCH

Whale Festival (Mendocino). Whale-watching walks, wine tasting, chowder tasting. Contact Mendocino Chamber of Commerce. Phone 707/961-6300 or 800/726-2780.

APRIL

Toyota Grand Prix (Long Beach). International race held on downtown streets. Phone 562/981-2600.

Monterey Wine Festival (Carmel). Approx 170 wineries participate in this food and wine-tasting festival. Phone 800/656-4282.

MAY

Cinco de Mayo (Los Angeles). El Pueblo de Los Angeles Historic Monument. Arts and crafts, music, and dancing. Contact Hollywood Visitors Information Center. Phone 213/689-8822.

JULY

San Jose America Festival (San Jose). Food booths, arts and crafts, rides and games, entertainment. Phone 408/298-6861.

FISHING AND HUNTING

Streams, rivers, canals, and lakes provide a great variety of freshwater fish. Salmon and steelhead trout run in great numbers in major coastal rivers north of San Francisco. Everything from barracuda to smelt may be found along or off the shore.

Hunting for deer, bear, and other big game is available in most national forests, other public lands, and some private lands (by permission) except in national and state parks, where firearms are prohibited. Waterfowl, quail, and dove shooting can be arranged at public management areas and in private shooting preserves. Tidepool collecting is illegal without special permit.

A fishing license is required for all persons 16 and older to fish in either inland or ocean waters. Some public piers in ocean waters allow fishing without a license (list available on request). A hunting license is required to hunt any animal. For information, contact the California Department of Fish and Game, 3211 S Street, Sacramento 95816. For general information phone 916/653-7664; for license information phone 916/227-2282.

Driving Information

Safety belts are mandatory for all persons anywhere in vehicle. Children under four years and under 40 pounds in weight must be in an approved safety seat anywhere in vehicle. Phone 916/657-7202.

American Century Celebrity Golf Championship (Lake Tahoe Area). Edgewood Tahoe Golf Course. More than 70 sports and entertainment celebrities compete for a $500,000 purse. Phone 800/AT-TAHOE.

Mozart Festival (San Luis Obispo). Recitals, chamber music, orchestra concerts, and choral music. Held at various locations throughout the county, include Mission San Luis Obispo de Tolosa and Cal Poly State University campus. Phone 805/781-3008.

AUGUST

California State Fair (Sacramento). California Exposition grounds. Includes traditional state fair activities, exhibits, livestock, carnival food, entertainment on ten stages, Thoroughbred racing, and one-mi monorail. Phone 916/263-FAIR.

SEPTEMBER

Los Angeles County Fair (Pomona). Fairplex. Thoroughbred racing, carnival, exhibits, free stage shows, food booths, monorail. Phone 909/865-4263.

Monterey Jazz Festival (Monterey). County Fairgrounds. Reserved seats only. Oldest jazz festival in the US. Phone 925/275-9255.

NOVEMBER

Hollywood Christmas Parade (Hollywood). Largest celebrity parade in the world. Features floats, marching band; over 50 of Hollywood's famous stars. Televised worldwide. Contact Hollywood Chamber of Commerce. Phone 323/469-2337.

DECEMBER

Christmas-Light Boat Parade (San Diego). San Diego Harbor, Shelter Island Yacht Basin. Mid-late Dec.

INTERSTATE HIGHWAY SYSTEM

Use the following list as a guide to access interstate highways in California. You should always consult a map to confirm driving routes.

Highway Number	Cities/Towns within ten miles
Interstate 5	Anaheim, Buena Park, Carlsbad, Costa Mesa, Del Mar, Dunsmuir, Fullerton, Garden Grove, Irvine, Lodi, Mount Shasta, Oceanside, Orange, Rancho Santa Fe, Red Bluff, Redding, Sacramento, San Clemente, San Diego, San Fernando Valley Area, San Juan Capistrano, Santa Ana, Stockton, Valencia, Willows, Yreka.
Interstate 8	Calexico, El Cajon, El Centro, Pine Valley, San Diego.
Interstate 10	Beaumont, Blythe, Claremont, Desert Hot Springs, Indio, Ontario, Palm Desert, Palm Springs, Pomona, Redlands, San Bernardino, Santa Monica, West Covina.
Interstate 15	Barstow, Corona, Escondido, Redlands, Riverside, San Bernardino, San Diego, Temecula, Victorville.
Interstate 40	Barstow, Needles.

Interstate 80	Auburn, Berkeley, Davis, Fairfield, Oakland, Sacramento, San Francisco, Truckee, Vacaville, Vallejo.
Interstate 110	Arcadia, Beverly Hills, Burbank, Culver City, Glendale, Long Beach, Los Angeles, Los Angeles Intl Airport Area, Marina del Rey, Pasadena, Redondo Beach, San Gabriel, San Marino, San Pedro, Torrance, Westwood Village.

Additional Visitor Information

For material on northern California, contact the San Francisco Information Center, 900 Market St, San Francisco 94102, phone 415/974-6900 or the Redwood Empire Association, 1925 13th Ave, #103, Oakland 94606-3161, phone 800/200-8334. For southern California, contact the Los Angeles Convention and Visitors Bureau, 633 W 5th St, Suite 6000, Los Angeles 90071, phone 213/624-7300; the San Diego Visitor Information Center, 11 Horton Plaza, 1st and F Sts, San Diego 92101, phone 619/236-1212, is also helpful. Serious hikers should consult *Sierra North* or *Sierra South,* available from the Wilderness Press, 1200 5th St, Berkeley 94710, or phone 800/443-7227. For general information, contact the California Division of Tourism, 801 K St, Suite 1600, Sacramento 95814, phone 916/322-2881 or 800/862-2543. The monthly magazine *Sunset* gives special attention to West Coast travel and life. Sunset Publishing Corporation also publishes the Sunset Travel Books, among which are: *Northern California* and *Southern California.* Contact Sunset Publishing Corporation, 80 Willow Rd, Menlo Park 94025-3691, phone 800/227-7346 outside California or 800/321-0372 in California.

THE BIG SUR COASTLINE

Hugging the rugged Big Sur coastline where cliffs fall to the sea, Highway 1 south of Monterey is often called the most scenic roadway in America. For sheer coastal beauty, it's hard to top. Development is sparse, so it's important to fill up on gas before starting out; a picnic lunch is a good option, too. From Monterey, it's less than 30 miles south to the most famous stretches of Big Sur, though the winding road and spectacular scenery call for taking it slow. Scenic turnouts dot the road along the way. Several state parks (Garrapata, Andrew Molera, Pfeiffer-Big Sur, and Julia Pfeiffer Burns) offer a combination of coastal access trails, waterfalls, and campgrounds. Rustic lodges and restaurants are also spread out along the route. Big Sur extends for about 90 miles south of Monterey, but for a one-day drive, a good turnaround point is the tiny hamlet of Lucia, about 50 miles south. The winding route is pitch black at night, so it's wise to return before dark. Those with two days can spend the night at Lucia in a modest lodge or continue south to San Simeon, where Hearst Castle perches high atop a mountain on the southern fringes of Big Sur. Those planning to tour Hearst Castle should reserve a time in advance and allow at least two hours. The town of Cambria, a few miles south of Hearst Castle, has plenty of lodging. Drivers have the option of returning to Monterey north on Highway 1 or looping back via Highway 101, a longer and less scenic (but potentially speedier) route that runs inland. To follow this option, take Highway 46 east off Highway 1 a few miles south of Cambria, reaching Highway 101 at Paso Robles. Continue north to Salinas, and take Highway 68 west to Monterey. **(APPROX 240 MI)**

Yosemite Valley

This tour takes the most scenic route into Yosemite Valley and includes the valley's most dramatic scenic points, as well as other beautiful stretches of the park. From Fresno, Highway 41 leads north toward the park. The route starts off flat but gets quite hilly and winding by the town of Oakhurst, the southernmost point on Highway 49. Follow Highway 49 northwest to the old mining town of Mariposa where Highway 140 heads north and then east toward Yosemite. On the way into the park, Highway 140 runs along a very pretty stretch of the Merced River, popular with rafters in summer. From the park's western entrance, follow the signs leading to Yosemite Valley. Expect heavy traffic on a weekend in the height of summer or over a holiday (cars are occasionally banned from the valley on peak summer holidays); the best times to visit are fall and spring. Snowy winters can be beautiful, but the roads may be slick and require four-wheel drive or tire chains; some high-elevation roads typically close. Southside and northside drives make a loop around the valley, passing spectacular waterfalls (best in spring) and granite monoliths such as Half Dome and El Capitan. There are plenty of pullouts where tourists can stop to take pictures or embark on a short hike. If you want to stay overnight in the valley, it would be wise to make reservations in advance; otherwise, lodging chances are slim here. When leaving the valley, take Highway 41 south. If the access road to Glacier Point is open (it closes in winter), and if you have an extra hour or two, follow the signs to Glacier Point for panoramic views of the valley, Yosemite Falls, and Half Dome. Continue south on Highway 41 through the park's Wawona section where the Mariposa Grove of Big Trees awaits; a short hike leads to several ancient giant sequoias. Highway 41 then leads south out of the park and back to Fresno. **(Approx 200 mi)**

Touring the Wine Country

Vineyards, wineries, restaurants, and all-around great scenery make this drive a must. From San Francisco, highways 101 north and 37 east lead to Route 121, which goes north and then east toward the Napa Valley. Highway 29 is the main route heading north, but rather than driving it in both directions, head to the gently curving, seldom-crowded Silverado Trail, which parallels 29 just a few miles away and retains a more rural atmosphere. (The start of the roadway begins in the town of Napa.) Follow the Silverado Trail north, passing dozens of boutique wineries and hillside vineyards, to the town of Calistoga, which has hot springs resorts and good restaurants and is an ideal place to spend the night. Return south on Highway 29, which is lined with many big-name, popular wineries, most of them open for tours and tastings. Along the way, the towns of St. Helena and Rutherford have numerous excellent restaurants. At Oakville, turn west across the mountains via the Oakville Grade; the winding road is steep at times, but the scenery is worth it. This route also serves as a shortcut to the Sonoma Valley. At Highway 12, turn south toward the town of Sonoma, near the town of Glen Ellen; Jack London State Park, where the famed writer/adventurer once lived, is nearby. The town of Sonoma has a large, attractive central square, which is the site of the state's northernmost historic Franciscan mission, as well as historic homes, excellent shops, wineries, and lodgings. Routes 12 and 121 (south), Highway 37 (west), and Highway 101 (south) lead back to San Francisco. **(Approx 150 mi)**

Postcards from Marin County

This tour packs in a remarkable amount of scenery: postcard views of San Francisco, the Pacific coastline, redwood forests, Tomales Bay, and the superb Point Reyes National Seashore. Allow a full day, especially if you want to stop and hike a bit. Cross over the Golden Gate Bridge to the Marin Headlands where Conzelman Road runs along the cliffsides and offers panoramas of the bridge and the San Francisco skyline. After the roadway loops back to Highway 101, take that north past Sausalito, then follow Highway 1 north toward the coast. First stop is Muir Woods, the state's most popular and accessible grove of virgin redwoods; short trails lead through the main groves. Continue north to Mount Tamalpais, and follow signs toward East Peak for picnic areas and dramatic views of the entire Bay Area. Farther north along Highway 1 is Point Reyes National Seashore. There are hiking trails near the Bear Valley Visitor Center (just off Highway 1). For a more complete tour of the park, go north about 22 miles on Sir Francis Drake Highway, through the resort town of Inverness (where there is lodging for overnight stays), all the way to the tip of the peninsula. There, a lighthouse is perched high over the Pacific (a top whale-watching site in the winter, though you may have to park and ride a shuttle bus at peak times on weekends). The entire peninsula is lined with often-deserted beaches, and there are forests, estuaries, wildlife, and rolling grasslands along the way. Doubling back to Highway 1, the town of Point Reyes Station offers several good restaurants. From there, follow the Point Reyes-Petaluma Road (and directional signs) across the rolling countryside to either Petaluma or Novato, both located on Highway 101, which heads south to San Francisco. **(Approx 90-120 mi)**

Santa Barbara to San Simeon

This route combines exceptional coastal and mountain scenery; several interesting towns, wineries, and vineyards; and historic sites including old missions and Hearst Castle. Two days are necessary to complete the entire route with sightseeing stops. From the popular coastal resort town of Santa Barbara, head north into the Santa Ynez Mountains via Route 154; the road passes Native American painted caves and a recreational lake. Follow Route 246 west through the Santa Ynez wine country to the Danish influenced town of Solvang, where shops abound. Continue on 246 to Highway 1; near that junction is La Purisima, one of the most interesting of the state's old Franciscan missions. Highway 1 then goes north to dune-swept Pismo Beach, where there are plenty of restaurants to stop at for lunch. Highway 1 (joining Highway 101) then veers back inland to the town of San Luis Obispo, site of another historic mission. If you have only one day, this is a good turnaround point, making for a 200-mile round-trip (return to Santa Barbara via Highway 101). If continuing, follow Highway 1 (not 101) north back to the coast at Morro Bay, which is a nice place to spend the night. The seafront is lined with restaurants, many with views of Morro Rock, a bird sanctuary known as the Gibraltar of the Pacific. The area has a number of good beaches; Montana de Oro State Park, a few miles south of Morro Bay, is one of the great undiscovered Central Coast gems. From Morro Bay, Highway 1 leads north to Hearst Castle. Tours of the castle require about two hours; reservations should be made in advance. To return, take Highway 46 east off Highway 1, then head to Highway 101; follow that south back to Santa Barbara. **(Approx 300 mi)**

Exploring Lake Tahoe

Circumnavigating North America's largest alpine lake offers perspectives on four different sides of Tahoe and allows access to historic sites, hiking trails, ski resorts, restaurants, and casinos. Starting in the resort center of South Lake Tahoe, highways 50 and 89 head west along the southern shore of the lake. From late spring through midfall, the Tallac Historic Site, a trio of opulent turn-of-the-century estates, is open for touring; beaches and nature trails are adjacent. Highway 89, turning north, leads to Emerald Bay, one of the most photographed sites in the state. The bay's emerald-green waters harbor tiny Fannette Island. A steep hiking trail leads a mile down to Vikingsholm, a replica of a medieval Scandinavian castle along Emerald Bay that is open for tours in summer. Farther north, Tahoe's rustic West Shore provides exceptional views of mountain peaks across the lake. State park shoreline campgrounds and hiking trails are exceptional. At Tahoe City, Highway 28 leads east around the lake's North Shore, site of numerous resorts, restaurants, and parks. At Crystal Bay, Highway 28 enters Nevada and then turns south, passing along the woodsy eastern shore back to South Lake Tahoe; casinos are clustered at Stateline, Nevada, just north of South Lake Tahoe. Though only 72 miles around, the lake's curvy roads require a minimum of three hours to navigate; a full day allows for several stops. In the winter, the three California sides of Tahoe are lined with ski resorts (some are located a few miles from the lake); four-wheel drive or tire chains may be necessary to negotiate snowy, icy roads at that time. **(Approx 72 mi; add approx 230 mi if starting in Sacramento)**

Through the Redwoods

This route takes in North Coast ocean scenery as well as redwoods, wineries, and state parks with forested hiking trails. It's important to get an early start, especially for a one-day tour. From San Francisco, follow Highway 101 north to the town of Cloverdale, then take Route 128 northwest to Mendocino, passing Anderson Valley wineries and Hendy Woods State Park (featuring redwoods) along the way. Much of the route is winding. At the coast, meet up with Highway 1 and follow it north to the artsy resort town of Mendocino, which resembles a New England fishing village perched upon cliff tops. Those with two days can spend the night here and linger at antique and art shops or at one of several nearby state parks. Those with only one day can return to San Francisco via Highway 20 east from the town of Fort Bragg (six miles north of Mendocino), a scenic route that leads to Highway 101, which then heads south to San Francisco. Total distance for the day is about 350 miles. Otherwise, continue north the next day on Highway 1 through Fort Bragg up to Leggett, where it is possible to drive through a redwood tree. At Leggett, take Highway 101 north to Humboldt Redwoods State Park, home of the world's greatest redwood forests. The 30-mile-long Avenue of the Giants runs north through the heart of the redwoods. After completing the Avenue of the Giants, reverse direction and follow Highway 101 south to San Francisco. **(Approx 500 mi)**

Russian River Country

This route combines rolling pastureland with spectacular coastal scenery and Russian River redwoods. Picturesque small towns dot the roadways. You can make the drive in one day or turn it into a leisurely two-day excursion. From San Francisco, follow Highway 101 north to Petaluma in Sonoma County. Then head west on Bodega Avenue and later Valley Ford Road, which cross through farmlands and old ranchos, to Highway 1 at the town of Valley Ford. Highway 1 then leads west and north to Bodega Bay, a coastal fishing village. Continue up the winding coastal road, perhaps stopping at one of the turnoffs to Sonoma Coast State Beach or to the town of Jenner, perched over the Pacific at the mouth of the Russian River. This is a good place to enjoy lunch with a spectacular view or to linger for an overnight stay. Next, head inland (east) for about 12 miles on Route 116 to Guerneville, a rustic Russian River resort town in the redwoods (Armstrong Redwoods State Reserve is just to the north). Bed-and-breakfasts and other lodging are available there. Route 116 heads southeast back to Highway 101, which then leads south to San Francisco. **(Approx 175 mi)**

Discovering Gold Country

This route combines California history with good scenery and a procession of colorful old towns. Allow plenty of time for negotiating the winding turns and for stops at historic sites along the way. From Sacramento, a 30-mile drive east along I-80 leads to Auburn, the gateway to Highway 49, which snakes north-south through the state's historic Gold Country. Old Town Auburn is well worth a stop. If you have more than one day, you can first head north from Auburn about 30 miles to Nevada City, an old mining town built on steep hills; nearby mines can be toured. The trip to Nevada City requires backtracking down Highway 49 again to Auburn. Those with only one day should forego Nevada City and turn south at Auburn onto Highway 49, proceeding to tiny Coloma, site of the Marshall Gold Discovery State Historic Park on the American River where the Gold Rush was ignited in 1848. The historic sites can be visited; it's also a prime picnic spot. Highway 49 then continues south through atmospheric 19th-century towns such as Placerville (or Hangtown), Amador City, Sutter Creek, Mokelumne Hill (once a top contender for state capital, but now a tiny burg), Angels Camp (site of Mark Twain's story *The Celebrated Jumping Frog of Calaveras County*), Sonora, and Jamestown. All these towns are lined with Victorian residences and hotels, restaurants, and antique shops. Those staying overnight in Sonora can visit Columbia State Historic Park the next morning; it's just off Highway 49 a few miles north of Sonora. The living history park re-creates the life of bygone times; you can pan for gold there, or tour nearby mines—an indispensable stop for families. To return to Sacramento, go north again on Highway 49 just past Amador City, then follow Highway 16 northwest about 35 miles to Sacramento.
(Approx 225 mi, not incl 60-mile round-trip to Nevada City)

Rim of the World Highway

Rugged lake and mountain scenery and crisp mountain air lie just a few hours east of Los Angeles. If you get an early start (to beat traffic), you can make this round-trip in a long day, but staying overnight in Big Bear makes for a more relaxed tour. From L.A., I-10 leads east to Redlands; from there, head northeast (routes 30 and 300) toward Running Springs. The roads rise steadily into the mountains and then wind along Highway 18, the Rim of the World Highway, which offers sweeping views south to forests and deserts on a clear day. Big Bear Lake lies about 15 miles east of Running Springs and is a popular public resort area lined with motels, lodges, restaurants, and places to go fishing and boating. Big Bear also has southern California's largest concentration of ski resorts. Weather and road conditions permitting, it's worthwhile to drive all the way around the lake, along both the more developed south shore and the rustic north shore. The road loops back onto the Rim of the World Highway going west, then drops steeply down to the flatlands and back to L.A. via I-10. **(Approx 275 mi)**

Joshua Tree National Park

Joshua Tree makes an easy day trip from the desert resort of Palm Springs and offers views of some of California's most dramatic high-desert landscapes where the Mojave Desert meets the Colorado River. From Palm Springs, a short drive on I-10 west and Highway 62 north leads to the western entrance of Joshua Tree in about an hour. The dramatic 30-mile-long Northern Loop passes thousands of Joshua trees, known for their distinctive-looking arms, as well as clusters of massive boulders and hiking trails that lead up mountains and through old rustlers' hideouts. A number of campgrounds lie along the route (bring water). Those with just a few hours can loop back to Highway 62 on the Northern Loop and head back west and south to Palm Springs. Those with more time can leave the Northern Loop at the Pinto Wye Junction and follow the signs toward Cottonwood Springs. The road leads southeast through the park, spanning two deserts and passing cholla and ocatillo cactus gardens and rugged hiking trails. The road reaches I-10 after 40 miles, just past Cottonwood Springs oasis; I-10 then leads west back to Palm Springs. **(Approx 150 mi; add approx 200 mi if starting in Los Angeles)**

Santa Cruz County Coastline

This route hugs the coastline from San Francisco to the beach resort of Santa Cruz, passing often-deserted golden-sand beaches, and then back up through redwood forests. From San Francisco, Highway 1 leads south through Pacifica toward Half Moon Bay, at times winding along the tops of sheer cliffs. The small fishing village of Princeton makes a good stop for seafood. The road later passes strikingly beautiful state beaches such as San Gregorio, Pomponio, and Bean Hollow; Pigeon Point Lighthouse, occupying a peninsula, is one of the state's most photographed sites. About 50 miles south of San Francisco is the Año Nuevo State Reserve where thousands of massive elephant seals migrate annually in winter to mate and give birth (reservations for walking tours are essential from mid-December through March; allow two to three hours). The seaside town of Santa Cruz, with beaches and an old-fashioned boardwalk and wharf, is 75 miles south of San Francisco. This is a good place to spend the night if making a multiday drive. Return north from Santa Cruz via Route 9, which climbs through the redwoods (with a possible winding side trip to Big Basin State Park, a redwood haven), and continue north on Route 35 at the Saratoga Gap (elevation 2,600 feet). Farther along, Route 84 leads back east to I-280, which usually offers a speedy return north to San Francisco.
(Approx 150 mi)

The Road to Julian

This route travels from San Diego to the mountain town of Julian and offers chances to hike in rugged state parks along the way. About 100 miles total, it involves some mountain driving and winding roads, so drivers should allow ample time. From San Diego, take I-8 (east) to Route 67 (north) to Highway 78 (east) to the picturesque hill town of Julian, a popular site for prowling through antique stores. Wineries and old mines are also nearby. Huge Anza-Borrego Desert State Park lies to the east (don't try to drive there unless you have two days for this tour). With restaurants and bed-and-breakfasts available, Julian is the best place to spend the night for those with more than one day. Highway 79 then heads south from Julian, passing Cuyamaca Reservoir and rugged Cuyamaca Rancho State Park, San Diego's nearest forest recreation and home to 6,500-foot Cuyamaca Peak. Highway 79 then continues south to I-8, which leads west back to San Diego. **(Approx 100 mi)**

Alturas

Pop 5,566 **Elev** 4,366 ft
Area code 530 **Zip** 96101
Information Chamber of Commerce, 522 S Main St; 530/233-4434

What to See and Do

Modoc County Historical Museum. More than 4,000 Native American artifacts, incl arrowheads, spear points, and many other items; exhibits of local history, incl antique gun collection. (May-Oct, daily) 600 S Main St. Phone 530/233-6328. ¢

Modoc National Forest. Scene of the Modoc Indian Wars, this forest of nearly two million acres is famous for its scenic trails through the South Warner Wilderness. In Medicine Lake Highlands Area there is a spectacular flow of jumbled black lava surrounding islands of timber; craters, cinder cones, and lava tube caves. For wildlife watchers, the Modoc National Forest is home to more than 300 species of wildlife; the Pacific Flyway for migratory waterfowl crosses directly over the forest, making this area a bird watcher's paradise. Swimming, stream and lake fishing; hunting. Winter sports area. Picnicking. Camping. Sections surrounding Alturas reached via US 395 and CA 139/299. Contact the Forest Supervisor, 800 W 12th St. Phone 530/233-5811.

Modoc National Wildlife Refuge. Nesting habitat for the Great Basin Canada goose; also ducks, sandhill cranes, other interesting birds. (Daily, daylight hrs; Dorris Reservoir Recreation Area closed during waterfowl hunting season; inquire about fees. Refuge closed to public fishing exc Dorris Reservoir Recreation Area.) 2 mi S on County 115. Phone 530/233-3572. **FREE**

Special Events

Fandango Days. July. Phone 520/233-4434.

Modoc-The Last Frontier Fair. In Cedarville. Phone 530/279-2315. Aug.

Motels/Motor Lodges

★★ **BEST WESTERN TRAILSIDE INN.** *343 N Main St (96161). 530/233-4111; fax 530/233-3180; toll-free 800/528-1234. www.bestwestern. com.* 38 rms, 2 story, 4 kits. May-Oct: S $50; D $50-$60; each addl $5; kit. units $10 addl; lower rates rest of yr. Crib $5. Pet accepted, some restrictions. TV; cable (premium). Pool. Complimentary coffee. Restaurant nearby. Ck-out 11 am. Business servs avail. In-rm modem link. Downhill/x-country ski 10 mi. Cr cds: A, C, D, DS, MC, V.

★ **HACIENDA MOTEL.** *201 E 12th St (96101). 530/233-3459.* 20 rms, 2 kits. S $29; D $31-$49; each addl $3; kit. units $5 addl; under 8 free. Pet accepted; $3. TV; cable (premium). Complimentary coffee in rms. Restaurant nearby. Ck-out 11 am. Downhill/x-country ski 10 mi. Refrigerators. Microwaves avail. Cr cds: A, C, D, DS, MC, V.

Anaheim

(E-5) *See also Buena Park, Corona, Los Angeles, Santa Ana*

Founded 1857 **Pop** 310,654 **Elev** 160 ft **Area code** 714
Information Anaheim/Orange County Visitor & Convention Bureau, 800 W Katella Ave, 92803; 714/765-8950
Web www.anaheimoc.org

Once part of a Spanish land grant, Anaheim was bought and settled by German colonists who came to this land to grow grapes and produce wine. The town takes its name from the Santa Ana River and the German word for "home." Today, Anaheim is known as the home of Disneyland.

What to See and Do

Disneyland. (see) On Harbor Blvd, off Santa Ana Fwy.

Disney's California Adventure. (see DISNEYLAND) Phone 714/781-4565.

Pacific Coast Sightseeing (Gray Line Anaheim, A Coach U.S.A. Company). For information contact 1213 E Howell Ave, 92805. Phone 714/978-8855.

Professional sports.

Anaheim Angels (MLB). Edison Field, 2000 Gene Autry Way. Phone 714/940-2000.

Mighty Ducks of Anaheim (NHL). Arrowhead Pond, 2695 Katella Blvd. Phone 714/704-2500.

Motels/Motor Lodges

★ **ANAHEIM BEST INN.** *1604 S Harbor Blvd (92802). 714/635-3630; fax 714/234-3422; res 800/237-8466. www.anaheiminn.com.* 58 units, 2 story, 8 suites. S $40-$99; D $49-$129; each addl $5; suites $99-$179; under 12 free. Crib $6. TV. Heated pool; whirlpool. Complimentary continental bkfst. Coffee in rms. Restaurant adj open 24 hrs. Ck-out 11 am. Coin lndry. Refrigerators, microwaves. Cr cds: A, C, D, DS, ER, JCB, MC, V.

D

★★ **BEST WESTERN STOVALL'S INN.** *1110 W. Katella Ave (92802). 714/778-1880; fax 714/778-3805; res 800/528-1234. www.stovallshotels.com.* 290 rms, 3 story. S, D $79-$129; each addl $6; under 18 free. Crib free. TV; cable (premium). 2 pools, 1 heated; wading pool, whirlpools. Complimentary coffee in rms. Restaurant adj 6 am-midnight. Bar 4 pm-midnight; closed Sun. Ck-out noon. Coin lndry. Meeting rm. Business servs avail. Gift shop. Free Disneyland transportation. Game rm. Refrigerators avail. Topiary garden. Cr cds: A, D, DS, MC, V.

D

★★ **CASTLE INN AND SUITES.** *1734 S Harbor Blvd (92802). 714/774-8111; fax 714/774-6024; toll-free 800/227-8530. www.castleinn.com.* 198 rms, 4 story, 46 suites. S, D $72-$82; suites $92-$102. Crib $6. TV; cable (premium). Heated pool; wading pool, whirlpool. Restaurant nearby. Ck-out 11 am. Coin lndry. Business servs avail. Gift shop. Valet serv. Free Disneyland transportation.

Refrigerators; microwaves in suites. Cr cds: A, C, D, DS, ER, MC, V.
D SC

★ **COMFORT INN & SUITES.** *300 E Katella Way (92802). 714/772-8713; fax 714/778-1235; toll-free 800/982-8239. www.comfortinn.com.* 80 kit. units, 3 story. June-Sept: S, D $69-$89; wkly rates; lower rates rest of yr. Crib $5. TV; cable (premium). Pool. Complimentary continental bkfst. Restaurant 6:30 am-9:30 pm. Ck-out noon, ck-in 3 pm. Business servs avail. Free Disneyland transportation. Sightseeing tours. Golf nearby. Microwaves. Private patios, balconies. Cr cds: A, D, DS, MC, V.
D

★★ **COMFORT INN MAINGATE.** *2200 S Harbor Blvd (92802). 714/750-5211; fax 714/750-2226; res 800/479-5210. www.visitmickey.com.* 66 rms, 2 story. S, D $49-$69; each addl $5; under 18 free. TV; cable. Heated pool; whirlpool. Complimentary continental bkfst. Coffee in rms. Restaurant nearby. Ck-out 11 am. Coin lndry. Business servs avail. Valet serv. Free Disneyland transportation. Refrigerators, microwaves avail. Cr cds: A, DS, MC, V.
D SC

★ **DAYS INN.** *1030 W Ball Rd (92802). 714/520-0101; fax 714/758-9406; toll-free 800/331-0055. www. daysinn.com.* 45 rms, 3 story. June-Aug: S, D $56-$99; each addl $8; under 18 free; higher rates hols; lower rates rest of yr. Crib free. TV; cable (premium). Heated pool; whirlpool. Complimentary continental bkfst. Coffee in rms. Restaurant opp 6-1 am. Ck-out 11 am. Coin lndry. Business servs avail. Airport, RR station, Disneyland transportation. Some refrigerators, wet bars, in-rm whirlpools. Cr cds: A, D, DS, MC, V.
D

★★ **FAIRFIELD INN.** *1460 S Harbor Blvd (92802). 714/772-6777; fax 714/999-1727; res 800/228-2800. www.anaheimfairfieldinn.com.* 467 rms, 9 story. S, D $64-$94. Crib free. TV; cable (premium). Heated pool; whirlpool. Complimentary coffee in rms. Restaurant 6 am-midnight. Ck-out noon. Coin lndry. Meeting rm. Business servs avail. Bellhops. Valet serv. Sundries. Gift shop. Free Disneyland transportation. Health club privileges. Refrigerators. Cr cds: A, D, DS, MC, V.
D

★★ **FAIRFIELD INN BY MARRIOTT.** *201 N via Cortez, Anaheim Hills (92807). 714/921-1100; fax 714/637-8790; toll-free 800/324-9909.www.marriott.com.* 163 rms, 4 story. S, D $69-$79; each addl $5; suites $109-$119; under 18 free. Crib free. TV; cable (premium). Heated pool; whirlpool. Complimentary continental bkfst. Coffee in rms. Restaurant adj 11-2 am. Ck-out noon. Coin lndry. Meeting rms. Business servs avail. Exercise equipt. Refrigerators avail. Cr cds: A, D, DS, JCB, MC, V.
D SC

★★ **HOLIDAY INN.** *1221 S Harbor Blvd (92805). 714/758-0900; fax 714/533-1804; res 800/545-7275. www.holiday-inn.com.* 254 rms, 5 story. S, D $109-$129; each addl $10; suites $175-$300; under 18 free. TV; cable. Heated pool; whirlpool, poolside serv. Coffee in rms. Restaurant 6:30 am-10 pm. Bar 5 pm-midnight. Ck-out noon. Coin lndry. Convention facilities. Business servs avail. Bellhops. Valet serv. Gift shop. Free Disneyland transportation. Game rm. Refrigerators avail. Cr cds: A, C, D, DS, ER, JCB, MC, V.
D SC

★ **HOWARD JOHNSON HOTEL - ANAHEIM RESORT.** *1380 S Harbor Blvd (92802). 714/776-6120; fax 714/533-3578; res 800/446-4656. www.hojoanaheim.com.* 318 rms in 6 buildings, 2, 4, and 7 story. S $81-$89; D $91-$105; suites $139-$149; under 18 free; package plans. Crib free. TV; cable. 2 heated pools; wading pool, whirlpool, poolside serv. Coffee in rms. Restaurant 6 am-11 pm. Ck-out noon. Coin lndry. Meeting rm. Business servs avail. Bellhops. Valet serv. Gift shop. Free Disneyland transportation. Game rm. Some refrigerators. Private patios, balconies. Cr cds: A, C, D, DS, JCB, MC, V.

★★ **JOLLY ROGER'S HOTEL.** *640 W Katella Ave (92802). 714/772-7621;*

fax 714/772-2308; toll-free 800/446-1555. www.tarsadia.com. 58 rms, 2 story. S, D $99-$129; under 17 free. Crib free. TV; cable (premium). Heated pool; wading pool. Coffee in rms. Restaurants 6:30 am-10 pm. Bar 11-2 am, Fri, Sat; entertainment Thurs-Sat. Ck-out 11 am. Coin lndry. Meeting rms. Business servs avail. Valet serv. Sundries. Gift shop. Barber, beauty shop. Airport, RR station, Disneyland transportation. Game rm. Refrigerators avail. Bathrm phone, wet bar in suites. Some patios, balconies. Cr cds: A, C, D, DS, MC, V.

D SC

★ **PARK VUE INN.** *1570 S Harbor Blvd (92802). 714/772-3691; fax 714/635-5305; res 800/334-7021. www.parkvueinn.com.* 86 units, 2 story. S $49-$75; D $59-$79; suites $75-$130; under 14 free. Crib $5. TV; cable (premium). Heated pool; wading pool. Complimentary continental bkfst. Coffee in rms. Restaurant adj open 24 hrs. Ck-out 11 am. Coin lndry. Business servs avail. Gift shop. Refrigerators; wet bar, microwave in suites. Sun deck. Cr cds: A, DS, MC, V.

SC

★★ **PEACOCK SUITES HOTEL.** *1745 S Anaheim Blvd (92805).*Fax *714/535-8255; res 800/522-6401. www.peacocksuitesresort.com.* 140 suites, 5 story. S, D $109-$179; under 16 free. Crib free. TV; cable (premium), VCR (movies). Covered heated pool; whirlpools. Complimentary continental bkfst, coffee in rms. Restaurant opp 7 am-10 pm. Ck-out 11 am. Coin lndry. Business servs avail. Gift shop. Valet serv. Free garage parking. Free Disneyland transportation. Health club privileges. Game rm. Refrigerators, microwaves. Sun deck. Cr cds: A, D, DS, ER, MC, V.

D

★★ **PENNY SLEEPER INN.** *1441 S Manchester Ave (92802). 714/991-8100; fax 714/533-6430; toll-free 800/854-6118. www.pennysleeperinn.com.* 189 rms, 2 story. S $59-$69; D $69-$79; suites $99-$119. Crib $6. TV; cable (premium). Heated pool. Complimentary continental bkfst. Restaurant nearby. Ck-out 11 am. Coin lndry. Business servs avail. Valet serv. Gift shop. Free Disneyland transportation. Game rm. Refrigerators, microwaves avail. Cr cds: A, C, D, DS, MC, V.

D SC

★★ **QUALITY HOTEL MAIN GATE.** *616 Convention Way (92802). 714/750-3131; fax 714/750-9027; res 800/231-6215. www.qualityhotel.com.* 284 units, 9 story, 100 suites. S $89.95-$139.95; D $99.95-$149.95; each addl $15; suites $99.95-$259.95; under 18 free. Crib free. Pet accepted. Parking $8. TV; cable (premium). Heated pool; poolside serv. Coffee in rms. Restaurants 6 am-2 pm; dining rm 5-10 pm. Bar 2 pm-midnight. Ck-out noon. Coin lndry. Convention facilities. Business servs avail. Bellhops. Free Disneyland transportation. Valet serv. Health club privileges. Gift shop. Barber, beauty shop. Game rm. Refrigerator, microwave in suites. Some balconies. Cr cds: A, C, D, DS, ER, JCB, MC, V.

D SC

★★★ **RADISSON MAIN GATE HOTEL.** *1850 S Harbor Blvd (92802). 714/750-2801; fax 714/971-4754; res 800/333-3333.* 314 rms, 5-8 story. S, D $119-$139; each addl $10; under 17 free; family rates. Crib free. TV; cable (premium). Heated pool; wading pool. Coffee in rms. Restaurant 6 am-2 pm, 5-10 pm. Bar noon-midnight. Ck-out noon. Coin lndry. Convention facilities. Business servs avail. Bellhops. Valet serv. Concierge. Gift shop. Airport, Disneyland transportation. Health club privileges. Game rm. Cr cds: A, D, DS, JCB, MC, V.

D

★★ **RAMADA INN.** *921 S Harbor Blvd (49770). 714/999-0684; fax 714/956-8839; res 800/235-3399.* 92 rms, 2 story. June-Aug: S, D $59-$79; each addl $6; suites $105-$145; under 16 free; higher rates hol wkends; lower rates rest of yr. Crib free. TV. Heated pool. Complimentary continental bkfst, coffee in rms. Restaurant adj 6 am-11 pm. Ck-out noon. Coin lndry. Business servs avail. Valet serv. Free Disneyland transportation. Refrigerators; microwaves avail. Cr cds: A, C, D, DS, JCB, MC, V.

D SC

★★ **RAMADA INN MAIN GATE/SAGA.** *1650 S Harbor Blvd (92802). 714/999-0684; fax 714/991-8219; toll-free 800/854-6097. www.ramada.com.* 185 rms, 2-4 story. S

$78-$98; D $88-$108; each addl $5; suites $90-$120; under 17 free. Crib free. TV; VCR avail (movies). Heated pool; whirlpool. Complimentary continental bkfst. Restaurant adj 11 am-10 pm. Ck-out 11 am. Coin lndry. Business servs avail. Valet serv. Shopping arcade. Free Disneyland transportation. Some wet bars; refrigerators avail. Cr cds: A, D, DS, JCB, MC, V.

D SC

★★ **RAMADA LIMITED.** *800 S Beach Blvd (92804). 714/995-5700; fax 714/826-6021; res 800/628-3400. www.ramada.com.* 72 rms, 3 story. S, D $55-$90; under 12 free. Crib $7. Pet accepted, some restrictions; $10/day. TV; cable (premium). Heated pool; whirlpool. Complimentary continental bkfst. Restaurant opp open 24 hrs. Ck-out noon. Meeting rm. Business servs avail. Coin lndry. Refrigerators, microwaves; some in-rm whirlpools. Cr cds: A, D, DS, JCB, MC, V.

D SC

★★ **RAMADA LIMITED SUITES.** *2141 S Harbor Blvd (92802). 714/971-3553; fax 714/971-4609; res 888/298-2054. www.ramada.com.* 94 units, 4 story, 73 suites. S, D $79-$119; each addl $5; under 18 free; wkly rates. Crib $5. TV; cable (premium), VCR avail (movies). Covered heated pool; whirlpool. Complimentary continental bkfst. Coffee in rms. Restaurant opp 6 am-midnight. Ck-out 11 am. Coin lndry. Business servs avail. Valet serv. Free Disneyland transportation. Refrigerators, microwaves. Cr cds: A, D, DS, MC, V.

D SC

★ **SUPER 8 MOTEL.** *915 Disneyland Dr (92802). Fax 714/778-0350; res 800/248-4400. www.super8.com.* 111 rms, 3 story. June-Aug: S, D $55-$65; under 12 free; lower rates rest of yr. TV; cable (premium). Heated pool; whirlpool. Complimentary continental bkfst. Restaurant opp 6-1 am. Ck-out 11 am. Coin lndry. Business servs avail. Free Disneyland transportation. Cr cds: A, C, D, DS, MC, V.

D SC

★ **TRAVELODGE.** *1700 E Katella Ave (92805). 714/634-1920; fax 714/634-0366; res 800/634-1920.* 72 rms, 2 story. S, D $42-$75; each addl (after 4) $5. Crib free. TV; cable (premium). Complimentary continental bkfst, coffee in rms. Restaurant opp open 24 hrs. Ck-out 11 am. Business servs avail. Valet serv. Coin lndry. Free Disneyland transportation. Pool; whirlpool. Refrigerators; some wet bars; microwaves avail. Cr cds: A, D, DS, JCB, V.

D SC

Hotels

★★ **CAROUSEL INN AND SUITES.** *1530 S Harbor Blvd (92802). 714/758-0444; fax 714/772-9965; toll-free 800/854-6767. www.carouselinnandsuites.com.* 131 units, 2-5 story, 26 suites. S, D $79-$89; suites $99-$139. Crib $5. TV; cable. Heated pool. Complimentary continental bkfst. Coffee in rms. Restaurant nearby. Ck-out 11 am. Coin lndry. Business servs avail. Gift shop. Valet serv. RR station, bus depot, Disneyland transportation. Game rm. Refrigerators, microwaves. Cr cds: A, DS, MC, V.

★★ **CONESTOGA HOTEL AT THE PARK.** *1240 S Walnut St (92802). 714/535-0300; fax 714/491-8953; toll-free 800/824-5459. www.conestogahotel.com.* 254 rms, 6 story. S $79-$99; D $89-$109; each addl $10; suites $150-$295; under 17 free; package plans. Crib free. TV; cable (premium). Heated pool; whirlpool, poolside serv. Complimentary coffee in rms. Restaurant 6:30 am-1 pm, 5:30-9:30 pm. Bar. Ck-out 11 am. Coin lndry. Convention facilities. Business servs avail. Concierge. Bellhops. Valet serv. Gift shop. Free Disneyland transportation. Game rm. Refrigerator, wet bar in suites; microwaves avail. Disneyland ¼ mi. Cr cds: A, D, DS, ER, JCB, MC, V.

D SC

★★★ **HILTON ANAHEIM.** *777 W Convention Way (92802). 714/750-4321; fax 714/740-4460. www.anaheim.hilton.com.* 1,574 units, 14 story. S $89-$300; D $119-$330; each addl $30; suites $800-$1,600; under 18 free; family rates. Crib free. Pet accepted. Covered parking: valet $11, garage in/out $6. TV; cable (premium). 2 heated pools, 1 indoor;

whirlpools, poolside serv. Coffee in rms. Restaurants 6 am-midnight. Bars 11-2 am; entertainment. Ck-out noon. Convention facilities. Business center. Concierge. Shopping arcade. Barber, beauty shop. Exercise rm; saunas, steam rms. Game rm. Some refrigerators. Some private patios, balconies. Luxury level. Cr cds: A, C, D, DS, ER, JCB, MC, V.

D

★★★ **HYATT REGENCY ORANGE COUNTY.** *100 Plaza Alicante (92803). 714/750-1234; fax 714/971-1421; res 800/233-1234. www.hyatt.com.* 396 rms, 17 story. S $99-$170; D $99-$195; each addl $25; suites $295-$895; under 17 free; Disneyland and Knott's Berry Farm packages. Parking $6, valet $8. Crib avail. TV; cable (premium), VCR avail. Heated pool; whirlpool, poolside serv. Restaurants 6 am-11:30 pm. Bars 3 pm-midnight. Ck-out noon. Convention facilities. Business center. Concierge. Shopping arcade. Airport, RR station, bus depot, Disneyland transportation. Lighted tennis. Golf driving range. Exercise equipt. Health club privileges. Game rm. Some bathrm phones, wet bars; whirlpool in suites. Some balconies. 17-story atrium with 60-ft palm trees provides tropical atmosphere. Cr cds: A, C, D, DS, JCB, MC, V.

★★★ **MARRIOTT ANAHEIM .** *700 W Convention Way (92802). 714/750-8000; fax 714/750-9100; toll-free 800/228-9290. marriotthotels.com/laxah.* 1,033 rms, 19 story. S $103-$180; D $123-$210; each addl $10; suites $200-$1,300; under 18 free. Crib free. Garage parking $9; valet $12. TV; cable (premium). 2 heated pools, 1 indoor/outdoor; whirlpools, poolside serv. Continental bkfst in lobby. Restaurants 6:30 am-11 pm; Fri, Sat to midnight. Bar 11-2 am. Ck-out noon. Coin lndry. Convention facilities. Business center. Concierge. Shopping arcade. Barber, beauty shop. Airport, Disneyland transportation. Exercise equipt; sauna. Game rm. Bathrm phone, refrigerator, wet bar in suites; microwaves avail. Some patios, balconies. Luxury level. Cr cds: A, D, DS, MC, V.

★★★ **SHERATON ANAHEIM HOTEL.** *900 S Disneyland Dr (92802). Fax 714/778-1700; fax 714/535-3889; res 800/325-3535. www.sheraton.com/anaheim.* 491 units, 3-4 story. June-Aug: S $170-$200; D $190-$220; each addl $20; suites $260-$280; under 18 free; lower rates rest of yr. Crib free. TV; cable (premium). Heated pool; whirlpool, poolside serv. Coffee in rms. Restaurants 6-1 am. Bar 11-1 am. Ck-out noon. Coin lndry. Convention facilities. Business servs avail. In-rm modem link. Concierge. Bellhops. Valet serv. Gift shop. Airport, Disneyland transportation. Game rm. Exercise equipt. Wet bar in suites. Disneyland 2 blks. Cr cds: A, C, D, DS, ER, JCB, MC, V.

D

Resorts

★★ **DISNEYLAND HOTEL.** *1150 W Cerritos Ave (92802). 714/778-6600; fax 714/956-6597; res 714/956-6425. www.disneyland.com.* 1,036 rms, 11-14 story. S, D $170-$225; each addl $15; suites $350-$2,000; under 18 free. Crib free. Parking $10. TV; cable. 3 heated pools; whirlpool. Playgrounds. Restaurants 6:30-1 am. Bars 11-2 am. Ck-out 11 am. Convention facilities. Business center. Concierge. Shopping arcade. Airport, bus depot, Disneyland transportation. Exercise equipt. Game rm. Refrigerators avail. Private patios, balconies. On 30 acres. Tropical gardens, waterfalls, fish ponds. Beach. Fantasy light show. Luxury level. Cr cds: A, C, D, DS, JCB, MC, V.

D

★★ **DISNEYLAND PARADISE PIER HOTEL.** *1717 Disneyland Dr (92802). 714/999-0990; fax 714/776-5763. www.disneyland.com.* 502 rms, 15 story. S, D $165-$225; each addl $15; suites $350-$1,000; under 18 free; seasonal packages. Parking $10. TV; cable, VCR avail. Heated pool; whirlpool, poolside serv. Restaurants 6:30 am-11 pm (see also YAMABUKI). Bars 11-1 am. Ck-out 11 am. Convention facilities. Business center. Concierge. Gift shop. Exercise equipt. Game rm. Refrigerators. Some private patios. Central atrium with skylight; observation elevator. Luxury level. Cr cds: A, D, DS, MC, V.

★★ DOLPHIN'S COVE RESORT. *465 W Orangewood Ave (92802). 714/980-0830; fax 714/980-0943; res 800/874-9900. www.dolphinscoveresort.com.* 136 suites, 2 story. Suites $150-$200. Crib $5. TV; cable, VCR (movies). Complimentary continental bkfst, coffee in rms. Restaurant nearby. Ck-out 11 am. Business servs avail. In-rm modem link. Bellhops. Gift shop. Coin lndry. Exercise equipt. Pool; whirlpool. Playground. Refrigerators, microwaves, wet bars. Balconies. Picnic tables, grills. Cr cds: A, D, DS, MC, V.
D

Sleeping Beauty Castle, Disneyland

All Suites

★★ COUNTRY SUITES. *22677 Oakcrest Cir, Yorba Linda (92827). 714/921-8688; fax 714/283-3927; toll-free 800/336-0632. www.countrysuites.com.* 112 rms, 4 story. S, D $97-$107; each addl $10; suites $127-$137; under 12 free. Crib free. TV; cable (premium). Complimentary full bkfst, coffee in rms. Restaurant adj 11 am-10 pm. Ck-out noon. Meeting rms. Business servs avail. Valet serv. Sundries. Coin lndry. Exercise equipt. Pool; whirlpool. In-rm whirlpools, refrigerators, microwaves, wet bars. Cr cds: A, C, D, DS, JCB, MC, V.
D

★★★ EMBASSY SUITES ANAHEIM. *3100 E Frontera St (92806). 714/632-1221; fax 714/632-9963; toll-free 800/362-2779. www.esanaheim.com.* 222 suites, 7 story. S $169-$179; D $179-$189; each addl $10; under 17 free. TV; cable (premium). Indoor pool; whirlpool. Complimentary full bkfst. Coffee in rms. Restaurant 11 am-10 pm. Bar to midnight. Ck-out noon. Meeting rms. Business servs avail. In-rm modem link. Gift shop. Free Disneyland transportation. Sauna. Health club privileges. Refrigerators, microwaves, wet bars. Private balconies. 7-story atrium courtyard with fountains, koi ponds, ducks, waterfalls. Cr cds: A, C, D, DS, MC, V.
D

Restaurants

★★★ ANAHEIM WHITE HOUSE. *887 S Anaheim Blvd (92805). 714/772-1381. www.anaheimwhitehouse.com.* Hrs: 11:30 am-2 pm, 5-10 pm; Sat, Sun from 5 pm. Closed hols. Res accepted. Northern Italian menu. Bar. A la carte entrees: lunch $10.50-$25, dinner $17.50-$28. Specializes in veal, pasta, fresh fish. Own desserts. Outdoor dining. Built 1909; restored estate fashioned after the White House. Totally nonsmoking. Cr cds: A, MC, V.
D

★★ FOXFIRE. *5717 E Santa Ana Canyon Rd, Anaheim Hills (92807). 714/974-5400. www.foxfirerestaurant.com.* Hrs: 11:30 am-2:30 pm, 5-9 pm; Fri to 10 pm; Sat 5-10 pm; Sun from 5 pm; Sun brunch 10 am-2 pm. Closed hols. Res accepted. Eclectic menu. Bar. A la carte entrees: lunch $6-$11, dinner $16-$25. Sun brunch $16.95. Children's menu. Specializes in steak, seafood. Own baking. Entertainment. Outdoor dining. Cr cds: A, D, MC, V.
D

★★ GUSTAV'S JAGERHAUS. *2525 E Ball Rd (92806). 714/520-9500. www.calendarlife.com.* Hrs: 7 am-9 pm; Fri to 10 pm; Sat 8 am-10 pm; Sun from 8 am. Closed Jan 1, Dec 25. Res accepted. German menu. Wine, beer. Bkfst $2.65-$6.50, lunch $4.50-$13.95, dinner $6.95-$15.75. Children's menu. Specializes in authentic German cooking. Own baking. Family-style neighborhood restaurant; many German knick-knacks displayed. Cr cds: A, DS, MC, V.
D

★ **HANSA HOUSE SMORGASBORD.** *1840 S Harbor Blvd (92802). 714/750-2411.* Hrs: 7-11 am, noon-3 pm, 4:30-9 pm; Sun brunch noon-3 pm. Bar. Buffet: bkfst $5.50, lunch $6.25, dinner $9.95. Sun brunch $7.50. Children's menu. Specialty: Swedish-American smorgasbord. Salad bar. Own baking. Patio dining. Scandinavian country decor. Family-owned. Cr cds: A, DS, MC, V.

★★★ **MR STOX.** *1105 E Katella Ave (92805). 714/634-2994. www.mrstox.com.* Hrs: 11:30 am-11 pm; Sat, Sun from 5:30 pm. Closed hols. Res accepted. Bar. Wine cellar. A la carte entrees: lunch $9.95-$15.95, dinner $15.95-$28.95. Specializes in fresh seafood, pasta. Own baking, herbs. Pianist. Valet parking. Family-owned. Totally nonsmoking. Cr cds: A, C, D, DS, MC, V.

D

★★ **PARIS RESTAURANT.** *1160 W Ball Rd (92802). 714/535-1622. www.cattlemanwharf.com.* Hrs: 11 am-2 pm, 5-10 pm; Sat from 5 pm; Sun 5-9 pm; Sun brunch 10 am-2 pm. Res accepted. Bar. Lunch $6.25-$12.50, dinner $12.75-$24.75. Sun brunch $18.50. Children's menu. Specializes in steak, seafood. 6 dining rms: Wine, Garden, Fountain, Tara, Library, Paulette. Different design in each rm. Totally nonsmoking. Cr cds: A, C, ER, MC, V.

D

★★ **YAMABUKI.** *1717 S West St (92802). 714/956-6755.www.disneyland.com.* Hrs: 11:30 am-2 pm, 5:30-10 pm; Sat, Sun from 5:30 pm. Res accepted. Japanese menu. Bar. Lunch $6.95-$12.95, dinner $9-$30. Children's menu. Specializes in sushi, tempura, teriyaki. Valet parking. Traditional Japanese decor; tatami rms avail. Original artwork. Cr cds: A, DS, MC, V.

D

Antioch

(F-3) *See also Concord, Martinez, Oakland, Vallejo*

Pop 91,800 **Elev** 25 ft **Area code** 925 **Zip** 94509

Information Chamber of Commerce, 301 W 10th St, Suite 1; 925/757-1800

Web www.antioch-coc.org

What to See and Do

Black Diamond Mines Regional Preserve. These 3,650 acres on flanks of Mt Diablo (see MOUNT DIABLO STATE PARK) contain coal, silica sand mines, and the Rose Hill Cemetery. Hiking, bicycle, bridle trails. Picnicking. Naturalist programs. Preserve (daily). From CA 4, S on Somersville Rd. Phone 925/757-2620. Per vehicle ¢¢

Contra Loma Regional Park. Approx 775 acres. Lake swimming (summer, daily), sand beach, fishing, boating; hiking, bicycling. Picnicking, concession. (Daily) From CA 4, S on Lone Tree Way to Golf Course Rd then right on Frederickson Ln to park entrance. Phone 925/757-0404. ¢¢

Special Event

Contra Costa County Fair. Fairgrounds, 10th and L sts. Phone 925/779-7937. Late May-early Jun. Phone 510/757-4400.

Motels/Motor Lodges

★★ **BEST WESTERN HERITAGE INN.** *3210 Delta Fair Blvd (94509). 925/778-2000; fax 925/778-6015; toll-free 800/422-2340.* 73 units, 3 story. S $63-$77; D $67-$82; each addl $5; suites $81-$99; under 12 free. TV; cable (premium). Pool; whirlpool. Complimentary continental bkfst. Restaurant adj open 24 hrs. Meeting rms. Business servs avail. Some refrigerators; microwaves avail. Cr cds: A, C, D, DS, MC, V.

D

★★ **RAMADA INN.** *2436 Mahogany Way (94509). 925/754-6600; fax 925/754-6828; res 800/272-6232.* 116 rms, 3 story, 10 suites. Apr-Sept: S, D $79-$99; each addl $10-$12; suites $115-$125; under 18 free; hol rates; lower rates rest of yr. Crib free. Pet accepted, some restrictions; $25. TV; cable (premium). Complimentary continental bkfst, coffee in rms. Restaurant adj 6 am-midnight. Ck-out noon. Meeting rms. Business servs avail. Coin lndry. Pool; whirlpool. Refrigerators; microwave, wet bar in suites. Grills. Cr cds: A, D, DS, MC, V.

D

Anza-Borrego Desert State Park (F-6)

Approximately 600,000 acres of desert wilderness are preserved here, relieved by an occasional spring-fed oasis and colorful canyons. CA 78 bisects the park, with Borrego Springs (see), park headquarters, and the visitor center to the north. Other improved roads are County S-2, S-3, and S-22. Anyone who wants to explore seriously must use a four-wheel drive vehicle; road condition information is available at the visitor center. Driving across sand can be rough on vehicles and passengers. The best time to visit is November-mid-May. Six hundred species of flowering plants in the park soften the somewhat austere landscape during the spring months. Elephant trees reach the northernmost limits of their range in Anza-Borrego Park; rare smoke trees and fan palms grow here around natural seeps and springs. The park provides a refuge for wildlife, including roadrunners, rare bighorn sheep, and kit foxes. There are nature, hiking, and bridle trails and picnic grounds. Improved campsites (trailer hookups in Borrego Springs) are scattered in the park; primitive camping (fee) is allowed throughout the park, and there is a horse campground. Naturalist programs, tours, campfire programs are offered weekends, November-May. Self-guided auto tour brochures are available at the visitor center (Oct-May, daily; rest of yr, wkends and hols), west of Borrego Springs. Standard fees. Phone 760/767-5311 or 760/767-4205 (visitor center). Day use **¢¢**; Camping **¢¢-¢¢¢¢¢**

Arcadia

See also Los Angeles, Pasadena

Pop 48,290 **Elev** 485 ft **Area code** 626
Information Chamber of Commerce, 388 W Huntington Dr, 91007; 626/447-2159 or 626/445-1400

Arcadia is known as the home of Santa Anita Park racetrack, a world-class thoroughbred racing facility.

What to See and Do

★ **The Arboretum of Los Angeles County.** More than 200 peacocks roam 127 acres; plants from many parts of the world. Water conservation garden; aquatic gardens and waterfalls. Historical area with Hugo Reid Adobe (1839), Queen Anne Cottage (1885). Greenhouses, library, demonstration home gardens. Tram tours. (Daily; closed Dec 25) 301 N Baldwin Ave, 6 mi N of San Bernardino Fwy and just S of Foothill Fwy. Phone 626/821-3222.

Santa Anita Park. Thoroughbred racing. (Late Dec-late Apr, Wed-Sun) 285 W Huntington Dr. Phone 626/574-7223. **¢¢**

Motels/Motor Lodges

★★ **HAMPTON INN.** *311 E Huntington Dr (91006). 626/574-5600; fax 626/446-2748; toll-free 800/426-7866. www.hampton-inn.com.* 131 rms, 4 story. S $75-$85; D $85-$95; under 18 free; higher rates Rose Bowl (3-day min). Crib free. Pet accepted; $5/day. TV; cable (premium). Heated pool. Complimentary continental bkfst, coffee in rms. Restaurant nearby. Ck-out noon. Meeting rm. Business servs avail. Valet serv. Health club privileges. Refrigerators, microwaves avail. Cr cds: A, C, D, DS, MC, V.

D SC

★★ **HOLIDAY INN.** *924 W Huntington Dr, Monrovia (91016). 626/357-1900; fax 626/357-1386. www.holiday-inn.com/hotels.* 174 rms, 10 story. S, D $89-$99; wkly, wkend rates; higher rates Rose Parade (4-day min). Crib free. Pet accepted. TV;

cable (premium). Heated pool; whirlpool. Complimentary continental bkfst, coffee in rms. Restaurant 6 am-10 pm. Bar 3-11 pm. Ck-out noon. Meeting rms. Business servs avail. Bellhops. Valet serv. Sundries. Coin lndry. Health club privileges. Refrigerators, microwaves avail. Cr cds: A, C, D, DS, JCB, MC.

D SC

Hotel

★★★ **EMBASSY SUITES.** *211 E Huntington Dr (91006). 626/445-8525; fax 626/445-8548; toll-free 800/362-2779. www.embassy-suites.com.* 192 suites, 7 story. S, D $129-$159; each addl $10; under 18 free. Crib free. TV; cable (premium). Indoor pool; whirlpool. Complimentary full bkfst. Coffee in rms. Restaurant 9:30 am-3 pm, 5-10 pm. Bar from noon. Ck-out 1 pm. Coin lndry. Meeting rms. Business servs avail. Gift shop. Free airport transportation. Sauna, steam rm. Health club privileges. Refrigerators, microwaves. 7-story atrium courtyard with fountains. Cr cds: A, C, D, DS, MC, V.

D SC

Extended Stay

★★ **RESIDENCE INN BY MARRIOTT - ARCADIA.** *321 E Huntington Dr (91006). 626/446-6500; fax 626/446-5824; res 800/331-3131.* 120 kit. suites, 2 story. Kit. suites $158-$188; higher rates Rose Bowl (4-day min). Crib free. Pet accepted; $50-$75 and $6/day. TV; cable (premium), VCR avail. Heated pool; whirlpool. Complimentary continental bkfst, coffee in rms. Restaurant nearby. Ck-out noon. Coin lndry. Meeting rm. Business servs avail. Valet serv. Free airport transportation. Health club privileges. Refrigerators, microwaves; some fireplaces. Some balconies. Picnic tables, grills. Cr cds: A, C, D, DS, JCB, MC, V.

D

Restaurants

★★★ **CHEZ SATEAU.** *850 S Baldwin Ave (91007). 626/446-8806.* Hrs: 11:30 am-2:30 pm, 5:30-9 pm; Fri, Sat to 10 pm; early-bird dinner 5:30-6:30 pm; Sun brunch 10:30 am-2:30 pm. Closed Mon; Jan 1, July 4. Res accepted. Continental menu. Bar. Wine list. Lunch $6.95-$12.50, dinner $9.75-$22.50. Prix fixe: dinner (5:30-6:30 pm) $17.75. Sun brunch $15.75. Specializes in fresh fish, seasonal dishes. Own pastries. Valet parking. French country decor. Totally nonsmoking.No cr dcs accepted.

★★ **THE DERBY.** *233 E Huntington Dr (91006). 626/447-8173. www.thederby.com.* Hrs: 11 am-10:15 pm; Fri to 11:15; Sat 4-11:15 pm; Sun 4-10:15 pm; early-bird dinner 4-6 pm. Closed Dec 25. Res accepted. Lunch $5.95-$16.95, dinner $10.50-$29.50. Children's menu. Specializes in steak, seafood, pasta. Own cheesecakes. Entertainment Wed-Sat. Free valet parking. Beamed ceiling, fireplaces. Portraits of famous thoroughbreds and jockeys. Family-owned. No cr cds accepted.

D

★★★ **LA PARISIENNE.** *1101 E Huntington Dr, Monrovia (91016). 626/357-3359. www.whatsuplaparisienne.com.* Hrs: 11:30 am-2 pm, 5:30-9:30 pm; Sat 5:30-10 pm. Closed Sun, hols. Res accepted. French menu. Bar. Wine list. Lunch $7.50-$16.95, dinner $16.95-$23.95. Specialties: bouillabaisse, duck with orange sauce, veal Normande. Own baking. French country atmosphere. Totally nonsmoking. Cr cds: A, C, D, DS, MC, V.

D SC

Atascadero

(C-2) *See also Morro Bay, Paso Robles, San Luis Obispo*

Founded 1913 **Pop** 23,138 **Elev** 855 ft **Area code** 805 **Zip** 93422

Information Chamber of Commerce, 6550 El Camino Real; 805/466-2044

Web www.atascaderocofc.com

In the foothills of the Santa Lucia Mountains, Atascadero was founded by St. Louis publisher E. G. Lewis, who also founded University City, Missouri. Lewis developed the town to be a self-sustaining community or colony.

What to See and Do

Atascadero Historical Society Museum. E. G. Lewis' original Atascadero Colony Administration Building (1918); Italian-Renaissance architecture. Houses displays on local history and Lewis' projects. (Mon-Sat; closed hols) Fee for some special events. 6500 Palma Ave. Phone 805/466-8341. **FREE**

Atascadero Lake Park. Fishing. Picnicking, playground. 2 mi W of US 101 on CA 41. Phone 805/461-5000. On premises is

Charles Paddock Zoo. Assortment of domestic, native, and exotic animals. (Daily; closed Jan 1, Thanksgiving, Dec 25) Phone 805/461-5080.

Special Event

Colony Days. Parade, activities, arts and crafts, displays, food booths. Third Sat Oct.

Auburn

(E-4) *See also Grass Valley, Placerville, Sacramento*

Settled 1848 **Pop** 10,592 **Elev** 1,297 ft **Area code** 530 **Zip** 95603

Information Auburn Area Chamber of Commerce, 601 Lincoln Way; 530/885-5616

Web www.auburnchamber.net

Here is a town with a split personality: the restored "old town" retains its gold rush boomtown flavor; the other Auburn, built on a hilltop, is a modern city. In 1848, a mining camp called North Fork Dry Diggins was renamed for Auburn, New York. It developed as a center for gold rush camps and survived when the railroad came through and orchards were planted after the gold gave out.

What to See and Do

Folsom Lake State Recreation Area. This 17,545-acre area offers swimming, waterskiing, fishing, boating (rentals, marina); bicycle, hiking, bridle trails, picnicking, concession, camping (dump station). Historic Folsom Powerhouse (Wed-Sun afternoons). Standard fees. Off Folsom-Auburn Rd, near the town of Folsom. Phone 916/988-0205.

Gold Country Museum. Exhibits depicting early days of Placer County; history of gold mining and lifestyle of gold miners. (Tues-Sun; closed hols) 1273 High St, at the Gold Country Fairgrounds. Phone 530/887-6500. ¢ Admission incl

Bernhard Museum Complex. Restored 14-rm house (1851), winery (1874), and art gallery. Living history programs. Guided tours (Tues-Sun; closed hols). 291 Auburn-Folsom Rd. Phone 530/889-6500.

Old Town. Walk along Lincoln Way, Sacramento, Commercial, and Court sts. Restored area. Chamber of Commerce has information. Phone 916/885-5616.

Special Events

Placer County Fair. 2 mi N off I-80, on Washington Blvd in Roseville. Phone 916/786-2023. June.

Gold Country Fair. Wkend after Labor Day wkend. Phone 530/823-4533.

Wild West Stampede. Gold Country Fairgrounds. Contact Chamber of Commerce for details. Phone 530/273-6217.

Motel/Motor Lodge

★★ AUBURN BEST INN AND SUITES. *1875 Auburn Ravine Rd (95603). 530/885-1800; fax 530/888-6424; toll-free 800/272-1444.* 80 rms, 2 story. S $54-$60; D $60-$66; each addl $6; suites $75-$100; under 13 free. Crib $6. TV; cable. Pool; whirlpool. Complimentary continental bkfst. Restaurant opp open 24 hrs. Ck-out 11 am. Coin lndry. Meeting rms. Cr cds: A, D, DS, MC, V.

Restaurants

★★ HEADQUARTER HOUSE. *14500 Musso Rd (95603). 530/878-1906.* Hrs: 11:30 am-10 pm; Sun 2-9:30 pm; Sun brunch 10 am-2 pm.

Res accepted. Continental menu. Bar. Lunch $4.25-$8.95, dinner $8.95-$21.95. Sun brunch $6.95-$10.95. Specializes in fresh local foods. Own desserts. Pianist evenings and Sun brunch. Totally nonsmoking. Cr cds: A, C, D, DS, ER, MC, V.

D

★ **LOU LA BONTE'S.** *13460 Lincoln Way (95603). 530/885-9193.* Hrs: 7 am-10:30 pm, Fri-Sun from 8 am. Continental menu. Bar. Bkfst $3.95-$9.95, lunch $5-$9.50, dinner $8.95-$21.95. Children's menu. Specializes in steak, seafood, beef. Dinner theater. Family-owned. Cr cds: A, D, DS, MC, V.

D SC

Avalon (Catalina Island)

(F-4) *See also Laguna Beach, Long Beach, Newport Beach, San Pedro (L.A.)*

Pop 2,918 **Elev** 20 ft **Area code** 310 **Zip** 90704

Information Catalina Island Visitors Bureau & Chamber of Commerce, PO Box 217; 310/510-1520

Web www.catalina.com

Avalon is the sport fishing and resort capital of 21-mile-long, 8-mile-wide Santa Catalina Island. The peaks of the island rise from the Pacific, 21 miles southwest of Los Angeles harbor. Scuba diving, kayaking, golf, tennis, horseback riding, swimming, and hiking are popular.

Discovered in 1542 by Juan Rodriguez Cabrillo, the Portuguese navigator, it was named by the Spanish explorer Sebastian Viscaino in 1602. Later, Russians and Aleuts used the island as a base to hunt sea otter. The town experienced a brief miniature gold rush in 1863. In 1919, William Wrigley, Jr., chewing gum magnate and owner of the Chicago Cubs major league baseball team, bought controlling interest in the Santa Catalina Island Company from the Banning brothers, who had incorporated the island. Wrigley established a program of conservation that still applies; today, 86 percent of Catalina Island is protected by the Santa Catalina Island Conservancy. Tourism is the island's only industry and source of revenue today.

Daily air or boat service to the island is available all year from Long Beach (see) and San Pedro; boat service only from Newport Beach.

What to See and Do

Catalina Island Museum. Permanent exhibits on history of the island; natural history and archaeology displays. (Daily) Casino Building. Phone 310/510-2414. ¢

Catalina tours and trips. Santa Catalina Island Company Discovery Tours offer boat and bus tours to several points of interest. Phone 310/510-2500.

Wrigley Memorial and Botanical Garden. Native trees, cactus, succulent plants, and flowering shrubs on 38 acres surround memorial to a man who contributed much to Catalina Island. (Daily) Tram may run here from Island Plaza (summer only; fee). 1400 Avalon Canyon Rd. Phone 310/510-2288. ¢

Motel/Motor Lodge

★ **EL TERADO TERRACE.** *230 Marilla St, Avalon (90704). 310/510-0831; fax 310/510-2370. www.hotelcatalina.com.* 18 rms, 2 story, 2 townhouses. No A/C. No rm phones. May-Oct: S, D $80-$330; each addl $10; suites $120; townhouses $170; lower rates rest of yr. TV; cable, VCR avail. Complimentary coffee in rms. Restaurant nearby. Ck-out 11 am. Free shuttle from boat dock. Whirlpool. Refrigerators, microwaves. Cr cds: A, DS, MC, V.

Hotels

★ **GLENMORE PLAZA HOTEL.** *120 Sumner St, Avalon (93301). 310/510-0017; fax 310/510-2833; toll-free 800/422-8462. www.glenmore.com.* 48 rms, 4 story, 2 suites. No elvtr. Apr-Oct: S, D $79-$175; suites $225-$450; wkends (2-day min); lower rates rest of yr. Crib avail. TV; cable. Complimentary continental bkfst. No rm serv. Ck-out 10:30 am. Free boat dock transportation. Built 1891. Cr cds: A, DS, MC, V.

★★★ **HOTEL METROPOLE.** *205 Crescent Ave, Avalon (90704). 310/510-1884; fax 310/510-2534; toll-free 800/300-8528. www.catalina.com/metropole.* 48 rms, 3 story. May-Oct: S, D $125-$355; 2-bedrm suite $795; under 12 free; lower rates rest of yr. Crib free. TV; cable (premium). Complimentary continental bkfst. No rm serv. Ck-out 11 am. Coin lndry. Meeting rms. Business servs avail. Shopping arcade. Rooftop whirlpool, sun deck. Health club privileges. Minibars; many in-rm whirlpools, fireplaces. Microwaves avail. Balconies. Ocean view. Totally nonsmoking. Cr cds: A, MC, V.

D SC

★★★ **HOTEL VISTA DEL MAR.** *417 Crescent Ave, Avalon (90704). 310/510-1452; fax 310/510-2917; toll-free 800/601-3836. www.hotelvistadelmar.com.* 15 rms. May-Oct: S, D $145-$175; lower rates rest of yr. Crib $5. TV; cable (premium), VCR. Complimentary continental bkfst. Coffee in rms. Ck-out 11 am. Business servs avail. Refrigerators, fireplaces. Some in-rm whirlpools. Microwaves avail. Swimming beach. Atrium courtyard. Cr cds: A, DS, MC, V.

Resort

★★ **HOTEL VILLA PORTOFINO.** *111 Crescent Ave, Avalon (90704). 310/510-0555; fax 310/510-0839; res 888/510-0555. www.hotelvillaportofino.com.* 34 rms, 3 story. No elvtr. June-Sept and wkends: S, D $190-$345; each addl $10; lower rates rest of yr. Crib $10. TV; cable (premium). Complimentary continental bkfst. Restaurant 5-10 pm. Bar to 11 pm. Ck-out 11 am. Sun deck. Some refrigerators. Some rms overlook bay. Cr cds: A, C, D, DS, MC, V.

B&Bs/Small Inns

★★★ **HOTEL ST LAUREN.** *231 Beacon St, Avalon (90704). 310/510-2299; fax 310/510-1369; res 800/645-2496. www.stlauren.com.* 42 rms, 6 story. May-mid-Oct: S $125-$198; D $198; each addl $20; package plans; lower rates rest of yr. Crib free. TV; cable. Complimentary continental bkfst. Restaurant nearby. Ck-out 11 am. Meeting rm. Victorian-style architecture. Ocean 1 blk. Cr cds: A, MC, V.

D

★★★★ **INN ON MOUNT ADA.** *398 Wrigley Rd, Avalon (90704). 310/510-2030; fax 310/510-2237. www.catalina.com/mtada.* This former home of William Wrigley, Jr., and his wife Ada was completed in 1921 and sits 350 feet above the town and harbor on a hilltop bearing her name. Rates incl a full breakfast, deli lunch, appetizers, and alcoholic beverages. The Georgian Colonial home has six antique-filled rooms overlooking Avalon Bay and the Pacific. 6 rms, 2 story. MAP, June-Oct and wkends: S, D $280-$510; each addl $75; lower rates rest of yr. TV; cable (premium), VCR avail (movies). Afternoon refreshments. Ck-out 11 am, ck-in 2 pm. Many fireplaces. Balconies. Totally nonsmoking. Cr cds: MC, V.

Restaurants

★ **ANTONIO'S PIZZERIA & CABARET.** *230 Crescent Ave, Avalon (90704). 310/510-0008.* Hrs: 8 am-11 pm; Fri, Sat to midnight. Italian, American menu. Bar. A la carte entrees: bkfst $3.95-$6.95. Lunch $5-$8, dinner $5-$20. Specializes in pizza, pastas. Outdoor dining. Early 1950s decor. 1955 Seeberg juke box at each table. Overlooks harbor. Cr cds: A, MC, V.

D

★★ **ARMSTRONG'S FISH MARKET AND SEAFOOD.** *306 Crescent Ave, Avalon (90704). 310/510-0113.* Hrs: 11 am-9:30 pm; Fri-Sun to 10 pm. Closed Thanksgiving, Dec 25. Bar. Lunch $5.95-$11.95, dinner $8.95-$24.95. Specializes in seafood cooked over mesquite wood. Outdoor dining. Deck overlooks harbor. Cr cds: A, MC, V.

D

★★ **BLUE PARROT.** *205 Crescent Ave, Avalon (90704). 310/510-2465.*

www.blueparrotcatalina.com. Hrs: 11 am-9 pm; Fri, Sat to midnight. No A/C. Bar. Complete meals: lunch $6.95-$7.95, dinner $11.95-$17.95. Children's menu. Specializes in steak, seafood, Cajun dishes. Polynesian decor. Harbor view. Cr cds: A, DS, MC, V.

★★ **CHANNEL HOUSE.** *205 Crescent Ave, Avalon (90704). 310/510-1617*. Hrs: 11 am-3 pm, 5-10 pm. Res accepted. Continental menu. Bar. Complete meals: lunch $6.95-$13.95, dinner $15.95-$24.95. Children's menu. Specializes in seafood, steak, lamb. Pianist Fri, Sat. Outdoor dining. Antique wooden bar. Cr cds: A, DS, MC, V.

D

Bakersfield (C-4)

Founded 1869 **Pop** 174,820 **Elev** 408 ft **Area code** 661

Information Chamber of Commerce, 1725 Eye St, 93301; 661/327-4421

Web www.bakersfield.org/chamber

Surrounded by oil wells and fields of cotton and grain, Bakersfield is an important trading center—the hub of a network of highways that carry its produce and products to major cities. Founded by Colonel Thomas Baker, the town awakened in 1885 when gold was discovered in the Kern River Canyon. Overnight it changed from a placid farm town to a wild mining community, complete with gunfights and gambling halls. A fire in 1889 destroyed most of the old town and resulted in considerable modernization. The discovery of oil in 1899 rekindled the gold rush hysterics. Unlike gold, oil has remained an important part of the city's economy. Bakersfield is the seat of Kern County (8,064 square miles; third-largest county in the state). Nearby vineyards produce 25 percent of California's wine, and surrounding fields provide a colorful flower display in spring. A Ranger District office of the Sequoia National Forest is located here.

What to See and Do

California Living Museum. Botanical garden and zoo house plants and animals native to California; natural history museum; interpretive tours. (Tues-Sun; closed Thanksgiving, Dec 25) 10500 Alfred Harrell Hwy, 12 mi NE via CA 178. Phone 661/872-2256. ¢¢

Colonel Allensworth State Historic Park. Park honoring the only California town founded, settled, and financed entirely by African Americans; now a ghost town with restored buildings. Camping. (Daily) 45 mi N along Hwy 43, at 4129 Palmer Ave, Allensworth-Earlimart. Phone 661/849-3433. ¢¢¢

Kern County Museum. Complete 16-acre outdoor museum of 60 restored or representational buildings incl Queen Anne-style mansion (1891), log cabin, wooden jail, hotel, drugstore; 1898 locomotive, oil-drilling rig, and horse-drawn vehicles. Main museum building contains changing exhibits on natural and cultural history of the area. (Daily) Phone 661/861-2132. ¢¢

Scenic drive. Many fine places for picnicking, camping, and fishing along the road. Go E on CA 178 and follow the Kern River through a rock-dotted canyon.

Tule Elk State Reserve. This 969-acre reserve is home for a small herd of elk native only to California. Picnic shelters. (Daily) 20 mi W via Stockdale Hwy, then S on Morris Rd to Station Rd, then ¼ mi W. Phone 661/764-6881. ¢¢

Special Event

Kern County Fair. Late Sept. Phone 661/833-4900.

Motels/Motor Lodges

★★ **BAKERSFIELD DAYS INN.** *4500 Buck Owens Blvd. (93308). 661/324-5555; fax 661/325-0106. www.daysinn.com*. 203 rms, 3 story. S $39-$52; D $46-$58; each addl $5; suites, kit. units $56-$64; under 18 free. Pet accepted; $10. TV; cable. Pool. Sauna. Ck-out 1 pm. Coin lndry. Meeting rms. Business servs avail. Valet serv. Sundries. Free airport, RR station, bus depot transportation. 9-hole golf course, $6 green fee. Refrigerator in suites. Some balconies. Cr cds: A, C, D, DS, MC, V.

★★ **BEST WESTERN.** *700 Truxton Ave (93301). 661/327-4064; fax 661/327-1247; res 800/528-1234.* 99 rms, 2 story. S $50-$60; D $55-$65; each addl $5; under 12 free. Crib free. Pet accepted; $3. TV; cable (premium). Pool. Complimentary continental bkfst. Restaurant 6:30 am-8 pm. Bar. Ck-out noon. Meeting rms. Exercise equipt. Refrigerators. Balconies. Cr cds: A, D, DS, MC, V.

★★ **CALIFORNIA INN.** *3400 Chester Ln (93309). 661/328-1100; fax 661/328-0433; res 800/707-8000.* 74 units, 3 story. S $39-$41; D $45-$49; each addl $4; suites $85; under 18 free. Crib $4. TV; cable (premium). Pool; whirlpool. Sauna. Complimentary continental bkfst, coffee in rms. Restaurant adj 6 am-11 pm. Ck-out noon. Coin lndry. Refrigerators; in-rm whirlpool in suites. Cr cds: A, C, D, DS, MC, V.

SC

★★ **COURTYARD BY MARRIOTT.** *3601 Marriott Dr (93308). 661/324-6660; fax 661/324-1185; res 800/321-2211.* 146 rms, 3 story. S, D $82; suites $95; wkly, wkend rates. Crib free. TV; cable (premium). Heated pool; whirlpool. Complimentary coffee in rms. Restaurant 6-10:30 am. Serv bar 4-10 pm. Ck-out 1 pm. Coin lndry. Meeting rms. Valet serv. Exercise equipt. Health club privileges. Some balconies. Cr cds: A, C, D, DS, MC, V.

★★★ **FOUR POINTS BY SHERATON HOTEL.** *5101 California Ave (93309). 661/325-9700 or661/325-9700; fax 661/323-3508; res 800/325-3535. www.fourpointshotels.com.* 198 rms, 2 story. S $99-$155; D $109-$165; each addl $10; suites $175-$300; under 17 free. Crib free. TV; cable (premium). Heated pool; whirlpool. Complimentary continental bkfst (Mon-Fri). Coffee in rms. Restaurant 6:30 am-10 pm. Bar 4-10 pm. Ck-out 1 pm. Meeting rms. Business servs avail. In-rm modem link. Bellhops. Valet serv. Airport, RR station, bus depot transportation. Exercise equipt. Some refrigerators. Private patios. Tropical decor; atrium. Extensive grounds. Cr cds: A, C, D, DS, ER, JCB, MC, V.

SC

★★ **HOLIDAY INN.** *4400 Hughes Ln (93304). 661/833-3000; fax 661/833-3736; res 800/636-1626. www.holidayinnexpressbak.com.* 108 rms, 4 story. S $81; D $86; each addl $5; under 18 free. Crib free. TV; cable (premium). Complimentary continental bkfst. Restaurant nearby. Ck-out 11 am. Meeting rms. Business center. In-rm modem link. Coin lndry. Pool; whirlpool. Game rm. Bathrm phones, refrigerators, microwaves; some in-rm whirlpools. Cr cds: A, C, D, DS, JCB, MC, V.

SC

★ **LA QUINTA INN.** *3232 Riverside Dr (93308). 661/325-7400; fax 661/324-6032; toll-free 800/687-6667.* 129 rms, 3 story. S $55-$65; D $62-$68; suites $110; under 18 free. Crib free. Pet accepted. TV; cable (premium). Heated pool. Complimentary continental bkfst, coffee in rms. Restaurant adj 5:30 am-10 pm. Ck-out noon. Business servs avail. Free airport transportation. Health club privileges. Cr cds: A, C, D, DS, MC, V.

SC

★★ **QUALITY INN.** *1011 Oak St (93304). 661/325-0772; fax 661/325-4646; toll-free 800/228-5050.* 90 units, 2 story. S $42-$60; D $50-$60; each addl $5; suites from $56; under 10 free. Crib free. Pet accepted, some restrictions. TV; cable (premium). Pool; whirlpool. Sauna. Complimentary continental bkfst, coffee in rms. Restaurant adj 6 am-11 pm. Ck-out noon. Coin lndry. Valet serv. Some private patios, balconies. Cr cds: A, C, D, DS, ER, JCB, MC, V.

SC

★ **SUPER 8.** *901 Real Rd (93309). 661/322-1012; fax 661/322-7636; res 800/800-8000.* 90 rms, 3 story. S $50-$54; D $54-$58; each addl $4; under 12 free. Crib free. TV; cable (premium). Pool. Complimentary coffee in lobby. Restaurant nearby. Ck-out 11 am. Cr cds: A, D, DS, MC, V.

★ **TRAVELODGE SOUTH.** *3620 Wible Rd (93309). 661/833-1000; fax 661/832-3212; res 800/578-7878.* 60 rms, 2 story. S $50; D $60; each addl $5; under 18 free. Crib free. TV; cable (premium). Complimentary continental bkfst, coffee in rms. Restaurant adj 5 am-midnight. Ck-out 11 am. Business servs avail. In-rm modem link. Coin lndry. Pool; whirlpool. Refrigerators; some in-rm whirlpools, microwaves, wet bars. Cr cds: A, C, D, DS, MC, V.

D

Guest Ranch

★★ **RANKIN RANCH.** *23500 Walkers Basin Rd, Caliente (93518). 661/867-2511; fax 661/867-0105. www.rankinranch.com.* 14 rms, 7 cabins. No rm phones. AP: S $160/person; D $150/person; children $35-$100; wkly rates; lower rates Apr-May and Sept-Oct. Closed 1st Sun Oct-wk before Easter. Crib free. Heated pool. Playground. Free supervised children's activities (mid-June-Labor Day). Complimentary coffee in rms. Dining rm, 3 sittings: 7:30-9 am, 12:30 pm, and 6:30 pm. Box lunches. Ck-out 1 pm, ck-in 3:30 pm. Grocery 5 mi. Meeting rms. Gift shop. Tennis. Boating. Hiking. Hay wagon rides. Lawn games. Soc dir. Square dancing. Rec rm. 31,000-acre working ranch (founded 1863) in Tehachapi Mountains. Cr cds: A, DS, MC, V.

D

Restaurants

★★ **MAMA TOSCA'S.** *6631 Ming Ave (93309). 661/831-1242.* Hrs: 11:30 am-2 pm, 5:30-10 pm; Sat from 5:30 pm. Closed Sun, hols. Res accepted. Italian, American menu. Bar. Lunch $6.95-$19.95, dinner $9.95-$30. Specialties: veal scallopini, eggplant Parmesan, rack of lamb. Vocalist, band Thurs-Sat. Parking. Cr cds: A, C, D, DS, MC, V.

D

★★ **ROSA'S.** *2400 Columbus (93306). 661/872-1606.* Hrs: 11 am-1:45 pm, 4-9:30 pm; Fri to 10 pm; Sat 4-10 pm; Sun 4-9:30 pm. Closed hols. Italian, American menu. Wine, beer. Lunch $3.85-$6.95, dinner $7.95-$14.95. Specialties: linguine with clams, fettucine Alfredo, lasagne. Patio dining. Italian village atmosphere. Family-owned. Totally nonsmoking. Cr cds: C, MC, V.

D

★ **WOOL GROWERS.** *620 E 19th St (93305). 661/327-9584.* Hrs: 11:30 am-2 pm, 6-9:30 pm. Closed Sun; Thanksgiving, Dec 25. Res accepted. Basque menu. Bar 10 am-11:30 pm. Complete meals: lunch $5.50-$11.50, dinner $10.50-$17.50. Children's menu. Specializes in French Basque dishes. Family-owned. Cr cds: A, C, DS, MC, V.

D

Barstow

See also Victorville

Founded 1880 **Pop** 21,472 **Elev** 2,106 ft **Area code** 760 **Zip** 92311

Information Desert Information Center, 831 Barstow Rd; 760/252-6060

In the heart of the beautiful high desert country, Barstow is a former frontier town that has become one of the fastest-growing cities in San Bernardino County. Once a desert junction for overland wagon trains and an outfitting station for Death Valley expeditions, Barstow thrives on nearby military installations and a $15-million tourist trade. It is the hub of three major highways that carry tourists into the Mojave Desert.

What to See and Do

Afton Canyon. Created in prehistoric times when Lake Manix broke through, chiseling a gorge through layers of multicolored rock. Primitive camping (fee). 40 mi E on I-15.

Calico Early Man Site. Archaeological digs; stone tool artifacts fashioned by early man approx 200,000 yrs ago are still visible in the walls of the excavations. Oldest evidence of human activity in the Western Hemisphere. Only New World site that Louis S. B. Leakey ever worked on; he served as project director until his death. Two master pits open for viewing; small museum. (Wed-Sun;

closed hols) Guided tours. 18 mi E via I-15, Minneola Rd exit, then 2¾ mi on graded dirt road. For further information contact California Desert Information Center, 831 Barstow Rd. Phone 760/252-6060. **FREE**

Calico Ghost Town Regional Park. Restored 1880s mining town. For six decades a dust-shrouded ghost town; privately restored in 1954. General store, old schoolhouse, the Maggie Mine, collection of paintings in "Lil's Saloon," print, pottery, basket, and leather shops; tramway, RR, mine tours; shooting gallery. (See SPECIAL EVENTS) Nearby are the Calico Mtns, which yielded $86 million in silver in 15 yrs. Camping (some hookups; fee). (Daily; closed Dec 25) 10 mi E via I-15, then 4 mi N on Ghost Town Rd. Phone 760/254-2122. **¢¢¢** East of Calico is

Odessa Canyon. Rock-studded landscape created by volcanic action. Erosion has etched striking rock formations. No cars.

Factory Merchants Outlet Mall. More than 90 outlet stores. (Daily) 2552 Mercantile Way. Phone 760/253-7342.

Mojave River Valley Museum. Rock and mineral displays, photographs, archaeology and RR displays, Native American exhibits. (Daily; closed hols) 270 E Virginia Way. Phone 760/256-5452. **Donation**

Mule Canyon and Fiery Gulch. Cathedral-like rocks, S-shaped formations, crimson walls, natural arches. No cars. 14 mi NE.

Rainbow Basin. Colorful geologic display of a syncline and hogbacks on the four-mi one-way drive. No motorhomes. 10 mi N on Old Irwin Rd.

Special Events

Calico Hullabaloo. Calico Ghost Town. World tobacco-spitting championships, old miner's stew cook-off, flapjack races, horseshoe pitching championships. Palm Sunday wkend. Phone 760/254-2122.

Calico Spring Festival. Calico Ghost Town. Fiddle and banjo contests, bluegrass music, gunfights, 1880s games, clogging hoedown. Mother's Day wkend. Phone 760/254-2122.

Calico Days. Calico Ghost Town. Country music, Wild West parade, national gunfight stunt championship, burro race, 1880s games. Columbus Day wkend. Phone 760/254-2122.

Calico Fine Arts Festival. Calico Ghost Town. Native American dance and works of art by many of the West's foremost artists displayed along Main St. First wkend Nov. Phone 760/254-2122.

Motels/Motor Lodges

★★ BEST WESTERN DESERT VILLA INN. *1984 E Main St (92311). 760/256-1781; fax 760/256-9265; res 800/528-1234.* 95 rms, 2 story, 8 kit. units. S $68-$78; D $70-$80; each addl $5; kit. units $73-$76; under 12 free. Crib free. TV; cable (premium). Pool; whirlpool. Complimentary continental bkfst. Coffee in rms. Restaurant 5-9 pm. Ck-out 11 am. Coin lndry. Gift shop. Refrigerators, microwaves avail. Cr cds: A, D, DS, ER, MC, V.

D

★ DAYS INN. *1590 Coolwater Ln (92311). 760/256-1737; fax 760/256-7771; toll-free 800/329-7466.* 113 rms, 2 story. S $26.90-$36.90; D $39-$49; under 12 free; wkly rates. Pet accepted. TV; cable (premium). Heated pool. Complimentary continental bkfst. Restaurant adj. Ck-out 11 am. Coin lndry. Some refrigerators. Cr cds: A, C, DS, MC, V.

D SC

Restaurant

★★ IDLE SPURS STEAK HOUSE. *690 Old Hwy 58 (92311). 760/256-8888. www.idlespurs.com.* Hrs: 11 am-9:30 pm; Sat 4-9:30 pm; Sun 3-9 pm. Closed hols. Res accepted. Bar to 11 pm. Lunch $6.50-$9.95, dinner $10.95-$24.95. Specialty: prime rib. Patio dining. Western decor. Cr cds: A, DS, MC, V.

D

Beaumont

See also Hemet, Palm Springs, Redlands, Riverside, San Bernardino

Pop 9,685 **Elev** 2,573 ft
Area code 909 **Zip** 92223
Information Chamber of Commerce, PO Box 637; 909/845-9541

What to See and Do

Edward-Dean Museum of Decorative Arts. European and Asian furniture, bronzes, porcelains, rugs, paintings from 17th and 19th centuries. (Fri-Sun; closed hols, also Aug) 9401 Oak Glen Rd, in Cherry Valley. Phone 909/845-2626. **¢¢**

Special Event

Cherry Festival. Stewart Park. First full wkend June. Phone 909/845-9541.

Berkeley

(G-3) *See also Oakland, San Francisco, San Rafael, Sausalito*

Settled 1841 **Pop** 102,724 **Elev** 152 ft
Area code 510
Information Berkeley Convention & Visitors Bureau, 2015 Center St, 94704; 510/549-8710
Web www.berkeleycvb.com

Berkeley is the home of the principal campus of the University of California. With an average monthly high temperature of 64°F, Berkeley regards itself as "one of America's most refreshing cities."

Named for George Berkeley, Bishop of Cloyne, an 18th-century Irish philosopher, the area was once a part of the vast Rancho San Antonio. Shortly after a group of developers bought the townsite, the College of California was founded—later to become the University of California.

The town's population was increased by refugees from the San Francisco earthquake and fire of 1906. In September of 1923, 25 percent of Berkeley was destroyed by fire. Quickly rebuilt, the city government instituted one of the most efficient fire-prevention systems in the country.

What to See and Do

Bade Institute of Biblical Archaeology. Devoted to archaeology of Palestine from 3200-600 B.C. Bible collection has documents from 5th-18th centuries (by appt only). Museum (Tues-Thurs; closed hols). Pacific School of Religion, 1798 Scenic Ave. Phone 510/848-0528. **FREE**

Berkeley Marina. Public fishing pier (free); bait and tackle shop; sportfishing boat; 950 berths, 25 visitor berths.Protected sailing basin; four-lane boat ramp (fee). Motel, restaurants. ½ mi W of Eastshore Fwy, I-80, at W end of University Ave, on San Francisco Bay. Phone 510/644-6376.

Berkeley Rose Garden. Collection of 4,000 roses; 200 varieties. (Daily; best blooms mid-May-Sept) Euclid Ave and Eunice St. Phone 800/847-4823. **FREE**

Grizzly Peak Blvd. A winding drive along the crest of hills behind the city; it offers views of most of San Francisco Bay and the surrounding cities.

Judah L. Magnes Museum. Artistic, historical, and literary materials, incl ceremonial objects and textiles, trace Jewish life and culture throughout the world; Western Jewish History Center houses documentation of Jewish contributions to the history of the American West; research library of rare and illustrated Jewish books and manuscripts; permanent collection and changing exhibits of traditional and contemporary Jewish artists and themes. (Mon-Thurs, Sun; closed Jewish hols) 2911 Russell St, one blk N of Pine and Ashby. Phone 510/549-6950. **Donation**

Lindsay Museum. Wildlife museum incl nation's oldest and largest wildlife rehabilitation center. Birds and animals that can't be released back into the wild are displayed in creative habitats. (Tues-Sun) 12 mi E at 1931 1st Ave, Walnut Creek. Phone 925/935-1978. **¢¢**

Tilden Regional Park. The park's 2,078 recreational acres incl swimming (fee), swimming beach, bathhouse, fishing at Lake Anza; nature, hiking, bicycle, bridle trails, 18-hole golf (fee), picnicking, concessions. Environmental Education Center, Little Farm, Jewel Lake. Merry-go-round, pony and steam train rides (fee); botanical garden of native California plants. Park connects with East Bay Skyline National Trail at Inspiration Point. (Daily) E on CA 24 to Fish Ranch Rd exit, then W to Grizzly Peak Blvd, right to park. Phone 510/562-7275. **FREE**

University of California. (1873) 30,370 students. Covers more than 1,200 acres in the foothills of the east shore of San Francisco Bay. Instruction in fields of learning from agriculture to zoology. The oldest of nine campuses, its white granite buildings are surrounded by groves of oak trees; its 307-ft campanile can be seen from a great distance (elevator, fee). 2 mi E of Eastshore Fwy, I-80, at E end of University Ave. Phone 510/642-5215. On or near the campus are

Art Museum. Incl Hans Hofmann paintings, outdoor sculpture garden, Pacific Film Archive film program; 11 exhibition galleries. (Wed-Sun) 2626 Bancroft Way. Phone 510/642-0808. ¢¢¢

Botanical Garden. Many unusual plants, incl native, Asian, Australian, and South American collections and a redwood grove; visitor center. (Daily; closed Dec 25) Tours (Sat-Sun). 200 Centennial Dr in Strawberry Canyon. Phone 510/643-2755. ¢¢

Hearst Greek Theatre. Gift of William Randolph Hearst; an amphitheater where leading pop and jazz artists perform. At east Gate. Phone 510/642-9988.

International House. This is a fine example of Mission-revival architecture. The dome is visible for miles. Built in 1930, this was the second such institution in the world. It serves as home and program center for 600 foreign and American students. (Daily) Bancroft Way at Piedmont Ave. Phone 510/642-9490.

Lawrence Hall of Science. Hands-on exhibits and activities for all ages. Classes, films, planetarium shows, discovery labs, special events, and programs on a variety of scientific topics. (Daily; closed school hols) Centennial Dr, S of Grizzly Peak Blvd. Phone 510/642-5132. ¢¢¢

Phoebe Apperson Hearst Museum of Anthropology. Changing exhibits on ancient and modern lands and people. (Wed-Sun; closed school hols) On Bancroft Way, at end of College Ave. In Kroeber Hall. Phone 510/643-7648. ¢

Wildcat Canyon Regional Park. On 2,421 acres. Hiking, jogging, bicycle, and bridle trails. Picnicking. Interpretive programs. Bird-watching. (Daily) N of Tilden Regional Park, access from Tilden Nature Area. Phone 510/635-0138. **FREE**

Motel/Motor Lodge

★ **CAMPUS MOTEL.** *1619 University Ave (94703). 510/841-3844; fax 510/841-8134.* 23 rms, 2 story, 1 kit. No A/C. S $50-$55; D $72-$80; suites $100.80; kit. unit $100.80. TV; cable (premium). Complimentary coffee in rms. Restaurant nearby. Ck-out 11 am. Business servs avail. University of California 5 blks. Cr cds: A, MC, V.

Hotels

★ **HOTEL DURANT.** *2600 Durant Ave (94704). 510/845-8981; fax 510/486-8336; res 800/238-7268. www.hoteldurant.com.* 140 rms, 6 story. No A/C. S $130-$160; D $150-$175; each addl $15; suites $275-$350; under 12 free. Crib free. Limited covered valet parking $5/day. TV; cable (premium). Complimentary continental bkfst. Restaurant 11 am-10 pm. Bar. Ck-out noon, ck-in 3 pm. Meeting rms. Business servs avail. Airport transportation. Health club privileges. Some refrigerators, wet bars. City landmark (1928). Cr cds: A, D, DS, MC, V.

★ **HOTEL SHATTUCK PLAZA.** *2086 Allston Way (94704). 510/845-7300; fax 510/644-2088; toll-free 800/805-9889. hotelshattuckplaza.com.* 175 rms, 5 story. No A/C. S $69-$90; D $79-$100; each addl $15; suites from $100; under 12 free. Crib $6. TV; cable (premium). Complimentary continental bkfst. Restaurant 7 am-3 pm; closed Sat, Sun. Ck-out noon. Meeting rms. Business servs avail. City landmark (1910). Cr cds: A, D, DS, MC, V.

D

★★★ **RADISSON HOTEL BERKELEY MARINA.** *200 Marina Blvd (94710). 510/548-7920; fax 510/548-7944; res 800/333-3333. www.radisson.com/berkeleyca.* 375 rms, 4 story. S, D $134-$180; each addl $15; suites $500-$750; under 12 free. Crib free. TV; cable (premium), VCR avail. 2 indoor pools; poolside serv. Restaurant 6 am-11 pm. Bar 11-2 am; Sun to midnight. Ck-out noon. Meeting rms. Business center. In-rm modem link. Gift shop. Exercise equipt; sauna. Dockage. Wet bar in suites; microwaves avail. Some balconies, private patios. Luxury level. Cr cds: A, C, D, DS, ER, JCB, MC, V.

D

B&B/Small Inn

★ **BANCROFT HOTEL.** *2680 Bancroft Way (94704). 510/549-1000; fax 510/549-1070; toll-free 800/549-1002. www.bancrofthotel.com.* 22 rms, 3 story. No A/C. S, D $99-$119; under 12 free; higher rates special events (min stay). Parking $6. TV; cable, VCR. Complimentary continental bkfst. Restaurant nearby. Ck-out noon, ck-in 3. Business servs avail. Luggage handing. Many balconies. Built 1928. Totally nonsmoking. Cr cds: A, D, MC, V.

★★ **ROSE GARDEN INN.** *2740 Telegraph Ave (94705). 510/549-2145; fax 510/549-1085; toll-free 800/992-9005. www.rosegardeninn.com.* 40 rms. No A/C. S, D $99-$165. TV; VCR avail. Complimentary full bkfst, afternoon refreshments, coffee. Ck-out noon, ck-in 2 pm. Business servs avail. Many fireplaces. Some private patios. Some rms in 2 restored Victorian mansions; antiques. Some private decks; English country garden. Cr cds: A, D, DS, MC, V.

D

Restaurants

★ **AJANTA.** *1888 Solano Ave (94707). 510/526-4373. www.ajantarestaurant.com.* Hrs: 11:30 am-2:30 pm, 5:30-9:30 pm; Fri-Sun to 9:30 pm. Closed Thanksgiving, Dec 25. Res accepted. Indian menu. Wine, beer. Lunch, dinner $11.25-$13.25. Complete meals: lunch, dinner $13.75-$14.75. Specials change monthly. Street parking. Indian artwork depicts scenes from Ajanta caves. Totally nonsmoking. Cr cds: A, C, DS, MC, V.

★★ **CAFE ROUGE.** *1782 4th St (94710). 510/525-1440. www.caferouge.net.* Hrs: 11:30 am-9:30 pm; Mon to 3 pm; Fri, Sat to 10:30 pm. Closed hols. Res accepted. French bistro menu. Bar. Lunch $8-$13, dinner $8-$20. Specializes in meats, homemade charcuterie. Outdoor dining. Authentic meat market setting. Cr cds: A, MC, V.

D

★★★ **CHEZ PANISSE RESTAURANT AND CAFE.** *1517 Shattuck Ave (94709). 510/548-5525. www.chezpanisse.com.* Hrs: Café (upper level) 11:30 am-3 pm, 5-10:30 pm; Fri, Sat 11:30 am-4 pm, 5-11:30 pm; Restaurant dining rm (main floor) 6-9:15 pm. Closed Sun; Dec 25. Res accepted in café; required in dining rm. Contemporary Mediterranean menu. Wine list. A la carte entrees: lunch $15-$17, dinner $16-$20. Prix fixe: dinner $35-$65. Street parking. Cr cds: A, C, DS, MC, V.

D

★★ **GINGER ISLAND.** *1820 4th St (94710). 510/644-0444.* Hrs: 11:30 am-10 pm; Fri, Sat 10:30 am to 11 pm; Sun from 10:30 am. Res accepted. Bar. A la carte entrees: lunch $8.25-$14.50, dinner $8.50-$17. Specializes in American cuisine with Asian influences. Parking. Outdoor dining. Two dining rms; skylights, light and airy feeling. Totally nonsmoking. Cr cds: A, D, DS, MC, V.

D

★ **LALIME'S CAFE.** *1329 Gilman St (94706). 510/527-9838. www.lalimes.com.* Hrs: 5:30-10 pm; Fri, Sat to 10 pm; Sun 5-9 pm. Closed hols. Res accepted. Eclectic, Mediterranean menu. Bar. A la carte entrees: dinner $12.75-$19.95. Complete meals: dinner $22-$37. Specializes in unique lamb dishes, seasonal fresh produce. Own desserts. Street parking. Two-level dining area housed in a cottage. Cr cds: A, D, MC, V.

D

★★★ **MAZZINI TARTTORIA.** *2826 Telegraph Ave (94705). 510/848-5599.* Menu changes daily. Hrs: 11:30 am-2:30 pm, 5-10 pm. Res accepted. Wine, beer. Lunch $6.95-$12.95; din-

ner $9.25-$19.95. Children's menu. Entertainment. Cr cds: A, MC, V.
D

★★ O CHAME. *1830 4th St (94710). 510/841-8783.* Menu changes seasonally. Hrs: 11:30 am-3 pm, 5:30-9 pm; Fri, Sat 5:30-9:30 pm. Closed Sun. Res acepted. Wine, beer. Lunch $8.50-$15.50; dinner $8.50-$19.50. Entertainment. Cr cds: A, D, MC, V.
D

★ SANTA FE BAR AND GRILL. *1310 University Ave (94702). 510/841-4740.* Hrs: 11:30 am-3 pm, 5-11 pm; Fri, Sat to midnight. Res accepted. Bar to 1 am. A la carte entrees: lunch $5.95-$12.95, dinner $9-$19.95. Specializes in chicken, beef, fish. Own baking. Pianist. In turn-of-the-century Santa Fe Railroad depot; historic landmark. Cr cds: A, C, D, ER, MC, V.
D

★★★ SKATES ON THE BAY. *100 Seawall Dr (94710). 510/549-1900. www.citysearch.com.* Hrs: 11:30 am-10 pm; Fri, Sat to 10:30 pm; Sun brunch 10:30 am-3 pm. Closed Thanksgiving, Dec 25. Res accepted. Bar. Lunch $6.95-$17.95, dinner $10.95-$28.95. Sun brunch $6.95-$15.95. Children's menu. Specializes in grilled meats, fresh seafood, pasta. Parking. Pier leads to entrance. View of Golden Gate Bridge. Cr cds: A, C, D, DS, ER, MC, V.
D

Beverly Hills

See also Hollywood (L.A.), Los Angeles

Pop 31,971 **Elev** 225 ft **Area code** 310

Information Visitors Bureau, 239 S Beverly Dr, 90212; 310/248-1015 or 800/345-2210

Web www.bhvb.org

Beverly Hills, an independent community 5.6 square miles in area, is conveniently located near downtown Los Angeles and many gorgeous beaches. It is famous for its exclusive residential districts, home to many movie and TV personalities. It boasts an international shopping area with the celebrated Rodeo Drive as its hub.

Hotels

★★★ AVALON HOTEL. *9400 W Olympic Blvd (90212). 310/277-5221; fax 310/277-4928. www.avalon-hotel.com.* 86 rms, 5 story, 2 suites. Mar-May; S, D $225; suites $425; each addl $35; under 18 free; lower rates rest of yr. Crib avail. Pet accepted, some restrictions, fee. Valet parking avail. Pool, lifeguard. TV; cable (premium), VCR avail, CD avail. Complimentary coffee in rms, newspaper. Restaurant 6 am-midnight. Rm serv 24 hr. Bar. Ck-out noon, ck-in 3 pm. Meeting rm. Business servs avail. Bellhops. Concierge. Dry cleaning. Exercise equipt. Golf, 18 holes. Tennis, 10 courts. Picnic facilities. Video games. Cr cds: A, C, D, JCB, MC, V.
D SC

★★★★★ THE BEVERLY HILLS HOTEL. *9641 Sunset Blvd (90210). 310/276-2251; fax 310/281-2905; toll-free 800/283-8885. www.beverlyhillshotel.com.* The pink facade and green scripted sign of this world-famous landmark is testament to its 1912 beginnings. But the flashback stops there. Renovated rooms, suites, and bungalows are as luxurious as their location would suggest, including personal butlers available upon request. Lounge in a cabana by the pool, dine in the Polo Lounge, or grab a limo to nearby Rodeo Drive. 203 rms, 37 suites, 21 bungalows with 53 rms, 1-4 story, 12 kits. S $325; D $355; suites $545-$4,700; 1-4 bdrm kit. bungalows $365-$3,595; under 12 free. Crib free. Valet parking $19. TV; cable (premium), VCR (movies). Pool; whirlpool, poolside serv. Restaurant (see POLO LOUNGE). Rm serv 24 hrs. Ck-out noon. Meeting rms. Business servs avail. In-rm modem link. Concierge. Beauty shop. Shopping arcade. Airport transportation. Lighted tennis, pro. Exercise equipt. Cr cds: A, C, D, JCB, MC, V.
D

★★★ HILTON HOTEL. *9876 Wilshire Blvd (90210). 310/274-7777; fax 310/285-1313; toll-free 800/445-8667. www.hilton.com.* 581 rms, 8 story. S, D $195-$335; each addl $20; suites $500-$1,500; family rates. Crib free. Pet accepted. Garage parking $20, valet parking $21. TV; cable (premium), VCR avail. 2 heated pools; wading pool, poolside serv. Restaurant 6:30-11 pm; dining rm 5:30-11 pm. Rm serv 24 hrs. Bars 11:30-2 am. Ck-out noon. Meeting rms. Business center. In-rm modem link. Concierge. Shopping arcade. Barber, beauty shop. Exercise equipt. Some bathrm phones, refrigerators. Patio, balconies. Lanai rms around pool. Cr cds: A, C, D, DS, ER, JCB, MC, V.

D SC

★★ LUXE HOTEL RODEO DRIVE. *360 N Rodeo Dr (90210). 310/273-0300; fax 310/859-8730. www.luxehotels.com.* 86 rms, 3 story. S, D $225-$275; each addl $25; suites $350; under 17 free. Crib free. Valet parking $15, in/out $12. TV; cable. Complimentary coffee in rms. Restaurant 9 am-10:30 pm. Ck-out noon. Airport transportation. Tennis privileges. Health club privileges. Some refrigerators. Cr cds: A, C, D, DS, ER, JCB, MC, V.

D SC

★★★★★ THE PENINSULA BEVERLY HILLS. *9882 S Santa Monica Blvd (90212). 310/551-2888; fax 310/788-2319; res 800/225-5549. www.peninsula.com.* Bright red flowers adorn the top of the entranceway of this French-Renaissance-style hotel near Rodeo Drive and Century City. The 196 rooms include 36 suites and 16 villas, the latter of which are clustered around a fountain courtyard. Tea in the Living Room, lunch at the Roof Garden, and the Dom Perignon Sunday brunch are some of the dining highlights. 196 units, 5 story, 32 suites, 16 villas (2 story, 1-2 bedrm). S, D $395; each addl $35; suites, villas $600-$3,000; under 12 free; wkend rates. Crib free. Valet parking $21. TV; cable (premium), VCR (movies). Rooftop pool; whirlpool, poolside serv. Complimentary beverages on arrival. Restaurant (see also THE BELVEDERE). Rm serv 24 hrs. Bar from 11:30 am; pianist. Meeting rms. Business center. In-rm modem link. Concierge. Gift shop. Airport transportation. Tennis privileges. 18-hole golf privileges, pro, putting green, driving range. Exercise equipt; sauna. Massage. Bathrm phones, minibars; many wet bars. Balconies. Cr cds: A, C, D, DS, ER, JCB, MC, V.

D

★★★★★ RAFFLES L'ERMITAGE BEVERLY HILLS. *9291 Burton Way (90210). 310/278-3344; fax 310/278-8247; toll-free 800/800-2113. www.lermitagehotel.com.* "The luxury of technology" is the motto of this business-savvy destination stepping confidently into the new millennium. The Mitsubishi 40-inch screen television, Bose speakers, and cellular phones are just the beginning. Oversized accommodations are designed for conducting in-room business and the Euro-Asian design has an urban minimalist feel. Visit the rooftop pool for a breathtaking 360-degree view. 124 rms, 8 story, 11 kit. suites. S, D, $385-$3,800. Crib free. Pet accepted, some restrictions. In/out garage parking $21. TV; cable (premium), DVD/CD (movies). Restaurant open 24 hrs. Rm serv 24 hrs. Bar 11-1 am. Meeting rms. Business servs avail. In-rm modem link. Concierge. Airport transportation. Exercise rm; sauna, steam rm. Massage. Pool; poolside serv. Bathrm phones, minibars. Balconies. Luxury level. Cr cds: A, C, D, DS, ER, JCB, MC, V.

D

★★★★ REGENT BEVERLY WILSHIRE. *9500 Wilshire Blvd (90212). 310/275-5200; fax 310/274-2851; toll-free 800/545-4000. www.regenthotels.com.* Located at the intersection of Wilshire Boulevard and

Shops along Rodeo Drive

Rodeo Drive, the Regent Beverly Wilshire is steps from one of the greatest streets of retail stores in the world. After a day of serious shopping, guests at the hotel can be pampered by a relaxing massage in the spa or by their personal room attendant, available to fulfill guests' every need. After a rejuvinating bath in the marble-lined bathroom, head to the bar, a premier see-and-be-seen spot in Beverly Hills. 395 rms, 10 and 12 story, 120 suites. S, D $345-$460; suites $560-$7,500; under 16 free. Pet accepted. Covered parking, valet $21. TV; cable (premium), VCR avail (movies). Pool; whirlpool, poolside serv. Restaurant (see THE DINING ROOM). Rm serv 24 hrs. Bar 11-2 am; entertainment. Ck-out noon. Convention facilities. Business center. In-rm modem link. Concierge. Gift shops. Beauty salon. Fitness center; sauna, steam rm. Massage. Bathrm phones, refrigerators. Some balconies. Cr cds: A, C, D, DS, ER, JCB, MC, V.

D

★★★ **RENAISSANCE BEVERLY HILLS.** *1224 S Beverwil Dr (90035). 310/277-2800; fax 310/203-9537; toll-free 800/468-3571.* 137 rms, 12 story, 21 suites. S, D $175-$225; suites $350-$1,000; family, wkend rates. Crib free. Covered parking $17. TV; cable (premium), VCR. Heated pool; poolside serv. Restaurant 7 am-10 pm. Rm serv 24 hrs. Bar 11-2 am. Ck-out noon. Meeting rms. Business center. In-rm modem link. Concierge. Exercise equipt. Health club privileges. Minibars. Balconies. Cr cds: A, C, D, DS, JCB, MC, V.

B&B/Small Inn

★★ **CARLYLE INN.** *1119 S Robertson Blvd (90035). 310/275-4445; fax 310/859-0496; toll-free 800/227-5953.* 32 rms, 5 story. S $110; D $120; each addl $10; suites $180-$200; under 10 free. Crib free. TV; cable, VCR (movies $3.50). Complimentary full bkfst; afternoon refreshments. Complimentary coffee in rms. Restaurant nearby. Ck-out noon, ck-in 2 pm. Business servs avail. In-rm modem link. Bellhops. Valet serv. Concierge serv. Exercise equipt. Whirlpool. Rms are on four levels of circular terraces overlooking a lush courtyard, terrace and spa. Cr cds: A, C, D, DS, JCB, MC, V.

D SC

All Suites

★★★ **BEVERLY HILLS PLAZA HOTEL.** *10300 Wilshire Blvd (90024). 310/275-5575; fax 310/278-3325; res 800/800-1234. www.complacestostay.com.* 116 suites, 5 story. S, D $155-$159. Crib avail. Pet accepted. TV; cable (premium), VCR avail. Heated pool; whirlpool, poolside serv. Restaurant 7 am-10 pm. Bar. Ck-out noon. Meeting rm. Business servs avail. In-rm modem link. Gift shop. Exercise equipt. Refrigerators, minibars. Many balconies. Garden; tropical plants. Cr cds: A, D, DS, JCB, MC, V.

D SC

Restaurants

★★★★ **THE BELVEDERE.** *9882 Little Santa Monica Blvd (90212). 310/788-2306. www.peninsula.com.* Inhabited by negotiating power brokers by day and romantics by night, The Belvedere is one of the premier choices for sophisticated hotel dining in Los Angeles. Servers manage to anticipate diners' every need, making every guest feel special. The California/French food with Asian overtones is well-prepared and uses many exotic ingredients that will awaken the palate. French, Continental menu. Hrs: 6:30 am-2:30 pm, 6-10:30 pm; Sun brunch 11 am-2:30 pm. Bar. Wine cellar. Res accepted. A la carte entrees: bkfst, lunch $16-$22, dinner $24-$31. Champagne brunch $52. Children's menu. Guitarist or harpist Sun brunch. Valet parking. Outdoor dining in partially covered terrace. Totally nonsmoking. Cr cds: A, MC, V.

D

★★★ **CRUSTACEAN.** *9646 Little Santa Monica Blvd (90210). 310/205-8990. www.antranbusinesscorp.com.* Hrs: 11:30 am-10:30 pm; Fri to 11:30 pm; Sat 5:30-11:30 pm. Closed Sun, hols. Res required. Asian, French menu. Bar. Wine list. A la carte entrees: lunch $11.95-$19.95, dinner $17.95-$34.95. Specialties: garlic-roasted crab, colossal royal prawns with garlic noodles, whole roasted dungeness crab. Pianist. Valet parking. Outdoor dining. Atmosphere is replica of 1930s French Colonial estate. Overlooks bamboo garden verandas. Cr cds: A, D, MC, V.

D

★★ **DA PASQUALE CAFE.** *9749 Santa Monica Blvd (90210). 310/859-3884.* Hrs: 11:30 am-3 pm, 5-10 pm; Fri to 11 pm; Sat 5-11 pm. Closed Sun, hols. Res accepted; required wkends. Italian menu. Wine, beer. A la carte entrees: lunch $7-$15, dinner $15-$30. Specializes in pizza, pasta, fish. Patio dining. Italian atmosphere. Totally nonsmoking. Cr cds: A, D, DS, MC, V.

D

★★ **DA VINCI.** *9737 Little Santa Monica Blvd (90212). 310/273-0960.* Hrs: 11:30 am-2:30 pm, 5:30-10:30 pm; Sat, Sun from 5:30 pm. Res accepted. Italian menu. Bar. A la carte entrees: lunch $10-$15, dinner $15-$30. Specialty: osso buco Milanese. Own pasta, desserts. Valet parking. Cr cds: A, DS, MC, V.

D

★ **DELMONICO'S SEAFOOD GRILLE.** *9320 W Pico Blvd (90035). 310/550-7737.* Specializes in lobster. Hrs: 11:30 am-10 pm; Sat 4-10 pm; Sun 10 am-10 pm. Res accepted. Wine list. Lunch $11.95-$25.95; dinner $11.95-$45.00. Brunch $18.95. Entertainment. Private booths. Cr cds: A, MC, V.

D

★★★ **THE DINING ROOM.** *9500 Wilshire Blvd (90212). 310/275-5200. www.regenthotels.com.* Continental menu. Specialities: egg white omelette with goat cheese, Maine lobster, cowboy steak, loin of lamb, veal chop. Hrs: 6:30 am-2:30 pm, 6-10 pm; Sun only 7 am-noon. Res accepted. Bar 11-1:30 am. Pianist. Extensive wine list. A la carte entrees: bkfst $13-$18, lunch $17-$28, dinner $19-$36. Prix fixe: dinner $40. Valet parking. Jacket required wkends. Fri, Sat dancing res required Cr cds: A, C, D, DS, ER, MC, V.

D

★★★★★ **GINZA SUSHIKO.** *218 N Rodeo Dr (90210). 310/247-8939.* If you can afford the extraordinarily high price tag, Ginza Sushiko is simply the only restaurant this side of Tokyo that can deliver such astonishing sushi. The decor is minimal, offering nothing to distract diners from the exquisite raw fish before them. To truly experience this exceptional restaurant, put yourself in the chef's hands and order omakase, letting him decide exactly what you will eat. The only downside is that Ginza Sushiko will make any other sushi restaurant pale by comparison. Japanese cuisine. Specialties: fugu platters, tuna in white miso, halibut ponzu. Hrs: 4-11 pm. Closed Sun, Mon. Res required. Prix fixe: $300. Valet parking. Jacket. Cr cds: MC, V.

D

★★★ **GRILL ON THE ALLEY.** *9560 Dayton Way (90210). 310/276-0615. www.thegrill.com.* Hrs: 11:30 am-11 pm; Fri, Sat to midnight; Sun 5-9 pm. Closed hols. Res accepted. Bar. A la carte entrees: lunch $12-$20, dinner $15-$30. Specializes in fresh seafood, steak, chops. Valet parking. Turn-of-the-century decor. Cr cds: A, D, MC, V.

D

★★★ **IL CIELO.** *9018 Burton Way (90211). 310/276-9990. www.ilcielo.com.* Hrs: 11:30 am-3 pm, 6-10:30 pm; Fri, Sat to 11 pm. Closed Sun, hols. Res accepted. Northern Italian menu. Beer. Wine list. A la carte entrees: lunch $10-$15, dinner $15-$25. Specializes in fresh seafood, veal. Own pasta, pastries. Valet parking. Outdoor dining. Gardens, fountains. Cr cds: A, D, MC, V.

D

★★ **IL PASTAIO.** *400 N Canon Dr (90210). 310/205-5444.* Hrs: 11 am-11 pm; Sun 5-10 pm. Closed hols. Italian menu. Bar. A la carte entrees: lunch $8.50-$13, dinner $9.50-$15. Specializes in pasta. Valet parking. Patio dining. Contemporary decor, artwork. Cr cds: A, D, MC, V.

D

★★★ **LA SCALA.** *410 N Canon Dr (90210). 310/275-0579. www.menuserve.com.* Hrs: 11:30 am-10 pm; Fri, Sat to 10:30 pm. Closed Sun, hols. Res accepted. Italian menu. Bar. Wine list. A la carte entrees: lunch $10-$20, dinner $15-$30. Specialties: cannelloni alla Gigi, minestrone, chopped salad. Valet parking. Outdoor dining. Totally nonsmoking. Cr cds: A, D, DS, MC, V.

D

★★★ LAWRY'S THE PRIME RIB. *100 N La Cienega Blvd (90211). 310/652-2827. www.lawrysonline.com.* Hrs: 5-10 pm; Fri to 11 pm; Sat 4:30-11 pm; Sun 4-10 pm. Closed Dec 25. Res accepted. Bar. Dinner $19.95-$27.95. Specialties: prime rib, fish, and lobster tails. Own desserts. Valet parking. Limited menu. Tableside serv. Cr cds: A, C, D, DS, ER, MC, V.

D

★★ THE MANDARIN. *430 N Camden Dr (90210). 310/859-0638.* Hrs: 11:30 am-10 pm; Fri to 11 pm; Sat 5-11 pm; Sun 5-10 pm. Closed hols. Res accepted. Chinese menu. Bar. A la carte entrees: lunch $15-$20, dinner $20-$25. Specialties: crispy chicken salad, Peking duck, steamed fillet of sea bass. Valet parking (dinner). Chinese decor. Totally nonsmoking. Cr cds: A, C, D, ER, MC, V.

D

★★★ MAPLE DRIVE. *345 N Maple Dr (90066). 310/274-9800. www.restaurant-pages.com/mapledrive.* Hrs: 11:30 am-2:30 pm, 6-10 pm. Closed Sun, hols. Res accepted. Bar. A la carte entrees: lunch $15-$22, dinner $16-$32. Specialties: fried calamari, tuna tartar, grilled swordfish. Pianist. Valet parking (dinner). Terrace dining. Exhibition kitchen. Changing display of artwork. Cr cds: A, C, D, DS, ER, MC, V.

D

★★★ MATSUHISA. *129 N La Cienega Blvd (90211). 310/659-9639.* Japanese menu. Hrs: 11:45 am-2:15 pm, 5:45-10:15 pm; Sat, Sun from 5:45 pm. Closed hols. Res accepted. Japanese menu. Wine, beer. Lunch $20-$30, dinner $40-up. Omakase dishes $50-$100. Specializes in gourmet seafood, sushi. Valet parking. Totally nonsmoking. Cr cds: A, D, MC, V.

D

★★ MCCORMICK & SCHMICK'S - BEVERLY HILLS. *206 N Rodeo Dr (90210). 310/859-0434. www.mccormickandschmicks.com.* Specializes in salmon, stuffed halibut, oysters. Hrs: 11:30 am-midnight; Sun to 10 pm. Res accepted. Wine, beer. Lunch $9-$15; dinner $13-$25. Children's menu. Entertainment. Cr cds: A, D, DS, JCB, MC, V.

D

★★ MR. CHOW. *344 N Camden Dr (90210). 310/278-9911. www.mrchow.com.* Specializes in Peking duck, drunken fish, green prawn. Hrs: Noon-2:30 pm, 6-11:30 pm. Res accepted. Wine, beer. Lunch $9.50-$17; dinner $19.50-$42. Entertainment. Cr cds: A, D, MC, V.

D

★★ P. F. CHANG'S. *121 N La Cienega Blvd (90048). 310/854-6467. www.pfchangs.com.* Specializes in Chang's spicy chicken, lemon pepper shrimp. Hrs: 11 am-11 pm; Fri, Sat to midnight. Wine, beer. Lunch, dinner $6.95-$12.95. Entertainment. Cr cds: A, D, MC, V.

D

★★★ POLO LOUNGE. *9641 Sunset Blvd (90210). 310/276-2251. www.beverlyhillshotel.com.* Hrs: 7-2 am; Sun brunch 11 am-3 pm. Res accepted. Bar. Wine cellar. A la carte entrees: bkfst $8-$14, lunch $14-$24, dinner $18-$28. Sun brunch $39. Specializes in Californian cuisine. Pianist. Valet parking. Outdoor dining. Cr cds: D, MC, V.

D

★★★ PREGO. *362 N Camden Dr (90210). 310/277-7346.* Hrs: 11:30 am-11:30 pm; Sun 5-11 pm. Closed Thanksgiving, Dec 25. Res accepted. Northern Italian menu. Bar. A la carte entrees: lunch $8-$18, dinner $15-$28. Specializes in homemade pasta, fresh fish, chicken. Valet parking evenings. Oak-burning pizza oven and mesquite grill. Cr cds: A, C, D, ER, MC, V.

D

★★★ RAFFLES L'ERMITAGE BEVERLY HILLS. *9291 Burton Way (90210). 310/278-3344. www.lermitagehotel.com.* Distinct Mediterranean cuisine. Specialties: foie gras, house-smoked salmon, duck confit, lamb porterhouse, and venison. Hrs: 6-11:30 am, 11:30 am-2:30 pm, 6:30-10:30 pm. Bkfst, lunch, dinner: $25-$38. Valet parking. Res accepted.

Children's menu. Bar. Cr cds: A, C, D, DS, ER, JCB, MC, V.

D

★★★ **REIGN.** *180 N Robertson Blvd (90211). 310/273-4463.* Soul cuisine menu. Hrs: 6-11 pm; Fri, Sat 6 pm-midnight; Sun brunch 11 am-3:30 pm. Wine, beer. Dinner $18-$27.50. Brunch $28. Entertainment: Jazz Sat. Cr cds: A, C, D, MC, V.

D

★ **R J'S THE RIB JOINT.** *252 N Beverly Dr (90210). 310/274-7427.* Hrs: 11:30 am-10 pm; Sat to 11 pm; Sun 3-10 pm; early-bird dinner Mon-Sat 3-6 pm. Res accepted. Southwestern menu. Bar. Lunch $7.50-$12, dinner $10-$25. Children's menu. Specializes in ribs, chicken, fish. Parking. Totally nonsmoking. Cr cds: A, C, D, DS, ER, MC, V.

★★★ **RUTH'S CHRIS STEAKHOUSE.** *224 S Beverly Dr (90212). 310/859-8744. www.ruthschris.com.* Specializes in BBQ shrimp, cowboy rib eye, creamed spinach. Hrs: 5-10 pm; Sun to 9:30 pm. Res accepted. Wine, beer. Dinner $23.95-$32.95. Entertainment. Cr cds: A, C, D, DS, MC, V.

D

★★★★ **SPAGO BEVERLY HILLS.** *176 N Canon Dr (90210). 310/385-0880. www.wolfgangpuck.com.* The celebrity scene remains white-hot at Wolfgang Puck's flagship restaurant, located in the heart of monied Beverly Hills. The dining room is as exciting to look at as the stunning people who are in it, though Puck's famous Californian cuisine still manages to attract attention. If what you want is a bona fide L.A. experience, Spago is still the place to be. Continental menu. Specializes in gourmet pizza, lobster ravioli, fresh fish. Hrs: 5:30-10:30 pm. Res accepted. Dinner $14.95-$28.95. Valet parking. Cr cds: A, C, D, DS, MC, V.

D

★★ **STINKING ROSE.** *55 N La Cienega Blvd (90211). 310/652-7673. www.thestinkingrose.com.* Hrs: 11 am-10 pm; Fri, Sat to midnight. Res accepted. Italian menu. Bar to 2 am. A la carte entrees: lunch $8-$11, dinner $8-$25. Specialties: 40-clove garlic chicken, bagna calda. Valet parking. Casual, eclectic decor. Cr cds: A, D, MC, V.

D

Unrated Dining Spot

ED DEBEVIC'S. *134 N La Cienega Blvd (90211). 310/659-1952. www.eddebevics.com.* Hrs: 11:30 am-10 pm; Fri, Sat to midnight. Closed Thanksgiving, Dec 25. Bar. Lunch, dinner $4.50-$7.95. Specializes in meatloaf, hamburgers, chicken. Own desserts. Valet parking. 1950s-style diner; memorabilia of the era. Staff provides entertainment: singing, dancing. Cr cds: A, C, D, DS, ER, MC, V.

D

Big Basin Redwoods State Park

(A-1) *See also Santa Cruz*

(23 mi N of Santa Cruz via CA 9, 236)

This 20,000-acre park is one of the most popular parks in California. The area was set aside as the state's first redwood preserve in 1902. Its redwood groves include trees 300 feet high. There are about 50 miles of hiking and riding trails, plus numerous picnic sites and campgrounds with full facilities (limit eight persons per site; reservations required in summer). Ranger-conducted nature programs, held in the summer, include campfire programs and guided hikes. Flora and fauna of the park are on display in exhibits at the nature lodge. Supplies are available at a concession and a store. Standard fees. Phone 831/338-8860.

Big Bear Lake

(E-6) *See also Lake Arrowhead, Redlands, Riverside, San Bernardino*

Pop 5,351 **Elev** 6,754 ft
Area code 909 **Zip** 92315

Information Big Bear Lake Resort Association, 630 Bartlett Rd;

909/866-6190, 909/866-7000, or 800/4-BIG-BEAR

Web www.bigbearinfo.com

This is a growing, year-round recreation area in the San Bernardino National Forest (see SAN BERNARDINO). Fishing, canoeing, parasailing, windsurfing, riding, golfing, bicycling, picnicking, hiking, and camping are available in summer; skiing and other winter sports are also popular in season.

What to See and Do

Alpine Slide at Magic Mountain. Incl Alpine bobsled-type ride (all yr), water slide (summer), and inner tubing (winter). Miniature golf (all yr). Video games; snack bar. (Daily) Approx ¼ mi W on CA 18. Phone 909/866-4626.

Big Bear Mountain Resort. Skiing, seasonal passes; also golf course and driving range; resort. N on I-215 (US 395), exit E on 10 Fwy, exit Orange Ave in Redlands, left at Hwy 38 (Lagonia Ave), left on Big Bear Blvd, left on Moonridge Rd. Phone 909/585-2519.

***Big Bear Queen* Tour Boat.** Paddlewheeler provides 90-min narrated tour of Big Bear Lake. Dinner and champagne cruises also avail. (Apr-Nov, daily) Big Bear Marina, Paine Rd at Lakeview Dr. Phone 909/866-3218.

Horseback riding.

Bear Mountain Riding Stables. One- to two-hr trail rides through San Bernardino National Forest; panoramic views of Big Bear Lake. Sunset hay rides avail (res required). (Memorial Day-Labor Day) Bear Mtn Ski Resort (see) at top of Lassen Dr. Phone 909/878-4677. ¢¢¢¢¢

Rockin' K Riding Stables. One- to four-hr trail rides through San Bernardino Natl Forest; views from highest elevations in Big Bear Valley. Sunset, twilight, moonlight, and overnight rides avail (res required for all). (May-Nov) 731 Tulip Ln. Phone 909/878-4677. ¢¢¢¢¢

Skiing.

Big Bear Mountain Ski Resort. Quad, high-speed quad, three triple, four double chairlifts, two Pomalifts; patrol, school, rentals; snowmaking; cafe, two restaurants, bar. Longest run 2½ mi; vertical drop 1,665 ft. (Mid-Nov-Apr, daily) Hiking, nine-hole golf course (May-mid-Oct, daily). 2 mi S off CA 18.

Snow Summit. Two high-speed quads, two quads, two triples, five double chairlifts; patrol, school, rentals, snowmaking; five restaurants, two bars. Longest run 1¼ mi; vertical drop 1,200 ft. (Mid-Nov-Apr, daily) Night skiing, snowboarding. Chairlift also operates in summer (May-early Sept). ½ mi S off CA 18. Phone 909/866-5766. ¢¢¢¢¢

Special Event

Old Miner's Days. Festival celebrating 19th-century frontier heritage, with cowboy music, parades, quick-draw contest, children's activities. Phone 909/866-4607. Three wkends July.

Motels/Motor Lodges

★ BIG BEAR LAKE INN. *39471 Big Bear Blvd (92315). 909/866-3477; fax 909/878-9187; toll-free 800/843-0103. www.bigbearlakecentral.com.* 52 rms, 2 story, 8 kit. units. S $39-$129; D $59-$149; under 12 free. TV; cable. Heated pool; whirlpool. Complimentary continental bkfst. Restaurant nearby. Ck-out 11 am. Meeting rm. Downhill/x-country ski 3½ mi. Refrigerators. Picnic tables. Cr cds: A, C, D, DS, MC, V.

★★ HOLIDAY INN BIG BEAR CHATEAU. *42200 Moonridge Rd (92315). 909/866-6666; fax 909/866-8988; toll-free 800/232-7466. www.holiday-inn.com/bigbearlake.* 80 rms, 3 story. S, D $99-$249; each addl $10; suites $150-$600. TV; cable. Heated pool; whirlpool. Restaurant 7 am-2 pm, 5-9 pm. Bar 5 pm-2 am; entertainment wkends. Ck-out noon. Meeting rms. Business servs avail. Bellhops. Downhill ski 1 mi. Fireplaces; microwaves avail. Balconies. European chateau-style decor. Cr cds: A, C, D, DS, MC, V.

★★ ROBIN HOOD INN. *40797 Lakeview Dr (92315). 909/866-4643; fax 909/866-4645; toll-free 800/990-9956. www.robinhoodinn.com.* 23 rms,

2 story, 5 suites. S, D $49-$159; suite $84-$199; higher rates hols. Pet accepted, some restrictions. TV; cable, VCR avail (free movies). Restaurant opp 6 am-11 pm. Ck-out 11 am. Meeting rm. Business servs avail. Downhill/x-country ski ½ mi. Whirlpool. Massage. Many refrigerators, some fireplaces, wet bars. Grill, picnic table, sun deck. Cr cds: A, MC, V.

Resorts

★ **GOLDMINE LODGE AND DOC'S GET AWAY.** *42268 Moonridge Rd and 402 Georgia St (92315). 909/866-5118; fax 909/866-3627; toll-free 800/641-2327. www.bigbear-goldmine-lodge.com.* 11 units, 2 story, 6 kit. suites. S, D $59-$89; kit. suites $69-$145; ski plans. Crib free. TV; cable (premium). Playground. Complimentary continental bkfst. Coffee in rms. Restaurant nearby. Ck-out 11 am. Downhill/x-country ski 1 mi. Whirlpool. Lawn games. Microwaves avail; fireplace in suites. Picnic tables, grills. Set amid pine forest in San Bernardino Mountains. Cr cds: A, DS, MC, V.

★★ **MARINA RESORT.** *40770 Lakeview Dr (92315). 909/866-7545; fax 909/866-6705; toll-free 800/600-6000. www.marinaresort.com.* 42 rms, 3 story, 3 kit. units. S, D $99-$135; each addl $8; kit. units $165-$295. Crib $6. TV; cable (premium). Heated pool; whirlpool. Complimentary continental bkfst, coffee in rms. Restaurant adj 5 am-11 pm. Ck-out 11 am. Business servs avail. Downhill/x-country ski 1 mi. Driving cage, putting green. Refrigerators; some fireplaces, in-rm whirlpools. Balconies, patios. Picnic tables, grills. Lawn games. Rms overlook lake. Private beach. Cr cds: A, DS, MC, V.

★★★ **NORTHWOODS RESORT & CONFERENCE CENTER.** *40650 Village Dr (92315). 909/866-3121; fax 909/878-2122; toll-free 800/866-3121. www.northwoodsresort.com.* 151 rms, 4 story, 9 suites. S, D $119-$149; each addl $10; suites $199-$499; under 18 free; ski plans; hol wkends (2-day min). Crib free. TV; cable. Heated pool; whirlpool, poolside serv. Coffee in rms. Restaurant 7 am-10 pm. Bar 3 pm-midnight. Ck-out noon. Meeting rms. Business servs avail. Bellhops. Concierge. Gift shop. Downhill/x-country ski 2 mi. Exercise equipt; sauna. Bicycles. Massage. Some fireplaces. Some wet bar, whirlpool, refrigerator in suites. Some patios, balconies. Cr cds: A, D, DS, MC, V.

D SC

B&Bs/Small Inns

★★★ **EAGLES NEST BED AND BREAKFAST.** *41675 Big Bear Blvd (92315). 909/866-6465; fax 909/866-6025; toll-free 888/866-6465. www.bigbear.com/enbb.* 5 rms, 2 story, 5 cottages. S, D $110-$130; wkly rates. Pet accepted, some restrictions. TV. Full bkfst. Coffee in rms. Whirlpool. Ck-out 11 am, ck-in 2 pm. Downhill/x-country ski ¼ mi. Refrigerators, microwaves in cottages. Fireplaces. Western decor; antiques. Cr cds: A, DS, MC, V.

★★★ **SWITZERLAND HAUS BED AND BREAKFAST.** *41829 Seitzerland Dr (92315). 909/866-3729; toll-free 800/335-3729. www.switzerlandhaus.com.* 5 rms, 4 with shower only, 2 story. No A/C. No rm phones. S, D $115-$145; each addl $20; suite $165-$175. TV; cable, VCR (movies). Complimentary full bkfst. Coffee in rms. Restaurant nearby. Ck-out 11 am, ck-in 2 pm. Downhill ski; x-country ski on site. Sauna. Fireplace. Refrigerator, microwave in suite. Totally nonsmoking. Cr cds: A, DS, MC, V.

Cottage Colony

★★ **WILDWOOD.** *40210 Big Bear Blvd (92315). 909/878-2178; fax 909/878-3036.* 5 rms in main building, 2 story, 14 kit. cottages. S, D $49-$85; kit. cottages $70-$180; wkly rates. Pet accepted; $10/day. TV; cable, VCR avail. Heated pool; whirlpool. Playground. Complimentary coffee in rms/cottages. Restaurant nearby. Ck-out 11 am. Downhill/x-country ski 3 mi. Many fireplaces. Lawn games. Picnic tables, grills. Cr cds: A, D, DS, MC, V.

Villa/Condo

★★ **ESCAPE FOR ALL SEASONS.** *41935 Seitzerland Dr (92315). 909/866-7504; fax 909/866-7507; toll-free 800/722-4366. www.bigbearescape.com.* 60 kit. suites, 2 story. Nov-Mar: kit. suites $120-$360; wkly rates; lower rates rest of yr. Crib avail. TV; cable (premium), VCR (free movies). Ck-out 10 am. Business servs avail. Mountain biking. Downhill/x-country ski adj. Microwaves, fireplaces. Most balconies. Cr cds: A, DS, MC, V.

Restaurant

★★ **BLUE WHALE LAKESIDE RESTAURANT.** *350 Alden Rd (92315). 909/866-5771. www.bluewhalelakeside.com.* Hrs: 3-10 pm; Fri to 11 pm; Sat noon-midnight; Sun 9 am-10 pm; Sun brunch to 2 pm. Res accepted. Bar. Lunch $5.75-$7.50, dinner $13.95-$19.95. Sun brunch $9.95. Children's menu. Specializes in fresh seafood, beef, regional items. Oyster/sushi bar (summer). Salad bar. Pianist wkends. Parking. Outdoor dining. Late 19th-century building. Boat dock; view of lake. Cr cds: A, DS, MC, V.

D

Big Sur

(B-1) *See also Carmel, Carmel Valley, Monterey, Pacific Grove*

Pop 1,000 **Elev** 155 ft **Area code** 831 **Zip** 93920

Information Pfeiffer-Big Sur State Park, Big Sur Station #1; 831/667-2315

Big Sur is 30 miles south of Monterey on CA 1, with the Santa Lucia Range on the east and the Pacific Ocean on the west.

A scenic drive along Highway 1 provides 90 miles of views along the rocky Big Sur bluffs, past redwood forests, canyons, waterfalls, secluded beaches, and sheer mountains. This route provides access to many state parks south of Carmel. **Garrapata State Park**, seven miles south of Carmel, offers hiking, mountain biking, fishing, coastal access, tide pools, canyons, and whale watching in winter. **Andrew Molera State Park**, 21 miles south of Carmel, is Big Sur's largest state park and offers hiking and beach access along rugged headlands. **Pfeiffer-Big Sur State Park** contains a coastal redwood forest. Recreational opportunities include swimming and hiking. Picnicking and camping facilities are available (fee for camping). There is also a lodge, gift shop, and store. Naturalist programs are offered. Standard fees. **Julia Pfeiffer Burns State Park**, 36 miles south of Carmel, has a dramatic 80-ft waterfall accessed by a short trail. Camping facilities (fee).

Resorts

★★★★ **POST RANCH INN.** *CA 1 (93920). 831/667-2200; fax 831/667-2824; toll-free 800/527-2200. www.postranchinn.com.* If serenity is what you're searching for, this one-with-nature retreat will surely please you. Experience Mickey Muennig's "organic architecture" in a complex of cottages and tree houses set on 96 art-strewn acres. The inventive Sierra Mar restaurant has spectacular views. All this is accomplished while keeping a responsible commitment to resource conservation and waste management. 30 rms. S, D $395-$695; each addl $50; 2-day min wkends. Heated pool. Complimentary continental bkfst, refreshments in rms. Restaurant (see also SIERRA MAR). Ck-out 1 pm, ck-in 4 pm. Business servs avail. Luggage handling. Exercise equipt. Massage. In-rm whirlpools, refrigerators, fireplaces. Free wine tasting Sat. Cr cds: A, MC, V.

D

★★★ **VENTANA INN & SPA.** *CA 1 (93920). 831/667-2331; fax 831/667-0573; toll-free 800/628-6500. www.ventanainn.com.* 62 rms, 1-2 story. S, D $450; each addl $50; suites $525-$850. TV; cable, VCR (movies). 2 heated pools; poolside serv (summer). Complimentary continental bkfst, afternoon refreshments. Dining rm. Picnics. Bar 11 am-midnight. Ck-out 1 pm, ck-in 4:30 pm. Luggage handling. Exercise equipt; sauna.

Massage. Wet bars; many fireplaces; some whirlpools. Balconies. Sun deck. Cr cds: A, C, D, DS, MC, V.

D

Restaurants

★★★★ **CIELO BIG SUR.** *CA 1 (93920). 831/667-2331. www.ventanainn.com.* Guests of the Ventana Inn walk on a lush wooded trail to reach Cielo. The restaurant boasts stunning views of the surrounding mountains and the Pacific Ocean and has a rustic feel, with a large stone fireplace and beamed ceilings supported by towering timbers. Many of the herbs and vegetables included on the menu are grown on the property and the wine list features extensive offerings from California's central coast. Specializes in California dishes. Own baking. Hrs: noon-3 pm, 6-9 pm; Fri-Sun and hols 11 am-3 pm, 6-9:30 pm. Winter hrs vary. Bar to midnight; Mon-Thurs to 11 pm. Res accepted (dinner). A la carte entrees: lunch $9.50-$17, dinner $8.50-$30. Outdoor dining (lunch). Totally nonsmoking. Cr cds: A, DS, MC, V.

D

★ **NEPENTHE.** *CA 1 (93920). 831/667-2345. www.nepenthebigsur.com.* Hrs: 11:30 am-10 pm. No A/C. Bar. Lunch $9.75-$15.75, dinner $9.25-$24.50. Specializes in roast chicken, steak, fresh fish. Parking. Outdoor dining. 40-mile view of Pacific coastline. Family-owned. Cr cds: A, MC, V.

D

★★★★ **SIERRA MAR RESTAURANT.** *CA 1 (93920). 831/667-2800.* Dramatically perched on the edge of a cliff hanging above the craggy shores of the Pacific Ocean over 1,000 feet below, Sierra Mar has one of the best views on the West Coast or anywhere else. While the romance of the incredible setting tends to steal the show, the California-inspired French fare does an admirable job of holding its own against such stunning competition. Eclectic California cuisine. Menu changes daily. Hrs: noon-4 pm, 5:30-9:30 pm. Bar. Extensive wine list. Res accepted. A la carte entrees: lunch $7-$18, dinner $29.50-$33.50. Prix fixe: dinner $63. Outdoor dining (lunch). Totally nonsmoking. Cr cds: A, MC, V.

D

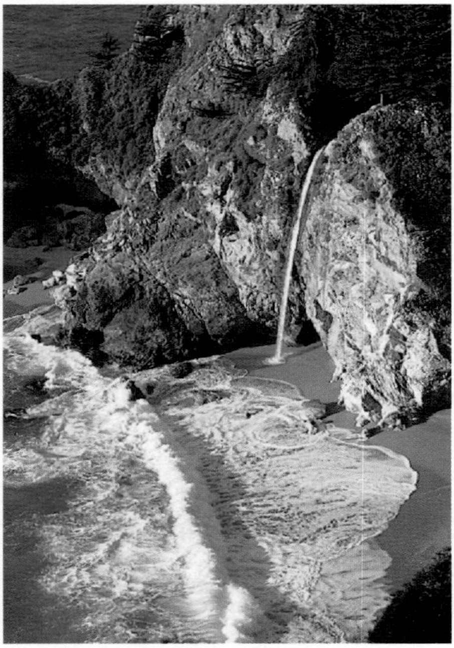

80-foot waterfall, Julia Pfeiffer State Park

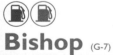

Bishop (G-7)

Pop 3,475 **Elev** 4,147 ft
Area code 760 **Zip** 93514

Information Bishop Area Chamber of Commerce and Visitors Bureau, 690 N Main St; 760/873-8405

Web www.bishopvisitor.com

What to See and Do

Ancient Bristlecone Pine Forest. These trees are estimated to be more than 4,600 yrs old, making them some of the oldest known living trees on earth. Naturalist programs. White Mtn Rd District Visitor Center (July 4-Labor Day, Mon-Fri). In the White and Inyo mountains of the Inyo National Forest (see). CA 168 E from Big Pine to

White Mtn Rd to Schulman Grove and Patriarch Grove. Contact visitor center, 798 N Main St. Phone 760/873-8405.

Laws Railroad Museum & Historical Site. Laws Post Office with old-fashioned equipment, 1883 depot, narrow-gauge locomotive, restored station agent's five-rm house; hand-operated gallows-type turntable used 1883-1960, when Laws was the northern terminus of the Laws-Keeler Branch of the Southern Pacific RR; water tower, pump house; mining exhibits; library and arts building, Western building, pioneer building, firehouse, bottle house, doctor's office, country store; Native American exhibit. (Daily, weather permitting; closed Jan 1, Thanksgiving, Dec 25) 5 mi NE on US 6, then ½ mi E on Silver Canyon Rd. Phone 760/873-5950. **Donation**

Special Events

Mule Days. Mule show and sale; concerts; barbecue; parade. Memorial Day wkend. Phone 760/872-4263.

Tri-County Fair, Wild West Rodeo. Labor Day wkend. Phone 760/872-4263.

Motels/Motor Lodges

★★ BEST WESTERN HOLIDAY SPA LODGE. *1025 N Main St (93514). 760/873-3543; fax 760/872-4777; toll-free 800/576-3543.* 89 rms, 1-2 story. S $60-$87; D $84-$97; each addl $5; higher rates hols. Crib $10. Pet accepted, some restrictions. TV; cable (premium). Pool; whirlpool. Complimentary coffee in rms. Ck-out noon. Coin lndry. X-country ski 20 mi. Fish cleaning, freezer facilities. Refrigerators, microwaves. Cr cds: A, C, D, DS, JCB, MC, V.
D SC

★ BISHOP THUNDERBIRD MOTEL. *190 W Pine St (93514). 760/873-4215; fax 760/873-6870; toll-free 800/828-2473.* 23 rms, 2 story. S $36-$55; D $44-$65; each addl $4. Crib $4. Pet accepted, some restrictions; $4. TV; cable (premium). Coffee in rms. Restaurant nearby. Ck-out 11 am. X-country ski 20 mi. Refrigerators, microwaves. Cr cds: A, C, D, DS, MC, V.
SC

★★ COMFORT INN. *805 N Main St (93514). 760/873-4284; fax 760/873-8563; toll-free 800/576-4080.* 52 rms, 2 story. S $64-$84; D $74-$84; each addl $5; suites $84-$90; higher rates hols. Crib $5. Pet accepted. TV; cable (premium). Heated pool; whirlpool. Complimentary continental bkfst, coffee in rms. Restaurant nearby. Ck-out 11 am. Coin lndry. Fish cleaning, freezer facilities. Refrigerators, microwaves; some wet bars. Picnic tables, grill. Cr cds: A, C, D, DS, MC, V.
D SC

★ MOTEL 6. *1005 N Main St (93514). 760/873-8426; fax 760/873-8060; res 800/662-1162.* 52 units, 2 story, 2 kits. S $39.95-$46; D $54-$64.95; each addl $10; kit. units $10 addl; higher rates: wkends, hols. Crib free. TV; cable (premium). Heated pool; whirlpool. Complimentary coffee in lobby. Restaurant opp open 24 hrs. Ck-out 11 am. Business servs avail. Fish clean and store area. Refrigerators. Cr cds: A, C, D, DS, MC, V.
D SC

B&Bs/Small Inns

★★ CHALFANT HOUSE BED & BREAKFAST. *213 Academy Ave (93514). 760/872-1790; fax 760/872-9221; toll-free 800/641-2996. www.chalfanthousebb.com.* 7 rms, 6 with shower only, 2 story, 2 suites, 1 kit. unit. No rm phones. S $70; D $95; each addl $15; suites $80-$90; kit. unit $90. Children over 8 yrs only. TV in some rms; cable, VCR avail (movies). Complimentary full bkfst. Restaurant nearby. Ck-out 7 am, ck-in 10 pm. Donwhill/x-country ski 15 mi. Picnic tables. Built in 1898; antiques. Totally nonsmoking. Cr cds: A, DS, MC, V.

★ THE MATLICK HOUSE BED AND BREAKFAST. *1313 Rowan Ln (93514). 760/873-3133; toll-free 800/898-3133.* 5 rms, 2 story. D $75-$85; under 6 free; wkly rates. Complimentary full bkfst. Restaurant nearby. Ck-out 11 am, ck-in 4 pm. Remodeled farmhouse built 1906; sitting rm with fireplace. Totally nonsmoking. Cr cds: A, DS, MC, V.

Restaurants

★★ **FIREHOUSE GRILL.** *635 N Main St (93514). 760/873-4888.* Hrs: 4:30-10 pm; early-bird dinner to 6 pm. Res accepted. Bar. Dinner $10-$18. Specializes in rack of lamb, fresh fish, choice of fresh meats. Cr cds: A, C, D, DS, ER, MC, V.

D

★ **INYO COUNTRY STORE AND RESTAURANT.** *177 Academy St (93514). 760/872-2552. www.inyocountrystore.ohgolly.com.* Hrs: 8 am-5 pm; Thurs-Sat to 9 pm. Closed Sun; Dec 25. Res accepted. Italian, American menu. Dinner $7.95-$19.95. A la carte entrees: bkfst, lunch $2.95-$8.95, dinner $4.95-$6.95. Specializes in lamb, steak. Gift shop; deli. Totally nonsmoking. Cr cds: A, C, DS, ER, MC, V.

D

★ **WHISKEY CREEK.** *524 N Main St (93514). 760/873-7174.* Hrs: 7 am-9 pm; June-Sept to 10 pm. Closed Dec 25. Res accepted. Bar. Bkfst $2.25-$9.95, lunch $4.50-$10.95, dinner $8.95-$19.95. Children's menu. Specializes in barbecue, beef, seafood. Outdoor dining. Country decor. Gift shop. Cr cds: A, C, D, DS, ER, MC, V.

D SC

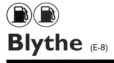

Blythe (E-8)

Settled 1910 **Pop** 8,428 **Elev** 270 ft **Area code** 760 **Zip** 92225

Information Chamber of Commerce, 201 S Broadway; 760/922-8166 or 800/443-5513

Thomas Blythe, an Englishman, came here with an idea of turning this portion of the Colorado River valley into another Nile River valley. The techniques of modern irrigation have allowed that dream to come true as a series of dams has converted the desert into rich farmland and a vast recreational area. There is still some mining in the Palo Verde valley, and rockhounding is good in some nearby areas.

What to See and Do

Canoe trips. One- to five-day self-guided trips on lower Colorado River. Fishing, boating, waterskiing, camping. Canoe rentals; delivery and pickup. For schedule and fee information contact Desert Canoe Rentals, 12400 14th Ave. Phone 760/922-8753.

Cibola National Wildlife Refuge. Large flocks of Canada geese, ducks, sandhill cranes, and wintering passerine birds. Swimming, fishing, boating; hunting, picnicking, visitor center (Mon-Fri; closed hols). 17 mi S of I-10, on Colorado River near Cibola, AZ. Phone 520/857-3253.

Indian Lore Monument. Giant intaglio pictographs. 15 mi N on US 95. Phone 760/922-8166.

Palo Verde Lagoon. A natural lake with fishing, picnicking, and camping facilities. 20 mi S on CA 78.

Riverfront camping. There are 30 camps for sports enthusiasts along the banks of the Colorado, Mayflower Park among them. Approx 30,000-50,000 people visit here each winter to hunt deer, duck, pheasant, quail, doves, and geese; and to fish for bass, crappie, bluegill, and catfish.

Special Events

Colorado River Country Music Festival. Bluegrass music. Third wkend Jan. Phone 909/684-6732.

Colorado River Country Fair. Mid-Apr.

Motels/Motor Lodges

★ **BEST VALUE INN.** *850 W Hobson Way (92225). 760/922-5145; fax 760/922-8422; res 888/315-2378. www.bestvalueinn.com.* 50 rms, 34 with shower only, 2 story. S $42-$75; D $49-$95; each addl $4; under 14 free; wkly rates. Crib free. Pet accepted, some restrictions; $25 deposit. TV; cable (premium). Pool. Complimentary continental bkfst, coffee in rms. Restaurant adj 5 am-11 pm. Ck-out 11 am. Refrigerators; microwaves avail. Picnic tables, grills. Cr cds: A, C, D, DS, MC, V.

D SC

★★ **BEST WESTERN SAHARA.** *825 W Hobson Way (92225). 760/922-5836; fax 760/922-5836; res 800/528-1234. www.bestwestern.com.* 47 rms. S

$59-$100; D $64-$110; each addl $5; under 12 free; higher rates special events. Crib free. Pet accepted. TV; cable, (premium), VCR. Pool; whirlpool. Complimentary continental bkfst, coffee in rms. Restaurant opp 5 am-11 pm. Ck-out noon. Refrigerators, microwaves. Cr cds: A, C, D, DS, MC, V.

★★ **HAMPTON INN.** *900 W Hobson Way (92225). 760/922-9000; fax 760/922-9011. www.hampton-inn.com.* 59 rms, 2 story. Jan-May: S $68-$80; D $72-$85; under 18 free; higher rates special events; lower rates rest of yr. Crib free. TV; cable (premium), VCR. Complimentary continental bkfst. Coffee in rms. Restaurant nearby. Ck-out 11 am. Meeting rm. Business servs avail. In-rm modem link. Coin lndry. Exercise equipt. Pool; whirlpool. Bathrm phones, refrigerators, microwaves. Cr cds: A, C, D, DS, MC, V.

D SC

★★ **LEGACY INN.** *903 W Hobson Way (92225). 760/922-4146; fax 760/922-8481; res 877/737-5342.* 48 rms, 2 story. S $48-$58; D $52-$65; each addl $5; under 18 free; higher rates special events. Crib free. Pet accepted. TV; cable (premium). Pool. Complimentary continental bkfst. Restaurant opp 5 am-11 pm. Ck-out noon. Refrigerators; microwaves avail. Cr cds: A, D, DS, MC, V.

Bodega Bay

(F-2) *See also Inverness, Santa Rosa*

Settled 1835 **Pop** 1,127 **Elev** 120 ft **Area code** 707 **Zip** 94923

Resorts

★★★ **BODEGA BAY LODGE & SPA.** *103 Coast Hwy 1 (94923). 707/875-3525; fax 707/875-2428; res 800/368-2468. www.woodsidehotels.com.* 78 rms, 2 story. No A/C. S, D $150-$375; each addl $10; under 18 free. Crib free. TV; cable. Heated pool; whirlpool. Complimentary coffee in rms. Restaurant (see also DUCK CLUB). Ck-out 11:30 am. Meeting rms. Business servs avail. In-rm modem link. Exercise equipt; sauna. Refrigerators, fireplaces; some wet bars; microwaves avail. Private patios, balconies. Overlooks ocean, beach. Cr cds: A, C, D, DS, MC, V.

D

★★ **BODEGA COAST INN.** *521 Coast Hwy (94923). 707/875-2217; fax 707/875-2964; toll-free 800/346-6999. bodegacoastinn.com.* 45 rms, 3 story. Apr-Nov: S, D $129-$179; each addl $10; under 18 free; lower rates rest of yr. Crib free. TV; cable (premium), VCR (movies $4.50). Complimentary continental bkfst, coffee in rms. Ck-out noon. Meeting rm. Business servs avail. Refrigerators; microwaves avail. Balconies. Bay view. Cr cds: A, C, D, DS, JCB, MC, V.

D

★★★ **INN AT THE TIDES.** *800 CA 1 (94923). 707/875-2751; fax 707/875-2669; toll-free 800/541-7788. www.innatthetides.com.* 86 rms, 2 story. No A/C. S, D $139-$159; each addl $20; under 12 free; golf plan. Crib free. TV; cable (premium). Pool; whirlpool. Complimentary continental bkfst. Restaurant (see also BAY VIEW). Rm serv 8-11 am, 5-9 pm. Bar from 5 pm; closed Mon, Tues. Ck-out 11 am. Meeting rms. Business servs avail. In-rm modem link. Exercise equipt; sauna. Refrigerators; some fireplaces. Some private patios. Opp Bodega Bay. Cr cds: A, D, DS, JCB, MC, V.

D SC

B&Bs/Small Inns

★★★ **INN AT OCCIDENTAL OF SONOMA WINE COUNTRY.** *3657 Church St, Occidental (95465). 707/874-1047; fax 707/874-1078; toll-free 800/522-6324. www.innatoccidental.com.* 14 rms, 3 story, 2 suites. S, D $175-$255; 2-day min wkends, hols. Children over 12 yrs only. Complimentary full bkfst; afternoon refreshments. Ck-out noon, ck-in 3 pm. Business servs avail. Luggage handling. Concierge serv. Rec rm. Many fireplaces. Totally nonsmoking. Cr cds: A, DS, MC, V.

D

★★★ **SONOMA COAST VILLA INN & SPA.** *16702 Coast Hwy 1, Bodega (94922). 707/876-9818; fax 707/876-9856; toll-free 888/404-2255. www.scvilla.com.* 12 rms, 6 with shower only. No A/C. May-Nov: S, D $245-$325; under 12 free; wkends, hols (2-day min). TV; VCR (free movies). Complimentary bkfst, coffee in rms. Ck-out 11 am, ck-in 3-6 pm. Business servs avail. Concierge serv. Pool; whirlpool. Game rm. Putting green. Refrigerators, fireplaces. Some in-rm whirlpools. On 60 acres. Totally nonsmoking. Cr cds: A, MC, V.

Restaurants

★★ **BAY VIEW.** *800 CA 1 (94923). 707/875-2751. www.innatthetides.com.* Hrs: 5-11 pm. Wed-Sun. Res accepted. Contemporary American menu. Bar. A la carte entrees: dinner $14.95-$26.50. Parking. View of bay. Cr cds: A, DS, MC, V.

SC

★★ **DUCK CLUB.** *103 CA 1 (94923). 707/875-3525. www.woodsidehotels.com.* Hrs: 6 am-9 pm. Res accepted. Wine, beer. Complete meal: bkfst $5-$12.95, dinner $10.95-$28.95. Children's menu. Specializes in seafood, duck. Casually elegant decor. Totally nonsmoking. Cr cds: A, D, DS, MC, V.

D

★★ **LUCA'S WHARF.** *595 CA 1 (94923). 707/875-3522. www.lucaswharf.com.* Hrs: 11 am-9:30 pm; wkends to 10 pm. Closed Thanksgiving, Dec 25. Bar. Lunch, dinner $6.95-$17. Children's menu. Specializes in fresh local seafood. Parking. Windows overlook bay and fishing boats. Totally nonsmoking. Cr cds: DS, MC, V.

D SC

Borrego Springs (F-6)

Pop 2,244 **Elev** 700 ft **Area code** 760 **Zip** 92004

Information Chamber of Commerce, 622 Palm Canyon Dr, PO Box 420; 760/767-5555 or 800/559-5524.

Web www.borregosprings.com

Artifacts from the area show that nomadic tribes lived here at least 5,000 years ago. Although prospectors and cattle ranchers had driven through the desert in the late 19th century, it wasn't until 1906 that the first permanent white settler arrived.

In the winter and spring, wildflowers transform the desert's valleys, canyons, and washes into a rainbow of colors, creating an oasis of this charming resort village in the midst of the desert.

What to See and Do

Anza-Borrego Desert State Park. (see) Approx 600,000 acres surrounding Borrego Springs. Hiking, nature and bridle trails, picnicking, camping. Visitor center with underground desert museum. Phone 760/767-5311. Day use ¢¢; Camping ¢¢¢¢; Museum **FREE**

Motels/Motor Lodges

★★ **BORREGO SPRING RESORT.** *1112 Tilting T Dr (92004). 760/767-5700; fax 760/767-6710. www.borregospringsresort.com.* 100 rms, 2 story, 36 suites. Nov-May: S, D $100; suites $125; under 10 free; golf plans; package plans; wkends 2-day min Nov-May; lower rates rest of yr. Crib free. Pet accepted; $100 deposit. TV; cable. Complimentary continental bkfst. Restaurant. Ck-out noon. Meeting rms. Business servs avail.

Whale watching off the California shoreline

In-rm modem link. Sundries. Coin lndry. Free airport transportation. Lighted tennis. 18-hole golf, greens fee $49-$59, pro, putting green, driving range. Exercise equipt. Pool; whirlpool. Refrigerators, microwaves, wet bars. Many balconies. Picnic tables, grills. Cr cds: A, DS, MC, V.

★★ **PALM CANYON RESORT.** *221 Palm Canyon Dr (92004). 760/767-5341; fax 760/767-4073; toll-free 800/242-0044.* 60 rms, 2 story. Nov-May: S, D $75-$150; under 12 free; lower rates rest of yr. Crib free. TV; cable; VCR avail. Pool; whirlpool. Complimentary coffee in rms. Ck-out noon. Coin lndry. Sundries. Gift shop. Grocery store. Some refrigerators. Cr cds: A, C, D, DS, MC, V.

D

Resort

★★★ **LA CASA DEL ZORRO.** *3845 Yaqui Pass Rd (92004). 760/767-5323; fax 760/767-4782; toll-free 800/824-1884.* This beautiful, small hotel is truly an oasis in the desert. A stream filled with colorful Japanese carp winds its way through the beautifully landscaped grounds. Many rooms are oversized and feature wood-burning fireplaces. Multibedroom casitas are also available. Several swimming pools and whirlpools dot the property. A well-equipped fitness/aerobic center, six lighted tennis courts, and a full-size pool are provided for guests' enjoyment. The semi-formal restaurant features creative California cuisine and a cordial, professional staff. 77 units, 19 cottages. Feb-Apr: S, D $105-$385; suites $260-$340; cottages $225-$825; under 8 free; lower rates rest of yr. Crib free. Valet parking. TV; cable (premium), VCR avail (movies, Nintendo avail). Supervised children's activities (hols and special occasions by prior arrangement). Restaurant (see also PRESIDIO). Bar 11-2 am; nightly entertainment. Ck-out noon, ck-in 4 pm. Conference facilities. Meeting rms. Business servs avail. Bellhops. Gift shop. 3 heated pools; lap pool, exercise pool, whirlpools. 6 lighted tennis cts, pro. Bicycles. Lawn games. Putting green. Fitness center. Salon, spa services. Massage. Some fireplaces; microwaves avail. 18-hole golf course nearby. Cr cds: A, C, D, DS, ER, MC, V.

D

B&Bs/Small Inns

★ **BORREGO VALLEY INN.** *405 Palm Canyon Dr (92004). 760/767-0311; fax 760/767-0900; toll-free 800/333-5710. www.borregovalleyinn.com.* 14 rms. Feb-May: S, D $115-$155; wkends 2-day min; lower rates rest of yr. TV; cable, VCR avail. Complimentary continental bkfst. Restaurant nearby. Business servs avail. In-rm modem link. Free airport transportation. Outdoor pool; whirlpool. Many refrigerators, microwaves, wet bars. Some fireplaces. Picnic tables, grills. Totally nonsmoking. Cr cds: A, C, D, DS, MC, V.

D

★★ **THE PALMS AT INDIAN HEAD.** *2220 Hoberg Rd (92004). 760/767-7788; fax 760/767-9717; res 800/519-2624. www.thepalmsatindianhead.com.* 10 rms, 2 story. No rm phones. Nov-May: S, D $99-$139; lower rates rest of yr. TV; cable, VCR avail. Restaurant 11 am-2 pm, 5-9 pm. Ck-out noon, ck-in 3 pm. Former Hoberg Resort Hotel. Totally nonsmoking. Cr cds: D, DS, MC, V.

Restaurants

★ **BERNARD'S.** *503 The Mall (92004). 760/767-5666.* Hrs: 11 am-10 pm. Closed Sun. Res accepted. Continental menu. Bar. Lunch $4.25-$8.25, dinner $8-$14.95. Specialties: Wiener schnitzel, roast pork. Casual decor. Totally nonsmoking. Cr cds: A, C, D, DS, ER, MC, V.

D

★ **D AND E'S.** *818 Palm Canyon Dr (92004). 760/767-4954.* Hrs: 5-9 pm. Closed Sun; Dec 25; also July, Aug. Res accepted. Wine, beer. Dinner $5-$12.50. Specializes in pasta, seafood. Casual decor. Cr cds: C, MC, V.

D

★★★ **LA PAVILION AT RAMS HILL.** *1881 Rams Hill Rd (92004). 760/767-5000.* Hrs: 11:30 am-3 pm, 5-9 pm; Mon to 2 pm; Sun to 2 pm (brunch). Res accepted. Continental menu. Bar 11 am-midnight. Lunch $5.95-$10.95, dinner $12.95-$28. Specialties: rack of lamb, filet mignon. Outdoor dining. Contemporary artwork. Cr cds: A, MC, V.

★★★ **PRESIDIO.** *3845 Yaqui Pass Rd (92004). 760/767-5323. www.lacasadelzorro.com.* Beautiful oil paintings of the old west Butterfield Stageline adorn the thick, white washed adobe walls of this sophisticated restaurant. Candlelight and sparkling table settings create a romantic atmosphere in which to enjoy chef Peter Brinckerhoff's creative California cuisine. The menu changes throughout the year taking advantage of the freshest seasonal ingredients.Hrs: 7 am-10 pm; Res accepted. Bar 11 am-midnight; Fri, Sat to 2 am. Extensive wine list. Bkfst $3.50-$11, lunch $6-$14, dinner $16-$28. Children's menu. Specializes in steak, fresh seafood. Cr cds: A, C, D, DS, ER, MC, V.

D SC

Bridgeport

(F-6) *See also Coleville, Lee Vining*

Pop 500 **Elev** 6,473 ft **Area code** 760 **Zip** 93517

A Ranger District office of the Toiyabe National Forest is located here.

What to See and Do

Bodie State Historic Park. Unrestored ghost town of the late 1800s. Between 1879 and 1881 more than 10,000 people lived here. Fires in 1892 and 1932 took their toll and now only about five percent of the town remains. A self-guiding brochure takes you through the main part of town; church (ca 1880), jail, two-rm school, Miners Union Hall (now a museum), hillside cemetery with monument to James A. Garfield. Picnicking. 7 mi S on US 395, then 13 mi E on partially unpaved road; not cleared in winter (only accessible on foot). Phone 760/647-6445. ¢¢

Yosemite National Park. (see). Approx 20 mi S via US 395, then 8 mi W via CA 120.

Motels/Motor Lodges

★ **SILVER MAPLE INN.** *310 Main St (93517). 760/932-7383. www.silvermapleinn.com.* 20 rms. No A/C. S $60-$65; D $60-$70; each addl $10. Crib free. Pet accepted. TV; cable (premium). Complimentary coffee in rms. Restaurant opp 6 am-10 pm. Ck-out 11 am. Lawn games. Picnic tables. Grills. Cr cds: A, DS, MC, V.

D

★★ **WALKER RIVER LODGE.** *100 Main St (93517). 760/932-7021; fax 760/932-7914; toll-free 800/388-6651. www.walkerriverlodge.com.* 36 rms, 1-2 story. Mid-Apr-Oct: S $70-$135; D $75-$150; each addl $10; kit. units $95-$200; lower rates rest of yr. Crib free. Pet accepted. TV; cable (premium). Heated pool; whirlpool. Complimentary coffee in rms. Restaurant opp 6 am-2 pm. Ck-out 11 am. Business servs avail. Gift shop. Refrigerators. Some balconies. Picnic tables, grills. Fish freezer. X-country ski 12 mi. Cr cds: A, C, D, DS, MC, V.

D SC

B&B/Small Inn

★★★ **CAIN HOUSE.** *340 Main St (93517). 760/932-7040; fax 760/932-7419; toll-free 800/433-2246. www.cainhouse.com.* 7 rms, 2 story. S $80; D $100. TV; cable (premium). Complimentary full bkfst, afternoon refreshments, coffee in rms. Restaurant nearby. Ck-out 11 am, ck-in 3 pm. Lawn games. Grills. Former residence of prominent local family. Totally nonsmoking. Cr cds: A, DS, MC, V.

Buena Park

See also Anaheim, La Habra, Long Beach, Whittier

Pop 68,784 **Elev** 74 ft **Area code** 714

Information Convention & Visitors Office, 6601 Brach Blvd, Suite 200, 90621; 714/562-3560 or 800/541-3953

Web www.buenapark.com

What to See and Do

Knott's Berry Farm. Re-created town of gold rush days; focus on the history, heritage, and culture of the West. Family entertainment park situated on 150 acres; incl rides, live entertainment, shops, food. This is the official home of Snoopy and the Peanuts characters. Farm is also noted for its berry preserves. (Daily; closed Dec 25) 8039 Beach Blvd, 2 mi S of Santa Ana Fwy (US 101, I-5) on CA 39. Phone 714/220-5200. ¢¢¢¢¢

Movieland Wax Museum. Museum houses more than 280 wax figures of Hollywood's greatest stars in more than 160 realistic movie sets; covers 70 yrs of movie history. Shop for favorite movie souvenirs and visit Chamber of Horrors. (Daily) 7711 Beach Blvd. Phone 714/522-1154. ¢¢¢¢¢ Incl admission to

Ripley's Believe It or Not Museum. Houses a collection of oddities and anthropological artifacts that allow visitors to experience first hand that truth is indeed stranger than fiction. (Daily) Opp Movieland. Phone 714/522-7045.

Motels/Motor Lodges

★★ **BEST WESTERN BUENA PARK INN.** *8580 Stanton Ave (90620). 714/828-5211; fax 714/826-3716; toll-free 800/646-1629.* 63 rms, 2 story, 3 suites. S, D $39-$59; suites $79-$99; under 18 free. Crib $5. TV; cable (premium). Heated pool. Complimentary continental bkfst. Restaurant adj 6 am-midnight. Ck-out noon. Coin lndry. Business servs avail. Some refrigerators; microwaves avail. Cr cds: A, C, D, DS, MC, V.

★ **COLONY INN.** *7800 Crescent Ave (90620). 714/527-2201; fax 714/826-3826; toll-free 800/982-6566. www.colonyinnbuenapark.com.* 90 units, 2 story, 8 suites. S $32-$39; D $39-$49; each addl $10; suites, family units $65; under 12 free. Crib free. TV; cable (premium). Heated pool; wading pool. Complimentary continental bkfst. Restaurant adj 6 am-11 pm. Ck-out 11 am. Coin lndry. Meeting rm. Cr cds: A, C, D, DS, JCB, MC, V.

D SC

★★ **COURTYARD BY MARRIOTT.** *7621 Beach Blvd (90620). 714/670-6600; fax 714/670-0360; res 800/321-2211.* 145 rms, 11 suites, 2 story. S, D $79-$89; suites $104-$114; under 18 free; wkly rates. Crib free. TV; cable (premium). Heated pool; whirlpool. Complimentary coffee in rms. Restaurant 6-10:30 am, 5-10 pm. Bar 4-10:30 pm. Ck-out 1 pm. Coin lndry. Meeting rms. Business servs avail. Valet serv. Sundries. Exercise equipt. Health club privileges. Refrigerators in suites; microwaves avail. Some patios, balconies. Cr cds: A, C, D, DS, MC, V.

D SC

★★ **DYNASTY SUITES.** *13530 E Firestone Blvd, Santa Fe Springs (90670). 562/921-8571; fax 562/921-2451; res 800/842-7899. www.dynastysuites.com.* 49 rms, 2 story. S, D $49.95-$99.95, each addl $5. TV; cable (premium), VCR avail (movies). Heated pool. Complimentary continental bkfst. Restaurant adj 6 am-midnight. Ck-out noon. Coin lndry. Business servs avail. Refrigerators, microwaves. Cr cds: A, D, DS, ER, MC, V.

D

★★ **FAIRFIELD INN.** *7032 Orangethorpe Ave (90621). 714/523-1488; fax 714/523-1488; toll-free 800/228-2800. www.fairfieldinn.com.* 133 rms, 3 story. S, D $50-$60. Crib free. TV; cable (premium). Heated pool. Complimentary continental bkfst. Restaurant opp 6 am-midnight; Fri, Sat to 2 am. Ck-out noon. Business servs avail. Valet serv. Disneyland transportation. Health club privileges. Some refrigerators, microwaves. Cr cds: A, C, D, DS, MC, V.

D SC

★★ **HOLIDAY INN BUENA PARK.** *7000 Beach Blvd (90620). 714/522-7000; fax 714/522-8646; res 800/465-4329. www.holidayinn.com/hotels/ia.* 245 rms, 4-5 story. S $119; D $129; each addl $10; suites $175-$350; under 17 free. Crib free. TV; cable (premium). Heated pool; wading pool, whirlpool. Complimentary coffee in rms. Restaurants 6:30 am-10 pm. Bar 11 am-midnight. Ck-out noon. Coin lndry. Meeting rms. Business servs avail. In-rm modem link. Bellhops. Valet serv. Gift shop. Exercise equipt. Health club privileges. Refrigerator avail. Some patios. Cr cds: A, C, D, DS, JCB, MC, V.

D SC

★ **RED ROOF INN.** *7121 Beach Blvd (90620). 714/670-9000; fax 714/522-7280; toll-free 800/538-0006. www.redroof.com.* 127 units, 4 story, 6 suites. S, D $49; each addl $4; suites $64-$70; under 19 free. Crib free. TV; cable (premium). Heated pool; whirlpool. Complimentary continental bkfst. Restaurant nearby. Ck-out 11 am. Meeting rms. Business servs avail. Health club privileges. Cr cds: A, C, D, DS, MC, V.

D SC

★ **SUPER 8.** *7930 Beach Blvd (90620). 714/994-6480; fax 714/994-3874; res 800/800-8000. www.super8.com.* 78 rms, 2 story, 40 kit. units. S $42-$50; D $44-$56; each addl $6; kit. units $42-$56; under 12 free; wkly rates. Crib free. TV; cable (premium). Heated pool; whirlpool. Complimentary continental bkfst, coffee in rms. Restaurant adj 24 hrs. Ck-out 11 am. Business servs avail. Sundries. Coin lndry. Refrigerators; many wet bars. Some balconies. Picnic tables, grills. Cr cds: A, C, D, DS, ER, JCB, MC, V.

★ **TRAVELODGE.** *7039 Orangethorpe Ave (90621). 714/521-9220; fax 714/521-6706. www.travelodgebuenapark.com.* 100 kit. units, 2 story, 12 suites. S $48-$58; D $52-$62; each addl $4; suites $115-$135; under 17 free; wkly rates. Crib free. TV; cable (premium). Pool; whirlpool. Sauna. Complimentary continental bkfst, coffee in rms. Restaurant opp 8-1 am. Ck-out 11 am. Meeting rm. Business servs avail. Valet serv. Sundries. Coin lndry. Health club privileges. Game rm. Refrigerators; wet bars; some microwaves. Picnic tables, grills. Cr cds: A, DS, MC, V.

D

Hotels

★★ **INN SUITES HOTEL.** *7555 Beach Blvd (90620). 714/522-7360; fax 714/523-2883; res 800/842-4242. www.innsuites.com.* 185 rms, 2 story, 27 suites. S, D $59-$69; each addl $10; suites $79-$175; under 18 free. Crib free. TV; cable (premium). Heated pool; whirlpool. Playground. Complimentary coffee in lobby. Ck-out noon. Meeting rms. Business servs avail. Valet serv. Coin lndry. Free Disneyland transportation. Game rm. Exercise equipt; sauna. Some refrigerators, microwaves. Picnic tables, grill. Cr cds: A, C, D, DS, MC, V.

SC

★★★ **NORWALK MARRIOTT.** *13111 Sycamore Dr, Norwalk (90650). 562/863-5555; fax 562/868-4486; res 800/228-9290. www.marriotthotels.com/laxnk.* 173 rms, 8 story, 27 suites. S, D $124; suites $158-$178; wkend rates. Crib free. TV; cable (premium). Heated pool; whirlpool, poolside serv. Complimentary coffee in rms. Restaurant 6 am-10:30 pm. Bar 4-11 pm. Ck-out noon. Meeting rms. Business servs avail. In-rm modem link. Gift shop. Free Disneyland transportation. Exercise equipt. Refrigerators; microwaves avail. Cr cds: A, C, D, DS, JCB, MC, V.

D

★★ **RADISSON RESORT KNOTT'S BERRY FARM.** *7675 Crescent Ave (90620). 714/995-1111; fax 714/828-8590. www.radisson.com.* 320 rms, 9 story, 8 suites. S, D $109; each addl $10; suites $199-$500; under 18 free. Crib free. TV; cable (premium). Heated pool; whirlpool, poolside serv. Coffee in rms. Restaurant 6 am-midnight. Bar 4 pm-2 am. Ck-out noon. Coin lndry. Convention facilities. Business servs avail. Concierge. Airport, Disneyland transportation. Game rm. Health club privileges. Some refrigerators. Cr cds: A, C, D, DS, JCB, MC, V.

D

★★★ **SHERATON HOTEL.** *12725 Center Court Dr, Cerritos (90703). 562/809-1500; fax 562/403-2080; toll-free 800/544-5064. www.sheraton.com.* 203 units, 8 story, 23 suites. S, D $85-$180; each addl $15; suites $160-$400; under 18 free. Crib free. Pet accepted, some restrictions; $25. TV; cable (premium). Heated pool; whirlpool, poolside serv. Coffee in rms. Restaurant 6:30 am-10 pm. Rm serv 6 am-11:30 pm. Bar noon-1 am. Ck-out noon. Meeting rms. Business center. In-rm modem link. Concierge. Gift shop. Free Disneyland transportation. Exercise equipt. Refrigerators; some bathrm phones. Atrium. Cr cds: A, C, D, DS, ER, JCB, MC, V.

D SC

All Suite

★★★ **EMBASSY SUITES.** *7762 Beach Blvd (90620). 714/739-5600; fax 714/521-9650; res 800/362-2779. www.embassy-suites.com.* 201 kit. suites, 4 story. S $159-$169; D $169-$179; each addl $15; under 18 free. Crib free. TV; cable (premium). Heated pool; whirlpool. Complimentary full bkfst. Coffee in rms. Restaurant 11:30 am-10 pm. Bar 5:30-11 pm. Ck-out noon. Coin lndry. Meeting rms. Business center. In-rm modem link. Valet serv. Gift shop. Free Disneyland transportation. Game rm. Exercise equipt. Health club privileges. Refrigerators, microwaves, wetbars. Balconies. Grills. Knott's Berry Farm 1 blk. Cr cds: A, C, D, DS, ER, JCB, MC, V.

D

Restaurant

★★ **RAJDOOT.** *11833 E Artesia Blvd, Artesia (90701). 562/860-6500.* Hrs: 11:30 am-2:30 pm, 5:30-10 pm; Fri, Sat to 10:30 pm. Closed Thanksgiving, Dec 25. Res accepted. Northern Indian menu. Bar. A la carte entrees: lunch, dinner $7.95-$14.95. Specialties: samundri khazana, chicken methi, garlic chicken tikka. Entertainment Fri, Sat. Indian palace atmosphere. Totally nonsmoking. Cr cds: A, MC, V.

D

Unrated Dining Spot

MEDIEVAL TIMES DINNER AND TOURNAMENT. *7662 Beach Blvd (90620). 714/521-4740. www.medievaltimes.com.* Hrs: show at 7 pm; Fri 6:30 pm and 8:45 pm; Sat 6 pm and 8:15; Sun varies. Res required. Bar. Complete meals: adults $34.95-$35.95, children $22.95. Medieval tournament competitions incl ring piercing, javelin throwing, sword fighting, jousting. Reproduction of 11th-century castle; medieval decor. Hall of Banners and Flags. Museum of Torture. Cr cds: A, DS, MC, V.

D SC

Burbank

Pop 93,643 **Elev** 598 ft **Area code** 818

Motel/Motor Lodge

★★ **SAFARI INN.** *1911 W Olive Ave (91506). 818/845-8586; fax 818/845-0054; res 800/767-1664. www.anabelle-safari.com.* 56 rms, 2 story. S, D $104; each addl $5; kit. suites $84-$114; under 18 free. Crib free. TV; cable (premium). Heated pool; whirlpool. Complimentary continental bkfst. Coffee in rms. Restaurant nearby. Ck-out noon. Business servs avail. Airport transportation. Refrigerators, microwaves avail. Cr cds: A, D, DS, MC, V.

D

Hotel

★★★ **HILTON BURBANK AIRPORT & CONVENTION CENTER.** *2500 N Hollywood Way (91505). 818/843-6000; toll-free 800/445-8667. www.burbankairport.hilton.com.* 486 rms, 8-9 story. S $144; D $164; each addl $15; suites $140-$480; under 19 free; family, wkend rates. Crib free. Pet accepted. TV; cable (premium). 2 heated pools; whirlpool, poolside serv. Complimentary coffee in rms. Restaurant 6 am-11 pm. Rm serv 24 hrs. Bar 11-2 am. Ck-out noon. Coin lndry. Convention facilities. Business center. Concierge. Gift shop. Free airport transportation. Exercise equipt; sauna. Health club privileges. Microwaves avail; refrigerator in suites. Cr cds: A, C, D, DS, JCB, MC, V.

D

Restaurant

★★ **MI PIACE.** *801 N San Fernando Blvd (91501). 818/843-1111.* Hrs: 11:30 am-11 pm; Fri, Sat to midnight. Closed Jan 1, Thanksgiving, Dec 25. Res accepted. Italian menu. Bar. A la carte entrees: lunch, dinner $5.75-$16.95. Specializes in southern Italian cuisine. Valet parking. Art Deco decor. Totally nonsmoking. Cr cds: A, D, MC, V.
D

Burlingame

(see San Francisco Airport Area)

Burney

(C-3) *See also Mount Shasta, Redding*

Pop 3,423 **Elev** 3,130 ft
Area code 530 **Zip** 96013

Information Chamber of Commerce, 37088 Main St, PO Box 36; 530/335-2111

All the attractions of outdoor living are in the area surrounding Shasta Lake, Mount Shasta (see), and Lassen Volcanic National Park (see).

What to See and Do

Lassen National Forest. (See SUSANVILLE) South and east of town. Phone 916/336-5521. In the forest is

Hat Creek Recreation Area. Fishing; picnicking, camping (fee). Geological sites incl Subway Cave, a lava tube; and Spattercone, a guided volcanic nature trail. Camping and fishing facilities for the disabled. 17 mi SE on CA 89. Phone 530/336-5521.

McArthur-Burney Falls Memorial State Park. These 853 acres encompass Burney Falls (in season, water bubbles from underground springs, flows ½-mi, then drops over a precipice in 129-ft twin falls). Swimming, fishing, boat launching; nature and hiking trails, picnicking, concession, camping. Naturalist program. Standard fees. 5 mi E on CA 299, then 6 mi N on CA 89. Phone 530/335-2777.

Calexico

(F-7) *See also El Centro*

Founded 1908 **Pop** 18,633 **Elev** 2 ft
Area code 760

Information Chamber of Commerce, 1100 Imperial Ave, PO Box 948, 92232; 760/357-1166

Web www.calexicochamber.ca.gov

Once a tent town of the Imperial Land Company, this community at the south end of the Imperial Valley is separated from its much larger sister city, Mexicali, Mexico, by only a fence. The town represents the marriage of two diverse cultures. It serves as a port of entry to the US. (For Border Crossing Regulations see MAKING THE MOST OF YOUR TRIP.)

Motel/Motor Lodge

★★ **QUALITY INN.** *801 Imperial Ave (92231).* Fax *760/357-3271. www.qualityinn.com.* 56 rms, 2 story. S $69; D $74; each addl $6; suites $80; kit. units $55-$62; under 12 free. TV; cable (premium). Pool. Restaurant 6 am-10 pm. Ck-out noon. Meeting rms. Free covered parking. Some refrigerators. Cr cds: A, C, D, DS, MC, V.
D

Calistoga

(F-3) *See also Napa, Petaluma, St. Helena, Santa Rosa, Sonoma*

Founded 1859 **Pop** 4,468 **Elev** 362 ft
Area code 707 **Zip** 94515

Information Chamber of Commerce, 1458 Lincoln Ave #9; 707/942-6333

Web www.napavalley.com/calistoga/

Samuel Brannan, a wealthy San Francisco entrepreneur, came here in 1859 and recognized that the natural hot-water geysers, mineral springs, and mineralized mud baths would support a resort community. Brannan considered the new resort the

Saratoga of California; thus Calistoga. He was also among those who cultivated grape vines on the surrounding hillsides. As a result, Calistoga is a thriving resort town and center of an important wine-producing area.

What to See and Do

Mount St. Helena. (4,344 ft). Extinct volcano where Robert Louis Stevenson honeymooned in 1880 and wrote "The Silverado Squatters." Robert Louis Stevenson State Park, on Mount St. Helena, has a monument (a statue of the author holding an open book) located near the site of the Silverado mine; ¾-mi hiking trail from parking lot. 8 mi N on CA 29.

Old Faithful Geyser of California. Approx 60-ft-high geyser is one of few, other than Yellowstone's Old Faithful, that erupts at regular intervals. Picnic area; snack bar; gift shop. (Daily; yearly avg eruption approx every 40 min) 1299 Tubbs Ln. Phone 707/942-6463. **¢¢¢**

Petrified Forest. Contains redwoods buried more than three million years ago by the eruption of Mount St. Helena. The trees were knocked down by a volcanic explosion and then buried in volcanic ash. Discovered around 1860, some trees are as large as 80 ft long and 12 ft in diameter, with details excellently preserved. Picnic area. (Daily) 8 mi W on Petrified Forest Rd. Phone 707/942-6667. **¢¢**

Sharpsteen Museum and Sam Brannan Cottage. History of Calistoga in diorama and shadow box form; changing exhibits incl hardware, hand mirrors, clothing, dolls, furniture. Restored cottage (1860) contains furniture of the period. (Daily; closed Thanksgiving, Dec 25) 1311 Washington St. Phone 707/942-5911. **FREE**

Sterling Vineyards. Access to winery by aerial tramway; self-guided tour; shop; wine tasting. Tour incl a considerable amount of walking. Under 16 must be accompanied by adult. Roof-top terrace picnic area. (Daily; closed Jan 1, Thanksgiving, Dec 25) 1111 Dunaweal Ln. Phone 707/942-3344. **¢¢¢**

Special Event

Napa County Fair. Fairgrounds, Oak St. July.

Motel/Motor Lodge

★★ COMFORT INN. *1865 Lincoln Ave (94515). 707/942-9400; fax 707/942-5262; toll-free 800/228-5150. www.callodging.com.* 54 rms, 2 story. Mar-Oct: S $65-$130; D $70-$155; each addl $7; under 18 free; lower rates rest of yr. Crib free. TV; cable (premium). Pool; whirlpool. Sauna. Complimentary continental bkfst. Restaurant opp 5-10 pm. Ck-out 11 am. Meetings rms. In-rm modem link. Some refrigerators, microwaves. Cr cds: A, C, D, DS, ER, JCB, MC, V.

Resorts

★ CALISTOGA SPA HOT SPRINGS. *1006 Washington St (94515). 707/942-6269; fax 707/942-4214. www.calistogaspa.com.* 57 rms with kits., 55 with shower only, 2 story. Mar-Oct: S $70-$90; D $85-$100; each addl $7; min stay wkends, hols; lower rates rest of yr. Crib $5. TV; cable. Heated pool; wading pool, whirlpool, lifeguard. Complimentary coffee in rms. Restaurant nearby. Ck-out 11 am. Meeting rms. Business servs avail. Exercise equipt; sauna. Massage. Picnic tables. Cr cds: MC, V.

★ DR. WILKINSON'S HOT SPRINGS RESORT. *1507 Lincoln Ave (94515). 707/942-4102; fax 707/942-4412. www.drwilkinson.com.* 42 units, 2 story, 16 kits. S, D $99-$169; each addl $12; kit. units $79-$149; package plans. Crib free. TV; cable. 3 heated pools, 1 indoor; whirlpool. Steam rm. Complimentary coffee in rms. Restaurant nearby. Ck-out noon. Meeting rm. Business servs avail. Massage. Many refrigerators. Victorian house (1877). Cr cds: A, MC, V.

B&Bs/Small Inns

★★ BRANNAN COTTAGE INN. *109 Wapoo Ave (94515). 707/942-4200; fax 707/942-2507. www.brannancottageinn.com.* 6 rms, 5 with shower only, 1-2 story, 2 suites. No rm phones. Apr-Nov: S, D $145; each addl $25; suites $160; wkends (2-day min); lower rates rest of yr. Children over 12 yrs only. TV in common rm; cable. Complimentary full bkfst; afternoon refreshments. Restaurant nearby. Ck-out 11 am, ck-in 2 pm. Luggage handling. Refrigerators. Built by original developer of Calistoga in 1862. Totally nonsmoking. Cr cds: A, MC, V.

★ CALISTOGA INN. *1250 Lincoln Ave (94515). 707/942-4101; fax 707/942-4914. www.napabeer.com.* 18 rms, all share bath, 2 story. No A/C. No rm phones. S, D $49-$65. Complimentary continental bkfst. Restaurant (also see CALISTOGA INN). Ck-out 11 am, ck-in 3 pm. Business servs avail. Street parking. Balconies. Built in 1900. On-site brewery in old watertower. Beer garden. Totally nonsmoking. Cr cds: A, MC, V.

★ CHRISTOPHER'S INN. *1010 Foothill Blvd (94515). 707/942-5755; fax 707/942-5755. www.chrisinn.com.* 22 rms, 5 with shower only, 2 story. Rm phones avail. S $125-$350; D $155-$395; suite $165-$350. TV; cable, VCR. Complimentary continental bkfst. Restaurant nearby. Ck-out 11 am, ck-in 2 pm. Meeting rm. Business servs avail. Concierge. Some in-rm whirlpools. Fireplaces. Picnic tables. Lawn games. Built 1918; renovated to incl modern amenities. English country decor; many antiques. Totally nonsmoking. Cr cds: A, V.

★★★ COTTAGE GROVE INN CALISTOGA. *1711 Lincoln Ave (94515). 707/942-8400; fax 707/942-2653; toll-free 800/799-2284. www.cottagegrove.com.* 16 rms. S, D $235-$295; each addl $5; wkends, hols (2-day min). Children over 12 yrs only. TV; cable, VCR (movies). Complimentary continental bkfst; afternoon refreshments. Ck-out 11 am, ck-in 3-7 pm. Business servs avail. In-rm modem link. Gift shop. Refrigerators, microwaves, wet bars, fireplaces. Totally nonsmoking. Cr cds: A, D, DS, MC, V.

D SC

★★ CULVER MANSION. *1805 Foothill Blvd (94515). 707/942-9476. www.culvermansion.com.* 4 rms, 2 story. No rm phones. S, D $140-$160. Children over 16 yrs only. Pool; whirlpool. Complimentary full bkfst; afternoon refreshments. Ck-out 11 am, ck-in 3-6 pm. Antiques. Built 1875. Totally nonsmoking. Cr cds: A, D, DS, MC, V.

D

★★ THE ELMS BED & BREAKFAST INN. *1300 Cedar St (94515). Fax 707/942-9476; res 707/942-9476. www.theelms.com.* 7 rms, 5 with shower only, 3 story. No elvtr. No rm phones. Mid-Mar-mid-Jan: S, D $110-$180; lower rates rest of yr. TV; cable. Complimentary full bkfst; afternoon refreshments. Restaurant nearby. Ck-out 11 am, ck-in 3-6 pm. Concierge serv. Luggage handling. Some in-rm whirlpools. Built in 1871; antiques. Totally nonsmoking. Cr cds: DS, MC, V.

★★★ FOOTHILL HOUSE BED AND BREAKFAST. *3037 Foothill Blvd (94515). 707/942-6933; fax 707/942-5692; toll-free 800/942-6933. www.foothillhouse.com.* 3 rms, 1 cottage. Rm phones on request. S $155; D $165; each addl $35. TV; cable, VCR avail (free movies). Complimentary full bkfst, coffee in rms. Ck-out 11 am, ck-in 3 pm. Lndry facilities avail. In-rm modem link. Refrigerators, fireplaces; some in-rm whirlpools. Private patios. Remodeled turn-of-the-century farmhouse. Individually decorated rms with country antiques. Sun deck. Fish pond. Totally nonsmoking. Cr cds: A, DS, MC, V.

★★ MEADOWLARK COUNTRY HOUSE AND INN. *601 Petrified Forest Rd (94515). 707/942-5651; fax 707/942-5023; res 800/942-5651. www.meadowlarkinn.com.* 7 rms, 2 story. Mar-Nov: S, D $185. TV in sitting rm; cable, VCR. Pool. Complimentary full bkfst. Ck-out 11:30 am, ck-in 3:30 pm. Business servs avail. Picnic tables. English country antiques. Totally nonsmoking. Cr cds: MC, V.

★ PINK MANSION. *1415 Foothill Blvd (94515). 707/942-0558; fax 707/942-0558; toll-free 800/238-7465. www.pinkmansion.com.* 6 rms, 3 story.

Mar-Nov: S, D $135-$225; each addl $20; lower rates rest of yr. TV; VCR (free movies). Indoor heated pool, whirlpool. Complimentary full bkfst; afternoon refreshments. Restaurant nearby. Ck-out 11 am, ck-in 3 pm. Rec rm. Microwaves avail. Balconies. Antiques. Library/sitting rm. Built 1875. Country garden. Totally nonsmoking. Cr cds: MC, V.

SC

★★ **MOUNT VIEW HOTEL AND SPA.** *1457 Lincoln Ave (94515). 707/942-6877; fax 707/942-6904; toll-free 800/816-6877. www.mountviewhotel.com.* 20 rms, 9 suites, 3 cottages. S, D $100-$225; each addl $25; suites, cottages $210-$225. TV; cable, VCR avail. Pool; whirlpool, poolside serv (summer). Complementary continental bkfst. Restaurant (see also CATAHOULA). Bar 5 pm-2 am. Ck-out noon. Business servs avail. Health club privileges. Some in-rm whirlpools. Some suites with balcony. Restored hotel (1917); National Historic Monument. Old World decor. Some antiques. Cr cds: A, DS, MC, V.

★★ **SCOTT COURTYARD.** *1443 2nd St (94515). 707/942-0948; fax 707/942-5102; toll-free 800/942-1515. www.scottcourtyard.com.* 3 suites. May-Oct: suites $175; lower rest of yr. Parking lot. Pool. TV; cable. Complimentary full bkfst, coffee in rms. Restaurant nearby. Ck-out 11 am, ck-in 3 pm. Golf, 9 holes. Tennis, 4 courts. Cr cds: A, DS, MC, V.

★★★ **SILVER ROSE INN AND SPA.** *351 Rosedale Rd (94515). 707/942-9581; fax 707/942-0841; res 800/995-9381. www.silverroseinn.com.* 20 rms, 2 story. S, D $165-$275; lower rates wkdays. 2 pools; 2 whirlpools. Complimentary continental bkfst, afternoon refreshments. Ck-out 11:30 am, ck-in 3-7 pm. Meeting rm. Business servs avail. In-rm modem link. Gift shop. Tennis. Putting green. Some in-rm whirlpools, fireplaces. Balconies. Picnic tables. Antiques. Library/sitting rms. Grounds surrounded by vineyards. Totally nonsmoking. Cr cds: A, DS, MC, V.

D

★★ **WINE WAY INN.** *1019 Foothill Blvd (94515). 707/942-0680; fax 707/942-4657; toll-free 800/572-0679. www.napavalley.com/wineway.* 6 rms, 4 with shower only, 2 story. No rm phones. S, D $110-$125; each addl $25. Crib free. Complimentary full bkfst. Restaurant nearby. Ck-out 11 am, ck-in 3 pm. Fireplace. Built 1915. Handmade quilts. Totally nonsmoking. Cr cds: A, DS, MC, V.

Restaurants

★★ **ALL SEASONS CAFE.** *1400 Lincoln Ave (94515). 707/942-9111.* Hrs: 11 am-3 pm, 6-10 pm. Closed Wed; Dec 24-25. Res accepted (dinner). Contemporary American menu. Bar 11 am-7 pm. A la carte entrees: lunch $5.95-$12.25, dinner $11.50-$19.50. Specializes in house-smoked poultry and fish. Own baking. Bistro-style cafe with rotating art display; wine shop on premises. Totally nonsmoking. Cr cds: DS, MC, V.

D

★★★ **BRANNAN'S GRILL.** *1374 Lincoln Ave (94515). 707/942-2233. www.brannansgrill.com.* Hrs: 11:30 am-10 pm. Res accepted. Eclectic menu. Bar. A la carte entrees: lunch $7.95-$15.95, dinner $10.95-$22.95. Specialties: voodoo shrimp, Creole-spiced pork chop, rotisserie chicken. Own desserts. Piano Fri-Sun. Street parking. Local crafter's and artisans' works displayed. Totally nonsmoking. Cr cds: A, MC, V.

D

★ **CALISTOGA INN.** *1250 Lincoln Ave (94515). 707/942-4101. www.napabeer.com.* Hrs: 11:30 am-10 pm. Wine, beer. A la carte entrees: lunch $5-$12, dinner $12-$18. Specializes in fresh seafood. Entertainment Tues-Sun. Outdoor dining. Totally nonsmoking. Cr cds: A, C, D, ER, MC, V.

D

★★ **CATAHOULA.** *1457 Lincoln Ave (94515). 707/942-2275. www.catahoularest.com.* Hrs: noon-2:30 pm, 5:30-10 pm; Fri-Sun 8:30 am-3:30 pm, 5:30-10:30 pm. Closed Dec 25; also 2 wks in Jan. Res accepted. Bar. Lunch $10-$13, dinner $15-$24. Specialties: spicy gumbo yaya, braised beef short ribs with garlic mashed potatoes. Casual, contemporary dining. Cr cds: DS, MC, V.

D

★★★ **CIN CIN.** *1440 Lincoln Ave (94515). 707/942-1008. www.cincin.citysearch.com.* Specializes in Mediterranean cuisine. Hrs: 5:30-9 pm; Fri, Sat 5:30-10 pm; Sat, Sun brunch 10 am-2 pm. Closed Mon; also Tues in winter. Res accepted. Dinner $14.50-$22. Brunch $6.50-$12. Entertainment. Cr cds: MC, V.

D

★ **HYDRO BAR AND GRILL.** *1403 Lincoln Ave (94515). 707/942-9777.* Hrs: 7 am-11 pm; Fri, Sat to midnight. Closed Dec 25. Bar. A la carte entrees: bkfst $4.95-$7.95, lunch $5-$11.50, dinner $8-$16. Children's menu. Specialties: seared salmon on buckwheat noodles, spinach salad with roasted shallot. Own desserts. Musicians Wed-Sun. Contemporary decor. Totally nonsmoking. Cr cds: DS, MC, V.

D

★ **PACIFICO.** *1237 Lincoln Ave (94515). 707/942-4400.* Hrs: 11 am-10 pm; Sat, Sun from 10 am; Sat, Sun brunch to 3 pm. Closed Thanksgiving, Dec 25. Mexican menu. Bar to 11 pm. Lunch $3.75-$7.50, dinner $5.95-$13.95. Sat, Sun brunch $3.75-$7.50. Children's menu. Specializes in authentic Mexican dishes. Cr cds: MC, V.

D

★ **SMOKE HOUSE CAFE.** *1458 Lincoln Ave (94515). 707/942-6060.* Specializes in BBQ smoked meats. Hrs: 8:30 am-10 pm; June-Aug wkends to 11 pm. Res accepted. Wine, beer. Lunch $7-$14; dinner $9-$17. Children's menu. Entertainment: Band wkends. Cr cds: MC, V.

D

★★ **WAPPO BAR AND BISTRO.** *1226 Washington St (94515). 707/942-4712. www.wappobar.com.* Hrs: 11:30 am-2:30 pm, 6-9:30 pm. Mon, Wed-Sun; closed Easter, Thanksgiving, Dec 25. Res required wkends. Wine, beer. A la carte entrees: lunch $10-$12, dinner $8-$17. Children's menu. Specialties: chili rellenos, duck carnitas with masa cakes, seared Chilean sea bass with mint chutney. Entertainment Sun. Outdoor dining on patio with fountain. Totally nonsmoking. Cr cds: A, MC, V.

D

Camarillo

(E-4) *See also Oxnard, Thousand Oaks, Ventura*

Pop 52,303 **Elev** 160 ft **Area code** 805 **Zip** 93010

Information Chamber of Commerce, 632 Las Posas Rd; 805/484-4383

Web www.ci.camarillo.ca.us

What to See and Do

Camarillo Factory Stores. Over 100 outlet stores. US 101, Las Posas Rd exit. Phone 805/445-8520.

Channel Islands Aviation. Offers trips to Santa Rosa Island, in the Channel Islands National Park; one-day scenic trips (Daily; closed Jan 1, Dec 25) Phone 805/987-1301. ¢¢¢¢¢

Motels/Motor Lodges

★★ **BEST WESTERN INN.** *295 Daily Dr (93010). 805/987-4991; fax 805/388-3679; res 800/528-1234.* 58 rms, 2 story. S $55; D $61-$63; each addl $5; under 12 free. Crib free. TV; cable (premium). Pool; whirlpool. Complimentary continental bkfst. Restaurant adj 6 am-10 pm. Ck-out 11 am. Meeting rms. Business servs avail. Cr cds: A, D, DS, JCB, MC, V.

D

★★★ **THE COUNTRY INN AT CAMARILLO.** *1405 Del Norte Rd (93010). 805/983-7171; fax 805/983-1838; res 800/456-4000.* 100 rms, 3 story. S, D $138; each addl $10; suites $159; under 12 free. TV; VCR (movies $4). Heated pool; whirlpool. Complimentary full bkfst. Ck-out noon. Lndry facilities. Business servs avail. In-rm modem link. Valet serv. Health club privileges. Refrigerators. Cr cds: A, D, DS, MC, V.

D

★★ **HOLIDAY INN.** *4444 Central Ave (93010). 805/485-3999; fax 805/485-1820. www.holiday-inn.com.*

110 rms, 3 story. S, D $89-$109; each addl $10; suites $120; under 12 free. Crib free. Pet accepted. TV; VCR (movies $4). Heated pool; whirlpool. Complimentary continental bkfst. Restaurant adj 8 am-10 pm. Ck-out noon. Coin lndry. Business servs avail. Valet serv. Refrigerators. Balconies. Cr cds: A, C, D, DS, MC, V.
D

Restaurants

★★ **MONEY PANCHO.** *3661 Las Posas Rd (93010). 805/484-0591.* Hrs: 10 am-9 pm. Res accepted. Mexican menu. Bkfst $4.45-$7.95, lunch $3.95-$7.95, dinner $7.95-$13.95. Children's menu. Specialties: sea and earth, marina rey, fajitas chicken rey. Guitar. Parking. Formal Mexican-style atmosphere and decor. Family-owned since 1975. Totally nonsmoking. Cr cds: A, DS, MC, V.
D SC

★★ **OTTAVIO'S.** *1620 Ventura Blvd (93010). 805/482-3810. www.ottavio.com.* Hrs: 11 am-10 pm; Sun to 9 pm; early-bird dinner Mon-Thurs, Sun 3-6 pm. Closed hols. Res accepted. Italian menu. Bar. Lunch $5.50-$10.50, dinner $7.50-$16.95. Specializes in pasta, veal, pizza. Italian decor. Family-owned. Totally nonsmoking. Cr cds: A, DS, MC, V.
D SC

Cambria

(C-2) *See also Morro Bay, San Simeon*

Pop 5,382 **Elev** 65 ft **Area code** 805 **Zip** 93428

Information Chamber of Commerce, 767 Main St; 805/927-3624

Web www.cambriachamber.org

Cambria's early commerce centered on lumbering, ranching, mining, and shipping. However, the town's shipping and whaling volume declined as trade relied on the railroad extending to San Luis Obispo. Today, Cambria is known as an artists' colony on California's central coast; there are many art galleries and gift and antique shops throughout town.

What to See and Do

Beach recreation. Rock and surf fishing at Moonstone Beach. Whale watching late Dec-early Feb. The large rocks at Piedras Blancas are a prime refuge for sea lions and sea otters.

Hearst-San Simeon State Historical Monument. (see) Approx 7 mi N on CA 1. Phone 800/444-4445.

Motels/Motor Lodges

★★ **BEST WESTERN FIRESIDE INN.** *6700 Moonstone Beach Dr (93428). 805/927-8661; fax 805/927-8584; toll-free 888/910-7100. www.firesideinn.com.* 46 rms. No A/C. S, D $69-$149; each addl $10; under 18 free; wkends, hols (2-day min). Crib free. TV; cable, VCR avail (movies). Heated pool; whirlpool. Complimentary continental bkfst, coffee in rms. Restaurant nearby. Ck-out 11 am. Business servs avail. In-rm modem link. Refrigerators, many fireplaces. Opp ocean. Cr cds: A, C, D, DS, ER, JCB, MC, V.
D SC

★ **CAMBRIA SHORES INN.** *6276 Moonstone Beach Dr (93428). 805/927-8644; fax 805/927-4070; toll-free 800/433-9179. www.cambriashores.com.* 24 rms. No A/C. Memorial Day-Labor Day, wkends, hols: S $125; D $135; lower rates rest of yr. Crib free. Pet accepted, some restrictions; $5. TV; cable. Complimentary continental bkfst, coffee in rms. Ck-out 11 am. Business servs avail. Refrigerators; microwaves avail. Ocean view; beach opp. Cr cds: A, DS, MC, V.

★★ **CASTLE INN BY THE SEA.** *6620 Moonstone Beach Dr (93428). 805/927-8605; fax 805/927-3179.* 31 rms. S, D $65-$150; each addl $5. Crib $5. TV; cable. Pool; whirlpool. Complimentary continental bkfst. Ck-out 11 am. Business servs avail. Many refrigerators. Ocean view; beach opp. Cr cds: A, DS, MC, V.

B&Bs/Small Inns

★★★ **BURTON DRIVE INN.** *4022 Burton Dr (93428). 805/927-5125; fax 805/927-9637. www.burtondrive*

inn.com. 10 suites, 2 story. No A/C. S, D $85-$150; each addl $10; wkend, hols (2-day min). TV; cable (premium). Complimentary continental bkfst, coffee in rms. Restaurant nearby. Ck-out 11 am, ck-in 2 pm. Refrigerators, microwaves. Comtemporary decor. Totally nonsmoking. Cr cds: A, DS, MC, V.

★★★ **J. PATRICK HOUSE BED AND BREAKFAST.** *2990 Burton Dr (93428). 805/927-3812; fax 805/927-6759; res 800/341-5258. www.jpatrickhouse.com.* 8 rms, 2 story. No A/C. No rm phones. S, D $150; wkends, hols (2-day min). Complimentary full bkfst. Ck-out 11 am, ck-in 3 pm. Health club privileges. Fireplaces. Each rm individually decorated; antiques, homemade quilts. Early American-style log house; garden with arbor; extensive grounds, landscaping. Totally nonsmoking. Cr cds: A, DS, MC, V.

★★★ **SQUIBB HOUSE.** *4063 Burton Dr (93428). 805/927-9600; fax 805/927-9606.* 5 rms, 2 story. No A/C. No rm phones. S, D $95-$155. Complimentary continental bkfst. Restaurant adj 11 am-10 pm. Ck-out 11 am, ck-in 3-6 pm. Wine tasting. Built in 1877; antiques. Totally nonsmoking. Cr cds: A, MC, V.

Villa/Condo

★★★ **MOONSTONE INN.** *5860 Moonstone Beach Dr (93428). 805/927-4815; fax 805/927-3944; toll-free 800/821-3764. www.cambriasbest.com/moonstoneinn.* 10 rms, 1-2 story. No A/C. May-Sept: S $85-$110; D $89-$110; each addl $10; lower rates rest of yr. TV; cable, VCR (free movies). Complimentary continental bkfst, coffee in rms. Restaurant nearby. Ck-out 11 am, ck-in 2 pm. Business servs avail. Whirlpool. Refrigerators, fireplaces. Antiques. On ocean; all rms with ocean view. Totally nonsmoking. Cr cds: A, C, D, DS, ER, JCB, MC, V.

SC

Restaurants

★★ **THE BRAMBLES DINNER HOUSE.** *4005 Burton Dr (93428). 805/927-4716. www.bramblesdinnerhouse.com.* Hrs: 4-9:30 pm; Sat to 10 pm; early-bird dinner Sun-Fri 4-6 pm, Sat 4-5:30 pm; Sun brunch 9:30 am-2 pm. Res accepted. Continental menu. No A/C. Bar. Dinner from $7.95. Sun brunch $8.95-$12.95. Children's menu. Specialties: prime rib with Yorkshire pudding, oak-broiled fresh salmon. Outdoor dining. Victorian decor; antiques. Totally nonsmoking. Cr cds: A, D, DS, MC, V.

D

★★ **ROBIN'S.** *4095 Burton Dr (93428). 805/927-5007. www.robinsrestaurant.com.* Hrs: 11 am-9 pm. Closed Thanksgiving, Dec 25. Res accepted. No A/C. Wine, beer. A la carte entrees: lunch $3.95-$10.95, dinner $7.95-$17.95. Specializes in vegetarian and Asian dishes with locally grown produce. Outdoor dining. Garden. Totally nonsmoking. Cr cds: MC, V.

Carlsbad

(F-5) *See also Escondido, La Jolla (San Diego), Oceanside, San Diego, San Juan Capistrano*

Pop 63,126 **Elev** 39 ft **Area code** 760

Information Convention & Visitors Bureau, PO Box 1246, 92018; 760/434-6093 or 800/227-5722

Web www.carlsbadca.org/

Named for Karlsbad, Bohemia (now in the Czech Republic), a famous European spa, this beach-oriented community is a playground for golfers, tennis players, waterskiers, and fishing enthusiasts.

What to See and Do

Legoland. Theme park inspired by the popular children's toy bricks offers displays and interactive exhibits. Incl a miniature landscape of five North American landmarks built with Legos. Rides, restaurants. (Daily) 1 Lego Dr. Phone 760/918-5346. ¢¢¢¢¢

South Carlsbad State Beach. Swimming, surfing, fishing. Improved camping (dump station). Standard fees. 3 mi S on Carlsbad Blvd. Phone 760/438-3143.

Special Events

Flower Fields at Carlsbad Ranch. Palomar Airport Rd. Phone 760/930-9123. Mid-Mar-Apr.

Carlsbad Village Street Faire. More than 800 art, craft and antique vendors; food, entertainment. First Sun May and first Sun Nov.

Motels/Motor Lodges

★★ HOLIDAY INN CARLSBAD-BY-THE-SEA. *850 Palomar Airport Rd (92008). 760/438-7880; fax 760/438-1015; res 800/465-4329. www.carlsbad holidayinn.com.* 145 rms, 2 story. Mid-May-Sept: S $119-$139; D $159-$169; under 12 free; lower rates rest of yr. Crib free. TV; cable (premium). Heated pool; whirlpool. Coffee in rms. Restaurant 6:30 am-10 pm. Bar 11 am-midnight; Fri, Sat to 2 am. Ck-out 11 am. Coin lndry. Meeting rms. Business servs avail. Valet serv. Free airport transportation. Some refrigerators. Private patios, balconies. Cr cds: A, C, D, DS, MC, V.

Capitol made of Legos at Legoland

★ INNS OF AMERICA. *751 Raintree Dr (92009). 760/931-1185; fax 760/931-0970; res 800/826-0778. www.innsofamerica.com.* 126 rms, 3 story. June-mid-Sept: S $63.90; D $68.90; lower rates rest of yr. Crib free. Pet accepted. TV; cable (premium). Heated pool. Complimentary continental bkfst. Restaurant adj 11:30 am-midnight; Sun brunch 9 am-1 pm. Ck-out 11 am. Coin lndry. Business servs avail. Cr cds: A, MC, V.

★ OCEAN PALMS BEACH RESORT. *2950 Ocean St (92008). 760/729-2493; fax 760/729-0579. www.ocean-palms. com.* 56 rms, 2 story, kit. suites. July-mid-Sept: S, D, kit. suites $84-$186; wkly rates; lower rates rest of yr. Crib $5. TV; cable, VCR avail (movies). Heated pool; whirlpool. Playground. Restaurant adj 7 am-10 pm. Ck-out 11 am. Gift shop. Coin lndry. Microwaves avail. Picnic tables, grills. Opp beach. Totally nonsmoking. Cr cds: A, DS, MC, V.

★★ RAMADA INN & SUITES CARLSBAD. *751 Macadamia Dr (92009). 760/438-2285; fax 760/931-7842; toll-free 800/644-9394. www. ramada.com.* 121 suites, 3 story. Suites $99-$139; under 18 free. Crib free. TV; cable (premium). Complimentary continental bkfst, coffee in rms. Restaurant nearby. Ck-out noon. Meeting rms. Business servs avail. In-rm modem link. Valet serv. Coin lndry. Health club privileges. Pool; whirlpool. Refrigerators, microwaves. Opp beach. Cr cds: A, D, DS, JCB, MC, V.

Resorts

★★ CARLSBAD INN BEACH RESORT. *3075 Carlsbad Blvd (92008). 760/434-7020; fax 760/729-4853; toll-free 800/235-3939. www.carlsbad inn.com.* 60 rms, 3 story, 27 kit. units. S, D $178; each addl $15; suites $205-$238; under 12 free. Crib free. TV; cable, VCR (movies). Heated pool; whirlpools. Supervised children's activities; ages 6-12. Complimentary coffee in rms. Restaurant adj 6:30 am-10 pm. Ck-out 11 am. Coin lndry. Meeting rms. Business servs avail. Exercise equipt; sauna. Lawn games. Putting green. Refrigerators; microwaves avail. Bathrm phone in suites. Picnic tables. Near beach. Cr cds: A, D, DS, MC, V.

D

★★★★ FOUR SEASONS RESORT AVIARA. *7100 Four Seasons Point (92009). 760/603-6800; fax 760/603-6801. www.fourseasons.com/aviara.* The sprawling grounds of this property contain golf courses, tennis courts, an excellent spa, and plenty of space for simply wandering amidst the pretty landscaping. Guest rooms are comfortable, but feel a bit more like executive offices than relaxed retreats. Service is attentive; the staff does all they can to accomodate guest requests. 331 rms, 5 story, 44 suites. S, D $355-$465; suites $500-$1,200; under 17 free; golf plans. Crib free. Pet accepted, some restrictions. TV; cable (premium), VCR avail. Pool; wading pool, whirlpool, poolside serv. Complimentary coffee in rms. Restaurants 6-10:30 pm (see also VIVACE). Rm serv 24 hrs. Bar to midnight; entertainment. Ck-out noon, ck-in 3 pm. Convention facilities. Business center. In-rm modem link. Bellhops. Valet serv. Concierge. Shopping arcade. Barber, beauty shop. Airport transportation. 6 lighted tennis courts, pro. 18-hole golf, greens fee $150; weekends $170. Putting green, driving range. Exercise rm; sauna, steam rm. Massage. Bathrm phones, minibars. Balconies. Cr cds: A, C, D, DS, ER, JCB, MC, V.

D

★★★ LA COSTA RESORT AND SPA. *2100 Costa Del Mar Rd (92009). 760/438-9111; fax 760/438-3758; toll-free 800/854-5000. www.lacosta.com.* 480 rms in hotel, 2-3 story, 2-3 bedrm houses. AP: S, D $335; suites $535-$2,400; golf, tennis, spa plans; MAP avail. Crib free. TV; cable (premium), VCR avail. 2 pools; whirlpool, poolside serv. Supervised children's activities. Restaurants 6:30 am-10 pm. Rm serv to 1 am. Snack bar. Bar. Ck-out noon, ck-in 4 pm. Meeting rms. Business center. In-rm modem link. Valet serv. Concierge. Shopping arcade. Airport transportation. Lighted tennis courts including clay, composition, and grass, pro. 36-hole golf, putting green, driving range. Soc dir. Exercise rm; sauna, steam rm. Spa. Minibars; wet bar in some suites. Some private patios. Cr cds: A, C, D, DS, JCB, MC, V.

D

Restaurants

★★★ BELLEFLEUR. *5610 Paseo del Norte (92008). 760/603-1919. www.bellefleur.com.* Hrs: 11 am-9 pm; Fri, Sat to 10 pm. Closed Jan 1, July 4, Dec 25. Res accepted. Contemporary American menu. Bar. Wine list. Lunch $9.25-$14.75, dinner $17-$22.75. Specializes in fresh, locally and regionally grown ingredients. Jazz and blues Tue, Thur. Parking. Outdoor dining. Winery. Totally nonsmoking. Cr cds: A, C, D, DS, MC, V.

D SC

★ SPIRITO'S. *300 Carlsbad Village Suite 208 (92008). 760/720-1132.* Hrs: 11 am-9 pm; Fri, Sat to 10 pm. Closed Easter, Thanksgiving, Dec 24, 25. Italian menu. Wine, beer. A la carte entrees: lunch, dinner $5-$14. Specializes in fresh pasta, pizzas. Outdoor dining. Totally nonsmoking. Cr cds: MC, V.

D

★★ TUSCANY. *6981 El Camino Real (92009). 760/929-8111.* Hrs: 11:30 am-10:30 pm; Sat, Sun 4:30-11 pm. Closed Thanksgiving. Res accepted. Italian menu. Bar. Lunch $6.95-$12.95, dinner $8.95-$18.95. Specializes in pasta, seafood, Northern Italian dishes. Entertainment Fri, Sat. Parking. Italian villa-style decor. Cr cds: A, D, MC, V.

D

★ VIGILUCCI'S TRATTORIA ITALIANA. *505 S Coast Hwy 101, Encinitas (92024). 760/942-7332.* Hrs: 11 am-3 pm, 5-10 pm; Sat, Sun 11 am-10:30 pm. Closed Jan 1, Thanksgiving, Dec 25. Res accepted. Italian menu. Bar. Lunch $5.95-$13.95, dinner $7.95-$17.95. Children's menu. Specializes in fresh fish, pasta. Outdoor dining. Totally nonsmoking. Cr cds: A, DS, MC, V.

D

★★★ VIVACE. *7100 Four Seasons Point (92009). 760/603-6999. www.fourseasons.com.* Hrs: 5:30-10:30 pm. Res accepted. Italian menu. Wine list. Dinner $14-$32. Children's menu. Specialties: osso buco, wood-grilled veal chop, lobster risotto.

Valet parking. Outdoor dining. Cr cds: A, D, DS, MC, V.
D

Carmel

(B-1) *See also Carmel Valley, Monterey, Pacific Grove, Pebble Beach*

Founded 1916 **Pop** 4,239 **Elev** 220 ft **Area code** 831

Information Carmel Business Association, San Carlos between 5th and 6th Sts, PO Box 4444, 93921; 831/624-2522

Web www.carmelcalifornia.org

Situated on the Bay of Carmel, the town sits at one of the loveliest spots along the California coast. A center for artists and writers since the turn of the century, Carmel fiercely protects its individuality. The architecture is a mixture of every style and whim of the literary and artistic populace, creating a unique and enchanting setting with endless activities for tourists.

What to See and Do

Antique and Art Galleries. More than 70 galleries display a wide variety of art and antiques in the Carmel area. A brochure, *The Guide To Carmel,* containing a list of galleries may be obtained from the Carmel Business Association, PO Box 4444, 93921. Phone 831/624-2522.

The Barnyard. Shopping area with 1½ acres of terraced flower gardens around rustic, old-style California barns housing a number of shops, galleries, and restaurants. CA 1, Carmel Valley Rd exit, then take first right and enter Barnyard from 26400 Carmel Rancho Blvd.

Beach areas. Carmel City Beach, located at the foot of Ocean Ave, has easy accessibility, white sands, and beautiful sunsets. **Carmel River State Beach**, south of Carmel on Scenic Rd, offers calm waters, tide pools, and an adj bird sanctuary. **FREE**

Biblical Garden. Founded in 1904. Stained-glass windows in the sanctuary depict Biblical and local scenes. Incl Gaza St. Galy mosaic, sundial on a granite boulder, mosaic cross in the garden. A 32-rank pipe organ provides quarterly concerts. Garden contains trees and plants mentioned in the Bible and indigenous to the Holy Land. (Daily) Church of the Wayfarer, Lincoln St and 7th Ave. Phone 831/624-3550. **FREE**

Mission San Carlos Borromeo del Rio Carmelo. Basilica founded by Frey Junipero Serra in 1770; his burial place. Oldest church in Carmel. Headquarters for the California missions. (Daily; closed Thanksgiving, Dec 25) 1 mi S off CA 1, then W to 3080 Rio Rd. Phone 831/624-3600. **Donation**

Pacific Repertory Theatre. Company performs dramas, comedies, and musicals in three venues: Golden Bough Playhouse, Circle Theatre, and outdoor Forest Theatre. (May-Oct, schedule varies) For location, fees, and schedule of plays, contact PO Box 222035, 93922. Phone 831/622-0700.

Point Lobos State Reserve. Sea Lion Rocks, Bird Island just offshore. Natural grove of Monterey cypress. Picnic area (no fires or stoves), naturalist programs. No dogs. (Day use only) 3 mi S on CA 1. Phone 831/624-4909. Per vehicle ¢¢

Rancho Cañada Golf Club. Two 18-hole championship courses; driving range. (Daily) Carmel Valley Rd, 1 mi E of CA 1. Phone 831/624-0111.

Seventeen-Mile Drive. From Carmel to Monterey (see MONTEREY).

Special Events

Monterey Wine Festival. Phone 800/656-4282. Early Apr.

Carmel Art Festival. Mid-May. Phone 831/642-2503.

Carmel Bach Festival. Sunset Center, San Carlos and 9th Sts. Concerts, recitals, lectures, special events. Contact PO Box 575, 93921. Phone 831/624-1521. Mid-July-early Aug.

Carmel Sand Castle Contest. Phone 831/626-1255. Oct.

Motels/Motor Lodges

★★ BEST WESTERN BAY VIEW INN. *6th Ave and Junipero St (93921). 831/624-1831; fax 831/625-2336. www.bestwestern.com/carmelbay viewinn.* 58 rms, 5 story. June-Oct: S,

D $79-$209; suites $169-$299; under 12 free; lower rates rest of yr. Crib $5. TV; cable. Pool. Complimentary continental bkfst. Restaurant opp 11-2 am. Ck-out 11 am. Business servs avail. Some refrigerators. Cr cds: A, D, DS, MC, V.

★★ **BEST WESTERN MISSION INN.** *3665 Rio Rd (93923). 831/624-1841; fax 831/624-8684; toll-free 800/348-9090.* 165 rms, 4 story. S, D $99-$199; each addl $10; suites $289-$359; under 13 free. Crib free. Pet accepted; $25. TV; cable (premium). Heated pool; whirlpools. Restaurant 7-10 am; wkends to 11 am, 5:30-9:30 pm. Bar. Ck-out noon. Meeting rms. Business servs avail. Bellhops. Refrigerators. Many balconies. Picnic sites. Cr cds: A, C, D, DS, MC, V.

★★ **BEST WESTERN TOWN HOUSE LODGE.** *5th and San Carlos sts (92135). 831/624-1261; fax 831/625-6783; res 800/528-1234. www.bestwestern.com/carmels.* 28 rms. Apr-Oct: S $110-$125; D $125-$160; each addl $6; lower rates rest of yr; under 12 free. TV; cable. Heated pool. Coffee in rms. Restaurant nearby. Ck-out 11 am. In-rm modem link. Some refrigerators. Sun deck. Cr cds: A, D, DS, MC, V.

★★ **CANDLE LIGHT INN.** *San Carlos, between 4th and 5th Aves (93921). 831/624-6451; fax 831/624-6732; res 800/433-4732. www.innsbythesea.com.* 20 rms, 2 story, 5 kit. units. No A/C. June-Oct, wkends: S, D $179-$219; each addl $15; under 13 free; wkends (2-day min); lower rates rest of yr. TV; cable, some VCRs. Heated pool. Complimentary continental bkfst. Coffee in rms. Ck-out noon. Business servs avail. Refrigerators; some fireplaces; microwaves avail. Cr cds: A, DS, MC, V.

★ **CARMEL RESORT INN.** *Carpenter and 1st Ave (93921). 831/624-3113; fax 831/624-5456; toll-free 800/454-3700.* 31 cottages, 2 kits. No A/C. June-Sept: S, D $89-$235; kits. $149-$235; under 6 free; lower rates rest of yr. Crib $10. TV; cable (premium). Complimentary continental bkfst. Coffee in rms. Ck-out 11 am. Whirlpool. Sauna. Refrigerators, microwaves; many fireplaces. Cr cds: A, D, DS, MC, V.

★★ **HORIZON INN.** *Junipero and 3rd St (93921). 831/624-5327; fax 831/626-8253; toll-free 800/350-7750.* 29 rms, 1-2 story, 6 kits; 6 suites (1 bedrm) in building opp. No A/C. S, D $89-$169; each addl $15; suites $180-$209. TV; cable. Heated pool. Complimentary continental bkfst. Coffee in rms. Restaurant nearby. Ck-out noon. Coin lndry. Business servs avail. Refrigerators; many fireplaces; microwaves avail. Some private patios, balconies. Some rms with ocean view. Cr cds: A, D, DS, MC, V.

★ **LOBOS LODGE.** *Ocean Ave and Monteverde St (93921). 831/624-3874; fax 831/624-0135. www.loboslodge.com.* 30 rms, 1-3 story. S, D $99-$129; each addl $25; suites $155-$195. TV; cable. Ck-out noon. Refrigerators, fireplaces. Private patios, balconies. Beach 4 blks. Cr cds: A, MC, V.

★★ **SVENDSGAARDS INN.** *San Carlos and 4th St (93921). 831/624-1511; fax 831/624-5667; res 800/433-4732. www.svendsgaardsinn.com.* 34 rms, 1-2 story, 14 kits. No A/C. June-Oct, wkends: S, D $119-$169; each addl $15; suites $199-$229; under 13 free; wkends (2-day min); lower rates rest of yr. TV; cable. Heated pool. Complimentary continental bkfst. Coffee in rms. Restaurant nearby. Ck-out noon. Business servs avail. Refrigerators; some fireplaces; microwaves avail. Country decor. Cr cds: A, DS, MC, V.

★★ **TALLY HO INN.** *Monte Verde St and 6th Ave (93921). 831/624-2232; fax 831/624-2661. www.tallyho-inn.com.* 14 rms, 1-2 story. No A/C. May-Oct: S, D $115-$250; lower rates mid-wk. Crib free. TV; cable. Complimentary continental bkfst. Restaurant opp from 7 am. Ck-out noon. Business servs avail. In-rm modem link. Some fireplaces, whirlpools. Some private patios. Landscaped gardens. Cr cds: A, C, D, DS, JCB, MC, V.

★★★ **TICKLE PINK COUNTRY INN CARMEL.** *155 Highlands Dr*

(93923). 831/624-1244; fax 831/626-9516; toll-free 800/635-4774. www.ticklepink.com. 34 rms in 2 buildings, 3, 4 story. No A/C. No elvtr. S, D $199-$269; each addl $25; suites $259-$309; cottage $259-$279; wkends (2-day min), special events (3-day min). TV; cable, VCR (movies). Complimentary continental bkfst. Coffee in rms. Restaurant adj 7 am-11 pm. Ck-out noon. Meeting rm. Business servs avail. Whirlpool. Refrigerators; some fireplaces, whirlpools. Many balconies. Scenic view of sea coast. Cr cds: A, MC, V.

D

★★ **THE VILLAGE INN.** *Ocean Ave and Junipero St (93921). 831/624-3864; fax 831/626-6763; toll-free 800/346-3864. www.carmelvillageinn.com.* 48 rms, 2 story. No A/C. May-Oct: S, D $79-$175; lower rates rest of yr. TV; cable (premium). Continental bkfst. Ck-out 11 am. Microwaves avail. Cr cds: A, MC, V.

D

Hotels

★★ **LA PLAYA HOTEL.** *Camino Real and 8th St (93921). 831/624-6476; fax 831/624-7966; toll-free 800/582-8900. www.laplayacarmel.com.* 75 rms, 3-4 story, 4 kit. cottages. S, D $195; each addl $15; suites $235-$395; kit. cottages $235-$525; under 12 free. Crib free. TV; cable. Heated pool; poolside serv. Restaurant 7 am-10 pm. Bar 11 am-midnight. Ck-out noon. Meeting rms. Business servs avail. Concierge. Valet parking. Health club privileges. Private patios. Renovated Mediterranean-style villa (1904). Cr cds: A, D, MC, V.

D

★★ **PINE INN.** *Ocean Ave and Monte Verde (93921). 831/624-3851; fax 831/624-3030; toll-free 800/228-3851. www.pine-inn.com.* 49 rms, 3 story, 6 suites. S, D $150; each addl $10; suites $230; under 18 free. Crib free. TV; cable. Restaurant 7 am-10 pm; wkends 8 am-11 pm. Bar. Ck-out 1 pm. Concierge. Meeting rms. Business servs avail. Some refrigerators. In historic (1889) building. Cr cds: A, C, D, DS, JCB, MC, V.

D

Resorts

★★★ **HIGHLANDS INN.** *120 Highlands Dr (93923). 831/620-1234; fax 831/626-1574; res 800/682-4811. www.hyatt.com.* 142 rms, 1-2 story, 100 suites. S, D $190-$435; each addl $25; suites $425-$575; 2-bedrm suites $550-$915; under 16 free. Crib free. TV; cable, VCR (movies). Heated pool; poolside serv. Coffee in rms. Restaurant 7 am-10 pm (see also PACIFIC'S EDGE). Bar 11-1 am; entertainment. Ck-out noon. Meeting rms. Business center. In-rm modem link. Concierge. Gift shop. Free airport transportation. Exercise equipt. Bicycles. Minibars; some whirlpools, fireplaces; full kit. in suites. Microwaves avail. Private patios, balconies. On 12 wooded acres; views of Pacific Ocean and Big Sur coast. Cr cds: A, C, D, DS, ER, JCB, MC, V.

D

★★★★ **QUAIL LODGE AND RESORT AND GOLF CLUB.** *8205 Valley Greens Dr (93923). 831/624-1581; fax 831/624-3726; res 800/538-9516. www.quail-lodge-resort.com.* Part of the Peninsula Group of luxury hotels, this resort is located on 850 Monterey Peninsula acres five minutes from Carmel-by-the-Sea. There's plenty to fill the days with a championship golf course, tennis courts, pools, and miles of hiking and biking trails dotting the countryside landscape. 100 units. S, D $225-$295; each addl $25; suites $405-$825; under 12 free; golf plan Sun-Thurs. Pet accepted. TV; cable (premium). 2 heated pools; whirlpool, poolside serv. Supervised children's activities by request (July-Sept). Complimentary afternoon refreshments, coffee in rms. Restaurants 6:30-10 pm. Rm serv 7 am-11 pm. Bars 11 am-midnight; entertainment. Ck-out 1 pm. Meeting rms. Business center. Bellhops. Concierge. Airport transportation. Tennis, pro. 18-hole golf, greens fee $145-$175, putting greens, driving range. Bicycles. Health club privileges. Lawn games. Some fireplaces, wet bars. Private patios, balconies. Cr cds: A, DS, MC, V.

D

B&Bs/Small Inns

★★★ **ADOBE INN.** *Dolores and 8th Ave (93921). 831/624-3933; fax 831/624-8636; res 800/388-3933. www.adobeinn.com.* 20 rms, 2 story, 1 suites. No A/C. S, D $225-$275; suites $240-$300. TV; cable, VCR avail. Heated pool. Sauna. Complimentary continental bkfst, coffee in rms. Restaurant adj 11:30 am-11:30 pm. Ck-out noon. Meeting rm. Free covered parking. Refrigerators. Balconies. Cr cds: A, C, D, DS, ER, JCB, MC, V.

D

★★ **BRIARWOOD INN.** *San Carlos St (93921). 831/626-9056; fax 831/626-8900; toll-free 800/999-8788. www.briarwood-inn-carmel.com.* 7 rms, 1 with shower only, 2 story, 5 suites. No A/C. S, D $125-$185; each addl $20; suites $225-$450; wkends (2-day min). TV; cable, VCR (movies). Complimentary continental bkfst, coffee in rms. Restaurant nearby. Ck-out 11 am, ck-in 2 pm. Refrigerators; some wet bars; microwaves avail. Totally nonsmoking. Cr cds: A, MC, V.

★★ **CARMEL GARDEN COURT INN.** *4th and Torres St (93921). 831/624-6926; fax 831/624-4935. www.carmelgardencourtinn.com.* 9 rms. No A/C. May-Oct: S, D $125-$245; suite $245-$425; wkends (2-day min). TV; cable, VCR (free movies). Complimentary continental bkfst; afternoon refreshments, coffee in rms. Restaurant nearby. Ck-out 11 am, ck-in 4-9 pm. Business servs avail. Refrigerators. Garden. Totally nonsmoking. Cr cds: A, MC, V.

★★★ **CARRIAGE HOUSE INN.** *Junipero, between 7th and 8th Aves (93921). 831/625-2585; fax 831/624-0974; res 800/433-4732. www.innsbythesea.com.* 13 rms, 2 story. No A/C. S, D $209-$279; suites $299; each addl $15; under 13 free; wkends (2-day min). TV; cable (premium), VCR. Complimentary continental bkfst; evening refreshments. Restaurant nearby. Ck-out noon, ck-in 3 pm. Business servs avail. Refrigerators, wet bars, fireplaces; some in-rm whirlpools. Antique furnishings. Totally nonsmoking. Cr cds: A, DS, MC, V.

SC

★★ **COBBLESTONE INN.** *Junipero Ave (93921). 831/625-5222; fax 831/625-0478; toll-free 800/833-8836. www.foursisters.com.* 24 rms, 2 story. S, D $95-$200; each addl $15; suites $175. TV; cable. Complimentary full bkfst; afternoon refreshments. Ck-out noon, ck-in 2 pm. Business servs avail. Refrigerators, fireplaces. English country decor; cobblestone courtyard. Cr cds: A, D, MC, V.

★★ **CRYSTAL TERRACE INN.** *24815 Carpenter St (93921). 831/624-6400; fax 831/624-5111; toll-free 800/600-4488.* 17 rms, 2 story. No A/C. May-Oct: S, D $150-$225; cottage $235-$275; higher rates special events; lower rates rest of yr. TV; cable (premium), VCR avail (movies). Complimentary continental bkfst; afternoon refreshments. Restaurant nearby. Ck-out 11 am, ck-in 3 pm. Business servs avail. Some refrigerators, microwaves, minibars, fireplaces. Some balconies. Built in 1927. Garden area. Totally nonsmoking. Cr cds: A, C, D, DS, ER, MC, V.

D

★★ **CYPRESS INN.** *Lincoln and 7th St (93921). 831/624-3871; fax 831/624-8216; toll-free 800/443-7443. www.cypress-inn.com.* 34 rms, 2 story. S, D $110-$350; each addl $15; lower rates Dec-Jan. Pet accepted; $17. TV; cable (premium). Complimentary continental bkfst, refreshments in rms. Bar 7 am-11 pm. Ck-out noon, ck-in 3 pm. Business servs avail. Luggage handling. Some refrigerators, fireplaces. Some verandas. Mediterranean facade; set in heart of Carmel Village. Cr cds: A, DS, MC, V.

D

★★ **DOLPHIN INN.** *San Carlos and 4th Ave (93921). 831/624-5356; fax 831/624-4891; res 800/433-4732. www.innsbythesea.com.* 26 rms, 2 story. No A/C. June-Oct, wkends: S, D $99-$169 each addl $15; suites $219-$229; under 13 free; wkends (2-day min); lower rates rest of yr. TV; cable. Heated pool. Complimentary continental bkfst. Coffee in rms. Ck-out noon. Business servs avail. Refrigerators; many fireplaces; microwaves avail. Cr cds: A, DS, MC, V.

★★ **GREEN LANTERN INN.** *Casanova St and 7th Ave (93921).*

831/624-4392; fax 831/624-9591; toll-free 888/414-4392. www.greenlantern inn.com. 18 rms, 2 story, 3 suites. No A/C. June-Sept: S, D $120-$190; suites $165-$190; under 16 free; wkends, hols (2-3-day min); lower rates rest of yr. Crib free. TV; cable. Complimentary full bkfst; afternoon refreshments. Restaurant nearby. Ck-out 11 am, ck-in 2 pm. Business servs avail. Cottage-style units. Refrigerators; some fireplaces. Totally nonsmoking. Cr cds: A, C, D, DS, JCB, MC, V.

★★ **HAPPY LANDING INN.** *Monte Verde St between 5th and 6th St (93921). 831/624-7917.* 5 rms, 2 suites. No A/C. No rm phones. S, D $95-$145; suites $185. Children over 12 yrs only. TV; cable. Complimentary full bkfst; afternoon refreshments. Restaurant nearby. Ck-out 11:30 am, ck-in 2 pm. Cathedral ceilings; antiques. Garden; gazebo; pond. 1925 Comstock cottage. Cr cds: MC, V.

★ **HOFSAS HOUSE.** *San Carlos between 3rd and 4th (93921). 831/624-2745; fax 831/624-0159; toll-free 800/221-2548. www.hofsashouse.com.* 38 rms, showers only, 4 story. No A/C. No elvtr. June-Sept: S, D $90-$130; suites $180; kit. units $110-$135; lower rates rest of yr. Crib $7.50. TV; cable, VCR avail (movies). Pool. Sauna. Complimentary continental bkfst. Restaurant nearby. Bar. Ck-out noon. Meeting rm. Cr cds: A, MC, V.

★★★ **MISSION RANCH.** *26270 Dolores St (93923). 831/624-6436; fax 831/626-4163; toll-free 800/538-8221.* 31 rms, 6 in farmhouse. No A/C. S, D $95-$275; each addl $15. TV; cable (premium). Complimentary continental bkfst, coffee in rms. Restaurant (see also MISSION RANCH). Bar; entertainment. Ck-out 11 am, ck-in 3 pm. Meeting rms. Business servs avail. Tennis, pro. Exercise equipt. Country decor; ranch atmosphere. Totally nonsmoking. Cr cds: A, MC, V.

D

★★ **NORMANDY INN.** *Ocean Ave and Monte Verde St (93921). 831/624-3825; fax 831/624-4614; res 800/343-3825. www.normandyinncarmel.com.* 45 rms, 2 story, 2 kit. suites, 3 kit cottages. June-Oct: S, D $98-$200; each addl $10; suites $165-$300; kit cottages $250-$400; lower rates rest of yr. TV; cable. Heated pool. Complimentary continental bkfst. Ck-out 11 am, ck-in 2 pm. Some fireplaces; refrigerators, microwaves avail. French country garden atmosphere. Cr cds: A, D, MC, V.

★★ **SANDPIPER INN AT THE BEACH CARMEL.** *2408 Bayview Ave (93923). 831/624-6433; fax 831/624-5964; toll-free 800/633-6433. www.sandpiperinn.com.* 16 rms, 2 story. No A/C. No rm phones. S, D $95-$200; each addl $20; hols, special events (3-day min), wkends (2-day min). TV in sitting rm; cable. Complimentary continental bkfst buffet; afternoon refreshments. Ck-out noon, ck-in after 3 pm. Business servs avail. Some fireplaces. Some rms with ocean view. Antiques. Cr cds: A, D, MC, V.

★ **STONEHOUSE INN.** *8th Ave and Monte Verde St (93921). 831/624-4569. www.carmelstonehouse.com.* 6 rms, 5 share bath, 2 story. No A/C. No rm phones. S, D $99-$199. Children over 12 yrs only. Complimentary full bkfst; evening refreshments. Ck-out noon, ck-in 3 pm. Built 1906. Antiques. Garden. Cr cds: A, MC, V.

★★ **SUNSET HOUSE BED & BREAKFAST.** *Camino Real, between Ocean Ave and 7th Aves (93921). 831/624-4884; fax 831/624-4884. www.sunset-carmel.com.* 5 rms, 4 with shower only. No A/C. S $190-$210; D $210-$230; each addl $20; under 5 free; wkly rates; wkends, hols (2-day min). Crib free. Pet accepted, some restrictions; $20. TV; cable (premium). Complimentary continental bkfst, coffee in rms. Restaurant nearby. Ck-out 11 am, ck-in 3-6 pm. Business servs avail. In-rm modem link. Refrigerators, fireplaces. Picnic tables. Fountain. Totally nonsmoking. Cr cds: MC, V.

SC

★★ **VAGABOND HOUSE INN.** *Dolores St and 4th Ave (93921).*

831/624-7738; fax 831/626-1243; toll-free 800/262-1262. vagabondshouse inn.com. 11 rms, 1-2 story. No A/C. S, D $115-$185; each addl $20. Pet accepted, $10. Over 12 yrs only. TV; cable (premium). Complimentary continental bkfst. Ck-out noon, ck-in 3 pm. Many fireplaces. Antiques. Courtyard garden. Cr cds: A, MC, V.

★★ **WAYSIDE INN.** *Mission St and 7th Ave (93921). 831/624-5336; fax 831/626-6974; res 800/433-4732. www.innsbythesea.com.* 21 rms, 2 story, 8 kits. No A/C. Mid-June-mid-Oct, wkends: S, D $179-$229; each addl $15; suites $219-$269; under 14 free; wkends (2-day min); lower rates rest of yr. Pet accepted. TV; cable. Complimentary continental bkfst. Coffee in rms. Restaurant nearby. Ck-out noon. Ck-in 3 pm. Business servs avail. Refrigerators; many fireplaces; microwaves avail. Some balconies. Colonial Williamsburg decor. Cr cds: A, DS, MC, V.

SC

Restaurants

★★ **ANTON AND MICHEL.** *Mission St (93921). 831/624-2406. www.carmelsbest.com.* Hrs: 11:30 am-3 pm, 5:30-9:30 pm. Res accepted. Continental menu. Bar 11 am-11 pm. A la carte entrees: lunch $7.75-$14.50, dinner $18.50-$39.50. Specialties: rack of lamb, fresh abalone, chicken Jerusalem. Garden view from main dining room. Cr cds: A, D, DS, MC, V.

D

★★ **CAFFE NAPOLI.** *Ocean Ave and Lincoln Ave (93923). 831/625-4033. www.caffenapoli.com.* Hrs: 11:30 am-10 pm. Closed Thanksgiving, Dec 25. Res accepted. No A/C. Italian menu. Wine, beer. A la carte entrees: lunch, dinner $9-$15. Specializes in pasta, pizza. Italian decor. Totally nonsmoking. Cr cds: C, MC, V.

D

★★ **CASANOVA.** *5th Ave and Mission (93923). 831/625-0501. www.casanovarestaurant.com.* Hrs: 11:30 am-3 pm, 5-10 pm; Fri, Sat to 10:30 pm; Sun brunch 10 am-3 pm, 5-10 pm. Closed Dec 25. Res accepted. No A/C. Wine cellar. Bar. French, Italian menu. Lunch $5.75-$13.75, dinner $19-$35. Sun brunch $7.25-$13.75. Specializes in southern French, northern Italian cuisine. Own baking, pasta. Outdoor dining. Cr cds: MC, V.

D

★ **COTTAGE RESTAURANT.** *Lincoln St (93921). 831/625-6260. www.cottagerestaurant.com.* Hrs: 7:30 am-3 pm; Thurs-Sat also 5-9 pm. Closed Dec 25. Res accepted. No A/C. Wine, beer. Bkfst $5.50-$9, lunch $5.75-$10.50, dinner $6.25-$14.95. Children's menu. Specialties: eggs Benedict, artichoke soup, Caesar salad. Country-style decor; stained-glass windows. Totally nonsmoking. Cr cds: MC, V.

D

★★ **FLYING FISH GRILL - KENNY'S.** *Carmel Plaza (93923). 831/625-1962.* Hrs: 5-10 pm. Closed Tues Nov-May. Res accepted. Dinner $13.75-$19.75. Specialties: black bean catfish, almond sea bass, seafood clay pot. Pacific Rim decor; fish motif incl artwork, papier mâche flying fish decorations. Cr cds: A, D, DS, MC, V.

★★ **THE FORGE IN THE FOREST AND GENERAL STORE.** *5th and Junipero (93921). 831/624-2233.* Specializes in rotisserie fowl. Hrs: 11:30 am-10 pm; Fri, Sat to 11 pm; Sun brunch 11:30 am-3 pm. Bar. Lunch $8.75-$18.95, dinner $8.95-$21.95. Sun brunch $10. Children's menu. Cr cds: A, C, D, DS, MC, V.

D

★★★ **FRENCH POODLE.** *Junipero and 5th Ave (93923). 831/624-8643.* Hrs: 5:30-9:30 pm. Closed Sun; Dec 25. Res accepted. Air-cooled. French menu. Dinner $16-$27. Extensive wine list. Specialties: sliced breast of duck in aged port wine sauce; les noisettes d'agneau au thym et a la moutarde de Dijon; abalone meuniere. Own desserts. Intimate dining. Chef-owned. Cr cds: A, D, MC, V.

D

★★ **GRILL ON OCEAN AVENUE.** *Ocean Ave (93921). 831/624-2569. www.carmelsbest.com.* Hrs: 11:30 am-10 pm. Res accepted. Bar. Lunch $7.75-$14.50, dinner $13.25-$20.75. Specializes in fresh seafood, grilled meats, pasta. Fireplace, artwork. Cr cds: A, D, DS, MC, V.

D

★★ **HOG'S BREATH INN.** *San Carlos and 5th (93921). 831/625-1044.* Hrs: 11:30 am-3 pm, 5-10 pm; Sun brunch 11 am-3 pm. Closed Dec 25. Bar 11-1:30 am. Lunch $5.50-$13.50, dinner $9-$22. Sun brunch $4.75-$12.95. Specializes in fresh seafood, steaks. Outdoor dining. Family-owned. Cr cds: A, D, DS, MC, V.
D

★★ **IL FORNAIO CUCINA ITALIANO.** *Ocean at Ponte Verde (93921). 831/622-5100. www.ilfornaio.com.* Specializes in turtei aragosta, agnello al timo. Hrs: 7 am-10 pm. Res accepted. Wine, beer. Lunch $9-$17, dinner $9-$25. Children's menu. Entertainment. Cr cds: A, C, D, ER, MC, V.
D

★★★ **LA BOHEME.** *Dolores and 7th Ave (93923). 831/624-7500. www.laboheme.com.* Hrs: 5:30-10 pm. Closed Easter, Thanksgiving, Dec 25. No A/C. European/country menu. Wine, beer. Dinner $21.75. Menu changes nightly. French village atmosphere. Cr cds: MC, V.

★★ **LE COQ D'OR.** *Mission St and 5th Ave (93923). 831/626-9319. www.lecoqdor.com.* Hrs: 5-9 pm; Fri-Sat to 9:30 pm. Res accepted. No A/C. French, German menu. Wine, beer. Complete meals: dinner $18.25-$23.50. Children's menu. Specialties: confit de canard, jaegerschnitzel, scallops in orange buerre blanc. Outdoor dining. Intimate atmosphere; French and German pottery, artwork. Patio dining. Cr cds: A, MC, V.

★★ **LITTLE NAPOLI.** *Dolores St (93921). 831/626-6335. www.caffe napoli.com.* Hrs: 11:30 am-10 pm. Closed Thanksgiving, Dec 25. Res accepted. No A/C. Italian menu. Wine, beer. A la carte entrees: $9-$15. Specializes in pizza, pasta. Italian decor; ceramics, color prints. Totally nonsmoking. Cr cds: C, MC, V.
D

★★ **LUGANO SWISS BISTRO.** *3670 The Barnyard (93923). 831/626-3779. www.swissbistro.com.* Hrs: 11:30 am-9 pm. Res accepted. Swiss, Continental menu. Bar. Lunch $5.75-$12.50, dinner $9.75-$17.50. Specializes in fondues. Outdoor dining. Alpine decor. Cr cds: A, D, MC, V.
D

★★ **MISSION RANCH.** *26270 Dolores (93923). 831/625-9040.* Hrs: 4:30-10 pm; Sat 11 am-3 pm; Sun brunch 9:30 am-1:30 pm. Closed Dec 25. Res accepted. No A/C. Bar 4 pm-12:30 am. Wine list. A la carte entrees: lunch $6-$10, dinner $7.75-$26.95. Sun brunch $18.95. Children's menu. Specializes in prime rib, fish. Pianist; jazz for Sun brunch. Parking. Outdoor dining. Rural ambiance with view of ocean, Fort Lobos. Totally nonsmoking. Cr cds: MC, V.
D

★★★ **PACIFIC'S EDGE.** *CA 1 (93921). 831/622-5445. www.hyatt.com.* Contemporary regional cuisine. Specialties: Monterey Bay spot prawns, butter-poached Maine lobster, roasted prime Colorado rack of lamb, truffle-roasted chicken breast. Hrs: 6-10 pm; Fri, Sat to 10:30 pm; Sun brunch 10 am-2 pm. Res acceptd. Bar 11-2 am. Extensive wine list. Prix fixe: dinner $56-$91. Sun brunch $29. Pianist Wed-Mon. Jazz Fri, Sat. Valet parking. Cr cds: A, C, D, DS, MC, V.
D

★ **PATISSERIE BOISSIERE.** *Mission St at Carmel Plaza (93923). 831/624-5008.* Hrs: 11 am-9 pm; Mon, Tues to 5 pm, Sat, Sun from 10 am. Closed Thanksgiving, Dec 25. Res accepted. California, French menu. Wine, beer. Lunch $6-$9.95, dinner $9.95-$16.95. Sat, Sun brunch $4.50-$7.95. Specialties: French onion soup, coquille St Jaques, salmon baked in parchment paper. Own pastries. Louis XV dining room. Cr cds: A, MC, V.
D

★★★ **RAFFAELLO CARMEL.** *Mission between Ocean and 7th (93923). 831/624-1541.* Hrs: 6-10 pm. Mon, Wed-Sun; closed first 2 wks Jan. Res accepted. Northern Italian menu. Beer. Wine cellar. Dinner $13.75-$23.50. Specialties: cannelloni alla Raffaello, fettucine alla Romana, salmone alle shallots. Own desserts.

Paintings; fireplace. Family-owned. Cr cds: A, D, MC, V.

D

★★ **RIO GRILL.** *101 Crossroads Blvd (93923). 831/625-5436. www.riogrill.com.* Hrs: 11:30 am-11 pm. Closed July 4, Thanksgiving, Dec 25. Res accepted. Bar to midnight. Wine cellar. A la carte entrees: lunch $9-$17, dinner $9-$17. Specializes in oakwood grilled chicken, fish, beef. Own pastries. Outdoor dining. Contemporary Southwestern adobe decor. Cr cds: A, DS, MC, V.

D

★★ **ROBATA GRILL AND SAKE BAR.** *3658 The Barnyard (93923). 831/624-2643.* Hrs: from 5 pm. Closed Thanksgiving, Dec 25. Japanese menu. Bar. Dinner $10.95-$30.95. Specializes in open hearth cooking, sushi. Parking. Japanese farmhouse decor. Cr cds: A, D, MC, V.

D

★★★ **ROBERT'S BOULEVARD BISTRO.** *217 Crossroads Blvd (93923). 831/624-9626.* Hrs: 11:30 am-2 pm, 5:30-10 pm; Sat, Sun from 5:30 pm. Tues-Sun; closed Thanksgiving, Dec 24, 25. Res accepted. French menu. Wine list. Dinner $17.95-$26.95. Complete meals: lunch $14.95. Specialties: rack of lamb, roast duckling, Holland Dover sole. Country French atmosphere; fireplaces. Cr cds: A, DS, MC, V.

D

★ **ROCKY POINT.** *CA 1 (93922). 831/624-2933. www.rocky-point.com.* Hrs: 9 am-9:30 pm. Res accepted. No A/C. Bar. Bkfst $4-$15, lunch $8-$15, dinner $19-$32. Specializes in steak, seafood. Parking. Full-window view of coastline; many outdoor tables and sitting benches. Totally nonsmoking. Cr cds: A, DS, MC, V.

D

★★★ **SANS SOUCI.** *Lincoln and 5th Ave (93923). 831/624-6220.* Hrs: 5:30-10 pm. Closed Wed. Res accepted. No A/C. French menu. Wine list. Dinner $16-$28. Specializes in lamb, duck, fresh seafood. French decor; fireplace. Family-owned. Cr cds: A, MC, V.

★★ **TERRACE GRILL AT LAPLAYA.** *8th Ave and Camino Real (93921). 831/624-6476. www.laplayacarmel.com.* Specializes in prime rib, grilled chicken panini. Hrs: 7 am-2:30 pm, 5:30-10 pm. Res accepted. Wine, beer. Lunch $8-$15; dinner $15-$20. Entertainment. Cr cds: A, C, D, MC, V.

D SC

Unrated Dining Spot

THUNDERBIRD BOOKSHOP CAFE. *3600 The Barnyard (93923). 831/624-9414.* Hrs: 10 am-8 pm. Closed hols. No A/C. Wine, beer. Lunch, dinner $3-$8.95. Specializes in sandwiches, pot pies, popovers. Outdoor dining. Glass-enclosed garden rm. Cr cds: A, DS, MC, V.

D SC

Carmel Valley

(B-1) *See also Carmel, Monterey*

Pop 4,407 **Elev** 400 ft **Area code** 831 **Zip** 93924

Resorts

★★★★ **BERNARDUS LODGE.** *415 Carmel Valley Rd (93924). 831/658-3400; fax 831/659-3529; toll-free 888/648-9463. www.bernardus.com.* It's obvious that this is an extension of the Bernardus Winery and Vineyard, from the in-room wine pantry to evening wine and cheese to the wine-based cuisine served in the restaurant. The mustard and rose adobe-style buildings are welcoming and the spa is magnificent. 56 rms, 2 story, 1 suite. June-Oct: S, D $445; suites $1,700; each addl $25; under 12 free; lower rates rest of yr. Crib avail. Valet parking. Pool. TV; cable (premium), VCR avail. Complimentary coffee in rms, newspaper. Restaurant 7 am-10 pm. Rm serv 24 hrs. Bar. Ck-out noon. Meeting rms. Business center. Concierge. Valet serv. Gift shop. Salon/barber shop. Exercise rm; sauna, steam rm. Golf. Tennis. Hiking trail. Cr cds: A, C, D, DS, JCB, MC, V.

D

★★★★ **CARMEL VALLEY RANCH.** *1 Old Ranch Rd (93923). 831/625-9500; fax 831/626-2574; toll-free 800/422-7635. www.wyndham.com.*

Delight in the vastness of this 1,700-acre estate set in secluded Monterey Peninsula countryside. The 144 suites, all with wood burning fireplaces, are clustered along the hillside. Play the Pete Dye championship golf course, visit the historic tennis clubhouse, and, at the end of the day, climb into your bed to enjoy the freshly-baked cookies left on your nightstand. 144 suites. July-Oct: S, D $325-$850; each addl $25; under 16 free; lower rates rest of yr. Crib free. Pet accepted. TV; cable (premium), VCR avail (movies). 2 heated pools; whirlpools, poolside serv. Restaurants 7 am-2 pm, 6-10 pm. Box lunches, snack bar. Rm serv 7 am-11 pm. Bar 11 am-midnight. Ck-out noon, ck-in 4 pm. Meeting rms. Business center. In-rm modem link. Concierge. Gift shop. Tennis, pro. 18-hole golf, pro, putting green, driving range, pro shop. Exercise rm; sauna. Entertainment Fri, Sat. Refrigerators, fireplaces. Private decks, balconies. Cr cds: A, D, DS, MC, V.

D

B&Bs/Small Inns

★★ **CARMEL VALLEY LODGE.** *8 Ford Rd (93924). 831/659-2261; fax 831/659-4558; toll-free 800/641-4646. www.valleylodge.com.* 31 units, 1-2 story, 8 kits. No A/C. July-Sept: S, D $119-$142; each addl $15; studios $164; kit units, cottages $186-$296; higher rates: hols, special events; wkends, hols (2-3-day min); lower rates rest of yr. Crib free. Pet accepted; $10/day. TV; cable, VCR avail. Heated pool; whirlpool. Complimentary continental bkfst, coffee in rms. Ck-out noon, ck-in after 2 pm. Meeting rm. Business servs avail. Exercise equipt; sauna. Fireplace in studios, cottages; some wet bars. Private patios, balconies. Cr cds: A, MC, V.

D

★★ **LOS LAURELES LODGE.** *313 Carmel Valley Rd (93924). 831/659-2233; fax 408/659-0481. www.loslaureles.com.* 30 units, 5 suites. No A/C. Apr-Oct: S, D $110-$250; suites $150-$450; under 17 free; wkends, hols (2-day min); lower rates rest of yr. TV; cable (premium). Heated pool; whirlpool. Restaurant May-Oct: 7:30 am-11 pm. Ck-out noon, ck-in 3 pm. Luggage handling. Business servs avail. Refrigerators; microwaves avail. Main building built in 1890s; once home of Muriel Vanderbilt. Cr cds: A, MC, V.

SC

Horses grazing under the warm California sun

★★★ **STONEPINE ESTATE RESORT.** *150 E Carmel Valley Rd (93924). 831/659-2245; fax 831/659-5160. www.stonepinecalifornia.com.* 14 suites, 2 story. No A/C. S, D $225-$750; each addl $50; 2-day min wkends, 3-day min hols. TV; cable. Heated pool. Children over 12 yrs only. Complimentary full bkfst; afternoon refreshments. Dining rm (by res). Ck-out noon, ck-in 3 pm. Business servs avail. Concierge serv. Luggage handling. Free airport transportation. Tennis. Exercise equipt. Lawn games. Refrigerators; some in-rm whirlpools. On 330 secluded acres with extensive equestrian facilities; built 1928. Cr cds: A, MC, V.

Restaurant

★★★★ **MARINUS.** *415 Carmel Valley Rd (93924). 831/658-3500. www.bernardus.com.* Marinus, at the Bernardus Lodge, is off to a great start under the capable direction of Executive Chef Cal Stamenov and Wine Director Mark Jensen. The inventive Californian cuisine is outstanding and the wine list holds great promise. California, French menu. Specializes in fish, lamb, lobster. Hrs: 11:30 am-2:30 pm, 5:30-10 pm. Res required. Wine, beer. Lunch $7-$19; dinner $12-$30. Entertainment; pianist. Cr cds: A, D, DS, MC, V.
D

★★ **WILL'S FARGO.** *W Carmel Valley Rd (93924). 831/659-2774. www.willsfargo.com.* Res accepted. No A/C. Bar from 5 pm. Dinner $13.95-$26.95. Specializes in steak, seafood, ribs. Own soups. Butcher shop. 1890s decor; old Western bar, fireplace. Cr cds: A, C, D, DS, MC, V.
D

Catalina Island

(see Avalon)

Channel Islands National Park (E-3)

(Off the coast of southern California)

Eight islands, extending over a range of 150 miles in the Pacific Ocean, make up this chain, of which five have been set aside by the government as Channel Islands National Park. Visitors can reach the National Park by commercial boat (see SANTA BARBARA and VENTURA). Anacapa Island, 14 miles south of Ventura, is actually a slender chain of three islands, five miles long with average width of ½ mile; Santa Barbara Island, 38 miles west of San Pedro, is roughly triangular with its greatest dimension being 1¼ miles. Santa Cruz Island (30 miles offshore), Santa Rosa Island (40 miles offshore), and San Miguel Island (45 miles offshore) are also part of the park. Santa Rosa may be reached by commercial flights (see CAMARILLO).

On Anacapa Island in early spring there is a spectacular display of wildflowers; a yellow table of the giant coreopsis, with its large flowers, is visible from a great distance. Sea mammals, including the California sea lion and harbor seal, are observed around the island's rocky shores. From January through March, the annual migration of gray whales passes close to Anacapa. The island also has a self-guided nature trail and a museum. Ranger-guided tours available all year. Scuba and skin diving are popular sports, as the islands are noted for their variety of marine life.

Santa Barbara Island is a marine terrace with steep cliffs, some rising to more than 500 feet. Numerous caves, coves, offshore pillars, and blowholes are also found. Because Santa Barbara is so isolated, sea mammals, including the huge elephant seal, are occasional visitors. Bird-watching is excellent on this island, and numerous species may be observed, including Xantus' murrelet, American kestrel, brown pelican, black oystercatcher, orange-crowned warbler, and others. Self-guided trails and ranger-conducted walking tours are available. Camping is permitted on Anacapa, Santa Barbara, Santa Rosa, Santa Cruz, and San Miguel Islands. Permits are issued in advance and may be obtained by calling 800/365-2267. No pets are permitted on the islands.

San Miguel Island (14 square miles) contains an outstanding number of natural features, including "caliche" or "fossil forests," which give the island landscape an eerie, almost alien appearance. It is the only island where six pinniped (seals and sea lions) species are found, more than are found in any other single location in the world. To land on the island a permit must be acquired from park headquarters prior to your visit.

Santa Rosa Island (53 square miles) is now owned by Channel Islands National Park. Visitors to the island must be accompanied by a park ranger. For camping, a permit is required (phone 805/658-5711). A landing permit is required only for ranger-led walks and hikes (arranged by appt). Santa Cruz Island (96 square miles) is divided between the National Park Service, which owns and manages the eastern 10 percent, and the Nature Conservancy, which owns and manages the western 90 percent. Information about public access to this island may be obtained from the Santa Cruz Nature Conservancy, 213 Stearns Wharf, Santa Barbara 93101; 805/962-9111. A visitor center (open all year) at 1901 Spinnaker Dr in Ventura offers information, exhibits, and audiovisual programs; 805/658-5730. For further information contact Park Superintendent, 1901 Spinnaker Dr, Ventura 93001; 805/658-5700 or 805/658-5730. **FREE**; Camping **¢¢**

Chester

(D-4) *See also Quincy, Susanville*

Pop 2,082 **Elev** 4,528 ft
Area code 530 **Zip** 96020

Information Chester/Lake Almanor Chamber of Commerce, 529 Main St, PO Box 1198; 530/258-2426 or 800/350-4838

The Lake Almanor area offers both summer and winter sports. Mount Lassen is 30 miles north and west. Fishing is good in the lake and surrounding streams and is served by many boat landings and ramps. Deer, bear, waterfowl, and birds are plentiful in season. There are many resorts, tent and trailer sites, and two scenic golf courses around the lake, as well as a number of improved campsites within five miles of Chester. Chester is also the home of the Collins Pine Sawmill, one of the largest in the state. A Ranger District office of the Lassen National Forest (see SUSANVILLE) is located here.

B&B/Small Inn

★★ BIDWELL HOUSE BED AND BREAKFAST. *1 Main St (96020). 530/258-3338. www.bidwellhouse.com.* 14 rms, 2 story, 1 cottage. No A/C. Rm phones avail. S, D $75-$150; cottage $150; hols (2-day min). TV avail. Complimentary full bkfst, coffee in rms. Restaurant 5:30-8 pm. Ck-out 11 am, ck-in 3-6 pm. Game rm. Some fireplaces. Antiques. Built in 1901. Flower and vegetable gardens. Totally nonsmoking. Cr cds: MC, V.
D SC

Chico

(D-3) *See also Oroville*

Settled 1843 **Pop** 40,079 **Elev** 200 ft
Area code 530

Information Chamber of Commerce, 300 Salem St, 95928; 530/891-5556 or 800/852-8570

Web www.chicochamber.com

Chico was originally settled in 1843 as Rancho Del Arroyo by General John Bidwell, a leading agriculturist of the 19th century as well as a gold miner, statesman, and a US congressman. Chico is now a city of diversified business, industry, and agriculture in an area that is said to produce 20 percent of the world's almonds.

What to See and Do

Bidwell Mansion State Historic Park. (1868). This is the 26-rm Victorian house of the founder of Chico (candidate for US president in 1892); first, second, and third floors restored. (Daily; closed Jan 1, Thanksgiving, Dec 25) 525 Esplanade. Phone 530/895-6144. **¢¢**

Bidwell Park. Ten-mi-long, 3,700-acre city park with stream; site of location shots for many movies, incl *The Adventures of Robin Hood*. Swimming pools; picnicking, 18-hole golf at northeast end of park; bridle, foot and nature trails; kiddie playland. ½ mi E on E 4th St. Phone 530/895-4972.

California State University, Chico. (1887) 15,000 students. On 115 tree-shaded acres; art galleries (Mon-Fri, Sun); "anthromuseum;" campus tour. Nearby is a 1,000-acre college farm. 400 W 1st St. Phone 530/898-4636.

Chico Museum. History museum housed in 1904 Carnegie Library; permanent and changing exhibits incl local history artifacts and photos, Chinese Temple. Programs, activities. (Wed-Sun afternoons) 141

Salem St, at Second St. Phone 530/891-4336. **Donation**

Self-guided nature tours. Detailed brochures with tour maps avail from Chamber of Commerce. Phone 530/891-5556.

Spring Blossom Tour. Forty-mi tour allows participants to view the wealth of blooming orchards and wildflowers in Butte County. Blossoms incl almond, prune, kiwi, pear, and iris. (Mid-Feb-June) **FREE**

Winter Migratory Waterfowl Tour. This 100-mi tour provides insight into importance of farmlands and wildlife preserves to migrating waterfowl in Butte County. Approx 150 bird species migrate here in winter. (Sept-Mar) **FREE**

Special Events

Bidwell Classic Marathon. First Sat Mar.

Silver Dollar Fair. Phone 530/895-4666. Five days late May.

Chico Chamber Expo. Phone 530/891-5556. Sept.

Motels/Motor Lodges

★★ BEST WESTERN HERITAGE INN. *25 Heritage Ln (95926). 530/894-8600; fax 530/894-8600; res 800/528-1234. www.bestwestern.com.* 101 rms, 3 story. S $64-$74; D $71-$82; each addl $7; under 12 free; higher rates: university graduation wkend, auto races. Crib free. TV. Pool; whirlpool. Complimentary continental bkfst. Ck-out 11 am. Meeting rm. Business servs avail. In-rm modem link. Health club privileges. Some refrigerators, wet bars. Cr cds: A, C, D, DS, MC, V.

★★ HOLIDAY INN. *685 Manzanita Ct (93923). 530/345-2491; fax 530/893-3040; res 800/465-4329. www.holiday-inn.com.* 172 rms, 5 story. S $85; D $93; each addl $6; suites $100-$160; under 19 free. Crib free. Pet accepted, some restrictions. TV; cable (premium). Pool; whirlpool. Restaurant 6 am-10 pm. Bar from 2 pm; entertainment. Ck-out 11 am. Coin lndry. Meeting rms. Business servs avail. In-rm modem link. Bellhops. Valet serv. Free airport, bus depot transportation. Health club privileges. Refrigerator in suites. Microwaves avail. Cr cds: A, C, D, DS, ER, JCB, MC, V.

D

★ VAGABOND INN. *630 Main St (95928). 530/895-1323; fax 530/343-2719; toll-free 800/522-1555. www.vagabond.com.* 42 rms, 2 story. S $34-$50; D $45-$75; higher rates special events; each addl $5; kit. units $8 addl; under 16 free. Crib free. Pet accepted. TV; cable (premium). Pool. Complimentary continental bkfst, coffee in rms. Restaurant adj open 24 hrs. Ck-out 11 am. Meeting rm. Business servs avail. Health club privileges. Cr cds: A, C, D, DS, MC, V.

SC

Chula Vista (G-6)

Pop 135,163 **Elev** 75 ft **Area code** 619

The name Chula Vista is Spanish for "beautiful view." Set between the mountains and the sea, the city lives up to its name.

What to See and Do

ARCO Olympic Training Center. The nation's first yr-round, warm-weather, multisport Olympic training facility. Narrated 1½-mi tours (hrly) show Olympic-hopeful athletes training for track and field, tennis, archery, kayaking, rowing, cycling, and soccer. (Daily) 4 mi S, at 1750 Wueste Rd. Phone 619/656-1500. **FREE**

Motels/Motor Lodges

★★ HOLIDAY INN EXPRESS. *4450 Otay Valley Rd (91911). 619/422-2600; fax 619/425-4605; res 800/628-2611. www.holiday-inn.com.* 118 rms, 3 story. May-Sept: S $69-$79; D $79-$89; each addl $5; under 17 free; lower rates rest of yr. Crib free. TV; cable (premium). Heated pool; whirlpool. Complimentary continental bkfst. Restaurant adj open 24 hrs. Ck-out noon. Coin lndry. Meeting rm. Business servs avail. In-rm modem link. Valet serv. Refrigerators, microwaves avail. Cr cds: A, C, D, DS, JCB, MC, V.

D SC

★★ RAMADA INN SOUTH CHULA VISTA. *91 Bonita Rd (91910). 619/425-9999; fax 619/425-8934; toll-free 800/272-6232. www.ramada.com.* 97 rms, 4 story. June-Sept: S $62-$72; D $70-$82; each addl $8; suites $72-$85; under 18 free; lower rates rest of yr. Crib free. TV; cable (premium). Heated pool; whirlpool. Restaurant adj 6:30 am-11 pm. Ck-out noon. Meeting rm. Business servs avail. Cr cds: A, C, D, DS, ER, JCB, MC, V.
D SC

★ RODEWAY INN. *778 Broadway (91910). 619/476-9555; toll-free 800/228-2000. www.rodewayinn.com.* 49 rms, 3 story. May-Sept: S $60-$70; D $70-$80; each addl $5; under 18 free; wkly rates; lower rates rest of yr. Crib $5. TV; cable (premium). Pool; whirlpool. Complimentary coffee in lobby. Restaurant nearby. Ck-out 11:30 am. Refrigerators, microwaves avail. Cr cds: A, C, D, DS, JCB, MC, V.
D SC

Restaurants

★★ BUON GIORNO. *4110 Bonita Rd, Bonita (91902). 619/475-2660.* Hrs: 11 am-10 pm; Fri, Sat to 11 pm; Sun 3-9 pm. Closed Jan 1, Thanksgiving, Dec 25. Res accepted. Italian menu. Bar to midnight. Lunch $5.95-$14.95, dinner $8.95-$22.95. Children's menu. Specializes in seafood, pasta. Pianist Thur-Sat. Old World Italian setting; prints of opera stars adorn walls. Cr cds: A, MC, V.
D

★ BUTCHER SHOP. *556 Broadway (91910). 619/420-9440.* Hrs: 11-1 am; Sun 2-10 pm. Closed Thanksgiving, Dec 25. Res accepted. Bar to 2 am. Lunch $7.95-$11.95, dinner $8.95-$25.95. Specializes in steak, prime rib. Entertainment Wed-Sat eves. Family-owned. Cr cds: A, DS, MC, V.
D

Claremont

See also Ontario, Pasadena, Pomona, Riverside

Pop 32,503 **Elev** 1,169 ft **Area code** 909 **Zip** 91711

Information Chamber of Commerce, 205 N Yale Ave; 909/624-1681

What to See and Do

The Claremont Colleges. A distinguished group of institutions comprised of Pomona College (1887) 1,500 students, Claremont Graduate School (1925) 1,800 students, Scripps College (1926) 550 students, Claremont McKenna College (1946) 900 students, Harvey Mudd College (1955) 650 students, and Pitzer College (1963) 700 students. College Ave between 1st St and Foothill Blvd (CA 66). Phone 909/621-8000. On campus are

Graduate School Art Building. Exhibits. (Daily, wkends by appt) 10th St and Columbia Ave. Phone 909/621-8071.

Montgomery Art Gallery. Exhibits. (Tues-Sun afternoons; closed school hols, June-Aug) 330 N College Ave. Phone 909/621-8283.

Rancho Santa Ana Botanic Garden. Native plants. (Daily; closed hols) 1500 N College Ave, N of Foothill Blvd. Phone 909/625-8767. **FREE**

Motel/Motor Lodge

★★ RAMADA INN & TENNIS CLUB. *840 S Indian Hill Blvd (91711). 909/621-4831; fax 909/621-0411; toll-free 800/322-6559. www.ramada.com.* 122 rms, 2 story. S $74; D $79; each addl $8; under 12 free. Crib free. Pet accepted. TV; cable (premium). Heated pool; wading pool, whirlpool. Complimentary continental bkfst. Restaurant opp open 24 hrs. Ck-out noon. Coin lndry. Meeting rms. Business servs avail. Valet serv. Lighted tennis. Health club privileges. Refrigerators. Picnic tables, grill. Cr cds: A, C, D, DS, MC, V.

Restaurant

★★ **YIANNIS.** *238 Yale Ave (91711). 909/621-2413.* Hrs: 11 am-10 pm. Closed Mon, hols. Greek menu. Bar. Lunch $5.85-$7.55. Complete meals: dinner $10.75-$14.95. Sun brunch $6.75. Specialties: moussaka, souvlakia. Own bread, baklava. Outdoor dining. Greek artifacts; colorful lamps. Family-owned. Cr cds: A, MC, V.
D

Clear Lake Area (Lake Co)

See also Healdsburg, Ukiah

Area code 707
Information Chamber of Commerce, 290 S Main St, PO Box 295, Lakeport 95453; 707/263-5092

This is a popular recreation area for fishing, hunting, swimming, boating, golfing, and other sports.

What to See and Do

Clear Lake State Park. Pomo Native Americans once occupied this area. Swimming, waterskiing, fishing, boating (ramp); nature and hiking trails. Picnicking. Camping (no hookups, dump station). Visitor center with wildlife dioramas, aquarium; nature films. Standard fees. 3 mi NE of Kelseyville on Soda Bay Rd. Phone 707/279-4293. **¢¢**

Special Events

Lake County Rodeo. Lake County Fairgrounds, Lakeport. July.

Lake County Fair and Horse Show. Lake County Fairgrounds. Phone 707/263-6181. Labor Day wkend.

Motels/Motor Lodges

★★ **ANCHORAGE INN.** *950 N Main St, Lakeport (95453). 707/263-5417; fax 707/263-5453.* 34 rms, 2 story, 20 kits. S $54; D $62; each addl $10; 1-2 bedrm suites and kit. units $64-$115; hol wkends (2-3 day min). TV; cable. Pool; whirlpool. Complimentary coffee in rms. Restaurant opp 6 am-9 pm. Ck-out 11 am. Coin lndry. Business servs avail. In-rm modem link. Sauna. Private patios; some balconies. Picnic tables, grills. Dockage. On Clear Lake. Cr cds: A, D, MC, V.

★★ **BEST WESTERN EL GRANDE INN.** *15135 Lakeshore Dr, Clearlake (95422). 707/994-2000; fax 707/994-2042; toll-free 800/528-1234. www.bestwestern.com/elgrandeinn.* 68 rms, 4 story. S $69; D $79-$89; each addl $7; suites $79-$95. Crib free. TV; cable (premium), VCR avail (movies). Indoor pool; whirlpool. Complimentary coffee in rms. Restaurant 7 am-1:30 pm, 5-9:30 pm. Bar 2 pm-midnight. Ck-out 11 am. Meeting rms. Business servs avail. In-rm modem link. Refrigerator in suites. Spanish-style lobby. All rms open to atrium. Cr cds: A, C, D, DS, MC, V.
D SC

★ **HIGHLANDS INN.** *13865 Lakeshore Dr, Clearlake (95422). 707/994-8982; fax 707/994-0613; toll-free 800/300-8982. www.high-lands.com.* 20 rms, 2 story. May-Sept S $55-$75; D $65-$85; each addl $5; suites $85-$95; higher rates hols; lower rates rest of yr. Crib $5. TV; cable. Pool. Complimentary coffee in rms. Ck-out 11 am. Coin lndry. Business servs avail. Refrigerators. Picnic tables. On lake. Grills. Cr cds: A, C, D, DS, MC, V.
D SC

Coleville

(F-6) *See also Bridgeport*

Pop 60 **Elev** 5,400 ft **Area code** 530 **Zip** 96107

Motel/Motor Lodge

★ **ANDRUSS MOTEL.** *106964 US 395 (96107). 530/495-2216. www.andruss.com.* 13 air-cooled rms, 4 kits. S $36-$42; D, kit. units $42-$52; each addl $4. Crib free. Pet accepted; $5. TV; cable (premium). Heated pool. Playground. Complimentary coffee in rms. Restaurant opp 6 am-10 pm. Ck-out 11 am. Lawn games. Picnic tables, grill. Fish cleaning, freezing facilities. Cr cds: A, DS, MC, V.
D

Coloma

(see Placerville)

Concord

(F-3) *See also Martinez, Oakland, Vallejo*

Pop 111,348 **Elev** 70 ft **Area code** 925

Information Contra Costa Convention & Visitors Bureau, 1333 Willow Path Rd, Suite 204, 94520; 925/685-1184

Web www.cccvb.com

What to See and Do

Chronicle Pavilion at Concord. Roofed, open-air performance and assembly facility, with lawn and reserved pavilion seating for 12,500; popular entertainment performances, sports, and special events (Apr-Oct). 2000 Kirker Pass Rd. Phone 925/363-5701.

Waterworld USA. Twenty-acre park incl attractions such as Breaker Beach Wavepool, Treasure Island kid's area, Lazy River, and The Big Kahuna, a six-story raft adventure. Also here are a multi-level activity pool and water-slides. (Late May-early Sept, daily) 1950 Waterworld Pkwy. ¢¢¢¢¢

Motels/Motor Lodges

★★ **BEST WESTERN HERITAGE INN.** *4600 Clayton Rd (94521). 925/686-4466; fax 925/825-0581; res 800/528-1234. www.bestwestern.com.* 126 rms, 2 story. S, D $65-$75; kit. units $85; under 18 free. Crib free. TV; cable (premium). Pool; whirlpool. Complimentary continental bkfst. Ck-out 11 am. Meeting rms. Business servs avail. In-rm modem link. Health club privileges. Refrigerators; some wet bars. Cr cds: A, D, DS, JCB, MC, V.

★★ **COMFORT INN.** *1370 Monument Dr (94520). 925/827-8998; fax 925/798-3374; res 800/228-5150. www.comfortinn.com.* 41 kit. units, 3 story. June-Sept: S, D $79-$94; each addl $5; wkly rates; lower rates rest of yr. TV; cable (premium), VCR (movies $4). Pool. Complimentary continental bkfst. Restaurant nearby. Ck-out 11 am. Coin lndry. Business servs avail. In-rm modem link. Exercise equipt. Patios, balconies. Cr cds: A, C, D, DS, MC, V.

Hotels

★★★ **HILTON.** *1970 Diamond Blvd (94520). 925/827-2000; fax 925/827-2113; toll-free 800/445-8667. www.concordhilton.com.* 330 rms, 11 story. S $159-$179; D $169-$189; each addl $10; suites $375-$475; family, wkend rates. Crib free. TV; cable (premium), VCR avail (movies). Pool; whirlpool. Coffee in rms. Restaurant 6:30 am-10 pm, wkends from 7 am. Bar 11 am-midnight; entertainment Mon-Fri. Ck-out noon. Convention facilities. Business servs avail. In-rm modem link. Gift shop. Exercise equipt. Cr cds: A, C, D, DS, JCB, MC, V.

★★★ **SHERATON CONCORD HOTEL AND CONFERENCE CENTER.** *45 John Glenn Dr (94520). 925/825-7700; fax 925/674-9567; toll-free 800/325-3535. www.sheraton.com.* 324 rms, 3 story. S $85-$139; D $85-$159; each addl $20; suites $175-$425; under 17 free. Crib free. Heated pool; whirlpool. TV; cable. Coffee in rms. Restaurant 6:30 am-2 pm, 5-10:30 pm. Bar noon-2 am; entertainment. Ck-out noon. Meeting rms. Business center. In-rm modem link. Concierge. Sundries. Gift shop. Indoor putting green. Exercise equipt. Health club privileges. Microwaves avail. Luxury level. Cr cds: C, D, DS, MC, V.

Corona

See also Ontario, Riverside

Established 1896 **Pop** 76,095 **Elev** 678 ft **Area code** 909 **Zip** 91719

Information Chamber of Commerce, 904 E 6th St; 909/737-3350

Web www.coronachamber.org

A Ranger District office of the Cleveland National Forest (see PINE VALLEY) is located in Corona.

What to See and Do

Glen Ivy Hot Springs. Natural hot mineral spa. Swimming, 15 outdoor mineral baths, massage, sauna, clay bath, outdoor poolside dining. Admission limited to guests over 16. (Daily; closed Jan 1, Thanksgiving, Dec 25) 25000 Glen Ivy Rd, 8 mi S via I-15 at Temescal Canyon Rd exit. Phone 909/277-3529. ¢¢¢¢¢

Motels/Motor Lodges

★★ **BEST WESTERN KINGS INN.** *1084 Pomona Rd (92882). 909/734-4241; fax 909/279-5371; toll-free 800/892-5464. www.bestwestern.com.* 87 rms, 2 story. S, D $59-$79; each addl $5; under 18 free. Crib free. TV; cable (premium), VCR avail (movies free). Heated pool; whirlpool. Complimentary continental bkfst. Restaurants adj 6 am-midnight. Ck-out noon. Meeting rm. Business servs avail. Health club priveleges. Valet serv. Some refrigerators. Microwaves avail. Cr cds: A, C, D, DS, MC, V.

D

★★ **THE COUNTRY INN.** *2260 Griffin Way (92879). 909/734-2140; fax 909/734-4056. www.countrysuites.com.* 102 rms, 2 story. S $79; D $89; each addl $10; under 12 free. Crib free. TV; cable (premium). Heated pool; whirlpool. Complimentary full bkfst. Restaurant opp 7 am-11 pm. Ck-out noon. Meeting rm. Business servs avail. Valet serv. Guest lndry. Refrigerators. Cr cds: A, C, D, DS, MC, V.

D

★★ **DYNASTY SUITES.** *3735 Iowa Ave (92882). 909/371-7185; fax 909/371-0401; res 800/842-7899. www.dynastysuites.com.* 56 rms, 2 story. S, D $49.95; each addl $5. Crib free. Pet accepted, some restrictions; $10/day. TV; cable (premium), VCR avail (movies). Complimentary continental bkfst. Restaurant adj 5-1 am. Ck-out noon. Meeting rms. Business servs avail. Valet serv. Health club privileges. Heated pool; whirlpool. Bathrm phones, refrigerators, microwaves; some in-rm whirlpools. Cr cds: A, C, D, DS, MC, V.

D SC

Corona del Mar

Elev 75 ft **Area code** 949 **Zip** 92625

This community is part of Newport Beach (see).

Restaurants

★★ **THE BUNGALOW.** *2441 E Pacific Coast Hwy, Corona Del Mar (92625). 949/673-6585. www.menusunlimited.com/thebungalow.* Hrs: 5-10 pm; Fri, Sat to 11 pm. Closed Memorial Day, July 4, Dec 25. Res accepted. Bar to 2 am. Dinner $13.95-$27.95. Specialties: fresh blackened rare ahi, fire-roasted Colorado rack of lamb. Valet parking. Outdoor dining. Garden patio; mahogany wood throughout. Totally nonsmoking. Cr cds: A, C, D, DS, MC, V.

D

★★★ **FIVE CROWNS.** *3801 E Pacific Coast Hwy (92625). 949/760-0331. www.lawrysonline.com.* Hrs: 5-10 pm; Sun 4-9:30 pm; Sun brunch 10:30 am-2:30 pm. Closed July 4, Dec 25. Res accepted. Bar. Wine list. A la carte entrees: dinner $14.50-$29.95. Sun brunch $11.50-$17. Specializes in beef, lamb, fresh fish. Valet parking. Patio, greenhouse dining. English-style inn, fireplaces. Cr cds: A, C, D, DS, MC, V.

D SC

★ **QUIET WOMAN.** *3224 E Pacific Coast Hwy (92625). 949/640-7440.* Hrs: 11:30 am-2:30 pm, 5-10 pm; Fri, Sat to 11 pm; Sun 5-11 pm. Closed hols. Bar to 1:30 am. Lunch $8-$14, dinner $14.50-$32.50. Specializes in lamb, fresh seafood. Entertainment Wed-Sat. English pub decor. Cr cds: A, MC, V.

D

Coronado (G-5)

Pop 26,540 **Elev** 25 ft **Area code** 619 **Zip** 92118

Known as the Crown City, Coronado lies across the bay from San Diego and is connected to the mainland by a long, narrow sandbar called the Silver Strand and by the beautiful Coronado Bridge. It is the site of the famous Hotel del Coronado (1888).

Motels/Motor Lodges

★ **CROWN CITY INN.** *520 Orange Ave (92118). 619/435-3116; fax 619/435-6750; toll-free 800/422-1173. www.crowncityinn.com.* 33 rms, 2 story. Mid-June-mid-Sept: S, D $106-$125; under 18 free; higher rates hols (3-day min); lower rates rest of yr. Crib $5. Pet accepted; $8. TV; cable (premium). Heated pool. Complimentary coffee in rms. Restaurant 8 am-2 pm, 5-9 pm. Ck-out 11 am. Coin lndry. Business servs avail. Health club privileges. Refrigerators, microwaves. Cr cds: A, C, D, DS, MC, V.

★★ **EL CORDOVA.** *1351 Orange Ave (92118). 619/435-4131; fax 619/435-0632; toll-free 800/229-2032. www.elcordovahotel.com.* 40 units, 2 story, 28 kits. Mid-June-mid-Sept: S, D $85-$95; suites $130-$295; studio rms $105-$135; wkly, monthly rates off-season; lower rates rest of yr. Crib free. TV; cable (premium). Heated pool. Restaurant 11 am-10 pm. Bar adj. Ck-out noon. Business servs avail. Health club privileges. Picnic tables, grills. Historic mansion (1902). Cr cds: A, D, DS, MC, V.

★ **LA AVENIDA INN.** *1315 Orange Ave (92118). 619/435-3191; fax 619/435-5024; res 800/437-0162. www.laavenidainn.com.* 29 rms, 2 story. July-Sept: S, D $105-$125; wkends (2-day min); lower rates rest of yr. Crib free. TV; cable (premium). Complimentary coffee in lobby. Restaurant adj 11 am-10 pm. Ck-out noon. Pool. Opp ocean. Cr cds: A, D, JCB, MC, V.

Hotel

★★ **GLORIETTA BAY INN.** *1630 Glorietta Blvd (92118). 619/435-3101; fax 619/435-6182; toll-free 800/283-9383. www.gloriettabayinn.com.* 100 units, 2 story, 33 kits. S, D $135-$225; each addl $10; suites, kit. units $185-$395. Crib free. TV; cable (premium). Heated pool; whirlpool. Complimentary continental bkfst. Ck-out 11 am. Coin lndry. Business center. In-rm modem link. Refrigerators; microwaves avail. Many private patios, balconies. Some rms overlook Glorietta Bay. Historic house (1908), part of Speckels mansion. Cr cds: A, D, DS, MC, V.

D SC

Resorts

★★★ **HOTEL DEL CORONADO.** *1500 Orange Ave (92118). 619/435-6611; fax 619/522-8262; res 619/522-8010. www.hoteldel.com.* 692 rms. S, D $205-$450; under 18 free. Crib free. TV; VCR avail. 2 heated pools; whirlpool, poolside serv. Supervised children's activities. Restaurants. Rm serv 24 hrs. Bar 7-2 am; entertainment. Ck-out noon, ck-in 4 pm. Convention facilities. Business center. In-rm modem link. Concierge. Spa, fitness center, sauna, massage. Lighted tennis. Minibars. Many private patios, balconies. Swimming beach; sail and power boat rentals avail at hotel docks. Cr cds: A, D, DS, JCB, MC, V.

D

★★★ **LOEWS CORONADO BAY RESORT.** *4000 Coronado Bay Rd (92118). 619/424-4000; fax 619/424-4400; toll-free 800/235-6397. www. loewshotels.com.* 440 guest rm. S, D $235; each addl $20; suites $425-$1,300; under 18 free; tennis plans. Crib free. Pet accepted. TV; cable, VCR avail. Supervised children's activities. Restaurants (see also AZZURA POINT). Rm serv 24 hrs. Bar 11-2 am; entertainment. Ck-out noon, ck-in 4 pm. Conference facilities. Meeting rooms. Business center. In-rm modem link. Bellhops. Valet serv. Concierge. Gift shop. Barber, beauty shop. Sports dir. 5 lighted tennis courts, pro. Beach, boats, water skiing, swimming. 3 pools;

whirlpools, poolside serv. Bicycle rentals. Lawn games. Game rm. Health club, sauna. Massage. Bathrm phones. Minibars. Refrigerators, microwaves avail. Balconies. All rooms offer views of San Diego Bay, ocean, marina. Private marina. Private access to beach Cr cds: A, C, D, DS, ER, JCB, MC, V.

D

★★★ **MARRIOTT RESORT CORONADO ISLAND.** *2000 2nd St (92118). 619/435-3000; fax 619/435-4183; res 800/228-9290. www.marriott.com.* Get hypnotized by the sparkling San Diego city lights at this 300-room bayfront resort five miles from the Gaslamp Quarter. The crisp white entranceway is a minimalist beginning to the 16 tropical acres that are home to waterfalls, exotic wildlife, and award-winning restaurants. For something special, reserve one of 28 villas with a private entrance and pool. 300 rms, 3 story, 28 villas. June-Sept: S, D $209-$229; suites, villas $325-$795; under 12 free. Crib free. Pet accepted. Covered parking $10; valet $14. TV; cable (premium), VCR avail. 3 pools; whirlpool, poolside serv. Restaurants 6:30 am-10 pm. Rm serv 24 hrs. Bar 11:30-1 am; entertainment Fri, Sat. Ck-out noon. Convention facilities. Business center. Concierge. Lighted tennis, pro, pro shop, tennis clinic. Scuba, snorkling, windsurfing classes. Bicycle rental. Exercise rm; sauna. Spa. Minibars; microwaves avail. Private patios. On bay; pier, 2 slips. Floral and wildlife tour. Cr cds: A, D, DS, JCB, MC, V.

Restaurants

★★★ **AZZURA POINT.** *4000 Coronado Bay Rd (92118). 619/424-4000.* Hrs: 6-10:30 pm; Fri, Sat to 11 pm. Res accepted. Mediterranean, California menu. Bar. Wine list. Dinner $22-$32. Children's menu. Specialties: scallop and prosciutto with porcini and white truffle essence, Pacific halibut with tomato-orange relish and garlic herbs. Valet parking. Panoramic view of the bay, ocean and city skyline. Jacket rec. Cr cds: A, DS, MC, V.

D

★★ **BRIGANTINE.** *1333 Orange Ave (92118). 619/435-4166. www.brigantine.com.* Hrs: 11:30 am-2:30 pm, 5-10:30 pm; Fri to 11:30 pm; Sat 5-11:30 pm; Sun 5-10:30 pm; early-bird dinner Sun-Thurs 5-7 pm. Res accepted. Bar to 2 am. Lunch $6.95-$12.95, dinner $8.95-$27.95. Children's menu. Specializes in fresh seafood, steak. Nautical decor. Family-owned. Cr cds: A, D, MC, V.

D

★★ **CHAMELEON CAFE.** *1301 Orange Ave (92118). 619/437-6677. www.chameleoncafe.com.* Hrs: 11 am-10 pm; Fri, Sat to 2 am. Closed Jan 1, Dec 25. Pacific Rim menu. Bar. Lunch $7.95-$14.95, dinner $8.95-$24.95. Children's menu. Specializes in fresh seafood. Street parking. Outdoor dining. Contemporary atmosphere. Totally nonsmoking. Cr cds: A, DS, MC, V.

D

★★★ **CHEZ LOMA.** *1132 Loma Ave (92118). 619/435-0661. www.chezloma.com.* Hrs: 5-10 pm; Sun brunch 10 am-2 pm. Closed hols. Res accepted. French menu. Bar. Wine cellar. Dinner $19-$29. Sun brunch $11.95. Specializes in duck, seafood. Own desserts. Historic landmark house (1889). Cr cds: A, C, D, MC, V.

D

★★★ **CROWN ROOM.** *1500 Orange Ave (92118). 619/435-6611.* Hrs: 7 am-9:30 pm; Fri, Sat to 10 pm; early-bird dinner Mon-Fri 5-6 pm. Res accepted. Serv bar. Wine cellar. Bkfst from $9.95, lunch from $10.95, dinner $18-$30. Prix fixe: dinner $26. Buffet: bkfst $34.95. Children's menu. Specializes in lamb, pasta, fresh fish. Own baking. Pianist Wed-Sat. Valet parking. Rotating menu. Historic 1888 structure; hand-tooled dome ceiling. Cr cds: A, C, D, DS, MC, V.

D

★★ **MEXICAN VILLAGE.** *120 Orange Ave (92118). 619/435-1822.* Hrs: 11 am-10 pm; Fri, Sat to 11 pm; Sun 8 am-noon. Mexican, American menu. Bar. Lunch $4.95-$8.95, dinner $5.95-$17.95. Children's menu. Specializes in Mexican pizza, romaine salad. Local landmark; opened 1945. Several dining rms; Mexican decor and artifacts. Cr cds: A, C, D, DS, MC, V.

D

★★ **PEOHE'S.** *1201 1st St (92118). 619/437-4474. www.peohes.com.* Hrs: 11:30 am-2:30 pm, 5:30-9:30 pm; Sat 5-10:30 pm; Sun brunch 10:30 am-2:30 pm. Res accepted. Bar. Lunch $6.95-$14.95, dinner $17-$29. Sun brunch $8-$15. Children's menu. Specialties: coconut crunchy shrimp, fresh Hawaiian fish. Parking. Outdoor dining. Tropical atmosphere with waterfalls and running streams; lush plants; ponds stocked with tropical fish. View of San Diego Harbor and skyline. Cr cds: A, C, D, DS, MC, V.
D

★★ **PRIMAVERA.** *932 Orange Ave (92118). 619/435-0454. www. primavera1st.com.* Hrs: 11 am-2:30 pm, 5-10:30 pm; Sat, Sun from 5 pm. Closed Jan 1, Dec 25. Res accepted. Northern Italian menu. Bar. Lunch $7.25-$12.95, dinner $12.95-$26.95. Specialties: osso buco Milanese, lamb chops al balsamico. Elegant, romantic Mediterranean decor; original artwork. Totally nonsmoking. Cr cds: A, D, DS, MC, V.
D

★★★ **PRINCE OF WALES.** *1500 Orange Ave (92118). 619/522-8818.* Hrs: 5:30-10 pm. Res accepted. Continental, contemporary American menu. Bar. Wine cellar. Dinner $21-$36. Specializes in seafood, pasta, lamb. Own baking. Valet parking. 1930s summer house atmosphere. Cr cds: A, DS, MC, V.
D

Corte Madera

(see San Francisco map) *See also San Francisco, San Rafael*

Pop 8,272 **Elev** 27 ft **Area code** 415 **Zip** 94925

Motel/Motor Lodge

★★ **BEST WESTERN CORTE MADERA INN.** *1815 Redwood Hwy (94925). 415/924-1502; fax 415/924-5419; res 800/528-1234. www. bestwestern.com.* 110 rms, 2 story. S $105-$115; D $115-$125; each addl $10; suites $145-$185; under 18 free. Crib free. TV; cable (premium). Heated pool; wading pool, whirlpools; lifeguard. Playground. Complimentary continental bkfst. Coffee in rms. Restaurant 8 am-11 pm; Fri, Sat 8:30 am-midnight. Ck-out noon. Coin lndry. Meeting rms. Business servs avail. In-rm modem link. Bellhops. Valet serv. Sundries. Exercise equipt. Massage. Refrigerators. Private patios, balconies. Picnic tables. Cr cds: A, C, D, DS, ER, JCB, MC, V.
D SC

Hotel

★★ **MARIN SUITES HOTEL.** *45 Tamal Vista Blvd (94925). 415/924-3608; fax 415/924-0761; toll-free 800/362-3372. www.marinsuites.com.* 100 suites, 3 story. S, D $119-$199; under 17 free. Crib free. TV; cable (premium), VCR avail. Pool. Complimentary continental bkfst. Restaurant adj 11:30 am-10:30 pm. Ck-out noon. Coin lndry. Exercise equipt; sauna. Refrigerators. Cr cds: A, C, D, DS, JCB, MC, V.
SC

Restaurants

★★ **CALIFORNIA CAFE.** *1736 Redwood Hwy (94925). 415/924-2233. www.calcafe.com.* Hrs: 11 am-9:30 pm; wkends to 10 pm; Sun brunch 11 am-3 pm. Closed Dec 25. Res accepted. Bar. A la carte entrees: lunch $5.95-$12.95, dinner $12.95-$21.95. Sun brunch $7.95-$12.95. Children's menu. Specializes in steaks, fresh fish, pasta. Outdoor dining. Modern artwork. Totally nonsmoking. Cr cds: A, DS, MC, V.
D

★★ **IL FORNAIO.** *223 Corte Madera Town Center (94925). 415/927-4400. www.ilfornai.com.* Hrs: 11:30 am-10 pm; Fri, Sat to 11 pm. Closed Thanksgiving, Dec 25. Res accepted. Italian menu. Bar. A la carte entrees: lunch, dinner $8.95-$21. Children's menu. Specialties: pollo tuscano, tiramisu. Own desserts. Parking. Outdoor dining. Bakery. Totally nonsmoking. Cr cds: A, D, MC, V.
D

★★★ **LARK CREEK INN.** *234 Magnolia Ave, Larkspur (94939). 415/924-7766.* California menu. Hrs: 11:30

am-2 pm, 5:30-9 pm; Fri, Sat to 10 pm. A la carte entrees: $16-$28. Res accepted. Menu changes daily. 1888 Victorian country inn. Cr cds: A, MC, V.

D

★★ **SAVANNA GRILL.** *55 Tamal Vista Blvd (94925). 415/924-6774. www.savannagrill.com.* Hrs: 11:30 am-10 pm; Sat, Sun 4-11 pm. Res accepted. Bar to midnight. A la carte entrees: lunch $6.95-$11, dinner $9.95-$15.50. Specializes in seafood. Outdoor dining. View of Mt Tamalpais. Cr cds: A, D, MC, V.

D

Costa Mesa

See also Huntington Beach, Irvine, Newport Beach, Santa Ana

Pop 96,357 **Elev** 101 ft **Area code** 714

Information Chamber of Commerce, 1700 Adams Ave, Suite 101, 92626; 714/885-9090

Web www.costamesa-chamber.com

What to See and Do

California Scenario. This 1½-acre sculpture garden is world-renowned sculptor Isamu Noguchi's tribute to California's environment. Flanked by two reflective glass buildings and two 40-ft-high concrete walls, the garden features tranquil walks, fountains, flowers, and native grasses and trees. Noguchi's *The Spirit of the Lima Bean* is the centerpiece. (Daily) South Coast Plaza Town Center, San Diego Fwy at Bristol St. Phone 714/384-5500. **FREE**

Special Events

Highland Gathering and Games. Orange County Fairgrounds. Scottish games, dancing; soccer, rugby; piping, drumming competition. Memorial Day wkend. Phone 714/708-3247.

Orange County Fair. Orange County Fairgrounds. Rodeo, livestock, exhibits, home arts, contests, photography, nightly entertainment, floriculture display, wine show, carnival, motorcycle races. Phone 714/708-3247. July.

Motels/Motor Lodges

★★ **BEST WESTERN NEWPORT MESA INN.** *2642 Newport Blvd (92627). 949/650-3020; fax 949/642-1220; res 800/528-1234. www.bestwestern.com/.* 97 rms, 3 story. S, D $59-$129; each addl $6; under 17 free; package plans. Crib free. TV; cable (premium). Heated pool; whirlpool. Sauna. Complimentary continental bkfst. Coffee in rms. Ck-out noon. Coin lndry. Meeting rms. Business servs avail. Some bathrm phones; some in-rm whirlpools. Some wet bars. Refrigerators avail. Balconies. Cr cds: A, C, D, DS, MC, V.

D SC

★★★ **COUNTRY INN AND SUITES BY AYRES.** *325 S Bristol St (92626). 714/549-0300; fax 714/662-0828; toll-free 800/322-9992. www.countrysuites.com.* 290 units in 2 buildings, 3 and 4 story, 32 suites. S $119; D $139; each addl $10; suites $150-$160; under 13 free; wkly rates; lower rates some wkends. Crib free. TV; cable (premium), VCR avail. 2 heated pools; whirlpools. Complimentary bkfst buffet. Coffee in rms. Restaurant 6:30 am-10 pm. Bar 11:30 am-11 pm. Ck-out noon. Coin lndry. Convention facilities. Business center. Bellhops. Valet serv. Concierge. Gift shop. Free airport transportation. Exercise equipt. Health club privileges. Refrigerators; many in-rm whirlpools; some microwaves. Fireplace in lobby, many antiques; open air courtyard with imported tile fountain. Cr cds: A, D, DS, MC, V.

D

★ **COZY INN.** *325 W Bay St (92627). 949/650-2055; fax 949/650-6281. www.cozyinn.com.* 29 rms, 2 story, 11 kits. June-mid-Sept: S $44-$49; D $52-$66; each addl $4; kit. units $10 addl; under 12 free; wkly rates; lower rates rest of yr. Crib $5. TV; cable (premium). Heated pool. Ck-out 11 am. Business servs avail. Refrigerators, microwaves avail. Cr cds: A, C, D, DS, MC, V.

D

★★ **HOLIDAY INN.** *3131 S Bristol St (92626). 714/557-3000; fax 714/957-8185; toll-free 800/221-7220. www.holiday-inn.com.* 233 rms, 3-5 story. S,

D $95; under 18 free; family rates; family rates. Crib free. TV; cable (premium). Heated pool; wading pool. Coffee in rms. Restaurant 6 am-2 pm, 5-10 pm. Bar 4-11:30 pm. Ck-out noon. Coin lndry. Meeting rms. Business servs avail. Bellhops. Valet serv. Free airport transportation. Exercise equipt; sauna. Refrigerators avail. Balconies, patios. Picnic tables. Cr cds: A, C, D, DS, JCB, MC, V.

★★ **RAMADA LIMITED.** *1680 Superior Ave (92627). 949/645-2221; fax 949/650-9125; toll-free 800/272-6232. www.ramadalimitednewport.com.* 140 rms, 35 suites, 3 story. Mid-May-mid-Sept: S, D $69-$79; each addl $5; suites $109-$169; under 17 free; lower rates rest of yr. Crib free. Pet accepted. TV; cable (premium). Heated pool; whirlpool. Complimentary continental bkfst. Restaurant nearby. Ck-out noon. Meeting rm. Valet serv. Coin lndry. Free airport transportation. Exercise equipt. Refrigerators; microwaves. Cr cds: A, C, D, DS, JCB, MC, V.

★ **VAGABOND INN.** *3205 Harbor Blvd (92626). 714/557-8360; fax 714/662-7596; toll-free 800/522-1555. www.vagabondinn.com.* 127 rms, 2 story, 5 suites. May-Sept: S, D $50-$80; each addl $5; suites $75-$110; under 18 free; lower rates rest of yr. Crib free. Pet accepted, some restrictions; $5/day. TV; cable (premium). Heated pool; whirlpool. Complimentary continental bkfst. Coffee in rms. Restaurant opp 24 hrs. Ck-out noon. Meeting rm. Business servs avail. Valet serv. Free airport transportation. Exercise equipt. Health club privileges. Refrigerators, microwaves avail. Some balconies. Mission-style building. Cr cds: A, C, D, DS, MC, V.

Hotels

★★ **HILTON COSTA MESA / ORANGE COUNTY.** *3050 Bristol Steet (92626). 714/540-7000; fax 714/540-9176; res 800/222-8733. www.doubletreehotels.com.* 484 rms, 7 story, 10 suites. S $149-$169; D $$169-$189; each addl $15; suites $425-$600; under 18 free. Crib free. Pet accepted. Self park $5. Valet parking $8. TV; cable (premium). Heated pool; whirlpool, poolside serv. Coffee in rms. 2 restaurants 6 am-midnight. Bar from 11 am; entertainment Fri-Sun. Ck-out noon. Convention facilities. Business center. In-rm modem link. Concierge. Gift shop. Barber, beauty shop. Free airport transportation. Tennis privileges. Golf privileges. Exercise equipt; sauna. Massage. Game rm. Refrigerators. Many private patios, balconies. Atrium lobby. Luxury level. Cr cds: A, C, D, DS, ER, JCB, MC, V.

★★★ **MARRIOTT SUITES COSTA MESA.** *500 Anton Blvd (92626). 714/957-1100; fax 714/966-8495. www.marriott.com.* 253 suites, 11 story. S, D $109-$139; wkend rates. Crib free. TV; cable (premium). Heated pool; whirlpool, poolside serv. Complimentary coffee in rms. Restaurant 6:30 am-10 pm. Rm serv 6 am-11 pm. Bar 11 am-11 pm. Ck-out noon. Coin lndry. Meeting rms. Business center. Gift shop. Free garage parking. Free airport transportation. Exercise equipt. Health club privileges. Refrigerators; microwaves avail. Wet bars. Many balconies. Cr cds: A, D, MC, V.

★★★ **WESTIN SOUTH COAST PLAZA.** *686 Anton Blvd (92626). 714/540-2500; fax 714/662-6695; res 800/301-1111. www.westin.com.* 390 rms, 17 story. S, D $200-$240; each addl $20; suites $285-$960; under 18 free; wkend package plans. Crib free. Pet accepted, some restrictions. Parking $7, valet $13. TV; cable (premium). Heated pool; poolside serv. Complimentary coffee in rms. Restaurant 6:30 am-10 pm. Rm serv 24 hrs. Bar noon-midnight; entertainment wkends. Ck-out 1 pm. Convention facilities. Business center. In-rm modem link. Gift shop. Free airport transportation. Lighted tennis. Exercise equipt. Health club privileges. Minibars; wet bar in some suites. South Coast Plaza retail center and village adj. Cr cds: A, D, DS, JCB, MC, V.

★★ **WYNDHAM GARDEN HOTEL - ORANGE COUNTY.** *3350 Ave of*

the Arts (92626). 714/751-5100; fax 714/751-0129. www.wyndham.com. 238, 35 suites, 6 story. S $129; D $139; each addl $10; suites $135-$145; under 12 free; wkly, wkend rates; higher rates special events. Pet accepted, some restrictions; $25. TV; cable . Heated pool; whirlpool. Coffee in rms. Restaurant 6:30 am-2:30 pm, 5-10 pm. Rm serv 5-10 pm. Bar 4:30 pm-midnight. Ck-out noon. Coin lndry. Meeting rms. Business servs avail. Free garage parking. Free airport transportation. Exercise equipt. Refrigerators, microwaves avail. Private patios, balconies. Fireplace in lobby; marble floors. Pool area overlooks lake. Cr cds: A, C, D, DS, JCB, MC, V.

D

Restaurants

★★ **DIVA.** *600 Anton Blvd (92626). 714/754-0600.* Hrs: 11:30 am-3 pm, 5-10 pm; Mon 5-9 pm; Fri to 11 pm; Sat 5-11 pm. Closed Sun, hols. Res accepted. Continental, eclectic menu. Bar. A la carte entrees: lunch $6-$18.95, dinner $6.50-$24.95. Specialties: killer vegetable plate, ahi towers with tomatillo sauce, light chocolate grand marnier with raspberry sauce. Valet parking. Outdoor dining. Theater-style decor. Cr cds: A, D, MC, V.

D

★★ **EL TORITO GRILL.** *633 Anton Blvd (92626). 714/662-2672.* Hrs: 11 am-10 pm; Fri, Sat to 11 pm; Sun brunch 10 am-2 pm. Closed Thanksgiving, Dec 25. Res accepted. Mexican, Southwestern menu. Bar to 11 pm; Fri, Sat to midnight. A la carte entrees: lunch, dinner $7.95-$16.95. Sun brunch $12.95. Specializes in grilled fresh fish, enchiladas, fajitas. Own tortillas, desserts. Valet parking. Southwestern decor. Totally nonsmoking. Cr cds: A, DS, MC, V.

D

★★★ **GOLDEN TRUFFLE.** *1767 Newport Blvd (92627). 949/645-9858.* Hrs: 11:30 am-2:30 pm, 5:30-10 pm. Tues-Sat; closed hols. Res accepted. French, Caribbean menu. Bar. Extensive wine list. A la carte entrees: lunch $7-$18, dinner $7-$19. Complete meals: lunch $18-$24, dinner $32-$45. Specialties: Jamaican jerk chicken salad, chipotle barbeque duck legs with potatoes, grilled lamb loin with horseradish lasagna. Jazz Thur (summer). Outdoor dining. Two distinct dining areas incl semi-formal rm and a casual bistro-style cafe with champagne display case. Cr cds: A, MC, V.

D

★★ **HABANA.** *2930 Bristol St (92626). 714/556-0176.* Hrs: 11:30 am-2:30 pm, 5-10 pm; Fri, Sat to 11 pm. Closed hols. Res accepted. Cuban, Caribbean menu. Bar. Lunch $7.95-$12.95, dinner $11.95-$17.95. Specialties: corn and black bean crab cakes, in-house smoked sea bass, plantain-crusted chicken breast. Own baking. Entertainment nightly. Outdoor dining. 1950s Caribbean decor. Cr cds: A, C, D, DS, MC, V.

D

★ **MEMPHIS SOUL CAFE.** *2920 Bristol St (92626). 714/432-7685.* Hrs: 11:30 am-2:30 pm, 5-10 pm; Fri, Sat to 10:30 pm; Sun from 5 pm; Sat, Sun brunch 10:30 am-2:30 pm. Closed hols. Res accepted. Bar. Lunch $4.50-$7.50, dinner $5.95-$16.50. Sat, Sun brunch $3.50-$11.75. Specialties: down-home gumbo, Southern crab cakes, center-cut pork chops. Jazz Thurs. Outdoor dining. Roadhouse cafe. Cr cds: A, D, MC, V.

D

★★★ **PINOT PROVENCE.** *686 Anton Blvd (92626). 714/444-5900. www.patinagroup.com/pinot.htm.* French Provencial menu, changes seasonally. Hrs: 6:30 am-10 pm; Fri, to 11 pm; Sun to 9:30 pm; Sat, Sun brunch 7 am-2:30 pm. Res accepted. Wine list. Lunch $7-$20; dinner $17-$25. Brunch $7-$18. Entertainment. Cr cds: A, D, DS, MC, V.

D

★★ **SCOTT'S SEAFOOD GRILL & BAR.** *3300 Bristol St (92626). 714/-979-2400. www.scottsseafood.com.* Hrs: 11 am-10 pm; Fri, Sat to 11 pm; Sun from 10 am; Sun brunch 10 am-3 pm. Closed hols. Res accepted. Bar. Wine list. Lunch $11.95-$35, dinner $11.95-$45. Sun brunch $21.95. Specializes in seafood, beef. Free valet parking. Outdoor dining. Southern plantation decor. Cr cds: A, D, DS, MC, V.

D

★ **TRATTORIA SPIGA.** *3333 Bear St (92626). 714/540-3365.* Hrs: 11 am-9 pm; Fri, Sat to 10 pm; Sun 11:30 am-7 pm. Closed hols. Res accepted. Italian menu. Bar. A la carte entrees: lunch, dinner $5.25-$13.95. Specialties: miniature ravioli with veal in meat Bolognese sauce, boneless breasts of chicken in mushroom marsala wine sauce, Italian-style thin crust pizza. Patio dining. Trattoria-style dining in inner courtyard of mall. Cr cds: A, C, D, DS, ER, MC, V.
D

Unrated Dining Spot

TEA AND SYMPATHY. *369 E 17th St (92627). 949/645-4860.* Hrs: 11 am-6 pm; Sun brunch to 4 pm. Closed Dec 25. British menu. Wine, beer. Lunch $4.75-$12.50. Sun brunch $6.95-$12.95. Traditional English tea room. Cr cds: A, DS, MC, V.
D

Crescent City

(A-1) *See also Redwood Highway*

Founded 1852 **Pop** 4,380 **Elev** 44 ft **Area code** 707 **Zip** 95531

Information Chamber of Commerce, Visitor Information Center, 1001 Front St; 707/464-3174 or 800/343-8300.

Web www.delnorte.org

The crescent-shaped beach that gives the city its name outlines a busy harbor. A party of treasure seekers discovered the harbor, and the city was laid out a year later.

What to See and Do

Battery Point Lighthouse. (1856). On Battery Point, at the end of A St; accessible only at low tide; museum. (Apr-Sept, Wed-Sun) Phone 707/464-3089. ¢

Del Norte County Historical Society Main Museum. Research center for local history; two-story lighthouse lens (1892), Native American and pioneer exhibits housed in former county jail. (May-Sept, Mon-Sat) 577 H Street. Phone 707/464-3922. ¢

Ocean World. Aquarium, shark petting tank, sea lion show. Gift shop. (Daily) 304 US 101S. Phone 707/464-4900. ¢¢¢

Point St. George. The *Brother Jonathan,* a side-wheeler, was wrecked here in 1865. Of 232 persons aboard, 203 died; they are buried in Brother Jonathan Cemetery, Pebble Beach Dr and 9th St N of beach.

★ **Redwood National and State Parks.** Stretches 46 mi north and south, incl 30 mi of coastline, and about 7 mi wide at its greatest width. Headquarters at 2nd and K sts has exhibits, information. Established in 1968; the 113,200-acre park, home of what is said to be the world's tallest tree, offers hiking, biking, and bridle trails; picnic areas; scenic drives; shuttle bus (summer); interpretive programs. Phone 707/464-6101 for details. Exhibits and information at Hiouchi Information Center, 10 mi E or at Redwood Information Center, 2 mi S of Orick (daily). S of town. Contact 1111 2nd St. **FREE** The three state parks located within the national park boundaries are

Del Norte Coast Redwoods State Park. Redwood trees grow on steep slopes just above the surf. Rhododendrons blanket the slopes, blooming in May and June. Nature, hiking trails. Picnicking. Camping (dump station). Standard fees. 7 mi S on US 101. Phone 707/464-6101. Day use ¢ Camping ¢¢¢¢

Jedediah Smith Redwoods State Park. Stout Memorial Grove, at the center of Mill Creek Flat, is about four mi from park entrance. Swimming, fishing; nature and hiking trails, picnicking, camping (dump station). Standard fees. 9 mi NE off US 101 on US 199. Phone 707/464-6101. Day use ¢ Camping ¢¢¢¢

Prairie Creek Redwoods State Park. These 14,000 acres are adorned by magnificent groves of coast redwoods. Gold Bluffs Beach was worked for gold in 1851, but most of it remained hopelessly mixed in vast amounts of sand and rock. Lush ferns cover the 50-ft walls of Fern Canyon and moss carpets the fallen tree trunks. Fishing; hiking on 75 mi of nature trails, picnicking. Educational displays in visitor center. Frequent

Prairie Creek Redwoods State Park

campfire programs and ranger-conducted hikes in summer. Two campgrounds: **Elk Prairie**, tent and trailer (res recommended); **Gold Bluffs Beach**, approx 3½ mi S via US 101 to Davison Rd (unpaved road; vehicle size and weight restriction). Standard fees. 33 mi S on US 101. Phone 707/464-6101. Day use ¢ Camping ¢¢¢¢

Trees of Mystery. Nature-based theme park with unusual trees, incl features Skytrail aerial gondola, End of the Trail Indian Museum, gift shop, 49-ft-high talking figure of Paul Bunyon standing next to Babe the Blue Ox. (Daily; closed Dec 25) 20 mi S in Klamath, at 15500 Hwy 101 N. Phone 707/482-2251. ¢¢¢¢

Special Event

World Championship Crab Races & Crustacean Festival. Del Norte County Fairgrounds. Phone 707/464-3174. President's Day wkend.

Motels/Motor Lodges

★★ **BAYVIEW INN.** *310 US 101 S (95531). 707/465-2050; fax 707/465-3690; toll-free 800/446-0583.* 65 rms, ½ with A/C, 3 story, 9 suites. S $45-$59; D $49-$64; suites $89-$99. TV; cable (premium). Complimentary coffee in rms. Restaurant open 24 hrs. Ck-out 11 am. Meeting rms. Business servs avail. Coin lndry. Some refrigerators, microwaves; in-rm whirlpool in suites. Opp harbor. Cr cds: A, D, DS, MC, V.

D

★★ **BEST VALUE INN.** *440 US 101 N (95531). 707/464-4141; fax 707/465-3274; toll-free 800/323-7917. www.bestvalueinn.com.* 62 rms, 2 story. No A/C. May-mid-Oct: S $52; D $62-$65; each addl $5; suites $75; lower rates rest of yr. Crib $5. TV; cable, VCR avail (movies). Complimentary coffee. Restaurant noon-9 pm. Bar 3 pm-midnight. Ck-out noon. Meeting rms. Business servs avail. Sundries. Whirlpool. Sauna. Some refrigerators. Cr cds: A, C, D, DS, MC, V.

SC

★★ **BEST WESTERN NORTHWOODS INN.** *655 US 101 S (95531). 707/464-9771; fax 707/464-9461; res 800/528-1234. www.bestwestern.com/northwoo.* 89 rms, 2 story. Late June-Sept: S $69-$99; D $79-$119; each addl $10; under 18 free; suites $150-$175; higher rates hols, special events; lower rates rest of yr. Crib $8. TV; cable (premium). 2 whirlpools. Complimentary full bkfst. Coffee in rms. Restaurant 6 am-9 pm. Bar 2 pm-midnight. Ck-out 11 am. Coin lndry. Meeting rms. Business servs avail. In-rm modem link. Sundries. Some refrigerators, microwaves. Cr cds: A, C, D, DS, MC, V.

D

★★ **CURLY REDWOOD LODGE.** *701 US 101 S (95531). 707/464-2137; fax 707/464-1655. www.curlyredwoodlodge.com.* 36 rms, 1-2 story. No A/C. June-Sept: S $39-$60; D $41-$65; each addl $5; suites $75-$86; lower rates rest of yr. TV; cable. Complimentary coffee. Restaurants opp 7 am-10 pm. Ck-out 11 am. Business servs avail. Building constructed of wood from a single curly redwood tree. Harbor opp. Family-owned. Cr cds: A, C, D, MC, V.

★★ **HOLIDAY INN EXPRESS.** *100 Walton St (95531). 707/464-3885; fax 707/464-5311; toll-free 800/465-4329. www.basshotels.com/holiday-inn.* 46 rms, 2 story, 6 suites. June-Sept: S $64-$80; D $66-$84; suites $125;

under 18 free; family rates; lower rates rest of yr. Crib free. TV; cable (premium). Complimentary continental bkfst. Restaurant opp 7 am-9 pm. Ck-out 11 am. Meeting rms. Business servs avail. In-rm modem link. Coin lndry. Refrigerators, microwaves; in-rm whirlpool in suites. Many balconies. Adj to bay. Cr cds: A, C, D, DS, JCB, MC, V.

D SC

★ **SUPER 8.** *685 US 101 S (95616). 707/464-4111; fax 707/465-8916; res 800/800-8000. www.super8.com.* 49 rms, 2 story. No A/C. Mid-June-Labor Day: S $65; D $69-$74; each addl $5; under 13 free; lower rates rest of yr. Crib free. Pet accepted, some restrictions; fee. TV; cable (premium). Complimentary coffee in rms. Restaurant adj 7 am-9 pm. Ck-out 11 am. Business servs avail. Coin lndry. Ocean opp. Cr cds: A, DS, MC, V.

D

Restaurant

★★ **HARBOR VIEW GROTTO.** *150 Starfish Way (95531). 707/464-3815.* Hrs: 11:30 am-10 pm; winter to 9 pm. Closed Jan 1, Thanksgiving, Dec 24, 25. Bar. Lunch $3.75-$9.95, dinner $7.95-$20.50. Specializes in seafood, steak, prime rib. View of harbor, ocean. Totally nonsmoking. Cr cds: DS, MC, V.

D

Crestline

(E-5) *See also Lake Arrowhead*

Pop 8,594 **Elev** 5,000 ft
Area code 909 **Zip** 92325
Information Chamber of Commerce, 24385 Lake Dr; 909/338-2706
Web www.crestlinechamber.net

What to See and Do

Lake Gregory Regional Park. Swimming beach (late June-Labor Day wkend), waterslide (fee), fishing, rowboats (rentals); picnicking, snack bars, park. Lake Dr at Gregory Rd, E of town. Phone 909/338-2233. ¢¢

Silverwood Lake State Recreation Area. Swimming, fishing, boating (rentals); nature and bicycle trails, picnicking, concession, camping (dump station). Visitor center. Standard fees. 12 mi E off I-15 on CA 138. Phone 760/389-2303.

Cucamonga

(see Rancho Cucamonga)

Culver City

Pop 38,793 **Elev** 94 ft **Area code** 310

Motel/Motor Lodge

★★ **RAMADA PLAZA HOTEL-LAX.** *6333 Bristol Pkwy (90230). 310/484-7000; fax 310/484-7074; toll-free 800/321-5575. www.ramadaplaza hotellax.com.* 260 rms, 12 story. S, D $79-$99; suites $250; under 18 free; wkend rates. Crib free. TV; VCR avail. Heated pool; whirlpool, poolside serv. Complimentary coffee in rms. Restaurant open 24 hrs. Rm serv 6 am-10 pm. Bar 11-1 am. Ck-out noon. Convention facilities. Business center. Gift shop. Free airport transportation. Exercise equipt. Health club privileges. Refrigerator in suites, wet bar. Cr cds: A, C, D, DS, JCB, MC, V.

D SC

Dana Point

(see Laguna Beach)

Davis

(F-3) *See also Napa, Sacramento, Vacaville*

Settled 1868 **Pop** 46,209 **Elev** 50 ft **Area code** 530 **Zip** 95616

Information Chamber of Commerce and Visitor Center, 130 G St, Suite B; 530/756-5160

Web www.davischamber.com

The pioneer settler Jerome C. Davis planted 400 acres of wheat, barley, orchards, and vineyards and pastured great herds of livestock here. Since then, Davis has remained the center of a rich agricultural area. The city is also known for its energy conservation programs and projects. A prime example is Village Homes Solar Village. Obtain a self-guided tour brochure at City Hall, 23 Russell Blvd.

What to See and Do

Davis Campus of the University of California. (1905) 23,000 students. Nearly 5,200 acres with College of Agricultural and Environmental Sciences, College of Engineering, College of Letters and Science, School of Veterinary Medicine, School of Law, Graduate School of Management, and School of Medicine. Art exhibits displayed in the Nelson and Union Memorial galleries and in the C. N. Gorman Museum. Tours. On CA 113, I-80. Phone 530/752-8111.

Special Event

Picnic Day. Sponsored by Associated Students of University of California at Davis. Incl parade, floats, exhibits, aquacade, dachshund races, concerts, horse show, rodeo, sheepdog trials. Phone 530/752-6320. Mid-Apr.

Motel/Motor Lodge

★★ **BEST WESTERN UNIVERSITY LODGE.** *123 B St (95616). 530/756-7890; fax 530/756-0245; res 800/528-1234. www.bestwestern.com.* 53 rms, 2 story, some kits. S $79; D $85; each addl $5. Crib $5. Pet accepted; $5. TV; cable (premium). Complimentary coffee in rms. Restaurant opp 6 am-11 pm. Ck-out noon. Exercise equipt. Whirlpool. Refrigerators. University of California 1 blk. Cr cds: A, C, D, DS, MC, V.

D

Hotel

★★ **HALLMARK INN.** *110 F St (95616). 530/753-3600; fax 530/758-8623; toll-free 800/753-0035. www.hallmarkinn.com.* 135 rms, 2-3 story. S, D $75-$90; each addl $10; suites $90-$160; under 12 free; higher rates special events. Crib free. TV; cable (premium). Heated pool. Complimentary full bkfst. Restaurant adj open 24 hrs. Ck-out noon. Meeting rms. Valet serv. Some refrigerators. Balconies. Cr cds: A, D, DS, MC, V.

Restaurants

★ **CAFE BERNARDO.** *234 D St (95616). 530/750-5101. www.paragarys com.* Hrs: 7 am-10 pm; Fri, Sat, Sun to 11 pm. Closed Thanksgiving, Dec 25. Bkfst $2.75-$5.50, lunch $4.75-$6.50, dinner $5.25-$9.50. Specialty: pizzettas. Street parking. Outdoor dining. Cafe style. Totally nonsmoking. Cr cds: MC, V.

D

★★ **SOGA'S.** *217 E St (95616). 530/757-1733.* Hrs: 11:30 am-2 pm, 5-9 pm; Fri to 10 pm; Sat from 5 pm. Closed Sun, Mon, hols. Res accepted. Wine, beer. Lunch $6-$9, dinner $12-$18. Specializes in roasted meats, seafood, pasta. Outdoor dining. Reminiscent of a 1930s home; fireplace. Totally nonsmoking. Cr cds: A, D, DS, MC, V.

D

Death Valley National Park (A-5)

(70 mi E of Lone Pine on CA 190)

Here, approximately 300 miles northeast of Los Angeles, are more than 5,200 square miles of rugged desert, peaks, and depressions—an unusual and colorful geography. The park is one vast geological museum, revealing secrets of ages gone by. Millions of years ago, this was part of the Pacific Ocean; then violent uplifts of the earth occurred, creating mountain ranges and draining water to the west. Today, 200 square miles of the valley are at or below sea level; the lowest point on the continent (282 feet below sea level) is here; Telescope Peak (11,049 feet) towers directly above it. The valley itself is about 140 miles long and 4 to 16 miles wide. The average rainfall is less than two inches a year. From October until May the climate is very pleasant. In summer it is extremely hot; a maximum temperature of 134°F in the shade has been recorded. If considered altogether, this is the lowest, hottest, driest area in North America.

Death Valley was named in 1849 when a party of gold hunters took a shortcut here and were stranded for several weeks awaiting help. The discovery and subsequent mining of borax, hauled out by the famous 20-mule teams, led to development of the valley as a tourist attraction.

The visitor center at Furnace Creek is open daily. Guided walks, evening programs and talks (Nov-Apr). Golden Age, Golden Eagle, Golden Access passports (see MAKING THE MOST OF YOUR TRIP). Phone 760/786-2331. Per vehicle **¢¢¢**

NOTE. It can be very dangerous to venture off paved roads in this area in the summer months. Carefully obey all National Park Service signs and regulations. Make sure your vehicle has plenty of gas and oil. Carry water when you explore this park, especially in hot weather. For further information contact Superintendent, Death Valley National Park, Death Valley 92328. Phone 760/786-2331.

What to See and Do

20-Mule-Team Canyon. Viewed from a twisting road om which RVs and trailers are not allowed. (This is an unpaved, one-way rd; watch carefully for the entrance sign.) Phone 760/786-2331.

Artist's Palette. A particularly scenic auto drive (nine mi one way), with spectacular colors. Because of difficult roads, RVs and trailers are advised not to drive here.

Badwater. At 279 ft below sea level, near the lowest spot on the North American continent; look for sea level sign. Phone 760/786-2331.

Camping. Developed and primitive camping in area; limited hookups. It is suggested that campers check with the visitors center for important information on camping facilities and road conditions. (Daily) Phone 760/786-2331. **FREE**

Charcoal kilns. Beehive-shaped stone structures, formerly used to make charcoal for nearby mines. **Note:** The last mile of the access road is unpaved. Phone 760/786-2331.

Dante's View. (5,475 ft) View of Death Valley with a steep drop to 279 ft below sea level at Badwater. Phone 760/786-2331.

Devil's Golf Course. Vast beds of rugged salt crystals. Phone 760/786-2331.

Golden Canyon. Offers a display of color ranging from deep red to rich gold. One-mi trail provides access. Phone 760/786-2331.

Natural Bridge. A bridge spanning a rugged canyon in the Black Mountains; one-mi walking trail. Phone 760/786-2331.

Rhyolite Ghost Town. This was the largest town in the mining history of

Moon setting over Panamint Range

Death Valley in the early 1900s; 5,000-10,000 people lived here then. The town bloomed from 1905-1910; by 1911 it was a ghost town. One structure still left standing from that era is the "bottle house," constructed of 12,000-50,000 beer and liquor bottles (depending on who does the estimating). Phone 760/786-2331.

Sand dunes. Sand blown by the wind into dunes 5 to 100 ft high. Phone 760/786-2331.

Scotty's Castle. A desert mansion (ca 1922-1931), designed and built to be viewed as a work of art, as well as a house. The furnishings are typical of the period; many were especially designed and hand crafted for this house. Living history tours are led by costumed interpreters. Phone 760/786-2331. ¢¢¢

Telescope Peak. Highest point in the Panamint Range (11,049 ft). (Although there is a 14-mi round-trip hiking trail, it is inaccessible in the winter months.) Phone 760/786-2331.

Ubehebe Crater. Colorful crater left by a volcanic steam explosion. Phone 760/786-2331.

Visitor Center. It is recommended that visitors stop here before continuing on for an orientation film, day-trip suggestions, help in organizing sightseeing routes, and important information on camping areas and road conditions. At Furnace Creek. Phone 760/786-2331.

Zabriskie Point. View of Death Valley and the Panamint Range from the rugged badlands of the Black Mtns. Phone 760/786-2331.

Motel/Motor Lodge

★ **STOVEPIPE WELLS VILLAGE.** *CA 190, Death Valley (92328). 760/786-2387; fax 760/786-2389. www.stovepipewells.com.* 83 rms, 5 buildings. No rm phones. S, D $58-$80; each addl $10; under 12 free. Crib $5. Pet accepted, some restrictions; $20 refundable. Heated pool. Restaurant 7 am-2 pm, 6:30-10 pm. Bar 4:30-11 pm. Ck-out 11 am. Sundries. Landing strip. Panoramic view of mountains, desert, dunes. Cr cds: A, D, DS, MC, V.

D

Resort

★★★ **FURNACE CREEK RANCH.** *CA 190, Death Valley (92328). 760/786-2345; fax 760/786-2423; toll-free 800/236-7916. www.furnacecreekresort.com.* 224 rms, 1-2 story. S, D $165-$270; each addl $14; under 18 free. TV; cable. Bar noon-midnight. Natural thermal spring water pool. Playground. Dining rms 6 am-10 pm. Ck-out noon, ck-in 4 pm. Grocery. Coin lndry. Package store. Gift shop. Lighted tennis. Golf, greens fee $40, pro, driving range. Volleyball, basketball courts. Museum. Some refrigerators. Cr cds: A, C, D, DS, JCB, MC, V.

D SC

★★ **FURNACE CREEK INN.** *CA 190, Death Valley (92328). 760/786-2345; fax 760/786-2307. www.furnacecreekresort.com.* 66 units, 4 story. Feb-Apr S, D $124-$129; each addl $15; suites $325; under 18 free; lower rates rest of yr. TV; cable. Natural thermal spring water pool; poolside serv. Restaurant 7-10:30 am, 11:30 am-2 pm, 5:30-10 pm (see also INN DINING ROOM). Bar noon-11 pm. Ck-out noon. Concierge. Gift shop. Lighted tennis. Golf privileges, greens fee $40, pro, driving range. Exercise equipt; sauna. Lawn games. Refrigerators. Private patios, balconies. 1920s-30s decor; native stone in many areas. Cr cds: A, C, D, DS, JCB, MC, V.

D SC

Restaurant

★★★ **INN DINING ROOM.** *CA 190 (92328). 760/786-2361. www.furnacecreekresort.com.* Hrs: 7-10:30 am, 11:30 am-2 pm, 5:30-10 pm; Sun brunch 11 am-2 pm. Res accepted. Continental menu. Bar noon-11 pm. Wine list. A la carte entrees: bkfst $9, lunch $8.50-$12.95, dinner $25. Sun brunch $17.95. Specializes in chicken, steak, seafood. Own baking. Valet parking. 1930s decor; beam ceilings. Jacket. Totally nonsmoking. Cr cds: A, DS, MC, V.

D

Del Mar

(F-5) *See also Carlsbad, La Jolla (San Diego), San Diego*

Pop 4,860 **Elev** 100 ft **Area code** 858 **Zip** 92014

Information Greater Del Mar Chamber of Commerce, 1104 Camino Del Mar; 858/793-5292

Web www.delmar.ca.us

This village-by-the sea community offers beautiful white beaches and brilliant sunsets. It is also an attractive area for year-round ballooning.

Special Events

Del Mar Fair. Fairgrounds. Name entertainment, carnival; livestock, trade, hobby and flower exhibits. Mid-June-early July. Phone 858/755-1141.

Del Mar Thoroughbred Club. County Fairgrounds. Thoroughbred horse racing. For prices, schedule, and information phone 858/755-1141; for ticket res phone 858/792-4242. Late July-mid-Sept.

Motels/Motor Lodges

★★ BEST WESTERN. *710 Camino del Mar (92014). 858/755-1501; fax 858/755-4704. www.bestwestern.com.* 95 rms, 2 story, 29 suites. June-Sept: S, D $109-$139; suites $149-$169; under 18 free; lower rates rest of yr. Crib free. TV; cable (premium). 2 pools; whirlpool. Complimentary continental bkfst. Restaurant adj 11-2 am. Ck-out noon. Coin lndry. Valet serv. Health club privileges. Some refrigerators, microwaves. Some balconies. Cr cds: A, D, DS, MC, V.

★★ CLARION CARRIAGE HOUSE DEL MAR INN. *720 Camino Del Mar (92014). 858/755-9765; fax 858/792-8196; toll-free 800/451-4515. www.clarioninn.com.* 81 rms, 3 story, 22 kits. Some A/C. June-Sept: S, D $115-$165; lower rates rest of yr. Crib $10. TV; cable (premium). Heated pool; whirlpool. Complimentary continental bkfst in rms; afternoon refreshments. Ck-out 11 am. Coin lndry. Meeting rm. Business servs avail. Health club privileges. Microwaves avail. Many balconies. Cr cds: A, C, D, DS, ER, JCB, MC, V.

★★ COUNTRY INN BY AYERS. *1661 Villa Cardiff Dr, Cardiff by the Sea, Cardiff (92007). 760/944-0427; fax 760/944-7708; res 800/322-9993. www.countrysuites.com.* 102 rms, 2 story. S, D $68-$125; each addl $8; under 12 free. Crib free. TV; cable (premium). Heated pool; whirlpool. Complimentary full bkfst. Ck-out noon. Meeting rms. Business servs avail. In-rm modem link. Health club privileges. Refrigerators; microwaves avail. Country French decor. Cr cds: A, C, D, DS, MC, V.

Hotel

★★★ HILTON DEL MAR NORTH SAN DIEGO. *15575 Jimmy Durante Blvd (92014). 858/792-5200; fax 858/792-9538; res 800/445-8667. www.hilton.com.* 245 units, 3 story. S $139-$219; D $159-$229; each addl $20; suites $279-$699; family rates; package plans. Crib free. TV; cable (premium). Pool; whirlpools, poolside serv. Complimentary coffee in rms. Restaurant 6 am-2 pm, 5-11 pm. Bar 11-1 am. Ck-out noon. Convention facilities. Business servs avail. In-rm modem link. Gift shop. Valet parking. Tennis privileges. Exercise equipt. Some refrigerators, microwaves, minibars. Cr cds: A, C, D, DS, MC, V.

Resort

★★★★ L'AUBERGE DEL MAR RESORT AND SPA. *1540 Camino Del Mar (92014). 858/259-1515; fax 858/755-4940; toll-free 800/553-1336. www.laubergedelmar.com.* This 120-room property, once the Hotel Del Mar in Hollywood's heyday, is a bastion of romance within walking distance of the beach and 20 minutes north of San Diego. All rooms have private balconies, many with views of the Pacific, and are decorated like beach cottages. You can dine on fine

Californian cuisine. 120 rms, 3 story. S, D $205-$395; each addl $25; suites $800-$1,300; package plans. Crib avail. Valet, underground parking (fee). TV; cable, VCR avail. 2 pools; poolside serv. Restaurant (see J. TAYLOR'S). Bar 11-1 am. Ck-out noon, ck-in 4 pm. Concierge. Business servs avail. Shopping arcade. Lighted tennis. Exercise rm; sauna, steam rm. Spa. Minibars; some fireplaces. Cr cds: A, C, D, DS, JCB, MC, V.

D SC

Restaurants

★★ **EPAZOTE.** *1555 Camino del Mar (92014). 858/259-9966. www.epazote.signonsandiego.com.* Hrs: 11:30 am-10 pm; Fri to 11 pm; Sat 11 am-11 pm; Sun from 10:30 am. Closed Dec 25. Res accepted. Southwestern menu. Bar. Lunch $6-$12, dinner $9.95-$19.95. Specialties: spit-roasted chicken, char-broiled salmon. Jazz Wed evening. Valet parking. Outdoor dining. View of ocean. Cr cds: A, MC, V.

D

★ **FISH MARKET.** *3333 Bristol Rd (92626). 714/708-2582. www.thefishmarket.com.* Specializes in cioppino, mesquite grilled fresh seafood. Oyster bar. Hrs: 11 am-9:30 pm; Fri, Sat to 10 pm. Res accepted. Wine, beer. Lunch $7-$29; dinner $10-$35. Children's menu. Entertainment. Cr cds: A, C, D, DS, MC, V.

D

★★ **IL FORNAIO.** *1555 Camino del Mar (92014). 858/755-8876. www.ilfornaio.com.* Hrs: 11:30 am-11 pm; Sat to midnight; Sun 10 am-11 pm. Closed Thanksgiving, Dec 25. Res accepted. Bar. Wine list. Lunch $12-$16, dinner $16-$26. Children's menu. Specializes in regional Italian dishes. Parking. Outdoor dining. Totally nonsmoking. Cr cds: A, C, D, MC, V.

D

★★ **JAKE'S DEL MAR.** *1660 Coast Blvd (92014). 858/755-2002. www.hulapie.com.* Hrs: 11:15 am-2:30 pm, 5-9:30 pm; Mon from 5 pm; Fri, Sat to 10 pm; Sun brunch 10 am-2:30 pm. Closed Dec 25. Res accepted. No A/C. Continental menu. Bar to midnight. A la carte entrees: lunch $6.95-$10.95, dinner $10-$19.95. Sun brunch $6.95-$11.95. Specializes in fresh seafood, lamb, steak. Own desserts. Valet parking. Patio dining. Ocean view. Cr cds: A, DS, MC, V.

D

★★★ **J. TAYLOR'S.** *1540 Camino del Mar (92014). 858/259-1515. www.laubergedelmar.com.* Hrs: 6:30-11 am, 11:30 am-2 pm, 5-10 pm; early-bird dinner 5-6:30 pm. Res accepted. Bar 11-1 am. Bkfst $4.95-$11.95, lunch $7-$12.95, dinner $12-$23. Prix fixe: dinner $29.95. Specializes in California cuisine with international flavor. Valet parking. Outdoor dining. Skylights. View of waterfall and gardens. Cr cds: A, D, DS, MC, V.

D

★ **PACIFICA DEL MAR.** *1555 Camino del Mar (92014). 858/792-0476. www.pacificadelmar.com.* Specializes in seafood. Hrs: 11:30 am-10 pm; Sat, Sun 11:30 am-10 pm. Res accepted. Wine, beer. Lunch $8-$14; dinner $13-$28. Children's menu. Entertainment. Ocean view. Cr cds: A, D, DS, MC, V.

D SC

★★ **PACIFIC COAST GRILL.** *437 S CA 101, Solana Beach (92075). 858/794-4632. www.pacificcoastgrills.com.* Hrs: 11:30 am-10 pm; Fri, Sat to 11 pm; Sun brunch 11:30 am-4 pm. Closed hols. Res accepted. Seafood menu. Bar. Lunch $6.95-$9.95, dinner $10.95-$18.95. Sun brunch $5.25-$9.95. Specialties: lobster tacos, steak-cut ahi, spicy pork tenderloin. Parking. Outdoor dining. Eclectic atmosphere; bright mosaic tiles in floor. Cr cds: A, D, DS, MC, V.

D

★★★ **TORREY PINES CAFE.** *2334 Carmel Valley Rd (92014). 858/259-5878. www.torreypinescafe.com.* Hrs: 11:30 am-2:30 pm, 5-9 pm; Fri to 10 pm; Sat 5-10 pm; Sun brunch 10 am-2 pm. Res accepted. Wine list. Lunch $4-$12.50, dinner $4-$19. Sun brunch $4.50-$8.50. Specialties: blackened catfish, lamb shank, osso buco. Outdoor dining. Overlooks Torrey Pines State Reserve Park. Totally nonsmoking. Cr cds: A, C, D, DS, MC, V.

D

Desert Hot Springs

(E-6) *See also Idyllwild, Indio, Palm Desert, Palm Springs*

Pop 11,668 **Elev** 1,070 ft
Area code 760 **Zip** 92240

Information Chamber of Commerce, 11-711 West Dr; 760/329-6403 or 800/346-3347

Web www.deserthotsprings.com

Resorts

★★ **DESERT HOT SPRINGS SPA HOTEL.** *10805 Palm Dr (92240). 760/329-6000; fax 760/329-6915; res 888/329-6000. www.dhsspa.com.* 50 rms, 2 story. Mid-Dec-May: S, D $99-$119; each addl $10; suites $109-$129; lower rates rest of yr. Crib $5. TV; cable (premium). 8 natural hot mineral pools (open to public); pool; 2 whirlpools, wading pool, poolside serv. Sauna. Restaurant 7 am-11 pm. Bar 10-1 am; entertainment Fri, Sat. Ck-out noon. Business servs avail. In-rm modem link. Sundries. Gift shop. Tennis privileges. 18-hole golf privileges. Refrigerators avail. Private patios, balconies. Cr cds: A, D, DS, MC, V.

D

★★★ **TWO BUNCH PALMS RESORT AND SPA.** *67-425 Two Bunch Palms Tr (92240). 760/329-8791; fax 760/329-1317; toll-free 800/472-4334. www.twobunchpalms.com.* 45 cottages. 2-day min: S, D $175-$295; suites $465-$570. Closed Aug. Adults only. TV; cable, VCR. 2 pools; whirlpool. Complimentary continental bkfst. Dining rm 8 am-9:30 pm. Box lunches, snacks. Bar. Ck-out noon, ck-in 3 pm. Business servs avail. Gift shop. Lighted tennis. Spa, sauna, massages. Bicycles avail. Refrigerators. Microwaves avail. 250 acres of rolling, wooded terrain incl a lake and offer a secluded, private getaway. Rock grotto pools are fed from natural mineral hot springs. Cr cds: A, MC, V.

D

Devils Postpile National Monument

(G-6) *See also Mammoth Lakes*

(56 mi NW of Bishop, off US 395)

Just southeast of Yosemite National Park (see) and surrounded by Inyo National Forest (see) is Devils Postpile National Monument. The monument is among the finest examples of columnar basalt in the world, formed approximately 100,000 years ago when basalt lava erupted in the area. These columns, standing 40 to 60 feet high, are protected by the National Park Service. The formation is a ½ mile hike from the ranger station. A short, steep trail leads to the top of the formation for a view of the ends of the columns, which have been polished by glaciers and resemble tilelike inlays. Pumice, a porous lava, and a nearby bubbling soda spring are evidence of recent volcanic activity.

Rainbow Falls is approximately two miles down the river trail from the Postpile. Here the San Joaquin River drops 101 feet—the foam-white water starkly contrasting with the dark cliffs. Its name was suggested by the rainbows that play across the falls in the afternoon. Fishing is per-

Devils Postpile National Monument

mitted with license; hunting is prohibited. Picnic area on grounds. A campground is maintained in the northeast section. Park (mid-June-mid-Oct, daily; closed rest of yr). Ranger station (daily; hrs may vary). Campfire programs and guided walks available; call for schedule. For further information contact PO Box 501, Mammoth Lakes 93546; 760/934-2289 (June-Oct) or 760/872-4881 (Nov-May). Camping per day **¢¢¢¢**

Disneyland

See also Anaheim, Buena Park, Los Angeles, Orange

(26 mi S of Los Angeles on Harbor Blvd, off Santa Ana Fwy in Anaheim)

The Walt Disney Company has sprinkled magic over 80 beautifully landscaped acres in Anaheim to create a fantasy that tantalizes adults as well as children. Park guests meet Mickey Mouse and the Disney characters and experience real-life adventures. Transportation ranges from horse-drawn streetcars to monorails; restaurant fare varies from pancakes to continental cuisine. Summer schedule includes name entertainment daily, dancing, fireworks, and parades. You'll need a minimum of eight hours to see Disneyland. Plan to rest up the next day.

Disneyland attractions are open daily (extended hrs during hols). Passport to Disneyland good for unlimited use of rides and attractions (except arcades). Guided tours. Facilities for the disabled include wheelchair rentals, ramps; tape cassettes for the visually impaired. Contact 1313 Harbor Blvd, PO Box 3232, Anaheim 92803; 714/781-4565. Passport (individual) $41; children ages 3-11 $31; under 3 yrs free.

What to See and Do

Adventureland. "Jungle Cruise" through tropical rivers of the world, with lifelike alligators, hippos, gorillas, monkeys, water buffalo and Indian elephants; Swiss Family Tree House. Enchanted Tiki Room shows musical fantasy with Audio-Animatronics: birds, flowers, talking and singing Tiki gods. The Indiana Jones Adventure thrill ride is also here.

California Adventure. The newest Disney theme park celebrates the history, culture, landscape, and industry of California. Located adj to Disneyland, this park features four main areas, each with a different California-related theme. **Sunshine Plaza** is the gateway to all areas of Disney's California Adventure, and incl a 50-ft-tall sun atop a perpetual wave fountain. Parade, lightshow (daily). **Golden State** area focuses on the diversity of people and landscape in California. Six areas explore the history, agriculture, and industry of the state: Condor Flats, Bountiful Valley Farm, Pacific Wharf, Bay Area, Grizzly Peak Recreation Area, and Golden Vine Winery. Hiking, climbing, art and music shows, wine tasting. **Paradise Pier** is a surfside boardwalk that features classic amusement park rides, diners, and shops. Rides incl California Screamin' rollercoaster, Sun Wheel Ferris wheel, Maliboomer 180-ft launch tower, Mulholland Madness ride, Golden Zephyr spinning spaceships, Orange Stinger ride, King Triton's Carousel, Games of the Boardwalk, and two floating interactive exhibits, Jumpin' Jellyfish and SS *rustworthy*. **Hollywood Pictures Backlot** lets visitors explore Hollywood Blvd during the 'Golden Age' of filmmaking. Incl Jim Henson's Muppet Vision 3-D, Disney animation, Hyperion Theater, and Superstar Limo. Musical theater, rides, films. (Daily) 1313 S Harbor Blvd. Phone 714/781-4565.

Critter Country. Home of "Splash Mountain" log flume ride, Country Bear Playhouse, a 15-min country and western revue featuring musical Audio-Animatronic bears and Davy Crockett Explorer Canoes.

Fantasyland. Favorite Disney classics come to life in exciting adventures. Major attractions incl It's a Small World, Pinocchio, Snow White, Dumbo, Peter Pan, and Alice in Wonderland.

Frontierland. Relive the Old West and capture the pioneer spirit with the *Mark Twain* sternwheel riverboat, keel boats, the Golden Horseshoe Stage and Big Thunder Mountain Railroad. FANTASMIC! is a special effects and character presentation (nightly anytime Disneyland is open after dark) on the Rivers of America, which flow between Frontierland and Tom Sawyer Island.

Main St, U.S.A. Revives turn-of-the-century nostalgia with steam-powered Disneyland RR, old-time cinema, Market House, 1900 emporium; an inspiring Audio-Animatronics presentation, "The Walt Disney Story," featuring "Great Moments with Mr. Lincoln."

Mickey's Toontown. A 3-D cartoon environment where guests can visit the homes of Mickey Mouse and his friends, incl Goofy's Bounce House and Chip 'n Dale's Tree Slide and Acorn Crawl. Other attractions incl The Jolly Trolley, Gadget's Go Coaster, and Roger Rabbit's Car Toon Spin.

New Orleans Square. Shops, cafes, nostalgic courtyards, a "Pirates of the Caribbean" cruise, and the Haunted Mansion.

Tomorrowland. This land of the future explores inner and outer space; features incl Space Mountain rollercoaster, Autopia, Submarine Voyage, a 2½-mi monorail; rocket ride; Star Tours is an exciting out-of-this-world trip through the galaxy.

Dunsmuir (B-3)

Pop 2,129 **Elev** 2,289 ft
Area code 530 **Zip** 96025

Information Chamber of Commerce, 4118 Pine St, PO Box 17; 530/235-2177 or 800/DUNSMUIR

Web www.dunsmuir.com

What to See and Do

Castle Crags State Park. On 4,250 acres. Named for nearby granite peaks up to 6,600 ft high. Fishing (exc in the Sacramento River and its tributaries). Picnicking, camping. 6 mi S off I-5. Phone 530/235-2684. ¢¢¢¢¢

Special Event

River Festival. Celebration of watershed stewardship. Exhibits, fishing clinics, demonstrations; art shows. Phone River Exchange Center, 530/235-2012. Late Apr.

Motel/Motor Lodge

★ CEDAR LODGE MOTEL. *4201 Dunsmuir Ave (96025). 530/235-4331; fax 530/235-4000. www.cedarlodgedunsmuir.com.* 16 rms, 6 kits. May-Oct: S $45; D $50; each addl $4; kit. units $10 addl; family units from $65; lower rates rest of yr. Crib $4. Pet accepted, some restrictions. TV; cable. Complimentary coffee in rms. Restaurant nearby. Ck-out 11 am. Downhill/x-country ski 16 mi. Private patios. Picnic tables, grill. Large exotic bird aviary. Near Sacramento River. Cr cds: A, DS, MC, V.

Resort

★★ RAILROAD PARK RESORT. *100 Railroad Park Rd (96025). 530/235-4440; fax 530/235-4470. www.rrpark.com.* 28 rms, 4 cabins. June-Sept: S, D $85-$100; each addl $8; cabins $70-$85. Pet accepted, some restrictions; $8. TV; cable. Pool; whirlpool. Complimentary coffee in rms. Restaurant 5-10 pm Wed-Sun. Bar from 4 pm. Ck-out 11 am. Coin lndry. Business servs avail. Sundries. Gift shop. Game rm. Lawn games. Refrigerators. Picnic tables, grills. RV hookups. Rooms in authentic railroad cars; ¼ mi from Sacramento River. Cr cds: A, DS, MC, V.

El Cajon (F-6)

Pop 88,693 **Elev** 435 ft **Area code** 619

Motels/Motor Lodges

★★ BEST WESTERN CONTINENTAL INN. *650 N Mollison Ave (92021). 619/442-0601; fax 619/442-0152; res 800/882-3781. www.bestwestern.com.* 97 rms, 2-3 story, 12 suites, 12 kits. Mid-June-mid-Sept: S, D $69-$105; each addl $5; suites $75-$150; kits. $75; under 18 free; lower rates rest of yr. Crib free. TV; cable (premium). Heated pool; whirlpool. Complimentary continental bkfst. Restaurant opp open 24 hrs. Ck-out

11 am. Coin lndry. Meeting rms. Business servs avail. Many refrigerators; some minibars, microwaves. Many balconies. Cr cds: A, C, D, DS, MC, V.

D SC

★ **EL CAJON TRAVELODGE.** *471 N Magnolia Ave (92020). 619/447-3999; fax 619/447-8403; res 800/578-7878. www.travelodge.com.* 49 rms, 3 story. S $55-$80; D $60-$90; each addl $5; under 17 free; higher rates hols. Crib free. Pet accepted, some restrictions; $15. TV; cable (premium), VCR avail. Complimentary continental bkfst, coffee in rms. Restaurant opp 6 am-10 pm. Ck-out 11 am. Business servs avail. In-rm modem link. Coin lndry. Pool. Refrigerators, microwaves. Cr cds: A, C, D, DS, MC, V.

D

★ **THRIFTLODGE.** *1220 W Main St (92020). 619/442-2576; fax 619/579-7562; res 800/578-7878.* 28 rms, 10 with shower only, 2 story. S $50-$99; D $71-$99; suite $89-$99; under 18 free; higher rates hols. Pet accepted, some restrictions; $20. TV; cable. Complimentary coffee in rms. Restaurant adj open 24 hrs. Ck-out noon. Business servs avail. In-rm modem link. Pool. Some refrigerators. Cr cds: A, D, DS, MC, V.

D SC

Hotel

★ **PLAZA INTERNATIONAL INN.** *683 N Mollison Ave (92021). 619/442-0973; fax 619/593-0772; toll-free 800/675-7105. www.plazainn.com.* 60 rms, 2 story. S $42; D $49; each addl $5; under 2 free. Crib avail. Parking lot. Pool, whirlpool. TV; cable. Complimentary coffee in rms. Restaurant nearby. Ck-out 11 am, ck-in 2 pm. Sauna. Golf, 18 holes. Cr cds: A, C, D, DS, MC, V.

Resort

★★★ **SINGING HILLS RESORT.** *3007 Dehesa Rd (92019). 619/442-3425; fax 619/442-9574; toll-free 800/457-5568. www.singinghills.com.* 102 rms, 1-2 story. S, D $93-$109; each addl $14; suites $121-$246; under 18 free. Crib free. TV; VCR avail. 2 heated pools; whirlpools. Complimentary coffee in rms. Restaurant 6 am-4 pm; dining rm 5:30-10 pm. Bar 10-2 am; entertainment Fri-Sat. Ck-out 1:30 pm. Coin lndry. Meeting rms. Business servs avail. Airport transportation. Lighted tennis, pro. Three 18-hole golf courses, greens fee $14-$45, 5 putting greens. Exercise equipt. Massage. Refrigerators; wet bar, some microwaves in suites. Private patios, balconies. View of mountains, valley and golf course. Cr cds: A, DS, MC, V.

D

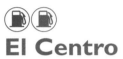

El Centro

(F-7) *See also Calexico*

Settled 1901 **Pop** 31,384 **Elev** 40 ft below sea level **Area code** 760 **Zip** 92243

Information Chamber of Commerce, 1095 S. 4th St; 760/352-3681

Web www.elcentrochamber.com

This busy marketplace in the center of the Imperial Valley is the largest town entirely below sea level in the United States. Water from the All-American Canal and Hoover Dam has turned arid desert into lush farmland, which produces great crops of sugar beets, melons, and lettuce. The Imperial Valley was once part of the Gulf of California; mountains east of El Centro are ringed with coral reefs. Other points of geological interest are Fossil Canyon, north of town, and Painted Gorge, northwest off I-8.

Motels/Motor Lodges

★★ **CALIPATRIA INN AND SUITES.** *700 N Sorensen Ave, Calipatria (92233). 760/348-2667; fax 760/348-7348; toll-free 800/830-1113.* 40 rms, 5 with shower only, 5 suites. S, D $52-$59; each addl $5; suites $67-$121; under 12 free; higher rates special events. Crib free. Pet accepted. TV; cable (premium), VCR avail. Complimentary continental bkfst. Restaurant nearby. Ck-out noon. Meeting rms. Business servs avail. In-rm modem link. Pool; whirlpool.

Many microwaves. Picnic tables, grills. Cr cds: A, DS, MC, V.

D

★ **EL DORADO MOTEL.** *1464 Adams Ave (92243). 760/352-7333; fax 760/352-4154; toll-free 800/874-5532.* 73 rms, 2 story, 6 kit. units. S, D $39-$45; each addl $4; kits. $39-$48; under 12 free; wkly rates. Pet accepted. TV; cable (premium). Pool. Complimentary continental bkfst. Restaurant adj 7 am-midnight. Ck-out 11 am. Some refrigerators. Cr cds: A, C, D, DS, MC, V.

D

★ **EXECUTIVE INN.** *725 W State St (92243). 760/352-8500.* 42 rms, 2 story, 5 kits. S, D $25-$50; kit. units $35-$50; each addl $2; suites $45-$60; under 12 free. Crib $5. Pet accepted, some restrictions. TV; cable. Pool. Complimentary continental bkfst. Restaurant nearby. Ck-out 11 am. Coin lndry. Some free covered parking. Some refrigerators; microwaves avail. Grills. Cr cds: A, D, DS, MC, V.

★★ **RAMADA INN.** *1455 Ocotillo Dr (92243). 760/352-5152; fax 760/337-1567; res 888/298-2054. www.ramada.com.* 147 rms, 2 story. S $59-$62; D $68-$74; each addl $6; suites $75-$90; under 18 free. Crib free. Pet accepted. TV; cable (premium), VCR avail. Heated pool, whirlpool. Complimentary coffee in lobby. Restaurant open 24 hrs. Rm serv 6 am-2 pm, 5-10 pm. Bar 3:30 pm-midnight. Ck-out noon. Coin lndry. Meeting rms. Free airport, bus depot transportation. Exercise rm. Microwaves avail. Cr cds: A, C, D, DS, JCB, MC, V.

D

★★ **VACATION INN.** *2015 Cottonwood Cir (92243). 760/352-9523; fax 760/353-7620; toll-free 800/328-6289.* 186 rms, 2 story. S, D $49-$54; suites $75-$95; higher rates special events. Crib free. Pet accepted; $25 deposit. TV; cable (premium). 2 heated pools; whirlpool, poolside serv. Restaurant (see also SCRIBBLES). Bar 5:30 am-midnight. Ck-out noon. Coin lndry. Meeting rms. Business servs avail. In-rm modem link. Some refrigerators; microwaves avail. Exercise equipt. Cr cds: A, C, D, DS, MC, V.

D SC

Resort

★★★ **BARBARA WORTH GOLF RESORT AND CONVENTION CENTER.** *2050 Country Club Dr, Holtville (92250). 760/356-2806; fax 760/356-4653; toll-free 800/356-3806. www.bwresort.com.* 103 rms, 2 story. S $70; D $76; each addl $6; kit. suites $135-$141; under 13 free; wkly, monthly rates; golf plans. Crib $6. TV; cable (premium). 2 heated pools; whirlpool. Coffee in rms. Restaurant (see also BARBARA WORTH GOLF RESORT AND CONVENTION CENTER). Bar 9 pm-midnight; Fri-Sun to 2 am. Ck-out noon. Meeting rms. 18-hole golf, greens fee $20-$28, putting green, driving range. Exercise equipt. Some refrigerators; microwaves avail. Private balconies. Cr cds: A, C, D, DS, JCB, MC, V.

D

Restaurants

★★ **BARBARA WORTH GOLF RESORT AND CONVENTION CENTER.** *2050 Country Club Dr, Holtville (92250). 760/356-2806.* Hrs: 6 am-10 pm; Sun brunch 10:30 am-2:30 pm. Closed Dec 25. Res accepted. Bar to midnight; Fri, Sat to 2 am. Bkfst $4.50-$6.95, lunch $3.50-$9.50, dinner $8.95-$20.95. Sun brunch $13.95. Children's menu. Specializes in beef, seafood. Outdoor dining. Garden atmosphere; large windows for outside view. Cr cds: A, D, DS, MC, V.

D

★★ **SCRIBBLES.** *2015 Cottonwood Cir (92243). 760/352-9523.* Hrs: 5:30 am-10 pm; Sun from 6 am. Closed Dec 25. Res accepted. Bar to 11 pm. A la carte entrees: bkfst $1.99-$8.95, lunch $4.50-$8.50, dinner $9.95-15.95. Children's menu. Specialties: prime rib, filet mignon. Totally nonsmoking. Cr cds: A, D, DS, MC, V.

D

Encino

(see Los Angeles)

Escondido

(F-6) *See also Carlsbad, La Jolla (San Diego), San Diego*

Pop 108,635 **Elev** 684 ft
Area code 760

Information San Diego North Convention and Visitors Bureau, 360 N Escondido Blvd, 92025; 760/745-4741 or 800/848-3336

Web www.sandiegonorth.com

A Ranger District office of the Cleveland National Forest (see PINE VALLEY) is located here.

What to See and Do

Escondido Heritage Walk. Escondido Historical Society history museum. Artifacts, books, preservation displays. Victorian ranch house; working blacksmith shop, early 1900s barn and windmill, 1888 Santa Fe RR depot, RR car with model train replica of the Oceanside to Escondido run (ca 1920). (Thurs-Sat; closed hols exc July 4) 321 N Broadway. Phone 760/743-8207. **Donation**

Palomar Observatory. Here are a 200-inch Hale telescope (second-largest in the US) and 48-inch and 60-inch telescopes. There is a visitors' gallery in the dome of the Hale telescope; Greenway Museum has photography from telescopes, exhibits explaining equipt. Self-guided tours. Gift shop. (Daily; closed Dec 24, 25) 35 mi NE on County S6. Phone 760/742-2119. **FREE**

San Diego Wild Animal Park. (See SAN DIEGO)

San Pasqual Battlefield State Historic Park and Museum. Interpretive displays of the Battle of San Pasqual, fought in Dec 1846, during the Mexican War. Fifty acres within deeply weathered granite foothills; self-guided native plant trail, hiking, picnicking. (Fri-Sun; closed Jan 1, Thanksgiving, Dec 25) 8 mi E on CA 78. Phone 760/737-2201. **FREE**

Welk Resort Center Theatre-Museum. Music Center houses memorabilia marking the milestones of Lawrence Welk's career. (Daily) Theater and dance performances (fee). At the Welk Resort (see RESORT). Phone 760/749-3448. **FREE**

Wineries.

Deer Park. Grape vineyard, winery, Napa Valley wine tasting rm (free) and deli; picnic areas. Also car museum with approx 90 antique convertibles and other vintage vehicles on display. (Daily; closed Thanksgiving, Dec 25) 8 mi N, at 29013 Champagne Blvd. Phone 760/749-1666. **¢¢¢**

Ferrara. Producers of wine and grape juice. Self-guided tours, wine tasting. (Daily; closed hols) 1120 W 15th Ave. Phone 760/745-7632. **FREE**

Orfila. Guided and self-guided tours, wine tasting rm; picnic area beneath grape arbor overlooks the vineyards and San Pasqual Valley. (Daily; closed hols) 13455 San Pasqual Rd. Phone 760/738-6500. **FREE**

Motels/Motor Lodges

★★ COMFORT INN. *1290 W Valley Pkwy (92029). 760/489-1010; fax 760/489-7847; toll-free 800/541-6012.* 93 rms, 3 story. S, D $89; under 18 free. Crib free. TV; cable. Pool; whirlpool. Complimentary continental bkfst. Restaurant adj 6 am-midnight. Ck-in 3 pm, ck-out noon. Meeting rms. In-rm modem link. Valet serv. Microwaves avail. Cr cds: A, D, DS, MC, V.

D SC

★★ SHERIDAN INN. *1341 N Escondido Blvd (92026). 760/743-8338; fax 760/743-0840. www.sheridan-inn.com.* 54 rms, 2 story, 32 suites. S, D, suites $69-$98; wkly rates. Crib free. TV; cable (premium). Heated pool; whirlpool. Complimentary continental bkfst. Restaurant opp 7 am-midnight. Ck-out noon. Health club privileges. Some refrigerators; microwaves avail. Cr cds: A, C, D, DS, MC, V.

D

Resorts

★★ **CASTLE CREEK INN RESORT AND SPA.** *29850 Circle R Way (92026). 760/751-8800; fax 760/751-8787; res 800/253-5341. www.castlecreekinn.com.* 30 rms, 2 story. S $119-$159; D $139-$159; 3-bedrm cottage $500; under 18 free. Crib free. Pet accepted, some restrictions. TV; cable. Pool. Complimentary continental bkfst. Restaurant 5-9 pm. Ck-out noon, ck-in 3 pm. Meeting rms. Tennis. Golf privileges. Exercise equipt; sauna. Cr cds: A, C, D, DS, MC, V.

D SC

★★★ **QUAIL'S INN HOTEL.** *1025 La Bonita Dr, San Marcos (92069). 760/744-0120; fax 760/744-0748; toll-free 800/447-6556. www.quailsinn.com.* 140 rms, 2 story. S, D $99; each addl $10; suites, kit. cottages $199-$300; under 12 free; package plans. Crib $10. Pet accepted, some restrictions; $10. TV; cable (premium), VCR avail. 2 heated pools; whirlpool. Restaurant adj 6:30 am-10 pm. Rm serv 7 am-8 pm. Ck-out noon. Meeting rms. Tennis privileges. Golf privileges. Exercise equipt. Boat rental. Some refrigerators; microwaves avail. Many private patios, balconies. On Lake San Marcos. Extensive grounds. Cr cds: A, C, D, DS, MC, V.

D

★★★ **WELK RESORT - SAN DIEGO.** *8860 Lawrence Welk Dr (92026). 760/749-3000; fax 760/749-9537; res 800/932-9355. www.welkresort.com.* 132 rms, 2-3 story. S, D $190; suites $160-$500; package plans. Pet accepted. TV; cable, VCR avail (movies). 2 heated pools; whirlpool. Supervised children's activities. Coffee in rms. Dining rm 7 am-9 pm. Bar 11 am-midnight. Ck-out noon. Meeting rms. In-rm modem link. Concierge. Shopping plaza. Beauty shop. 3 lighted tennis courts. 2 18-hole golf courses, putting green. Exercise equipt. Massage. Dinner theater. Semi-private patios, balconies. Some refrigerators. Cr cds: A, DS, MC, V.

D

B&B/Small Inn

★★★ **ZOSA GARDENS BED AND BREAKFAST.** *9381 W Lilac Rd (92026). 760/723-9093; fax 760/723-3460; res 800/711-8361. www.zosagardens.com.* 10 rms, 3 share bath, 1 guest house. No rm phones. S, D $100-$195; each addl $10; guest house $175-$250; hols 2-day min. Premium cable TV in some rms; VCR avail (movies). Complimentary full bkfst. Ck-out noon, ck-in 2 pm. Lighted tennis. Heated pool; whirlpool. Microwaves avail. Picnic tables, grills. Totally nonsmoking. Cr cds: A, C, D, DS, MC, V.

D SC

Restaurants

★★★ **150 GRAND CAFE.** *150 W Grand Ave (92029). 760/738-6868. www.150grandcafe.com.* Hrs: 11:30 am-3 pm, 5-9 pm; Fri to 9:30 pm; Sat 5-9:30 pm. Closed Sun, hols. Res accepted. Bar. Lunch $6-$12, dinner $14-$22. Specialties: open-faced seafood ravioli, roasted pork tenderloin. Guitarist Fri-Sat. Outdoor dining. Cr cds: A, D, MC, V.

D

★★ **SANDCRAB CAFE.** *2229 Micro Pl (92029). 760/480-2722.* Hrs: 11 am-9 pm; Fri, Sat to 10 pm. Closed Dec 25. Seafood menu. Bar. Lunch $2-$9.95, dinner $10.50-$18. Children's menu. Specializes in shellfish. Totally nonsmoking. Cr cds: MC, V.

D

★★ **SIRINO'S.** *113 W Grand Ave (92025). 760/745-3835.* Hrs: 11:30 am-2 pm, 4:30-9:30 pm; Sat from 4:30 pm; early bird dinner 4:30-5:30 pm. Tues-Sat; closed hols, last 2 wks Feb. Res required (dinner). Continental menu. Bar. Lunch $8-$18, dinner $14-$22. Specializes in lamb, duck. Outdoor dining. Cr cds: A, C, D, DS, MC, V.

D

Eureka

(C-1) *See also Trinidad*

Founded 1850 **Pop** 27,025 **Elev** 44 ft **Area code** 707 **Zip** 95501

Information Chamber of Commerce, 2112 Broadway; 707/442-3738 or 800/356-6381

Web www.eurekachamber.com

The largest fishing fleet north of San Francisco Bay makes the city of Eureka its main port. Lumbering is the city's major industry.

What to See and Do

Arcata Architectural Tour. Self-guided walking or driving tour to many Victorian structures, covering 35 city blocks. City of Arcata, 8 mi N on US 101.Obtain city map at Arcata Chamber of Commerce, 1635 Heindon Rd. Phone 707/822-3619.

Clarke Memorial Museum. Regional history, collection of Karuk, Hupa, Wiyot, and Yurok basketry and ceremonial regalia; firearms, Victorian furniture and decorative art. Guided tours by appt. (Tues-Sat afternoons; closed hols, also Jan) Third and E St. Phone 707/443-1947. **Donation**

Ferndale Architectural Tour. Ferndale's Victorian architecture is superior; the entire village has been declared a State Historic Landmark. 20 mi S. Call for a driving tour. Phone 707/786-4477. **FREE**

Ferndale Museum. Local history displays of "Cream City." (June-Sept, Tues-Sun; rest of yr, Wed-Sun; closed hols, Jan) 12 mi S on US 101, then 5 mi W in Ferndale, at 3rd and Shaw Sts. Phone 707/786-4466. **Donation**

Fort Humboldt State Historic Park. Ulysses S. Grant was stationed at Fort Humboldt in 1854. Logging and military exhibits. Tours. Picnicking. (Daily; closed Jan 1, Thanksgiving, Dec 25) 3431 Fort Ave. Phone 707/445-6567. **FREE**

Fortuna Depot Museum. Train memorabilia, barbed wire collection, fishing and logging displays. In 1893 train depot. (June-Aug, daily; rest of yr, Thurs-Sun afternoons; closed Dec 25) 18 mi S on US 101 in Fortuna, Rohner Park. Phone 707/725-7645. **FREE**

Humboldt Bay Harbor Cruise. 1¼-hr trips. (May-Sept, three departures daily: two afternoon, one evening) Special charter rest of yr. Foot of C St. Phone 707/445-1910. **¢¢¢**

Humboldt Bay Maritime Museum. Pacific and northcoast maritime heritage displays; marine artifacts. (Daily; closed hols) 1410 Second St. Phone 707/444-9440. **Donation**

Old Town. Designated a National Historic District, this section of town has original buildings of early Eureka. Also here is a gazebo, cascading water fountain, sculptured benches, commercial and residential Victorian buildings; antique and specialty shops; horse and buggy rides (fee); restaurants. All situated on waterfront of Humboldt Bay. Cruises of the bay are avail. 1st, 2nd, and 3rd Sts, C to G Sts.

Romano Gabriel Wooden Sculpture Garden. A colorful collection of folk art, constructed of wood in the mid-1900s. (Daily) 315 2nd St, in Old Town section. **FREE**

Sequoia Park Zoo. Area surrounded by 46 acres of redwoods; duck pond, gardens, picnic facilities, snack bar, children's playground. (Tues-Sun) Glatt and W Sts. Phone 707/442-6552. **FREE**

Six Rivers National Forest. On 1,111,726 acres. The Klamath, Eel, Trinity, Van Duzen, and Mad rivers provide excellent fishing. Hunting, camping, picnicking. Resorts and lodges located in and near forest. Standard fees. Reached via US 101, 199, CA 36, 96, 299. Contact Forest Supervisor's Office, 1330 Bay Shore Way. Phone 707/442-1721. Located within the forest is

Smith River National Recreation Area. (305,337 acres) This is the heart of one of the largest wild and scenic river systems (315 mi) in the US. Offers whitewater rafting, wilderness hiking, bird-watching, nature study, world-class steelhead fishing, hunting, and camping. For information contact Gasquet Ranger Station, Box 228, Gasquet 95543-0228. Phone 707/457-3131.

Woodley Island Marina. Mooring for commercial fishing boats and recreational craft; cafe and shops; site of *The Fisherman* memorial statue and Table Bluff Lighthouse. 1 mi W via US 101, Samoa Bridge exit (CA 255).

EUREKA'S VICTORIAN ARCHITECTURE

The old-time lumber town of Eureka, situated along the coast in redwood country 270 miles north of San Francisco, displays its heritage in striking renovated Victorian homes and commercial buildings near the waterfront. Eureka has more Victorians per capita—over 10,000—than any other California city. This walking tour can take anywhere from one hour to several depending on your pace. Along the way, you'll encounter a number of gaudily decorated gingerbread Victorians, including a lumber baron's mansion reputed to be the most photographed Victorian house in the world. To get an overview of the area's cultural history, start your walk in Old Town Eureka at the compact but excellent Clarke Memorial Museum (240 E Street); the lumberjacks, seafarers, pioneers, and Native Americans from Eureka's past are all represented here. Now walk two blocks west to C Street and turn south. Over the next 14 or so blocks you'll encounter some of Eureka's finest examples of Victorian architecture, including the Moorish arches at 1228 C Street, the columns at 1461 C Street, and the Eastlake-style ornamentation and gardens at 1406 C Street, now a bed-and-breakfast inn. After viewing the Victorians along the 1600 block of C Street, backtrack a few blocks to Hillsdale Street; turn right (east) and note the Eastlake, Queen Anne, and Carpenter Gothic styles at 216, 220, 233, 258, 261, and 303 Hillsdale. Turn left (north) on E Street, walk to 9th Street, and turn right two blocks to G Street. The Queen Anne at 904 G Street and the Italianate Victorian at 828 G Street are worth special attention. Continue north to 3rd Street and head right (east) on 3rd until you reach M Street. The famous Carson Mansion, at 143 M Street, is an incredibly ostentatious three-story, green Victorian that dates back to 1884. Lumber baron William Carson employed 100 men for two years to build it. The mansion is built of redwood and combines elements of Queen Anne, Eastlake, and Italianate styles; few visitors can resist photographing it. Though not open to the public, it's perfectly acceptable to gawk out front. Across the street, at 202 M Street, is a combination Queen Anne-Eastlake Victorian known as the "Pink Lady," which Carson built for his son as a wedding present in 1889. To conclude the tour, walk back west down 2nd Street to take advantage of Old Town's shops, restaurants, and galleries.

Special Events

Jazz Festival. Various locations in town. Last wkend Mar. Phone 707/445-3378.

Rhododendron Festival. Varied events throughout Humboldt County incl parades, races, art exhibits, contests, entertainment. Usually last wkend Apr. Phone 707/443-6580.

Cross-Country Kinetic Sculpture Race. A three-day, 35-mi x-coutnry race over land, water, beaches, and highways. Participants race on their self-powered, artistically sculptured vehicles. Memorial Day wkend. Phone 707/786-4477.

Motels/Motor Lodges

★★ BEST WESTERN HUMBOLDT BAY INN. *232 W 5th St (95501). 707/443-2234; fax 707/443-3489; res 800/528-1234. www.humboldtbayinn.com.* 115 rms, some A/C, 2 story. Mid-May-mid-Oct: S,D $79-$95; each addl $5; suites $90-$150; lower rates rest of yr. Crib free. TV; cable (premium), VCR avail (free movies). Heated pool; whirlpool. Coffee in rms. Restaurant 6 am-10 pm. Ck-out noon. Coin lndry. Meeting rms. Business servs avail. In-rm modem link. Sundries. Free bus depot transportation. Game rm. Some refrigerators. Cr cds: A, C, D, DS, ER, JCB, MC, V.
D SC

★ EUREKA TRAVELODGE. *4 Fourth St (95501). 707/443-6345; fax 707/443-1486; res 800/578-7878. www.travelodge.com.* 46 rms, 2 story. No A/C. S $37-$55; D $38-$73; each addl $5; under 12 free. Crib free. Pet accepted. TV; cable (premium). Heated pool. Coffee in rms. Restaurant nearby. Ck-out 11 am. Business servs avail. Sundries. Cr cds: A, D, DS, MC, V.

★★ QUALITY INN. *1209 Fourth St (95501). 707/443-1601; fax 707/444-*

8365; res 800/228-5151. 60 rms, 2 story. No A/C. June-mid-Oct: S, D $75-$150; each addl $10; suites $100-$200; lower rates rest of yr. Crib $5. Pet accepted. TV; cable (premium). Heated pool; wading pool, whirlpool. Complimentary continental bkfst, coffee in rms. Restaurant opp 7 am-11 pm. Ck-out noon. Meeting rms. Business servs avail. Sauna. Cr cds: A, D, DS, MC, V.

★★ **RED LION HOTEL.** *1929 Fourth St (95501). 707/445-0844; fax 707/445-2752; res 800/733-5466. www.redlion.com.* 178 rms, 3-4 story. S $79-$89; D $89-$99; suites $125-$175; under 18 free; wkend rates. Crib free. Pet accepted. TV; cable (premium), VCR avail. Heated pool; whirlpool. Coffee in rms. Restaurant 6 am-10 pm. Bar; entertainment wkends. Ck-out noon. Meeting rms. Business servs avail. In-rm modem link. Bellhops. Valet serv. Sundries. Free airport transportation. Balconies. Cr cds: A, C, D, DS, ER, JCB, MC, V.

Hotel

★★ **EUREKA INN.** *518 7th St (95501). 707/442-6441; fax 707/442-0637; toll-free 800/862-4906. www.eurekainn.com.* 104 rms, 4 story. No A/C. S, D $104-$129; suites $149-$289; each addl $10; under 16 free. Crib free. Pet accepted. TV; cable. Heated pool; whirlpool. Saunas. Restaurant 6:30 am-10 pm. Bar 11-2 am; entertainment Thurs-Sat. Ck-out noon. Meeting rms. Business servs avail. Free airport, bus depot transportation. Some bathrm phones. Fireplace in lobby. Historic Tudor-style building (1922). Cr cds: A, C, D, DS, MC, V.

B&Bs/Small Inns

★★★ **ABIGAIL'S ELEGANT VICTORIAN MANSION.** *1406 C St (95501). 707/444-3144; fax 707/442-5594. www.eureka-california.com.* 4 rms, 3 share bath, 2 story, 1 suite. No A/C. Rm phones avail. June-Sept: S $85-$125; D $95-$145; each addl $35-$50; suite $135-$185; MAP avail; lower rates rest of yr. Premium cable TV in common rm; VCR avail (movies). Complimentary full bkfst. Restaurant nearby. Ck-out 11 am, ck-in 3-6 pm. Business servs avail. Luggage handling. Valet serv. Coincierge serv. Guest lndry. Free RR station, bus depot transportation. Bicycles. Sauna. Massage. Game rm. Lawn games. Picnic tables. Built in 1886; Victorian decor, antiques. Totally nonsmoking. Cr cds: MC, V.

★★★ **CARTER INN AND CARTER HOUSE BED AND BREAKFAST.** *1033 3rd St (95501). 707/444-8062; fax 707/444-8067; toll-free 800/404-1390. www.carterhouse.com.* 5 rms, 4 story. S, D $125-$145; suites $165-$275. TV; cable, VCR (free movies). Children over 10 yrs only. Complimentary full bkfst; afternoon refreshments. Ck-out 11 am, ck-in 3-6 pm. Business servs avail. In-rm modem link. Valet serv. Game rm. Golf privileges. Health club privileges. Massage. Suite with whirlpool, fireplace. Re-created 1884 San Francisco Victorian house. Antiques, Oriental rugs; marble fireplaces. Totally nonsmoking. Cr cds: A, C, D, DS, JCB, MC, V.

★★★ **DALY INN.** *1125 H St (95501). 707/445-3638; fax 707/444-3636; toll-free 800/321-9656. www.dalyinn.com.* 5 rms, 2 share bath, 2 story, 2 suites. No A/C. No rm phones. May-Oct: S $70-$75; D $80-$85; each addl $20; suites $140-$150; hols (2-3-day min); lower rates rest of yr. TV in den; cable (premium), VCR (movies). Complimentary full bkfst; afternoon refreshments. Ck-out 11 am, ck-in 4-7 pm. Guest lndry. Business servs avail. Lawn games. Picnic tables. Built in 1905. Surrounded by gardens. Totally nonsmoking. Cr cds: A, DS, MC, V.

★★★ **GINGERBREAD MANSION.** *400 Berding St, Ferndale (95536). 707/786-9667; fax 707/786-4381; toll-free 800/952-4136. www.gingerbread-mansion.com.* 11 rms, 3 story. Some with rm phones. S $90-$120; D $120-$140; each addl $40; suites $160-$350. TV in some rms. Complimentary full bkfst; afternoon refreshments. Ck-out 11 am, ck-in 2-7 pm. Business servs avail. Restored Victorian mansion (ca 1899); English gardens; in

Victorian Village; community setting. Elaborate bathrms; many fireplaces; formal dining rm. Totally nonsmoking. Cr cds: A, MC, V.

★★ **OLD TOWN BED AND BREAKFAST INN.** *1521 3rd St (95501). 707/443-5235; fax 707/443-5235; toll-free 888/508-5235. www.geocities.com/oldtownbandb.* 6 rms, 2 story. No A/C. S $70-$130; D $80-$140; each addl $15. Complimentary full bkfst. Ck-out 11 am, ck-in 4-7 pm. Business servs avail. Whirlpool. Some fireplaces. Built 1871, oldest lodging in town; Greek Revival Victorian home with antique furnishings. Garden. Bay 1½ blks. Totally nonsmoking. Cr cds: C, D, DS, MC, V.

SC

Restaurants

★★★ **RESTAURANT 301.** *301 L St (95501). 707/444-8062. www.carterhouse.com.* Hrs: 6-9 pm. Res accepted. Wine, beer. Dinner $9.95-$24. Prix fixe $39-$49, 8-course dinner $55. Children's menu. Wine cellar. Specialties: Humboldt Bay oysters, rack of lamb, Pacific salmon. Own desserts. Own garden vegetables. Original art; view of bay. Totally nonsmoking. Cr cds: A, C, D, DS, MC, V.

D

★★ **SEA GRILL.** *316 E St (95501). 707/443-7187. www.theseagrill.com.* Hrs: 11 am-2 pm, 5-9:30 pm; Mon, Sat from 5 pm. Mon-Sat; closed hols, also 2 wks early Nov. Res accepted. Bar. Lunch $4.95-$10.95, dinner $12.95-$20.95. Children's menu. Specializes in fresh local seafood, steaks, prime rib. Salad bar. Restored Victorian building (ca 1870). Antique bar. Totally nonsmoking. Cr cds: D, DS, MC, V.

D SC

Fairfield

(F-3) *See also Vacaville, Vallejo*

Pop 77,211 **Elev** 15 ft **Area code** 707 **Zip** 94533

This is the home of Travis Air Force Base and the seat of Solano County.

What to See and Do

Western Railway Museum. Take a two-mi ride on electric streetcars and interurbans, with occasional steam and diesel operation. Museum collection incl 100 vintage RR cars and trains operating on demonstration RR; bookstore, gift shop; picnic area. (Early July-Labor Day, Wed-Sun; Sept-June, Sat, Sun, hols; closed Jan 1, Thanksgiving, Dec 25) Museum admission incl unlimited rides. 12 mi E on CA 12. Phone 707/374-2978. ¢¢¢

Motels/Motor Lodges

★★ **BEST WESTERN CORDELIA INN.** *4373 Central Pl (94585). 707/864-2029; fax 707/864-5834; toll-free 800/422-7575. www.bestwestern.com.* 60 rms, 2 story. S $68-$80; D $72-$84; each addl $6; under 18 free. Crib free. TV; cable. Pool; whirlpool. Complimentary continental bkfst, coffee in rms. Restaurant nearby. Ck-in 3 pm, ck-out noon. Coin lndry. Business servs avail. In-rm modem link. Valet serv. Refrigerators, microwaves avail. Cr cds: A, C, D, DS, MC, V.

D SC

★★ **HAMPTON INN.** *4441 Central Pl, Suisun City (94585). 707/864-1446; fax 707/864-4288; res 800/426-7866. www.hampton-inn.com/hi/fairfield-napa.* 57 rms, 3 story. S $74-$79; D $84-$89; suites $145; lower rates winter. Crib free. TV; cable (premium), VCR avail (movies). Heated pool. Complimentary continental bkfst. Ck-out noon. Coin lndry. Meeting rms. Business servs avail. In-rm modem link. Exercise equipt. Microwaves avail. Cr cds: A, C, D, DS, MC, V.

D SC

★★ **HOLIDAY INN SELECT.** *1350 Holiday Ln (94533). 707/422-4111; fax 707/428-3452.* 142 rms, 4 story. S, D $89-$139; each addl $10; suites $225; under 12 free; higher rates some special events. Crib free. TV; cable (premium). Pool; wading pool. Coffee in rms. Restaurant 6:30 am-2 pm, 5-10 pm. Bar 4 pm-midnight. Ck-out noon. Meeting rms. Business servs avail. In-rm modem link. Coin lndry. Bellhops. Valet serv. Exercise equipt. Health club privileges. Microwaves avail. Some patios, balconies. Cr cds: A, D, DS, ER, JCB, MC, V.

D

Restaurants

★★ FUSILLI RISTORANTE. *620 Jackson St (94533). 707/428-4211.* Hrs: 11:30 am-2:30 pm, 5-9 pm; Sat 5-9:30 pm. Closed Sun; Easter, Thanksgiving, Dec 25. Res accepted. Italian menu. Wine, beer. A la carte entrees: lunch, dinner $8.25-$18. Specializes in woodburning oven pizza. Own bread, pasta. Modern decor. Totally nonsmoking. Cr cds: A, MC, V.

D

★ OLD SAN FRANCISCO EXPRESS. *4560 Central Way (94585). 707/864-6453.* Hrs: 4 pm-9 pm; Fri, Sat to 10:30 pm. Closed Mon. Res accepted. Bar. Complete meals: dinner $5.95-$15.95. Children's menu. Specializes in pastas, seafood, beef. Comprised of 11 RR cars connected together to form 2 large dining areas; some cars form private dining rms. Cr cds: A, MC, V.

D

Fallbrook

(F-6) *See also Temecula*

Settled 1880s **Pop** 22,095 **Elev** 685 ft **Area code** 760 **Zip** 92028

Motels/Motor Lodges

★★ BEST WESTERN FRANCISCAN INN. *1635 S Mission Rd (92028). 760/728-6174; fax 760/731-6404; toll-free 800/528-1234.* 50 rms, 1-2 story, 27 kits. S, D $60-$75; each addl $5; kit. units $65-$80; under 12 free. Crib $5. TV; cable. Heated pool; whirlpool. Complimentary continental bkfst. Coffee in rms. Ck-out 11 am. Meeting rm. Microwaves avail. Cr cds: A, C, D, DS, MC, V.

SC

★ FALLBROOK LODGE. *1608 S Mission Rd (92028). 760/723-1127; fax 760/723-2917.* 36 units, 2 story, 8 kits. S, D $55-$70; each addl $5; kits. $60-$90; under 17 free; wkly rates. TV; cable. Complimentary continental bkfst. Restaurant opp 7:30 am-9 pm. Ck-out 11 am. Some balconies. Cr cds: A, DS, MC, V.

D SC

Resort

★★★ PALA MESA RESORT. *2001 Old Hwy 395 (92028). 760/728-5881; fax 760/723-8292; toll-free 800/722-4700. www.palamesa.com.* 133 rms, 1-2 story. S, D $150; suites $250-$350; under 18 free; package plans. Crib free. TV; cable, VCR avail. Heated pool; whirlpool. Coffee in rms. Dining rm 6 am-10 pm. Rm serv to 11 pm. Bar 11-2 am; entertainment Fri-Sun. Ck-out noon, ck-in 4 pm. Meeting rms. Business servs avail. In-rm modem link. Lighted tennis. 18-hole golf, pro, putting green, driving range. Exercise equipt. Massage. Refrigerators. Cr cds: A, C, D, DS, MC, V.

D

Restaurant

★★ CASK 'N CLEAVER. *3757 S Mission Rd (92028). 760/728-2818. www.caskncleaver.com.* Hrs: 5-9 pm; Fri, Sat to 10 pm; Sun from 4:30 pm. Closed hols. Res accepted. Bar. Dinner $10-$19. Children's menu. Specialties: deep-fried avocado, mesquite pepper steak, prime rib. Music Sat. Parking. Outdoor dining. Totally nonsmoking. Cr cds: A, DS, MC, V.

D

Felton

(see Santa Cruz)

Fort Bragg

(D-2) *See also Mendocino, Ukiah, Willits*

Founded 1884 **Pop** 6,078 **Elev** 75 ft **Area code** 707 **Zip** 95437

Information Fort Bragg-Mendocino Coast Chamber of Commerce, 332 N

Main St, PO Box 1141; 707/961-6300 or 800/726-2780

Web www.mendocinocoast.com

The town is a lumber, agricultural, recreational, and fishing center that stands on the edge of the rocky coastline where the military post of Fort Bragg was set up in 1857. When the fort was abandoned in 1867, the land was opened for purchase, and a lumber town sprang up. It was rebuilt after the earthquake of 1906. Driftwood and shell hunting are popular on nearby beaches.

What to See and Do

Forest Tree Nursery. Greenhouse with two million redwood and Douglas fir seedlings for reforestation on local timberland. Nature trail. Picnic tables. Visitor center (Mon-Fri; closed hols). Georgia-Pacific Corp, foot of Walnut St on CA 1. Phone 707/961-3209. **FREE**

Jughandle Ecological Staircase. Nature trail climbs from sea level to pygmy forest; 500,000 yrs of geological history. 5 mi S. Phone 707/937-5804.

MacKerricher State Park. Approx 10 mi of beach and ocean access. Fishing (nonmotorized boat launching). Nature, hiking trails. Picnicking. Camping (dump station; fee). 3 mi N on CA 1. Phone 707/937-5804. ¢¢¢¢

Mendocino Coast Botanical Gardens. Approx 47 acres of rhododendrons, heathers, perennials, fuchsias, coastal pine forest, and ocean bluffs. Cafe; gift shop, nursery; picnic areas; self-guided tours. (Daily) 2 mi S on CA 1. Phone 707/964-4352. ¢¢¢

Noyo. Fishing village with picturesque harbor; public boat launching; charter boats avail. ½ mi S on CA 1 at mouth of Noyo River. Phone 707/964-4719.

The "Skunk Train." Originally a logging RR, the California Western Railroad train, affectionately known as "the Skunk," runs 40 mi through redwoods along the Noyo River and over the Coastal Range to Willits (see). Full-day round trips avail aboard either diesel-powered motor cars or a diesel-pulled train (all yr). Half-day round trips avail from Fort Bragg (Mar-Nov, daily; rest of yr, wkends). Half-day and full-day trips avail from Willits (second Sat June-second Sat Sept; inquire for schedule). Foot of Laurel St. Contact California Western Railroad, Box 907. Phone 707/964-6371.

Special Events

Whale Festival. Whale-watching cruises and walks; whale run; beerfest; chowder tasting. Mar. Phone 707/961-6300.

Rhododendron Show. More varieties of rhododendrons are grown here than anywhere else in the world. Apr. Phone 707/964-3282.

Salmon Barbecue. S Noyo Harbor. Sat nearest July 4. Phone 707/964-2781.

The "Skunk Train"

Paul Bunyan Days. Logging competition, gem and mineral show; parade (Mon); fuchsia show, arts and crafts. Labor Day wkend. Phone 707/961-6300.

Winesong. More than 20 vintners pour for wine tasting, food tasting, music, wine auction. Sat after Labor Day. Phone 707/961-4688.

Whale Watch. Nov-Mar. Phone 888/942-8284.

Motels/Motor Lodges

★★ **HARBOR LITE LODGE.** *120 N Harbor Dr, Fort Bragg (95437). 707/964-0221; fax 707/964-8748; toll-free 800/643-2700. www.harborlitelodge.com.* 79 rms, 2-3 story, 9 suites. No A/C. May-Oct, hols, wkends: S, D $64-$125; each addl $6; suites $92-$110; lower rates rest of yr. Crib $6. TV; cable (premium). Complimentary coffee. Restaurant nearby. Ck-out noon. Meeting rms. Sauna. Refrigerator in suites. Balconies. Footpath to beach. Most rms with harbor view. Cr cds: A, C, D, DS, MC, V.

D

★★ **PINE BEACH INN & SUITES.** *16801 N CA 1 (94537). 707/964-5603; fax 707/964-8381. www.pinebeachinn.com.* 50 rms, 1-2 story. No A/C. Apr-Oct: S, D $65-$170; lower rates rest of yr. Crib free. TV; cable. Restaurant 7-10:30 am, 5:30-9 pm; closed Nov-Feb. Bar from 5 pm. Ck-out noon. Meeting rms. Tennis. Private beach. Private patios, balconies. Some rms with ocean view. Cr cds: A, D, MC, V.

★★ **SURF MOTEL.** *1220 S Main St (95437). 707/964-5361; fax 707/964-3187; toll-free 800/339-5361. www.surfmotelfortbragg.com.* 54 rms, 2 kit. units. No A/C. Late May-mid-Oct: S $42-$62; D $60-$75; each addl $6; kit. units from $90; lower rates rest of yr. Crib $6. TV; cable. Coffee in rms. Restaurant nearby. Ck-out 11 am. Business servs avail. Picnic tables, grill. Gardens. Cr cds: A, C, D, DS, JCB, MC, V.

★ **TRADEWINDS LODGE.** *400 S Main St (95821). 707/964-4761; fax 707/964-0372. www.fortbragg.org.* 92 rms, 2 story. No A/C. Memorial Day-Sept: S $59-$79; D $69-$89; each addl $8; suites $120; under 12 free; lower rates rest of yr. Crib $8. TV; cable (premium). Indoor pool; whirlpool. Restaurant 4 am-midnight. Bar from noon. Ck-out 11 am. Coin lndry. Meeting rms. Business servs avail. In-rm modem link. Gift shop. Free RR station transportation. Some refrigerators. Bicycle rentals. Cr cds: A, D, DS, MC, V.

D

B&Bs/Small Inns

★★ **CLEONE GARDENS INN.** *24600 N CA 1 (95437). 707/964-2788; fax 707/964-2523; toll-free 800/400-2189. www.cleonegardensinn.com.* 10 rms, 1-2 story, 4 kits, 1 cottage. No A/C. Some rm phones. S, D $76-$140; each addl $10; kit cottage $108. TV; cable. Pet accepted, some restrictions; $4. Ck-out 11 am, ck-in 1:30 pm. Business servs avail. Whirlpool. Health club privileges. Walking trails. Some refrigerators, fireplaces. Antiques. Private patios, balconies. Picnic tables, grills. On 9½ acres; gazebo. Near beach. Cr cds: A, MC, V.

★★★ **GREY WHALE INN BED AND BREAKFAST.** *615 N Main St (95437). 707/964-0640; fax 707/964-4408; toll-free 800/382-7244. www.greywhaleinn.com.* 14 rms, 4 story. No A/C. S $80-$120; D $96-$120; each addl $25; hols, wkends (2-3-day min). TV; VCR avail. Complimentary bkfst buffet. Restaurant nearby. Ck-out noon, ck-in 1-8 pm. Meeting rm. Business servs avail. Game rm. Rec rm. Some fireplaces. Some private patios, balconies. Library. Antiques. Some rms with ocean view. Mendocino coast landmark since 1915. Totally nonsmoking. Cr cds: A, DS, MC, V.

D

★★★ **LODGE AT NOYO RIVER.** *500 Casa Del Norte (95437). 707/964-8045; fax 707/964-9366; toll-free 800/628-1126. www.noyolodge.com.* 16 rms, 1-2 story, 8 suites. No A/C. No rm phones. S $85-$115; D $99-$115; suites $149-$179. TV in suites; cable. Complimentary full bkfst. Ck-out 11 am, ck-in 3 pm. Balconies. Picnic tables. Sitting rm; antiques. Built 1868; located on 2½ acres overlooking Noyo River, Noyo Harbor Fishing Village. Totally nonsmoking. Cr cds: A, MC, V.

D

Restaurants

★★★ **RENDEZVOUS.** *647 N Main St (95437). 707/964-8142. www.rendezvousinn.com.* Hrs: 5:30-8:30 pm; Fri, Sat to 9 pm. Wed-Sun; closed Dec 25. Res accepted. Country French menu. Wine cellar. Dinner $12.75-$19.75. Specialties: pepper steak Rendezvous, wild game. Music Sat. Parking. In restored 1908 redwood home; fireplace. Totally nonsmoking. Cr cds: DS, MC, V.

★★★ **RESTAURANT.** *418 N Main St (95437). 707/964-9800.* Hrs: 5-9 pm; Thur, Fri 11:30 am-2 pm, 5-9 pm; Sun brunch 10 am-1 pm. Closed Wed; Dec 25. Res accepted. No A/C. Continental menu. Beer. Wine list. Lunch $6.50-$8.50, dinner $9.75-$18.50. Sun brunch $4.50-$6.75. Children's menu. Specializes in seasonal dishes. Own baking. Jazz Fri, Sat evenings and Sun brunch. Totally nonsmoking. Cr cds: MC, V.

D

★★ **THE WHARF.** *32260 N Harbor Dr (95437). 707/964-4283. www.mcn.org/a/wharf.* Hrs: 11 am-10 pm. Res accepted. Bar to 2 am. Lunch $3.25-$8.95, dinner $9.25-$19.95. Children's menu. Specializes in fresh seafood, steak. Outdoor dining. View of harbor, fishing boats. Totally nonsmoking. Cr cds: DS, MC, V.

Fort Ross State Historic Park

(F-2) *See also Bodega Bay, Guerneville, Healdsburg*

(12 mi N of Jenner on CA 1)

This was once an outpost of the Russian empire. For nearly three decades the post and fort set up by the Russian-American Company of Alaska was an important center for the Russian sea otter trade. The entire "Colony Ross of California" was purchased by Captain John A. Sutter in 1841.

Here are reconstructions of the Russian Orthodox chapel (ca 1825), the original seven-sided and eight-sided blockhouses, the Commandant's house, officers' barracks, and stockade walls. Interpretive exhibits at Fort and visitor center. (Daily; closed Jan 1, Thanksgiving, Dec 25) Phone 707/865-2391 or 707/847-3286. Per vehicle ¢¢¢

What to See and Do

Salt Point State Park. Located here are Pygmy forest, Gerstle Cove marine reserve. Hiking, riding trails. Picnicking. Camping. Standard fees. 18 mi N of Jenner. Nearby is

Kruse Rhododendron State Reserve. Here are 317 acres of coastal vegetation. Trails. Rhododendrons bloom Apr-May. 2 mi N of park entrance. Phone 707/847-3286.

Sonoma Coast State Beach. On 4,200 acres along coastline. Sandy beaches, rocky headlands, sand dunes. Diving, fishing, hiking, picnicking, camping. (Daily) 12 mi S, between Jenner and Bodega Bay. ¢¢¢¢¢

Motels/Motor Lodges

★ **SALT POINT LODGE.** *23255 Hwy 1, Jenner (95450). 707/847-3234; fax 707/847-3354; toll-free 800/956-2427. www.saltpoint.com.* 16 rms. No A/C. S, D $60-$147; each addl $10. Crib free. TV; cable (premium), VCR avail. Restaurant 9 am-9 pm, wkends 9 am-10 pm; Dec-Apr hrs vary. Bar. Ck-out 11 am. Whirlpool. Sauna. Sun deck. Some fireplaces. Balconies. Ocean view. Cr cds: A, DS, MC, V.

★★ **TIMBER COVE INN.** *21780 N Hwy 1, Jenner (95450). 707/847-3231; fax 707/847-3704; res 800/987-8319. www.timbercoveinn.com.* 51 rms, 26 with shower only, 2 story. No A/C. No rm phones. S, D $110-$390; wkends, hols (2-day min). Restaurant 7:30 am-3 pm, 4:30-9:30 pm; Fri-Sun to 10 pm. Ck-out 11 am. Gift shop. Many fireplaces; some in-rm whirlpools. Many balconies. Picnic tables. On ocean. Cr cds: A, MC, V.

SC

Fremont

(G-3) *See also Livermore, Oakland, San Jose, Santa Clara*

Pop 173,339 **Elev** 53 ft **Area code** 510

Information Chamber of Commerce, 39488 Stevenson Pl #100, 94538; 510/795-2244

Web www.fremontbusiness.com

At the southeast end of San Francisco Bay, this young town was created in 1956 from five Alameda County communities whose origins goes back to the days of the Ohlone.

What to See and Do

Mission San Jose. (1797) The reconstructed adobe church was originally built in 1809 and destroyed by an earthquake in 1868. A portion of the padres' living quarters that survived holds a museum. Original baptismal font, historic vestments, and mission-era artifacts. (Daily; closed hols) 43300 Mission Blvd. Phone 510/657-1797. **Donation**

Regional parks. Contact East Bay Regional Park District, 2950 Peralta Oaks Court, PO Box 5381, Oakland 94605-0381. Phone 510/562-PARK.

Ardenwood Regional Preserve and Historic Farm. A 208-acre 1890s working farm. Patterson House (tours). Horse-drawn wagon, haywagon rides, farming demonstrations, and rail car tour. Picnic area. (Tues-Sun) I-880, CA 84 Decoto exit, right on Ardenwood Blvd to park entrance. Phone 510/796-0663. **¢¢**

Coyote Hills. Wetlands preserved on 966 acres. Hiking, bicycle trails, picnicking. Guided tours of 2,000-yr-old Native American shell mounds (Sun); freshwater marsh; nature programs; access to Alameda Creek Trail, San Francisco Bay National Wildlife Refuge. (Daily) 8000 Patterson Ranch Rd. Phone 510/795-9385. **¢¢**

Sunol Regional Wilderness. Hiking trails, picnicking, camping (fee). Nature center and program; backpack area by reservation. Rugged terrain incl Maguire Peaks (1,688 ft), Flag Hill (1,360 ft). Connects with Ohlone Wilderness Trail (permit required). NE on I-680 to Calaveras Rd, then S to Geary Rd. Phone 501/636-1684. **¢¢**

San Francisco Bay National Wildlife Refuge. Offers 25 mi of shoreline, boardwalks, and hiking trails. This was the nation's first urban wildlife refuge and is still its most popular. Houses more than a million birds during spring and fall migrations, also home to harbor seals. Exhibits and family programs. (Daily) Visitor center at 1 Marshlands Rd. Phone 510/792-0222. **FREE**

Special Event

Fremont Festival of the Arts. 4th wkend July.

Motels/Motor Lodges

★★ BEST WESTERN GARDEN COURT INN. *5400 Mowry Ave (94538). 510/792-4300; fax 510/792-2643; res 800/528-1234. www.bestwestern.com.* 122 rms, 2-3 story. S, D $139; under 14 free; wkend rates. Crib $10. Pet accepted, some restrictions; $50 ($25 refundable). TV; cable (premium). Pool; whirlpool. Complimentary continental bkfst. Restaurant 11:30 am-10 pm. Bar. Ck-out noon. Meeting rms. Business servs avail. Valet serv. Sauna. Health club privileges. Some private patios, balconies. Cr cds: A, C, D, DS, ER, JCB, MC, V.

D SC

★★ COURTYARD BY MARRIOTT. *47000 Lakeview Blvd (94538). 510/656-1800; fax 510/656-2441. www.marriott.com.* 146 rms, 3 story. S, D $179; suites $199; under 12 free. Crib avail. TV; cable (premium). Indoor pool. Complimentary coffee in rms. Restaurant 6:30 am-2 pm, 5-10 pm, Fri from 5 pm, Sat to noon. Bar 4-11 pm. Ck-out 1 pm. Coin lndry. Meeting rms. Business servs avail. Sundries. Exercise equipt. Some refrigerators. Some balconies. Cr cds: A, C, D, DS, ER, JCB, MC, V.

D

Hotels

★★★ FREMONT MARRIOTT. *46100 Landing Pkwy (94538). 510/413-3700. www.marriott.com.* 357 rms, 10 story. S, D $145-$330; each addl $15; under 17 free. Crib avail. Pet accepted. Valet parking. Indoor pool. TV; cable (premium), VCR avail. Complimentary coffee in rms, newspaper. Restaurant 6 am-10:30 pm. Bar. Ck-out 11 am. Meeting rms. Business center. Valet serv. Gift shop. Exercise rm. Golf. Some refrigerators, minibars. Cr cds: A, C, D, DS, MC, V.

★★★ HILTON HOTEL. *39900 Balentine Dr, Newark (94560). 510/490-8390; fax 510/651-7828; toll-free 800/445-8667. www.hilton.com.* 315 rms, 7 story. S $99-$189; D $109-$199; each addl $15; suites $199-$375; family rates; wkend rates. Crib free. Pet accepted. TV; cable (premium). Heated pool; poolside serv. Restaurant 6 am-10 pm. Bar 11-2 am; entertainment. Ck-out noon. Meeting rms. Business center. Gift shop. Exercise equipt; sauna. Massage. Some refrigerators. Some private patios, balconies. Cr cds: A, D, DS, MC, V.

B&B/Small Inn

★★ LORD BRADLEY'S INN. *43344 Mission Blvd (94539). 510/490-0520; fax 510/490-3015; toll-free 877/567-3272. www.lordbradleysinn.com.* 8 rms, 2 story. Some A/C. Some rm phones. S, D $99-$155. Children over 11 yrs only. Complimentary continental bkfst. Restaurant nearby. Ck-out noon, ck-in 3 pm. Free guest lndry. Built in 1868 as Solon Washington Hotel; survived earthquakes and fires that destroyed much of Mission San Jose; antique furnishings. Cr cds: A, DS, MC, V.

D

All Suite

★★★ W SUITES NEWARK. *8200 Gateway Blvd, Newark (94560). 510/494-8800. www.whotels.com.* 174 suites, 10 story. S, D $199-$550; each addl $25. Crib avail. Pet accepted. Valet parking. Indoor pool. TV; cable (premium), VCR avail. Complimentary coffee in rms, newspaper. Restaurant 6 am-midnight. Bar. Ck-out noon. Meeting rms. Business center. Valet serv. Exercise rm. Spa. Refrigerators, minibars. Cr cds: A, C, D, DS, MC, V.

D

Extended Stay

★★ RESIDENCE INN BY MARRIOTT. *5400 Farwell Pl (94536). 510/794-5900; fax 510/793-6587; toll-free 800/331-3131.* 80 kit. suites, 2 story. Kit. suites $209-$249; wkly, monthly rates. Crib free. Pet accepted, some restrictions; $75 and $10/day. TV; cable (premium). Heated pool; whirlpool. Complimentary continental bkfst. Restaurant adj 6 am-midnight. Ck-out noon. Coin lndry. Meeting rms. Business servs avail. Valet serv. Health club privileges. Private patios, balconies. Picnic tables, grills. Cr cds: A, C, D, DS, JCB, MC, V.

D SC

Fresno (B-3)

Founded 1874 **Pop** 354,202 **Elev** 296 ft **Area code** 559

Information Convention & Visitors Bureau, 848 M St, 93721; 559/233-0836 or 800/788-0836

Web www.fresnocvb.org

Fresno was founded when the population of Millerton moved in a body from that town to the railroad line. In the geographic center of the state and heart of the San Joaquin Valley—the great central California "Garden of the Sun"—Fresno and Fresno County are enjoying tremendous growth. The county claims the greatest agricultural production of any in the United States, handling more than $3 billion annually. The world's largest dried fruit packing plant (Sun Maid) is here.

What to See and Do

California State University, Fresno. (1911) 19,000 students. Farm, arboretum, California wildlife habitat exhibits; tours. Cedar and Shaw Aves, 9 mi NE of CA 99. Phone 559/278-4240.

The Discovery Center. Participatory natural and physical science exhibits for families; outdoor exhibits, cactus garden; picnicking, Native American rm. (Tues-Sun) 1944 N Winery Ave. Phone 559/251-5533.

Forestiere Underground Gardens. Former home of Italian immigrant Baldasare Forestiere has ten acres of underground tunnels filled with citrus plants, grape vines, rose bushes, and other flora. (Apr-Nov, Wed-Sun) 5021 W Shaw. Phone 559/271-0734. ¢¢¢

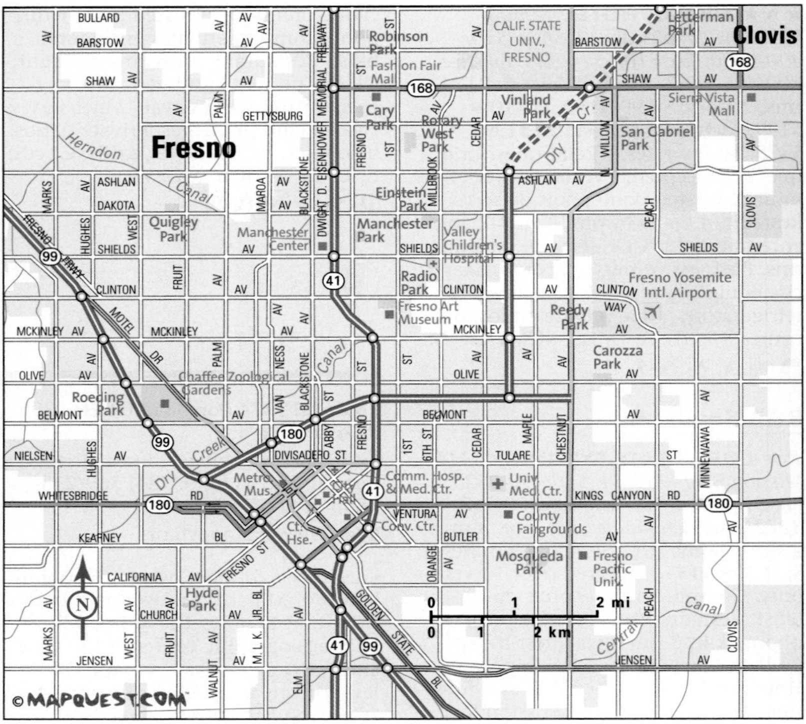

Fresno Metropolitan Museum. Displays on the heritage and culture of the San Joaquin Valley; hands-on science exhibits; touring exhibits. (Tues-Sun; closed hols) 1515 Van Ness Ave. Phone 559/441-1444. ¢¢¢

Kearney Mansion Museum. (1900-1903). Historic mansion has been restored; contains many original furnishings, incl European wallpapers and art nouveau light fixtures. Servant's quarters adj houses ranch kitchen and museum gift shop. Narrated 45-min tour of mansion. (Fri-Sun afternoons; closed Jan 1, Easter, Dec 25) 7160 W Kearney Blvd, 7 mi W via CA 99, exit Fresno St, entrance is ½ mi on the right; located in 225-acre Kearney Park. Phone 559/441-0862. ¢¢

Kingsburg. Settled by Swedes, their colorful influence remains in this town. Swedish architectural design on buildings, dala horses and flags decorate streets. **Historical Society Museum** at 2321 Sierra St. 18 mi S via CA 99. Contact Kingsburg Chamber of Commerce, 1475 Draper St, Kingsburg 93631. Phone 559/897-1111.

Millerton Lake State Recreation Area. 14,107 acres. Swimming, waterskiing (lifeguards), fishing, boat launching; hiking and riding trails, picnicking, concession, store nearby, camping (dump station). Standard fees. 21 mi NE via CA 41, Friant Rd. Phone 559/822-2332. ¢¢¢

Roeding Park. Variety of trees and shrubs on 157 acres ranging from high mountain to tropical species. Boating (rentals). Tennis. Camellia garden, picnic areas; children's storyland (fee); playland (fee/ride); amphitheater. (Daily) W Belmont Ave at CA 99. In the park is

Chaffee Zoological Gardens. This 18-acre zoo has more than 650 animals representing 200 species. Incl reptile house, elephant exhibit, humming bird and butterfly exhibits; also tropical rain forest exhibit containing plants and animal species found primarily in South American regions. (Daily) At the S end of the park, near Belmont Ave. Phone 559/498-2671. ¢¢¢

Sequoia & Kings Canyon National Parks. (see) Approx 55 mi E on CA 180.

Sierra National Forest. Nearly 1.3 million acres ranging from rolling foothills to rugged, snow-capped mountains, two groves of giant sequoias, hundreds of natural lakes, 11 major reservoirs, and unique geological formations. The topography can be rough and precipitous in higher elevations, with deep canyons and many beautiful meadows along streams and lakes; five wilderness areas. Rafting, boating, sailing, fishing; hunting, downhill and x-country skiing, picnicking, camping. Standard fees. Sections NE & E reached via CA 41, 99, 168. Contact Forest Supervisor, 1600 Tollhouse, Clovis 93611. Phone 559/297-0706.

Sierra Summit Ski Area. Three triple, two double chairlifts, four surface lifts; patrol, school, rentals; snowmaking; snack bar, cafeteria, restaurant, bar; lodge. (Mid-Nov-mid-Apr, daily) Twenty-five runs; longest run 2¼ mi; vertical drop 1,600 ft. Half-day rates (wkends and hols). 65 mi NE on CA 168, in Sierra National Forest. Phone 209/233-0900. ¢¢¢¢¢

Wild Water Adventures. Water park with rides, slides, and picnicking. Has one of the West's largest wave pools, plus water slides for teens and a water play area for children. (Mid-June-mid-Aug, daily; May-mid-June, wkends and hols) 11413 E Shaw Ave, Clovis. Phone 559/299-9453. ¢¢¢¢¢

Woodward Park. Approx 300 acres. Authentic Japanese garden (wkends only; summer wkday evenings, fee); fishing ponds for children under 16; jogging course; picnic area; bird sanctuary. (Daily) Audubon Dr & CA 41. Phone 559/498-1551.

Yosemite National Park. (see) 89 mi NE on CA 41.

Special Events

Fresno County Blossom Trail. This 62-mi self-guided driving tour features the beauty of California agriculture during peak season (weather permitting). Highlights of the trail are fruit orchards, citrus groves, vineyards, and historical points of interest. The Visitors Bureau has maps, information. Phone 559/237-2294. Peak season late Feb-mid-Mar.

Clovis Rodeo. In Clovis, NE corner of Fresno. Parade. Phone 559/299-8838. Late Apr.

Swedish Festival. In Kingsburg. Parade, pancake bkfst, smorgasbord, entertainment, arts and crafts, carnival, Maypole, folk dancing. Third wkend May. Phone 559/897-5821.

Highland Gathering and Games. Coombs Ranch. Scottish athletics, dancing contests, bagpipe competition. Mid-Sept. Phone 559/226-8549.

The Big Fresno Fair. Phone 559/453-3247. Oct.

Skiing California's alpine meadows

Motels/Motor Lodges

★★ **BEST WESTERN VILLAGE INN.** *3110 N Blackstone (93703). 559/226-2110; fax 559/226-0539; res 800/528-1234.* 152 rms, 2 story. S $50-$54; D $56-$60; each addl $4; under 12 free. Crib $6. TV; cable (premium). Pool; whirlpool. Complimentary continental bkfst, coffee in rms. Restaurant adj open 24 hrs. Ck-out noon. Business servs avail. In-rm modem link. Cr cds: A, C, D, DS, MC, V.

★★ **CHATEAU INN BY PICCADILLY INNS.** *5113 E McKinley Ave (93727). 559/456-1418; fax 559/456-4643; toll-free 800/445-2428. www.piccadilly-inn.com.* 78 rms, 2 story. S $71; D $77; each addl $6; under 18 free. Crib free. TV; cable, VCR (free movies). Pool. Complimentary coffee in rms. Restaurant adj 6 am-10 pm. Ck-out 1 pm. Business servs avail. Free airport transportation. Bathrm phones; some refrigerators. Cr cds: A, C, D, DS, JCB, MC, V.

D SC

★ **INNS OF AMERICA.** *2570 S East St (93706). 559/486-1188; fax 559/486-2743. www.innsamerica.com.* 121 rms, 2 story. S $31.90-$36.90; D $43.90-$47.90; each addl $5. Pet accepted. TV; cable (premium). Heated pool. Restaurant adj 24 hrs. Ck-out 11 am. Coin lndry. Cr cds: A, MC, V.

D

★★★ **THE SAN JOAQUIN SUITE HOTEL.** *1309 W Shaw Ave (93711). 559/225-1309; fax 559/225-6021; toll-free 800/775-1309. www.sanjoaquinhotel.com.* 68 suites, 3 story, 18 kit. units. Suites $89-$135; kit. units $135-$195; under 5 free; wkly, monthly rates. Crib free. TV; cable (premium), VCR avail. Pool; whirlpool. Coffee in rms. Restaurant nearby. Ck-out noon. Coin lndry. Meeting rms. Business center. In-rm modem link. Bellhops. Concierge. Free covered parking. Free airport, RR station transportation. Refrigerators, microwaves. Balconies. Cr cds: A, C, D, DS, MC, V.

D SC

Hotels

★★ **DOUBLETREE.** *1055 Van Ness Ave (93721). 559/485-9000; fax 559/485-3210; res 800/222-8733. www.hilton.com.* 193 rms, 9 story. S $74-$109; D $79-$129; each addl $10; suites $179-$525; wkend rates. Crib free. TV; cable (premium). Complimentary coffee in rms. Heated pool; whirlpool. Restaurant 11 am-10 pm. Bar. Ck-out noon. Meeting rms. Business servs avail. In-rm modem link. Free airport transportation. Cr cds: A, D, DS, MC, V.

D

★★ **FOUR POINTS BY SHERATON HOTEL.** *3737 N Blackstone Ave (93726). 559/226-2200; fax 559/222-7147; res 800/325-3535. www.sheraton.com.* 204 rms, 2 story. S $85-$96; D $90-$101; each addl $5; suites $175; wkend rates; under 17 free. Crib $5. TV; cable (premium), VCR avail. Heated pool; whirlpool, poolside serv. Complimentary coffee in rms. Restaurant 6:30 am-10 pm. Bar 10-1 am. Ck-out noon. Meeting rms. Business servs avail. In-rm modem link. Bellhops. Valet serv. Coin lndry. Free airport, RR station, bus depot transportation. Exercise equipt. Health club privileges. Refrigerators, bathrm phones. Private patios. Cr cds: A, C, D, DS, ER, JCB, MC, V.

D

★★★ **PICCADILLY INN AIRPORT.** *5115 E McKinley Ave (93727). 559/251-6000; fax 559/251-6956; toll-free 800/468-3587. www.piccadilly-inn.com.* 185 rms, 2 story. S, D $80-$130; suites $185-$235; under 18 free; wkend rates. Crib free. TV; cable, VCR avail. Pool; whirlpool, poolside serv. Complimentary coffee in rms. Restaurant 6 am-2 pm; dining rm 11 am-2 pm, 5-10 pm; Sat from 5 pm; Sun 5-9 pm. Bar 5-11 pm. Ck-out 1 pm. Coin lndry. Meeting rms. Bellhops. Valet serv. Gift shop. Free airport transportation. Exercise equipt. Health club privileges. Bathrm phones; some refrigerators. Private patios, balconies. Cr cds: A, C, D, DS, JCB, MC, V.

D

★★★ **PICCADILLY INN UNIVERSITY.** *4961 N Cedar Ave (93726). 559/224-4200; fax 559/227-2382; toll-free 800/468-3587. www.piccadilly-inn.com.* 190 rms, 3 story. S $94- $130; D $104-130; each addl $10; suites $185-$195; under 18 free. TV; cable. Pool; whirlpool. Complimentary continental bkfst (Mon-Fri). Coffee in rms. Restaurant nearby. Ck-out 1 pm. Coin lndry. Meeting rms. Bellhops. Valet serv. Airport, RR station, bus depot transportation. Exercise equipt. Health club privileges. Bathrm phones; some refrigerators. Private patios. Cr cds: A, C, D, DS, JCB, MC, V.

D SC

★★★ **RADISSON.** *2233 Ventura St (93721). 559/268-1000; fax 559/441-2954; res 800/333-3333.* 321 rms, 8 story. S, D $79-$129; each addl $10; suites $105-$205; under 18 free. Crib free. Pet accepted. TV; cable, VCR avail. Indoor/outdoor pool; whirlpool, poolside serv. Restaurant 6 am-2 pm, 5-10 pm. Bar noon-11 pm. Ck-out noon. Convention facilities. Business servs avail. Gift shop. Beauty shop. Free airport, RR station transportation. Exercise equipt; sauna. Eight-story atrium lobby. Cr cds: A, C, D, DS, ER, MC, V.

D

Restaurants

★ **GEORGE'S.** *2405 Capitol St (93721). 559/264-9433.* Hrs: 6 am-3 pm; Sat from 7 am. Closed Sun; hols. Armenian menu. Wine, beer. Bkfst $2.95-$7.50, lunch $3.50-$7.75. Specialties: lamb shank, shish kebab.

D

★★ **RIPE TOMATO.** *5064 N Palm Ave (93704). 559/225-1850.* Hrs: 11:30 am-2:30 pm, 6-10 pm. Closed Sun, Mon; hols. Res accepted. French Provençal menu. Bar. Lunch $8.95-$13.95, dinner $16.95-$27.95. Specializes in roast duck, salmon. Outdoor dining. Cr cds: A, DS, MC, V.

D

Fullerton

See also Anaheim, Buena Park

Pop 114,144 **Elev** 155 ft
Area code 714 or 657

Motel/Motor Lodge

★ **HOWARD JOHNSON EXPRESS INN.** *1000 S Euclid St (92832).* 714/871-7200*; fax 714/871-3929; res 800/225-7343.* 59 rms, 2 story. S $49-$89; D $55-$95; each addl $6; under 18 free; wkly rates. Crib $10. TV; cable (premium), VCR avail (movies). Complimentary continental bkfst. Restaurant nearby. Ck-out 11 am. Business servs avail. Coin lndry. Disneyland transportation. Health club privileges. Heated pool. Many refrigerators; microwaves avail. Cr cds: A, D, DS, MC, V.

SC

Hotels

★★ **FOUR POINTS BY SHERATON FULLERTON.** *1500 S Raymond Ave (92831). 714/635-9000; fax 714/520-5831; res 888/635-9000. www.four-points-hotel.com.* 256 rms, 3-6 story. S, D $85; each addl $10; suites $159-$300; under 13 free. Crib free. TV; cable (premium). Heated pool; poolside serv. Coffee in rms. Restaurant 6 am-10 pm. Bar 4 pm-midnight. Ck-out noon. Coin lndry. Convention facilities. Business center. Valet serv. Free Disneyland transportation. Exercise equipt. Refrigerators avail. Some balconies. Cr cds: A, D, DS, JCB, MC, V.

D

★★★ **MARRIOTT.** *2701 E Nutwood Ave (92831). 714/738-7800; fax 714/738-0288; res 800/468-3571. www.marriott.com.* 224 rms, 6 story. S, D $149-$178; suites $275. Crib avail. Pet accepted, some restrictions. TV; cable (premium). Heated pool; whirlpool, poolside serv. Coffee in rms. Restaurant 6:30 am-11 pm. Bar from 11 am. Ck-out noon. Meeting rms. Business center. Exercise equipt; sauna. Bathrm phone, wet bar, refrigerator in suites. Some patios. Luxury level. Cr cds: A, D, DS, JCB, MC, V.

D

★★★ **RADISSON HOTEL.** *222 W Houston Ave (92832). 714/992-1700; fax 714/992-4843; res 800/333-3333. www.radisson.com/fullertonca.* 289 rms, 4 and 7 story. S, D $139; suites $145; each addl $10; under 18 free. Crib free. TV; cable (premium). Heated pool; wading pool, poolside serv. Restaurant 6 am-2 pm, 4-10 pm. Bar 4 pm-midnight. Ck-out noon. Coin lndry. Convention facilities. Business servs avail. Bellhops. Gift shop. Free RR station, Disneyland transportation. Exercise equipt. Game rm. Some balconies. Cr cds: A, D, DS, JCB, MC, V.

D SC

All Suite

★★ **CHASE SUITE HOTEL.** *2932 E Nutwood Ave (92631). 714/579-7400; fax 714/528-7945; toll-free 888/433-9406. www.woodfinsuitehotels.com.* 96 rms, 5 story. S $119; D $129; each addl $10; under 18 free. Crib free.

TV; cable (premium). Heated pool. Complimentary continental bkfst, coffee in rms. Restaurant adj 6 am-11 pm. Ck-out noon. Coin lndry. Meeting rms. Business servs avail. Exercise equipt. Health club privileges. Bathrm phones, refrigerators, in-rm whirlpools; microwaves avail. Some balconies. Grill. Cr cds: A, C, D, DS, JCB, MC, V.

D

Restaurants

★★★ **THE CELLAR.** *305 N Harbor Blvd (92832). 714/525-5682.* Hrs: from 5:30 pm. Closed Sun, Mon; hols. Res accepted. French menu. Bar. Wine cellar. A la carte entrees: dinner $17.50-$33.50. Specializes in lamb, duckling, fresh seafood. Own baking, ice cream. Valet parking. Grotto decor. In cellar of former hotel (1922). Totally nonsmoking. Cr cds: A, C, D, DS, MC, V.

D

★★★ **LA VIE EN ROSE.** *240 S State College Blvd, Brea (92821). 714/529-8333. www.lavieenrose.com.* Hrs: 11:30 am-2 pm, 5:30-9 pm. Closed Sun; hols. Res accepted. French country menu. Bar. Wine list. A la carte entrees: lunch $9.75-$17.50, dinner $19.75-$31. Complete meal: three course dinner $35. Specialties: sauteed shrimp with lobster sauce, sauteed duck breast and leg confit with a dark cherry demi glace, grilled filet mignon with bearnaise sauce. Parking. French country decor; Norman (France) farmhouse replica. Totally nonsmoking. Cr cds: A, MC, V.

D

★★ **MULBERRY STREET.** *114 W Wilshire Ave (92832). 714/525-1056.* Hrs: 11 am-3 pm, 5-10 pm; Fri, Sat to 11 pm; Sun from 5 pm. Closed hols. Res accepted. Italian menu. Bar to 1 am; Fri, Sat to 2 am. Lunch $4.50-$10.95, dinner $8.95-$22.95. Specializes in fresh seafood, homemade pasta. Own baking. Cr cds: A, D, DS, MC, V.

D

★★★ **SUMMIT HOUSE.** *2000 E Bastanchury Rd (92835). 714/671-4111.* Hrs: 11:30 am-2:30 pm, 5-9 pm; Fri to 10 pm; Sat 5-10 pm; Sun from 5 pm. Closed hols. Res accepted. Continental menu. Bar. Wine list. Lunch $8.95-$16.95, dinner $17.95-$26.95. Specializes in roast prime rib, chef's creations. Own desserts. Pianist. Valet parking. Outdoor dining. Hilltop restaurant; Old-World English country-inn decor. View of Orange County. Cr cds: A, D, DS, MC, V.

D

Garberville

Pop 900 **Elev** 533 ft **Area code** 707 **Zip** 95440

What to See and Do

Avenue of the Giants. A 33-mi roadway running parallel to US 101 through Humboldt Redwoods State Park. Roadside attractions incl drive-through tree and other "novelty" redwoods. (Daily) From Phillipsville N to Pepperwood. **FREE**

Humboldt Redwoods State Park. (see) Approx 15 mi N off US 101.

King Range National Conservation Area. Approx 60,000 acres on the coast incl King Peak (4,087 ft). Saltwater fishing on 26 mi of coastline, inland stream fishing (subject to state regulations); hunting, hiking, picnicking, improved camping (fee/car/night). 15 mi W off US 101. Phone 707/825-2300.

Richardson Grove State Park. (see) 8 mi S on US 101.

Motels/Motor Lodges

★★ **HUMBOLDT REDWOODS INN.** *987 Redwood Dr (95542). 707/923-2451; fax 707/923-2451.* 21 rms, 2 story. Memorial Day-Sept: S $50-$75; D $55-$85; each addl $10; suites $100-$125; higher rates special events; lower rates rest of yr. TV; cable (premium). Pool. Complimentary coffee in rms. Restaurant nearby. Ck-out 11 am. Business servs avail. Cr cds: A, D, DS, JCB, MC, V.

★★ **SHERWOOD FOREST MOTEL.** *814 Redwood Dr (95542). 707/923-2721; fax 707/923-3677. www.sherwoodforestmotel.com.* 32 rms. May-Oct: S $56; D $60-$62; each addl $5; suites, kit. units $80-$88; lower rates rest of yr. Crib $6. Pet accepted. TV; cable (premium). Heated pool; whirlpool. Coffee in rms. Restaurant adj 6 am-3 pm. Ck-out 11 am. Coin lndry. Business servs avail. Free airport transportation. Refrigerators. Picnic tables, grills. Fish cleaning, fish storage facilities. Cr cds: A, DS, MC, V.

Resort

★★★ **BENBOW INN.** *445 Lake Benbow Dr (95542). 707/923-2124; fax 707/923-2897; toll-free 800/355-3301. www.benbowinn.com.* 55 rms, 2-4 story. S, D $120-$180; each addl $20; suites $190-$315. Closed Jan-Mar. TV in some rms; cable, VCR avail (free movies). Pool privileges. Complimentary afternoon refreshments. Coffee in rms. Restaurant (see also BENBOW INN). Bar 4 pm-midnight (seasonal); entertainment. Ck-out noon, ck-in 2 pm. Bellhops. Business servs avail. Free airport, bus depot transportation. Nine-hole golf, greens fee $18, putting green. Boats. Lawn games. Classic vintage movies nightly. Some refrigerators, fireplaces. On lake; private beach. Woodland setting. Tudor mansion resort hotel (1926); antiques. Totally nonsmoking. Cr cds: A, DS, MC, V.

Restaurant

★★★ **BENBOW INN.** *445 Lake Benbow Dr (95542). 707/923-2125. www.benbowinn.com.* Hrs: 8-11 am, noon-1:30 pm (seasonal), 6-9 pm; Sun brunch 8 am-1:30 pm. Closed Jan-Mar. Res accepted. Wine cellar. A la carte entrees: bkfst $4.50-$8.50, lunch $6.50-$10, dinner $12.95-$22. Children's menu. Specializes in fresh pasta, fresh fish, lamb. Own desserts. Pianist. Patio dining. Tudor decor; antiques. Totally nonsmoking. Cr cds: A, DS, MC, V.

Garden Grove

See also Anaheim, Orange, Santa Ana

Pop 143,050 **Elev** 90 ft **Area code** 714

What to See and Do

Crystal Cathedral. The all-glass church resembles a four-pointed crystal star. Designed by Philip Johnson; set on 36 acres of landscaped grounds. Guided tours. (Mon-Sat; closed hols) 13280 Chapman Ave. Phone 714/971-4000. **Donation**

Motel/Motor Lodge

★★ **BEST WESTERN PLAZA INTERNATIONAL INN.** *7912 Garden Grove Blvd (92641). 714/894-7568; fax 714/894-6308; res 800/528-1234.* 100 rms, 2 story. Late May-late Sept: S $39-$79; D $44-$89; each addl $3; under 18 free; higher rates hols; lower rates rest of yr. Crib $8. TV; cable (premium), VCR avail. Pool. Sauna. Coffee in rms. Restaurant opp 7 am-11 pm. Ck-out 11 am. Meeting rm. Business servs avail. Refrigerators, microwaves avail. Cr cds: A, C, D, DS, JCB, MC, V.

Restaurant

★★ **LA FAYETTE.** *12532 Garden Grove Blvd (92843). 714/537-5011.* Hrs: 11:30 am-2 pm, 6-10 pm. Closed Sun; hols. Res accepted. French menu. Bar. Lunch $8-$19, dinner

Crystal Cathedral

$16-$28. Specializes in fresh fish, rack of lamb, veal. Pianist wkends. Classical French decor; original artwork. Family-owned since 1972. Totally nonsmoking. Cr cds: A, C, D, MC, V.
D

Gilroy

(A-1) *See also Salinas, San Jose*

Pop 31,487 **Elev** 200 ft
Information Gilroy Chamber of Commerce, 7471 Monterey St, 95020; 408/842-6437
Web www.gilroy.org

What to See and Do

Fortino Winery. Small family winery. Tours, wine tasting rm, picnic area. (Daily; closed Easter, Thanksgiving, Dec 25) 5 mi W via CA 152, at 4525 Hecker Pass Hwy. Phone 408/842-3305. **FREE**

Henry W. Coe State Park. Approx 68,000 acres. Highlights incl unusually large manzanita shrubs and a botanical island formed of ponderosa pines. Hiking, backpacking, horseback riding, and mountain biking. Primitive drive-in campsites (no electric). Pine Ridge Museum displays ranch life in the late 1880s (Sat, Sun). Guided walks and eve programs (Mar-June, wkends). Standard fees. 9 mi N on US 101, then 13 mi E of Morgan Hill on E Dunne Ave. Phone 408/779-2728. Per vehicle ¢

Outlets at Gilroy. Approx 150 outlet stores. (Daily) 8155 Arroyo Circle. Phone 408/842-3729.

Special Event

Gilroy Garlic Festival. Located at Christmas Hill Park. Features Gourmet Alley, a giant open-air kitchen; cooking demonstrations and contests; food and beverage booths; arts and crafts; entertainment. Phone 408/842-1625. Last full wkend July.

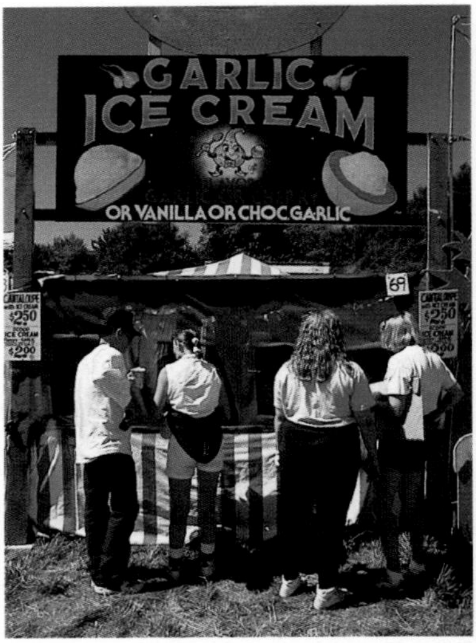

Tasty treats at the Gilroy Garlic Festival

Glendale (E-4)

Pop 180,038 **Elev** 571 ft
Area code 818

Motels/Motor Lodges

★★ BEST WESTERN EAGLE ROCK INN. *2911 Colorado Blvd (90041). 323/256-7711; fax 323/255-6750; res 800/528-1234. www.bestwestern.com/eagleroc.* 50 rms, 3 story. S $70-$90; D $80-$100; each addl $5; under 12 free; higher rates Rose Bowl activities. Crib $5. TV; cable (premium), VCR (free movies). Heated pool; whirlpool. Complimentary continental bkfst. Restaurant adj 11 am-10 pm. Ck-out noon. Business servs avail. Refrigerators, microwaves avail. Cr cds: A, D, DS, MC, V.
D SC

★★ BEST WESTERN GOLDEN KEY. *123 W Colorado St (91204). 818/247-0111; fax 818/545-9393; res 800/528-1234. www.bestwestern.com/goldenkeygle.* 55 rms, 3 story. S; D $99-$129; each addl $5; under 18 free; higher rates Rose Bowl. Crib $5. TV; cable (premium), VCR (free movies). Heated pool; whirlpool. Complimentary continental bkfst, coffee in rms. Restaurant opp 6 am-10 pm. Ck-out noon. Meeting rms. Business servs avail. In-rm modem link. Valet serv. Sundries. Health club privileges. Refrigerators, microwaves. Cr cds: A, D, DS, JCB, MC, V.

★ **VAGABOND INN.** *120 W Colorado St (91204). 818/240-1700; fax 818/548-8428; toll-free 800/522-1555. www.vagabondinn.com.* 52 rms, 3 story. S, D $53-$85; each addl $5; under 18 free; higher rates: special events, Rose Bowl (3-day min). Crib $5. Pet accepted, some restrictions; $5/day. TV; cable (premium). Heated pool. Complimentary continental bkfst. Coffee in rms. Restaurant adj. Ck-out noon. Some refrigerators; microwaves avail. Cr cds: A, C, D, DS, MC, V.

Restaurant

★★ **FAR NIENTE.** *204-1/2 N Brand Blvd (91203). 818/242-3835.* Hrs: 11:30 am-10:30 pm; Sat 5:30-11 pm; Sun 5-9:30 pm. Closed hols. Res accepted. Northern Italian menu. Bar. Lunch, dinner $7-$21. Specialties: penne Far Niente, ravioli. Own pasta, ice cream. Piano bar. Cr cds: A, DS, MC, V.

D

Grass Valley

(E-4) *See also Nevada City*

Settled 1849 **Pop** 9,048 **Elev** 2,411 ft **Area code** 530

Information Chamber of Commerce, 248 Mill St, 95945-6783; 530/273-4667 or 800/655-4667 (CA)

Web www.gvncchamber.org

Immigrants followed their half-starved cattle to this spot, not knowing that under the thick grass were rich quartz deposits that were to make the Grass Valley area the richest gold mining region in California—the Mother Lode country. The stamp mills, cyanide tanks, and shafts are no longer in operation. Located on the edge of the Tahoe National Forest, Grass Valley has become a recreation center and retirement haven.

A Ranger District office of the Tahoe National Forest is located here.

What to See and Do

Empire Mine State Historic Park. At one time, this historic hardrock gold mine was the largest and richest in California. Baronial cottage with formal gardens among 784 acres. Hiking, picnicking, visitor center, mining exhibits. Tours (daily; closed Dec 25). Standard fees. 10791 E Empire St. Phone 530/273-8522.

Lola Montez House. Facsimile of 1851 Grass Valley house once owned by Lola Montez; singer, dancer, and *paramour* of the rich and famous. Now houses Grass Valley/Nevada County Chamber of Commerce. 248 Mill St. Phone 530/273-4667.

Mining Museum-North Star Powerhouse. Hard rock mining display and artifacts; 30-ft Pelton water wheel; stamp mill; largest operational Cornish pump in the US. (May-Oct, daily) Allison Ranch Rd. Phone 530/273-4255. **FREE**

"Rough and Ready" Town. Gold strike named after General Zachary Taylor, "Old Rough and Ready." At one time the miners tried to secede from the Union and form the independent Republic of Rough and Ready. 4 mi W on CA 20.

Special Events

Blue Grass Festival. Fairgrounds, McCourtney Rd. Phone 530/273-6217. Mid-June.

Nevada County Fair. Fairgrounds, McCourtney Rd. Rodeo, horse show, livestock, loggers Olympics. Phone 530/273-6217. Four days mid-Aug.

Cornish Christmas. In Old Town. Street fair. Cornish treats, musicians, entertainment, vendors. Phone 530/272-8315. Late Nov-early Dec.

Motel/Motor Lodge

★ **HOLIDAY LODGE.** *1221 E Main St (95945). 530/273-4406; fax 530/477-2878; toll-free 800/742-7125. www.holidaylodgegrassvalley.homestead.com.* 36 rms, 1-2 story. Mid-Apr-mid-Oct: S, D $48-$85; gold panning, hol rates; lower rates rest of yr. Crib $6.

Pet accepted, some restrictions; $20 deposit. TV; cable. Pool. Continental bkfst. Coffee in rms. Restaurant nearby. Ck-out 11 am. Some balconies. Cr cds: A, C, D, DS, MC, V.
SC

Restaurant

★★ **SCHEIDEL'S.** *10100 Alta Sierra Dr (95949). 530/273-5553.* Hrs: 5:30-8:30 pm; Sun 4-9 pm. Closed Mon, Tues; also Jan. German, American menu. Bar. Dinner $9.95-$18.95. Children's menu. Specialties: Wiener schnitzel, German-marinated sauerbraten. Bavarian decor. Family-owned. Cr cds: MC, V.
D

Gualala (E-2)

Pop 1,200 **Elev** 67 ft **Area code** 707 **Zip** 95445

Information Redwood Coast Chamber of Commerce, PO Box 199; 800/778-5252

Web www.redwoodcoastchamber.com

Because of its relative isolation and quiet atmosphere, the area attracts many visitors. Favorite local activities include steelhead, abalone, and silver salmon fishing; canoeing and swimming in the Gualala River; and camping. A debate on the origin of the name "Gualala" has persisted for more than 100 years. Some say it derived from the native Pomo word *qhawala-li,* meaning "water coming down place," while others maintain that it is a Spanish rendering of Valhalla.

What to See and Do

Point Arena Lighthouse and Museum. This 115-ft-tall lighthouse (1908) and Fog Signal Building (1869) houses historical artifacts and photographs. Viewing at top of lighthouse through a two-ton lens. (Daily; closed Thanksgiving, Dec 25, also wkdays in Dec and Jan) 15 mi N on CA 1. Phone 707/882-2777. ¢¢

Hotel

★★ **SEA RANCH LODGE.** *60 Sea Walk Dr, The Sea Ranch (95497). 707/785-2371; fax 707/785-2917; toll-free 800/732-7262. www.searanchlodge.com.* 19 rms, 2 story. No A/C. S, D $205-$395; each addl $15; under 6 free; package plans. Crib $5. Coffee in rms. Restaurant 8-10 am, 11:30 am-2:30 pm, 6:30-9 pm. Bar 11 am-midnight. Ck-out noon. Meeting rms. Business servs avail. Gift shop. 18-hole golf, greens fee $35-$55, pro, pro shop, putting green, driving range. Some fireplaces. On bluff overlooking ocean; 5,500 acres in historic Sea Ranch. Totally nonsmoking. Cr cds: A, MC, V.

B&Bs/Small Inns

★★★ **BREAKERS INN.** *PO Box 389, 39300 S Hwy 1 (95445). 707/884-3200; fax 707/884-3400. www.breakersinn.com.* 27 rms, 3 story. No A/C. No elvtr. S, D $135-$235; under 5 free; lower rates mid-wk. Crib $10. TV; cable, VCR avail. Complimentary continental bkfst. Coffee in rms. Restaurant 8 am-2:30 pm, 5:30-9 pm. Ck-out 11 am, ck-in 3 pm. Bellhops. Golf privileges. Some refrigerators. Some balconies. Fireplaces; some in-rm whirlpools. Cr cds: A, DS, MC, V.

★★ **NORTH COAST COUNTRY INN.** *34591 S Hwy 1 (95445). 707/884-4537; fax 707/884-1833; toll-free 800/959-4537. www.northcoastcountryinn.com.* 6 rms, 4 kit. units. No A/C. S, D $150-$195; hols, wkends (2-3-day min). Children over 12 yrs only. TV in common rm. Complimentary full bkfst. Ck-out 11 am, ck-in 2 pm. Gift shop. Free airport transportation. Whirlpool. Refrigerators, fireplaces. Private decks. Antiques, handmade quilts. Forested setting overlooking Mendocino coast. Totally nonsmoking. Cr cds: A, MC, V.

★★★ **SAINT ORRES.** *36601 Hwy 1 S (95445). 707/884-3303; fax 707/884-1840. www.saintorres.com.* 8 rms, 3 baths, 15 cottages. No A/C. No rm phones. S, D $60-$75; cottages $85-$225. Complimentary bkfst. Restaurant (see also ST. ORRES). Ck-out noon, ck-in 3 pm. Whirlpool, sauna at cottages. Balconies. Fireplace in most cottages. Built by local craftsmen with local materials. The house is similar to a Russian dacha, with onion-domed towers; stained glass, woodwork. Most rms with ocean view. Beach opp. Cr cds: MC, V.

★★★ WHALE WATCH INN BY THE SEA. *35100 S Hwy 1 (95445). 707/884-3667; fax 707/884-4815; toll-free 800/942-5342. www.whalewatchinn.com.* 18 rms, 1-2 story, 5 kits. No A/C. Some rm phones. S $170. Complimentary full bkfst. Ck-out 11 am, ck-in 3 pm. Business servs avail. Many in-rm whirlpools. Fireplaces. Private patios. 2 acres on ocean bluff. Totally nonsmoking. Cr cds: A, MC, V.

Restaurant

★★★ ST. ORRES. *36601 S CA 1 (95445). 707/884-3335. www.saintorres.com.* Hrs: 6-9 pm; Sat 5:15-10 pm. Closed Wed Oct-May. No A/C. Res accepted; required wkends. Wine, beer. Prix fixe: dinner $30. Specializes in lamb, fresh fish, wild game. Own baking. Natural wood, stained glass. Totally nonsmoking. Cr cds: MC, V.

Guerneville

(F-2) *See also Bodega Bay, Healdsburg, Santa Rosa*

Pop 1,966 **Elev** 56 ft **Area code** 707

Information Russian River Region Visitors Bureau, 13250 River Rd, 95448; 707/869-9212 or 800/253-8800

Web www.russianriver.org

With swimming, golfing, fishing, canoeing, and hiking nearby, this scenic area is popular for recreational vacations.

What to See and Do

Armstrong Redwoods State Reserve. Named for Colonel James Boydston Armstrong of Ohio, who settled here with his family in 1874. Nature, hiking, riding trails, picnicking. Standard fees. 2 mi N off CA 116. Phone 707/865-2391. **¢¢**

Korbel Champagne Cellars. Produces wine, champagne and brandy. Guided tours; century-old cellars; champagne, wine tasting; garden tours in summer (one in morning, one in afternoon). (Daily; closed hols) 13250 River Rd. Phone 707/824-7000. **FREE**

Special Events

Russian River Blues Festival. Johnson's Beach. Phone 707/869-3940. Early June.

Russian River Jazz Festival. Johnson's Beach. Phone 707/869-3940. Wkend after Labor Day.

Resort

★★★ APPLEWOOD INN & RESTAURANT. *13555 Hwy 116 (95446). 707/869-9093; fax 707/869-9170; toll-free 800/555-8509. www.applewoodinn.com.* 16 rms, 3 story. A/C some rms. S, D $165; suites $295. TV; cable (premium). Pool; whirlpool. Complimentary full bkfst. Restaurant (see also APPLEWOOD). Ck-out noon, ck-in 3 pm. Business servs avail. In-rm modem link. Library. Antiques. Some fireplaces. Private patios, balconies. Picnic tables. County historical landmark. Totally nonsmoking. Cr cds: A, DS, MC, V.

B&B/Small Inn

★★ RIDENHOUR RANCH HOUSE INN. *12850 River Rd (95446). 707/887-1033; fax 707/869-2967; toll-free 888/877-4466. www.ridenhourranchhouseinn.com.* 6 rms, 3 story, 2 cottages. S, D $130; cottages $145. Complimentary full bkfst. Ck-out 11 am, ck-in 3-9 pm. Business servs avail. Dinner avail. Library. Antiques, handmade quilts. Balconies. Gardens. Picnic tables. Totally nonsmoking. Cr cds: A, MC, V.

Restaurant

★★ APPLEWOOD. *13555 CA 116 (95446). 707/869-9093. www.apple*

woodinn.com. Sittings: 6:30 and 7:15 pm; Fri, Sat also 8 pm. Closed Sun, Mon. Res required. No A/C. Regional California menu. Wine, beer. Complete meals: dinner $40-$45. Specializes in fresh local meat, fowl, fish. In Mediterranean-style, historic inn; own vegetable and herb garden. Totally nonsmoking. Cr cds: A, DS, MC, V.

D

Half Moon Bay

(G-3) *See also San Mateo*

Pop 8,886 **Elev** 69 ft **Area code** 650 **Zip** 94019

Motel/Motor Lodge

★★ HOLIDAY INN EXPRESS. *230 S Cabrillo Hwy (94019). 650/726-3400; fax 650/726-1256; res 800/465-4329. www.basshotels.com/holiday-inn.* 52 rms, 2 story. July-Aug: S, D $119-$139; each addl $10; under 18 free; higher rates: hols, special events; lower rates rest of yr. Crib free. Pet accepted; $10. TV. Complimentary continental bkfst. Restaurant nearby. Ck-out noon. Business servs avail. In-rm modem link. Cr cds: A, D, DS, MC, V.

Resorts

★★★ HALF MOON BAY LODGE AND CONFERENCE CENTER. *2400 S Cabrillo Hwy (94019). 650/726-9000; fax 650/726-7951; toll-free 800/368-2468. www.woodsidehotels.com.* 81 rms, 2 story. No A/C. Mar-Nov: S, D $195; each addl $10; suites $235; under 18 free; lower rates rest of yr. Crib free. TV; cable (premium). Heated pool; whirlpool. Complimentary continental bkfst, coffee in rms. Restaurants adj 6 am-10 pm. Ck-out 11:30 am. Meeting rms. Business servs avail. Exercise equipt. Refrigerators; many wet bars; some fireplaces. Balconies. Overlooks golf course. Totally nonsmoking. Cr cds: A, C, D, DS, ER, JCB, MC, V.

D

THE RITZ-CARLTON, HALF MOON BAY. *(Too new to be rated.) One Miramontes Point Rd (94019). 650/712-7000. www.ritz-carlton.com.* 261 rms, 5 story, 22 suites. S, D $350-$550; suites $745-$2,500. Crib avail. Valet parking avail. TV; cable (premium), VCR avail, CD avail. Complimentary newspaper. Restaurant. 24-hr rm serv. Bar. Ck-out noon, ck-out 3 pm. Conference center, meeting rms. Business center. Bellhops. Concierge serv. Dry cleaning. Gift shop. Exercise rm, sauna, steam rm. Bike rentals. Video games.

B&Bs/Small Inns

★★★ CYPRESS INN. *407 Mirada Rd (94019). 650/726-6002; fax 650/712-0380; toll-free 800/832-3224. www.cypressinn.com.* 12 rms, 2-3 story. S, D $215-$305. TV; cable. Complimentary full bkfst; afternoon refreshments. Restaurants nearby. Ck-out 11:30 am, ck-in 3 pm. Meeting rm. Business servs avail. Massage. Health club privileges. Fireplaces. Balconies. Colorful collection of folk art. Oceanfront location with five mi of sandy beach. All rms have ocean view. Totally nonsmoking. Cr cds: A, DS, MC, V.

D

★★ GOOSE AND TURRETS BED AND BREAKFAST INN. *835 George St, Montara (94037). 650/728-5451; fax 650/728-0141. www.goose.montara.com.* 5 rms, 2 shower only. No A/C. No rm phones. S, D $85-$120; each addl $20. Crib $20. Complimentary full bkfst; afternoon refreshments. Restaurant nearby. Ck-out noon, ck-in 4-7 pm. Concierge. Lawn games. Built in 1908; antiques. Totally nonsmoking. Cr cds: A, D, DS, MC, V.

★★★ MILL ROSE INN. *615 Mill St (94019). 650/726-8750; fax 650/726-3031; toll-free 800/900-7673. www.millroseinn.com.* 4 rms, 1 with shower only, 2 story, 2 suites. No A/C. S, D $165; each addl $25; suites $255-$285; wkends (2-day min). TV; cable (premium), VCR (movies). Whirlpool. Complimentary full bkfst, coffee in rms. Restaurants nearby. Ck-out 11 am, ck-in 3-9 pm. Meeting rm. Business servs avail. Bellhops Concierge serv. Exercise equipt.

Health club privileges. Refrigerators. Picnic tables. English country gardens. Totally nonsmoking. Cr cds: A, C, D, DS, MC, V.

★★ **OLD THYME INN.** *779 Main St (94019). 650/726-1616; fax 650/726-6394; toll-free 800/720-4277. www.oldthymeinn.com.* 7 rms, 2 story. No A/C. No rm phones. S, D $155; suite $165-$220. TV; VCR avail (free movies). Complimentary full bkfst; afternoon refreshments. Restaurants nearby. Ck-out 11 am, ck-in 3-7 pm. Business servs avail. Health club privileges. Some in-rm whirlpools, fireplaces. Picnic tables. Library/sitting rm. Herb garden. Built 1899. Totally nonsmoking. Cr cds: A, C, D, DS, MC, V.

★★ **RANCHO SAN GREGORIO.** *5086 La Honda Rd, San Gregorio (94074). 650/747-0810; fax 650/747-0184. www.san-gregorio-lodging.com.* 4 rms, 2 story. No A/C. 1 rm with phone. S, D $85-$155; each addl $15. Crib free. Some VCRs (free movies). Complimentary full bkfst; afternoon refreshments. Ck-out noon, ck-in 3 pm. Business servs avail. Game rm. Lawn games. Picnic tables, grills. Overlooks historic San Gregorio Valley. Spanish mission-style home located on 15 acres; cactus courtyard; gazebo. Totally nonsmoking.

★★★ **SEAL COVE INN.** *221 Cypress Ave, Moss Beach (94038). 650/728-4114; fax 650/728-4116; toll-free 800/995-9987. www.sealcove.com.* 8 rms, 2 suites, 2 story. No A/C. S, D $190-$215; each addl $30; suites $270; 2-day min hols. TV; VCR (300 movies avail). Complimentary full bkfst; afternoon refreshments. Restaurants nearby. Ck-out 11 am, ck-in 3 pm. Meeting rm. Business servs avail. Refrigerators, minibars. Balconies second floor only. Nightly turn-down service. Picnic tables. Totally nonsmoking. Views of garden and Pacific Ocean. Cr cds: A, MC, V.

D

★★ **ZABALLA HOUSE.** *324 Main St (94019). 650/726-9123; fax 650/726-3921. www.zaballahouse.com.* 9 rms, 2 story, 3 suites. No rm phones. S, D $140-$275; each addl $10. Pet accepted; $10. TV; cable in some rms. Complimentary bkfst buffet; afternoon refreshments. Restaurant nearby. Ck-out 11 am, ck-in 3-7 pm. Business servs avail. Oldest building in town still standing (1859); some antiques. Some in-rm whirlpools, fireplaces. Totally nonsmoking. Cr cds: A, DS, MC, V.

D

Restaurants

★★ **MOSS BEACH DISTILLERY.** *140 Beach Way, Moss Beach (94038). 650/728-5595. www.mossbeachdistillery.com.* Hrs: noon-9 pm; Sun brunch 10 am-2:45 pm. California menu. Bar. Lunch $11.95-$16.95, dinner $16.95-$25. Sun brunch $22.95. Specializes in seafood, steaks. Terrace dining overlooking ocean. Displays on colorful history of restaurant (1927) incl Prohibition and resident ghost. Totally nonsmoking. Cr cds: A, C, D, DS, MC, V.

D

★ **PASTA MOON.** *315 Main St (94019). 650/726-5125. www.pastamoon.com.* Hrs: 11:30 am-2:30 pm, 5:30-9:30 pm; Fri to 10 pm; Sat noon-3 pm, 5:30-10 pm; Sun (brunch) 11 am-3 pm, 5:30-10 pm. Closed Thanksgiving, Dec 25. Res accepted. No A/C. Italian menu. Bar. A la carte entrees: lunch $8-$13, dinner $10-$20. Sun brunch $6-$13. Children's menu. Specializes in seafood, game. Own pasta, baking. Exhibition kitchen features wood-burning oven. Totally nonsmoking. Cr cds: A, D, DS, MC, V.

D

Hanford

(B-3) *See also Visalia*

Pop 30,897 **Elev** 246 ft **Area code** 559 **Zip** 93230

Information Hanford Visitor Agency, 200 Santa Fe, Suite D; 559/582-0483

Web www.hanfordchamber.com

China Alley, the century-old Chinatown, has been saved by Chef Wing's family. Two outstanding restaurants were the reason that presidents Eisenhower and Truman, Mao Tse-tung and Chiang Kai-shek suggested that others eat in this historic town. One of these restaurants, Imperial Dynasty, remains open (see RESTAURANT).

Motels/Motor Lodges

★ **DOWNTOWN MOTEL.** *101 N Redington St (93230). 559/582-9036.* 29 rms, 2 story. S $36; D $38; each addl $2. TV; cable (premium). Restaurant nearby. Ck-out 11 am. Cr cds: A, D, DS, MC, V.

★★★ **INN AT HARRIS RANCH.** *24505 W Dorris, Coalinga (93210). 559/935-0717; fax 559/935-5061; toll-free 800/942-2333. www.harrisranch.com.* 153 rms, 3 story. S, D $89-$104; each addl $8; suites $101-$250; under 12 free. Crib free. Pet accepted; $10/day. TV; cable (premium). Heated pool; whirlpools. Complimentary coffee in rms. Restaurant 6 am-11 pm. Bar from 11 am. Ck-out noon. Coin lndry. Meeting rms. Bellhops. Sundries. Exercise equipt. Minibars. Private patios, balconies. Private 2,800-ft paved and lighted airstrip on site. Cr cds: A, C, D, DS, MC, V.

D SC

B&B/Small Inn

★★ **IRWIN STREET INN.** *522 N Irwin St (93230). 559/583-8000; fax 866/583-7378; toll-free 888/583-8080. www.irwinstreet.com.* 30 rms in 4 Victorian-style buildings, 2 story, 3 suites. S, D $69-$89; suites $125-$150; under 12 free. Crib avail. Pet accepted. TV; cable (premium), VCR avail. Wading pool. Continental bkfst. Restaurant 6:30 am-9 pm; Sun to 2 pm. Ck-out noon, ck-in 3 pm. Balconies. Historic buildings (late 1800s), restored; many antiques. Totally nonsmoking. Cr cds: A, DS, MC, V.

D SC

Restaurant

★★★ **IMPERIAL DYNASTY.** *406 China Alley (93230). 559/582-0196.* Hrs: 4:30-10 pm. Closed Mon; Jan 1, Thanksgiving, Dec 25; also one wk in Feb. Res accepted. Continental menu. Bar. Wine cellar. Complete meals: dinner $9.95-$29.95, gourmet dinner (one wk advance notice) $60. Specialties: tournedos of beef bordelaise, escargots a la Bourguignonne, rack of lamb. Gourmet societies meet here; special meals prepared. In historic Chinese community; many original Chinese works of art, artifacts. Family-owned. Cr cds: A, MC, V.

D

Hayward

(G-3) *See also Fremont, Oakland, San Francisco Airport Area*

Pop 111,498 **Elev** 111 ft
Area code 510

What to See and Do

Garin Regional Park. Secluded 1,520 acres in the Hayward hills with vistas of south Bay Area. Fishing at Jordan Pond; bird-watching, hiking, riding trails, picnicking. Interpretive programs at visitor center; historic farm equipment (wkends). S on CA 238 to Garin Ave E. Phone 510/562-PARK. Per vehicle ¢¢

Dry Creek Pioneer Regional Park. On 1,563 acres. Bird-watching, hiking, riding trails, picnicking. Interpretive programs. Enter via Garin Regional Park. Phone 510/562-PARK.

Hayward Area Historical Society Museum. Displays incl fire engines, costumes, California and local artifacts. Changing exhibits. (Mon-Sat; closed hols) 22701 Main St. Phone 510/581-0223. ¢

McConaghy Estate. (1886) Twelve-rm Victorian farmhouse with period furnishings; carriage house; tank house. During Dec, farm house is decorated for Christmas in 1886. Picnic and play areas in adj Kennedy Park. (Thurs-Sun; closed hols, Jan) 18701 Hesperian Blvd. Phone 510/276-3010. ¢¢

Motels/Motor Lodges

★★ COMFORT INN. *24997 Mission Blvd (94544). 510/538-4466; fax 510/581-8029; toll-free 800/835-6159. www.comfortinn-hay.com.* 62 rms, 2 story. S $82; D $87; each addl $5; suites $100-$125; under 18 free. Crib $5. TV; cable (premium). Complimentary continental bkfst. Restaurant nearby. Ck-out 11 am. Coin lndry. Meeting rms. Business servs avail. In-rm modem link. Refrigerators. Cr cds: A, C, D, DS, JCB, MC, V.
D

★★ EXECUTIVE INN. *20777 Hesperian Blvd (94541). 510/732-6300; fax 510/783-2265. www.haywoodhotels.com.* 146 rms, 3 story, 23 suites. S, D $79-$99; each addl $10; suites $105-$125; under 17 free; wkend rates. TV; cable (premium). Heated pool. Complimentary continental bkfst, coffee in rms. Restaurant nearby. Ck-out noon. Coin lndry. Meeting rms. Valet serv. Sundries. Free airport transportation. Exercise equipt. Some balconies. Cr cds: A, D, DS, JCB, MC, V.
D

Restaurants

★★ RUE DE MAIN. *22622 Main St (94541). 510/537-0812. www.ruedemain.com.* Hrs: 11:30 am-2:15 pm, 5:30-10 pm; Mon to 2:15 pm; Sat from 5:30 pm. Closed Sun (exc Mother's Day); hols. Res accepted. French menu. Lunch $9-$14. A la carte entrees: dinner $15-$22. Specialty: medaillons de veau. Own pastries. Contemporary French decor; murals of French city scenes. Cr cds: A, D, MC, V.
D

Healdsburg

(F-2) *See also Bodega Bay, Guerneville, Santa Rosa*

Pop 9,469 **Elev** 106 ft **Area code** 707 **Zip** 95448

Information Chamber of Commerce & Visitors Bureau, 217 Healdsburg Ave; 707/433-6935 or 800/648-9922 (CA)

Web www.healdsburg.org

What to See and Do

Canoe trips. One-day to five-day trips on Russian River (Apr-Oct). Equipment and transportation provided. Contact Trowbridge Canoe Trips. Phone 707/433-7247 or 800/640-1386.

★ Healdsburg area wineries. More than 60 wineries are located in the northern Sonoma County region; most are open to the public for wine tasting. A map listing the wineries and other area attractions is avail from the Chamber of Commerce & Visitors Bureau. Phone 707/433-7247. Among them are

Chateau Souverain. Wine tasting, restaurant (Fri-Sun). 5 mi N on US 101, Independence Ln exit, in Geyserville. 400 Souverain Rd, Geyserville 95441. **FREE**

Simi Winery. Winery dates from the turn of the century. Guided tours; wine tasting. (Daily; closed hols) 16275 Healdsburg Ave. Contact PO Box 698. Phone 800/746-4880. **FREE**

Warm Springs Dam/Lake Sonoma. Earth-filled dam, anadromous fish hatchery operated by California Department of Fish and Game and the Army Corps of Engineers. Park overlook provides scenic views of lake and nearby wine country. Swimming, fishing, boating (marina); hiking and bridle trails. Picnic facilities at marina, at Yorty Creek, and near visitor center. Primitive and improved camping. Visitor center. (Wed-Sun; closed hols) 11 mi W via US 101, exit on Dry Creek Rd. Contact Visitor Center, 3333 Skaggs Springs Rd, Geyserville 95441; Phone 707/433-9483. Camping ¢¢¢¢

Special Event

Healdsburg Harvest Century Bicycle Tour. Road and mountain bikes tour through Alexander, Russian River, and Dry Creek valleys. Phone707/433-6935. Mid-July.

Motels/Motor Lodges

★★ **BEST WESTERN DRY CREEK INN.** *198 Dry Creek Rd (95448). 707/433-0300; fax 707/433-1129; toll-free 800/222-5784. www.drycreekinn.com.* 102 rms, 3 story. Apr-Oct: S, D $69-$169; each addl $10; under 12 free; lower rates rest of yr. Crib free. Pet accepted; $10. TV; cable (premium). Pool; whirlpool. Complimentary continental bkfst. Restaurant adj. Ck-out noon. Guest lndry. Business servs avail. In-rm modem link. Exercise equipt. Some refrigerators. Cr cds: A, C, D, DS, MC, V.

D

★★ **GEYSERVILLE INN.** *21714 Geyserville Ave, Geyserville (95441). 707/857-4343; fax 707/857-4411; toll-free 877/857-4343. www.geyservilleinn.com.* 38 rms, 2 story. Apr-Oct: S, D $99-$139; each addl $10; under 10 free; wkends (2-day min); lower rates rest of yr. Crib $10. TV; cable. Complimentary continental bkfst. Restaurant 9 am-5 pm. Ck-out 11 am. Business servs avail. In-rm modem link. Concierge. Gift shop. Pool; whirlpool. Many fireplaces. Some balconies. Surrounded by vineyards. Totally nonsmoking. Cr cds: A, DS, MC, V.

D SC

B&Bs/Small Inns

★★★ **BELLE DE JOUR INN.** *16276 Healdsburg Ave (95448). 707/431-9777; fax 707/431-7412. www.belledejourinn.com.* 5 cottages. S, D $150-$300. Complimentary full bkfst. Ck-out 11 am, ck-in 4-7 pm. Business servs avail. In-rm modem link. Many refrigerators, in-rm whirlpools, fireplaces. Balconies. Picnic tables. Hilltop setting on six acres. Totally nonsmoking. Cr cds: A, D, MC, V.

★★ **CAMELLIA INN.** *211 North St (95448). 707/433-8182; fax 707/433-8130; res 800/727-8182. www.camelliainn.com.* 9 rms, 2 story. No A/C. Some rm phones. S, D $179. Crib free. Heated pool. Complimentary full bkfst; eve refreshments. Ck-out 11 am, ck-in 3-6 pm. Business servs avail. In-rm modem link. Valet serv. Some in-rm whirlpools, fireplaces. Victorian house; antique furnishings. Town's first hospital. Totally nonsmoking. Cr cds: A, DS, MC, V.

★★ **GRAPE LEAF INN.** *539 Johnson St (95448). 707/433-8140; fax 707/433-3140. www.grapeleafinn.com.* 7 rms, 2 story. No rm phones. S, D $125-$250; each addl $35. Complimentary full bkfst; afternoon refreshments. Restaurant nearby. Ck-out 11 am, ck-in 4-6 pm. Some in-rm whirlpools. Picnic tables. Antiques. Sitting rm. Skylights. Victorian house (1900). Totally nonsmoking. Cr cds: DS, MC, V.

★★ **HAYDON STREET INN.** *321 Haydon St (95448). 707/433-5228; fax 707/433-6637; toll-free 800/528-3703. www.haydon.com.* 8 rms, 2 story. No rm phones. S $110; D $180; each addl $25. TV in sitting rm. Complimentary full bkfst; afternoon refreshments. Restaurant nearby. Ck-out 11 am, ck-in 3:30-6:30 pm. Business servs avail. Some in-rm whirlpools. Balconies. Picnic tables. Antiques. Sitting rm. Queen Anne/Victorian house (1912). Totally nonsmoking. Cr cds: DS, MC, V.

SC

★★★ **HEALDSBURG INN ON THE PLAZA.** *110 Matheson St (95448). 707/433-6991; fax 707/433-9513; toll-free 800/431-8663. www.healdsburginn.com.* 10 rms. S, D $255-$285; each addl $35. TV; cable, VCR (free movies). Complimentary full bkfst; afternoon refreshments. Ck-out 11 am, ck-in 3 pm. Business servs avail. Many fireplaces. Former Wells Fargo Express building, built 1901; antiques, artwork, stained glass. Enclosed solarium. Cr cds: DS, MC, V.

★★★ **HONOR MANSION.** *14891 Grove St (95448). 707/433-4277; fax 707/431-7173; toll-free 800/554-4667. www.honormansion.com.* 6 rms, 2 with shower only, 2 story. 1 rm phone. Mar-Dec: S, D $170-$250; suites $250-$270; each addl $25; 2-3-day min wkends, hols; lower rates rest of yr. TV in parlor; cable. Pool. Complimentary full bkfst; afternoon refreshments. Restaurant nearby. Ck-out 11 am, ck-in 3-7 pm. Bellhops. Concierge serv. Lawn games. Minibars. Microwaves avail. Picnic tables. Italianate

Victorian house built in 1883. Totally nonsmoking. Cr cds: DS, MC, V.

★★★ **MADRONA MANOR.** *1001 Westside Rd (95448). 707/433-4231; fax 707/433-0703; toll-free 800/258-4003. www.madronamanor.com.* 21 rms, 2-3 story, 3 suites. S, D $165-$285; suites $295-$445; under 6 free. Crib $15. Pool. Complimentary full bkfst. Restaurant (see also MADRONA MANOR). Ck-out 11 am, ck-in 3 pm. Business servs avail. Bellhops. Concierge serv. Many fireplaces. Balconies. Picnic area. Antiques. Sitting rm. Built 1881. Extensive gardens. Fountain. Cr cds: A, C, D, DS, MC, V.

D

Restaurants

★★ **BISTRO RALPH.** *109 Plaza St (95448). 707/433-1380.* Hrs: 11:30 am-2:30 pm; 5:30-closing. Closed Thanksgiving, Dec 25. Res accepted. Wine, beer. A la carte entrees: lunch $6-$12, dinner $12-$18. Specialties: Campbell Ranch lamb, Caesar salad. Outdoor dining. Contemporary and casual atmosphere. Totally nonsmoking. Cr cds: MC, V.

D

★ **CATELLI'S THE REX.** *241 Healdsburg (95448). 707/433-6000. www.catellistherex.com.* Hrs: noon-2 pm, 5-9 pm; Fri to 9:30; Sat 5-9:30; Sun from 5 pm. Closed Mon; hols. Res accepted. Italian menu. Bar 11:30 am-9 pm. Lunch $6.95-$11.95, dinner $12.95-$24.95. Children's menu. Specialties: fresh seafood, lobster ravioli. Outdoor dining. Family-owned. Totally nonsmoking. Cr cds: DS, MC, V.

D

★★★ **CHATEAU SOUVERAIN.** *400 Souverain Rd, Geyserville (95441). 707/433-3141. www.chateausouverain.com.* Hrs: 11:30 am-2:30 pm, 5:30-8:30 pm. Closed Mon-Thurs; Thanksgiving, Dec 24, 25; also Jan. Res required. Country French menu. Wine cellar. A la carte entrees: lunch $10.75-$13.75, dinner $14-$19.95. Specialties: wild mushroom penne pasta with rock shrimp, roast leg of lamb, fresh ancho chile pepper tagliarini. Outdoor dining. View of valley, vineyards. Totally nonsmoking. Cr cds: A, DS, MC, V.

D

★ **EL FAROLITO.** *128 Plaza St (95448). 707/433-2807.* Hrs: 10:30 am-9 pm. Closed Jan 1, Easter, Thanksgiving, Dec 25. Res accepted. Mexican menu. Wine, beer. Bkfst $6-$7, lunch, dinner $6.50-$7.50. Children's menu. Specializes in carnitas. Cr cds: A, DS, MC, V.

★★ **FELIX AND LOUIE'S.** *106 Matheson St (95448). 707/433-6966.* Hrs: 11:30 am-9 pm, Fri, Sat to 11 pm. Closed Dec 25. Italian, American menu. Bar to midnight. A la carte entrees: lunch $7.95-$14, dinner $9.95-$21. Children's menu. Specializes in wood-burning oven pizza. Own pasta. Parking. Outdoor dining. Totally nonsmoking. Cr cds: MC, V.

D

★ **LOTUS.** *109 Plaza St #A (95448). 707/433-5282.* Hrs: 11:30 am-2:30 pm, 5-9:30 pm. Closed Mon; Thanksgiving, Dec 25. Res accepted. Thai menu. Wine, beer. A la carte entrees: lunch $5.95-$8.50, dinner $8.50-$13.95. Specialties: pad thai, plamuk gapow. Thai decor. Totally nonsmoking. Cr cds: A, DS, MC, V.

D

★★ **MADRONA MANOR.** *1001 Westside Rd (95448). 707/433-4231. www.madronamanor.com.* Hrs: 6-9 pm. Res accepted. Prix-fixe: dinner $40-$48. Specializes in wine country cuisine. Outdoor dining. Dining rms overlook extensive gardens. Formal dining in Victorian mansion. Totally nonsmoking. Cr cds: MC, V.

D

★ **RAVENOUS.** *117 North St (95448). 707/431-1770.* Hrs: 11:30 am-2:30 pm, 5-9 pm; Fri, Sat to 9:30 pm. Closed Mon, Tues; Easter, Thanksgiving, Dec 25. Wine, beer. A la carte entrees: lunch $7.50-$11.50, dinner $12.50-$16. Specialties: roast pork tenderloin, Ravenous burger, duck breast. Totally nonsmoking. Cr cds: A, MC, V.

D

★ **WESTERN BOOT STEAK HOUSE.** *9 Mitchell Ln (95448). 707/433-6362.* Hrs: 11:30 am-9 pm, Fri to 10 pm; Sat 4-10 pm, Sun 4-9 pm. Closed hols. Res accepted. Wine, beer. Lunch $4.95-$9.95, dinner $7.95-$23. Children's menu. Specializes in steak, ribs, seafood. Parking. Cr cds: A, MC, V.

D

Hearst-San Simeon State Historical Monument (Hearst Castle)

(C-2) *See also Cambria, San Simeon*

Information Hearst Castle, 750 Hearst Castle Rd, San Simeon 93452; 805/927-2020 or 800/444-4445 (res)

Web www.hearstcastle.org

Crowning La Cuesta Encantada—the Enchanted Hill—is a princely domain of castle, guest houses, theater, pools, and tennis courts created by William Randolph Hearst as his home and retreat. After his death in 1951, the estate was given to the state as a memorial to the late publisher's mother, Phoebe Adderson Hearst. For years Hearst Castle could be glimpsed by the public only through a telescope at the nearby village of San Simeon, but today it is open to the public. A "carefully planned, deliberate attempt to create a shrine of beauty," it was begun in 1919 under the direction of noted architect Julia Morgan. An army of workers built the castle with its twin towers and surrounded it with formal Mediterranean gardens; construction continued for 28 years. And, though three guest houses and 115 rooms of the main house were completed, there was still much more Hearst had hoped to build.

Items collected by Hearst can be viewed in the castle and on the grounds. Features of the castle itself are the Refectory, an unbelievable "long, high, noble room" with a hand-carved ceiling and life-size statues of saints, silk banners from Siena, and 15th-century choir stalls from a Spanish cathedral; the Assembly Room, with priceless tapestries; and the lavish theater where the latest motion pictures were shown.

The estate includes three luxurious "guest houses"; the Neptune Pool, with a colonnade leading to an ancient Roman temple facade and an array of marble statuary; an indoor pool, magnificent gardens, fountains, walkways and, of course, the main house of 115 rooms.

Visitors may explore an exhibit on the life and times of William Randolph Hearst inside the Visitor Center at the bottom of the hill. Also here is an iWERKS giant-screen theater showing "Hearst Castle: Building the Dream," a 40-minute film detailing the rich history and architectural precedents of Hearst and his estate (phone 805/927-6811). Food and gift concessions are also located here. There is an area to observe artifact restoration in progress; entrance to the exhibit is free.

Parking is available in a lot near CA 1, where buses transport visitors to the castle. Access to the castle and grounds is by guided tour only. Tour One takes in the grounds, a guest house, the pools, and the lower level of the main house; Tour Two visits the upper levels of the main house, which include Hearst's private suite; Tour Three covers the north wing and a guest house and includes a video about the construction of the castle; Tour Four (available April-October) is spent mostly outside in the gardens and around the pools but also includes behind-the-scenes areas such as the wine cellar and two floors of the largest guest house. Evening tours are available for selected evenings in the spring and fall; evening tours take in the highlights of the estate and include a living history program developed to give visitors a glimpse of life at the "Castle" in the early 1930s. All tours include the outdoor and indoor pools.

Day tours take approximately one hour and 45 minutes; evening tours take approximately two hours and 15 minutes. No pets. Reservations are recommended and are available up to eight weeks in advance by calling 800/444-4445. Tickets are also available at the ticket office in the visitor center. Tours entail much walking and stair climbing; wheelchairs can be accommodated under certain con-

Hearst Castle, San Simeon

ditions and with ten days advance notice by calling 805/927-2020; strollers cannot be accommodated. (Daily; closed Jan 1, Thanksgiving, Dec 25) ¢¢¢¢

Hemet

(E-6) *See also Palm Springs, Riverside*

Founded 1890 **Pop** 36,094 **Elev** 1,596 ft **Area code** 909

Located in the beautiful San Jacinto Valley, Hemet was once the largest producer of alfalfa and herbs in the country. Today it is near the hub of an area that includes ocean, desert, mountains, lakes, health resorts, and springs, along with neighboring historic Native American reservations and large cattle ranches, all within an hour's drive.

What to See and Do

San Jacinto Valley Museum. Permanent and temporary exhibits of genealogy, Native American archaeology, and a variety of historical items of San Jacinto Valley. (Thurs-Sat, afternoons; closed Jan 1, Thanksgiving, Dec 25) 181 E Main St, 3 mi N in San Jacinto. Phone 909/654-4952. **FREE**

Special Events

Ramona Pageant. Ramona Bowl is a 6,662-seat outdoor amphitheater built into the side of a mountain. Beautiful setting among the rolling hills, where most of the action of Helen Hunt Jackson's story takes place. More than 350 persons participate in this romance of early California, presented annually since 1923. Contact Ramona Pageant Association, 27400 Ramona Bowl Rd, 92544. Phone 800/645-4465. Three wkends late Apr-early May.

Farmers Fair. Lake Perris Fairgrounds, 10 mi W on CA 74 in Perris. Competitions and exhibits, food, activities, entertainment. Phone 909/657-4221. Mid-Oct.

Motels/Motor Lodges

★★ **BEST WESTERN HEMET.** *2625 W Florida Ave (92545). 909/925-6605; res 800/528-1234.* 68 rms, 2 story, 29 kits. S $49; D $52-$100; each addl $6; suites $89; kit. units $52-$100; wkly, monthly rates; higher rates: Ramona Pageant, special events. Crib $4. Pet accepted, some restrictions; $10. TV; cable (premium). Heated pool; whirlpool. Complimentary bkfst. Coffee in rms. Restaurant adj open 24 hrs. Ck-out 11 am. Coin lndry. Business servs avail. Health club privileges. Lawn games. Refrigerators; microwaves avail. Grills. Cr cds: A, C, D, DS, ER, JCB, MC, V.

D

★ **HEMET SUPER 8.** *3510 W Florida Ave (92545). 909/658-2281; fax 909/925-6492; res 800/800-8000.* 70 rms, 3 story. Oct-Apr: S $38.88; D $46.88; each addl $4; suites $54.88; under 12 free; lower rates rest of yr. Crib free. TV; cable (premium), VCR avail. Pool; whirlpool. Complimentary continental bkfst. Restaurant nearby. Ck-out 11 am. Business servs avail. Health club privileges. Refrigerators; microwaves avail. Cr cds: A, C, D, DS, JCB, MC, V.

D

★ **TRAVELODGE.** *1201 W Florida Ave (92543). 909/766-1902; fax 909/766-7739; res 800/578-7878.* 46 rms, 2 story. S $38; D $43; suites $38-$43. Crib $5. Pet accepted, some restrictions; $5. TV; cable (premium), VCR avail. Pool; whirlpool. Complimentary continental bkfst. Restaurant opp 6 am-10 pm. Ck-out noon. Meeting rms. Coin lndry. Health club privileges. Refrigerators; microwaves avail. Cr cds: A, C, D, DS, ER, JCB, MC, V.
D

Restaurant

★★ **DATTILO.** *2288 E Florida Ave (92544). 909/658-4248.* Hrs: 11 am-9 pm; Sat from 4 pm; Sun to 8 pm. Closed Mon; hols. Italian menu. Bar. Bkfst $2.99-$5.99, lunch $3.99-$6.99, dinner $5.99-$19.99. Children's menu. Specialties: lasagna, ravioli, rack of lamb. Cr cds: A, D, DS, MC, V.
D

Hollywood (L.A.)

See also Los Angeles

Elev 385 ft **Area code** 213,323

Information Chamber of Commerce, 7018 Hollywood Blvd, 90028; 323/469-8311; or Hollywood Convention & Visitors Information Center, 685 S. Figueroa St; 213/689-8822

Web www.hollywoodchamber.net

Known as the "Entertainment Capital of the World," Hollywood is the birthplace of the motion picture industry and home to much of the movie and television industry today. Often thought of as a separate city, Hollywood is actually a neighborhood of Los Angeles.

What to See and Do

Barnsdall Art Park. Named after socialite Aline Barnsdall, who commisioned Frank Lloyd Wright to build her home and later gave the property to the city of Los Angeles. (Daily) 4808 Hollywood Blvd. Phone 213/485-8665. **FREE** Within the park are

Hollyhock House. Built by Wright from 1919-1921, the house was given its name for Aline Barnsdall's favorite flower. Extensive outdoor courtyards and terraces were designed by Wright to extend living spaces to outdoors. Closed for renovation through 2003. Phone 213/662-7272. ¢

Municipal Art Gallery. Features work by regional and local artists. Phone 213/485-4581. ¢

Hollywood Boulevard. "Main Street" of moviedom. Hollywood and Vine is one of the most famous intersections in the world.

Hollywood Bowl. Huge outdoor amphitheater, where 250,000 hear "Symphony Under the Stars" each summer. 2301 N Highland Ave, just SW of Hollywood Fwy. Phone 323/850-2000.

Hollywood Entertainment Museum. Showcases contributions of film, TV, radio, and recording industries through state-of-the-art exhibits and shows. Traces Hollywood's evolution as "Entertainment Capital." Incl complete set from *Cheers,* also the "bridge" from *Starship Enterprise.* (Labor Day-Memorial Day, Mon, Tues, Thurs-Sun; rest of yr, daily; closed hols) 7021 Hollywood Blvd. Phone 323/465-7900. ¢¢¢

Hollywood Forever Cemetery. Crypts of Tyrone Power, Cecil B. De Mille, Rudolph Valentino, Douglas Fairbanks, Sr., Nelson Eddy, and Norma Talmadge, as well as other famous stars, statesmen, and industrialists. (Daily) On the grounds at 6000 Santa Monica Blvd. Phone 323/469-1181. **FREE**

Hollywood Heritage Museum. Dedicated to preserving the history of Hollywood's silent film era. Site of Hollywood's first feature-length Western, *The Squaw Man,* in 1913. Costumes, props, photographs, early movie artifacts. Gift shop. (Sat and Sun; closed hols) 2100 N Highland Blvd. Phone 323/874-4005. ¢¢

Hollywood Wax Museum. More than 170 famous people of the past and present re-created in wax. Presidents, movie stars, Western scenes; theater. (Daily) 6767 Hollywood Blvd. Phone 323/462-8860. ¢¢¢

Mann's Chinese Theatre. Historic movie palace; scene of spectacular opening nights for decades. Theatre's famous cement forecourt has stars' footprints, hand prints, and autographs (since 1927). 6925 Hollywood Blvd, between Highland and LaBrea. Phone 323/464-8111.

Universal Studios Hollywood. (See LOS ANGELES) Phone 818/622-3801.

Walk of Fame. The world's most famous sidewalk, with more than 2,000 stars embedded in charcoal and coral-colored terrazzo strip along Hollywood's main business district. Honors celebrities from film, television, radio, recording, and live stage. From LaBrea to Gower along Hollywood Blvd, and from Yucca to Sunset along Vine St. Phone 323/469-8311. **FREE**

Westwood Memorial Cemetery. (See WESTWOOD VILLAGE)

Special Events

Easter Sunrise Services. Hollywood Bowl. Interdenominational service with music of select choral groups. Phone 323/850-2000.

Hollywood Christmas Parade. Features floats, marching bands; over 50 of Hollywood's famous stars. Televised world wide. Sun after Thanksgiving.

Motels/Motor Lodges

★★ **BEST WESTERN INN.** *6141 Franklin Ave (90028). 323/464-5181; fax 323/962-0536; res 800/528-1234.* 86 rms, 3-4 story. S $79-$89; D $89-$119; each addl $5; under 12 free; wkly rates; higher rates Rose Bowl. Crib $5. Pet accepted, some restrictions; $25. Heated pool. TV; cable (premium). Restaurant 7 am-10 pm. Ck-out noon. Business servs avail. Sundries. Coin lndry. Some refrigerators, microwaves wet bars. Cr cds: A, C, D, DS, MC, V.

D

★★ **RAMADA - HOLLYWOOD / UNIVERSAL STUDIOS.** *1160 N Vermont Ave, Hollywood (90029). 323/660-1788; fax 323/660-8069; res 800/272-6232. www.ramadahollywood.com.* 130 rms, 8 with shower only, 4 story. S $99-$109; D $99-$129; suites $99-$139; kit. units $159-$199; under 18 free; family rates; package plans. Crib free. Parking fee. TV; cable (premium). Complimentary continental bkfst. Restaurant 6:30 am-11 pm. Bar from 3 pm. Ck-out noon. Meeting rms. Business servs avail. Bellhops. Valet serv. Sundries. Gift shop. Coin lndry. Exercise equipt; steam rms, saunas. Heated pool. Game rm. Many refrigerators, microwaves. Many balconies. Cr cds: A, C, D, DS, ER, JCB, MC, V.

D SC

★★ **RAMADA INN.** *8585 Santa Monica Blvd, West Hollywood (90069). 310/652-6400; fax 310/652-2135; res 800/272-6232. www.ramada-wh.com.* 175 rms, 4 story, 44 suites. S, D $109-$149; each addl $15; suites $159-$279; under 16 free. Crib free. TV; cable (premium), VCR avail. Heated pool. Coffee in rms. Restaurant 6:30 am-11:30 pm. Bar. Ck-out noon. Coin lndry. Business servs avail. Shopping arcade. Airport transportation. Health club privileges. Bathrm phones, refrigerators; some wetbars; microwaves avail. Some balconies. Cr cds: A, C, D, DS, JCB, MC, V.

D SC

★ **SUPER 8 - HOLLYWOOD.** *1536 N Western Ave (90027). 323/467-3131; fax 323/467-5258; res 800/800-8000.* 54 rms, 4 story. S $47-$57; D $57-$64; each addl $5. TV; cable (premium). Complimentary continental bkfst. Restaurant nearby. Ck-out 11 am. Business servs avail. Some refrigerators. Cr cds: A, C, D, DS, JCB, MC, V.

D

Hotels

★★★ **THE ARGYLE HOTEL.** *8358 Sunset Blvd, West Hollywood (90069). 323/654-7100; fax 323/654-9287; toll-free 800/225-2637. www.argylehotel.com.* 64 rms, 15 story, 44 suites. S $240; D $300; suites $545-$1200; wkend rates. Crib free. Valet parking $18. TV; cable (premium), VCR (movies). Heated pool; poolside serv. Complimentary coffee in lobby. Restaurant (see also FENIX). Rm serv 24 hrs. Bar 11-1:30 am. Ck-out 1 pm. Meeting rms. Business servs avail. In-rm modem link. Concierge. Exercise rm; sauna. Massage. Bathrm phones, refrigerators, minibars; some in-rm whirlpools, wet bars; microwaves avail. Some balconies. Cr cds: A, D, DS, MC, V.

D

★★ **CHATEAU MARMONT.** *8221 Sunset Blvd, Hollywood (90046). 323/656-1010; fax 323/655-5311; res 800/242-8328.* 63 rms, 7 story, 54 kits. S $220; D $290; suites $240-$1,200; cottages, kits. $260; villas $600; monthly rates. Pet accepted. TV; cable (premium), VCR. Heated pool; poolside serv. Restaurant 6-2 am. Rm serv 24 hrs. Ck-out noon. Meeting rm. Business servs avail. In-rm modem link. Garage, valet parking. Exercise equipt. Refrigerators, minibars. Private patios, balconies. Neo-Gothic chateau-style building; old Hollywood landmark. Cr cds: A, D, MC, V.

★★ **HOLLYWOOD ROOSEVELT HOTEL.** *7000 Hollywood Blvd, Hollywood (90028). 323/466-7000; fax 323/462-8056; res 800/950-7667.* 320 rms, 2-12 story, 47 suites. S, D $159-$199; each addl $20; suites $299-$1,500; under 18 free. Crib free. Valet parking $9.90. TV; cable (premium), VCR avail. Heated pool; whirlpool, poolside serv. Coffee in rms. Restaurant 6 am-11 pm. Rm serv to 1 am. Bars 11-1 am; entertainment. Convention facilities. Business servs avail. Concierge. Gift shop. Exercise equipt. Massage. Minibars; some bathrm phones; refrigerators, microwaves avail. Site of first Academy Awards presentation. Cr cds: A, C, D, DS, ER, JCB, MC, V.

D

★★★ **HYATT WEST HOLLYWOOD.** *8401 Sunset Blvd, West Hollywood (90069). 323/656-1234.* 262 rms, 14 story; 21 suites. S, D $155-$350; each addl $25; under 17 free. Crib avail. Pet accepted. Valet parking. Heated pool. TV; cable (premium), VCR avail. Complimentary coffee in rms, newspaper. Restaurant 6 am-10:30 pm. Bar. Ck-out noon. Meeting rms. Business center. Valet serv. Gift shop. Exercise rm. Some refrigerators, minibars. Cr cds: A, C, D, DS, MC, V.

★★ **LE MONTROSE SUITE HOTEL.** *900 Hammond St, West Hollywood (90069). 310/855-1115; fax 310/657-9192; toll-free 800/776-0666. www.lemontrose.com.* 132 kit. suites, 5 story. Suites $270-$575; under 18 free. Crib free. Covered parking $15. Pet accepted. TV; cable (premium), VCR avail. Pool; whirlpool, poolside serv. Restaurant 5 am-10:45 pm. Rm serv 24 hrs. Ck-out noon. Meeting rm. Business servs avail. In-rm modem link. Concierge. Lighted tennis, pro. Exercise rm; sauna. Massage. Bathrm phones, refrigerators, fireplaces; many wet bars; microwaves avail. Some balconies. Art Nouveau decor. Cr cds: A, D, DS, JCB, MC, V.

D

★★★ **MONDRIAN.** *8440 Sunset Blvd, West Hollywood (90069). 323/650-8999; fax 323/650-5215; toll-free 800/525-8029. www.mondrianhotel.com.* 245 rms, 12 story. S, D $225-$445; under 12 free. Covered parking $20. TV; cable (premium), VCR. Heated pool; whirlpool, poolside serv. Restaurant 7 am-11:30 pm. Rm serv 24 hrs. Bar 11-2 am. Ck-out noon. Business center. In-rm modem link. Concierge. Exercise equipt; sauna. Minibars, wet bars. Some balconies. Contemporary decor. Cr cds: A, D, MC, V.

D

★★★ **SUNSET MARQUIS HOTEL & VILLAS.** *1200 N Alta Loma Rd, West Hollywood (90069). 310/657-1333; fax 310/652-5300; toll-free 800/858-9758. www.sunsetmarquishotel.com.* 114 suites, 10 with kit., 3 story, 12 villas. Suites, kit. units $260-$450; each addl $30; villas $450-$1,200; under 12 free. Crib free. Valet parking $15. TV; cable (premium), VCR avail (movies). 2 heated pools; whirlpool, poolside serv. Restaurant 7 am-10 pm. Rm serv 24 hrs. Bar. Ck-out 1 pm. Meeting rm. Business center. In-rm modem link. Concierge. Butler serv avail. Exercise equipt; sauna, steam rm. Massage. Refrigerators; microwaves avail; some in-rm steam baths; wet bar in suites; bathrm phones in villas. Private patios, balconies. Recording studio. Cr cds: A, C, D, DS, MC, V.

D

All Suite

★★ **WYNDHAM BEL AGE HOTEL.** *1020 N San Vicente Blvd, West Holly-*

wood (90069). 310/854-1111; fax 310/854-0926. www.wyndham.com. 200 suites, 10 story. S, D $229-$259; each addl $25; under 18 free; wkend rates. Valet parking $18. TV; cable (premium), VCR avail. Heated pool; poolside serv. Restaurants 7 am-11 pm. Rm serv 24 hrs. Bar 11-2 am; jazz Thurs-Sat, Sun brunch. Ck-out 1 pm. Convention facilities. Business servs avail. In-rm modem link. Concierge. Shopping arcade. Barber, beauty shop. Exercise equipt. Bathrm phones, wet bars; microwaves avail. Private patios, balconies. Cr cds: A, C, D, DS, ER, JCB, MC, V.

D SC

Restaurants

★★★ **AGO.** *8478 Melrose Ave, West Hollywood (90069). 323/655-6333.* Specializes in bistecca alla fiortina, baby rack of lamb, tagliatella with artichokes. Hrs: noon-2:30 pm, 6-11 pm; Fri, Sat to 11:30 pm; Sun 6-10 pm. Res accepted. Wine, beer. Lunch, dinner $9-$38. Entertainment. Jacket. Cr cds: A, C, D, JCB, MC, V.

D

★★ **ALTO PALATO TRATTORIA.** *755 N La Cienega Blvd (90069). 310/657-9271. www.alto-palato.com.* Hrs: 6-11 pm; Fri noon-2:30 pm, 6-11 pm; Sun 5-10:30 pm. Closed Jan 1, Thanksgiving, Dec 25. Res accepted. Italian menu. Bar. A la carte entrees: lunch, dinner $9.50-$29. Specialties: wood-fired pizza, pumpkin gnocchi, sauteed breast of chicken. Own pasta, desserts. Valet parking. Outdoor dining. Two-story; Italian cafe atmosphere. Cr cds: A, C, D, DS, ER, MC, V.

D

★★ **ANTONIO'S.** *7470 Melrose Ave, West Hollywood (90046). 323/655-0480.* Hrs: 11 am-11 pm; Sat from noon; Sun noon-10 pm. Closed Mon; Thanksgiving, Dec 25. Res accepted. Mexican menu. Bar. A la carte entrees: lunch, dinner $8.50-$15.95. Specialties: pollo Yucateco, blue corn tamales with spinach. Strolling musicians wkend evenings. Valet parking. Outdoor dining. Colorful Mexican decor. Family-owned. Cr cds: A, MC, V.

D

★★ **ASIA DE CUBA.** *8440 Sunset Blvd, West Hollywood (90069). 323/848-6000.* Combination of Asian and Cuban food menu. Specializes in calamari salad, tuna pica, miso glazed salmon. Hrs: 7 am-3:30 pm, 5:30-11:30 pm; Thurs-Sat to 1 am; Sun to 10:30 pm. Res accepted. Wine list. Lunch $30; dinner $55. Entertainment. City view. Cr cds: A, C, D, MC, V.

D

★★ **CA'BREA.** *346 S La Brea Ave (90036). 323/938-2863.* Hrs: 11:30 am-2:30 pm, 5:30-10 pm; Fri, Sat to 11:30 pm. Closed Sun. Res accepted. Northern Italian menu. Bar. A la carte entrees: lunch, dinner $8.95-$22.95. Specializes in authentic Venetian dishes. Own pasta, desserts. Valet parking. Patio dining. Italian cafe decor. Totally nonsmoking. Cr cds: A, D, DS, MC, V.

D

★★ **CHAYA BRASSERIE.** *8741 Alden Dr, West Hollywood (90048). 310/859-8833.* Specializes in chaya ribeye steak, sliced roasted venison. Hrs: 11:30 am-2:30 pm, 6-10:30 pm. Res accepted. Wine, beer. Lunch $13.50-$16.50; dinner $16.50-$27.50. Entertainment. Cr cds: A, C, D, ER, MC.

D

★★ **CHIANTI RISTORANTE AND CUCINA.** *7383 Melrose Ave (90046). 323/653-8333.* Hrs: Cucina 11:30 am-11:30 pm; Fri, Sat to midnight; Sun 4-11 pm. Chianti 5:30-11:30 pm; Fri, Sat to midnight; Sun 5-10:30 pm. Closed Thanksgiving, Dec 25. Res accepted. Northern Italian menu. Bar. A la carte entrees: Cucina: lunch, dinner $6.75-$18.95; Chianti: lunch, dinner $10.95-$24.50. Specializes in fresh seafood, pasta. Own baking. Valet parking. Two distinct dining areas. Totally nonsmoking. Cr cds: A, D, MC, V.

D

★★ **DAN TANA'S.** *9071 Santa Monica Blvd, West Hollywood (90069). 310/275-9444.* Hrs: 5 pm-1 am; Sun to 12:30 am. Closed Thanksgiving, Dec 25. Res required. Northern Italian menu. Bar. A la carte entrees: dinner $15-$39. Specializes in NY prime steak, whitefish. Valet parking.

2 dining areas. New York-style Italian restaurant with fireplace. Family-owned. Totally nonsmoking. Cr cds: A, C, D, DS, MC, V.

★★★ **FENIX.** *8358 Sunset Blvd, West Hollywood (90069). 323/848-6677. www.argylehotel.com.* French, California menu. Specializes in tuna in rice paper, gulf red snapper, duck. Hrs: 7 am-2:30 pm, 6-11 pm; Fri, Sat to midnight; Sun brunch 10 am-3 pm. Res accepted. Bar. Extensive wine list. A la carte entrees: bkfst $7.95-$10.50, lunch $7-$16.50, dinner $16.50-$25. Sun brunch $16-$21. Valet parking. Outdoor dining. Cr cds: A, D, DS, MC, V.

D

★★★ **INDOCHINE.** *8225 Beverly Blvd, Hollywood (90048). 323/655-4777.* French flair menu. Specializes in crispy filet of salmon with lemongrass braised cabbage, grilled whole prawn with ginger, scallions and angel hair noodles. Hrs: 6-11 pm. Res accepted. Wine, beer. Dinner $12-$20. Entertainment. Cr cds: A, D, MC, V.

D

★★ **THE IVY.** *113 N Robertson Blvd (90048). 310/274-8303.* Specializes in grilled vegetable salad, crab cakes, cajune shrimp. Hrs: 11:30 am-10 pm; Sun from 11 am. Res required. Wine, beer. Lunch $18-$27; dinner $22-$35. Entertainment. Cr cds: A, C, D, DS, MC, V.

D

★★★ **JOZU.** *8360 Melrose Ave, West Hollywood (90069). 323/655-5600. www.jozu.com.* Hrs: Mon-Fri 6-10 pm, Sat 5:30-11 pm, Sun 5:30-9:30 pm. Prices $18-$27. Bar. California menu with Asian influence. Specialties: Chilean sea bass, tomato and crab salad with green mangoes and musaman curry vinaigrette, lobster with beet salad and chili lime vinaigrette. Cr cds: A, D, DS, MC, V.

D

★★★ **LA BOHEME.** *8400 Santa Monica, West Hollywood (90069). 323/848-2360. www.calendarline.com/laboheme.* Specializes in New Zealand snapper, filet of beef, roasted rack of lamb. Hrs: 5:30-10 pm; Fri, Sat 5-11 pm. Res accepted. Wine, beer. Dinner $17-$29. Entertainment. Cr cds: A, D, DS, MC, V.

D

★★★ **LE COLONIAL.** *8783 Beverly Blvd, West Hollywood (90048). 310/289-0660.* Specializes in vegetarian, beef. Hrs: 11 am-10 pm. Res required. Wine, beer. Lunch $14-$18; dinner $18-$28. Entertainment. Cr cds: A, D, MC, V.

D

★★ **LE DOME.** *8720 Sunset Blvd (90069). 310/659-6919.* Hrs: noon-midnight; Sat from 6 pm. Closed Sun; hols. Res accepted. French, continental menu. Bar. Wine list. A la carte entrees: lunch $11.75-$19.75, dinner $14-$30. Specializes in fresh fish, prime beef. Own desserts. Valet parking. Outdoor dining. Art Noveau decor. Cr cds: A, D, MC, V.

D

★ **LE PETIT FOUR.** *8654 Sunset Blvd, Hollywood (90069). 310/652-3863. www.lepetitfour.com.* Hrs: 11-1 am; Sat 9-2 am; Sun from 9 am; Sun brunch to 6 pm. Closed Dec 25. Res accepted. Continental menu. Bar. A la carte entrees: lunch, dinner $5.50-$17.50. Sun brunch $4.50-$10.25. Specializes in fresh fish, pasta, salad. Own baking, ice cream. Outdoor dining. Sidewalk dining area has bistro atmosphere. Cr cds: A, D, MC, V.

D

★★ **LOLA'S.** *945 N Fairfax Ave, West Hollywood (90046). 213/736-5652. www.lolasla.com.* Hrs: 5:30 pm-2 am. Closed Thanksgiving, Dec 24, 25. Res accepted. Bar. Dinner $6-$16.50. Specialties: grilled pork chop, baked macaroni and cheese, chocolate kiss cake. Own desserts. Valet parking. Skylights, chandeliers. Totally nonsmoking. Cr cds: A, D, MC, V.

D

★★★★ **L'ORANGERIE.** *903 N La Cienega Blvd, Hollywood (90069). 310/652-9770. www.orangerie.com.* A bit of Versailles' luxurious aura seems to inhabit Southern California in the form of this opulent, formal French dining room—a favored choice among Angelenos for special occasions for 20 years. The current chef, young and talented Ludovic Lefebvre, has kept the menu very French while adding contemporary touches evidenced in dishes like beef tenderloin roasted with six peppers and grilled Maine lobster with sesame and sumac. Service is formal, and be prepared, the L'Orangerie experience comes at a price. Contemporary French menu. Specialties: eggs in the shell with caviar; whole roasted rock lobster; fideos with small shellfish in cinnamon butter, lamb medallion with cardamom, paste of caper, and grape; baby bell pepper stuffed with eggplant and artichokes; peach tart with verbena ice cream. Hrs: 6-11 pm. Closed Mon. Extensive wine list. Bar. Res required. A la carte entrees: $32-$45. Degustation menu: $85, vegetarian: $50. Valet parking. Jacket required, tie optional. Terrace and patio dining on the courtyard. Cr cds: A, C, D, DS, ER, MC, V.

D

★★★ **MORTON'S.** *8764 Melrose Ave (90069). 310/276-5205 www.mortons.com.* Hrs: noon-3 pm, 6-11 pm; Sat from 6 pm. Closed Sun; hols. Res accepted. Bar to 1 am. Wine cellar. A la carte entrees: lunch $11-$19, dinner $20-$29. Specialties: tuna sashimi, grilled marinated lamb loin, lime grilled free-range chicken. Own desserts. Valet parking. Modern decor. Totally nonsmoking. Cr cds: A, D, DS, MC, V.

D

★ **MUSSO & FRANK GRILL.** *6667 Hollywood Blvd, Hollywood (90028). 323/467-5123.* Hrs: 11 am-11 pm. Closed Sun, Mon; hols. Res accepted. Continental menu. Bar. A la carte entrees: lunch, dinner $4.95-$29.50. Specialties: bouillabaisse Marseillaise, homemade chicken pot pie. Own desserts. Menu changes daily. Historic restaurant opened 1919. Famed "Round Table" of Saroyan, Thurber, Faulkner, and Fitzgerald met here.

Walk of Fame, Los Angeles

Totally nonsmoking. Cr cds: A, C, D, MC, V.

D

★★ **PALM.** *9001 Santa Monica Blvd (90069). 310/550-8811. www.thepalm.com.* Hrs: noon-10:30 pm; Sat from 5 pm; Sun 5-9:30 pm. Closed hols. Res accepted. Bar. A la carte entrees: lunch $10-$18, dinner $15-$30. Specializes in steak, lobster. Valet parking. Several dining areas. Hollywood celebrity caricatures cover walls. Totally nonsmoking. Cr cds: A, D, DS, MC, V.

D

★★★★ **PATINA.** *5955 Melrose Ave, Newport Beach (90038). 323/467-1108.* Los Angeles's premier chef, Joachim Splichal, is responsible for this excellent California/French restaurant where everything from plate presentations to decor to service is meant to impress. Look for dishes that make the most of California's exceptional array of ingredients interpreted through Splichal's French lens. Add a major wine list to complete the picture. California French menu. Hrs: 6-9:30 pm; also Tues noon-2 pm. Bar. Lunch $16-$18, dinner $29-$34. Res required. Jacket. Cr cds: A, D, DS, MC, V.

D

★★ **SONORA CAFE.** *180 S La Brea Ave (90036). 323/857-1800. www.sonoracafe.com.* Hrs: 11:30 am-10 pm; Fri to 11 pm; Sat 5:30-11 pm; Sun 5-9 pm. Closed hols. Res accepted. Southwestern menu. Bar. Wine list. Lunch $9.95-$16.95, dinner $14.25-$24.95. Specialties: Prince Edward Island mussels, Texas barbecue pork chops, wood-grilled sea scallops. Own desserts. Valet parking. Outdoor dining. Southwestern dcor; original Southwestern and early American artwork; fireplace. Cr cds: A, C, D, DS, ER, MC, V.

D

★★★ **YUJEAN KANG'S.** *8826 Melrose Ave, West Hollywood (90069). 310/288-0806.* Hrs: noon-2:30 pm, 5:30-11 pm; Sat, Sun from 5:30 pm. Closed Thanksgiving. Res accepted. Chinese menu. Bar. Wine cellar. Lunch $8-$13, dinner $13.95-$18.95. Specialties: Chilean sea bass in spicy sesame sauce, crispy flank steak, lamb loin. Valet parking. Asian decor; antiques. Totally nonsmoking. Cr cds: A, D, DS, MC, V.

Unrated Dining Spot

HOLLYWOOD HILLS COFFEE SHOP. *6145 Franklin Ave, Hollywood (90028). 323/467-7678.* Specializes in huevos rancheros, meatloaf, green corn tamale. Hrs: 7 am-10 pm. Res accepted. Wine, beer. Bkfst $6.95-$10.95; lunch, dinner $6.95-$10.95. Children's menu. Entertainment. Cr cds: A, DS, MC, V.

Humboldt Redwoods State Park

(C-1) *See also Garberville, Redwood Highway*

(45 mi S of Eureka via US 101)

Park encompasses more than 52,000 acres, including 17,000 acres of old growth coastal redwoods. The Avenue of the Giants, site of redwoods over 300 feet tall, parallels US 101 and passes through the park. The South Fork of the Eel River follows the Avenue through the park. Recreation includes swimming, fishing, nature hiking, mountain biking, and camping. Humboldt Redwoods State Park has a visitor center located next to park headquarters. Park headquarters is at Burlington, 2 mi S of Weott on the Avenue. Campfire and nature programs are offered (summer). Standard fees. Contact PO Box 100, Weott 95571; 707/946-2409.

Pacific Lumber Company. A cooperative agreement in the late 1920s between the Pacific Lumber Company and the Save-the-Redwoods League led to the establishment of Humboldt Redwoods State Park. Nearly 20,000 acres of magnificent groves once owned by Pacific Lumber are now permanently protected in parks. In Scotia, tour Pacific Lumber's mill, said to be the world's largest redwood operation (Monday-Friday); 707/764-2222 for tour schedule. A museum (open summer months) features historic photographs and memorabilia from days gone by. **FREE**

Huntington Beach

(E-5) *See also Costa Mesa, Newport Beach*

Pop 181,519 **Elev** 28 ft **Area code** 714

Motels/Motor Lodges

★★ COMFORT SUITES. *16301 Beach Blvd (92647). 714/841-1812; fax 714/841-0214; toll-free 800/717-4040. www.comfortsuites.com.* 102 suites, 3 story. S, D $59-$79; each addl $5; under 18 free. Crib free. TV; cable. Heated pool; whirlpool. Complimentary continental bkfst. Ck-out 11 am. Coin lndry. Meeting rm. Exercise equipt. Refrigerators. Balconies. Cr cds: A, D, DS, MC, V.

D

★★ RAMADA LIMITED. *17205 Pacific Coast Hwy, Sunset Beach (90742). 714/840-2431; fax 562/592-4093; toll-free 800/654-8904.* 50 rms, 2 story. S, D $89-$119; each addl $10; under 12 free. TV; cable (premium). Complimentary continental bkfst. Ck-out 11 am. Business servs avail. Whirlpool. Refrigerators. Private patios, balconies. Beach opp. Cr cds: A, DS, MC, V.

D SC

Hotel

★★ HOTEL HUNTINGTON BEACH. *7667 Center Ave (92647). 714/891-0123; fax 714/895-4591; res 877/891-0123. www.hbhotel.com.* 224 rms, 8 story. S, D $105-$115; each addl $10; suites $195; under 18 free. Crib free. TV; cable (premium). Indoor pool; whirlpool. Coffee in rms. Restaurant 6:30 am-10 pm. Bar 5-11 pm. Ck-out noon. Business servs avail. Gift shop. Airport transportation. Exercise equipt. Health club privileges. Cr cds: A, C, D, DS, JCB, MC, V.

D SC

Resort

★★★ **THE HILTON WATERFRONT BEACH RESORT.** *21100 Pacific Coast Hwy (92648). 714/845-8000; fax 714/845-8424; toll-free 800/822-7873. waterfrontbeachresort.hilton.com.* 290 rms, 12 story, 36 suites. S, D $199-$239; suites $339-$579; under 18 free; wkend rates. Crib free. Garage, valet parking $10. TV; cable (premium), VCR avail. Heated pool; whirlpool, poolside serv. Supervised children's activities (mid-June-Labor Day). Complimentary coffee in rms. Restaurant 6:30 am-11 pm. Bar 11-1:30 am; entertainment Mon-Sat. Ck-out noon. Meeting rms. Business center. In-rm modem link. Concierge. Gift shop. Free airport transportation. Lighted tennis. Golf privileges. Bicycle rentals. Exercise equipt. Minibars; bathrm phone in suites; microwaves avail. Balconies. All rms with ocean view. Luxury level. Cr cds: A, C, D, DS, ER, JCB, MC, V.

D

Restaurant

★★★ **TROQUET.** *3333 Bristol (92626). 714/708-6865.* French menu. Specializes in foie gras, John Dory, Angus strip steak, petit filet, chocolate soufflé. Hrs: 11:30 am-9 pm; Fri, Sat to 10 pm. Res accepted. Wine list. Lunch $15-$20; dinner $45-$70. Valet parking. Cr cds: A, MC, V.

D

Idyllwild

See also Palm Desert, Palm Springs

Pop 2,853 **Elev** 5,500 ft
Area code 909 **Zip** 92549
Information Chamber of Commerce, 54295 Village Center Dr; 909/659-3259 or 888/659-3259
Web www.idyllwild.org

Idyllwild, located in the San Jacinto Mountains amidst pine and cedar forests with towering mountains providing the backdrop, is a small alpine village at the gateway to thousands of acres of national forest, state, and county parks. This popular resort and vacation area provides fishing in backcountry streams and lakes, hiking, rock climbing, and riding. A Ranger District office of the San Bernardino National Forest (see SAN BERNARDINO) is located here.

What to See and Do

Mount San Jacinto State Park. On 3,682 acres. Nature and hiking trails. Picnicking, camping (res recommended in summer). Interpretive programs. Standard fees. On CA 243. Phone 909/659-2607.

Riverside County parks.

Hurkey Creek. Camping (fee), picnicking (fee), play area, hiking. Pets on leash. 6 mi SE via CA 243, 74, near Lake Hemet. Phone 909/659-2050.

Idyllwild. Camping (fee); res phone 909/659-2656. Picnicking (fee), play area; hiking. Pets on leash. Visitor center with museum. 1 mi W at end of County Park Rd. Phone 909/659-3850.

Motel/Motor Lodge

★ **WOODLAND PARK MANOR.** *55350 S Circle Dr (92549). 909/659-2657; fax 909/659-2988; toll-free 877/659-2657. www.woodlandparkmanor.com.* 11 cottages, 6 with kit. No A/C. S, D $75; kit. units $95-$150; wkday rates. TV; VCR (free movies). Heated pool. Playground. Complimentary coffee in rms. Restaurant nearby. Ck-out 11 am. Lawn games. Fireplaces; microwaves avail. Picnic tables, grill. Sun decks. Scenic, mountainous area. Cr cds: MC, V.

B&Bs/Small Inns

★★ **FERN VALLEY INN.** *25240 Fern Valley Rd (92549). 909/659-2205; fax 909/659-2630. www.fernvalleyinn.com.* 11 cottage rms, 5 with kit. No A/C. S, D, studio rm $65-$105; each addl $10; kit. units $85-$105; wkday rates. TV; cable. Pool. Complimentary coffee in rms. Restaurant nearby. Ck-out 11 am, ck-in 2 pm. Refrigerators, fireplaces; microwaves avail. Private patios. Rms furnished with antiques, brass beds, handmade quilts. Totally nonsmoking. Cr cds: A, DS, MC, V.

D

★★ **FIRESIDE INN.** *54540 N Circle Dr (92549). 909/659-2966; fax 909/659-4286; toll-free 877/797-3473. www.thefireside-inn.com.* 8 rms, 4 with shower only, 2 suites, 1 cabin, 6 kit. units. 1 A/C rm. No rm phones. S, D $75; each addl $10; suites $85; cabin $100; under 5 free. Pet accepted, some restrictions. TV; cable (premium), VCR. Complimentary coffee in rms. Restaurant nearby. Ck-out 11 am, ck-in 2 pm. Refrigerators; microwaves avail. Picnic tables. In wooded area near village center. Cr cds: A, C, D, DS, JCB, MC, V.

★★ **PINE COVE INN.** *23481 Hwy 243 (92549). 909/659-5033; fax 909/659-5034; toll-free 888/659-5033. www.thepinecoveinn.com.* 10 rms, 3 with shower only, 2 story. No A/C. No rm phones. S $70-$100; D $65-$80; each addl $10; under 12 free; wkly rates; wkends, hols (2-3-day min). TV and VCR in sitting rm. Complimentary full bkfst. Ck-out noon, ck-in 1 pm. Business servs avail. Refrigerators, microwaves. Picnic tables. Cr cds: A, DS, MC, V.

★★ **QUIET CREEK INN.** *26345 Delano Dr (92549). 909/659-6110; fax 909/659-4287. www.quietcreekinn.com.* 12 units, 5 suites, 5 studio rms, 2 cabins. No rm phones. Suites $88; studio rms $75, cabins $125-$150. TV, VCR avail. Complimentary coffee. Restaurant nearby. Ck-out 11 am. Meeting rms. Business servs avail. Game rm. Lawn games. Refrigerators, fireplaces; microwaves avail. Private patios, balconies. Picnic tables, grills. Cr cds: A, JCB, MC, V.

D

★★★ **STRAWBERRY CREEK INN.** *26370 Hwy 243 (92549). 909/659-3202; toll-free 800/262-8969. www.strawberrycreekinn.com.* 9 rms, 5 in main house, 1 kit. cottage. Some rm phones. S, D $89-$109; kit. cottages for 2, $150; each addl (in cottage) $10-$20; wkends (2-day min); wkday rates. TV in some rms; VCR. Complimentary full bkfst; afternoon refreshments. Restaurant nearby. Ck-out 11 am, ck-in 2-6 pm. Business servs avail. Large rambling home nestled in the mountains, surrounded by pine and oak trees; Strawberry Creek at edge of property. Totally nonsmoking. Cr cds: DS, MC, V.

D

Restaurants

★★ **GASTROGNOME.** *54381 Ridgeview (92549). 909/659-5055. www.gastrognome.com.* Hrs: 11:30 am-2:30 pm, 5-9 pm; Fri, Sat to 10 pm; Sun 4-9 pm; Sun brunch 11 am-4 pm. Res accepted. Bar. A la carte entrees: lunch $6.95-$9.95, dinner $10.95-$33.95. Sun brunch $14.95. Specializes in seafood, lamb, pastas. Outdoor dining. Cabin setting, fireplace, stained glass. Cr cds: D, DS, MC, V.

D

★★ **VERCOLLINI'S.** *26290 CA 243 (92549). 909/659-5047.* Hrs: 5-9 pm. Closed Mon-Wed; Dec 25; also Dec 1-15. Eclectic menu. Wine, beer. Dinner: $10.95-$25.95. Children's menu. Specialties: beef Wellington, New Orleans jambalaya, scampi linguini. Chef-owned. Cr cds: MC, V.

D

Indio

(E-6) *See also Desert Hot Springs, Idyllwild, Palm Desert, Palm Springs*

Founded 1876 **Pop** 36,793 **Elev** 14 ft below sea level **Area code** 760

Information Chamber of Commerce, 82-503 Hwy 111, 92201; 760/347-0676 or 800/44-INDIO

Web www.indiochamber.org

Founded as a railroad construction camp, the town took its name from the large number of Native Americans nearby. Few settlers came until the All-American Canal and its 500 miles of pipeline turned the Coachella Valley into an area so fertile that it now produces 59 types of crops, including 95 percent of all American dates. The groves in the valley are the thickest in the Western Hemisphere. Today, Indio is a marketing and transportation hub for this agricultural outpouring. It is also known for its variety of festivals (see SPECIAL EVENTS).

What to See and Do

All-American Canal. Brings water 125 mi from Colorado River. North, east, and west of the city.

Fantasy Springs Casino. Gaming and entertainment center offers off-track betting, video gaming machines, 1,200-seat bingo rm, and more than 35 card tables. Also entertainment shows and dining. (Daily, open 24 hrs) 84-245 Indio Springs Pkwy. Phone 760/342-5000. ¢¢¢¢¢

General George S. Patton Memorial Museum. Once the desert training headquarters on approx 18,000 sq mi in the California, Arizona, and Nevada deserts. General Patton selected this site to prepare his soldiers for combat in North Africa. Patton memorabilia, artifacts; desert survival displays; natural science exhibits. (Daily; closed Thanksgiving, Dec 25) 30 mi E on US 60, I-10, at Chiriaco Summit. Phone 760/227-3483. ¢¢

Joshua Tree National Park. (see) 25 mi E on I-10.

Salton Sea State Recreation Area. (see) 24 mi S via CA 111 to nearest shoreline.

Special Events

Indio Desert Circuit Horse Show. The largest hunter/jumper horse show west of the Mississippi River. Phone 800/44-INDIO. Six wks Jan-Mar.

Riverside County Fair and National Date Festival. County Fairgrounds on CA 111 between Oasis and Arabia Sts. Fair and pageant done in Arabian Nights style. For schedule phone 760/863-8247. Mid-late Feb.

Indio International Tamale Festival. Celebration of traditional Latin American fare. Tamales prepared in various ways; traditional dance, music, entertainment. Carnival, petting zoo, arts and crafts, holiday parade. Phone 760/347-0676 or 800/44-INDIO. First wkend Dec.

Motels/Motor Lodges

★★ BEST WESTERN DATE TREE HOTEL. *81909 Indio Blvd (92201). 760/347-3421; fax 760/347-3421; toll-free 800/292-5599.* 121 rms, 2 story. Jan-Apr: S, D $59-$98; each addl $6; suites, kit. units $79-$165; under 18 free; wkly rates; higher rates special events; lower rates rest of yr. Crib $10. Pet accepted, some restrictions. TV; cable. Heated pool; whirlpool. Playground. Complimentary continental bkfst. Restaurant adj open 24 hrs. Ck-out noon. Coin lndry. Business servs avail. In-rm modem link. Exercise equipt. Game rm. Lawn games. Refrigerators; microwaves avail. Balconies. Picnic tables, grills. Surrounded by palm trees, cactus gardens. Cr cds: A, C, D, DS, MC, V.

★★ QUALITY INN. *43505 Monroe St (92201). 760/347-4044; res 800/228-5151. www.qualityinn.com.* 63 rms, 2 story. Dec-May: S $59-$99; D $64-$129; under 18 free; higher rates: late Dec, Bob Hope Classic, Date Festival, Fri, Sat Dec-May; lower rates rest of yr. Crib $6. TV; cable (premium). Heated pool; whirlpool. Continental bkfst. Restaurant nearby. Ck-out 11 am. Business servs avail. Many refrigerators; microwaves avail. Cr cds: A, D, DS, MC, V.

D

Inverness

(F-2) *See also Bodega Bay, San Rafael*

Pop 1,422 **Elev** 20 ft **Area code** 415 **Zip** 94937

What to See and Do

★ Point Reyes National Seashore. More than 70,000 acres on Point Reyes peninsula. Shipwrecks and explorers, incl Sir Francis Drake, who is believed to have landed here, brighten the history of this area; traders, whalers, fur hunters, and ranchers followed. The weather is changeable—in winter, be prepared for rain in the inland areas; in summer, fog and brisk winds on the beaches. The area is especially beautiful during the spring flower season (Feb-June). Access is possible to most beaches; wading at Drakes Beach; surf fishing. There are more than 150 mi of trails to upland country. Picnic areas are scattered throughout the park. Four hike-in campgrounds with limited facilities (by res only, fee); no pets exc at some Point Reyes beaches. Visitor center at Drakes Beach (Sat, Sun, hols); interpretive programs and information at Bear Valley headquarters (daily). For tours of the Point Reyes Lighthouse, Phone 415/669-1534. **FREE**

Samuel P. Taylor State Park. On 2,800 acres of wooded countryside with many groves of coastal redwoods. Historic paper mill site. Hiking and bridle trails, picnicking, camping (yr-round, by res only). Standard fees. 2 mi S on CA 1 to Olema, then 6 mi E on Sir Francis Drake Blvd. Phone 415/488-9897. Per vehicle day use ¢¢

Tomales Bay State Park. Virgin groves of Bishop pine and more than 300 species of plants grow on 1,018 acres. Swimming, sand beach, fishing; hiking, picnicking. Standard fees. 3 mi NW on Sir Francis Drake Blvd, 2 mi N on Pierce Point Rd. Phone 415/669-1140. ¢¢

B&Bs/Small Inns

★★ BLACKTHORNE INN. *266 Vallejo Ave (94937). 415/663-8621; fax 415/663-8635. www.blackthorneinn.com.* 4 rms, 4 story. S, D $225-$375. Complimentary buffet bkfst; afternoon refreshments. Ck-out 11 am, ck-in 4-7 pm. Business servs avail. Whirlpool. Balconies. Rustic structure resembles tree house; decks on four levels; wooded canyon setting. Totally nonsmoking. Cr cds: MC, V.

★★★ MANKA'S INVERNESS LODGE. *30 Callendar Way (94937). 415/669-1034; fax 415/669-1598; toll-free 800/585-6343. www.mankas.com.* 14 rms, 4 with shower only, 2 story, 4 kit. cabins. No A/C. Rm phone in 3 cottages. S, D $185-$465; under 12 free; wkly rates; 2-day min stay wkends; lower rates winter wkdays. Crib free. Pet accepted, some restrictions; $50. TV; cable, VCR. Restaurant (see also MANKA'S INVERNESS LODGE). Ck-out 11 am, ck-in 4 pm. Business servs avail. In-rm modem link. Hiking. Some refrigerators, some balconies, some fireplaces; microwaves avail. Turn-of-the-century hunting lodge and cabins. Totally nonsmoking. Cr cds: MC, V.

★★ OLEMA INN. *10000 Sir Francis Drake Blvd, Olema (94950). 415/663-9559; fax 415/663-8783.* 6 rms, 2 with shower only, 2 story. No A/C. No rm phones. S, D $105-$115; lower rates wkdays. Complimentary continental bkfst. Restaurant (see also OLEMA INN). Bar; entertainment Fri, Sun. Ck-out 11:30 am, ck-in after 2 pm. Country inn built in 1876. Totally nonsmoking. Cr cds: A, D, DS, MC, V.

D

★★ POINT REYES SEASHORE LODGE. *10021 Hwy 1, Olema (94950). 415/663-9000; fax 415/663-9030; toll-free 800/404-5634. www.pointreyesseashore.com.* 21 rms, 7 with shower only, 3 suites. No A/C. Mar-Nov: S, D $105-$195; each addl over 12 yrs $15; under 13, $5; suites $175-$195; cottage $195-$250. TV in sitting rm; cable, VCR avail (free movies). Complimentary continental bkfst. Restaurant adj 11:30 am-9 pm. Ck-out noon, ck-in 3-6 pm. Business servs avail. Concierge serv. Rec rm. Many in-rm whirlpools, fireplaces. Some refrigerators, wet bars. Some balconies. Rustic; resembles turn-of-the-century lodge. Cr cds: A, DS, MC, V.

D

★★ TEN INVERNESS WAY. *10 Inverness Way (94937). 415/669-1648; fax 415/669-7403. www.teninvernessway.com.* 5 rms, 3 story. No rm phones. S, D $125-$152; each addl $15; suite $180. Complimentary full bkfst; afternoon refreshments. Ck-out 11 am, ck-in 3-7 pm. Whirlpool. Refrigerator avail. Library. Antiques, handmade quilts. Built 1904. Totally nonsmoking. Cr cds: DS, MC, V.

D SC

Restaurants

★ GRAY WHALE PUB AND PIZZERIA. *12781 Sir Francis Drake Blvd (94937). 415/669-1244. www.pointreyes.org.* Hrs: 11 am-9 pm; Sat, Sun from 8:30 am; fall hrs vary. Closed Thanksgiving, Dec 25. No

A/C. Beer, wine. A la carte entrees: lunch, dinner $5.35-$19.30. Specializes in specialty pizzas, pasta, salads. Outdoor dining overlooking Tomales Bay. Small cafe atmosphere. Totally nonsmoking. Cr cds: MC, V.
D

★★ **MANKA'S INVERNESS LODGE.** *30 Callendar Way (94937). 415/669-1034. www.mankas.com.* Hrs: 5:30-8:30 pm; Thurs, Fri 6-9 pm. Closed Tues, Wed. Res accepted. Wine, beer. Dinner $25-$35. Children's menu. Specializes in fish, wild game, regional foods. Built as a hunting lodge (1917). Totally nonsmoking. Cr cds: MC, V.

★★ **OLEMA INN.** *10000 Sir Francis Drake Blvd, Olema (94950). 415/663-9559.* Hrs: 11:30 am-3 pm, 5-9 pm; Sun brunch 11 am-3 pm. Res accepted. No A/C. Wine, beer. Lunch $6.50-$13.50, dinner $14-$19.50. Specialties: rack of lamb, bouillabaisse. Classical guitarist Sun brunch, Fri. Outdoor dining on patio. Overlooks garden. Totally nonsmoking. Cr cds: A, MC, V.
D

★ **STATION HOUSE CAFE.** *11180 Hwy 1, Point Reyes Station (94956). 415/663-1515.* Hrs: 8 am-9 pm; Fri, Sat to 10 pm. Closed Thanksgiving, Dec 25. Res accepted. Bar; Fri, Sat to 11 pm. A la carte entrees: bkfst $4-$7.50, lunch $6-$9, dinner $9-$18.50. Specializes in oysters, beef, chicken. Entertainment Fri-Sun, hols. Garden dining. Cr cds: DS, MC, V.
D

Inyo National Forest

(A-3) *See also Bishop*

(Sections E and W of Bishop, via US 395)

In this 2,000,000 acre area are seven wilderness areas — John Muir, Golden Trout, Ansel Adams, Boundary Peak, South Sierra, Inyo Mountains, and Hoover — with hundreds of lakes and streams. Impressive peaks include Mount Whitney (14,496 feet) and the famous Minarets, a series of jagged, uniquely weathered peaks in the Sierra Nevada. Devils Postpile National Monument (see) is also within the boundaries of the forest. The Ancient Bristlecone Pine Forest (4,600 years old), 600-million-year-old fossils, views of one of the world's great fault scarps (the eastern Sierra Nevada), and a unique high-elevation alpine desert (10,000-14,000 ft) are all east of US 395 in the White Mountains. Palisade Glacier (the southernmost glacier in the United States) is west of US 395 (west of the town of Big Pine), on the boundary of John Muir Wilderness and Kings Canyon National Park. There are 83 campgrounds; many of them are accessible to the disabled (inquire for details).

The Mammoth Lakes Area (see MAMMOTH LAKES) includes Mammoth Lakes Basin, Inyo Craters, Earthquake Fault, Hot Creek, and many historic and archaeological features. Ranger naturalists conduct guided tours during the summer and offer ski tours during the winter; evening programs take place in the visitor center all year.

Deer; bear; tule elk; bighorn sheep; rainbow, brown, and golden trout; and a variety of birds abound in the forest. Swimming, fishing, hunting, boating, riding, picnicking, hiking, camping, and pack trips are available. Winter sports include nordic skiing, snow play areas, snowmobiling, and downhill skiing on Mammoth Mountain (see MAMMOTH LAKES) and June Mountain (see JUNE LAKE). For further information contact the White Mountain Ranger Station, 798 N Main St, Bishop 93514; phone 760/873-2500.

Irvine

(E-5) *See also Costa Mesa, Laguna Beach, Newport Beach, Santa Ana*

Pop 110,330 **Elev** 195 ft
Area code 949

Information Chamber of Commerce, 17755 Sky Park East, Suite 101, 92614; 949/660-9112

Web www.irvinechamber.com

The land on which the community of Irvine lies was once the property of the Irvine Ranch. In the heart of Orange County, Irvine is a totally planned community.

What to See and Do

University of California, Irvine. (1965). 17,000 students. Undergraduate, graduate, and medical schools on 1,489-acre campus. Taped and guided tours of campus (daily). 2 mi W of I-405, closest off-ramp Jamboree. Phone 949/824-5011. **FREE**

Wild Rivers. One of Southern California's biggest water parks (20 acres), with rides designed for children, teens, and adults. (Mid-June-mid-Sept, daily; mid-May-mid-June and late Sept, wkends) 8770 Irvine Center Dr. Phone 949/768-9453. **¢¢¢¢¢**

Hotels

★★ **ATRIUM HOTEL.** *18700 Macarthur Blvd (92612). 949/833-2770; fax 949/757-1228; toll-free 800/854-3012. www.atriumhotel.com.* 214 units, 3 story. S, D $138-$169; each addl $10; suites $179; under 18 free. Crib free. TV; cable. Heated pool; poolside serv. Complimentary coffee in rms. Restaurant 6 am-midnight. Bar 3:30 pm-2 am; entertainment. Ck-out 11:30 am. Coin lndry. Meeting rms. Business servs avail. Bellhops. Valet serv. Gift shop. Barber, beauty shop. Free airport transportation. Exercise equipt. Wet bar, refrigerator in suites; microwaves avail. Patios, balconies. Cr cds: A, D, DS, MC, V.

D

★★★ **CROWNE PLAZA.** *17941 Von Karman Ave (92614). 949/863-1999; fax 949/752-7423; res 800/227-6963. www.crowneplaza.com.* 335 rms, 14 story. S $159; D $169; each addl $10; suites $300; family rates; lower rates wkends. Crib free. TV; cable (premium). Indoor pool; whirlpool, poolside serv. Coffee in rms. Restaurant 6 am-10 pm. Bar 11:30 am-midnight. Ck-out noon. Coin lndry. Convention facilities. Business center. Gift shop. Free airport transportation. Exercise equipt; sauna. Health club privileges. Refrigerators avail. Sun deck. Luxury level. Cr cds: A, C, D, DS, ER, JCB, MC, V.

D

★★★ **EMBASSY SUITES.** *2120 Main St (92614). 949/553-8332; fax 949/261-5301; res 800/456-3950.* 293 suites, 10 story. S, D $115-$250; each addl $10. Crib free. TV; cable (premium). Indoor pool; whirlpool. Complimentary full bkfst. Coffee in rms. Restaurant 11 am-11 pm. Bar 11 am-11 pm. Ck-out 1 pm. Meeting rms. Business servs avail. Gift shop. Free airport transportation. Game rm. Exercise equipt; sauna. Health club privileges. Refrigerators; microwaves avail. Sun deck. 10 story triangular atrium. Cr cds: A, D, DS, ER, JCB, MC, V.

D

★★★ **HYATT REGENCY.** *17900 Jamboree Blvd (92614). 949/975-1234; fax 949/852-1574; toll-free 800/233-1234. www.hyatt.com.* 536 units, 14 story. S, D $104-$205; each addl $25; suites $250-$3,000; under 18 free. Crib free. TV; cable (premium), VCR avail. Heated pool; whirlpool, poolside serv. Restaurants 6 am-11 pm. Bars 11-1 am. Ck-out noon. Convention facilities. Business center. Concierge. Gift shop. Free airport transportation. Lighted tennis, pro. Golf privileges. Exercise equipt; sauna. Massage. Health club privileges. Refrigerators avail. Some private patios, balconies. Luxury level. Cr cds: A, C, D, DS, MC, V.

D

★★★ **MARRIOTT.** *18000 Von Karman Ave (92612). 949/553-0100; fax 949/261-7059; res 800/228-9290.* 485 rms, 17 story. S, D $119-$199; suites $259-$789. Crib free. Pet accepted, some restrictions. Parking $5, valet $8. TV; cable (premium). Indoor/outdoor heated pool; whirlpool, poolside serv. Coffee in rms. Restaurants 6 am-midnight. Rm serv 6-1 am. Bars 11-2 am; Mon-Fri entertainment. Ck-out noon. Coin lndry. Convention facilities. Business center. Concierge. Barber, beauty shop. Free airport transportation. Lighted tennis, pro. Exercise equipt. Health club privileges. Massage. Game rm. Refrigerators avail. Some balconies. Luxury level. Cr cds: A, C, D, DS, MC, V.

D

Restaurants

★ **CHANTECLAIR.** *18912 MacArthur Blvd (92612). 949/752-8001.* Hrs: 11:30 am-2:30 pm, 6-10 pm; Sat from 5:30 pm; Sun 10 am-2 pm, 5-9 pm. Res accepted. Country French cuisine. Bar. Wine cellar. A la carte entrees: lunch $6.95-$15.95, dinner $21.95-$31.95. Sun brunch $21.95-$24.95. Specialties: herb-crusted rack of lamb with sweet mustard, sauteed imported Dover sole. Own desserts. Pianist. Free valet parking. Outdoor dining. Country French decor. Eight theme dining areas. Fireplaces; atrium; garden. Cr cds: A, C, D, DS, ER, MC, V.
D

★★ **CHICAGO JOE'S.** *1818 N Main St (92614). 949/261-5637. www.ocretailers.com.* Hrs: 11 am-midnight; Sun from 4:30 pm; early-bird dinner 4:30-6:30 pm. Closed hols. Res accepted. Bar. Lunch $7.95-$12.95, dinner $9.95-$25.95. Specialties: mesquite-grilled rack of lamb, Alberta beef. Own baking. Oyster bar. Turn-of-the-century Chicago decor. Totally nonsmoking. Cr cds: A, MC, V.
D

★★ **MCCORMICK AND SCHMICK'S.** *2000 Main St (92614). 949/756-0505. www.mccormickandschmicks.com.* Hrs: 11 am-11 pm; Sat from 5 pm; Sun 5-10 pm. Res accepted. Bar. Lunch $4.90-$16.95, dinner $4.90-$21.95. Specializes in fresh seafood, salads, prime beef. Own desserts. Outdoor dining. Beveled, stained glass windows; wildlife artwork. Microbrewery. Cr cds: A, DS, MC, V.
D

★★ **P.F. CHANG'S.** *61 Fortune Dr (92618). 949/453-1211. www.pfchangs.com.* Specializes in Chang's Spicy Chicken Stir Fry. Hrs: 11 am-11 pm; Fri, Sat to midnight. Wine list. Lunch, dinner $5-$13. Entertainment. Cr cds: A, D, MC, V.
D

★★★ **RUTH'S CHRIS STEAKHOUSE.** *2961-A Michelson Dr (92612). 949/252-8848. www.ruthschris.com.* Specializes in steaks. Hrs: 5-10 pm; Fri to 10:30 pm; Sat 4:30-10:30 pm; Sun 4:30-9:30 pm. Res accepted. Wine list. Dinner $23.95-$32.95. Entertainment. Cr cds: A, D, DS, MC, V.
D

Jackson

(F-4) *See also Lodi, Sacramento*

Pop 3,545 **Elev** 1,235 ft
Area code 209 **Zip** 95642

A Ranger District office of the El Dorado National Forest (see PLACERVILLE) is located in Jackson.

What to See and Do

Amador County Museum. Exhibits pertaining to gold country displayed in 1859 house; tours of Kennedy Mine model exhibit (fee). (Wed-Sun; closed hols) 225 Church St. Phone 209/223-6386. **Donation**

Indian Grinding Rock State Historic Park. Site of reconstructed Miwok village with Native American petroglyphs, bedrock mortars. Interpretive trail, picnicking, camping. Regional museum. Standard fees. 11½ mi NE via CA 88, Pine Grove-Volcano Rd. Phone 209/296-7488. Per vehicle ¢

Motels/Motor Lodges

★★ **BEST WESTERN AMADOR INN.** *200 S Hwy 49 (95642). 209/223-0211; fax 209/223-4836; res 800/528-1234.* 118 rms, 2 story. S $54-$76; D $64-$86; each addl $10; kit. units $15 addl; under 16 free. Crib free. TV; cable (premium). Coffee in rms. Pool. Restaurant adj open 24 hrs. Bar 9 am-11 pm. Ck-out noon. Meeting rms. Business servs avail. In-rm modem link. Some refrigerators, fireplaces. Cr cds: A, D, DS, JCB, MC, V.
D

★ **JACKSON GOLD LODGE.** *850 N Hwy 49 and 88 (95642). 209/223-0486; fax 209/223-2905; toll-free 888/777-0380.* 36 rms, 2 story, 8 kits. S, D $48-$85; each addl $5; kit. units $79. Crib $5. Pet accepted, some restrictions; $10. TV; cable. Pool. Complimentary continental bkfst, coffee in rms. Ck-out 11 am. Cr cds: A, DS, MC, V.

B&Bs/Small Inns

★★★ FOXES IN SUTTER CREEK. *77 Main St, Sutter Creek (95685). 209/267-5882; fax 209/267-0712; toll-free 800/987-3344. www.foxesinn.com.* 7 rms, 1-2 story. No rm phones. S, D $135-$195; wkends, hols (2-day min). Some TV; cable. Complimentary full bkfst. Ck-out 11 am, ck-in 3-6 pm. Covered parking. Former Brinn House, built during the Gold Rush (1857). Antique furnishings. Totally nonsmoking. Cr cds: DS, MC, V.

★★★ GATE HOUSE INN. *1330 Jackson Gate Rd (95642). 209/223-3500; fax 209/223-1299; toll-free 800/841-1072. www.gatehouseinn.com.* 5 air-cooled rms, 1-2 story, 1 cottage. No rm phones. S $105; D $110; suite $145; wkly rates. Children over 12 yrs only. Pool. Complimentary full bkfst; afternoon refreshments. Restaurant nearby. Ck-out 11 am, ck-in 2:30 pm. Business servs avail. Gift shop. Some fireplaces. Victorian architecture and furnishings. Built 1903. Beautiful gardens. Totally nonsmoking. Cr cds: A, C, D, DS, JCB, MC, V.

★★ GREY GABLES BED AND BREAKFAST INN. *161 Hanford St, Sutter Creek (95685). 209/267-1039; fax 209/267-0998; toll-free 800/473-9422. www.greygables.com.* 8 rms, 3 story. S, D $145-$200; each addl $20; wkends, hols (2-day min). Complimentary full bkfst; afternoon refreshments. Restaurant adj 5:30-9:30 pm. Ck-out 11 am, ck-in 3 pm. Business servs avail. Fireplaces. Picnic tables, grills. Built in 1897; renovated in 1994. Totally nonsmoking. Cr cds: A, D, DS, MC, V.

★★ HANFORD HOUSE B&B INN. *61 Hanford St, Sutter Creek (95685). 209/267-0747; fax 209/267-1825; toll-free 800/871-5839. www.hanfordhouse.com.* 9 rms, 2 story. S $89-125; D $129. Complimentary bkfst; afternoon refreshments. Restaurant nearby. Ck-out 11 am, ck-in 2:30 pm. In-rm modem link. Rooftop deck; shaded patio. Totally nonsmoking. Cr cds: DS, MC, V.

★★ IMPERIAL HOTEL. *14202 CA 49, Amador City (95601). 209/267-9172; res 800/242-5594. www.imperialamador.com.* 6 rms, 2 story. Mar-Dec: S $85-$100; D $90-$105; each addl $15; wkends, hols 2-day min; lower rates rest of yr. Children over 5 yrs only. Complimentary full bkfst; refreshments. Restaurant 5-9 pm. Ck-out noon, ck-in 3 pm. In-rm modem link. Some balconies. Built in 1879 (goldrush era). Cr cds: A, DS, MC, V.

★★ SUTTER CREEK INN. *75 Main St, Sutter Creek (95685). 209/267-5606; fax 209/267-9287. www.suttercreekinn.com.* 18 rms, 7 with shower only, 1-2 story, 2 suites. No rm phones. S, D $82-$185; each addl $25, suites $155-$175. TV in some rms; cable. Complimentary full bkfst; afternoon refreshments. Ck-out 11 am, ck-in 2:30 pm. Business servs avail. Some fireplaces. 1859 house; many antiques. Landscaped grounds; gardens. Totally nonsmoking. Cr cds: MC, V.

★★★ WEDGEWOOD INN. *11941 Narcissus Rd (95642). 209/296-4300; fax 209/296-4301; toll-free 800/933-4393. www.wedgewoodinn.com.* 6 rms, 1-2 story. Some rm phones. S, D $110-$185. Complimentary full bkfst; afternoon refreshments. Ck-out 11 am, ck-in 3-6 pm. Whirlpool in suites. Microwaves avail. Lawn games. Some balconies. Picnic tables. Extensively furnished with antiques. Landscaped gardens; gazebo. Victorian replica building in scenic Sierra foothills. Totally nonsmoking. Cr cds: A, DS, MC, V.

Unrated Dining Spot

ROSEBUD'S CLASSIC CAFE. *26 Main St (95642). 209/223-1035.* Hrs: 7 am-4 pm. Closed Dec 25. Res accepted. Bkfst $4-$10, lunch $5-$9. Children's menu. Specialties: omelets, Philly cheesesteak sandwich. Own pies. Street parking. Scottie dog motif. Totally nonsmoking. Cr cds: MC, V.

Joshua Tree National Park

(E-6) *See also Desert Hot Springs, Indio, Palm Desert*

(Entrances: 25 mi E of Indio on I-10 or S of Joshua Tree, Yucca Valley, and Twentynine Palms on CA 62)

Covering more than 1,236 square miles, this park preserves a section of two deserts: the Mojave and the Colorado. Particularly notable is the variety and richness of desert vegetation. The park shelters many species of desert plants. The Joshua tree, which gives the park its name, was christened thus by the Mormons because of its upstretched "arms." A member of the Lily family, this giant yucca attains heights of more than 40 feet. The area consists of a series of block mountains, ranging in altitude from 1,000 to 5,800 feet and separated by desert flats. The summer gets very hot, and the temperature drops below freezing in the winter. Water is available only at the Black Rock Canyon Visitor Center/Campground, Cottonwood Campground, the Indian Cove Ranger Station, and the Twenty-nine Palms Visitor Center. Pets on leash only; pets are not permitted on trails. Guided tours and campfire programs (February-May and October-December). Picnicking permitted in designated areas and campgrounds, but no fires may be built outside the campgrounds. For additional information, contact 74485 National Park Dr, Twentynine Palms 92277; phone 760/367-5500. Per vehicle ¢¢¢

What to See and Do

Camping. Restricted to nine campgrounds with limited facilities; bring own firewood and water. Thirty-day limit, July-Sept; 14-day limit rest of yr. Cottonwood, Black Rock Canyon, and Indian Cove Campgrounds (fee); other campgrounds free. Group camping at Cottonwood, Indian Cove, and Sheep Pass. Campgrounds are operated on a first-come, first-served basis except for Indian Cove, Sheep Pass, and Black Rock Canyon. Phone 800/365-2267.

Hidden Valley Nature Trail. One-mi loop; access from picnic area across Hidden Valley Campground. Valley enclosed by wall of rocks.

Keys View. (5,185 ft) Sweeping view of Coachella valley, desert, and mountain. A paved path leads off the main road.

Lost Palms Canyon. Eight-mi round-trip hike. Reached by four-mi trail from Cottonwood Spring. Shelters largest group of palms (120) in the park. Day use only.

★ **Oasis Visitor Center.** Exhibits; self-guided nature trail through the Oasis of Mara, discovered by a government survey party in 1855. (Daily) Park headquarters, just N of park at Twentynine Palms entrance.

Stands of Joshua trees. In Queen and Lost Horse valleys.

Special Event

Pioneer Days. Twentynine Palms, 5 mi N. Carnival, parade, rodeo, food, games. Outhouse Race, Best-Legs Contest for men, children's day. Phone 760/367-3445. Third wkend Oct.

Joshua Tree National Park

Motels/Motor Lodges

★★ BEST WESTERN GADEN INN AND SUITES. *71487 Twentynine Palms Hwy, Twentynine Palms (92277). 760/367-9141; fax 760/367-2584.* 84 rms, 2 story, 12 kit. suites. S, D $65; each addl $10; kit. suites $85-$110; under 12 free. Crib free. TV. Heated pool; whirlpool. Complimentary continental bkfst. Restaurant nearby. Ck-out noon. Business servs avail. Health club privileges. Some refrigerators; microwaves avail. Grill. Cr cds: A, C, D, DS, MC, V.

D

★★ CIRCLE C LODGE. *6340 El Rey Ave, Twentynine Palms (92277). 760/367-7615; fax 760/361-0247. www.circleclodge.com.* 12 kit. units. S $70; D $85; each addl $10. TV; cable (premium), VCR. Heated pool; whirlpool. Continental bkfst. Restaurant nearby. Ck-out 11 am. Meeting rm. Business servs avail. Refrigerators, microwaves. Picnic tables, grills. Cr cds: A, D, MC, V.

D

★ DESERT VIEW MOTEL. *57471 Primrose Dr, Yucca Valley (92284). 760/365-9706; fax 760/365-6021. www.desertviewmotel.com.* 14 rms. S $40; D $45.50; each addl $5; under 12 free. Crib free. TV; cable (premium). Heated pool. Complimentary continental bkfst. Restaurant nearby. Ck-out 11 am. Business servs avail. Refrigerators avail. Cr cds: A, D, DS, MC, V.

SC

Hotel

★★ OASIS OF EDEN INN AND SUITES. *56377 Twentynine Palms Hwy, Yucca Valley (92284). 760/365-6321; fax 760/365-9592; toll-free 800/606-6686. www.oasisofeden.com.* 39 rms, 1-2 story, 20 suites, 6 kit. units. Jan-May: S $49-$69; D $59-$69; each addl $5; suites, kit. units $54.75-$95.75; family, wkly, monthly rates; lower rates rest of yr. Crib free. Pet accepted, some restrictions; $10. TV; cable (premium), VCR (movies $3). Heated pool; whirlpool. Complimentary continental bkfst. Restaurant opp 7 am-10 pm. Ck-out 11 am. Meeting rms. Business servs avail. Golf privileges. Refrigerators; microwaves avail. Theme rms with in-rm whirlpools avail. Cr cds: A, C, D, DS, ER, JCB, MC, V.

D SC

B&B/Small Inn

★★ JOSHUA TREE INN. *61259 Twentynine Palms Hwy, Joshua Tree (92252). 760/366-1188; fax 760/366-3805; toll-free 800/366-1444. www.joshuatreeinn.com.* 10 rms, shower only, 1 with A/C, 2 suites. Oct-mid-June: S $55-$95; D $65-$135; suites $125-$150; each addl $10; under 10 free; wkly, monthly rates; lower rates rest of yr. Pet accepted, some restrictions; $10. TV; cable (premium), VCR avail. Pool. Playground. Complimentary full bkfst; afternoon refreshments. Dining rm by res. Ck-out noon, ck-in 2 pm. Business servs avail. In-rm modem link. Concierge serv. Bellhops. Airport transportation. Some refrigerators; microwaves avail. Picnic tables. Cr cds: A, C, D, MC, V.

SC

June Lake

(G-6) *See also Lee Vining, Mammoth Lakes*

Pop 425 **Elev** 7,600 ft **Area code** 760 **Zip** 93529

Web www.junemountain.com

What to See and Do

June Mountain Ski Area. Two detachable quad, five double chairlifts, high-speed tram; patrol, school, rentals; snowboarding; cafeteria, bar, day care center. Longest run 2½ mi; vertical drop 2,590 ft. Half-day rates. (Mid-Nov-Apr, daily) W of US 395. Phone 760/934-2224. ¢¢¢¢¢

Lake Recreation. Fishing, sailing, windsurfing, swimming; hiking, scenic drives. (Daily) US 395 N from Mammoth Lakes, then Rte 158 W.

Motel/Motor Lodge

★ BOULDER LODGE MOTEL. *2282 Hwy 158 (93529). 760/648-7533; fax*

760/648-7330; toll-free 800/458-6355. www.boulderlodge.com. 60 rms, 2 story, 8 suites, 30 kits., 10 cabins. No A/C. S, D $52-$78; each addl $8-$10; suites $90-$250; kit. units $75-$175; cabins $50-$105; 5-bedrm house $260-$300; wkly rates; ski plans; wkday rates in winter; higher rates: July-Labor Day and hols. Crib $8. TV; cable. Complimentary coffee in rms. Indoor pool; whirlpool. Sauna. Playground. Restaurant nearby. Ck-out 11 am. Business servs avail. Tennis. Downhill/x-country ski 1 mi. Game rm. Fish cleaning and freezing facilities. Overlooking June Lake. Picnic tables, grill. Cr cds: A, DS, MC, V.

D

Restaurant

★★ **SIERRA INN.** *Hwy 158 (93529). 760/648-7774.* Hrs: 5-10 pm. Closed Nov-mid-Dec and Easter to opening day of fishing season. Res accepted. Bar to midnight. Dinner $8.95-$19.95. Dinner buffet: (Sat) $14.95. Children's menu. Specializes in steak, fresh seafood. Salad bar. View of mountains, lake. Outdoor dining. Cr cds: A, DS, MC, V.

SC

Kernville (C-4)

Pop 1,656 **Elev** 2,650 ft
Area code 760 **Zip** 93238

Information Chamber of Commerce, 11447 Kernville Rd, PO Box 397; 760/376-2629

A Ranger District office of the Sequoia National Forest (see PORTERVILLE) is located in Kernville. Trout fishing is enjoyed in nearby Kern River.

What to See and Do

Greenhorn Mountain Park. Park has 90 campsites with barbecue pits, 115 picnic tables, camping supplies. Camping limited to 14 days, no res; pets on leash only. 12 mi W via CA 155 in Sequoia National Forest. Phone 760/379-5646. ¢¢¢

Isabella Lake. Swimming, waterskiing, fishing; boating (marinas). More than 700 improved campsites with showers, rest rms (site/night). Auxiliary (primitive) camp area (free). S of town. For information contact Sequoia National Forest, Lake Isabella Visitors Center, PO Box 3810, Lake Isabella, 93240-3810; Phone 760/379-5646.

River rafting. Kern River Tours. Rafting trips down the Lower Kern River, a Class III-IV river. (May-Sep) Box 3444, Lake Isabella, 93240. Phone 760/379-4616. ¢¢¢¢¢

Special Events

Whiskey Flat Days. Gold Rush days celebration. Phone 760/376-2629. Mid-Feb.

Kernville Rod Run. Show for pre-1949 cars. Oct.

Motels/Motor Lodges

★★ **KERNVILLE INN.** *11042 Kernville Rd (93238). 760/376-2206; fax 760/376-3735; toll-free 877/393-7900.* 26 rms, 1-2 story, 8 kit. units. S $49-$59; D $59-$74; each addl $10; kit. units $64-$99; wkends, hols (2-3 day min). TV; cable (premium). Complimentary coffee in lobby. Restaurant adj 6 am-9 pm. Ck-out 11 am. Coin lndry. Downhill/x-country ski 15 mi. Pool. Picnic tables. Cr cds: A, DS, MC, V.

★★ **WHISPERING PINES LODGE.** *13745 Sierra Way (93238). 760/376-3733; fax 760/376-6513; toll-free 877/241-4100. www.kernvalley.com/whisperingpines.* 17 rms, 5 kit. units. S, D $99-$159; each addl $15. TV; cable; VCR (movies). Pool. Complimentary full bkfst, coffee in rms. Ck-out 11 am. Downhill ski 14 mi. Some fireplaces, in-rm whirlpools. Balconies. Refrigerators. Picnic tables, grills. On river. Totally nonsmoking. Cr cds: A, D, DS, MC, V.

D

B&B/Small Inn

★★ **KERN RIVER INN BED AND BREAKFAST.** *119 Kern River Dr (93238). 760/376-6750; fax 760/376-6643; toll-free 800/986-4382. www.*

virtualcities.com/ca/kernriverinn.htm. 6 air-cooled rms, 2 story. No rm phones. Apr-Oct: S $89; D $99-$109; each addl $15; wkends (Memorial Day-Labor Day: 2-day min); lower rates rest of yr. Cable TV in common rm; VCR avail (movies). Complimentary full bkfst; afternoon refreshments. Restaurant nearby. Ck-out 11 am, ck-in 3-6 pm. Business servs avail. Bellhops. Downhill/x-country ski 15 mi. Some in-rm whirlpools, fireplaces. Opp river. Antiques. Totally nonsmoking. Cr cds: A, MC, V.
D SC

Restaurant

★ **JOHNNY MCNALL'S FAIRVIEW LODGE.** *Star Rte 1, Box 95 (93238). 760/376-2430.* Hrs: 5-10 pm; Sun 4-9 pm. Closed Dec-Feb. Bar 4:30-11 pm. Complete meals: dinner $7.50-$29.95. Children's menu. Specializes in steak, seafood. Western decor. Hamburger stand mid-Apr-Sept, lunch. Totally nonsmoking. Cr cds: A, MC, V.
D

King City (C-3)

Pop 7,634 **Elev** 330 ft **Area code** 831 **Zip** 93930

Information Chamber of Commerce, 203 Broadway St; 831/385-3814

Web www.kingcitychamber.com

What to See and Do

Los Padres National Forest. Contains the Santa Lucia Mtns, which feature the southernmost groves of coastal redwoods and the only natural stands of bristlecone fir. The 164,575-acre Ventana Wilderness was almost completely burned in a 1977 fire, but vegetation in the fire area reestablished itself and provides an excellent opportunity to witness the changing conditions. Fishing; hiking, camping. West of town is the forest's northernmost section. (Daily) For further information contact the District Ranger Office, 406 S Mildred, 831/385-5434; or the Forest Supervisor, 6144 Calle Real, Goleta 93117, phone 805/683-6711. ¢¢¢¢

Mission San Antonio de Padua. Founded in 1771 as the third in the chain of missions. Restoration incl gristmill, waterwheel, wine vat; tannery; museum; Padres Garden. (Daily; closed hols) 24 mi SW on County G14 in Jolon. Phone 831/385-4478. **Donation**

Pinnacles National Monument. (see)

Special Event

Mission San Antonio de Padua Fiesta. Special Mass and music, barbecue, dancing. Phone 831/385-4478. Second Sun June.

Motels/Motor Lodges

★ **COURTESY INN.** *4 Broadway Cir (93930). 831/385-4646; fax 831/385-6024; toll-free 800/350-5616.* 28 rms, 35 suites. S, D $54-$110; each addl $6; suites $59-$135; under 14 free. Crib free. Pet accepted, some restrictions; $10. TV; cable (premium), VCR (movies $2.50). Pool; whirlpool. Complimentary continental bkfst. Coffee in rms. Restaurant adj 6 am-10 pm. Ck-out noon. Coin lndry. Meeting rm. Business servs avail. In-rm modem link. Refrigerators, microwaves; whirlpool suites avail. Grill. Cr cds: A, C, D, DS, MC, V.
D

★ **KEEFER'S INN.** *615 Canal St (93930). 831/385-4843; fax 831/385-1254.* 47 rms, 1-2 story. S $43-$53; D $48-$58; each addl $5; under 12 free. Crib $5. TV; cable (premium). Pool; whirlpool. Complimentary continental bkfst. Restaurant 7 am-9:30 pm. Ck-out 11 am. Coin lndry. Business servs avail. Refrigerators; microwaves avail. Grill. Cr cds: A, D, DS, MC, V.
D

Kings Canyon National Park

(see Sequoia & Kings Canyon National Parks)

Laguna Beach

See also Costa Mesa, Irvine, Newport Beach, San Juan Capistrano

Pop 23,170 **Elev** 40 ft **Area code** 949

Information Chamber of Commerce, 357 Glenneyre St, 92651; 949/494-1018

Web www.lagunabeachchamber.org

Artists have contributed to the quaint charm of this seaside town. Curio, arts and crafts, and antique shops make leisurely strolling a pleasure. There is swimming and surfing at beautiful beaches.

What to See and Do

Laguna Playhouse. Theater company presents dramas, comedies, musicals, children's theater. Main stage (Sept-May, Tues-Sun; closed Jan 1, Dec 25). 606 Laguna Canyon Rd.

Special Events

Festival of Arts & Pageant of the Masters. 650 Laguna Canyon Rd. All pageant seats reserved. Exhibits by 160 artists; *tableaux vivants;* entertainment; restaurant. Grounds: daily. For information on ticket prices and reservations, contact festival box office, phone 800/487-FEST. July-Aug. Phone 949/494-1145.

Sawdust Fine Arts and Crafts Festival. 935 Laguna Canyon Rd. Nearly 200 Laguna Beach artists showcase their work. Phone 714/494-3030. Daily, July-Aug. Phone 949/494-3030.

Motels/Motor Lodges

★★ **ALISO CREEK INN.** *31106 S Pacific Coast Hwy (92677). 949/499-2271; fax 949/499-4601; toll-free 800/223-3309. www.alisocreekinn.com.* 62 suites, 1-2 story. No A/C. July-Aug: S, D $145-$290; each addl $10; lower rates rest of yr. Crib $5. TV; cable (premium). Heated pool; wading pool. Restaurant 11 am-10 pm. Bar to 1 am. Ck-out noon. Coin lndry. Meeting rms. Business servs avail. Nine-hole golf, pro, putting green. Some in-rm whirlpools; microwaves avail. Private patios, balconies. In secluded area of Aliso Canyon. Near beach; fishing pier. Cr cds: A, D, DS, MC, V.

D SC

★★ **BEST WESTERN LAGUNA BRISAS SPA HOTEL.** *1600 S Coast Hwy (92651). 949/497-7272; fax 949/497-8306; res 800/624-4442. www.bestwestern.com.* 66 rms, 4 story. June-Sept: S, D $139-$359; each addl $10; under 16 free; 2-day min: wkends, July, Aug, hols; lower rates rest of yr. Crib free. Pet accepted, some restrictions. TV; cable (premium), VCR avail. Heated pool; whirlpool. Complimentary continental bkfst, coffee in rms. Restaurant nearby. Ck-out noon. Coin lndry. Meeting rms. Business center. Health club privileges. Massage. In-rm whirlpools, refrigerators; microwaves avail. Balconies. Ocean view sun deck. Cr cds: A, C, D, DS, ER, JCB, MC, V.

D SC

★★ **BEST WESTERN LAGUNA REEF INN.** *30806 S Pacific Coast Hwy (92651). 949/499-2227; fax 949/499-5575; res 800/922-9905.* 43 rms, 2 story, 7 kits. July-Sept: S, D $120-$175; each addl $10; kit. units $175; wkly rates; lower rates rest of yr. TV; cable, VCR (free movies). Heated pool; whirlpool. Sauna. Complimentary continental bkfst. Restaurant nearby. Ck-out noon. Some refrigerators; microwaves avail. Botanical garden. Cr cds: A, D, DS, MC, V.

D

★★ **COURTYARD BY MARRIOTT LAGUNA HILLS.** *23175 Ave de la Carlota, Laguna Hills (92653). 949/859-5500; fax 949/454-2158; toll-free 800/321-2211.* 136 rms, 5 story. S, D $94-$104; suites $114-$129. Crib free. TV; cable (premium). Heated pool; whirlpool. Complimentary coffee in rms. Restaurant 6:30-10:30 am. Bar. Ck-out 1 pm. Coin lndry. Meeting rms. Business servs avail. In-rm modem link. Exercise equipt. Valet serv. Refrigerator in suites; microwaves avail. Balconies. Cr cds: D, MC, V.

D

★★ DANA POINT INN AND SUITES. *34280 Pacific Coast Hwy, Dana Point (92629). 949/248-1000; toll-free 800/232-3262. www.danapoint inn.com.* 86 rms, 3 story, 60 suites. May-Sept: S, D $79; each addl $5; suites $85; under 16 free; higher rates hols; lower rates rest of yr. Crib $10. TV; cable (premium). Complimentary continental bkfst. Restaurant opp open 24 hrs. Ck-out 11 am. Meeting rms. Business servs avail. In-rm modem link. Coin lndry. Exercise equipt; sauna. Pool. Some in-rm whirlpools; refrigerators, microwaves avail. Many balconies. Cr cds: A, C, D, DS, JCB, MC, V.

★★ HOLIDAY INN. *25205 La Paz Rd, Laguna Hills (92653). 949/586-5000; fax 949/457-0610; toll-free 800/282-1789. www.holiday-inn.com.* 147 rms, 4 story. S, D $119-$129; each addl $10; under 18 free. Crib free. TV; cable. Pool; poolside serv. Coffee in rms. Restaurant 6 am-10 pm. Bar; entertainment. Ck-out 1 pm. Meeting rms. Business servs avail. In-rm modem link. Bellhops. Valet serv. Free airport transportation. Health club privileges. Microwaves avail. Cr cds: A, D, DS, MC, V.

SC

★★ HOLIDAY INN EXPRESS. *34744 S Coast Hwy, Dana Point (92624). 949/240-0150; fax 949/240-4862; res 800/465-4329.* 30 rms, 3 story. May-Sept: S, D $149-$199; each addl $10; under 18 free; lower rates rest of yr. Crib free. TV; cable (premium). Complimentary continental bkfst, coffee in rms. Restaurant adj noon-10 pm. Ck-out 11:30 am. Business servs avail. Free covered parking. Health club privileges. Whirlpool. Sauna. Refrigerators, wet bars; microwaves avail. Some balconies. Most rms with ocean view. Cr cds: A, D, DS, MC, V.

★★★ INN AT LAGUNA BEACH. *211 N Pacific Coast Hwy (92651). 949/497-9722; fax 949/497-9972; toll-free 800/544-4479. www.innatlaguna beach.com.* 70 rms, 5 story. Memorial Day-Labor Day: S, D $179-$459; each addl $20; under 18 free; wkday rates; lower rates rest of yr. Crib free. TV; cable, VCR (movies). Heated pool; whirlpool. Complimentary continental bkfst. Coffee in rms. Restaurant adj 8 am-10 pm. Ck-out noon. Meeting rms. Business servs avail. In-rm modem link. Bellhops. Massage. Health club privileges. Minibars; microwaves avail. Some private balconies. On ocean; beach. Cr cds: A, D, DS, MC, V.

★ VACATION VILLAGE HOTEL. *647 S Coast Hwy (92651). 949/494-8566; fax 714/494-1386; toll-free 800/843-6895.* 133 rms in 5 buildings, 3-5 story, 70 kits. July-Labor Day (2-day min): S, D $88-$235; each addl $10; suites $190-$325; kit. units $95-$205; family, wkly rates Sept-Memorial Day; winter wkends (2-day min); some lower rates rest of yr. Crib free. Pet accepted, some restrictions. TV; cable. 2 heated pools; whirlpool. Complimentary coffee in rms. Restaurant 8 am-10 pm. Bar. Ck-out 11 am. Meeting rm. Bellhops. Some covered parking. Health club privileges. Game rm. Refrigerators; microwaves avail. Some balconies. Sun deck. On beach. Cr cds: A, C, D, DS, MC, V.

SC

Hotels

★ HOTEL LAGUNA. *425 S Coast Hwy (92651). 949/494-1151; fax 949/497-2163; toll-free 800/524-2927. www.menbytes.com/hotellaguna.* 65 rms, 3 story. No A/C. June-Labor Day: S, D $100-$220; lower rates rest of yr. Crib $10. TV; cable (premium). Complimentary continental bkfst; afternoon refreshments. Restaurant 7 am-10 pm. Bar 11-2 am; entertainment. Ck-out noon. Meeting rms. Business servs avail. Barber, beauty shop. Massage. On ocean; private beach. Cr cds: A, C, D, DS, MC, V.

SC

★★★ SURF AND SAND HOTEL. *1555 S Pacific Coast Hwy (92651). 949/497-4477; fax 949/497-1092; toll-free 888/869-7569. www.surfand sandresort.com.* 164 rms, 9 story. No A/C. Mid-June-mid-Oct: S, D $270-$305; suites $500-$1,000; lower rates rest of yr. Crib avail. Covered parking, valet. TV; cable (premium). Heated pool; poolside serv. Supervised children's activities (July-Aug); ages 3-12. Restaurant 7 am-10 pm; Fri, Sat to 11 pm. Bar 11 am-midnight; Fri, Sat to 1 am. Ck-out noon.

Meeting rms. Business servs avail. In-rm modem link. Concierge. Shopping arcade. Beauty shop. Massage. Health club privileges. Refrigerators, minibars; some in-rm whirlpools, fireplaces. Private patios; balcony rms overlook ocean. On beach. Cr cds: A, C, D, DS, MC, V.

D SC

Resorts

★★★ **LAGUNA CLIFFS MARRIOTT RESORT.** *25135 Park Lantern, Dana Point (92629). 949/661-5000; fax 949/661-5358; res 800/228-9290. www.marriott.com.* 346 rms, 3 and 4 story. S, D $199-$269; suites $300-$1,200; under 16 free; seasonal rates avail. Crib free. TV; cable (premium), VCR avail. 2 heated pools; whirlpool, poolside serv. Coffee in rms. Restaurant 6 am-11 pm. Picnics. Bar 11-2 am; entertainment. Ck-out noon, ck-in 3 pm. Grocery, package store ¼ mi. Coin lndry ½ mi. Convention facilities. Business center. In-rm modem link. Bellhops. Valet serv. Gift shop. Lighted tennis, pro. Golf privileges, greens fee $80-$125, pro, putting green, driving range. Bicycle rentals. Exercise equipt; sauna. Health club privileges. Massage. Minibars; some wet bars. Some balconies. Opp beach. Park. Located on the cliffs above the bay, with 42 acres of lawn and parkland. Cr cds: A, C, D, DS, MC, V.

D

★★ **LAGUNA RIVIERA HOTEL.** *825 S Pacific Coast Hwy (92651). 949/494-1196; fax 949/494-8421; toll-free 800/999-2089. www.laguna-riviera.com.* 41 rms, 5 story, 20 kits. No elvtr. Some A/C. Mid-June-mid-Sept: S, D $132-$167; each addl $10; suites $94-$177; studio rms, kit. units $81-$180; wkends (2-day min); lower rates rest of yr. Crib $5. TV; cable (premium). Indoor pool; whirlpool. Complimentary continental bkfst. Restaurant nearby. Ck-out noon. Sauna. Rec rm. Some fireplaces; microwaves avail. Balconies. Sun decks, terraces. Oceanfront. Cr cds: A, C, D, DS, JCB, MC, V.

D

★★★★ **THE RITZ-CARLTON, LAGUNA NIGUEL.** *One Ritz-Carlton Dr, Dana Point (92629). 949/240-2000; fax 949/240-0829; res 800/241-3333. www.ritzcarlton.com.* It's no wonder this resort has been recognized for its romantic atmosphere given its location on a dramatic bluff overlooking the Pacific. If your timing is right, you might join the more than 4,000 couples that have celebrated weddings, proposals, and anniversaries on the breathtaking grounds. Dining options are numerous, with the Ocean Terrace being the most popular sunset spot. 393 rms, 4 story. May-Sept: S, D $395-$595; suites $480-$3,700; lower rates rest of yr. Crib free. Valet parking $20. TV; cable (premium), VCR avail. 2 pools; poolside serv. Supervised children's activities; ages 6-12. Restaurants 6:30 am-midnight (see also THE DINING ROOM). Afternoon tea in library 2:30-5 pm. Rm serv 24 hrs. Bars; entertainment. Ck-out noon, ck-in 4 pm. Convention facilities. Business center. In-rm modem link. Bellhops. Valet serv. Concierge. Shopping arcade. Barber, beauty shop. Airport transportation; shuttle serv to beach. Tennis, pro. Eighteen-hole golf privileges, pro, putting green. Swimming beach. Lawn games. 2-mi bicycle path. Exercise rm; sauna, steam rm. Massage. Bathrm phones, refrigerators, minibars; microwaves avail; fireplace in some suites. Balconies. Luxury level. Cr cds: A, C, D, DS, MC, V.

D

THE ST. REGIS MONARCH BEACH. *(Too new to be rated.) One Monarch Beach Resort Dr, Dana Point (92629). 949/487-0244.* 400 rms, 6 story; 74 suites. S, D $325-$800; suites $950-$3,000; each addl $25; under 17 free. Crib avail. Pet accepted. Valet parking. Pool. TV; cable (premium), VCR avail. Restaurant 6 am-11 pm. Bar. Ck-out noon. Meeting rms. Business center. Valet serv. Gift shop. Exercise rm. Spa. Minibars, refrigerators, patios. Tuscan-style architecture. Cr cds: A, D, DS, JCB, MC, V.

B&Bs/Small Inns

★★★ **BLUE LANTERN INN.** *34343 St of the Blue Lantern, Dana Point (92629). 949/661-1304; fax 949/496-1483; toll-free 800/950-1236.*

www.foursisters.com. 29 units, 3 story, 3 suites. S, D $140-$210; each addl $15; suites $275-$500; under 2 free; package plans. Crib free. TV; cable (premium). Complimentary full bkfst; afternoon refreshments. Restaurants nearby. Ck-out noon, ck-in 3 pm. Business servs avail. Bellhops. Exercise equipt. In-rm whirlpools, refrigerators, fireplaces. Many rms have private sun decks. Located on a bluff overlooking yacht harbor; some rms have view of the coast. Park adj. Totally nonsmoking. Cr cds: A, D, MC, V.

D

★ **CASA LAGUNA INN.** *2510 S Pacific Coast Hwy (92651). 949/494-2996; fax 949/494-5009; toll-free 800/233-0449. www.casalaguna.com.* 20 rms, 3 story, 6 kit. suites. S, D $105-$120; suites $175-$225; wkly rates. Crib $5. Pet accepted. TV; cable, VCR avail. Heated pool. Complimentary continental bkfst; afternoon refreshments. Ck-out 11 am, ck-in 2 pm. Some refrigerators; microwaves avail. Balconies. Elaborate grounds; garden. Spanish architecture, individually decorated rms. Panoramic ocean views. Cr cds: A, DS, MC, V.

SC

★★ **EILER'S INN.** *741 S Coast Hwy (92651). 949/494-3004; fax 949/497-2215. www.eilersinn.com.* 12 rms, 2 story. No A/C. No rm phones. May-Sept: S, D $120-$145; suites $195; lower rates rest of yr. Complimentary continental bkfst; afternoon refreshments. Restaurant adj 7 am-11:30 pm. Ck-out noon, ck-in 2 pm. Bellhops. Business servs avail. Tennis privileges. Health club privileges. Totally nonsmoking. Cr cds: A, DS, MC, V.

★ **LAGUNA HOUSE.** *539 Catalina St (92651). 949/497-9061; toll-free 800/248-7348.* 8 kit. suites, 2 with shower only, 3 story. No A/C. Late May-mid-Sept: kit. suites $125-$185; under 18 free; wkly, wkend, hol rates; wkends (2-day min); lower rates rest of yr. Crib free. TV; cable, VCR (free movies). Complimentary coffee in rms. Restaurant nearby. Ck-out 11 am, ck-in 3 pm. Microwaves. Picnic tables. Beach cottage atmosphere; courtyard with fountain and outdoor furniture. Cr cds: A, MC, V.

D SC

All Suite

★★ **DOUBLETREE GUEST SUITES.** *34402 Pacific Coast Hwy, Dana Point (92629). 949/661-1100; fax 949/443-9761; toll-free 800/634-4586.* 196 rms, 4 story. Mid-June-mid-Aug: S, D $109-$169; under 18 free; monthly rates; lower rates rest of yr. Crib free. Garage parking $5. Pool. Complimentary coffee in rms. Restaurant 6:30 am-10 pm. Bar. Ck-out noon. Meeting rms. Business servs avail. In-rm modem link. Gift shop. Valet serv. Exercise equipt. Massage. Refrigerators, microwaves. Cr cds: A, C, D, DS, ER, JCB, MC, V.

D SC

Restaurants

★★ **BEACH HOUSE INN.** *619 Sleepy Hollow Ln (92651). 949/494-9707. www.thebeachhouseinn.com.* Hrs: 8 am-9:30 pm; Fri, Sat to 10:30 pm. Closed Thanksgiving, Dec 25. Res accepted. No A/C. Bar. Bkfst $4.95-$9.95, lunch $7.95-$13.95, dinner $12.95-$26.95. Children's menu. Specializes in fresh fish, seafood, steak. Oyster bar. Valet parking. Outdoor dining. On beach; view of ocean. Cr cds: A, D, DS, MC, V.

D

★★ **CEDAR CREEK INN.** *384 Forest Ave (92651). 949/497-8696. www.eatatcedarcreek.com.* Hrs: 11 am-11:30 pm; Sun brunch to 3 pm. Closed hols. Res accepted. Bar. A la carte entrees: lunch $5.95-$12.95, dinner $9.75-$23.95. Sun brunch $6.75-$12.95. Children's menu. Specializes in rack of lamb, beef, fresh fish. Own desserts. Entertainment Tues-Sun. Parking. Old World atmosphere; patio dining, skylit ceilings, stained-glass windows, stone fireplace. Family-owned. Cr cds: A, MC, V.

D

★ **THE COTTAGE.** *308 N Pacific Coast Hwy (92651). 949/494-3023.* Hrs: 7 am-3 pm, 5-10 pm; Fri, Sat to 11 pm. Res accepted. Wine, beer. Bkfst $4.35-$9.95, lunch $4.95-$8.95, dinner $8.95-$16.95. Children's menu. Specializes in fresh seafood.

Parking. Outdoor dining. Turn-of-century landmark home; many dining areas, fireplaces. Cr cds: A, D, DS, MC, V.

D

★★★★ **THE DINING ROOM.** *1 Ritz Carlton Dr (92629). 949/240-2000. www.ritzcarlton.com.* Dine underneath glittering chandeliers at this ultimate special occasion spot, where the romance of the surrounding landscape infiltrates the formal dining room in every way. Chef Yvon Goetz enhances the mood with his signature modern Mediterranean cuisine that exploits the freshest ingredients possible. Service is designed to pamper guests and take them far away from the daily grind. Contemporary, French Mediterranean menu. Specializes in fresh seafood, prime meats. Menu changes seasonally. Hrs: 6:30-9:30 pm. Closed Sun, Mon. Res required Fri, Sat. Dinner: 3-course $50. Prix-fixe dinner: 5-course $85-$135. Valet parking. Jacket required. Cr cds: A, D, MC, V.

D

★★★★ **FIVE FEET RESTAURANT.** *328 Glenneyre St (92651). 949/497-4955. www.fivefeetrestaurant.com.* Despite being a bit cramped and noisy, Five Feet continues to impress diners with unusual Pacific Rim cuisine in a stylish, upbeat setting. The menu manages to incorporate a little of everything, as evidenced in a signature dish of catfish in a Chinese-style braised sauce. Servers manage to be warm and efficient while navigating the crowded room. Hrs: 5-10 pm; Fri, Sat to 11 pm. A la carte entrees: $40-$45. Beer, wine. Res accepted. Cr cds: A, C, D, DS, ER, MC, V.

D

★★ **KING'S FISH HOUSE.** *24001 Avenida de la Carlota, Laguna Hills (92653). 949/586-1515. www.kingsfishhouse.com.* Specializes in crab, lobster, oysters. Hrs: 11 am-10 pm; Fri, Sat to 11 pm; Sun to 9 pm. Closed hols. Res accepted. Wine list. Lunch $6.95-$32.50; dinner $9.95-$32.50. Children's menu. Blues band Fri, Sat. Cr cds: A, D, DS, JCB, MC, V.

D

★★★ **LAS BRISAS DE LAGUNA.** *361 Cliff Dr (92651). 949/497-5434.* Hrs: 8 am-3:30 pm; 5-10 pm; Sat 4:30-11 pm; Sun brunch 9 am-3 pm; June-Labor Day open 4-11 pm daily. Closed Dec 25. Res accepted. Mexican, continental menu. Bar 11-1 am. Lunch $8.50-$12.95, dinner $11.55-$24.95. Buffet: bkfst $7.25. Sun brunch $18.95. Specialties: marisco en banderilla, filete de calamar. Valet parking. Overlooks Laguna Beach and ocean. Cr cds: A, DS, MC, V.

D

★ **MARK'S.** *858 S Pacific Coast Hwy (92651). 949/494-6711. www.markslaguna.com.* Hrs: 5-10:30 pm; Mon, Fri, Sat to 11 pm. Closed Dec 25. Res accepted. Bar. Dinner $11-$17.50. Specialties: basil garlic rigatoni, tournedos of salmon. Valet parking. Outdoor dining. Art Deco decor; local artists' works displayed. Cr cds: A, MC, V.

D

★★★ **PARTNERS BISTRO.** *448 S Pacific Coast Hwy (92651). 949/497-4441.* Hrs: 5:30-10 pm; Fri to 10:30 pm; Sat to 11 pm; Sun from 5 pm. Closed Dec 25. Res accepted. French, American menu. Bar. Wine list. Dinner $11-$23. Specialties: rack of lamb, salmon en papillote, spinach en croute. Parking. Outdoor dining. Elegant decor. Totally nonsmoking. Cr cds: A, C, D, ER, MC, V.

D

★★ **RUMARI.** *1826 S Pacific Coast Hwy (92651). 949/494-0400.* Hrs: 5-9:30 pm; Fri, Sat to 10:30 pm. Closed Dec 25. Res accepted. Italian menu. Bar. Dinner $11-$25. Specialty: linguine nere del mare al cartoccio. Outdoor dining. Italian decor. Totally nonsmoking. Cr cds: A, C, D, DS, ER, MC, V.

D

★ **SAN SHI GO.** *1100 S Pacific Coast Hwy (92651). 949/494-1551.* Hrs: 11:30 am-2 pm, 5-10 pm; Fri, Sat to 11 pm; Sun 3-10 pm. Closed July 4, Thanksgiving, Dec 25. Res accepted. Japanese menu. Wine, beer. A la carte entrees: lunch $5-$11.50, dinner $7.95-$16.95. Specializes in sushi. Parking. Ocean view. Cr cds: A, D, MC, V.

D SC

★★★ SAVANNAH CHOP HOUSE. *32441 St of the Golden Lantern, Laguna Niguel (92677). 949/493-7107. www.culinaryadventures.com.* Hrs: 5-10 pm. Res accepted. Bar 5 pm-midnight. Dinner $11.95-$26.95. Children's menu. Specializes in American cuisine with Southwestern flair. Outdoor dining. View of ocean. Totally nonsmoking. Cr cds: A, MC, V.
D

Unrated Dining Spot

A LA CARTE. *1915 S Coast Hwy (92651). 949/497-4927.* Hrs: 10 am-8 pm; Sun 11 am-5 pm. Closed Jan 1, Dec 25. No A/C. A la carte entrees: lunch $4-$6.50, dinner $4.99-$8.99. Specializes in gourmet meals to go. Counter serv. Outdoor dining on patio. Cr cds: MC, V.
D

La Habra

See also Buena Park, Whittier

Pop 51,266 **Elev** 298 ft **Area code** 562 **Zip** 90631

Restaurant

★★★ CAT AND THE CUSTARD CUP. *800 E Whittier Blvd (90631). 562/694-3812. www.catandcustard cup.com.* Hrs: 11:30 am-2:30 pm, 5:30-9 pm; Sat to 10:30 pm; Sun 5-9 pm. Closed July 4, Dec 25. Res accepted. California cuisine. Bar. A la carte entrees: lunch $9.25-$14.75, dinner $15.75-$25.75. Specialties: North Atlantic salmon, sauteed venison. Own pastries. Pianist Tues-Sun. Patio dining. Antiques. Cr cds: A, D, MC, V.
D

La Jolla (San Diego)

(F-5) *See also San Diego*

Area code 858 **Zip** 92037

Information La Jolla Town Council, PO Box 1101; 858/454-1444

This resort community is known as the "Jewel of San Diego." Sandstone bluffs laced with white sand and sparkling ocean suggest the look of the French Riviera. La Jolla is also a recognized center for scientific research.

What to See and Do

★ Birch Aquarium at Scripps. At Scripps Institution of Oceanography, University of California, San Diego; situated on a hilltop, with a spectacular view of the ocean. Visitors can explore the "blue planet," from the depths of the ocean to the far reaches of outer space, at this impressive interpretive center. This facility presents undersea creatures in realistic habitats, and allows visitors to experience the frontiers of marine science through interactive museum exhibits. Tidepool exhibit. Bookshop. Beach and picnic areas nearby. (Daily; closed Thanksgiving, Dec 25) 2300 Expedition Way (entrance at N Torrey Pines). Phone 858/534-3474. ¢¢¢

Kellogg Park. Swimming, skin diving, surfing, bathing beach, small boat landing; boardwalk, picnic areas. (Daily) At La Jolla Shores Beach, foot of Avenida de la Playa.

Museum of Contemporary Art. Permanent collection and changing exhibits of contemporary painting, sculpture, design, photography, and architecture. Sculpture garden; bookstore; films, lecture programs. (Mon, Tues, Thurs-Sun; closed Jan 1, Thanksgiving, Dec 25) 700 Prospect St. Phone 858/454-3541. ¢¢

Scripps Park at La Jolla Cove. Oceanfront landscaped park with swimming beach, scuba and skin diving areas; picnic areas. (Daily) Phone 619/221-8900.

Torrey Pines State Reserve. Wilderness park on 2,000 acres. Home to the rare and elegant Torrey Pine trees, mi of unspoiled beaches, and a lagoon that is vital to migrating seabirds. Incl eight mi of hiking trails, a visitor center and museum (daily), guided nature walks (wkends and hols), and educational programs. 12000 N Torrey Pines Rd. Phone 858/755-2063. ¢

University of California, San Diego. (1960). 18,000 students. Scattered around campus is an outdoor collection of contemporary sculpture. Campus tours. On La Jolla Village Dr and N Torrey Pines Rd, near I-5. Phone 858/534-2230.

Wind'n'sea Beach. Surfing area; also bathing beach. (Daily) At foot of Palomar St.

Motels/Motor Lodges

★★ **ANDREA VILLA INN.** *2402 Torrey Pines Rd (92037). 858/459-3311; fax 858/459-1320; toll-free 800/411-2141. www.andreavilla.com.* 49 rms, 2 story, 20 kits. Mid-June-mid-Sept: S, D $105-$125; kit. units $119-$165; monthly rates; lower rates rest of yr. Crib free. Pet accepted; $25. TV; cable (premium). Heated pool; whirlpool. Complimentary continental bkfst. Ck-out noon. Coin lndry. Business servs avail. Health club privileges. Microwaves avail. Sun deck. Cr cds: A, D, DS, MC, V.

★★ **BEST WESTERN.** *7830 Fay Ave (92037). 858/459-4461; fax 858/456-2578; res 800/462-9732. www.bestwestern.com.* 132 rms, 5 story. July-Aug: S, D $119-$199; each addl $10; suites from $350; under 12 free; lower rates rest of yr. Crib free. TV; cable. Heated pool; whirlpool. Complimentary continental bkfst. Restaurant 6 am-10 pm. Rm serv from 7 am. Ck-out noon. Coin lndry. Meeting rms. Business servs avail. In-rm modem link. Bellhops. Valet serv. Health club privileges. Some refrigerators; microwaves avail. Balconies. Ocean view from some rms. Cr cds: A, D, DS, MC, V.

D

★★ **INN AT LA JOLLA.** *5440 La Jolla Blvd (92037). 858/454-6121; fax 858/459-1377.* 44 rms, 1-2 story, 19 kit. suites. No A/C. Mid-June-mid-Sept: S, D $79-$99; each addl $10; kit. suites $99-$109; under 18 free; lower rates rest of yr. TV; cable (premium). Heated pool; whirlpool. Complimentary continental bkfst. Restaurant nearby. Ck-out 11 am. Putting green. Many refrigerators. Cr cds: A, D, DS, MC, V.

★ **LA JOLLA BEACH TRAVELODGE.** *6750 La Jolla Blvd (92037). 858/454-0716; fax 858/454-1075; res 800/578-7878. www.lajollatravelodge.com.* 44 rms, 29 with shower only, 3 story. No elvtr. June-Sept: S $54-$89; D $64-$129; under 17 free; wkly rates; lower rates rest of yr. Crib free. TV; cable (premium). Heated pool; whirlpool. Complimentary coffee in rms. Restaurant adj 6 am-midnight. Ck-out noon. Coin lndry. In-rm modem link. Health club privileges. Refrigerators; microwaves avail. Cr cds: A, C, D, DS, ER, JCB, MC, V.

★★ **LA JOLLA COVE SUITES.** *1155 Coast Blvd (92037). 858/459-2621; fax 858/459-2621; res 888/525-6552. www.lajollacove.com.* 90 rms, 6 story. No A/C. June-Aug: S, D $115-$195; each addl $15; suites $195-$325; under 18 free; lower rates rest of yr. Crib $15. TV; cable (premium). Pool; whirlpool. Complimentary coffee in rms. Restaurant nearby. Ck-out 11 am. Meeting rms. Business servs avail. Valet serv. Coin lndry. Health club privileges. Putting green. Refrigerators; microwaves avail. Cr cds: A, D, DS, MC, V.

D

★ **LA JOLLA SHORES INN.** *5390 La Jolla Blvd (92037). 619/454-0175; fax 619/551-7520.* 39 rms, 2 story, 4 suites, 8 kits. No A/C. Mid-May-Sept: S, D $79-$99; each addl $10; suites $99-$119; kit. units $99-$109; under 18 free; lower rates rest of yr. Crib free. TV; cable (premium). Heated pool. Complimentary coffee. Restaurant nearby. Ck-out 11 am. Many refrigerators. Cr cds: A, C, D, DS, MC, V.

SC

★ **SEA LODGE OCEANFRONT HOTEL.** *8110 Camino Del Oro*

(92037). 858/459-8271; fax 858/456-9346; res 800/237-5211. www.thelodge.com. 128 rms, 3 story. June-Sept: S, D $205-$339; each addl $15; suites $409-$479; under 12 free; lower rates rest of yr. TV; cable (premium). Heated pool; wading pool, whirlpool, poolside serv. Coffee in rms. Restaurant 7 am-10 pm. Bar 10:30 am-11 pm. Ck-out noon. Coin lndry. Meeting rms. Business servs avail. In-rm modem link. Bellhops. Valet serv. Covered parking. Tennis; pro. Exercise equipt; sauna. Massage. Refrigerators; microwaves avail. Private patios, balconies. On ocean. Cr cds: A, D, DS, MC, V.

D

★ **TRAVELODGE.** *1141 Silverado St (92037). 858/454-0791; fax 858/459-8534; res 800/578-7878.* 30 rms, 23 with shower only, 3 story. July-Aug: S, D $79-$150; wkly rates; higher rates hols, special events; lower rates rest of yr. Crib free. TV; cable (premium). Coffee in rms. Restaurant nearby. Ck-out noon. Refrigerators avail. Sun decks. Picnic tables. Cr cds: A, C, D, DS, JCB, MC, V.

Hotels

★★★ **EMPRESS HOTEL.** *7766 Fay Ave & Silverado St (92037). 858/454-3001; fax 858/454-6387; res 888/369-9900. www.empress-hotel.com.* 73 rms, 5 story. S, D $119-$189; kit. suites $325; under 18 free. Crib free. Valet parking $5. TV; cable. Complimentary continental bkfst. Coffee in rms. Restaurant 11:30 am-2 pm, 5:30-10 pm. Bar 11:30-1:30 am. Ck-out noon. Meeting rms. Business servs avail. In-rm modem link. Exercise equipt; sauna. Whirlpool. Health club privileges. Refrigerators. Sun deck. Cr cds: A, C, D, DS, MC, V.

D SC

★★★ **EMBASSY SUITES LA JOLLA.** *4550 La Jolla Village Dr (92122). 858/453-0400; fax 858/453-4226. www.embassysuites.com.* 335 suites, 12 story. Suites $195-$295; each addl $10; under 18 free. Crib free. TV; cable (premium), VCR avail. Indoor pool; whirlpool. Complimentary full bkfst, coffee in rms. Restaurant 11 am-11 pm. Bar to 1 am. Ck-out noon. Coin lndry. Meeting rms. Business servs avail. In-rm modem link. Gift shop. Exercise equipt; sauna. Health club privileges. Game rm. Refrigerators, microwaves, wet bars. Cr cds: A, C, D, DS, MC, V.

D

★★ **THE GRAND COLONIAL.** *910 Prospect St (92037). 858/454-2181; fax 858/454-5679; res 800/826-1278. www.thegrandecolonial.com.* 75 air-cooled rms, 4 story, 11 suites. S, D $189-$349; suites $209-$429. Crib free. Pet accepted. TV; cable. Pool. Complimentary coffee in lobby. Restaurant 7 am-2:30 pm, 5-10 pm; Fri, Sat to 11 pm. Ck-out noon. Meeting rms. Business servs avail. Health club privileges. Refrigerators avail. Cr cds: A, C, D, JCB, MC, V.

D

★★ **HOTEL LA JOLLA.** *7955 La Jolla Shores Dr (92037). 858/459-0261; fax 858/459-7649; res 800/426-0670. www.hotellajolla.com.* 108 rms, 11 story. July-Aug: S $159-$179; D $179-$199; each addl $20; suites $350; under 18 free; package plans; lower rates rest of yr. TV; cable (premium), VCR avail. Heated pool; whirlpool. Coffee in rms. Restaurant (see also CRESCENT SHORES GRILL). Bar 11-1 am; entertainment wkends. Ck-out noon. Meeting rms. Business servs avail. Concierge. Exercise equipt; sauna. Refrigerators, minibars. Balconies. Cr cds: A, C, D, DS, MC, V.

D SC

★★★ **HOTEL PARISI.** *1111 Prospect St (92037). 858/454-1511; fax 858/454-1531; toll-free 877/472-7474. www.hotelparisi.com.* 20 rms, 2 story. S, D $275-$395. Valet parking avail. TV; cable (premium), VCR avail. Complimentary continental bkfst, newspaper, coffee in rms. Restaurant 11:30 am-10 pm; Fri, Sat to 11 pm. Rm serv 5-10 pm. Bar. Ck-out noon. Meeting rm. Business servs avail. Bellhops. Concierge. Massage. Balconies. Feng Shui design.

★★★★ **HYATT REGENCY LA JOLLA AT AVENTINE.** *3777 La Jolla Village Dr (92122). 858/552-1234; fax 858/552-6066; res 800/552-1234.* A landmark hotel with an impressively sleek facade. Located in the Golden Triangle, the property is attached to a 32,000-square-foot Sporting Club and Spa and is adjacent to the

Restaurant Village. 32,000 square feet of meeting space is available. 419 rms, 16 story. S, D $175-$250; each addl $35; suites $325-$2,500; under 18 free. Crib avail. Garage parking $12, valet $16. TV; cable (premium), VCR avail. Pool; whirlpool. Restaurant 6 am-midnight. Bar from noon. Ck-out noon. Convention facilities. Business center. In-rm modem link. Concierge. Gift shop. Tennis. Health club privileges. Massage. Minibars; microwaves avail. Luxury level. Cr cds: A, C, D, DS, JCB, MC, V.

★★★ **LA VALENCIA.** *1132 Prospect St (92037). 858/454-0771; fax 858/456-3921; toll-free 800/451-0772. www.lavalencia.com.* 100 rms, 7 story, 7 kits. S, D $250-$500; each addl $15; suites $600-$900. Crib $10. TV; cable, VCR avail. Heated pool; whirlpool, poolside serv. Coffee in rms. Restaurant 6:30 am-11 pm. Rm serv 24 hrs. Bar; entertainment Mon-Sat. Ck-out noon. Meeting rms. Business servs avail. Exercise equipt; sauna. Health club privileges. Bathrm phones; many refrigerators, minibars. Some private patios, balconies. Gardens. Beach opp. Cr cds: A, C, D, DS, JCB, MC, V.

★★★ **RADISSON.** *3299 Holiday Ct (92037). 858/453-5500; fax 858/453-5550; res 800/333-3333. www.radisson.com/lajollaca.* 200 rms in 4 buildings, 2 story. S $135; D $145; each addl $10; under 18 free. TV; cable (premium), VCR (movies). Heated pool; whirlpool, poolside serv. Coffee in rms. Restaurant 6:30 am-10 pm. Bar; entertainment Tues-Sat. Ck-out noon. Meeting rms. Business servs avail. In-rm modem link. Bellhops. Free airport, RR station, bus depot transportation. Exercise equipt. Refrigerators; microwaves avail. Cr cds: A, C, D, DS, MC, V.

★★★ **SAN DIEGO MARRIOTT LA JOLLA.** *4240 La Jolla Village Dr (92037). 858/587-1414; fax 858/546-8518; res 800/228-9290.* 360 rms, 15 story. S, D $119-$174; suites $275-$650; under 18 free; wkend rates. Crib free. Pet accepted. Covered parking $8/day, valet $12. TV; cable (premium), VCR avail. Indoor/outdoor pool; whirlpool. Complimentary coffee in rms. Restaurant 6:30 am-10:30 pm. Bar. Ck-out noon. Coin Indry. Convention facilities. Business servs avail. In-rm modem link. Exercise rm; sauna. Game rm. Tennis privileges. Refrigerators avail. Private patios, balconies. Luxury level. Cr cds: A, D, DS, MC, V.

Resorts

★★★★ **HILTON LA JOLLA TORREY PINES.** *10950 N Torrey Pines Rd (92037). 858/558-1500; fax 858/450-4584; res 877/414-8020. www.hilton.com.* Set on a bluff above La Jolla, this luxury hotel overlooks the sea and the 18th fairway of the Torrey Pines golf course. It offers fine amenities for both business and leisure travelers. Unwind poolside, take a walk on the hiking trails, or enjoy a picnic by the sea. 400 rms, 4 story. S, D $175-$215; each addl $20; suites $450-$2,500; under 18 free. Crib free. Valet parking $12; in/out $9. TV; cable (premium), VCR avail. Pool; whirlpool, poolside serv. Supervised children's activities (Memorial Day-Labor Day); ages 3-12. Restaurant (see TORREYANA GRILLE). Rm serv 24 hrs. Bar 11-2 am; pianist. Ck-out noon, ck-in 3 pm. Convention facilities. Business center. In-rm modem link. Concierge. Butler serv. Gift shop. Lighted tennis. Exercise equipt; sauna. Health club privileges. Bicycle rentals. Bathrm phones, minibars; microwaves avail. Wet bar in some suites. Balconies. Cr cds: A, C, D, DS, ER, JCB, MC, V.

D SC

★ **LA JOLLA BEACH & TENNIS CLUB.** *2000 Spindrift Dr (92037). 858/454-7126; fax 858/456-3805. www.ljbtc.com.* 33 rms, 2 story, 57 suites. June-Sept: S, D $79; suites $79; each addl $20; lower rates rest of yr. Crib avail. Parking lot. Pool, lap pool, children's pool. TV; cable (premium), VCR avail, CD avail. Complimentary coffee in rms, newspaper, toll-free calls. Restaurant 7:30 am-9 pm. Bar. Ck-out noon, ck-in 4 pm. Meeting rms. Business servs avail. Bellhops. Dry cleaning. Coin lndry. Gift shop. Salon/barber avail. Exercise equipt. Golf. Tennis, 12 courts. Beach access. Supervised children's activities. Cr cds: A, C, D, DS, MC, V.

D

B&Bs/Small Inns

★★★ BED AND BREAKFAST INN AT LA JOLLA. *7753 Draper Ave (92037). 858/456-2066; fax 858/456-1510; toll-free 800/582-2466. www.innlajolla.com.* 15 rms, 2 story. Rm phones avail. S, D $159-$379. TV in sitting rm and penthouse; VCR avail. Complimentary full bkfst; afternoon refreshments. Ck-out 11 am, ck-in 3-5 pm. Some refrigerators. Beach nearby. Cubist-style house built 1913; gardens. Cr cds: A, DS, MC, V.

★★ PROSPECT PARK INN. *1110 Prospect St (92037). 858/454-0133; fax 858/454-2056. www.prospectparkinn.com.* 22 units, 4 story, 6 kits. S, D $120-$185; suites $275-$325; wkly, monthly rates off season. Crib free. TV; cable (premium). Complimentary continental bkfst, coffee in rms. Restaurant adj 7 am-11 pm. Ck-out 11 am, ck-in 3 pm. Business servs avail. In-rm modem link. Health club privileges. Refrigerators; microwaves avail. Balconies. Library. Most rms have ocean view. Totally nonsmoking. Cr cds: A, C, D, DS.

Extended Stay

★★ RESIDENCE INN BY MARRIOTT. *8901 Gilman Dr (92037). 858/587-1770; fax 858/552-0387; toll-free 800/876-1778.* 287 kit. suites, 2 story. Kit. suites $180-$299; wkly rates. Crib free. Pet accepted; $100 and $10/day. TV; cable (premium). 2 heated pools; 5 whirlpools. Complimentary continental bkfst. Restaurant nearby. Ck-out noon. Coin lndry. Meeting rms. Business servs avail. In-rm modem link. Valet serv. Airport transportation. Health club privileges. Lawn games. Refrigerators, microwaves, fireplaces. Grills. Cr cds: A, D, MC, V.

D

Restaurants

★ ASHOKA. *8008 Girard Ave (92037). 858/454-6263.* Hrs: 5:30-9:30 pm; Fri, Sat to 10:30 pm. Closed Mon. Res accepted. Indian menu. Wine, beer. Dinner $8.95-$17.95. Specializes in tandoori dishes, curries, authentic Indian cuisine. Dining rm overlooks La Jolla Cove. Cr cds: A, DS, MC, V.

★★★ AZUL. *1250 Prospect St (92037). 858/454-9616. www.azul-lajolla.com.* Specializes in salmon, rack of lamb, fresh local ingredients. Hrs: 11:30 am-2:30 pm, 5-9 pm; Fri, Sat to 10 pm; Sun brunch 10 am-2:30 pm. Res accepted. Wine, beer. Lunch $9-$14; dinner $17-$29. Brunch $13-$17. Children's menu. Entertainment. Ocean view. Cr cds: A, C, D, MC, V.

D

★★ BIRD ROCK CAFE. *5656 La Jolla Blvd (92037). 858/551-4090.* Hrs: 5-10 pm. Closed July 4, Thanksgiving, Dec 25. Res accepted. Bar. Dinner $8-$19. Specializes in seafood. Outdoor dining. Casual decor. Totally nonsmoking. Cr cds: A, C, D, DS, ER, MC, V.

D

★★ BROCKTON VILLA. *1235 Coast Blvd (92037). 858/454-7393. www.brocktonvilla.com.* Hrs: 8 am-9 pm; Mon to 5 pm; Sun brunch to 3 pm. Closed Thanksgiving, Dec 25. Res accepted. No A/C. Beer, wine. Bkfst $2-$8, lunch $5-$8, dinner $11-$19. Sun brunch $4.50-$7.50. Specialties: coast toast, shrimp and chicken salad, rack of lamb. Outdoor dining. Hillside cottage overlooking cove and Scripps Park; abalone shell fireplace. Totally nonsmoking. Cr cds: A, DS, MC, V.

★★ CAFE JAPENGO. *8960 University Center Ln (92122). 858/450-3355. www.aventine.com.* Hrs: 11:30 am-2:30 pm, 5:30-10:30 pm; Fri to 11:30 pm; Sat 5:30-11:30 pm; Sun 5:30-10:30 pm. Closed Easter, Thanksgiving, Dec 25. Res accepted. Pacific Rim menu. Bar. Wine list. A la carte entrees: lunch $10-$16, dinner $10-$30. Specializes in fresh seafood. Sushi bar. Valet parking. Japanese art and designs adorn walls. Cr cds: A, DS, MC, V.

D

★★ THE COTTAGE. *7702 Fay Ave (92037). 858/454-8409. www.cottagelajolla.com.* California menu. Hrs:

7:30 am-3 pm; June-Aug: Sun, Mon to 9 pm. Res accepted. Wine, beer. Lunch $5.95-$10.95; dinner $8.95-$18.95. Children's menu. Entertainment. Cr cds: A, DS, MC, V.

D

★★ **CRAB CATCHER.** *1298 Prospect St (92037). 858/454-9587.* Hrs: 11:30 am-3 pm, 5:30-10 pm; Fri, Sat to 10:30 pm; Sun brunch 10:30 am-3 pm. Res accepted. Bar 11:30 am-midnight. A la carte entrees: lunch $8-$17, dinner $15-$30. Sun brunch $11-$18. Children's menu. Specializes in fresh fish, steak, pastas. Outdoor dining. View of cove. Cr cds: A, D, DS, MC, V.

D

★★ **CRESCENT SHORES GRILL.** *7955 La Jolla Shores Dr (92037). 858/459-0541. www.hotellajolla.com.* Hrs: 6:30 am-10 pm; Fri, Sat to 11 pm; Sun brunch 10:30 am-2:30 pm. Res accepted. Regional American menu. Bar 11:30 am-midnight. Bkfst $4.75-$9.95, lunch $7.50-$13.50, dinner $12-$25. Sun brunch $4-$16. Specializes in grilled swordfish, grilled paillard of veal. Entertainment Thurs-Sat. On 11th floor overlooking ocean; open bistro kitchen. Cr cds: A, DS, MC, V.

D

★★★ **FLEMING'S PRIME STEAKHOUSE & WINE BAR.** *8970 University Center Ln (92122). 858/535-0078.* Steakhouse menu. Specializes in grilled swordfish, grilled paillard of veal. Hrs: 5-10 pm; Fri, Sat to 11 pm. Res accepted. Wine list. Dinner $16-$29. Entertainment. Massive tempered reserve wine rm, fireplace, display kitchen. Cr cds: A, D, MC, V.

D

★★★ **GEORGE'S AT THE COVE.** *1250 Prospect Pl (92037). 858/454-4244. www.georgesatthecove.com.* Hrs: 11:30 am-2:30 pm, 5:30-10 pm; Fri, Sat 11:30 am-3 pm, 5-11 pm. Res accepted. Extensive wine list. Lunch $8.95-$14.50, dinner $19.50-$30. Specializes in fresh seafood, California cuisine. Own baking. Valet parking. Outdoor dining. View of cove. Cr cds: A, C, D, DS, ER, MC, V.

D

★★ **LA BRUSCHETTA.** *2151 Avenida de la Playa (92037). 858/551-1221.* Hrs: 11:30 am-3 pm, 5:30-11 pm. Closed Jan 1, Thanksgiving, Dec 25. Res accepted. Italian menu. Wine, beer. Lunch $4.95-$15, dinner $8.95-$22.95. Children's menu. Specializes in regional Italian cuisine. Parking. Outdoor dining. Italian decor. Totally nonsmoking. Cr cds: A, C, D, ER, MC, V.

D

★★ **MANHATTAN.** *7766 Fay Ave (92037). 858/459-0700.* Specializes in pasta. Hrs: 11:30 am-2 pm, 5-10:30 pm. Res accepted. Wine, beer. Lunch $9.95-$16.95; dinner $15.95-$28.95. Entertainment. Ten saltwater aquariums, singing waiter. Cr cds: A, D, DS, MC, V.

D

★★★ **MARINE ROOM.** *2000 Spindrift Dr (92037). 858/459-7222. www.marineroom.com.* Hrs: 11:30 am-2:30 pm, 6-10 pm; Sun brunch 10 am-2 pm. Res accepted. Bar to midnight. A la carte entrees: lunch $7-$14, dinner $19.50-$35. Sun brunch $24.95. Specializes in fresh seafood. Entertainment. On beach; view of ocean, cliffs. Family-owned. Cr cds: A, C, D, DS, ER, MC, V.

D

★★ **P. F. CHANGS.** *4540 La Jolla Village Dr (92122). 858/458-9007. www.pfchangs.com.* Traditional Chinese cuisine. Specializes in Chef Roy's Favorite Chicken, Szechwan Chicken Chow Fun. Hrs: 11 am-11 pm; Fri, Sat to midnight. Res accepted. Wine list. Lunch $6.95-$8.95; dinner $5.95-$13.95. Entertainment. Cr cds: A, D, MC, V.

D

★★★ **PIATTI RISTORANTE.** *2182 Avenida de la Playa (92037). 858/454-1589.* Hrs: 11:30 am-10 pm; Fri, Sat to 11 pm; Sat, Sun brunch 11 am-3 pm. Res accepted. Italian menu. Bar. A la carte entrees: lunch $9.95-$13.95, dinner $9-$17. Sat, Sun brunch $7-$9. Specialties: il pollo arrosto, pappardelle fantasia, cannelloni and "Mamma Concetta". Outdoor dining. Patio area has fountain. Cr cds: A, D, MC, V.

D

★★★ **ROPPONGI.** *875 Prospect St (92037). 858/551-5252. www.roppongiusa.com.* Asian fusion menu. Hrs: lunch Mon-Fri 11:30 am, Sat-Sun 10:30 am. Dinner Sun-Thurs until 10 pm, Fri, Sat to 11pm. Prices: lunch $6-$14; dinner $14-$25. Bar. Reserv pref. Valet. Outdoor dining. Cr cds: A, C, D, DS, ER, MC, V.
D

★★ **SAMMY'S CALIFORNIA WOOD-FIRED PIZZA.** *702 Pearl St (92037). 858/456-5222. www.sammyspizza.com.* Hrs: 11:30 am-10 pm; Fri, Sat to 11 pm. Closed Thanksgiving, Dec 25. Bar. Lunch, dinner $5.95-$9.95. Children's menu. Specializes in wood-fired pizzas. Outdoor dining. Casual dining. Totally nonsmoking. Cr cds: A, C, D, ER, MC, V.
D

★★★ **SANTE.** *7811 Herschel Ave (92037). 858/454-1315. www.santeristorante.com.* Hrs: 11:30 am-2:30 pm, 5-11:30 pm; Sat, Sun from 5 pm. Closed Jan 1, Dec 25. Res accepted (dinner). Italian menu. Bar. Wine list. Lunch $8.95-$15, dinner $10-$24. Specialties: veal with marsala and shiitake mushroom sauce, fresh Dover sole. Pianist Thurs-Sat. Street parking. Outdoor dining. Gated entry; Italian decor. Cr cds: A, DS, MC, V.
D

★★ **SKY ROOM RESTAURANT.** *1132 Prospect St (92037). 858/454-0771. www.lavalencia.com.* Specializes in sauteed English Channel dover sole, whole sweet butter poached Maine lobster. Hrs: 6-9 pm. Res required. Wine, beer. Dinner $28-$38. Entertainment. Jacket. Cr cds: A, C, D, DS, MC, V.
D

★★★ **TAPENADE.** *7612 Fay Ave (92037). 858/551-7500. www.tapenaderestaurant.com.* French cuisine. Hrs: Tues-Fri noon-2:30 pm; Tues-Sun 5:30-10 pm. Closed Mon, hols. Lunch $9-$16, dinner $10-$26. Res recommended. Bar. Summer entertainment. Totally nonsmoking. Cr cds: A, D, MC, V.
D

★★★ **TOP O' THE COVE.** *1216 Prospect Pl (92037). 858/454-7779. www.topofthecove.com.* Hrs: 11:30 am-10:30 pm; Sun brunch 10:30 am-2:30 pm. Res accepted. No A/C. Bar. Wine cellar. A la carte entrees: lunch $10-$18, dinner $25-$32. Specializes in Pacific Rim and European cuisine. Own pastries. Pianist Sat, Sun. Valet parking. Outdoor dining. In converted cottage (1896); rare Moreton fig trees at front entrance. Second-floor cafe overlooks La Jolla cove. Cr cds: A, C, D, ER, MC, V.
D

★★★ **TORREYANA GRILLE.** *10950 N Torrey Pines Rd (92037). 858/450-4571.* Hrs: 6:30 am-10:30 pm; Sun brunch 10:30 am-2 pm. Res accepted. Bar 11-2 am. Bkfst $4.95-$14.50, lunch $8.95-$14.75, dinner $11.50-$29. Sun brunch $28.95. Children's menu. Specialties: filet mignon, steamed shelled Maine lobster. Entertainment Thurs-Sat. Valet parking. Outdoor dining. Elegant atmosphere. Cr cds: A, C, D, DS, ER, MC, V.
D

★★ **TRATTORIA ACQUA.** *1298 Prospect St (92037). 858/454-0709. www.trattoriaacqua.com.* Specializes in halibut, lobster ravioli, baby lamb chops. Hrs: 11:30 am-2:30 pm, 5-9:30 pm; Fri, Sat to 10:30 pm. Res accepted. Wine, beer. Lunch $10.50-$17; dinner $13-$27. Entertainment. Cr cds: A, DS, MC, V.
D

★★★ **TUTTO MARE.** *4365 Executive Dr (92121). 858/597-1188.* Hrs: 11:30 am-10:30 pm; Tues-Thurs to 11 pm; Fri to midnight; Sat 5 pm-midnight; Sun 5-10 pm. Closed July 4, Thanksgiving, Dec 25. Res accepted. Italian menu. Bar. Lunch $8-$16, dinner $8-$18. Specializes in wood-fired oven-baked fish, charcoal-grilled meat and fish. Entertainment. Open cooking area. Cr cds: A, D, DS, MC, V.
D

Unrated Dining Spots

DAILY'S FIT AND FRESH. *8915 Towne Centre Dr (92122). 858/453-1112.* Hrs: 10:30 am-9 pm; Sun 11 am-8 pm. Closed hols. Lunch, dinner $3.89-$5.89. Children's meals. Specializes in low-calorie and low-fat entrees. Outdoor dining. Casual dining with emphasis on nutritional food. Totally nonsmoking. Cr cds: A, DS, MC, V.

D SC

FRENCH PASTRY SHOP. *5550 La Jolla Blvd (92037). 858/454-9094. www.frenchpastryshop.com.* Hrs: 7:30 am-11 pm. Closed Jan 1, Dec 25. Continental menu. Bkfst $3.25-$6.75, lunch $3.50-$11.95, dinner $6.75-$14.95. Specializes in pâte, chocolates. Own baking. Outdoor dining. Cr cds: MC, V.

D

Lake Arrowhead

(E-6) *See also Big Bear Lake*

Pop 6,539 **Elev** 5,191 ft
Area code 909 **Zip** 92352
Information Chamber of Commerce, PO Box 219; 909/337-3715
Web www.lakearrowhead.net

This area specializes in year-round sports, with water sports in the summer and snow skiing in the winter. The lake, which is 2½ miles long and about one mile wide, is slightly north of the breathtaking Rim of the World Highway (CA 18), which is a Scenic Byway, in the San Bernardino National Forest (see SAN BERNARDINO).

What to See and Do

Arrowhead Queen. Enjoy a 50-min narrated boat cruise on Lake Arrowhead, past architectural points of interest and historical sites. (Daily; hrly departures) On the waterfront at Lake Arrowhead Village. Phone 909/336-6992. ¢¢¢

Lake Arrowhead Children's Museum. Offers a hands-on interactive setting for children; learning through play and activities. (Daily; closed Thanksgiving, Dec 25) Lower Peninsula, Lake Arrowhead Village. Phone 909/336-3093. ¢¢

Snow Valley Ski Resort. Five triple, eight double chairlifts; patrol, school, rentals; snowmaking; cafeteria, restaurant, bar. Twenty-five runs; longest run 1¼ mi; vertical drop 1,141 ft. (Mid-Nov-Apr) Snowboarding. Summer activities incl hiking, mountain biking, backpacking, camping, outdoor concerts. Indoor playland for children. 14 mi SE on CA 18, 30; 5 mi E of Running Springs. Phone 909/867-2751. ¢¢¢¢¢

Motel/Motor Lodge

★ LAKE ARROWHEAD TREE TOP LODGE. *27992 Rainbow Dr (92352). 909/337-2311; fax 909/337-1403; toll-free 800/358-8733. www.arrowheadtree top.com.* 20 rms, 1-2 story, 7 kits. S, D $59-$164; suites, kit. units $80-$139; fireplace units $74-$129. Pet accepted, some restrictions; $8/day. TV; cable, VCR avail (movies $2). Heated pool. Complimentary coffee in lobby. Ck-out 11 am. Refrigerators; some fireplaces. Patios, balconies. Picnic tables, grill. Private nature trail. Cr cds: A, D, DS, MC, V.

D

Resort

★★★ LAKE ARROWHEAD RESORT. *27984 Hwy 189 (92352). 909/336-1511; fax 909/336-1378; toll-free 800/800-6792. www.lakearrow headresort.com.* 177 rms, 3 story. S, D $89-$189; each addl $15; suites $299-$399; under 18 free; package plans. Crib free. TV; cable. Heated pool; whirlpools, poolside serv. Supervised children's activities (June-Aug daily, Sept-May Fri eve, Sat and Sun only); ages 4-12. Complimentary coffee in rms. Restaurants 7 am-11 pm. Bar 4-11 pm, wkends to 1 am. Ck-out noon. Meeting rms. Business servs avail. Bellhops. Concierge. Gift shop. Barber, beauty shop. Valet parking. Airport transportation. Lighted tennis. Downhill/x-country ski 20 mi. Exercise rm; sauna, steam rm. Massage. Boating, waterskiing; fishing equipt avail. Game rm. Racquetball courts. Lawn games. Bicycle rentals. Minibars; many refrigerators; fireplace in some suites. Many balconies. On lake with private beach. Cr cds: A, C, D, DS, MC, V.

D SC

B&Bs/Small Inns

★★ **CHATEAU DU LAC.** *911 Hospital Rd (92352). 909/337-6488; fax 909/337-6746; res 800/601-8722. www.lakearrowhead.com/chateaudulac.* 5 rms, 1 with shower only, 3 story. S $125-$150; D $125. TV; cable, VCR (free movies). Complimentary full bkfst. Restaurant nearby. Ck-out 11 am, ck-in 2 pm. Downhill ski 15 mi; x-country ski 12 mi. Some in-rm whirlpools, fireplaces. Some balconies. Country French decor. Totally nonsmoking. Cr cds: A, C, D, DS, JCB, MC, V.

★★ **ROMANTIQUE LAKEVIEW LODGE.** *28051 Hwy 189 (92352). 909/337-6633; fax 909/337-5966. www.lakeviewlodge.com.* 9 units, 2 story, 2 suites. No rm phones. Late June-early Jan: S, D $75-$160; suites $110-$225; lower rates rest of yr. Adults only. TV; cable, VCR (free movies). Complimentary continental bkfst. Restaurant nearby. Ck-out 11 am, ck-in 2-9 pm. Downhill ski 10 mi; x-country ski 10 mi. Many fireplaces. Reconstructed lodge was once a private home; antique furnishings; Victorian-style decor. Lush pine garden. Lake nearby. Totally nonsmoking. Cr cds: A, DS, JCB, MC, V.

D

Restaurant

★★ **ROYAL OAK.** *27187 Hwy 189, Blue Jay (92317). 909/337-6018.* Hrs: 11:30 am-2:30 pm, 5-9 pm; Sun, Mon from 5 pm. Closed Easter, Thanksgiving, Dec 25. Res accepted. Bar to 11 pm; Fri, Sat to midnight. Lunch $6.50-$12.95, dinner $14.95-$29.95. Specializes in beef, seafood, veal. Own desserts. Pianist Wed, Fri, Sat; jazz Thurs. English Tudor decor. Family-owned. Totally nonsmoking. Cr cds: A, DS, MC, V.

D

Lake County

(see Clear Lake Area)

Lake Tahoe Area (E-5)

Area code 530 (CA), 702, 775 (NV)

Information Lake Tahoe Visitors Authority, 1156 Ski Run Blvd, South Lake Tahoe 96150; 530/544-5050 or 800/AT-TAHOE (reservations)

Lake Tahoe is one of the most magnificent mountain lakes in the world, with an area of about 200 square miles, an altitude of approximately 6,230 feet, and a maximum depth of more than 1,600 feet. Mostly in California, partly in Nevada, it is circled by paved highways edged with campgrounds, lodges, motels, and resorts. The lake, with some fine beaches, is surrounded by forests of ponderosa, Jeffery and sugar pine, white fir, juniper, cedar, aspen, dogwood, and cottonwood, as well as a splendid assortment of wildflowers.

Heavenly Ski Resort, Lake Tahoe

The Sierra Nevada, here composed mostly of hard granite, is a range built by a series of roughly parallel block faults along its eastern side, which have tipped the mountainous area to the west, with the eastern side much steeper than the western. Lake Tahoe lies in a trough between the Sierra proper and the Carson Range, similarly formed and generally regarded as a part of the Sierra, to its east.

There are spectacular views of the lake from many points on the surrounding highways. Eagle Creek, one of the thousands of mountain streams that feed the lake, cascades 1,500 feet over Eagle Falls into Emerald Bay at the southwestern part of the lake. Smaller mountain lakes are scattered around the Tahoe area; accessibility varies. Tahoe and El Dorado National Forests stretch north and west of the lake, offering many recreational facilities.

Public and commercial swimming (there are 29 public beaches), boating, and fishing facilities are plentiful. In winter the area is a mecca for skiers. There is legalized gambling on the Nevada side.

Note. Accommodations around Lake Tahoe are listed under South Lake Tahoe, Tahoe City, and Tahoe Vista. In this area many motels have higher rates in summer and during special events and holidays. Reservations advised.

What to See and Do

Boat rides.

Hornblower Cruises. *Tahoe Queen,* paddlewheeler, cruise boat to Emerald Bay (all yr, three departures daily, res required). Foot of Ski Run Blvd in South Lake Tahoe. Phone 530/541-3364. ¢¢¢¢¢

MS *Dixie II* Cruises. Tours of Lake Tahoe and Emerald Bay aboard paddlewheeler; sightseeing, bkfst and dinner cruises avail. Champagne brunch cruise (Sun). Leaves Zephyr Cove marina, 4 mi NE of Stateline, NV on US 50. Res recommended. Phone 775/588-3508. ¢¢¢¢¢

Lake Tahoe Historical Society Museum. Displays of Lake Tahoe's Native American history, Frémont's discovery, and development as a resort center. (Late June-Labor Day, daily; rest of yr, wkends) 3058 US 50. Phone 530/541-5458. ¢

Ponderosa Ranch and Western Theme Park. Cartwright House seen in the *Bonanza* television series. Frontier town with 1870 country

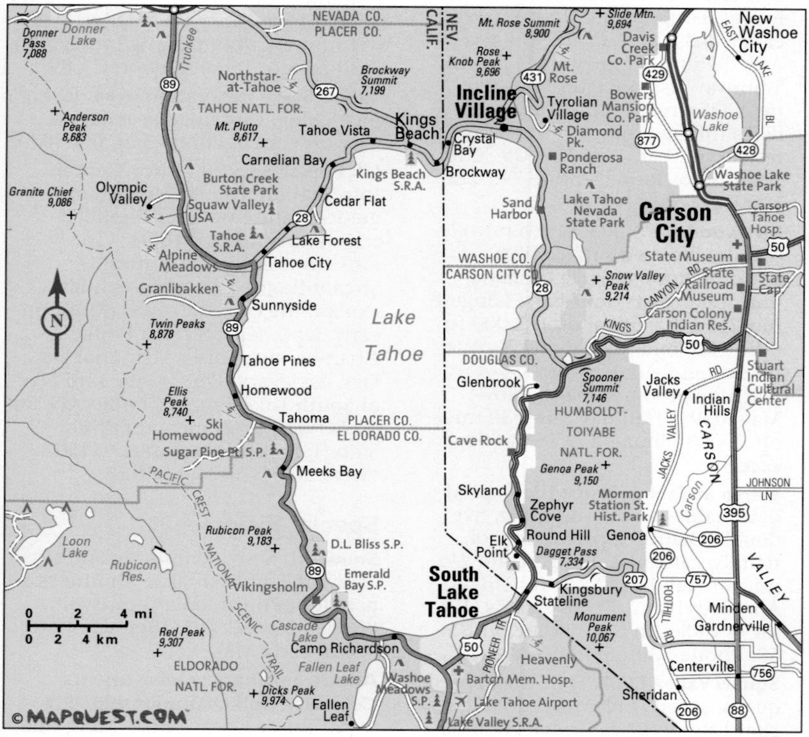

church; vintage autos; bkfst hayrides (fee); amusements. Convention facilities. (Apr-Oct, daily) On Tahoe Blvd (NV 28). Phone 775/831-0691. ¢¢¢

Riding. Camp Richardson Corral. One- and two-hr rides, bkfst and steak rides (May-Oct, daily); pack rides (July-Sept, daily); sleigh rides (Dec-Mar). For further information contact PO Box 8335, South Lake Tahoe 96158. Phone 530/541-3113. ¢¢¢¢

Ski areas.

Alpine Meadows. Quad, two triple, seven double chairlifts, one Pomalift; patrol, school, rentals; snowmaking; children's snow school; snack bar, cafeteria, restaurant, bars. Longest run 2½ mi; vertical drop 1,800 ft. Snowboarding. (Mid-Nov-late May, daily) 6 mi NW of Tahoe City off CA 89. Phone 530/583-4232. ¢¢¢¢

Heavenly Ski Resort. Aerial Tramway to 8,200 ft. Two detachable quad, seven triple, ten double chairlifts, six surface lifts; patrol, school, rentals; snowmaking; snack bar, cafeteria, restaurant, bars; six lodges. Longest run 5½ mi; vertical drop 3,500 ft. (Mid-Nov-mid-Apr, daily) X-country trails nearby. Tramway also operates May-Sept (fee). Observation platform, sun deck; hiking trail; picnic area; restaurant, bar. 1 mi E of US 50 in South Lake Tahoe. Phone 775/586-7000. ¢¢¢¢

Kirkwood. Two quads, seven triple, one double, two surface lifts; patrol, school, rentals; cafeteria, four restaurants, four bars. Longest run 2½ mi; vertical drop 2,000 ft. (Mid-Nov-mid-May, daily) X-country skiing. Rentals, lessons; machine-groomed trails. (Nov-May; daily) Half-day rates. 30 mi S off CA 88. Phone 209/258-6000. ¢¢¢¢

Sierra at Tahoe. Three high-speed detachable quads, one triple, five double chairlifts; patrol, school, rentals; cafeterias. Longest run 2½ mi; vertical drop 2,212 ft. (Nov-Apr, daily) Shuttle bus service. 12 mi W of South Lake Tahoe on US 50. Phone 530/659-7453. ¢¢¢¢

Squaw Valley USA. Four high-speed quads, seven triple, nine double chairlifts, aerial cable car, gondola, five surface lifts; patrol, school, rentals; snack bars, cafeterias, restaurants, bars. Longest run 3½ mi; vertical drop 2,850 ft. (Mid-Nov-mid-May, daily) X-country skiing (25 mi); rentals (Mid-Nov-May, daily). Tram also operates yr-round (daily and eve). Also bungee jumping. 5 mi NW of Tahoe City off CA 89. Phone 530/583-6985. ¢¢¢¢

State parks/recreation areas.

D.L. Bliss State Park. Sand beach; hiking, incl Balancing Rock nature trail and start of Rubicon trail; camping (fee). 17 mi S of Tahoe City on CA 89. Phone 530/525-7277 or 530/525-7232. ¢¢¢

Emerald Bay State Park. Swimming, fishing; picnicking, vamoping. Closed in winter. Standard fees. 22 mi S of Tahoe City on CA 89. Phone 530/525-7232 or 530/525-7277. ¢¢¢ In Emerald Bay State Park is

Grover Hot Springs state Park. Hot mineral pool, swimming; camping. 29 mi S of South Lake Tahoe on CA 89. Phone 530/694-2248.

Vikingsholm. Old Scandinavian architecture and furnishings. Tours (mid-June-Labor Day, daily). Steep 1 mi walk from parking lot (CA 89). 10 mi S of Tahoe City on CA 89.

Tahoe State Recreation Area. Pier, picnicking, camping. Near Tahoe City on CA 28. Phone 530/583-3074.

US Forest Service Visitor Center. Information, campfire programs, guided nature walks; self-guided trails and auto tape tours. Visitors look into Taylor Creek from the Stream Profile Chamber; exhibits explain life cycle of trout. (Mid-June-early Sept, daily; Stream Profile Chamber open after Memorial Day-Oct, days vary) On CA 89, 3 mi NW of South Lake Tahoe. Contact US Forest Service, 870 Emerald Bay Rd, Suite 1, South Lake Tahoe 96150. Phone 530/573-2600. **FREE**

Special Events

Snowfest. Snow sculpture contests, snowshoe and ski races, children's parade, carnival, polar bear swim. Phone 530/583-7625. Ten days late Feb or early Mar..

American Century Investments Celebrity Golf championship. Edgewood Tahoe Golf Course. More than 70 sports and entertainment celebrities compete for a $500,000 purse. Phone 530/544-5050. July.

Great Gatsby Festival. Event at Tallac Historic Site re-creating the 1920s, with vintage clothing, music, cars, and children's games. Phone 530/541-5227. Aug.

Lancaster

(D-4) *See also Palmdale*

Pop 97,291 **Elev** 2,355 ft
Area code 661
Information Chamber of Commerce, 554 W Lancaster Blvd, 93534; 661/948-4518
Web www.lancasterchamber.org

What to See and Do

Edwards Air Force Base. Landing site for the NASA space shuttle program. Free 90-min walking tours (two departures daily, 7:30 am-4 pm, Mon-Fri; res required. Also 90-min bus tours (Fri only). 10 mi N via CA 14 to Rosamond, then 10 mi E on Rosamond Blvd. Phone 661/258-3460.

Special Events

Wildflower Season. California State Poppy Reserve. 15101 W Lancaster Rd. Phone 661/942-0662. Usually late Mar-May.

Antelope Valley Fair and Alfalfa Festival. Eleven days (Mon-Fri, 8 am-5 pm). Fairgrounds. Phone 661/948-6060. Usually late Aug-Labor Day.

Motel/Motor Lodge

★★ BEST WESTERN ANTELOPE VALLEY INN. *44055 N Sierra Hwy (93534). 661/948-4651; fax 661/948-4651; res 800/810-9430.* 148 units, 1-3 story. S $65; D $73; each addl $7; suites $125; under 12 free. Crib free. Pet accepted. TV; cable. Heated pool; poolside serv, whirlpool. Playground. Complimentary full bkfst. Restaurant 5 am-11 pm. Rm serv 6 am-10 pm. Bar 5 pm-1:30 am. Ck-out 1 pm. Meeting rms. Business servs avail. In-rm modem link. Valet serv. Barber, beauty shop. Health club privileges. Many refrigerators. Cr cds: A, C, D, DS, MC, V.
D

Restaurant

★ EL TAPATIO. *1006 E Ave J (93535). 661/948-9673.* Hrs: 11 am-10 pm; Sun brunch 10 am-2 pm. Closed Thanksgiving, Dec 25. Res accepted. Mexican, American menu. Serv bar. Lunch $4.75-$6.45, dinner $4.95-$12.95. Sun brunch $7.25. Children's menu. Specialties: fajitas, tamales, rellenos. Mexican decor. Cr cds: A, DS, MC, V.
D

Lassen Volcanic National Park

(C-4) *See also Chester, Red Bluff, Redding*

(44 mi E of Redding via CA 44; 51 mi E of Red Bluff via CA 36, 89)

This 165-square-mile park was created to preserve the area including Lassen Peak (10,457 feet), a volcano last active in 1921. Lassen Park, in

Bumpass Hell, Lassen Volcanic State Park

the southernmost part of the Cascade Range, contains glacial lakes, virgin forests, mountain meadows, and snow-fed streams. Hydrothermal features, the Devastated Area, and Chaos Jumbles can be seen from Lassen Park Road. Boiling mud pots and fumaroles (steam vents) can be seen a short distance off the road at Sulphur Works. At Butte Lake, colorful masses of lava and volcanic ash blend with the forests, meadows, and streams. The peak is named for Peter Lassen, a Danish pioneer who used it as a landmark in guiding immigrant trains into the northern Sacramento Valley.

The Devastated Area, after being denuded in 1915 by a mudflow and a hot blast, is slowly being reclaimed by small trees and flowers. The Chaos Crags, a group of lava plugs, were formed some 1,100 years ago. Bumpass Hell, a colorful area of mud pots, boiling pools, and steam vents, is a three-mile round-trip hike from Lassen Park Road. Clouds of steam and sulfurous gases pour from vents in the thermal areas. Nearby is Lake Helen, named for Helen Tanner Brodt, first white woman to climb Lassen Peak (1864). At the northwest entrance is a visitor center (late June-Labor Day, daily) where one may find information on the park's human, natural, and geological history. There are guided walks during the summer; self-guided nature trails and evening talks at some campgrounds. Camping (fee/site/night) at eight campgrounds; two-week limit except at Lost Creek and Summit Lake campgrounds (seven-day limit); check at the Ranger Stations for regulations.

Lassen Park Road is usually open mid-June to mid-October, weather permitting. Sulphur Works (south) and Manzanita Lake (northwest) entrances are open during winter months for winter sports.

Some facilities for the disabled (visitor center, comfort station, and amphitheater at Manzanita Lake; other areas in park). For information and descriptive folder contact the Superintendent, PO Box 100, Mineral 96063; phone 530/595-4444.

Lava Beds National Monument (A-4)

(30 mi SW of Tulelake, off CA 139)

Seventy-two square miles of volcanic formations are preserved here in the extreme northeast part of the state. Centuries ago rivers of molten lava flowed here. In cooling, they formed a strange and fantastic region. Cinder cones dot the landscape—one rising 476 feet from its base. Winding trenches mark the collapsed roofs of lava tubes, an indicator of the 380 caves beneath the surface. Throughout the area are masses of lava hardened into weird shapes. Spatter cones may be seen where vents in the lava formed vertical tubelike channels, some only three feet in diameter but reaching downward 100 feet.

Outstanding caves include Sentinel Cave, named for a lava formation in its passageway; Catacombs Cave, with passageways resembling Rome's catacombs; and Skull Cave, with a broad entry cavern reaching approximately 80 feet in diameter. (The name comes from the many skulls of mountain sheep that were found here.) The National Park Service provides ladders and trails in the 24 caves easily accessible to the public.

One of the most costly Native American campaigns in history took place in this rugged, otherworldly setting. The Modoc War of 1872-73 saw a small band of Native Americans revolt against reservation life and fight a series of battles with US troops. Although obliged to care for their families and live off the country, the Modocs held off an army almost ten times their number for more than five months.

There is a campground at Indian Well (fee/site/night, water available mid-May-Labor Day) and picnic areas at Fleener Chimneys and Captain Jacks Stronghold (no water). Guided walks, audiovisual programs, cave trips, and campfire programs are held daily, mid-June-Labor Day. Headquarters has a visitor center (daily). No gasoline is available in the park—fill gas tank before entering. Golden

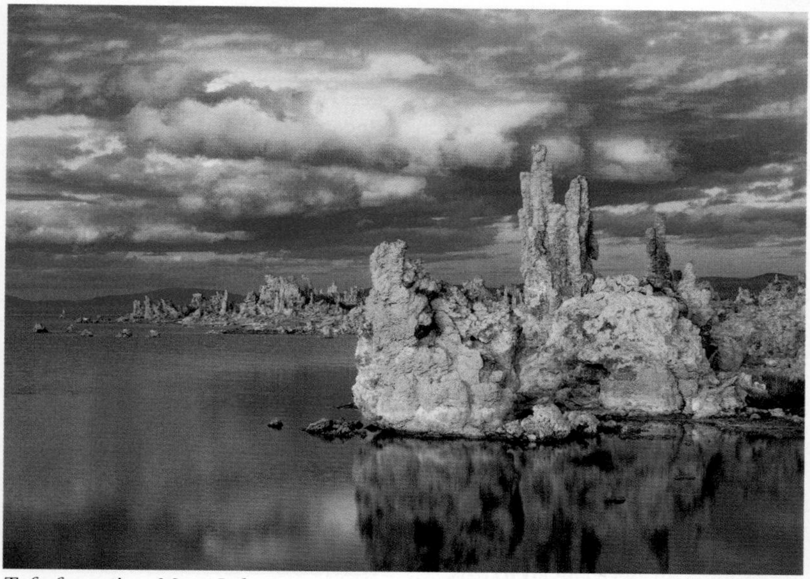

Tufa formation, Mono Lake

Eagle, Golden Age, and Golden Access passports accepted (see MAKING THE MOST OF YOUR TRIP). For further information, contact PO Box 867, Tulelake 96134; phone 530/667-2282. Per vehicle **¢¢**

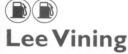

Lee Vining

(F-6) *See also Bridgeport, June Lake*

Settled 1923 **Pop** 600 **Elev** 6,781 ft **Area code** 760 **Zip** 93541

A Ranger District office of the Inyo National Forest (see) is located here.

What to See and Do

Mono Lake. Located in the Mono Basin National Forest Scenic Area, Mono Lake is one of North America's oldest lakes. It contains 250 percent more salt than the ocean, and millions of migratory waterfowl feed on brine shrimp and brine flies. Stratified limestone rock formations, or tufa, surround the lake. Samuel Clemens wrote about the lake and its islands, volcanoes, and gulls in *Roughing It.* (Daily) South Tufa area offers a visitor center with exhibits, movie; guided tours of lake area (all yr, one tour Sat and Sun; fee). Summer interpretive programs (July and Aug). NE of town. Lake access on W side. For more information contact the Visitor Center. PO Box 29. Phone 760/647-6595. **FREE**; South Tufa area and tour **¢¢**

Yosemite National Park. (see) W on CA 120.

Motel/Motor Lodge

★ YOSEMITE GATEWAY MOTEL. *51340 Hwy 395 (93541). 760/647-6467; fax 760/647-1108; toll-free 800/282-3929. www.thesierraweb.com/lodging.* 18 rms, 6 A/C, 1-2 story. May-Oct: S, D $69-$95; lower rates rest of yr. Crib $3. TV; cable. Whirlpool. Complimentary coffee in rms. Restaurant opp 6 am-10 pm. Ck-out 10 am. Downhill ski 11 mi; x-country ski 4 mi. Sun deck. View of Mono Lake. Cr cds: A, DS, MC, V.

Livermore

(G-3) *See also Fremont, Oakland, Pleasanton, San Jose, Santa Clara*

Pop 56,741 **Elev** 486 ft **Area code** 925 **Zip** 94550

Information Chamber of Commerce, 2157 First St; 925/447-1606

Web www.livermorechamber.org

What to See and Do

Del Valle Regional Park. Centerpiece of these 3,997 acres is a five-mi-long lake. Swimming, windsurfing, lifeguards in summer, fishing, boating (launch, rentals; 10 mph limit); nature trails, picnicking, camping (all yr, fee; 150 sites; dump station, showers, 20 water/sewage hookups). Visitor center. From I-580, S on N Livermore, E on Tesla Rd, right on Mines Rd, S on Del Valle Rd to park entrance. Phone 925/373-0332. **¢¢¢¢¢**

Lawrence Livermore National Laboratory's Visitor Center. Research center operated by University of California for the US Department of Energy. Multimedia presentation of the laboratory's major programs. Interactive and audio displays and computers allow for hands-on activities. (Tues-Fri, afternoons; closed hols) 5 mi E via East Ave to Greenville Rd. Phone 925/422-4599. **FREE**

Shadow Cliffs Regional Recreation Area. Formerly a gravel quarry on 255 acres. Swimming, bathhouse, fishing, boating (rentals); hiking and riding trails, picnicking. Giant water slide (Apr-Labor Day; fee). Between Livermore and Pleasanton; from I-580, S on Santa Rita Rd, left onto Valley Ave, then left onto Stanley Blvd to park entrance. Phone 925/846-3000. **¢¢**

Wineries.

Concannon Vineyard. (1883) Picnic facilities. Tours; wine tasting. Horse carriage tours avail; inquire for details. (Daily; closed hols) 4590 Tesla Rd, 3 mi S of I-580 via N Livermore Ave. Phone 925/456-2500. **FREE**

Wente Brothers Winery. Guided tours, tasting (daily; closed hols). Picnic facilities by request. 5565 Tesla Rd, 2½ mi SE via S Livermore Ave. Phone 925/456-2400. **FREE**

Special Events

Wine and Honey Festival. Celebration focusing on wine, honey, and bees. Early May.

Rodeo. PRCA sanctioned. Second wkend in June.

Restaurant

★★★ WENTE VINEYARDS. *5050 Arroyo Rd (94550). 925/456-2450. www.wentevineyards.com.* Continental cuisine. Hrs: 11:30 am-2:30 pm; 5:30 pm-9:30 pm. Dinner prices $16-$30. Res recommended. Serv bar. Valet. Cr cds: A, C, D, ER, MC, V.

D

Lodi

(F-4) *See also Sacramento, Stockton*

Pop 51,874 **Elev** 51 ft **Area code** 209

Information Lodi District Chamber of Commerce, 35 S School St, PO Box 386, 95240; 209/367-7840

Web www.lodichamber.com

Located in the northernmost county in the San Joaquin Valley, Lodi is surrounded by vineyards and a rich agricultural area. Lodi is home to the flame Tokay grape and more than ten wineries.

What to See and Do

Camanche Recreation Area, South Shore. Swimming, waterskiing, fishing, boating (rentals, marina); tennis, picnic facilities, concession, groceries, camping (fee; hookups); cottages. 24 mi E off CA 12. Phone 209/763-5178. Day use **¢¢¢**; Camping **¢¢¢¢¢**

Lodi Lake Park. Major recreational facility for a wide area. Swimming beach, boating (rentals, ramp); nature area, discovery center, picnicking. (Daily) 1 mi W of US 99 on Turner Rd. Phone 209/333-6742. **¢¢**

Micke Grove Park & Zoo. Japanese garden, camellia and rose gardens; picnicking; historical museum. Zoo and park (daily; closed Dec 25). 11793 N Micke Grove Rd, 5 mi S, just off CA 99, Armstrong Rd exit. Phone 209/953-8800. Park per vehicle **¢-¢¢**; Zoo **¢**

Special Events

Lodi Spring Wine Show. Festival Grounds, 413 E Lockeford St. Wine and food tastings from California wineries and food establishments. Art and flower shows; cooking demonstrations. Phone 209/369-2771. Late Mar.

Lodi Grape Festival and Harvest Fair. Festival Grounds, 413 E Lockeford St. County fair with exhibits, entertainment, carnival. Phone 209/369-2771. Late Sept.

Motels/Motor Lodges

★★ BEST WESTERN ROYAL HOST INN. *710 S Cherokee Ln (95240). 209/369-8484; fax 209/369-0654; res 800/528-1234.* 48 rms, 2 story. S $45-$52; D $50-$62; each addl $8; suites $75. Crib $6. TV; cable (premium). Heated pool. Complimentary continental bkfst, coffee in rms. Restaurant adj 8 am-11 pm. Ck-out 11 am. Refrigerators; some microwaves. Cr cds: A, D, DS, MC, V.

D

★★ HOLIDAY INN. *1140 S Cherokee Ln (95240). 209/334-6422; fax 209/368-7967; toll-free 800/432-7613. www.holiday-inn.com.* 95 rms, 2 story. S, D $79; each addl $6; under 12 free. Crib free. TV; VCR avail. Pool; whirlpool. Complimentary continental bkfst. Restaurant nearby. Ck-out 11 am. Coin lndry. Meeting rms. Exercise equipt; sauna. Some refrigerators. Cr cds: A, C, D, DS, MC, V.

D SC

B&B/Small Inn

★★ WINE AND ROSES COUNTRY INN. *2505 W Turner Rd (95242). 209/334-6988; fax 209/334-6570. www.winerose.com.* 10 rms, 2 story. S, D $145; each addl $15; suite $195; under 4 free. Crib free. TV; VCR avail. Continental breakfast; afternoon refreshments. Restaurant (see also WINE AND ROSES). Ck-out 11 am, ck-in 3 pm. Business servs avail. Lawn games. Some balconies. Picnic tables. Historic inn, built 1902; individually decorated rms; fireplace in sitting rm. Situated on 5 acres, with shade trees and flower and herb gardens. Approx 1 mi from lake; swimming. Totally nonsmoking. Cr cds: A, C, D, DS, MC, V.

D

Restaurant

★★ WINE AND ROSES. *2505 W Turner Rd (95242). 209/334-6988. www.winerose.com.* Hrs: 11:30 am-1:30 pm, 6-9 pm; Tues to 1:30 pm; Sat from 6 pm; Sun brunch 10:30 am-2 pm. Closed Mon; Dec 25. Res accepted. Serv bar. Lunch $7.25-$11.95, dinner $13.95-$23.95. Sun brunch $13.95. Specialties: fresh poached salmon with citrus salsa, rack of lamb. Entertainment Fri and Sat (summer). Garden dining. Totally nonsmoking. Cr cds: A, C, D, DS, ER, MC, V.

D

Lompoc

(D-2) *See also Santa Maria, Solvang*

Settled 1874 **Pop** 37,649 **Elev** 104 ft **Area code** 805 **Zip** 93436

Information Chamber of Commerce, 111 South I St; 805/736-4567

Web www.lompoc.com

Lompoc is known as "The City of Murals in the Valley of Flowers." More than two dozen murals showcase the works of internationally acclaimed muralists such as Roberto Delgado and Dan Sawatsky. Lompoc is also the flower seed capital of the world; most of the world's flower seeds come from here. From May through September, the city is bordered by over a thousand acres of vivid zinnias, marigolds, sweet peas, petunias, stock, and other blossoms. Vandenberg AFB is ten miles west of here.

What to See and Do

La Purisima Mission State Historic Park. The 11th in a chain of 21 Franciscan missions. Founded in 1787, moved in 1812. Restored in current setting. Native American artifacts, mission relics. Guide map at museum. Craft demonstrations in summer. Picnicking. Living history tours summer and fall; write for schedule, fees. (Daily, mid-morning-mid-afternoon; closed Jan 1, Thanksgiving, Dec 25) For further information contact 2295 Purisima Rd. 3 mi NE at jct Purisima Rd and Mission Gate Rd. Phone 805/733-3713. ¢

Mural Walk. More than 24 giant murals, painted by world class artists, adorn the exterior walls of buildings in old downtown. Contact Chamber of Commerce for brochure.

Special Events

Greenhouse Tour. Spectacular display of flowers by Bodger Seed Company. Phone 805/737-0595. Second Sat Apr.

Flower Festival. Floral parade, flower exhibits, arts and craft show, entertainment, bus tours of 1,200 acres of flower fields. Phone 805/736-4567. June.

Mural celebrating ethnic diversity, Lompoc

Motel/Motor Lodge

★★ **QUALITY INN.** *1621 N H St (90802). 805/735-8555; fax 805/735-8566; res 800/224-6530.* 218 rms, 4 story, 92 kits. S, D $74-$84; suites $85-$129; each addl $6; under 18 free. Crib free. Pet accepted; $25. TV; cable (premium). Heated pool; whirlpool. Full bkfst buffet. Coffee in rms. Ck-out noon. Coin lndry. Meeting rm. Business servs avail. Valet serv. Driving range. Health club privileges. Massage. Many refrigerators. Cr cds: A, C, D, DS, MC, V.

Hotel

★★★ **EMBASSY SUITES.** *1117 N H St (93436). 805/735-8311; fax 805/735-8459; toll-free 800/362-2779.* 155 suites, 3 story. Suites $107-$199; each addl $10; under 18 free. Crib free. TV; cable (premium), VCR avail. Heated pool; whirlpool. Complimentary full bkfst; evening refreshments. Coffee in rms. Ck-out noon. Coin lndry. Meeting rms. Business servs avail. In-rm modem link. Valet serv. Exercise equipt. Refrigerators. Balconies. Cr cds: A, D, DS, JCB, MC, V.

Lone Pine (B-5)

Pop 1,818 **Elev** 3,733 ft
Area code 760 **Zip** 93545

Information Chamber of Commerce, 126 S Main, PO Box 749; 760/876-4444

Web www.lone-pine.com

Dating from the early 1860s, Lone Pine has catered to tourists and outfits hiking trips to nearby Mount Whitney (14,495 feet, tallest peak in the contiguous United States). A 13-mile drive due west to the base of Mount Whitney leads through the unusual Alabama Hills.

A Ranger District office of the Inyo National Forest (see) is located here.

What to See and Do

Alabama Hills Recreation Area. Site of Indian Wars in the 1860s; named for Southern warship *Alabama.* These hills are a favorite film location for TV and movie companies because of the unique rock formations and Sierra backdrop. Contact Chamber of Commerce for details. 2 mi W via Whitney Portal Rd. Phone 760/876-4444.

The Commander's House. (1872) Victorian house, built for commander of Camp Independence and moved to present location in 1889; eight rms of antique furniture, some made by soldiers at camp. (Late May-early Sept, Sat and Sun afternoons, also by appt) 16 mi N on US 395, 303 N Edwards in Independence. Phone 760/878-0364. **Donation**

Death Valley National Park. (see) 70 mi E on CA 190.

Eastern California Museum. Little Pine Village; Native American baskets and artifacts; pioneer artifacts, photographs; natural history. (Mon, Wed-Sun; closed hols) 16 mi N via US 395, W on Center St in Independence. Phone 760/878-0364. **Donation**

Special Event

Lone Pine Film Festival. Celebration of movies made on location in Lone Pine. Fri eve concert; bus tour of movie locations; films; movie memorabilia; arts and crafts. Phone 760/876-4314. Oct.

Motel/Motor Lodge

★★★ **DOW VILLA MOTEL.** *310 S Main St (93545). 760/876-5521; fax 760/876-5643; toll-free 800/824-9317. www.dowvillamotel.com.* 39 rms, 2 story. S, D $58-$80; each addl $5; suites $75; golf packages. Crib free. Pet accepted, some restrictions. TV; cable (premium), VCR avail. Heated pool; whirlpool. Complimentary coffee in rms. Restaurant open 24 hrs. Ck-out noon. Refrigerators. Some in-rm whirlpools. Motel for motion picture casts since the early 1920s. Cr cds: A, C, D, DS, MC, V.

D SC

B&B/Small Inn

★ **WINNEDUMAH COUNTRY INN.** *211 N Edwards, Independence (93526). 760/878-2040; fax 760/878-2833. www.winnedumah.com.* 24 air-cooled rms, 7 share bath, 2 story. Many rm phones. May-Oct: S $45-$55; D $55-$65; each addl $5-$8; wkend rates; lower rates rest of yr. Cable TV in common rm. Complimentary continental bkfst. Restaurant nearby. Ck-out 11 am, ck-in after 2 pm. Business servs avail. Bellhops. Valet serv. Concierge serv. Downhill/x-country ski 10 mi. Built in 1927; movie stars and crews used this inn in the 1920s and 1940s. Totally nonsmoking. Cr cds: A, D, DS, JCB, MC, V.

Long Beach

(E-4) *See also Anaheim, Buena Park, Los Angeles, Santa Ana*

Founded 1881 **Pop** 429,433 **Elev** 29 ft **Area code** 562

Information Long Beach Area Convention & Visitors Bureau, One World Trade Center, 3rd Floor, 90831; 562/436-3645 or 800/452-7829

A multibillion-dollar redevelopment program helped Long Beach become one of southern California's most diverse waterfront destinations, recapturing the charm it first attained as a premier California seaside resort in the early 1900s. Projects involving hotels and major attractions, along with shopping, commercial, and residential area development, contributed to the revitalization of both the downtown and the waterfront. A 21½-mile light rail system, the Metro Blue Line, connects Long Beach and Los Angeles.

Founded by British-born W. E. Willmore as the "American Colony" of Willmore City, the name change to Long Beach was prompted by a desire to advertise its 5½-mile-long, 500-foot-wide beach. Earlier in this century, prosperity came with the elegant hotels and summer houses of the wealthy, and later with the discovery of oil. Today, the state's largest beach city derives its economic security from the aerospace, harbor, oil, and tourism industries. McDonnell-Douglas is its largest employer.

What to See and Do

Alamitos Bay. Seven mi of inland waterways for swimming, sunning, windsurfing, boating. 205 Marina Dr. Phone 562/570-3215.

California State University, Long Beach. (1949) 32,000 students. On the 320-acre campus are: monumental sculptures created by artists, from here and abroad, who participated in the first International Sculpture Symposium held in the US (1965); art museum with displays and exhibits; the Earl Burns Miller Japanese Garden. Campus tours (Mon-Fri, by appt). 1250 Bellflower Blvd. Phone 562/985-4111.

El Dorado East Regional Park and Nature Center. A 450-acre park with four fishing lakes, boat rentals; archery range, nature and hiking trails, picnicking. Museum and visitors center (free). (Tues-Sun) 7550 E Spring St, at I-605. Phone 562/570-1745. **¢¢**

General Phineas Banning Residence Museum. Restored Greek-revival house (1864); exhibits tell of Banning's role in the development of Los Angeles. Docent tours (Tues-Thurs, Sat, Sun). 401 E M St in Wilmington. **Donation**

Long Beach Aquarium of the Pacific. Aquarium focusing on the Pacific Rim, with more than 10,000 ocean animals. (Daily; closed Dec 25) 100 Aquarium Way. Phone 562/590-3100. **¢¢¢¢**

Long Beach Convention & Entertainment Center. A 111-acre multipurpose complex houses major sporting arena, convention/exhibition complex, and two traditional performing theaters. Terrace Theater has proscenium stage and Center Theater. Resident companies incl Long Beach Symphony, Opera, Civic Light Opera, and Classical Ballet. 300 E Ocean Blvd, at end of Long Beach Fwy. Phone 562/436-3636.

Long Beach Museum of Art. Changing contemporary exhibitions housed in 1912 mansion overlooking the Pacific Ocean. Permanent collection incl American art, German expressionists, video art. Facilities incl contemporary sculpture garden; education gallery; Media Arts Center. (Tues-Sun; closed hols) 2300 E Ocean Blvd. Phone 562/439-2119. **¢¢**

Long Beach Sport Fishing. Entertainment/fishing complex with full range of sportfishing vessels for half-day, three-quarter-day, full-day, and night fishing excursions; restaurants; fish market; bar. Whale watching (Jan-Mar). 555 Pico Ave, in port of Long Beach. Phone 562/432-8993. **¢¢¢¢¢**

Marinas.

Alamitos Bay Marina. Slips for 2,005 pleasure craft; guest docking. On grounds is Seaport Village; restaurants, shops. (Daily) 205 Marina Dr. Phone 562/570-3215.

Municipal Beach. Lifeguards at many areas in summer. (Daily) S of Ocean Blvd from Alamitos Marina. Phone 562/436-3645.

★ ***Queen Mary Seaport.*** This historic ship, which made more than 1,000 transatlantic crossings, is permanently docked here. Now a 365-rm hotel and tourist attraction, it is the centerpiece of a 55-acre site that incl the MegaBungee, one of the tallest free-standing bungee towers, and the Queen's Marketplace, with a number of eateries open for bkfst, lunch, and dinner and opportunities for shopping. Guided and self-guided tours avail; res accepted for dining and guided tours (fee). (Daily) Located at the S end of the Long Beach Fwy (710), at 1126 Queens Hwy. Phone 562/435-3511. **¢¢¢¢¢**

Rancho Los Alamitos. Guided tours of adobe ranch house (ca 1800) with antique furnishings; six barns and outbuildings, incl a blacksmith shop; five acres of gardens. (Wed-Sun afternoons; closed hols) 6400 Bixby Hill Rd. Phone 562/431-3541. **Donation**

Rancho Los Cerritos. (1844) One of original California land grants that became Long Beach. Renovated Monterey colonial-style adobe building served as headquarters for sheep ranchers in 1870s; historic garden; orientation exhibit. Special events throughout the yr (fee). Picnic area. (Wed-Sun afternoons; closed hols; guided tours on the hr, wkends) 4600 Virginia Rd. Phone 562/570-1755. **FREE**

Shoreline Village. This seven-acre shopping, dining, and entertainment complex recaptures the look and charm of a turn-of-the-century California seacoast village. Special features incl a collection of unique shops, galleries, and restaurants, a historic carousel, and a complete marine center with daily harbor cruises and seasonal whale watch excursions. Alternative transportation to Shoreline Village is avail via the free Promenade Tram from downtown Long Beach, the Runabout Shuttle (also from downtown

Long Beach), and the Water Taxi that transports passengers between Shoreline Village and the downtown marina. (Daily) 419 Shoreline Village Dr., adj to the Downtown Shoreline Marina at the foot of Pine Ave, just S of the Convention Center. Phone 562/435-2668. **FREE**

Sightseeing cruises.

Catalina Express. Departs from *Queen Mary*. Res recommended Phone 800/481-3470. ¢¢¢¢¢

Special Events

Toyota Grand Prix. International race held on downtown streets. Phone 562/436-9953. Usually three days Apr.

Long Beach Blues Festival. Phone 562/424-0013. Aug or Sept.

Jazz Festival. Rainbow Lagoon Park. Phone 562/436-7794. Mid-Aug.

Boat Parades. Dec.

Motels/Motor Lodges

★★ BEST WESTERN GOLDEN SAILS HOTEL. *6285 E Pacific Coast Hwy (90803). 562/596-1631; fax 562/594-0623; toll-free 800/762-5333. www.bestwestern.com.* 172 rms, 4 story. S, D $118-$138; each addl $10; under 12 free. Crib free. TV; cable (premium), VCR avail. Pool; whirlpool, poolside serv. Complimentary full bkfst. Restaurant 6 am-10 pm. Bar 10-2 am; entertainment. Ck-out noon. Coin lndry. Meeting rms. Business servs avail. In-rm modem link. Valet serv. Free airport transportation. Exercise equipt. Refrigerators; some in-rm whirlpools; microwaves avail. Private patios, balconies. Marina adj. Cr cds: A, C, D, DS, MC, V.

SC

★★ COURTYARD BY MARRIOTT. *500 E 1st St (90802). 562/435-8511; fax 562/901-0296; toll-free 800/321-2211. www.marriott.com.* 216 rms, 9 story. S, D $109; wkend rates; higher rates: Grand Prix, special events. Crib free. TV; cable (premium). Heated pool; whirlpool. Restaurant 6:30-10 am, 5-10 pm. Rm serv 5-10 pm. Ck-out 1 pm. Coin lndry. Meeting rms. Business servs avail. In-rm modem link. Free garage parking. Valet serv. Exercise equipt. Balconies. Near beach, convention center. Cr cds: A, C, D, DS, MC, V.

D SC

★★ GUEST HOUSE. *5325 E Pacific Coast Hwy (90804). 562/597-1341; fax 562/597-1664; toll-free 800/990-9991. www.guesthouselb.net.* 143 rms, 2 story. S, D $109; each addl $10; suites $109-$149; under 18 free; wkly rates; higher rates Grand Prix. Crib free. Pet accepted. TV; cable (premium), VCR avail. Heated pool. Coffee in rms. Restaurant 7 am-10 pm. Bar to 2 am. Ck-out noon. Coin lndry. Meeting rms. Business servs avail. In-rm modem link. Valet serv. Airport transportation. Health club privileges. Some in-rm whirlpools, refrigerators; microwaves avail. Cr cds: A, D, DS, MC, V.

D

The luxurious Queen Mary

★ INN OF LONG BEACH. *185 Atlantic Ave (90802). 562/435-3791; fax 562/436-7510; toll-free 800/230-7500. www.innoflongbeach.com.* 46 rms, 2 story. S $48-$62; D $55-$70; each addl $5; suite $125; under 12 free; higher rates Grand Prix. Crib free. TV; cable (premium), VCR avail. Heated pool; whirlpool. Complimentary continental bkfst. Restaurant nearby. Ck-out noon. Business servs avail. In-rm modem link. Refrigerators avail. Balconies. Cr cds: A, D, DS, MC, V.

Hotels

★★★ HILTON LONG BEACH. *2 World Trade Center (90831). 562/983-3400; fax 562/983-1200; toll-free 800/445-8667. www.longbeachhilton.com.* 393 rms, 15 story. S $135-$200; D $155-$220; each addl $25; suites $450-$1,400; family rates; higher rates Grand Prix. Crib free. Pet accepted, some restrictions. Garage parking $8, valet $10. TV; cable (premium). Pool; whirlpool. Restaurant 6 am-midnight. Bar 4 pm-2 am. Ck-out noon. Convention facilities. Business center. In-rm modem link. Concierge. Gift shop. Beauty shop. Free airport transportation. Exercise rm; steam rm. Minibars; some wet bars; refrigerators avail. Balconies. Opp ocean; most rms have ocean view. Cr cds: A, C, D, DS, ER, JCB, MC, V.

★★★ HYATT REGENCY. *200 S Pine Ave (90802). 562/491-1234; fax 562/624-6115; res 800/233-1234. www.hyatt.com.* 521 rms, 17 story. S $189; D $209; each addl $25; suites $325-$1,000; under 18 free. Crib free. Covered, garage, valet parking $10; self-park $8. TV; cable (premium), VCR avail. Heated pool; whirlpool, poolside serv. Restaurant 6 am-11 pm. Bar 11-2 am. Ck-out noon. Convention facilities. Business center. In-rm modem link. Concierge. Gift shop. Exercise equipt. Opp harbor. Luxury level. Cr cds: A, C, D, DS, JCB, MC, V.

★★★ MARRIOTT LONG BEACH . *4700 Airport Plaza Dr (90815). 562/425-5210; fax 562/425-2744; res 800/228-9290. www.marriotthotels.com/lgblb.* 311 rms, 8 story. S, D $99-$179; each addl $15; suites $350; under 13 free; wkend rates. TV; cable (premium), VCR avail. 2 pools, 1 indoor; whirlpool, poolside serv. Coffee in rms. Restaurants 6:30 am-11 pm. Bar noon-2 am. Ck-out noon. Convention facilities. Business center. In-rm modem link. Concierge. Gift shop. Free airport transportation. Golf privileges. Exercise equipt. Massage. Luxury level. Cr cds: A, C, D, DS, JCB, MC, V.

★★★ RENAISSANCE LONG BEACH HOTEL. *111 E Ocean Blvd (90802). 562/437-5900; fax 562/499-2509; res 800/228-9898.* 374 rms, 12 story. S $159; D $174; each addl $15; suites $175-$1,250; under 18 free; wkly rates; higher rates Grand Prix. Valet parking $8, garage $6. TV; cable (premium). Heated pool; poolside serv. Restaurant 6 am-11 pm. Bar to midnight. Ck-out noon. Convention facilities. Business center. In-rm modem link. Concierge. Gift shop. Free airport transportation. Exercise equipt; sauna. Minibars. Balconies. Luxury level. Cr cds: A, C, D, DS, ER, JCB, MC, V.

★★ WESTCOAST HOTELS LONG BEACH. *700 Queensway Dr (90802). 562/435-7676; fax 562/435-3788; toll-free 800/426-0670. www.westcoasthotels.com.* 195 rms, 5 story. S $130-$140; D $150-$160; each addl $10; under 16 free. Crib free. TV; cable. Heated pool. Complimentary coffee in rms. Restaurant 6:30 am-10 pm; Fri-Sun 7 am-11 pm. Bar 11 am-11 pm. Ck-out noon. Meeting rms. Business servs avail. Gift shop. Free airport transportation. Two lighted tennis courts. Exercise equipt. Health club privileges. Massage. Private patios, balconies. City, ocean view, bayside rms avail. Cr cds: A, C, D, DS, MC, V.

★★★ WESTIN LONG BEACH. *333 E Ocean Blvd. (90802). 562/436-3000; fax 562/436-9176; toll-free 888/627-8403. www.westin.com.* 460 rms, 16 story. S, D $199-$209; each addl $20; suites $359-$1,000; under 17 free; wkend rates; higher rates Grand Prix. Crib free. Pet accepted. Garage $8, valet parking $10. TV; cable (premium), VCR avail. Heated pool; whirlpool, poolside serv. Complimentary coffee in rms. Restaurant 6:30 am-10:30 pm. Rm serv 24 hrs. Bar 11-2 am. Ck-out noon. Convention facilities. Business center. In-rm modem link. Concierge. Gift shop. Exercise equipt; sauna. Minibars; some bathrm phones. Opp ocean. Cr cds: A, D, DS, MC, V.

B&Bs/Small Inns

★★★ THE SEAL BEACH INN AND GARDENS. *212 5th St, Seal Beach (90740). 562/493-2416; fax 562/799-0483; toll-free 800/443-3292. www.sealbeachinn.com.* 24 rms, 2 story, 14 kits. S, D $165. Crib $5. TV. Pool. Complimentary full bkfst. Restaurants nearby. Ck-out 11 am, ck-in 4-10 pm. Meeting rms. Business servs avail. Some in-rm whirlpools, fireplaces; microwaves avail. Some balconies. Ocean 300 yds. Restored inn (1923). Totally nonsmoking. Cr cds: A, C, D, DS, JCB, MC, V.

D

★★ THE TURRET HOUSE VICTORIAN BED AND BREAKFAST. *556 Chestnut Ave (90802). 562/983-9812; fax 562/437-4082; toll-free 888/488-7738. www.turrethouse.com.* 5 air-cooled rms, 3 story. S, D $120; higher rates special events. Premium cable TV in common rm. Complimentary full bkfst. Restaurant nearby. Ck-out 11 am, ck-in 3-9 pm. Street parking. Built in 1906; Victorian decor. Totally nonsmoking. Cr cds: A, DS, MC, V.

Restaurants

★ ANNELIESE'S BAVARIAN INN. *5730 E 2nd St (90803). 562/439-4089.* Hrs: 11 am-2 pm, 4-9 pm; Sat, Sun from 4 pm. Closed Tues; hols. Res accepted. German menu. Wine, beer. Lunch $5.95-$11.95, dinner $12.95-$14.95. Specialties: sauerbraten, Wiener schnitzel, rouladen. Bavarian decor. Cr cds: A, MC, V.

D

★★ KING'S FISH HOUSE. *100 W Broadway (90802). 562/432-7463. www.calendarlive.com/kingsfishhouse.* Hrs: 11:15 am-10 pm; Fri, Sat to 11 pm; Sun to 9 pm; Sat, Sun brunch to 4 pm. Closed Thanksgiving, Dec 25. Res accepted. Seafood menu. Bar. Lunch $11-$13, dinner $15-$20. Sat, Sun brunch $9-$11. Children's menu. Specialties: sake-kasu Chilean sea bass, New Orleans barbecue shrimp. Blues music Wed, Sun. Street parking. Outdoor dining. Cr cds: A, DS, MC, V.

D

★ L'OPERA RISTORANTE. *101 Pine Ave (90802). 562/491-0066. www.lopera.com.* Specializes in agnolotti al gorgonzola. Hrs: 11:30 am-11 pm; Fri to midnight; Sat 5 pm-midnight; Sun 5-10 pm. Res accepted. Wine, beer. Lunch $10-$25; dinner $12-$28. Entertainment: Opera wkend. Cr cds: A, D, DS, MC, V.

D

★★★ MUM'S. *144 Pine Ave (90802). 562/437-7700. www.mumsrestaurant.com.* Hrs: 11:30 am-midnight; Fri, Sat to 2 am; Sun to 11 pm. Closed Thanksgiving, Dec 25. Res accepted. Bar 11:30-1 am. A la carte entrees: lunch $6.95-$13.95, dinner $8.95-$20.95. Specializes in California cuisine. Sushi bar. Jazz Tues-Sun. Valet parking. Patio dining. Cr cds: A, D, MC, V.

D

★★ PARKER'S LIGHTHOUSE. *435 Shoreline Village Dr (90802). 562/432-6500. www.selectrestaurant.com.* Hrs: 11 am-11:30 pm; Fri, Sat to 1 am; Sun 10 am-11 pm; Sun brunch to 1 pm. Closed Dec 25. Res accepted. Bar. Wine list. Lunch $6.95-$13.95, dinner $11.95-$19.95. Sun brunch $17.95. Specializes in mesquite-grilled fresh fish, seafood platter, prime Angus beef. Blues Sun. Patio dining. Landmark building overlooks *Queen Mary* and marina. Cr cds: A, C, D, DS, ER, MC, V.

D

★★ THE YARD HOUSE. *401 Shoreline Dr (90802). 562/628-0455. www.yardhouse.com.* Hrs: 11:30 am-midnight; Thurs-Sat to 2 am; Sun from 11 am. Closed Dec 25. Res accepted. Bar. Wine list. Lunch $5-$15, dinner $7-$30. Children's menu. Specializes in pizza, steak, seafood. Outdoor dining. One dining area is formal, the other is casual and features the world's largest selection of draft beer. Totally nonsmoking. Cr cds: A, C, ER, MC, V.

D

Los Angeles (E-4)

Founded 1781 **Pop** 3,485,398 **Elev** 330 ft **Area code** 213, 310, 323, 569 or 818 (San Fernando Valley)

Information Convention and Visitors Bureau, 633 W Fifth St, Suite 6000, 90071; 213/624-7300

Web www.lacvb.com

Occupying a land area of 463½ square miles, Los Angeles has spilled over from the plain into the canyons and foothills. Like an empire in miniature, it boasts mountains and deserts, canyons formed by skyscrapers and by rock, a Mediterranean climate, and working ranches. The city has spread out and around the independent communities of Beverly Hills, Santa Monica, Culver City, Universal City, and Inglewood. The Los Angeles city limits are twisting and confusing. Street maps are available at any Exxon and Mobil service station.

Imagine a sprawling formation made up of a thousand pieces from a thousand different jigsaw puzzles. Illuminate it with klieg lights and flashing neon signs, garnish it with rhinestones, oranges, and oil wells—and you have Los Angeles.

The city has many faces: excitement, tranquility, tall buildings, cottages, ultramodern electronics plants, off-beat religious sects, health fads, sunshine, smog, movie stars and would-be stars, artists, writers, libraries, museums, art galleries, superhighways, and real estate booms.

Los Angeles presents a distilled, concentrated picture of the United

States. People are drawn to its glamour, riches, excitement, and sunshine—all of which have encouraged a general informality. Beneath the glitter and salesmanship there is a pioneer spirit. Although no further geographic frontiers exist, many writers, researchers, scientists, and artists have settled in this area to explore scientific and intellectual frontiers.

Los Angeles is a young city with ancient roots. Along with modern architecture, exuberant growth, and a cultural thirst, it has retained a Spanish serenity and historical interest. On September 4, 1781, Don Felipe de Neve, Governor of California, marched to the site of the present city and with solemn ceremonies founded El Pueblo de Nuestra Señora La Reina de Los Angeles de Porciuncula -"The Town of Our Lady the Queen of the Angels of Porciuncula"—now popularly shortened to "Los Angeles."

The little pueblo slumbered until 1846, when the seizure of California by the United States converted it into a vigorous frontier community. The Gold Rush of 1849 fanned its growth; for a time lawlessness became so prevalent that the city was referred to as Los Diablos—The Devils. The railroads reached it in 1885 and 1886 and, helped by a fare war, brought a tidal wave of new settlers. By 1890, a land boom developed and the population figure reached 50,000, with oil derricks appearing everywhere. The piping in of water from the Owens Valley in 1913 paved the way for expansion and doubling of the population in the 1920s. In the half century between 1890 and 1940, the city grew from 50,395 to 1,504,277—a gain of more than 2,000 percent. The war years added new industries and brought new waves of population which continued throughout the 1980s. Currently, the city's economic assets are invested in "growth" industries such as electronics, machinery, chemicals, oil, printing, publishing, tourism, and entertainment.

The city's geographic scope makes it almost essential that visitors drive their own car, or rent one, for sightseeing in areas other than the downtown section and Westwood. Parking facilities are ample.

Additional Visitor Information

Los Angeles Magazine, available at newsstands, has up-to-date information on cultural events and articles of interest to visitors.

The Los Angeles Convention and Visitors Bureau, 633 W Fifth St, Suite 6000, 90071; phone 213/624-7300, handles written inquiries and has general information brochures available in English, French, German, Japanese, and Spanish. Printed tourist guides are available at two visitor information centers: Downtown at 685 S Figueroa St, phone 213/689-8822; and in Hollywood, 6541 Hollywood Blvd, phone 213/236-2311. In addition, multilingual counselors are on staff at each information center to assist visitors.

Transportation

Airport. See LOS ANGELES INTERNATIONAL AIRPORT AREA.

Car Rental Agencies. See IMPORTANT TOLL-FREE NUMBERS.

Public Transportation. Buses (Metropolitan Transit Authority), phone 213/626-4455.

Rail Passenger Service. Amtrak 800/872-7245.

What to See and Do

Amateur Athletic Foundation. Resource Center contains more than 35,000 print and nonprint volumes, multipurpose pavilion, audio and video exhibits, Olympic awards and memorabilia. (Mon-Fri; closed hols) 2141 W Adams Blvd; 5 mi SW via Santa Monica Fwy, Western Ave exit. Phone 323/730-9600. **FREE**

Angels Flight Railway. A Victorian-era funicular takes riders on a 70-second climb up or down a 300-ft incline via two wooden cable cars. (Daily) Hill St between 3rd and 4th Sts. Phone 213/626-1901.

Autry Museum of Western Heritage. Museum devoted to the Wild West and Hollywood depictions of it. Exhibits incl Wyatt Earp, Custer, Billy the Kid, Native Americans, Pony Express riders, mountain men, and pioneers. Children's Discovery

HISTORIC DISTRICT AND OLVERA STREET

Though Los Angeles isn't known as a walking city, the only way to see the historic district where the city was born, El Pueblo de Los Angeles State Historic Park, is on foot. The historic area is located in the heart of downtown L.A., west of Alameda Street, south of Cesar Chavez Avenue, and north of Arcadia Street and the Hollywood Freeway. This is the place to discover that Los Angeles really does have a history that predates the 20th century—all the way back to 1781, when Spaniards and Mexicans settled here. Much of the area has been or is being restored. The tour continues to adjacent pedestrian-only Olvera Street, where you'll find Mexican-style street markets, restaurants, cafes, and occasional festivals.

Start at the visitor center in the 1887-vintage Sepulveda House at 622 North Main Street to pick up free self-guided walking tour brochures. Now walk a short distance down Main Street and cross east into the Pueblo's historic focal point, the Plaza de Los Angeles, located between Main and Los Angeles streets. In the early 1800s, the plaza was the site of bullfights and bear fights; folkloric performances now take place there on Sundays. The city's first firehouse, dating from 1884, is located on the south side of the plaza; it now serves as a small fire-fighting museum of the era. The Pico House, once known as southern California's finest hotel, stands nearby. Walking northeast from the Plaza, you'll enter Olvera Street. Continue on Olvera to the Avila Adobe, L.A.'s oldest surviving house (built in 1818), which has been restored in the style of an 1840s ranching family. Then browse the markets of Olvera Street, and stop to eat at one of the Mexican restaurants. La Golondrina (W-17 Olvera Street), housed in the city's first brick building, is particularly atmospheric with an open-air patio and mariachi music. For a smaller meal, you can find delicious tacos at one of several casual stands. Allow at least two hours for the walk, assuming a few stops to tour historic sites, but distances are fairly short. If you want to extend your walking tour of downtown, you can head north up Spring Street (west of Main Street), to nearby Chinatown, which is centered along North Broadway.

Center. (Tues-Sun) 4700 Western Heritage Dr. Phone 323/667-2000. ¢¢¢

Beach areas. There are mi of oceanfront in Los Angeles County within 35 mi of downtown Los Angeles. Beaches incl Malibu, Santa Monica, Ocean Park, Venice, Manhattan, Redondo, Long Beach, and others. Redondo Beach has a horseshoe pier and yacht harbor.

Central Library. (1926) A classic, Egyptian-style structure renovated after a 1986 fire. Incl a children's story theater inside and a 1½-acre garden outside. (Daily) 630 W 5th St. Phone 213/228-7000. **FREE**

Descanso Gardens. On 165 acres with ten-acre native plant garden. Ornamental camellia gardens, more than 100,000 plants in bloom Dec-Mar, peaking in mid-Feb. Azalea and rhododendron display Mar-Apr; five-acre rose garden in bloom May-Oct; iris and lilacs in spring; annuals in summer. (Daily, closed Dec 25) Tram tours (Tues-Sun). Hospitality House with changing artwork (daily). Oriental Pavilion with teahouse (Sat, Sun). 1418 Descanso Dr, just S of Foothill Blvd in La Cañada/Flintridge. Phone 818/952-4400. ¢¢

Disneyland. (see) 26 mi SE via Santa Ana Fwy in Anaheim.

Downtown. Contains, among others, these facilities:

ARCO Plaza. Bi-level, subterranean shopping center; art shows, exhibits; restaurants, specialty and service shops. 505 S Flower St.

Broadway Plaza. Designed after an Italian Renaissance shopping galleria. 7th & Hope Sts.

Chinatown. Quaint shops and Chinese restaurants on "Street of the Golden Palace." N Broadway near College St. Phone 310/441-0690.

City Hall. First tall building constructed in southern California. Observation deck (27th floor) in the tower. (Mon-Fri; closed hols) 200 N Spring St. Phone 213/485-2121.

Grand Central Market. City' s oldest (1917) and largest open-air market offers fresh produce and goods from California and around the world. Parking at Hill and 3rd Sts. Phone 213/624-2378.

Hall of Justice. County law enforcement headquarters. 211 W Temple St.

Little Tokyo. Japanese restaurants, art and crafts shops, flower exhibits. 1st St between Main and San Pedro Sts. Phone 310/441-4101.

Los Angeles Mall. Mall complex; shops, restaurants; triforium; music and light presentation. Spring St across from City Hall. Phone 213/974-3288.

Museum of Contemporary Art (MOCA). Seven-level museum devoted to art created since the early 1940s. The building, most of which is below street level, features 11 pyramidial skylight forms and a 53-ft barrel-vaulted structure housing the library and boardroom and serving as the entrance to the exhibits below. Paintings, photographs, drawings, sculptures, and "transmedia." (Tues-Sun; closed Jan 1, Thanksgiving, Dec 25) Free admission Thurs eves. 250 S Grand Ave, at California Plaza. Phone 213/621-2766. ***¢¢¢***

Music Center of Los Angeles County. Performing arts center contains Dorothy Chandler Pavilion, Ahmanson Theatre, Mark Taper Forum. Daily performances by renowned music, dance, and theater companies. (See SPECIAL EVENTS). Free guided tours. 135 N Grand Ave, at First St. Phone 213/972-7211.

Wells Fargo History Museum. More than 140 yrs of Wells Fargo history depicted by displays and exhibits, incl Dorsey gold collection, stagecoaches, treasure boxes, reward posters, 19th-century tools, archival documents, photographs, Western art objects, and a reproduction of a Wells Fargo office (ca 1860); audiovisual presentations. (Mon-Fri; closed hols) 333 S Grand Ave, Plaza Level. Phone 213/253-7166. **FREE**

World Trade Center. Retail stores, restaurants, banks, golf driving ranges, tennis center, travel and tour services. Concourse mural depicts the history of world trade. 350 S Figueroa St. Phone 213/680-2673.

El Pueblo de Los Angeles Historic Monument. Marks area close to where original pueblo of Los Angeles was founded in 1781. Much of the park has been restored; additional building restorations are underway that will also reflect the history and atmosphere of old Los Angeles. Exhibit on "History of Water in Los Angeles." 125 Paseo de la Plaza Phone 213/485-6855. **FREE** The park incl

Avila Adobe. The oldest existing house in Los Angeles (ca 1820), damaged by an earthquake in 1971, now restored as an example of 1840s lifestyle in honor of Los Angeles' Hispanic heritage. (Daily) Phone 213/628-1274. **FREE**

Guided walking tours. Leave from Sepulvada House (see). **FREE**

Nuestra Señora La Reina de Los Angeles. (1818-1822). Our Lady Queen of the Angels. The restored Old Plaza Catholic Church is still an active parish. Contains fine old statuary. (Daily) Phone 213/629-3101.

Old Plaza Firehouse. Built as Los Angeles' first firehouse in 1884; restored as a museum with photographs and fire-fighting equipment of 19th century. (Tues-Sun) 134 Paseo de la Plaza Phone 213/625-3741. **FREE**

Olvera Street. Preserved as a picturesque Mexican street market with stalls, shops, and restaurants selling traditional food and merchandise. It has several annual celebrations, which incl Blessing of the Animals (Sat before Easter), Cinco de Mayo (May 5), the city's birthday (Sept 4), Mexican Independence Day (Sept 15) and Los Posadas (Dec 16-24). (Daily) Phone 213/628-1274. **FREE**

Sepulveda House. (1887). Partially restored Victorian business block; also houses **Visitor Center** (Mon-Sat). Offers 18-min film on early history of Los Angeles and the park (shown upon request). 622 S Main St Phone 213/628-1274.

Elysian Park. Covers 575 acres with beautiful landscaping. Picnicking, playground, tennis courts, and ballfields. Dodger Stadium, home of L.A. Dodgers baseball team, is located here. (Daily) Near intersection of Pasadena and Golden State Fwys. **FREE**

Exposition Park. Park incl sunken rose garden, picnic grounds. Sports arena, Los Angeles Swimming Stadium. Figueroa St and Exposition Blvd. Phone 213/748-4772. Park is also the setting for

California Science Center. Hands-on exhibits on science, mathematics, economics, the urban environment, energy, and health. Hall of Health; Aerospace Hall; earthquake simulator; IMAX theater offers films (fee). (Daily) 700 State Dr, adj to the Coliseum. **FREE**

Los Angeles Memorial Coliseum and Sports Arena. Home field for USC teams. Also scene of soccer, concerts, track events, and many others. Seating capacity of 92,516. 3911 S Figueroa St. Phone 213/747-7111. **¢¢**

Natural History Museum of Los Angeles County. Permanent science exhibits feature mammal, bird, insect, and marine life as well as dinosaurs, other prehistoric fossils, and extinct creatures. Minerals and metals display incl extensive collection of cut gems. History gallery incl features on US history; 400 yrs of life in California; displays of pre-Columbian cultures. Docent tours (one tour every afternoon exc first Tues of each month). Cafeteria. Parking fee. (Daily; closed hols) Free admission first Tues of month. 900 Exposition Blvd. **¢¢¢**

Farmers Market. Historic landmark with outdoor food stalls, restaurants, and shops. (Daily; closed hols) Corner of 3rd and Fairfax Ave. Phone 323/933-9211.

☆ **The Getty Center.** Approx 110-acre campus dedicated to visual arts and humanities situated in the Santa Monica Mtns. Tram takes visitors up hill to central plaza with grand staircase leading to J. Paul Getty Museum, which features six 2-story pavilions; an open courtyard with changing exhibits; and a permanent collection of pre-20th-century European paintings, drawings, illuminated manuscripts, sculpture and decorative arts, and 19th- and 20th-century American and European photographs. The campus also has an auditorium, museum bookstore, restaurant, cafes, and extensive gardens and terraces with views of city and ocean. (Tues-Sun; closed hols) Parking res required. 1200 Getty Center Dr, Suite 1000. Phone 310/440-7300.

☆ **Griffith Park.** More than 4,000 mountainous acres with swimming pool (fee); bridle paths, four golf courses (fee), tennis courts (fee), baseball fields, and many picnic grounds. (Daily) N end of Vermont

The Getty Center, Los Angeles

Ave, bordered by Ventura Fwy on N, Golden State Fwy on E, Los Feliz Blvd entrances on S. Phone 323/662-5874. Also in park are merry-go-round, miniature railroad, refreshment stands, and

Greek Theatre. Scene of summer season of musical events in open-air setting. 2700 N Vermont Ave Phone 323/665-5857.

Griffith Observatory and Planetarium. Incl Hall of Science (summer, daily; winter, Tues-Sun; closed Thanksgiving, Dec 24, 25; fee). Planetarium has frequent shows (Tues-Sun in winter; under age 5 admitted only 1:30 pm shows and special children's shows). Telescope (Tues-Sun eves in winter). Laserium Light concerts (phone 818/901-9405); bookshop. 2800 E Observatory Ave. Phone 213/664-1191 (recording) for planetarium show schedule. Planetarium shows ***¢¢***; Light concerts ***¢¢¢***

Los Angeles Zoo. On 113 landscaped acres; animals grouped by continental origin; reptile house, aviary, aquatic section; koala house; children's zoo; animal rides. Tram service. Picnic areas, concessions. (Daily; closed Dec 25) 5333 Zoo Dr, in center of park. Phone 323/644-4273. ***¢¢¢***

Travel Town. Transportation museum with antique trains, steam engines, planes, fire engines, cable cars. Picnic areas, concession. (Daily; closed Dec 25) 5200 W Zoo Dr. Phone 323/662-5874. **FREE**

In the area are

Cabrillo Marine Aquarium. (see SAN PEDRO) Phone 310/548-7562.

Hollywood. (see) Reached via Hollywood Fwy.

Knott's Berry Farm. (see BUENA PARK). Phone 714/220-5200.

Los Angeles Maritime Museum. (see SAN PEDRO). Phone 310/548-7618.

Mission San Fernando Rey de España. (see SAN FERNANDO).

Ports o'Call Village. (see SAN PEDRO). Phone 310/831-0287.

Six Flags California. (see VALENCIA)

Trips to Catalina Island. (see LONG BEACH). Also from Los Angeles International Airport. Phone 310/510-1520.

Japanese American National Museum. Permanent exhibits document Japanese life in America; temporary exhibits focus on Japanese-American culture, such as WWII internment camps. (Tues-Sun) Phone 213/625-0414. ***¢¢***

Los Angeles County Museum of Art. This outstanding museum consists of five buildings. The Robert Anderson Building houses the 20th-century art collection and traveling exhibitions; the Ahmanson Building houses small changing exhibits and the museum's permanent collection, incl paintings, sculptures, graphic arts, costumes, textiles, and decorative arts of different cultures and periods, dating from prehistoric to modern times; the Hammer Building has major changing exhibits; the Leo S. Bing Center has music, film, and theater programs; two cafes and educational services; and the Pavilion for Japanese Art displays Japanese paintings, sculpture, lacquerware, screens, scrolls, and prints. (Mon, Tues, Thurs-Sun; closed Thanksgiving, Dec 25) Free admission second Tues each month. 5905 Wilshire Blvd, 2 blks E of Fairfax Ave. Phone 323/857-6000. ***¢¢¢***

★ **Los Angeles State and County Arboretum.** (see ARCADIA) Phone 626/821-3222.

Lummis Home and Garden State Historical Monument. Picturesque stone-faced house of Charles F. Lummis (1859-1928), author, historian, librarian, and archaeologist; surrounded by model two-acre water-conserving garden. Also headquarters for Historical Society of Southern California. (Fri-Sun afternoons; closed hols) 200 E Ave 43, adj to Pasadena Frwy (CA 110). Phone 323/222-0546. **FREE**

Mulholland Drive. Runs along crest of Santa Monica Mtns. For a look at the Los Angeles hills and canyons and views of the city and San Fernando Valley, this drive is unsurpassed. Reached by Laurel Canyon Blvd, Hollywood Blvd, Coldwater Canyon Dr, Beverly Glen Blvd, and other roads.

Museum of Tolerance. Unique museum focuses on two central themes: the Holocaust and the history of racism and prejudice in the

American experience. (Mon-Fri, Sun) 9786 W Pico Blvd, The Simon Wiesenthal Center Phone 310/553-8403. ¢¢¢

Page Museum at the La Brea Discoveries. Houses more than one million prehistoric specimens recovered from the La Brea asphalt deposits or "tar pits." More than 30 exhibits, incl reconstructed skeletons; murals, theaters. (Daily; closed hols) Free admission first Tues of each month. 5801 Wilshire Blvd, in Hancock Park. Phone 323/934-PAGE. ¢¢¢

Paramount Film and Television Studios. Two-hr walking tour of studios (Mon-Fri; no tours hols) and tapings of situation comedies and talk shows (seasonal; usually Tues or Fri eves). Walking tour given twice daily. Minimum age 10 yrs for studio tour and 18 yrs for television tapings. For taping schedule write to Paramount Promotional Services, 5555 Melrose Ave. (Mon-Fri) 5555 Melrose Ave, between Van Ness Ave & Gower St. Phone 323/956-1777. ¢¢¢¢

Petersen Automotive Museum. The world's largest automobile museum. Over 200 rare and classic autos; auto culture. (Tues-Sun) 6060 Wilshire Blvd. Phone 323/930-2277. ¢¢¢

Professional sports.

Los Angeles Clippers (NBA). Staples Center, 1111 S Figueroa St. Phone 213/742-7555.

Los Angeles Dodgers (MLB). Dodger Stadium, 1000 Elysian Park Ave. Phone 323/224-1500.

Los Angeles Galaxy (MLS). The Rose Bowl, 1001 Rose Bowl Dr, in Pasadena.

Los Angeles Kings (NHL). Staples Center, 1111 S Figueroa St.

Los Angeles Lakers (NBA). Staples Center, 1111 S Figueroa St. Phone 213/742-7333.

Los Angeles Sparks (WNBA). Staples Center, 1111 S Figueroa St. Phone 310/426-6031.

Rodeo Drive. Street lined with chic boutiques; famous for window-shopping and "star-gazing." (Daily) Between Wilshire and Santa Monica Blvds. Phone 310/248-1000.

San Antonio Winery. Winery, gift shop, wine tasting; restaurant. Self-guided tours. (Daily; closed hols) 737 Lamar St. Phone 323/223-1401. **FREE**

Six Flags California. (see VALENCIA)

South Coast Botanic Garden. Hillside and coastal plants on 87 acres of filled land. (Daily; closed Dec 25) 26300 Crenshaw Blvd, 1 mi S of Pacific Coast Hwy in Palos Verdes Peninsula. Phone 310/544-6815. ¢¢

Southwest Museum. Prehistoric to contemporary Native American art and artifacts; research library. (Tues-Sun; closed hols) 234 Museum Dr, at Marmion Way, Pasadena Fwy, Ave 43 exit. Phone 323/221-2164. ¢¢¢

State historic parks.

Los Encinos. Early California ranch; exhibits of ranch life contained in nine-rm adobe. Blacksmith shop, spring, and small lake. Picnicking. Grounds (Wed-Sun 10 am-5 pm). 16756 Moorpark St, in Encino. Phone 818/784-4849. **FREE**

Will Rogers. Home contains Rogers memorabilia, western art, Native American artifacts; audio tour and film. Hiking and riding trails (horses not avail). Picnicking. (Daily; closed Jan 1, Thanksgiving, Dec 25) Polo games (Sat afternoons, Sun mornings, weather permitting). 15 mi W, 1501 Will Rogers State Park Rd, in Pacific Palisades. Phone 310/454-8212. ¢¢¢

"The Stack". A four-level junction of freeways. Motorists are likely to arrive in central Los Angeles on one of them. The high-speed, six- and eight-lane roads cut across town: Hollywood Fwy to Hollywood and San Fernando Valley; Harbor Fwy to the south; Santa Ana Fwy to the southeast; San Bernardino Fwy to the east; Pasadena Fwy to Pasadena.

TV production studios.

CBS Television City. West Coast studios of CBS Television and source of many of its network telecasts. Write for free tickets well in advance (specify dates and shows preferred) and enclose a stamped, self-addressed envelope. Tickets may also be picked up at Information Window (daily) on a first-come, first-served basis. Age limits for admittance vary and are specified on tickets; children under 12 not admitted to any broadcast; ages 12-15 with adult only. (Mon-Fri) 7800 Beverly Blvd, at Fairfax Ave, 90036. **FREE**

NBC Studios Tour. Free tickets to a taping of one of NBC's TV shows; free parking. Age limits are specified on face of tickets. For tour information phone 818/840-3537 (24 hrs). 3000 W Alameda Ave, Burbank 91523 Phone 818/840-4444. ¢¢¢

Sony Pictures Studio Tour. View current movie and television filming in action. Sets from films, incl *Men in Black* and *The Wizard of Oz*, and game shows, incl *Jeopardy*. (Mon-Fri) 10202 W Washington Blvd, Culver City. Phone 323/520-8687. ¢¢¢¢¢

UCLA Mildred Mathias Botanical Garden. Collection of plants, trees and shrubs. Parking (fee). (Daily; closed school hols, also Jan 2, day after Thanksgiving, Dec 24) Guided tour of campus from visitor center (wkdays). Hilgard and Le Conte Aves. Phone 310/825-1260. **FREE**

Universal Studios Hollywood. Offers a full day of behind-the-scenes views of Hollywood's largest and busiest studio; 45-min tram ride through 420-acre production area where motion pictures and television films are made. Experience the excitement of Jurassic Park—The Ride, *Backdraft* Live, fly with *E.T.*, face *King Kong*, and feel Earthquake, the Big One; also, take "the greatest ride in history" on *Back to the Future*, The Ride. Tours (daily; closed Thanksgiving, Dec 25). 100 Universal City Plaza, ½ blk N of Hollywood Fwy in Universal City. Phone 818/508-9600. ¢¢¢¢¢

Universities.

Fowler Museum of Cultural History, UCLA. Changing exhibits on cultures around the world. Museum store. (Wed-Sun afternoons, also Thurs eves) Free admission Thurs. Parking (fee). Enter campus from Sunset Blvd, at the Westwood Plaza entrance, and inquire about parking availability at the information kiosk. Located near the center of the campus. Phone 310/825-4361. ¢¢

University of California, Los Angeles (UCLA). (1919) 34,000 students. Tours (Mon-Fri). Art gallery, botanical garden, Franklin D. Murphy Sculpture Garden. Parking (fee). 405 Hilgard Ave. Phone 310/825-4321. Also here is

University of Southern California. (1880) 29,500 students. This is the oldest and largest private university in the western US. Points of interest on campus incl Fisher Gallery, 823 Exposition Blvd (Sept-Apr, Tues-Sat; May-Aug, by appt) Phone 213/740-4561; Hancock Memorial Museum. 551 University Ave. Phone 213/740-5144.

Inspecting the killer shark from "Jaws," Universal Studios

Watts Towers. Eight spires made of reinforced steel covered with cement, assembled without welding, nuts, or bolts, and encrusted with 70,000 bits of tile, crockery, and bottles. Built solely by the late Simon Rodia over a 33-yr period, described as "paramount achievement of 20th-century American folk art." Two of the towers rise 100 ft. Call for information about tower tours. Also art center (free) at 1727 E 107th St (Tues-Sun). 1765 E 107th St, S of Century Blvd, E of Harbor Fwy in Watts. Phone 213/847-4646.

Special Events

Chinese New Year. Phone 213/617-0396. Feb.

Cinco de Mayo Celebration. El Pueblo de Los Angeles Historic Monument. Arts and crafts, music and dancing. Early May.

Greek Theatre in Griffith Park. Musical events. Phone 323/665-1927. Mid-June-late Sept.

Lotus Festival. Echo Park Lake, Park and Glendale Aves. 3900 Chevy Chase Dr. Celebrates various Asian and Pacific Island Cultures. Mid-July.

Nisei Week. Little Tokyo. Japanese cultural exhibits. Phone 213/687-7193. Aug.

Los Angeles County Fair. Fairplex, 1101 W McKinley Ave in Pomona (see). Largest in the nation. Early-late Sept.

Los Angeles Music Center Opera. Music Center of Los Angeles County, Dorothy Chandler Pavilion, 135 N Grand Ave. Phone 213/972-8001. Early Sept-June.

Fiesta Broadway. Street party with music, dancing, food. Phone 310/914-0015. Sunday before Cinco de Mayo.

Horse racing.

Hollywood Park. Century Blvd and Prairie Ave in Inglewood. Phone 310/419-1500. Late Apr-late July, early Nov-late Dec.

Santa Anita Park. (see ARCADIA) Phone 626/574-7223.

Motels/Motor Lodges

★★ COURTYARD BY MARRIOTT. *10320 W Olympic Blvd (90064). 310/556-2777; fax 310/203-0563; toll-free 800/321-2211. www.courtyard.com.* 134 rms, 4 story. S, D $124-$159; each addl $10; suites $139-$159; wkend rates. TV; cable (premium). Coffee in rms. Restaurant 6-10:30 am. Bar 4:30 pm-midnight. Ck-out noon. Guest lndry. Meeting rm. Business servs avail. In-rm modem link. Bellhops. Valet serv. Free covered parking. Exercise equipt. Whirlpool. Health club privileges. Minibars; microwaves avail. Balconies. Cr cds: A, C, D, DS, MC, V.

D

★★ COURTYARD BY MARRIOTT AT LAX. *6161 W Century Blvd (90045). 310/649-1400; fax 310/649-0964; toll-free 800/321-2211. www.courtyard.com.* 134 rms, 4 story. S, D $149-$189; each addl $15; suites $169-$225. TV; cable (premium). Complimentary coffee in rms. Ck-out noon. Guest lndry. Meeting rms. Business servs avail. In-rm modem link. Valet serv. Exercise equit. Minibars; microwaves avail. Balconies. Cr cds: A, D, DS, JCB, MC, V.

★★ HOLIDAY INN BRENTWOOD BEL AIR. *170 N Church Ln (90049). 310/476-6411; fax 310/472-1157.* 211 rms, 17 story. S, D $119-$169; each addl $10; suites $210; under 19 free; hol, wkend, wkly rates; higher rates special events. Crib free. TV; cable (premium), VCR avail. Pool; whirlpool. Coffee in rms. Restaurant 6:30 am-11 pm. Bar 11 am-midnight. Ck-out noon. Coin lndry. Meeting rms. Business servs avail. In-rm modem link. Concierge. Exercise equipt. Refrigerators avail. Balconies. Cr cds: A, C, D, DS, MC, V.

D

★★ HOLIDAY INN EXPRESS. *10330 W Olympic Blvd, Century City (90064). 310/553-1000; fax 310/277-1633; toll-free 800/553-1005. www.holiday-inn.com.* 47 rms, 3 with shower only, 4 story, 14 suites. S, D $119; suites $119; under 18 free. Crib free. Valet parking $7.50, in/out $7.50. TV; cable (premium), VCR (movies). Complimentary continental bkfst, coffee in rms. Restaurant nearby. Ck-out noon. Meeting rms. Bellhops. Refrigerators, microwaves. Cr cds: A, C, D, DS, ER, JCB, MC, V.

D SC

★★ HOLIDAY INN LA DOWNTOWN. *750 Garland Ave (90017). 213/628-9900; fax 213/628-1201; res 800/465-5329. www.holiday-inn.com.* 205 rms, 6 story. S, D $89-$129; under 18 free. Crib free. Pet accepted. TV; cable (premium), VCR avail. Pool. Complimenatry coffee in rms. Restaurant 6 am-2 pm, 5-10 pm. Bar 4:30-midnight. Ck-out noon. Coin lndry. Meeting rms. Business servs avail. In-rm modem link. Gift shop. Bellhops. Valet serv. Airport transportation. Exercise equipt. Cr cds: A, D, DS, JCB, MC, V.

D

★★ HOLIDAY INN LOS ANGELES CITY CENTER. *1020 S Figueroa St (90015). 213/748-1291; fax 213/748-6028; toll-free 888/336-3745. www.holiday-inn.com.* 195 rms, 9 story. S, D $109-$139; each addl $10; under

18 free. Crib free. Pet accepted, some restrictions. TV; cable (premium), VCR avail. Heated pool. Restaurant 6:30 am-1 pm, 5-10 pm. Bar noon-midnight. Ck-out noon. Coin lndry. Meeting rms. Business servs avail. Gift shop. Exercise equipt; sauna. Cr cds: A, C, D, DS, JCB, MC, V.

Hotels

★★★ BEVERLY PLAZA HOTEL. *8384 W Third St (90048). 323/658-6600; fax 323/653-3464. www.beverlyplazahotel.com.* 98 rms, 5 story. S, D $192-$249; under 18 free. TV; cable (premium), VCR avail. Valet parking $13. Heated pool; whirlpool, poolside serv. Restaurant (see also CAVA). Rm serv 24 hrs. Bar 11 am-midnight. Ck-out noon. Exercise equipt; sauna. Cr cds: A, D, DS, ER, JCB, MC, V.

★★★★ THE CENTURY PLAZA HOTEL AND SPA. *2025 Ave of the Stars (90067). 310/277-2000; fax 310/551-3355; toll-free 800/228-3000. www.centuryplazala.com.* 1,046 rms, 19-30 story. S $290; D $295; each addl $25; suites $500-$3,000. Tower: S $320; D $345; suites $750-$5,400; each addl $25; under 18 free. TV; cable (premium), VCR avail. Pet accepted. Pool; whirlpool, poolside serv (summer). Rm serv 24 hrs. Bars 11 pm-2 am; entertainment. Ck-out 1 pm. Lndry facilities. Convention facilities. Business center. In-rm modem link. Concierge. Barber, beauty shop. Valet parking. Tennis privileges. Exercise equipt. Health club privileges. Massage. Bathrm phones. Balconies. Cr cds: A, C, D, DS, ER, JCB, MC, V.

★★★★ FOUR SEASONS HOTEL LOS ANGELES. *300 S Doheny Dr (90048). 310/273-2222; fax 310/859-3824; toll-free 800/332-3442. www.fourseasons.com.* You'll find understated luxury at this 179-room, 106-suite hotel tucked into a calm residential neighborhood one mile from Rodeo Drive. The cloistered garden is perfect for outdoor receptions in addition to the nearly 10,000 square feet of available indoor meeting space. Hide away in a poolside cabana overlooking Beverly Hills or dine in the rich atmosphere of the Gardens restaurant. 285 rms, 16 story. S, D $340; suites $525-$4,300; family, wkend rates. Pet accepted. TV; cable (premium), VCR avail. Pool; whirlpool, poolside serv. Restaurant 6:30 am-11 pm (see also GARDENS). Afternoon tea. Bar 11-1 am; pianist. Ck-out noon. Convention facilities. Business center. In-rm modem link. Concierge. Gift shop. Underground parking. Exercise equipt. Massage. Bathrm phones, refrigerators. Balconies. Cr cds: A, C, D, DS, JCB, MC, V.

★★★★ HOTEL BEL AIR. *701 Stone Canyon Rd (90077). 310/472-1211; fax 310/476-5890; res 800/648-4097. www.hotelbelair.com.* Incognito celebrities and visiting dignitaries have long found sanctuary at this Spanish-style villa nestled in the hills of Bel-Air. Many of the rooms have working fireplaces, perfect for a romantic rendezvous, and all are decorated in a Mediterranean mode with terra cotta floors and private patios or gardens. The opulent restaurant will cap off any special occasion. 92 rms. S $426; D $451; suites $550-$2,500. TV; cable (premium), VCR (movies). Pool; poolside serv. Restaurant (see THE RESTAURANT). Rm serv 24 hrs. Bar 10-2 am; entertainment. Ck-out 1 pm. Meeting rms. Business servs avail. In-rm modem link. Concierge. Valet parking. Airport transportation. Exercise equipt. Massage. Health club privileges. Bathrm phones; some wood-burning fireplaces. Private patios. Cr cds: A, C, D, ER, JCB, MC, V.

★★★ HOTEL SOFITEL. *8555 Beverly Blvd (90048). 310/278-5444; fax 310/657-2816. www.sofitel.com.* 311 rms, 10 story. S, D $280-$320; each addl $30; suites $375-$500; under 18 free; wkend rates. Crib free. Valet parking $17.50. TV; cable (premium), VCR avail. Heated pool; poolside serv. Restaurant 6:30 am-11 pm. Rm serv 24 hrs. Bar 11-2 am; entertainment. Ck-out 1 pm. Convention facilities. Business servs avail. In-rm modem link. Concierge. Shopping arcade. Exercise equipt; sauna. Bathrm phone, minibar, wet bar in suites. Some balconies. Contemporary Mediterranean-style hotel features a blend of French and Californian cultures. Cr cds: A, C, D, MC, V.

D

★★★ **HYATT REGENCY.** *711 S Hope St (90017). 213/683-1234; fax 213/629-3230; toll-free 800/233-1234. www.hyatt.com.* 485 rms, 26 story. S $175-$215; D $200-$240; each addl $25; suites $225-$750; under 18 free; wkend rates; package plans. Crib free. Garage parking; valet $15. TV; cable (premium), VCR avail. Restaurants 6 am-11 pm. Bar 11:30-1 am; entertainment. Ck-out noon. Convention facilities. Business center. In-rm modem link. Concierge. Shopping arcade. Barber, beauty shop. Exercise equipt. Some minibars. Luxury level. Cr cds: A, C, D, DS, ER, JCB, MC, V.

D SC

★★★★ **LE MERIDIEN AT BEVERLY HILLS.** *465 S La Cienega Blvd (90048). 310/247-0400; fax 310/246-2166; res 800/645-5687. www.forte-hotels.com.* This stylishly modern hotel offers everthing for visitors in town on business and vacationers alike with close proximity to downtown and Rodeo Drive. A variety of room types, all with a sleek look, are available, many with private balconies. Pangaea, located in the hotel, is a stylish newcomer to L.A.'s dining scene. 310 units, 7 story. S $310-$330; D $315-$415; each addl $25; suites $600-$1,800; under 12 free. Crib $25. Pet accepted. Valet parking $16. TV; cable (premium), VCR avail. Pool. Complimentary coffee in rms. Restaurants 6 am-10 pm. Rm serv 24 hrs. Bar 3 pm-1 am; entertainment. Ck-out 1 pm. Business center. In-rm modem link. Concierge. Gift shop. Exercise equipt. Massage. Bathrm phones, Japanese soaking tubs, minibars. Balconies. Cr cds: A, C, D, DS, ER, JCB, MC, V.

D

★★★ **LOS ANGELES MARRIOTT DOWNTOWN.** *333 S Figueroa St (90071). 213/617-1133. www.marriott.com.* 469 rms, 15 story. S, D $175-$350; each addl $25; under 17 free. Crib avail. Pet accepted. Valet parking. Pool. TV; cable (premium), VCR avail. Complimentary coffee in rms, newspaper. Restaurant 6 am-10:30 pm. Bar. Ck-out noon. Meeting rms. Business center. Valet serv. Gift shop. Exercise rm. Golf. Some refrigerators, minibars. Cr cds: A, C, D, DS, MC, V.

D

★★ **LUXE SUMMIT HOTEL BEL-AIR.** *11461 W Sunset Blvd (90049). 310/476-6571; fax 310/471-6310; res 800/468-3541. www.luxehotels.com.* 162 rms, 2 story. S, D $149-$239; each addl $20; suites $199-$499; under 18 free; wkend rates. TV; cable (premium), VCR avail. Heated pool; poolside serv. Restaurant 6:30 am-11 pm. Bar. Ck-out noon. Meeting rms. Business servs avail. In-rm modem link. Gift shop. Valet parking. Airport transportation. Tennis, pro. Exercise equipt. Bathrm phones, refrigerators, minibars; microwaves avail. Private patios, balconies. Cr cds: A, C, D, DS, JCB, MC, V.

D SC

★★★ **NEW OTANI HOTEL AND GARDEN.** *120 S Los Angeles St (90012). 213/629-1200; fax 213/622-0980; res 800/421-8795. www.newotani.com.* 434 rms, 21 story. S $189; D $204; each addl $25; suites $475-$1,800; under 12 free. Crib free. Covered parking $13.75/day, valet $18.15/day. TV; cable (premium), VCR avail. Restaurants 6 am-9:30 pm. Bars 10-1 am. Ck-out noon. Meeting rms. Business center. Concierge. Shopping arcade. Barber. Exercise equipt. Japanese health spa. Bathrm phones, minibars. Japanese-style decor, garden. Cr cds: A, C, D, DS, ER, JCB, MC, V.

D

★★★ **OMNI LOS ANGELES HOTEL.** *251 S Olive St (90012). 213/617-3300; fax 213/617-3399; res 800/843-6664. www.omnihotels.com.* 439 rms, 17 story. S $230; D $260; each addl $30; suites $395-$1650; under 14 free; package plans; higher rates special events. Crib free. Pet accepted, some restrictions. Valet parking $21. TV; cable (premium), VCR avail (movies). Restaurant (see also GRAND CAFE). Rm serv 24 hrs. Bar 1 pm-1 am; piano. Ck-out noon. Convention facilities. Business center. In-rm modem link. Concierge. Shopping arcade. Barber, beauty shop. Exercise equipt; sauna. Massage. Heated pool; poolside serv.

Bathrm phones, minibars; microwaves avail. Luxury level. Cr cds: A, C, D, DS, ER, JCB, MC, V.
D

★★ **OXFORD PALACE.** *745 S Oxford Ave (90005). 213/389-8000; fax 213/389-8500. www.oxfordhotel.com.* 86 rms, 4 story, 9 suites. S $89-$139; D $94-$149; each addl $20; suites $110-$239. TV; cable, VCR (movies $3). Restaurants 7 am-2:30 pm, 5:30-10:30 pm. Bar 9-2 am. Ck-out 11 am. Meeting rms. Business center. Shopping arcade. Garage parking. Health club privileges. Minibars. Some balconies. Cr cds: A, D, MC, V.
D

Aztec dancers on Olvera Street

★★★ **PARK HYATT LOS ANGELES.** *2151 Ave of the Stars (90067). 310/277-1234; fax 310/785-9240; res 800/233-1234. www.hyatt.com.* 367 rms, 17 story, 189 suites. S $299-$349; D $324; suites $349-$2,500; under 18 free; wkend rates. Valet parking $17. TV; cable (premium), VCR avail (movies). 2 pools, 1 indoor; whirlpool, poolside serv. Restaurant (see PARK GRILL). Rm serv 24 hrs. Bar 11:30-1:30 am; pianist. Ck-out noon. Meeting rms. Business center. In-rm modem link. Concierge. Shopping arcade. Tennis privileges. Golf privileges. Exercise equipt; sauna, steam rm. Massage. Bathrm phones, refrigerators, minibars; microwaves avail. Private patios, balconies. Cr cds: A, C, D, DS, JCB, MC, V.
D

★★★ **RADISSON WILSHIRE PLAZA.** *3515 Wilshire Blvd (90010). 213/381-7411; fax 213/386-7379; res 800/333-3333. www.radisson.com/losangelesca_wilshire.* 380 rms, 12 story. S, D $129-$149; each addl $10; suites $275-$575; under 18 free. Crib free. Valet parking $13. TV; cable (premium). Heated pool; poolside serv. Restaurants 6 am-11 pm. Bar 11-1 am; entertainment Mon-Fri. Ck-out noon. Convention facilities. Business center. In-rm modem link. Concierge. Barber, beauty shop. Exercise equipt. Minibars. Cr cds: A, C, D, DS, JCB, MC, V.
D

★★★ **REGAL BILTMORE HOTEL.** *506 S Grand Ave (90071). 213/624-1011; fax 213/612-1545; toll-free 800/245-8673. www.millennium-hotels.com.* 683 rms, 12 story. S, D $225-$275; each addl $30; suites $390-$2,000; under 18 free; wkend rates. Valet parking $17.60. Pool; whirlpool. TV; cable (premium), VCR avail. Restaurants 6:30 am-11 pm (see also BERNARD'S). Rm serv 24 hrs. Bars 11-2 am. Ck-out noon. Convention facilities. Business servs avail. In-rm modem link. Shopping arcade. Beauty shop. Exercise rm; sauna. Massage. Health club privileges. Wet bar in most suites; some bathrm phones. Luxury level. Cr cds: A, C, D, DS, ER, JCB, MC, V.
D SC

★★★★ THE ST. REGIS, LOS ANGELES. *2055 Ave of the Stars (90067). 310/277-6111.* The new St. Regis Los Angeles is a warm and intimate, urban hotel right in the heart of Los Angeles' Century City area It's close to shopping, theater, and the business districts. The hotel boasts upscale amenities and has a wonderful fitness center. The decor is contemporary and formal without being fussy. Service is attentive and friendly. 257 rms, 30 story, 40 suites. S, D $300-$750; suites $550-$2,500. Crib avail. Valet parking avail. TV; cable (premium). Pool. Restaurant 6 am-10 pm. Rm serv 24 hrs. Bars; entertainment. Ck-out noon, ck-in 3 pm. Meeting rms. Business center. In-rm modem link. Bellhops. Valet serv. Concierge. Airport transportation. Exercise rm; sauna, steam rm. Spa. Cr cds: A, D, DS, JCB, MC, V.

★★★ THE WESTIN BONAVENTURE HOTEL. *404 S Figueroa St (90071). 213/624-1000; fax 213/612-4800; res 800/937-8461.* 1,354 rms, 35 story. S $170-$190; D $190-$230; suites $195-$2,500; under 18 free. Crib free. Garage $18.15/day. TV; cable (premium), VCR avail. Heated pool; poolside serv. Restaurants 5:30 am-midnight. Rm serv 24 hrs. Bars 11-2 am. Ck-out noon. Convention facilities. Business center. In-rm modem link. Concierge. Shopping arcade. Barber, beauty shop. Exercise equipt. Health club privileges. Six-story atrium lobby. Cr cds: A, C, D, DS, JCB, MC, V.

D

★★★ WILSHIRE HOTEL AND CENTRE. *930 Wilshire Blvd (90017). 213/688-7777; fax 213/612-3989; toll-free 888/773-2888. www.wilshiregrand.com.* 900 rms, 16 story. S $169-$209; D $189-$229; each addl $25; suites $375-$1,200. Crib free. Garage $18.50. TV; cable (premium). Heated pool; whirlpool, poolside serv. Coffee in rms. Restaurants 6:30 am-11 pm (see also SEOUL JUNG). Bar 10 am-midnight; pianist. Ck-out noon. Convention facilities. Business center. In-rm modem link. Concierge. Shopping arcade. Barber, beauty shop. Exercise equipt. Minibars. Luxury level. Cr cds: A, C, D, DS, ER, JCB, MC, V.

D SC

W LOS ANGELES. (Too new to be rated) *930 Hilgard Ave (90024). 310/208-8765. www.whotels.com.* 258 rms, 16 story. S, D $289-$319; under 17 free. Crib avail. Pet accepted. TV; cable (premium). Indoor pool. Restaurant 6:30 am-10 pm. Business center. Exercise rm. Massage.

★★★ WYNDHAM CHECKERS. *535 S Grand Ave (90071). 213/624-0000; fax 213/626-9906. www.wyndham.com.* 188 rms, 12 story. S $240-$249; D $269; each addl $20; suites $380-$950; under 18 free; wkend rates. Crib free. Valet parking $20. TV; cable (premium), VCR avail. Heated pool; whirlpool, poolside serv. Restaurant (see also CHECKERS). Rm serv 24 hrs. Bar 11:30 am-11:30 pm. Meeting rms. Business center. In-rm modem link. Concierge. Airport transportation. Exercise equipt; sauna, steam rm. Massage. Bathrm phones, minibars. Library. Opened in 1927. Cr cds: A, C, D, DS, ER, JCB, MC, V.

D SC

★★★ WYNDHAM COMMERCE. *5757 Telegraph Rd, Commerce (90040). 323/887-8100. www.wyndham.com.* 201 rms, 7 story; 20 suites. S, D $145-$330; each addl $15; under 17 free. Crib avail. Pool. TV; cable (premium), VCR avail. Complimentary coffee in rms, newspaper. Restaurant 6 am-10:30 pm. Bar. Ck-out 11 am. Meeting rms. Business center. Valet serv. Gift shop. Exercise rm. Some refrigerators, minibars. Cr cds: A, C, D, DS, MC, V.

All Suites

★★★ SUMMERFIELD SUITES BY WYNDHAM. *1000 Westmount Dr, West Hollywood (90069). 310/657-7400; fax 310/854-6744; toll-free 800/833-4353. www.summerfieldsuites.com.* 95 kit. suites, 4 story. S, D $210-$255; under 12 free; monthly rates. Crib free. Pet accepted. Covered parking $12. TV; cable (premium), VCR (movies $5). Pool. Complimentary continental bkfst. Ck-out noon. Coin lndry.

Meeting rm. In-rm modem link. Exercise equipt; sauna. Health club privileges. Refrigerators, microwaves, fireplaces. Balconies. Cr cds: A, D, DS, JCB, MC, V.

D

Extended Stay

★★ **RESIDENCE INN BY MARRIOTT MANHATTAN BEACH.** *1700 N Sepulveda Blvd, Manhattan Beach (90266). 310/546-7627; fax 310/545-1327; res 800/331-3131.* 176 kit. suites, 2 story. S $99-$178; D $150-$218; each addl $10; under 12 free; wkly, monthly rates. Crib free. Pet accepted, some restrictions. TV; cable (premium). Heated pool; whirlpool. Complimentary continental bkfst. Restaurant nearby. Ck-out noon. Meeting rm. Business servs avail. In-rm modem link. Valet serv. Free airport transportation. Microwaves. Balconies. Cr cds: A, C, D, DS, MC, V.

D

Restaurants

★★ **72 MARKET STREET OYSTER BAR AND GRILL.** *72 Market St, Venice (90291). 310/392-8720. www.72marketst.com.* Specialties: tuna tartare, meat loaf, chili. Oyster bar. Hrs: 11:30 am-2:30 pm, 6-10 pm; Fri to 11 pm; Sat 6-11 pm; Sun 5:30-9 pm. Res accepted. Bar. A la carte entrees: lunch $8-$12, dinner $15-$24. Own baking. Pianist. Valet parking. Two dining rms: high-tech; chic supper club. Celebrity haunt. Rotating art exhibit. Cr cds: A, D, MC, V.

D

★ **ANNA'S.** *10929 W Pico Blvd (90064). 310/474-0102.* Hrs: 11:30 am-11 pm; Fri to midnight; Sat 4 pm-midnight; Sun from 4 pm. Closed Thanksgiving, Dec 25. Res accepted. Italian menu. Bar. Lunch $5.50-$13, dinner $6.95-$22. Specialties: chicken cacciatore, linguine Sorrento. Valet parking. Family-owned. Totally nonsmoking. Cr cds: A, DS, MC, V.

D

★★★ **A THOUSAND CRANES.** *120 S Los Angeles St (90012). 213/629-1200.* Specializes in Japanese entrees. Hrs: 7-10 am, 11:30 am-2 pm, 6-9:30 pm; Sun brunch 11 am-2 pm. Res accepted. Wine, beer. Lunch $16-$23; dinner $26-$90. Children's menu. Entertainment. Overlooks hotel and waterfall and gardens. Cr cds: A, D, DS, JCB, MC, V.

D SC

★★ **BERNARD'S.** *506 S Grand Ave (90071). 213/612-1580.* Hrs: 11:30 am-2:30 pm, 6-10 pm; Fri to 10:30 pm; Sat 6-10:30 pm. Closed Sun; hols. Res accepted. Continental menu. Wine cellar. A la carte entrees: lunch $13-$21, dinner $17-$30. Specializes in seafood. Own baking. Entertainment. Valet parking. Cr cds: A, D, DS, MC, V.

D

★★★ **CAFE DES ARTISTES.** *1534 N McCadden Pl (90028). 323/469-7300. www.cafedesartistes.com.* Specializes in pork chops, macaroni and cheese, seafood platter. Hrs: 11:30 am-3 pm, 5:30 pm-midnight; Thurs-Sat 5:30 pm-2 am; Sun 5:30 pm-midnight; Sun brunch 11:30 am-3 pm. Res accepted. Wine, beer. Lunch $7-$16; dinner $9-$18. Brunch $7-$16. Entertainment. Cr cds: A, D, DS, MC, V.

D

★★★ **CAFE PINOT.** *700 W 5th St (90071). 213/239-6500.* Hrs: 11:30 am-2:30 pm, 5:30-9 pm; Sat, Sun 5-10 pm. Closed hols. Res accepted. Seasonal menu. Bar. Wine list. Lunch $13-$20, dinner $15.75-$19.95. Specialties: rotisserie chicken, suckling pig, Peking duck ravioli. Valet parking (dinner). Outdoor dining. French bistro atmosphere. Cr cds: A, C, D, DS, ER, MC, V.

D

★★★ **CAMPANILE.** *624 S La Brea Ave (90036). 323/938-1447. www.campanilerestaurant.com.* Hrs: 11:30 am-2:30 pm, 6-10 pm; Fri to 11 pm; Sat 8 am-1:30 pm, 5:30-11 pm; Sun 8 am-1:30 pm. Closed Memorial Day, Thanksgiving, Dec 25. Res accepted. California, Italian menu. Bar. Bkfst $6-$15, lunch $12-$18, dinner $20-$35. Specialties: seared wild salmon, risotto, prime rib. Own baking. Valet parking. Charlie Chaplin's original offices. Malibu tile, fountain; skylights. Cr cds: A, C, D, DS, ER, MC, V.

D

★★ **CAVA.** *8384 W 3rd St (90048). 323/658-8898. www.calendarlive.com/cava.* Hrs: 6:30 am-11 pm; Fri, Sat to midnight. Res accepted. Contemporary Spanish menu. Bar. A la carte entrees: bkfst $4.50-$9.75, lunch, dinner $7.50-$17.95. Specialties: pescado Vera Cruz, pollo diablo, paella Valenciana. Jazz Tues, Fri, Sat eves. Valet parking. Outdoor dining. Contemporary decor. Cr cds: A, C, D, DS, ER, MC, V.

D

★★★ **CHECKERS.** *535 S Grand Ave (90071). 213/624-0000.* Hrs: 6 am-9 pm; Sat, Sun brunch 10 am-2 pm. Res accepted. Bar. Wine list. Bkfst $8-$15, lunch $10-$25, dinner $25-$40. Sat, Sun brunch $10-$18. Specializes in fresh seafood dishes. Valet parking. Outdoor dining. Intimate dining in formal setting. High tea. Totally nonsmoking. Cr cds: A, C, D, DS, MC, V.

D SC

★★★ **CIAO TRATTORIA.** *815 W 7th St (90017). 213/624-2244. www.ciaotrattoria.com.* Hrs: 11 am-10 pm; Sat, Sun from 5 pm. Closed hols. Res accepted. Italian menu. Bar. A la carte entrees: lunch $10.95-$15.50, dinner $14.50-$22. Specialties: chicken cacciatore, farfalle gustose, veal saltimbocca. Valet parking. In historic Fine Arts Building. Intimate, European atmosphere. Cr cds: A, DS, MC, V.

D

★★★ **CICADA.** *617 S Olive St (90014). 213/488-9488.* Specializes in duck ravioli, seared John Dory with braised artichoke. Hrs: 11:30 am-2:30 pm, 5:30-9:30 pm. Closed Sun. Res accepted. Wine, beer. Lunch $12-$22; dinner $16-$30. Jazz. Cr cds: A, D, DS, JCB, MC, V.

D

★★ **CIUDAD.** *445 S Figueroa (90071). 213/486-5171. www.ciudad-la.com.* Cuban chicken, Brazilian seafood stew, lobster salad. Hrs: 11:30 am-10 pm; Sat, Sun 4:30-11 pm. Res accepted. Wine, beer. Lunch $8-$15; dinner $10-$20. Entertainment. Cr cds: A, D, DS, JCB, MC, V.

D

★★★★ **DIAGHILEV.** *1020 N San Vincente Blvd (90069). 310/854-1111. www.wyndham.com.* Love seats, long-

HOLLYWOOD BOULEVARD

In the first half of the 20th century, Hollywood Boulevard was a legendary place replete with glamorous stars and nightclubs; in the latter part of the century, as film studios deserted Hollywood for other parts of greater L.A., it fell into decline. But now the once-glittering boulevard is making a comeback. Walking is the best way to see its sights, which include renowned theaters, old-time restaurants and hotels, and much of the Hollywood Walk of Fame. Start at the celebrated corner of Hollywood and Vine. The Walk of Fame heads north on Vine up to Sunset Boulevard. You can also view the famous circular Capitol Records Building, located at 1750 North Vine Street, designed to resemble a stack of records. Needless to say, this building predated the CD era. Return to Hollywood Boulevard and walk west, continuing to follow the Walk of Fame; keep your eyes open for the stars of Marilyn Monroe, Charlie Chaplin, Clark Gable, Jack Nicholson, Elvis Presley, and Mickey Mouse. But don't forget to look up either—in the hills to the north, you should be able to spot the 50-foot-high letters of the Hollywood Sign. Meanwhile, at eye level, you'll pass several vintage theaters, each more ornate (and gaudy) than the last, including the Pantages (6233 Hollywood Boulevard), the Egyptian (6712), and El Capitan (6838). Most legendary of all is Mann's Chinese (6925), where stars ranging from Shirley Temple to Harrison Ford have left their handprints and footprints (and, in Lassie's case, pawprints) in the cement in the theater's courtyard. Next to Mann's is the new Academy of Motion Pictures Arts and Sciences Complex, which is helping to put the "Hollywood" back into Hollywood. And just across the street is the venerable Hollywood Roosevelt Hotel (7000 Hollywood Boulevard), where Hollywood's golden years are chronicled in a photo exhibit on the mezzanine. At the end of your stroll, head to Musso and Frank Grill at 6667 Hollywood Boulevard, an oldtime Hollywood hangout that retains its vintage flavor; it's a good place to eat or have a drink at the splendid bar.

stemmed roses, balalaika music, and impeccable service abound at this Franco-Russian hotspot, perfect for a romantic evening, or perhaps the Big Question. Don't miss the flavored vodka, the chicken Kiev, or the caviar. Located in the Wyndham Bel Age Hotel. Franco-Russian menu. Specialties: braised leg of duck, filet of salmon with sturgeon mousse, braised veal chop. Hrs: 6-11 pm. Closed Sun, Mon; Jan 1. Res accepted. Bar. A la carte entrees: dinner $20-$50. Complete meal: dinner $75. Elegant dining. Jacket. Cr cds: A, C, D, DS, ER, MC, V.

D

★★ **EL CHOLO.** *1121 W Western Ave (90006). 323/734-2773. www.elcholo.com.* Hrs: 11 am-10 pm; Fri, Sat to 11 pm; Sun to 9 pm. Closed July 4, Thanksgiving, Dec 25. Res accepted. Mexican menu. Bar. Lunch, dinner $6.45-$13.95. Specialties: fajitas, green corn tamales, margaritas. Valet parking. Family-owned since 1927. Casual dining. Cr cds: A, D, MC, V.

D

★★ **ENGINE CO. NO. 28.** *644 S Figueroa St (90017). 213/624-6996. www.engineco.com.* Specializes in grilled meats. Hrs: 11:15 am-9 pm; Sat, Sun 5-9 pm. Res required. Wine, beer. Lunch, dinner $10-$22. Children's menu. Entertainment. Cr cds: A, C, D, MC, V.

D

★★ **EUROCHOW.** *1099 Westwood Blvd (90024). 310/209-0066. www.eurochow.com.* Chinese menu. Specializes in eurochow pizza, prawns with xo sauce, spaghetti. Hrs: 11:30 am-2:30 pm, 5:30 pm-midnight; Thurs-Sat to 1 am. Res accepted. Wine, beer. Lunch $10-$19.75; dinner $10-$20. Entertainment. Cr cds: A, D, JCB, MC, V.

D

★★★ **FOUR OAKS.** *2181 N Beverly Glen (90077). 310/470-2265. www.fouroaksrestaurant.com.* Hrs: 11:30 am-2 pm, 6-10 pm; Sun, Mon from 6 pm; Sun brunch 10:30 am-2 pm. Closed hols. Res accepted. Modern French, American menu. Bar. A la carte entrees: lunch $15-$22, dinner $22-$27. Sun brunch $32. Menu changes seasonally; emphasizes natural ingredients. Own desserts. Valet parking. Patio dining. Mediterranean decor. Built 1890. Cr cds: A, D, MC, V.

★★★ **GARDENS.** *300 S Doheny Dr (90048). 310/273-2222. www.fourseasons.com.* Mediterranean menu. Specializes in steak, lamb, seafood. Own baking, ice cream. Hrs: 7 am-11 pm; Sun brunch 10 am-2:30 pm. Bar 11-1 am. Wine cellar. Res accepted. A la carte entrees: bkfst $5.95-$18, lunch $8.95-$18, dinner $18-$35. Sun brunch $42. Children's menu. Valet parking. Outdoor dining. Cr cds: A, C, D, DS, ER, MC, V.

D

★ **GRAND CAFE.** *624 S Grand Ave (90017). 213/622-0474. www.omnihotels.com.* Hrs: 6:30-10:30 pm; early-bird dinner 5:30-7:30 pm (seasonal). Res accepted. Pan-Asian menu. Bar 1 pm-1 am. Wine list. A la carte entrees: bkfst $10-$15, lunch $14-$17, dinner $20-$30. Buffet: bkfst $17.95, lunch $14.95. Children's menu. Specialties: Dungeness crab cake salad, proscuitto and grab cheese wrapped tiger prawns, pecan-crusted halibut. Valet parking. Outdoor dining. Cr cds: A, D, DS, MC, V.

D

★★ **IL FORNAIO.** *301 N Beverly Dr (90210). 310/550-8330. www.ilfornaio.com.* Specializes in pollo toscano, pizza. Hrs: 6:30 am-11 pm; Sat 7:30 am-midnight; Sun 7:30 am-11 pm. Res accepted. Wine, beer. Lunch, dinner $9.95-$24.95. Children's menu. Entertainment. Cr cds: A, D, MC, V.

D

★★ **KASS BAH.** *9010 Melrose Ave (90069). 310/274-7664.* Continental menu. Specializes in tuna tartar. Hrs: 7 pm-2 am. Closed Sun. Res accepted. Wine list. Dinner $15-$30. Cr cds: A, MC, V.

D

★★ **LA CACHETTE.** *10506 Santa Monica Blvd (90025). 310/470-4992.* Hrs: 11:30 am-2:30 pm, 6-10 pm; Fri to 10:30 pm; Sat 5:30-10:30 pm; Sun 5:30-9 pm. Closed hols. Res accepted. French menu. Bar service. A la carte entrees: lunch $12-$18, dinner $18-$29. Specialties: shellfish bouillabaisse, double-roasted muscovy duck, grilled swordfish. Intimate dining. Totally nonsmoking. Cr cds: A, C, DS, MC, V.

D

★★ LA GOLONDRINA MEXICAN CAFE. *17 Olvera St (90012). 213/628-4349. www.lagolondrina.com.* Hrs: 10 am-9 pm; Fri, Sat to 10 pm; Sun from 9 am. Closed Jan 1, Dec 25. Res accepted. No A/C. Mexican menu. Bar. Bkfst $4.25-$8.95, lunch, dinner $4.25-$13.95. Children's menu. Specialties: carnitas, costillas en adobado. Own breads. Mexican guitarists. Outdoor dining. Historical landmark; first brick building in Los Angeles (1855). Family-owned since 1924. Cr cds: A, C, D, DS, MC, V.

D SC

★ LA SERENATA DE GARIBALDI. *1842 E 1st St (90039). 323/265-2887.* Specializes in fisherman's soup, fish taco, Mexican sea bass in cilantro sauce. Hrs: 11 am-10 pm; Fri to 11 pm; Sat, Sun 10 am-11 pm. Res accepted. Wine, beer. Lunch $7-$11; dinner $9-$21. Sun brunch, $6-$9. Entertainment: Mariachi band. Cr cds: A, D, DS, MC, V.

D

★★ LES DEUX CAFES. *1638 N Las Palmas Ave, Hollywood (90028). 323/465-0509.* Specializes in French entrees. Hrs: 11:30 am-2:30 pm, 6:30-11:30 pm; Sun 6-11:30 pm. Res required. Wine, beer. Lunch $9-$20; dinner $20-$30. Entertainment. Cr cds: A, MC, V.

D

★★ LES FRERESTAIX. *1911 Sunset Blvd (90026). 213/484-1265. www.taixfrench.com.* Hrs: 11 am-10 pm; Sun noon-9 pm. Closed hols. Res accepted. Country French menu. Bar. Wine list. Complete meals: lunch $6.95-$16.95, dinner $7.95-$24.50. Children's menu. Specialty: escargots a la Bourguignonne. Own soups. Valet parking. Family-owned since 1927. Cr cds: A, DS, MC, V.

D

★★★ LINQ. *8338 W Third St (90048). 323/655-4555.* Specializes in soy mirin glazed Chilean sea bass. Hrs: 11 am-3 pm, 6 pm-1:30 am. Res accepted. Wine, beer. Lunch $6-$23; dinner $8.50-$28. Entertainment. Waterfalls, 2 fireplaces, black marble on walls. Cr cds: A, D, DS, JCB, MC, V.

D

★★ LOCANDA VENETA. *8638 W Third St (90048). 310/274-1893. www.locandaveneta.com.* Hrs: 11:30 am-2:30 pm, 5:30-10:30 pm; Fri to 11 pm; Sat 5:30-11 pm. Closed Sun. Res accepted. Northern Italian menu. Beer. Wine list. A la carte entrees: lunch, dinner $10-$25. Specializes in seafood, pasta. Own baking. Valet parking. Patio dining. Windows open to street; open kitchen. Cr cds: A, D, DS, MC, V.

★★★ LUCQUES. *8474 Melrose Ave (90069). 323/655-6277.* Mediterranean menu. Specializes in grilled veal chops with sweet corn, stewed leeks and morel butter, and brazed beef short ribs with greens, pearl onions, and horseradish crème. Menu changes bimonthly. Hrs: 5-10 pm. Closed Mon. Res accepted. Bar. Dinner $18-$25. Valet parking. Lodge décor. Cr cds: A, D, MC, V.

D

★★ MADEO. *8897 Beverly Blvd (90048). 310/859-0242.* Hrs: noon-3 pm, 6:30-11 pm; Sat, Sun from 6:30 pm. Closed Dec 25. Res accepted. Italian menu. Bar. A la carte entrees: lunch $10-$30, dinner $30-$50. Specialties: branzino, leg of veal. Own pastries. Valet parking. Wood-burning oven. Cr cds: A, DS, MC, V.

D

★★★ MOJO. *930 Hilgard Ave (90024). 310/443-7820. www.whotels.com.* Specializes in chicken rostizado, hot paprika prawns. Hrs: 6:30-11 pm. Res accepted. Wine, beer. Dinner $21-$30. Entertainment. Cr cds: A, D, DS, JCB, MC, V.

D

★★ NICK & STEF'S. *330 S Hope St (90071). 213/680-0330.* Specializes in steak, broiled Northern haibut. Hrs: 11:30 am-2:30 pm, 5:30-9 pm; Sat, Sun 5-9 pm. Res accepted. Wine, beer. Lunch $11-$27; dinner $19-$32. Entertainment. Cr cds: A, C, D, DS, JCB, MC, V.

D

★★ PACIFIC DINING CAR. *1310 W 6th St (90017). 310/483-6000. www.pacificdiningcar.com.* Steakhouse menu. Specializes in T-bone steaks,

seafood mix grill, ribeye steak. Open 24 hrs. Res accepted. Wine list. Lunch $14-$25; dinner $25-$39. Entertainment. Cr cds: A, C, D, MC, V.
D

★★ **PARK GRILL.** *2151 Ave of the Stars (90067). 310/277-1234. www.hyatt.com.* Hrs: 6:30 am-10:30 pm; Sat, Sun from 7 am; Sun brunch 10:30 am-2 pm. Res accepted. Continental menu. Bar 11:30-1:30 am. Wine cellar. A la carte entrees: bkfst $8-$17, lunch $12-$20, dinner $17-$30. Buffet: bkfst $17. Sun brunch $25. Seasonal menu; changes monthly. Own baking. Valet parking. Cr cds: A, C, D, DS, MC, V.
D

A Los Angeles landmark

★ **PATINETTE AT MOCA.** *250 S Grand Ave (90012). 213/626-1178.* Hrs: 11 am-4:30 pm; Thurs to 8 pm. Closed Mon; hols. A la carte entrees: lunch, dinner $5.95-$9.25. Specializes in salads, sandwiches, light entrees. Outdoor dining on terrace. Totally nonsmoking. Cr cds: A, D, DS, MC, V.
D

★★ **P. F. CHANG'S.** *2041 Rosecrans Ave, El Segundo (90245). 310/607-9062. www.pfchangs.com.* Specializes in Chang's spicy chicken. Hrs: 11 am-11 pm; Fri, Sat to midnight. Wine, beer. Lunch, dinner $6.95-$12.95. Entertainment. Cr cds: A, D, MC, V.
D

★★★ **PINOT HOLLYWOOD.** *1448 N Gower St (90028). 323/461-8800.* Hrs: 11:30 am-10:30 pm; Sat 5:30-11 pm. Closed Sun; hols. Res accepted. French menu. Bar to 1:30 am. Extensive wine list. Lunch $7.25-$16.50, dinner $14.25-$19.95. Children's menu. Specializes in beef, chicken. Valet parking. Outdoor dining. French bistro decor. Cr cds: A, C, D, DS, MC, V.
D

★★★ **POSTO.** *14928 Ventura Blvd, Sherman Oaks (91403). 818/784-4400.* Hrs: 11:30 am-2:30 pm, 5-10 pm; Sat from 5 pm. Closed Sun; hols. Res accepted. Italian menu. Bar. Wine cellar. A la carte entrees: lunch, dinner $8-$26. Specialties: veal osso buco, risotto lobster, filet mignon with onions. Valet parking. Original artwork. Cr cds: A, MC, V.
D

★★ **R23.** *923 E 2nd St (90013). 213/687-7178.* Japanese menu. Specializes in sushi. Hrs: noon-2 pm, 6-10 pm. closed Sun. Res accepted. Lunch $8-$10; dinner $15-$19.50. Entertainment. Cr cds: A, D, MC, V.

★★★ **THE RESTAURANT.** *701 Stone Canyon Rd (90077). 310/472-1211.* Hrs: 7-10:30 am, 11:30 am-2:30 pm, 6:30-10:30 pm; Sun brunch 11 am-2:30 pm. Res accepted. French, Californian menu. Bar. Complete meals: bkfst $8-$13. A la carte entrees: lunch $15-$26.50, dinner $28-$36. Sun brunch $37.50. Specializes in seasonal dishes. Own pastries. Valet parking. Herb garden. Chef's tableside dining. Cr cds: A, C, D, DS, ER, MC, V.
D

★ **THE RESTAURANT GETTY CENTER.** *1200 Getty Center Dr (90049). 310/440-7300. www.getty.edu.* Menu changes seasonally. Hrs: 11 am-9 pm. Res accepted. Wine, beer. Lunch $14-$16; dinner $20-$35. Entertainment. To eat in the restaurant, you must make res to park your car in parking lot. Cr cds: A, MC, V.
D

★★★ SADDLE PEAK LODGE. *419 Cold Canyon Rd, Calabasas (91302). 818/222-3888. www.saddlepeaklodge.com.* Specializes in elk tenderloin rossini, musquovy duck breast, buffalo. Hrs: 5:30-9:30 pm. Closed Mon, Tues. Res required. Wine, beer. Dinner $25-$39. Entertainment. Jacket. Cr cds: A, C, D, JCB, MC, V.
D

★★ SEOUL JUNG. *930 Wilshire Blvd (90017). 213/688-7880. www.thewilshiregrand.com.* Hrs: 11:30 am-2 pm, 5:30-9:30 pm. Res accepted. Korean menu. Bar. Wine list. A la carte entrees: lunch, dinner $12-$25. Specialties: marinated short ribs, noodle casserole. Valet parking. Elegant dining; many Korean artifacts. Totally nonsmoking. Cr cds: A, C, D, DS, ER, MC, V.
D

★ SISLEY ITALIAN KITCHEN. *10800 W Pico Blvd (90064). 310/446-3030.* Hrs: 11:30 am-10 pm; Fri, Sat to 10:30 pm; Sun to 9 pm. Res accepted. Italian, California menu. Bar. A la carte entrees: lunch $5.95-$10.95, dinner $7.50-$12. Specialty: cioppino. Valet parking. Italian cafe decor. Cr cds: A, D, DS, MC, V.
D

★★★ TAM-O-SHANTER INN. *2980 Los Feliz Blvd (90039). 323/664-0228. www.lawrysonline.com.* Hrs: 11 am-3 pm, 5-10 pm; Fri, Sat to 11 pm; Sun 10:30 am-2:30 pm (brunch), 4-10 pm. Closed Dec 25. Bar. A la carte entrees: lunch $8.95-$14.95, dinner $9.95-$22.95. Sun brunch $9.50-$17.95. Children's menu. Specialties: prime rib and Yorkshire pudding, creamed spinach, roast duckling. Free valet parking. Scottish motif. Family-owned since 1922. Cr cds: A, D, DS, MC, V.
D

★★ TRAXX. *800 N Alameda (90012). 213/625-1999.* Specializes in beef tenderloin, monkfish. Hrs: 11:30 am-9 pm; Sat 5:30-10 pm. Closed Sun. Res accepted. Wine, beer. Lunch $9-$16; dinner $12-$25. Entertainment. Cr cds: A, MC, V.
D

★★★★ WATER GRILL. *544 S Grand Ave (90071). 213/891-0900. www.kingsseafood.com.* From the exceptional oyster bar to the ever-changing selection of line-caught fish, Water Grill delivers impeccable seafood. Far from a simple shoreside grill, creatures from the sea are creatively prepared by chef Michael Cimarusti, who isn't afraid to make unusal combinations such as a dish of bluefish tuna with sweetbread ravioli. Also impressive is the understated setting. Seafood cuisine. Hrs: 10 am-11 pm; Mon, Tues 5-9 pm; Sat 5-10 pm; Sun 4-9 pm. Bar. Lunch, dinner $24-$34. Res accepted. Jacket requested. Valet parking. Cr cds: A, C, D, DS, MC, V.
D

Unrated Dining Spots

BARBARA'S AT THE BREWERY. *620 Moulton Ave, Suite 110 (90031). 323/221-9204. www.barbarasatthebrewery.com.* Specializes in pizza, soups, gourmet entrees. Hrs: 11 am-3 pm, 5-10 pm. Closed Sun. Res accepted. Wine, beer. Lunch, dinner $5.95-$12.95. Entertainment. Cr cds: A, MC, V.
D

CASSELL'S. *3266 W 6th St (90020). 213/480-8668.* Hrs: 10:30 am-4 pm. Closed Sun; hols. A la carte entrees: lunch $4.60-$5.80. Specializes in prime beef hamburgers. Old-style hamburger diner. Cr cds: A, MC, V.
D SC

FRED 62. *1850 N Vermont Ave (90027). 323/667-0062.* Specializes in pancakes, hamburgers. Hrs: Open 24 hrs. Wine list. Lunch $5.62-$9.62; dinner $5.62-$13.62. Entertainment. Jukebox; counter, diner atmosphere. Cr cds: A, C, D, DS, JCB, MC, V.
D

HARD ROCK CAFE. *8600 Beverly Blvd (90048). 310/276-7605. www.hardrock.com.* Hrs: 11:30-12:30 am. Closed Labor Day, Thanksgiving, Dec 25. Bar. Lunch, dinner $5.95-$15. Children's menu. Specialties: lime barbecued chicken, grilled hamburgers. Valet parking. Extensive rock 'n roll memorabilia collection. Cr cds: A, C, D, DS, MC, V.
D

OFF VINE. *6263 Leland Way (90028). 323/962-1900.* Specializes in Blackened turkey, pork chops, dessert souffles. Hrs: 5:30-10:30 pm; Fri, Sat

to 11:30 pm; Sun 5-10 pm; Sun brunch 10:30 am-2:30 pm. Res accepted. Wine list. Lunch $8.95-$16.45; dinner $10.95-$19.95. Brunch $7.95-$13.95. Entertainment. Outdoor dining garden, fireplace. Cr cds: A, D, DS, MC, V.
D

PHILIPPE THE ORIGINAL. *1001 N Alameda St (90012). 213/628-3781. www.philippes.com.* Hrs: 6 am-10 pm. Closed Thanksgiving, Dec 25. Wine, beer. A la carte entrees: bkfst $1-$4.50, lunch, dinner $4-$7. Specializes in French dip sandwiches, salads, baked apples. Own baking. Since 1908; old-style dining hall. Totally nonsmoking. Cr cds: A, MC, V.
D

ROAST TO GO. *317 S Broadway, #C-8 (90013). 213/625-1385.* Hrs: 9 am-6 pm; Sun from 10 am. Closed hols. Mexican menu. Bkfst, lunch, dinner $1.50-$7. Children's menu. Specializes in tacos, charbroiled chicken. Parking. Family-owned since 1952. Cr cds: A, MC, V.
D

UNCLE BILL'S PANCAKE HOUSE. *1305 Highland Ave, Manhattan Beach (90266). 310/545-5177.* Hrs: 6 am-3 pm; wkends, hols from 7 am. Closed Jan 1, Thanksgiving, Dec 25. Bkfst $3.25-$5.95, lunch $3.50-$6.50. Specializes in potatoes Stroganoff, strawberry waffles, homemade muffins. Small, cozy atmosphere. Converted 1908 house. Cr cds: A, MC, V.
D

Los Angeles International Airport Area

See also Los Angeles

Services and Information

Information. 310/646-5252.

Lost and Found. 310/417-0440.

Airlines. Aero California, Aerolineas Argentinas, Aeromexico, Aeroperu, Air Canada, Air France, Air New Zealand, Air Pacific, Alaska Airlines, Alitalia, All Nippon, American West, American, American Trans Air, AOM French Airlines, Asiana Airlines, Avianca, Aviateca, British Airways, Canadian Airlines International, Carnival Air Lines, Cathay Pacific, China Airlines, China Eastern, Continental, Delta, EgyptAir, El Al, EVA Airways, Frontier, Garuda Indonesia, Hawaiian Airlines, Iberia, Japan Airlines, KLM, Korean Air, LACSA, Lan Chile, LTU, Lufthansa, Malaysia Airlines, Mexicana, Midwest Express, Northwest, Philippine Airlines, Qantas, Reno Air, Singapore Airlines, Southwest, Swissair, TACA, Thai Airways, Tower Air, Transaero Airlines, TWA, United, USAir, Vanguard, Varig, Virgin Atlantic, Western Pacific Airlines.

Heliport. Helitrans, LA Helicopter.

Motel/Motor Lodge

★★ HAMPTON INN LAX. *10300 La Cienega Blvd, Inglewood (90304). 310/846-3200; fax 310/645-6925; res 800/426-7866. www.hamptoninn.com.* 148 rms, 7 story. S, D $69-$99; under 18 free. Crib free. Pet accepted, some restrictions. TV; cable (premium). Complimentary continental bkfst. Restaurant nearby. Ck-out noon. Meeting rms. In-rm modem link. Valet serv. Free airport transportation. Exercise equipt. Cr cds: A, C, D, DS, JCB, MC, V.
D

★★ QUALITY INN. *5249 W Century Blvd (90045). 310/641-8241; fax 310/641-8214; res 800/266-2200.* 278 rms, 10 story. S, D $89-$129; each addl $10; under 18 free; wkend rates. Pet accepted. TV; cable (premium), VCR avail. Pool; poolside serv. Restaurant 6 am-10 pm. Bar 5-11 pm. Ck-out noon. Convention facilities. Business center. Free airport transportation. Exercise equipt. Cr cds: A, C, D, DS, ER, JCB, MC, V.
D SC

★ TRAVELODGE HOTEL AT LAX AIRPORT. *5547 W Century Blvd (90045). 310/649-4000; fax 310/649-0311; toll-free 800/421-3939. www.travelodgelax.com.* 147 rms, 2 story. S, D $74-$99; each addl $8; under 18 free. Crib $4. Pet accepted. TV; cable (premium), VCR. Pool. Coffee in rms. Restaurant open 24 hrs. Rm serv 6 am-10 pm. Bar 10-2 am. Ck-out noon. Coin lndry. Bellhops. Valet serv. Gift shop. Free airport transportation. Exercise equipt. Some private patios, balconies. Cr cds: A, C, D, DS, ER, JCB, MC, V.

Hotels

★★ **BARNABEY'S HOTEL.** *3501 Sepulveda Blvd, Manhattan Beach (90266). 310/545-8466; fax 310/545-8621; res 800/552-5285.* 120 rms, 3 story. S $155; D $170-$185; under 12 free; hol, wkend rates. Crib $15. Overnight valet parking $8. TV; cable (premium), VCR avail. Pool. Complimentary full bkfst. Coffee in rms. Restaurant 6:30 am-10 pm. Bar 11 am-midnight; entertainment. Ck-out noon. Meeting rms. In-rm modem link. Gift shop. Free airport transportation. Health club privileges. Microwaves avail. European-style decor; antiques. Cr cds: A, C, D, DS, JCB, MC, V.

★★★ **CROWNE PLAZA.** *5985 W Century Blvd (90045). 310/642-7500; fax 310/417-3608; toll-free 888/315-3700. www.crowneplaza.com.* 615 rms, 15 story. S, D $99-$149; suites $350-$550; under 12 free; wkend rates. Crib free. Garage $9. TV; cable (premium). Heated pool; whirlpool. Coffee in rms. Restaurant 6 am-11 pm. Bar 11-2 am; entertainment Tues-Thurs. Ck-out noon. Coin lndry. Business servs avail. Concierge. Gift shop. Free airport transportation. Exercise equipt; sauna. Luxury level. Cr cds: A, C, D, DS, ER, JCB, MC, V.

★★ **DOUBLETREE CLUB HOTEL LAX.** *1985 E Grand Ave, El Segundo (90245). 310/322-0999; fax 310/322-4758; res 310/322-0999.* 215 rms, 7 story. S $102; D $112; each addl $10; suites $125; under 12 free. Crib $10. TV; cable (premium). Heated pool; whirlpool, poolside serv. Restaurant 6-10 am, 11 am-2 pm, 5-10 pm. Bar. Ck-out 1 pm. Meeting rms. Business servs avail. In-rm modem link. Free airport transportation. Exercise equipt. Cr cds: A, D, JCB, MC, V.

★★★ **EMBASSY SUITES.** *1440 E Imperial Ave, El Segundo (90245). 310/640-3600; fax 310/322-0954.* 349 suites, 5 story. S, D $119-$169; each addl $15; under 18 free; wkend rates. Pet accepted, some restrictions. Parking $6/day. TV; cable (premium). Indoor pool; whirlpool. Complimentary full bkfst. Restaurant 11 am-10 pm. Bar to 2 am. Ck-out noon. Meeting rms. Business center. In-rm modem link. Gift shop. Free airport transportation. Exercise equipt. Refrigerators, microwaves. Balconies. Sun deck. Spanish mission architecture. Near beach. Cr cds: A, C, D, DS, JCB, MC, V.

★ **FURAMA HOTEL LOS ANGELES.** *8601 Lincoln Blvd (90045). 310/670-8111; fax 310/337-1883; toll-free 800/225-8126. www.furama-hotels.com.* 760 rms, 12 story. S, D $79-$99; each addl $10; suites $250-$350; under 18 free. Crib free. TV; cable (premium). Pool. Restaurants 6 am-11 pm. Bar 3 pm-2 am; entertainment. Ck-out noon. Meeting rms. Barber, beauty shop. Free airport transportation. Exercise equipt. Some private patios. Garden patio. Golf, tennis opp. Luxury level. Cr cds: A, DS, JCB, MC, V.

★★★ **HILTON LOS ANGELES AIRPORT.** *5711 W Century Blvd (90045). 310/410-4000; fax 310/410-6250. www.hilton.com.* 1,234 rms, 17 story. S $119-$169; each addl $20; suites $150-$900; family, wkend rates. Valet parking $14, garage $10. Pet accepted. TV; cable (premium), VCR avail. Heated pool; whirlpools, poolside serv. Restaurants open 24 hrs. Bar 11-2 am. Ck-out noon. Convention facilities. Business center. In-rm modem link. Gift shop. Coin lndry. Free airport transportation. Exercise rm; sauna. Some bathrm phones; refrigerators avail. Some private patios. Luxury level. Cr cds: A, C, D, DS, ER, JCB, MC, V.

★★★ **MANHATTAN BEACH MARRIOTT.** *1400 Parkview Ave, Manhattan Beach (90266). 310/546-7511; fax 310/939-1486.* 385 rms, 7 story. S, D $170-$185; suites $250-$1,000; under 16 free; higher rates special events. Crib free. Valet parking $10; garage $9. TV; cable (premium), VCR avail. Complimentary coffee in rms.

Restaurant 6 am-10 pm. Bar noon-midnight. Ck-out noon. Convention facilities. Business center. In-rm modem link. Concierge. Gift shop. Free airport transportation. 9-hole golf par 3, greens fee $7, pro, putting green. Exercise equipt; sauna. Massage. Heated pool; whirlpool, poolside serv. Minibars; some bathrm phones. Some balconies. Luxury level. Cr cds: A, D, DS, JCB, MC, V.

D

★★★ **MARRIOTT.** *5855 W Century Blvd (90045). 310/641-5700; fax 310/939-1486.* 1,010 rms, 18 story. S, D $135-$160; suites from $189; family, wkend rates. Crib free. Pet accepted, some restrictions. Parking $10, valet $12. TV; cable (premium), VCR avail. Heated pool; whirlpool, poolside serv. Restaurants 6 am-midnight. Bars; entertainment. Ck-out 1 pm. Coin lndry. Convention facilities. Business center. In-rm modem link. Concierge. Shopping arcade. Beauty shop. Free airport transportation. Exercise equipt. Some bathrm phones, refrigerators. Balconies. Luxury level. Cr cds: A, C, D, DS, ER, JCB, MC, V.

D

★★ **RADISSON HOTEL AT LOS ANGELES AIRPORT.** *6225 W Century Blvd (90045). 310/670-9000; fax 310/670-8110. www.radisson.com.* 591 rms, 12 story. S, D $144; each addl $20; suites $350-$600; under 18 free; wkend rates. TV; cable (premium). Heated pool; whirlpool, poolside serv. Restaurant 6 am-11 pm; dining rms 11 am-10:30 pm. Bars 11-2 am, entertainment Mon-Sat. Ck-out noon. Convention facilities. Business center. In-rm modem link. Concierge. Gift shop. Garage parking. Free airport transportation. Exercise equipt. Sun deck. Luxury level. Cr cds: A, C, D, DS, JCB, MC, V.

D

★★ **RENAISSANCE.** *9620 Airport Blvd (90045). 310/337-2800; fax 310/216-6681.* 499 rms, 11 story, 56 suites. S, D $160-$200; each addl $10; suites $225; under 16 free; wkend rates. Valet parking $14, garage $11. TV; cable (premium), VCR avail. Heated pool; whirlpool, poolside serv. Restaurants 6-10:30 am, 11:30 am-2:30 pm, 5-11 pm. Rm serv 24 hrs. Bar. Meeting rms. Business center. In-rm modem link. Concierge. Gift shop. Free airport transportation. Tennis privileges. Golf privileges. Exercise equipt; sauna. Massage. Health club privileges. Minibars. Cr cds: A, C, D, DS, JCB, MC, V.

D

★★★ **SHERATON GATEWAY HOTEL LAX.** *6101 W Century Blvd (90045). 310/642-1111; fax 310/410-1267; res 800/325-3535.* 804 rms, 15 story. S $150-$190; D $170-$210; each addl $20; suites $185-$505; under 18 free; wkend rates. Crib free. Valet parking $15. TV; cable (premium), VCR avail. Heated pool; whirlpool, poolside serv. Restaurants 6-11 pm. Bar 11-2 am; entertainment. Ck-out noon. Convention facilities. Business center. In-rm modem link. Concierge. Gift shop. Free airport transportation. Exercise equipt. Minibars; microwaves avail. Luxury level. Cr cds: A, D, DS, JCB, MC, V.

D

★★ **WESTIN.** *5400 W Century Blvd (90045). 310/216-5858; fax 310/417-4545; res 800/937-8461. www.westin.com.* 723 rms, 12 story. S, D $129-$159; each addl $20; suites $275-$1,500; under 18 free; wkend rates. Covered parking $10. Pet accepted. TV; cable (premium). Heated pool; whirlpool. Restaurant (see also CHARISMA CAFE). Rm serv 24 hrs. Bar 10-2 am; entertainment. Ck-out noon. Convention facilities. Business center. In-rm modem link. Gift shop. Free airport transportation. Guest lndry. Exercise equipt; sauna. Minibars; bathrm phones in suites; microwaves avail. Balconies. Luxury level. Cr cds: A, C, D, DS, ER, JCB, MC, V.

D

All Suite

★★★ **SUMMERFIELD SUITES BY WYNDHAM.** *810 S Douglas Ave, El Segundo (90245). 310/725-0100; fax 310/725-0900; res 800/833-4353. www.summerfieldsuites.com.* 122 kit. suites, 3 story. Jan-Aug: kit. suites $150-$220; family rates; package plans; lower rates rest of yr. Crib free. Pet accepted, some restrictions; $75-

$250. TV; cable (premium), VCR (movies). Complimentary continental bkfst, coffee in rms. Restaurant nearby. Bar. Ck-out noon. Meeting rms. Business servs avail. In-rm modem link. Concierge. Gift shop. Grocery store. Drugstore. Coin lndry. Free airport transportation. Exercise equipt. Health club privileges. Pool; whirlpool. Playground. Picnic tables, grills. Cr cds: A, D, DS, JCB, MC, V.

D

Restaurants

★★ **CHARISMA CAFE.** *5400 W Century Blvd (90045). 310/216-5858. www.westin.com.* Hrs: 6 am-11 pm. Res accepted. Eclectic menu. Bar. Bkfst $4.95-$14.50, lunch $10.50-$14.50, dinner $12.50-$22.50. Children's menu. Specialty: fire-roasted chicken. Salad bar. Valet parking. International decor; large windows. Totally nonsmoking. Cr cds: A, DS, MC, V.

D SC

★★ **LIDO DI.** *1550 Rosecrans, Manhattan Beach (90266). 310/536-0730.* Hrs: 11 am-10:30 pm; Sat, Sun 5-10:30 pm. Closed hols. Res accepted. Italian menu. Bar. A la carte entrees: lunch $9-$11.50, dinner $9-$22. Children's menu. Specialties: filet mignon; charbroiled chicken, sun-dried tomato and spinach pasta; baked halibut. Parking. Outdoor dining. Casual dining; Italian atmosphere. Cr cds: A, D, MC, V.

D

★★★ **MANGIAMO.** *128 Manhattan Beach Blvd, Manhattan Beach (90266). 310/318-3434.* Hrs: 5:30-10:30 pm. Closed hols. Res accepted. Italian menu. Bar. Wine cellar. A la carte entrees: dinner $12-$21. Children's menu. Specialties: rack of lamb, swordfish, penne with vodka sauce. Street parking. Italian decor; Italian atmosphere. Totally nonsmoking. Cr cds: A, MC, V.

D

★★ **MANHATTAN BAR AND GRILL.** *1019 Manhattan Beach Blvd, Manhattan Beach (90266). 310/546-4545.* Hrs: 11:30 am-2:30 pm, 5-9:30 pm; Fri, Sat to 10:30 pm. Closed Sun; hols. Res accepted. Italian menu. Bar to midnight. A la carte entrees: lunch $6.95-$11.95, dinner 48.95-$20. Children's menu. Specializes in seafood, veal, pasta. Piano Thurs-Sat. Parking. Outdoor dining. Intimate dining. Family-owned since 1978. Totally nonsmoking. Cr cds: A, MC, V.

D

★★ **MCCORMICK AND SCHMICK'S.** *2101 Rosecrans Ave, El Segundo (90245). 310/416-1123. www.mccormickandschmicks.com.* Hrs: 11 am-11 pm. Res accepted. Seafood menu. Bar to 1 am. Wine list. A la carte entrees: lunch $4.95-$9.95, dinner $9.95-$19.95. Children's menu. Specialties: crab cakes, cedar plank salmon, stuffed halibut. Valet parking. Outdoor dining. Victorian/Art Deco decor. Cr cds: A, D, DS, MC, V.

D

★ **REEDS.** *2640 N Sepulveda Blvd, Manhattan Beach (90266). 310/546-3299.* Hrs: 11:30 am-2:30 pm, 5:30-10 pm. Closed hols. Res accepted. French menu. Wine list. Lunch $7.95-$17.95, dinner $12.95-$19.95. Children's menu. Specialties: filet mignon, rack of lamb with rosemary sauce, sea bass with potato crust in miso sauce. Piano Tues-Sun. Parking. Outdoor dining. Intimate atmosphere. Totally nonsmoking. Cr cds: A, DS, MC, V.

D SC

★★ **TALIA'S.** *1148 Manhattan Ave, Manhattan Beach (90266). 310/545-6884.* Hrs: 5:30-10:30 pm; Sun brunch 8 am-2 pm. Closed hols. Res accepted. Italian menu. A la carte entrees: dinner $12-$18. Sun brunch $4-$7. Children's menu. Specialties: osso buco, seared ahi, tortellini vico. Intimate dining. Family-owned since 1977. Cr cds: A, C, D, DS, ER, MC, V.

D

★★ **WOLFGANG PUCK'S CAFE.** *2121 E Rosecrans, El Segundo (90245). 310/607-9653. www.wolfgangpuck.com.* Hrs: 11 am-10 pm; Fri, Sat to 11 pm; Sun brunch 11 am-3 pm. Closed Jan 1, Thanksgiving, Dec 25. Res accepted. Contemporary American menu. Bar. Lunch $15-$18, dinner $18-$22. Sun brunch $13.50. Children's menu. Specialties: wood-burning pizzas, Chinois chicken salad, sesame ahi tuna. Valet parking. Outdoor dining. Totally nonsmoking. Cr cds: A, D, MC, V.

D

Los Gatos

See also San Jose, Saratoga

Founded ca 1870 **Pop** 27,357
Elev 385 ft **Area code** 408 **Zip** 95030

Information Town of Los Gatos Chamber of Commerce, 349 N Santa Cruz Ave; 408/354-9300

Web www.losgatosweb.com

Free-roaming wildcats inspired the name "La Rinconada de Los Gatos," the corner of the cats. Today, two sculptured cats, Leo and Leona, guard the town entrance at Poets Canyon.

What to See and Do

Forbes Mill Museum of Regional History. Historic landmark; former grain mill. (Wed-Sun) 75 Church St. Phone 408/395-7375. **Donation**

Los Gatos Museum of Art & Natural History. Natural history exhibits; art displays, art history. In restored firehouse. (Wed-Sun afternoons; closed hols) Tait and Main. Phone 408/354-2646. **Donation**

Old Town. Shops, restaurants, art galleries, flowered garden walkways, housed in what was once an elementary school (1921). 50 University Ave.

Youth Science Institute. Located in Vasona Lake County Park, this Junior Museum houses aquaria with local and native fish, reptiles, and amphibians. Native plant trail. Museum (Mon-Fri); park (daily). Parking fee. 296 Garden Hill Dr. Phone 408/356-4945. **Donation**

Motels/Motor Lodges

★★ **LODGE AT VILLA FELICE.** *15350 S Winchester Blvd (95030). 408/395-6710; fax 408/354-1826; toll-free 800/662-9229.* 33 rms, 2 story. S, D $130-$150; each addl $10; suites $160-$240; under 16 free. Crib free. TV; cable (premium), VCR avail. Heated pool; whirlpool. Complimentary continental bkfst. Ck-out noon. Meeting rms. Business servs avail. Sundries. Refrigerators; some in-rm saunas. Private patios, balconies. On mountain; view of Lake Vasona. Cr cds: A, D, MC, V.

D

★★ **LOS GATOS LODGE.** *50 Los Gatos-Saratoga Rd (95032). 408/354-3300; fax 408/354-5451; toll-free 800/231-8676. www.losgatoslodge.com.* 129 rms, 2 story. S $135; D $135; under 16 free. Crib free. Pet accepted, some restrictions. TV; cable. Heated pool; whirlpool. Coffee in rms. Restaurant 7 am-2 pm, 5-10 pm. Bar 10:30-2 am; entertainment Fri, Sat. Ck-out noon. Coin lndry. Meeting rms. Business servs avail. Sundries. Putting green. Lawn games. All rms have private patio or deck. Cr cds: A, C, D, DS, MC, V.

D

Hotel

★★★ **TOLL HOUSE HOTEL.** *140 S Santa Cruz Ave (95030). 408/395-7070; fax 408/395-3730; toll-free 800/238-6111. www.tollhousehotel.com.* 97 rms, 3 story. S $182; D $192; suites $250; under 16 free. Crib free. TV; cable (premium). Coffee in rms. Complimentary continental bkfst. Restaurant 6:30-9:30 pm; Fri, Sat to 10 pm. Rm serv 5-10 pm. Bar. Ck-out noon. Meeting rms. Business center. In-rm modem link. Garage parking. Free airport transportation. Exercise equipt. Health club privileges. Some refrigerators. Private patios, balconies. Cr cds: A, C, D, DS, MC, V.

D SC

B&B/Small Inn

★★ **LA HACIENDA INN.** *18840 Los Gatos-Saratoga Rd (95030). 408/354-9230; fax 408/354-7590. www.lahaciendainn.com.* 20 rms, 3 kits. S, D $150; each addl $10; suites, kit. units $105-$150; under 6 free. Crib free. TV; cable (premium), VCR avail (free movies). Pool; whirlpool. Complimentary continental bkfst. Restaurant 11 am-2:30 pm, 5-11 pm. Ck-out noon. Meeting rm. Business servs avail. In-rm modem link. Guest lndry. Refrigerators; some fireplaces. Private patios. Beautifully landscaped grounds. Totally nonsmoking. Cr cds: A, C, D, DS, JCB, MC, V.

Restaurant

★★ **LOS GATOS BREWING COMPANY.** *130 N Santa Cruz Ave (95030). 408/395-9929. www.lgbrewingco.com.* Hrs: 11:30 am-10 pm; Fri, Sat to 11 pm; Sun brunch 11:30 am-3 pm. Closed Dec 25. Res accepted. Contemporary American menu. Bar. A la carte entrees: lunch $7.50-$12.95, dinner $7.95-$18.95. Sun brunch $6.95-$10.50. Children's menu. Specialties: spit-roasted chicken, fusilli pasta. Parking. In microbrewery. Totally nonsmoking. Cr cds: A, C, D, DS, MC, V.
D

Madera

(A-3) *See also Fresno*

Pop 29,281 **Elev** 270 ft **Area code** 559 **Zip** 93637

Motel/Motor Lodge

★★ **MADERA VALLEY INN BEST WESTERN.** *317 N G St (93637). 559/673-5164; fax 559/661-8426; res 800/528-1234. www.bestwestern.com.* 93 rms, 5 story. S $65; D $75; each addl $4; suites $85; under 12 free. Crib free. TV; cable (premium). Complimentary coffee in rms. Restaurant 6 am-9 pm. Bar 11:30-2 am. Ck-out noon. Meeting rms. Bellhops. Health club privileges. Free airport transportation. Refrigerators. Cr cds: A, D, DS, MC, V.

Malibu

Pop 7,000 **Elev** 25 ft **Area code** 310 **Zip** 90265

What to See and Do

Beach areas. Surfrider, Malibu Lagoon, Topanga Canyon, and Zuma beaches offer surfing and swimming Phone 310/457-2527 (Surfrider), 818/880-0350 (Malibu Lagoon), 310/456-8800 (Topanga Canyon), or 310/457-9891 (Zuma). **FREE**

Pepperdine University. (1937) 2,300 students. On 830 acres, campus incl School of Law as well as college of arts, sciences, and letters; cultural arts center and Weisman Museum of Art (Tues-Sun). 24255 Pacific Coast Hwy. Phone 310/506-4000.

Santa Monica Mountains National Recreation Area. (See SANTA MONICA) Phone 805/370-2301.

Motel/Motor Lodge

★★ **MALIBU COUNTRY INN.** *6506 Westward Beach Rd (90265). 310/457-9622; fax 310/457-1349.* 16 rms, 1 story. No A/C. Apr-Sept: S, D $165; under 7 free; lower rates rest of yr. Crib free. TV; cable. Heated pool. Complimentary continental bkfst, coffee in rms. Restaurant. Business servs avail. Ck-out noon. Refrigerators. Balconies. 1940s Cape Cod-style building with three acres of garden; located on a bluff overlooking Zuma Beach. Cr cds: A, C, D, DS, MC, V.
D

Hotels

★★ **CASA MALIBU INN ON THE BEACH.** *22752 Pacific Coast Hwy (90265). 310/456-2219; fax 310/456-5418; toll-free 800/831-0858.* 21 rms, 1-2 story, 6 kits. Some A/C. June-Sept: S, D $90-$99; each addl $15; kit. units $12 addl (3-day min); lower rates rest of yr. Crib $15. TV. Coffee in rms. Restaurant nearby. Ck-out noon. In-rm modem link. Valet serv. Health club privileges. Golf privileges. Tennis privileges. Refrigerators. Some balconies, fireplaces. Cr cds: A, MC, V.

★★ **MALIBU BEACH INN.** *22878 Pacific Coast Hwy (90265). 310/456-6444; fax 310/456-1499; toll-free 800/462-5428. www.malibubeachinn.com.* 47 rms, 3 story. June-Sept: S, D $179-$219; each addl $15; suites $275-$325. TV; cable, VCR (movies $5). Complimentary continental bkfst, coffee in rms. Restaurants nearby. Ck-out noon. Business servs avail. In-rm modem link. Gift shop. Health club privileges. Minibars, fireplaces; some in-rm whirlpools. Balconies. Tile-roofed, Mediterranean-style hotel on beach. Cr cds: A, C, D, MC, V.

D SC

Restaurants

★★ **GEOFFREY'S.** *27400 Pacific Coast Hwy (90265). 310/457-1519.* Hrs: noon-10 pm; Sat 11 am-11 pm; Sun 10:30 am-9:30 pm. Res accepted. Bar. Wine list. A la carte entrees: lunch $8-$20, dinner $30-$45. Specialties: grilled stuffed lamb chop, grilled Norwegian salmon, eggs Benedict en croissant. Valet parking. Patio dining. Panoramic view of ocean. Cr cds: A, MC, V.

D

★★★ **GRANITA.** *23725 W Malibu Rd (90265). 310/456-0488. www.wolfgangpuck.com.* Hrs: 6-10 pm; Sat, Sun 11 am-2 pm, 5:30-10 pm. Closed Jan 1, Thanksgiving, Dec 24, 25. Res accepted; required wkends. California cuisine. Bar. Wine list. A la carte entrees: brunch $11-$19, dinner $22-$32. Specialties: grilled big-eye tuna, crisp potato galette with gravlax, dill cream, and fresh chives. Entertainment Wed. Outdoor dining. Unique interior with underwater ocean fantasy theme. Cr cds: A, C, D, DS, MC, V.

D

★ **MOONSHADOWS.** *20356 W Pacific Coast Hwy (90265). 310/456-3010. www.moonshadowsmalibu.com.* Hrs: 11 am-11 pm; Fri, Sat to midnight; Sun to 10 pm. Closed Thanksgiving, Dec 25. Bar. Lunch $4.95-$12.95, dinner $15.95-$22.95. Specializes in steak, lobster, fresh fish of the day. Salad bar. Valet parking. Overlooks ocean. Cr cds: A, DS, MC, V.

★★★ **NOBU.** *3835 Cross Creek Rd (90265). 310/317-9140.* Specializes in seafood. Hrs: 11:45 am-2 pm, 5:45-10 pm. Res required. Wine, beer. Lunch $12-$20; dinner $18-$30. Entertainment. Cr cds: A, D, MC, V.

D

Mammoth Lakes

(G-6) *See also Bishop, June Lake*

Pop 4,785 **Elev** 7,800 ft
Area code 760 **Zip** 93546
Information Mammoth Lakes Visitor Bureau, CA 203, PO Box 48; 760/934-2712 or 888/GO-MAMMOTH
Web www.visitmammoth.com

Spectacular scenery and a variety of recreational opportunities are found in this region of rugged peaks, numerous lakes, streams, and waterfalls, alpine meadows, and extensive forests. Much of the outstanding scenery was created by volcanos or carved by glaciers.

What to See and Do

Devils Postpile National Monument. (see)

Fishing, boating, rentals. **Crowley Lake**, 6 mi S on US 395. **Sherwin Creek** (fishing, camping), 3 mi SE of ranger station. **Convict Lake**, 4 mi SE of Mammoth Junction, 2 mi W of US 395. SW on Lake Mary Rd are **Twin Lakes** (camping), **Lake Mary** (camping), **Coldwater** (camping), **Lake George** (camping), **Pine City** (camping). Fees charged at recreation sites. All campgrounds first-come, first-served basis (self-registration). For further details and information on other areas contact the Mammoth Ranger District, Box 148. Phone 760/924-5500. ¢¢¢

Hot Creek Fish Hatchery. Most of the five million fish planted in eastern Sierra lakes and rivers are bred here. (Daily) S on US 395 to Hot Creek Fish Hatchery exit, then Owens River Rd. Phone 760/934-2664. **FREE**

Hot Creek Geological Site. Hot springs and fumaroles in a river setting surrounded by mountains. Boardwalks lead through a steep canyon for viewing volcanic features. Fly-fishing for trout is popular upstream from the hot springs. S on US 395 to Hot Creek Fish Hatchery exit, then Owens River Rd. Phone 760/924-5500. **FREE**

Mammoth Adventure Connection. In the summer, Mammoth Mtn is transformed into a bike park. Park activities also incl hiking, ropes course, and rock climbing. Ride the gondola to the top of the mountain and bike down on a variety of trails, suited to various skills and ages. Helmets are required within park boundaries. (July-Sept, daily, weather permitting) Fee for activities. Phone 760/934-0606.

Mammoth Mountain Ski Area. Eight quad, seven triple, 11 double chairlifts, two gondolas, surface lift; patrol, school, rentals; cafeterias, restaurants. More than 150 runs; longest run 3 mi; vertical drop 3,100 ft. (Nov-June, daily) Gondola ride (daily). In Inyo National Forest. Phone 760/934-0745. ¢¢¢¢¢

Mammoth Visitor Center Ranger Station. Visitor summer activities (July 4-Labor Day wkend) incl interpretive tours, evening programs, and Jr.-Ranger programs (6-12 yrs). Visitor center (yr-round). All family campgrounds (exc ½ of Sherwin Creek, which requires res) on first-come, first-served basis; group camping and Sherwin Creek camping reservable through National Forest recreation res (800/280-CAMP). Shady Rest campground open in winter (tent camping only). Self-registration for backpackers during nonquota season; wilderness permits required all yr. Quota season last Fri in June-mid-Sept. Res may be made six months to two days in advance by contacting Wilderness Reservations, PO Box 430, Big Pine 93513. Phone 888/374-3773. At the edge of town, surrounded by Inyo National Forest. Contact Mammoth Ranger District, Box 148. Phone 760/924-5500. ¢¢¢

Pack trips. For wilderness camping.

Mammoth Lakes Pack Outfit. 4 mi SW on Lake Mary Rd near Lake Mary. Phone 760/934-2434.

McGee Creek Pack Station. 12 mi SW. Contact Rte 1, Box 162. Phone 760/878-2207.

Red's Meadow Pack Station and Resort. 15 mi W on Minaret Hwy. Contact Box 395; Phone 760/934-2345.

Motels/Motor Lodges

★ **ALPINE LODGE.** *6209 Minaret Rd (93546). 760/934-8576; fax 760/934-8007.* 131 rms, 3 story, 12 kit. cottages. No A/C. Nov-Apr: S, D $100-$116; lower rates rest of yr. Package plans. Complimentary coffee in rms. Crib free. TV; cable (premium). Restaurant nearby. Ck-out 11 am. Business servs avail. Downhill/x-country ski 1 mi. Whirlpool. Sauna. Some refrigerators. Some balconies. Cr cds: A, DS, MC, V.

★ **ECONO LODGE WILDWOOD INN.** *3626 Main St (93546). 760/934-6855; fax 760/934-8208; toll-free 800/228-5050. www.econolodge.com.* 32 rms, 2 story. No A/C. S $49-$99; D $59-$99; ski plans. Pet accepted. TV; cable (premium). Heated pool; whirlpool. Continental bkfst. Coffee in rms. Restaurant nearby. Ck-out 10 am. Business servs avail. Downhill/x-country ski 3 mi. Some refrigerators, microwaves. Mountain view from some rms. Cr cds: A, C, D, DS, MC, V.

★★ **QUALITY INN.** *3537 Main St (93546). 760/934-5114; fax 760/934-5165; res 800/626-1900. www.qualityinn.com.* 59 rms, 2 story. No A/C. S, D $69-$150; each addl $10; under 18 free. Crib free. TV; cable (premium). Complimentary continental bkfst, coffee in rms. Restaurant nearby. Ck-out 11 am. Business servs avail. Garage parking. Downhill/x-country ski 2 mi. Whirlpool. Refrigerators, microwaves. Cr cds: A, C, D, DS, MC, V.

★★ **SHILO INN.** *2963 Main St (93546). 760/934-4500; fax 760/934-7594; toll-free 800/222-2244. www.shiloinns.com.* 70 rms, 4 story. Mid-Nov-mid-Apr: S, D $109-$149; under 12 free; lower rates rest of yr. Crib free. Pet accepted, some restrictions; $7. TV; cable (premium), VCR avail. Indoor pool. Complimentary continental bkfst, coffee in rms. Restaurant adj 5 am-10 pm. Ck-out noon. Coin lndry. Meeting rm. Business servs avail. Garage parking. Free airport transportation. Downhill/x-country ski 5 mi. Exercise equipt; sauna. Bathrm phones, refrigerators, microwaves, wet bars. Cr cds: A, D, DS, MC, V.

Hotel

★★★ **MAMMOTH MOUNTAIN INN.** *1 Minaret Rd (93546). 760/934-2571; fax 760/934-0701; toll-free 800/228-4947. www.mammothmountain.com.* 213 rms, 3 story, 50 kit. condos. Nov-Apr: S, D $99-$125; suites $195-$490; family, mid-wk rates; ski plans; lower rates rest of yr. Crib $10. TV; cable (premium). Supervised children's activities; ages 1-12. Complimentary coffee in rms. Restaurant 7:30 am-9:30 pm. Box lunches. Snack bar. Barbecues. Bar from 10 am. Ck-out 11 am. Grocery store. Coin lndry. Meeting rms. Business servs avail. Bellhops. Concierge. Gift shop. Covered parking. Free airport transportation. Downhill/x-country ski on site. Sleighing. Horseback riding. Haywagon rides. Bicycles. Entertainment. Whirlpools. Game rm. Fish/hike guides. Some balconies. Picnic tables. Cr cds: A, MC, V.

D

B&B/Small Inn

★ **CINNAMON BEAR INN.** *113 Center St (93546). 760/934-2873; fax 760/924-2873; res 800/845-2873.* 18 rms, 2 story. No A/C. Some rm phones. Nov-Mar: S, D $49-$139; ski plans; higher rates hols; lower rates rest of yr. TV; cable (premium). Complimentary full bkfst; afternoon refreshments. Restaurant nearby. Ck-out 10 am, ck-in 2 pm. Business servs avail. Downhill ski 10 mi; x-country ski on site. Some refrigerators. Built in 1955. Cr cds: A, DS, MC, V.

SC

Manhattan Beach

(see Los Angeles)

Marina del Rey

See also Los Angeles, Santa Monica

Pop 7,431 **Elev** 10 ft **Area code** 310 **Zip** 90292

Information Chamber of Commerce, 13246 Fiji Way; 310/821-0555

Web www.marinadelrey.com

With its name, could this community next to Venice be anything but boat-oriented? The 6,000-slip facility attracts many boating and sportfishing enthusiasts. Sail and power boat rentals, ocean cruises, and fishing expenditions are available. In addition, there are waterfront biking and jogging trails.

What to See and Do

Fisherman's Village. Modeled after a turn-of-the-century New England fishing town and located on the main channel of the largest man-made small craft harbor in the country, this area and its well-known lighthouse have appeared in many television and movie productions. Cobblestone walks complement the nautical atmosphere and provide a panoramic view of the marina; boat rentals, fishing charters, harbor cruises; shops, boutiques, and restaurants. Entertainment throughout the yr (weather permitting), incl free jazz concerts (Sun). (Daily) 13755 Fiji Way. Phone 310/823-5411.

Motels/Motor Lodges

★★ **COURTYARD BY MARRIOTT.** *13480 Maxella Ave (90292). 310/822-8555; fax 310/823-2996; res 800/628-0908. www.courtyard.com/laxcm.* 276 rms, 5 story. S, D $159; each addl $10; suites $179; under 12 free; wkend rates. Crib free. TV; cable (premium), VCR avail. Heated pool; whirlpool, poolside serv. Restaurant 6:30-11 am. Bar 11-1 am. Ck-out noon. Meeting rms. Business servs avail. In-rm modem link. Bellhops. Tennis opp. Exercise equipt. Health club privileges. Minibars; microwaves avail. Private patios, balconies. Cr cds: A, C, D, DS, JCB, MC, V.

D SC

★★ FOGHORN HARBOR INN. *4140 Via Marina (90292). 310/823-4626; fax 310/578-1964; res 800/423-4940. www.foghornhotel.com.* 23 rms, 2 story. June-Aug: S, D $109-$159; each addl $10; under 10 free; lower rates rest of yr. Crib free. TV; cable (premium), VCR (movies). Complimentary continental bkfst. Restaurant adj 11:30 am-midnight. Ck-out 11:30 am. Free airport transportation. Refrigerators; microwaves avail. Swimming beach. Cr cds: A, D, DS, MC, V.

D SC

★★ MARINA DEL REY HOTEL. *13534 Bali Way (90292). 310/301-1000; fax 310/301-8167; toll-free 800/882-4000. www.marinadelrey hotel.com.* 160 rms, 3 story. S $139-$210; D $149-$220; each addl $20; suites $350-$400; under 18 free. TV; cable (premium), VCR avail. Heated pool; poolside serv. Restaurant 6 am-11 pm. Rm serv 24 hrs. Bar 10-2 am. Ck-out noon. Meeting rms. Business center. In-rm modem link. Gift shop. Free airport transportation. Charter boats. Some bathrm phones. Private patios, balconies. On waterfront; view of marina. Cr cds: A, C, D, MC, V.

D SC

Hotels

★★★ MARINA BEACH MARRIOTT. *4100 Admiralty Way (90292). 310/301-3000; fax 310/448-4870; res 800/228-9290. www.marriott.com.* 370 rms, 9 story. S, D $225-$250; suites $268-$1,200; under 18 free; wkend packages. Valet parking $10. TV; cable (premium), VCR avail. Pool; poolside serv. Restaurant 6 am-11 pm. Bar 10-1:30 am; entertainment. Ck-out noon. Convention facilities. Business center. In-rm modem link. Concierge. Gift shop. Tennis privileges. Exercise equipt. Health club privileges. Bathrm phones, refrigerators. Balconies. Opp beach. Luxury level. Cr cds: A, C, D, DS, ER, JCB, MC, V.

D

★★★★ THE RITZ-CARLTON, MARINA DEL REY. *4375 Admiralty Way (90292). 310/823-1700; fax 310/823-2403; toll-free 800/241-3333. www.ritzcarlton.com.* You can stare out at the Pacific and count the yachts at this world-class resort on the edge of the largest man-made marina. Los Angeles International Airport and the energy of Santa Monica and Beverly Hills are all nearby. Choose one of 46 club rooms on the hotel's top two floors if you crave even more luxury than this deluxe chain's norm. 306 rms, 12 story. S, D $280-$470; suites $550-$2,500; wkend rates. Crib free. TV; cable (premium), VCR avail. Valet parking $21. Pool; whirlpool, poolside serv. Supervised children's activities; ages 5-13. Restaurant. Rm serv 24 hrs. Bar 11-1 am; pianist eves. Ck-out noon. Convention facilities. Business center. In-rm modem link. Concierge. Shopping arcade. Lighted tennis, pro. Golf privileges. Bicycle rental. Exercise rm. Massage. Bathrm phones, refrigerators, minibars. Balconies. Luxury level. Cr cds: A, C, D, DS, ER, JCB, MC, V.

D SC

B&B/Small Inn

★★★ INN AT PLAYA DEL REY. *435 Culver Blvd, Playa Del Rey (90293). 310/574-1920; fax 310/574-9920. www.innatplayadelrey.com.* 21 rms, 3 story. S, D $95-$245; under 18 free. Crib avail. Garage parking. TV; cable (premium), VCR (free movies). Complimentary full bkfst. Restaurant adj 7 am-11 pm. Ck-out noon. Meeting rm. Business servs avail. In-rm modem link. Concierge serv. Some in-rm whirlpools; microwaves avail. Some balconies. Overlooks Ballona Wetlands bird sanctuary.

Restaurants

★★★ THE DINING ROOM. *4375 Admiralty Way (90292). 310/823-1700. www.ritzcarlton.com.* Specializes in fish, pastry desserts. Hrs: 6-10 pm. Res accepted. Dinner a la carte entrees: $30-$58. Valet parking. Jacket. View of harbor. Elegant dining. Cr cds: A, C, D, DS, ER, MC, V.

D

★ ROCK. *13455 Maxella Ave (90292). 310/822-8979. www.rockenwagner.com.* Specializes in marinated flank steak, pastachio crusted salmon, sauteed sand dabs. Hrs: 11:30 am-2:30 pm, 5:30-10:30 pm; Fri, Sat to 11:30 pm. Res accepted. Wine, beer. Lunch

$8.50-$14.25; dinner $10-$20. Children's menu. Cr cds: A, D, MC, V.
D

Martinez

(see San Francisco map) *See also Concord, Oakland, Vallejo*

Pop 31,808 **Elev** 23 ft **Area code** 510 **Zip** 94553

What to See and Do

Briones Regional Park. Covers 5,484 acres of rolling hills and wooded ravines. John Muir Nature Area at north end. Hiking on many trails incl two self-guided nature trails, horseback riding. Picnicking. Archery range. Connects with Briones to Mt Diablo Trail. (Daily) N entrance 2 mi S of Arnold Industrial Hwy (CA 4) via Alhambra Valley Rd. Phone 510/635-0135. ¢¢

John Muir National Historic Site. House built in 1882 was the home of the conservationist, author, and advocate of the National Park system. Visitor center, film, self-guided tours (Daily; closed Jan 1, Thanksgiving, Dec 25). Guided tour (Wed-Sun). Martinez Adobe (1849) is also on the grounds. 4202 Alhambra Ave. Phone 925/228-8860. ¢

Marysville

(E-3) *See also Oroville*

Settled 1842 **Pop** 12,324 **Elev** 63 ft **Area code** 530 **Zip** 95901

Information Yuba-Sutter Chamber of Commerce, 429 10th St, PO Box 1429; 530/743-6501

Marysville is at the confluence of the Yuba and Feather rivers. The river town was once the third-largest community in the state. Hydraulic mining has raised the Yuba River bed so that it is above, rather than below, the city. The river is contained by huge levees. Named for a survivor of the Donner Party, the town was the head of river navigation—the point where miners continued upriver by foot to the gold diggings.

What to See and Do

Bok Kai Temple. Chinese temple, built in 1879, honors Bok Kai, river god of good fortune. Caretaker will open temple for visitors; guided tours may be arranged by appt (daily). D St on the Levee. Phone 530/743-6501. **Donation**

Special Events

Bok Kai Festival. Parade, street entertainment, Lion Dances, martial arts demonstrations; one-mi run; climaxed by firing of the "Lucky Bombs." Phone 530/743-1004. Late Feb-early Mar.

Stampede Days. Riverfront Park. Stampede and rodeo sponsored by the Flying U Rodeo; parade, activities. Phone 530/695-2727. Memorial Day wkend.

California Prune Festival. Yuba-Sutter Fairgrounds in Yuba City. Food, wine tasting, music, art displays, children's activities. Usually second wkend Sept.

Beckwourth Frontier Days. In commeration of when James Beckwourth passed through here in the 1850s. Costumed participants re-create the life as it was then; events incl muzzle loaders; wagon train. First wkend Oct.

Motel/Motor Lodge

★★ **BEST WESTERN INN.** *1001 Clark Ave, Yuba City (95991). 530/674-8824; fax 530/674-0563; res 800/562-5700.* 125 rms, 2-3 story. S $64-$75; D $64-$85; each addl $4; suites $89-$150. TV; cable. Pool; whirlpool. Complimentary coffee in rms. Restaurant 6 am-10 pm. Bar 4 pm-midnight. Ck-out noon. Meeting rms. Business servs avail. Some refrigerators, in-rm whirlpools, fireplaces, balconies. Cr cds: A, C, D, DS, MC, V.
D SC

Mendocino

(E-1) *See also Fort Bragg, Ukiah, Willits*

Founded 1852 **Pop** 1,100 **Elev** 125 ft **Area code** 707 **Zip** 95460

Information Fort Bragg-Mendocino Coast Chamber of Commerce, 332 N Main St, PO Box 1141, Fort Bragg 95437; 707/961-6300 or 800/726-2780

Web www.mendocinocoast.com

Once a remote lumber port, Mendocino has evolved into a cultural center and popular vacation spot. The town's 19th-century legacy is reflected in its Cape Cod/New England architecture.

What to See and Do

Kelley House Museum & Library. (1861) Displays feature antique photographs, exhibits of local artifacts, and private collections. (Sept-May, Fri-Sun; June-Aug, daily) 45007 Albion St. Phone 707/937-5791. ¢

Mendocino Art Center. Classes in ceramics, textiles, painting, drawing, printmaking, and sculpture. Exhibition/sales gallery, art library, gardens; theatrical productions and arts and crafts fairs. (Daily; closed Jan 1, Dec 25) 45200 Little Lake St, PO Box 765. Phone 707/937-5818. **FREE**

State parks.

Mendocino Headlands. Incl 1850s building (Ford House Visitor Center) containing exhibits on town and local history (daily; fee); Phone 707/937-5397. **FREE**

Russian Gulch. Swimming beach, entry point for skin divers, fishing; hiking and bicycle trails, picnicking, camping (Apr-Dec). Standard fees. 2 mi N via CA 1. Phone 707/937-5804.

Van Damme. In the SE portion of this 2,190-acre park is Pygmy Forest, where poor soil conditions inhibit tree growth. Some trees, nearly 200 yrs old, have trunks only ¼ inch in diameter. Fishing, beach with access for divers and boaters; nature and hiking trails, picnicking, camping. Standard fees. 3 mi S via CA 1. Phone 707/937-5804.

Special Events

Crab and Wine Days Festival. Phone 707/961-6300.Last wk Jan, first wk Feb.

Whale Festival. Whale watching walks, wine tasting, chowder tasting. Phone 707/961-6300. Mar.

Mendocino Music Festival. Chamber, symphonic, choral, opera and jazz concerts. Phone 707/937-2044. Ten days July.

Mendocino Christmas Festival. Tour of inns; events. Phone 707/961-6300. First two wks Dec.

B&Bs/Small Inns

★★★ **ALBION RIVER INN.** *3790 N Hwy 1, Albion (95410). 707/937-1919; fax 707/937-2604; toll-free 800/479-7944. www.albionriverinn.com.* 20 rms. No A/C. S, D $180. Complimentary full bkfst, coffee, wine in rms. Restaurant (see also ALBION RIVER INN). Ck-out noon, ck-in 3 pm. Business servs avail. Fireplaces, refrigerators; some in-rm whirlpools. Ten landscaped acres on cliff above ocean; flower gardens. Individually decorated rms; antiques. View of ocean. Totally nonsmoking. Cr cds: A, C, D, DS, MC, V.

D

★★★ **BLACKBERRY INN.** *44951 Larkin Rd (95460). 707/937-5281; toll-free 800/950-7806.* 17 rms, 2 kit. units. No A/C. Some rm phones. S $90-$140; D $95-$145; each addl $5; kit. units $145; mid-wk rates in winter. TV; cable. Complimentary continental bkfst. Coffee in rms. Ck-out 11 am, ck-in 2 pm. Many fireplaces; some refrigerators, in-rm whirlpools. Ocean view. Cr cds: MC, V.

D

★★★ **ELK COVE INN.** *6300 S Hwy 1, Elk (95432). 707/877-3321; fax 707/877-1808; res 800/275-2967. www.elkcoveinn.com.* 14 rms. No A/C. No rm phones. D $108-$128; suites $248-$278; lower mid-wk rates (winter). Children over 12 yrs only. TV in sitting rm; VCR (free movies). Complimentary full bkfst. Coffee in rms. Bar. Ck-out 11 am, ck-in 2-6 pm. Business servs avail. Library; sitting rm. Antiques. Some fireplaces. Picnic tables, grills. Gazebo. Former executive guest house (1883). Overlooks ocean; private beach access. Totally nonsmoking. Cr cds: A, DS, MC, V.

★★★ **HARBOR HOUSE INN.** *5600 S Hwy 1, Elk (95432). 707/877-3203; fax 707/877-3452; toll-free 800/720-7474. www.theharborhouseinn.com.* 10 rms, 2 story, 4 cottages. No A/C. No rm phones. MAP: S $270-$345; D $315-$385; each addl $55; mid-wk rates Jan-Mar. Children over 12 yrs only. Ck-out noon, ck-in 2 pm. Lawn games. Many fireplaces. Library. Antiques, original artwork, piano. Gardens, private beach. Built in 1916 for lumber company executive. Totally nonsmoking. Cr cds: A, MC, V.

D

★★★ **HEADLANDS INN.** *Albion and Howard Sts (95460). 707/937-4431; fax 707/937-0412; toll-free 800/354-4431. www.headlands inn.com.* 7 rms, 3 story. No A/C. No rm phones. S, D $90-$195; lower rates winter mid-wk. TV in cottage; VCR. Complimentary full bkfst; afternoon refreshments. Restaurant nearby. Ck-out 11 am, ck-in 3-6 pm. Business servs avail. Street parking. Fireplaces. Sitting rms; antiques. Victorian house (1868) built as town

MENDOCINO

A thriving lumber town way back in the 1850s, a quiet backwater a century after that, and now a popular artists' colony and resort town, the entire village of Mendocino is listed on the National Historic Register. It's a great place for strolling, with wide, quiet streets leading past old water towers, sea captains' homes, inns, galleries, shops, and restaurants. Much of the town is surrounded by Mendocino Headlands State Park, where cliffs overlooking the ocean are honeycombed by some three miles of trails. During the November to March migration season, you might spot California grey whales off the coast. The village itself is small enough that you could wander almost all of its streets in an hour or two, or make a day of it by browsing through the small museums and shops. Start your walk on Main Street at the corner of Evergreen, on the eastern edge of town not far from Highway 1. Stroll west along Main Street, where you'll pass the Sweetwater Inn, which incorporates one of Mendocino's remaining water towers that provided fresh water to settlers' homes here nearly 150 years ago. (Of the town's 80-plus 19th-century water towers, only a dozen survive today.) Look for another tower just beyond, at the corner of Main and Howard streets. Continuing along Main, stop into the Ford House, an 1854 home that serves as the interpretive center for the Mendocino Headlands State Park; a small museum with local artifacts and nature displays is inside. Walk the rest of Main Street, which is lined with inns, restaurants, and galleries, and turn right at Woodward Street to Albion Street. Turn right again on Albion and walk east. About halfway down the first block on the northern side of the road is the Kwan Tai temple, the oldest Chinese temple along the North Coast. In the next block, between Kasten and Lansing streets, look for the MacCallum House Inn (45020 Albion), which combines Victorian architecture with rooms located in a converted water tower. On the other side of Albion (45007) is the Kelley House Museum, where old photos reveal more Mendocino history. At the end of the block, turn left up Lansing Street, then right on Ukiah past Howard Street. On the south side of Ukiah on the block between Howard and Evergreen streets is the Sweetwater Gardens (955 Ukiah), another inn that incorporates a water tower. Nearby, the well-known Cafe Beaujolais serves candlelight dinners that rank with the best along the entire North Coast. Backtrack along Ukiah to Lansing Street, and go right up to Little Lake Street. Turn left and go one block west to the corner of Ford Street. There you'll find Blair House, an inn better known as Jessica Fletcher's house in the fictitious Cabot Cove, Maine, on the long-running television series *Murder, She Wrote*, starring Angela Lansbury. Mendocino's weather-beaten architecture, often compared to that of New England, managed to fool millions of viewers. From here, if you still have energy, walk west along just about any street to pick up a trail leading out to the Mendocino Headlands and enjoy the sea views and salt air.

barber shop overlooks English garden, ocean. Totally nonsmoking. Cr cds: A, MC, V.

★★★ HERITAGE HOUSE INN. *5200 N Hwy 1 (95456). 707/937-5885; fax 707/937-0318; res 800/235-5885. www.heritagehouseinn.com.* 66 rms, 1-2 story, 10 suites. No A/C. No rm phones. S, D $125-$300; each addl $20; suites $225-$350; under 6 free; wkends, hols (2-3 day min). Complimentary coffee in rms. Restaurant 8-11 am, 6-8:30 pm. Ck-out noon, ck-in 2 pm. Business servs avail. Bellhops. Concierge serv. Gift shop. Many fireplaces, refrigerators; some wet bars. On ocean. Built in 1877; on 37 acres. Cr cds: A, MC, V.

D SC

★★★ HILL HOUSE INN OF MENDOCINO. *10701 Palette Dr (95460). 707/937-0554; fax 707/937-1123; toll-free 800/422-0554. www.hillhouseinn.com.* 44 rms, 2 story, 4 suites. No A/C. S, D $110-$175; suites $195-$300. TV; cable. Complimentary coffee in rms. Dining rm 7:30-10:30 am, 11:30 am-9 pm. Bar. Ck-out noon, ck-in 3 pm. Meeting rms. Business servs avail. Private patios, balconies. Picnic tables. Library. Victorian decor. Overlooks ocean. On 2½ acres. Cr cds: A, DS, MC, V.

D

★★ INN AT SCHOOLHOUSE CREEK. *7051 N Hwy 1, Littleriver (95456). 707/937-5525; fax 707/937-2012; toll-free 800/731-5525. www.schoolhousecreek.com.* 13 rms, 4 suites, 3 kit. units, 1 guest house. No A/C. Some rm phones. Mid-May-Sept: S, D $125; each addl $10-$15; suites $115-$150; kit. units $140-$175; guest house $150-$180; wkends, hols (2-3 day min); lower rates rest of yr. Crib $10. Pet accepted, some restrictions; $15-$25. TV; cable (premium), VCR (movies). Complimentary continental bkfst, coffee in rms. Restaurant nearby. Ck-out 11 am, ck-in 2 pm. Business servs avail. Concierge serv. Gift shop. Lawn games. Fireplaces; some refrigerators. Balconies. Built in 1862; on 8½ acres; gardens, meadows, forests. Totally nonsmoking. Cr cds: A, DS, MC, V.

★★★ JOSHUA GRINDLE INN. *44800 Little Lake Rd Box 647 (95460). 707/937-4143; toll-free 800/474-6353. www.joshgrin.com.* 10 rms, 1 guest house, 1-2 story. No A/C. Rm phones avail. S, D $100-$195; guest house $200-$250; wkly rates; wkends (2-day min). Complimentary full bkfst; afternoon refreshments. Ck-out 11 am, ck-in 1 pm. Free airport transportation. Lawn games. Antiques. Many fireplaces. New England country atmosphere. Two-acre English-style garden. Antique pump organ. Built 1879 by local banker. Overlooks ocean. Totally nonsmoking. Cr cds: A, DS, MC, V.

★★★ MENDOCINO HOTEL. *45080 Main St (95460). 707/937-0511; fax 707/937-0513; toll-free 800/548-0513.* 51 rms, 38 with bath, 1-3 story. S, D $85-$185; each addl $20; suites $190-$275; lower rates wkdays. TV in some rms; cable. Dining rm 8 am-9:30 pm. Bar. Ck-out noon, ck-in 4 pm. Meeting rms. Business servs avail. Bellhops. Some fireplaces. Some balconies. Antiques. Built 1878. Some rms with ocean view. Cr cds: A, MC, V.

D

★★★ THE STANFORD INN BY THE SEA. *Hwy 1 at Comptche Ukiah Rd (95460). 707/937-5615; fax 707/937-0305; toll-free 800/331-8884. www.stanfordinn.com.* 40 rms, 2-3 story, 2 kits. No A/C. S, D $215-$242; kit. suites $275-$365. Crib $5. Pet accepted; fee. TV; cable (premium), VCR (movies $4). Indoor pool; whirlpool. Complimentary full bkfst. Coffee in rms. Restaurant 8-10 am; Thurs-Sat 8-10 am, 6-8:30 pm; Sun 8 am-1 pm, 6-8:30 pm. Ck-out noon, ck-in 4 pm. Business center. In-rm modem link. Bellhops. Concierge. Free airport transportation. Exercise equipt; sauna. Refrigerators, fireplaces. Private patios, balconies. Bike, canoe rentals. Antiques. Big River llamas on grounds. Tropical greenhouse. Organic gardens, nursery. On ten acres of meadow, forest overlooking ocean, river. Totally nonsmoking. Cr cds: A, C, D, DS, MC, V.

D

★★★ WHITEGATE INN. *499 Howard St (95460). 707/937-4892; fax 707/937-1131; res 800/531-7282.*

www.whitegateinn.com. 7 rms, 2 story, 1 guest house. No A/C. No rm phones. July-Oct and wkends: S, D $139-$159; each addl $25; guest house $189-$229; under 10 free (in cottage); wkends, hols 2-3 day min; lower rates rest of yr. Children over 10 yrs only (in inn). TV; cable. Complimentary full bkfst. Restaurant nearby. Ck-out 11 am, ck-in 3-6 pm. Business servs avail. Bellhops. Concierge serv. Gift shop. Street parking. Fireplaces. Picnic tables. Built in 1883; old world atmosphere; antique organ. Totally nonsmoking. Cr cds: A, C, D, DS, JCB, MC, V.

Restaurants

★★★ **ALBION RIVER INN.** *3790 N CA 1, Albion (95410). 707/937-1919. www.albionriverinn.com.* Hrs: 5:30-9:30 pm; wkends 5-10 pm. Res accepted. No A/C. Coastal country menu. Bar 4:30 pm-midnight. Dinner $14-$21. Specializes in fresh seafood, pasta, local produce. Pianist Fri, Sat. Original art. On ocean. Totally nonsmoking. Cr cds: A, C, D, DS, ER, MC, V.

D

★★★ **CAFE BEAUJOLAIS.** *961 Ukiah St (95460). 707/937-5614. www.cafebeaujolais.com.* Hrs: 5:45-9 pm. Closed Dec 25. Res accepted. No A/C. French, California menu. Beer. Wine list. Dinner $16.95-$18.50. Specializes in French cuisine. Own bread. Victorian atmosphere. Totally nonsmoking. Cr cds: DS, MC, V.

D

Menlo Park

(see San Francisco map) *See also Palo Alto, Redwood City, San Francisco, Santa Clara, Saratoga*

Founded 1854 **Pop** 28,040 **Elev** 70 ft **Area code** 650 **Zip** 94025

What to See and Do

Allied Arts Guild. Unique complex of shops set on a portion of the once vast Rancho de las Pulgas. Original barn and sheep sheds were preserved and new builidgs constructed in Colonial Spanish design; formal gardens, paths, and courtyards. (Mon-Sat; closed hols) 75 Arbor Rd, at Cambridge. Phone 650/325-3259.

Filoli House and Gardens. (1917) This 654-acre estate contains the Georgian-style residence built for William B. Bourn II and 16-acre formal gardens. The gardens are an Italian Renaissance-style of parterres, terraces, lawns, and pools. The house was featured in the television series "Dynasty." House and garden: guided tours (mid-Feb-Oct, Tues-Sat), res required; self-guided tours, no res required. Three-mi guided nature hike (Sat), res required. N on El Camino Real to Woodside Rd (CA 84), then 4 mi W to Cañada Rd, then 5 mi N, in Woodside. Phone 650/364-8300. ¢¢¢

Stanford Linear Accelerator Center (SLAC). This 426-acre national facility houses a two-mi-long linear accelerator that generates the highest energy electron beams in the world. 2½-hr tour consists of orientation, slide show and bus tour. (Limited hrs; res required) 2575 Sand Hill Rd, E of I-280. Phone 650/926-2204. **FREE**

Sunset Publishing Corporation and Gardens. Publishers of *Sunset* magazine and books. Self-guided tour of gardens. (Mon-Fri; closed hols) Willow and Middlefield Rds. Phone 650/321-3600. **FREE**

Motels/Motor Lodges

★★ **MENLO PARK INN.** *1315 El Camino Real (94025). 650/326-7530; fax 650/328-7539; toll-free 800/327-1315. www.menloparkinn.com.* 30 rms, 2 story. S $105-$115; D, suites $115-$125; each addl $7; under 18 free. Crib free. TV; cable (premium), VCR. Complimentary continental bkfst. Restaurant nearby. Ck-out 11 am. Business servs avail. In-rm modem link. Refrigerators. Cr cds: A, C, D, DS, MC, V.

D SC

★★★ **STANFORD PARK.** *100 El Camino Real (94025). 650/322-1234; fax 650/322-0975; toll-free 800/368-2468. www.stanfordparkhotel.com.* 155 rms, 8 suites. 3-4 story. S, D $295-$335; each addl $15; suites $360-

$400; under 12 free. Crib free. Valet parking. TV; cable, VCR avail. Restaurant (see also DUCK CLUB). Rm serv 24 hrs. Bar 11 am-midnight. Ck-out noon. Complimentary coffee in the lobby. Concierge. Meeting rms. Business center. In-rm modem link. Bellhops. Heated swimming pool, whirlpool. Fitness center, sauna. Bathrm phones, minibars, some refrigerators. Some balconies. Cr cds: A, C, D, DS, JCB, MC, V.

D SC

Restaurants

★★ **DUCK CLUB.** *100 El Camino Real (94025). 650/322-1234. www.woodsidehotels.com.* Hrs: 6 am-2 pm, 6-10 pm; Sun brunch 10 am-2 pm. Res accepted. Bar 11 am-midnight. Wine list. Bkfst $6.75-$14, lunch $8.95-$15.75, dinner $9.50-$24.95. Sun brunch $26.99. Children's menu. Specializes in fresh seafood, pasta, American regional cuisine. Own baking. Piano bar. Valet parking. Cr cds: A, C, D, DS, ER, MC, V.

D

★★ **LEFT BANK.** *635 Santa Cruz Ave (94025). 650/473-6543.* Specializes in French entrees. Hrs: 11:30 am-11 pm; Mon, Sun 5-10 pm. Res accepted. Wine, beer. Lunch $9-$20, dinner $11-$22. Children's menu. Entertainment. Cr cds: A, C, MC, V.

D

★★ **LE POT AU FEU.** *1149 El Camino Real (94025). 650/322-4343.* Hrs: 5:30-9:30 pm; Sun to 9 pm. Closed Mon; hols. Res accepted. Country French menu. Wine, beer. A la carte entrees: dinner $15.95-$19.95. Specialties: brie puff pastry with Riesling wine sauce and onion marmalade, beef Wellington, filet mignon with truffle cognac sauce. Patio dining. Two dining rms; country inn ambience. Cr cds: A, C, D, MC, V.

D

★★★ **WILD HARE.** *1029 El Camino Real (94025). 650/327-4273. www.thewildhare.com.* Specializes in wild game, bison steak, roasted duck. Hrs: 11:30 am-2:30 pm, 5:30-11 pm; Fri, Sat 5:30-11 pm; Sun 5-10 pm. Res accepted. Wine, beer. Lunch $8-$14, dinner $14-$30. Entertainment. Cr cds: A, D, MC, V.

D

Merced (G-5)

Pop 56,216 **Elev** 172 ft **Area code** 209 **Zip** 95340

Information Conference & Visitors Bureau, 690 W 16th St; 209/384-7092 or 800/446-5353

Web www.yosemite-gateway.org

The Gateway to Yosemite National Park (see), Merced is the center of a rich agricultural area with dairy and beef production as well as peach, almond, tomato, and alfalfa crops. Publishing, canneries, and metal and plastic manufacturers contribute to its economic base.

What to See and Do

Castle Air Museum. Displays 44 vintage military aircraft; indoor military museum; inquire for guided tours. Restaurant. Museum (daily; closed hols) 8 mi N, adj to Castle aviation park at Sante Fe and Buhach Rd. Phone 209/723-2178. ¢¢

Lake Yosemite Park. Swimming, sailing, waterskiing, fishing, boating; picnicking. (Daily for sightseeing and fishing) Fee for group facility use and boat launching. 5714 N Lake Rd, 5 mi NE on G St, 2 mi E on Bellvue Rd, then ½ mi N on N Lake Rd to park entrance. Phone 209/385-7426. ¢¢

Merced County Courthouse Museum. Restored courthouse with collection of antique dolls, quilts, historical exhibits. (Wed-Sun afternoons) Courthouse Park, N and 21st Sts. Phone 209/723-2401. **FREE**

Merced Multicultural Arts Center. Three-story building contains theater, lobby, retail galleries, photo gallery, traveling exhibits, and six visual and performing arts studios. (Mon-Fri; wkends by appt; closed hols) 645 W Main St. Phone 209/388-1090. **FREE**

Merced River Development Project. S of CA 132. **Exchequer Dam.** Rises 490 ft to impound Lake McClure (82-mi shoreline). **McClure Point, Barrett Cove, Horseshoe Bend, and**

Bagby Recreation Areas. McSwain Dam stands 80 ft high; impounds Lake McSwain (12½-mi shoreline). All areas offer swimming, showers, rest rms, waterskiing, fishing, boating (launching facilities; fee), marinas; picnicking, concessions, camping (fee; electricity addl). Contact Merced Irrigation District, Parks Dept, 9090 Lake McClure Rd, Snelling 95369. Phone 209/378-2520.

Special Events

West Coast Antique Fly-in. Antique and experimental aircraft. First full wkend June.

Merced County Fair. County Fairgrounds. Mid-July. Phone 209/722-1507.

Central Valley Band Review. High school and junior high school band competitions. Nov.

Motel/Motor Lodge

★★ **BEST WESTERN INN.** *1213 V Street (95340). 209/723-3711; fax 209/722-8551.* 98 rms, 2 story. S $59-$64; D $64-$69; each addl $5; under 18 free. Crib free. Pet accepted. TV; cable (premium). Pool. Complimentary continental bkfst, coffee in rms. Restaurant 6 am-11 pm. Bar noon-11 pm, wkends to midnight. Ck-out noon. Meeting rm. Business servs avail. Some refrigerators, microwaves. Cr cds: A, C, D, DS, JCB, MC, V.

SC

Restaurant

★★ **EAGLES NEST.** *2000 E Childs Ave (95340). 209/723-1041.* Hrs: 6 am-10 pm; Sun brunch 9 am-2 pm. Res accepted; required hols. Bar 10 am-midnight. Bkfst $1.95-$7, lunch $5.95-$8.95, dinner $5.49-$15.95. Sun brunch $9.95. Children's menu. Specialties: angel hair pasta, stuffed teriyaki chicken. Outdoor dining. Nature-themed decor; etched glass depicts nature scenes. Cr cds: A, D, DS, MC, V.

D SC

Millbrae

(see San Francisco Airport Area)

Mill Valley

(see San Francisco map) *See also San Francisco, San Rafael*

Pop 13,038 **Elev** 80 ft **Area code** 415 **Zip** 94941

Information Mill Valley Chamber of Commerce, 85 Throckmorton Ave; 415/388-9700

What to See and Do

Mount Tamalpais State Park. This park is one of the favorite retreats of San Franciscans. The mountain rises 2,571 ft above sea level and provides a spectacular view of the entire bay area. A winding road climbs to a spot near the summit. Trails and bridle paths wind through the woods to attractive picnic areas; hike-in camping (fee; no vehicles). Muir Woods National Monument (see) is at the foot of the mountain. The Mountain Theatre, located just N of the park, presents plays in a natural amphitheater (May-Sept). Standard fees. 6 mi W on Panoramic Hwy. Phone 415/388-2070. Day use per vehicle ¢¢

Motel/Motor Lodge

★★ **HOLIDAY INN EXPRESS.** *160 Shoreline Hwy (94941). 415/332-5700; fax 415/331-1859.* 100 rms, 2 story. June-Oct: S, D $100-$130; each addl $8; under 18 free; lower rates rest of yr. Crib free. TV; cable (premium), some VCRs. Pool, wading pool. Complimentary continental bkfst. Ck-out noon. Meeting rms. Business servs avail. In-rm modem link. Valet serv. Exercise equipt. Private patios, balconies. Cr cds: A, D, DS, MC, V.

D

B&Bs/Small Inns

★★★ **CASA DEL MAR.** *37 Belvedere, Stinson Beach (94970). 415/868-2124; fax 415/868-2305; toll-free 800/552-2124. www.stinsonbeach.*

com. 6 rms, 4 with shower only, 3 story. No A/C. No elvtr. No rm phones. S, D $140-$235; each addl $20. Complimentary full bkfst; afternoon refreshments. Restaurant nearby. Ck-out 11 am, ck-in 4 pm. Concierge serv. Game rm. Refrigerators. Some balconies. Totally nonsmoking. Cr cds: A, MC, V.

★★★ **MILL VALLEY INN.** *165 Throckmorton Ave (94941). 415/389-6608; fax 415/389-5051; toll-free 800/595-2100. www.millvalleyinn.com.* 25 rms, 3 story, 2 cottages. S, D, cottages $160; each addl $20; under 18 free; wkly rates; spa plans; wkends, hols (2-3-day min). Crib free. TV; cable. Complimentary continental bkfst. Restaurant nearby. Ck-out 11 am, ck-in 4 pm. Concierge serv. Meeting rm. Business servs avail. In-rm modem link. Health club privileges. Some balconies, fireplaces. Stucco building, sun terrace in back. Original pieces in guest rms by North Bay craftspeople. Totally nonsmoking. Cr cds: A, D, DS, JCB, MC, V.

D

★★ **MOUNTAIN HOME INN.** *810 Panoramic Hwy (94941). 415/381-9000; fax 415/381-3615. www.mtnhomeinn.com.* 10 rms, 3 story. No A/C. S, D $175-$325; each addl $29. Complimentary full bkfst. Dining rm 11:30 am-3:30 pm, 5:30-9:30 pm (see also MOUNTAIN HOME INN). Ck-out 11 am, ck-in 3 pm. Business servs avail. Some fireplaces. Private patios, balconies. Scenic view. On road to Mt Tamalpais. Cr cds: A, MC, V.

D

Restaurants

★★ **BUCKEYE ROADHOUSE.** *15 Shoreline Hwy (94941). 415/331-2600.* Hrs: 11:30 am-10:30 pm; Fri-Sat to 11 pm; Sun brunch 10:30 am-3 pm. Closed Dec 25. Res accepted. No A/C. Bar. Lunch, dinner $7-$25. Sun brunch $7-$12. Children's menu. Specializes in steak, fresh crab, ribs. Free valet parking. Outdoor dining. Roadhouse first opened in 1937; flower gardens. Totally nonsmoking. Cr cds: C, D, DS, MC, V.

D

★★ **FRANTOIO.** *152 Shoreline Hwy (94941). 415/289-5777. www.frantoio.com.* Hrs: 11:30 am-10 pm; Fri, Sat to 11 pm; Sun from 5 pm. Closed July 4, Thanksgiving, Dec 25. Res accepted. Italian menu. Bar. Lunch $7.95-$18, dinner $10-$20. Specializes in grilled meat and fish, pasta. Outdoor dining. Pianist. Contemporary decor, olive oil press operating Oct-Mar. Totally nonsmoking. Cr cds: A, D, DS, MC, V.

D

★ **MOUNTAIN HOME INN.** *810 Panoramic Way (94941). 415/381-9000. www.mtnhomeinn.com.* Hrs: 11:30 am-3:30 pm, 5:30-9:30 pm; Sat, Sun from 8 am; Sat, Sun brunch 11:30 am-3:30 pm. Closed Mon Nov-Apr; Dec 25. Res accepted; required Fri, Sat. No A/C. Bar. Bkfst, lunch $7.50-$12.25, dinner $11.50-$18. Sat, Sun brunch $7-$12. Specialties: lamb shanks, teriyaki-marinated flank steak. Outdoor dining (exc dinner). Views of bay and mountains. Cr cds: A, MC, V.

D

★★ **ROBATA GRILL AND SUSHI.** *591 Redwood Hwy (94941). 415/381-8400. www.robatagrill.com.* Hrs: 11:30 am-2 pm, 5:30-9:30 pm; Fri to 10 pm; Sat 5:30-10 pm; Sun from 5:30 pm. Closed hols. Res accepted. Japanese menu. Wine, beer. Lunch, dinner $10-$25. Specializes in sushi, robata grilled dishes. Japanese decor; sushi bar. Totally nonsmoking. Cr cds: A, D, DS, MC, V.

D

Modesto

(G-4) *See also Oakdale, Stockton*

Founded 1870 **Pop** 164,730 **Elev** 91 ft **Area code** 209 **Zip** 95353

Information Convention & Visitors Bureau, 1114 J Street, PO Box 844; 209/571-6480 or 800/266-4282

Web www.modestocvb.org

A processing, shipping, and marketing center for the rich farmlands of the central San Joaquin Valley and Stanislaus County, Modesto was named for a San Francisco banker who was too modest to publicize his own name. Nearby Don Pedro Dam provides the irrigation and power that is the key to the area's prosperity. Modesto is a gateway to Yosemite National Park (see) and the Gold Country.

What to See and Do

Caswell Memorial State Park. On 274 acres. Swimming, fishing; nature, hiking trails; picnicking, camping. Standard fees. 15 mi N via CA 99, S on Austin Rd. Phone 209/599-3810.

Don Pedro Lake Recreation Area. Approx 37 mi E, N of CA 132 (see SONORA). Phone 209/852-2396.

Great Valley Museum of Natural History. Exhibits of natural plant and animal habitats and complete ecosystems. Also children's discovery rm. (Tues-Sat) 1100 Stoddard Ave. Phone 209/575-6196. ¢

McHenry Museum. Historical exhibits in period rms; schoolrm, doctor's office, blacksmith shop. (Tues-Sun, afternoons) 1402 I Street. Phone 209/577-5366. **FREE** One blk NE is the

McHenry Mansion. (1883). Restored Victorian mansion built for one of Modesto's first families. Period furnishings. (Tues-Sun, afternoons; closed hols) 15th and I streets. Phone 209/577-5344. **FREE**

Turlock Lake State Recreation Area. On 3,000 acres. Swimming, waterskiing, fishing, boating; picnicking, camping. Standard fees. 23 mi E on CA 132, just off 132 on Lake Rd. Phone 209/874-2008.

Special Events

International Festival. Graceada Park. Oct.

Riverbank Cheese & Wine Exposition. 6 mi E on CA 108 in Riverbank. Street festival with food booths, arts and crafts, antiques, entertainment. Tasting of local wines and cheeses. Phone 209/869-4541. Oct.

Motels/Motor Lodges

★★ **COURTYARD BY MARRIOTT.** *1720 Sisk Rd (95350). 209/577-3825; fax 209/577-1717; res 800/321-2211.* 126 units, 2 story, 11 suites. S, D $99; each addl $10; suites $105-$195; under 18 free. Crib $5. TV; cable (premium). Heated pool, whirlpool, poolside serv. Complimentary coffee in rms. Restaurant 6:30-9:30 am, 5-9 pm. Rm serv 5-9 pm. Ck-out noon. Meeting rms. Business servs avail. Free airport transportation. Exercise equipt. Some refrigerators. Wet bar in suites. Cr cds: A, C, D, DS, MC, V.
D SC

★★ **HOLIDAY INN.** *1612 Sisk Rd (95350). 209/521-1612; fax 209/527-5074; toll-free 800/465-4329. www.holiday-inn.com.* 186 rms, 2 story. S, D $109-$129; suites $150; under 19 free. Crib free. TV; cable. Complimentary coffee in rms. 2 pools, 1 indoor, whirlpool. Playground. Restaurant 6:30 am-2 pm, 5-10 pm. Bar noon-1:30 am; entertainment. Ck-out noon. Meeting rms. Business servs avail. Coin lndry. Lighted tennis. Putting green. Exercise equipt. Rec rm. Cr cds: A, C, D, DS, ER, JCB, MC, V.
D SC

★ **VAGABOND INN.** *1525 McHenry Ave (95350). 209/521-6340 or 209/521-6340; fax 209/575-2015.* 99 rms, 2 story. S, D $60-$70; each addl $5; under 18 free. Crib free. Pet accepted; $5. TV; cable (premium). Heated pool. Complimentary continental bkfst. Restaurant adj open 24 hrs. Ck-out noon. Business servs avail. Cr cds: A, D, DS, MC, V.
D

Hotel

★★★ **DOUBLETREE HOTEL MODESTO.** *1150 9th St (95354). 209/526-6000; fax 209/526-6096; res 800/222-8733.* 258 rms, 10 story. Jan-Nov: S $114; D $134; each addl $15; suites $250-$500; under 18 free; family rates; package plans; lower rates rest of yr. Crib free. Pet accepted; $100 deposit. Valet parking $7. TV; cable. Complimentary coffee in rms. Restaurant 6 am-midnight. Bar 11-2 am; entertainment Fri, Sat. Ck-out noon. Convention facilities. Business servs avail. In-rm modem link. Gift shop. Beauty shop. Free airport, RR station, bus depot transportation. Exercise equipt; sauna. Pool, whirlpool. Bathrm phones; some in-rm whirlpools. Some balconies. Cr cds: A, C, D, DS, MC, V.
D SC

Monterey

(B-1) *See also Carmel, Pacific Grove, Pebble Beach, Salinas*

Founded 1770 **Pop** 31,954 **Elev** 40 ft **Area code** 831 **Zip** 93940

Information Monterey Peninsula Visitors & Convention Bureau, 401 Camino El Estero, PO Box 1770; 831/649-1770

Web www.monterey.com

The calm harbor, red-roofed white stucco houses, white sand beach, Monterey cypress, and Monterey pine all existed in the days when Monterey was the Spanish heart of California. A mélange of Mexican, New England, sea, mission, and ranch makes Monterey uniquely Californian in its culture and history. The Spanish explorer Sebastian Vizcaino sailed into the bay in 1602 and named it for the Count of Monte-Rey, Viceroy of Mexico. The spot was rediscovered in 1770 when Fray Crespi, Fray Junipero Serra, and Gaspar de Portola took possession, founding the Presidio and the Mission San Carlos Borromeo del Rio Carmelo (see CARMEL). The King of Spain recognized it as the capital of California in 1775, but in 1822 it became part of the Mexican Republic. Soon after, American whalers and traders began to arrive. Commodore Sloat raised the American flag in 1846, ending years of opposition to Mexican rule. Delegates to a constitutional convention in 1849 met in Monterey and drew up California's first constitution. The city became a whaling center; fisheries, canneries, and specialized agriculture developed. The sardine fisheries and canneries, in particular, inspired the novels *Cannery Row* and *Sweet Thursday* by John Steinbeck. Now, with the sardines gone and the canneries silent, the row has been taken over by an aquarium, gourmet restaurants, and art galleries, while Fisherman's Wharf offers fishing and sightseeing trips and the bay's famous sea otters; nearby is the Maritime Museum of Monterey.

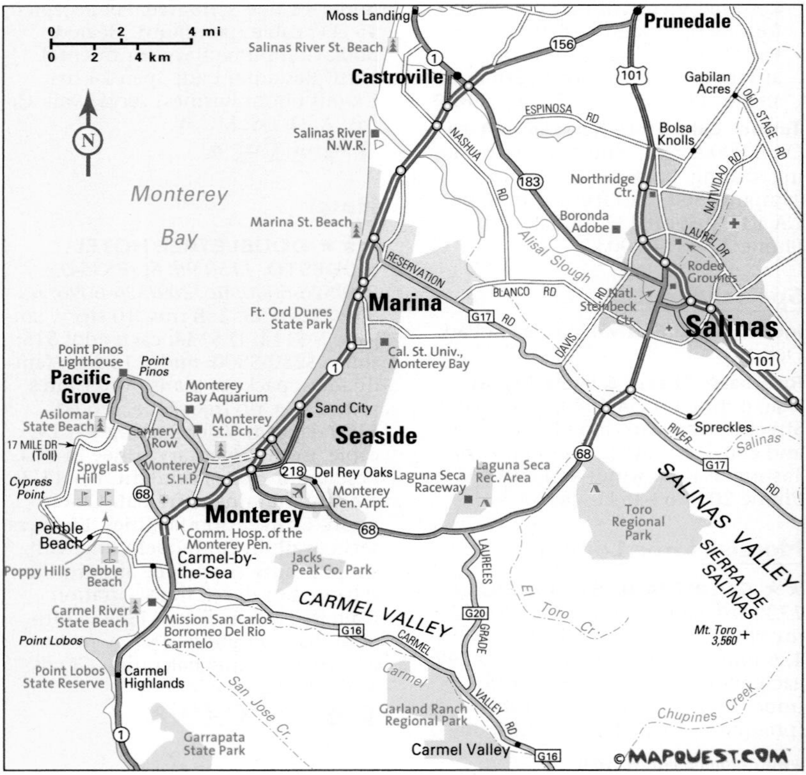

What to See and Do

Cannery Row. Mile-long strip overlooking the waterfront lined with combination of historic buildings (many related to John Steinbeck and his writings), entertainment, shops, restaurants, hotels. (Daily) Phone 831/373-1902. **FREE**

Colton Hall Museum. (1849) and **Old Monterey Jail** (1854). Built as a town hall and public school by the Reverend Walter Colton, alcalde (mayor or judge) of Monterey District during the American occupation of California, 1846-1848. Classic Revival design of stone and adobe mortar. The first constitution of California (in Spanish and English) was written here. Changing exhibits. The jail, a single-story addition of granite, was added to the building in 1854 at which time Colton Hall served as the Monterey County Courthouse. (Daily; closed Jan 1, Thanksgiving, Dec 25) Pacific St, between Madison and Jefferson Sts, in Civic Center, second floor. Phone 831/646-5640. **FREE**

Fisherman's Wharf. Restaurants, shops, tour boat departure area. On Monterey Harbor.

La Mirada. Original residence of Jose Castro, prominent Californian during the Mexican period, and later Frank Work, who added a collection of art and antiques to the 2½-acre estate. Garden and house tours (Wed-Sun). 720 Via Mirada. Phone 831/372-3689. **¢¢**

Marina. Berths for 420 vessels up to 50 ft long; two launching ramps. Municipally owned. (Office closed Jan 1, Thanksgiving, Dec 25) Foot of Figueroa St. Phone 831/646-3950.

Maritime Museum of Monterey. Seven major theme areas provide exhibits on maritime and naval history of the area, incl sailing ship era and whaling industry; ship models, maritime artifacts, interactive exhibits; paintings; research library; model workshop for restoration and building replicas of historic vessels. The jewel of the museum collection is the 16-ft-tall intricately crafted first order Fresnel Lens from the old lighthouse at Point Sur. Also here is a 100-seat theater featuring an orientation film and reenactments. (Tues-Sun; closed Jan 1, Thanksgiving, Dec 25) Located in the Stanton Center at #5 Custom House Plaza, adj to Fisherman's Wharf. Phone 831/373-AHOY. **¢¢**

Monterey Bay Aquarium. One of the largest aquariums in the US; 100 exhibits of the sea life and habitats along the shores of California's Monterey Bay incl sea otters, sharks, and a three-story-tall kelp forest. The Outer Bay exhibit has daily live video broadcasts, "Live from Monterey Canyon," of work in progress transmitted from waters up to 3,300 ft deep to a screen in the aquarium auditorium (Mon and Tues afternoons). (Daily; closed Dec 25) 886 Cannery Row. Phone 831/648-4888. **¢¢¢¢¢**

Monterey Museum of Art. Displays early California and American art, folk, ethnic and tribal art, Asian art. Photography exhibits; changing exhibitions of major American artists. Docent-guided tour avail (Sun afternoon). (Wed-Sun; closed Jan 1, Thanksgiving, Dec 25) 559 Pacific St. Phone 831/372-5477. **¢¢**

Monterey State Historic Park. Day ticket valid in all historic buildings in state historic park. (Park and building hrs may vary) Phone 831/649-7118. **¢¢**

Boston Store. (1845). Restored general store built by Thomas Larkin and operated by Joseph Boston & Co. Houses a general merchandise store operated by the Montery History and Art Association. (Thurs-Sun; closed Jan 1, Thanksgiving, Dec 25) Scott and Olivier Sts. Phone 831/649-7118. **FREE**

Casa Soberanes. (1842). Adobe house containing displays of Monterey history from 1840-1970. Excellent example of adobe construction; walls are 38 inches thick. Local art collection. (Daily) Guided tours (inquire for schedule). Admisson incl in day ticket. 336 Pacific St.

Cooper-Molera House. (1827). Largest complex in the park. Built by John Rogers Cooper, half-brother of Thomas Larkin. (Daily; inquire for hrs) Admission incl in day ticket. Corner of Polk and Munras. Phone 831/649-7118.

Custom House. (1827) Old Mexican custom house exhibit re-creates a cargo of the 1840s. Commodore Sloat raised the American flag over this adobe building in 1846, bringing 600,000 square mi into the Union. (Daily; closed hols) Custom House Plaza. Phone 831/649-7118. **FREE**

Larkin House. (1830s). Consulate for Thomas Larkin, first and only US consul to Mexican California (1843-1846). Large collection of antiques. (Daily) Guided tours (inquire for schedule). Admission incl in day ticket. 510 Calle Principal, at Jefferson St.

Pacific House. (1847) A museum of California history and Holman Native American artifact collection. (Daily; closed hols) Custom House Plaza. Phone 831/649-7118. **FREE**

Robert Louis Stevenson House. Preserved as a state historic monument with large collection of Stevenson memorabilia. Stevenson lived here for four months while visiting his future wife. (Daily) Guided tours (hrs vary, inquire for schedule). Admission incl in day ticket. 530 Houston St.

"Path of History" tour. Leads to many old buildings of distinction. These are marked with a plaque explaining the history and architecture. Several buildings are open to the public. Some of these buildings and a number of others are part of the Monterey State Historic Park. Obtain map at the Monterey Peninsula Visitor and Convention Bureau, Camino El Estero and Franklin Sts.

Presidio of Monterey. Home of Defense Language Institute. Developed in 1902 as cantonment for troops returning from the Philippine Insurrection. Monument to John Drake Sloat, commander of American troops that captured Monterey (1846); statue in honor of Fray Junipero Serra. There are 12 historic sites and monuments on Presidio Hill; brochure and map avail. Hrs vary. Pacific St, N of Scott St. Phone 831/242-5104. **FREE**

Royal Presidio Chapel. Founded June 3, 1770, the only presidio chapel remaining in California; in continuous use since 1795. Facade is considered most ornate of all California missions. (Daily) San Carlos Cathedral, 550 Church St, between Camino El Estero and Figueroa St. Phone 831/373-2628. **FREE**

★ **Seventeen-Mile Drive.** A famous scenic drive between Monterey and Carmel (see) along Pacific Coast past Seal Rock, Lone Cypress, Cypress Point, and Spyglass Hill and Pebble Beach golf courses. This private community in Del Monte Forest is known around the world for its natural beauty. Road may be entered at several points; follow the red-and-yellow center lines and the Seventeen-Mile Drive signs. Toll **¢¢¢**

Sightseeing tours.

Gray Line bus tours. Contact 350 8th St, San Francisco 94103. Phone 415/558-9400.

Special Events

AT&T-Pebble Beach National Pro-Amateur Golf Championship. Takes place on Pebble Beach, Cypress, and Spyglass courses. Late Jan or early Feb.

Monterey County Fair. Fairgrounds and Exposition Park. 2004 Fairground Rd, corner of Fairground Rd and Garden Rd. Phone 831/372-5863. Aug.

Monterey Jazz Festival. County Fairgrounds. Reserved seats only. Phone 925/275-9255. Mid-Sept.

Motels/Motor Lodges

★★ BAY PARK HOTEL. *1425 Munras Ave (93940). 831/649-1020; fax 831/373-4258; toll-free 800/338-3564. www.bayparkhotel.com.* 80 rms, 3 story. No elvtr. June-Sept: S, D $99-$155; each addl $10; under 18 free; lower rates rest of yr. Crib free. Pet accepted; $5/day. TV, cable. Heated pool, whirlpool. Coffee in rms. Restaurant 7 am-9 pm. Bar 4-10 pm; entertainment Sat. Ck-out noon. Meeting rms. Business servs avail. Sundries. Some refrigerators. Cr cds: A, C, D, DS, MC, V.

D

★★ BEST WESTERN MONTEREY BEACH HOTEL. *2600 Sand Dunes Dr (93940). 831/394-3321; fax 831/393-1912; res 800/528-1234. www.montereybeachhotel.com.* 196 rms, 4 story. June-Oct: S, $119-$169; D $129-$179; under 13 free; lower rates rest of yr. Crib free. Pet accepted;

IN THE FOOTSTEPS OF STEINBECK: MONTEREY'S CANNERY ROW

In 1945, John Steinbeck published one of his best-loved novels, *Cannery Row*, which chronicled the lives and fortunes of characters in the rough-and-tumble neighborhood encompassing the sardine factories along the Monterey shoreline. Steinbeck, born in nearby Salinas but living in Monterey, described the area then as "a poem, a stink, a grating noise, a quality of light, a tone, a habit, a nostalgia, a dream." On this walking tour, you'll find a new Cannery Row, but one that retains some of its old flavor (minus the stink and noise, unless you happen to stand too close to a sea lion). When the sardines were fished out by the late 1940s, the area fell into decay. However, the old canneries and warehouses were subsequently renovated and transformed into shops, restaurants, hotels, and attractions. If you start at the far end of the Row, near the boundary with the town of Pacific Grove, you can visit the Monterey Bay Aquarium (886 Cannery Row), itself fashioned from what was once the largest sardine factory along the Row. The aquarium's indoor-outdoor design is a perfect setting for its displays of sea otters, sharks, and jellyfish. Continue down Cannery Row past sites Steinbeck celebrated in his book: La Ida's Cafe (once a house of ill repute) at 851 Cannery Row; Lee Chong's Heavenly Flower Grocery (once a general store, bank, and gambling hall) at 835 Cannery Row; and Ed "Doc" Ricketts's lab at 800 Cannery Row, where the Steinbeck hero collected sea specimens. (None of the original businesses remain, however.) Proceed down Cannery Row to Steinbeck's Spirit of Monterey Wax Museum (at 700 Cannery Row), which features wax figures and scenes and narration by "Steinbeck" and is a fun way to absorb some of the area's history. Cannery Row extends for about a mile in all. Farther along, you'll pass several restaurants and cafes where you can have lunch or a drink. Cannery Row ends at the Coast Guard pier, but continue the pretty seaside walk along the Monterey Peninsula Recreation Trail to Fisherman's Wharf, where boats once unloaded tons of sardines. The Wharf now caters mainly to tourists, but there are several good seafood restaurants and places to pick up snacks and watch sea lions. Leaving the Wharf, walk south a short distance to Custom House Plaza; there you'll find the Maritime Museum of Monterey, which contains exhibits on Monterey's seafaring past, from early explorers up to the sardine-fishing days of Steinbeck's time.

$25. TV; cable (premium). Pool, whirlpool. Coffee in rms. Restaurant 7 am-1:45 pm, 5:30-10 pm. Bar 4-11 pm. Ck-out noon. Meeting rms. Business servs avail. Bellhops. Exercise equipt. Some refrigerators. Ocean view; beach access. Cr cds: A, C, D, DS, ER, JCB, MC, V.

D SC

★★ **BEST WESTERN VICTORIAN INN.** *487 Foam St (93940). 831/373-8000; fax 831/373-4815; res 800/232-4141.* 68 rms, 3 story. S, D $139-$309; each addl $10; under 18 free; higher rates special events. Pet accepted; $100 deposit, $25 fee. TV; cable, VCR (movies). Complimentary continental bkfst. Coffee in rms. Ck-out noon. Meeting rm. Business servs avail. Whirlpool. Bathrm phones, refrigerators, fireplaces. Private patios, balconies. Victorian furnishings. Two blks from bay. Cr cds: A, C, D, DS, JCB, MC, V.

D

★★ **CANNERY ROW INN.** *200 Foam St (93940). 831/649-8580; fax 831/649-2566; toll-free 800/876-8580.* 32 rms, 2 story. No A/C. S, D $79-$240. TV; cable. Complimentary continental bkfst, coffee in rms. Ck-out noon. Business servs avail. Covered parking. Whirlpool. Refrigerators, fireplaces. Balconies. Cr cds: A, DS, MC, V.

D SC

★★ **CYPRESS GARDENS INN.** *1150 Munras Ave (93940). 831/373-2761; fax 831/549-1329; res 800/433-4732. www.magnussonhotel.com.* 46 rms, 2 story. No A/C. Late June-Oct: S, D $99-$129; each addl $10; suite $199; under 13 free; lower rates rest of yr. Crib free. Pet accepted. TV; cable (premium). Heated pool, whirlpool. Coffee in rms. Complimentary continental bkfst. Ck-out noon. Business servs avail. Refrigerators, fireplace in suite, microwaves avail. Private patios, balconies.

★ **CYPRESS TREE INN.** *2227 N Fremont St (93940). 831/372-7586; fax 831/372-2940; toll-free 800/464-8303. www.cypresstreeinn.com.* 55 rms, 2 story, 12 kits. No A/C. S $48-$149; D $52-$179; each addl $6; suites $95-$180. Crib $6. TV; cable. Ck-out 11 am. Coin lndry. Business servs avail. Whirlpool. Sauna. Refrigerators, some whirlpools, fireplaces in suites. Private patios, some balconies. Grill. Cr cds: A, D, DS, MC, V.

D

★ **EL ADOBE INN.** *936 Munras Ave (93940). 831/372-5409; fax 831/375-7236.* 26 rms, 2 story. No A/C. Late June-Oct: S, D $89-$129; each addl $10; under 13 free; lower rates rest of yr. Crib free. Pet accepted. TV; cable (premium). Swimming privileges. Whirlpool. Complimentary continental bkfst. Coffee in rms. Ck-out noon. Business servs avail. Refrigerators. Sun deck. Cr cds: A, DS, JCB, MC, V.

Sea lions, Monterey

★★ **HOLIDAY INN EXPRESS.** *443 Wave St (93940). 831/372-1800; fax 831/372-1969; res 800/465-4329. www.hiexpress.com/montereyca.* 43 rms, 3 story. No A/C. May-Oct: S, D $95-$229; each addl $10; under 19 free; higher rates Fri, Sat; lower rates rest of yr. Crib free. TV; cable (premium). Complimentary continental bkfst, coffee in rms. Ck-out noon. Business servs avail. Covered parking. Whirlpool. Totally nonsmoking. Cr cds: A, C, D, DS, JCB, MC, V.

D

★★ **MARIPOSA INN.** *1386 Munras Ave (93940). 831/649-1414; fax 831/649-5308; toll-free 800/824-2295.* 50 rms, 3 story. No A/C. S, D $79-$125; each addl $10; suites $89-$195; under 18 free; golf plans. TV; cable (premium). Heated pool, whirlpool. Coffee in rms. Complimentary continental bkfst. Restaurant nearby. Ck-out noon. Business servs avail. Refrigerator in suites; microwaves avail. Cr cds: A, C, D, DS, MC, V.

D SC

★★ **MONTEREY BAY INN.** *242 Cannery Row (93940). 831/373-6242; fax 831/373-7603; res 800/424-6242.* 47 rms, 4 story. No A/C. May-Oct: S, D $199-$349; under 12 free; lower rates rest of yr. Crib free. TV; cable, VCR (movies). Whirlpools. Complimentary continental bkfst, coffee in rms. Restaurant nearby. Ck-out noon. Meeting rms. Business servs avail. Covered parking. Exercise equipt; sauna. Minibars. Balconies. On bay. Cr cds: A, C, D, DS, JCB, MC, V.

D

★ **OTTER INN.** *571 Wave St (93940). 831/375-2299; fax 831/375-2352; toll-free 800/385-2299.* 33 rms, 4 story. No A/C. July-Aug: S, D $89-$249; suites $179-$269. Crib free. TV; cable. Complimentary continental bkfst, coffee in rms. Restaurant nearby. Ck-out noon. Business servs avail. Whirlpool. Covered parking. Refrigerators. Near beach. Cr cds: A, DS, MC, V.

D SC

★★ **SAND DOLLAR INN.** *755 Abrego St (93940). 831/372-7551; fax 831/372-0916; toll-free 800/982-1986. www.sanddollarinn.com.* 63 rms, 3 story. June-Sept: S, D $69-$99; each addl $10; suites $115-$125; under 12 free; wkends (2-day min); higher rates special events; lower rates rest of yr. Crib free. TV; cable, VCR avail (movies). Heated pool; whirlpool. Complimentary continental bkfst. Coffee in rms. Restaurant nearby. Ck-out noon. Business servs avail. Coin lndry. Some refrigerators, fireplaces. Some private patios, balconies. Cr cds: A, C, D, JCB, MC, V.

D

★★ **WAY STATION INN.** *1200 Olmsted Rd (93940). 831/372-2945; fax 831/375-6267; toll-free 831/858-0822.* 46 rms, 2 story. No A/C. S $99-$189; D $79-$209; each addl $10; suites $99-$239. TV; cable. Complimentary continental bkfst. Restaurant 11 am-10 pm. Bar. Ck-out 11 am. Meeting rms. Refrigerators. Cr cds: A, C, D, DS, MC, V.

D SC

Hotels

★★★ **DOUBLETREE HOTEL MONTEREY.** *2 Portola Plz (93940). 831/649-4511; fax 831/649-4115; res 800/222-8733. www.doubletreemonterey.com.* 380 rms, 7 story. No A/C. June-Oct: S $125-$165; D $145-$185; each addl $20; suites $250-$750; under 18 free; lower rates rest of yr. Crib free. TV; cable (premium). Heated pool; whirlpool, poolside serv. Restaurants 6 am-10 pm; Fri, Sat to 11 pm. Bar 11-1:30 am. Ck-out noon. Convention facilities. Business center. Concierge. Shopping arcade. Valet, self-parking. Exercise rm. Cr cds: A, D, DS, MC, V.

D SC

★★★ **HILTON MONTEREY.** *1000 Aguajito Rd (93940). 831/373-6141; res 800/445-8667. www.monterey.hilton.com.* 204 rms, 3 story. May-Oct: S $119-$159; D $129-$169; each addl $10; suites $250-$500; kit. unit $250-$450; under 18 free; higher rates special events; lower rates rest of yr. Crib free. TV; cable (premium), VCR avail. Complimentary coffee in rms. Restaurant 6:30 am-2 pm, 5-10 pm. Ck-out noon. Business servs avail. In-rm modem link. Bellhops. Valet serv. Concierge. Gift shop. Coin lndry. Free airport transportation. Tennis. Exercise equipt; sauna. Pool. Some refrigerators, microwaves. Balconies. Picnic tables, grills. Cr cds: A, C, D, DS, ER, JCB, MC, V.

D

★★★ **HOTEL PACIFIC.** *300 Pacific St (93940). 831/373-5700; fax 831/373-6921; res 800/232-4141. www.hotelpacific.com.* 105 suites, 4 story. May-Oct: S, D $199-$349; each addl $10; under 12 free; lower rates rest of yr. Crib avail. TV; cable, VCR (movies). Whirlpools. Complimentary continental bkfst; evening refreshments. Coffee in rms. Ck-out noon, ck-in 4 pm. Meeting rms. Business servs avail. Luggage handling. Covered parking. Refrigerators, fireplaces. Private patios, balconies. Spanish decor; original art, antiques, fireplace in lobby. Gardens; fountains. Cr cds: A, C, D, DS, JCB, MC, V.

D

★★★ **HYATT REGENCY MONTEREY.** *1 Golf Course Dr (93940). 831/372-1234; fax 831/375-3960; toll-free 800/233-1234. www.montereyhyatt.com.* 575 rms, 4 story. No A/C. S, D $89-$300; suites $275-$2,500; higher rates special events. Crib free. TV; cable (premium), VCR avail. 2 heated pools; whirlpool, poolside serv. Supervised children's activities (summer and hols; rest of yr on request). Coffee in rms. Restaurant 6:30 am-10 pm. Bar 4 pm-1 am; wkends from noon. Ck-out noon. Convention facilities. Business center. Concierge. Beauty salon. 6 tennis courts, pro. 18-hole golf, greens fee $70-$90, putting green. Bicycles. Exercise equipt. Refrigerators avail. Situated on 23 landscaped acres. Luxury level. Cr cds: A, C, D, DS, MC, V.

D

★★★ **MONTEREY MARRIOTT.** *350 Calle Principal (93940). 831/649-4234; fax 831/372-2968; toll-free 800/228-9290.* 341 rms, 10 story. July-Sept: S, D $209-$300; suites $250-$600; under 18 free; lower rates rest of yr. Crib free. Pet accepted, some restrictions; $10/day. Valet parking $12. TV; cable (premium). Heated pool; whirlpool. Coffee in rms. Restaurants 6:30-1 am. Ck-out noon. Meeting rms. Business center. Concierge. Gift shop. Barber, beauty shop. Exercise equipt. Refrigerators, microwaves avail; bathrm phone in suites. Cr cds: A, D, DS, JCB, MC, V.

D

★★★ **MONTEREY PLAZA HOTEL.** *400 Cannery Row (93940). 831/646-*

1700; fax 831/646-5937; toll-free 800/368-2468. www.woodsidehotels.com. 285 rms, 4 story. S, D $175-$350; each addl $30; suites $385-$800; under 12 free; package plans. Garage, valet parking $12. TV; cable. Coffee in rms. Restaurant (see also THE DUCK CLUB). Bar 11:30 am-midnight. Ck-out noon. Business center. Concierge. Exercise equipt. Minibars. Some bathrm phones. Some private patios, balconies. Library on Monterey Bay; beach access. Located on oceanfront on historic Cannery Row. Totally nonsmoking. Cr cds: A, C, D, DS, JCB, MC, V.

D SC

B&Bs/Small Inns

★★★ JABBERWOCK BED AND BREAKFAST. *598 Laine St (93940). 831/372-4777; fax 831/655-2946; toll-free 888/428-7253.* 7 rms, 2 share bath, 3 story. No A/C. No rm phones. S, D $115-$225. Complimentary full bkfst; afternoon refreshments. Ck-out noon, ck-in 3 pm. Business servs avail. Some fireplaces; 1 in-rm whirlpool. Library; antiques. ½-acre gardens; waterfalls. Former convent. Cr cds: A, D, MC, V.

★★★ MERRITT HOUSE INN. *386 Pacific St (93940). 831/646-9686; fax 831/646-5392; toll-free 800/541-5599. www.merritthouseinn.com.* 25 rms, 2 story. Mar-Nov: S, D $89-$160; each addl $15; suites $195-$220; under 10 free; lower rates rest of yr. Crib avail. TV; cable (premium). Continental bkfst. Restaurants nearby. Ck-out noon, ck-in 3 pm. Business servs avail. Refrigerators. Some patios, balconies. Suites in adobe house (1830). Garden. Totally nonsmoking. Cr cds: A, C, D, DS, MC, V.

D

★★★ THE MONTEREY HOTEL. *406 Alvarado St (93940). 831/375-3184; fax 831/373-2899; toll-free 800/727-0960. www.montereyhotel.com.* 39 rms, 4 story, 6 suites. No A/C. S, D $119-$169; suites $199-$279; seasonal rates avail. Crib free. Valet parking $10. TV; cable (premium). Complimentary continental bkfst; afternoon refreshments. Ck-out noon, ck-in 3 pm. Meeting rms. Some refrigerators, wet bars. Fireplace in some suites. Cr cds: A, C, D, DS, MC, V.

D SC

★★★ OLD MONTEREY INN. *500 Martin St (93940). 831/375-8284; fax 831/375-6730; toll-free 800/350-2344. www.oldmontereyinn.com.* The breathtaking views on the drive south from San Francisco are only the beginning. Perfect for golfers visiting nearby courses or those wanting a romantic escape, this ten-unit historic inn is set amidst striking gardens. Extra in-room comforts abound with featherbeds, down comforters, terry robes, and candles. A pleasant breakfast and "sunset wine hour" make this a first-rate escape. 9 rms, 1 cottage. No A/C. No rm phones; cordless phone avail. S, D $260; cottage $350; each addl $50. TV avail. Complimentary full bkfst; afternoon refreshments. Ck-out noon, ck-in 3-7 pm. Business servs avail. Many fireplaces. Totally nonsmoking. Cr cds: MC, V.

★★★ SPINDRIFT INN. *652 Cannery Row (93940). 831/646-8900; fax 831/646-5342; res 800/232-4141. www.spindriftinn.com.* 42 rms, 4 story. No A/C. May-Oct: S, D $159-$409; under 12 free; higher rates special events; lower rates rest of yr. Parking $6. TV; cable, VCR (movies). Complimentary continental bkfst; afternoon refreshments. Restaurant adj. Rm serv 11 am-9:30 pm. Ck-out noon, ck-in 4 pm. Business servs avail. Luggage handling. Concierge serv. Valet parking. Bathrm phones, refrigerators, honor bars, fireplaces. Some balconies. Roof-top garden; views of Monterey Bay. Cr cds: A, C, D, DS, JCB, MC, V.

D

All Suite

★★★ EMBASSY SUITES HOTEL ON MONTEREY BAY. *1441 Canyon Del Rey Blvd, Seaside (93955). 831/393-1115; fax 831/393-1113; res 800/362-2779.* 225 suites, 12 story. Apr-Oct: S $129-$189; D $149-$209; each addl $20; under 18 free; higher rates special events; lower rates rest of yr. Crib free. TV; cable. Indoor pool; whirlpool. Complimentary full bkfst. Coffee in rms. Restaurant 11 am-2 pm, 5-10 pm. Bar to midnight.

Ck-out noon. Meeting rms. Business center. Coin lndry. Gift shop. Free airport transportation. Exercise equipt; sauna. Game rm. Refrigerators, microwaves. Cr cds: A, C, D, DS, MC, V.

D

Restaurants

★ **ABALONETTI SEAFOOD TRATTORIA.** *57 Fisherman's Wharf (93940). 831/373-1851. www.pisto.com.* Hrs: 11 am-10 pm; wkends to 11 pm. Closed Dec 25. Res accepted. No A/C. Italian, seafood menu. Bar 11 am-10 pm. A la carte entrees: lunch $6.95-$14.95, dinner $10.95-$21.95. Children's menu. Specializes in grilled fish, seafood pasta, pizza baked in wood-burning oven. Outdoor dining. Exhibition kitchen. Harbor view. Cr cds: A, C, D, DS, MC, V.

D

★ **AMARIN.** *807 Cannery Row (93940). 831/373-8811.* Hrs: 11 am-9 pm. Closed Thanksgiving, Dec 25. Res accepted. No A/C. Thai menu. Wine, beer. Lunch $5.95-$7.95, dinner $8.95-$12.95. Specialties: pad Thai, masaman, basil squid. Contemporary Thai decor. Totally nonsmoking. Cr cds: A, MC, V.

★★ **CAFE FINA.** *47 Fisherman's Wharf (93940). 831/372-5200. www.cafefina.com.* Hrs: 11:30 am-2:30 pm, 5-10 pm; Sat-Sun 11:30 am-3 pm, 5-10 pm. Closed Thanksgiving, Dec 25. Res accepted. No A/C. Seafood menu. Bar. A la carte entrees: lunch $7.25-$17.95, dinner $10-$35. Specializes in fresh Monterey Bay seafood, pasta, meat dishes. Collection of family photos displayed. View of bay. Cr cds: A, C, D, DS, MC, V.

★★ **CHART HOUSE.** *444 Cannery Row (93940). 831/372-3362. www.chart-house.com.* Hrs: 5-10 pm; Fri to 11 pm; Sat 4-11 pm; Sun from 4 pm. Res accepted. Bar. Dinner $12.95-$34.95. Specializes in fresh seafood, steak, prime rib. Salad bar. Parking. Bay view. Cr cds: A, D, DS, MC, V.

D

★★★ **CIBO RISTORANTE ITALIANO.** *301 Alvarado St (93940). 831/649-8151. www.cibo.com.* Hrs: 5-10 pm; Fri, Sat to 10:30 pm. Res accepted. Italian menu. Bar to 1 am; Sat, Sun to 1:30 am. Dinner $8.25-$19.95. Specializes in veal, seafood, pasta. Entertainment Tues-Sun from 9 pm. Neo-classic decor. Cr cds: A, D, MC, V.

D

★★ **DOMENICO'S.** *50 Fisherman's Wharf (93940). 831/372-3655. www.restauranteur.com/domenico.* Hrs: 11 am-9 pm. Closed Dec 25. Res accepted. Bar. A la carte entrees: lunch $7.95-$20.95, dinner $14.95-$25.95. Children's menu. Specializes in seafood, pasta. Lobster tank. Oyster bar. Casual decor. Overlooks harbor. Cr cds: A, D, DS, MC, V.

D

★★★ **THE DUCK CLUB.** *400 Cannery Row (93940). 831/646-1700. www.woodsidehotels.com.* Hrs: 6:30-11 am, 5:30-10 pm; Sat, Sun 6:30 am-noon, 5:30-10 pm. Res accepted. Contemporary American menu. Wine list. A la carte entrees: bkfst $7.25-$14, dinner $19-$32. Children's menu. Specializes in duck, seafood, pasta. Valet parking. Large windows provide ocean views. Totally nonsmoking. Cr cds: A, C, D, DS, MC, V.

D

★ **EL TORITO.** *600 Cannery Row (93940). 831/373-0611.* Hrs: 11 am-10 pm; Fri, Sat to 11 pm; Sun 9 am-10 pm; Sun brunch 10 am-2 pm. Closed Thanksgiving, Dec 25. Res accepted. Mexican menu. Bar. Lunch $3.59-$10.99, dinner $3.59-$12.99. Sun brunch $10.99. Children's menu. Specializes in fajitas. Parking. Overlooks Monterey Bay. Totally nonsmoking. Cr cds: A, D, DS, MC, V.

D SC

★★★ **FRESH CREAM.** *99 Pacific St, Building 100C (93940). 831/375-9798. www.freshcream.com.* Hrs: 6-10 pm. Res accepted; required wkends. French menu. Bar. Wine cellar. Dinner $22.95-$32.95. Specialties: roast duck, rack of lamb. Street parking. Five dining rms, all with harbor view. Cr cds: A, D, DS, MC, V.

D

★★ **INDIAN SUMMER.** *220 Olivier St (93940). 831/372-4744. www.restauranteur.com/indiansummer.* Authentic Indian menu. Specializes in tandoori chicken, shahi paneer, chicken tikka. Hrs: 11 am-2:30 pm, 5:30-10:30 pm. Res accepted. Wine, beer. Lunch $9.95, dinner $8.95-$19.95. Entertainment. Dine on the heated patio with a garden setting. Cr cds: A, C, D, DS, ER, JCB, MC, V.

D SC

★★ JOHN PISTO'S WHALING STATION. *763 Wave St (93940). 831/373-3778. www.pisto.com.* Hrs: 5-10 pm. Closed hols. Res accepted. Bar. A la carte entrees: dinner $15-$40. Children's menu. Specializes in prime steak, seafood. Totally nonsmoking. Cr cds: A, DS, MC, V.

D

★★ MONTRIO. *414 Calle Principal (93940). 831/648-8880. www.montrio.com.* Hrs: 11:30 am-10 pm; wkends to 11 pm. Closed Thanksgiving, Dec 25. Res accepted. Bar. Wine list. Lunch $6-$11, dinner $6-$22. Children's menu. Specializes in chicken, beef, lamb. Eclectic decor in former firehouse (1910); open kitchen features wood-burning rotisserie. Totally nonsmoking. Cr cds: A, MC, V.

D

★★ PARADISO TRATTORIA. *654 Cannery Row (93940). 831/375-4155. www.pisto.com.* Hrs: 11 am-9 pm; Fri, Sat to 10:30 pm. Closed Dec 25. Res accepted. Mediterranean menu. Bar. A la carte entrees: lunch $8-$14, dinner $10-$20. Children's menu. Specializes in steak, local seafood, pasta. Oyster bar. Casual decor. Large fish tanks. Wood burning pizza oven. Cr cds: A, C, D, DS, MC, V.

D

★ RAPPA'S SEAFOOD. *101 Fisherman's Wharf (93940). 831/372-7562.* Hrs: 11 am-9:30 pm; Fri, Sat to 10 pm; winter hrs vary. Closed Thanksgiving, Dec 25. Res accepted. Italian menu. Bar. A la carte entrees: lunch $5.95-$14.75, dinner $8.95-$28.50. Specialties: cioppino, bouillabaisse, fresh fish. Casual dining. Scenic view of bay. Family-owned. Cr cds: A, C, D, DS, MC, V.

D

★ SANDBAR AND GRILL. *Fisherman's Wharf #2 (93940). 831/373-2818.* Hrs: 11:30 am-10:30 pm; wkends 10:30 am-11 pm. Bar to 2 am. Lunch $6.95-$12, dinner $9.95-$19.95. Sat, Sun brunch $6.95-$9.95. Specializes in seafood. Pianist in bar Tues-Sat. At waterfront; seals, otters often swimming in view. Cr cds: A, D, DS, MC, V.

★★★ SARDINE FACTORY. *701 Wave St (93940). 831/373-3775. www.sardinefactory.com.* Hrs: 5-10:30 pm; Fri, Sat to 11 pm; Sun 5-10 pm. Closed wk of Dec 25. Res accepted. Bar. Wine cellar. A la carte entrees: dinner $17-$29. Specializes in fresh seafood, pasta, steak. Parking. Four separate dining rms; two wine cellar rooms. Historic building originally built as canteen for sardine workers. Cr cds: A, D, DS, MC, V.

D

★★ STOKES ADOBE. *500 Hartnell St (93940). 831/373-1110. www.stokesadobe.com.* Hrs: 11:30 am-10 pm; Fri, Sat to 10:30 pm. Closed Dec 25. Res accepted. No A/C. California, Mediterranean menu. Bar to midnight. Wine list. Lunch $3-$11, dinner $3-$18.25. Children's menu. Specialties: lavender-infused pork chop, pan-roasted halibut with spring vegetable risotto, cassoulet with duck confit. Historic Mission-style building. Totally nonsmoking. Cr cds: A, D, MC, V.

D

★★★ TARPY'S ROADHOUSE. *2999 Monterey-Salinas Hwy (93940). 831/647-1444. www.tarpys.com.* Hrs: 11:30 am-10 pm; Sun brunch 11:30 am-3 pm. Closed July 4, Thanksgiving, Dec 25. Res accepted. Bar. A la carte entrees: lunch $6.55-$23.95, dinner $6.55-$29.95. Sun brunch $6-$12. Specializes in game, chicken, steak. Parking. Outdoor dining. Located in historic country stone house; dining area is former wine tasting room. Fireplaces. Cr cds: A, DS, MC, V.

D

Morro Bay

(C-2) *See also Atascadero, Paso Robles, Pismo Beach, San Luis Obispo*

Pop 9,664 **Elev** 200 ft **Area code** 805 **Zip** 93442

Information Chamber of Commerce, 880 Main St, PO Box 876; 805/772-4467 or 800/231-0592

Web www.morrobay.com

At the harbor entrance to this seaport town is Morro Rock, a 576-foot volcanic dome discovered by Juan Rodriguez Cabrillo in 1542. A large commercial fishing fleet sails from here and many boats dock along the Embarcadero. Morro Bay is a designated State and National Estuary; other natural features are Morro Bay Heron Rookery, Montana de Oro State Park, Morro Strand State Beach, and Los Osos Oaks Reserve.

What to See and Do

Harbor cruises. One-hr narrated tours of bay on sternwheeler *Tiger's Folly II,* departing from Harbor Hut Dock. 1205 Embarcadero. Phone 805/772-2257. ¢¢¢

Montana de Oro State Park. Spectacular scenery along seven miles of shoreline, with tide pools, beaches, camping. Hiking trails up 1,350-ft Valencia Peak. Popular for whale watching and viewing harbor seals and sea otters along shore. 8 mi S on Pecho Valley Rd in Los Osos. Phone 805/528-0513. ¢¢¢

Morro Bay Aquarium. Displays 300 live marine specimens. (Daily) 595 Embarcadero. Phone 805/772-7647. ¢

Morro Bay State Park. Approx 2,400 acres on Morro Bay. Fishing, boating; 18-hole golf course (fee), picnicking, cafe, hiking, tent and trailer camping (showers, dump station; water and electric hookups). Standard fees. S of town. Phone 805/772-7434. On White Point is

Museum of Natural History. Films, slide shows, displays; nature walks. (Daily; closed Jan 1, Thanksgiving, Dec 25) State Park Rd. Phone 805/772-2694.

Morro Rock. A 576-ft-high volcanic boulder often called "The Gibraltar of the Pacific," now a bird sanctuary. Drive to the base of the rock for optimum viewing. (Daily) Phone 805/772-4467.

Special Event

Winter Bird Festival. Celebration of migrating birds incl birding and natural history field trips; workshops, guest speakers; banquet, ice cream social; art exhibit. Phone 800/231-0592. Four days mid-Jan.

Motels/Motor Lodges

★★ **BAY VIEW LODGE.** *225 Harbor St (93442). 805/772-2771; fax 805/772-0411; toll-free 800/742-8439. www.californiabay.com.* 22 rms, 2 story. No A/C. June-Sept, wkends: S $60-$80; D $65-$92; each addl $6; higher rates graduation wkend; lower rates rest of yr. Crib $4. TV; cable (premium), VCR (movies $2). Coffee in rms. Restaurant nearby. Ck-out 11 am. Coin lndry. Whirlpool. Refrigerators, fireplaces. Ocean view from some rms. Bay 1 blk. Cr cds: A, MC, V.

★★ **BEST WESTERN EL RANCHO.** *2460 N Main St (93442). 805/772-2212; fax 805/772-2212.* 27 rms. S, D $49-$89; each addl $7; under 12 free. Crib $5. Pet accepted; $10. TV; cable, VCR (free movies). Heated pool. Restaurant 7 am-10 pm. Ck-out 11 am. Coin lndry. Business servs avail. Refrigerators; microwaves avail. Grill. Redwood lobby, etched glass door. Ocean view. Cr cds: A, C, D, DS, MC, V.

★★ **BLUE SAIL INN.** *851 Market Ave (93442). 805/772-7132; fax 805/772-8406; res 888/337-0707. www.bluesail inn.com.* 48 rms, 1-2 story. No A/C. S, D $75-$145; suites $95-$115. Crib $6. TV; cable (premium). Complimentary coffee in rms. Restaurant adj 7 am-10 pm. Ck-out 11 am. Business servs avail. In-rm modem link. Covered parking. Whirlpool. Refrigerators. Some wet bars, fireplaces. Balconies. Bay view. Cr cds: A, D, DS, MC, V.

D

★★ **BREAKERS MOTEL.** *780 Market Ave (93442). 805/772-7317; fax 805/772-4771; res 800/932-8899. www.morrobay.com/breakersmotel.* 25 rms, some A/C, 2-3 story. No elvtr. S, D $95-$120; each addl $10. Crib $4. TV; cable (premium). Heated pool; whirlpool. Complimentary coffee in rms. Restaurant opp 7 am-10 pm. Ck-out noon. Business servs avail. Refrigerators; some fireplaces. Bay view from many rms. Cr cds: A, C, D, DS, MC, V.

★ **DAYS INN.** *1095 Main St (93442). 805/772-2711; fax 805/772-2711.* 46 rms, 2 story. No A/C. Memorial Day-Sept: S, D $60-$125; each addl $6; lower rates rest of yr. Pet accepted, some restrictions; $10. TV; cable (premium). Complimentary continental bkfst. Coffee in rms. Restaurant opp open 24 hrs. Ck-out 11 am. Business servs avail. Whirlpool. Some refrigerators. Patios, balconies. Cr cds: A, C, D, DS, JCB, MC, V.

D

★ **SUNSET TRAVELODGE.** *1080 Market Ave (93442). 805/772-1259; fax 805/772-8967; toll-free 800/578-7878.* 31 rms, 1-2 story. No A/C. S, D $45-$98; each addl $8; under 18 free; higher rates wkend, hols, special events. Crib free. Pet accepted; deposit required. TV; cable (premium). Heated pool. Complimentary continental bkfst. Coffee in rms. Restaurant nearby. Ck-out 11 am. Business servs avail. In-rm modem link. Refrigerators. Microwaves avail. Sundeck. Cr cds: A, D, DS, MC, V.

SC

★★ **TWIN DOLPHIN.** *590 Morro Ave (93442). 805/772-4483.* 31 rms, 3 story. S, D $65-$130; each addl $10. Crib $6. TV; cable (premium). Complimentary continental bkfst. Restaurant nearby. Ck-out 11 am. Meeting rm. Covered parking. Whirlpool. Refrigerators avail. Balconies. Cr cds: DS, MC, V.

D

Hotels

★ **ASCOT SUITES.** *260 Morro Ave (93442). 805/772-4437; fax 805/772-8860; toll-free 800/887-6454. www.ascotinn.com.* 25 rms, 2 story, 3 suites. No A/C. May-Oct: S, D $99-$200; each addl $5; suites $65-$168; under 15 free; lower rates rest of yr. TV; cable (premium). Complimentary continental bkfst, coffee in rms. Restaurant adj 7 am-10 pm. Ck-out 11 am. Business servs avail. In-rm modem link. Beauty shop. Some refrigerators. Cr cds: A, C, D, DS, ER, MC, V.

D

★★ **LA SERENA INN.** *990 Morro Ave (93442). 805/772-5665; fax 805/772-1044; toll-free 800/248-1511. www.laserenainn.com.* 37 rms, 3 story, 5 suites. S, D $100; each addl $10; suites $125-$160. Crib $10. TV; cable (premium). Complimentary continental bkfst. Restaurant nearby. Ck-out 11 am. Meeting rm. Business servs avail. In-rm modem link. Covered parking. Sauna. Refrigerators, microwaves. Balconies. Ocean view. Cr cds: A, DS, MC, V.

D

Resort

★★★ **INN AT MORRO BAY.** *60 State Park Rd; 19 Country Club Rd (93442). 805/772-5651; fax 805/772-4779; toll-free 800/321-9566. www.innatmorrobay.com.* 98 rms, 2 story. No A/C. S, D $95-$275; cottage $350. Crib free. TV; cable (premium). Heated pool; poolside serv. Restaurant 7 am-2 pm, 5-9 pm; summer to 10 pm. Bar 11 am-midnight; entertainment wkends. Ck-out noon. Meeting rms. Business servs avail. Health club privileges. Golf privileges. Massage. Many refrigerators, fireplaces. Private patios, balconies. Guest bicycles. On Morro Bay. Cr cds: A, C, D, DS, MC, V.

D

B&B/Small Inn

★★★ **BEACHWALKER INN.** *501 S Ocean Ave, Cayucos (93430). 805/995-2133; fax 805/995-3139; toll-free 800/750-2133. www.beachwalkerinn.com.* 24 rms, 2 story, 12 kit. units. No A/C. Mid-June-mid-Sept: S, D $90-$120; each addl $10; kit. units $105-$225; under 12 free; family rates; package plans; wkends, hols (2-3 day min); higher rates hols; lower rates rest of yr. Crib free. TV; cable (premium), VCR avail (movies). Complimentary continental bkfst, coffee in rms. Restaurant nearby. Ck-out 11 am, ck-in 2 pm. Business servs avail. Gift shop. Fireplaces. Some balconies. Picnic tables. Opp beach. Totally nonsmoking. Cr cds: A, C, D, DS, JCB, MC, V.

D

Restaurants

★★★ **GALLEY.** *899 Embarcadero (93442). 805/772-2806.* Hrs: 11 am-9 pm. Closed late Nov-Dec 25. Res accepted. Beer. Wine cellar. Lunch $3.95-$11. Complete meals: dinner from $13.75. Children's menu. Specializes in fresh fish. Overlooks Morro Bay and Morro Rock. Family-owned since 1966. Totally nonsmoking. Cr cds: A, DS, MC, V.

★★ **ROSE'S LANDING.** *725 Embarcadero (93442). 805/772-4441.* Hrs: 11:30 am-9 pm; Fri, Sat 11 am-10 pm; Sun 11-9 pm. Res accepted. Bar 11:30 am-10 pm; Fri, Sat to midnight. Lunch $5.95-$9.95, dinner $9.95-up. Children's menu. Specializes in steak, seafood, pasta. Entertainment (summer). Patio dining. View of bay. Cr cds: A, C, D, DS, MC, V.

D

Mother Lode Country

(D-3) *See also Auburn, Grass Valley, Jackson, Nevada City, Placerville, Sonora, Truckee*

Three hundred eighteen miles long and only a few miles wide, this strip of land stretching through nine counties from the Sierra foothills was the scene of the gold rush of the mid-19th century. Discovery of gold at Coloma in 1848 touched off a wave of migration to the West that accelerated the development and population of all the western states by several decades. The enormous gold-bearing quartz vein was surface-mined until the end of the century; a few mines still exist, but it is now necessary to penetrate deep into the earth. In this narrow stretch of country have developed frontier and mining camp legends that are part of the warp and woof of the American West.

Today the scenic Mother Lode country is dotted with ghost towns, old mine shafts, rusting machinery, and ancient buildings. Recreational gold panning is a favorite pastime. CA 49, a delightful but not high-speed highway, connects many of the towns where the 49ers panned for gold. Many picnic and camping areas can be found here. Map available from Chamber of Commerce offices throughout Mother Lode Country. Contact the El Dorado County Chamber of Commerce, 542 Main St, Placerville 95667. Phone 530/621-5885.

Mountain View

(see San Francisco map) *See also Palo Alto, Santa Clara*

Pop 67,460 **Elev** 97 ft **Area code** 650

Motels/Motor Lodges

★★ **COUNTY INN.** *850 Leong Dr (94043). 650/961-1131; fax 650/965-9099; res 800/223-9901. www.countyinn.com.* 52 rms, 2 story. S $149; D $169; each addl $10; under 12 free; wkend, hol rates. Closed Dec 24-Jan 2. Crib free. TV; cable (premium), VCR (free movies). Heated pool. Complimentary continental bkfst, coffee in rms. Restaurant adj open 24 hrs. Ck-out noon. Coin lndry. Business servs avail. In-rm modem link. Sundries. Valet serv. Health club privileges. Minibars. Cr cds: A, C, D, DS, MC, V.

★★ **HOLIDAY INN EXPRESS HOTEL & SUITES - TOWNCENTER.** *93 W El Camino Real (94040). 650/967-6957; fax 650/967-4834; res 800/465-4329. www.hitowncenter.com.* 58 rms, 2 story. May-Dec: S, D $145-$165; each addl $10; suites $145-$160; under 12 free; higher rates special events; lower rates rest of yr. Crib free. TV; cable (premium), VCR (movies). Heated pool, whirlpool. Complimentary continental bkfst, coffee in rms. Restaurant adj open 24 hrs. Ck-out 11 am. Coin lndry. Valet serv. Exercise equipt. Refrigerators. Cr cds: A, C, D, DS, ER, JCB, MC, V.

D SC

★★ **MOUNTAIN VIEW INN.** *2300 W El Camino Real (94040). 650/962-9912; fax 650/962-9011; res 800/528-*

1234. 72 units, 2-3 story, 2 suites. No elvtr. S $125; D $135; each addl $5; suites, kit. units $235; under 12 free. TV; cable (premium). Pool; whirlpool. Complimentary continental bkfst, coffee in rms. Restaurant nearby. Ck-out 11 am. Coin lndry. Meeting rm. Business servs avail. In-rm modem link. Exercise equipt; sauna. Refrigerators. Cr cds: A, D, DS, MC, V.
D

Extended Stay

★★ **RESIDENCE INN BY MARRIOTT.** *1854 W El Camino Real (94040). 650/940-1300; fax 650/969-4997; toll-free 800/331-3131*. 112 kit. suites, 2 story. S, D $229-$259; wkly, wkend, monthly rates. Pet accepted; $50-$75 and $10/day. TV; cable (premium). Heated pool; whirlpool. Complimentary continental bkfst. Restaurant nearby. Ck-out noon. Coin lndry. Meeting rm. Business servs avail. Valet serv. Health club privileges. Refrigerators. Picnic tables, grills. Cr cds: A, C, D, DS, JCB, MC, V.
D SC

Restaurants

★★ **AMBER INDIA.** *2290 El Camino Real (94040). 650/968-7511. www.amber-india.com*. Hrs: 11:30 am-2:30 pm, 5-10 pm; Sun brunch 11:30 am-2:30 pm. Closed Thanksgiving, Dec 25. Res accepted. East Indian menu. Bar. A la carte entrees: lunch, dinner $7.25-$24.95. Complete meal: lunch, dinner $17.95-$22.95. Lunch buffet $8.95; Sun brunch $9.95. Parking. Indian decor. Cr cds: A, D, DS, MC, V.
D SC

★★★ **CHEZ T.J.** *938 Villa St (94041). 650/964-7466. www.cheztj.com*. Hrs: 5:30-9 pm. Closed Sun, Mon; Jan 1, Thanksgiving, Dec 25. Res required. No A/C. French, California menu. Complete meals: dinner $50-$65. Specializes in choice beef, fresh seafood. Outdoor dining. Intimate dining in Victorian house; original art, woodburning fireplace. Totally nonsmoking. Cr cds: A, D, DS, MC, V.

Mount Diablo State Park

(see San Francisco map) *See also Fremont, Livermore, Pleasanton, Santa Clara*

(5 mi E of I-680, Danville, on Diablo Rd)

A spiraling road leads to the summit of Mt Diablo (3,849 ft), the highest peak in the San Francisco Bay Area. From here, on a clear day, one can see 200 miles in each direction. The mountain is dotted with rock formations containing fossilized shells. Hiking trails wind from ridge to ridge throughout the more than 19,000 acres of the park. Near the south entrance are unusual rock formations known as the Devil's Slide and the Wind Caves. There are more than 100 miles of unpaved roads and 68 miles of trails available to hikers and horseback riders. Also available are picnic and camping facilities. Standard fees. Phone 510/837-2525.

Mount Shasta

(B-3) *See also Dunsmuir, Redding, Yreka*

Pop 3,460 **Elev** 3,554 ft
Area code 530 **Zip** 96067

Information Chamber of Commerce or the Visitors Bureau, 300 Pine St; 530/926-3696, 530/926-4865, or 800/926-4865

Web www.mtshastachamber.com

Set in Strawberry Valley, Mount Shasta offers a central location to fishing in nearby lakes and streams and year-round outdoor activities in the surrounding area. City water from a nearby spring is so pure that it is untreated.

A Ranger District office of the Shasta-Trinity National Forest (see REDDING) is located in Mount Shasta.

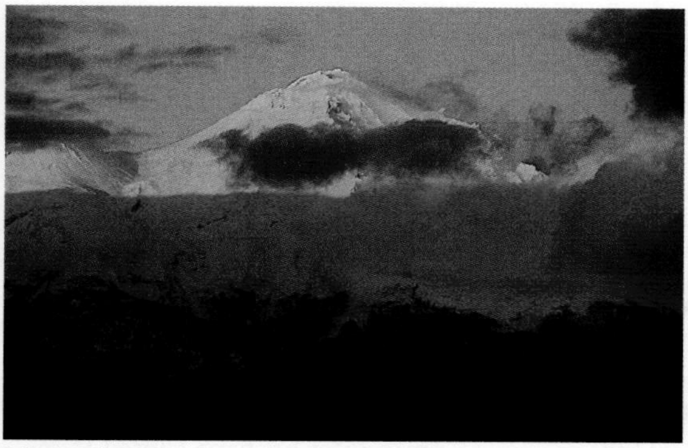

Mount Shasta

What to See and Do

Campgrounds. The US Forest Service maintains the following:

Castle Lake. Six units. Swimming, fishing; picnicking. No trailers. 12 mi SW, ½ mi from Castle Lake. **Sims Flat.** Fishing. 20 mi S, 1 mi E of I-5. 19 units. **McBride Springs.** Nine units. 5 mi E of Mt Shasta. All closed winters. Fee at Sims and McBride. For additional information on these and other campgrounds contact the Shasta-Trinity National Forest, 204 Alma St. Phone 530/926-4511.

Lake Siskiyou. Box Canyon Dam impounds the Sacramento River, creating a 430-acre lake for fishing and swimming. 2½ mi SW, off I-5. On W shore of lake is

Lake Siskiyou Camp-Resort. Swimming beach, fishing, boating (rentals, ramp, marina); hiking, picnicking, snack bar, store, camping (tent and RV sites; hookups, rentals; dump station). Contact PO Box 276. Phone 888/926-2618. ¢¢¢¢¢

Mount Shasta. Perpetually snow-covered double peak volcano towering to 14,162 ft. Five glaciers persist on the slopes, feeding the McCloud and Sacramento rivers. A scenic drive on Everitt Memorial Hwy climbs from the city of Mt Shasta up the slope to 7,840 ft for a magnificent view. White pine, the famous Shasta lily, and majestic stands of red fir are found at various elevations. E of I-5, in Shasta-Trinity National Forest (see REDDING).

Mount Shasta Ski and Board Park. Three triple chairlifts, one surface lift; patrol, school, rentals; cafeteria, bar. Thirty-one runs; longest run 1.75 mi; vertical drop 1,400 ft. (Thanksgiving-mid-Apr, daily) Night skiing (Wed-Sat), snowboarding. Park open for mountain biking, chairlift rides, climbing tower, and volcanic exhibit (mid-June-Labor Day, daily). 10 mi SE on CA 89. Phone 530/926-8610.

State Fish Hatchery. Raises trout; in continuous operation since 1888. Self-guided tour of trout ponds. Picnic tables, restrms. (Daily) ½ mi W off I-5, Central Mt Shasta exit. Phone 530/926-2215. **FREE** Adj is

Sisson Museum. Features exhibits on area history, mountain climbing, fish hatchery, and local Native American culture. (Daily; closed Easter, Dec 25, also Jan-Feb) Also annual quilt show. Phone 530/926-5508. **FREE**

Motels/Motor Lodges

★★ **BEST WESTERN.** *111 Morgan Way (96067). 530/926-3101; fax 916/926-3542; res 800/528-1234.* 95 rms, 2-3 story. S $69-$79; D $79-$94; each addl $5; suites $89-$154. Crib free. TV; cable. Indoor pool; whirlpool. Restaurant 5:30 am-10 pm; Sun to 9 pm. Bar from 10 am. Ck-out noon. Meeting rms. Business servs avail. In-rm modem link. Downhill/x-country ski 10 mi. View of Mt Shasta. Cr cds: A, C, D, DS, MC, V.

D

★★ **FINLANDIA MOTEL.** *1612 S Mt Shasta Blvd (96067). 530/926-5596.* 23 rms, 14 A/C, 1-2 story, 3 kits. S $34; D $38-$56; suites $48-$75. Crib $4. TV; cable. Whirlpool. Ck-out 11 am. Free bus depot transportation. Downhill ski 9 mi; x-country ski 8 mi. Picnic table, grill. Many lake, mountain views. Cr cds: A, C, D, DS, MC, V.

D

★★ **STRAWBERRY VALLEY INN.** *1142 S Mt Shasta Blvd (96067). 530/926-2052; fax 530/926-0842.* 25 rms, 7 suites. No A/C. S $45.50-$52.50; D $55.50-$72.50; each addl $6; suites $67-$75; under 10 free; ski plans. TV; cable. Complimentary continental bkfst. Restaurant nearby. Ck-out 11 am. In-rm modem link. Downhill/x-country ski 10 mi. Picnic tables. Totally nonsmoking. Cr cds: A, D, DS, MC, V.
D

★ **SWISS HOLIDAY LODGE.** *2400 S Mt Shasta Blvd (96067). 530/926-3446; fax 530/926-3091.* 21 air-cooled rms, 2 story. S $36-$42; D $42-$62; each addl $5; suite $95. Crib $5. Pet accepted; $5. TV; cable (premium). Heated pool; whirlpool. Complimentary continental bkfst, coffee in rms. Ck-out 11 am. Downhill/x-country ski 10 mi. Refrigerators avail. Picnic tables, grills. View of Mt Shasta. Cr cds: A, DS, MC, V.

Resort

★★★ **MOUNT SHASTA RESORT.** *1000 Siskiyou Lake Blvd (96067). 530/926-3030; toll-free 800/958-3363.* 50 cottages, 2 story. May-Sept: S $108-$128; D $155-$178; package plans; wkends, hols 2-3 day min; lower rates rest of yr. Crib free. TV; cable. Complimentary coffee in rms. Restaurant 7 am-9 pm; winter hrs from 11 am. Bar 11 am-9 pm. Ck-out 11 am, ck-in 3 pm. Meeting rms. Business servs avail. In-rm modem link. Lighted tennis, pro. 18-hole golf, greens fee $42, putting green, driving range. Downhill/x-country ski 10 mi. Tobogganing. Camping. Spa. Refrigerators, microwaves, fireplaces. Totally nonsmoking. Cr cds: A, C, D, DS, MC, V.
D

B&B/Small Inn

★★ **MCCLOUD HOTEL BED AND BREAKFAST.** *408 Main St, McCloud (96057). 530/964-2822; fax 530/964-2844; res 800/964-2823. www.mccloud hotel.com.* 17 rms, 2 story, 4 suites. No rm phones. S, D $74-$88; each addl $10; suites $134-$148; package plans; hols 2-day min. Adults only. TV in common rm. Complimentary full bkfst. Restaurant adj 5-9 pm. Ck-out 11 am, ck-in 3-7 pm. Business servs avail. Luggage handling. Concierge serv. Gift shop. Downhill/x-country ski 4 mi. Massage. In-rm whirlpool in suites. Picnic tables. Built in 1915. Totally nonsmoking. Cr cds: A, DS, MC, V.
D

Restaurant

★★ **PIEMONT.** *1200 S Mt Shasta Blvd (96067). 530/926-2402.* Hrs: 5-9:30 pm; Fri, Sat to 10 pm; Sun from 1 pm; winter hrs vary. Closed Mon; Thanksgiving, Dec 24-25; also Tues Jan and Feb. Res accepted. Italian, American menu. Bar. Complete meals: dinner $8.25-$16.50. Children's menu. Specializes in pasta, chicken, steak. Own pasta. Family-owned since 1940. Totally nonsmoking. Cr cds: A, DS, MC, V.
D

Muir Woods National Monument

(see San Francisco map) *See also Corte Madera, Mill Valley, San Francisco, Sausalito*

(17 mi N of San Francisco, off CA 1)

This was the first area in the National Park system to preserve an old growth stand of redwoods *(Sequoia sempervirens),* the tallest species of tree on earth. Every effort has been made to preserve this area as closely as possible to what it was when the first European settler saw it in 1850. The monument lies at the south foot of Mt Tamalpais. Two parcels of land, totaling more than 465 of the monument's 553 acres, were donated to the United States by William and Elizabeth Thacher Kent and named in honor of John Muir, famous traveler and naturalist. The first parcel of land was donated in 1908.

Charred stumps and deep scars on living trees are proof that fires regularly occurred prior to 1850. During mid-December to mid-March, depending on winter rains, visitors may see mature salmon and steelhead trout fighting their way up Redwood Creek to spawn. There are six miles of trails; visitors must stay on trails. The following are not permitted: pets, picnicking, fishing, camping, hunting, and possession of firearms. There are 1½ miles of flat, asphalt trail suitable for wheelchairs and strollers. The park is open every day, 8 am to sunset. Visitor Center, snack bar, and gift shop (daily). Because the area is so popular, during the summer months it is best to drive there before 11 am or after 5 pm. Limited parking for oversize vehicles and large RVs. Contact the Site Manager, Muir Woods National Monument, Mill Valley 94941. Phone 415/388-2595. Park ¢

Napa

(F-3) *See also Calistoga, St. Helena, Sonoma, Yountville*

Pop 61,842 **Elev** 17 ft **Area code** 707

Information Chamber of Commerce, 1556 First St, 94559; 707/226-7455. Conference & Visitors Bureau, 1310 Napa Town Center, 94559; 707/226-7459

Web www.napavalley.com/napa/

As gateway to the fertile Napa Valley, an area renowned for its fine wines, the town of Napa is a popular stopping-off point for tourists.

What to See and Do

Hot-air ballooning. Hot-air balloon trips (approx an hr in air) above the Napa Valley vineyards. Contact Balloons Above the Valley, 5091 Solano Ave. Phone 707/253-2222. ¢¢¢¢¢

✪ **Napa Valley Wine Train.** Scenic trips aboard turn-of-the-century Pullman cars and 1950s diesel Steamliners. The three-hr, 36-mi round-trip journey departs from Napa to St. Helena and passes through Napa Valley vineyards. Lunch, brunch, and dinner also served (fee). Res for wkends recommended one month in advance. Contact 1275 McKinstry St, 94559. Phone 707/253-2111. ¢¢¢¢¢

Wineries. There are over 240 wineries in Napa Valley and most of them are open to the public. Among these are

Artesa Winery. Tour the wine-making operations from an elevated walkway or enjoy the view from the visitor center and terrace. There is also an adj gallery and museum. (Daily) Phone 707/224-1668. **FREE**

Bouchaine Vineyards. A 38-acre estate two mi south of downtown Napa. Produces vintage Pinot Noir and Chardonnay. (Daily) Phone 707/252-9065. **FREE**

Carneros Creek Winery. Founded in 1972, it's known for Pinot Noir and stock of rare older wines. (Daily) Phone 707/253-WINE. ¢¢

Domaine Carneros by Taittinger. The majestic hilltop chateau makes this one of the most spectacular to view. The house specialty is sparkling wine. (Daily) Phone 707/257-0101. **FREE**

Hess Collection Winery. Offers self-guided tours and a gallery of contemporary art. (Daily) Phone 707/255-1144. **FREE**

Luna Vineyards. The Tuscan villa will make you believe you're in Italy, while visiting this winery known for its varieties of Pinot Grigio, Merlot, and Sangiovese. (Daily) Phone 707/255-5862. ¢¢

Pine Ridge Winery. After your tour, stay for a picnic beneath the pines. The barrel-aging caves run for ½ mi. (Daily) Phone 707/252-9777. **FREE**

William Hill Winery. Appts are necessary for a tour of this vineyard specializing in Chardonnay, Cabernet Sauvignon, and Merlot. (Daily) Phone 707/224-4477. **FREE**

Motels/Motor Lodges

★★ BEST WESTERN INN AT THE VINES. *100 Soscol Ave (94559). 707/257-1930; res 800/528-1234. www.innatthevines.com.* 68 rms, 3 story. Apr-Nov: S $90-$160; D $100-$160; each addl $10; suites $175-$200; lower rates rest of yr. Crib free. TV; cable (premium). Heated pool; whirlpool. Coffee in rms. Restaurant open 24 hrs. Ck-out 11 am. Business servs avail. Meeting rm. Health club privileges. Refrigerators. Private patios, balconies. Cr cds: A, C, D, DS, ER, JCB, MC, V.

D SC

★ **CHABLIS INN.** *3360 Solano Ave (94558). 707/257-1944; fax 707/226-6862; toll-free 800/443-3490.* 34 rms, 2 story, 7 kits. Apr-Oct: S, D $100-$125; kit. units $75-$85; each addl $5; under 14 free; higher rates Fri, Sat, hols; lower rates rest of yr. Crib $5. TV; cable (premium). Heated pool; whirlpool. Complimentary continental bkfst, coffee in rms. Restaurant nearby. Ck-out noon. Business servs avail. Refrigerators. Picnic tables. Cr cds: A, C, D, DS, MC, V.

D

Hotels

★ **CHATEAU HOTEL.** *4195 Solano Ave (94558). 707/253-9300; fax 707/253-0906; toll-free 800/253-6272. www.napavalleychateauhotel.com.* 115 rms, 2 story. Apr-Oct: S, D $100-$140; each addl $10; suites $155-$190; under 12 free; lower rates rest of yr. Crib free. TV; cable (premium). Heated pool; whirlpool. Coffee in rms. Restaurant nearby. Ck-out noon. Meeting rms. Business servs avail. Some refrigerators. Cr cds: A, C, D, DS, MC, V.

D SC

★★ **EMBASSY SUITES NAPA VALLEY.** *1075 California Blvd (94559). 707/253-9540; fax 707/253-9202; res 800/362-2779. www.embassynapa.com.* 205 suites, 3 story. May-Oct: S, D $159-$274; each addl $10; under 18 free; lower rates rest or yr. Crib free. TV; cable (premium). 2 pools, 1 indoor; whirlpool. Sauna, steam rm. Complimentary full bkfst, coffee in rms. Restaurants 11 am-10 pm. Bar to 1 am; entertainment. Ck-out noon. Meeting rms. Business servs avail. In-rm modem link. Health club privileges. Concierge. Refrigerators, wet bars. Cr cds: A, C, D, DS, JCB, MC, V.

D

★★ **JOHN MUIR INN.** *1998 Trower Ave (94558). 707/257-7220; fax 707/258-0943; toll-free 800/522-8999. www.johnmuirnapa.com.* 59 units, 3 story. Apr-Oct: S $115-$135; D $135; each addl $10; suites $120-$160; kits. $95-$110; under 14 free; mid-wk rates. Crib free. TV; cable (premium), VCR avail (movies). Pool, whirlpool. Complimentary continental bkfst, coffee in rms. Restaurant nearby. Meeting rms. Business servs avail. In-rm modem link. Valet serv. Some refrigerators. Microwaves avail. Cr cds: A, C, D, DS, JCB, MC, V.

D

★★★ **NAPA VALLEY MARRIOTT.** *3425 Solano Ave (94558). 707/253-7433; fax 707/258-1320; toll-free 800/228-9290.* 187 rms, 2 story. Mar-Nov: S, D $125-$193; suites $260-$470; lower rates rest of yr. TV; cable (premium). Heated pool; whirlpool, poolside serv. Coffee in rms. Restaurant 6:30 am-10 pm. Bar. Ck-out noon. Meeting rms. Business center. In-rm modem link. Bellhops. Valet serv. Sundries. Gift shop. Lighted tennis. Refrigerators avail. Some private patios, balconies. Cr cds: A, C, D, DS, ER, JCB, MC, V.

D SC

Resort

★★★ **SILVERADO COUNTRY CLUB & RESORT.** *1600 Atlas Peak Rd (94558). 707/257-0200; fax 707/257-2867; toll-free 800/532-0500.*

Ballooning over Napa Valley

www.silveradoresort.com. 420 rms, 1 and 2 story, 280 suites. Mar-late Nov: S, D $180-$340; kit. suites $290-$1,300; each addl $15; hol, golf, tennis pkgs; lower rates rest of yr. Crib free. TV; cable (premium), VCR avail. 9 pools, some heated; whirlpool. Restaurant 5:30 am-5 pm; dining rms 5:30-11 pm (see also VINTNERS COURT). Bar 11-1 am; Fri, Sat to 2 am; entertainment. Ck-out noon, ck-in 4 pm. Coin lndry. Conference facilities. Business center. In-rm modem link. Concierge. Sundries. Valet parking. Golf, tennis pro shops. Lighted tennis $13, pro. 36-hole golf, greens fee $120 (incl cart), pro, putting greens, driving range. Refrigerators, minibars, fireplaces. Private patios, balconies. Cr cds: A, C, D, DS, ER, JCB, MC.

D

B&Bs/Small Inns

★★★ **BEAZLEY HOUSE.** *1910 1st St (94559). 707/257-1649; fax 707/257-1518; toll-free 800/559-1649. www.beazleyhouse.com.* 11 rms, 2 story. S $125; D $180; each addl $25. Complimentary full bkfst; evening refreshments. Ck-out 11:30 am, ck-in 3:30-6:30 pm. Meeting rm. Business servs avail. Health club privileges. Built 1902; antiques; library. Totally nonsmoking. Cr cds: A, MC, V.

D

★ **COUNTRY GARDEN INN.** *1815 Silverado Trl (94558). 707/255-1197; fax 707/255-3112. www.countrygardeninn.com.* 10 rms, 2 story. No rm phones. Apr-Nov, wkends: D $150-$225; each addl $25; lower rates rest of yr. Children over 16 yrs only. Complimentary full bkfst; evening refreshments. Ck-out 11:30 am, ck-in 3 pm. Business servs avail. Meeting rm. Lawn games. Fireplaces; some in-rm whirlpools. Private patios, balconies. Picnic tables. View of river. Built 1855; antiques. On 1½ acres of woodland; rose garden; aviary. Totally nonsmoking. Cr cds: A, MC, V.

D

★★★★ **LA RESIDENCE.** *4066 St. Helena Hwy (94558). 707/253-0337; fax 707/253-0382; toll-free 800/253-9203. www.laresidence.com.* A short distance off the highway this bed and breakfast offers rooms done in a country decor. Guests will enjoy the gorgeous gardens and pool area. All should take advantage of a wonderful breakfast and wine and cheese served later in the garden. 20 rms, 2-3 story. Mar-Nov: S $175-$195; D $210; each addl $20; suites $225-$275; lower rates rest of yr. TV avail. Heated pool, whirlpool. Complimentary full bkfst. Ck-out 11 am, ck-in 2 pm. Meeting rm. Business servs avail. In-rm modem link. Luggage handling. Balconies. Antiques, fireplaces. Gothic Revival architecture. Built 1870. Cr cds: A, D, DS, MC, V.

★★ **THE OLD WORLD INN.** *1301 Jefferson St (94559). 707/257-0112; fax 707/257-0118; res 707/257-0112.* 8 rms, 2 story, 1 cottage. S, D $125-$160; cottage $215. Complimentary full bkfst; afternoon refreshments. Ck-out 11:30 am, ck-in 3-6 pm. Whirlpool. Some fireplaces. Built ca 1900; Scandinavian country decor; antiques. Garden. Totally nonsmoking. Cr cds: A, DS, MC, V.

Restaurants

★★ **BISTRO DON GIOVANNI.** *4110 St. Helena Hwy (CA 29) (94558). 707/224-3300.* Hrs: 11:30 am-10 pm; wkends to 11 pm. Closed Jan 1, Thanksgiving, Dec 25. Res accepted. Italian, French menu. Bar. A la carte entrees: lunch, dinner $8.95-$16.95. Children's menu. Specialties: fritto misto, grilled portabello mushrooms, seared filet of salmon. Parking. Outdoor dining. Terrace overlooking vineyard. Mexican tile floors, original artwork. Cr cds: A, D, DS, MC, V.

D

★★ **CELADON.** *1040 Main St #104 (94559). 707/254-9690.* Hrs: 11:30 am-2 pm, 5-9 pm; Sat 5-9 pm. Closed Sun; also hols. Continental menu. Wine, beer. A la carte entrees: lunch $12-$15, dinner $15-$28. Specialties: flash-fried calamari with spicy chipotle chili glaze, steak frites, Asian-inspired noodle bowl. Parking. Outdoor dining. On creek. Totally nonsmoking. Cr cds: A, D, MC, V.

D

★★ **CHANTERELLE.** *804 1st St (94559). 707/253-7300.* Hrs: 11 am-4 pm, 5-9:30 pm; Sun to 9 pm; Sun brunch 10:30 am-2:30 pm. Closed Jan 1. Res accepted. Mediterranean menu. Bar. Lunch $5.50-$12.95, dinner $11-$19. Complete meals: dinner $34. Sun brunch $15.50-$18.50. Specializes in beef, chicken. Cr cds: A, MC, V.
D

★ **JONESY'S FAMOUS STEAK HOUSE.** *2044 Airport Rd (94558). 707/255-2003.* Hrs: 11:30 am-9 pm; Sun to 8 pm. Closed Mon; Dec 25. Res accepted. Bar. Lunch, dinner $6.75-$16.95. Children's menu. Specializes in steak, seafood, salads. View of planes landing and taking off at airport. Totally nonsmoking. Cr cds: A, D, DS, MC, V.
D

★★ **LA BOUCANE.** *1778 2nd St (94559). 707/253-1177.* Hrs: 5:30-10:30 pm. Closed Sun; hols; also two wks in Jan. Res accepted; required wkends. Dinner $14-$21. Specialties: salmon poached in cream and champagne, rack of lamb, roast duckling. Parking. House built 1885. Cr cds: MC, V.

★★★ **NAPA VALLEY WINE TRAIN.** *1275 McKinstry St (94559). 707/253-2111. www.winetrain.com.* Sittings: 11 am and 6 pm; Sat, Sun noon and 5:30 pm; Mon 11 am; Sat, Sun brunch 8:30 am. Closed Dec 25; also 1st wk Jan. Res required. Bar. Wine list. A la carte entrees: lunch $27.50. Prix fixe: lunch $65-$77, dinner $70-$85. Sat, Sun brunch $57. Children's menu. Specializes in beef, chicken, fish. Eight vintage (ca 1915) railroad cars carry diners 36 mi through vineyards to St. Helena and back to Napa; turn-of-the-century decor. Totally nonsmoking. Cr cds: A, C, D, DS, MC, V.
D SC

★★ **RUFFINO'S.** *645 1st St (94559). 707/255-4455.* Hrs: 5-10 pm; Sun 4-9:30 pm. Closed Mon; Jan 1, Thanksgiving, Dec 24-25. Res accepted. Italian menu. Bar. Dinner $7.95-$16.95. Children's menu. Specializes in steak, veal, pasta. Totally nonsmoking. Family-owned. Cr cds: A, C, D, MC, V.
D

★★ **VINTNERS COURT.** *1600 Atlas Peak Rd (94558). 707/257-0200. www.silveradoresort.com.* Hrs: 6-10:30 pm; Fri to 9:30 pm; Sun brunch 10 am-3 pm. Closed Mon. Res accepted. Bar. A la carte entrees: dinner $21-$27. Fri seafood buffet $33.50. Sun brunch $23.50. Children's menu. Specialties: wok-fried Chilean sea bass, braised lamb shank. Pianist nightly. Valet parking. Overlooks golf course. Totally nonsmoking. Cr cds: A, C, D, DS, MC, V.
D SC

Unrated Dining Spot

CAFE LUCY - LE PETITE BISTRO. *1408 Clay St (94558). 707/255-0110.* Specializes in French dishes. Hrs: 11 am-3 pm, 5:30-9:30 pm. Closed Sun, Mon. Res accepted. Wine, beer. Lunch $2.95-$10.95; dinner $10-$14. Entertainment. Cr cds: MC, V.
D

Needles

Founded 1882 **Pop** 5,191 **Elev** 488 ft **Area code** 760 **Zip** 92363

Information Chamber of Commerce, 100 G St; 760/326-2050

Founded as a way station for the Santa Fe Railroad, this town took its name from the needlelike peaks visible 15 miles away in Arizona. The town has a variety of trees and desert plant life. Nearby are many mines and ghost towns. With marinas on the Colorado River and recreational areas under development, the area is attracting anglers, boaters, and campers.

What to See and Do

Moabi Regional Park. Swimming beach and lagoon, waterskiing, fishing, boating (boat rentals, launches, marina); camping (fee; hookups, hot showers), lndry, general store. Peninsula, riverfront camping. Pets on leash only. Water, rest rms only. Fee per vehicle. 11 mi SE via I-40, on the Colorado River. Phone 760/326-3831.

Providence Mountains State Recreation Area. Spectacular scenery incl 300-square-mi area of desert. Two of the Mitchell Caverns are open to the public—El Pakiva and Tecopa; both contain fine examples of stalactites and stalagmites. El Pakiva has rare shields or palettes (round platelike protrusions from the walls). Cavern tours (Labor Day-Memorial Day, daily; rest of yr, wkends; fee). Visitors are advised to bring adequate clothing, food, and water. There are trails to the surrounding area near the visitor center. Developed & RV camping (fee). Park open all yr. Contact the Ranger Office, Box 1, Essex 92332. 40 mi W on I-40, then 17 mi NW on Essex Rd. Phone 760/928-2586. Parking per vehicle ¢¢ Camping ¢¢¢¢ Cavern tours ¢¢

Restaurant

★ **HUNGRY BEAR.** *1906 W Needles Hwy (92363). 760/326-2988.* Hrs: 5:30 am-10:30 pm. Closed Dec 25. Bar noon-2 am. Bkfst $3-$7, lunch $3.95-$7, dinner $4.95-$14.95. Children's menu. Specializes in steak, seafood. Own desserts. Salad bar. Route 66 motif in dining rm. Cr cds: A, D, DS, MC, V.
D SC

Nevada City

See also Auburn, Grass Valley, Marysville, Oroville

Settled 1849 **Pop** 2,855 **Elev** 2,525 ft **Area code** 530 **Zip** 95959

Information Chamber of Commerce, 132 Main St; 530/265-2692 or 800/655-6569 (CA & NV)

Web www.ncgold.com

Two years after gold was discovered here, 10,000 miners were working every foot of ground within a radius of three miles. The gravel banks are said to have yielded $8 million in gold dust and nuggets in two years. Of the major gold rush towns, Nevada City remains one of the most picturesque, its residential areas dotted with multigabled frame houses. Principal occupations are lumbering, tourism, government, electronics, and craft shops. The gold mines were closed in 1956.

A Ranger District office of the Tahoe National Forest is located here.

What to See and Do

Firehouse No. 1. (1861) On display are Donner Party relics, Joss House altar, Maidu artifacts and furniture, clothing, and photos of early settlers. (Daily; closed Jan 1, Thanksgiving, Dec 25; Wed in winter) 214 Main St. Phone 530/265-5468. **Donation**

Historic Miners Foundry. (1856). Group of stone, brick, and frame buildings. The Pelton Wheel was originally tested and manufactured here (1878). Special events, theater, and concerts are held here. 325 Spring St. Phone 530/265-5383.

Malakoff Diggins State Historic Park. Gold mining town on 3,000 acres. Museum with hydraulic mining exhibits (May-Oct, daily; rest of yr, wkends). Swimming, fishing; hiking and bridle trails, picnicking, camping, cabins. Standard fees. 15 mi NE off CA 49 at Tyler-Foote Crossing. Phone 530/265-2740. Day use per vehicle ¢¢

National Hotel. Three stories, with balconies and balustrades reaching over the sidewalks. Victorian furnishings. Conducted a prosperous bar business during 1860s and 1870s. Still operates dining rm (see RESTAURANT) and saloon. 211 Broad St. Phone 530/265-4551.

Nevada Theatre. (1865). The Foothill Theatre Company performs several productions in this historic theater. (Mar-Dec) 401 Broad St. Phone 812/530-2658.

Walking tours. Booklets describing historical buildings and sites may be obtained at the Chamber of Commerce.

Special Events

International Teddybear Convention. Phone 530/265-5804. First wkend Apr.

Nevada City Classic Bicycle Tour. A 40-mi senior race and a 20-mi junior race through the city's hilly streets. Phone 530/265-2692. June.

Constitution Day Parade. Phone 530/265-2692. Second wkend Sept.

Fall Color Spectacular. Colorful maples, aspens, fruit trees, poplars, firs, cedars, and pines. Phone 530/265-2692. Mid-Oct-mid-Nov.

Victorian Christmas. Street fair with costumes, crafts, music, entertainment. Phone 530/265-2692. Three Wed nights and Sun preceding Christmas.

B&Bs/Small Inns

★★ EMMA NEVADA HOUSE. *528 E Broad St (95959). 530/265-4415; fax 916/265-4416; toll-free 800/916-3662.* 6 rms, 2 story. S, D $100-$150; each addl $20; wkends, hols (Apr-Dec: 2-day min); higher rates special events. Children over 10 yrs only. TV in some rms. Complimentary full bkfst. Restaurant nearby. Ck-out 11 am, ck-in 3-6 pm. Luggage handling. Concierge serv. Some in-rm whirlpools, fireplaces. Built in 1856; antiques. Totally nonsmoking. Cr cds: A, D, MC, V.

★★ FLUME'S END BED AND BREAKFAST. *317 S Pine St (95959). 530/265-9665; toll-free 800/991-8118. www.flumesend.com.* 6 rms, 3 story. S, D $80-$140. TV in lobby; cable. Complimentary full bkfst; afternoon refreshments. Restaurant nearby. Ck-out 11 am, ck-in 2-6 pm. Balconies. Picnic tables. Victorian inn built 1861. On stream; historic water flume on property. Gold rush ambience. Totally nonsmoking. Cr cds: MC, V.

D

★★ GRANDMERE'S BED & BREAKFAST INN. *449 Broad St (95959). 530/265-4660; fax 530/265-4561.* 7 rms, 4 with shower only, 3 story. S, D $100-$165; wkends, hols (Apr-Dec: 2 day min). Adults only. Complimentary full bkfst; afternoon refreshments. Restaurant nearby. Ck-out 11 am, ck-in 3-6 pm. Luggage handling. Concierge serv. Some balconies. Picnic tables. Built in 1856; country French decor; large garden. Totally nonsmoking. Cr cds: A, MC, V.

★★ RED CASTLE. *109 Prospect St (95959). 530/265-5135; res 800/761-4766.* 7 rms, 4 story. No rm phones. S, D $70-$150; higher rates wkends (2-day min). Children over 12 yrs only. Complimentary full bkfst; afternoon refreshments. Restaurant nearby. Ck-out 11 am, ck-in 2-4 pm. Balconies. Built in 1860, historic inn is fine example of domestic Gothic; restored and furnished with antiques and period pieces. Terraced gardens; fountain pool. Totally nonsmoking. Cr cds: MC, V.

SC

Restaurants

★★ FRIAR TUCK'S. *111 N Pine St (95959). 530/265-9093. www.friartucks.com.* Hrs: 5-9 pm. Closed hols. Res accepted. Continental menu. Bar. Dinner $16-$23. Children's menu. Specialties: fondue dinners, rack of lamb, roast duck. Guitar. Street parking. Totally nonsmoking. Cr cds: A, MC, V.

D

★ KIRBY'S CREEKSIDE. *101 Broad St (95959). 530/265-3445.* Hrs: 11:30 am-2:30 pm, 5-9:30 pm; Fri, Sat to 10 pm; Sun (brunch) 10:30 am-2:30 pm, 5-8:30 pm. Closed Jan 1, Dec 25. Res accepted. French menu. Bar 4:30 pm-midnight. A la carte entrees: lunch $6-$12, dinner $11-$25. Complete meal: dinner $33-$60. Children's menu. Specialties: veggie sampler, free-range chicken, culinary adventures. Sun brunch $6-$13. Parking. Outdoor dining. On creek. Totally nonsmoking. Cr cds: A, DS, MC, V.

D

★★ NATIONAL HOTEL VICTORIAN DINING ROOM. *211 Broad St (95959). 530/265-4551.* Hrs: 7 am-2:30 pm, 5:30-9:30 pm; Sat to 3 pm; Sun brunch 7 am-3 pm. Res accepted. Continental menu. Bar 10-2 am. Bkfst, lunch $3.95-$8.95, dinner $11.95-$18.95. Sun brunch $7.25-$14.95. Children's menu. Specialty: prime rib. Own desserts. Entertainment Fri, Sat; pianist Sat, Sun in summer. Victorian decor. In historic hotel (1852). Totally nonsmoking. Cr cds: A, MC, V.

D

Newport Beach

(E-5) *See also Huntington Beach, Irvine, Laguna Beach, Long Beach*

Pop 66,643 **Elev** 25 ft **Area code** 949 **Zip** 92660

Information Newport Harbor Area Chamber of Commerce, 1470 Jamboree Rd; 949/729-4400

Web www.newportbeach.com

This seaside community, sometimes referred to as the American Riviera, is famous for elegant waterfront villas, smart shops and restaurants, and beautiful Pacific Coast scenery. With a six-mile-long beach and a fine harbor, it offers a variety of water activities. Vacation attractions are largely clustered around the Balboa peninsula, a six-mile finger of land running east and west. Behind it is Newport Harbor, with 12 miles of waterways and eight islands.

What to See and Do

Balboa Fun Zone. Amusement area at the pier. Ferris wheel, kiddie rides, video games, arcade. (Hours vary) 600 E Bay Ave. Phone 949/673-0408. **FREE**

Orange County Museum of Arts. Permanent and changing exhibits of modern and contemporary art, with an emphasis on California art since WWII. Bookshop; Sculpture Garden Cafe (Tues-Fri). Museum (Tues-Sun; closed hols). Admission free on Tues. 850 San Clemente Dr. Phone 949/759-1122. **¢¢**

Sherman Library & Gardens. Botanical gardens set amidst fountains and sculpture. Historical library has a research center for the study of Pacific Southwest. (Daily; closed Jan 1, Thanksgiving, Dec 25) 5 mi S via Pacific Coast Hwy, Dahlia Ave exit to 2647 E Coast Hwy in Corona del Mar. Phone 949/673-2261. **¢**

Special Events

Taste of Newport. Mid-Sept. Phone 714/729-4400.

Christmas Boat Parade. Newport Beach Harbor. Late Dec. Phone 949/729-4400.

Motel/Motor Lodge

★★ BEST WESTERN BAY SHORES INN. *1800 W Balboa Blvd (92663). 949/675-3463; fax 949/675-4977; toll-free 800/222-6675. www.bestwestern.com.* 21 rms. Mid-June-early Sept: S, D $109-$169; each addl $10; suite $369-$389; under 10 free; lower rates rest of yr. Crib free. TV; VCR (free movies). Complimentary continental bkfst. Restaurant nearby. Ck-out 11 am. Business servs avail. In-rm modem link. Sun deck. Some ocean, bay views. Cr cds: A, C, D, DS, MC, V.

Hotels

★★★★ FOUR SEASONS HOTEL NEWPORT BEACH. *690 Newport Center Dr (92660). 949/759-0808; fax 714/759-0568; res 800/332-3442. www.fourseasons.com.* A characteristically elegant setting perfect for both business and recreation, this property welcomes guests with a creamy, marble-filled lobby and is minutes from beaches and seaside golf courses. Dining options include the Pavilion and the more casual Gardens Lounge and Cafe. The magnificent ballroom is perfect for special events. The renowned Pelican Hill Golf Club is only a 15-minute drive from here. 285 rms, 96 suites, 20 story. S $375-$415; each addl $30; suites $485-$3,300; under 18 free; wkend rates. Pet accepted, some restrictions. Valet parking $14.50/day. TV; cable (premium), VCR avail (movies). Outdoor heated pool, whirlpool, poolside serv. Restaurants 6:30 am-10 pm (see PAVILION and GARDENS LOUNGE AND CAFE). Rm serv 24 hrs. Bar 11 pm-1 am; entertainment. Ck-out noon, ck-in 3 pm. Complimentary coffee in lobby. Conference facilities. Business center. In-rm modem link. Concierge. Gift shop. Beauty shop. Airport transportation. 2 lighted tennis courts, pro. Golf privileges. Bicycles. Fitness center, spa, sauna. Massage. Bathrm phones. Minibars. Microwaves in suites. Balconies.

Oceanfront views avail. Cr cds: A, DS, MC, V.

★★★ HYATT NEWPORTER. *1107 Jamboree Road (92660). 949/729-1234; fax 949/644-1552; res 800/233-1234. www.hyattnewporter.com.* 410 rms, 2 and 3 story, four 3-bedrm villas. S, D $179-$234; each addl $25; suites $250-$400; villas for 1-6 $750-$900; under 18 free. Crib free. Pet accepted, some restrictions. TV; cable (premium). 3 pools, 1 heated; whirlpools, poolside serv. Dining rm 6 am-10:30 pm. Rm serv 24 hrs. Bar 11-2 am; entertainment. Ck-out noon, ck-in 4 pm. Convention facilities. Business center. In-rm modem link. Valet serv. Concierge. Gift shop. Barber, beauty shop. Free airport transportation. Lighted tennis privileges, pro. 18-hole golf privileges, 9-hole golf. Exercise equipt. Health club privileges. Bicycle rentals. Lawn games. Wet bar in suites. Villas have fireplaces, private pool. Private patios, balconies. 26 acres, beautiful landscaping, lush gardens, overlooking bay and harbor. Ocean 1 mi. Cr cds: A, C, D, DS, ER, JCB, MC, V.

★★★ NEWPORT BEACH MARRIOTT HOTEL AND TENNIS CLUB. *900 Newport Center Dr (92660). 949/640-4000; fax 949/640-5055; toll-free 800/228-9290.* 578 rms, 16 story. S, D $139-$180; 1-2-bedrm suites $350-$750; under 12 free; wkend, tennis package plans. Crib free. Pet accepted. TV; cable (premium). 2 heated pools; whirlpool, poolside serv. Restaurant 6:30 am-10 pm. Bar 4 pm-2 am. Ck-out noon. Coin lndry. Convention facilities. Business center. In-rm modem link. Gift shop. Valet parking. Free airport transportation. 8 lighted tennis courts, pro, tennis club. Exercise rm. Health club privileges. Refrigerators avail. Private patios, balconies. Beautiful landscaping. Shopping center opp. Luxury level. Cr cds: A, C, D, DS, JCB, MC, V.

★★ PORTOFINO BEACH HOTEL. *2306 W Ocean Front (92663). 949/673-7030; fax 949/723-4370; toll-free 800/571-8749. www.portofino beachhotel.com.* 15 rms, 5 villas, 2 story, 3 suites. S $99-$199; D $299-$399; under 16 free. TV. Complimentary continental bkfst. Dining rm 5:30-11 pm. Rm serv from 6 pm. Ck-out noon, ck-in 3 pm. Business servs avail. Some fireplaces. Restored ocean-front hotel; library/sitting rm; many antiques. Cr cds: A, C, D, DS, JCB, MC, V.

★★★ RADISSON HOTEL NEWPORT BEACH. *4545 MacArthur Blvd (92660). 949/833-0570; fax 949/833-0187; res 888/333-3333.* 334 rms, 7 and 10 story. S, D $129-$139; suites $350-$400; under 18 free. Crib free. TV; cable (premium). Heated pool; whirlpool, poolside serv. Restaurant 6:30 am-10 pm. Bar 5 pm-midnight; Fri, Sat to 2 am. Ck-out 1 pm. Convention facilities. Business servs avail. In-rm modem. Gift shop. Free airport transportation. 2 lighted tennis courts. Health club privileges. Balconies. Luxury level. Cr cds: A, C, D, DS, ER, MC, V.

★★★ THE SUTTON PLACE HOTEL. *4500 MacArthur Blvd (92660). 949/476-2001; fax 949/476-0153; toll-free 800/243-4141. www.suttonplace.com.* 435 rms, 10 story. S, D $190-$250; each addl $25; suites $310-$875; under 16 free; wkend rates. TV; cable (premium), VCR avail (movies). Pool; whirlpool, poolside serv. Restaurant 6:30 am-10:30 pm. Rm serv 24 hrs. Bars 4 pm-2 am; entertainment. Ck-out noon. Meeting rms. Business center. In-rm modem link. Concierge. Gift shop. Free airport transportation. Lighted tennis, pro. Exercise equipt; sauna. Massage. Health club privileges. Bathrm phones, minibars. Some balconies. European decor. Luxury level. Cr cds: A, C, D, DS, V.

B&B/Small Inn

★★ DORYMAN'S OCEANFRONT INN. *2102 W Ocean Front (92663). 949/675-7300; fax 949/675-7300; res 800/634-3303.* 10 rms, 4 suites. S, D $160-$180; suites $220-$300. TV; cable, VCR avail. Complimentary continental bkfst, coffee in rms. Ck-out noon, ck-in 3 pm. Business servs avail. In-rm modem link. Fireplaces; microwaves avail. French and American antiques; sitting rm; sun deck. On ocean with pier opp. Cr cds: A, MC, V.

SC

All Suite

★★★ **NEWPORT BEACH MARRIOTT SUITES.** *500 Bayview Cir (92660). 949/854-4500; fax 949/854-3937; toll-free 800/228-9290. www.marriott.com.* 250 suites, 9 story. S, D $115-$185; wkend rates mid-Sept-mid-May. Crib free. Pet accepted. TV; cable (premium). Pool; whirlpool, poolside serv. Coffee in rms. Restaurant 6:30 am-10 pm. Bar 6 am-11 pm. Ck-out noon. Meeting rms. Business servs avail. In-rm modem link. Free airport transportation. Exercise equipt; sauna. Refrigerators; microwaves avail. Private balconies. Cr cds: A, C, D, DS, JCB, MC, V.

Restaurants

★★ **21 OCEANFRONT.** *2100 W Ocean Front (92663). 949/673-2100.* Hrs: 5:30-10 pm; Fri, Sat to 11 pm. Closed hols. Res accepted. Bar from 4 pm. Wine list. A la carte entrees: dinner $22-$60. Specializes in seafood, pasta, prime meats. Valet parking. Elegant dining overlooking ocean and pier. Jacket. Totally nonsmoking. Cr cds: A, C, D, DS, MC, V.

★★★ **ACCENTS.** *4500 MacArthur Blvd (92660). 949/476-2001.* Specializes in New York steak, sea bass. Hrs: 11 am-10 pm; Sun 6-11 am; Sun brunch 10:30 am-3:30 pm. Res accepted. Wine, beer. Lunch $12-$19, dinner $17-$26. Children's menu. Entertainment: jazz band Sat. Cr cds: A, C, D, DS, MC, V.

D

★★ **AMELIA'S.** *311 Marine Ave, Balboa Island (92662). 949/673-6580.* Hrs: 11:30 am-2:30 pm, 5-10 pm; Sun brunch 10 am-3:30 pm. Closed hols. Res accepted. Italian, seafood menu. Wine, beer. Lunch $5-$9, dinner $9-$18. Sun brunch $4-$9. Specialties: crab-stuffed abalone, baby calamari with fresh bay scallops. Wood-beamed ceilings; antique mirrors. One of the original restaurants in Orange County. Cr cds: A, C, D, DS, ER, MC, V.

D

★★ **BISTRO 201.** *3333 W Coast Hwy (92663). 949/631-1551.* Hrs: 11:30 am-10 pm; Fri to 11 pm; Sat 5-11 pm; Sun from 5 pm; Sun brunch 10:30 am-3 pm. Closed Jan 1, Labor Day. Res accepted. Bar. Lunch $8.95-$18, dinner $11.95-$23.95. Children's menu. Specialties: rack of lamb, roasted sea bass, grilled duck. Flemenco Thurs-Sat; Caribbean music Sun brunch. Outdoor dining. On marina. Totally nonsmoking. Cr cds: A, C, D, DS, MC, V.

D

★★ **CHIMAYO GRILL.** *327 Newport Ctr Dr (92660). 949/640-2700. www.culinaryadventures.com.* Hrs: 11:30 am-10 pm; Fri, Sat to 11 pm. Closed Thanksgiving, Dec 25. Southwestern menu. Bar. A la carte entrees: lunch $4.45-$15.45, dinner $5-$21. Children's menu. Specializes in beef, chicken. Outdoor dining. Several fireplaces, original artwork. Totally nonsmoking. Cr cds: A, D, DS, MC, V.

D

★★ **EL TORITO GRILL.** *951 Newport Ctr Dr (92660). 949/640-2875. www.eltoritogrill.com.* Hrs: 11 am-10 pm; Fri, Sat to 11 pm; Sun brunch 10 am-2:30 pm. Closed Thanksgiving, Dec 25. Res accepted. Southwestern menu. Bar to midnight. Lunch $6.95-$10.95, dinner $7.95-$15.95. Sun brunch $11.95. Children's menu. Specializes in tortillas, mesquite-grilled items. Valet parking. Outdoor dining. Southwestern atmosphere. Cr cds: A, D, DS, MC, V.

D

★★★ **FLEMING'S STEAKHOUSE.** *455 Newport Center Dr (92660). 949/720-9633.* Specializes in 40 oz porterhouse, 16 lobster tails, center cut filet. Hrs: 5-10 pm; Fri, Sat to 11 pm. Res accepted. Wine, beer. Dinner $14-$30. Children's menu. Entertainment. Cr cds: A, D, MC, V.

D

★★ **KOTO.** *4300 Von Karman Ave (92660). 949/752-7151.* Hrs: 11:30 am-2:30 pm, 5:30-10:30 pm; Fri to 11 pm; Sat 5:30-11 pm; Sun brunch 11 am-2:30 pm. Closed July 4, Thanks-

giving, Dec 25. Res accepted. Japanese menu. Bar. A la carte entrees: lunch $12-$15, dinner $15-$25. Complete meals: lunch $38, dinner $26-$50. Sun brunch $18.95. Specializes in sushi. Japanese tea house overlooking lake, gardens. Totally nonsmoking. Cr cds: A, D, DS, MC, V.
D

★★ NEWPORT BEACH BREWING COMPANY. *2920 Newport Blvd (92663). 949/675-8449. www.nbbrewco.com.* Hrs: 11:30 am-11:30 pm; Fri to 1 am; Sat 9:30-1 am; Sun 9:30 am-11:30 pm. Closed Thanksgiving, Dec 25. Bar. Bkfst $2.99-$9.99, lunch $3.95-$9.95, dinner $5.85-$12.99. Children's menu. Specializes in salads, wood-fired oven pizzas. Brewery in historic Cannery Village. Cr cds: A, D, DS, MC, V.
D

★★★ PASCAL. *1000 N Bristol St (92660). 949/752-0107. www.pascalnewportbeach.com.* Hrs: 11:30 am-2:30 pm, 6-9:30 pm; Fri to 10 pm; Sat 6-10 pm; Mon to 2:30 pm. Closed Sun; hols. Res accepted. French Provençal menu. Bar. Wine cellar. A la carte entrees: lunch $7-$14, dinner $11-$25. Prix fixe: dinner $46. Specialties: Chilean sea bass, New York steak, mustard rabbit. Outdoor dining. Cr cds: A, D, MC, V.
D

★★★★ PAVILION. *690 Newport Center Dr, Hollywood (92660). 949/760-4920. www.fshr.com.* This formal dining room with exquisite flower arrangements delivers a level of sophistication in line with its locale in the Four Seasons hotel. The menu reflects the best of what the area has to offer, transformed by the creativity of the kitchen team. California cuisine. Specializes in fish, lamb, grilled veal chops. Own pastries, bread. Hrs: 6:30 am-2:30 pm, 6-10:30 pm. Bar 11:30-2 am. Res accepted. A la carte entrees: bkfst $12-$19.75, lunch $9.75-$15.95, dinner $24.95-$28.50. Prix fixe: dinner $32.50-$39.50. Valet parking. Outdoor dining. Overlooks garden. Cr cds: A, C, D, DS, MC, V.
D

★★ P.F. CHANG'S CHINA BISTRO. *1145 Newport Ctr Dr (92660). 949/759-9007. www.pfchangs.com.* Hrs: 11:30 am-11 pm; Fri, Sat to midnight. Closed Thanksgiving, Dec 25. Chinese menu. Bar. A la carte entrees: lunch $6.95-$12.95, dinner $8.95-$14.95. Specialties: spicy chicken, orange peel chicken, dan dan noodles. View of bay. Totally nonsmoking. Cr cds: A, D, MC, V.
D

★★★ THE RITZ. *880 Newport Ctr Dr (92660). 949/720-1800. www.ritzrestaurant.com.* Hrs: 11:30 am-3 pm, 6-10 pm; Fri, Sat 5:30-11 pm; Sun 5-9 pm. Res accepted. Continental menu. Bar. Wine cellar. A la carte entrees: lunch $8-$14, dinner $18-$34. Specialties: bouillabaisse, roast duck, rack of lamb. Own baking. Pianist. Valet parking. Elegant decor. Cr cds: A, D, MC, V.
D

★★ SAPORI. *1080 Bayside Dr (92660). 949/644-4220.* Hrs: 11:30 am-10 pm; Fri, Sat to 11 pm. Closed hols. Res accepted. Italian menu. Bar. A la carte entrees: lunch $7.50-$17.95, dinner $8.50-$22. Specializes in seafood, gourmet pizza, pasta. Outdoor dining. Cr cds: A, C, D, DS, MC, V.
D

★★ SUSHI BAR AT AYSIA. *2901 Pacific Coast Hwy (92663). 949/722-4128.* Specializes in catfish, Alaskan snow crablegs, pineapple and fried rice. Hrs: 5:30-10 pm; Fri, Sat to 11 pm. Res accepted. Wine, beer. Dinner $8-$10. Entertainment. Cr cds: A, DS, MC, V.
D

★ TALE OF THE WHALE. *400 Main St, Balboa (92661). 949/673-4633. www.taleofthewhale.com.* Hrs: 7 am-11 pm; Sat, Sun brunch to 3:45 pm. Closed Dec 25. Bar 10-2 am. Bkfst, lunch $4.95-$11.95, dinner $10.95-$29.95. Sat, Sun brunch $3.95-$11.95. Specializes in seafood. Entertainment Thurs-Sun. Valet parking. In historic Balboa Pavilion (1905) overlooking bay. Cr cds: A, C, D, DS, ER, MC, V.
D

★★ TUTTO MARE. *545 Newport Ctr Dr (92660). 949/640-6333.* Hrs: 11:30 am-11 pm; Fri, Sat to midnight; Sun to 10 pm; Sun brunch to 3 pm. Closed hols. Res accepted. Italian

menu. Bar. A la carte entrees: lunch, dinner $4.95-$22.95. Sun brunch $18.95. Specializes in seafood. Guitarist Thurs, Sun brunch. Outdoor dining. Tropical atmosphere; fresh floral arrangements. Totally nonsmoking. Cr cds: A, C, D, DS, MC, V.
D

★★ **VILLA NOVA.** *3131 W Coast Hwy (92663). 949/642-7880. www.villanovarestaurant.com.* Hrs: 5 pm-midnight; Fri to 1 am; Sat 4 pm-1 am; Sun 4 pm-midnight. Closed Thanksgiving, Dec 25. Res accepted. Italian menu. Bar. Wine cellar. A la carte entrees: dinner $9.95-$25. Children's menu. Specializes in veal, homemade pasta, seafood. Entertainment. Valet parking. Outdoor dining. Courtyard entry; resembles Italian villa. Original artwork; autographed celebrity photos. Cr cds: A, C, D, DS, MC, V.
D

North Hollywood (L.A.)

See also Hollywood (L.A.), Los Angeles

Elev 385 ft **Area code** 818

This community is a neighborhood of Los Angeles, but is regarded by many as a separate entity.

Motels/Motor Lodges

★★ **BEST WESTERN MIKADO HOTEL.** *12600 Riverside Dr (91607). 818/763-9141; fax 818/752-1045; res 800/528-1234. www.bestwestern.com/mikadoho.* 58 rms, 2 story. S, D $119-$129; suite $150; each addl $10; under 12 free. Crib free. TV; cable (premium). Pool, whirlpool. Complimentary full bkfst. Restaurant 11:30 am-2 pm, 5:30-9:30 pm; Fri, Sat 5:30-10 pm; Sun 5-9 pm. Bar. Ck-out 1 pm. Business servs avail. Bathrm phones; refrigerators avail. Some balconies. Cr cds: A, C, D, DS, ER, JCB, MC, V.
D SC

★★ **HOLIDAY INN BEVERLY GARLAND'S.** *4222 Vineland Ave (91602). 818/980-8000; fax 818/766-0112; res 800/238-3759. www.beverlygarland.com.* 255 rms, 6-7 story. S, D $99-$159; each addl $10; suites $215-$395; under 18 free; wkend rates. Crib free. TV; cable (premium). Heated pool, wading pool, poolside serv. Playground. Coffee in rms. Restaurant 6 am-11 pm. Bar 11 am-11 pm. Ck-out noon. Convention facilities. Business servs avail. Bellhops. Valet serv. Concierge. Gift shop. Airport transportation. Lighted tennis, pro. Health club privileges. Private patios, balconies. Cr cds: A, C, D, DS, ER, JCB, MC, V.
D SC

Hotels

★★★ **HILTON UNIVERSAL CITY & TOWERS.** *555 Universal Terrace Pkwy, Uviversal City (91608). 818/506-2500; fax 818/509-2031; res 800/445-8667. www.hilton.com.* 469 units, 24 story. S, D $225-$260; each addl $30; suites $250-$1,395; under 18 free. Crib free. Garage parking $10, valet $14. TV; cable (premium), VCR avail. Heated pool, whirlpool, poolside serv. Coffee in rms. Restaurant 6:30 am-11 pm; pianist Fri-Sun. Rm serv 24 hrs. Bar 11-1:30 am. Ck-out noon. Convention facilities. Business servs avail. In-rm modem link. Gift shop. Exercise equipt. Bathrm phones, minibars. Some suites with vaulted, skylit ceiling; panoramic view of city. Luxury level. Cr cds: A, C, D, DS, JCB, MC, V.
D

★★★ **SHERATON UNIVERSAL HOTEL.** *333 Universal Terrace Pkwy, Universal City (91608). 818/980-1212; fax 818/985-4980; res 800/325-3535. www.sheraton.com.* 442 rms, 20 story. S, D $129-$159; each addl $20; suites $250-$2,000; under 18 free. Crib free. Garage $14; valet parking $16. TV; cable (premium), VCR avail. Heated pool, whirlpool, poolside serv. Coffee in rms. Restaurant 6 am-10:30 pm. Bar 11-2 am. Ck-out noon. Convention facilities. Business center. In-rm modem link. Concierge. Exercise equipt. Game rm. Minibars. Some private patios, balconies. Overlooks San Fernando Valley and Hollywood Hills. Luxury level. Cr cds: A, C, D, DS, ER, JCB, MC, V.

D SC

Restaurant

★ WOLFGANG PUCK'S CAFE. *1000 Universal Center Dr, Universal City (91608). 818/985-9653. www.wolfgangpuck.com.* Hrs: 11 am-11 pm; Fri, Sat to 11:30 pm. Wine, beer. A la carte entrees: lunch $7.95-$9.50, dinner $9.95-$18.95. Specializes in wood-burning oven pizza, rotisserie chicken. Patio dining. Ultramodern decor; kinetic wall art. Cr cds: A, D, MC, V.

D

Oakdale

See also Modesto

Pop 11,961 **Elev** 155 ft **Area code** 209 **Zip** 95361

Information Chamber of Commerce, 590 S Yosemite Ave; 209/847-2244

Web www.ci.oakdale.ca.us

Oakdale's birth is linked to gold and the railroad. An important town along the freight lines to the Mother Lode towns, it was founded by the Stockton & Visalia Railroad Co in 1871. Beef and dairy cattle and a variety of produce support the area now, as do major industries Hershey Chocolate and Hunt-Wesson Foods.

What to See and Do

Hershey Chocolate USA. Visitors' Reception Center and 30-min factory tours. (Mon-Fri; closed hols) No cameras. 1400 S Yosemite Ave. Phone 209/848-8126. **FREE** Opp is

> **Oakdale Cowboy Museum.** Pays tribute to local rodeo champions, farmers, ranchers, and working cowboys. Housed in historic Depot Building. Tours. (Mon-Fri) 355 F St #1. Phone 209/847-7049. **FREE**

Woodward Reservoir. Swimming, waterskiing, fishing, boating (moorings, marina); duck hunting, picnicking, concession (Apr-mid-Sept), camping, showers. (Daily) 5 mi N at 14528 26-Mile Rd. Phone 209/847-3304. ¢¢¢¢¢

Special Events

PRCA Rodeo. Second wkend Apr. Phone 209/847-2244.

Chocolate Festival. Third wkend May. Phone 209/847-2244.

California Dally Team Roping Championships. Oakdale Saddle Club Rodeo grounds, CA 120. July. Phone 209/847-1641.

Motel/Motor Lodge

★★ RAMADA INN. *825 East F St (94612).209/847-8181; res 800/272-6232. www.ramada.com.* 70 rms, 2 story. Apr-Sept: S $71-$83; D $77-$89; each addl $6; suites $126-$197; under 18 free; lower rates rest of yr. Crib free. TV; cable (premium), VCR avail (movies). Heated pool, whirlpool. Coffee in rms. Restaurant 5:30 am-11 pm. Bar 11 am-midnight. Ck-out noon. Meeting rms. Cr cds: A, C, D, DS, MC, V.

D

Oakhurst

Pop 8,051 **Elev** 2,300 ft **Area code** 559 **Zip** 93644

Information Yosemite-Sierra Visitors Bureau, 40637 CA 41; 559/683-4636

Web www.yosemite-sierra.org

Motels/Motor Lodges

★★ BEST WESTERN YOSEMITE GATEWAY INN. *40530 Highway 41 (93644). 559/683-2378; fax 559/683-3813; res 800/528-1234. www.pacificplazahotels.com.* 118 rms, 2 story, 16 suites, 11 kits. Early May-mid-Oct: S $44-$79; D $56-$96; each addl $6; suites $129; kit. units $5-$10 addl; wkly rates off-season; higher rates late Dec; lower rates rest of yr. Crib $2. Pet accepted. TV; cable (premium), VCR avail (movies). Indoor pool, whirlpool. Sauna. Restaurant adj 7-10:30 am, 5-9:30 pm. Bar. Ck-out 11 am. Coin lndry. Meeting rm. Some refrigerators. Balconies. Picnic table, grill. Cr cds: A, C, D, DS, JCB, MC, V.

D

★★ **COMFORT INN.** *40489 Hwy 41 (93644). 559/683-8282; fax 559/658-7030; res 800/228-5150.* 114 rms, 2 story. Apr-Nov: S $80; D $85; each addl $6; suites $125; kit. unit $225; under 18 free; lower rates rest of yr. Crib $5. Pet accepted, some restrictions; $6. TV; cable (premium), VCR avail (movies). Complimentary continental bkfst, coffee in rms. Restaurant adj 11-2 am. Ck-out 11 am. Gift shop. Pool; whirlpool. Refrigerators. Cr cds: A, C, D, DS, ER, JCB, MC, V.

D

★★ **SHILO INN YOSEMITE.** *40644 Hwy 41 (93644). 559/683-3555; fax 559/683-3386; toll-free 800/222-2244. www.shiloinns.com.* 80 rms, 4 story. Apr-Sept: S, D $59-$149; each addl $10; under 13 free; lower rates rest of yr. TV; cable (premium), VCR avail. Pool, whirlpool. Complimentary continental bkfst. Coffee in rms. Restaurant adj 7 am-9 pm. Ck-out noon. Coin lndry. Exercise equipt; sauna, steam rm. Bathrm phones, refrigerators. Some patios, balconies. Cr cds: A, D, DS, MC, V.

D SC

Hotel

★★★★★ **CHATEAU DU SUREAU.** *48688 Victoria Ln (93644), 1/4 mi S of jct CA 49 and CA 41. 559/683-6800; fax 559/683-0800. www.chateaudu sureau.com.* Minutes away from Yosemite, a fairy tale awaits in the foothills of the Sierra Nevadas at Chateau du Sureau. Everything from the European-style stucco building to the life-sized chess board will evoke a felling of being transported to another place and time. Each guest room is individiually decorated and named for restorative herbs that can be found growing on the property. Erna's Elderberry House has long been a destination for serious diners. 10 rms, 2 story. S, D $325-525 and 12% serv charge. TV in sitting rm; cable, VCR avail. Pool. Complimentary full bkfst, coffee in rms. Restaurant (see ERNA'S ELDERBERRY HOUSE). Ck-out noon, ck-in 2 pm. Concierge serv. Exercise equipt. Lawn games. Balconies. Totally nonsmoking. 2 rms also available in adjoining building (Villa Sureau) $2,500, w/24 hour butler service. Cr cds: A, DS, MC, V.

D

B&B/Small Inn

★★ **HOUNDS TOOTH INN.** *42071 State Hwy 41 (93644). 209/642-6600; fax 559/658-2946; toll-free 888/642-6610. www.houndstoothinn.com.* 12 rms, 8 with shower only, 2 story. S, D $95; each addl $20; under 12 free; hols 2-day min. TV; cable (premium). Complimentary full bkfst; refreshments. Restaurant nearby. Ck-out noon, ck-in 3-5 pm. Business servs avail. Concierge serv. X-country ski 10 mi. Some in-rm whirlpools. Totally nonsmoking. Cr cds: A, DS, MC, V.

D

Restaurant

★★★★ **ERNA'S ELDERBERRY HOUSE.** *48688 Victoria Ln (93644). 559/683-6860. www.chateausureau.com.* Erna Kubin-Clanin named her romantic restaurant for the plentiful elderberry bushes that surround the restaurant and adjoining inn. Each night chef James Overbaugh plans a prix fixe menu based on seasonal ingredients that can include everything from Pacific salmon gratin to a salad of baby greens to beef in a red wine sauce. The wine list will impress with many rare California bottlings and a surprising number of wines from Austria, Erna's native land. French, California cuisine. Menu changes daily. Menu recited. Own baking. Hrs: 11:30 am-1 pm, 5:30-8:30 pm; Sun brunch 11 am-1 pm. Closed Mon, Tues. Bar. Wine cellar. Res accepted. Complete meals: lunch $4.50-$14.50. 6-course prix-fixe dinner; $68/person. Sun brunch $28.50. Cr cds: A, DS, MC, V.

D

Oakland

(G-3) *See also Berkeley, Hayward, San Francisco, San Francisco Airport Area, San Mateo, Sausalito*

Founded 1850 **Pop** 372,242 **Elev** 42 ft **Area code** 510 **Zip** 94612

Information Oakland Chamber of Commerce, 475 14th St, Suite 120; 510/874-4800 or 800/262-5526

Web www.oakland.net

Oakland lies just across the bay from San Francisco. The port of Oakland has excellent facilities and caters to heavy Pacific trade. More than 1,500 factories help make Alameda County a leading manufacturing center. The Bay Area Rapid Transit system (BART) links suburban areas and Oakland with San Francisco. Once part of the Rancho San Antonio, 48,000-acre domain of former Spanish cavalry sergeant Luis Maria Peralta, it was acquired as a townsite by Horace W Carpentier, who named it for the evergreen oaks that marked the landscape.

What to See and Do

Camron-Stanford House. (1876). Once the home of the Camron family and later the Stanford family, this building served as the Oakland Public Museum from 1910 until 1967. Today the house operates as a resource center and museum with authentic period furnishings, sculpture, and paintings. Slide program; library. Guided tours. (Wed and Sun) Free admission first Sun of each month. 1418 Lakeside Dr, on the shores of Lake Merritt. Phone 510/444-1876. **¢¢**

Chabot Observatory and Science Center. This 70,000-sq-ft complex incl the nation's largest public telescope, a state-of-the-art planetarium, Omnimax theater, and hands-on science exhibits. Also incl a six-acre environmental education area and nature trail and education facilities. Call for schedule and pricing. 10,000 Skyline Blvd. Phone 510/530-3480.

Dunsmuir House and Gardens. (1899) A 37-rm Colonial-revival mansion; 40 acres of trees, lawns, shrubs, and gardens; special events (Apr-Dec). Guided tours. 2960 Peralta Oaks Ct. Phone 510/615-5555. **¢¢**

East Bay Regional Park District. Organization maintains more than 75,000 acres in 50 parks and recreation areas in Alameda and Contra Costa counties. Facilities incl swimming, fishing, boating; archery, riding, picnic grounds, campgrounds, and other pastimes. Most parks are open daily. Headquarters at 2950 Peralta Oaks Court. Phone 510/635-0135. The park system incl

Anthony Chabot Regional Park & Lake Chabot. Park offers 4,927 acres for hiking and riding, horse rentals; marksmanship range for rifle, pistol, and trapshooting; 18-hole golf course. Camping: motor home and tent camping (fee). Park entrances along Skyline Blvd, between Redwood and Golf Links Rd and along Redwood Rd E of Skyline Blvd; stables and hiking along Skyline Blvd. At Lake Chabot there are fishing and boating facilities (rentals); bicycle trails and picnic areas. Park: E and S via 35th Ave and Redwood Rd; Lake Chabot: S on I-580 to Fairmont Ave, then E to Lake Chabot Rd and left to parking area. Phone 510/562-2267. **¢¢** Adj is

Martin Luther King, Jr. Regional Shoreline. On 1,219 acres, near Oakland Intl Airport. Sunning beach, fishing, boating (two-lane launching ramp); hiking trails, bird-watching, picnicking, children's playfields, beach cafe. Nature study. S on I-880 to Hegenberger exit, then NW on Doolittle Dr. Phone 510/635-0135. **FREE**

Redwood Regional Park. Redwood groves, evergreens, chaparral, and grassland on 1,830 acres. Hiking; nature study. Picnicking, playfields, children's playground. Creek with native rainbow trout. E of Skyline Blvd on Redwood Rd. Per vehicle Phone 510/562-7275. **¢¢**

★ **Jack London Square.** Colorful waterfront area where the author worked. **Heinold's First and Last Chance Saloon**, 56 Jack London Square, at the foot of Webster St, is where London spent much of his time and wrote his most famous novels. Several restaurants and the reconstructed cabin in which the author weathered the Klondike winter of 1898 reflect characters and situations from his life and books. Adj is **Jack London Village,** foot of Alice St. Shops, restaurants, marina area. (Daily) Formed by Clay, Franklin, Embarcadero, and the Oakland Estuary. Phone 510/814-6000.

Joaquin Miller Park. Site of the "Hights," former house of Joaquin Miller, "Poet of the Sierras." Four monuments erected by Miller to Moses, General Frémont, Robert and Elizabeth Browning, and a funeral pyre for himself. Fountain and statuary from 1939 World's Fair. Park is also site of Woodminster Amphitheater, scene of Woodminster Summer Musicals (see SEASONAL EVENT). Hiking and picnic areas. (Daily) Joaquin Miller Rd. Phone 510/238-3187. **FREE**

Kaiser Center. This complex was founded by industrialist Henry J. Kaiser and remains the home of Kaiser Aluminum & Chemical Corporation. The Kaiser Building is of aluminum and glass construction. Changing art exhibits on mezzanine; remarkable 3½-acre rooftop garden with trees, shrubs, flowers, pool, and fountains. Cafeterias, restaurants. (Mon-Fri; closed hols) 300 Lakeside Dr. Phone 510/271-6146. **FREE**

Lake Merritt. In heart of downtown Oakland. Largest natural body of saltwater in the world completely within any city (155 acres), surrounded by drives and handsome buildings. Boat rentals (daily; fee), sightseeing launch (wkends, hols). Sailing lessons, day camps. Special events incl sailing regattas. 568 Bellevue. Phone 510/444-3807. ¢ Adj lake is

Children's Fairyland. Everything child-size, with tiny buildings depicting fairyland tales. Many contain live animals and birds. Carousel, Ferris wheel, train and trolley rides, children's bumper boats, and puppet theater (fee for some activities). (Oct-Apr, Fri-Sun; Apr-June, Wed-Sun; June-Sept, daily; Sept-Oct, Wed-Sun; closed Jan 1, Thanksgiving, Dec 25) Bellevue and Grand Aves. Phone 510/452-2259. ¢¢¢

Lakeside Park. Approx 120 acres. Picnic areas, free children's play area; lawn bowling, putting greens; trail and show gardens, duck-feeding area; bandstand concerts (summer, Sun, and hols). Parking free (exc Feb-Oct, wkends and hols). Vehicle entrance at Bellevue and Grand Aves. Phone 510/238-3187. Also here are

Rotary Nature Center. North America's oldest wildlife refuge (1870); nature and conservation exhibits; native birds; films, illustrated lectures, or walks (wkends); animal feeding area. (Daily) Phone 510/238-3739. **FREE**

Trial and Show Gardens. Demonstration Gardens; incl cactus, fuchsia, dahlia, chrysanthemum, Polynesian, palm, herb, and Japanese gardens. (Daily; closed Jan 1, Thanksgiving, Dec 25) 666 Bellevue Ave. **FREE**

Oakland Museum of California. Galleries, gardens cover four city blocks; exhibits on natural science, history, and art interpret land and people of California. Great Hall exhibits. (Wed-Sun; closed hols) 1000 Oak St, near Lake Merritt. Phone 510/238-2200. ¢¢

Oakland Zoo in Knowland Park. Situated on 525 acres, the zoo houses 330 native and exotic animals, a children's petting zoo and "Simba Pori," a 1½-acre habitat with a pride of six lions, and Siamang Island. Also here are children's rides and picnic areas. Free parking first Mon of each month exc hols. (Daily; closed Thanksgiving, Dec 25) 9777 Golf Links Rd. Phone 510/632-9523. ¢¢

Paramount Theatre. Impressive, restored 1931 art-deco movie palace, home of Oakland Ballet. Hosts organ pops series and a variety of musical performances. 90-min tours start from Box Office (first and third Sat of each month; no tours hols). 2025 Broadway. Phone 510/465-6400. ¢

Professional Sports.

Golden State Warriors (NBA). Arena at Oakland, 7000 Coliseum Way. Phone 510/986-2200.

Oakland Athletics (MLB). Oakland Coliseum, 7000 Coliseum Way. Phone 510/638-4900.

Oakland Raiders (NFL). Oakland Coliseum, 7000 Coliseum Way. Phone 510/864-5000.

Skyline Blvd. On top of Berkeley-Oakland Hills; superb views of entire East Bay area.

USS *Potomac*. Originally built in 1934 as the Coast Guard cutter *Elec-*

tra, this was Franklin D. Roosevelt's beloved "Floating White House." The fully restored, 165-ft steel vessel is now owned and operated as a floating museum by the Potomac Association; it is a National Historic Landmark. Dockside tours (Wed, Fri, Sun; groups by appt only). Narrated two-hr educational cruises around Treasure Island and San Francisco Bay (Mar-Nov, departures first and third Thurs and second and fourth Sun of each month). Res required for cruises. Franklin D. Roosevelt Pier, Jack London Sq. Phone 510/627-1215. Tours ¢¢ Cruises ¢¢¢¢¢

Special Event

Woodminster Summer Musicals. Joaquin Miller Park. July-Sept. Phone 510/531-9597.

Motels/Motor Lodges

★★ BEST WESTERN INN AT THE SQUARE. *233 Broadway (94607). 510/452-4565; fax 510/452-4634; res 800/528-1234. www.innatthesquare.com.* 102 rms, 50 with shower only, 2-3 story, no ground floor rms. S, D $114; each addl $10; under 12 free. Crib free. TV; cable (premium). Heated pool. Complimentary continental bkfst. Restaurant nearby. Ck-out noon. Business servs avail. In-rm modem link. Exercise equipt; saunas. Health club privileges. Garage. Refrigerators avail. Some balconies. Cr cds: A, C, D, DS, JCB, MC, V.

D SC

★★ CLARION SUITES, LAKE MERRITT HOTEL. *1800 Madison St (94612). 510/832-2300; fax 510/832-7150; toll-free 800/933-4683. www.lakemerritthotel.com.* 50 units, 6 story, 41 suites. S, D $159; each addl $10; suites $149-$179; under 17 free. Valet parking $9. Pet accepted; $150. TV; cable, VCR avail. Complimentary continental bkfst, coffee in rms. Restaurant 11 am-10 pm; Sat, Sun by res. Bar. Ck-out 11 am. Meeting rms. Business servs avail. In-rm modem link. Concierge. Health club privileges. Refrigerators, microwaves. Restored Mediterranean/Art Deco landmark (1927) offers views of Lake Merritt. Cr cds: A, C, D, DS, JCB, MC, V.

D

★ CORAL REEF MOTEL & SUITES. *400 Park St, Alemeda (94501). 510/521-2330; fax 510/521-4707; res 510/521-2330. www.alemedamotels.com.* 93 kit units, 1-2 story. S $89; D $96; each addl $7; suites $89-$96; under 6 free; wkly, monthly rates. Crib free. TV; cable. Heated pool. Complimentary continental bkfst. Restaurant opp. Ck-out 11 am. Coin lndry. Business servs avail. Balconies. Cr cds: A, C, D, DS, MC, V.

SC

★★ HAMPTON INN. *8465 Enterprise Way (94621). 510/632-8900; fax 510/632-4713; toll-free 877/547-7667.* 152 rms, 3 story. S, D $89-$99; under 18 free. Crib free. TV; cable (premium). Heated pool, whirlpool. Complimentary continental bkfst. Restaurant nearby. Business servs avail. In-rm modem link. Valet serv. Sundries. Free airport transportation. Health club privileges. Refrigerators avail. Cr cds: A, D, DS, V.

D

★★ HOLIDAY INN. *500 Hegenberger Rd (94621). 510/562-5311; fax 510/636-1539; toll-free 800/465-4329. www.holiday-inn.com.* 293 rms, 2-6 story. S, D $169; each addl $10; suite $199-$249; under 18 free. Crib free. TV; cable (premium), VCR avail. Pool. Restaurant 6 am-1:30 pm, 5-10 pm. Bar 4 pm-midnight. Ck-out noon. Coin lndry. Meeting rms. Business servs avail. In-rm modem link. Bellhops. Sundries. Gift shop. Airport transportation. Exercise equipt. Cr cds: A, C, D, DS, JCB, MC, V.

D SC

★★ MARINA VILLAGE INN. *1151 Pacific Marina, Alameda (94501). 510/523-9450; fax 510/523-6315; toll-free 800/345-0304.* 51 rms, 2 story. S $83-$123; D $91-$133; each addl $8; under 12 free; wkend rates. Crib free. TV; cable (premium). Heated pool. Complimentary continental bkfst, coffee in rms. Restaurant adj 11 am-9:30 pm. Ck-out noon. Business servs avail. In-rm modem link. Sundries. Valet serv. Refrigerators; microwaves avail. Balconies. On waterfront; berthing avail. Cr cds: A, C, D, DS, MC, V.

D SC

Hotels

★★★ **HILTON HOTEL.** *1 Hegenberger Rd (94621). 510/635-5000; fax 510/383-4062; res 800/415-8667.* 363 rms, 3 story. S $129-$149; D $149-$169; each addl $20; suites $350-$500; wkend rates. Crib free. TV; cable (premium), VCR avail. Heated pool, poolside serv. Coffee in rms. Restaurants 6 am-10 pm. Bar 10:30-2 am; entertainment. Ck-out noon. Meeting rms. Business center. In-rm modem link. Bellhops. Gift shop. Free airport transportation. Exercise equipt. Some bathrm phones; refrigerators avail. Private patios. Cr cds: A, C, D, DS, MC, V.

★★★ **OAKLAND MARRIOTT CITY CENTER.** *1001 Broadway (94607). 510/451-4000; fax 510/835-3466. www.marriott.com.* 479 rms, 21 story. S, D $178; each addl $20; suites $325-$750; wkend plans. Crib free. TV; cable. Heated pool, whirlpool. Restaurants 6:30 am-10:30 pm. Bar 4:30 pm-1 am. Convention facilities. Business servs avail. In-rm modem link. Concierge. Gift shop. Exercise equipt. Health club privileges. Refrigerator in suites. Cr cds: A, C, D, DS, ER, JCB, MC, V.

★ **WASHINGTON INN.** *495 Tenth St (94607). 510/452-1776; fax 510/452-4436. www.thewashingtoninn.com.* 47 units, 4 story, 8 suites. S, D $128; suites $159-$179. Valet parking $17. TV; cable. Complimentary bkfst. Restaurant 7 am-9:30 pm. Bar 11 am-11 pm; closed Sun. Ck-out noon. Meeting rm. Business servs avail. In-rm modem link. Health club privileges. Wet bars. Renovated 1913 hotel with turn-of-the-century bar. Cr cds: A, D, DS, MC, V.

★★ **WATERFRONT PLAZA HOTEL.** *10 Washington St (94607). 510/836-3800; fax 510/830-5695; toll-free 800/729-3638.* 144 rms, 5 story, 27 suites. S, D $175-$195; suites $250-$325; under 16 free; wkend packages. Crib free. Valet parking, in/out $10. TV; cable (premium), VCR. Heated pool. Coffee in rms. Restaurant (see also JACK'S BISTRO). Rm serv 6:30 am-midnight. Bar 10-2 am. Ck-out noon. Meeting rms. Business center. In-rm modem link. Concierge. Exercise equipt; sauna. Bathrm phones, minibars; some fireplaces. Balconies. Many rms with view of San Francisco skyline. 2 boat slips avail. Cr cds: A, C, D, DS, MC, V.

Palm trees

B&B/Small Inn

★★ **GARRATT MANSION.** *900 Union St, Alameda (94501). 510/521-4779; fax 510/521-6796. www.garrattmansion.com.* 7 air-cooled rms, 2 share baths, 3 story. No elvtr. Some rm phones. S $110; D $125; each addl $10-$15; suite $130. Complimentary full bkfst; afternoon refreshments. Restaurant nearby. Ck-out 11 am, ck-in 3 pm. Concierge. Game rm. Microwaves avail. Built in 1893; antiques, stained-glass windows. Totally nonsmoking. Cr cds: A, D, MC, V.

Restaurants

★★★ **BAY WOLF.** *3853 Piedmont Ave (94611). 510/655-6004. www.baywolf.com.* Hrs: 11:30 am-2 pm, 6-9 pm; Sat, Sun from 5:30 pm. Closed hols. Res accepted. No A/C. Mediterranean menu. Bar. A la carte entrees:

lunch $9-$13, dinner $14-$18. Specializes in duck, regional dishes. Street parking. Outdoor dining. Contemporary decor with several dining areas, including front porch. Family-owned. Totally nonsmoking. Cr cds: A, MC, V.

★★ **BUCCI'S.** *6121 Hollis St, Emeryville (94608). 510/547-4725.* Specializes in fresh grilled salmon, tuna, lamb dishes. Hrs: 11:30 am-2:30 pm, 5:30-9:30 pm; Sat from 5:30 pm. Closed Sun. Res accepted. Wine, beer. Lunch $7-$11, dinner $9-$17. Entertainment. Cr cds: MC, V.

D

★★ **CHEF PAUL'S.** *4179 Piedmont Ave (94611). 510/547-2175. www.chefpaul.citysearch.com.* Hrs: 5 pm-midnight. Closed Mon. Res accepted. Eclectic French-Swiss menu. Wine list. A la carte entrees: dinner $8-$14. Complete meal: dinner $29-$36. Specializes in seafood, tasting menu, vegetarian menu. Outdoor dining. Elegant atmosphere. Chef-owned. Cr cds: A, DS, MC, V.

D SC

★ **EL TORITO.** *67 Jack London Sq (94607). 510/835-9260. www.eltorito.com.* Hrs: 11 am-11 pm; Fri, Sat to midnight; Sun 9:30 am-10 pm; Sun brunch to 2 pm. Closed Thanksgiving, Dec 25. Res accepted. Mexican menu. Bar 11 am-11:30 pm, Sun 10 am-midnight. Lunch $6-$9, dinner $7-$13. Sun brunch $10.99. Children's menu. Specializes in tacos, fajitas, chili rellenos. Outdoor dining. Spanish decor. Cr cds: A, D, DS, MC, V.

D SC

★★ **IL PESCATORE.** *57 Jack London Sq (94607). 510/465-2188.* Hrs: 11:30 am-10 pm; Sat from 11 am; Sun 3-9 pm, Sun brunch 10:30 am-3 pm. Closed Jan 1, Thanksgiving, Dec 25. Res accepted. Italian menu. Bar. Lunch $10.25-$14, dinner $10.25-$22. Sat, Sun brunch $10-$17. Specializes in pasta, seafood. Outdoor dining. On waterfront. Cr cds: A, MC, V.

D

★★ **JACK'S BISTRO.** *1 Broadway (94607). 510/444-7171. www.waterfrontplaza.com.* Hrs: 6:30 am-10 pm; Sun brunch 7 am-2:30 pm. Res accepted. Mediterranean menu. Bar 10-2 am. Bkfst, lunch, dinner $8.25-$19.95. Sun brunch $6.50-$12.75. Specializes in pasta, pizza, rotisserie chicken. Own baking. Pianist; musicians Fri, Sat. Valet parking. Outdoor dining. Waterfront views; murals. Totally nonsmoking. Cr cds: A, D, DS, MC, V.

D

★ **QUINN'S LIGHTHOUSE.** *51 Embarcadero Cove (94606). 510/536-2050. www.quinnslighthouse.com.* Hrs: 11:30 am-2 pm, 5:30-9 pm; Fri to 10 pm; Sat 5:30-10 pm; Sun 11:30 am-3 pm, 4:30-9 pm. Closed Jan 1. Res accepted. No A/C. Bar. Lunch $5.95-$13.95, dinner $5.95-$15. Sun brunch $5.95-$11. Children's menu. Specializes in prawn dishes, pasta, steak. Parking. Outdoor dining. In historic Oakland Harbor Lighthouse (1890); nautical decor. Cr cds: MC, V.

D

★★ **SCOTT'S SEAFOOD.** *2 Broadway (94607). 510/444-3456. www.scottsrestaurants.com.* Hrs: 11 am-10 pm; Fri, Sat to 11 pm; Sun to 9 pm; Sun brunch to 3 pm. Closed Dec 25. Res accepted. Bar. Lunch, dinner $12.95-$29. Sun brunch $12.95-$19.95. Specialties: grilled Petrale sole, Norwegian salmon. Pianist. Jazz trio Sun brunch. Valet parking. Patio dining. On estuary; view of harbor, San Francisco. Cr cds: A, C, D, DS, MC, V.

D

★ **SILVER DRAGON.** *835 Webster St (94607). 510/893-3748.* Hrs: 11:30 am-9 pm. Closed Thanksgiving, Dec 25. Cantonese menu. Bar. Lunch $5-$8, dinner $12-$18. Specialties: Peking duck, stuffed crab claws, crispy-skin chicken. Cr cds: A, MC, V.

D

★ **SOIZIC.** *300 Broadway (94607). 510/251-8100. www.soizicbistro.com.* Hrs: 11:30 am-2:30 pm, 5:30-9 pm; Sat from 5:30. Closed Mon; hols. Res accepted. No A/C. Modern French menu. Bar. A la carte entrees: lunch, dinner $9.50-$15. Specializes in fresh fish, seasonal sorbets, ginger custard. Own desserts. Street parking. Bistro-style atmosphere in former warehouse building; eclectic art collection. Totally nonsmoking. Cr cds: A, MC, V.

D

★★★ TRADER VIC'S. *9 Anchor Dr, Emeryville (94608). 510/653-3400.* Hrs: 11:30 am-2:30 pm, 5-9:30 pm; Fr, Sat to 10:30 pm; Sun 4:30-9:30 pm. Closed hols. Res accepted. Bar. A la carte entrees: lunch $11-$17, dinner $15-$25. Specialties: peach blossom duck, fresh seafood, Indonesian rack of lamb. Entertainment. Valet parking. Tropical decor. Bay view. Family-owned. Cr cds: A, D, DS, MC, V.

D

Oceanside

(F-5) *See also Carlsbad, Escondido, San Clemente*

Pop 128,398 **Elev** 47 ft **Area code** 760

Information Chamber of Commerce, Visitor Information Center, 928 N Coast Hwy, 92054; 800/350-7873

Web www.oceansidechamber.com

Camp Pendleton, a US Marine base, borders this city on the north. I-5 goes through the camp property for about 18 miles.

What to See and Do

Antique Gas & Steam Engine Museum. Agricultural museum on 40 acres of rolling farmland, featuring early farming equipment, steam and gas engines. Special shows third and fourth wkends in June and Oct (fee). (Daily; closed Dec 25) 2040 N Santa Fe Ave. 7 mi E via Oceanside Blvd, in Vista. Phone 760/941-1791. ¢¢

California Surf Museum. Learn about the sport and lifestyle of the surfer through various exhibits and presentations. Tours (by appt). (Mon, Thurs-Sun; closed hols) 223 N Coast Hwy. Phone 760/721-6876. **FREE**

Mission San Luis Rey de Francia. (1798). Founded by Father Lasuén, it was named for Louis IX, crusader and ruler of France from 1226 to 1270. It was 18th of the chain. "King of Missions," largest of the 21 early California missions, it has a large collection of Spanish vestments, cloister gardens, Native American cemetery, first pepper tree (1830), and other historic artifacts. Picnicking. Self-guided tours. Museum (daily; closed Jan 1, Thanksgiving, Dec 25). 4050 Mission Ave. 4½ mi E on CA 76 in San Luis Rey. Phone 760/757-3651. ¢¢

Oceanside Harbor and Marina. Mecca for sportfishing, whale watching, boating, and other water-oriented activities. Marina has slips ranging in length from 25 to 51 ft. Transient moorings and limited RV beach camping avail. Seaport Village offers restaurants and gift shops. 1540 Harbor Dr N. Phone 760/435-4000.

Motels/Motor Lodges

★★ BEST WESTERN MARTY'S VALLEY INN. *3240 Mission Ave (92054). 760/757-7700; fax 760/439-3311; toll-free 800/747-3529. www.bestwestern.com.* 111 rms, 2 story. June-mid-Sept: S $70-$75; D $79-$95; each addl $5; suite $125; under 12 free; lower rates rest of yr. Crib $7. TV; cable (premium). Pool. Complimentary continental bkfst. Restaurant adj 11 am-11 pm. Bar to 2 am. Ck-out noon. Meeting rms. Business servs avail. In-rm modem link. Refrigerators, microwaves avail. Cr cds: A, C, D, DS, MC, V.

D SC

★★ BEST WESTERN OCEANSIDE INN. *1680 Oceanside Blvd (92054). 760/722-1821; fax 760/967-8969; toll-free 800/443-9995. www.bestwestern.com.* 80 rms, 2 story. S, D $89; each addl $10; suites $99-$119. Crib free. TV; cable (premium), VCR avail (movies). Heated pool; whirlpool. Complimentary continental bkfst, coffee in rms. Ck-out noon. Guest lndry. Meeting rms. Business servs avail. Valet serv. Sundries. Exercise equipt; saunas. Some bathrm phones; refrigerator in suites. Private patios, balconies. Cr cds: A, C, D, DS, MC, V.

★ OCEANSIDE DAYS INN. *3170 Vista Way (92056). 760/757-2200; fax 760/757-2389; res 800/329-7466.* 44 rms, 2 story. S, D $69-$79; each addl $5; wkly rates. Crib $5. TV; cable (premium). Heated pool. Complimentary continental bkfst. Ck-out 11 am. Tennis. 18-hole golf, greens fee

$72, pro. Refrigerators, microwaves avail. Private patios, balconies. Cr cds: A, C, D, DS, JCB, MC, V.

D

Restaurant

★ **LA PALOMA.** *116 Escondido Ave, Vista (92084). 760/758-7140. www.sandiegoinsider.com.* Hrs: 11 am-10 pm; Sat, Sun from 1 pm; early-bird dinner Sun-Thurs 4-7 pm. Closed Jan 1, Dec 25. Res accepted. Mexican menu. Bar. Lunch $5.95-$9, dinner $7.95-$18.95. Specializes in innovative gourmet Mexican cuisine. Parking. Outdoor dining. Intimate atmosphere and dining. Cr cds: A, DS, MC, V.

D SC

Ojai

(D-3) *See also Oxnard, Santa Barbara, Ventura*

Pop 7,613 **Elev** 746 ft **Area code** 805 **Zip** 93023

Information Ojai Valley Chamber of Commerce & Visitors Center, 150 W Ojai Ave; 805/646-8126

Web www.the-ojai.org/

The Ojai Valley was first farmed by citrus and cattle ranchers after the Civil War. In the 1870s, publicity in Eastern newspapers initiated its popularity as a tourist haven and winter resort. Attracted by its quiet, rural beauty and proximity to urban centers, many artists, writers, and other creative people make their home in the Ojai Valley.

A Ranger District office of the Los Padres National Forest (see SANTA BARBARA) is located here.

What to See and Do

Lake Casitas Recreation Area. Fishing; boating (rentals, trailer rentals). Picnicking, concession. Camping (fee; for res phone 805/649-1122; hookups); trailer storage (fee). Pets on leash only (fee); no firearms. Nearby are beaches, golf courses, and tennis courts. (Daily) 5 mi W on CA 150. Contact 11311 Santa Ana Rd, Ventura 93001. Phone 805/649-2233.

Ojai Center for the Arts. Rotating exhibitions of local artists; live theater productions. (Tues-Sun) 113 S Montgomery. Phone 805/646-0117.

Ojai Valley Museum. Permanent and changing exhibits explore environmental, cultural, and historical factors that shaped the Ojai Valley; research library. (Wed-Sun; closed hols) 130 W Ojai Ave. Phone 805/640-1390. **FREE**

Special Events

Tennis Tournament. Libbey Park. Oldest amateur tennis tournament in the same location in the US (since 1895). Phone 805/646-7241. Late Apr.

Ojai Festivals. Libbey Park. Outdoor concerts. Phone 805/646-2094. Wkend after Memorial Day. Phone 805/646-9455.

Ojai Shakespeare Festival. Libbey Park. Outdoor evening and matinee performances of two Shakespeare plays, with pre-show Madrigal entertainment. Phone 805/646-9455. Aug.

Ojai Studio Artists Tour. Recognized artists open their studios to the public. Phone 805/646-8126. Oct.

Motels/Motor Lodges

★★ **BEST WESTERN CASA.** *1302 E Ojai Ave (93023). 805/646-8175; fax 805/646-8247; res 800/528-1234.* 44 rms, 2 story. Mid-May-mid-Sept: S $75-$120; D $80-$120; each addl $10; under 12 free; lower rates rest of yr. TV; cable, VCR avail (movies $1). Heated pool, whirlpool. Complimentary continental bkfst. Coffee in rms. Restaurant nearby. Ck-out noon. Business servs avail. In-rm modem link. Some refrigerators; microwaves avail. Cr cds: A, C, D, DS, MC, V.

D

★★ **HUMMINGBIRD INN.** *1208 E Ojai Ave (93023). 805/646-4365; fax 805/646-0625; res 800/228-3744. www.hummingbirdinnofojai.com.* 31 rms, 2 story. June-Oct: S $79-$118; D $89-$125; under 12 free; higher rates special events; lower rates rest of yr. Crib free. Pet accepted, some restrictions; $10. TV; cable (premium). Complimentary continental bkfst. Restaurant nearby. Ck-out 11 am. Pool, whirlpool. Refrigerators, microwaves avail. Cr cds: A, DS, MC, V.

Resort

★★★ OJAI VALLEY INN AND SPA. *905 Country Club Blvd (93023). 805/646-5511; fax 805/646-7969; res 800/422-6524.* 209 units, 3 story. S, D $210-$290; suites, cottages $345-$850; family rates. Pet accepted; $25. TV; cable (premium). 3 heated pools; whirlpools, poolside serv. Playground. Supervised children's activities; ages 3-12. Coffee in rms. Restaurant (public by res): 6:30 am-10 pm. Box lunches, snack bar, picnics. Rm serv 24 hrs. Bar 11:30 am-midnight. Ck-out noon, ck-in 4 pm. Meeting rms. Business center. In-rm modem link. Concierge. Sports dir. Lighted tennis, pro. 18-hole golf, greens fee from $80, pro, putting green, driving range. Bicycles. Lawn games. Hiking, horseback riding, mountain biking. Aviary. Children's petting zoo. Soc dir; entertainment. Exercise rm; sauna, steam rm. Refrigerators, minibars; some fireplaces. Many private patios, balconies. On 220 acres. Mountain views. Cr cds: A, C, D, DS, MC, V.

D

Restaurants

★★★ L'AUBERGE. *314 El Paseo St (93023). 805/646-2288. www.tales.com/ca/l'aubergerestaurant.* Hrs: 5:30-9 pm; Sat, Sun brunch 11 am-2:30 pm. Res accepted. Country French, Belgian menu. Beer. Wine list. A la carte entrees: dinner $16.50-$21. Sat, Sun brunch $8.75. Children's menu. Specializes in frogs' legs, sweetbreads, fish. Own desserts. Outdoor dining. In old house; country French decor. Cr cds: A, MC, V.

★★★ RANCH HOUSE. *102 Besant Rd (93023). 805/646-2360. www.theranchhouse.com.* Hrs: dinner sittings 6-8:30 pm; Sun sittings 11 am-7:30 pm; Sun brunch to 2 pm. Closed Mon, Tues; Jan 1, Dec 24, 25. Res accepted. Continental menu. Beer. Wine cellar. A la carte entrees: dinner $18.95-$24.95. Sun brunch $18.95. Children's menu. Specializes in garden dining, grilled fish. Own baking. Outdoor dining. Wine terrace. Bakery. Family-owned. Cr cds: A, C, D, DS, MC, V.

D

Ontario

(E-5) *See also Claremont, Pomona*

Founded 1882 **Pop** 133,179 **Elev** 988 ft **Area code** 909

Information Convention and Visitors Authority, 2000 Convention Center Way, 91764; 909/937-3000 or 800/455-5755

Web www.ontariocvb.org

What to See and Do

California Speedway. Two-mi asphalt track is home to professional auto racing, incl NASCAR Winston Cup Series and PPG CART World Series races. (Dates vary) I-10 W to Cherry Ave, N to Randall Ave entrance.

Industrial tour. Graber Olive House. Tour of sorting, canning, packaging areas. Mini-museum, gourmet food, and gift shop. (Daily; closed hols) 315 E 4th St. Phone 909/983-1761. **FREE**

Museum of History and Art, Ontario. Regional history and fine arts exhibits. (Wed-Sun afternoons; closed hols) 225 S Euclid Ave. Phone 909/983-3198. **FREE**

Ontario Mills. California's largest entertainment and outlet mall; 1.7 million sq ft with over 200 shops, incl an enormous Dave & Buster's with Million Dollar Midway, D & B Speedway, casino, billiards, golf simulator, and dining room. Also here are 30 standard movie theaters (fees); American Wilderness zoo and aquarium (fee), featuring five regions, each with native plants and animals in indoor re-creations of their natural ecosystems. Also adventure simulator ride; large food court. (Daily) 1 Mills Cir. Phone 909/484-8300. **FREE**

Planes of Fame Air Museum. Exotic collection of more than 60 operable historic military aircraft, including Japanese Zero, ME-109G, B-17. Aircraft rides. (Daily; closed Thanksgiving, Dec 25) 5 mi S via Euclid Ave, 7000 Merrill Ave in Chino. Phone 909/597-3722. **¢¢¢**

Prado Regional Park. Fishing; nonpower boat rentals. Horseback riding (rentals; fee), golf, picnicking, camping. (Daily; closed Dec 25) 8 mi S via Euclid Ave; 6 mi S of Pomona Frwy. Phone 909/597-4260. Per vehicle ¢¢

Raging Waters. Huge 50-acre water park with 50 million gallons of water in use. Largest flume ride in US; highest two-person tube ride. Million-gallon wave cove. Separate waterplay area for young kids. (Late Apr-late May, Mid-Sept-mid-Oct, wkends; May-Sept, daily) Phone 909/592-8181 or 909/592-6453. ¢¢¢¢

Motels/Motor Lodges

★★ **BEST WESTERN AIRPORT.** *209 N Vineyard Ave (91764). 909/937-6800; fax 909/937-6815; res 800/528-1234. www.bestwestern.com.* 150 rms, 2 story. S $55-$60; D $60-$70; each addl $5; under 12 free. Crib free. Pet accepted; $10. TV; cable (premium). Heated pool, whirlpool. Complimentary continental bkfst, coffee in rms. Restaurant adj open 24 hrs. Ck-out noon. Coin lndry. Meeting rms. Valet serv. Free airport transportation. Exercise equipt. Some refrigerators; microwaves avail. Cr cds: A, D, DS, MC, V.

★★ **COUNTRYSIDE SUITES.** *204 N Vineyard (91764). 909/937-9700; fax 909/937-2070; res 800/248-4661. www.countrysuites.com.* 107 units, 2 story, 2 suites. S, D $69-$150; suites $150-$250; under 13 free; wkly rates. Crib free. TV; cable (premium), VCR avail (movies). Heated pool, whirlpool. Complimentary full bkfst, coffee in rms. Restaurant adj open 24 hrs. Ck-out noon. Coin lndry. Meeting rms. Business servs avail. Valet serv. Free airport transportation. Exercise equipt. Refrigerators; wet bars, microwaves. Cr cds: A, D, DS, MC, V.

D

★★★ **COUNTRY SUITES.** *1945 E Holt Blvd (91761). 909/390-7778; fax 909/983-4777; res 800/248-4661. www.countrysuites.com.* 167 units, 3 story, 2 suites. S, D $70-$165; each addl $15; suites $150-$250; wkly rates. Crib free. TV; cable (premium). Heated pool, whirlpool. Complimentary full bkfst, coffee in rms. Restaurant 11:30 am-2:30 pm, 4:30-10 pm; Sat, Sun from 4:30 pm. Rm serv from 4:30 pm. Ck-out noon. Meeting rms. Business servs avail. Bellhops. Valet serv. Coin lndry. Free airport transportation. Exercise equipt. Refrigerators, microwaves, wet bars; some in-rm whirlpools. Grills. Cr cds: A, C, D, DS, MC, V.

D

★★ **FAIRFIELD INN.** *3201 Centre Lake Dr (91761). 909/390-9855; fax 909/390-9835; toll-free 800/228-2800. www.marriott.com.* 117 rms, 3 story. S, D $59.64; under 18 free. Crib free. TV; cable (premium). Heated pool. Complimentary continental bkfst. Restaurant adj 11 am-9 pm. Ck-out noon. Meeting rm. Business servs avail. In-rm modem link. Valet serv. Free airport transportation. Cr cds: A, C, D, DS, MC, V.

D SC

★★ **HOLIDAY INN.** *3400 Shelby St (91764). 909/466-9600; fax 909/941-1445; toll-free 800/642-2617. www. holiday-inn.com.* 150 kit. suites, 3 story. S, D $109. Suites $99-$119; 1-bedrm suites $109-$129; each addl $10; under 18 free; wkly rates. Crib free. Pet accepted, some restrictions. TV; cable (premium), VCR avail. Heated pool, whirlpool. Complimentary full bkfst, coffee in rms. Restaurant 6:30-10 am, 11 am-2 pm, 6-10 pm. Bar 4-10 pm. Ck-out noon. Coin lndry. Meeting rms. Business servs avail. Valet serv. Sundries. Gift shop. Free airport transportation. Exercise equipt; sauna. Game rm. Microwaves. Some patios. Grill. Cr cds: A, C, D, DS, JCB, MC, V.

D

★ **ONTARIO AIRPORT COMFORT INN.** *514 N. Vineyard Ave (91764). 909/937-2999; fax 909/937-2978.* 130 rms, 3 story. S, D $55-$65; each addl $5; under 12 free. Crib free. TV; cable (premium). Pool, whirlpool. Complimentary continental bkfst. Restaurant adj open 24 hrs. Ck-out 11 am. Free airport transportation. Health club privileges. Cr cds: A, C, D, DS, MC, V.

D

Hotels

★★★ **DOUBLETREE.** *222 N Vineyard Ave (91764). 909/937-0900; fax 909/937-1999.* 339 rms, 3-4 story. S, D $124-$144; each addl $15; suites $375-$650; under 18 free; wkend

rates. Crib free. TV; cable (premium), VCR avail. Heated pool; whirlpool, poolside serv. Coffee in rms. Restaurants 6 am-11 pm; dining rm 11:30 am-2 pm, 5-10 pm; Sat 5-11 pm; Sun 9 am-2 pm, 5-10 pm. Bars 11-2 am; entertainment. Ck-out 1 pm. Convention facilities. Business servs avail. Bellhops. Valet serv. Gift shop. Free airport transportation. Exercise equipt. Microwaves avail. Balconies, patios. Luxury level. Cr cds: A, C, D, DS, ER, JCB, MC, V.
D SC

★★★ **HILTON AIRPORT.** *700 N Haven (91764). 909/980-0400; fax 909/941-6781; toll-free 800/654-1379. www.hilton.com.* 309 rms, 10 story. S, D $129-$159; suites $265. Crib free. TV; cable (premium). Heated pool; whirlpool, poolside serv. Complimentary coffee in rms. Restaurant 5 am-midnight. Bar 11-1 am. Ck-out noon. Convention facilities. Business servs avail. In-rm modem link. Concierge. Gift shop. Free airport transportation. Exercise equipt. Some balconies. Luxury level. Cr cds: A, C, D, DS, JCB, MC, V.
D SC

★★★ **ONTARIO AIRPORT MARRIOTT.** *2200 E Holt Blvd (91761). 909/975-5000; fax 909/975-5050; res 800/228-9290. www.marriotthotels.com/ontca.* 299 rms, 3 story. S, D $109-$149; suites $250; wkend rates. Crib free. TV; cable (premium). Heated pool, whirlpool, poolside serv. Restaurants open 24 hrs. Bars 11 am-midnight. Ck-out noon. Convention facilities. Business servs avail. In-rm modem link. Concierge. Gift shop. Free airport transportation. Lighted tennis. Exercise rm; sauna, steam rm. Racquetball, basketball courts. Cr cds: A, C, D, DS, ER, JCB, MC, V.
D SC

★★★ **SHERATON ONTARIO AIRPORT HOTEL.** *429 N Vineyard Ave (91764). 909/937-8000; fax 909/937-8028; res 800/325-3535. www.sheraton.com/ontario.* 170 units, 6 story, 3 suites. S, D $79-$119; each addl $10; suites $175; under 12 free. Crib free. TV; cable (premium). Heated pool, whirlpool. Complimentary full bkfst, coffee in rms. Restaurant 5-10 pm. Bar. Ck-out 1 pm. Meeting rms. Business servs avail. In-rm modem link. Free airport transportation. Exercise equipt. Refrigerators; microwaves avail. Cr cds: A, C, D, DS, MC, V.
D SC

Extended Stay

★★ **RESIDENCE INN BY MARRIOTT ONTARIO AIRPORT.** *2025 Convention Center Way (91764). 909/937-6788; fax 909/937-2462; res 800/331-3131.* 200 kit. units, 2 story. S, D $124; Kit. units $145-$165. Pet accepted; $50-$75 and $6/day. TV; cable (premium), VCR avail. Heated pool, whirlpool. Complimentary continental bkfst. Coffee in rms. Restaurant nearby. Ck-out noon. Coin lndry. Meeting rm. Business servs avail. Valet serv. Free airport transportation. Exercise equipt. Health club privileges. Paddle tennis. Refrigerators, microwaves; some fireplaces. Some balconies. Picnic tables, grills. Cr cds: A, D, DS, MC, V.
D SC

Restaurant

★★★ **ROSA'S.** *425 N Vineyard Ave (91764). 909/937-1220. www.rosasitalian.com.* Hrs: 11:30 am-10 pm; Sat from 5 pm; Sun 5-9 pm. Closed hols. Res accepted. Italian menu. Bar. Wine cellar. A la carte entrees: lunch $7-$18, dinner $11.50-$24. Specializes in fresh fish, pasta. Own pasta, desserts. Pianist. Mediterranean villa atmosphere. Cr cds: A, D, MC, V.
D

Orange

See also Anaheim, Santa Ana

Founded 1868 **Pop** 110,658 **Elev** 187 ft **Area code** 714

Information Chamber of Commerce, 439 E Chapman Ave, 92866; 714/538-3581

Web www.orangechamber.org

What to See and Do

Tucker Wildlife Sanctuary. Twelve-acre refuge for native plants and birds, incl several species of hummingbirds (seasonal); observation porch, nature trails, museum displays, picnic areas. (Daily) 29332 Modjeska Canyon Rd. Phone 714/649-2760. **¢**

Motel/Motor Lodge

★★★ COUNTRY INN BY AYRES. *3737 W Chapman Ave (92868). 714/978-9168; fax 714/385-1528; toll-free 888/268-7974. www.countrysuites.com.* 129 rms, 6 story. S, D $89; wkend rates. Crib free. TV; cable (premium). Complimentary full bkfst, coffee in rms. Restaurant 11:30 am-2:30 pm, 5-9 pm. Ck-out noon. Meeting rms. Business servs avail. Bellhops. Valet serv. Sundries. Coin lndry. Free Disneyland transportation. Exercise equipt. Pool, whirlpool. Cr cds: A, D, DS, MC, V.

D

Hotels

★★★ DOUBLETREE HOTEL. *100 The City Dr (92868). 714/634-4500; fax 714/978-2370; toll-free 800/528-0444. www.doubletreehotels.com.* 454 units, 20 story. S, D $190; each addl $10; suites $250-$575; under 18 free. Crib free. Parking $6, valet $8. TV; cable (premium). Heated pool, whirlpool, poolside serv. Coffee in rms. Restaurants 6 am-10 pm. Bar from 4 pm. Ck-out noon. Convention facilities. Business center. Concierge. Free Disneyland transportation. Lighted tennis. Exercise equipt. Bathrm phone, refrigerator in some suites. Cr cds: A, C, D, DS, ER, JCB, MC, V.

D SC

★★★ HILTON SUITES. *400 N State College Blvd (92868). 714/938-1111; fax 714/938-0930; res 714/704-2345. www.anaheimsuites.hilton.com.* 230 suites, 10 story. S $79-$165; D $99-$185. Suites $140-$180; each addl $20; family rates. Crib free. TV; cable (premium), VCR (movies free). Indoor pool, whirlpool. Complimentary full bkfst, coffee in rms. Restaurant 11:30 am-1:30 pm, 5:30-10 pm; wkend hrs vary. Rm serv 5:30-10 pm. Bar 4 pm-midnight. Ck-out noon. Meeting rms. Business center. In-rm modem link. Gift shop. Free Disneyland transportation. Exercise equipt; sauna. Refrigerators, microwaves. Some balconies. 10-story triangular atrium. Cr cds: A, C, D, DS, JCB, MC, V.

D

All Suite

★★ HAWTHORN SUITES. *720 The City Dr S (92668). 714/740-2700; fax 714/971-1692; res 800/527-1133. www.hawthorn.com.* 123 suites, 3 story. Suites $160-$230. Crib free. TV; cable (premium). Heated pool, whirlpool. Complimentary full bkfst, coffee in rms. Ck-out noon. Coin lndry. Meeting rms. Business center. Valet serv. Sundries. Gift shop. Health club privileges. Refrigerators, microwaves, wet bars. Grill. Cr cds: A, D, DS, MC, V.

D

Extended Stay

★★ RESIDENCE INN BY MARRIOTT. *3101 WChapman Ave (92868). 714/978-7700; fax 714/978-6257; res 800/331-3131.* 104 kits, 2 story. S $104; D $114; family, wkly rates. Crib free. Pet accepted, some restrictions; $75. TV; cable (premium), VCR avail. Heated pool, whirlpool. Complimentary continental bkfst, coffee in rms. Restaurant nearby. Ck-out noon. Coin lndry. Meeting rms. Business servs avail. Valet serv. Airport, RR station, bus depot transportation. Free Disneyland transportation. Health club privileges. Basketball, volleyball. Microwaves. Some balconies, fireplaces. Picnic tables, grills. Cr cds: A, C, D, DS, MC, V.

D

Restaurants

★★★ HOBBIT. *2932 E Chapman Ave (92869). 714/997-1972.* One sitting: 7:30 pm; Sun 7 pm. Closed Mon; hols. Res required. Contemporary continental menu. Bar. Wine cellar. Complete meal: 7-course dinner $55. Menu changes wkly. Own baking. Parking. Two dining rms in Spanish-style house; mahogany staircase, antique fireplace. Jacket. Family-owned. Cr cds: MC, V.

D

★★ **LA BRASSERIE.** *202 S Main St (92868). 714/978-6161. www.calendarlive.com/labrasserie.* Hrs: 11:30 am-2 pm, 5-10 pm; Sat from 5 pm. Closed Sun; hols. Res accepted. Continental menu. Bar. Wine list. Lunch $8.95-$13.95, dinner $16.95-$28.95. Specializes in veal, fresh fish. Own desserts. Parking. French country-style decor; many antiques, fireplace. Totally nonsmoking. Cr cds: A, MC, V.
D

★★ **YEN CHING.** *574 S Glassell St (92666). 714/997-3300.* Hrs: 11:30 am-2:30 pm, 4:30-9:30 pm; Fri to 10:30 pm; Sat noon-10:30 pm; Sun noon-9:30 pm. Res accepted. Chinese menu. Wine, beer. Lunch $5.99-$7.80, dinner $8.75-$14.30. Complete meals: dinner $14.95. Specializes in Mandarin dishes. Parking. Totally nonsmoking. Cr cds: A, DS, MC, V.
D

Oroville

(D-4) *See also Chico, Marysville*

Settled 1850 **Pop** 11,960 **Elev** 174 ft **Area code** 530 **Zip** 95965

Information Chamber of Commerce, 1789 Montgomery St; 530/538-2542 or 800/655-GOLD

Web www.oroville-ca.com

Water-oriented recreation, tourism, and hunting predominate in Oroville—where the lure of gold once held sway and "too many gambling houses to count" catered to the wants of miners. Miners' Alley is a historic remnant of those days when Oroville was the second-largest city in California.

Oroville, in addition to being the portal to the Sierra's great watershed, the Feather River, also has orange and olive groves, which thrive in the area's thermal belt. Fruit and olive processing, as well as lumber, contribute much to the community's economy.

A Ranger District office of the Plumas National Forest (see QUINCY) is located in Oroville.

What to See and Do

Chinese Temple. (1863). The "Temple Beside the River," largest of the authentic temples in California, has a tapestry hall and display rm. It is all that remains of a Chinatown that was second in size only to San Francisco's. (Daily; closed mid-Dec-Jan) 1500 Broderick St, at Elma. Phone 530/538-2496. ¢

Feather Falls. Sixth-highest in US. 3½-mi trail leads to a 640-ft drop of the Fall River into the canyon just above the Middle Fork of the Feather River in Feather Falls Scenic Area. Allow 4-6 hrs for round trip and carry drinking water. 25 mi NE in Plumas National Forest (see QUINCY). Phone 530/538-2200.

Feather River Fish Hatchery. Raises salmon and steelhead. Underwater viewing chamber (Sept-Jan); hatchery (daily). 5 Table Mountain Blvd, on N bank of Feather River. Phone 530/538-2222. **FREE**

Historic Judge C. F. Lott House. (1856). Authentically restored; period furnishings. Picnic area. (Mon, Fri, Sun afternoons; closed mid-Dec-Jan) 1067 Montgomery St, in Lott-Sank Park. Phone 530/538-2497. ¢

Lake Oroville State Recreation Area. In several sections. **Forebay-South.** Powerboats allowed (fee for boat launch); no camping. (Daily; fee) 3 mi W, CA 70 Grand Ave exit. **Forebay-North.** Swimming, bathhouse; no powerboats. (Daily; fees) 1 mi W, CA 70 Garden Dr exit. **Loafer Creek Campground.** Swimming; camping (fee). (Daily, Apr-Oct) All three recreation areas have fishing, boat ramps; hiking trails, picnicking. Standard fees. 9 mi E via CA 162. Two marinas: **Lime Saddle** and **Bidwell Canyon**. Also camping facilities at Bidwell Canyon (campground all yr; full RV hookup; fees). **Spillway.** Wayside camping; launch ramp. (Daily; fees) 7 mi E via CA 162, N via Canyon Dr, 3 mi W across dam. Res for both campgrounds avail through MISTIX. Phone 800/444-7275.

Oroville Dam & Reservoir. This 770-ft-high earth-filled dam impounds Lake Oroville with a 167-mi shoreline. The dam is a vital part of the $3.2-billion California State Water Project. 7 mi E on CA 162, then 3 mi

N on Canyon Dr. Phone 530/538-2200. **FREE**

Visitor Center & Overlook. Exhibits, slide shows, films; observation tower. (Daily; closed Jan 1, Thanksgiving, Dec 25) 9 mi E on CA 162, 2½ mi N on Kelly Ridge Rd. Phone 530/538-2219. **FREE**

Special Events

Old Time Fiddlers' Contest. Northern California Regional Championship. Phone 530/589-4844. Usually late Apr.

Feather Fiesta. Parades. Car show. Pancake bkfst. Early May. Phone 530/534-7690.

Bidwell Bar Days. Gold panning, pioneer arts and crafts. May. Phone 530/538-2219.

Motels/Motor Lodges

★★ BEST WESTERN GRAND MANOR INN. *1470 Feather River Blvd (95965). 530/533-9673; fax 530/533-5862; res 800/626-1900. www.bestwestern.com.* 54 rms, 3 story. S, D $64-$84; suites $87-$125; under 12 free. Crib $6. Pet accepted, some restrictions. TV; cable. Pool, whirlpool. Complimentary continental bkfst, coffee in rms. Restaurant nearby. Ck-out 11 am. Coin lndry. Meeting rm. Business servs avail. In-rm modem link. Exercise equipt; sauna. Refrigerators. Many balconies. Cr cds: A, D, DS, MC, V.

★ VILLA MOTEL. *1527 Feather River Blvd (95965). 530/533-3930; fax 530/533-1200.* 20 rms. S $50; D $55-$60; each addl $5. Crib free. TV; cable. Pool. Coffee in rms. Restaurant nearby. Ck-out 11 am. Cr cds: A, C, D, MC, V.

B&B/Small Inn

★★★ LAKE OROVILLE BED AND BREAKFAST. *240 Sunday Dr, Berry Creek (95916). 530/589-0700; fax 530/589-4761; res 800/589-4761. www.now2000.com/lakeorovile.* 6 rms. S, D $75-$135; each addl $10; hols (2-3 day min). Pet accepted, some restrictions. TV avail; VCR avail (movies). Complimentary full bkfst. Restaurant nearby. Ck-out 11:30 am, ck-in 3-6 pm. Business servs avail. Luggage handling. 18-hole golf privileges. Bicycles avail. Game rm. Rec rm. Many in-rm whirlpools; microwaves avail. Some balconies. Picnic tables, grills. Lake view. Hiking trails. On 40 acres. Totally nonsmoking. Cr cds: A, D, MC, V.

Restaurant

★★ DEPOT. *2191 High St (95965). 530/534-9101. www.oroville-city.com/depot.* Hrs: 11 am-2:30 pm, 4-9:30 pm; Fri to 10 pm; Sat 4-10 pm; Sun 3:30-9 pm; early-bird dinner Mon-Sun 4-5:30 pm. Closed Dec 25. Bar 11-2 am. Lunch $4.75-$8.50, dinner from $5.95. Children's menu. Specialties: chicken Cordon Bleu, prime rib. Salad bar. Outdoor dining. In 1908 Western Pacific railroad depot. Family-owned. Cr cds: A, DS, MC, V.

Oxnard

(E-3) *See also Ventura*

Pop 142,216 **Elev** 52 ft **Area code** 805 **Zip** 93030

Information Tourism Bureau, 200 W Seventh St; 805/385-7545 or 800/2-OXNARD

Web www.oxnardtourism.com

What to See and Do

Carnegie Art Museum. Regional and international visual and fine arts. (Thurs-Sun) 424 South C St. Phone 805/385-8157. **¢¢**

CEC/Seabee Museum. Enter on Ventura Rd at Sunkist St, S of Channel Islands Blvd. Memorabilia of the US Navy Seabees, who are the construction battalions of the Navy; uniforms, Antarctic display, South Pacific artifacts, underwater diving display, outrigger canoes, WWII dioramas, weapons, flags. (Daily; closed hols) Naval Construction Battalion Center, Channel Islands Blvd, and Ventura Rd, SW off US 101 in Port Hueneme. Phone 805/982-5165. **FREE**

Channel Islands Harbor. Public recreation incl boating, fishing, swimming, beaches; parks, barbecue and picnic facilities, playgrounds, tennis courts; charter boat and bicycle rentals. Also here is

Fisherman's Wharf. A New England-style village with specialty shops, restaurants, and transient docking for pleasure boaters. Phone 800/269-6273.

Channel Islands National Park. (see). HQ at 1901 Spinnaker Dr, Ventura 93001.

Gull Wings Children's Museum. (Tues-Sun) 418 W 4th St. Phone 805/483-3005. ¢¢

Ventura County Maritime Museum. (Daily) 2731 S Victoria Ave. Phone 805/984-6260. **Donation**

Special Events

Point Mugu Airshow. Pacific Coast Hwy (CA 1) or I-101 (Ventura Fwy) W to Las Posas exit. Military aircraft demonstration, parachutists, and displays; civilian/foreign aerobatics. Phone 805/989-8786. Late Apr.

California Strawberry Festival. Strawberry Meadows at College Park. Waiters' race, wine tasting, entertainment, crafts, strawberry foods. Phone 888/288-9242. Third wkend May.

Motels/Motor Lodges

★★ CASA SIRENA HOTEL AND MARINA. *3605 Peninsula Rd (93035). 805/985-6311; fax 805/985-4329; res 800/447-3529. www.casasirenahotel.com.* 273 rms, 2-3 story. Some A/C. S, D $120-$149; each addl $10; suites $179-$275; kit. units $179; package plans. Crib free. Pet accepted. TV; cable. Heated pool, whirlpool. Playground. Coffee in rms. Restaurant 6:30 am-10 pm. Rm serv to 9:30 pm. Bar 10-1:30 am; Sun to 11:30 pm. Ck-out noon. Convention facilities. Business servs avail. In-rm modem link. Valet serv. Sundries. Barber, beauty shop. Free airport, RR station, bus depot transportation. Lighted tennis. Putting green. Exercise equipt; sauna. Game rm. Refrigerators. Private patios, balconies. Marina. View of harbor. Park adj. Cr cds: A, C, D, DS, MC, V.

D SC

★★★ COUNTRY INN AND SUITES. *350 E Hueneme Rd, Port Hueneme (93041). 805/986-5353; fax 805/986-4399.* 135 kit. units, 3 story. S, D $128; each addl $10; suites $138-$168; under 12 free. Crib avail. Pet accepted. TV; cable, VCR (movies $4). Pool, whirlpool. Complimentary full bkfst. Ck-out noon. Coin lndry. Business servs avail. In-rm modem link. Refrigerators. Near ocean. Nautical decor. Cr cds: A, C, D, DS, ER, JCB, MC, V.

D

Hotels

★★★ EMBASSY SUITES. *2101 Mandalay Beach Rd (93035). 805/984-2500; fax 805/984-8339; res 800/362-2779.www.embassy-suites/mandalaybeach.com.* 250 suites, 3 story. S, D $159-$750; each addl $15; under 18 free. TV; cable (premium). Pool, whirlpool, poolside serv. Complimentary full bkfst. Coffee in rms. Restaurant 11:30 am-2:30 pm, 5-10 pm. Bar 11-2 am. Ck-out noon. Guest lndry. Convention facilities. Business servs avail. In-rm modem link. Garage parking. Gift shop. Free airport transportation. Exercise equipt. Lighted tennis. Bicycle rentals. Refrigerators. Some private patios, balconies. 8 acres; on beach. Cr cds: A, C, D, DS, MC, V.

D SC

★★★ RADISSON HOTEL OXNARD. *600 E Esplanade Dr (93030). 805/485-9666; fax 805/485-2061.* 160 rms, 6 story. S, D $109; each addl $10; suites $129-$169; under 18 free. Crib free. Pet accepted; $25. TV; cable (premium). Pool; whirlpool. Restaurant 6:30 am-10 pm. Bar 11-2 am; Fri, Sat to midnight; entertainment. Ck-out noon. Meeting rms. Business servs avail. In-rm modem link. Valet serv. Shopping arcade. Barber, beauty shop. Free airport transportation. Health club privileges. Refrigerators. Some balconies. Cr cds: A, D, DS, MC, V.

D

Extended Stay

★★ RESIDENCE INN BY MARRIOTT RIVERSIDE. *2101 W Vineyard Ave (93030). 805/278-2200; fax 805/983-4470; res 800/331-3131.* 252 kit. suites, 1-2 story. S $109; D $139; under 17 free; golf, tennis packages. Crib free. TV; cable (premium). 2 heated pools, whirlpools, poolside serv. Complimentary bkfst buffet, coffee in rms. Ck-out noon. Coin lndry. Convention facilities. Business servs avail. In-rm modem link. Free airport, RR station, bus depot transportation. Lighted tennis, pro. 18-hole golf, pro, greens fee, driving range. Exercise equipt. Some wood-burning fireplaces. Balconies. Picnic tables, grills. Located on 15 acres; gazebo. Cr cds: A, C, D, DS, MC, V.
D

Restaurant

★ MONEY PANCHO. *155 E 7th St (93030). 805/483-1411.* Hrs: 8 am-10 pm. Res accepted. Mexican menu. Bkfst $4.45-$7.95, lunch $3.95-$7.95, dinner $7.95-$13.95. Children's menu. Specialties: sea and earth, marina rey, fajitas chicken rey. Guitar Mon, Fri, Sat. Parking. Mexican-style atmosphere and decor. Totally nonsmoking. Cr cds: A, D, DS, MC, V.
D SC

Pacific Beach (San Diego) (F-5)

Area code 858 **Zip** 92109

This community is an integral part of San Diego, but is regarded by many as a separate entity.

Motels/Motor Lodges

★★ OCEAN PARK INN. *710 Grand Ave. 858/483-5858; fax 858/274-0823; toll-free 800/231-7735. www.oceanparkinn.com.* 73 rms, 3 story. May-Sept: S $134-$184; D $124-$204; each addl $10; suites $179-$219; under 12 free; lower rates rest of yr. Crib free. TV; cable (premium). Heated pool; whirlpool. Complimentary continental bkfst. Restaurant adj 7 am-9 pm. Ck-out 11 am. Business servs avail. Valet serv. Refrigerators; microwave in suites. Balconies. On beach. Cr cds: A, C, D, DS, MC, V.
D

★★★ PACIFIC TERRACE INN. *610 Diamond St (92109). 858/581-3500; fax 858/274-3341; toll-free 800/344-3370. www.pacificterrace.com.* 73 rms, 3 story, 42 kits. S, D $195-$255; each addl $10; suites, kit. units $255-$560. Crib free. TV; cable (premium). Heated pool; whirlpool. Complimentary continental bkfst, coffee in rms. Restaurant nearby. Rm serv 6:30 am-11 pm. Ck-out 11 am. Meeting rm. Business servs avail. In-rm modem link. Bellhops. Covered parking. Health club privileges. Refrigerators; microwaves avail. Bathrm phone in suites. Private patios, balconies. On beach. Cr cds: A, D, DS, MC, V.
D

Hotel

★★★ CATAMARAN RESORT HOTEL. *3999 Mission Blvd (92109). 858/488-1081; fax 858/539-8601; res 800/288-0770.* 313 rms, 2-12 story, 120 kits. S, D $150-$275; each addl $15; suites $315-$400. Crib free. TV; cable (premium). Supervised children's activities (June-Labor Day). Heated pool; whirlpool, poolside serv. Complimentary coffee in rms. Restaurant 6:30 am-10 pm; Fri, Sat to 11 pm. Bar 11-2 am; entertainment. Ck-out noon. Meeting rms. Business center. In-rm modem link. Concierge. Exercise equipt. Sailboats. Beach activities. Many refrigerators. Private patios, balconies. Opp ocean. On Mission Bay. Cr cds: A, C, D, DS, MC, V.
D SC

Restaurants

★★ CHATEAU ORLEANS. *926 Turquoise, Pacific Beach (92109). 858/488-6744. www.chateauorleans.com.* Hrs: 6-10 pm. Closed Sun; hols. Res accepted. Cajun menu. Wine, beer. Dinner $10.95-$22. Children's menu. Specializes in Creole and Cajun dishes. Blues/jazz Thurs-Sat evenings. Intimate, casual dining. Cr cds: A, D, DS, MC, V.
D

★ **GREEN FLASH.** *701 Thomas Ave, Pacific Beach (92109). 858/270-7715.* Hrs: 8 am-10 pm; Sat, Sun from 7:30 am; Sun brunch to 3 pm; early-bird dinner Sun-Thurs exc hols 4:30-6:30 pm. Bar to 2 am. Bkfst $2.50-$9.95, lunch $5.95-$12.95, dinner $8.95-$39.95. Sun brunch $2.50-$12.95. Children's menu. Specializes in fresh seafood, prime rib. Outdoor dining. Intimate dining with view of beach and boardwalk. Family-owned. Cr cds: A, C, D, ER, MC, V.
D

★★ **LAMONT ST GRILL.** *4445 Lamont St, Pacific Beach (92109). 858/270-3060.* Hrs: 5:30-10 pm; Fri, Sat to 11 pm; Sun 5-10 pm. Closed Jan 1, July 4, Dec 24, 25. Res accepted. Bar. Dinner $9.95-$18.95. Specializes in beef, pork, fresh fish. Outdoor dining. Converted bungalow with intimate dining; garden courtyard. Totally nonsmoking. Cr cds: A, DS, MC, V.
D

Pacific Grove

(B-1) *See also Carmel, Carmel Valley, Monterey, Pebble Beach*

Pop 16,117 **Elev** 0-300 ft
Area code 831 **Zip** 93950

Information Chamber of Commerce, Central and Forest Aves, PO Box 167; 831/373-3304 or 800/656-6650

Web www.pacificgrove.org

What to See and Do

Asilomar State Beach and Conference Center. A 105-acre beach-front conference center, historical landmark, and park. Recreational facilities, meeting rms, accommodations. (Daily) 800 Asilomar Blvd. Phone 831/372-8016.

Monarch Grove Sanctuary. Grove of Monterey pines where Monarch butterflies typically migrate each yr to spend the winter. Monarchs are typically visible Oct-Mar; best chance to see them flying around is when temperatures warm up by mid-morning (otherwise, they cluster in the trees). (Daily) Enter from Ridge Rd off

Monarch butterfly enjoying a flower

Lighthouse Ave. Phone 831/375-0982. **FREE**

Ocean View Blvd. Five-mile scenic road along rocky, flower-bordered shoreline.

Pacific Grove Museum of Natural History. Natural history of Monterey County, incl birds, shells, mammals, Native American exhibits; native plants garden. (Tues-Sun; closed hols) (See SPECIAL EVENTS) Central and Forest Aves. Phone 831/648-3116. **FREE**

Point Piños Lighthouse. (1855) Oldest continuously operating lighthouse on Pacific Coast. (Jan-late Nov, Thurs-Sun afternoons) Asilomar Ave at Lighthouse Ave. Phone 831/648-3116.

Special Events

Good Old Days. Parade, fair, entertainment, quilt show, contests. Apr. Phone 831/373-3304.

Wildflower Show. Pacific Grove Museum of Natural History. Mid-Apr.

Feast of Lanterns. Lantern-lit processions on land and sea, barbecue; pageant. Late July. Phone 831/372-7625.

Butterfly Parade. Celebrates arrival of thousands of Monarch butterflies. Oct. Phone 831/646-6540.

Marching Band Festival. Parade, field show; competition of statewide high school championship bands. Early Nov. Phone 831/646-6595.

Christmas at the Inns. Tour of old Victorian inns decorated for the holidays. Usually second Tues Dec.

Motels/Motor Lodges

★★ **BEST WESTERN.** *1111 Lighthouse Ave (93950). 831/646-8885; fax 831/375-5567; res 800/922-9060.* 49 units, 2 story, 5 suites. S, D $70-$200; each addl $10-$20; suites $140-$550; under 18 free; higher rates: hols, special events. Crib $10. TV; cable (premium). Heated pool, whirlpool. Sauna. Complimentary continental bkfst, coffee in rms. Restaurant nearby. Ck-out noon. Meeting rms. Business servs avail. Refrigerator in suites; microwaves avail. Cr cds: A, C, D, DS, ER, JCB, MC, V.
D SC

★ **DAYS INN AND SUITES.** *660 Dennett Ave (93950). 831/373-8777; fax 831/373-2698; toll-free 800/329-7466.* 30 rms, 3 story, 11 kits. No A/C. May-Nov: S, D $135-$225; each addl $10; children under 17 free; wkends (2-day min); higher rates special events; lower rates rest of yr. Crib free. TV; cable (premium). Complimentary continental bkfst, coffee in rms. Ck-out 11 am. Microwaves. Cr cds: A, C, D, DS, MC, V.
D SC

★★ **DEER HAVEN INN.** *740 Crocker Ave (93950). 831/373-1114; fax 408/655-5048; toll-free 800/525-3373.* 27 rms, 2 story. No A/C. July-Oct: S, D $79-$139; each addl $10; 2-day min wkends; higher rates special events; lower rates rest of yr. Crib $10. TV; cable. Complimentary continental bkfst, coffee in rms. Restaurant nearby. Ck-out 11 am. Coin lndry. Business servs avail. Cr cds: A, DS, MC, V.
SC

★ **THE LARCHWOOD-DEER HAVEN INN.** *740 Crocker Ave (93950). 831/373-1114; fax 408/655-5048; toll-free 800/525-3373.* 22 kit. units, 2 story. No A/C. July-Oct: S, D $89-$229; under 6 free; lower rates rest of yr. Crib $10. TV; cable. Whirlpool; sauna. Complimentary continental bkfst. Restaurant nearby. Ck-out 11 am. Coin lndry. Totally nonsmoking. Cr cds: A, DS, MC, V.
SC

B&Bs/Small Inns

★★★ **CENTRELLA INN.** *612 Central Ave (93750). 831/372-3372; fax 831/372-2036; res 800/233-3372. www.centrellainn.com.* 26 rms, 11 with shower only, 3 story, 9 suites; 5 guest houses. No A/C. No rm phones. June-Oct: S, D $179-$209; each addl $15; suites $189-$199; guest houses $209-$229; under 13 free; wkends, hols (2-day min); lower rates rest of yr. Children over 12 yrs only in main house. TV; cable, VCR avail (movies). Complimentary continental bkfst, afternoon refreshments. Restaurant nearby. Ck-out noon, ck-in 3 pm. Business servs avail. Concierge serv. Street parking. Refrigerator in suites; wet bar, fireplace in guest house. Cr cds: A, DS, MC, V.
SC

★★ **THE GATEHOUSE INN.** *225 Central Ave (93950). 831/649-8436; fax 831/648-8044; res 800/753-1881. www.sueandlewinns.com.* 9 rms, 2 story. No A/C. S, D $153. Complimentary full bkfst, afternoon refreshments. Ck-out noon, ck-in 2 pm. Business servs avail. Victorian inn (1884) with view of Monterey Bay. Totally nonsmoking. Cr cds: A, D, DS, MC, V.
D

★★★ **GOSBY HOUSE INN.** *643 Lighthouse Ave (93950). 831/375-1287; fax 831/655-9621; toll-free 800/527-8828. www.foursisters.com.* 22 rms, 20 with bath. No A/C. S, D $90-$160; each addl $15. Complimentary bkfst buffet; evening refreshments. Picnic lunches. Ck-out noon, ck-in 2 pm. Business servs avail. Some fireplaces. 2-story Queen Anne/Victorian mansion built in 1887 by cobbler from Nova Scotia. Wine cellar. Cr cds: A, D, JCB, MC, V.

★★★ **GREEN GABLES INN.** *104 5th St (93950). 831/375-2095; fax 831/375-5437; toll-free 800/722-1774. www.foursisters.com.* 11 rms, 7 with bath, 2 story, 6 rms in main building, 5 rms in carriage house. No A/C. S, D $120-$240. TV in some rms; VCR avail. Complimentary full bkfst; afternoon refreshments. Ck-out noon, ck-in 2 pm. Business servs avail. In-rm whirlpools avail. Victorian mansion (1888); on Monterey Bay. Cr cds: A, MC, V.

D

★★★ **THE INN AT 213 SEVENTEEN MILE DRIVE.** *213 17 Mile Dr (93950). 831/642-9514; fax 831/642-9546; res 800/526-5666. www.innat213-17miledr.com.* 14 rms, 2 story. May-Oct: S $240; lower rates rest of yr. Parking lot. TV; cable. Complimentary full bkfst, newspaper. Restaurant nearby. Ck-out noon, ck-in 3 pm. Beach access. Hiking trail. Cr cds: A, MC, V.

D

★★★ **THE MARTINE INN.** *255 Ocean View Blvd (93950). 831/373-3388; fax 831/373-3896; res 800/852-5588. www.martineinn.com.* 23 rms, 3 story. S, D $150-$295; each addl $35. Complimentary full bkfst; afternoon refreshments. Ck-out 11 am, ck-in 2 pm. Meeting rms. Business servs avail. Game rm. Refrigerators; some fireplaces. Victorian, Mediterranean-style home built 1899. Antiques. On Monterey Bay. Cr cds: A, DS, MC, V.

D

★★ **PACIFIC GROVE INN.** *581 Pine Ave (93950). 831/375-2825; toll-free 800/732-2825.* 16 rms, in 2 houses, 3 story. June-Oct: S, D $99.50-$169.50; lower rates rest of yr. TV; cable. Complimentary continental bkfst. Ck-out noon, ck-in 3 pm. Refrigerators, fireplaces; microwaves avail. Restored Queen Anne-style house (1904). Totally nonsmoking. Cr cds: A, C, D, DS, MC, V.

D SC

★★ **ROSEDALE INN.** *775 Asilomar Blvd (93950). 831/655-1000; fax 831/655-0691; toll-free 800/822-5606. www.rosedaleinn.com.* 16 rms, 3 kit. units. No A/C. June-Sept: S, D $115-$135; under 18 free; lower rates rest of yr. Crib free. TV; cable (premium), VCR (movies $2). Complimentary continental bkfst, coffee in rms. Restaurant nearby. Ck-out 11 am. In-rm whirlpools, refrigerators, microwaves, fireplaces. Cr cds: A, D, DS, MC, V.

D SC

★★★ **SEVEN GABLES INN.** *555 Ocean View Blvd (93950). 831/372-4341; res 831/372-4341. www.pginns.com.* 10 rms, 3 story. No A/C. No rm phones. S $155-$275; D $165-$375; wkends, hols (2-3-day min). Children over 12 yrs only. Complimentary full bkfst; afternoon refreshments. Restaurant nearby. Ck-out noon, ck-in 2:30-10 pm. At edge of Monterey Bay overlooking Lover's Point beach. Cr cds: MC, V.

D

Restaurants

★★ **CYPRESS GROVE.** *663 Lighthouse Ave (93950). 831/375-1743.* Hrs: 11 am-3 pm, 5-10 pm; Sat, Sun brunch 11 am-3 pm. Closed Mon. Res accepted. French, Californian menu. Lunch $8.95-$11.95, dinner $14.95-$24.95. Specializes in sauteed foie gras, roasted quail with morels, ahi tuna tartar. Own pastries. French provincial decor; fireplace. Totally nonsmoking. Cr cds: A, MC, V.

★★★ **FANDANGO.** *223 17th St (93950). 831/372-3456. www.fandangorestaurant.com.* Hrs: 11 am-3:30 pm, 5-9:30 pm; Sun 10 am-2:30 pm, 5-9:30 pm. Res accepted. No A/C. Mediterranean menu. Bar. Lunch $8.25-$14.75, dinner $11.75-$28.75. Specializes in fresh seafood, paella, rack of lamb. Outdoor dining. Casual southern European decor; fireplaces. Cr cds: A, C, D, DS, MC, V.

D

★ **FISHWIFE.** *1996 1/2 Sunset Dr (93950). 831/375-7107. www.fishwife.com.* Hrs: 11 am-10 pm; Sun from 10 am; Sun brunch to 4 pm. Closed Thanksgiving, Dec 25. Res accepted. Caribbean menu. Wine, beer. Lunch $5.95-$9.25, dinner $8.25-$13.25. Sun brunch $5.95-$8.95. Children's menu. Specialties: sea garden salad with Cajun spices, prawns Belize. Caribbean decor. Cr cds: A, DS, MC, V.

★★★ **OLD BATH HOUSE.** *620 Ocean View Blvd (93950). 831/375-5195.* Hrs: 5-10:30 pm; Sat, Sun from 4 pm. Res accepted. No A/C. Continental menu. Bar 4 pm-midnight. Dinner $16.50-$28.50. Specializes in unique seafood, game, beef dishes, fresh Dungeness crab. Own pastries. In 1930s Victorian-style building overlooking Lover's Point. Cr cds: A, C, D, DS, MC, V.

★★ **PASSION FISH.** *701 Lighthouse Ave (93950). 831/655-3311. www.passionfish.net.* Hrs: 5-9 pm; Fri, Sat to 10 pm. Closed Tues; Thanksgiving, Dec 25. Res accepted. Californian menu. Wine, beer. A la carte entrees: dinner $12-$19. Specializes in seafood, slow-roasted meats, vegetarian dishes. Tropical, Southwestern atmosphere. Cr cds: A, D, DS, MC, V.
D

★ **PEPPERS MEXICALI CAFE.** *170 Forest Ave (93950). 831/373-6892.* Hrs: 11:30 am-10 pm; Fri, Sat to 10:30 pm; Sun 4-10 pm. Closed Tues; hols. Res accepted. Mexican, Latin American menu. Beer, wine. Lunch, dinner $5.75-$10.95. Specializes in fresh seafood, fajitas. Own tamales, chips, salsa. Southwestern decor; Latin American artifacts. Cr cds: A, C, D, DS, MC, V.

★★ **TASTE CAFE AND BISTRO.** *1199 Forest Ave (93950). 831/655-0324. www.tastecafebistro.com.* Hrs: 5-9 pm; Fri, Sat to 10 pm. Closed Mon; Easter, July 4, Thanksgiving; also mid-Dec-early Jan. Res accepted. Dinner $15-$25. Children's menu. Specializes in fish, lamb, chicken. Contemporary bistro decor. Totally nonsmoking. Cr cds: A, MC, V.
D

★ **TINNERY AT THE BEACH.** *631 Ocean View Blvd (93950). 831/646-1040.* Hrs: 8 am-midnight; Sat, Sun to 1 am. No A/C. Bar. Bkfst $5.50-$9.99, lunch $6.50-$12.99, dinner $10.99-$23.99. Children's menu. Specializes in seafood, pizza, steak, ribs. Parking. Outdoor dining. Entertainment Wed-Sat. Ocean view. Cr cds: A, D, DS, MC, V.
D

★ **VIVO'S.** *1180 Forest Ave (93950). 831/375-3070.* Hrs: 5-10 pm. Closed Thanksgiving, Dec 25. Res accepted. Italian menu. Wine, beer. Dinner $10.50-$14.95. Children's menu. Specialties: seafood pasta, lasagna. Totally nonsmoking. Cr cds: A, D, DS, MC, V.
D

Palmdale

(D-4) *See also Lancaster*

Pop 68,842 **Elev** 2,659 ft
Area code 661 **Zip** 93550

Information Chamber of Commerce, 38260 10th St E; 661/273-3232

Web www.cityofpalmdale.org

The Angeles National Forest is west and south of town (see PASADENA).

Motel/Motor Lodge

★★ **RAMADA INN.** *300 W Palmdale Blvd (93551). 661/273-1200; fax 661/947-9593; toll-free 800/272-6232.* 135 rms, 4 story. S, D $53-$75; each addl $5; under 13 free. Crib free. Pet accepted, some restrictions; $50. TV; cable (premium), VCR avail. Pool, whirlpool. Complimentary full bkfst. Restaurant 6 am-9 pm; wkends from 7 am. Bar 5 pm-1 am; Fri, Sat to 1:30 am; closed Sun. Ck-out noon. Coin lndry. Meeting rms. Business center. Valet serv. Exercise equipt. Refrigerators avail. Cr cds: A, C, D, DS, MC, V.
D SC

Palm Desert (E-6)

Pop 23,252 **Elev** 243 ft **Area code** 760 **Zip** 92260

Information Chamber of Commerce, 73710 Fred Waring Dr Suite 114; 760/346-6111 or 800/873-2428

What to See and Do

The Living Desert. This 1,200-acre wildlife and botanical park contains interpretive exhibits from the world's deserts. Animals incl mountain lions, zebras, bighorn sheep, coyotes, cheetas, reptiles, and birds. Native American exhibits; picnic areas, nature trails; gift shop; cafe; nursery. Special programs on wkends. (Daily; closed Dec 25) 47-900 S Portola Ave. Phone 760/346-5694.

Palms to Pines Highway. Scenic CA 74 goes S and W toward Idyllwild and Hemet (see both). 47-900 S Portola Ave.

Special Event

Bob Hope Chrysler Classic. Golf pros and celebrities play at four country clubs at Bermuda Dunes, La Quinta, Palm Desert, and Indian Wells. Phone 760/346-8184. Mid-Jan.

Motels/Motor Lodges

★★ **FAIRFIELD INN.** *72-322 US Hwy 111 (92260). 760/341-9100; fax 760/773-3515; toll-free 800/633-8300.* 112 rms, 3 story. Mid-Jan-May: S, D $69-$124; each addl $7; suites $130; under 18 free; lower rates rest of yr. Crib free. TV; cable (premium). Heated pool, whirlpool. Complimentary continental bkfst. Restaurant nearby. Ck-out 11 am. Meeting rm. Business servs avail. Free airport transportation. Putting green. Some refrigerators. Private patios, balconies. Cr cds: A, C, D, DS, MC, V.

D SC

★★ **HOLIDAY INN EXPRESS.** *74-675 US 111 (92260). 760/340-4303; fax 760/340-3723; res 800/465-4329.* 129 rms, 3 story. Jan-May: S, D $109; suites $95-$209; under 18 free; lower rates rest of yr. Crib free. TV; cable (premium), VCR avail (movies). Heated pool, whirlpool. Coffee in rms. Complimentary California bkfst. Restaurant adj. Ck-out noon. Coin Indry. Business servs avail. In-rm modem link. Valet serv. Tennis. Exercise equipt. Health club privileges. Lawn games. Some refrigerators. Balconies. Picnic tables. Cr cds: A, C, D, DS, MC, V.

D SC

★★ **INTERNATIONAL LODGE.** *74380 El Camino (96620). 760/346-6161; fax 760/568-0563; toll-free 800/874-9338.* 50 kit. units, 50 with shower only, 2 story. Jan-Mar: S, D $110; under 3 free; wkly, monthly rates; hols (2-day min); lower rates rest of yr. TV; cable, some VCRs. 2 heated pools, whirlpool. Complimentary coffee in rms. Restaurant nearby. Ck-out noon. Coin Indry. Business servs avail. Balconies. Cr cds: A, DS, MC, V.

★★ **VACATION INN HOTEL AND SUITE.** *74-715 US Hwy 111 (92260). 760/340-4441; fax 760/773-9413; toll-free 800/231-8675. www.vacation-inn.com.* 130 rms, 3 story. Jan-May: S, D $99-$116; each addl $10; under 17 free; lower rates rest of yr. Crib free. TV; cable (premium). Heated pool, whirlpool. Continental bkfst, coffee in rms. Restaurant nearby. Ck-out noon. Meeting rm. Business servs avail. Free airport transportation. Tennis. Putting green. Refrigerators; microwaves avail. Private patios, balconies. Cr cds: A, C, D, DS, JCB, MC, V.

D

Hotel

★ **THE INN AT DEEP CANYON.** *74-470 Abronia Trl (92260). 760/346-8061; fax 760/341-9120; res 800/253-0004. www.inn-adc.com.* 32 rms, 2 story, 15 kit. units. Mid-Dec-May: S $109-$139; D $119-$149; kit. units $109-$129; wkly rates, golf plans; lower rates rest of yr. Crib free. Pet accepted, some restrictions; $20 deposit. TV; cable. Complimentary continental bkfst, coffee in rms. Restaurant nearby. Ck-out noon. Business servs avail. Golf privileges. Pool. Refrigerators. Cr cds: A, DS, MC, V.

D

Resorts

★★★★ **DESERT SPRINGS MARRIOTT RESORT & SPA.** *74855 Country Club Dr (92260). 760/341-2211; fax 760/341-1872; toll-free 800/331-3112. www.desertspringsresort.com.* This enormous business hotel and spa complex boasts over 50,000 square feet of meeting space, 13 restaurants, tennis, golf, workout facilities, and much more. All of the guest rooms are comfortable, and there is the added bonus of having a hopping night club on the premises. 884 rms, 8 story. Late Dec-Memorial Day: S, D $205-$498; suites $600-$2,000; golf, tennis, spa plans; lower rates rest of yr. Crib free. Garage, valet parking (fee). TV; cable (premium). 5 heated pools, whirlpools, poolside serv. Supervised children's activities; ages 4-12. Dining rms 6:30 am-10 pm (see also TUSCANY). Box lunches, snack bar, picnics. Bar 11-2 am. Ck-out noon, ck-in 4 pm. Convention facilities. Business center. In-rm modem link. Concierge. Shopping arcade. José Eber Salon. Sports dir. 20 hard tennis courts, 7 lighted, 3 clay, 2 grass. 36-hole golf, greens fee $145, pro, putting course, putting green, driving range. Boats. Lawn games. Act dir; entertainment. Exercise rm; spa. Minibars; microwaves avail. Private patios, balconies. Cr cds: A, C, D, DS, JCB, MC, V.

D

HYATT GRAND CHAMPIONS RESORT. *(Unrated due to renovations.) 44-600 Indian Wells Ln, Indian Wells (92210). 760/341-1000; fax 760/568-2236. www.grandchampions.hyatt.com.* Located at the base of the imposing San Jacinto mountains, the Hyatt Grand Champions offers something for everyone. There are five heated pools, tennis, and golf, not to mention shopping nearby. Guest rooms are all split-level suites with marble bathrooms. 318 rms, 5 story, 19 villas (1-2 bedrm). Jan-May: S, D $154-$430; each addl $25; villas $810-$1,020; under 18 free; golf, tennis plans; lower rates rest of yr. Crib free. Valet parking (fee). TV; cable (premium), VCR avail. 4 pools, whirlpool, wading pool, poolside serv. Supervised children's activities; ages 3-12. Complimentary coffee in rms. Dining rm 6:30 am-10 pm. Box lunches, snack bar, picnics. Rm serv 6-2 am. Bar 11-1 am. Ck-out 1 pm, ck-in 4 pm. Convention facilities. Business center. In-rm modem link. Beauty shop. Sports dir. 12 tennis courts, incl 2 clay, 2 grass, 8 hard surface, pro, pro shop. 36-hole golf, greens fee $130-$180, pro, putting green, driving range, pro shop. Bicycles. Lawn games. Entertainment. Exercise rm; sauna, steam rm. Spa. Some refrigerators, minibars, fireplaces. Private patios, balconies. Butler serv in villas 6 am-11 pm. Luxury level. Cr cds: A, C, D, DS, ER, JCB, MC, V.

D SC

★★★ INDIAN WELLS RESORT HOTEL. *76-661 Hwy 111, Indian Wells (92210). 760/345-6466; fax 760/772-5083; toll-free 800/248-3220. www.indianwellsresort.com.* 155 rms, 3 story. Mid-Jan-Apr: S $79-$289; D $89-$299; suites $390-$430; under 18 free; golf plans; wkend, long-stay rates; lower rates rest of yr. Crib avail. TV; VCR avail (movies). Heated pool, whirlpool, poolside serv. Restaurant 6:30 am-2 pm, 5-10 pm; wkends to 11 pm. Box lunches. Bar 10:30 am-midnight; entertainment wkends. Ck-out noon, ck-in 3 pm. Gift shop. Grocery 1 mi, coin lndry 3 mi. Bellhops. Valet serv. Concierge. Meeting rms. Business servs avail. In-rm modem link. Airport transportation. Tennis. 27-hole golf privileges, greens fee $175, putting green, driving range. Bicycles. Exercise equipt; bicycles, treadmill. Health club privileges. Massage. Minibars. Balconies. Cr cds: A, D, DS, MC, V.

D

★★★ RENAISSANCE ESMERALDA RESORT. *44-400 Indian Wells Ln, Indian Wells (92210). 760/773-4444; fax 760/773-9250; res 800/468-3571. www.renaissancehotels.com.* 560 units, 7 story. Jan-May: S, D $119-$320; each addl $25; suites $600-$2,500; under 18 free; packege plans; lower rates rest of yr. Crib free. Pet accepted, some restrictions. TV; cable (premium). 2 pools, whirlpool, wading pool, poolside serv. Supervised children's activities; ages 3-12. Dining rms 6:30 am-10 pm (see also SIROCCO). Rm serv 6 am-1 am. Bar noon-2 am; entertainment. Ck-out noon, ck-in 3 pm. Coin lndry. Meeting rms. Business center. In-rm modem link. Bellhops. Valet serv. Concierge. Gift shops. Airport transportation. Sports dir. Lighted tennis, pro. 36-hole golf, greens fee $100-$110, pro, putting green, driving range. Tennis and golf clinics; equipt rentals. Private beach. Hiking. Lawn games. Game rm. Exercise rm; sauna, steam rm. Massage. Bathrm phones, minibars; some wet bars. Some suites with woodburning fireplace. Balconies. Cr cds: A, C, D, DS, JCB, MC, V.

D

★★★ SHADOW MOUNTAIN RESORT. *45-750 San Luis Rey (92260). 760/346-6123; fax 760/346-6518; toll-free 800/472-3713. www.shadow-mountain.com.* 125 units, 1-2 story. Mid-Feb-mid-Apr, maj hols: S, D $122-$218; each addl $15; condos and villas $240-$520; under 18 free;

lower rates rest of yr. Crib $15. TV; cable, VCR avail (movies $4). 4 heated pools, whirlpools, poolside serv. Supervised children's activities (wkends Dec-May), ages 5-12. Ck-out 11 am, ck-in 3 pm. Coin lndry. Meeting rms. Business center. In-rm modem link. Valet serv. Concierge. 16 tennis courts, 6 lighted, pro, pro shop. 18-hole golf privileges. Exercise equipt; sauna. Massage. Lawn games. Bicycle rentals. Private patios, balconies. Home of the Desert Tennis Academy. Cr cds: A, D, MC, V.

B&B/Small Inn

★★★ **TRES PALMAS BED AND BREAKFAST.** *73-135 Tumbleweed Ln (92260). 760/773-9858; fax 760/776-9159; toll-free 800/770-9858. www.innformation.com/ca/trespalmas.* 4 rms. No rm phones. Mid-Oct-mid-June: S, D $100-$150; each addl $20; wkly rates; wkends, hols (2-day min); lower rates rest of yr. Children over 10 yrs only. TV; cable. Pool. Complimentary continental bkfst. Restaurant nearby. Ck-out 11 am, ck-in 3-8 pm. Southwestern decor. Totally nonsmoking. Cr cds: A, MC, V.

All Suite

★★★ **EMBASSY SUITES.** *74-700 US Hwy 111 (92260). 760/340-6600; fax 760/340-9519; toll-free 800/362-2779. www.embassy-suites.com.* 198 suites, 3 story. Jan-May: S, D $189-$249; each addl $15; exec suites $259-$289; under 12 free; lower rates rest of yr. Crib free. TV; cable (premium), VCR avail (movies). Heated pool, whirlpool, poolside serv. Complimentary full bkfst. Coffee in rms. Restaurant 11:30 am-2:30 pm, 5-10 pm. Bar to 2 am; entertainment. Ck-out noon. Meeting rms. Business servs avail. In-rm modem link. Exercise equipt. Health club privileges. Lighted tennis. Putting green. Gift shop. Refrigerators; microwaves avail. Some balconies. Courtyard. Cr cds: A, C, D, DS, MC, V.

D SC

Restaurants

★★ **CEDAR CREEK INN.** *73-445 El Paseo (92260). 760/340-1236.* Hrs: 11 am-10 pm. Closed Dec 25. Bar. Lunch $7.95-$11.95, dinner $11.95-$22.95. Specializes in fresh fish, prime rib, steak. Own soups. Outdoor dining. Extensive dessert menu. Cr cds: A, MC, V.

D SC

★★ **CUISTOT.** *73-111 El Paseo (92260). 760/340-1000.* Hrs: 11:30 am-2:30 pm, 6-10 pm. Closed Mon, hols, also Aug. Res accepted. French California menu. Bar. Wine cellar. A la carte entrees: lunch $8.75-$18.95, dinner $17.95-$28.75. Specializes in veal chop, rack of lamb, fresh fish. Cr cds: A, D, MC, V.

D

★★★ **HAMILTON'S.** *44-600 Indian Wells Ln, Indian Wells (92210). 760/340-4499.* Mediterranean cuisine. Specialties: lamp chops, lobster, steak. Hrs: Tues-Sat 6-10 pm. Bar to 2 am. Closed Sun, Mon. Prices: Dinner $18-$32. Exotic, Casablanca-like ambience. Outdoor seating. View of mountains. Fireplaces. Cr cds: A, MC, V.

D

★★ **JILLIAN'S.** *74-155 El Paseo (92262). 760/776-8242. www.desertdiningguide.com/jillians.html.* Hrs: 6 pm-close. Closed Jan 1, Dec 25; also mid-June-Sept. Res required. Bar. Wine cellar. Dinner $17-$31. Specializes in rack of lamb, salmon in parchment, pasta. Pianist, vocalist. Valet parking. Outdoor dining in courtyard. Semi-formal decor in 4 dining areas. Cr cds: A, C, D, DS, MC, V.

D

★★ **KAISER GRILLE.** *74-225 CA 111 (92260). 760/779-1988. www.kaisergrille.com.* Hrs: 5-9:30 pm; early-bird dinner 5-6 pm. Closed hols. Res accepted. Bar. A la carte entrees: dinner $8.95-$19.50. Specialties: hazelnut salmon, blackened prime rib, pasta. Valet parking. Outdoor dining. Open kitchen. Cr cds: A, D, DS, MC, V.

D

★ **LA QUINTA CLIFFHOUSE.** *78-250 CA 111, La Quinta (92260). 760/360-5991.* Hrs: 11:30 am-2 pm,

5-9 pm; Fri, Sat to 9:30 pm; Sun brunch (seasonal) 10 am-2 pm. Closed Dec 25, July 4. Res accepted. Bar. Lunch $5.95-$11.95, dinner $12.95-$19.95. Children's menu. Specializes in fresh seafood, steak, pasta. Valet parking. Outdoor dining. Situated on a hillside. 3 separate dining areas, 2 with valley view. Southwestern decor, western artifacts, memorabilia. Cr cds: A, D, DS, MC, V.

D

★★ **LE DONNE CUCINA ITALIANA.** *72-624 El Paseo (92260). 760/773-9441.* Hrs: 5-9:30 pm. Closed Sun; Jan 1, Dec 25. Res accepted. Italian menu. Wine. A la carte entrees: dinner $8.50-$15.95. Children's menu. Specialties: veal marsala, linguine with mussels and clams, fettuccine with lobster tail. Own baking. Outdoor dining. Italian decor; murals. Totally nonsmoking. Cr cds: A, DS, MC, V.

D

★★★ **LE PAON.** *45640 CA 74 (92260). 760/568-3651. www.desert concierge.com.* Hrs: 6-10 pm; wkends to 11 pm. Closed Thanksgiving. Res accepted. French, continental menu. Bar to 2 am. Wine cellar. A la carte entrees: dinner $16-$35. Specializes in veal, poultry, seafood. Pianist, vocalist. Valet parking. Outdoor dining. Elegant dining; rose garden. Cr cds: A, D, MC, V.

D

★ **LE SAINT GERMAIN.** *74985 US 111, Indian Wells (92210). 760/773-6511.* Hrs: lunch 11:30 am-2:30 pm, dinner 5:30 pm-10:00 pm. Res preferred. French menu. Bar. Wine cellar. Dinner $18-$32. Specializes in seafood, lamb, veal. Pianist. Valet parking. Oil painting of Paris. Cr cds: A, C, D, DS, ER, MC, V.

D

★★ **LG'S PRIME STEAKHOUSE.** *74-225 Hwy 111 (92260). 760/779-9799. www.lgsprimesteakhouse.com.* Hrs: from 5:30 pm. Res accepted. Bar. A la carte entrees: dinner $18.95-$45.95. Specializes in 6 varieties of steak, fresh fish, chicken. Valet parking. Pueblo-style structure with 4 separate dining areas; Southwestern decor, artifacts. Cr cds: A, D, DS, MC, V.

D

★ **NEST.** *75-188 Hwy 111, Indian Wells (92210). 760/346-2314.* Hrs: 5-10:30 pm. Closed hols. Continental menu. Bar to 12:30 am. Dinner $9.50-$21.95. Specializes in fresh fish, pasta. Entertainment. Parking. Newspaper menu. Bistro atmosphere, Parisian decor. Cr cds: A, C, D, DS, ER, MC, V.

D

★★ **PALOMINO.** *73-101 Hwy 111 (92260). 760/773-9091.* Hrs: 5-10 pm; Fri, Sat to 11 pm. Closed July 4, Dec 25. Res accepted. Mediterranean menu. Bar. Wine list. A la carte entrees: dinner $7.95-$24.95. Children's menu. Specialties: grilled salmon, spit-roasted garlic chicken, oven-roasted garlic prawns. Valet parking. Outdoor dining. Cr cds: A, C, D, DS, MC, V.

D

★ **PASTA ITALIA.** *44-491 Town Ctr Way (92260). 760/341-1422.* Hrs: 11:30 am-2:30 pm, 5-10 pm; Fri, Sat to 10:30 pm; Sun 5-10 pm. Res accepted. Italian menu. Bar. Lunch $5.95-$8.95, dinner $6.95-$15.95. Specializes in pasta, non-cholesterol dishes, tiramisu. Own desserts. Entertainment. Parking. Outdoor dining. Old World trattoria atmosphere. Family-owned. Cr cds: A, MC, V.

D

★★★ **RISTORANTE MAMMA GINA.** *73-705 El Paseo (92260). 760/568-9898.* Hrs: 11:30 am-2 pm, 5:15-10 pm; Fri, Sat to 10:30 pm; Sun from 5:15 pm. Closed Easter, Thanksgiving, Dec 25. Res accepted. Northern Italian menu. Bar. A la carte entrees: lunch $6.90-$13.90, dinner $12.90-$26.90. Specializes in pasta, veal. Valet parking. Contemporary and Italian decor. Cr cds: A, D, V.

D

★★★ **RUTH'S CHRIS STEAK HOUSE.** *74040 CA 111 (92260). 760/779-1998. www.ruthschris.com.* Steakhouse menu. Specializes in swordfish, salmon, Maine lobster. Hrs: 5-10 pm; Sat, Sun 4:30-10 pm. Res accepted. Wine list. Dinner $22.95-$30. Entertainment. Cr cds: A, C, D, DS, MC, V.

D

★★ **SIROCCO.** *44-400 Indian Wells Ln (92260). 760/773-4444. www.*

renaissancehotels.com. Hrs: 11:30 am-2:30 pm, 6-10 pm; Sat, Sun from 6 pm. Closed June-Sept. Res accepted. Mediterranean cuisine. Bar. Wine cellar. A la carte entrees: lunch $8.95-$16.95, dinner $12-$36. Specialties: shellfish cioppino, sauteed Maine lobster. Own baking. Valet parking. Classical Mediterranean decor. Two display wine rooms at entry. Overlooks golf course. Cr cds: A, C, D, DS, MC, V.

D

★★★ **TUSCANY.** *74855 Country Club Dr (92260). 760/341-2211.* Northern Italian cuisine. Hrs: Sun-Thurs 5:30-10 pm, Fri-Sat to 11pm. Dinner $19-$36. Res reqd. Children's menu. Outdoor dining by request. Bar. Wine cellar (dine in/wine tasting). Valet. Cr cds: A, D, DS, MC, V.

D

Palm Springs (E-6)

Founded 1876 **Pop** 40,181 **Elev** 466 ft **Area code** 760

Information Palm Springs Desert Resort Convention and Visitors Bureau, 69-930 CA 111, Suite 201, Rancho Mirage, 92270; 760/770-9000 or 800/967-3763

Web www.desert-resorts.com

Discovered in 1774 by a Spanish explorer, this site was dubbed Agua Caliente (hot water). One hundred years later it was the location of a stagecoach stop and a drowsy, one-store railroad town. Today, after a second hundred years, Palm Springs is known as "America's premier desert resort." Originally the domain of the Cahuilla, the city has been laid out in a checkerboard pattern, with nearly every other square mile still owned by the tribe.

What to See and Do

Indian Canyons. The remains of the ancient Cahuilla people incl rock art, mortars ground into the bedrock, pictographs, and shelters built atop high cliff walls. Hiking trails throughout the canyons which are also home to bighorn sheep and wild ponies. Rangers give interpretive walks. (Daily) Phone 707/327-6555. ¢¢¢

Moorten's Botanical Garden. Approx 3,000 varieties of desert plants; nature trails. World's first "cactarium" contains several hundred species of cactus and desert plants from around the world. Guide maps to desert wildflowers. (Mon, Tues, Thurs-Sun; closed hols) 1701 S Palm Canyon Dr. Phone 760/327-6555. ¢¢

Oasis Waterpark. This 22-acre water park has 13 water slides, inner tube ride, wave pool, and beach sand volleyball courts. (Mar-Labor Day, daily; early Sept-late Oct, wkends) 5 mi S off I-10, at 1500 Gene Autry Trail. Phone 760/327-0499. ¢¢¢¢¢ Also here is

Uprising Rock Climbing Center. The only outdoor rock-climbing gym in the US. Offers training and climbing for all ages. Night climbing. (Daily) 1500 S Gene Autry Trail. Phone 760/320-6630. ¢¢¢¢¢

Palm Canyon. Approx 3,000 native palm trees line a stream bed. Magnificent views from the canyon floor or from points above the canyon. Picnic tables. (Daily) 6½ mi S on S Palm Canyon Dr, in the Palm Springs Indian Canyons. Phone 760/325-5673. ¢¢¢

Palm Springs Aerial Tramway. World's longest double-reversible, single-span aerial tramway. Two 80-passenger cars make 2½-mi trip ascending to 8,516-ft elevation on Mt San Jacinto. Picnicking, camping in summer; cafeteria at summit. (Daily) 2 mi N on CA 111, then 4 mi W on Tramway Rd. Phone 760/325-1449. ¢¢¢¢¢

Palm Springs Air Museum. Vintage, WWI aircrafts on display. Also period photographs and video documentaries. (Daily) Phone 760/778-6262. ¢¢¢

Palm Springs Desert Museum. Natural science and art exhibits; performing arts; features art of the American West, contemporary art and Native American basketry, film retrospectives. (Tues-Sun; closed Jan 1, Thanksgiving, Dec 25) Free admission first Fri each month. 101 Museum Dr. Phone 760/325-0189. ¢¢¢

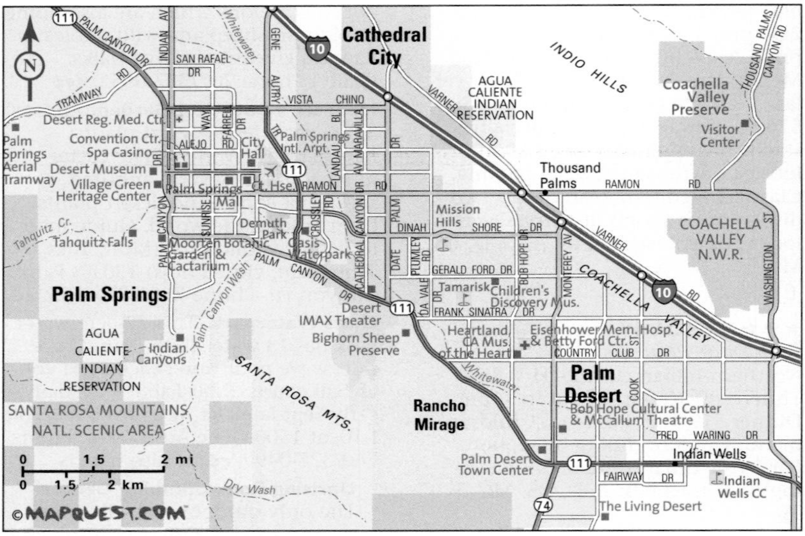

Tahquitz Creek Palm Springs Golf Resort. There are 87 other courses within a 15-mi radius of the city, making this area the "Winter Golf Capital of the World." (Daily) 1885 Golf Club Dr, 3 mi SE on CA 111. Phone 760/328-1005 or 760/328-1956. ¢¢¢¢¢

Village Green Heritage Center. Consists of two 19th-century houses exhibiting artifacts from early Palm Springs. **McCallum Adobe** (ca 1885) is the oldest building in city and houses extensive collection of photographs, paintings, clothes, tools, books, and Native American ware. **The Cornelia White House** (ca 1890) was constructed of rail ties from the defunct Palmdale Railway and is furnished with authentic antiques. (Mid-Oct-May, Wed-Sun; rest of yr, by appt; closed hols) 221 S Palm Canyon Dr. Phone 760/323-8297. ¢

Motels/Motor Lodges

★★ **BEST WESTERN INN.** *1633 S Palm Canyon Dr (92264). 760/325-9177; fax 760/325-9177; toll-free 800/222-4678. www.innatpalmsprings.com.* 72 rms, 3 story. Late Dec-mid-June: S, D $98-$149; each addl $10; under 12 free; higher rates: hols, wkends; lower rates rest of yr. Crib $10. TV; cable. Heated pool, whirlpool. Complimentary continental bkfst. Restaurant nearby. Ck-out noon. Business servs avail. In-rm modem link. Health club privileges. Refrigerators; some microwaves. Cr cds: A, C, D, DS, ER, JCB, MC, V.

★★ **BEST WESTERN LAS BRISAS.** *222 S Indian Canyon Dr (92262). 760/325-4372; fax 760/320-1371; res 800/528-1234.* 90 rms, 3 story. Jan-May: S, D $85-$159; each addl $10; suites $99-$169; under 17 free; lower rates rest of yr. Crib free. TV; cable. Pool, whirlpool, poolside serv. Complimentary full bkfst. Coffee in rms. Restaurant nearby. Bar noon-midnight. Ck-out noon. Coin lndry. Business servs avail. Health club privileges. Refrigerators; microwaves avail. Cr cds: A, C, D, DS, MC, V.

★ **CHANDLER INN.** *1530 N Indian Canyon Dr (92262). 760/320-8949; fax 760/320-8949.* 21 rms, 2 story, 5 kit. units. Nov-May: S, D $79-$98; kit. units $98; wkly rates; golf plans; wkends, hols (2-, 3-day min). Pet accepted, some restrictions; $20 deposit. TV; cable, VCR avail (movies). Complimentary continental bkfst. Restaurant nearby. Ck-out 11 am. Business servs avail. Golf privileges. Pool; whirlpool. Refrigerators. Cr cds: A, C, D, JCB, MC, V.

★★ **THE CHASE HOTEL AT PALM SPRINGS.** *200 W Arenas Rd (92262). 760/320-8866; fax 760/323-1501; toll-*

free 877/532-4273. www.chasehotel palmsprings.com. 24 kit. units, 16 with shower only, 1-2 story. Mid-Dec-early June: S, D $75-$125; each addl $15; wkends, hols (2-day min); higher rates: hols, special events; lower rates rest of yr. TV. Complimentary continental bkfst. Restaurant adj 7 am-10 pm. Ck-out noon. Business servs avail. Bellhops. Concierge. Tennis privileges. Pool. Lawn games. Refrigerators; many microwaves. Some balconies. Cr cds: A, C, D, MC, V.

D

★★ **COMFORT SUITE.** *69-151 E Palm Canyon Dr, Cathedral City (92234). 760/324-5939; fax 760/324-3034; toll-free 800/329-7466. www.soramanagement.com.* 94 kit. suites, 3 story. Jan-May: kit. suites $95-$159; under 16 free; higher rates wkends; lower rates rest of yr. Crib free. Pet accepted. TV; cable (premium). Heated pool, whirlpool. Complimentary continental bkfst. Restaurant opp open 24 hrs. Ck-out noon. Coin lndry. Meeting rms. Business servs avail. Valet serv. Free airport transportation. Golf privileges. Cr cds: A, C, D, DS, JCB, MC, V.

D SC

★★ **COURTYARD BY MARRIOTT.** *1300 Tahquitz Canyon Way (92262). 760/322-6100; fax 760/322-6091; res 800/321-2211.* 149 rms, 3 story. Mid-Dec-May: S, D $149; suites $169; under 18 free; lower rates rest of yr. Crib free. TV; cable (premium). Heated pool. Complimentary coffee in rms. Restaurant 6:30-10:30 am. Bar 4-11 pm. Ck-out noon. Coin lndry. Meeting rms. Business servs avail. In-rm modem link. Valet serv. Free airport transportation. Exercise equipt. Refrigerators, microwaves avail. Balconies. Cr cds: A, D, DS, MC, V.

D

★★ **EL RANCHO LODGE.** *1330 E Palm Canyon Dr (92264). 760/327-1339.* 19 rms, 5 kit. suites. Oct-May: S, D $61-$80; kit. suites $131; lower rates rest of yr. TV; cable. Heated pool, whirlpool. Complimentary continental bkfst. Restaurant opp open 24 hrs. Ck-out noon. Coin lndry. Refrigerators; many microwaves. Some private patios. Cr cds: A, DS, MC, V.

★★ **HAMPTON INN.** *2000 N Palm Canyon Dr (92262). 760/320-0555; fax 760/320-2261; res 800/436-7866.* 96 rms, 2 story. Jan-May: S, D $79-$99; under 18 free; higher rates: special events, hols, wkends; lower rates rest of yr. Crib free. TV; cable (premium). Heated pool, whirlpool. Complimentary continental bkfst. Restaurant nearby. Ck-out noon. Meeting rms. Business servs avail. In-rm modem link. Valet serv. Health club privileges. Some refrigerators; microwaves avail. Spanish-style architecture. Cr cds: A, C, D, DS, MC, V.

D

★ **HOWARD JOHNSON RESORT.** *701 E Palm Canyon Dr (92264). 760/320-2700; fax 760/320-1591; res 800/446-4656.* 205 rms, 2 story. Mid-Dec-May: S $65; D $70; higher rates: Easter, Memorial Day, Labor Day; lower rates rest of yr. Crib free. TV; cable. Heated pool, whirlpool. Restaurant open 24 hrs. Bar 10 am-midnight. Ck-out noon. Coin lndry. Business servs avail. Cr cds: A, C, D, DS, MC, V.

★★★ **LA SIESTA VILLAS.** *247 W Stevens rd (92262). 760/325-2269; fax 760/778-6533. www.adpark.com/lasiestavillas.* 10 villas (1-2-bedrm). Mid-Dec-May: villas $125-$225 (2-day min); wkly, monthly rates; lower rates rest of yr. Adults only. TV; cable, VCR. Heated pool, whirlpool. Restaurant nearby. Ck-out noon. Business servs avail. Concierge. Covered parking. Fireplaces. Private patios. Tropical setting. Cr cds: A, MC, V.

SC

★★ **L'HORIZON GARDEN HOTEL.** *1050 E Palm Canyon Dr (92264). 760/323-1858; fax 760/327-2933; res 800/377-7855.* 22 rms, 19 with shower only, 7 kit. units. Mid-Dec-early July: S, D $115; kit. units $140; monthly rates; wkends (2-day min); lower rates rest of yr. TV; cable, VCR avail. Complimentary continental bkfst. Restaurant opp open 24 hrs. Ck-out noon. Business servs avail. Tennis privileges. Golf privileges.

Pool, whirlpool. Picnic tables, grills. Totally nonsmoking. Cr cds: A, D, DS, MC, V.

★ **MOTEL 6.** *660 S Palm Canyon Dr (92264). 760/327-4200; fax 760/320-9827; toll-free 800/466-8356.* 149 rms, shower only, 3 story. Sept-mid-Apr: S $34.99; D $40.99; each addl $3; under 17 free. Crib free. Pet accepted, some restrictions. TV; cable (premium). Heated pool. Restaurant nearby. Ck-out noon. Coin lndry. Business servs avail. Cr cds: A, C, D, DS, MC, V.

D SC

★★ **PLACE IN THE SUN.** *754 E San Lorenzo Rd (87123). 760/325-0254; fax 760/327-9303; toll-free 800/779-2254.* 16 kit. units, 3 with shower only, 11 suites. Mid-Dec-May: S, D $59-$79; each addl $12; suites $99-$149; higher rates hols (2-day min); lower rates rest of yr. Crib $10. Pet accepted, some restrictions; $10. TV; cable. Heated pool. Restaurant nearby. Ck-out noon. Coin lndry. Meeting rms. Free airport transportation. Health club privileges. Lawn games. Refrigerators, microwaves. Cr cds: A, MC, V.

SC

★★ **QUALITY INN.** *1269 E Palm Canyon Dr (92264). 760/323-2775; fax 760/416-1014; toll-free 800/228-5050. www.qualityinn.com.* 145 rms, 2 story, 8 suites. Late Dec-May: S, D $65-$105; suites $95-$155; under 18 free; lower rates rest of yr. Crib avail. TV; cable. Heated pool, wading pool, whirlpool. Complimentary coffee in rms. Restaurant adj open 24 hrs. Ck-out noon. Coin lndry. Meeting rm. Business servs avail. In-rm modem link. Free airport transportation. Many refrigerators. Grill. Cr cds: A, C, D, DS, ER, JCB, MC, V.

D SC

★★ **SHILO INN.** *1875 N Palm Canyon Dr (92262). 760/320-7676; fax 760/320-9543; toll-free 800/222-2244. www.shiloinns.com.* 124 rms, 2 story. Jan-May: S, D $85-$159; each addl $12; kit. units $140-$155; under 12 free; wkly, monthly rates; lower rates rest of yr. Crib free. TV; cable, VCR avail (movies). Heated pools, whirlpool. Complimentary continental bkfst. Coffee in rms. Ck-out noon. Coin lndry. Meeting rm. Business servs avail. Valet serv. Free airport transportation. Exercise equipt; sauna, steam rm. Health club privileges. Bathrm phones, refrigerators; microwaves avail. Private patios, balconies. Cr cds: A, C, D, DS, MC, V.

D SC

★ **SUPER 8 LODGE.** *1900 N Palm Canyon Dr (92262). 760/322-3757; fax 760/323-5290; res 800/800-8000. www.innworks.com.* 61 rms, 2 story. Late Dec-May: S $68; D $73; each addl $5; suites $90-$110; under 12 free; lower rates rest of yr. Crib $4. Pet accepted; $10. TV; cable. Heated pool, whirlpool. Complimentary continental bkfst. Restaurant nearby. Ck-out 11 am. Coin lndry. Business servs avail. Refrigerators. Cr cds: A, D, DS, MC, V.

★ **TRAVELODGE.** *333 E Palm Canyon Dr (92264). 760/327-1211; fax 760/320-4672; res 800/578-7878. www.ids2.com/tl.* 157 rms, 2 story. Jan-mid-June: S, D $55-$79; each addl $10; higher rates: special events, hols, wkends; lower rates rest of yr. Crib free. TV; cable (premium). Heated pools, whirlpool. Complimentary coffee in rms. Restaurants nearby. Ck-out noon. Coin lndry. Business servs avail. Lawn games. Many refrigerators; microwaves avail. Private patios, balconies. Cr cds: A, C, D, DS, ER, JCB, MC, V.

D SC

★★ **VAGABOND INN.** *1699 S Palm Canyon Dr (92264). 760/325-7211; fax 760/322-9269; toll-free 800/522-1555.* 120 rms, 3 story. Jan-May: S, D $39-$99; higher rates: hols (2-day min), date festival, golf classics; lower rates rest of yr. Crib $6. TV. Heated pool, whirlpool. Sauna. Complimentary coffee in rms. Restaurant nearby. Ck-out noon. Business servs avail. Refrigerators avail. Cr cds: A, C, D, DS, ER, MC, V.

SC

Hotels

★★★ **HYATT REGENCY SUITES PALM SPRINGS.** *285 N Palm Canyon Dr (92262). 760/322-9000; fax 760/322-6009; res 800/223-1234. www.palmsprings.hyatt.com.* 192 suites, 6 story. Jan-Apr: suites $205-

$425; under 18 free; mid-wk rates; lower rates rest of yr. Crib free. TV; cable (premium), VCR avail (movies). Pool, whirlpool, poolside serv. Restaurants 7 am-10 pm; Fri-Sun to 11 pm. Bar 11-1 am; entertainment Fri, Sat. Ck-out noon. Meeting rms. Business servs avail. Concierge. Valet parking. Airport transportation. Tennis privileges. Golf privileges. Exercise equipt. Massage. Bathrm phones, refrigerators, wet bars; microwaves avail. Private patios, balconies. Cr cds: A, C, D, DS, ER, JCB, MC, V.

D

★★ **RAMADA RESORT INN.** *1800 E Palm Canyon Dr (92264). 760/323-1711; fax 760/327-6941; toll-free 800/245-6904. www.ramadapalmsprings.com.* 254 rms, 3 story. Feb-May: S, D $59-$109; each addl $15; suites $125-$200; under 18 free; higher rates: wkends, hols; lower rates rest of yr. Crib free. Pet accepted. TV. Heated pool, whirlpools, poolside serv. Coffee in rms. Restaurant 7 am-10 pm. Bar 11 am-midnight; entertainment wkends. Ck-out noon. Coin lndry. Meeting rms. In-rm modem link. Gift shop. Free airport transportation. Tennis privileges. Golf privileges. Exercise equipt; sauna. Refrigerators; wet bar in suites. Microwaves avail. Balconies. Cr cds: A, C, D, DS, MC, V.

D SC

★★ **WYNDHAM PALM SPRINGS.** *888 Tahquitz Canyon Way (92262). 760/322-6000; fax 760/322-5351; toll-free 800/996-3426. www.wyndham.com.* 410 units, 5 story, 158 suites. Jan-June: S, D $89-$279; each addl $25; suites $230-$250; under 17 free; lower rates rest of yr. Crib free. Pet accepted; $25. TV; cable. Pool, wading pool, whirlpool, poolside serv. Coffee in rms. Restaurant 6:30 am-11 pm. Bar 11-1:30 am. Ck-out noon. Convention facilities. Business center. In-rm modem link. Concierge. Gift shops. Barber, beauty shop. Free valet parking. Free airport transportation. Tennis privileges. Golf privileges. Exercise equipt; sauna. Private patios, balconies. Covered walkway to convention center. Cr cds: A, C, D, DS, ER, JCB, MC, V.

D

Resorts

★★★ **DORAL PALM SPRINGS RESORT.** *67-967 Vista Chino at Landau Blvd, Cathedral City (92234). 760/322-7000; fax 760/322-6853; toll-free 888/386-4677. www.doralpalmsprings.com.* 285 rms, 4 story, 45 condos (1-3 bedrm). Jan-late Apr: S, D $69-$169; each addl $15; suites $150-$400; condos $135-$350; under 18 free; wkly, monthly rates in condos; golf plans; higher rates wkends; lower rates rest of yr. Crib free. TV; cable (premium). Heated pool, whirlpool, poolside serv. Dining rm 6:30 am-11 pm. Bar 10-2 am; entertainment. Ck-out noon, ck-in 3 pm. Grocery, package store 1 mi. Convention facilities. Concierge. Gift shop. Barber, beauty shop. Free airport transportation. Lighted tennis, pro. 27-hole golf, greens fee $85-$95, pro, putting greens, driving range. Lawn games. Exercise equipt; sauna. Massage. Health club privileges. Refrigerators. Private patios, balconies. On 347 acres; panoramic mountain view. Cr cds: A, C, D, DS, ER, JCB, MC, V.

D

★★★ **HILTON PALM SPRINGS RESORT.** *400 E Tahquitz Canyon Way (92262). 760/320-6868; fax 760/320-2126; res 800/345-6565. www.hiltonpalmsprings.com.* 260 rms, 3 story. Dec-May: S, D $140-$235; each addl $20; suites $265-$685; studio rms $155; kit. condos $235-$345; under 18 free; lower rates rest of yr. Crib free. Pet accepted. TV; cable (premium), VCR avail (movies). Heated pool, 2 whirlpools, poolside serv. Children's activities (Sept-May, hols); ages 3-12. Coffee in rm. Restaurant 6 am-10 pm. Bar 4 pm-2 am. Ck-out noon. Convention facilities. Business center. In-rm modem link. Concierge. Gift shop. Barber, beauty shop. Valet parking. Free airport transportation. Exercise equipt; sauna. 6 lighted tennis courts, pro, pro shop. Golf privileges. Refrigerators, minibars; microwaves avail. Private patios, balconies. Cr cds: A, D, DS, MC, V.

D SC

★★★ **LA MANCHA PRIVATE RESORT AND VILLAS.** *444 N Avenida Caballeros (92262). 760/323-1773; fax 760/323-5928; toll-free 800/255-1773. www.la-mancha.com.*

53 kit. villas, 1-2 story, 13 minisuites. Dec-Apr: minisuites $99-$185; villas $250-$895; extended-stay rates; tennis, golf, plans; lower rates rest of yr. Crib $25. TV; cable, VCR avail (movies). Pool, whirlpool, poolside serv. Dining rm 7:30 am-2:30 pm, 5:30-9:30 pm. Box lunches, picnics. Bar 8 am-9:30 pm. Ck-out noon, ck-in 3 pm. Grocery, coin lndry, package store 1 mi. Meeting rms. Business center. In-rm modem link. Concierge. Gift shop. Free airport transportation. Lighted tennis, pro. Golf privileges, putting green. Bicycles. Lawn games. Exercise rm; sauna. Microwaves avail. Some fireplaces. Private patios, balconies. Grills. Most villas with private pool, whirlpools and/or spa; some villas with private tennis court. Extensive landscaped grounds; Spanish Colonial decor. Cr cds: A, D, DS, JCB, MC, V.

D

★★★ **LA QUINTA RESORT CLUB.** *49-499 Eisenhower Dr, La Quinta (92253). 760/598-3828. www.laquintaresort.com.* 590 rms, 3 story. S, D $170-$400; each addl $25. Crib avail. Pool. TV; cable (premium), VCR avail. Complimentary coffee, newspaper in rms. Restaurant 5:30 am-10 pm. Bar. Ck-out noon. Meeting rms. Business center. Gift shop. Exercise rm. Spa. Golf. Cr cds: A, C, D, DS, MC, V.

★★★ **MARRIOTT'S RANCHO LAS PALMAS RESORT & SPA.** *41000 Bob Hope Dr, Rancho Mirage (92270). 760/568-2727; fax 760/568-5845; res 800/228-9290.* 450 rms, 2 story. Jan-Apr: S, D $280-$300; suites $330-$1,000; under 18 free; golf, tennis plans; lower rates rest of yr. Pet accepted, some restrictions. TV; cable (premium), VCR avail (movies). 2 pools, whirlpool, wading pool, poolside serv. Playground. Supervised children's activities; under age 12. Restaurants 6:30 am-11 pm. Box lunches, snack bar. Bar 11-2 am. Ck-out noon, ck-in 4 pm. Convention facilities. Business center. In-rm modem link. Concierge. Gift shop. Barber, beauty shop. Lighted tennis, pro. Tennis school. 27-hole golf, greens fee $99-$109, pro, putting green, driving range. Bicycle rentals. Soc dir. Exercise equipt. Health club privileges. Some refrigerators, minibars; microwaves avail. Private patios, balconies. Cr cds: A, D, DS, MC, V.

D

★★★ **MERV GRIFFIN'S RESORT & GIVENCHY SPA.** *4200 E Palm Canyon Dr (92253). 760/770-5000.* 136 rms, 3 story. S, D $250-$650; each addl $25. Crib avail. 2 Pools. TV; cable (premium), VCR avail. Complimentary coffee, newspaper in rms. Restaurant 6 am-10 pm. Bar. Ck-out noon. Meeting rms. Business center. Gift shop. Fitness center. Spa.

Aerial tramway, Palm Springs

Golf. Tennis. Cr cds: A, C, D, DS, MC, V.

★★★ MIRAMONTE RESORT. *45000 Indian Wells Ln, Indian Wells (92210). 760/341-2200. www.miramonte-resort.com.* 222 rms, 3 story. S, D $250-$550; each addl $25. Crib avail. 2 Pools. TV; cable (premium), VCR avail. Complimentary coffee, newspaper in rms. Restaurant 5:30 am-10 pm. Bar. Ck-out noon. Meeting rms. Business center. Gift shop. Fitness center. Spa. Golf. Tennis. Cr cds: A, C, D, DS, MC, V.

★★★ PALM SPRINGS MARQUIS RESORT. *150 S Indian Canyon Dr (92262). 760/322-2121; fax 760/322-2380; toll-free 800/223-1050. www.psmarquis.com.* 166 rms, 101 kit. suites, 3 story. Jan-Apr: S, D $130-$290; suites $199-$750; wkly, monthly rates; golf, tennis packages; lower rates rest of yr. Underground, valet, overnight parking $7.50. Crib free. TV; cable, VCR avail (movies). 2 pools, wading pool, whirlpool, poolside serv. Supervised children's activities; ages 2-12. Restaurants 6:30 am-11 pm. Rm serv 24 hrs. Bar 11-2 am; entertainment wkends. Ck-out noon. Convention facilities. Business center. In-rm modem link. Concierge. Gift shop. Free airport transportation. Lighted tennis, pro. Golf privileges. Exercise equipt. Massage. Bathrm phones; microwaves avail. Private patios, balconies. View of San Jacinto Mountains. Eight-acre resort. Cr cds: A, C, D, DS, MC, V.

D SC

★★★ PALM SPRINGS RIVIERA RESORT & RACQUET CLUB. *1600 N Indian Canyon Dr (92262). 760/327-8311; fax 760/778-2560; res 760/327-8311. www.psriviera.com.* 477 rms, 2-3 story. Mid-Jan-mid-May: S, D $139-$189; each addl $20; suites $215-$860; under 18 free; lower rates rest of yr. Crib free. Pet accepted. TV; cable. 2 heated pools, whirlpools, poolside serv. Restaurant 6:30 am-10 pm. Bar 11-2 am; entertainment. Ck-out noon. Convention facilities. In-rm modem link. Bellhops. Valet serv. Concierge. Sundries. Gift shop. Beauty shop. Free valet parking. Free airport transportation. Lighted tennis. Golf privileges. Exercise equipt. Massage. Health club privileges. Bicycle rentals. Lawn games. Bathrm phones, refrigerators; microwaves avail. Some wet bars. Balconies. Cr cds: A, C, D, DS, ER, JCB, MC, V.

D

★★★★ THE RITZ-CARLTON, PALM SPRINGS. *68-900 Frank Sinatra Dr, Rancho Mirage (92270). 760/321-8282; fax 760/770-7605; toll-free 800/241-3333.* Dramatic views of the desert are seen from every angle of this premier Palm Springs property. Set amidst towering palms, the property provides a private retreat with tennis, croquet, and access to 18 championship golf courses. Most guests indulge in one of the many spa treatments available, all of which are provided by a professional staff. Gourmet French fare is available in The Dining Room, and creative Southwestern cuisine, befitting the desert locale, can be had at Miranda. 240 rms, 3 story. Jan-mid-Apr: S, D $295-$495; each addl $25; suites $425-$1,000; lower rates rest of yr. TV; cable (premium), VCR avail (movies). Pool, whirlpool, poolside serv. Supervised children's activities; ages 4-12. Restaurants 7 am-11 pm (see also THE DINING ROOM). Afternoon tea 2:30-5 pm. Rm serv 24 hrs. Bar 10:30-1 am. Ck-out noon, ck-in 3 pm. Convention facilities. Business center. In-rm modem link. Shopping arcade. Barber, beauty shop. Valet serv. Concierge. Underground valet parking. Lighted tennis, pro, pro shop. 18-hole golf privileges, greens fee $65-$170. Lawn games. Exercise rm; sauna. Massage. Spa. Bathrm phones. Minibars. Private patios, balconies. Luxury level. Cr cds: A, C, D, DS, ER, JCB, MC, V.

D

★★★ SPA HOTEL AND CASINO. *100 N Indian Canyon Dr (92262). 760/325-1461; fax 760/325-3344; toll-free 800/854-1279. www.spa-hotel.com.* 230 rms, 5 story. Jan-mid-June: S, D $69-$219; each addl $20; suites from $250; under 18 free; lower rates rest of yr. Crib $10. TV; cable, VCR avail (movies). 3 pools, 2 hot mineral pools, whirlpool, poolside serv. Restaurant 7 am-10 pm. Rm serv 24 hrs. Bar 10-2 am. Ck-out noon. Meeting rms. Business center. Bellhops.

Concierge. Sundries. Gift shop. Barber, beauty shop. Free airport transportation. Tennis privileges. 18-hole golf privileges. Exercise equipt; sauna, steam rm. Solarium. Some bathrm phones, refrigerators; microwaves avail. Private patios, balconies. Cr cds: A, D, DS, JCB, MC, V.

★★★ **WESTIN MISSION HILLS.** *71333 Dinah Shore Dr, Rancho Mirage (92270). 760/328-5955; fax 760/770-2199; res 800/937-8461. www.westin.com.* 512 units in 16 buildings, 2 story. Jan-May: S, D $179-$475; each addl $25; suites $430-$1,250; under 18 free; golf, tennis plans; lower rates rest of yr. Crib free. TV; cable (premium), vcr avail (movies). 3 pools, whirlpool, poolside serv, lifeguard (main pool); 60-ft waterslide. Playground. Supervised children's activities; ages 4-12. Dining rms 6 am-11 pm. Box lunches, snack bar. Rm serv 24 hrs. Bars 10-2 am; entertainment. Ck-out noon, ck-in 4 pm. Convention facilities. Business center. In-rm modem link. Bellhops. Valet serv. Concierge. Shopping arcade. Beauty shop. Sports dir. 7 lighted tennis courts, pro, pro shop. Pete Dye and Gary Player championship 18-hole golf courses, pro, 6 putting greens, 2 double-sided practice ranges, pro shop. Bicycle rentals. Lawn games. Soc dir. Game rm. Exercise equipt; steam rm. Health and fitness center. Massage. Minibars; refrigerators avail. Cr cds: A, C, D, DS, ER, JCB, MC, V.

B&Bs/Small Inns

★★ **BALLANTINES HOTEL.** *1420 N Indian Canyon Dr (92262). 760/320-1178; fax 760/320-5308; toll-free 800/780-3464. www.palmsprings.com/ballantines.* 14 rms, 6 kits. Oct-May: S, D $149-$189; kit. units $90; monthly rates; lower rates rest of yr. Adults only. TV; VCR avail. Heated pool. Complimentary continental bkfst. Ck-out noon. Refrigerators, microwaves. Cr cds: A, MC, V.

★★ **CASA CODY BED AND BREAKFAST INN.** *175 S Cahuilla Rd (92262). 760/320-9346; fax 760/325-8610; toll-free 800/231-2639.* 23 rms, 21 kit. suites. Late Dec-late Apr: S, D $79-$199; each addl $10; monthly, wkly rates; lower rates rest of yr. Crib $10. Pet accepted. TV; cable, VCR avail (free movies). 2 heated pools, whirlpool. Complimentary continental bkfst. Restaurant nearby. Ck-out 11 am, ck-in 2 pm. Business servs avail. Health club privileges. Refrigerators, microwaves; many fireplaces. Many private patios. Cr cds: A, C, D, DS, MC, V.

★★★ **ESTRELLA INN.** *415 S Belardo Rd (92262). 760/320-4117; fax 760/323-3303; toll-free 800/237-3687. www.estrella.com.* 67 rms, 6 shower only, 2 story, 8 suites. Jan-Apr: S, D $150; each addl $15; suites $225-$275; villas $250-$275; under 12 free; wkly rates; tennis, golf plans; lower rates rest of yr. Crib free. Pet accepted; $10. TV; VCR avail. 3 heated pools. Complimentary bkfst, coffee in rms. Restaurant nearby. Ck-out noon, ck-in 3 pm. Business servs avail. Luggage handling. Concierge serv. Free airport transportation. Health club privileges. Lawn games. Refrigerators, microwaves. Patios, balconies. Built 1929. Cr cds: A, C, D, MC, V.

★★★ **INGLESIDE INN.** *200 W Ramon Rd (92264). 760/325-0046; fax 760/325-0710; res 760/325-0046. www.inglesideinn.com.* 30 rms. Oct-May: S, D $175; suites $295-$600; villas $125-$375; lower rates rest of yr. TV; cable, VCR avail. Heated pool, whirlpool, poolside serv. Complimentary continental bkfst, coffee in rms. Restaurant (see also MELVYN'S AT THE INGLESIDE). Bar; entertainment. Ck-out noon, ck-in 2 pm. Business servs avail. Valet serv. Concierge serv. In-rm whirlpools, refrigerators; some fireplaces; microwaves avail. Some private patios. Hacienda atmosphere; courtyard, fountain. Rms individually decorated; many antiques. Cr cds: A, C, D, DS, MC, V.

★★★ **KORAKIA PENSIONE.** *257 S Patencio Rd (92262). 760/864-6411; fax 760/864-4147.* 20 rms, 15 with kits, 6 with shower only, 2 story. Sept-July: S, D $79-$239; each addl $30; 2-day min wkends. Heated pool. Complimentary continental bkfst. Restaurant nearby. Ck-out noon.

Business servs avail. Luggage handling. Concierge serv. Tennis privileges. Golf privileges. Refrigerators; some fireplaces. Balconies. Picnic tables. Moorish-style architecture; built 1924, set against San Jacinto Mountains, antiques.

★★★ **ORCHID TREE INN.** *261 S Belardo Rd (92262). 760/325-2791; fax 760/325-3855; toll-free 800/733-3435. www.orchidtree.com.* 40 rms, 19 with shower only, 1 and 2 story, 33 kit units. Nov-May: S $79-$125; D $99-$140; each addl $15; suites $135-$295; lower rates rest of yr. TV; cable, VCR avail. 3 pools, 2 whirlpools. Complimentary continental bkfst. Ck-out noon, ck-in 3 pm. Luggage handling. Concierge serv. Business servs avail. Health club privileges. Game rm. Tennis, shuffleboard. Many refrigerators, microwaves avail. Cr cds: A, C, D, DS, MC, V.

★★★ **VILLA ROYALE INN.** *1620 Indian Trail (92264). 760/327-2314; fax 760/322-3794; toll-free 800/245-2314. www.villaroyale.com.* 33 rms, 19 suites. Oct-May: S, D $100-$150; each addl $25; suites $150-$295; lower rates rest of yr. Adults only. TV; cable. 2 pools, whirlpool. Dining rm (see also EUROPA). Bar 5-11 pm. Ck-out noon, ck-in 2 pm. Meeting rms. Business servs avail. Health club privileges. Massage. Many refrigerators; some fireplaces. Private patios. Located on 3½ acres with series of interior couryards. Rms decorated with objets d'art from Morocco, France, England, Holland, Spain, and Greece. European atmosphere. Cr cds: A, C, D, DS, MC, V.

D

★★★★ **THE WILLOWS HISTORIC PALM SPRINGS INN.** *412 W Tahquitz Canyon Way (92262). 760/320-0771; fax 760/320-0780; res 800/966-9597. www.thewillows palmsprings.com.* The eight guestrooms of this restored Mediterranean villa have been host to many stars over their long history. Antiques, hardwood floors, and rich fabrics all add to the unique character of each room and the relaxing grounds are reserved for guests only. Included are a full gourmet breakfast, afternoon refreshments, and an evening wine and hors d'oeuvres reception. 8 rms, 2 story. Oct-May: S, D $395-$525; wkends, hols 2-day min; lower rates rest of yr. TV; VCR avail. Pool, whirlpool. Complimentary full bkfst; afternoon refreshments. Restaurant nearby. Ck-out noon, ck-in 4 pm. Business servs avail. In-rm modem link. Luggage handling. Valet serv. Concierge serv. Bathrm phones, refrigerators; some fireplaces. Totally nonsmoking. Cr cds: A, D, DS, MC, V.

D

Villa/Condo

★★★ **SUNDANCE VILLAS.** *303 Cabrillo Rd (92262). 760/325-3888; fax 760/323-3029; toll-free 800/455-3888. www.palmsprings.com/hotels/sundance.* 19 kit. villas. Mid-Dec-May: villas $295-$375; wkly rates; lower rates rest of yr. Crib $80/wk. TV; cable (premium), VCR. Pool, whirlpool. Restaurant nearby. Ck-out noon. Business servs avail. Valet serv. Concierge. Free airport transportation. Lighted tennis. Golf privileges. Wet bars, microwaves, fireplaces. Patios. Grills. Cr cds: A, C, D, DS, MC, V.

D

Restaurants

★★ **BLUE COYOTE.** *445 N Palm Canyon Dr (92262). 760/327-1196.* Hrs: 11 am-10 pm; Fri, Sat to 11 pm. Closed Thanksgiving, Dec 25. Mexican, Southwestern menu. Bar. Lunch $5.50-$14.95, dinner $8.95-$20.95. Specialties: pollo cilantro, filete jalapeño. Parking. Outdoor dining. Cantina ambiance. Cr cds: A, D, MC, V.

D

★★ **CEDAR CREEK INN.** *1555 S Palm Canyon Dr (92264). 760/325-7300. www.cedarcreekinnps.com.* Hrs: 11 am-10 pm. Res accepted. Bar to 11 pm. Lunch $6.95-$12.95, dinner $11.95-$24.95. Specialties: chicken papaya salad, rack of lamb, homemade desserts. Entertainment Wed-Sun. Parking. Outdoor dining. Old

World country garden atmosphere. Cr cds: A, D, DS, MC, V.

D

★★★★ **THE DINING ROOM.** *68-900 Frank Sinatra Dr, Rancho Mirage (92270). 760/321-8282. www.ritzcarlton.com.* This sophistacated room, located in the middle of the Palm Springs desert, is outfitted with excellent quality, tasteful furnishings. The Mediterranean cuisine, seafood, and fresh pastas, is always excellent and is accompanied by live jazz piano and polished service. There is also a fantastic Sunday brunch. French, Mediterranean menu. Specialties: Chilean sea bass (seasonal), Dover sole, foie gras, rack of lamb, duck. Hrs: 6:30-10 pm. Closed Mon, Tues. Bar 10:30-1 am. Extensive wine list. Res accepted. Prix fixe: 2-course dinner $39, 3-course dinner $49, 4-course dinner $56. Children's menu. Pianist. Valet parking. Oil paintings; crystal chandeliers. Jacket, tie. Cr cds: C, D, DS, ER, MC, V.

D

★★★ **EUROPA.** *1620 Indian Trl (92264). 760/327-2314. www.villaroyale.com.* Hrs: 5:30-10 pm; Sun brunch 11:30 am-2 pm. Closed Mon. Res accepted. Continental menu. Bar. Wine cellar. A la carte entrees: dinner $13-$28. Sun brunch $20. Specialties: salmon in parchment, roast rack of lamb. Parking. Outdoor dining. Intimate setting. Cr cds: A, D, DS, MC, V.

★★ **FLOWER DRUM.** *424 S Indian Canyon Dr (92262). 760/323-3020.* Hrs: 11:30 am-3 pm, 4:30-10 pm; Fri, Sat to 10:30 pm; early-bird dinner 4:30-6:30 pm. Res accepted. Chinese menu. Bar to 10 pm. A la carte entrees: lunch $4.95-$12.95, dinner $8.95-$28. Specializes in chicken, duck, seafood. Chinese costumed dancing. Hosts Chinese New Year's Celebration (Jan-Feb). Goldfish stream. Rock gardens. Cr cds: A, MC, V.

D

★★ **GREAT WALL.** *362 S Palm Canyon Dr (92262). 760/322-2209.* Hrs: 11:30 am-3 pm, 4:30-10 pm. Res accepted. Chinese menu. Bar. A la carte entrees: lunch $4.95-$6.95, dinner $6.25-$14.95. Specialties: Chinese chicken salad, house pan-fried noodle, sesame chicken. Outdoor dining. Asian decor; authentic Chinese watercolors; large tapestry of the Great Wall. Cr cds: A, C, D, DS, MC, V.

D

★★ **LAS CASUELAS NUEVAS.** *70050 US 111, Rancho Mirage (92270). 760/328-8844.* Hrs: 11 am-9:30 pm; Fri, Sat to 10 pm; Sun brunch 10 am-2 pm. Closed Thanksgiving, Dec 25. Res accepted. Mexican menu. Bar. Lunch $6.50-$11.50, dinner $9.50-$16.95. Sun brunch $15.95. Children's menu. Specialties: crab enchiladas, pollo en mole, chicken fajitas. Entertainment wkends. Valet parking. Patio dining. Cr cds: A, DS, MC, V.

D

★★ **LAS CASUELAS TERRAZA.** *222 S Palm Canyon Dr (92262). 760/325-2794.* Hrs: 11 am-closing; Sun from 10 am. Closed Thanksgiving, Dec 25. Res accepted. Mexican menu. Bar. Lunch $5.75-$11, dinner $6.95-$14.95. Children's menu. Specialties: Oaxacan black bean tostada, shrimp enchiladas, fajitas. Nightly entertainment. Parking. Outdoor dining. Antique bar. Mexican decor. Cr cds: A, D, DS, MC, V.

D

★★★ **LE VALLAURIS.** *385 W Tahquitz Canyon Way (92262). 760/325-5059. www.levallauris.com.* Hrs: 11:30 am-2:30 pm, 5:30-11 pm. Res accepted. French/California menu. Bar to midnight. Wine cellar. A la carte entrees: lunch $10-$18.50, dinner $22-$30. Specializes in veal, lamb, seafood. Own pastries. Pianist. Valet parking. Menu changes daily. Outdoor dining. Cr cds: A, C, D, DS, MC, V.

D

★★ **LYONS ENGLISH GRILLE.** *233 E Palm Canyon Dr (92264). 760/327-1551.* Hrs: 4-11 pm; early-bird dinner 4:30-6 pm. Res accepted. English menu. Bar. Dinner $10.95-$21.95. Specializes in steak, prime rib, fresh seafood. Own desserts. Pianist. Valet parking. Old English decor; stained glass. Family-owned. Cr cds: A, D, MC, V.

D

★★★ **MELVYN'S.** *200 W Ramon Rd (92264). 760/325-2323. www.inglesideinn.com.* Hrs: 11:30 am-3 pm, 6-11 pm; Sat, Sun brunch 9 am-3 pm. Res accepted. Continental menu. Bar 10-2 am. Wine cellar. Lunch $8.95-$16, dinner $16.95-$28. Sat, Sun brunch $13.95-$16.95. Specialties: veal Ingleside, chicken Charlene, steak Dianne. Pianist, vocalist. Valet parking. Historic building; 2 main dining areas, garden rm. Jacket (dinner). Cr cds: A, MC, V.

D

★★ **OLYMPIA GREEK RESTAURANT.** *42434 Bob Hope Dr, Rancho Mirage (92270). 760/340-3066.* Hrs: 11:30 am-2 pm, 5-10 pm. Closed July-Aug. Res accepted. Greek, Continental menu. Bar. Lunch $5.95-$9.95, dinner $11.95-$25.95. Specialties: rack of lamb, moussaka, shrimp a la Mykonos. Belly dancer. Greek decor. Cr cds: A, D, DS, V.

D

★ **PALMIE.** *276 N Palm Canton Dr (92262). 760/320-3375.* Hrs: from 5:30 pm. Closed Sun; Jan 1-2; Aug-mid Sept. Res accepted. French menu. Bar. A la carte entrees: dinner $14.50-$23. Specialties: lamb shank, ravioli, cheese souffle. Outdoor dining. Cr cds: A, D, MC, V.

D

★★ **ROCK GARDEN CAFE.** *777 S Palm Canyon Dr (92264). 760/327-8840.* Hrs: 7 am-midnight; early-bird dinner 5-8 pm. Res accepted. Bar. Bkfst $3.50-$5, lunch $5-$7, dinner $7-$15. Children's menu. Specializes in seafood, ribs, Greek salad. Pianist Wed-Sun. Parking. Outdoor dining. Cr cds: A, C, D, DS, MC, V.

D

★★ **ST. JAMES AT THE VINEYARD.** *265 S Palm Canyon Dr (92262). 760/320-8041. www.palmsprings.com/dine/stjames.* Hrs: 5-10 pm; Fri, Sat to 11 pm. Closed Aug. Eclectic menu. Bar. A la carte entrees: dinner $16-$32. Specializes in seafood, pasta, curries. Cr cds: A, D, DS, MC, V.

D

★★ **SORRENTINO'S SEAFOOD HOUSE.** *1032 N Palm Canyon Dr (92262). 760/325-2944.* Hrs: 5-10 pm; off-season 5:30-10 pm. Closed Thanksgiving. Res accepted. Italian/seafood menu. Bar. Complete meals: dinner $10.95-$25. Specializes in seafood, veal, steak. Pianist. Parking. Outdoor dining. Family-owned since 1944. Cr cds: A, MC, V.

D

★★★★ **WALLY'S DESERT TURTLE.** *71-775 Hwy 111, Rancho Mirage (92270). 760/568-9321. www.wallys-desert-turtle.com.* A fanciful setting, which some may call dated, with 20 ft high, hand-painted murals, gilt chairs, and twinkling chandeliers provides a unique backdrop for interesting, French-inspired food. Dishes incorporate international ingredients like tiger prawns with saffron basmati rice, or scallops with Szechuan peppercorn, but the feeling remains decidedly Old World. There are many glittering private rooms that can accomodate private parties. Continental menu. Specializes in Dover sole, rack of lamb, duck. Hrs: 6-10 pm; also Fri 11:30 am-2 pm. Closed mid-June-Sept. Bar. Wine cellar. Res accepted. A la carte entrees: lunch $13-$20, dinner $18-$36. Pianist. Valet parking. Two-level dining with elevated terrace. Jacket. Cr cds: A, D, DS, MC, V.

D

★★★ **WILDE GOOSE.** *67-938 E Palm Canyon Dr (92234). 760/328-5775. www.calendarlive.com/wildegoose.* Hrs: from 5:30 pm. Res accepted. Continental menu. Bar. Dinner $12.95-$34.95. Specializes in beef, seafood, wild game. Pianist Fri, Sat. Valet parking. European country inn decor. Cr cds: A, C, D, DS, MC, V.

D

Palm Springs Area

What was once one of the country's favorite vacation towns has become one of America's most popular resort regions. Tourism experienced a remarkable boom in the years since the first Hollywood celebrities built their winter houses here. The beautiful scenery and ideal weather that attracted those first vacationers are still present, but as the area's popularity has increased they have been accompanied by an ever growing number of hotels, inns, resorts, shopping malls, golf courses, recreation sites, and performing arts facilities. No longer is the area solely a retreat for the famous and wealthy. Although there are more luxurious restaurants, resorts, and stores than ever before, it is now also quite easy to take full advantage of the area's attractions while on a restricted budget. The more than three million people who visit each year come mostly to relax, soak up the sun, and enjoy the climate. It is also possible to enjoy everything from cross-country skiing atop Mount San Jacinto to camping among the tall cactus at Joshua Tree National Park (see). The following towns, all within a short distance of the city of Palm Springs, provide this great variety of recreation: Desert Hot Springs, Idyllwild, Indio, Palm Desert, and Palm Springs (see all).

Palo Alto

(see San Francisco map) *See also Fremont, Redwood City, Santa Clara, Saratoga*

Founded 1889 **Pop** 55,900 **Elev** 23 ft **Area code** 650

Information Chamber of Commerce, 325 Forest Ave, 94301; 650/324-3121

Web www.batnet.com/pacc

A tall and ancient redwood tree stands at the northwest entrance to the city. Nearly two centuries ago, Spanish explorers used it as a landmark, calling it El Palo Alto ("tall tree"). Stanford University is a major economic factor. The city is also one of the nation's most important electronics development and research centers.

What to See and Do

Junior Museum & Zoo. Displays introduce children to art, science, history, and anthropology through a variety of media; hands-on exhibits, and workshops. Zoo on grounds. (Tues-Sun; closed hols) 1451 Middlefield Rd. Phone 650/329-2111. **FREE**

Lucy Evans Baylands Nature Interpretive Center. Nature preserve at edge of salt marsh. Naturalist-guided walking tours; slide shows; bicycling; bird-watching. (Tues-Sun; closed Thanksgiving, Dec 25) 2775 Embarcadero Rd, E of US 101. Phone 650/329-2506. **FREE**

☒ **Stanford University.** (1891) 13,549 students. Founded by Senator and Mrs. Leland Stanford in memory of their only son, it has become one of the great universities of the world. Near El Camino Real (CA 82). Phone 650/723-2300. Features of the campus incl

Hoover Tower. Library houses collection begun by President Herbert Hoover during WWI. At 250 ft high, the carillon platform on 14th floor offers panoramic view of campus and peninsula (daily; closed school hols). Information desk (daily; closed school hols). Phone 650/723-2053. **¢**

Stanford Guide Service. Located in Memorial Hall and in Hoover Tower (daily; closed school hols). Free one-hr campus tours leave information booth (twice daily; closed school hols). Maps and brochures are at both locations. Phone 650/723-2560.

Stanford Medical Center. A $21-million cluster of buildings on a 56-acre site, designed by internationally famous architect Edward Durell Stone. Tours (Thurs). Phone 650/723-7167.

Stanford Stadium. Home of Stanford Cardinals football. Phone 650/329-2506.

Thomas Welton Stanford Art Gallery. Changing exhibits. (Tues-Sun; closed hols) Phone 650/723-3469. **FREE**

Trees. For which Palo Alto is famous. **El Palo Alto.** "The Tall Tree" that gives city its name. Palo Alto Ave near Alma St. Also, 60 varieties along Hamilton Ave, blocks between 100 and 1500. Phone 650/723-7167.

Winter Lodge. Only outdoor ice rink in the US west of the Sierra Nevada Mountains. Skate rentals. (Oct-mid-Apr; closed hols) 3009 Middlefield Rd. Phone 650/493-4566. **¢¢¢**

Motels/Motor Lodges

★ **COUNTRY INN MOTEL.** *4345 El Camino Real (94306). 650/948-9154; fax 650/949-4190.* 27 rms, 12 A/C, 1-2 story, 13 kits. S, D $50-$70; each addl $6; kit. units $10 addl. Crib $5. TV; cable (premium). Heated pool. Complimentary continental bkfst. Restaurant adj open 24 hrs. Ck-out 11 am. In-rm modem link. Cr cds: A, DS, MC, V.

★★★ **CREEKSIDE INN.** *3400 El Camino Real (94306). 650/493-2411; fax 650/493-6787; toll-free 800/492-7335. www.creekside-inn.com.* 136 rms, 2-4 story, 14 kits. S, D $125-$155; each addl $5; kit. units $165-$200. Crib avail. TV; cable (premium), VCR avail (movies $5). Heated pool. Coffee in rms. Restaurant 6 am-10:30 pm; Sat, Sun from 7 am. Bar 11 am-10:30 pm. Ck-out noon. Coin lndry. Business servs avail. In-rm modem link. Valet serv. Convenience store. Exercise equipt. Refrigerators. Private patios, balconies. Totally nonsmoking. Cr cds: A, D, DS, JCB, MC, V.

★★ **STANFORD TERRACE INN.** *531 Stanford Ave (94306). 650/857-0333; fax 650/857-0343; toll-free 800/729-0332. www.stanfordterraceinn.com.* 80 units, 2-3 story, 14 kits. S $160; D $185; each addl $10; kit. suites $190-$310; under 12 free. TV; cable (premium). Pool. Complimentary continental bkfst. Coffee in rms. Restaurant nearby. Ck-out noon. Coin lndry. Meeting rms. Business servs avail. Free garage parking. Exercise equipt. Refrigerators, minibars. Stanford Univ opp. Cr cds: A, D, DS, MC, V.

★★ **TOWN HOUSE INN.** *4164 El Camino Real (94306). 650/493-4492; fax 650/493-3418; toll-free 800/458-8696.* 38 rms, 15 with shower only, 2 story, 7 suites, 9 kit. units. S $69; D $85; each addl $6-$10; suites $89-$170; kit. units $90-$100; under 12 free; wkly rates. Crib free. TV; cable (premium), VCR. Whirlpool. Complimentary continental bkfst, coffee in rms. Restaurant nearby. Ck-out 11 am. Exercise equipt. Refrigerators. Cr cds: A, C, D, MC, V.

Hotels

★★★ **DINAH'S GARDEN HOTEL.** *4261 El Camino Real (94306). 650/493-2844; fax 650/856-4713; toll-free 800/227-8220. www.dinahshotel.com.* 107 rms, 1-3 story, 41 suites. D $154-$265; suites $180-$430. Crib free. TV; cable (premium), VCR avail. 2 pools, heated; poolside serv. Coffee in rms. Restaurant 6:30 am-11 pm. Ck-out noon. Coin lndry. Business servs avail. Valet serv. Sundries. Exercise equipt; sauna. Refrigerators. Many private patios, terraces. On 9 acres; lagoons. Cr cds: A, D, DS, MC, V.

★★★ **GARDEN COURT HOTEL.** *520 Cowper St (94301). 650/322-9000; fax 650/324-3609. www.gardencourt.com.* 62 rms, 4 story, 13 suites. S, D $265; each addl $20; suites $300-$475. Crib free. Valet parking $12. TV; cable (premium), VCR (free movies). Restaurant 7 am-11 pm. Rm serv 24 hrs. Bar 11:30 am-midnight. Ck-out noon. Meeting rms. Business servs avail. In-rm modem link. Concierge. Exercise equipt. Bicycles. Minibars, some in-rm whirlpools, fireplaces. Balconies. Open-air, flower-laden courtyard reminiscent of a European village square. Cr cds: A, C, D, DS, MC, V.

★★★ **HYATT RICKEYS.** *4219 El Camino Real (94306). 650/493-8000; fax 650/424-0836; res 800/223-1234. www.hyatthotels.com.* 344 units, 1-6 story. S $229-$259; D $254-$284; suites $280-$650; under 18 free; wkend rates. Crib free. TV; cable (premium). Pool. Coffee in rms. Restaurant 6:30 am-10 pm. Bar 11-1:30 am. Ck-out noon. Convention facilities. Business center. In-rm modem link. Exercise equipt. Barber, beauty shop. Lawn games. Putting green. Fireplace in many suites; refrigerators avail. Some balconies. On 22 acres with gardens, pond. Cr cds: A, D, DS, MC, V.

★★★ **SHERATON PALO ALTO.** *625 El Camino Real (94301). 650/328-2800; fax 650/327-7362; res 800/325-3535. www.sheraton.com.* 343 units, 4 story, 6 kits. S, D $239; each addl $10; suites $259-$399; kit. units $179; under 18 free; wkend rates. Crib free. TV; cable (premium). Pool. Coffee in rm. Restaurant 6 am-11 pm. Bar 11 am-midnight. Ck-out noon. Coin lndry. Meeting rms. Business center. Bellhops. Valet serv.

Concierge. Exercise equipt. Some bathrm phones, in-rm whirlpools; refrigerators avail. Some private patios, balconies. Cr cds: A, C, D, DS, JCB, MC, V.

D

★★★ **WESTIN.** *675 El Camino Real (94301). 650/321-4422.* 184 rms, 6 story. S, D $175-$275; each addl $25; under 17 free. Crib avail. Pet accepted. Heated pool. TV; cable (premium), VCR avail. Complimentary coffee, newspaper in rms. Restaurant 6 am-10 pm. Ck-out noon. Meeting rms. Business center. Gift shop. Exercise rm. Some refrigerators, minibars. Cr cds: A, C, D, DS, MC, V.

B&B/Small Inn

★★ **COWPER INN.** *705 Cowper St (94301). 650/327-4475; fax 650/329-1703. www.cowperinn.com.* 14 rms, 6 with shower only, 2 share bath, 3 A/C, 3 story, 2 suites, 2 kit. units. S, D, suites, kit. units $65-$130; each addl $10. TV; cable. Complimentary continental bkfst. Restaurant nearby. Ck-out 11 am, ck-in 2 pm. Business servs avail. Victorian house built in 1893. Totally nonsmoking. Cr cds: A, DS, MC, V.

Restaurants

★ **BLUE CHALK CAFE.** *630 Ramona St (94301). 650/326-1020.* Hrs: 11:30 am-2:30 pm, 5-10 pm. Closed Sun; Jan 1, Thanksgiving, Dec 25. Res accepted. Southern regional menu. Bar. A la carte entrees: lunch $5.95-$11.50, dinner $6.95-$16.25. Children's menu. Specialties: pan-seared catfish, grilled jumbo prawns over grits, Carolina fritters. Outdoor dining. Casual dining; billiards and shuffleboard avail. Totally nonsmoking. Cr cds: A, DS, MC, V.

D

★★★ **EVVIA.** *420 Emerson St. (94301). 650/326-0983.* Hrs: 11:30 am-2:30 pm, 5:30-10 pm; Fri to 11 pm; Sat 5-11 pm; Sun 5-9 pm. Closed hols. Res accepted. Greek menu. Bar. A la carte entrees: lunch $9.95-$15.95, dinner $13.50-$26.95. Specialties: lamb chops, whole striped bass, moussaka. Valet parking. Greek, Mediterranean decor. Totally nonsmoking. Cr cds: A, D, DS, MC, V.

D

★★ **L'AMIE DONIA.** *530 Bryant St (94301). 650/323-7614.* Hrs: 5:30-10 pm; Fri, Sat to 10:30 pm. Closed Mon, Sun; hols; also Jan, last wk June-1st 2 wks in July. Res accepted. French menu. Wine, beer. A la carte entrees: dinner $15-$25. Complete meal: dinner $30. Specialties: beef tongue salad, rabbit, tarte tatin. Street parking. Outdoor dining. French bistro atmosphere; rotating artworks by one artist. Totally nonsmoking. Cr cds: A, DS, MC, V.

D

★★ **SCOTT'S SEAFOOD.** *2300 E Bayshore Rd (94303). 650/856-1046. www.scottsseafood.com.* Hrs: 7 am-9:30 pm; Sat from 5 pm; Sun 5-9 pm; early-bird dinner 4-6 pm. Closed hols. Res accepted. Bar. A la carte entrees: lunch, dinner $7.95-$51. Specializes in seafood, steak. Parking. Patio dining. Cape Cod decor. Family-owned. Cr cds: A, D, DS, MC, V.

D

★★★ **SPAGO.** *265 Lytton Ave (94301). 650/833-1000. www.wolfgangpuck.com.* Hrs: 11:30 am-10 pm; Sat, Sun 5:30-10:00 pm. Closed hols. Res accepted. Continental, contemporary, and Mediterranean menu. Bar. Wine list. A la carte entrees: lunch $9-$16.50, dinner $19.50-$29.50. Valet parking. Outdoor dining. Totally nonsmoking. Cr cds: A, C, D, DS, MC, V.

D

★★ **ZIBIBBO.** *430 Kipling St (94301). 650/328-6722.* Hrs: 11:30 am-10:30 pm; Mon to 10 pm; Fri to 11 pm; Sat 11 am-11 pm; Sun 11 am-10 pm. Closed hols. Res accepted. Mediterranean menu. Bar 11 am-1 am. A la carte entrees: lunch $5.95-$13.95, dinner $9.95-$19.95. Sun brunch $4.95-$11.95. Specialties: rotisserie chicken rosemary, non-skillet mussels. Valet parking (dinner). Outdoor dining. Totally nonsmoking. Cr cds: A, DS, MC, V.

D

Pasadena

(E-5) *See also Claremont, Glendale, Los Angeles Area, Pomona, San Marino*

Founded 1874 **Pop** 131,591 **Elev** 865 ft **Area code** 626

Information Convention & Visitors Bureau, 171 S Los Robles, 91101; 626/795-9311

Web www.pasadenacal.com

Home of the world-famous Tournament of Roses, Pasadena was first chosen as a health refuge for weary Midwesterners and later as a winter retreat for Eastern millionaires. Today it is a cultural center and scientific and industrial frontier because of its many research, development, and engineering industries, including NASA's Jet Propulsion Laboratory. The name "Pasadena" comes from the Ojibwa language; it means "Crown of the Valley."

What to See and Do

Angeles National Forest. Approx 700,000 acres, incl San Gabriel and Sheep Mtn wildernesses. More than 100 camp and picnic grounds; many streams and lakes for fishing; hiking, winter sports. N, E, and S via US 210, CA 2, 118, 39, I-5. Contact Office of Information, 701 N Santa Anita Ave, Arcadia 91006. Phone 626/574-5200. ¢¢ Also here is

Crystal Lake Recreation Area. Fishing; nature and hiking trails, picnicking, store, tent and trailer camping (fee). Amphitheater programs (summer). Visitor Center has maps and interpretive materials (Sat, Sun). Long trailers (over 22 ft) and recreational vehicles not recommended (steep roads). Phone 626/910-2848.

The Gamble House. (1908) Exemplary of the mature California bungalow designs of American architects Greene and Greene; interiors of teakwood, mahogany, maple, and cedar; gardens. One-hr guided tour. (Thurs-Sun afternoons; closed hols) 4 Westmoreland Pl. Phone 626/793-3334. ¢¢¢

Kidspace. Hands-on museum for kids, incl TV studio, indoor beach, computer center, theater, and build-it area. (Tues-Sun) 390 S Molino Ave. Phone 626/449-9144. ¢¢

Norton Simon Museum of Art. Paintings, tapestries, and sculpture from Renaissance to mid-20th century; sculptures of Southeast Asia and India. (Mon, Wed-Sun, mid-afternoon-early eve; closed Jan 1, Thanksgiving, Dec 25) 411 W Colorado Blvd. Phone 626/449-6840. ¢¢

Pacific Asia Museum. Changing exhibits of traditional and contemporary Asian and Pacific Basin art; Chinese Imperial Palace-style building and Chinese courtyard garden; research library; bookstore. Docent tours avail. (Wed-Sun) 46 N Los Robles Ave. Phone 626/449-2742. ¢¢

Pasadena Historical Society. Housed in 18-rm Fenyes Estate (1905); contains original furnishings, antiques, paintings, and accessories. The mansion gives a glimpse of the elegant lifestyle that existed on Orange Grove Blvd at the turn of the century. Mansion, Finnish Folk Art Museum, and library archives have extensive photo and San Gabriel Valley historic collections. Tours. (Thurs-Sun afternoons; closed hols) 470 W Walnut St. Phone 626/577-1660. ¢¢

Rose Bowl. One of the country's most famous football stadiums, seats 98,636. Home of UCLA Bruins football team; scene of annual Rose Bowl game and other events throughout the yr. Rosemont Ave off Arroyo Blvd between I-210 and CA 134. Phone 626/577-3100.

Special Event

Tournament of Roses. Spectacular floral parade on Colorado Blvd attracts more than a million people. Afternoon capped at the Rose Bowl. Special tournament events during preceding wk. Phone 626/449-4100. Jan 1.

Motels/Motor Lodges

★★ BEST WESTERN COLORADO INN. *2156 E Colorado Blvd (91107). 626/793-9339; fax 626/568-2731; res 800/528-1234.* 77 rms, 3 story. S $52-$60; D $60-$65; each addl $8; under 12 free; Rose Parade (3-day min). Crib free. TV; cable (premium).

Exotic float at the Tournament of Roses

Heated pool, whirlpool. Complimentary continental bkfst. Restaurant nearby. Ck-out 11 am. Coin lndry. Meeting rm. Business servs avail. Refrigerators; some bathrm phones; microwaves avail. Some balconies. Cr cds: A, D, DS, MC, V.

D

★★ **COMFORT INN.** *2462 E Colorado Blvd (91107). 626/405-0811; fax 626/796-0966; res 800/228-5150. www.comfortinn.com.* 50 rms, 3 story. S, D $67; each addl $6; under 18 free; Rose Parade 3-day min. Crib free. TV; cable (premium), VCR (free movies). Heated pool, whirlpool. Sauna. Complimentary continental bkfst, coffee in rms. Ck-out noon. Coin lndry. Business servs avail. Valet serv. Refrigerators, microwaves. Cr cds: A, C, D, DS, ER, JCB, MC, V.

D

★★ **SAGA MOTOR HOTEL.** *1653 E. Colorado Blvd (91106). 626/795-0431; fax 626/792-0559; toll-free 800/793-7242.* 70 rms, 3 story. S $53-$79; D $55-$89; each addl $6; suites $69-$99; Rose Parade (3-day min). Crib free. TV; cable (premium). Heated pool. Complimentary continental bkfst. Ck-out noon. Business servs avail. Valet serv. Cr cds: A, C, D, DS, MC, V.

D

Hotels

★★★ **DOUBLETREE HOTEL.** *191 N Los Robles Ave (91101). 626/792-2727; fax 626/792-3755; res 800/222-8733. www.doubletreehotels.com.* 350 rms, 12 story. S, D $139-$199; each addl $20; suites $300-$1,200; under 16 free; wkend rates. Crib free. Garage parking $5; valet $10. TV; cable (premium). Heated pool, whirlpool, poolside serv. Coffee in rms. Restaurants 6:30 am-11 pm. Rm serv 24 hrs. Bars 11-1 am; entertainment Tues-Sat. Ck-out noon. Convention facilities. Business servs avail. Concierge. Gift shop. Airport transportation. Exercise rm; sauna, steam rm. Refrigerators, microwaves avail. Some balconies. City hall adj. Luxury level. Cr cds: A, C, D, DS, ER, JCB, MC, V.

D SC

★★★ **HILTON.** *168 S Los Robles Ave (91101). 626/577-1000; fax 626/584-3148; res 800/445-8667.* 291 rms, 13 story. S $120-$180; D $135-$195; each addl $15; suites $200-$500; under 18 free; family, wkend rates; Rose Parade (4-day min). Crib free. Valet $10/day, garage $5/day. TV; cable (premium). Heated pool, whirlpool. Coffee in rms. Restaurant 6 am-10 pm. Bar 11-1 am. Ck-out noon. Convention facilities. Business center. Gift shop. Barber, beauty shop. Exercise equipt. Minibars; some bathrm phones. Some balconies. Cr cds: A, C, D, DS, ER, JCB, MC, V.

D

★★★ **SHERATON PASADENA HOTEL.** *303 E Cordova St (91101). 626/449-4000; fax 626/584-1390; res 800/325-3535. www.sheratonpasadena.com.* 320 rms, 5 story. S, D $109-$179; each addl $15; suites $229-$350; under 19 free; Rose Parade (4-day min). Pet accepted, some restrictions. Garage $5. TV; cable (premium). Heated pool; poolside serv. Coffee in rms. Restaurant 6 am-2 pm, 5-10 pm. Bar 2 pm-1 am. Ck-out noon. Convention facilities. Business servs avail. Bellhops. Gift shop. Lighted tennis. Health club privileges. Some patios, balconies. Cr cds: A, C, D, DS, JCB, MC, V.

D

Resort

★★★★ **THE RITZ-CARLTON, HUNTINGTON HOTEL & SPA.** *1401 S Oak Knoll Ave (91106).*

626/568-3900; fax 626/568-3700; res 800/241-3333. www.ritz-carlton.com. Located just 20 minutes from downtown Los Angeles, this historic retreat feels like it's miles from anything. Excellent spa and salon services are designed to pamper guests, yet extensive business services provide business travelers with everything they need to suceed. The fitness center provides everything from virtual reality bikes to climbing equipment. 392 rms, 3-8 story, 16 suites, 7 cottages. S, D $245-$2,000; suites, cottages $350-$5,000; under 18 free; package plans. Crib free. Valet parking $19. TV; cable (premium), VCR avail. Heated pool, whirlpool, poolside serv. Restaurants 6 am-10 pm; (see also THE GRILL). Rm serv 24 hrs. Bar to midnight; Fri, Sat to 2 am; entertainment. Ck-out noon. Convention facilities. Business center. Concierge. Gift shop. Spa. Lighted tennis, pro. Golf privileges. Lawn games. Bicycle rental. Bathrm phones, minibars; many balconies. Luxury level. Cr cds: A, C, D, DS, ER, JCB, MC, V.

D

B&B/Small Inn

★★★ **ARTIST'S INN.** *1038 Magnolia St, South Pasadena (91030). 626/799-5668; fax 626/799-3678; res 888/799-5668.* 5 rms, 1 with shower only, 2 story. S, D $110-$165; each addl $20; wkends (2-day min); higher rates Rose Parade (4-day min). Children over 9 yrs only. TV avail. Complimentary full bkfst; afternoon refreshments. Restaurant nearby. Ck-out noon, ck-in 3-6 pm. 1890s Victorian style; antiques. Cr cds: A, DS, MC, V.

Restaurants

★★ **BECKHAM GRILL.** *77 W Walnut St (91103). 626/796-3399.* Hrs: 11:30 am-2:30 pm, 5-9:30 pm; Fri, Sat 5-10 pm; Sun 5-9:30 pm. Closed hols. Res accepted. Bar 11 am-11:30 pm; Fri, Sat 5 pm-midnight. Lunch $6.95-$13.75, dinner $11.95-$17.95. Specializes in prime rib, fresh seafood. Own baking. Valet parking. Outdoor dining. English inn decor; antiques. Cr cds: A, D, DS, MC, V.

D SC

★★★ **BISTRO 45.** *45 S Mentor Ave (91106). 626/795-2478. www.bistro45.com.* Hrs: 11:30 am-2:30 pm, 6-10 pm; Sat 5:30-11 pm; Sun 5-9 pm. Closed Mon; Jan 1, Thanksgiving, Dec 25. Res accepted. French menu. Bar. Wine list. A la carte entrees: lunch $11.45-$15.45, dinner $16.45-$25.45. Own pastries. Valet parking. Patio dining. Seasonal menu. Art Deco atmosphere. Cr cds: A, D, MC, V.

D

★★ **CAFE SANTORINI.** *64-70 W Union St (91103). 626/564-4200. www.cafesantorini.com.* Hrs: 11 am-11 pm; Fri, Sat to midnight. Closed hols. Italian, Mediterranean menu. Bar. Lunch $6.50-$9.95, dinner $8.95-$17.95. Specialties: grilled calamari, red curry paella. Own baking. Top-40, salsa music Fri and Sat. Outdoor dining on rooftop with garden terrace. Relaxed Mediterranean atmosphere. Cr cds: A, D, DS, MC, V.

D

★ **CROCODILE CAFE.** *140 S Lake Ave (91101). 626/449-9900.* Hrs: 11 am-10 pm; Fri, Sat to midnight. Closed Thanksgiving, Dec 25. California eclectic cuisine. Bar. A la carte entrees: lunch, dinner $6.75-$16.95. Specializes in pizza, salads, grilled items. Patio dining. Contemporary room open to kitchen. Cr cds: A, D, MC, V.

D

★★★ **THE GRILL.** *1401 S Oak Knoll Ave (91106). 626/568-3900. www.ritz-carlton.com.* Dine on perfectly prepared grilled meats and seafood at this clubby dining room located within the excellent Huntington Hotel. Service is top-notch, and servers will gladly accomodate any special request. A perfect spot for entertaining clients. French cuisine. Hrs: 6:30 am-10 pm. Res accepted. A la carte entrees: bkfst, lunch, dinner $20-$35. Children's menu. Outdoor dining. Valet parking. Jacket. Cr cds: A, C, D, DS, MC, V.

D

★ **HUGO MOLINA.** *1065 E Green St (91106). 626/449-7820. www.hugomolina.com.* California Eclectic with

Latin and Caribbean flair menu. Specializes in crab cakes, stuffed filet, Lamb chops. Hrs: 11 am-2 pm, 5-10 pm; Sat, Sun from 5 pm. Closed hols. Res accepted. Wine list. Lunch $4-$14, dinner $16-$23. Entertainment. Cr cds: A, D, DS, MC, V.

D

★★ **MCCORMICK & SCHMICK SEAFOOD.** *111 N Los Robles (91101). 626/405-0064. www.mccormickand schmicks.com.* Specializes in halibut, Atlantic salmon, crab, and shrimp cake. Hrs: 11:30 am-11 pm; Sun 10 am-10 pm. Res accepted. Wine, beer. Lunch $6-$15, dinner $7-$23. Children's menu. Entertainment. Cr cds: A, D, DS, JCB, MC, V.

D

★★ **MI PIACE.** *25 E Colorado Blvd (91105). 626/795-3131. www.citysearch. com/pas/mipiace.* Hrs: 11:30 am-11 pm; Fri, Sat to midnight. Closed Thanksgiving, Dec 25. Res accepted. Italian menu. Bar. A la carte entrees: lunch, dinner $5.50-$15.95. Specializes in traditional Southern Italian dishes. Valet parking. Outdoor dining. Casual trattoria atmosphere. Cr cds: A, D, MC, V.

D

★★ **MIYAKO.** *139 S Los Robles Ave (91101). 626/795-7005.* Hrs: 11:30 am-2 pm, 5:15-9 pm; Fri, Sat 5:15-9:30 pm; Sun 4-9 pm. Closed July 4, Thanksgiving, Dec 25. Res accepted. Japanese menu. Bar. Lunch $6.95-$13.95, dinner $7.95-$17.95. Children's menu. Specializes in shrimp tempura, beef sukiyaki, teriyaki dishes. Parking. Japanese and Western seating. Boat dinners. Family-owned. Totally nonsmoking. Cr cds: A, MC, V.

★★★ **OYE.** *69 N Raymond Ave (91103). 626/796-3286.* Hrs: 5:30-10:30 pm. Closed hols. Res accepted. Asian-Cuban menu. Bar. Wine list. A la carte entrees: dinner $15-$18. Specialties: calle zanja eggroll, crispy sea bass la charada, pa'canton giant prawns. Valet parking. Supper club atmosphere; tropical decor. Totally nonsmoking. Cr cds: A, C, D, DS, MC, V.

★★★ **PARKWAY GRILL.** *510 S Arroyo Pkwy (91105). 626/796-3399.* American regional menu. Specializes in whole fried catfish, prime tenderloin beef, roasted Chinese air-dried duck. Hrs: 11:30 am-2:30 pm, 5:30-11 pm; Fri, Sat to midnight. Closed hols. Res accepted. Wine list. Lunch $11-$20, dinner $17-$29. Entertainment: pianist. Daily harvest from own organic vegetable/herb garden. Cr cds: A, C, D, MC, V.

D

★ **PEPPER MILL.** *77 W Walnut St (91101). 626/796-3399.* Hrs: 11:30 am-9:30 pm; Mon to 9 pm; Fri, Sat to 10 pm; Sun 10:30 am-9 pm; early-bird dinner 3-5:30 pm; Sun brunch 10:30 am-3 pm. Closed Thanksgiving, Dec 25. Res accepted. Continental menu. Bar. Lunch $6.25-$14.50, dinner $7.95-$21.95. Sun brunch $9.50-$10.95. Children's menu. Specializes in prime rib, steak, seafood. Salad bar. Own desserts. Patio dining. Cr cds: A, MC, V.

D SC

★★★ **RAYMOND.** *1250 S Fair Oaks Ave (91105). 626/441-3136.* Hrs: 11:30 am-2:30 pm, 6-9:30 pm; Fri to 10 pm; Sat 5:45-10 pm; Sun 4:30-8 pm; Sat brunch 11 am-2:30 pm; Sun brunch 10 am-2:30 pm. Closed Mon; Jan 1, July 4, Dec 25. Res accepted. Bar. Wine cellar. A la carte entrees: lunch $10-$17, dinner $28-$32. Complete meals: lunch $15, dinner $28-$45. Specialties: Long Island roast duckling, grilled king salmon. Menu changes weekly. Own desserts. Patio dining. Turn-of-the-century caretaker's cottage; wood floors, lace curtains, fireplace. Cr cds: A, D, DS, MC, V.

D

★★ **SALADANG.** *363 S Fair Oaks Ave (91105). 626/793-8123.* Hrs: 10 am-10 pm. Closed hols. Res accepted. Thai menu. Wine, beer. Lunch, dinner $5.95-$15.95. Complete meals: lunch $6.95. Specialties: miang salmon, Saladang spicy noodles. Parking. Work by local artists; casual ambience. Art Deco decor. Totally nonsmoking. Cr cds: A, MC, V.

D

★★★ **SHIRO.** *1505 Mission St, South Pasadena (91030). 626/799-4774.* Hrs: 6-9 pm; Fri, Sat to 10 pm; Sun 5:30-9 pm. Closed Mon; hols; also 3 wks in Sept. Res accepted. Continental menu. Wine, beer. Dinner $16-$25.50. Specialties: tuna steak with shimeji and shiitake mushrooms in sesame sauce, whole sizzling catfish with ponzu sauce and fresh cilantro. Daily menu. Bistro atmosphere. Totally nonsmoking. Cr cds: A, MC, V.

D

★★ **TWIN PALMS.** *101 W Green St (91105). 626/577-2567. www.twin-palms.com.* Hrs: 11:30 am-midnight; Fri, Sat to 1:30 am; Sun brunch 10:30 am-3 pm. Closed Dec 25. Res accepted. California coastal menu. Bar. A la carte entrees: lunch $8-$14, dinner $9-$29. Sun brunch $21.95-$24.95. Extensive salad selection. Own baking. Entertainment. Patio dining. In converted warehouse; California resort atmosphere. Cr cds: A, D, DS, MC, V.

D

★★★ **XIOMARA.** *69 N Raymond Ave (91103). 626/796-2520. www.citysearch.com/pas/xiomara.* Hrs: 11:30 am-2:30 pm, 5:30-10:30 pm; Sat, Sun from 5:30 pm. Closed hols. Res accepted. Continental menu. Bar. A la carte entrees: lunch $9-$15, dinner $17-$25. Complete meals: 3-course lunch $9.50, dinner (Mon) $20. Specialties: rock shrimp tamal, Chilean sea bass, churrasco Nicaraguense. Valet parking. Outdoor dining. Bistro atmosphere. Original artwork. Cr cds: A, D, DS, MC, V.

D

★★★ **YUJEAN KANG'S.** *67 N Raymond Ave (91103). 626/585-0855. www.ladinig.com/yujeankangs.* Hrs: Mon-Thurs, Sun 11:30 am-2:30 pm, 5-9:30 pm. Fri, Sat to 10 pm. Closed Thanksgiving. Res accepted. Chinese menu. Beer, wine. Lunch $6.95-$8.50, dinner $7.95-$17.95. Specialties: tea-smoked duck, crisp beef with Chinese baby bok choy. Own ice cream. Totally nonsmoking. Cr cds: A, D, DS, MC, V.

D

Unrated Dining Spot

MAISON AKIRA. *713 E Green St (91101). 626/796-9501.* Specializes in miso marinated Chilean sea bass, baby rack of lamb. Hrs: 11:30 am-2 pm, 6-9 pm; Fri to 10 pm; Sat 6-10 pm; Sun 5-8 pm. Res accepted. Wine, beer. Lunch $9.50-$14.50, dinner $15-$24. Entertainment. Cr cds: A, D, JCB, MC, V.

D

Paso Robles

(C-2) *See also Atascadero*

Pop 18,600 **Elev** 721 ft **Area code** 805 **Zip** 93446

Information Chamber of Commerce, 1225 Park St; 805/238-0506 or 800/406-4040

Web www.pasorobleschamber.com

Franciscan Fathers named this city for the great oak trees in the area, at the southern end of the fertile Salinas River Valley. Lying between mountains on the west and barley and grape fields on the east, Paso Robles is also noted for its almond tree orchards.

What to See and Do

Lake Nacimiento Resort. Swimming, waterskiing, fishing, boating (dock, landing, dry storage, rentals), marina (all yr, daily); picnicking, lodge, cafe, general store, camping (fee). Park (daily). 17 mi NW on Lake Nacimiento Dr (G14), off US 101. Phone 805/238-3256. ¢¢¢¢¢

Lake San Antonio Recreation Area. Swimming, waterskiing, fishing, boating (marina, launching, rentals); picnicking, snack bar, grocery, lndry, camping (fee); trailer facilities (off-season rates mid-Sept-mid-May). Pets on leash only; fee. Fee for activities. (Daily) 28 mi NW off US 101, between Nacimiento and Lockwood on Interlake Rd. Phone 805/472-2311. ¢¢

Mission San Miguel Arc Angel. (1797). Sixteenth in chain of 21 Franciscan missions; interior is in excellent condition; frescoes by Esteban Munras and his Native American helpers (1821); museum. Picnic facilities. (Daily; closed hols) 7 mi N via US 101, Mission St in San Miguel. Phone 805/467-3256.

Wineries. For a brochure describing many of the 35 wineries in the Paso

Robles appellation, tours and tasting rms, contact the Chamber of Commerce.

Special Events

Wine Festival. Wine tasting, winemaker dinner concerts, and open houses. Third Sat May. Phone 805/238-0506.

California Mid-State Fair. Rodeo, horse show, amusements, entertainment. Aug. Phone 805/239-0655.

Motels/Motor Lodges

★★ ADELAIDE INN. *1215 Ysabel Ave (93446). 805/238-2770; fax 805/238-3497; toll-free 800/549-7276. www.adelaideinn.com.* 67 rms, 1-2 story. May-mid-Oct: S $45-$60; D $59-$65; each addl $5; lower rates rest of yr. Crib $3. TV; cable (premium), VCR avail (movies). Heated pool, whirlpool. Playground. Complimentary coffee in rms. Restaurant nearby. Ck-out noon. Coin lndry. Meeting rm. Business servs avail. In-rm modem link. Valet serv. Sundries. Free airport, RR station, bus depot transportation. Health club privileges. Putting green. Refrigerators; microwaves avail. Picnic tables, grills. Cr cds: A, C, D, DS, JCB, MC, V.

D SC

★★ BEST WESTERN BLACK OAK MOTOR LODGE. *1135 24th St (93446). 805/238-4740; fax 805/238-0726; toll-free 800/528-1234. www.bestwestern.com/blackoakmotorlodge.* 110 units, 2 story. May-mid-Oct: S, D $57-$79; each addl $6; suites $104-$115; lower rates rest of yr. Crib $3. TV; cable, VCR avail (movies $2). Pool, whirlpool. Sauna. Playground. Complimentary coffee in rms. Restaurant 6 am-10 pm. Ck-out noon. Coin lndry. Business servs avail. In-rm modem link. Valet serv. Free airport transportation. Refrigerators. Picnic table, grills. Cr cds: A, C, D, DS, JCB, MC, V.

D SC

★ MELODY RANCH MOTEL. *939 Spring St (93446). 805/238-3911; toll-free 800/909-3911.* 19 rms. May-mid-Sept: S $36-$44; D $42-$50; higher rates special events; lower rates rest of yr. Crib $2. TV; cable. Heated pool. Complimentary coffee in rms. Restaurant adj 7 am-10 pm. Ck-out noon. Picnic table. Cr cds: A, C, D, DS, MC, V.

D

Restaurant

★ F. MCLINTOCK'S SALOON. *1234 Park St (93446). 805/238-2233.* Hrs: 11:30 am-9 pm; Fri to 10 pm; Sat 8 am-10 pm; Sun 8 am-9 pm. Closed Jan 1, Thanksgiving, Dec 25. Bar. Bkfst $3.75-$8.25, lunch $4.50-$9.25, dinner $5-$16.50. Children's menu. Specializes in steak. Street parking. Unique ranch era decor. Totally nonsmoking. Cr cds: A, DS, MC, V.

D

Pebble Beach

(B-1) *See also Carmel, Monterey, Pacific Grove*

Pop 5,000 **Elev** 0-37 ft **Area code** 831 **Zip** 93953

Pebble Beach is noted for its scenic beauty, the palatial houses of its residents, and the Pebble Beach golf courses, where the annual National Pro-Amateur Golf Championship is held (see MONTEREY).

Hotel

★★★★ CASA PALMERO PEBBLE BEACH. *1518 Cypress Dr (93953).* 800/654-8598; *fax 831/622-6650. www.pebblebeach.com.* This elegant, yet intimate 24-room inn is situated on the fabled grounds of Pebble Beach Golf Club. The Mediterranean inspired, formerly private estate offers luxurious public rooms with an emphasis on comfort. Each of the beautifully appointed, spacious guestrooms features a wood-burning fireplace, an oversized soaking tub, and separate shower. Ground floor spa rooms open to a private patio with whirlpool. Pebble Beach Spa is just a few steps away. Guests have access to all the facilities of the two sister properties, The Lodge at Pebble Beach and the Inn at Spanish Bay. In addition, a Continental breakfast, choice of newspaper, and complimentary evening beverages and snacks are provided. 24 rms, 2 story, 3 suites. S $600; D $850; suites

$1750. Crib avail. Valet parking avail. Pool, whirlpool. TV; cable (premium), VCR avail, CD avail. Complimentary continental bkfst, coffee in rms, newspaper, toll-free calls. Restaurant nearby. 24-hr rm serv. Bar. Ck-out noon, ck-in 2 pm. Meeting rms. Fax servs avail. Bellhops. Dry cleaning. Gift shop. Salon/barber avail. Exercise priviliges, sauna, steam rm. Beach access. Bike rentals. Video games. Cr cds: A, D, DS, JCB, MC, V.

D

Resorts

★★★★ **THE INN AT SPANISH BAY.** *2700 Seventeen Mile Dr (93953). 831/647-7500; fax 831/644-7955; toll-free 800/654-9300. www.pebble-beach.com.* This premier golf resort boasts some of the best facilities for golfers to be had in the United States, including a knowledgeable professional staff of caddies and golf pros. Those not interested in putting can indulge in spa treatments, horseback ride, play tennis at the tennis and beach club, or relax by the water. 270 units, 4 story. S, D $388-$517; suites $745-$2,385; under 18 free; golf, tennis plans. Serv charge $17 per day per rm. Crib free. TV; cable, VCR avail. Heated pool, whirlpool, poolside serv. Dining rm 6:30 am-10 pm. Box lunches, picnics. Rm serv 24 hrs. Bar 10-2 am. Ck-out noon, ck-in 4 pm. Lndry facility. Convention facilities. Business center. In-rm modem link. Concierge. Shopping arcade. Free valet parking. Lighted tennis. 72-hole golf, greens fee $75-$295 (incl cart), pro, putting green. Private beach. Bicycle rentals. Equestrian center. Hiking trails. Exercise rm; sauna. Massage. Health club privileges. Minibars, fireplaces; microwaves avail. Private patios, balconies. Picnic tables, grills. Complimentary shuttle service to the lodge and golf courses. Cr cds: A, C, D, DS, JCB, MC, V.

D

★★★★ **THE LODGE AT PEBBLE BEACH.** *Seventeen Mile Dr (93953). 831/624-3811; fax 831/625-8598; toll-free 800/654-9300.* The Lodge at Pebble Beach is a golfer's paradise, with seven championship courses that overlook the shores of the Pacific. The owners made the intelligent move of recently adding a full-service spa, providing non-golfers with somthing to do other than looking at the stellar views. Club XIX is a fine dining destination, though there are many dining options on the property. Though this property is beginning to show signs of wear and tear, it remains a favored destination in the area. 161 rms, 1-3 story. S, D $395-$575; suites $730-$2,080; under 18 free. Serv charge $15/day. Crib free. Pet accepted. TV; cable (premium), VCR avail. Heated pool, waking pool, whirlpool, poolside serv. Supervised children's activities (June-Aug). Restaurants. Box lunches, snacks. Rm serv 24 hrs. Bar 11-1 am. Ck-out noon, ck-in 4 pm. Convention facilities. Business serv avail. In-rm modem link. Valet serv. Concierge. Shopping arcade. Barber, beauty shop. Valet parking. Free airport transportation. Tennis. 4 golf courses, par-3 golf, greens fee $165-$295, putting green, 2 driving ranges. Private beach. Exercise rm; sauna, steam rm. Massage. Fireplaces; refrigerators, microwaves avail; some wet bars. Private patios, balconies. Cr cds: A, C, D, DS, ER, JCB, MC, V.

D

Spyglass Course, Pebble Beach

Restaurants

★★★★ **CLUB XIX.** *Seventeen Mile Dr (93953). 831/624-3811. www.pebble-beach.com.* Guests can dine on the lovely brick patio, kept warm by two fireplaces, to take full advantage of the view of Carmel Bay and the 18th green of the famous Pebble Beach links. The formal French fare includes dishes like pan seared foie gras with beluga lentils and a cassoulet of lobster and duck confit. Each night there is also a vegetarian tasting menu. Contemporary French menu. Specializes in filet mignon, sea bass, rack of lamb. Own baking. Hrs: 11:30 am-3:30 pm, 6-10 pm. Bar. Wine cellar. Res accepted. A la carte entrees: lunch $10-$19, dinner $27-$38. Parking. Outdoor dining. Cr cds: A, C, D, DS, ER, MC, V.

D

★★★ **ROY'S AT PEBBLE BEACH.** *2700 Seventeen Mile Dr (93953). 831/647-7423.* Hrs: 6:30 am-10 pm. Res accepted. Eclectic menu. Bar 11 am-11 pm. Wine list. A la carte entrees: bkfst $7.95-$11.95, lunch $8.25-$22.95, dinner $13.95-$25.95. Children's menu. Specializes in seafood, steak, pasta. Valet parking. Outdoor dining. Modern decor. View of ocean, golf course. Cr cds: A, MC, V.

D

★★★ **STILLWATER BAR AND GRILL.** *Seventeen Mile Dr (93953). 831/625-8524. www.pebble-beach.com.* Hrs: 7 am-2:30 pm, 6-10 pm; Sun brunch 10 am-2:30 pm. Res accepted. Bar 10 am-midnight. Wine cellar. A la carte entrees: bkfst $10-$14, lunch $9.95-$19, dinner $18-$28. Sun brunch buffet $30. Children's menu. Specializes in seafood from Pacific Northwest. View of golf course, Carmel Bay. Totally nonsmoking. Cr cds: A, C, D, DS, ER, MC, V.

Petaluma

(F-2) *See also Guerneville, Napa, Santa Rosa, Sonoma*

Pop 43,184 **Elev** 12 ft **Area code** 707 **Zip** 94952

Information Petaluma Visitors Program, 800 Baywood Dr, 94954; 707/769-0429

Web www.petaluma.org

What to See and Do

The Great Petaluma Mill. Refurbished historic grain mill housing shops intermingled with remnants of the riverboat era of the building. (Daily; closed Dec 25) 6 Petaluma Blvd N. **FREE**

Marin French Cheese Company. Manufacturer of soft ripening cheeses, incl Camembert, Brie, Breakfast, and Schloss. Guided tours (daily; closed Jan 1, Thanksgiving, Dec 25). 7500 Red Hill Rd, ¼ mi S of jct Novato Blvd and Petaluma-Point Reyes Rd. Phone 707/762-6001. **FREE**

Petaluma Adobe State Historic Park. Restored adobe ranch house, built 1834-1845 for General M. G. Vallejo, combines Monterey Colonial style with the traditional Spanish-Mexican plan. (Daily; closed Jan 1, Thanksgiving, Dec 25) 3325 Adobe Rd, 3 mi E of US 101 on CA 116. Phone 707/762-4871. ¢

Petaluma Historical Museum and Library. Built with a grant from Andrew Carnegie in 1906, the museum contains one of California's only free-standing glass domes. Permanent and changing exhibits of Petaluma history. (Wed-Sun; closed hols) 20 Fourth St. Phone 707/778-4398. **FREE**

Petaluma Village Factory Outlets. More than 50 name brand outlet stores in village-style setting. (Daily) 2200 Petaluma Blvd N. Phone 707/778-9300.

Special Events

Sonoma-Marin Fair. Agricultural fair, carnival, rodeo, entertainment. Phone 707/763-0931. Five days late June.

World Wrist Wrestling Championships. Phone 707/778-1430. Second Sat Oct.

Motels/Motor Lodges

★★ **BEST WESTERN INN.** *200 S McDowell Blvd (94954). 707/763-0994; fax 707/778-3111; toll-free 800/297-3846.* 75 rms, 38 with shower only, 2 story. S $68-$100; D $92-$116; each addl $6; under 12 free; higher rates special events. Crib free. TV; cable (premium). Heated pool. Complimentary coffee in lobby. Restaurant adj 6:30 am-11 pm. Ck-out 11 am. Coin lndry. Business servs avail. In-rm modem link. Cr cds: A, C, D, DS, MC, V.

D SC

★★ **QUALITY INN.** *5100 Montero Way (94954). 707/664-1155; fax 707/664-8566; toll-free 800/228-5151. www.lokhotels.com.* 110 rms, 2 story, 4 suites. S, D $79-$152; each addl $5; suites $110-$180; under 18 free. Crib $5. TV; cable (premium). Heated pool, whirlpool. Sauna. Complimentary continental bkfst. Coffee in rms. Restaurant adj open 24 hrs. Ck-out noon. Coin lndry. Meeting rm. Business servs avail. Valet serv. Refrigerators; microwaves avail. Cr cds: A, C, D, DS, ER, JCB, MC, V.

D

Restaurants

★★ **BUONA SERA.** *148 Kentucky St (94952). 707/763-3333.* Hrs: 5-9 pm; Fri, Sat to 10 pm. Closed hols. Res accepted. Italian menu. Wine, beer. Dinner $13.95-$19.95. Children's menu. Specializes in pasta, fresh seafood. Italian trattoria decor. Cr cds: A, MC, V.

D

★ **DE SCHMIRE.** *304 Bodega Ave (94952). 707/762-1901.* Hrs: 5:30-10 pm; Sun to 9 pm. Closed hols. Res accepted. No A/C. Continental menu. Wine, beer. A la carte entrees: dinner $14-$20. Children's menu. Specialties: ahi tuna baked in nut crust, chicken Zanzibar, chicken Dijonaise. Parking. European bistro atmosphere; open kitchen. Eclectic mix of European, California, Pacific rim cuisine. Cr cds: A, D, DS, MC, V.

D

★ **GRAZIANO'S.** *170 Petaluma Blvd N (94952). 707/762-5997. www.sterba.com/graziano.* Hrs: 5-9:30 pm; Fri, Sat 5:30-10 pm. Closed Mon; hols. Res accepted. Italian menu. Bar. Dinner $10-$25.50. Specializes in fresh fish, rack of lamb. Open kitchen. Totally nonsmoking. Cr cds: A, MC, V.

D

Pine Valley

(F-6) *See also El Cajon, San Diego*

Settled 1869 **Pop** 1,297 **Elev** 3,736 ft **Area code** 619 **Zip** 92062

What to See and Do

Cleveland National Forest. Surrounds town. Nearly 420,000 acres; dense chaparral environment with conifers at higher levels, treelike manzanitas, Palomar Observatory (see ESCONDIDO). Fishing; hiking, riding, nature trails, guided walks, picnicking, camping. Incl Laguna Mountain Recreation Area, 10 mi NE of I-8 on County S1. Fees at developed recreation sites. Contact Forest Supervisor, 10845 Rancho Bernardo Dr, Suite 200, San Diego 92127-2107. Phone 858/673-6180.

Pinnacles National Monument

(B-2) *See also King City, Salinas*

(35 mi S of Hollister, off CA 25 or 35 mi NE of King City, off US 101; also 11 mi E of Soledad, off US 101)

Geologic activity formed a large volcano 23 million years ago—Pinnacles is the eroded remnant. The volcano formed where two plates of the earth's crust grind together along the San Andreas fault; one portion has remained near the point of origin, while the other has shifted 195 miles northward. The former section now lies between Gorman and Lancaster; the latter section, traveling at a rate of two centimeters a year, is the Pinnacles—an area of three square miles eroded by wind, rain, heat, frost, and chemical action. Also here are the canyons of Bear Gulch and Chalone Creek, containing talus caves or "covered canyons," formed by large blocks of rock that have slipped from the steep walls. In all, the monument covers 25 square miles, is four miles wide, and seven miles long. It has a variety of bird life, including the prairie falcon, turkey vulture, and golden eagle.

Hiking is the main activity, with well-defined trails (some strenuous). High Peaks Trail follows the spectacular cliffs and pinnacles; the North Chalone Peak Trail reaches 3,305 feet, the highest point in the monument. Trails in the caves area are shorter but equally interesting.

There are picnic areas with barbecue grills on both the east and west sides. Visitors must bring their own fuel. No wood fires permitted during high fire season (usually June-Oct). Pets on leash only; not permitted on trails. There is limited camping on west side (June-Jan only) and there is a private campground outside east entrance (phone 831/389-4462). A service station and camper store are also available there. Interpretive programs on east side (mid-Feb-Memorial Day, wkends). There is no through road; access to the east entrance is via Hollister, off CA 25 or via King City, off US 101. The west entrance is reached via Soledad, off US 101. Visitor center on east side. For campground and visitor information phone 831/389-4485. Golden Eagle Passport (see MAKING THE MOST OF YOUR TRIP). Per vehicle **¢¢**

Pismo Beach

(D-2) *See also San Luis Obispo, Santa Maria*

Pop 7,669 **Elev** 33 ft **Area code** 805 **Zip** 93449

Information Conference & Visitors Bureau, 760 Mattie Rd; 805/773-7034 or 800/443-7778 (CA)

Web www.pismobeach.org

This town is famous for its 23 miles of scenic beach. Ocean fishing, dunes, swimming, surfing, diving, golf, horseback riding, and camping make the area popular with vacationers. Pismo Beach is also in a growing wine region. It is the last Pacific oceanfront community where autos can still be driven on the beach (access ramps are at two locations along the beach). A more dramatic and rugged coastline is found at Shell Beach, to the north, which has been incorporated into Pismo Beach.

What to See and Do

Lopez Recreational Area. On lake created by Lopez Dam. Swimming, waterskiing, water slide, windsurfing, fishing, boating; hiking, picnicking, primitive camping, tent and trailer sites (hookups, dump station; fee). Summer campfire programs, boat tours. 12 mi SE via US 101, Grand Ave exit. Phone 805/788-2381. Day use, per vehicle **¢¢**

Monarch Butterfly Grove. The state's largest winter site for Monarch butterflies; they can be seen in the grove located at the North Beach Campground (Oct-Feb, daily; dependent on butterfly migration). Pismo State Beach, 1 mi S via CA 1, North Beach Campground exit. Phone 805/489-1869. **FREE**

Oceano Dunes State Vehicular Recreation Area. Operated by the state park system to provide location for off-highway vehicle use (vehicle access to the beach is not common in California). (Daily) 2 mi S via CA 1, Pier Ave exit. Phone 805/473-7220. **¢¢¢**

Wineries of the Edna Valley & Arroyo Grande Valley. Several wineries, many with public tasting rms and offering tours, may be found along the county roads of Edna Valley and Arroyo Grande Valley; approx 5-8 mi NE and SE via CA 227 off US 101. Many are free; fee at some. Contact the Chamber of Commerce for winery maps. Phone 800/443-7778.

Special Event

Pismo Beach Clam Festival. Well-known festival held annually at Pismo Beach pier. Incl parade, clam chowder contest, sand sculpture contest, rubber duckie regatta, a clam dig, carnival rides, and food booths. Mid-Oct. Phone 805/773-4382. **¢¢**

Motels/Motor Lodges

★★ BEST WESTERN CASA GRANDE INN. *850 Oak Park Rd, Arroyo Grande (93420). 805/481-7398; fax 805/481-4859; res 800/475-9777.* 114 rms, 2-3 story, 21 suites. June-mid-Sept: S $75-$90; D $85-$120; each addl $10; suites $100-$140; family rates; hols (2-day min); lower rates rest of yr. Crib free. TV; cable (premium), VCR avail. Pool, whirlpool. Complimentary continental bkfst; afternoon refreshments. Restaurant noon-10 pm. Bar. Ck-out 11 am. Meeting rms. Business servs avail. Coin lndry. Exercise equipt; sauna. Game rm. Many refrigerators; some wet bars; microwaves avail. Some balconies. Adj shopping mall. Cr cds: A, C, D, DS, MC, V.

D

★★★ KON TIKI INN. *1621 Price St (93449). 805/773-4833; fax 805/773-6541; toll-free 888/566-8454. www.kontikiinn.com.* 86 rms, 3-4 story. Mid-Mar-early Oct: S, D $92-$104; each addl $7; lower rates rest of yr. Crib $7. TV; cable (premium). Heated pool, whirlpools. Complimentary continental bkfst. Restaurant 11:30 am-2 pm. Bar. Ck-out noon. Coin lndry. Meeting rms. Business servs avail. In-rm modem link. Lighted tennis. Exercise rm; sauna. Massage. Refrigerators; some fireplaces. Private patios, balconies. On ocean; stairway to beach. Cr cds: A, DS, JCB, MC, V.

D SC

★★★ SEA CREST RESORT MOTEL. *2241 Price St (93449). 805/773-4608; fax 805/773-4525; toll-free 800/782-8400. www.sea-crest.com.* 160 rms, 4 story. Memorial Day-Labor Day: S, D $79-$109; each addl $10; suites $125-$175; lower rates rest of yr. Crib $5. TV; cable (premium). Heated pool, whirlpools. Coffee in rms. Restaurant 8 am-10 pm. Ck-out noon. Coin lndry. Meeting rms. Business servs avail. Lawn games. Refrigerators. Private patios, balconies. Picnic tables, grills. On beach; ocean view from some rms, walkway to beach. Sun deck. Cr cds: A, C, D, DS, JCB, MC, V.

D SC

★★ SEA GYPSY MOTEL. *1020 Cypress St (93449). 805/773-1801; fax 805/773-9286; toll-free 800/592-5923. www.seagypsymotel.com.* 77 units, 3 story, 47 kits. S $35-$105; D $40-$105; each addl $10; suites $75-$190. Crib free. TV; cable. Heated pool, whirlpool. Complimentary coffee in lobby. Ck-out noon. Coin lndry. Business servs avail. In-rm modem link. Refrigerators. Private patios, balconies. On ocean, sand beach. Cr cds: A, DS, MC, V.

★★★ SEA VENTURE RESORT. *100 Ocean View Ave (93449). 805/773-4994; fax 805/773-0924; toll-free 800/662-4545. www.seaventure.com.* 51 rms, 3 story. Memorial Day-Labor Day: S, D $139-$349; each addl $15; 3-bedrm cottage $300-$650; under 18 free; wkends, hols (2-day min); higher rates: hols, special events; lower rates rest of yr. Crib free. TV; cable, VCR (movies). Pool. Complimentary continental bkfst, coffee in rms. Restaurant 4-9 pm; Sun 9 am-2 pm. Bar. Ck-out noon. Meeting rms. Business servs avail. In-rm modem link. Bellhops. Valet serv. Concierge. Gift shop. Free garage parking. 18-hole golf privileges, greens fee $20. Massage. Health club privileges. Bathrm phones, refrigerators, minibars, wet bars, fireplaces; many in-rm whirlpools. Many balconies. On beach. Totally nonsmoking. Cr cds: A, C, D, DS, MC, V.

D

★★★ SPYGLASS INN SHELL BEACH. *2705 Spyglass Dr, Shell Beach (93449). 805/773-4855; fax 805/773-5298; toll-free 800/824-2612. www.spyglassinn.com.* 82 rms, 1-2 story. S, D $59-$159; each addl $6; suites, kit. units $89-$179; under 12 free; higher rates wkends. TV; cable, VCR (movies $3). Pool, whirlpool. Coffee in rms. Restaurant 7 am-2 pm, 4-9:30 pm. Bar 10-2 am; entertainment Fri-Sat. Ck-out 11 am. Meeting rm. Business servs avail. Refrigerators. Many private patios, balconies with ocean view. Cr cds: A, C, D, DS, ER, MC, V.

D

Hotels

★★★ THE CLIFFS RESORT. *2757 Shell Beach, Shell Beach (93449). 805/773-5000; fax 805/773-0764; toll-*

free 800/826-7827. 165 rms, 5 story, 27 suites. S, D $145-$200; suites $275-$375; under 18 free; wkend packages; golf plans. Crib free. TV; cable, VCR avail. Heated pool; whirlpool, poolside serv. Complimentary coffee in lobby. Restaurant 7 am-9:30 pm; Fri, Sat to 10 pm. Bar 11-2 am; entertainment. Ck-out noon. Coin lndry. Meeting rms. Business servs avail. In-rm modem link. Valet serv. Gift shop. Valet parking. Free airport, RR station, bus depot transportation. Exercise rm; sauna. Lawn games. Some refrigerators. Whirlpool in suites. Private patios, balconies. On cliff overlooking beach. Cr cds: A, C, D, DS, ER, JCB, MC, V.

D

★★ **SANDCASTLE INN.** *100 Stimson Ave (93449). 805/773-2422; fax 805/773-0771; toll-free 800/822-6606. www.sandcastleinn.com*. 60 rms, 3 story. Memorial Day-Labor Day: S, D $89-$169; suites $175-$250; under 12 free; lower rates rest of yr. Crib free. TV; cable, VCR (movies). Complimentary continental bkfst, coffee in rms. Ck-out 11 am. Business servs avail. Whirlpool. Refrigerators; some fireplaces. Patios, balconies. On beach. Cr cds: A, D, DS, MC, V.

D SC

All Suite

★★★ **OXFORD SUITES RESORT.** *651 Five Cities Dr (93449). 805/773-3773; fax 805/773-5177; toll-free 800/982-7848. www.oxfordsuites.com*. 133 suites, 2 story. S, D $79-$129; each addl $10; under 10 free. Crib free. Pet accepted; $10. TV; cable, VCR (movies $3). Heated pool, wading pool, whirlpool. Complimentary full bkfst. Ck-out noon. Coin lndry. Meeting rm. Business servs avail. Valet serv. Gift shop. Refrigerators, microwaves. Cr cds: A, C, D, DS, MC, V.

D

Restaurants

★★ **F. MCLINTOCK'S.** *750 Mattie Rd (93448). 805/773-1892. www.mclintocks.com*. Hrs: 4-10 pm; Sat 3-10:30 pm; Sun 9 am-9:30 pm; early-bird dinner Mon-Fri 4-6 pm, Sat 3-5 pm; Sun noon-5 pm; Sun brunch 9-11:30 am. Closed hols. Res accepted Mon-Thurs, Sun. Bar. Complete meals: dinner $9.50-$30.95. Sun brunch $9.95-$13.95. Children's menu. Specializes in steak, seafood, oak pit barbecue. Guitarist (seasonal). Unique ranch-era decor incl 6-foot-high stuffed buffalo, old farm implements, blacksmith, and branding gear. Cr cds: A, DS, MC, V.

D

★★ **ROSA'S.** *491 Price St (93449). 805/773-0551*. Hrs: 11:30 am-2 pm, 4-9:30 pm; Sat, Sun 4-10 pm. Closed Thanksgiving, Dec 25. Italian menu. Bar. Lunch $5.45-$10.25, dinner $7.95-$17.45. Children's menu. Specializes in pasta, seafood, chicken. Parking. Patio dining. Extensive floral display. Totally nonsmoking. Cr cds: A, D, DS, MC, V.

D

Placerville

(E-4) *See also Auburn, Sacramento*

Founded 1848 **Pop** 8,355 **Elev** 1,866 ft **Area code** 530 **Zip** 95667

Information El Dorado County Chamber of Commerce, 542 Main St; 530/621-5885 or 800/457-6279

Web www.eldoradocounty.org

This one-time rough-and-tough gold town was first known as Dry Diggins (because the gravel had to be carried to water to be washed for gold) and later as Hangtown (because of the number of hangings necessary to keep law and order). At one time the town rivaled San Francisco and nurtured three notables: Mark Hopkins, railroad magnate; Philip D. Armour, meat-packing magnate; and John Studebaker, automobile magnate. A few mines still function, but lumbering, agriculture, and recreation are the main industries.

What to See and Do

El Dorado County Historical Museum. Displays and exhibits of early Gold Rush days, when Miwok, Maidu, and Washoe inhabited the area. (Wed-Sun; closed hols) 104 Placerville Dr. Phone 530/621-5865. **FREE**

El Dorado National Forest. Approx 786,000 acres. Incl the 105,364-acre

Mokelumne Wilderness, located between CA 4 and CA 88, and the popular 63,475-acre Desolation Wilderness, located immediately W of Lake Tahoe. Campgrounds have varying fees and facilities; all are closed in winter. 25 mi E via US 50. Contact the Information Center, 3070 Camino Heights Dr, Camino 95709. Phone 530/644-6048.

Gold Bug Mine. Municipally owned double-shaft gold mine with exposed vein; restored gold stampmill. Picnic area. Guided tours avail (res required, fee). (Mid-Apr-Oct, daily; rest of yr, wkends) In Hangtown's Gold Bug Park. Phone 530/642-5207. ¢¢

Marshall Gold Discovery State Historic Park. Marks place where James Marshall found flecks of gold in tailrace of Sutter's Mill in Jan of 1848. By the next yr more than $10 million in gold had been taken from the American River's South Fork. Park incl Gold Discovery Museum (daily; closed Jan 1, Thanksgiving, Dec 25), Marshall's cabin and monument where he is buried, Thomas House Museum, operating replica of Sutter's mill, blacksmith shop, and several other buildings. Fishing; nature and hiking trails, picnicking, concession. Park (daily). 8 mi NW on CA 49 in Coloma. Phone 530/622-3470. ¢

Special Events

El Dorado County Fair. Fairgrounds, SW on US 50. June.

Wagon Train Week. Celebrations each night along wagon train trek (US 50) from Nevada to Placerville. Sat celebrations at fairgrounds; parade on Sun. Mid-June.

Motels/Motor Lodges

★★ **BEST WESTERN.** *3361 Coach Ln, Cameron Park (95682). 530/677-2203; fax 530/676-1422; toll-free 800/601-1234.* 62 rms, 1-2 story. S $51-$65; D $56-$70; each addl $5; suites $75-$104; under 16 free; family rates. Crib free. Pet accepted. TV; cable (premium), VCR avail. Complimentary continental bkfst, coffee in rms. Restaurant adj 6-2 am. Ck-out noon. Meeting rms. Business center. Coin lndry. Golf privileges. Health club privileges. Outdoor pool. Some refrigerators, microwaves. Some balconies. Grills. Cr cds: A, C, D, DS, MC, V.

D

★★ **BEST WESTERN INN.** *6850 Greenleaf Dr (95667). 530/622-9100; res 800/528-1234.* 105 rms, 3 story. No elvtr. S $60-$70; D $71-$82; each addl $10; suites from $138; under 12 free. Crib free. Pet accepted; $10. TV; cable. Heated pool, whirlpool. Coffee in rms. Restaurant adj. Ck-out 11 am. Meeting rms. Business servs avail. Some patios, balconies. Cr cds: A, D, DS, MC, V.

D

B&B/Small Inn

★★ **COLOMA COUNTRY INN.** *345 High St, Coloma (95613). 530/622-6919. www.colomacountryinn.com.* 6 rms, 2 share bath, 2 story, 2 suites, 1 guest house. No rm phones. S, D $90-$110; suites $130-$180; guest house $310; package plans; hols (2-day min). Complimentary full bkfst; afternoon refreshments. Restaurant nearby. Ck-out 11 am, ck-in 4 pm. Playground. Lawn games. Refrigerator in suites. Picnic tables, grills. Built in 1852. Totally nonsmoking.

Restaurant

★ **LYON'S.** *1160 Broadway (95667). 530/622-2305.* Hrs: open 24 hrs; Sat, Sun brunch 9 am-3 pm. Bar. Bkfst $2.99-$8, lunch $5.99-$8.99, dinner $8.99-$12.99. Sat, Sun brunch $6.99-$8.99. Children's menu. Specialties: prime rib, Yankee pot roast, sizzling steak platters. Parking. Children eat free on Tuesdays. Totally nonsmoking. Cr cds: A, DS, MC, V.

D SC

Pleasanton

(G-3) *See also Fremont, Hayward, Livermore, Oakland*

Settled 1851 **Pop** 50,553 **Elev** 352 ft **Area code** 925 **Zip** 94566

Information Tri-Valley Convention & Visitors Bureau, 260 Main St; 925/846-8910 or 888/874-9253

Named for the friend of an early settler, Pleasanton was once called "the most desperate town in the West," for its many bandits and desperados. Phoebe Apperson Hearst founded the PTA in Pleasanton.

What to See and Do

Alameda County Fairgrounds. Exhibit area; 9-hole golf course. Events and activities. Oldest racetrack west of the Mississippi River. Thoroughbred racing during county fair (see ANNUAL EVENT); satellite-broadcast races yr-round. 4501 Pleasanton Ave, I-680 at Bernal Ave. Phone 925/426-7600.

Blackhawk Auto Museum. Display of 110 classic and rare automobiles, many custom-built. Modern sculpture building; library. (Wed-Sun; closed New Year's Day, Thanksgiving, Dec 25) 7 mi N on I-680 to Crow Canyon Rd in San Ramon, then 4 mi E to Camino Tassajara, then 1 blk E, turn left on Blackhawk Plaza Dr. Phone 925/736-2277. **¢¢¢** Admission incl

Berkeley Museum of Art, Science, and Culture. Houses university collections of anthropology, paleontology, and changing art exhibits. (Wed-Sun) Combination ticket with Auto Museum. Phone 925/736-2277.

Eugene O'Neill National Historic Site. Winner of the Nobel Prize and four Pulitzer Prizes, O'Neill wrote some of his finest works at Tao House, incl the autobiographical *Long Day's Journey Into Night* and *A Moon For the Misbegotten*. A blend of Chinese philosophy and Spanish-style architecture, Tao House was to be O'Neill's "final home and harbor." The house commands a spectacular view of the hills and orchards of the San Ramon Valley and Mt Diablo. Tours (Wed-Sun, morning and afternoon; by res only). Shuttle service provided from Danville. 7 mi W of I-680, near Danville. Phone 280/945-2692. **FREE**

Special Event

Alameda County Fair. Fairgrounds, jct I-680 and I-580, Bernal Ave exit. Horse racing, exhibitions, carnival, theatrical shows. Phone 925/426-7600. Late June-mid-July.

Motel/Motor Lodge

★★ COURTYARD BY MARRIOTT. *5059 Hopyard Rd (94588). 925/463-1414; fax 925/463-0113; toll-free 800/321-2211. www.marriott.com.* 145 rms, 2-3 story, 14 suites. S, D $59-$159; each addl $10; suites $149; wkly, wkend rates. Crib free. TV; cable (premium). Heated pool, whirlpool. Complimentary coffee in rms. Restaurant 6:30-10 am; wkends 7-11:30 am. Bar 5:30-10:30 pm. Ck-out 1 pm. Coin lndry. Meeting rms. Business servs avail. Valet serv. Sundries. Exercise equipt. Refrigerator in suites. Some balconies. Cr cds: A, D, DS, MC, V.

D

Hotels

★★★ CROWNE PLAZA. *11950 Dublin Canyon Rd (94588). 925/847-6000; fax 925/463-2585; res 800/227-6963.* 244 rms, 6 story. S $149-$169; D $159-$179; each addl $10; under 18 free; wkend rates. Crib free. Pet accepted, some restrictions; $50 deposit. TV; cable (premium). Heated pool, whirlpool. Complimentary coffee in rms. Restaurant 6 am-10 pm. Bar noon-midnight. Ck-out noon. Coin lndry. Convention facilities. Business servs avail. Gift shop. Exercise equipt. Refrigerators avail. Cr cds: A, C, D, DS, ER, JCB, MC, V.

D

★★★ HILTON PLESANTON AT THE CLUB. *7050 Johnson Dr (94588). 925/463-8000; fax 925/463-3801; toll-free 800/445-8667. www.pleasanton hilton.com.* 294 rms, 5 story. S $79-$239; D $94-$254; each addl $10; suites $300-$600; family, wkend rates. Crib free. Pet accepted, some restrictions; $15. TV; cable (premium), VCR avail. Heated pool, poolside serv. Restaurant 6:30 am-10:30 pm. Bar 11-1:30 am. Ck-out noon. Meeting rms. Business center. Gift shop. Barber, beauty shop. Valet parking. Indoor tennis, pro. Exercise rm; sauna. Bathrm phones. Luxury level. Cr cds: A, C, D, DS, ER, JCB, MC, V.

D SC

★★ WYNDHAM GARDEN HOTEL. *5990 Stoneridge Mall Rd (94588). 925/463-3330; fax 925/463-3315. www.wyndham.com.* 171 rms, 6 story.

S $139; D $149; each addl $10; suites $550; under 18 free; wkend, hol rates. TV; cable (premium). Heated pool, whirlpool. Complimentary coffee in rms. Restaurant 6:30 am-10 pm; Fri, Sat 7 am-10 pm. Bar. Ck-out noon. Meeting rms. Business servs avail. In-rm modem. Exercise equipt; sauna. Refrigerator in suites. Cr cds: A, C, D, DS, ER, JCB, MC, V.

D

B&B/Small Inn

★★ **EVERGREEN BED AND BREAKFAST.** *9104 Longview Dr (94588). 925/426-0901; fax 925/426-9568. www.evergreen-inn.com.* 4 rms, 1 with shower only, 2 story. S, D $145; each addl $20. TV; cable, VCR avail. Whirlpool. Complimentary full bkfst. Restaurant nearby. Ck-out 11 am, ck-in 3 pm. Guest lndry. Luggage handling. Concierge serv. Some in-rm whirlpools. Totally nonsmoking. Cr cds: A, MC, V.

SC

All Suite

★ **CANDLEWOOD SUITES.** *5535 Johnson Dr (94588). 925/463-1212; fax 925/463-6080; res 888/226-3539. www.candlewoodsuites.com.* 126 suites, 4 story. S, D $109-$129; under 18 free; package plans. Crib free. Pet accepted; $75 and $10/day. TV; cable (premium), VCR (movies). Complimentary coffee in rms. Restaurant adj open 24 hrs. Rm serv 5-9 pm. Ck-out noon. Business servs avail. In-rm modem link. Sundries. Guest lndry. Exercise equipt. Pool privileges, whirlpool. Refrigerators, microwaves. Cr cds: A, D, DS, MC, V.

Extended Stay

★★ **RESIDENCE INN BY MARRIOTT.** *11920 Dublin Canyon Rd (94588). 925/277-0500. www.marriott.com.* 135 rms, 3 story. S, D $155-$275; each addl $25; under 17 free. Crib avail. Heated pool. TV; cable (premium), VCR avail. Complimentary coffee, newspaper in rms. Restaurant nearby. Ck-out noon. Coin lndry. Exercise rm. Refrigerators. Cr cds: A, C, D, DS, MC, V.

Restaurant

★★ **GIRASOLE.** *3180 Santa Rita Rd (94566). 925/484-1001. www.girasole grill.com.* Hrs: 11 am-9 pm; Fri, Sat to 10 pm; Sun 4-9 pm. Closed hols. Res accepted. Italian, American menu. A la carte entrees: lunch $5.50-$14.95, dinner $9.50-$18.95. Children's menu. Specialties: scoozzi, Absolut prawns, Tuscan pork. Parking. Outdoor dining. Totally nonsmoking. Cr cds: A, MC, V.

D SC

Pomona

(E-5) *See also Claremont, Ontario, Pasadena*

Pop 131,723 **Elev** 850 ft
Area code 909

Information Pomona Chamber of Commerce, 485 N Garey Ave, 91767; 909/622-1256

Web www.pomonachamber.org

What to See and Do

California State Polytechnic University, Pomona. (1938) 19,000 students. Kellogg West Continuing Education Center has conference facilities (daily). 3801 W Temple Ave. Phone 909/869-7659. On campus is the renowned

> **Kellogg Arabian Horse Center.** Also houses Equine Research Center. One-hr performances (Oct-June, first Sun each month; no shows Easter). Stable (daily; free). Phone 909/869-2224. ¢¢

Historical Society of Pomona Valley. (1850-1854). Grounds, furnished 13-rm adobe house illustrate romantic "Days of the Dons." Native American artifacts, baskets. (Sun 2-5 pm or by appt; closed hols) 491 E Arrow Hwy, 1 mi N on Garey Ave off San Bernardino Fwy. Phone 909/623-2198. **Donation** Located here are

Adobe de Palomares. 491 E Arrow Hwy, 1 mi N on Garey Ave off San Bernardino Fwy

La Casa Primera. Corner of Park and McKinley Ave. Phone 909/623-2198.

Pomona School of Fine Arts. Classes in fine arts, exhibits. 242 S Garey Ave. Phone 909/868-0900.

Special Event

Los Angeles County Fair. Fairplex, 1101 W McKinley Ave. Thoroughbred racing, carnival, exhibits, free stage shows, food booths, monorail. Contact PO Box 1456, 91769. Phone 909/623-3111. Mid-Sept-early Oct.

Motels/Motor Lodges

★★ **BEST WESTERN DIAMOND BAR.** *259 Gentle Springs Ln, Diamond Bar (91765). 909/860-3700; fax 909/860-2110; res 800/528-1234.* 96 rms, 2 story. S, D $55-$61; each addl $5; suites $125; under 12 free; family, wkly rates. Crib $5. TV; cable (premium). Pool, whirlpool. Complimentary continental bkfst. Restaurant nearby. Ck-out noon. Meeting rms. Business servs avail. Valet serv. Coin lndry. Health club privileges. Some wet bars. Cr cds: A, D, DS, MC, V.
D

★★ **HOLIDAY INN SELECT.** *21725 E Gateway Dr, Diamond Bar (91765). 909/860-5440; fax 909/860-8224; toll-free 800/988-3587. www.holiday-inn.com.* 176 rms, 6 story. S, D $119-$129; each addl $10; under 18 free. Crib free. TV; cable (premium). Heated pool, whirlpool, poolside serv. Restaurant 6 am-10 pm. Bar 4-10 pm. Ck-out noon. Meeting rms. Business servs avail. Some balconies. Cr cds: A, C, D, DS, JCB, MC, V.
D SC

★★ **SHILO HILLTOP SUITES.** *3101 Temple Ave (91768). 909/598-7666; fax 909/598-5654; res 800/222-2244. www.shiloinns.com.* 129 units, 69 suites, 3 story. S, D $99-$120; suites $159; each addl $15; under 12 free. Crib free. TV; cable (premium), VCR (movies). Heated pool, whirlpool, poolside serv. Complimentary full bkfst, coffee in rms. Restaurant 6 am-10 pm; Fri, Sat to 11 pm. Bar 11-2 am; entertainment Tues-Sat. Ck-out noon. Coin lndry. Meeting rms. Business servs avail. In-rm modem link. Bellhops. Valet serv. Sundries. Free airport transportation. Exercise equipt; sauna, steam rm. Health club privileges. Bathrm phones, refrigerators, microwaves, wet bars. Cr cds: A, C, D, DS, MC, V.
D SC

Restaurant

★★ **D'ANTONIO'S RISTORANTE.** *808 N Diamond Bar Blvd, Diamond Bar (91765). 909/860-3663. www.athand.com.* Hrs: 11 am-10 pm; Fri to 11 pm; Sat noon-11 pm; Sun noon-10 pm. Closed hols. Res accepted. Italian menu. Wine, beer. Lunch $5.95-$13.95, dinner $8.45-$22.95. Specializes in steak, seafood, chicken. Own desserts. Outdoor dining. Cr cds: A, C, D, DS, MC, V.
D

Porterville (B-4)

Pop 29,563 **Elev** 459 ft **Area code** 559 **Zip** 93257

What to See and Do

Sequoia National Forest. Precipitous canyons, spectacular views of the Sierra Nevada, and more than 30 groves of giant sequoias on 1,139,000 acres. Largest tree of any National Forest is here; the Boole Tree stands 269 feet and is 90 ft in circumference. (The General Sherman Tree in Sequoia National Park is a few ft taller.) The forest contains the 303,290-acre Golden Trout, 130,995-acre Dome Land, 10,610-acre Jennie Lake, 63,000-acre South Sierra, 88,290-acre Kiavah, and the 45,000-acre Monarch wilderness areas. Activities incl swimming, lake and stream fishing for trout, whitewater rafting in the Kern and Kings rivers; hunting, hiking, riding, and backpacking trails in wilderness areas (permit required). X-country skiing, snowshoeing, and snowmobiling in winter. Picnicking. Camping (for res phone 877/444-6777) at 50 areas; 14-day/month limit; no electric hookups or other utility connections;

campgrounds (fees vary). Contact Forest Supervisor, 900 W Grand Ave. 20 mi E via CA 190. Phone 559/784-1500.

Quincy

(D-4) *See also Chester*

Pop 4,271 **Elev** 3,432 ft
Area code 530 **Zip** 95971
Information Plumas County Visitors Bureau, PO Box 4120; 800/326-2247
Web www.plumas.ca.us

What to See and Do

Plumas County Museum. Period rms, changing historical displays, artifacts, and photographs featured in main gallery; permanent exhibit of baskets woven by area's native Maidu. Mezzanine gallery features contemporary cultural displays by county artisans, historical exhibits, and Western Pacific and local RR collections. Archival collection of Plumas County documents. (May-Sept, daily; rest of yr, Mon-Fri) 500 Jackson St. Phone 530/283-6320. ¢

Plumas National Forest. Beautiful 1½ million-acre forest in Feather River Country. Feather Falls (640-ft drop), sixth-highest waterfall in US, accessible by 3.5-mi trail (see OROVILLE). CA 70, which runs approx 150 mi through the forest, is a designated National Scenic Byway. Groomed x-country skiing, snowmobile trails. Interpretive trails; hiking, backpacking. Fishing, boating; hunting (deer, bear, game birds), picnicking, camping (Apr-Oct, fee). Contact the Forest Supervisor, 159 Lawrence St, PO Box 11500. Phone 877/444-6777 or 530/283-2050.

Special Event

Plumas County Fair. Plumas County Fairgrounds. Held annually since 1859. Horse shows, stock car races, Pacific Coast Loggers Championship Show, country/western entertainment, parade, pageant, 4-H livestock auction. Phone 530/283-6272. Second wk Aug.

Motels/Motor Lodges

★ **LARIAT LODGE.** *2370 E Main St (95971). 530/283-1000; fax 530/283-2154; toll-free 800/999-7199.* 20 rms. 12 A/C. S, D $42-$54; each addl $6; family units $58-$68. TV; cable (premium). Heated pool. Complimentary continental bkfst, coffee in rms. Restaurant nearby. Ck-out 11 am. X-country ski 17 mi. Some refrigerators, microwaves. Cr cds: A, DS, MC, V.

D

★ **RANCHITO MOTEL.** *2020 E Main St (95971). 530/283-2265; fax 530/283-2316.* 30 rms, 4 kits. No A/C. S $44; D $51-$56; each addl $9; kit. units for 1-5, $53-$90. Crib free. TV; cable. Complimentary coffee in rms. Restaurant nearby. Ck-out 11 am. X-country ski 17 mi. Private patios. Picnic tables. Some adobe buildings; Spanish decor. Shaded gardens, brook, 2 wooded acres. Cr cds: A, DS, MC, V.

D

Restaurants

★★ **MOON'S.** *501 Cresent St (95971). 530/283-0765.* Hrs: 4-10 pm. Closed Mon; hols. Res accepted. Italian, American menu. Wine, beer. Dinner $8.25-$17.95. Specializes in fresh fish, vegetarian dishes, Angus beef. Own desserts. Patio dining. Restored early 1900s building. Totally nonsmoking. Cr cds: MC, V.

D

★★★ **OLSEN'S CABIN.** *589 Johnsville Rd, Gray Eagle (96103). 530/836-2801.* Hrs: 6-9:30 pm; Closed Sun, Mon; also Tue, Wed Nov-Apr. Res accepted. Bar. Complete meals: dinner $16-$19. Children's menu. Specializes in seafood, steaks, chops. Salad bar. Own baking. In historic log cabin. Gift shop. Family-owned. Totally nonsmoking. Cr cds: MC, V.

D

Rancho Bernardo

(see San Diego)

Rancho Cordova

(E-4) *See also Sacramento*

Pop 48,731 **Elev** 126 ft **Area code** 916

Information Cordova Chamber of Commerce, 3328 Mather Field Rd, 95670; 916/361-8700

Web www.ranchocordova.org

Motels/Motor Lodges

★★ BEST WESTERN HERITAGE INN. *11269 Point East Dr (95742). 916/635-4040; fax 916/635-7198; res 800/528-1234.* 123 rms, 3 story. S, D $89; each addl $5; under 12 free. TV; cable (premium). Pool. Complimentary full bkfst. Restaurant 6-9:30 am, 5-10 pm. Bar 5-9:30 pm. Ck-out 11 am. Meeting rms. Business servs avail. Valet serv. Some in-rm whirlpools, refrigerators. Cr cds: A, C, D, DS, ER, JCB, MC.

D SC

★★ COMFORT INN. *3240 Mather Field Rd (95670). 916/363-3344; toll-free 800/638-7949.* 110 rms, 4 story. S $65; D $70; suites $90-$95; under 14 free. Pet accepted; $100 deposit. TV; cable (premium). Pool, whirlpool. Complimentary continental bkfst. Coffee in rms. Restaurant nearby. Ck-out noon. Coin lndry. Meeting rms. Some refrigerators. Cr cds: A, C, D, DS, ER, JCB, MC, V.

D SC

★★ COURTYARD BY MARRIOTT. *10683 White Rock Rd (95670). 916/638-3800; fax 916/638-6776; toll-free 800/321-2211. www.marriott.com.* 144 rms, 3 story. S, D $109; suites $124; under 18 free; wkend rates. TV; cable (premium). Heated pool, whirlpool. Restaurant 6:30-10 am. Rm serv 5-10 pm. Bar 4-11 pm. Ck-out noon. Coin lndry. Meeting rms. Valet serv. Sundries. Exercise equipt. Some refrigerators. Private patios, balconies. Cr cds: A, D, DS, MC, V.

D

★ INNS OF AMERICA. *12249 Folsom Blvd (95670). 916/351-1213; fax 916/351-1817; res 800/826-0778. www.innsofamerica.com.* 124 rms, 3 story. S $50-$60; D $59-$65; each addl (up to 4) $5. Pet accepted, some restrictions. TV; cable (premium). Pool. Complimentary continental bkfst. Restaurant adj 11 am-11 pm. Ck-out 11 am. Coin lndry. Cr cds: A, MC, V.

D

Hotel

★★★ MARRIOTT HOTEL. *11211 Point East Dr (95742). 916/638-1100; fax 916/638-5803. www.marriott.com.* 262 rms, 11 story. S $160; D $170; each addl $10; suites $250-$300; under 17 free; wkend rates. TV; cable (premium). Heated pool, whirlpool, poolside serv. Complimentary coffee in rms. Restaurant 6 am-10:30 pm. Bar 11-2 am; Sun to 11 pm. Ck-out noon. Convention facilities. Business center. In-rm modem link. Concierge. Gift shop. Airport, RR station, bus depot transportation. Exercise equipt. Luxury level. Cr cds: A, C, D, DS, ER, JCB, MC, V.

D

All Suite

★★ HALLMARK SUITES. *11260 Point East Dr (95742). 916/638-4141; fax 916/638-4287; toll-free 800/444-1089. www.hallmarksuites.com.* 159 suites, 32 kit. units, 3 story. S $119; D $129, kit. units $95-$199; under 18 free; wkend rates. Crib free. TV; cable. Heated pool, whirlpool. Complimentary full bkfst. Restaurant nearby. Rm serv (lunch, dinner). Bar 5-11 pm. Ck-out noon. Coin lndry. Meeting rms. Valet serv. Gift shop. Exercise equipt. Bathrm phones, refrigerators. Some private patios. Cr cds: A, D, DS, MC, V.

D

Restaurant

★★★ SLOCUM HOUSE. *7992 California Ave, Fair Oaks (95628). 916/961-7211. www.slocum-house.com.* Hrs: 11:30 am-2 pm, 5:30-10 pm;

Sun brunch 10:30 am-2 pm. Closed Mon; Jan 1. Res accepted. Contemporary American menu. Bar. Wine list. A la carte entrees: lunch $8.50-$12.95, dinner $17.95-$23.95. Sun brunch $13.95. Specializes in seafood, wild game. Jazz quartet Fri-Sat in summer. Outdoor dining. Historic 1920s luxury house; Art Deco decor; original marble/oak fireplace. Hillside setting, among trees and flowers. Cr cds: A, C, D, DS, MC, V.
D

Rancho Cucamonga

See also Claremont, Ontario, Pomona

Pop 101,409 **Elev** 1,110 ft
Area code 909 **Zip** 91730
Information Chamber of Commerce, 7945 Vineyard Ave, Suite D-5; 909/987-1012
Web www.ranchochamber.org

The original residents, the Serrano, called this area Cucamonga or "sandy place." Later, it was part of the vast Rancho de Cucamonga. Violent deaths and long legal battles caused the eventual sale of the land to several wine and citrus industries in 1871.

What to See and Do

Casa de Rancho Cucamonga (Rains House). Oldest burned-brick house in San Bernardino County (ca 1860); was home to wealthy and socially prominent John and Merced Rains. (Wed-Sun) 8810 Hemlock St, just north of Vineyard. Phone 909/989-4970. ¢

Special Event

Grape Harvest Festival. Wine tasting, grape stomping contest, carnival, displays, entertainment. Early Oct.

Motel/Motor Lodge

★★ BEST WESTERN HERITAGE INN. *8179 Spruce Ave (91730). 909/466-1111; fax 909/466-3876; res 800/528-1234. www.bestwestern.com.* 116 rms, 6 story. S $79-$89; D $84-$94; each addl $8; suites $99-$104; under 13 free. Crib free. TV; cable (premium). Heated pool, whirlpool. Complimentary continental bkfst. Coffee in rms. Restaurant nearby. Ck-out noon. Meeting rms. Business servs avail. Valet serv. Exercise equipt. Refrigerators; wet bars in suites; microwaves avail. Cr cds: A, C, D, DS, MC, V.
D

Restaurant

★★ MAGIC LAMP INN. *8189 E Foothill Blvd (91730). 909/981-8659.* Hrs: 11:30 am-2:30 pm, 5-10 pm; Sat-Sun from 5 pm; early-bird dinner Tues-Thurs 4:30-6:30 pm. Closed Mon; Dec 25 and 26. Res accepted. Continental menu. Bar. Lunch $6.95-$11.95, dinner $9.95-$26.50. Lunch buffet (Tues-Fri): $8.25. Children's menu. Specializes in prime rib, fresh seafood. Own soup. Entertainment Wed-Sat. Parking. Family-owned since 1955. Cr cds: A, D, MC, V.
D

Rancho Santa Fe

(F-5) *See also Del Mar*

Pop 5,000 **Elev** 245 ft **Area code** 858 **Zip** 92067

Resorts

★★★ MORGAN RUN RESORT & CLUB. *5690 Cancha De Golf (92091). 858/756-2471; fax 858/756-3013; toll-free 800/378-4653. www.morganrun.com.* 89 Rrs, 2 story. May-Oct: S, D $159-$179; each addl $15; suites $239-$259; golf plans; lower rates rest of yr. Crib free. Tv; cable (premium). Pool, poolside serv. Complimentary coffee in rms. Restaurant 6:30 am-9 pm. Bar 10 am-midnight. Ck-out noon, ck-in 4 pm. Meeting rms. Valet serv. Lighted tennis, pro.

27-hole golf course, greens fee $85, pro, putting green, driving range. Exercise equipt. Some refrigerators; microwaves avail. Cr cds: A, D, MC, V.

D

★★★★ **RANCHO VALENCIA RESORT.** *5921 Valencia Circle (92067). 858/756-1123; fax 858/756-0165. www.ranchovalencia.com.* At this casually elegant retreat in the rolling hills you can choose from 43 suites in 20 casitas or splurge for the Hacienda, a three-suite 5,000-square-foot adobe house with a private pool. Everything from tennis to golf to spa service is here to rejuvenate the mind and body. The Clubhouse restaurant serves gourmet California-Pacific Rim cuisine. 43 suites. S, D $420-$4,000; 2-bedrm suites $900-$1,050; 3-bedrm hacienda from $4,000; tennis, golf plans. Crib free. Pet accepted; $75/day. TV; cable (premium), VCR. Pool, poolside serv. Complimentary coffee in rms. Restaurant (see VALENCIA). Box lunches, picnics. Bar from 10 am. Ck-out noon, ck-in 4 pm. Guest lndry. Meeting rms. Business servs avail. In-rm modem link. Bellhops. Valet serv. Gift shop. 18 tennis courts, pro. 18-hole golf privileges. Bicycle rentals. Lawn games. Social dir. Exercise equipt. Massage. Bathrm phones, refrigerators, minibars, wet bars, fireplaces; microwaves avail. Cr cds: A, D, DS, MC, V.

D

B&B/Small Inn

★★★ **THE INN AT RANCHO SANTA FE.** *5951 Linea Cielo (92067). 858/756-1131; fax 858/759-1604; toll-free 800/843-4661. www.theinnat ranchosantafe.com.* 89 units in lodge, cottages. S, D $130-$210; each addl $20; suites $275-$520. Crib $20. Pet accepted. TV; VCR avail. Heated pool, poolside serv. Restaurant 7:30-10:30 am, noon-2:30 pm, 6:30-9:30 pm. Box lunches. Bar 11 am-11 pm. Ck-out noon, ck-in 3 pm. Grocery 2 blks. Meeting rms. Business servs avail. Bellhops. Tennis. 18-hole golf privileges. Exercise equipt. Massage. Lawn games. Some in-rm whirlpools; refrigerators, wet bars, fireplaces; microwaves avail. Many private patios. On 22 acres of landscaped grounds. Beach house in Del Mar avail for day use. Cr cds: A, C, D, MC, V.

D

Restaurants

★★★ **DELICIAS.** *6106 Paseo Delicias (92067). 858/756-8000.* Hrs: noon-2 pm, 6-10 pm; Tues from 6 pm. Closed Sun, Mon; Jan 1, July 4, Dec 25. Res accepted. Contemporary American menu. Bar to 11 pm. Wine list. A la carte entrees: lunch $8-$15, dinner $16-$30. Specialties: smoked salmon pizza, Chinese duck. Outdoor dining. French country style decor. Outdoor fireplace. Cr cds: A, D, MC, V.

D

★★★ **MILLE FLEURS.** *6009 Paseo Delicias (92067). 858/756-3085.* French menu. Menu changes daily. Own pastries. Hrs: 11:30 am-2 pm, 6-10 pm; Sat from 5:30 pm; Sun from 6 pm. Closed Jan 1, Dec 25. Res required Fri, Sat. Bar 11:30 am-midnight; Sat from 5:30 pm; Sun from 6 pm. Wine list. Lunch $9-$25, dinner $28-$35. Pianist Tues-Sat. Outdoor dining. Cr cds: A, D, MC, V.

D

★★★ **VALENCIA.** *5921 Valencia Cir (92067). 858/759-6216. www.ranch ovalencia.com.* Hrs: 7 am-10 pm. Res sugested. Bar. A la carte entrees: bkfst $10-$17, lunch $12-$17, dinner $20-$32. Sun brunch $11-$15. Children's menu. Specialties: sauteed ahi tuna roll, roasted rack of lamb. Classical guitarist Fri, Sat. Valet parking. Outdoor dining. Overlooks gardens and tennis courts. Cr cds: A, D, MC, V.

D

Red Bluff

(C-3) *See also Redding*

Pop 12,363 **Elev** 340 ft **Area code** 530 **Zip** 96080

Information Red Bluff-Tehama County Chamber of Commerce, 100 Main St, PO Box 850; 530/527-6220

Web www.discoverredbluff.com

A marketing center for the products of the upper Sacramento Valley, the town is named for the reddish sand

and gravel cliffs in the vicinity. The first settlers came for gold, but found wealth in wheat fields and orchards instead. As river steamers discharged passengers and freight, the city also became a transportation center for the mines around it. Now lumbering, agriculture, and wood products are important industries. One notable pioneer of Red Bluff, William Ide, led the Bear Flag Revolt against Mexico.

What to See and Do

City River Park. Swimming pool (June-Aug, Mon-Sat; fee); boat ramp; picnic areas, playgrounds. Band concerts (summer, Mon). On the Sacramento River, between Reeds Creek Bridge and Sycamore St. Phone 530/527-8177. **FREE**

Fishing. In Sacramento River. Steelhead, salmon, trout. Sam Ayer Park and Dog Island Fishing Access, 1 mi N on Sacramento River. Footbridge to 11-acre island; nature trails, picnicking. Phone 530/527-8177. **FREE**

Kelly-Griggs House Museum. (1880s). Renovated Victorian house with period furnishings; Pendleton Gallery of Art; Chinese and Native American artifacts; historical exhibits. Map of auto tours of Victorian Red Bluff avail (fee). (Thurs-Sun, afternoons; closed hols) 311 Washington St, at Ash St. Phone 530/527-1129. **FREE**

Lassen Volcanic National Park. (see). 45 mi E on CA 36.

William B. Ide Adobe State Historic Park. Restored version of adobe house of William B. Ide, only president of the California Republic. Collection of household artifacts. Picnicking. Demonstrations on process of adobe brickmaking, pioneer crafts in summer. (Daily; closed Jan 1, Thanksgiving, Dec 25) 21659 Adobe Rd. 2 mi NE off I-5 Wilcox Rd exit. Phone 530/529-8599. Per vehicle **¢**

Special Events

Red Bluff Roundup. PRCA approved. One of the biggest three-day rodeos in the West. Mid-Apr. Phone 530/527-1000.

Tehama District Fair. Four days late Sept. Phone 530/527-5920.

Motels/Motor Lodges

★★ BEST INN AND SUITES. *90 Sale Ln (96080). 530/529-7060; fax 530/529-7077; res 800/626-1900. www.bestinn.com.* 67 rms, 3 story. Mid-May-Jan: S $63; D $69-$91; each addl $6; suites $85-$91; under 12 free; lower rates rest of yr. Crib $6. Tv; cable (premium). Pool, whirlpool. Complimentary continental bkfst, coffee in rms. Restaurant adj 6 am-10 pm. Ck-out 11 am. Exercise equipt. Meeting rms. Coin lndry. Refrigerators. Cr cds: A, D, DS, MC, V.

★★ LAMPLIGHTER LODGE. *210 S Main St (96080). 530/527-1150; fax 530/527-5878; toll-free 800/521-4423.* 51 rms, 1-2 story, 3 family units. S $34-$38; D $44-$48; each addl $4; family units, suites $56-$65. Crib $4. TV; cable (premium). Pool. Complimentary continental bkfst. Restaurant 6:30 am-9 pm. Ck-out 11:30 am. Business servs avail. In-rm modem link. Cr cds: A, C, D, DS, MC, V.

B&B/Small Inn

★★ JETER VICTORIAN INN. *1107 Jefferson St (96080). 530/527-7574.*5 rms, 2 share bath, 4 story, 1 guest house. Some rm phones. S, D $65-$140; guest house $95-$115; special events 2-day min. Children over 14 yrs only. Cable TV in some rms. Complimentary full bkfst; refreshments. Restaurant nearby. Ck-out 11:30 am, ck-in 3:30 pm. Luggage handling. Street parking. Picnic tables. Built in 1881; Victorian decor and atmosphere; antiques. Garden. Totally nonsmoking. Cr cds: MC, V.

Restaurant

★ PEKING CHINESE RESTAURANT. *860 Main St (96080). 530/527-0523.* Hrs: 11 am-10 pm; Sat, Sun from noon. Closed Thanksgiving, Dec 25. Res accepted. Chinese, American menu. Bar. Lunch $3.95-$5.50, dinner $5.50-9. Complete meals: dinner $6.50-$9.95. Specialties: Mongolian beef, lemon chicken, Kung Pao chicken. Chinese decor. Cr cds: A, MC, V.

D

Redding

(C-3) *See also Burney, Mount Shasta, Red Bluff, Weaverville*

Founded 1872 **Pop** 66,462 **Elev** 557 ft **Area code** 530

Information Convention and Visitors Bureau, 777 Auditorium Dr, 96001; 530/225-4100 or 800/874-7562

Web www.ci.redding.ca.us/cnvb/cnvbhome.htm

The hub city of northern California's vast scenic Shasta-Cascade Region is located at the top of the Sacramento Valley, in the shadow of Mount Shasta—with the rugged Coast Range on the west, the Cascades on the north and east, and the Sierra Nevada to the southeast. The city was founded when the California and Oregon Railroad chose the site as its northern terminus; it became the county seat in 1888. Lumber and tourism are its principal industries. The Sacramento River flows directly through the city, providing popular pastimes such as fishing, rafting, and canoeing.

What to See and Do

Carter House Natural Science Museum. Live wildlife exhibits incl owls, hawks, turtles, bees, and beetles. Various hands-on discovery activities for children. (Tues-Sun; closed hols) Phone 530/243-5457.

Coleman National Fish Hatchery. Chinook (king) salmon and steelhead trout are raised here to help mitigate the loss of spawning area due to construction of Shasta Dam. (Daily) S on I-5 to Cottonwood, 5 mi E on Balls Ferry Rd to Ash Creek Rd, 1 mi to Gover Rd, 2½mi to Coleman Fish Hatchery Rd. Phone 530/365-8622. **FREE**

Lake Redding-Caldwell Park. An 85-acre park; boat ramp, swimming pool. Picnic facilities. Falls of the lake are lighted in summer. Rio Dr, N on Market St, on N shore of Sacramento River. Phone 530/225-4095. **FREE** In Caldwell Park is the

Redding Museum of Art & History. Rotating fine arts and regional history exhibits. (Tues-Sun; closed hols) 56 Quartz Hill Rd. Phone 530/243-8801. **FREE**

Lake Shasta Caverns. Stalactites, stalagmites, flowstone deposits; 58∞F. Guided tour incl boat ride across McCloud Arm of Lake Shasta and bus ride up mountain to cavern entrance. (Daily; closed Thanksgiving, Dec 25) 16 mi N on I-5, then 1½ mi E on Shasta Cavern Rd. Phone 530/238-2341 or 800/795-CAVE. ¢¢¢¢¢

Lassen Volcanic National Park. (see). 44 mi E on CA 44.

Paul Bunyan's Forest Camp. Forestry and ecology exhibits. Also hosts a popular summer butterfly house. (Tues-Sun; closed hols) Phone 530/243-8960.

Shasta State Historic Park. Remains of gold rush town with several well-preserved original buildings; historical museum; art gallery. Picnicking. (Daily; closed Jan 1, Thanksgiving, Dec 25) 6 mi W on CA 299. Phone 530/243-8194. ¢

Shasta-Trinity National Forest. More than two million acres contain portions of the Trinity Alps Wilderness, Mt Shasta Wilderness, Castle Crags Wilderness, Chanchelulla Wilderness, and the Yolla Bolly-Middle Eel Wilderness. Picnicking; camping (fee). N, E, and W via CA 299, I-5. Phone 530/244-2978. **FREE**

Turtle Bay. A developing museum-arboretum complex along the Sacramento River. Live wildlife exhibits, aquariums, cultivated gardens, and a pedestrian bridge over the Sacramento River. (Museum, Tues-Sun; arboretum, daily) 800 Auditorium Dr. Phone 530/243-8960. ¢¢

Waterworks Park. Water theme park with three giant serpentine slides, Raging River inner tube ride, activity pool, kiddie water playground. (Memorial Day-Labor Day, daily) Jct I-5 and CA 299 E. Phone 530/246-9550. ¢¢¢¢

Whiskeytown-Shasta-Trinity National Recreation Area, Whiskeytown Unit. Water sports, fishing, boating (marinas); picnicking, snack bars, camping (fee), campfire programs. 8 mi W via

CA 299. Phone 530/242-3400. ¢¢ Contains areas surrounding

Lewiston Dam and Lake. Regulator and diversion point for water to Whiskeytown Dam near Shasta. 17 mi NW on CA 299, then 6 mi N on unnumbered roads.

Shasta Dam and Power Plant. Three times as high as Niagara Falls: 602 ft high, 3,460 ft long. Roadway and sidewalks along the crest; view of Mt Shasta. Visitor center. Waters of three rivers back up to form Shasta Lake, 35 mi long with a 365-mi shoreline. Houseboating is popular here; boats are avail for rent at several local marinas. Guided tours daily; schedule may vary. (Daily) 5 mi W of I-5. Schedule may vary. Phone 530/275-4463. Tours **FREE**

Trinity Dam and Lake. Large earthfill dam (465 ft high) creates lake, known locally as Trinity Lake, 20 mi long with 145-mi shoreline. 22 mi NW via CA 299 W. Phone 530/623-2121.

Whiskeytown Dam and Lake. Part of the Central Valley Project; forms lake with a 36-mi shoreline. Camping (fee). Information center NE of dam at jct CA 299 and Kennedy Memorial Dr. Contact Box 188, Whiskeytown 96095. 17 mi NW on CA 299, then 6 mi N on unnumbered roads. Phone 530/246-1225.

Special Events

Children's Lawn Festival. Caldwell Park. Children and adults participate in various activities incl weaving, bread baking, cow milking, and acorn grinding; also Native American games. Phone 530/225-4095. Late Apr or early May.

Rodeo Week. Third wk May. Phone 530/241-5731.

Renaissance Festival & Jousting Tournament. Memorial Day wkend.

Shasta District Fair. 11 mi S on US 99, I-5 in Anderson. Phone 530/378-6789. June.

Motels/Motor Lodges

★★ **BEST WESTERN HILLTOP INN.** *2300 Hilltop Dr (96002). 530/221-6100; fax 916/221-2867; res 800/336-4880. www.bestwestern.com.* 114 rms, 2 story. S $79-$99; D $89-$109; each addl $10; suites $95-$150; under 18 free. Crib free. TV; cable (premium), VCR avail. Heated pool, wading pool, whirlpool. Complimentary full bkfst buffet, coffee in rms. Restaurant 11 am-11 pm. Bar 11 am-midnight. Ck-out noon. Coin lndry. Meeting rms. Business servs avail. In-rm modem link. Valet serv. Health club privileges. Many refrigerators. Cr cds: A, C, D, DS, MC, V.

D SC

★★ **BEST WESTERN HOSPITALITY.** *532 N Market St (96003). 530/241-6464; fax 530/244-1998; res 800/528-1234.* 61 rms, 2 story. S $44-$64; D $50-$70; each addl $6; suite $99; under 18 free. TV; cable. Pool. Complimentary full bkfst, coffee in rms. Restaurant 6:30 am-8:30 pm. Ck-out 11 am. Coin lndry. Business servs avail. Cr cds: A, D, DS, MC, V.

D

★★ **BRIDGE BAY RESORT.** *10300 Bridge Bay Rd (96003). 530/275-3021; fax 530/275-8365; res 800/752-9669. www.sevencrown.com.* 40 rms, 1-2 story, 8 kit. suites; 2-day min suites. May-Sept: S $89; each addl $6; suites $120-$160; under 12 free; lower rates rest of yr. Crib $5. Pet accepted; $25 deposit, $5/day. TV; cable. Complimentary coffee in lobby. Restaurant 7 am-2 pm, 5-9 pm. Bar 4 pm-midnight. Ck-out 11 am. Meeting rms. Business servs avail. Gift shop. Grocery store. Pool. Cr cds: DS, MC, V.

D

★★ **LA QUINTA INN.** *2180 Hilltop Dr (96002). 530/221-8200; fax 530/223-4727; toll-free 800/687-6667. www.laquinta.com.* 133 rms, 3 story. S, D (up to 4) $60; suites $99; under 18 free. Crib free. Pet accepted, some restrictions. TV; cable. Pool, whirlpool. Complimentary continental bkfst. Coffee in rms. Restaurant 5 pm-midnight. Ck-out noon. Coin lndry. Meeting rms. Business servs avail. In-rm modem link. Valet serv. Exercise equipt. Private patios, balconies. Cr cds: A, C, D, DS, MC, V.

D SC

★★ **RED LION HOTEL.** *1830 Hilltop Dr (96002). 530/221-8700; fax 530/221-0324. www.redlion.com.* 193 rms, 2 story. May-Sept: S, D $79-$105;

each addl $15; suites $250; under 18 free; package plans; lower rates rest of yr. Crib free. Pet accepted. TV; cable, VCR avail (movies). Pool, wading pool, whirlpool, poolside serv. Complimentary coffee in rms. Restaurant 6 am-11 pm; dining rm 11:30 am-1:30 pm, 5-10 pm; Fri, Sat to 11 pm. Bar 11-2 am; entertainment Thurs-Sat. Ck-out 1 pm. Meeting rms. Business servs avail. In-rm modem link. Bellhops. Valet serv. Sundries. Free airport, RR station, bus depot transportation. Exercise equipt. Health club privileges. Private patios, balconies. Cr cds: A, C, D, DS, JCB, MC, V.

D

★★ **RIVER INN MOTOR HOTEL.** *1835 Park Marina Dr (96001). 530/241-9500; fax 530/241-5345; toll-free 800/995-4341.* 79 rms, 2-3 story. No elvtr. S, D $55-$65; each addl $5; under 12 free. Crib $5. Pet accepted; $5. TV; cable (premium). Pool, whirlpool. Coffee in rms. Restaurant 7 am-7 pm. Bar 11-2 am. Ck-out 11 am. Business servs avail. Sauna. Refrigerators; some wet bars. Private patios, balconies. Picnic tables. Cr cds: A, C, D, DS, MC, V.

D SC

B&B/Small Inn

★★★ **O'BRIEN MOUNTAIN INN.** *18026 O'Brien Inlet Rd, O'Brien (96051). 530/238-8026; fax 530/238-2027; toll-free 888/799-8026. www.obrienmtn.com.* 4 rms, 2 shower only. No rm phones. S, D $155-$225; each addl $25; hols 2-day min. Complimentary full bkfst, coffee in rms. Restaurant nearby. Ck-out 11 am, ck-in 4-6 pm. Business servs avail. Luggage handling. Concierge serv. Game rm. Lawn games. Built in 1963; antiques. On 47 acres. Totally nonsmoking. Cr cds: A, C, D, DS, MC, V.

Redlands

(E-5) *See also Big Bear Lake, Lake Arrowhead, Ontario, Riverside, San Bernardino*

Founded 1888 **Pop** 60,394 **Elev** 1,302 ft **Area code** 909

Information Chamber of Commerce, One E Redlands Blvd, 92373; 909/793-2546

Web www.redlandschamber.org

Named for the color of the earth in the area and known for many years as the Navel Orange Center, Redlands still handles a large volume of citrus fruits, but has diversified its industry in recent years to achieve greater economic prosperity and stability.

What to See and Do

Asistencia Mission de San Gabriel. (1830). Restored adobe with Native American and early pioneer exhibits, historic scenes of the valley; cactus garden; wishing well, bell tower, wedding chapel, and reception rm. (Wed-Sat, also Sun afternoons; closed Jan 1, Thanksgiving, Dec 25) 26930 Barton Rd, 2 mi W. Phone 909/793-5402. **FREE**

Kimberly Crest House and Gardens. (1897) French chateau-style house and accompanying carriage house on 6.5 acres. Former house of John Kimberly, founder of the Kimberly-Clark Corporation. Structure is representative of the "Mansion Era" of Southern California; 1930s furnishings. Italian gardens and citrus grove on grounds. Guided tours. (Thurs-Sun afternoons; closed hols, also Aug) 1325 Prospect Dr. Phone 909/792-2111. **¢¢**

Lincoln Memorial Shrine. George Grey Barnard's Carrara marble bust of Lincoln; murals by Dean Cornwell; painting by Norman Rockwell; manuscripts, books, artifacts relating to Lincoln and the Civil War. (Tues-Sat; closed hols) 125 W Vine St, in Smiley Park. Phone 909/798-7632. **FREE**

Pharaoh's Lost Kingdom. Family theme park features race car complex

Modern windmills

with Indy, Grand Prix, and kiddy cars; water park with wave pools and multiple water slides and flumes; 14 amusement rides; miniature golf; arcade, indoor playground, gift shop, restaurant, amphitheater. (Daily) 1101 California St, at I-10. Phone 909/335-PARK. ¢¢¢¢¢

Prosellis Bowl. Also known as the Redlands Bowl; the free concerts held here every Tues and Fri in summer have earned it the name Little Hollywood Bowl. Eureka and Vine Sts. Phone 909/793-7316.

San Bernardino County Museum. Mounted collection of birds and bird eggs of Southern California; reptiles, mammals. Pioneer and Native American artifacts; rocks and minerals; paleontology. Changing art exhibits. On grounds are steam locomotive, garden of cacti and succulents. (Tues-Sun; closed Jan 1, Thanksgiving, Dec 25) 2024 Orange Tree Ln. Phone 909/307-2669. ¢¢

Motels/Motor Lodges

★★ BEST WESTERN SANDMAN MOTEL. *1120 W Colton Ave (92374). 909/793-2001; fax 909/792-7612; res 800/528-1234. www.bestwestern.com.* 65 rms, 2 story, 6 kits. S $59; D $45; each addl $4; kit. units $5 addl; under 12 free. Pet accepted, some restrictions. TV; cable (premium). Heated pool, whirlpool. Complimentary continental bkfst. Restaurant adj 6 am-midnight. Ck-out 11 am. Business servs avail. Some refrigerators; microwaves avail. Cr cds: A, C, D, DS, MC, V.

D

★ SUPER 8. *1160 Arizona St (92374). 909/335-1612; fax 909/792-8779; res 800/800-8000. www.super8.com.* 78 rms, 2 story. S $37-$50; D $42-$65; each addl $5; under 12 free. Crib $5. TV; cable (premium), VCR avail. Complimentary continental bkfst. Restaurant opp open 24 hrs. Ck-out 11 am. Meeting rm. Business servs avail. Valet serv. Coin lndry. Pool. Some refrigerators, microwaves. Cr cds: A, C, D, DS, ER, JCB, MC, V.

D SC

Restaurant

★★★ JOE GREENSLEEVES. *220 N Orange St (92374). 909/792-6969.* Hrs: 11:30 am-2 pm, 5-9:30 pm; Sun from 5 pm. Closed hols. Res accepted. Wine list. Lunch $5.95-$11.75, dinner $13.25-$25. Specializes in fresh fish, steak, chops. Own desserts. Nautical atmosphere; large, cedar-carved replica of sloop on display. Totally nonsmoking. Cr cds: A, MC, V.

D

Redondo Beach

Pop 60,167 **Elev** 59 ft **Area code** 310
Information Visitors Bureau, 200 N Pacific Coast Hwy, 90277; 310/374-2171 or 800/282-0333
Web www.visitredondo.com

This is a recreation and vacation center featuring a 2½-mile beach and the popular King Harbor, which houses 1,700 craft.

What to See and Do

Redondo Beach Pier. Largest pier on California coast (72,000 sq ft). Fishing, cruises, collection of shops and restaurants featuring goods and foods from all over the world. Western end of Torrance Blvd. Phone 800/280-0333.

Motels/Motor Lodges

★★ **BEST WESTERN SUNRISE AT REDONDO BEACH MARINA.** *400 N Harbor Dr (90277). 310/376-0746; fax 310/376-7384; toll-free 800/334-7384. www.bestwestern-sunrise.com.* 111 rms, 3 story. S, D $82-$114; each addl $10; suites $135-$145; under 12 free; wkend rates. Crib free. TV; cable. Heated pool, whirlpool. Complimentary coffee in rms. Restaurant 6:30 am-10:30 pm. Ck-out noon. Meeting rms. Business servs avail. Valet serv. Refrigerators. Opp ocean. Cr cds: A, C, D, DS, ER, JCB, MC, V.

D

★★ **HOTEL HERMOSA.** *2515 Pacific Coast Highway, Hermosa Beach (90254). 310/318-6000; fax 310/318-6936; res 800/331-9979. www.hotelhermosa.com.* 81 units, 3 story, 8 suites. S, D $69-$125; each addl $10; suites $99-$109; under 12 free. Crib free. TV; cable (premium). Heated pool. Complimentary continental bkfst, coffee in rms. Restaurant nearby. Ck-out 11 am. Coin lndry. Meeting rms. Business servs avail. In-rm modem link. Free garage parking. Exercise equipt. Bathrm phones, refrigerators; some wet bars. Attractive landscaping; Japanese garden. Cr cds: A, C, D, DS, JCB, MC, V.

D

★ **REDONDO PIER LODGE.** *206 S Pacific Coast Hwy (90277). 310/318-1811; fax 310/379-0190; toll-free 800/841-9777.* 37 rms, 3 story, 2 suites. S $59-$69; D $65-$77; each addl $6; suites $90-$98; under 17 free. Crib free. TV; cable (premium). Heated pool, whirlpool. Complimentary continental bkfst. Coffee in rms. Restaurant nearby. Ck-out 11 am. Refrigerators. Cr cds: A, C, D, DS, ER, JCB, MC, V.

D SC

Hotel

★★★ **CROWNE PLAZA REDONDO BEACH.** *300 N Harbor Dr (90277). 310/318-8888; fax 310/376-1930. www.crowneplaza.com.* 340 rms, 5 story. S, D $179; each addl $20; suites $275-$625; under 19 free. Crib free. Valet parking $9. TV; cable (premium). Pool, poolside serv. Restaurant 6 am-10 pm. Rm serv 24 hrs. Ck-out noon. Coin lndry. Convention facilities. Business center. In-rm modem link. Concierge. Gift shop. Lighted tennis. Exercise equipt. Health club privileges. Refrigerators. Private patios, balconies. Opp ocean. Large deck overlooks harbor. Luxury level. Cr cds: A, C, D, DS, ER, JCB, MC, V.

D

★★ **PALOS VERDES INN.** *1700 S Pacific Coast Hwy (90277). 310/316-4211; fax 310/316-4863; toll-free 800/421-9241.* 110 rms, 4 story. May-Sept: S $96-$110; D $106-$120; each addl $10; under 12 free; lower rates rest of yr. Crib free. TV; cable (premium). Heated pool, whirlpool. Restaurant 7 am-midnight (see also CHEZ MELANGE). Bar from 10 am. Ck-out noon. Meeting rms. Business servs avail. In-rm modem link. Bellhops. Valet serv. Health club privileges. Refrigerator in suites. Many balconies. Cr cds: A, C, D, DS, JCB, MC, V.

D SC

★★★ **THE PORTOFINO HOTEL AND YACHT CLUB.** *260 Portofino Way (90277). 310/379-8481; fax 310/372-7329; toll-free 800/468-4292. www.hotelportofino.com.* 163 rms, 3 story, 23 suites. S, D $165-$210; each addl $10; suites $245-$275; under 12 free; wkend, package plans. Crib free. TV; cable (premium), VCR avail. Heated pool, whirlpool, poolside serv. Restaurant 6 am-10 pm. Bar 11-1:30 am. Ck-out noon. Meeting rms. Business center. In-rm modem link. Bellhops. Valet serv. Gift shop. Exercise equipt. Refrigerators, minibars; microwaves avail. On ocean. Cr cds: A, C, D, DS, JCB, MC, V.

D SC

Restaurant

★★ **LE BEAUJOLAIS.** *522 S Pacific Coast Hwy (90277). 310/543-5100. www.quickpages.com.* Hrs: 11:30 am-3 pm, 5-10 pm; Fri, Sat to 11 pm; Sat, Sun brunch 10 am-3 pm. Res accepted. French menu. Serv bar. Lunch $5.95-$15.95, dinner $16.95-$26.95. Sat, Sun brunch $10.95. Specializes in rack of lamb, duck, fresh fish. Harpist Thur, Fri, Sun. Intimate dining. Elegant decor. Cr cds: A, D, DS, MC, V.

D

Redwood City

(G-3) *See also Palo Alto, San Francisco Airport Area, San Mateo*

Settled 1854 **Pop** 66,072 **Elev** 15 ft **Area code** 650

Information Redwood City San Mateo County Chamber of Commerce, 1675 Broadway, 94063; 650/364-1722

In the center of the booming commercial and industrial peninsula area, Redwood City has the only deepwater bay port south of San Francisco on the peninsula. Once a Spanish ranch, it was settled by S. M. Mezes, who called it Mezesville; lumbermen who cut the nearby virgin redwoods renamed it Redwood City. It was incorporated in 1867 and is the seat of San Mateo County.

What to See and Do

Lathrop House. Victorian house and furnishings. (Tues-Thurs; closed hols, Aug, late Dec) 627 Hamilton St. Phone 650/365-5564. **FREE**

Marinas. Port of Redwood City Yacht Harbor. Phone 650/306-4150. **Docktown Marina,** foot of Maple St, phone 650/365-3258. **Pete's Harbor,** Uccelli Blvd, at foot of Whipple Ave, phone 650/366-0922. 675 Seaport Blvd.

Methuselah Redwood. Tree more than 1,500 yrs old, measures 55 ft in circumference. Trunk has been blackened by repeated fires. Junipero Serra Fwy via Woodside Rd exit, W on CA 84 to Skyline Blvd, 4 mi N.

Special Event

San Mateo County Fair & Floral Fiesta. Phone 650/574-FAIR. Aug. Phone 650/574-3247.

Motels/Motor Lodges

★★ BEST WESTERN EXECUTIVE SUITE. *25 Fifth Ave (94063). 650/366-5794; fax 650/365-1429; res 800/528-1234.* 28 rms, 2 story, 5 suites. S $99; D $110; each addl $10; suites $145. TV; cable (premium), VCR. Complimentary continental bkfst, coffee in rms. Restaurant nearby. Ck-out 11 am. Coin lndry. Business servs avail. Exercise equipt. Bathrm phones, refrigerators, microwaves; some minibars. Cr cds: A, D, DS, MC, V.

D

★★ COMFORT INN-REDWOOD CITY. *1818 El Camino Real (94063). 650/599-9636; fax 650/396-6481; res 800/228-5150.* 52 rms, 3 story, 11 kit. suites. May-Nov: S $118; D $128; each addl $10; suites $145-$155; under 16 free; lower rates rest of yr. TV; cable (premium), VCR. Pool. Sauna. Complimentary full bkfst. Restaurant nearby. Ck-out 11 am. Meeting rm. Business servs avail. In-rm modem link. Free garage parking. Refrigerators, microwaves. Cr cds: A, C, D, DS, JCB, MC, V.

D

★ DAYS INN. *2650 El Camino Real (94061). 650/369-9200; fax 650/363-8167; toll-free 800/329-7466.* 68 rms, 2 story. S, D $70-$80; each addl $5. Crib free. TV; cable (premium), VCR avail. Heated pool; whirlpool. Complimentary continental bkfst. Restaurant nearby. Ck-out 11 am. Coin lndry. Meeting rm. Business servs avail. Exercise equipt. Refrigerators, microwaves. Some private patios, balconies. Picnic tables. Gazebo. Cr cds: A, C, DS, MC, V.

D SC

★★★ THE LODGE AT SKYLONDA. *16350 Skyline Blvd, Woodside (94062). 650/851-4500; fax 650/788-7872; res 800/851-2222.* 16 rms, 3 story. No A/C. Rm phones on request. S $425-$525; D $298-$362; package plans; wkends 2-day min. Complimentary full bkfst. Restaurant nearby. Meeting rms. Business servs avail. Bellhops. Gift shop. Airport transportation. Exercise rm; sauna. Indoor pool; whirlpool. Game rm. Rec rm. Lawn games. Balconies. In redwood forest. Totally nonsmoking. Cr cds: A, DS, MC, V.

D

Hotel

★★★ **HOTEL SOFITEL.** *223 Twin Dolphin Dr (94065). 650/598-9000; fax 650/598-0459; toll-free 800/763-4835.* 319 units, 9 story. S $290; D $310; each addl $20; suites $329-$470; under 12 free. Crib free. TV; cable (premium), VCR avail. Pool. Restaurant 6 am-11 pm. Rm serv 5:30-2 am. Bar 10-2 am; entertainment exc Sun. Ck-out noon. Convention facilities. Business servs avail. In-rm modem link. Concierge. Gift shop. Free airport transportation. Exercise equipt. Minibars. Elegant atmosphere; Baccarat chandeliers. Cr cds: A, C, D, JCB, MC, V.

D SC

Redwood Highway

(A-1) *See also Crescent City, Eureka*

Information Redwood Empire/North Coast Visitors Services, 2801 Leavenworth, 2nd Floor, San Francisco, 94133; 888/678-8506

US 101 runs for 387 miles from San Francisco to the wine country of Sonoma and Mendocino counties, through scenic countryside where 97 percent of the world's coastal redwoods grow. Redwoods can be seen in Marin County at Muir Woods National Monument (see), which has six miles of hiking trails and no vehicle access. The bulk of the giant redwood trees, *Sequoia sempervirens,* are from Leggett north to the Oregon state line. The Humboldt Redwoods State Park (see) runs on both sides of the highway; many of the major groves are here, incl the spectacular Avenue of the Giants north of Phillipsville, south of Pepperwood. A guidebook with maps is available from the Redwood Empire/North Coast Visitors Services (fee). Other concentrations of redwoods are at **Grizzly Creek Redwoods State Park,** 18 miles E of US 101 on CA 36, camping (standard fees), picnicking, swimming, fishing; and at Redwood National and State Parks (see CRESCENT CITY), which takes in Prairie Creek Redwoods State Park, 6 miles north of Orick on US 101, Del Norte Coast Redwoods State Park, 7 miles south of Crescent City, and Jedediah Smith Redwoods State Park, 9 miles northeast of Crescent City. The highway has several spectacular overlooks of the Pacific Ocean and the north coast of California.

The Redwood Highway, a major thoroughfare from the Golden Gate Bridge north, has four lanes for more than 260 miles and two lanes with many turnabouts for the remainder. Lodging is usually available, but heavy summer traffic makes it wise to plan ahead.

Richardson Grove State Park

(D-1) *See also Garberville*

(8 mi S of Garberville on US 101)

One of California's beautiful redwood parks, Richardson Grove covers a 1,000-acre tract along the south fork of the Eel River. Swimming, fishing (Oct-Jan); hiking trails, picnicking, camping. Visitor center, store (summer); nature programs offered daily in summer. Standard fees. Phone 707/247-3318.

Riverside

(E-5) *See also San Bernardino*

Founded 1870 **Pop** 226,505 **Elev** 858 ft **Area code** 909

Information Greater Riverside Chambers of Commerce, 3985 University Ave, 92501; 909/683-7100

Web www.riverside-chamber.com

In 1873, a resident of the new town of Riverside obtained from the US Department of Agriculture two cuttings of a new type of orange, a mutation that had suddenly developed in Brazil. These cuttings were the origin of the vast navel orange groves that make this the center of the "Orange Empire."

What to See and Do

California Museum of Photography. Large collection of photographic equipment, prints, stereographs, memorabilia. Interactive gallery, walk-in camera; library. (Tues-Sun; closed hols) 3824 Main St. Phone 909/787-4787. **FREE**

Castle Amusement Park. Features 80-yr-old Dentzel carousel with hand-carved animals; antique cars. Ride Park with 30 rides and attractions (Fri-Sun). Four 18-hole miniature golf courses and video arcade (daily). Fee for activities. 3500 Polk St, 92505, CA 91 between Tyler and La Sierra exits. Phone 909/785-3000.

Chinese Memorial Pavilion. Dedicated to Chinese pioneers of the West and those who contributed to the growth of Riverside. 3581 7th St, on Riverside Public Library grounds.

Heritage House. (1891). Restored Victorian mansion. (Sept-June, Thurs, Fri, Sun; rest of yr, Sun) 8193 Magnolia Ave. Phone 909/689-1333. **FREE**

Mount Rubidoux Memorial Park. According to legend, the mountain was once the altar of Cahuilla and Serrano sun worship. A cross rises on the peak in memory of Fray Junipero Serra, founder of the California missions. The World Peace Tower stands on the side of the mountain. Hiking. (Daily, weather permitting: vehicular traffic prohibited) W end of 9th St at Mount Rubidoux Dr 1/2 mi W. Phone 909/955-4310. **FREE**

Orange Empire Railway Museum. More than 150 rail vehicles and pieces of off-rail equipment; railroad and trolley memorabilia; picnicking. Trolley rides (Sat, Sun. hols; fee). (Daily; closed Thanksgiving, Dec 25) 2201 South A Street, 14 mi S via I-215 in Perris. Phone 909/657-2605. **FREE**

Parent Washington Navel Orange Tree. Propagated from one of the two original trees from Bahia, Brazil. Planted in 1873, all navel orange trees stem from this tree or from its offspring. Magnolia and Arlington Aves.

Riverside Art Museum. Changing exhibits of historical and contemporary sculpture, painting, and graphics; lectures, demonstrations, juried shows, sales gallery. Housed in 1929 Mediterranean-style YWCA building designed by Julia Morgan. (Mon-Sat; closed hols) Corner of Lime St and Mission Inn Ave. Phone 909/684-7111. ¢

Riverside Municipal Museum. Area history, anthropology, and natural history displays; changing exhibits. (Tues-Sun; closed hols) 3580 Mission Inn Ave. Phone 909/826-5273. **FREE**

University of California at Riverside. (1954) 8,800 students. Centers around 161-ft Carillon Tower; Botanic Garden featuring flora from all parts of the world. 900 University Ave. Phone 909/787-1012.

Special Event

Easter Sunrise Pilgrimage. Mt Rubidoux Memorial Park. First nonsectarian sunrise service in US; continuous since 1909. Easter Sun.

Motels/Motor Lodges

★★ COMFORT INN RIVERSIDE. *1590 University Ave (92507). 909/683-6000; fax 909/782-8052.* 116 rms, 2 story. S, D $45-$50; under 18 free. Crib free. TV; cable (premium). Heated pool. Complimentary continental bkfst, coffee in rms. Restaurant nearby. Ck-out noon. Meeting rms. Business servs avail. Health club privileges. Valet serv. Refrigerators, microwaves avail. Cr cds: A, C, D, DS, MC, V.

D

★★ COURTYARD BY MARRIOTT. *1510 University Ave (92507). 909/276-1200; fax 909/787-6783; res 800/321-2211. www.courtyard.com/ralcy.* 163 rms, 6 story. S, D $95; under 18 free. Crib free. TV; cable (premium). Heated pool; whirlpool. Complimentary coffee in lobby. Bkfst avail 6:30-10 am. Bar 5-11 pm. Ck-out 1 pm. Meeting rms. Business servs avail. In-rm modem link. Valet serv. Exercise equipt. Refrigerators avail. Some balconies. Cr cds: A, C, D, DS, MC, V.

D SC

★★ DYNASTY SUITES. *3735 Iowa Ave (92507). 909/369-8200; fax*

909/341-6486; res 800/842-7899. www.dynastysuites.com. 34 rms, 2 story. S, D $42.95-$47.95; each addl $5; suites $89.95. TV; cable (premium), VCR avail (movies). Heated pool. Complimentary continental bkfst. Restaurant nearby. Ck-out noon. Business servs avail. Refrigerators; microwaves avail. In-rm whirlpool in suites. Cr cds: A, C, D, DS, MC, V.

D

★★ **HOLIDAY INN.** *3400 Market St (92501). 909/784-8000; fax 909/369-7127; toll-free 877/291-7519. www.holiday-inn.com.* 292 rms, 12 story. S $99-$119; D $89-$129; each addl $10; suites $129-$236; under 18 free. Crib free. TV; cable (premium). Heated pool; whirlpool, poolside serv. Coffee in rms. Restaurant 6:30 am-11 pm. Bar 11:30 am-midnight. Ck-out noon. Convention facilities. Business center. Gift shop. Free covered parking. Free airport transportation. Exercise equipt. Health club priveleges. Some wet bars; refrigerators, microwaves avail. Some balconies. Cr cds: A, C, D, DS, MC, V.

D SC

Hotels

★★ **MISSION INN.** *3649 Mission Inn Ave (92501). 909/784-0300; fax 909/683-1342; toll-free 800/843-7755. www.missioninn.com.* 235 rms, 15 with shower only, 5 story. S $139-$175; D $149-$185; each addl $15; suites $400-$800; under 15 free; package plans. TV; cable (premium), VCR avail. Heated pool; whirlpool, poolside serv. Restaurants 6:30 am-10 pm. Bars 11-2 am; entertainment Thurs-Sat. Meeting rms. Business center. In-rm modem link. Concierge. Gift shop. Beauty shop. Free airport transportation. Exercise equipt. Massage. Minibars; some balconies. Gazebo. Historic building was originally a 2-story, 12-rm boarding house (1876); expanded over the years. Renovated, unique Spanish-style architecture; courtyard fountains, gardens; stained-glass windows; many antiques. 2 wedding chapels, mission bells. Cr cds: A, C, D, DS, MC, V.

D SC

Restaurants

★★ **CIAO BELLA.** *1630 Spruce St (92507). 909/781-8840.* Hrs: 11:30 am-10:30 pm; Fri to 11 pm; Sat 5-11 pm; Sun 5-10 pm. Res accepted. Northern Tuscany menu. Bar. Wine list. A la carte: lunch $6.95-$13.95, dinner $7.25-$15.50. Specializes in fresh pasta, seafood. Parking. Outdoor dining. Cr cds: A, C, DS, ER, MC, V.

D

★★ **GERARD'S.** *9814 Magnolia Ave (92503). 909/687-4882. www.dineatgerards.com.* Hrs: 5-9:30 pm; Sun to 8:30 pm. Closed Mon; most hols. Res accepted. French, continental menu. Wine, beer. Dinner $12.95-$21.95. Specialties: pepper-steak/filet mignon flambe, bouillabaise/shellfish stew au safran. Own desserts. Country French decor; intimate dining area. Family-owned since 1969. Totally nonsmoking. Cr cds: A, DS, MC, V.

D

★★ **MARKET BROILER.** *3525 Merrill St (92506). 909/276-9007.* Hrs: 11 am-10 pm; Fri, Sat to 11 pm. Closed Thanksgiving, Dec 24, 25. Bar. Lunch $4.95-$8.95, dinner $6.95-$21.95. Children's menu. Specializes in mesquite-grilled fresh seafood, chicken, steaks. Nautical decor, tropical fish aquariums; seafood market on premises. Totally nonsmoking. Cr cds: A, C, D, DS, ER, MC, V.

D

Roseville

(E-4) *See also Rancho Cordova, Sacramento*

Pop 44,685 **Elev** 160 ft **Area code** 916 **Zip** 95678

What to See and Do

Folsom Premium Outlets. More than 70 outlet stores. (Daily) US 50, Folsom Blvd exit, 13000 Folsom Blvd, in Folsom. Phone 916/985-0312.

Motel/Motor Lodge

★★ **FIRST CHOICE INN.** *4420 Rocklin Rd, Rocklin (95677). 916/624-4500; fax 916/624-5982; toll-free*

800/462-2400. www.firstchoiceinn.com. 129 rms, 3 story. Apr-Sept: S $68-$73; D $75-$80; each addl $7; suites, kit. units $85-$125; under 12 free; lower rates rest of yr. Crib free. Pet accepted; $20/wk ($100 deposit). TV; cable (premium), VCR avail. Pool; whirlpool. Complimentary full bkfst; afternoon refreshments. Complimentary coffee in rms. Restaurant adj open 24 hrs. Ck-out noon. Coin lndry. Meeting rms. Business center. In-rm modem link. Valet serv. Exercise equipt. Refrigerators, microwaves; minibar in suites. Picnic tables. Grill. Cr cds: A, D, DS, JCB, MC, V.

D

Hotel

★★★ ROCKLIN PARK HOTEL. *5450 China Garden Rd, Rocklin (95677). 916/630-9400; fax 916/630-9448; res 888/630-9400. www.rocklinpark.com.* 33 rms, 2 story. S, D $155; suite $225; wkend rates. Crib free. TV; cable (premium), VCR avail (movies). Complimentary continental bkfst. Restaurant 11 am-10 pm. Bar; jazz Fri (summer). Ck-out noon. Meeting rms. Concierge. Airport transportation. Pool; whirlpool, poolside serv. Refrigerator, microwave in suite. Some balconies. Cr cds: A, C, D, DS, MC, V.

D

Restaurant

★ ROSY'S. *4950 Pacific St, Rocklin (95677). 916/624-1920.* Hrs: 7 am-3 pm; Fri, Sat to 9 pm. Closed Dec 25. Res accepted. Bar. Wine, beer. Bkfst $4-$7.50, lunch $6-$9, dinner $6-$15. Children's menu. Specializes in burgers, omelettes, sandwiches. Parking. Outdoor dining. Football memorabilia. Totally nonsmoking. Cr cds: A, DS, MC, V.

D SC

Sacramento

(F-4) *See also Davis, Rancho Cordova*

Settled 1839 **Pop** 369,365 **Elev** 25 ft **Area code** 916

Information Convention and Visitors Bureau, 1303 J Street, Suite 600, 95814; 916/264-7777.

Web www.sacramentocvb.org/cvb/

Capital of the state since 1854, Sacramento is known to flower lovers as the "Camellia Capital of the World." It is the marketing center for 11 counties in the Sacramento Valley, producing a cash farm income approaching 11 percent of the state's income.

Modern Sacramento started when Captain John A. Sutter established New Helvetia, a colony for his Swiss compatriots. Sutter built a fort here and immigrants came. He prospered in wheat raising, flour milling, distilling, and in a passenger and freight boat service to San Francisco. The discovery of gold at Coloma in 1848 (see PLACERVILLE) brought ruin to Sutter. Workers deserted to hunt gold, and he soon lost possession of the fort. The next year his son, who had been deeded family property near the boat line terminus, laid out a town there, naming it Sacramento City. At the entrance to the gold rush country, its population rocketed to 10,000 within seven months. Chosen as California's capital in 1854, the new capitol building was constructed at a cost of more than $2.6 million over a 20-year period.

Transportation facilities were important in the city's growth. In 1860, the Pony Express made Sacramento its western terminus. Later, Sacramento's "Big Four"—Mark Hopkins, Charles Crocker, Collis P Huntington, and Leland Stanford—financed the building of the Central Pacific Railroad over the Sierras. Deepwater ships reach the city via a 43-mile-long channel from Suisun Bay. Sacramento's new port facilities handle an average of 20 ships a month carrying import and export cargo from major ports around the world.

What to See and Do

Blue Diamond Growers Visitors Center & Retail Store. 20-min video (Mon-Sat). 1701 C Street at 16th St. Phone 916/446-8439. **FREE**

Cal Expo. Multipurpose facility for variety of activities incl various consumer shows, auto racing, and concerts. (See SPECIAL EVENTS) 5 mi NE at 1600 Exposition Blvd, borders Business Loop I-80.

California State University, Sacramento. (1947) 25,000 students. A replica of the Golden Gate bridge serves as a footbridge across the river. 6000 J St, on the banks of the American River on the E side of campus. Take Hwy 50 to exit Power Inn and follow the signs. Phone 916/278-6156.

Crocker Art Museum. Original restored Victorian Gallery (1872), reconstructed Mansion Wing and Herold Wing housing E. B. Crocker collection; European and American paintings; master drawings; Asian art; decorative arts; changing exhibits. Museum bookstore/gift shop. (Tues-Sun; closed hols) 216 O St at 2nd St. Phone 916/264-5423. ¢¢

Discovery Museum. Regional history exhibits, incl gold ore specimens and restored artifacts; hands-on exhibits; video computers; working print shop. (Tues-Sun; closed hols) 101 I St, in Old Sacramento. Phone 916/264-7057. ¢¢

Golden State Museum. Museum about California's past, present, and future; exhibits look at "Place," "People," "Promise," and "Politics." (Tues-Sun; closed hols) 1020 O Street. Phone 916/653-7524.

Gold Rush District State Parks. (ca 1850-1870) Adj to central business district between I-5 and I St bridge. This 28-acre area of historic buildings along the banks of the Sacramento River, known as the old Sacramento Historic District, has been restored to its 1850-1870 period of the Pony Express, the arrival of the Central Pacific Railroad, and the gold rush. Special events held throughout the yr. The area also has shops and restaurants. Most buildings closed Jan 1, Thanksgiving, Dec 25. For recorded information, incl the Governor's Mansion and Sutter's Fort State Historic Park, State Indian Museum, State Railroad Museum, the Leland Stanford Mansion, and Woodland Upper House State Park, phone 916/324-0539. **FREE** Incl

California State Railroad Museum and Railtown State Historic Park. The largest part of this complex is the **Museum of Railroad History**, which houses 21 pieces of rolling stock and a total of 40 exhibits covering all aspects of railroading. (Daily; closed Jan 1, Thanksgiving, Dec 25) 125 I St in Old Sacramento. Phone 916/445-6645. Also part of the State Railroad Museum, and incl in museum admission fee, is the

Central Pacific Passenger Depot. 930 Front St. (Same days as railroad museum) 2618 K Street at 26th St.

Governor's Mansion. Once owned by Joseph Steffens, father of Lincoln Steffens, a turn-of-the-century journalist. Every governor from 1903 through 1967 lived here. Guided tours (daily 10 am-5 pm; closed Jan 1, Thanksgiving, Dec 25). 16th and H Sts. Phone 916/323-3047.

Hastings Building. Western terminus of the Pony Express and original home of the California Supreme Court. 2nd and J Sts.

Old Eagle Theatre. Docent-led programs on Sacramento history. Front and J Sts. Phone 916/445-4209.

State Indian Museum. Displays incl dugout canoes, weapons, pottery, basketry; changing exhibits. (Hrs same as park) Films (Sat and Sun). 2618 K St at 26th St. Phone 916/324-7405.

★ **Sutter's Fort State Historic Park.** Restored in the late 1800s. Exhibits depict Sutter's life; kitchen. Special craft and living history demonstration days. (Daily; closed Jan 1, Thanksgiving, Dec 25) Admission incl self-guided audio tour. 2701 L St at 27th St. Phone 916/445-4422.

Professional sports.

Sacramento Kings (NBA). ARCO Arena, One Sports Pkwy, 95834. Phone 916/928-6900.

Sacramento Monarchs (WNBA). ARCO Arena, Phone 916/419-WNBA.

State Capitol. The Capitol provides a unique combination of past and present under one roof. It has been the home of California's lawmaking branch of government since the Capitol opened in 1869. The main building has been restored to recreate its turn-of-the-century ambience and to ensure its safety. The Legislature still meets in the restored Senate and Assembly chambers. Nine historic offices incl exhibits from the State Library and State Archives. The more modern east annex contains the offices of the legislators and the governor. The building is surrounded by a 40-acre park with hundreds of varieties of trees, shrubs, and flowers. Free guided tours of building (daily, on the hour). Park tours (June-Sept, daily). Capitol (daily; closed Jan 1, Thanksgiving, Dec 25). 10th and L Sts. Phone 916/324-0333. **FREE**

Towe Ford Museum. Extensive collection of American automobiles. (Daily; closed Jan 1, Thanksgiving, Dec 25) 2200 Front St. Phone 916/442-6802. **¢¢¢**

William Land Park. Wading pool (summer, daily); fishing (children under 16 only). Nine-hole golf course. Picnic facilities, supervised playground, ballfields. Amusement area near zoo has pony, amusement rides (summer, daily). **Sacramento Zoo,** in the park at Land Park Dr and Sutterville Rd, has more than 340 specimens representing more than 150 species of exotic animals displayed in a 15-acre botanical garden setting (daily, mid-morning-mid-afternoon; closed Dec 25). Fairytale Town children's theme park (Jan-Feb, wkends; rest of yr, daily). Fee for activities. Freeport Blvd between 13th Ave and Sutterville Rd. Phone 916/277-6060 or 264/520-0916. Fairytale Town **¢¢**

Special Events

Sacramento Jazz Jubilee. Venues throughout city. Cabaret, concert, and jam sessions. Phone 916/372-5277. Memorial Day wkend.

Music Circus. Music Circus Tent at 15th and H Sts, box office at 1419 H St. Community Center Theatre at 14th and L Sts. Summer professional musical theater. Phone 916/557-1999. July-Sept.

California State Fair. California Exposition grounds. Incl traditional state fair activities; exhibits, livestock, carnival food, entertainment on ten stages, thoroughbred racing and one-mi monorail. Phone 916/263-FAIR. Last two wks Aug. Phone 916/263-3247.

Festival de la Familia. In Old Sacramento. The "Festival of the Family" celebrates Latino culture with music, entertainment, food, arts and crafts, and children's activities. Last Sun Apr. Phone 916/552-5252.

Motels/Motor Lodges

★★ BEST WESTERN HARBOR INN AND SUITES. *1250 Halyard Dr, West Sacramento (95691). 916/371-2100; fax 916/373-1507; res 800/371-2101. www.bestwestern.com.* 138 rms, 2-4 story, 19 suites. S, D $69-$79; each addl $5; suites $84-$94; under 12 free. Crib free. Pet accepted; $10. TV; cable (premium). Heated pool; 2 whirlpools. Complimentary continental bkfst, coffee in rms. Restaurant adj 7 am-11 pm. Ck-out 11 am. Meeting rms. Business servs avail. Valet serv. Some refrigerators, in-rm whirlpools. Private patios, balconies. Cr cds: A, C, D, DS, MC, V.

D SC

★★ CLARION HOTEL. *700 16th St (95814). 916/444-8000; fax 916/442-8129; toll-free 800/443-0880. www.clarionhotel.com.* 238 rms, 2-4 story. S, D $86-$94; each addl $20; suites $135-$265; under 18 free; wkend rates. Crib free. Pet accepted; $50 deposit. TV; cable (premium), VCR avail. Pool; poolside serv. Complimentary coffee in rms. Restaurant 6:30 am-2 pm, 5-10 pm. Bar 11-1 am. Ck-out noon. Meeting rms. Business servs avail. In-rm modem link. Bellhops. Valet serv. Sundries. Airport transportation. Health club privileges. Some refrigerators. Some private patios, balconies. Cr cds: A, C, D, DS, ER, JCB, MC, V.

D SC

★ DAYS INN DISCOVERY PARK. *350 Bercut Dr (95814). 916/442-6971; fax 916/444-2809; res 800/329-7466.*

www.daysinn.com. 99 rms, 2 story. S $69-$99; D $79-$109; each addl $5; under 12 free. Crib free. TV; cable (premium). Pool; whirlpool. Complimentary continental bkfst, coffee in rms. Restaurant adj open 24 hrs. Ck-out 11 am. Meeting rms. Coin lndry. Valet serv. Some refrigerators, wetbars. Some private patios and balconies. Cr cds: A, D, DS, MC, V.

D

★★ **GOVERNORS INN.** *210 Richards Blvd (95814). 916/448-7224; fax 916/448-7382; toll-free 800/999-6689. www.governorsinn.net.* 133 rms, 3 story. Jan-Nov: S $79; D $89; each addl $10; suites $96-$106; under 12 free; higher rates jazz festival; lower rates rest of yr. Crib $5. TV; cable (premium). Complimentary continental bkfst, coffee in rms. Restaurant opp open 24 hrs. Ck-out 11 am. Meeting rms. Business servs avail. In-rm modem link. Valet serv. Free airport, RR station, bus depot transportation. Exercise equipt. Pool; whirlpool. Refrigerator, wet bar in suites. Balcony in suites. On river. Cr cds: A, D, DS, MC, V.

D

★★ **HOLIDAY INN.** *300 J St (95814). 916/446-0100; fax 916/446-0117; res 800/465-4329. www.holiday-inn.com.* 364 rms, 16 story. S $122; D $132; each addl $10; suites $225-$550; under 12 free. Crib free. TV; cable (premium), VCR avail. Pool; sauna. Coffee in rms. Restaurant 6 am-2 pm; dining rm 6-11 pm. Bar 11-1 am; entertainment Tues-Sat. Ck-out noon. Convention facilities. Business servs avail. In-rm modem link. Concierge. Gift shop. Exercise equipt. Health club privileges. Some refrigerators. Luxury level. Cr cds: A, D, DS, JCB, MC, V.

D

★ **LA QUINTA INN.** *4604 Madison Ave (95841). 916/348-0900; fax 916/331-7160; res 800/687-6667. www.laquinta.com.* 127 rms, 3 story. S, D $59-$79; each addl $5; suites $131; under 18 free. Crib free. Pet accepted, some restrictions. TV; cable (premium). Pool. Continental bkfst. Restaurant adj open 24 hrs. Ck-out noon. Coin lndry. Meeting rms. Business servs avail. In-rm modem link. Health club privileges. Fireplace in lobby. Cr cds: A, D, DS, V.

D

★ **LA QUINTA INN.** *200 Jibboom St (95814). 916/448-8100; fax 916/447-3621; toll-free 800/531-5900. www.laquintainn.com.* 165 rms, 3 story. S, D $70-$75; under 18 free. TV; cable (premium). Pool. Complimentary continental bkfst, coffee in rms. Restaurant nearby. Ck-out noon. Guest lndry. Meeting rms. Business servs avail. In-rm modem link. Free airport, RR station, bus depot transportation. Exercise equipt. On Sacramento River. Cr cds: A, C, D, DS, V.

D SC

★★ **RED LION HOTEL SACRAMENTO.** *1401 Arden Way (95815). 916/922-8041; fax 916/922-0386. www.redlion.com.* 376 rms, 2-3 story. S, D $125-$148; each addl $15; suites $150-$395; under 18 free. Crib free. Pet accepted, some restrictions; $25. TV; cable (premium). 3 pools, whirlpool, poolside serv. Restaurant 6 am-10 pm. Bar 11-2 am; entertainment Tues-Sat. Ck-out noon. Coin lndry. Meeting rms. Bellhops. Sundries. Gift shop. Valet parking. Putting green. Exercise equipt. Some bathrm phones, in-rm whirlpools, refrigerators. Private patios, balconies. Cr cds: A, C, D, DS, ER, JCB, MC, V.

D

★ **SUPER 8 MOTEL.** *9646 Micron Ave (95827). 916/361-3131; fax 916/361-9674; res 800/800-8000.* 93 rms, 3 story. S $39; D $45-$50; each addl $5; under 13 free; higher rates special events. Crib $5. TV; cable. Complimentary coffee in lobby. Restaurant opp 6 am-10 pm. Ck-out 11 am. Coin lndry. Pool. Cr cds: A, D, DS, MC, V.

D SC

★ **VAGABOND INN.** *909 3rd St (95814). 916/446-1481; fax 916/448-0364; res 800/522-1555. www.vagabondinns.com.* 108 rms, 3 story. S $73-$83; D $83-$93; each addl $5; under 17 free. Crib free. Pet accepted, some restrictions; $5/day. TV; cable (premium). Heated pool. Complimentary continental bkfst, coffee in rms. Restaurant adj open 24 hrs. Ck-out noon. Meeting rm. Valet serv. Free airport, RR station, bus depot transportation. Some refrigerators, microwaves. Cr cds: A, D, DS, MC, V.

★ **VAGABOND INN.** *1319 30th St (95816). 916/454-4400; fax 916/736-2812; res 800/522-1555. www.vagabondinns.com.* 81 rms, 3 story. S, D $45-$65; each addl $5; under 18 free. Crib free. Pet accepted, some restrictions; $5/day. TV; cable. Pool. Coffee in lobby. Restaurant adj open 24 hrs. Ck-out noon. Cr cds: A, D, DS, MC, V.

Hotels

★★★ **DOUBLETREE HOTEL.** *2001 Point West Way (95815). 916/929-8855; fax 916/924-0719; res 800/222-8733.* 448 rms, 4 story. S, D $119-$199; each addl $15; suites $200-$500; under 18 free. Crib free. Pet accepted, some restrictions; $50. TV; cable (premium), VCR avail. Pool; poolside serv, whirlpool. Restaurant 6 am-midnight. Bar 11-2 am. Ck-out noon. Meeting rms. Business center. In-rm modem link. Bellhops. Valet serv. Gift shop. Free airport, RR station, bus depot transportation. Exercise equipt. Health club privileges. Bathrm phone, refrigerator, minibar, whirlpool in suites. Balconies. Cr cds: A, D, DS, MC, V.

★★★ **HILTON SACRAMENTO ARDEN WEST.** *2200 Harvard St (95815). 916/922-4700; fax 916/922-8418; toll-free 800/445-8667. www.sacramentoardenwest.hilton.com.* 330 rms, 12 story. S $129-$159; D $139-$169; each addl $10; suites $275-$525; wkend rates. Crib free. TV; cable (premium), VCR avail. Heated pool; whirlpool, poolside serv. Coffee in rms. Restaurant 6 am-10 pm. Bar noon-midnight. Ck-out noon. Convention facilities. Business servs avail. In-rm modem link. Gift shop. Exercise equipt; sauna. Some balconies. Luxury level. Cr cds: A, C, D, DS, ER, JCB, MC, V.

★★★ **HYATT REGENCY.** *1209 L St (95814). 916/443-1234; fax 916/321-6631; res 800/233-1234. www.hyatt.com.* 500 rms, 15 story. S $190; D $215; each addl $25; suites $225-$895; under 18 free; wkly, wkend rates. Crib free. Valet parking $12/day, garage $7/day. TV; cable (premium), VCR avail. Heated pool; poolside serv. Complimentary coffee in rms. Restaurant 6 am-midnight. Bar 11-2 am; entertainment Tues-Sat. Ck-out noon. Convention facilities. Business servs avail. In-rm modem link. Concierge. Airport, RR station, bus depot transportation. Exercise equipt; whirlpool. Minibars. Balconies. Luxury level. Cr cds: A, D, DS, MC, V.

★★★ **RADISSON.** *500 Leisure Ln (95814). Fax 916/922-2020; res 800/333-3333. www.radissonsac.com.* 307 rms, 2 story. S, D $69-$129; each addl $10; suites $159-$448; under 18 free; wkend rates. Crib avail. Pet accepted, some restrictions; $100 deposit. TV; cable, VCR avail. Pool; whirlpool, poolside serv. Complimentary coffee in rms. Restaurant 6:30 am-10 pm. Rm serv 24 hrs. Bar 11-2 am; entertainment. Ck-out noon. Convention facilities. Business center. Bellhops. Valet serv. Concierge. Sundries. Gift shop. Exercise equipt. Some refrigerators, minibars. Balconies. On small, private lake. Cr cds: A, C, D, DS, JCB, MC, V.

★★★ **THE STERLING HOTEL.** *1300 H St (95814). 916/448-1300; fax 916/448-8066; toll-free 800/365-7660. www.sterlinghotel.com.* 17 rms, 3 story. S $159; D $179. Crib free. TV; cable (premium). Complimentary coffee in sitting rm. Dining rm (see also CHANTERELLE). Serv bar. Ck-out 11 am, ck-in 3 pm. Meeting rms. Business servs avail. In-rm modem link. Health club privileges. In-rm whirlpools. Some refrigerators. Some balconies. Individually decorated rms. Totally nonsmoking. Cr cds: A, C, D, MC, V.

SC

B&Bs/Small Inns

★★★ **AMBER HOUSE BED AND BREAKFAST INN.** *1315 22nd St (95816). 916/444-8085; fax 916/552-6529; toll-free 800/755-6526. www.amberhouse.com.* 14 rms in 3 houses, 2 story. S $149-$159; D $149-$279.

TV; cable (premium), VCR. Complimentary full bkfst. Ck-out noon, ck-in 4 pm. Business servs avail. In-rm modem link. Whirlpool in most rms. Bicycles. Health club privileges. Houses built 1895 and 1913; rms individually decorated; antiques; library. Totally nonsmoking. Cr cds: A, C, D, DS, MC, V.

★★★ **INN AT PARKSIDE.** *2116 6th St (95818). 916/658-1818; fax 916/658-1809; toll-free 800/995-7275. www.innatparkside.com.* 7 rms, 3 story, 2 suites. No elvtrs. S, D $110-$130; each addl $10; suites $275. TV; cable, VCR (movies). Complimentary full bkfst. Restaurant nearby. Ck-out noon, ck-in 3-8 pm. Business servs avail. In-rm modem link. Concierge serv. Microwaves avail; in-rm whirlpool, fireplace in suites. Picnic tables. Built in 1936 by Chinese ambassador and used as cultural center. Totally nonsmoking. Cr cds: A, MC, V.

D

★★ **VIZCAYA.** *2019 21st St (95818). 916/455-5243; fax 916/455-6102; toll-free 800/456-2019.* www.*sterlinghotel.com.* 9 rms, 3 story. S $139, D $149. TV; cable (premium). Complimentary full bkfst. Ck-out 11 am, ck-in 3 pm. Business servs avail. Street parking. Some in-rm whirlpools, fireplaces. Picnic tables. Landscaped gardens, Victorian gazebo. Built 1899; Italian marble in bathrms. Sitting rm; antiques. Brick patio. Totally nonsmoking. Cr cds: A, D, MC, V.

D SC

All Suite

★★ **HAWTHORN SUITES.** *321 Bercut Dr (95814). 916/441-1200; fax 916/444-2347; res 800/527-1133. www.hawthorn.com.* 272 suites, 3 story. S $109; D $119; each addl $10; under 12 free; wkend rates. Crib free. Pet accepted, some restrictions. TV; cable (premium), VCR avail. Heated pool; whirlpool. Complimentary full bkfst, coffee in rms. Restaurant 7 am-11 pm. Bar 4 pm-1 am. Ck-out noon. Coin lndry. Convention facilities. Business servs avail. Bellhops. Valet serv. Sundries. Free RR station, bus depot transportation. Exercise equipt. Health club privileges. Refrigerators, microwaves. Cr cds: A, D, DS, MC, V.

D

Extended Stay

★★ **RESIDENCE INN BY MARRIOTT - CAL EXPO.** *1530 Howe Ave (95825). 916/920-9111; fax 916/921-5664; res 800/331-3131. residenceinn.com/sacex.* 176 kit. units, 2 story. Kit. units $139-$199; each addl $10; under 12 free; wkly rates. Crib free. Pet accepted; $60-$100 and $10/day. TV; cable (premium). Pool; whirlpools. Complimentary continental bkfst. Ck-out noon. Coin lndry. Meeting rm. Business servs avail. In-rm modem link. Valet serv. Sundries. Health club privileges. Balconies. Cr cds: A, C, D, DS, MC.

D

Restaurants

★★★ **BIBA.** *2801 Capitol Ave (95816). 916/455-2422. www.ristorante-biba.com.* Hrs: 11:30 am-2:30 pm, 5:30-10:30 pm; Fri to 10:30 pm; Sat 5:30-10:30 pm. Closed Sun; also hols. Res accepted. Italian menu. Bar. Wine cellar. Lunch $8-$14, dinner $16-$20. Specializes in pasta, veal, rabbit. Pianist Tues-Sat. Street parking. Totally nonsmoking. Cr cds: A, C, D, ER, MC, V.

D

★★ **CHANTERELLE.** *1300 H St (95814). 916/442-0451. www.sterlinghotel.com.* Hrs: 5:30-8:30 pm. Res accepted. California, French menu. Setups. Wine list. Dinner $12.50-$21. Specialty: veal with chanterelle mushrooms. Own baking. Totally nonsmoking. Cr cds: A, MC, V.

D

★★★ **FIREHOUSE.** *1112 2nd St (95814). 916/442-4772.* Hrs: 11:30 am-2 pm, 5:30-9 pm; Fri to 10 pm; Sat 5-10 pm; Sun 5-9 pm. Closed hols. Res accepted. Contemporary American menu. Bar 11:30 am-10 pm. A la carte entrees: lunch $6.95-$14.95, dinner $12.95-$34.95. Specialties: filet mignon, artichokes and asparagus. Courtyard dining (lunch). Antiques, crystal. In Old Sacramento; restored landmark firehouse (1853). Family-owned. Cr cds: A, MC, V.

D

★★★ **FRANK FAT'S.** *806 L St (95814). 916/442-7092.* Hrs: 11:30 am-2 pm, 5:30-10 pm; Sat 5:30-10 pm; Sun 5-10 pm. Closed July 4, Thanksgiving, Dec 25. Res accepted. Chinese menu. Bar. Wine cellar. Lunch $10-$15, dinner $15-$25. Specialties: honey-cured walnut prawns, clams in black bean sauce, Frank Fat's NY steak. Parking. Totally nonsmoking. Cr cds: A, MC, V.
D

★★ **LEMON GRASS.** *601 Munroe St (95825). 916/486-4891.* Hrs: 11:30 am-2 pm, 5:30-9:30 pm; Fri, Sat 5-10 pm; Sun 5-9 pm. Closed hols. Vietnamese, Thai menu. Bar. Lunch $5-$15, dinner $9-$18. Specializes in grilled seafood. Parking. Outdoor dining. Original art. Cr cds: A, D, MC, V.
D

★★★ **MORTON'S OF CHICAGO.** *521 L St (95814). 916/442-5091. www.mortons.com.* Hrs: 5:30-11 pm; Sun 5-10 pm. Closed hols. Res accepted. Bar. Wine cellar. A la carte entrees: dinner $20-$30. Specializes in prime aged beef, live Maine lobster, fresh seafood. Valet parking. Chicago club atmosphere. Totally nonsmoking. Cr cds: A, C, D, ER, MC, V.
D

★★ **MUM'S VEGETARIAN.** *2968 Freeport Blvd (95818). 916/444-3015.* Hrs: 11:30 am-2 pm, 5:15-9 pm; Mon 11:30 am-2 pm; Fri to 9:30 pm; Sat 5:15-9:30 pm; Sun 4-8 pm; Sat, Sun brunch 9:30 am-2 pm. Closed Jan 1, Dec 25. Res accepted. Vegetarian menu. Bar. Lunch $4.50-$7.50, dinner $9.75-$12.50. Sat, Sun brunch $5.75-$8. Children's menu. Specialties: Mum's shepherd's pie, avocado rarebit, herbed polenta torta. Parking. Outdoor dining. Totally nonsmoking. Cr cds: A, MC, V.
D

★★ **PILOTHOUSE.** *1000 Front St (95814). 916/441-4440. www.deltaking.com.* Hrs: 11:30 am-2 pm, 5-10 pm; Sun brunch 10 am-2 pm. Res accepted. Bar. A la carte entrees: lunch $5.95-$10.95, dinner $11.95-$21.95. Sun brunch $16.95. Children's menu. Specializes in fresh fish, grilled meats, pasta. Valet parking. Authentic period decor. Totally nonsmoking. Cr cds: A, MC, V.
D

★★ **RISTORANTE PIATTI.** *571 Pavilions Ln (95825). 916/649-8885.* Hrs: 11 am-10 pm; Fri, Sat to 11 pm. Closed Dec 25. Res accepted. Italian menu. Bar. A la carte entrees: lunch, dinner $7.50-$17.95. Children's menu. Specializes in roasted chicken, wood-fired pizza, fresh pasta. Valet parking. Outdoor dining. Mediterranean decor. Totally nonsmoking. Cr cds: A, DS, MC, V.

★ **RUSTY DUCK.** *500 Bercut Dr (95814). 916/441-1191.* Hrs: 11:30 am-10 pm; Fri to 11 pm; Sat 4:30-11 pm; Sun 10 am-3 pm, 4:30-10 pm; early-bird dinner 4:30-6:30 pm. Res accepted. Bar; Fri, Sat to 1:30 am. Lunch $5.95-$12.95, dinner $9.95-$32.95. Children's menu. Specializes in fresh fish, prime rib, pasta. Own pies, cheesecake. Parking. Rustic hunting lodge decor; fireplace. Cr cds: A, C, DS, MC, V.
D

★★ **SILVA'S SHELDON INN.** *9000 Grant Line Rd, Elk Grove (95624). 916/686-8330.* Hrs: 5-9:30 pm; Fri, Sat to 10 pm; Sun 5-8:30 pm. Closed Mon; hols; also wk of Jan 1 and wk of July 4. Bar from 5 pm. Complete meals: dinner $10-$17. Children's menu. Specializes in fresh fish, steak, Portuguese bean soup. Parking. Outdoor dining. In turn-of-the-century building. Totally nonsmoking. Cr cds: MC, V.
D

Unrated Dining Spot

RICK'S DESSERT DINER. *2322 K St (95816). 916/444-0969.* Hrs: 10 am-11 pm; Fri, Sat to 1 am; Sun from noon. Closed hols. A la carte: $.90-$3.95. Specializes in desserts. Specialties: Chocolate OD, white chocolate almond torte. Outdoor dining. 1950s decor. Totally nonsmoking.
D

St. Helena

(F-3) *See also Calistoga, Napa, Santa Rosa, Yountville*

Founded 1853 **Pop** 4,990 **Elev** 257 ft **Area code** 707 **Zip** 94574

Information Chamber of Commerce, 1010 Main St, Suite A; 707/963-4456

Web www.sthelena.com

What to See and Do

Lake Berryessa. Artificial lake formed by Monticello Dam; 165 mi of shoreline. Swimming, waterskiing, fishing; picnicking, concession areas, camping. Oak Shores has car top boat launch. Contact Lake Berryessa Recreation Office, Bureau of Reclamation, 5520 Knoxville Rd, Spanish Flat Station, Napa 94558. 4 mi S on CA 29 to Rutherford, then E on CA 128. Phone 707/966-2111.

Silverado Museum. Approx 8,500 items of Robert Louis Stevenson memorabilia; first and variant editions of author's works, original letters, and manuscripts; paintings, sculptures, photographs. Special exhibits. (Tues-Sun, afternoons; closed hols) 1490 Library Ln. Phone 707/963-3757. **FREE**

Wineries.

Beaulieu Vineyard. Winery founded at the turn of the century. Tours and tastings (daily; closed hols). Select tasting rm (fee). Web www.bv-wine.com 4 mi S on CA 29, at 1960 S St. Helena Hwy, in Rutherford. Phone 707/967-5200. **FREE**

Beringer Vineyards. Established 1876. Underground cellars; Rhine House (1883). Tours with wine tasting (daily; closed hols). Web www.beringer.com. 2000 Main St, N on CA 29. Phone 707/963-4812. **FREE**

Charles Krug Winery. Established 1861. Tours and wine tasting. Select tasting rm (fee). (Daily; closed hols) 2800 Main St. Phone 707/967-2000.

Franciscan Vineyards. Wine tasting and sales. (Daily; closed hols) 15 mi N via CA 29 in Rutherford, at 1178 Galleron Rd. Phone 707/963-7111. **¢¢**

Louis M. Martini Winery. Guided tours. Wine tasting. (Daily; closed hols) Web www.louismartini.com 254 S St. Helena Hwy. Phone 707/963-2736. **FREE**

Merryvale Vineyards. Tasting rm within restored 1930s building; 2,000- and 3,000-gallon oak casks on display. Merryvale produces distinct Chardonnays as well as Bordeaux-style red wine. Tours (daily, by appt; closed hols). Web www.merryvale.com. 1000 Main St. Phone 707/963-7777. **¢¢**

Vineyards of Napa Valley

Motel/Motor Lodge

★★ **EL BONITA.** *195 Main St (94574). 707/963-3216; fax 707/963-8838; toll-free 800/541-3284.* 42 rms, 27 kits. June-Oct: S, D $95-$165; suites $199-$219; lower rates rest of yr. Crib $5. Pet accepted, some restrictions; $5. TV; cable (premium). Pool; whirlpool, sauna. Complimentary continental bkfst, coffee in rms. Restaurant nearby. Ck-out 11:30 am. Business servs avail. Refrigerators; some in-rm whirlpools. Cr cds: A, C, D, DS, MC, V.

D

Resorts

★★★★ **AUBERGE DU SOLEIL.** *180 Rutherford Hill Rd, Rutherford (94573). 707/963-1211; fax 707/963-8764; res 800/348-5406. www.aubergedusoleil.com.* This stunning retreat, located in the heart of the Napa Valley, provides a tranquil respite from the harried workaday world. Guests can enjoy a full menu of excellent spa treatments, blow off steam by playing tennis, find solitude in the serene sculpture garden, dine on world-class cuisine, or simply luxuriate in a plush guest room with exceptional showers and tubs. The staff are proud of the attractive Mediterranean-style setting, making this property worthy of its moniker: the inn of the sun. 52 rms, 2 story, 2 cottages. Apr-Nov: S, D $300-$1,500; cottages from $525-$2,000; lower rates rest of yr. TV; cable (premium), VCR (movies). Pool; poolside serv. Dining rm (see also AUBERGE DU SOLEIL). Rm serv 24 hrs. Bar 11 am-11 pm. Ck-out noon, ck-in 3 pm. Meeting rm. Business servs avail. In-rm modem link. Luggage handling. Valet serv. Gift shop. Beauty shop. Tennis, pro. Bicycles avail. Exercise equipt; steam rm. Massage. Refrigerators, fireplaces. Private patios, balconies. Cr cds: A, C, D, DS, JCB, MC, V.

D

★★★★ **MEADOWOOD RESORT HOTEL.** *900 Meadowood Ln, St. Helena (94574). 707/963-3646; fax 707/963-3532; toll-free 800/458-8080.* Like staying at an elegant country estate, Meadowood provides the ultimate care in tailoring a stay to suit guests' individual interests. The staff will arrange winery visits and tastings, provide personal trainers and private yoga instruction, arrange spa visits, or recommend outdoor activities on the exquisite property and beyond. Dining options range from formal gourmet meals with excellent wine to poolside dining. 99 units, 51 suites. July-mid-Nov: S $335-$525; D $335-$525; each addl $25; suites $570-$2,175; under 12 free; lower rates rest of yr. Crib free. TV; cable (premium), VCR avail (movies). 2 pools; whirlpool, poolside serv. Coffee in rms. Dining rm (see also THE RESTAURANT AT MEADOWOOD). 3 bars 10:30 am-midnight. Ck-out noon, ck-in 4 pm. Meeting rms. Business center. 7 tennis courts, pro. 9-hole golf, pro, putting green. Croquet facilities, pro. Bicycle rentals. Exercise rm; sauna, steam rm. Spa. Refrigerators, minibars; many fireplaces; microwaves avail. Private patios, balconies. Cr cds: A, C, D, DS, MC, V.

D

★ **WHITE SULPHUR SPRINGS RETREAT AND SPA.** *3100 White Sulphur Springs Rd (94574). 707/963-8588; fax 707/963-2890; toll-free 800/593-8873. whitesulphursprings.com.* 28 rms in 2 buildings, 14 share bath, 14 full baths, 9 cottages, 4 with kit. No A/C (5 cottages with A/C). No rm phones. S, D $126-$151; each addl $15; cottages $135; kit. cottages $185; wkend rates. Crib free. Pool; whirlpool. Complimentary continental bkfst. Ck-out 11 am, ck-in 3 pm. Meeting rms. Business servs avail. Hiking. Massage. Lawn games. Microwaves avail. Picnic tables, grills. Rustic inn in secluded canyon surrounded by forests; a hot sulphur spring (87º) flows out of the mountains into a rock-lined outdoor soaking pool. Totally nonsmoking. Cr cds: MC, V.

B&Bs/Small Inns

★★ **ADAGIO INN.** *1417 Kearney St, St Helena (94574). 707/963-2238; fax 707/963-5598; res 800/823-2466. adagiolnn.com.* 4 rms, 2 story, 1 suite. May-mid-Nov: S, D $139-$195; each addl $30; wkends (2-day min); wkly rates; lower rates rest of yr. TV; VCR. Complimentary full bkfst, afternoon refreshments. Restaurant nearby. Ck-out 11 am, ck-in 4 pm. Business servs avail. Street parking. Victorian house (1904) with wrap-around porch; library/sitting rm furnished with antiques. Totally nonsmoking. Cr cds: MC, V.

★★★ **HARVEST INN.** *1 Main St (94574). 707/963-9463; fax 707/963-4402; toll-free 800/950-8466. www.harvestinn.com.* 54 rms, 1-2 story. Apr-Oct: S, D $269-$319; suites $319-$499; wkends (2-day min); lower rates rest of yr. Crib free. Pet accepted, some restrictions; $75. TV; cable, VCR avail (movies). 2 heated pools; whirlpools. Complimentary continental bkfst, coffee in rms. Ck-out 11 am, ck-in after 4 pm. Meeting rms. Business servs avail. In-rm modem link. Refrigerators, bathrm phones, fireplaces, wet bars. Some private patios, balconies. Overlooks vineyards. Cr cds: A, D, DS, MC, V.

D

★★ **HOTEL SAINT HELENA.** *1309 Main St (94574). 707/963-4388; fax 707/963-5402; toll-free 888/478-4355.* 18 units, 14 with bath, 2 story (no ground floor units). S, D $145-$275; each addl $20; mid-wk rates. TV in most rms; cable (premium). Complimentary continental bkfst. Restaurant adj 8:30 am-10 pm. Ck-out noon, ck-in 3 pm. Business servs avail. Victorian structure (1881). Cr cds: A, MC, V.

★★★ **INN AT SOUTHBRIDGE.** *1020 Main St, Saint Helena (94574). 707/967-9400; fax 707/967-9486; toll-free 800/520-6800. www.placestostay.com.* 21 Rms, 2 Story. Mid-June-mid-Nov: S, D $245-$355; Suites $455; Under 18 Free; lower rates rest of yr. Crib free. TV; Cable, VCR (movies). Pool. Complimentary continental bkfst. Restaurant 11:30 am-10 pm. Ck-out noon, Ck-In 4 pm. Concierge serv. Luggage handling. Business servs avail. Tennis, golf, and health club privileges. Refrigerators. Some balconies. Cr cds: A, C, D, ER, JCB, MC, V.

D SC

★★ **OLIVER HOUSE.** *2970 Silverado Trail North (94574). 707/963-4089; fax 707/963-5566; toll-free 800/682-7888. www.oliverhouse.com.* 4 suites, 2 story. Rm phones avail. Apr-Nov: suites $145-$295; each addl $15; wkends (2-day min); lower rates rest of yr. Complimentary full bkfst. Ck-out 11 am, ck-in 4-6 pm. Business servs avail. Lawn games. Balconies. Country-Swiss house with antique furnishings; fireplaces. Totally nonsmoking. Cr cds: A, DS, MC, V.

★★ **RANCHO CAYMUS.** *1140 Rutherford Rd, Rutherford (94573). 707/963-1777; fax 707/963-5387; toll-free 800/845-1777. www.ranchocaymus.com.* 26 suites, 2 story, 5 kits. Apr-Nov: suites $175-$185; kit. units $265-$315; wkends (2-day min); lower rates rest of yr. TV. Complimentary continental bkfst. Ck-out noon, ck-in 3 pm. Business servs avail. Health club privileges. Refrigerators; some in-rm whirlpools, fireplaces. Private patios, balconies. Spanish-style architecture. Cr cds: A, C, D, MC, V.

D

★★ **VINEYARD COUNTRY INN.** *201 Main St (94574). 707/963-1000; fax 707/963-1794. www.vineyardcountryinn.com.* 21 suites, 2 story. Mid-May-mid-Nov: S, D $155-$230; each addl $15; under 5 free; wkends (2-day min), hols (3-day min). TV. Heated pool; whirlpool. Complimentary buffet bkfst. Restaurant nearby. Ck-out 11 am. Business servs avail. Refrigerators. Some balconies, patios. Cr cds: A, C, D, MC, V.

D

★★★ **THE WINE COUNTRY INN.** *1152 Lodi Ln (94574). 707/963-7077; fax 707/963-9018. www.winecountryinn.com.* 25 units, 2-3 story. Aug-mid-Oct: S $125-$248; D $145-$268; each addl $20; suites $206-$268; lower rates rest of yr. Closed Dec 25. Pool; whirlpool. Complimentary full bkfst; afternoon refreshments. Ck-out noon, ck-in 3 pm. Gift shop. Many fireplaces; some in-rm whirlpools, refrigerators. Private patios, balconies. Handmade quilts in many rms; antiques. View of vineyards. Cr cds: MC, V.

Restaurants

★★★★ **AUBERGE DU SOLEIL.** *180 Rutherford Hill Rd, Rutherford (94573). 707/963-1211. www.aubergedusoleil.com.* You'll almost feel like you are dining in an airy, open wine barrel as you sit underneath the red-hued timbered ceiling, which is appropriate considering Auberge du Soleil's incredible locale overlooking Rutherford Hill, not to mention the stellar wine list. The excellent food is decidedly Californian, with plenty of influences from France evidenced in the many Provencal-style dishes on the menu. All of the elements of fine dining come together here, which has kept the restaurant a mecca for diners for two decades. Specializes in foie gras, duck club, pan roasted chilean sea bass. Hrs: 7-11 am, 11:30 am-2:30 pm, 6-9:30 pm. Res required. Extensive wine list. Lunch $15-$23; dinner $26-$36. Entertainment. Cr cds: A, D, DS, MC, V.

D

★★ **BRAVA TERRACE.** *3010 St. Helena Hwy N (94574). 707/963-9300. www.bravasthelena.com.* Hrs: noon-9 pm. Closed Wed Nov-Apr; Thanksgiving, Dec 25; also 10 days Jan. Res accepted. Contemporary American menu. Bar. A la carte entrees: lunch, dinner $7.95-$22. Specialties: cassoulet, penne pasta, coq au vin. Parking. Outdoor dining. Large stone fireplace. Totally nonsmoking. Cr cds: A, D, DS, MC, V.

D

★★★ **GREYSTONE.** *2555 Main St (94574). 707/967-1010.* Hrs: 11:30 am-9 pm; Fri, Sat to 10 pm. Closed hols; Jan 1-15; also Tues, Wed Dec-Mar. Res accepted. Mediterranean menu. Bar. Wine cellar. A la carte entrees: lunch, dinner $15-$23. Children's menu. Specialties: Greystone paella, tapas. Outdoor dining. View of vineyard. Totally nonsmoking. Cr cds: A, D, DS, MC, V.

D

★★ **PINOT BLANC.** *641 Main St (94574). 707/963-6191.* Hrs: 11:30 am-10 pm. Country French menu. Bar. A la carte entrees: lunch $8.25-$19.95, dinner $14.50-$22.95. Children's menu. Daily menu and specials. Own baking. Outdoor dining. Fireplace. Totally nonsmoking. Cr cds: A, D, DS, MC, V.

D

★★★ **THE RESTAURANT AT MEADOWOOD.** *900 Meadowood Ln (94574). 707/963-3646. www.meadowood.com.* Hrs: 6-9:30 pm; Sun brunch 10 am-2 pm. Res accepted. French, American menu. Bar open 5:30-12am on weekends. Wine cellar. A la carte entrees: dinner $26-$32. Complete meals: dinner $45-$75. Sun brunch $34. Specializes in vegetarian items, seafood. Own baking. Valet parking on weekends. Outdoor dining. Jacket required. Cr cds: A, D, DS, MC, V.

D

★★★★ **TERRA.** *1345 Railroad Ave (94574). 707/963-8931. www.terrarestaurant.com.* Chef/owner Hiro Sone makes the most of his surroundings, turning out what he calls Napa Valley cuisine at his sophisticated restaurant dominated by a rustic stone wall. Napa Valley can mean a ragout of sweetbreads, or it can incorporate a range of Asian ingredients like shiso or sake. As expected, the wine list focuses on the Napa Valley, and service is professional. Southern French, northern Italian menu. Specialties: petit ragout of sweetbreads with prosciutto, broiled sake-marinated sea bass with shrimp dumplings. Own pastries. Hrs: 6-9 pm; Fri, Sat to 10 pm. Closed Tues; hols. Wine, beer. Res required. A la carte entrees: dinner $15-$25. Street parking. Totally nonsmoking. Cr cds: D, MC, V.

D

★ **TOMATINA.** *1016 Main St (94574). 707/967-9999.* Hrs: 11:30 am-10 pm. Closed Dec 25. Italian menu. Bar. A la carte entrees: lunch, dinner $6.95-$19.95. Children's menu. Specialty: pizza wraps. Parking. Outdoor dining. Modern artwork. Totally nonsmoking. Cr cds: D, DS, MC, V.

D

★★★ **TRA VIGNE.** *1050 Charter Oak Ave (94574). 707/963-4444.* Hrs: 11:30 am-10:30 pm; Fri, Sat to 11 pm. Closed July 4, Thanksgiving, Dec 25. Res accepted. Northern Italian menu. Bar. A la carte entrees: lunch, dinner $4.95-$17.50. Specializes in fresh pasta, grilled dishes. Own desserts. Parking. Outdoor dining. Patio. Totally nonsmoking. Cr cds: C, D, MC, V.

D

Salinas

(B-1) *See also Big Sur, Carmel, Monterey, Pacific Grove*

Pop 108,777 **Elev** 53 ft **Area code** 831

Information Salinas Valley Chamber of Commerce, 119 E Alisal St, PO Box 1170, 93901; 831/424-7611

Web www.salinaschamber.com

Birthplace of novelist John Steinbeck, many of whose works, incl *East of Eden* (1952), *Tortilla Flat* (1935), and *Of Mice and Men* (1937), are set in the Salinas Valley area.

What to See and Do

Hat in Three Stages of Landing. Sculpture by Claes Oldenburg. Concept of a straw hat tossed out of the rodeo grounds (adj) in three stages of landing on the field. Community Center, 940 N Main St.

National Steinbeck Center Museum. (Daily) One Main St. Phone 831/796-3833. ¢¢¢

Pinnacles National Monument. (see). Approx 25 mi S via US 101, then 11 mi E via CA 146.

Steinbeck House. Former home of famous Salinas native John Steinbeck. Gift shop. Lunch open 11:30-2 (two seatings daily). (Daily; closed three wks late Dec-early Jan) 132 Central Ave. Phone 831/424-2735. ¢¢¢¢

Special Events

California Rodeo. Parades, dancing, entertainment, competitions, barbecue. Third wk July. Rodeo Grounds, 1034 N Main St, ¼ mi N off US 101. Phone 800/771-8807.

Steinbeck Festival. Sponsored by National Steinbeck Center Foundation. Bus and walking tours of Steinbeck country; films, plays, readings, and lectures about the author. Early Aug. Phone 831/796-3833.

California International Airshow. Aerobatic displays, formation parachute jumping, precision close-formation flying by top US and international performers, incl the US Navy's Blue Angels. Sept. Airport Blvd exit off US 101, at airport. Phone 888/845-7469.

Motels/Motor Lodges

★★ **COMFORT INN.** *144 Kern St (93905). Fax 831/758-8850; res 800/221-2222.* 32 rms, 2 story. S $59-$149; D $69-$149; suite $89-$149; each addl $8; under 16 free; higher rates some wkends. Crib $8. TV; cable (premium). Complimentary continental bkfst, coffee in rms. Restaurant nearby. Ck-out 11 am. Business servs avail. Refrigerators, microwaves avail; bathrm phones. Cr cds: A, C, D, DS, ER, JCB, MC, V.

D

★★ **LAUREL INN MOTEL.** *801 W Laurel Dr (93906). 831/449-2474; fax 831/449-2476; toll-free 800/354-9831.* 145 rms, 2 story, 4 suites. S $52-$130; D $58-$130. Crib $4. TV; cable (premium). Heated pool; whirlpool, sauna. Coffee in lobby. Restaurant adj 5:30 am-midnight. Bar from 11 am. Ck-out noon. Meeting rms. Business servs avail. Some refrigerators, fireplaces. Cr cds: A, C, D, DS, MC, V.

D SC

★ **VAGABOND INN.** *131 Kern St (93905). 831/758-4693; fax 831/758-9835; toll-free 800/522-1555. www.vagabondinns.com.* 70 rms, 2 story. S $52-$65; D $62-$85; each addl $5; under 18 free. Crib free. Pet accepted, some restrictions; $5. TV; cable (premium). Heated pool. Complimentary continental bkfst. Restaurant adj. Ck-out noon. Cr cds: A, D, DS, MC, V.

D

Restaurants

★ **PUB'S PRIME RIB.** *227 Monterey St (93901). 831/424-2261.* Hrs: 11 am-10 pm; Sat noon-10 pm; Sun 3-9 pm. Closed hols. Res accepted. Bar. Complete meals: lunch $7-$10, dinner $12.95-$20.95. Children's menu. Specialties: prime rib, skirt steak, sweet-

breads. Own desserts. Cr cds: A, C, D, DS, ER, MC, V.
D

★ **SMALLEY'S ROUNDUP.** *700 W Market St (93901). 831/758-0511. www.smalleysroundup.com.* Hrs: 11:30 am-1:30 pm, 5-8:30 pm; Sat 5-9 pm; Sun 4-8:30 pm. Closed Mon; hols; also wk of July 4, wk of Dec 25. Res accepted. Wine, beer. Lunch, dinner $5.99-$20.99. Children's menu. Specializes in steak, chicken, ribs. Totally nonsmoking. Cr cds: DS, MC, V.

★★ **SPADO'S.** *66 W Alisal (93901). 831/424-4139. www.spados.com.* Hrs: 11 am-2:30 pm, 5-9 pm; Sat 5-9 pm; Sun 4-8 pm. Closed Jan 1, July 4, Dec 25. Res accepted (dinner). Italian menu. Wine, beer. A la carte entrees: lunch $5.50-$9.50, dinner $7.95-$12.95. Children's menu. Specializes in lamb, brick-oven pizzas. Outdoor dining. Contemporary decor. Totally nonsmoking. Cr cds: A, C, D, DS, ER, MC, V.
D

Salton Sea State Recreation Area

(F-7) *See also Indio*

(N shore of Salton Sea, CA 111 at State Park Rd)

The Salton Sea, located in the Colorado Desert, is a popular inland boating and fishing area. In 1905, the Colorado River flooded through a broken canal gate into the Salton Basin, creating a vast new lake. Anglers catch corvina, croakers, sargo, and tilapia year round. A launch ramp is available and can accommodate any trailer boat. The recreation area covers 17,913 acres and has areas for swimming and waterskiing. There are nature trails for birdwatching, interpretive programs (Nov-May), picnic grounds, and 148 developed campsites (dump station, hookups), plus two miles of primitive camping at Corvina Beach, Salt Creek, and Bombay Beach campgrounds. Standard fees. (Daily) Phone 760/393-3052 or 760/393-3059.

San Bernardino

(E-5) *See also Anaheim, Lake Arrowhead, Redlands, Riverside*

Founded 1810 **Pop** 164,164
Elev 1,049 ft **Area code** 909
Information San Bernardino Area Chamber of Commerce, 546 W 6th St, 92410; or PO Box 658, 92402; 909/885-7515

Set amid mountains, valleys, and deserts, San Bernardino is a mixture of Spanish and Mormon cultures. The city takes its name from the valley and mountains discovered by a group of missionaries in 1810 on the feast of San Bernardino of Siena. In 1851, a group of Mormons bought the Rancho San Bernardino and laid out the city, modeled after Salt Lake City. The group was recalled by Brigham Young six years later but the city continued to thrive. The area has a vast citrus industry. In April the fragrance and beauty of orange blossoms fill the nearby groves.

What to See and Do

Glen Helen Regional Park. Approx 500 acres. Swimming (fee), two flume water slides (fee), fishing (fee); nature trail, picnicking, playground. Group camping (fee). (Daily; closed Jan 1, Dec 25) 2555 Glen Helen Pkwy, 10 mi N, 1 mi W of I-215. Phone 909/387-7540. ¢¢

Skiing. Mountain High Ski Area. Two quad, three triple, six double chairlifts; patrol, school, rentals, snowmaking; concession areas, cafeterias. Longest run 1½ mi; vertical drop 1,600 ft. (Mid-Nov-mid-Apr, daily) Night skiing. Shuttle bus operates between east and west areas (free). 20 mi N on I-215 (US 395), then 9 mi NW on CA 138, then 8 mi SW, off CA 2 in Wrightwood. Phone 619/249-5477. ¢¢¢¢¢

Rim of the World Highway. (CA 18). Scenic 45-mi mountain road leading to Big Bear Lake, Snow Summit, Running Springs, Lake Arrowhead, Blue Jay, and Skyforest. Beaches on the lakes, fishing, hiking and riding trails, picnic grounds.

San Bernardino National Forest. One of the most heavily used national forests in the country; stretches east from San Bernardino to Palm Springs. Incl the popular San Gorgonio Wilderness at the forest's east edge by Redlands, the small Cucamonga Wilderness in the west end of the San Bernardino Mountains, and the San Jacinto Wilderness in the San Jacinto Mountains (permits required for wildernesses). Boating, fishing, hunting; hiking, horseback riding, skiing, off-road vehicle trails, picnicking, camping (fees charged; res for camping accepted, as well as first-come, first-served basis). 10 mi N via I-215, CA 18, 30, 38, 330. Phone 824/924-0890. ¢¢¢¢¢

Special Events

National Orange Show. Fairgrounds, Mill and E Sts. Marks completion of winter citrus crop harvest. Held annually since 1915. Exhibits, sports events, entertainment. Contact National Orange Show Fairground; 909/888-6788. Apr or May.

Renaissance Faire. Glen Helen Regional Park, 10 mi N on I-215, exit Devore Rd. Re-creates an Elizabethan experience with costumed performers, booths, food, and games. Late Apr-mid-June, wkends. Phone 909/880-0122.

Motels/Motor Lodges

★★ **LA QUINTA INN.** *205 E Hospitality Ln (92408). 909/888-7571; fax 909/884-3864; toll-free 800/687-6667. www.laquinta.com.* 153 rms, 3 story. S $65-$70; D $73-$78; suites $120-$150; each addl $8; under 18 free. Crib free. Pet accepted, some restrictions. TV; cable (premium). Heated pool. Complimentary continental bkfst, coffee in rms. Restaurant adj 11 am-midnight. Ck-out noon. Business servs avail. Valet serv. Health club privileges. Refrigerators, microwaves avail. Cr cds: A, C, D, DS, MC, V.
D SC

★ **LEISURE INN AND SUITES.** *777 W 6th St (92410). 909/889-3561; fax 909/884-7127.* 57 rms, 2 story. S $32.95-$40; D $40-$45; each addl $4; suites $48-$52. Crib $4. TV; cable (premium). Pool; whirlpool. Sauna. Complimentary continental bkfst. Restaurant nearby. Ck-out 11 am. Meeting rm. Guest lndry. Refrigerators; microwaves avail. Grills. Cr cds: A, D, DS, MC.

Hotels

★★★ **HILTON SAN BERNARDINO.** *285 E Hospitality Ln (92408). 909/889-0133; fax 909/381-4299; toll-free 800/446-1065. www.hilton.com.* 250 rms, 6-7 story. S, D $99-$175; each addl $10; suites $175-$325; under 18 free. Crib free. TV; cable (premium). Heated pool; whirlpool, poolside serv. Coffee in rms. Restaurant 6:30 am-3 pm, 5-10 pm; Sun 7 am-3 pm, 5-9 pm. Bar 11:30-1 am. Ck-out noon. Convention facilities. Business servs avail. Gift shop. Free airport transportation. Exercise equipt. Health club privileges. Bathrm phones, refrigerators; whirlpool in some suites. Cr cds: A, D, DS, MC, V.
D

★★★ **RADISSON HOTEL CONVENTION CENTER.** *295 N E St (92401). 909/381-6181; fax 909/381-5288; res 800/333-3333. www.radisson.com/sanbernardinoca.* 231 units, 12 story, 24 suites. S $120; D $140; each addl $10; suites $220-$350; under 17 free. Crib free. TV; cable (premium). Coffee in rms. Restaurant 6:30-9 am, 11:30 am-2 pm, 5-10 pm. Bar from 4 pm; Sat from 5 pm; closed Sun. Ck-out noon. Meeting rms. Business center. Gift shop. Florist. Garage parking. Free airport, railroad station, bus depot transportation. Exercise equipt; whirlpool. Some refrigerators. Convention center adj. Cr cds: A, C, D, DS, MC, V.
D

Restaurant

★★ **LOTUS GARDEN.** *111 E Hospitality Ln (92408). 909/381-6171.* Hrs: 11:30 am-9:30 pm; Fri, Sat to 10:30 pm. Res accepted. Chinese menu. Bar. A la carte entrees: lunch, dinner $7.25-$14.95. Complete meals: lunch

$5.95-$8.75, dinner $10.55-$14.75. Buffet: lunch $5.75. Children's menu. Specializes in Mandarin dishes. Parking. Chinese decor; exterior resembles a Chinese temple. Totally nonsmoking. Cr cds: A, C, D, DS, ER, MC, V.
D

San Clemente

(F-5) *See also Anaheim, Laguna Beach, San Juan Capistrano*

Pop 41,100 **Elev** 200 ft **Area code** 949 **Zip** 92672

Information Chamber of Commerce, 1100 N El Camino Real; 949/492-1131

Web www.scchamber.com

What to See and Do

San Clemente State Beach. Swimming, lifeguard, fishing; hiking trail, picnicking, trailer hookups, camping. Camping res necessary. (Daily) Califia Ave, off I-5. Phone 949/492-3156. ¢¢¢¢¢

Swimming. Municipal Pier & Beach. Swimming, surfing; picnicking, playground; fishing, bait and tackle shop at end of pier. (Daily; lifeguards) ½ mi W of I-5. Phone 949/361-8219. **FREE**

Special Event

San Clemente Fiesta. Street festival. Second Sun Aug. Phone 949/492-1131.

Motels/Motor Lodges

★★ HOLIDAY INN SAN CLEMENTE. *111 S Ave De La Estrella (92672). 949/361-3000; fax 949/361-2472; toll-free 800/469-1161. www.sanclemente.com/holidayinn.* 72 rms, 3 story, 19 suites. S, D $119-$169; suites $139-$199; under 18 free; wkly, monthly rates. Crib free. Pet accepted; $10. TV; cable (premium), VCR avail. Heated pool. Restaurant 7 am-2 pm, 6-9 pm. Bar. Ck-out noon. Meeting rms. Business servs avail. In-rm modem link. Bellhops. Free garage parking. Health club privileges. Massage. Refrigerators; some wet bars; microwaves avail. Balconies. Cr cds: A, C, D, DS, V.

★ SAN CLEMENTE BEACH TRAVELODGE. *2441 S El Camino Real (92672). 949/498-5954; fax 949/498-6657; res 800/578-7878. www.travelodge.com.* 23 rms, 3 suites. June-mid-Sept: S $49-$79; D $69-$89; each addl $4; suites $95-$145; lower rates rest of yr. Crib $4. TV; cable (premium), VCR avail (movies). Complimentary continental bkfst. Restaurant nearby. Ck-out 11 am. Free covered parking. Refrigerators, microwaves. Many private patios, balconies. Cr cds: A, D, DS, MC, V.

San Diego

(F-5)

Founded 1769 **Pop** 1,110,549 **Elev** 42 ft **Area code** 619

Information Convention and Visitors Bureau, 401 B Street, Suite 1400, 92101; 619/232-3101. Visitors Center; 619/236-1212

Web www.sandiego.org

Suburbs Carlsbad, Chula Vista, Coronado, Del Mar, El Cajon, Escondido, Oceanside, Rancho Santa Fe, San Ysidro.

The southernmost city in California gains a Mexican flavor from its proximity to Mexico's border town of Tijuana. Like many California cities, San Diego stretches from the Pacific Ocean eastward over lovely rolling hills of 1,591 feet. It is a warm city where the sun nearly always shines; this balmy year-round climate encourages outdoor living. Within San Diego County are mountains as high as 6,500 feet, 70 miles of beaches, a desert area, resorts, flowers, palm trees, and a lively cultural program. Several universities are located here.

For many years San Diego has been an important Navy center. Many Navy personnel, as well as others, retire here. It is a growing oceanography center and is also noted for avocado producing, electronics, ship, aircraft, and missile building, manufacturing, education, health and biomedical research, and tourism.

San Diego was "the place where California began" when the Portuguese conquistador Juan Rodriguez Cabrillo landed here in 1542. Since the first mission in California was built in San Diego in 1769, the city has grown steadily under the Spanish, Mexicans, and Americans.

Additional Visitor Information

For towns in the San Diego area see map. These towns and their accommodations are listed alphabetically.

The San Diego Convention & Visitors Bureau, International Visitor Information Center, 401 B St, Ste 1400, 92101, phone 619/236-1212, offers general information brochures in English, French, German, Japanese, Portuguese, and Spanish. *San Diego Magazine* may be obtained at newsstands and has up-to-date information on cultural events and articles of interest to visitors.

Transportation

Car Rental Agencies. See IMPORTANT TOLL-FREE NUMBERS.

Public Transportation. Buses, trolleys downtown, to East County, and to Tijuana (San Diego Transit), phone 619/233-3004.

Rail Passenger Service. Amtrak 800/872-7245.

Airport Information

San Diego International Airport/ Lindbergh Field. San Diego International Airport. Information 619/ 231-2100; lost and found 619/ 686-8002; weather 619/289-1212; cash machines, E Terminal.

What to See and Do

★ **Balboa Park.** Center of city on 1,200 acres. Art galleries, museums, theaters, restaurants, recreational facilities, and miles of garden walks, lawns, flowers, subtropical plants, and ponds. Off Park Blvd are

House of Pacific Relations. Thirty-one nations offer cultural and art exhibits in 15 California/Spanish-style cottages. (Sun) 2125 Park Blvd, in Balboa Park. Phone 619/234-0739. **FREE**

Mingei International Museum of World Folk Art. The museum moved into this 14,000-sq-ft facility in July 1996. Seven galleries contain exhibits of arts of people from all cultures of the world. Many art forms are shown in different collections and changing exhibitions such as costumes, jewelry, dolls and toys, utensils, painting, and sculpture. Also here is a theater, library, collections research center, and educational facilities. (Tues-Sun; closed hols) 1439 El Prado, in Central Plaza (Plaza de Panama) Phone 619/239-0003. **¢¢**

Museum of Photographic Arts. Changing exhibitions featuring 19th-century, early-mid-20th century, and contemporary works by world-renowned photographers. (Daily; closed hols) Free guided tours (Sun). 1649 El Prado, Casa de Balboa. Phone 619/238-7559. **¢¢¢** In same building is

Old Globe Theatre. One of three unique theaters of the Simon Edison Centre for the Performing Arts; productions staged incl classical and contemporary comedy and drama of diverse styles in the 581-seat Old Globe Theatre, the 225-seat Cassius Carter Centre Stage, and the 612-seat outdoor Lowell Davies Festival Theater. Performances (Tues-Sun eves, also Sat and Sun matinees). Web www.oldglobe.org. Phone 221/719-2112. **¢¢¢¢¢**

Reuben H. Fleet Science Center and Space Theater. Space Theater features Omnimax theater with large-format, educational science films, and multimedia shows. Science Center is a museum of natural phenomena; more than 50 permanent exhibits engage the visitor in active exploration. Admission incl participatory exhibits in Science Center. (Daily) On Park Blvd at Bay Theater Way. Phone 619/238-1233. **¢¢¢¢**

San Diego Aerospace Museum. Aerospace Historical Center. Full-scale original and reproduced aircraft; moon rock exhibit. (Daily; closed Jan 1, Thanksgiving, Dec 25) www.aerospacemuseum.org.

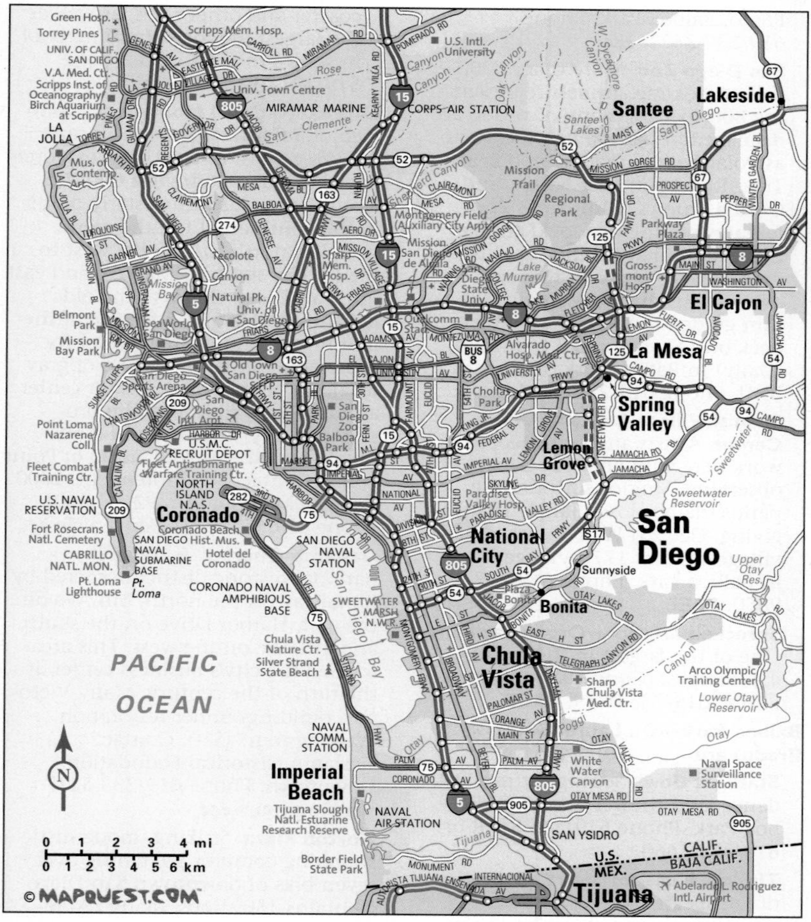

2001 Pan American Plaza, in Balboa Park. Phone 619/234-8291. ¢¢¢

San Diego Hall of Champions Sports Museum. Exhibits on more than 40 sports in the area; theater, gift shop, Breitbard Hall of Fame, and San Diego sports archives. (Daily; closed Jan 1, Thanksgiving, Dec 25) 2131 Pan American Plaza, Balboa Park. Phone 619/234-2544. ¢¢

San Diego Museum of Art. European and American paintings and decorative arts; Japanese, Chinese, and other Asian art, contemporary sculpture. (Tues-Sun; closed Jan 1, Thanksgiving, Dec 25) Free admission third Tues of month. Web www.sdmart.com. 1450 El Prado in Balboa Park at the Plaza de Panama. Phone 619/232-7931. ¢¢¢

San Diego Museum of Man. Exhibits on California and Hopi Native Americans, ancient Egypt, Mayan culture, early man, mummies; human reproduction; changing exhibits. (Daily; closed Jan 1, Thanksgiving, Dec 25) 1350 El Prado, Balboa Park. Phone 619/239-2001. ¢¢¢

San Diego Natural History Museum. Exhibits of flora and fauna and minerology of southwestern US and Baja California; seismograph, Foucault pendulum; traveling exhibits; classes, nature outings. (Daily; closed Jan 1, Thanksgiving, Dec 25) 1788 El

Prado, Balboa Park. Phone 619/232-3821. ¢¢¢

San Diego Zoo. More than 3,200 rare and exotic animals representing 800 species, many of which are displayed in natural habitats such as Polar Bear Plunge, Hippo Beach, Tiger River, Sun Bear Forest, and Gorilla Tropics. **Children's Zoo** features petting paddock, animal nursery, animal exhibits at children's eye level. Walk-through aviaries. Animal shows daily; 40-min guided tour aboard double-deck bus; Skyfari aerial tramway. (Daily) In Balboa Park off of Park Blvd. Phone 619/234-3153. ¢¢¢¢¢

Spanish Village Arts and Crafts Center. Artists and craftspeople work here with amateur critics observing. Studios surrounding patios (daily; closed Jan 1, Thanksgiving, Dec 25) Web www.spanishvillageart.com. 1770 Village Place in Balboa Park. Phone 619/233-9050. **FREE**

Spreckels Outdoor Organ Pavilion. One of the largest in the world; 4,445 pipes. (Concerts: Sun, hols) Phone 619/226-0819. **FREE**

Balboa Park—On Laurel St (El Prado) are

Starlight Bowl. Setting for musical, dance, and theater events. In Balboa Park. Phone 619/544-STAR or 619/239-1660.

Timken Museum of Art. Collection of European Old Masters, 18th- and 19th-century American paintings, and Russian icons. (Tues-Sat, also Sun afternoons; closed hols, also Sept) Web www.gort.ucsd.edu/sj/timken. 1500 El Prado. Phone 619/239-5548. **FREE**

Balboa Park recreational facilities incl

Golf. Municipal courses. 18- and 9-hole courses; pro shop, restaurant, driving range, three putting greens; rental carts. (Daily) Near 26th and A Sts.

Beach areas. Ocean Beach (off I-8 and Sunset Cliffs Blvd); Mission and Pacific beaches (adj to each other off I-5 at Garnet Ave exit); Coronado Beach (off Orange Ave on Coronado); and Silver Strand Beach (Palm Ave exit on I-5, then W to Hwy 75; follow signs). Mission Beach also incl

Belmont Park. Seaside amusement park incl a vintage wooden roller coaster and other rides, as well as the largest indoor swimming pool in southern California. Phone 619/491-2988.

Cabrillo National Monument. Commemorates arrival on what is now the West Coast of the US by explorer-navigator Juan Rodriguez Cabrillo. From the most southwesterly point in the continental US, the view stretches north to La Jolla, west to the Pacific, south to Mexico, and east into San Diego County. The old lighthouse (1855) is a feature of the monument and vantage point for observing annual migration of gray whales (Dec-mid-Mar). Visitor center and museum; slide and film programs. (Daily) 10 mi W of I-8 on Catalina Blvd (CA 209), at tip of Point Loma. Contact Superintendent, 1800 Cabrillo Memorial Dr, 92106-3601. Phone 619/557-5450. Per vehicle ¢¢

Gaslamp Quarter. A 16½-blk national historic district bordered by Broadway on the north, 6th Ave on the east, Harbor Drive on the south, and 4th Ave on the west. This area formed the city's business center at the turn of the century. Many Victorian buildings under restoration. Walking tours (Sat). Contact Gaslamp Historical Foundation. Downtown. Phone 619/233-5227. Walking tours ¢¢¢

Horton Plaza. Striking, modernistic shopping complex stretching over seven blks of downtown San Diego. Contains 150 shops, many restaurants and snack shops, street entertainers, excellent views from the top. (Daily) Bound by Broadway, G Street, and 1st and 4th Aves. Phone 619/238-1596.

Hotel del Coronado. (1888) A National Historic Landmark. One of America's most famous hotels; a vintage Victorian architectural masterpiece of turrets and gingerbread. Has hosted 13 US Presidents. Said to be "haunted" by the ghost of Kate Morgan, a broken-hearted woman who checked into the hotel in Nov 1892 and was found dead in her rm five days later of a gunshot wound to the head. A number of people claim to have seen Morgan's ghost in that rm. Guided tours. 1500 Orange Ave, Coronado. Phone 619/435-6611. ¢¢¢¢

Mission Basilica San Diego de Alcala. (1769) First California mission.

Restored, still used for services. Museum has relics of early days of mission; audio tours incl mission and grounds. (Daily; closed Thanksgiving, Dec 25) 10818 San Diego Mission Rd. Phone 619/281-8449. Museum ¢¢

Mission Bay Park. Aquatic park on 4,600 acres. Swimming, lifeguards (summer, daily), waterskiing in Fiesta and Sail bays, fishing, boating, sailing (rentals, ramps, landings, marinas), sportfishing fleet; golf, picnicking, camping. (Daily) Web www.infosandiego.com. N of San Diego River, reached via I-5. For details, res and regulations, send self-addressed, stamped envelope to Visitor Information Center, 2688 E Mission Bay Dr, 92109. Phone 619/276-8200. **FREE** In park is

Sea World. This 150-acre marine park on Mission Bay features several shows and more than 20 exhibits and attractions. Special Shamu show. (Daily) Web www.seaworld.com. Sea World Dr, exit W off I-5. Phone 619/226-3901. ¢¢¢¢¢

Museum of Contemporary Art, San Diego. Permanent and changing exhibits of contemporary painting, sculpture, design, photography, and architecture. Bookstore. (Tues-Sun; closed Jan 1, Thanksgiving, Dec 25) 1001 Kettner Blvd. Phone 619/234-1001. **FREE**

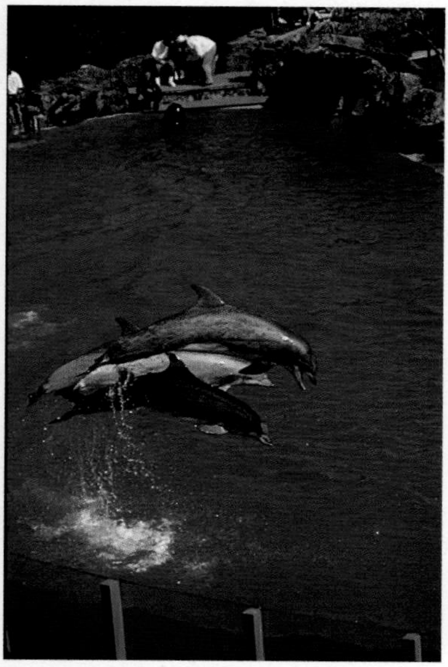

Sea World, San Diego

Naval ship tour. The public is invited to tour a ship as guests of the Commanding Officer. (Sat and Sun, when ships are in port) (May be temporarily closed when military deems security measures are necessary.) Broadway Pier, Broadway, and Harbor Dr. Contact the Naval Base Public Affairs Office. Phone 619/532-1430. **FREE**

Old Town. Historic section of city with many restored or reconstructed buildings; old adobe structures, restaurants, shops. Guided walking tours (daily). Around the plaza at Mason St and San Diego Ave. Old Town incl Old Town San Diego State Historic Park and

Presidio Park. Site of the first mission in California. Mounds mark the original Presidio and fort. Presidio Dr off Taylor St. Inside is

Serra Museum. Landmark of San Diego; the museum stands on top of the hill recognized as the site where California's first mission and presidio were established in 1769. The museum interprets the Spanish and Mexican periods of San Diego's history. (Fri-Sun; closed hols) 2727 Presidio Dr. Phone 619/297-3258. ¢¢

Whaley House. (1856) Once housed "The Tanner Troupe" theater company, and later served as the San Diego County Courthouse until the records were transferred to "New Town" on Mar 31, 1871. Restored and refurnished; on grounds are replica of Old Town drugstore; herb and rose gardens. (Daily; closed hols) 2482 San Diego Ave, at Harney St. ¢¢

Old Town San Diego State Historic Park. This is an area within Old Town that is bounded by Congress, Wallace, Twigg and Juan Sts. Visitor center, 4002 Wallace St (daily; closed Jan 1, Thanksgiving, Dec 25) Use Hwy 5 and Hwy 8. Park off Pacific Hwy between Taylor and Twig sts Phone 619/220-5422. **FREE** Incl

Casa de Estudillo. (1820-1829) Restored example of one-story adobe town house; period furnishings. (Daily; closed Jan 1, Thanksgiving, Dec 25) 4001 Mason St.

San Diego *Union* Historical Restoration. Restored birthplace of the San Diego newspaper that first came off the press in 1868. (Daily; closed Jan 1, Thanksgiving, Dec 25) 2626 San Diego Ave. **FREE**

Seeley Stable. Restoration of stables built in 1869 to serve US mail stage line; display of horse-drawn vehicles, historic Western artifacts. (Daily; closed Jan 1, Thanksgiving, Dec 25) Calhoun St. Phone 619/220-5422. **FREE**

Professional sports.

San Diego Chargers (NFL). Qualcomm Stadium. 9449 Friars Rd. Phone 619/874-4500.

San Diego Padres (MLB). Qualcomm Stadium. 9449 Friars Rd.

San Diego Bay and the Embarcadero. Port for active Navy ships, cruise ships, commercial shipping, and tuna fleet. Sailing, powerboating, waterskiing, and sportfishing at Shelter Island, Harbor Island, the Yacht Harbor, and America's Cup Harbor. Phone 619/234-9153.

The San Diego Children's Museum. A "please-touch" museum where kids can paint, create, and act in plays. (Tues-Sat) 200 W Island Ave. Phone 619/233-5437. ¢¢¢

San Diego Maritime Museum and *Star of India*. Restored bark *Star of India* (1863) built at Ramsey on the Isle of Man and launched as the *Euterpe;* sailed under the British, Hawaiian (before it was part of the US), and United States flags. It sailed for the first time in 50 yrs on July 4, 1976. Also here are the steam ferry *Berkeley* (1898), with nautical exhibits, and the luxury steam yacht *Medea* (1904). (Daily) 1306 N Harbor Dr (Embarcadero). Phone 619/234-9153. ¢¢¢

San Diego Wild Animal Park. Operated by the Zoological Society of San Diego as a preservation area for endangered species. More than 2,400 African and Asian animals roam freely on the 2,100-acre preserve; five-mi guided Wgasa Bush Line monorail tour; Africa-inspired Nairobi Village featuring animal shows, hiking trail, animal and botanical exhibits. (Daily) 30 mi NE via I-15 to Via Rancho Pkwy exit, follow signs, in Escondido (see). Phone 760/747-8702. ¢¢¢¢¢

Seaport Village. A 14-acre shopping, dining, and entertainment complex on San Diego Bay. Incl 75 specialty shops and restaurants; restored 1890 Looff Carousel; horse-drawn carriage rides; ¼-mi boardwalk along the waterfront. (Daily) Market St at Kettner Blvd, adj to Embarcadero Marina Park. Phone 619/235-4014.

Sightseeing.

Corporate Helicopters of San Diego. Sky tours offer views of city's attractions and natural beauty. For tours, fees, and schedules, phone 858/505-5650.

Gray Line bus tours. Contact 1775 Hancock, Suite 130, 92110. Phone 619/491-0011.

San Diego-Coronado Ferry. Hrly departures from Broadway Pier to Ferry Landing Marketplace in Coronado. (Daily) Phone 619/234-4111. ¢

San Diego Harbor Excursion. One-hr (12-mi) narrated tour highlights Harbor Island, Coronado, and the Navy Terminals at North Island and 32nd St. Two-hr (25-mi) narrated tour incl the above plus Shelter Island, Ballast Point (where Cabrillo is believed to have first landed in 1542), the harbor entrance, the ship yards, and the Navy's submarine base. (Daily) 1050 N Harbor Dr. Phone 619/234-4111 or 800/442-7847. One-hr tour ¢¢¢¢ Two-hr tour ¢¢¢¢¢

San Diego Scenic Tours. Narrated bus and harbor tours. Choose from four-hr San Diego City Tour, City and Harbor Tour, San Diego-La Jolla Tour, Tijuana Tour. Also Full-Day Tijuana Tour, and the ultimate full-day San Diego, Harbor and Tijuana Tour or Tijuana-San Diego-LaJolla Tour. (Daily) For res and to arrange hotel pickup, phone 858/273-8687. ¢¢¢¢¢

San Diego Trolley. The 15-mi South Line takes visitors to the United States/Mexico border; 17-mi East Line takes visitors to El Cajon. Lines merge at the Imperial and 12th Transfer Center. Departures every 15 min from Santa Fe Depot at Kettner Blvd and C St; tickets also avail at 5th and Broadway. (Daily) Phone 619/233-3004.

Scenic drive. Many of the attractions noted above may be seen on a 59-mi loop marked by blue and yellow seagull signs. The drive takes 2½-3 hrs, incl waterfront, Shelter Island, Cabrillo National Monument, Point Loma, Old Town, and the top of Mt Soledad, which has a magnificent view of entire area.

Villa Montezuma/Jesse Shepard House. (1887) Lavish Victorian mansion built for Jesse Shepard, musician and author, during the city's "Great Boom" (1886-1888). More than 20 stained glass windows reflect Shepard's interest in art, music, and literature; incl restored kitchen, antiques. Guided tours (Fri-Sun, last tour leaves at 3:45 pm). 20th and K sts. Phone 619/239-2211. ¢¢

Whale-watching trips. For three months each yr (mid-Dec-mid-Feb), California gray whales make their way from Alaska's Bering Sea to the warm bays and lagoons of Baja, passing only a mi or so off the San Diego shoreline. As many as 200 whales a day have been counted during the peak of the migration period. Trips to local waters and Baja lagoons are scheduled by the San Diego Natural History Museum, PO Box 1290, 92112. For information on other whale-watching trips, inquire at local sport fishing companies or at the International Visitors Information Center; 619/236-1212. Phone 619/232-3821. ¢¢¢¢¢

White Water Canyon. The area's biggest water park. Incl 16 slides, wave pool, tubing river, children's play area, ball field, volleyball pit, picnic facilities. (May-Sept, daily) 2052 Otay Valley Rd in Chula Vista. Phone 619/H2O-PARK. ¢¢¢¢¢

Special Events

Corpus Christi Fiesta. Mission San Antonio de Pala. 41 mi N via CA 163, I-15, then 7 mi E on CA 76. Open-air mass, procession; games, dances, entertainment; Spanish-style pit barbecue; held annually since 1816. First Sun June.

Festival of Bells. Mission Basilica San Diego de Alcala. Commemorates July 16, 1769 founding of mission. Wkend mid-July.

Cabrillo Festival. Cabrillo National Monument. Celebration of discovery of the west coast. Phone 619/557-5450. Last wkend Sept-early Oct.

Christmas on the Prado. Spreckels Outdoor Organ Pavilion and throughout Balboa Park. Fifty-ft-tall lighted tree, Nativity scenes; special programs. First wkend Dec.

Christmas-Light Boat Parade. San Diego Harbor, Shelter Island Yacht Basin. Mid-late Dec.

Mother Goose Parade. Family-oriented parade features characters and floats representing Mother Goose rhymes. Sun before Thanksgiving. Phone 619/444-8712.

Motels/Motor Lodges

★★ **BEST WESTERN BAYSIDE INN.** *555 W Ash St (92101). 619/233-7500; fax 619/239-8060; toll-free 800/314-1818. www.baysideinn.com.* 122 rms, 14 story. July-early Sept: S, D $89-$129; each addl $10; under 12 free; lower rates rest of yr. Crib $6. TV; cable (premium). Pool; whirlpool. Complimentary continental bkfst, coffee in rms. Restaurant adj 6 am-2 pm, 5-9 pm. Ck-out noon. Business servs avail. In-rm modem link. Free airport, RR station tranportation. Health club privileges. Cr cds: A, C, D, DS, ER, JCB, MC, V.

D

★★ **BEST WESTERN ISLAND PALMS.** *2051 Shelter Island Dr (92106). 619/222-0561; fax 619/222-9760; res 877/484-3725. www.islandpalms.com.* 97 rms, 80 with shower only, 2 story, 29 kit. units. S, D $129-$169; each addl $10; kits. $209-$269; under 18 free; wkly rates. Crib free. TV; cable (premium). Pool; whirlpool, poolside serv. Complimentary coffee in rms. Restaurant 6:30 am-10 pm. Bar 10:30 am-midnight; Fri, Sat to 2 am. Ck-out noon. Coin lndry. Meeting rms. Business servs avail. In-rm modem link. Valet serv. Exercise equipt. Refrigerators; microwaves avail. Many balconies. On bay. Near airport. Cr cds: A, C, D, DS, MC, V.

D SC

★★ **BEST WESTERN SEVEN SEAS LODGE.** *411 Hotel Cir S (92108). 619/291-1300; fax 619/291-6933; res 800/528-1234.* 307 rms, 2 story, 9 kit. units. S, D $79-$89; under 18 free.

OLD TOWN SAN DIEGO

This short walk leads through intriguing Old Town, an amalgam of Old Town State Historic Park and adjacent areas containing restored or replicated 19th-century historic structures, small museums, and lively restaurants and shops. The area—which has the flavor of a low-key historic theme park (but without the rides and tacky touristy elements)—pays homage to San Diego's first settlers from the Mexican and early American eras. It lies north of downtown San Diego at Juan Street, near the intersection of I-5 and I-8. You could spend an hour or a day here, depending on how long you wish to linger at the museums and shops; on certain days you may encounter living history presentations, with demonstrations of blacksmithing and tortilla-making. From the parking lot at Juan and Mason streets, walk down Mason a block or so to Old Town Plaza in the middle of the State Historic Park. The dirt streets that line the plaza help transport you back to the days before San Diego became known for surfers and the US Navy. At the Robinson-Rose House on the north side of the plaza, you can pick up brochures and view depictions of Old Town in the early 1800s. Turn right and head along the southwestern edges of the plaza to view some old adobes dating from the 1820s and 1830s. Back on Mason Street, don't miss the Mason Street School, a one-room schoolhouse dating from 1865 where you can sit at the wooden desks and assess the punishments listed on the board for acting up. Nearby is the McKinstry Dentist Office, where the primitive dental tools will make you glad for the invention of floss. At the Wells Fargo History Museum you can view an 1868 stagecoach, a telegraph machine, and gold samples. A bit farther up Mason Street is the Casa de Estudillo, Old Town's largest original adobe, which is furnished in the mid-19th-century style of a wealthy rancher. At Calhoun Street, go right to see the Casa de Bandini, which dates from 1829 and now houses a good Mexican restaurant. Just down the street is the Seeley Stables, with a nice stagecoach exhibit. Turning right on Twiggs Street, you'll come upon the old office of the *San Diego Union* newspaper. Take a left turn on San Diego Avenue to the Whaley House Museum, which has a nice collection of early California artifacts. Complete your walk around Old Town by going back on San Diego Avenue to Old Town Plaza and walking northwest to Calhoun Street. There you'll come upon the Bazaar del Mundo, a colorful collection of Mexican-flavored shops and open-air restaurants, including the festive Casa de Pico.

Crib free. TV; cable (premium). Heated pool; whirlpool, poolside serv. Playground. Complimentary coffee in rms. Restaurant 6 am-10 pm. Bar noon-2 am. Ck-out noon. Coin lndry. Meeting rms. In-rm modem link. Bellhops. Valet serv. Free airport, RR station, bus depot transportation. Some refrigerators; microwaves avail. Some balconies. Cr cds: A, C, D, DS, ER, JCB, MC, V.

D

★★ **COMFORT INN AND SUITES.** *2485 Hotel Cir Pl (92108). 619/881-6200; fax 619/297-6179; res 800/228-5150. www.comfortinn.com.* 200 rms, 4 story. July-early Sept: S, D $89-$109; suites $99-$139; under 18 free; lower rates rest of yr. Crib free. TV; cable (premium). Heated pool; whirlpool. Complimentary continental bkfst, coffee in rms. Restaurant nearby. Ck-out noon. Coin lndry. Business servs avail. In-rm modem link. Free covered parking. Exercise equipt. Some refrigerators, in-rm whirlpools; microwaves avail. Cr cds: A, D, DS, MC, V.

D

★ **DAYS INN.** *543 Hotel Cir S (92108). 619/297-8800; fax 619/298-6029; toll-free 800/345-9995. www.daysinnhc.com.* 280 rms, 3 story, 49 kit. units. S, D $85-$89; kit. units $85-$109; under 18 free; wkly rates; higher rates wkends, special events. Crib free. TV; cable (premium). Heated pool; whirlpool. Coffee in rms. Restaurant 6:30 am-9 pm. Ck-out noon. Coin lndry. Business servs avail. Bellhops. Valet serv. Sundries. Barber, beauty shop. Health club privileges. Free airport, RR station, bus depot transportation. Refrigerators; microwaves avail. Cr cds: A, C, D, DS, JCB, MC, V.

D SC

★ **GOOD NITE INN.** *4545 Waring Rd (92120). 619/286-7000; fax*

619/286-8403; toll-free 800/648-3466. www.good-nite.com. 94 rms, 2 story. S, D $39-$55; each addl $6; under 18 free. Crib free. Pet accepted. TV; cable (premium). Heated pool. Restaurant adj 10 am-9 pm; Sat-Sun from 7 am. Ck-out 11 am. Coin lndry. Meeting rm. Refrigerators, microwaves avail. Private patios, balconies. Cr cds: A, D, DS, JCB, MC, V.

D SC

★★ **GOOD NITE INN.** *225 Bay Blvd (91910). 619/425-8200; fax 619/426-7411; toll-free 800/648-3466. www.goodnite.com.* 118 rms, 2 story. Mid-May-mid-Sept: S $43-$49; D $49-$55; each addl $6; under 18 free; lower rates rest of yr. Crib free. Pet accepted, some restrictions. TV; cable (premium). Heated pool. Complimentary coffee in lobby. Restaurant 6 am-10 pm. Ck-out 11 am. Some refrigerators, microwaves. Cr cds: A, C, D, DS, JCB, MC, V.

D SC

★★ **HAMPTON INN KEARNY MESA.** *5434 Kearny Mesa Rd (92111). 858/292-1482; fax 858/292-4410; res 800/426-7866. www.hampton-inn.com.* 150 rms, 5 story. June-Aug: S, D $84-$99; under 18 free; lower rates rest of yr. Crib free. TV; cable (premium). Heated pool. Complimentary continental bkfst, coffee in rms. Restaurant adj 7 am-11 pm. Ck-out 11 am. Coin lndry. Meeting rms. Business servs avail. In-rm modem link. Valet serv. Health club privileges. Some refrigerators; microwaves avail. Cr cds: A, D, DS, MC, V.

D

★★ **HOLIDAY INN.** *3737 Sports Arena Blvd (92110). 619/226-3711; fax 619/224-9248; toll-free 800/511-6909. www.holiday-inn.com.* 316 rms, 3 story, 192 suites. May-Sept: S, D $89-$139; each addl $10; suites $149-$189; under 19 free; hols 2-day min; higher rates bowl game; lower rates rest of yr. Crib free. TV; cable (premium). Complimentary coffee in rms. Restaurant adj 6 am-10 pm. Ck-out noon. Meeting rms. Business servs avail. In-rm modem link. Concierge. Gift shop. Coin lndry. Health club privileges. Heated pool; whirlpool, poolside serv. Many bathrm phones; microwaves avail; refrigerator, microwave in suites. Cr cds: A, C, D, DS, JCB, MC, V.

D

★★ **HOLIDAY INN BAYSIDE.** *4875 N Harbor Dr (92106). 619/224-3621; fax 619/224-3629; res 800/345-9995. www.holinnbayside.com.* 237 rms, 2-5 story. S, D $129-$149; each addl $10; suites $179-$219; under 18 free. Crib free. TV; cable (premium). Heated pool. Complimentary coffee in rms. Restaurant adj 6 am-10 pm. Bar 2 pm-2 am. Ck-out noon. Coin lndry. Meeting rms. Business center. In-rm modem link. Bellhops. Valet serv. Sundries. Free airport, RR station, bus depot transportation. Exercise equipt. Putting green. Lawn games. Refrigerators. Some private patios, balconies. Opp marina. Cr cds: A, C, D, DS, JCB, MC, V.

D SC

★★ **HOLIDAY INN HARBORVIEW.** *1617 First Ave (92101). 619/239-9600; fax 619/233-6228; res 800/465-4329. www.holiday-inn.com.* 218 rms, 16 story. Late Mar-Sept: S $169; D $184; under 18 free; hols 2-day min; lower rates rest of yr. Crib free. Garage parking $3. TV; cable (premium). Complimentary coffee in rms. Restaurant 6 am-10 pm. Bar. Ck-out noon. Meeting rms. Business servs avail. In-rm modem link. Concierge. Coin lndry. Free airport transportation. Exercise equipt. Pool; poolside serv. Refrigerators, microwaves avail. Luxury level. Cr cds: A, C, D, DS, ER, MC, V.

SC

★★ **HOLIDAY INN MISSION VALLEY STADIUM NORTH.** *3805 Murphy Canyon Rd (92123). 858/278-9300; res 800/465-4329. www.holiday-inn.com.* 174 rms, 4 story, 19 suites. S, D $89-$129; each addl $10; suites $119-$149; under 18 free. Crib free. TV; cable (premium). Pool; whirlpool. Coffee in rms. Restaurant 6:30 am-2 pm, 5-10 pm. Bar. Ck-out noon. Coin lndry. Meeting rms. Business servs avail. In-rm modem link. Free garage parking. Exercise equipt. Refrigerators; microwaves avail. Wet bar in suites. Most suites with balcony. Cr cds: A, C, D, DS, MC, V.

D

★★ HOLIDAY INN ON THE BAY. *1355 N Harbor Dr (92101). 619/232-3861; fax 619/235-0117; res 800/877-8920. www.holiday-inn.com.* 600 rms, 14 story. S, D $169.95-$189.95; each addl $10; suites $250-$800; under 18 free. Crib free. Pet accepted, some restrictions. Parking $12/day. TV; cable (premium). Heated pool. Coffee in rms. Restaurant 6:30 am-11 pm. Bar 11-2 am. Ck-out noon. Convention facilities. Business center. In-rm modem link. Shopping arcade. Free airport transportation. Exercise equipt. Health club privileges. Some bathrm phones; refrigerators avail. Balconies. Many bay view rms. Outside glass-enclosed elvtr. Cruise ship terminal opp. Cr cds: A, C, D, DS, JCB, MC, V.

D SC

★★ HOLIDAY INN RANCHO. *17065 W Bernardo Dr (92127). 619/485-6530; fax 619/485-7819; res 800/465-4329. www.holiday-inn.com.* 179 rms, 2-3 story, 16 kits. S, D $99-$119; each addl $10; suites $119-$179; under 19 free. Crib free. TV; cable (premium). Heated pool; whirlpool. Complimentary full bkfst, coffee in rms. Restaurant opp 11 am-midnight. Ck-out noon. Coin lndry. Meeting rms. Business servs avail. In-rm modem link. Some covered parking. Exercise equipt; sauna. Health club privileges. Some refrigerators, in-rm whirlpools; microwaves avail. Many private patios, balconies. Cr cds: A, D, DS, MC, V.

★ LA QUINTA INN. *10185 Paseo Montril (92129). 858/484-8800; fax 858/538-0476.* 120 rms, 4 story. S, D $58-$69; each addl $8; under 18 free. Crib free. Pet accepted. TV; cable (premium). Heated pool. Complimentary continental bkfst, coffee in rms. Restaurant adj 6 am-midnight. Ck-out noon. In-rm modem link. Cr cds: A, D, DS, MC, V.

D

★ OLD TOWN INN. *4444 Pacific Hwy (92110). 619/260-8024; fax 619/296-0524; toll-free 800/643-3025. www.oldtown-inn.com.* 84 rms, 41 with shower only, 1-3 story. June-Sept: S $60-$90; D $70-$100; each addl $5; suites $111; kit units $62-$77; under 12 free; wkly rates; higher rates hols (3-day min); lower rates rest of yr. Crib $5. Pet accepted; $5. TV; cable (premium). Complimentary continental bkfst. Restaurant nearby. Ck-out 11 am. Coin lndry. Refrigerators avail. Cr cds: A, C, D, DS, ER, JCB, MC, V.

D SC

★★ RAMADA INN. *5550 Kearny Mesa Rd (92111). 858/278-0800; fax 858/277-6585; res 800/272-6232. www.ramadasandiego.com.* 150 rms, 2 story. June-Sept: S $79; D $129; each addl $10; suites $99-$159; under 17 free; lower rates rest of yr. Crib free. Pet accepted; $75. TV; cable. Complimentary continental bkfst, coffee in rms. Restaurant 6-2 am. Bar; entertainment Sat. Ck-out noon. Meeting rms. Business servs avail. Valet serv. Coin lndry. Pool; whirlpool. Refrigerators; some microwaves. Cr cds: A, C, D, DS, MC, V.

D

★★ RAMADA INN AND SUITES. *830 6th Ave (92101). 619/531-8877; fax 619/231-8307; toll-free 800/664-4400. www.ramada.com.* 99 rms, 35 with shower only, 10 story. June-mid-Sept: S $89-$119; under 18 free; hols 2-day min; lower rates rest of yr. Crib free. Valet parking $8. TV; cable (premium). Complimentary continental bkfst, coffee in rms. Restaurant 7 am-10 pm. Bar from 10 am. Ck-out noon. Meeting rms. Business servs avail. In-rm modem link. Concierge. Exercise equipt. Refrigerator, microwave, minibar in suites. Totally nonsmoking. Cr cds: A, C, D, ER, MC, V.

★★ RAMADA LIMITED. *641 Camino Del Rio S (92108). 619/295-6886; fax 619/296-9661; toll-free 800/624-1257. www.ramadamission valley.com.* 170 rms, 3 story, 58 kit. suites. May-Sept: S $69-$109; D $79-$119; each addl $10; kit. suites $99-$129; under 18 free; higher rates special events; lower rates rest of yr. Crib free. TV; cable (premium), VCR avail (movies). Complimentary continental bkfst, coffee in rms. Restaurant nearby. Ck-out 11 am. Meeting rms. Business servs avail. In-rm modem link. Sundries. Coin lndry. Free airport, RR station, bus depot transportation. Health club privileges. Many refrigerators; microwave,

minibar in kit. suites. Cr cds: A, D, DS, JCB, MC, V.
D SC

★★ **RAMADA LTD OLD TOWN.** *3900 Old Town Ave (92110). 619/299-7400 or 619/299-7400; fax 619/299-1619; res 800/272-6232. www.ramada.com.* 125 rms, 3 story. Mid-May-mid-Sept: S, D $99-$109; each addl $10; suites $129-$169; under 18 free; lower rates rest of yr. Crib free. TV; cable (premium). Heated pool; whirlpool. Complimentary continental bkfst, coffee in rms. Restaurant opp 11 am-10 pm. Ck-out noon. Coin lndry. Meeting rms. Business servs avail. In-rm modem link. Covered parking. Free airport, RR station transportation. Health club privileges. Refrigerators, microwaves; some wet bars. Some balconies. Cr cds: A, D, DS, JCB, MC, V.

★★ **RAMADA PLAZA HOTEL.** *2151 S Hotel Cir (92108). 619/291-6500; fax 619/294-7531; toll-free 800/532-7201.* www.*ramadaplaza-hc.com.* 182 rms, 4 story. S, D $89-$109; each addl $5; under 18 free. Crib free. TV; cable (premium). Heated pool; whirlpool. Complimentary coffee in rms. Restaurant 6:30 am-2:30 pm, 5-10 pm. Bar 5-11 pm. Ck-out noon. Coin lndry. Meeting rms. Business servs avail. In-rm modem link. Bellhops. Valet serv. Some covered parking. Exercise equipt. Health club privileges. Game rm. Refrigerators avail. Cr cds: A, C, D, DS, JCB, MC, V.
D SC

★ **RODEWAY INN.** *833 Ash St (92101). 619/239-2285; fax 619/235-6951; res 800/228-2000. www.showhotel.com/rodeway/9210101.* 45 rms, 4 story. S, D $89; each addl $5-$15; under 18 free. Crib free. TV; cable (premium). Complimentary continental bkfst. Restaurant opp 6 am-3 pm. Ck-out noon. Coin lndry. Business servs avail. In-rm modem link. Valet serv. Sauna. Whirlpool. Health club privileges. Some refrigerators; microwaves avail. Some balconies. Cr cds: A, C, D, DS, ER, JCB, MC, V.
D SC

★ **TRAVELODGE.** *16929 W Bernardo Dr (92127). 858/487-0445; fax 858/673-2062; toll-free 800/578-7878.* 49 rms, 2 story. Mid-May-mid-Sept: S, D $59-$75; each addl $7; under 16 free; lower rates rest of yr. Crib free. TV; cable (premium). Complimentary continental bkfst, coffee in rms. Restaurant nearby. Ck-out 11 am. Pool. Refrigerators, microwaves avail. Cr cds: A, C, D, DS, JCB, MC, V.
D SC

★ **TRAVELODGE.** *1201 Hotel Cir S (92108). 619/297-2271; fax 619/542-1510; res 800/578-7878.* 101 rms, 2 story. June-Sept: S, D $65-$79; each addl $10; under 18 free; higher rates special events; lower rates rest of yr. Crib free. TV; cable (premium), VCR avail (movies). Complimentary coffee in rms. Restaurant 6:30 am-11 pm, Sun 7 am-1 pm. Ck-out noon. Business servs avail. In-rm modem link. Health club privileges. Pool. Cr cds: A, D, DS, MC, V.
D SC

★ **VAGABOND INN.** *625 Hotel Cir S (92108). 619/297-1691; fax 619/692-9009; res 800/522-1555. www.vagabondinns.com.* 88 rms, 2 story. Mid-May-mid-Sept: S, D $65-$100; each addl $5; under 18 free; lower rates rest of yr. Crib free. Pet accepted; $10. TV; cable (premium). 2 heated pools; whirlpool. Complimentary continental bkfst. Restaurant adj open 24 hrs. Ck-out noon. Business servs avail. In-rm modem link. Cr cds: A, D, DS, MC, V.

Hotels

★★ **BAY CLUB HOTEL AND MARINA.** *2131 Shelter Island Dr (92106). 619/224-8888; fax 619/225-1604; toll-free 800/672-0800. www.bayclubhotel.com.* 105 rms, 2 story. S $149; D $159; each addl $10; suites $199-$299; under 12 free; package plans. Crib $10. TV; cable (premium), VCR avail. Heated pool; whirlpool, poolside serv. Complimentary full bkfst,coffee in rms. Restaurant 6:30 am-10 pm. Bar 10 am-midnight. Ck-out noon. Meeting rms. Business servs avail. Bellhops. Valet serv. Concierge. Sundries. Covered parking. Free airport, RR station, bus depot transportation. Exercise equipt. Refrigerators; microwaves avail. Private patios, balconies. On bay; marina. Fishing from nearby pier. Cr cds: A, C, D, DS, ER, JCB, MC, V.

D

★★ CLARION BAYVIEW HOTEL. *660 K Street (92101). 619/696-0234; fax 619/231-8199; res 800/252-7466. www.clarionbayview.com.* 312 rms, 21 story, 48 suites. Late May-early Sept: S $109-$169; D $119-$179; each addl $15; suites $159-$189; under 18 free; lower rates rest of yr. Crib free. Covered parking $9/day. TV; cable, VCR avail. Coffee in rms. Restaurant 6:30 am-10 pm. Bar 11-2 am; entertainment Fri, Sat. Ck-out noon. Coin lndry. Meeting rms. Business center. In-rm modem link. Gift shop. Exercise equipt; whirlpool. Sauna. Massage. Game rm. Some bathrm phones. Balconies. View of San Diego Bay. Cr cds: A, D, DS, ER, V.

D

★★★ DOUBLETREE HOTEL SAN DIEGO MISSION VALLEY. *7450 Hazard Center Dr (92108). 619/297-5466; fax 619/297-5499; res 800/222-8733. www.doubletreesandiego.com.* 300 rms, 11 story. S, D $149; each addl $10; under 18 free. Crib free. Pet accepted. TV; cable. 2 pools, 1 indoor; whirlpool, poolside serv. Complimentary coffee in rms. Restaurant 6:30 am-10:30 pm. Bar 5 pm-2 am; entertainment. Ck-out noon. Convention facilities. Business servs avail. In-rm modem link. Gift shop. Garage parking; valet. Free airport, RR station, bus depot transportation. Lighted tennis. Exercise equipt; sauna. Minibars. Microwaves avail. Some bathrm phones, wet bars in suites. Some balconies. Luxury level. Cr cds: A, C, D, DS, ER, JCB, MC, V.

D

★★ FOUR POINTS BY SHERATON RANCHO BERNARDO. *11611 Bernardo Plz Ct (92128). 858/485-9250; fax 858/451-7948; toll-free 800/528-0444. www.fourpoints.com.* 209 rms, 4 story. S, D $200-$280; each addl $10; suites $400; under 10 free; wkend rates. Crib free. TV; cable. Heated pool; whirlpool. Restaurant 6-9 am, 5-10 pm; Sat, Sun from 7 am. Bar from 5 pm. Ck-out 1 pm. Meeting rms. Business servs avail. In-rm modem link. Exercise equipt. Microwaves avail. Cr cds: A, C, D, DS, ER, JCB, MC, V.

D SC

★★★ HILTON SAN DIEGO AIRPORT. *1960 Harbor Island Dr (92101). 619/291-6700; fax 619/293-0694; toll-free 800/578-7878. www.hilton.com.* 207 rms, 9 story. S $189; D $204; each addl $10; suites $225-$375; under 18 free. Crib free. TV; cable (premium). Heated pool; whirlpool. Complimentary coffee in rms. Restaurant 6:30 am-2 pm, 5:30-10 pm. Bar 11-1 am. Ck-out noon. Meeting rms. Business servs avail. In-rm modem link. Concierge. Gift shop. Free airport transportation. Exercise equipt; sauna. Some in-rm whirlpools, refrigerators. Balconies. Cr cds: A, D, DS, ER, JCB, MC, V.

D

★★★ HILTON SAN DIEGO RESORT. *1775 E Mission Bay Dr (92109). 619/276-4010; fax 619/275-8944; toll-free 800/345-6565. www.hiltonhotels.com.* 357 rms, 8 story. S $169-$269; D $179-$279; each addl $20; suites $450-$710; family, wkend rates. Crib free. Pet accepted; $50. TV; cable (premium), VCR avail. Heated pool; wading pool, whirlpool, poolside serv. Playground. Supervised children's activities; ages 6-12. Complimentary coffee in rms. Restaurant 6:30 am-10 pm. Bar 10:30-1 am; entertainment. Ck-out noon. Coin lndry. Convention facilities. Business center. In-rm modem link. Gift shop. Beauty shop. Valet parking. Lighted tennis, pro. Putting greens. Exercise rm; sauna. Massage. Rec rm. Lawn games. Many bathrm phones, refrigerators, minibars; microwaves avail. Private patios, balconies. Dock; boats. On beach. Cr cds: A, C, D, DS, ER, JCB, MC, V.

D

★ HORTON GRAND HOTEL. *311 Island Ave (92101). 619/544-1886; fax 619/544-0058; toll-free 800/542-1886. www.hortongrand.com.* 132 rms, 4 story. S, D $119-$200; each addl $20; suites $189-$259; under 12 free. Crib $20. Some covered parking, valet $10. TV; cable. Restaurant 7 am-10 pm. Tea 2:30-5:30 pm. Bar 4 pm-midnight. Ck-out noon. Meeting rms. Business servs avail. Free airport transportation. Health club privileges. Fireplaces; refrigerator, microwave in suites. Some balconies. Victorian building; built 1886. Antiques, oak staircase. Chinese Museum and Tea Room. Skylight in lobby; bird cages. Oldest building in San Diego. Cr cds: A, C, D, MC, V.

★★★ **HYATT REGENCY.** *1 Market Pl (92101). 619/232-1234; fax 619/239-5678; res 800/233-1234. www.hyatt.com.* 875 units, 40 story, 56 suites. S, D $265-$290; suites from $500; under 18 free. Crib free. Garage parking $12-$18. TV; cable (premium), VCR avail. Pool; whirlpool, poolside serv. Coffee in rms. Restaurants 6 am-10 pm (see also SALLY'S). Rm serv 24 hrs. Bar noon-1:30 am. Ck-out noon. Convention facilities. Business center. In-rm modem link. Concierge. Shopping arcade. 4 tennis courts. Exercise rm; sauna, steam rm. Massage. Some refrigerators, minibars. Located on San Diego Bay; panoramic view of harbor and marina. Luxury level. Cr cds: A, C, D, DS, MC, V.

★★★ **HYATT REGENCY ISLANDIA.** *1441 Quivira Road (92109). 619/224-1234; fax 619/224-0348; res 800/233-1234. www.islandia.hyatt.com.* 422 rms, 17 story. S, D $159-$304; suites $359-$3,300; under 18 free. Crib free. TV; cable (premium). Heated pool; whirlpool, poolside serv. Supervised children's activities (June-Sept). Restaurant 6 am-10 pm; Fri-Sun to 11 pm. Bar 11:30-2 am; entertainment Thurs-Sat. Ck-out noon. Convention facilities. Business center. In-rm modem link. Concierge. Exercise equipt. Some refrigerators. Many private patios, balconies. Bicycle rentals. Marina; sport fishing; sailboat charters. Whale watching (Dec-Mar). Cr cds: A, C, D, DS, ER, JCB, MC, V.

★ **J STREET INN.** *222 J St (92101). 619/696-6922; fax 619/696-1295.* 221 rms, 4 story. Rm phones avail. S, D $39.95-$60; under 10 free; package plans. Parking $5. TV; cable. Complimentary coffee in rms. Restaurant nearby. Ck-out 1 pm. Exercise equipt. Refrigerators, microwaves. Balconies. Near bay, airport. Cr cds: A, D, DS, MC, V.

★★★ **MISSION VALLEY HILTON.** *901 Camino Del Rio S (92108). 619/543-9000; fax 619/543-9358; res 800/733-2332. www.hilton.com.* 350 rms, 14 story. S $189-$219; D $199-$229; each addl $10; suites $250-$450; under 18 free. Crib free. Pet accepted, some restrictions; $25. TV; cable (premium). Heated pool; whirlpool, poolside serv. Coffee in rms. Restaurant 6:30 am-10:30 pm. Bar 11-1 am. Ck-out noon. Convention facilities. Business center. In-rm modem link. Some covered parking. Exercise equipt; sauna. Health club privileges. Refrigerators. Large entrance foyer. Cr cds: A, C, D, DS, MC, V.

★★★ **RADISSON HOTEL SAN DIEGO.** *1433 Camino Del Rio S (92108). 619/260-0111; fax 619/497-0813; res 800/333-3333. www.radisson.com/sandiegoca.* 260 rms, 13 story. S, D $99-$129; each addl $15; under 18 free; wkend rates. Crib free. TV; cable, VCR avail. Heated pool; whirlpool. Restaurant 6:30 am-10 pm. Bar 4 pm-1:30 am. Ck-out noon. Convention facilities. Business servs avail. In-rm modem link. Free airport transportation. Exercise equipt. Health club privileges. Some balconies. Luxury level. Cr cds: A, C, D, DS, ER, JCB, MC, V.

★★ **REGENCY PLAZA HOTEL.** *1515 Motel Circle S (92108). 619/291-8790; fax 619/260-0147; toll-free 800/619-1549.* 217 rms, 8 story, 32 suites. June-Sept: S $99; D $159; each addl $10; suites $119-$179; under 18 free; higher rates special events; lower rates rest of yr. Crib free. TV; cable (premium), VCR avail (movies). Complimentary coffee in rms. Restaurant 7 am-2 pm, 5-10 pm; Fri, Sat to 11 pm. Bar. Ck-out noon. Meeting rms. Business servs avail. In-rm modem link. Concierge. Gift shop. Coin lndry. Lighted tennis privileges, pro. 48-hole golf privileges. Exercise equipt. Health club privileges. Pool; whirlpool, poolside serv. Game rm. Bathrm phones, refrigerators; microwave, wet bar in suites. Balconies. Cr cds: A, C, D, DS, JCB, MC, V.

★★★ **SAN DIEGO MARRIOT HOTEL & MARINA.** *333 W Harbor Dr (92101). 619/234-1500; fax 619/234-8678; res 800/228-9290. www.sdmarriott.com.* 1,355 rms, 26 story. S, D $290-$310; each addl $20; suites from $425; under 18 free. Crib free. Pet accepted, some restrictions. TV; cable (premium). Pool; whirlpool, poolside serv. Coffee in rms. Restaurant 6:30 am-11 pm. Rm serv 24 hrs. Bar 11-2 am; entertainment. Ck-out noon. Coin lndry. Meeting rms. Business center. In-rm modem link. Concierge. Shopping arcade. Barber, beauty shops. Six lighted tennis courts, pro. Exercise rm; sauna. Game rm. Bathrm phones; some refrigerators. Some balconies. Luxurious; large chandeliers in lobby. Bayside; marina. Luxury level. Cr cds: A, C, D, DS, ER, JCB, MC, V.

★★★ **SAN DIEGO MARRIOTT MISSION VALLEY.** *8757 Rio San Diego Dr (92108). 619/692-3800. www.marriott.com.* 350 rms, 17 story. S, D $195-$295; each addl $25; under 17 free. Crib avail. Heated pool. TV; cable (premium), VCR avail. Complimentary coffee, newspaper in rms. Restaurant 6 am-10:30 pm. Bar. Ck-out noon. Meeting rms. Business center. Valet serv. Gift shop. Exercise rm. Some refrigerators, minibars. Cr cds: A, C, D, DS, MC, V.

★★★★ **SHERATON SAN DIEGO HOTEL & MARINA.** *1380 Harbor Island Dr (92101). 619/291-2900; fax 619/692-2337; res 877/734-2726. www.sheraton.com.* This bayfront resort is convenient to the airport and local attractions and has 1,045 rooms and 50 suites with spectacular views of the bay, marina, and cityscape. With 80,000 square feet of meeting space, several outdoor event spaces, and a separate 18,700 square foot exhibit space, it's perfect for meetings and conventions. The five restaurants and lounges all have waterfront views. 1,044 rms in 2 buildings, 12 story. S, D $265-$285; each addl $20; suites $375-$1,100; under 18 free. Crib free. TV; cable (premium), VCR avail. 3 pools; whirlpool, 2 wading pools, poolside serv. Complimentary coffee in rms. Restaurant 6 am-10 pm. Rm serv 24 hrs. Bar 11-1 am. Ck-out noon. Coin lndry. Convention facilities. Business center. In-rm modem link. Concierge. Shopping arcade. Free airport transportation. Lighted tennis, pro. Exercise rm; sauna. Spa. Massage. Bicycle rentals. Minibars; microwaves avail. Bathrm phone in suites. Balconies. Cr cds: A, C, D, DS, ER, JCB, MC, V.

★★★ **U.S. GRANT HOTEL.** *326 Broadway (92101). 619/232-3121; fax 619/239-9517; res 619/232-3121. www.usgranthotel.com.* 280 rms, 11 story, 60 suites. S $205-$225; D $215-$245; each addl $20; suites $215-$1,500. Crib free. Pet accepted. Valet parking $14. TV; cable (premium), VCR avail. Coffee in rms. Restaurant 6:30-10:30 pm. Bar 11-2 am; entertainment Fri, Sat. Ck-out noon. Business center. In-rm modem link. Concierge. Gift shop. Free airport transportation. Exercise equipt. Massage. Bathrm phones, minibars. Antiques, artwork, period chandeliers and fixtures. 1910 landmark has been restored to its original elegance. Luxury level. Cr cds: A, D, DS, JCB, MC, V.

★★★ **THE WESTGATE HOTEL.** *1055 Second Ave (92101). 619/238-1818; fax 619/557-3737; toll-free 800/221-3802. www.westgatehotel.com.* 223 units, 19 story, some kits. S, D from $194; each addl $10; suites from $500; under 18 free; wkend rates. Valet parking $12/day. Crib free. TV; cable (premium), VCR avail. Irons and ironing boards in evey rm. Complimentary coffee in lobby. Restaurants 6 am-11 pm (see also LE FONTAINEBLEAU). Rm serv 24 hrs. Bar 11-1 am; entertainment. Ck-out noon. Meeting rms. Business servs avail. In-rm modem link. Concierge. Free airport, RR station, bus depot transportation. Exercise equipt. Bathrm phones, minibars; microwaves avail. Cr cds: A, C, D, DS, MC, V.

★★★ **WESTIN HOTEL AT HORTON PLAZA.** *910 Broadway Cir (92101). 619/239-2200; fax 619/239-0509; res 800/993-7846. www.westin.*

com. 450 rms, 16 story. S, D $129-$289; each addl $15; suites $250-$1,500; under 18 free; wkend, wkday packages. Crib free. Covered parking $12; valet $18. TV; cable (premium), VCR avail. Heated pool; whirlpool, poolside serv. Restaurant 6:30 am-11 pm. Rm serv 24 hrs. Bar to 2 am. Ck-out noon. Convention facilities. Business center. In-rm modem link. Concierge. Exercise equipt; sauna. Bathrm phones, refrigerators, minibars; microwaves avail. Some balconies. Connected to Horton Plaza. Luxury level. Cr cds: A, C, D, DS, ER, JCB, MC, V.

D SC

★★ WYNDHAM EMERALD PLAZA. *400 W Broadway (92101). 619/239-4500; fax 619/239-3274. www.wyndham.com.* 436 rms, 25 story. S, D $194-$248; each addl $20; suites $380-$2,000; under 18 free. Crib free. Garage $16. TV; cable (premium), VCR avail. Heated pool; whirlpool, poolside serv. Restaurant 6 am-10 pm. Bar 11-1 am; entertainment Wed-Sat. Ck-out noon. Convention facilities. Business center. In-rm modem link. Concierge. Shopping arcade. Free airport transportation. Exercise rm; steam rm, sauna. Massage. Bathrm phones, minibars. Cr cds: A, C, D, DS, ER, JCB, MC, V.

D

★★ WYNDHAM SAN DIEGO. *5975 Lusk Blvd (92121). 858/558-1818. www.wyndham.com.* 350 rms, 17 story. S, D $195-$295; each addl $25; under 17 free. Crib avail. Heated pool. TV; cable (premium), VCR avail. Complimentary coffee, newspaper in rms. Restaurant 6 am-10:30 pm. Bar. Ck-out noon. Meeting rms. Business center. Valet serv. Gift shop. Exercise rm. Some refrigerators, minibars. Cr cds: A, C, D, DS, MC, V.

Resorts

★★ DANA INN AND MARINA. *1710 W Mission Bay Dr (92109). 619/222-6440; fax 619/222-5916; res 800/345-9995. www.danainn.com.* 196 rms, 2 story. S, D $125-$146; each addl $10; under 18 free. Crib free. TV; cable (premium). Heated pool; whirlpool, poolside serv. Coffee in rms. Restaurant 7 am-10 pm. Bar. Ck-out noon. Coin lndry. Business servs avail. Bellhops. Valet serv. Free airport, RR station, bus depot transportation. Tennis. Marina. Boat launch adj. Cr cds: A, C, D, DS, JCB, MC, V.

SC

Panda bears, San Diego Zoo

★★★ DOUBLETREE GOLF RESORT. *14455 Penasquitos Dr (92129). 619/672-9100; fax 858/672-9166; toll-free 800/622-9223. www. doubletreehotels.com.* 172 rms, 3 story, 6 suites. S, D $119-$189; each addl $10; suites $189; under 12 free; golf, tennis, fitness plans. Crib free. Pet accepted, some restrictions; $150. TV; cable (premium). 2 pools; whirlpool, poolside serv, lifeguard (summer). Supervised children's activities (June-early Sept); ages 6-12. Complimentary coffee in rms. Dining rms 6:30 am-10 pm. Bar 11-1 am. Ck-out noon, ck-in 3 pm. Convention facilities. Business servs avail. In-rm modem link. Bellhops. Beauty shop. Five lighted tennis courts, pro. 18-hole golf, greens fee $48-$60, pro, putting green. Exercise rm; saunas, steam rm. Microwaves avail. Private patios, balconies. On 130 acres. Cr cds: A, C, D, DS, ER, JCB, MC, V.

★★★ HANALEI HOTEL. *2270 Hotel Circle N (92108). 619/297-1101; fax 619/297-6049; toll-free 800/882-0858. www.hanaleihotel.com.* 416 rms, 8 story. June-Sept: S, D $79-$169; suite $225-$375; under 18 free; hols (2-day min); lower rates rest of yr. Crib free. Pet accepted, some restrictions; $25 deposit. TV; cable (premium). Pool; whirlpool, poolside serv. Restaurant 6:30 am-10 pm; Sat, Sun to 11 pm. Bar. Ck-out noon. Coin lndry. Meeting rms. Business center. In-rm modem link. Concierge. Tennis privileges. Golf privileges. Exercise equipt. Health club privileges. Lawn games. Some refrigerators. Balconies. Cr cds: A, D, DS, MC, V.

★★★ HANDLERY HOTEL RESORT. *950 Hotel Circle N (92128). 619/298-0511; fax 619/298-9793; toll-free 800/676-6567. www.handlery.com.* 217 rms, 2 story. S $129; D $139; each addl $10; suites $175-$250; under 14 free. Crib free. Pet accepted, some restrictions, $25. TV; cable. 3 pools (1 lap pool); whirlpool, poolside serv. Coffee in rms. Restaurant 6:30 am-10 pm. Rm serv 7 am-9 pm. Bars 11-2 am. Ck-out noon. Lndry facilities. Meeting rms. Business center. In-rm modem link. Bellhops. Valet serv. Sundries. Gift shop. Barber, beauty shop. Tennis, pro. Exercise rm. Massage. Some balconies. Cr cds: A, C, D, DS, JCB, MC, V.

★★ HUMPHREY'S HALF MOON INN. *2303 Shelter Island Dr (92106). 619/224-3411; fax 619/224-3478; toll-free 800/345-9995. www.halfmoon inn.com.* 182 rms, 2 story, 30 kit. units. Late May-early Sept: S $149-$159; D $159-$169; each addl $10; kit. suites $219-$299; under 18 free; lower rates rest of yr. Crib free. TV; cable (premium), VCR avail. Heated pool; whirlpool, poolside serv. Complimentary coffee in rms. Restaurant 6:30 am-10 pm. Bar 11-2 am; entertainment. Ck-out noon. Coin lndry. Meeting rms. Business servs avail. In-rm modem link. Bellhops. Concierge. Sundries. Free airport, RR station transportation. Bicycles. Health club privileges. Lawn games. Refrigerators. Many private patios, balconies. South Sea island decor. Gardens. Cr cds: A, D, DS, MC, V.

★★ QUALITY RESORT MISSION VALLEY-SAN DIEGO. *875 Hotel Cir S (92108). 619/298-8282; fax 619/295-5610; res 800/228-5151. www.quality resort.com.* 202 rms, 2 story. June-Aug: S $99-$109; D $89-$119; suites $139-$169; under 18 free; lower rates rest of yr. Crib free. TV; cable. Pool; poolside serv. Coffee in rms. Restaurant adj open 24 hrs. Bar 11 am-11 pm. Ck-out noon. Meeting rms. In-rm modem link. Beauty shop. Valet serv. Coin lndry. Lighted tennis. Exercise equipt; sauna. Massage. Lawn games. Microwave in suites. Some balconies. Cr cds: A, C, D, DS, MC, V.

★★★ RANCHO BERNARDO INN. *17550 Bernardo Oaks Dr (92128). 858/675-8500; fax 858/675-8501; toll-free 800/542-6096. www.jcresorts.com.* 285 rms, 3 story. Mid-Sept-mid-May: S, D $239-$260; suites $289-$800; under 12 free; golf, tennis plans; lower rates rest of yr. TV; cable (premium), VCR avail. 2 pools; 7 whirlpools, poolside serv. Supervised children's activities (Aug and hols); ages 5-15. Complimentary afternoon refreshments Wed and Sat. Dining rms 6 am-10 pm (see also EL BIZCOCHO). Snack bar. Rm serv to midnight. Bars 11-1 am. Ck-out 1 pm, ck-in 4 pm. Convention facilities. Business center. In-rm modem link. Concierge. Sundries. Gift shop. Airport transportation. Lighted tennis, pro. Three 18-hole, one 27-hole golf courses, pro, putting green, driving range. Volleyball. Bicycles. Exercise equipt; sauna, steam rm. Massage. Many minibars; some bathrm phones; microwaves avail. Private patios, balconies. Cr cds: A, D, DS, MC, V.

★★ SAN DIEGO PARADISE POINT RESORT. *1404 W Vacation Rd (92109). 858/274-4630; fax 858/581-5929; toll-free 800/344-2626. www. paradisepoint.com.* 462 cottage rms, 153 kits. May-Aug: S, D $180-$230; each addl $15; suites $245-$395; kit. units $190-$240; lower rates rest of yr. Crib free. Pet accepted. TV; cable (premium). 5 pools, 2 heated; wading pool, whirlpool, poolside serv. Supervised children's activities (June-Aug); ages 3-18. Complimentary coffee in rms. Dining rms 7 am-11 pm. Bars 11-2 am; entertainment Tues-Sun. Ck-out noon, ck-in 4 pm. Coin lndry. Convention facilities. Business center. In-rm modem link. Valet serv. Concierge. Gift shop. Lighted tennis, pro. Putting green. Exercise equipt; sauna, steam rm. Health club privileges. Bicycles. Game rm. Lawn games. Boats. Some bathrm phones, refrigerators; microwaves avail. Private patios. On beach. Botanical walk. Cr cds: A, D, DS, MC, V.

★★ **SHELTER POINTE HOTEL AND MARINA.** *1551 Shelter Island Dr (92106). 619/221-8000; fax 619/221-5953; toll-free 800/566-2524. www.shelterpointe.com.* 211 rms, 3 story, 32 suites, 5 kit. units. May-Sept: S, D $139-$169; each addl $20; suites $195-$225; kit. units $450; under 12 free; hols 3-day min; higher rates bowl games; lower rates rest of yr. Crib free. TV; cable (premium). Complimentary coffee in rms. Restaurant (see also EL EMBARCADERO). Bar 11 am-11 pm. Ck-out noon. Meeting rms. Business servs avail. In-rm modem link. Concierge. Gift shop. Coin lndry. Free airport transportation. Lighted tennis, pro. Exercise rm; sauna. Massage. Pools; whirlpools, poolside serv. Playground. Supervised children's activities (May-Sept); from age 5. Some microwaves, wet bars; refrigerator in suites. Balconies. Picnic tables, grills. On ocean. Cr cds: A, D, DS, JCB, MC, V.

B&Bs/Small Inns

★★ **BALBOA PARK INN.** *3402 Park Blvd (92103). 619/298-0823; fax 619/294-8070; toll-free 800/938-8181. www.balboaparkinn.com.* 26 rms, 2 story, 17 kit. suites. S, D $80-$210; kit. suites $99-$200; under 11 free. Crib $5. TV; cable (premium). Complimentary continental bkfst, coffee in rms. Ck-out noon. Free guest lndry. Refrigerators; some in-rm whirlpools, microwaves. Many patios, balconies. Sun deck. Each rm has a distinctly different theme and decor. Cr cds: A, D, DS, MC, V.

★★ **ELSBREE HOUSE BED AND BREAKFAST.** *5054 Narragansett Ave (92107). 619/226-4133 or 619/226-4133; fax 619/224-4133; res 800/510-6975.www.oceanbeach-online.com/elsbree/b&b.* 6 rms, 1 condo, 2 story. No A/C. No rm phones. 2-4-day min: S, D $125-$135 (2-day min); condo $285 (4-day min); wkly rates. TV in sitting rm. Complimentary continental bkfst. Restaurant nearby. Ck-out 11 am, ck-in 3 pm. Balconies. New England-style house near ocean. Totally nonsmoking. Cr cds: MC, V.

★★★ **HERITAGE PARK INN.** *2470 Heritage Park Row (92110). 619/299-6832; fax 619/299-9465; toll-free 800/995-2470. www.heritageparkinn.com.* 12 rms, 5 with shower only, 2 story, 1 suite. No A/C. S, D $125; each addl $20; suite $250; under 12 free; wkends, hols (2-day min). TV; VCR (movies avail). Complimentary full bkfst; afternoon refreshments. Restaurant nearby. Ck-out 11 am, ck-in 3 pm. In-rm modem link. Free airport transportation. Victorian house (1889) moved to this site. Many antiques. Totally nonsmoking. Cr cds: A, C, D, DS, MC, V.

★★★ **JULIAN GOLDRUSH HOTEL.** *2032 Main St, Julian (92036). 760/765-0201; fax 760/765-0327; toll-free 800/734-5854. www.julianhotel.com.* 14 air-cooled rms, 12 with shower only, 2 cottages. Sept-May: S $49; D $72-$82; cottages $120-$185; wkends 2-day min; lower rates rest of yr. Complimentary full bkfst; refreshments. Restaurant adj 7 am-9 pm. Ck-out noon, ck-in 2 pm. Street parking. Built in 1897. Totally nonsmoking. Cr cds: A, MC, V.

★★ **JULIAN WHITE HOUSE BED AND BREAKFAST.** *3014 Blue Jay Dr, Julian (92036). 760/765-1764; res 800/948-4687. www.julian-whitehouse-bnb.com.* 4 rms, 1 with shower only; 1 suite. No rm phones. S, D $90-$135; each addl $25; suite $145; under 5 free; wkends, hols (2-day min). Closed Dec 24, 25. Complimentary full bkfst. Ck-out noon, ck-in 4 pm. Business servs avail. In-rm modem link. Some fireplaces. Totally nonsmoking. Cr cds: MC, V.

★★★ **ORCHARD HILL COUNTRY INN.** *2502 Washington St, Julian (92036). 760/765-1700; fax 970/765-0290; res 800/716-7242. www.orchardhill.com.* 22 rms, 2 with shower only, 12 deluxe rms. S, D $160-$170; each addl $25; deluxe rms $210-$265; ; 2-day min wkends. TV; cable, VCR (movies). Complimentary full bkfst, coffee in rms; afternoon refreshments. Ck-out noon, ck-in 3 pm. Business servs avail. Gift shop. Some in-rm whirlpools; refrigerator, wet bar, fireplace in deluxe rms. Balconies on deluxe rms. Totally nonsmoking. Cr cds: A, MC, V.

All Suites

★★ **BEST WESTERN HACIENDA HOTEL.** *4041 Harney St (92110). 619/298-4707; fax 619/298-4771; res 800/528-1234.* 169 suites, 2-3 story. June-Aug: S, D $135-$150; each addl $10; under 16 free; lower rates rest of yr. Crib free. TV; cable, VCR (movies). Heated pool; whirlpool, poolside serv. Complimentary coffee in rms. Restaurants 6:30 am-10 pm. Bar 11 am-midnight. Ck-out noon. Meeting rms. Business servs avail. Bellhops. Valet serv. Concierge. Covered parking. Free airport, RR station, bus depot transportation. Exercise equipt. Refrigerators, microwaves. Some private patios, balconies. Grills. Spanish architecture. Cr cds: A, C, D, DS, MC, V.

D

★★★ **EMBASSY SUITES.** *601 Pacific Hwy (92101). 619/239-2400; fax 619/239-1520; res 800/362-2779. www.essandiegobay.com.* 337 suites, 12 story. Mid-June-mid-Sept: suites $159-$239; under 18 free; lower rates rest of yr. Crib free. Covered parking $10. TV; cable (premium). Indoor pool; whirlpool. Complimentary full bkfst, coffee in rms. Restaurant 11 am-midnight. Bar to midnight. Ck-out noon. Coin lndry. Meeting rms. Business center. In-rm modem link. Concierge. Gift shop. Barber, beauty shop. Free airport transportation. Exercise equipt; sauna. Refrigerators, microwaves. Some balconies. Cr cds: A, C, D, DS, ER, JCB, MC, V.

★★ **QUALITY SUITES.** *9880 Mira Mesa Blvd (92131). 858/530-2000; fax 858/530-0202; res 800/221-2222.* www.*qualitysuitessandiego.com.* 132 suites, 4 story. S $89-$149; D $99-$159. Early June-mid-Sept: suites $105-$199; each addl $10; under 18 free; lower rates rest of yr. Crib free. TV; cable (premium), VCR. Heated pool. Complimentary continental bkfst. Coffee in rms. Ck-out noon. Meeting rms. Business servs avail. In-rm modem link. Health club privileges. Microwaves. Cr cds: A, D, DS, ER, MC, V.

D SC

★★★ **RADISSON SUITES HOTEL RANCHO BERNARDO.** *11520 W Bernardo Ct (92127). 858/451-6600; fax 858/592-0253; res 800/333-3333. www.radisson.com.* 176 suites, 3 story. S, D $119-$179; each addl $10; under 12 free; golf plans. Crib free. Pet accepted, some restrictions. TV; cable (premium), VCR (movies). Heated pool; whirlpool. Complimentary full bkfst, coffee in rms. Restaurant 6-9:30 am, 5-11 pm. Bar 5-11 pm. Ck-out noon. Coin lndry. Meeting rms. Business servs avail. In-rm modem link. Tennis and Golf privileges. Exercise rm. Health club privileges. Minibars, microwaves. Cr cds: A, C, D, DS, JCB, MC, V.

D

★★★ **SAN DIEGO MARRIOTT SUITES.** *701 A St (92101). 619/696-9800; fax 619/696-1555; res 800/228-9290. www.marriotthotels.com.* 264 suites, 27 story. S, D $129-$255; under 18 free. Crib free. Pet accepted, some restrictions; $50. Garage $10, valet parking $15. TV; cable (premium). Indoor pool; whirlpool. Coffee in rms. Restaurant 6:30 am-10 pm. Bar 11:30 am-midnight. Ck-out noon. Meeting rms. In-rm modem link. Gift shop. Exercise equipt; sauna. Health club privileges. Minibars; refrigerators, microwaves avail. Cr cds: A, C, D, DS, JCB, MC, V.

D

Conference Center

★★ TOWN AND COUNTRY RESORT & CONVENTION CENTER. *500 Hotel Cir N (92108). 619/291-7131; fax 619/291-3584; res 800/772-8527. www.towncountry.com.* 1,000 rms, 1-10 story. S $95-$175; D $110-$190; each addl $15; suites $350-$675; under 18 free. Crib free. Parking $8. TV; cable (premium). 4 pools, 1 heated; whirlpool, poolside serv. Coffee in rms. Restaurant 6-1 am. Bar 11-2 am; entertainment. Ck-out noon. Convention facilities. Business center. In-rm modem link. Concierge. Barber. Lighted tennis privileges, pro. Golf privileges; driving range adj. Health club privileges. Some refrigerators; microwaves avail. Some private patios, balconies. On 35 acres. Cr cds: A, C, D, DS, ER, JCB, MC, V.

D

Restaurants

★★ AFGHANISTAN KHYBER PASS. *523 University Ave (92103). 619/294-7579.* Hrs: 11 am-2:30 pm, 5-10 pm; Sun from 5 pm. Res accepted. Afghan menu. Wine, beer. Lunch $6.95-$11.95, dinner $10.95-$15.95. Specializes in shish kebab, curries. Interior designed as an Afghan cave. Cr cds: A, C, D, DS, ER, MC, V.

D

★★ ANTHONY'S FISH GROTTO. *11666 Avena Pl (92128). 858/451-2070. www.gofishanthonys.com.* Hrs: 11:30 am-8:30 pm. Closed hols. Res accepted. Bar. Lunch $4.75-$8.95, dinner $7.50-$26. Children's menu. Specializes in fresh seafood. Parking. Outdoor dining. Overlooks Webb Lake Park. Family-owned. Cr cds: A, DS, MC, V.

D

GASLAMP QUARTER AND HARBORFRONT

This tour combines the best aspects of San Diego's downtown area, an historic area now thriving with shops and restaurants, with the scenic waterfront—all best appreciated on foot. Start at the International Visitor Information Center at 1st Avenue and F Street in Horton Plaza, a multilevel open-air complex of shops and snack bars. The colorful architecture alone is worth a look. Walk east down F Street to 4th Avenue, where you'll come upon the Gaslamp Quarter, a $16\frac{1}{2}$-block historic district with renovated Victorian-era architecture. Bounded by 4th Avenue, 6th Avenue, Broadway, and L Street, the Gaslamp Quarter is just two blocks wide and eight blocks long. This is a good place to wander among antique shops, art galleries, cafes, restaurants, and nightspots (in the evenings, especially on weekends, it can be quite lively; you may want to return to experience some of the nightlife). Walk east for two blocks on F Street, turning right at 6th Avenue; walk three blocks south to Island Avenue and make another right so you're walking west. If you have children in tow, you may want to stop at the Children's Museum of San Diego (200 West Island Avenue), a "please touch" museum where kids and parents can create their own art and enjoy hands-on exhibits. Now walk north a block to Market Street and cross West Harbor Drive to Kettner Boulevard, where you'll find Seaport Village, an attractive open-air complex of shops and other entertainment, including an old-fashioned carousel. There are good seaside views here, which continue as you walk south on Kettner to Embarcadero Marina Park—a lovely area filled with sights of green grass, kites flapping in the breeze, and sailboats skimming across the bay. Continue back up to Harbor Drive and follow it north along the waterfront, also known as the Embarcadero. At the Broadway Pier, near the intersection of North Harbor Drive and Broadway, you'll see the San Diego-Coronado Ferry port (ferries leave hourly for Coronado, which is just across the way). Harbor cruise boats also depart from here. A bit past the pier is the Maritime Museum—a collection of three historic ships berthed in the harbor, including the striking *Star of India*, an 1863 windjammer that is the oldest iron sailing ship still afloat. The ships are available for tours. Depending on stops, the entire walking tour can take anywhere from two to four hours or more.

★★ ATHENS MARKET TAVERNA. *109 W F St (92101). 619/234-1955. www.athensmarket.net.* Hrs: 11:30 am-10 pm; Sat 4-10:30 pm. Closed Sun, hols. Res accepted. Greek menu. Bar to midnight. Lunch $5.50-$14.50, dinner $11.75-$22.75. Specializes in lamb, fish, vegetarian specials. Cr cds: A, C, D, DS, ER, MC, V.

D

★★★ BACI. *1955 W Morena Blvd (92110). 619/275-2094.* Hrs: 11:30 am-2 pm, 5:30-10 pm; Sat from 5:30 pm. Closed Sun; hols. Res required Fri, Sat. Northern Italian menu. Bar. Wine list. A la carte entrees: lunch $7.95-$16.95, dinner $11.95-$23.50. Specializes in seafood, veal, pasta. Own baking, pasta. Intimate atmosphere; many art pieces, prints. Cr cds: A, DS, ER, MC, V.

D

★★ BAYOU BAR AND GRILL. *329 Market St (92101). 619/696-8747. www.signonsandiego.com.* Hrs: 11:30 am-3 pm, 5-10 pm; Fri, Sat to 11 pm; Sun brunch 11:30 am-3 pm. Closed Jan 1, Thanksgiving, Dec 25. Res accepted. Cajun, Creole menu. Bar. Lunch $5.95-$11.95, dinner $11.95-$16.95. Sun brunch $12.95. Specializes in beef, chicken. Outdoor dining. Casual dining in New Orleans atmosphere. Cr cds: A, DS, MC, V.

D

★★ BELLA LUNA. *748 5th Ave (92101). 619/239-3222. www.bellalunasandiego.com.* Hrs: 11:30 am-2:30 pm, 5-11 pm; Fri- Sat to midnight. Closed Jan 1, Dec 25. Res accepted. Italian menu. Bar. Lunch $4.95-$12.95, dinner $5.95-$18.95. Specializes in pasta, seafood. Valet parking. Patio dining. Original artwork with moon motif; ceiling painted to look like sky. Cr cds: A, D, DS, MC, V.

D

★★ BENIHANA. *477 Camino del Rio S (92108). 619/298-4666.* Hrs: 11:30 am-2 pm, 5-10 pm; Fri to 11 pm; Sat 1-11 pm; Sun 1-10 pm. Res accepted. Japanese menu. Bar. Lunch $6.75-$15.75, dinner $14-$35.75. Children's menu. Specializes in Japanese steak and seafood. Sushi bar. Valet parking. Japanese village settings. Cr cds: A, C, D, DS, ER, MC, V.

D

★★★ BLUE POINT. *565 Fifth Ave (92101). 619/233-6623. www.cohnrestaurants.com.* Hrs: 5-10 pm; Fri, Sat to 11 pm; Sun to 9 pm. Closed Dec 25. Res accepted. Bar. Extensive wine list. Dinner $15.95-$23.95. Specialties: miso-marinated bass, fresh Maine lobster with macadamia nut butter, grilled Hawaiian ahi. Oyster bar. Valet parking. Outdoor dining. Oil paintings. Cr cds: A, D, DS, MC, V.

D

★ THE BRIGANTINE. *2444 San Diego Ave (92110). 619/298-9840. www.brigantine.com.* Specializes in seafood. Hrs: 11:30 am-9:30 pm; Fri, Sat to 10 pm; Sun brunch 10 am-2:30 pm. Res accepted. Wine, beer. Lunch $7.95-$11.95; dinner $11.95-$35. Brunch $6.95-$11.95. Children's menu. Entertainment. Cr cds: A, D, MC, V.

D SC

★★★ BUSALACCHI'S. *3683 5th Ave (92103). 619/298-0119. www.signonsandiego.com.* Hrs: 11:30 am-2:15 pm, 5-10 pm; Fri, Sat to 10:15 pm. Closed hols. Res accepted. Italian menu. Bar. A la carte entrees: lunch $7.25-$19.95, dinner $10.95-$26.95. Specializes in Sicilian dishes. Valet parking. Outdoor dining. Victorian-style house. Cr cds: A, C, D, DS, ER, MC, V.

★ CAFE COYOTE. *2461 San Diego Ave (92110). 619/291-4695.* Hrs: 7:30 am-10 pm; Fri, Sat to 11 pm. Closed Dec 25. Res accepted. Mexican, American menu. Bar. Bkfst $3.50-$6.95, lunch, dinner $3.95-$9.95. Children's menu. Specialties: blue corn pancakes, carnitas, carne asada. Own tortillas. Entertainment Thurs-Sun on patio. Parking. Outdoor dining. Pictures, statues of Southwestern wildlife. Cr cds: A, C, D, DS, ER, MC, V.

D

★★ CAFE PACIFICA. *2414 San Diego Ave (92110). 619/291-6666. www.cafepacifica.com.* Hrs: 5:30-10 pm; Sun 5-9:30 pm; early-bird dinner 5:30-6:30 pm. Res accepted. Bar. Dinner $14-$22. Specializes in fresh fish. Near Old Spanish Cemetery. Cr cds: A, C, D, DS, ER, MC, V.

D

★★★ CALIFORNIA CUISINE. *1027 University Ave (92103). 619/543-0790. www.californiacuisine.com.* Hrs: 11

am-10 pm; Sat, Sun from 5 pm. Closed Mon; Jan 1, Thanksgiving, Dec 25. Res accepted. California menu. Wine, beer. Lunch $7-$14, dinner $12.75-$19.75. Specializes in fresh seafood, pasta, salad. Outdoor dining. Menu changes daily. Original paintings. Cr cds: A, C, D, DS, ER, MC, V.

D

★★ **CASA DE BANDINI.** *2754 Calhoun St (92110). 619/297-8211.* Hrs: 11 am-9:30 pm; Sun 10 am-8:30 pm; winter to 9 pm. Closed Thanksgiving, Dec 25. Mexican menu. Bar. Lunch, dinner $5.95-$15.50. Children's menu. Specializes in seafood. Mariachi band. Parking. Outdoor dining. Early California atmosphere, garden patio with fountain. Adobe building (1829) once served as headquarters for Commodore Stockton. Cr cds: A, DS, MC, V.

D SC

★★ **CHIEU-ANH.** *16769 Bernardo Center Dr (92128). 858/485-1231.* Hrs: 11 am-2 pm, 5-9 pm; Sat, Sun 5-9:30 pm. Closed Mon; Dec 25. Res accepted. Vietnamese menu. Wine, beer. Lunch $5.95-$7.45, dinner $9.50-$14.95. Specializes in rice noodles, clay pot dishes. Contemporary decor. Cr cds: A, DS, MC, V.

D

★★ **CROCE'S.** *802 5th Ave (92101). 619/233-4355. www.croces.com.* Hrs: 5 pm-midnight. Closed Thanksgiving, Dec 25. Res accepted. Contemporary American menu. Bar to 2 am. Dinner $12.95-$21.95. Specializes in seafood. Jazz. Valet parking. Outdoor dining. Tribute to famous singer, composer Jim Croce. Cr cds: A, D, DS, MC, V.

★★★ **DAKOTA GRILL AND SPIRITS.** *901 5th Ave (92101). 619/234-5554. www.cohnrestaurants.com.* Hrs: 11:30 am-2:30 pm, 5-10 pm; Fri, Sat to 11 pm, Sun 5-9 pm. Closed Thanksgiving, Dec 25. Res accepted. Bar. Lunch $5.95-$10.95, dinner $10.95-$21.95. Specializes in barbecue ribs, mesquite-broiled meat, seafood. Pianist Wed-Sat. Valet parking. Balcony, patio dining. Original artwork. Cr cds: A, C, D, DS, ER, MC, V.

D

★★ **DOBSON'S.** *956 Broadway Cir (92101). 619/231-6771.* Hrs: 11:30 am-3 pm, 5:30-10 pm; Thur, Fri to 11 pm; Sat 5:30-11 pm. Closed hols. Res accepted. Continental menu. Bar to 1:30 am. Lunch $7-$11.25, dinner $15-$26. Prix fixe: dinner $21.95. Specializes in fresh seafood, veal. Own sourdough bread. Covered parking. Cr cds: A, D, MC, V.

D

★★ **EDGEWATER GRILL.** *861 W Harbor Dr (92101). 619/232-7581. www.edgewatergrill.com.* Hrs: 8 am-10 pm; Fri, Sat to 10:30 pm. Res accepted. Seafood menu. Bar. Lunch $6.95-$22.95, dinner $8.25-$22.95. Children's menu. Specialties: pan-roasted salmon, ruby red ahi. Parking. Outdoor dining. View of harbor. Cr cds: A, DS, MC, V.

D

★★★ **EL BIZCOCHO.** *17550 Bernardo Oaks Dr (92128). 858/675-8500.* Hrs: 6-10 pm; Fri, Sat to 10:30 pm; Sun brunch 10 am-2 pm. Res accepted. Classical French menu. Bar. Extensive wine list. A la carte entrees: dinner $23-$40. Sun brunch $24. Specializes in seasonal cuisine. Pianist. Valet parking. Jacket required (exc brunch), tie optional. Cr cds: A, C, D, DS, ER, MC, V.

D

★ **FAIROUZ CAFE AND GALLERY.** *3166 Midway Dr (92110). 619/225-0308. www.alnashashibi.com.* Hrs 11 am-9 pm; Fri, Sat to 10 pm. Closed Jan 1. Res required Fri, Sat. Mediterranean menu. Bar. Lunch $3.95-$7, dinner $5-$13.95. Buffet: lunch $5.25, dinner $10.95. Specialties: hommos taboleh, kabobs. Parking. Cr cds: A, MC, V.

D

★★★ **FIO'S.** *801 5th Ave (92101). 619/234-3467. www.fiositalian.com.* Hrs: 5-10:30 pm; Fri, Sat to 11:30 pm; Sun to 10 pm. Closed Dec 25. Res accepted. Italian menu. Bar. Wine cellar. Dinner $11.95-$24.95. Specializes in pasta. Outdoor dining. European decor; original artwork depicting Palio of Siena. Cr cds: A, C, D, DS, ER, MC, V.

D

★★ **FORTUNE COOKIE.** *16425 Bernardo Center Dr (92128). 858/451-8958.* Hrs: 11 am-9 pm; Fri, Sat to 10 pm; Sun 4:30-9 pm. Closed Thanksgiving. Res accepted. Chinese menu. Bar. Lunch $6.45-$12.95, dinner $8.95-$19.95. Specialties: kung pao chicken, stir-fried sea bass, Taiwanese ribeye steak. Parking. Totally nonsmoking. Cr cds: A, DS, MC, V.

D

★★ FRENCH MARKET GRILLE. *15717 Bernardo Hts Pkwy, Rancho Bernardo (92128). 858/485-8055.* Hrs: 11 am-9 pm. Res accepted. French, American menu. Lunch $8-$12, dinner $15-$20. Specialties: coq au vin, beef bourguignon, lamb shank on artichoke ravioli and white beans. Opera Tues. Outdoor dining. Intimate dining. Cr cds: A, C, D, DS, ER, MC, V.

D

★ GRANT GRILL. *326 Broadway (92101). 619/232-3121. www.usgranthotel.com.* Specializes in prime rib, duck a l'orange. Hrs: 6:30-10 am, 11 am-2 pm, 5:30-10 pm; Fri, Sat to 10:30 pm, Sat, Sun brunch 11 am-2 pm. Res accepted. Wine list. Lunch $7.95-$18; dinner $18-$25. Brunch $6.95-$18. Entertainment: Latin Caribbean Jazz. New York style restaurant; hotel is a historical building. Cr cds: A, D, DS, MC, V.

D

★★★ GREYSTONE - THE STEAKHOUSE. *658 Fifth Ave (92101). 619/232-0225. www.greystonesteakhouse.com.* Specializes in steak, seafood, pasta. Hrs: 5-10 pm. Res accepted. Wine, beer. Dinner $18.95-$34.95. Entertainment. In a historical theater building, in gaslamp district. Cr cds: A, D, DS, MC, V.

D

★★ HARBOR HOUSE. *831 W Harbor Dr (92101). 619/232-1141.* Hrs: 11 am-11 pm. Res accepted. Bar from 11 am. A la carte entrees: lunch $8.95-$22.95, dinner $14.95-$23.95. Children's menu. Specializes in fresh seafood. Oyster bar. Parking. View of harbor, boat docks, Coronado Bay Bridge. Cr cds: A, DS, MC, V.

D

★★ HOB NOB HILL. *2271 1st Ave (92101). 619/239-8176. www.hobnobhill.com.* Hrs: 7 am-9 pm. Closed Dec 25. Res accepted. Wine, beer. Bkfst $2.35-$10.95. Complete meals: lunch $5.65-$8.55, dinner $5.65-$13.45. Children's menu. Specializes in Eastern fried scallops, lamb shanks, roast turkey. Family-owned. Cr cds: A, C, D, DS, ER, MC, V.

D

San Diego Bay and skyline

★ HUMPHREY'S BY THE BAY. *2241 Shelter Island Dr (92106). 619/224-3577. www.humphreysbythebay.com.* Hrs: 6:30 am-2 pm, 5:30-10 pm; Fri 5:30-11 pm; Sat 7 am-3 pm, 5:30-11 pm; Sun 7 am-2 pm, 5:30-10 pm; Sun brunch 10 am-2 pm. Res accepted. Seafood menu. Bar 11 am-midnight. Bkfst $3.95-$7.95, lunch $6.95-$12.95, dinner $14.95-$24.95. Sun brunch $24.95. Children's menu. Specializes in seafood, prime beef, pasta. Entertainment. Parking. View of bay. Cr cds: A, DS, MC, V.

D

★★ IMPERIAL HOUSE. *505 Kalmia St (92101). 619/234-3525.* Hrs: 11 am-4 pm, 5-9 pm; Mon to 2 pm; Fri, Sat to 11 pm; early-bird dinner Tues-Fri 5-6:30 pm. Closed Sun; hols. Res accepted. Continental menu. Bar to 11 pm; Fri, Sat to 12:30 am. A la carte entrees: lunch $7-$11, dinner $11-$22. Specializes in rack of lamb, pepper steak, seafood. Pianist Wed-Sat.

Valet parking. Old World decor. Family-owned. Cr cds: A, D, DS, MC, V.
D

★★ **ITRI.** *835 4th Ave (92101). 619/234-6538.* Hrs: 11 am-3 pm, 5-11 pm. Closed Sun, hols. Res accepted. Italian menu. Wine, beer. Lunch $9-$11, dinner $10-$25. Specialties: lamb shank, portobello itrano, pollo al profumi di bosco. Street parking. Outdoor dining. Italian country atmosphere and decor. Totally nonsmoking. Cr cds: A, C, D, DS, ER, MC, V.
D

★ **JACK AND GIULIO'S.** *2391 San Diego Ave (92110). 619/294-2074. www.jackandgiulios.com.* Hrs: 11:30 am-2 pm, 5-9:30 pm; Fri, Sat to 10:30 pm. Closed Easter, Thanksgiving, Dec 25. Italian menu. Wine, beer. Lunch, dinner $4.95-16.95. Children's menu. Specialties: scampi guilio, tortelloni verdi. Outdoor dining. Italian bistro atmosphere. Cr cds: A, DS, MC, V.
D

★★ **JASMINE.** *4609 Convoy St (92111). 858/268-0888.* Hrs: 10 am-11 pm. Res accepted. Chinese menu. Bar. Lunch $5.95-$18, dinner $9-$25. Specializes in dim sum, live seafood. Parking. Large dining rm with movable walls. Cr cds: A, DS, MC, V.

★ **KARL STRAUSS' BREWERY AND GRILL.** *1157 Columbia St (92101). 619/234-2739. www.karlstrauss.com.* Hrs: 11:30 am-10 pm; Thur-Sat to 1 am. Closed hols. Res accepted. Bar. Lunch $6-$11, dinner $7-$16. Specializes in hamburgers, fresh fish, German-style sausage. Brews own beer; some seasonal varieties. View of microbrewery from restaurant. Cr cds: A, MC, V.
D

★★ **KELLY'S STEAKHOUSE.** *500 Hotel Cir N (92108). 619/291-7131.* Hrs: 4 pm-midnight; early-bird dinner 4-6 pm. Closed Easter, Thanksgiving, Dec 25. Bar to 2 am; Sat, Sun from 4 pm. Dinner $10.50-$23.95. Specializes in barbecued ribs, steak, prime rib. Entertainment. Parking. Waterfalls. Cr cds: A, C, D, DS, ER, MC, V.
D

★★★★ **LAUREL.** *505 Laurel St (92101). 619/239-2222. www.laurelrestaurant.com.* Located in the glassed-in atrium of a modern building, Laurel serves well-prepared Provencal food that is designed to complement the extensive wine list that focuses on the Rhone region of France. Dishes, prepared by chef Douglas Organ, run the gamut of Southern French flavors from the seasonal risotto to Provencal chicken cooked in a clay pot. French Mediterranean menu. Specialities: Moroccan-spiced braised lamb shank, pan-roasted venison with sauteed red grapes, grilled yellowfin tuna with warm green lentil salad, warm peach tart with raspberry sorbet. Hrs: 5-10 pm; Fri, Sat to 11 pm. Bar. Res accepted. A la carte entrees: dinner $15-$28. Extensive wine list. Nightly entertainment. Valet parking $6. Contemporary decor. Cr cds: A, C, D, DS, ER, MC, V.
D

★★ **LA VACHE AND COMPANY.** *420 Robinson St (92103). 619/295-0214. www.lavacheandco.com.* Hrs: 11:30 am-2:30 pm, 5-11 pm; Fri-Sat to midnight. Closed Dec 25. Res accepted. Country French menu. Wine, beer. Lunch $5-$10, dinner $5-$18.50. Specializes in beef, chicken. Outdoor dining. Casual European decor. Totally nonsmoking. Cr cds: A, C, D, DS, ER, MC, V.
D

★★★ **LE FOUNTAINEBLEAU.** *1055 2nd Ave (92101). 619/238-1818. www.westgatehotel.com.* Hrs: 11:30 am-2 pm, 6-10 pm; Sun brunch 10 am-2 pm. Res accepted. Continental menu. Bar. Wine cellar. Lunch, dinner $16-$30. Sun brunch $28.95. Children's menu. Specializes in seafood, veal. Pianist. Valet parking. Lavish French period setting; antiques. Cr cds: A, D, DS, MC, V.
D

★★ **LINO'S.** *2754 Calhoun St (92110). 619/299-7124.* Hrs: 11 am-9 pm; Fri, Sat to 10 pm. Closed Jan 1, Thanksgiving, Dec 25. Res accepted. Italian menu. Bar. Lunch $4.50-$8.95, dinner $5.50-$14.95. Specializes in veal, chicken, shrimp. Own pasta. Parking. Outdoor dining. Cr cds: A, DS, MC, V.

D

★★ **MIXX.** *3671 5th Ave (92103). 619/299-6499.* Hrs: 5-10 pm; Fri, Sat to 11 pm. Closed Jan 1, Thanksgiving, Dec 25. Res accepted. Contemporary American menu. Bar. Dinner $9.95-$17.95. Specialties: pan-roasted trout, grilled lamb rack chops. Entertainment Wed-Sat. Intimate dining. Unique dish presentation. Totally nonsmoking. Cr cds: A, MC, V.

D

★★ **MONTANA'S AMERICAN GRILL.** *1421 University Ave (92103). 619/297-0722.* Hrs: 5 pm-9:30 pm; Fri, Sat to 10:30 pm; Sun 5-9 pm. Closed hols. Res accepted. Bar. Lunch $7.95-$10.95, dinner $8.95-$19.95. Specializes in BBQ ribs, skirt steak. Valet parking. Contemporary decor. Totally nonsmoking. Cr cds: A, D, DS, MC, V.

D

★ **NATI'S.** *1852 Bacon St (92107). 619/224-3369.* Hrs: 11 am-8 pm; Fri, Sat to 8 pm; winter to 8 pm. Closed hols. Mexican menu. Bar. Bkfst $3.95-$6.75, lunch, dinner $4.95-$8.75. Specializes in chiles rellenos, sour cream tostadas, carne asada. Parking. Outdoor dining. Cr cds: MC, V.

D

★★ **NICK'S AT THE BEACH.** *809 Thomas Ave (92109). 858/270-1730.* Hrs: 11-2 am; Sun brunch 10 am-2 pm. Closed Dec 25. Bar. Lunch, dinner $5.95-$14.95. Sun brunch $4.95-$9.95. Children's menu. Specializes in fresh seafood. Casual atmosphere. Totally nonsmoking. Cr cds: D, DS, MC, V.

D

★ **OLD TOWN MEXICAN CAFE AND CANTINA.** *2489 San Diego Ave (92110). 619/297-4330. www.oldtownmexcafe.com.* Hrs: 7-2 am. Closed Thanksgiving, Dec 25. Mexican menu. Bar to 2 am. A la carte entrees: bkfst $2.95-$7.25, lunch, dinner $2.75-$13. Specialties: carnitas, Old Town pollo, Mexican-style ribs. Own tortillas. Children's menu. Parking. Patio dining. Cr cds: A, D, DS, MC, V.

D

★★ **PANDA INN.** *506 Horton Plaza (92101). 619/233-7800. www.pandainn.com.* Hrs: 11 am-10 pm; Fri, Sat to 10:30 pm. Closed Thanksgiving. Res accepted. Mandarin menu. Bar. Lunch $6.25-$10.45, dinner $6.50-$19.95. Specialties: sweet and pungent shrimp, orange-flavored beef. Parking. Outdoor dining. Several dining areas, all with Chinese art, one with whole-ceiling skylight; pandas depicted in stained-glass windows. Cr cds: A, D, MC, V.

D

★★ **THE PRADO AT BALBOA PARK.** *1549 El Prado (92101). 619/557-9441. www.pradobalboa.com.* Latin, Italian fusion menu. Specializes in Italian. Hrs: 11 am-3 pm, 5-9 pm; Mon from 5 pm. Res accepted. Wine, beer. Lunch $10-$17; dinner $10-$22. Children's menu. Entertainment. In historic building in Balboa Park. Cr cds: A, C, D, DS, JCB, MC, V.

D

★★★ **PREGO.** *1370 Frazee Rd (92108). 619/294-4700. www.prego.signonsandiego.com.* Hrs: 11:30 am-11 pm; Sat 5-11 pm; Sun 4-10 pm. Closed hols. Res accepted. Italian menu. Bar. Wine list. A la carte entrees: lunch, dinner $8.50-$21.50. Specialties: grilled veal chops, lobster/prosciutto filled pasta, fresh fish of the day. Valet parking. Outdoor dining. Italian artwork. Cr cds: A, DS, MC, V.

D

★★★ **RAINWATER'S.** *1202 Kettner Blvd (92101). 619/233-5757. www.rainwaters.com.* Hrs: 11:30 am-midnight; Sat from 5 pm; Sun 5-11 pm. Closed July 4, Thanksgiving, Dec 25. Res accepted. Bar. Wine list. Lunch $7-$15, dinner $19-$40. Specializes in fresh seafood, prime steaks. Own pastries. Valet parking. Outdoor dining. Cr cds: A, C, D, ER, MC, V.

D

★ **RED SAILS INN.** *2614 Shelter Island Dr (92106). 619/223-3030.* Hrs: 7 am-11 pm; early-bird dinner Sun-Thurs 5-7 pm. Closed Dec 25. Res accepted. Bar. Bkfst $1.95-$8.95, lunch $5.95-$9.95, dinner $9.95-$21.95. Children's menu. Specializes in steak, seafood. Street parking. Outdoor dining. On marina; boating memorabilia. Family-owned since 1975. Cr cds: DS, MC, V.

D

★★★ **RUTH'S CHRIS STEAK HOUSE.** *1355 N Harbor Dr (92101). 619/233-1422. www.ruthschris.com.* Hrs: 5-10 pm; Fri, Sat to 10:30 pm. Closed Thanksgiving, Dec 25. Res accepted. Bar. A la carte entrees: dinner $18.95-$29.95. Specializes in steak, lobster. Contemporary decor. Cr cds: A, C, D, DS, ER, MC, V.

D

★★★ **SALLY'S.** *One Market Pl (92101). 619/687-6080.* Hrs: 11:30 am-11 pm. Closed Dec 25. Res accepted. Mediterranean menu. Bar. Lunch $8-$15, dinner $18-$32. Specializes in seafood. Outdoor dining. Contemporary decor. Cr cds: A, DS, MC, V.

D

★★★ **SALVATORE'S.** *750 Front St (92101). 619/544-1865.* Hrs: 5-10 pm. Res accepted. Italian menu. Bar. Wine list. A la carte entrees: dinner $15-$24. Specializes in Northern Italian dishes. Parking. Original artwork. Cr cds: A, D, MC, V.

D

★★ **SAN DIEGO PIER CAFE.** *885 W Harbor Dr (92101). 619/239-3968.* Hrs: 11 am-10 pm; Fri, Sat to 11 pm. Serv bar. Bkfst $4.25-$8.95, lunch $5.50-$13.95, dinner $9.95-$18.95. Children's menu. Specializes in fresh fish broiled. Outdoor dining. On harbor pier. Cr cds: A, DS, MC, V.

D

★★ **TAKA.** *614 5th Ave #M (92101). 619/338-0555.* Hrs: 5:30-10 pm; Fri, Sat to 11:30 pm. Closed Jan 1, Dec 25. Res accepted. Japanese menu. Bar. Dinner $6-$24. Specializes in seafood, sushi. Valet parking. Outdoor dining. Japanese decor. Totally nonsmoking. Cr cds: A, DS, MC, V.

D

★★★ **THEE BUNGALOW.** *4996 W Point Loma Blvd (92107). 619/224-2884. www.theebungalow.com.* Hrs: 5:30-9:30 pm; Fri, Sat 5-10 pm; Sun 5-9 pm. Closed July 4, Dec 26. Res accepted. Extensive wine list. Continental menu. Dinner $9.95-$22. Specializes in roast duck, rack of lamb, fresh seafood. Parking. In converted house. Many special wine dinners planned throughout the year. Cr cds: A, MC, V.

D

★★ **TOM HAM'S LIGHTHOUSE.** *2150 Harbor Island Dr (92101). 619/291-9110. www.tomhamslighthouse.com.* Hrs: 11:15 am-3:30 pm, 5-10:30 pm; Sat 4:30-11 pm; Sun 4-10 pm; early-bird dinner Mon-Fri 5-6 pm, Sun 4-6 pm; Sun brunch 10 am-2 pm. Closed Jan 1, Dec 25. Res accepted. Bar 11-2 am. Lunch $6.95-$14.95, dinner $9.95-$24.50. Sun brunch $11.95. Children's menu. Specializes in steak, seafood. Salad bar (lunch). Entertainment Wed-Sat. Parking. Early California, Spanish decor. View of bay, San Diego skyline. Official Coast Guard No. 9 beacon. Family-owned. Cr cds: A, DS, MC, V.

D SC

★★ **TOP OF THE MARKET.** *750 N Harbor Dr (92101). 619/232-3474. www.thefishmarket.com.* Hrs: 11 am-10 pm; Sun brunch 10 am-2 pm. Closed Thanksgiving, Dec 25. Res accepted. Bar to 10 pm. Lunch $9.50-$31.75, dinner $13-$34.25. Sun brunch $16.50. Children's menu. Specializes in seafood. Oyster, sushi bar. Parking. Outdoor dining. Pictures of turn-of-the-century fishing scenes. Retail fish market lower floor. Cr cds: A, DS, MC, V.

D

★★ **TRATTORIA LA STRADA.** *702 5th Ave (92101). 619/239-3400. www.trattorialastrada.com.* Hrs: 11 am-11 pm. Res accepted. Italian menu. Bar. Lunch $10.95-$19.95, dinner $11.95-$21.95. Specialties: osso buco alla milanese, salmone ai carciofi e basilico. Outdoor dining. Italian bistro atmosphere. Cr cds: A, C, D, DS, ER, MC, V.

D

★★ **VINCINO MARE.** *1702 India St (92101). 619/702-6180.* Hrs: 11:30 am-2 pm, 5-10 pm; Fri to 11 pm; Sat 5-11 pm; Sun 5-10 pm. Closed hols. Res accepted. Italian, seafood menu. Wine, beer. Lunch $9.50-$15.95, dinner $12.95-$18.95. Specialties: involtini di pesce spada, blackened ahi, paella. Valet parking. Outdoor din-

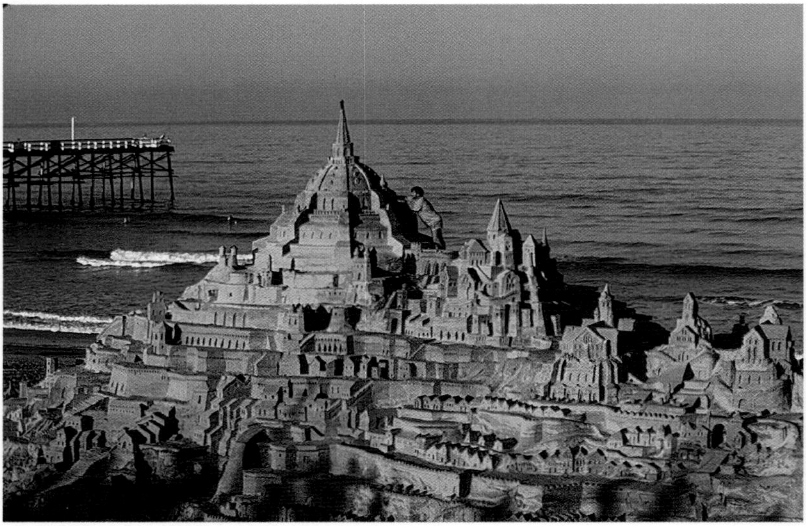

Elaborate sand castle

ing. Italian seaside trattoria decor. Totally nonsmoking. Cr cds: A, C, D, DS, ER, MC, V.

D

★★★ **WINESELLAR AND BRASSERIE.** *9550 Waples St, Suite 115 (92121). 858/450-9576. www.winesellar.com.* Hrs: 5:30-10 pm; Sun to 9 pm. Closed Mon; hols. Res accepted; required Fri-Sun. Contemporary French menu. Wine list. A la carte entrees: dinner $20-$38. Menu changes seasonally. Intimate, formal dining. Cr cds: A, C, D, DS, ER, MC, V.

Unrated Dining Spots

AESOP'S TABLES. *8650 Genesee Ave (92122). 858/455-1535.* Hrs: 11 am-10 pm; Mon to 9 pm; Sun from 4 pm. Closed hols. Greek, Middle Eastern menu. Bar. Lunch $4-$9.95, dinner $5-$12.95. Patio dining. Cr cds: A, DS, MC, V.

D

CITY DELICATESSEN. *535 University Ave (92103). 619/295-2747.* Hrs: 7 am-midnight; Fri, Sat to 2 am. Closed Dec 25; Yom Kippur. Jewish-style delicatessen. Wine, beer. A la carte entrees: bkfst, lunch $4.50-$8.50, dinner $4.50-$9.95. Children's menu. Own baking. Delicatessen and bakery. Cr cds: A, C, D, DS, ER, MC, V.

D

CORVETTE DINER. *3946 5th Ave (92103). 619/542-1001.* Hrs: 11 am-11 pm; Fri, Sat to midnight. Closed Jan 1, Dec 24 eve, 25. Bar. Lunch $4.85-$7.95, dinner $5.50-$9.95. Specializes in hamburgers, chicken-fried steak. DJ. 1950s-style diner with soda fountains. Corvette in center of room. Cr cds: A, C, D, DS, ER, MC, V.

D

DICK'S LAST RESORT. *345 4th Ave (92101). 619/231-9100. www.dickslastresort.com.* Hrs: 11-1:30 am. Closed Dec 25. Res accepted. Bar to 2 am. Lunch $3.25-$8.95, dinner $6.95-$14.95. Children's menu. Specialties: beef and pork ribs, crab, chicken. Entertainment. Valet parking Fri, Sat. Outdoor dining. Large warehouse setting. Casual dining. Cr cds: A, C, D, DS, ER, MC, V.

D

D.Z. AKIN'S. *6930 Alvarado Rd (92120). 619/265-0218.* Hrs: 7 am-9 pm; Fri, Sat to 11 pm. Closed July 4, Thanksgiving, Dec 25; some Jewish hols. Bkfst $3.50-$6, lunch $6-$8, dinner $8-$12. Specializes in delicatessen items. Own pastries. Parking. Cr cds: A, MC, V.

D

EL INDIO MEXICAN. *3695 India St (92103). 619/299-0333. www.elindio.net.* Hrs: 7 am-9 pm. Mexican menu. Bkfst $3-$4, lunch, dinner $5-$7.

Outdoor dining. Cafeteria-style. Tortilla factory in kitchen. Family-owned. Cr cds: MC, V.
D SC

GREEK CORNER. *5841 El Cajon Blvd (92115). 619/287-3303.* Hrs: 11 am-9:30 pm. Greek, Middle Eastern menu. Wine, beer. Lunch, dinner $4-$10. Specializes in Greek dishes, Middle Eastern vegetarian dishes. Parking. Outdoor dining. Greek cafe-style dining. Cr cds: A, MC, V.
D

LORNA'S ITALIAN KITCHEN. *3945 Governor Dr (92122). 858/452-0661.* Hrs: 11 am-9:30 pm; Fri to 10:30 pm; Sat 4-10:30 pm; Sun 4-9 pm. Closed hols. Italian menu. Wine, beer. Lunch $4.50-$8.50, dinner $6.50-$14.50. Children's menu. Specializes in pasta, salad. Italian bistro decor. Totally nonsmoking. Cr cds: A, C, D, DS, ER, MC, V.
D

SAFFRON. *3731 India St (92103). 619/574-0177.* Hrs: 11 am-9 pm; Sun 11 am-8 pm. Closed Jan 1, Thanksgiving, Dec 25. Thai menu. A la carte entrees: lunch, dinner $3.75-$12. Specialties: Thai grilled chicken. Picnic baskets avail. Cr cds: MC, V.
D SC

San Fernando

Pop 22,580 **Elev** 1,061 ft
Area code 818

Information Chamber of Commerce, 519 S Brand Blvd, 91340; 818/361-1184

A Ranger District office of the Angeles National Forest (see PASADENA) is located here.

What to See and Do

Mission San Fernando Rey de España. (1797). Restored 17th mission of chain; collections of Native American artifacts, furniture, woodcarvings, gold-leaf altars. A 35-bell carillon rings with an ancient melody sung by Native Americans in mission days. Guided tours (Sat afternoons). (Daily; closed Thanksgiving, Dec 25) 15151 San Fernando Mission Blvd. Phone 818/361-0186. Also here, and incl in admission, is the

Archival Center. Located in the west garden of the mission, the center houses ecclesiastical and historical documents; medals and mitres; relics of early California missionaries; changing exhibits. (Mon and Thurs afternoons) Phone 818/361-0186.

San Fernando Valley Area

North and west of Los Angeles (see) and bounded by the Santa Monica, Santa Susana, and San Gabriel mountains is the area known as the San Fernando Valley. The Los Angeles River, which flows through the valley, has its source in the mountains. Once primarily an agricultural area, the San Fernando Valley has diversified into a haven for light industry and commuters to Los Angeles.

The valley was explored by the Spanish in 1769; they found "a very pleasant and spacious valley... with many live oaks and walnuts." The arrival of the Southern Pacific railroad in 1876, linking Los Angeles to San Francisco, temporarily boosted agricultural production. However, production decreased following World War II, when the land was divided into housing tracts. At one time, the valley gained 15,000-20,000 new residents per year, rivaling the spectacular growth of Los Angeles.

The following towns and Los Angeles neighborhoods in the San Fernando Valley area are included in the *Mobil Travel Guide*. For additional information on any of them, see the individual alphabetical listing: North Hollywood, San Fernando, Studio City, Van Nuys, Woodland Hills.

San Francisco (G-3)

Founded 1776 **Pop** 723,959 **Elev** 63 ft
Area code 415

Information Convention & Visitors Bureau, 900 Market St, PO Box 429097, 94102-9097; 415/391-2000

Web www.sfvisitor.org

Suburbs Berkeley, Corte Madera, Hayward, Mill Valley, Oakland, San Mateo, San Rafael, Sausalito, Tiburon. (See individual alphabetical listings.)

Nearly everyone who comes to San Francisco falls in love with it. A city of sea, hills, parks, cable cars, a bustling waterfront, bridges that span mighty spaces—all freshened by clean Pacific breezes and warmed by a cooperative sun and a romantic fog—San Francisco is alive and lovely. Heart of a great Pacific empire, it is the true capital of the West.

This city of precipitous hills stretches seven miles across in each direction, rimmed on three sides by water. Its awe-inspiring bay, 500 square miles, equal in beauty to the Bay of Naples, constitutes one of the most nearly perfect natural harbors on earth. Rome has its seven hills; San Francisco was built on 43 hills. The city encompasses a total of 129.4 square miles, of which only 46.6 square miles are land. Within its boundaries are islands—Yerba Buena, Treasure Island, and Alcatraz—plus the Farallon group 32 miles west, part of the city since 1872.

San Francisco is one of nature's few "air-conditioned cities"—relatively warm in winter and cool in summer. Weather Bureau statistics show sunshine in 66 out of every 100 possible hours. The average mean temperatures for San Francisco are 50°F in winter; 55°F in spring; 62°F in summer; and 60°F in fall.

Gateway to the Orient, San Francisco is a melting pot of cultures. Its population is descended from peoples of almost every nation of the world and every state of the Union. Leading national groups are Italian, German, Irish, Chinese, English, Russian, Latin American, Japanese, Korean, and Filipino. More than 500 churches, temples, and meetinghouses conduct services in 23 different tongues. Fifty periodicals are published in 13 languages.

San Francisco is an important financial center and headquarters of one of the largest banks in the world (Bank of America). Although no longer considered the air hub of the West (Los Angeles now holds that title), the city still plays a major role in the nation's air travel: San Francisco International Airport, a $250-million air gateway to the world, is located 14½ miles south off Bayshore Freeway and US 101. The San Francisco Bay Area ranks second on the West Coast in waterborne commerce. The Port of San Francisco is a $100-million public utility with a 7½-mile stretch of ship-berthing space, 229 acres of covered and open wharf area, and a total of 43 piers. More than 1,500 San Francisco firms engage in international trade.

Hellenic in its setting and climate, European in its intellectual and cultural scope, American in its vigor and informality, and Asian in its tranquility, San Francisco is indeed an exciting "Baghdad by the Bay." Author and raconteur Gene Fowler said, "Every man should be allowed to love two cities—his own and San Francisco."

San Francisco's lusty history began with early Portuguese, English, and Spanish explorers penetrating the Bay. In 1775 the Spanish ship *San Carlos* sailed through the Golden Gate to drop the first anchor off San Francisco. On March 28, 1776, a mission site was selected and dedicated to St. Francis of Assisi. The little village of Yerba Buena developed near the mission, but slumbered until 1836, when the port grew into an important trading post.

In 1846, the USS *Portsmouth* dropped anchor in the cove; Captain John B. Montgomery and 70 men came ashore and hoisted the Stars and Stripes, marking the end of Mexican rule. The next year, the village changed its name to San Francisco, taking its cue from the mission.

A year later, gold was discovered in Sutter's millrace on the American River at Coloma. This had tremendous impact on San Francisco; few of the inhabitants remained, and, as the news spread around the world, a torrent of people and ships descended on the city. A year later, 6,000 miners were digging and San Francisco was a wild tent city of 20,000 rough, tough transients. An average of 50 sailing ships a month anchored in San Francisco Bay; many were deserted by crews eager for gold.

A few farsighted men realized that fortunes could be made in San Francisco as well as in the gold camps. Their foresight is reflected today in many of the city's distinguished stores.

Meanwhile, thirsty for gold, the East was migrating to California. With the aid of imported Chinese labor, 2,000 miles of railroad track crossed the nation's two greatest mountain ranges to join East and West. Shipping to Asia flourished and small industries prospered.

Young and raw, San Francisco spent the last half of the 19th century as an exciting mix of growing metropolis, frontier, and boom town. Then, on April 18, 1906, came the great earthquake (8.6 on the Richter scale) and fire. Raging unchecked for three days, the fire wiped out the entire business area and burned out 497 blocks of buildings in the heart of the city. Losses amounted to some 2,500 lives and nearly $350 million. With the ashes still warm, the city started rebuilding; it was largely completed by 1915, when the city celebrated the opening of the Panama Canal with the Panama Pacific International Exposition.

The opening of the San Francisco-Oakland Bay Bridge in 1936, followed by the Golden Gate Bridge in 1937 and the completion of the Bay Area Rapid Transit System (BART) have tied the cities of the Bay Area together.

A significant historical event took place April 25-June 26, 1945, when

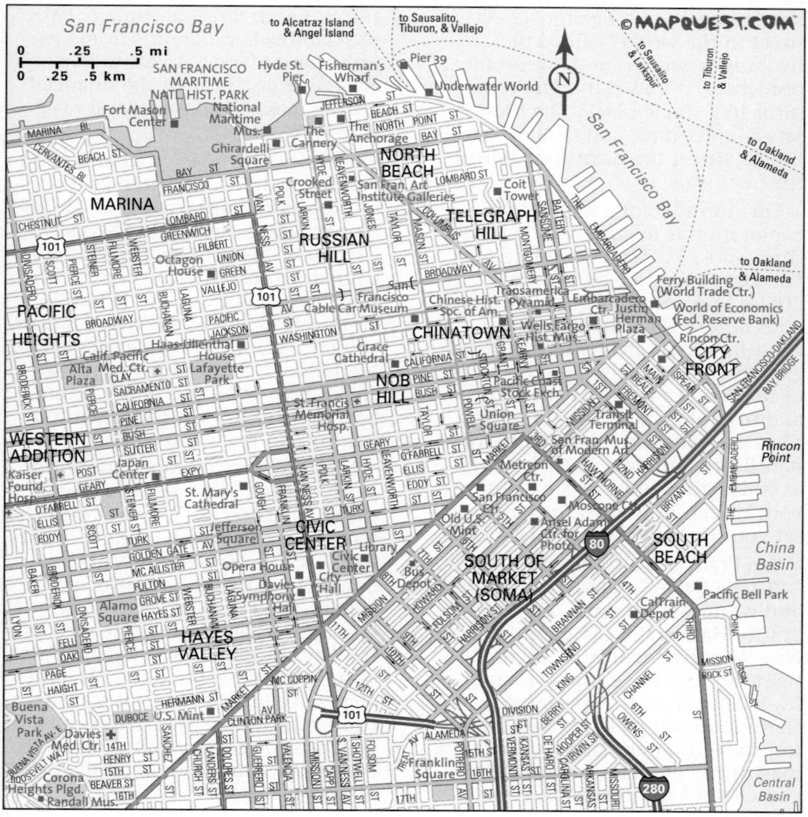

delegates from the nations of the world assembled here to found the United Nations. San Francisco became the birthplace of the UN—another facet of its cosmopolitan personality.

In sightseeing, dining, nightlife, shopping, and all other tourist adventures, San Francisco is rivaled—and perhaps not exceeded—only by New York City.

From the Twin Peaks area, the center of the city, Market Street bisects the eastern segment of San Francisco, ending at the Ferry Building and the Embarcadero. The business section, "the Wall Street of the West," is a cluster of skyscrapers extending from Kearny Street to the waterfront and south of Market Street from New Montgomery Street north to Jackson Street. Chinatown, Nob Hill, Telegraph Hill, and Fisherman's Wharf fan out north of Market Street. Russian Hill gives a panoramic view of San Francisco Bay. Here is Lombard Street, known as "the crookedest street in the world"—lined by hydrangea gardens and handsome residences, it makes nine hairpin turns in a single block. The Presidio, several museums, and Golden Gate Bridge are on the northwest side of the peninsula.

One formula for a systematic exploration is to start with a guided three-and-a-half-hour "around San Francisco" sightseeing bus tour. (These tours can be booked through your hotel.) Note the places you want to visit at greater length, then explore in detail. Use your own car or rent one to reach outlying areas and to explore across the bridges. The San Francisco hills are not for fainthearted drivers, but they're not as bad as they look. Be sure to turn your wheels in toward the curb and set your brake when parking.

San Francisco also has its scenic "49-Mile Drive," marked with blue and white seagull signs. This begins at City Hall in the Civic Center (Van Ness Ave and McAllister St), then twists around the entire city and leads to most of the spectacular sights. You can pick this up and follow its signs at any point or obtain a map of the drive from the San Francisco Visitor Information Center, lower level of Hallidie Plaza, Powell and Market Sts.

San Francisco's famous cable cars (designated a National Historic Landmark) were the brainchild of Andrew Hallidie. The inaugural run was made down Clay from Jones Street on August 2, 1873. The century-old cable car system was temporarily shut down in 1982 for renovations. The $60-million project was completed in June 1984.

These cable cars offer a thrilling roller-coaster experience (fare $2). The natives hop on and off with abandon, but visitors are advised to be more cautious. Also, avoid rush hours. There are three lines: Powell-Mason and Market Streets goes up Powell, over Nob Hill, along Columbus Avenue to Taylor and down to Bay Street at Fisherman's Wharf; the Powell-Hyde cable runs from Powell and Market Streets, up Powell to Jackson Street, west on Jackson to Hyde, north on Hyde over Russian Hill to Beach Street at Aquatic Park; the California cable runs from California and Market Streets to Van Ness Avenue, through the financial district, past Chinatown, and over Nob Hill.

The city's diverse restaurants number nearly 3,300. The gold of the mining camps attracted some of the finest chefs in the world to San Francisco and this heritage persists today. Chinatown features the exotic cuisine of Asia; Fisherman's Wharf is famous for seafood. Mexican, Italian, French, Armenian, Russian, Japanese, Vietnamese, East Indian, American are all here—you can make a culinary trip around the world without leaving San Francisco.

Nightlife in San Francisco is only partly carried on in the tradition of the "Barbary Coast" days. One of the most famous cocktail lounges in the world is "The Top of the Mark" (Mark Hopkins Inter-Continental Hotel). The Fairmont, across the street, offers an equally fine view of the city, as do several other high-rise hotels and office buildings. The theaters have long, successful seasons. In sports, the San Francisco Giants play in spring and summer and both college and professional football are played in the fall.

Additional Visitor Information

San Francisco Magazine, available at newsstands, has up-to-date information on cultural events and articles of interest to visitors.

The San Francisco Convention and Visitors Bureau, PO Box 429097, 94102-9097, phone 415/391-2000, handles written inquiries. Tourist guides may be obtained by mail (postage and handling fee) or at the San Francisco Visitor Information Center, Hallidie Plaza, Powell and Market Sts on lower plaza level. Phone 415/391-2001 for a daily recording of events.

Transportation

Airport. See SAN FRANCISCO AIRPORT AREA.

Car Rental Agencies. See IMPORTANT TOLL-FREE NUMBERS.

Public Transportation. In San Francisco—cable cars, streetcars, subway trains, buses (San Francisco Municipal Railway), phone 415/673-6864; from San Francisco across bay—ferries (Golden Gate Bus Transit), phone 415/923-2000; from San Francisco to Bay Area towns—buses (AC Transit), phone 510/839-2882.

Rail Passenger Service. Amtrak 800/872-7245.

Airport Information

San Francisco Airport Area. For additional accommodations, see SAN FRANCISCO AIRPORT AREA, which follows SAN FRANCISCO.

What to See and Do

Acres of Orchids (Rod McLellan Co). Largest orchid and gardenia nursery in the world; scientific laboratories show cloning. Guided tours (twice daily: mid-morning and early afternoon). Visitor center (daily; closed hols). 1450 El Camino Real (CA 82), in South San Francisco. Phone 415/362-1520. **FREE**

Angel Island State Park. A beautiful, woodsy park occupying San Francisco Bay's largest island, once known as the "Ellis Island of the West"; hiking and biking trails with panoramic views of the bay, plus historic sites and camping. Contact Box 866, Tiburon 94920. Island accessible only by ferry (or private boat) from San Francisco, Tiburon, or Vallejo. Phone 415/435-1915.

Cable Car Museum. Three antique cable cars, incl the world's first. Also features machinery that powers the cables. Underground viewing area, artifacts, mechanical explanation of operations, vintage photographs, 16-min film on cable car operation. Museum shop. (Daily; closed Jan 1, Thanksgiving, Dec 25) 1201 Mason St. Phone 415/474-1887. **FREE**

San Francisco cable car

California Academy of Sciences, Natural History Museum & Aquarium. Incl Morrison Planetarium (shows daily; closed Thanksgiving, Dec 24, 25); Steinhart Aquarium and the Fish Roundabout; African Safari Hall, Cowell Hall (main entrance), Wild California, Earth and Space Hall, Hall of Human Cultures, Gem and Mineral Hall, and "Life Through Time," a hall devoted to the evidence for evolution. Also Far Side of Science Gallery, featuring more than 160 cartoons by Gary Larson. Cafeteria. (Daily) Admission free first Wed of month. Golden Gate Park. Located on Music Concourse Dr. Phone 415/750-7145. **¢¢¢**

California Palace of the Legion of Honor. Dramatically designed art museum incl top-flight collection of

European paintings and sculpture. (Tues-Sun) Located in San Francisco's Lincoln Park; features a commanding view of the Golden Gate Bridge. 100 34th Ave (enter at 34th Ave and Clement St). Phone 415/863-3330.

Cartoon Art Museum. One of three museums in the US dedicated to preserving cartoon art. Museum displays a wide range of cartoon art dating back to the 18th century. Incl original William Hogarth drawing from 1730, as well as original *Peanuts* and *Calvin and Hobbes* strips. 814 Mission St. Phone 415/227-8666. **¢¢**

Civic Center. Eleven-sq-blk cluster of buildings bounded by Franklin, 7th, Golden Gate, and Hayes Sts. Incl

Bill Graham Civic Auditorium. Seats 7,000. Opp is Phone 415/974-4060.

Brooks Hall. Under Civic Center Plaza; connected to Civic Auditorium by ramp and escalators; 90,000 sq ft of exhibit space. Phone 415/974-4060.

City Hall. Classic building with dome more than 13 ft taller than that of the Capitol in Washington, DC. Phone 415/554-4000.

The Federal and State Buildings. Also part of the Civic Center group.

Louise M. Davies Symphony Hall. This $30-million concert hall opened in 1980; capacity of 2,743.

Chinatown and North Beach

This tour covers two of the most walkable neighborhoods in San Francisco, Chinatown and North Beach—places where it's much easier to enjoy the sights if you're on foot. Begin at the Chinatown gate—topped with dragons—at Bush Street and Grant Avenue, where you'll wind past Chinatown's exotic herb and tea shops, Buddhist temples, neon-lit cafes, colorful produce markets, and dim sum restaurants. Walk north for four blocks past the curio shops along commercially oriented Grant Avenue, the gaudiest (and least authentic) stretch of Chinatown. At Clay Street, go left and walk a short block to Waverly Place, then turn right on Waverly. The Tin How Temple, located at 125 Waverly, is the oldest Buddhist temple in the country; climb to the third floor to smell the incense and see the lanterns and carved deities. At the end of Waverly Place, cross Washington Street and jog left into narrow Ross Alley, where the tiny Golden Gate Fortune Cookie Factory (number 56) sits near the end of the block. You can watch fortune cookies being made, then choose between regular fortunes and X-rated ones. Turn left on Jackson Street until you reach Stockton Street, then go right. You'll pass a series of colorful markets stocked with exotic produce and fresh fish. Walk north on Stockton to Broadway, which forms a rough boundary between Chinatown and North Beach, the Italian-flavored district known for its many cafes, bakeries, family-style restaurants, and night spots. Walk east on Broadway to Columbus Avenue, North Beach's main thoroughfare. Go right on Columbus to City Lights Books (261 Columbus), San Francisco's most famous bookstore. Founded by poet Lawrence Ferlinghetti, City Lights was a leading center of Beat life in the 1950s, nurturing authors such as Jack Kerouac and Allen Ginsberg. Just down the block (255 Columbus) is Vesuvio, an atmospheric cafe of the Beat era. Now turn around and walk back up Columbus, heading northwest, where you'll pass many of the area's best-known cafes and restaurants. Mario's Bohemian Cigar Store, a tiny cafe and bar at the corner of Columbus and Union Street, offers a pleasant stop for lunch or cappuccino. Across the street is Washington Square, North Beach's main plaza, where green grasses attract sunbathers, Frisbee tossers, and art shows. On the north side of the square (666 Filbert Street) is the twin-spired Italianate Sts. Peter and Paul Church, one of the area's foremost landmarks. The square is lined with restaurants, bakeries, and cafes. Those looking for further exercise can climb Telegraph Hill for great views from Coit Tower (you can follow the path from Greenwich Street off Grant Avenue, one block north of Filbert). After riding the elevator to the top of the tower, walk down the other side of Telegraph Hill, via the Filbert or Greenwich stairways that descend steeply through hidden gardens and offer stunning views of the bay. The steps will bring you to the Embarcadero, where streetcars run north toward Fisherman's Wharf or south toward the Ferry Building.

(See SPECIAL EVENTS) Van Ness Ave and Grove St. Phone 415/864-6000.

Performing Arts Center. Second-largest performing arts center in US, with a total seating capacity of 7,233. Van Ness Ave and Grove St.

San Francisco Public Library. In Apr 1996, the library opened its expanded seven-story facility across the street from its previous location. Special Collections Department features rare books and many volumes on California and San Francisco (tours daily). (Daily; closed hols) 100 Larkin St between Grove and Fulton Sts, housed in the Civic Center. Phone 415/557-4400.

War Memorial/Opera House. Opened in 1932, it was here that the UN was established in 1945 and the Japanese Peace Treaty Conference was held in 1951. First civic-owned opera house in the country. (See SPECIAL EVENTS) Van Ness Ave and Grove St. Phone 415/864-3330.

Cow Palace. World famous exhibit center and arena, seating 14,700. Used for sports events, exhibits, and concerts. (See SPECIAL EVENTS) Geneva Ave, 1 mi W off Bayshore Blvd.

Exploratorium. Hands-on museum dedicated to providing insights into scientific and natural phenomena. More than 700 participatory exhibits on science, art, and human perception. Changing exhibits. (Memorial Day-Labor Day, daily; rest of yr, Tues-Sun; closed Thanksgiving, Dec 25) Free admission first Wed of month. Web www.exploratorium.edu. 3601 Lyon St, housed in the Palace of Fine Arts. ¢¢¢

Ferry Building. Ferries to Sausalito and Larkspur leave from Ferry Plaza end of building (Pier ½); ferries to Oakland, Alameda, Vallejo, and Tiburon leave from terminal at N end. Also here is a waterfront promenade. Embarcadero at the foot of Market St. Ferries ¢¢

Fort Mason Center. Multicultural complex for all ages located in what was once the Army's western headquarters and port of embarkation. Incl four theaters and a gourmet vegetarian restaurant. A National Historic Landmark, Fort Mason Center boasts spectacular views of the Golden Gate Bridge and the hills of Marin. Laguna St and Marina Blvd. Phone 415/441-3400.

☆ The Golden Gate Bridge. Connecting San Francisco with Marin County. One of famous sights of the world, conceded to be the most beautiful bridge on the globe because of its setting and design. Auto toll collected southbound only. Phone 415/921-5858.

☆ Golden Gate National Recreation Area. Within the 74,000 acres of the recreation area are most of the shoreline of San Francisco, the countryside extending 20 mi N in Marin County and a 1,047-acre parcel in San Mateo County to the south. The Golden Gate Bridge connects the two segments of the park. The most popular visitor areas are the former penitentiary on Alcatraz Island, the historic Cliff House, Fort Point National Historic Site, Muir Woods National Monument (see), and the cultural-entertainment center, Fort Mason Center. The area has 28 mi of shoreline with many beaches, lagoons, rugged headlands, meadows, fortifications, valleys, hillsides, picnic facilities, and 100 mi of trails within the area Congress designated in 1972 as one of the first urban national parks. (Hrs vary, but most areas are always open during the day.) Contact Golden Gate National Recreation Area, Fort Mason, Building 201, San Francisco 94123. Phone 415/556-0560. Some of the park areas incl

Alcatraz Island. Once a famous maximum security federal penitentiary, closed in 1963. Former inmates incl Al Capone, "Machine Gun" Kelly, public enemy #1 Al Karpis, and Robert Stroud, the "Birdman of Alcatraz." Boats leave Pier 41 near Fisherman's Wharf every ½-hr (all yr; advance ticket purchase recommended). Tours incl long uphill walk. Self-guided tour; slide show; taped audio tour (fee). In San Francisco Bay, 1¼ mi from shore. Phone 415/705-5555. Ferry ¢¢¢¢

Baker Beach. Sandy beach on the western shore of the Presidio. Phone 415/556-0560. **FREE**

China Beach. Wind-protected cove with swimming beach. **FREE**

Fort Mason. Old Army Post, once the Army's western headquarters, is now headquarters for the Golden Gate National Recreation Area. Jogging, bicycling, and exercise courses. Fort Mason Center, Building C.

Fort Point National Historic Site. This restored Civil War-era fort houses an exhibit explaining story of the fort; also a museum with military artifacts. Guided tours. (Daily; closed Jan 1, Thanksgiving, Dec 25) Long Ave and Marine Dr, under southern end of Golden Gate Bridge in the Presidio. Phone 293/339-4129.

Golden Gate Promenade. Bay shoreline between Fort Point and Fort Mason provides an area to walk, run, and observe; also off-leash dog walking permitted.

Mount Tamalpais State Park. (See MILL VALLEY) (Daily) Some day-use parking fees. 4 mi N via CA 1, then right turn on Panoramic Hwy, 5 mi to park headquarters. Phone 415/388-2070.

Muir Beach. Protected cove in the ocean coastline, picnicking. (Daily) Marin County. Phone 415/331-1540. **FREE**

Ocean Beach. 3½ mi of beach on San Francisco's Pacific shore. **FREE**

Seal Rocks & Cliff House. Restaurants at the Cliff House (1909) overlook the ocean, the Marin Coast to the north, and the Seal Rocks habitat of sea lions. Visitor information center (limited hrs). Phone 415/386-3330. **FREE**

Stinson Beach. North to Bolinas. (Daily) In Marin County, off Hwy 1. Phone 415/868-0942. **FREE**

Tennessee Valley and Beach and Bonita Cove. Secluded, protected beach on ocean. Approx 1½-mi walk from parking. (Daily) Marin County. Phone 415/331-1540.

Golden Gate Park. Once a 1,017-acre sand waste, from 1887 the area was developed by John McLaren, master botanist and landscaper, into one of the most beautiful parks in the world. Park contains more than 10,000 trees and shrubs, a restored Dutch windmill, statues and monuments, 11 gardens, two waterfalls, 11 lakes, and 40 picnic areas. Also, McLaren Rhododendron Dell (free), a conservatory on Kennedy Dr near Arguello Blvd (daily; fee), a Music Concourse near Fulton St and 8th Ave entrance (band concerts: Sun, hols, weather permitting), the Strybing Arboretum and Botanical Garden, King Dr and 9th Ave (daily, free). Fee for some activities. Bounded by Lincoln Way, Stanyan and Fulton Sts, and Great Hwy. Phone 415/831-2700. Other park attractions incl

Buffalo paddock. A ten-acre enclosure with bison.

Japanese Tea Garden. Oriental landscaping; incl a teahouse, gift shop, pagoda, Buddha, several ponds, streams, footbridges. In spring, cherry blossoms, azaleas, and flowering shrubs are in bloom. (Daily) Phone 415/668-0909. **¢¢**

Mary Connolly Children's Playground. Innovative play equipment, Herschel Spillman Carrousel (1912-1914) (fee); picnic area. Near King Dr and 3rd Ave.

Prayerbook Cross. (1894) Commemorates first prayer service in English language held on Pacific Coast, conducted by Sir Francis Drake's chaplain. Kennedy Dr.

Sports. Nine-hole golf course (fee), three lawn bowling greens, 21 tennis courts (fee), three fly and plug casting pools, two indoor and two outdoor handball courts; archery field; horseshoe courts; trotting track, bicycle track, running trails, baseball diamonds (fee). 47th Ave off Fulton St. Phone 415/751-8987.

Spreckels Lake. Used primarily for sailing model boats. Kennedy Dr and 36th Ave. Phone 415/556-0560.

Stow Lake. Surrounds Strawberry Hill. View of park and city. One-hr boat rentals (fee): electric motorboat, rowboat, pedal boat. Stow Lake Dr off Kennedy Dr, near 16th Ave.

Haas-Lilienthal House. (1886) Queen Anne-style Victorian house. One-hr guided tour (Wed, Sun). 2007 Franklin St, between Washington and Jackson Sts. Phone 415/441-3004. **¢¢**

Haight-Ashbury. Intersection made famous by the "Flower Power/Summer of Love" days in the late 1960s; actually the name of the entire district just east of Golden Gate Park.

Offers many second-hand clothing stores and shops specializing in retro fashions and items. Haight and Ashbury Sts; district runs from Stanyan St to about Lyon St, and from Oak St up to Ashbury Heights.

Japan Center. The focal point of an expanding Japantown, this three-sq-blk complex houses Japanese restaurants, baths, bookstores, shops; movie complex, art galleries, and hotel. Peace Pagoda has five-tiered roof. Peace Plaza, paved in slate, has Japanese gardens, reflecting pools, and is the site of traditional Japanese entertainment during spring and summer festivals. (Daily; most businesses closed Jan 1-3, Thanksgiving, Dec 25) On Post St, between Fillmore, Geary, and Laguna Sts, 1 mi W of Union Square. Phone 415/922-6776.

Lombard Street. The "Crookedest Street in the World" curves several times while snaking its way down one steep blk from Russian Hill. 1000 blk of Lombard St between Hyde and Leavenworth Sts.

Marina Green. An eight-blk-long stretch of greenery running from Fort Mason past the Marina Small Craft Harbor. Offers views of the Bay, Alcatraz, the Golden Gate Bridge. Also kite flying, skating, jogging, volleyball. Marina Blvd between Baker and Buchanan Sts. Phone 415/831-2700. **FREE**

Metreon. A futuristic Sony Entertainment Complex. Incl 15 movie screens, IMAX theater, shops, restaurants, and family attractions. Mission and 4th Sts. Phone 800/638-7366. **FREE**

The Mexican Museum. Pre-Hispanic, Colonial, Folk, contemporary Mexican, and Mexican-American art. Permanent and changing exhibits. Gift shop. (Wed-Sun, afternoons; closed hols and late Dec) Free admission first Wed of month. Fort Mason Center, Building D, Laguna St and Marina Blvd. Phone 415/202-9700.

Mission District Murals. Hundreds of murals painted on walls around the Mission District. Self-guided tours (daily); guided tours (wkends). Balmy Alley in the Mission District, and nearby area. Phone 415/285-2287. ¢¢¢

Mission Dolores. (1776) Fountainhead from which the city grew. Mission San Francisco de Asís was sixth in a chain of missions established by Franciscan fathers under the direction of Junipero Serra. (It is now known as Mission Dolores, the name being taken from nearby Laguna de Nuestra Señora de los Dolores.) Cornerstone of present mission building was laid in 1782. Many pioneers are buried in ancient cemetery beside the church. (Daily; closed Thanksgiving, Dec 25) 16th and Dolores Sts. Phone 415/621-8203. ¢

M.H. deYoung Memorial Museum. Features 17th- to 20th-century American art. Paintings from collection of John D. Rockefeller III; British art; tribal rugs from Central Asia; African, Oceanic and ancient art. Cafe. (Tues-Sun) Free admission first Wed of month. Golden Gate Park. Phone 415/863-3330. ¢¢¢ In the west wing is the

Asian Art Museum. The Avery Brundage Collection; art from China, India, Japan, Korea, and southeast, central, and western Asia; traveling exhibitions; displays rotate often. (Tues-Sun) Free admission first Wed of month. Web www.asianart.org. Phone 415/379-8801. ¢¢¢

Museo ItaloAmericano. Dedicated to researching, collecting, and displaying the works of Italian and Italian-American artists. Promotes educational programs for the appreciation of Italian art and culture. Gift shop. (Wed-Sun, afternoons; closed hols) Free admission first Wed of month. Phone 415/673-2220. ¢¢

Museum of Craft & Folk Art. Promotes the understanding and appreciation of human expression, ranging from utilitarian objects to contemporary art, through innovative exhibits of craft and folk art from cultures past and present. Gift shop. (Tues-Sun, closed hols) Free admission first Wed of month. Fort Mason Center, Building A. Phone 415/775-0990. ¢¢

Palace of Fine Arts. Monumental Greco-Romanesque rotunda with Corinthian colonnades; built for the 1915 Panama-Pacific International Exposition; has been restored. Surrounded by duck lagoon and park. Houses Exploratorium. 3301 Lyon St. Grounds **FREE**

Professional sports.

San Francisco 49ers (NFL). 3COM Park, at Candlestick Point. Phone 408/562-4949.

San Francisco Giants (MLB). Pacific Bell Park at China Basin. Phone 415/972-2000.

Randall Museum. Incl live animal rm (Tues-Sat, limited hrs). 199 Museum Way, between Roosevelt Way, 14th and 17th Sts. Phone 415/554-9600. **FREE**

Ripley's Believe It or Not Museum. Oddities collected from US and abroad; video displays; walk-through kaleidoscope. (Daily) 175 Jefferson St, at Taylor St and Fisherman's Wharf. Phone 415/771-6188. ¢¢¢

San Francisco African American Historical & Cultural Society. Dedicated to providing accurate accounts of the culture and history of African Americans through permanent and changing exhibitions featuring African and African American culture, arts, and crafts. Gift shop. (Wed-Sun afternoons; closed hols) Free admission first Wed of month. Fort Mason Center, Building C. Phone 415/441-0640. ¢

San Francisco Maritime National Historical Park. Adj to Fort Mason, at the N end of Fisherman's Wharf. Phone 415/556-3002. Incl

Aquatic Park. Cove contains a swimming beach and municipal pier for fishing. Here are most of the historic ships. Phone 415/556-3002.

Hyde Street Pier Historic Ships. Collection of five historic merchant ships, incl SV *Balclutha,* a sailing ship built in 1886 and restored as a Cape Horn trader. (Daily; closed federal hols) Foot of Hyde St. Phone 415/556-3002. ¢¢

National Maritime Museum. Collection of ship models, relics, and gear; figureheads, scrimshaw, photographs of historic Pacific Coast vessels and early San Francisco. (Daily; closed federal hols) Foot of Polk St. Phone 415/556-3002. **FREE**

San Francisco Museum of Modern Art. 20th-century art on permanent exhibit, also traveling exhibitions; concerts, lectures, special events. Gift shop, cafe. (Mon, Tues, Thurs-Sun; closed hols) Free admission first Tues of month. 151 Third St. Phone 415/357-4000. ¢¢¢

San Francisco Museum of Modern Art Rental Gallery. Exhibition program of 11 shows each yr that feature the works of California artists. The work of more than 1,300 Northern California artists also is avail for rental and sale. (Tues-Sat, afternoons) Phone 415/441-4777.

San Francisco-Oakland Bay Bridge. Stretches 8½ mi to the East Bay cities. Double-decked, with five lanes on each; the upper deck is one-way westbound, the lower deck one-way eastbound. Tunnels through Yerba Buena Island in midbay. Auto toll collected westbound only.

San Francisco Zoo. Zoo with over 1,000 animals, incl unique Primate Discovery Center with 14 species of rare and exotic monkeys. Also here, Prince Charles, a rare white tiger; African wild dogs; Koala Crossing, Gorilla World, African Scene, and Insect Zoo. Children's Zoo with barnyard and nursery (fee); 25-min train tour on the Zebra Zephyr; carousel. Nature trail in summer. Zoo (daily). Fee for activities. Sloat Blvd at 45th Ave. Phone 415/753-7080. ¢¢¢

Sightseeing tours.

CCInc Auto Tape Tours. These 90-min cassettes offer mi-by-mi self-guided tours to Monterey (139 mi) along Skyline Blvd, atop Santa Cruz Mtns, to Henry Cowell Redwoods, Monterey's Fisherman's Wharf, and Cannery; to Sacramento (166 mi) with a visit to Sausalito, Muir Woods, wineries in the Napa Valley, the historic state capital; to the Wine Country (160 mi) through Sausalito, Muir Woods, a winery tour, dramatic re-creation of the great San Francisco earthquake. Fourteen different tour tapes of California are avail. Tapes may be purchased directly from CCInc. Phone 201/236-1666. ¢¢¢¢

Gray Line bus tours. Contact 350 8th St, 94103. Phone 415/558-9400.

San Francisco Bay cruises. Red & White Fleet. Bay cruises. (Daily) Fisherman's Wharf, at Pier 43½. Phone 877/855-5506. **Blue & Gold Fleet.** Offers 1¼-hr cruise. (Daily) Adj to Fisherman's Wharf. Pier 41. Phone 415/705-5555. **Hornblower Dining Yachts.** Luxury dining yachts cruise San Francisco Bay. Flagship is the *California Horn-*

blower, a 183-ft, 1,000-passenger vessel with three decks. Luncheon. dinner/dance, wkend champagne brunch, and special event cruises avail. Res required. Pier 33 , along the Embarcadero. Phone 415/788-8866, ext 6, or 800/ON-THE-BAY. Phone 415/447-0597. ¢¢¢¢¢

Special areas.

The Cannery. Complex of shops, restaurants, and markets housed in old fruit-processing factory; informal entertainment on the mall. 2801 Leavenworth St, at Beach St.

Chinatown, San Francisco

Chinatown. A "little Cathay" with more than 80,000 people. Largest community of its kind outside Asia. Grant Ave, its main thoroughfare, has been called the "Street of 25,000 Lanterns." Points of interest incl **St. Mary's Square,** Bufano's stainless steel statue of Sun Yat-sen, founder of Republic of China. Nearby is Old St. Mary's Church (1853). Also see the **Chinese Culture Center.** Art exhibitions, Chinese cultural performances, gift shop; docent-guided walks through the Chinese community. Gallery (Tues-Sat; closed hols). Chinese Heritage Walk (Tues-Fri; fee). Also Culinary/Luncheon Walk (Wed; fee). 750 Kearny St, third floor. Phone 415/986-1822. **FREE**

Cow Hollow. Originally the location of a milk-producing area populated mostly by cows, this has been developed into an area of specialty shops, art galleries, and bookshops. Many shops are in restored Victorian houses. Numerous restaurants in area. Union St between Van Ness Ave and Lyon St.

The Embarcadero. Wide thoroughfare paralleling waterfront behind the docks from China Basin to Fisherman's Wharf, about 3½ mi. Between Montgomery St and the Ferry Building is the new Embarcadero Center. On the Embarcadero at the foot of Market St is the Ferry Building. Phone 415/352-0810.

☆ **Fisherman's Wharf.** Center of multimillion-dollar commercial fishing industry and location of many seafood restaurants. Foot of Taylor St. Phone 415/705-5500.

Ghirardelli Square. Charming shopping-restaurant complex with live theater on site of Ghirardelli Chocolate factory. Informal entertainment; arts and crafts, women's and children's fashions, sports clothes, ski equipment, and many other interesting stores and buildings. North Point, Beach, and Larkin Sts, W of Fisherman's Wharf. Phone 415/775-5500.

Jackson Square. Historic District; many buildings date back to the mid-1800s. Incl One Jackson Pl (formerly a paper warehouse)—a compound of shops, showrooms, and gaslit courtyards. Washington, Jackson, and Pacific Sts from Montgomery to Battery St.

Market Street. San Francisco's best-known street, lined with business establishments and center for municipal transportation. Runs from Ferry Building to base of Twin Peaks.

Montgomery Street. Called the "Wall Street of the West," it's the West's financial hub. Tall buildings form a canyon beginning at Market St and extending to within a blk of the Embarcadero.

Nob Hill. Home to Grace Cathedral (replica of Notre Dame in Paris) and Huntington Park (site of many art shows, also features replica of a 16th-century Roman fountain). A 376-ft crest at Sacramento and Jones Sts.

Pier 39, San Francisco

Pier 39. Approx 110 specialty shops, ten restaurants, bay cruises, motorized cable car, city tours, free entertainment, waterfront park, 350-berth marina. Re-creates early San Francisco Barbary Coast. Shops (daily); restaurants (daily). On Embarcadero two blks E of Fisherman's Wharf. Phone 415/981-7437.

The Presidio. Wooded tract of 1,450 acres, fortified since 1776 and now a national park. The present Officer's Club contains sections of the first building to be erected in San Francisco. Markers indicate points of historical interest; hiking. 102 Montgomery St. Phone 415/561-4323. **FREE**

Sigmund Stern Memorial Grove. Natural amphitheater enclosed by eucalyptus trees. Free outdoor concerts in summer (see SPECIAL EVENTS). Picnic tables and barbecue pits nearby. Sloat Blvd and 19th Ave.

Telegraph Hill. (284 ft). Topped by 210-ft Coit Memorial Tower, monument to Volunteer Firefighters of 1850s and 1860s. Murals decorating first and second floors can also be seen from the outside. Elevator to top. (Daily; closed Thanksgiving, Dec 25) The hill itself is occupied by artists' studios and expensive homes. Lombard above Kearny St. **FREE**

Union Square. Public park above four-story subsurface parking garage, first of its kind in the nation. Square is in midst of city's fashionable downtown shopping center. Stores (daily). Bounded by Geary, Powell, Post, and Stockton Sts.

S.S. *Jeremiah O'Brien*. The last surviving intact Liberty ship. At Pier 45. Phone 415/441-3101.

Twin Peaks. The thrilling experience it provides comes not only from the breathtaking panorama, but also from the breezes that whip the hilltops. The north peak is 903 ft, the south peak 910 ft. Many apartment buildings and homes dot the hillsides. Near center of city. Phone 415/391-2000.

Washington Square. Plaza in the heart of North Beach, San Francisco's Italian district and one of its restaurant/nightlife capitals. Surrounded by cafes, restaurants, bakeries, and Italian businesses. Popular spot for sunbathing and art shows. Sts. Peter and Paul church borders one end of the square. Close to Telegraph Hill.

Wax Museum at Fisherman's Wharf. New 100,000-sq-ft museum (replacing the old museum, torn down in 1998) contains wax reproductions of celebrities and famous artistic masterpieces. (Daily) 145 Jefferson St. Phone 415/885-4834. **¢¢¢¢**

Wells Fargo Bank History Museum. Artifacts and displays dating from the Gold Rush to the 1906 earthquake to present-day banking; Concord Stagecoach. (Mon-Fri; closed hols) 420 Montgomery St. Phone 415/396-2619. **FREE**

Yerba Buena Gardens. Parklike complex contains museums, gardens, cafes, the Martin Luther King, Jr., Memorial Fountain, and the Rooftop at Yerba Buena Gardens, a children's center with ice rink, carousel, and high-tech arts studio (Zeum). (Daily) Bounded by Mission, 3rd, 4th, and Folsom Sts. Phone 415/777-2800.

Special Events

Chinese New Year. Largest and most colorful celebration of this occasion held in US. Wk-long activities incl Golden Dragon Parade, lion dancing, carnival, cultural exhibits. Contact Chinese Chamber of Commerce, 730 Sacramento St, 94108. Late Jan-mid-Feb. Chinatown. Phone 415/982-3000.

San Francisco Ballet. War Memorial/Opera House, on corner of Van Ness Ave and Grove St. Phone 425/865-2000. Repertory season early Feb-early May; *Nutcracker,* Dec. Phone 415/865-2000.

Cherry Blossom Festival. Japanese music, dancing, flower arranging, doll and sword exhibits, bonsai show, martial arts, calligraphy, origami, Akita dog exhibit, tea ceremony, children's village, arts and crafts, films, food bazaar, parade. Two wkends Apr. Japan Center. Phone 415/563-2313.

Carnaval. Memorial Day wkend. Mission District. Phone 415/826-1401.

Stern Grove Midsummer Music Festival. Sun afternoons. Mid-June-late Aug. Sigmund Stern Memorial Grove, 19th Ave and Sloat Blvd. Phone 415/252-6252.

Pop concerts. Check newspapers for schedule. July. Bill Graham Civic Auditorium, Grove St at Larkin St. Phone 415/974-4000.

Ala Carte, Ala Park. Sharon Meadow, Golden Gate Park. About 50 local restaurants sell samples of their cooking. Phone 415/383-9378. Labor Day wkend.

San Francisco Opera. Some summer presentations and 14 wks beginning early Sept. War Memorial/Opera House, corner of Van Ness Ave and Grove St. Phone 941/024-1586.

San Francisco Symphony Orchestra. Obtain tickets in lobby and at major ticket agencies. Also special events. Sept-July. Louise M. Davies Symphony Hall, Van Ness Ave and Grove St Phone 415/864-6000.

Grand National Rodeo, Horse & Stock Show. Cow Palace, on Geneva Ave at Old Bay Shore. Phone 415/469-6065. Late Oct-early Nov.

Bay to Breakers Footrace. From south of Market St through Golden Gate Park to Ocean Beach. Some 100,000 people run, walk, jog, or ride in strollers from San Francisco Bay to Ocean Beach, about 7 ½ mi. Many participants run in colorful costumes; some, in just their birthday suits. Sun morning mid-May. Phone 415/777-7773 or 415/808-5000.

Motels/Motor Lodges

★★ **BEST WESTERN.** *364 9th St (94103). 415/621-2826; fax 415/621-0833; toll-free 800/528-1234.* 57 rms, 2 story. No A/C. May-Oct: S, D $99-$109; each addl $10; under 18 free; lower rates rest of yr. Crib free. TV; cable. Heated pool. Complimentary coffee in rms. Restaurant 7 am-2 pm. Ck-out noon. Coin lndry. Business servs avail. In-rm modem link. Refrigerators; microwaves avail. Cr cds: A, C, D, DS, ER, JCB, MC, V.
SC

★★ **BEST WESTERN AMERICANIA.** *121 7th St (94103). 415/626-0200; fax 415/863-2529; res 800/444-5816. www.renesonhotels.com.* 143 rms, 4 story, 17 suites. No A/C. Apr-Oct: S, D $115-$166; each addl $10; suites $159-$229; under 17 free; lower rates rest of yr. Crib free. TV; cable (premium). Heated pool. Coffee in rms. Restaurant 6:30 am-10 pm. Bar 11 am-midnight. Ck-out noon. Coin lndry. Meeting rms. Business servs avail. In-rm modem link. Valet serv. Exercise equipt; sauna. Some refrigerators; microwaves avail. Cr cds: A, C, D, DS, ER, JCB, MC, V.

★★ **BEST WESTERN CANTERBURY HOTEL.** *750 Sutter St (94109). 415/474-6464; fax 415/474-5856; res 800/528-1234. www.canterbury-hotel.com.* 250 rms in 2 buildings, 4 and 10 story. S $125-$155; D $135-$170; each addl $15; suites $200-$250; under 4 free; wkend, honeymoon plans. Valet parking $22. TV; cable (premium). Pool privileges. Restaurant (see also MURPHY'S). Bar. Ck-out noon. Meeting rms. Business servs avail. In-rm modem link. Gift shop. Health club privileges. Cr cds: A, D, DS, JCB, MC, V.
D SC

★★ **BEST WESTERN MIYAKO INN.** *1800 Sutter St (94115). 415/921-4000; fax 415/923-1064; res 800/528-1234.* 125 rms, 8 story. S $99-$119; D $109-$129; each addl $10; suites $175-$275; under 18 free. Crib free. TV; cable. Garage parking $10. Restaurant 7 am-10 pm. Bar to midnight.

Ck-out noon. Business servs avail. Bellhops. Valet serv. Gift shop. Health club privileges. Balconies. Cr cds: A, C, D, DS, ER, JCB, MC, V.

D

★★ **BEST WESTERN TUSCAN INN.** *425 Northpoint St (94133). 415/561-1100; fax 415/561-1199; toll-free 800/648-4626. www.tuscaninn.com.* 221 rms, 12 suites, 4 story. S, D $188-$218; each addl $10; suites $238-$258; under 16 free; package plans. Crib free. Garage $17/day. TV; cable, VCR avail. Complimentary coffee. Restaurant 7 am-10 pm. Bar. Ck-out 11 am. Meeting rms. Business servs avail. Concierge. Health club privileges. Minibars. European-style boutique hotel following the tradition of a classic inn. 3 blks from Pier 39. Cr cds: A, C, D, DS, JCB, MC, V.

D SC

★★ **BUENA VISTA MOTOR INN.** *1599 Lombard St (94123). 415/923-9600; fax 415/441-4775; toll-free 800/835-4980.* 50 rms, 3 story. Mid-Apr-mid-Oct: S, D $119; under 12 free; suite $175; lower rates rest of yr. Crib free. TV. Complimentary coffee in rms. Ck-out noon. Business servs avail. Cr cds: A, C, D, DS, MC, V.

D

★★ **CHELSEA MOTOR INN.** *2095 Lombard St (94123). 415/563-5600; fax 415/567-6475.* 60 rms, 3 story, no ground floor rms. S $82-$94; D $86-$98; each addl $10; under 5 free. Crib free. TV; cable. Complimentary coffee in rms. Restaurant nearby. Ck-out noon. Free covered parking. Health club privileges. Cr cds: A, D, MC, V.

D

★★ **CLARION HOTEL.** *761 Post St (94109). 415/673-6040; fax 415/563-6739; res 800/252-7466. www.hotelbedford.com.* 144 rms, 17 story. No A/C. S, D $149-$189; each addl $10; 2-bedrm family unit $179; under 18 free. Crib free. Valet parking $18. TV; cable. Coffee in rms. Restaurant 6 am-midnight. Bar. Ck-out noon. Meeting rms. Business servs avail. In-rm modem link. Refrigerators, minibars. Cr cds: A, C, D, DS, JCB, V.

SC

★ **COLUMBUS MOTOR INN.** *1075 Columbus Ave (94133). 415/885-1492; fax 415/928-2174.* 45 rms, 5 story. Mid-May-mid-Oct: S, D $110-$130; each addl $10; suites $155; lower rates rest of yr. Crib free. TV; cable. Complimentary coffee in rms. Restaurant nearby. Ck-out noon. Business servs avail. Free covered parking. Cr cds: A, MC, V.

D

★★ **COMFORT INN.** *2775 Van Ness Ave (94109). 415/928-5000; fax 415/441-3990; res 800/228-5150.* 138 rms, 11 story. Mid-June-Oct: S $99-$139; D $109-$149; each addl $10; under 19 free; lower rates rest of yr. Crib free. Garage parking in/out $15. TV; cable. Complimentary continental bkfst. Ck-out noon. Business servs avail. In-rm modem link. Microwaves avail. Cr cds: A, D, DS, JCB, MC, V.

D

★★ **COMFORT INN AND SUITES.** *121 E Grand Ave (94080). 650/589-7100; fax 650/589-7766.* 169 suites, 3 story. S $129; D $139; each addl $10; under 18 free. TV; cable (premium). Complimentary continental bkfst. Coffee in rms. Ck-out noon. Business servs avail. In-rm modem link. Valet serv. Free airport, RR station transportation. Whirlpool. Health club privileges. Refrigerators, microwaves. Grill. Cr cds: A, C, D, DS, JCB, MC, V.

D SC

★ **COVENTRY MOTOR INN.** *1901 Lombard St (94123). 415/567-1200; fax 415/921-8745.* 69 rms, 3 story. S $84-$96; D $88-$116; each addl $10; under 6 free. Crib free. TV; cable. Complimentary coffee in rms. Restaurant nearby. Ck-out noon. Business servs avail. Free covered parking. Cr cds: A, D, MC, V.

D

★ **COW HOLLOW MOTOR INN AND SUITES.** *2190 Lombard St (94123). 415/921-5800; fax 415/922-8515; res 415/921-5800.* 117 rms, 2-4 story, 12 suites. Mid-May-mid-Oct: S $82-$102; D $86; each addl $10; suites $185-$265; under 5 free; lower rates rest of yr. Crib free. TV; cable. Coffee in rms. Restaurant adj 7 am-2:30 pm. Ck-out noon. Business servs avail. Free covered parking. Health club privileges. Cr cds: A, D, MC, V.

D

★★ **DAYS INN.** *2600 Sloat Blvd (94116). 415/665-9000; fax 415/665-5440; res 800/329-7466.* 33 rms, 2 story. July-mid-Sept: S $70-$90; D $85-$95; suites $95-$130; under 12 free; lower rates rest of yr. Crib free. TV; cable. Complimentary continental bkfst. Restaurant nearby. Ck-out 11 am. Business servs avail. Refrigerators, microwaves. Cr cds: A, C, D, DS, MC, V.

D

★ **FRANCISCO BAY MOTEL.** *1501 Lombard St (94123).* 415/474-3030; *fax 415/474-3030; res 800/410-7007. www.citysearch.com/sfo/franciscobay.* 39 rms, 4 story. Mid-May-mid-Sept: S $75-$125; D $85-$135; each addl $10; lower rates rest of yr. TV; cable, VCR avail. Complimentary continental bkfst, coffee in rms. Restaurant nearby. Ck-out 11 am. Some refrigerators. Cr cds: A, C, D, DS, ER, JCB, MC, V.

D SC

★★ **HOLIDAY INN.** *1300 Columbus Ave (94133). 415/771-9000; fax 415/771-7006; toll-free 800/465-4329. www.hiwharf.com.* 585 rms, 2-5 story. June-Nov: S, D $169-$249; each addl $15; suites $400-$500; lower rates rest of yr. Crib free. Parking $13. TV; cable (premium), VCR avail. Heated pool; poolside serv. Restaurants open 24 hrs. Bar 4-11:30 pm. Ck-out noon. Coin lndry. Meeting rms. Business center. In-rm modem link. Bellhops. Valet serv. Sundries. Some refrigerators. Cr cds: A, C, D, DS, JCB, MC, V.

D SC

★★ **HOLIDAY INN CIVIC CENTER.** *50 Eighth St (94103). 415/626-6103; fax 415/552-0184; toll-free 800/243-1135. www.holiday-inn.com.* 394 rms, 14 story. S, D $109-$199; each addl $15; suites $250-$350; under 19 free; wkend rates. Garage $16. Crib free. TV; cable (premium). Heated pool. Restaurant 6-11 am, 5-10 pm. Bar 5 pm-midnight. Ck-out noon. Coin lndry. Meeting rms. Business servs avail. In-rm modem link. Gift shop. Health club privileges. Balconies. Cr cds: A, D, DS, JCB, MC, V.

★★ **HOLIDAY INN GOLDEN GATEWAY.** *1500 Van Ness Ave (94109). 415/441-4000; fax 415/776-7155.* 499 rms, 26 story. May-Oct: S, D $115-$220; each addl $15; suites $185-$460; under 19 free; lower rates rest of yr. Crib free. Parking in/out $16. TV; cable. Heated pool. Restaurant 6 am-10:30 pm. Bar. Ck-out noon. Convention facilities. Business servs avail. In-rm modem link. Gift shop. Exercise equipt. Some refrigerators. On cable car line. Cr cds: A, C, D, DS, ER, JCB, MC, V.

D

★ **LOMBARD MOTOR INN.** *1475 Lombard St (94123). 415/441-6000; fax 415/441-4291; toll-free 800/835-3639.* 48 rms, 3 story. May-Sept: S $88-$92; D $88-$108; each addl $5; under 5 free; lower rates rest of yr. Crib free. TV. Complimentary coffee in rms. Ck-out noon. Business servs avail. Cr cds: A, D, MC, V.

★ **NOB HILL MOTOR INN.** *1630 Pacific Ave (94109). 415/775-8160; fax 475/673-8842; toll-free 800/343-6900.* 29 rms, 12 with shower only, 2 story. Mid-May-Oct: S $105-$125; D $115-$135. Complimentary continental bkfst. Restaurant adj 5-10:30 pm. Ck-out 11 am. Concierge. Free garage parking. Refrigerators; some microwaves. Cr cds: A, C, D, DS, MC, V.

★ **PACIFIC HEIGHTS INN.** *1555 Union St (94123). 415/776-3310; fax 415/776-8176; toll-free 800/523-1801. www.pacificheightsinn.com.* 40 rms, 2 story, 17 kits. No A/C. S $89-$110; D $98-$125; suites $95-$150; family rates. Crib free. TV; cable. Complimentary continental bkfst, coffee in rms. Restaurant opp open 24 hrs. Ck-out noon. Business servs avail. In-rm modem link. Bellhops. Refrigerators; some in-rm steam and whirlpool baths. Microwaves avail. Cr cds: A, C, D, DS, MC, V.

★★ **THE PHOENIX INN.** *601 Eddy St (94109). 415/776-1380; fax 415/885-3109; res 800/738-7477.* 44 rms, 2 story. No A/C. May-Oct: S, D $119; suites $149-$159; under 12 free. Crib free. TV; cable, VCR avail (free movies). Heated pool; poolside serv. Complimentary continental bkfst. Restaurant 6 pm-midnight. Bar to 2 am. Ck-out noon. Business servs avail. Concierge. Sundries. Free parking. Health club privileges. Some refrigerators. Private patios, balconies. Cr cds: A, D, DS, MC, V.

D

★★ **RAMADA PLAZA HOTEL.** *2620 Jones St (94133). 415/885-4700; fax 415/771-8945; res 800/228-8408. www.ramada.com.* 232 rms, 4 story. May-Oct: S $190-$260; D $190-$270; each addl $15; suites $275-$500; under 17 free; lower rates rest of yr. Crib free. Garage in/out $10. TV; cable, VCR avail. Restaurant 6:30-11 am, 5-10 pm. Bar 5 pm-midnight. Ck-out noon. Meeting rms. Business servs avail. In-rm modem link. Valet serv. Sundries. Gift shop. Refrigerator in suites. Cr cds: A, C, D, DS, ER, JCB, MC, V.

D SC

★ **ROYAL PACIFIC MOTOR INN.** *661 Broadway (94133). 415/781-6661; fax 415/781-6688; toll-free 800/545-5574.* 74 rms, 12 A/C, 5 story. Apr-Nov: S, D $75-$93; each addl $5; suites $95-$105; lower rates rest of yr. Crib $10. TV. Complimentary coffee in rms. Restaurant nearby. Ck-out noon. Coin lndry. Business servs avail. Parking. Sauna. Refrigerators avail. Some balconies. Cr cds: A, C, D, MC, V.

★ **SAN FRANCISCO BAYSIDE TRAVELODGE.** *2011 Bayshore Blvd (94134). 415/467-8811; fax 415/468-3097; res 800/578-7878. www.sftravelodge.com.* 103 rms, 27 with shower only, 2 story. No A/C. S $75; D $98; each addl $8; under 5 free. TV; cable. Complimentary coffee in lobby. Restaurant open 24 hrs. Ck-out 11:30 am. Meeting rms. Business servs avail. Coin lndry. Indoor/outdoor pool. Sauna. Some balconies. Cr cds: A, C, D, DS, ER, JCB, MC, V.

★★ **THE SUITES AT FISHERMAN'S WHARF.** *2655 Hyde St (94109). 415/771-0200; fax 415/346-8058; toll-free 800/227-3608.* 24 kit. suites, 3 story. No A/C. S $219-$259; D $319; each addl $10; under 12 free. Garage in/out $15. TV; cable, VCR avail. Complimentary continental bkfst. Ck-out 10 am. Coin lndry. Business servs avail. Concierge. Refrigerators, microwaves avail. Private rooftop patio; some balconies. Ghirardelli Square 1 blk. Totally nonsmoking. Cr cds: A, D, DS, MC, V.

★ **VAGABOND INN.** *2550 Van Ness Ave (94109). 415/776-7500; fax 415/776-5689; toll-free 800/522-1555.* 132 rms, 5 story. No A/C. S, D $89-$159; each addl $5; suites, kit. units $109-$195; under 19 free; higher rates special events. Crib free. TV; cable (premium). Heated pool. Complimentary continental bkfst, coffee in rms. Ck-out noon. Meeting rm. Business servs avail. In-rm modem link. Valet serv. Some refrigerators. Some balconies. Cr cds: A, C, D, DS, MC, V.

D SC

★★ **WHARF INN.** *2601 Mason St (94133). 415/673-7411; fax 415/776-2181; toll-free 800/548-9918. www.wharfinn.com.* 51 rms, 3-4 story. No A/C. June-Oct: S, D $119-$179; kit. suite $275-$375; lower rates rest of yr. Crib free. TV; cable (premium). Complimentary coffee in lobby. Restaurant nearby. Ck-out 11 am. Concierge. Some balconies. Cr cds: A, D, DS, MC, V.

Hotels

★★ **AMSTERDAM HOTEL.** *749 Taylor St (94108). 415/673-3277; fax 415/673-0453; toll-free 800/637-3444. www.amsterdamhotel.com.* 34 rms, 3 story. No elvtr. S $89-$99; D $99-$109; each addl $10; under 11 free. Crib free. Garage $13 in/out. TV; cable. Complimentary continental bkfst. Restaurant nearby. Ck-out 11 am, ck-in noon. Business servs avail. Garden/patio for guests. Cr cds: A, MC, V.

★★★ **ARGENT HOTEL.** *50 3rd St (94103). 415/974-6400; fax 415/543-8268; toll-free 877/222-6699. www.argenthotel.com.* 667 rms, 36 story. S, D $230-$285; each addl $25; suites $380-$1,500; under 12 free. Crib free. Valet, garage parking $27. TV; VCR avail. Coffee in rms. Restaurant 6:30 am-10 pm; Fri, Sat to 10:30 pm. Bar 11-1:30 am. Ck-out noon. Convention facilities. Business center. In-rm modem link. Concierge. Gift shop. Tennis privileges. Exercise equipt;

RELIVING THE GOLD RUSH DAYS

This walking tour takes you down streets that gave birth to the city of San Francisco back in the Gold Rush days. It's an easy walk that starts at the center of the shopping district, passes through parts of the Financial District and Chinatown, and ends in the historic Barbary Coast areas near North Beach. Start at Union Square, the heart of downtown San Francisco, which dates from the 1850s and is bounded by Geary, Post, Powell, and Stockton streets. (The plaza in the center of the square has been undergoing reconstruction that should be completed by late 2002.) On the east (Stockton) side of the square, walk down little Maiden Lane, the ironically named former "red light" district of the Gold Rush era. Maiden Lane is closed to cars, so its two blocks are a pleasant place to stroll amid the shops and cafes where brothels once stood. At the end of Maiden Lane, go left up Kearny Street and then right on Bush Street, where Sam's Grill (374 Bush Street) offers excellent seafood and classic San Francisco atmosphere. Or check out the outdoor tables along Belden Place (turn left just before Sam's Grill), which is lined with Mediterranean-style restaurants. At the end of Belden Place, turn right down Pine Street to Montgomery Street. You'll find the Wells Fargo History Museum, open weekdays only, at 420 Montgomery between California and Pine streets. This excellent museum paints a fascinating portrait of Gold Rush San Francisco, with a re-created Wells Fargo office (complete with telegraph machine) and a century-old stagecoach. Walk back north on Montgomery to Commercial Street, and go left. Now on the fringes of Chinatown, Commercial Street was once a haven of Gold Rush-era merchants. Note the plaque at 608 Commercial Street, marking the site of the first US Branch Mint in 1854; it's also the location of the Pacific Heritage Museum, open weekdays only and well worth a stop. Continue on Commercial to Kearny, and turn right; after a short block you'll see Portsmouth Square, the oldest section of San Francisco, on your left. Now the central square of Chinatown, it blossomed from a sleepy plaza to the dynamic center of the city during the Gold Rush of the late 1840s and early 1850s. Turn right again on Clay Street (walking east back to Montgomery); the intersection of Clay and Montgomery marks the spot where the Pony Express ended its route during its fabled 2,000-mile runs of 1860-1861. Continue north on Montgomery past the Gold Rush-era Belli Building (722 Montgomery Street), and turn right on Jackson Street, lined with ornately decorated Gold Rush buildings, many of which are now antique shops. Note little Hotaling Place, where San Francisco Bay once lapped the shoreline before landfill extended the city borders. At Balance Street, go left into narrow Gold Street, site of San Francisco's first gold assaying office. Explore Gold Street, then continue east to Sansome Street, and take a left to Pacific Avenue. You'll pass rows of brick buildings that were built following the earthquake of 1906; these once served as Barbary Coast-era dancehalls, theaters, and saloons. You can now return to Union Square via Chinatown if you wish, or walk to adjoining North Beach.

sauna. Health club privileges. Massage. Bathrm phones, minibars; microwaves avail. Cr cds: A, D, DS, JCB, MC, V.

★★ **ATHERTON HOTEL.** *685 Ellis St (94109). 415/474-5720; fax 415/474-8256; toll-free 800/474-5720. www.hotelatherton.com.* 74 rms, 6 story. No A/C. S $79-$109; D $89-$119; each addl $10; under 12 free. Crib free. TV; VCR avail. Complimentary coffee in lobby. Restaurant 7 am-11 pm. Bar 5 pm-2 am. Ck-out noon. Meeting rm. Business servs avail. Cr cds: A, C, D, DS, MC, V.

★★ **BERESFORD ARMS HOTEL.** *701 Post St (94102). 415/673-2600; fax 415/474-0449; res 800/533-6533. www.beresford.com.* 96 rms, 8 story, 40 kit. units. No A/C. S $129-$139; D $139-$149; each addl $10; suites $140-$175, under 12 free. Crib free. Pet accepted, some restrictions. Valet parking $16 in/out. TV; cable, VCR (movies $5). Complimentary continental bkfst. Ck-out noon. Business servs avail. In-rm modem link. No rm serv. Health club privileges.

Refrigerators; some bathrm phones, in-rm whirlpools, minibars; microwaves avail. Cr cds: A, C, D, DS, JCB, MC, V.

D SC

★ **BERESFORD HOTEL.** *635 Sutter St (94102). 415/673-9900; fax 415/474-0449; res 800/533-6533. www.beresford.com.* 114 rms, 7 story. No A/C. S $125-$135; D $135-$145; each addl $10; family units $129-$139; under 12 free. Crib free. Pet accepted, some restrictions. Garage parking $16 in/out. TV; cable, VCR avail. Complimentary continental bkfst. Restaurant 7 am-2 pm, 5:30-10 pm; Sun, Mon to 2 pm. No rm serv. Bar 7-1 am, Sun to 2 pm. Ck-out noon. Business servs avail. In-rm modem link. Health club privileges. Refrigerators, minibars. Cr cds: A, C, D, DS, JCB, MC, V.

SC

★★★★ **CAMPTON PLACE HOTEL.** *340 Stockton St (94108). 415/781-5555; fax 415/955-5536; toll-free 800/235-4300. www.camptonplace.com.* This small luxury hotel offers greater intimacy than many of its larger counterparts around the city. Rooms are carefully designed for comfort with separate seating areas, wood paneling, several bed types available, and plush, goosedown pillows. 110 rms, 9 suites, 17 story. S, D $355-$475; suites $550-$2,000. Pet accepted, some restrictions $35. Valet parking $26/day. Complimentary coffee in lobby. TV; cable, VCR avail (movies). Restaurant (see also CAMPTON PLACE). Rm serv 24 hrs. Bar 10 am-11 pm; Fri, Sat to midnight. Ck-out noon; ck-in 3 pm. Meeting rms. Business servs avail. In-rm modem link. Concierge. Valet serv. Health club avail. Bathrm phones, minibars. Views of Union Square and Financial District. Cr cds: A, C, D, JCB, MC, V.

D

★ **CARLTON HOTEL.** *1075 Sutter St (94109). 415/673-0242; fax 415/673-4904; toll-free 800/922-7586. www.carltonhotel.com.* 165 rms, 9 story. No A/C. S, D $109-$165; each addl $20; under 12 free. Crib free. TV; cable. Complimentary afternoon refreshments, coffee in rms. Restaurant 7-11 am, 5-9 pm. Ck-out 1 pm. Meeting rm. Business servs avail. Health club privileges. Minibars. Cr cds: A, C, D, DS, JCB, MC, V.

D

★ **CARTWRIGHT HOTEL.** *524 Sutter St (94102). 415/421-2865; fax 415/398-6345; res 800/227-3844. www.cartwrighthotel.com.* 114 rms, 34 A/C, 8 story. S, D $139-$169; suites $189-$229; under 3 free. Crib free. Valet parking in/out $21. TV; cable, VCR avail. Complimentary afternoon refreshments. Ck-out noon. Meeting rm. Business servs avail. In-rm modem link. Health club privileges. Game rm/library. Many refrigerators. Antiques. Originally opened 1915. Cr cds: A, C, D, DS, JCB, MC.

SC

★★ **CATHEDRAL HILL HOTEL.** *1101 Van Ness Ave (94109). 415/776-8200; fax 415/441-2841; res 800/622-0855. www.cathedralhillhotel.com.* 400 rms, 8 story. S $179-$199; D $189-$209; each addl $20; suites $200-$400; under 18 free; wkend rates. Crib free. Garage parking $15 in/out. TV; cable, VCR avail. Heated pool. Restaurant 6:30 am-10 pm. Bar 11-1 am. Ck-out noon. Convention facilities. In-rm modem link. Concierge. Shopping arcade. Barber, beauty shop. Health club privileges. Bathrm phones; some refrigerators. Balconies; some private patios. Cr cds: A, C, D, DS, JCB, MC, V.

D

★★ **CHANCELLOR HOTEL ON UNION SQUARE.** *433 Powell St (94102). 415/362-2004; fax 415/362-1403; toll-free 800/428-4748. www.chancellorhotel.com.* 137 rms, 16 story. No A/C. S $99-$140; D $99-$155; each addl $15; suites $230. Crib free. TV; cable (premium). Restaurant 7 am-3 pm, 5-9:30 pm. Bar 11-1 am. Ck-out noon. Meeting rm. Business servs avail. In-rm modem link. Health club privileges. Gift shop. Tallest building in the city when constructed (1914) after the San Francisco earthquake in 1906. Cr cds: A, D, DS, JCB, MC, V.

SC

THE CLIFT. (Unrated, renovation in progress) *495 Geary St (94102). 415/775-4700; fax 415/441-4621; toll-free 800/652-5438. www.clifthotel.com.* 329 rms, 17 story. S, D $255-$385; each addl $30; suites $395-$1260;

under 18 free; wkend rates. Crib free. Pet accepted. Valet parking $25. TV; cable (premium), VCR avail. Restaurant (see also FRENCH ROOM). Rm serv 24 hrs. Bar 11-2 am; pianist 5:30 pm-1:30 am. Ck-out 1 pm. Valet serv 24 hrs. Concierge. Business center. In-rm modem link. Exercise equipt. Bathrm phones, refrigerators, minibars; microwaves avail. Cr cds: A, D, MC, V.

D

★★ COMMODORE HOTEL SAN FRANCISCO. *825 Sutter St (94109). 415/923-6800; fax 415/923-6804; res 800/738-7477. www.basshotels.com.* 113 rms, 6 story. No A/C. July-Oct: S, D $149-$225; each addl $10; under 12 free; hols (2-day min); lower rates rest of yr. Crib free. Garage, in/out parking $15. TV; cable, VCR avail. Restaurant 7 am-2 pm. No rm serv. Bar 5 pm-2 am. Ck-out noon. Meeting rm. Business servs avail. In-rm modem link. Concierge. Health club privileges. Some refrigerators. Cr cds: A, C, D, DS, ER, JCB, MC, V.

D SC

★★★ CROWNE PLAZA UNION SQUARE. *480 Sutter St (94108). 415/398-8900; fax 415/989-8823; res 800/465-4329. www.crowneplaza.com.* 400 rms, 30 story. S, D $279-$299; each addl $15; suites $250-$750; under 19 free; wkend rates. Crib free. Parking in/out $23. TV; cable (premium), VCR avail. Restaurant 6:30-11:30 am, 5-11 pm. Bar. Ck-out noon. Convention facilities. Business center. Valet serv. Gift shop. Exercise equipt. Refrigerator in suites. Cr cds: A, C, D, DS, JCB, MC, V.

D SC

★★★ THE DONATELLO. *501 Post St (94102). 415/441-7100; fax 415/885-8891; toll-free 800/227-3184. www.travelweb.com.* 94 rms, 14 story. S, D $189-$280; each addl $25; suites $325-$525; under 12 free; wkend rates. Crib free. Garage, in/out $24. TV; cable (premium), VCR avail (movies $2). Restaurant 6:30 am-11 pm (see also ZINGARI). Bar 11 am-midnight. Ck-out noon. Meeting rms. Business center. In-rm modem link. Concierge. Exercise equipt; sauna. Whirlpool. Bathrm phones; some refrigerators. Italian Renaissance decor; antiques; classic elegance. Cr cds: A, C, D, DS, MC, V.

D

★★★ EL DRISCO HOTEL. *2901 Pacific Ave (94115). 415/346-2880.* 100 rms, 10 story. 43 rms, 6 story; 19 suites. S, D $205-$325; each addl $25; under 17 free. Crib avail. TV; cable (premium), VCR avail. Complimentary continental bkfst, coffee and newspaper in rms. Ck-out noon. Exercise rm. Some refrigerators, minibars. Cr cds: A, C, D, DS, MC, V.

★★ ESSEX HOTEL. *684 Ellis St (94109). 415/474-4664; fax 415/441-1800; toll-free 800/453-7739.* 96 rms, 7 story. No A/C. S $69-$79; D $79-$89; each addl $10; suites $99; under 12 free. TV. Complimentary coffee in lobby. Ck-out noon. Some balconies. Civic Center 3 blks. Cr cds: A, MC, V.

★★★★ THE FAIRMONT SAN FRANCISCO. *950 Mason St (94108). 415/772-5000; fax 415/722-5013; res 800/527-4727. www.fairmont.com.* Following a recent renovation, this majestic Nob Hill hotel has been restored to its former grandeur. The grand lobby and public spaces are impressive. Guest rooms offer classic elegant decor with soothing colors and elegant fabrics, and afford outstanding views of the city and bay from the tower. Many rooms feature large marble bathrooms with separate tub and shower. The formal, attentive service matches the updated environment. 596 rms, 8 and 24 story. S, D $229-$319; each addl $30; suites $350-$8,000; under 13 free; wkend rates. Crib free. Garage, in/out $27/day, valet. TV; cable, VCR (movies). Restaurant 6 am-11 pm. Rm serv 24 hrs. Bars; entertainment. Ck-out 1 pm. Convention facilities. Business center. In-rm modem link. Concierge. Shopping arcade. Barber, beauty shop. Free financial district transportation. Exercise rm; sauna. Whirlpool. Massage. Bathrm phones, minibars; microwaves avail. Some suites with private patio. Outside glass-enclosed elvtr to Fairmont Crown Room. Panoramic view of city; rooftop garden. Cr cds: A, C, D, DS, ER, JCB, MC, V.

FOUR SEASON. (Too new to be rated) *757 Market St (94103). 415/633-3000.* 277 rms, 10 story. S, D $325-$800; suites $950-$3,000; each addl $25; under 17 free. Crib avail. Valet parking. TV; cable (premium), VCR avail. Restaurant 6 am-11 pm. Bar. Ck-out noon. Meeting rms. Business center. Valet serv. Gift shop. Exercise rm. Minibars, refrigerators. Cr cds: A, D, DS, JCB, MC, V.

★★ THE GALLERIA PARK. *191 Sutter St (94104). 415/781-3060; fax 415/781-7302; toll-free 800/792-9639. www.galleriapark.com.* 177 rms, 8 story. S, D $159-$239; suites $250-$450; family, wkend rates. Garage in/out $25. TV; cable (premium). Restaurant 7 am-11 pm. Bar. Ck-out noon. Meeting rms. Business center. In-rm modem link. Concierge. Shopping arcade. Exercise equipt. Refrigerators, mini bars. Atrium lobby with unique sculptured fireplace. Cr cds: A, C, D, DS, JCB, MC, V.

★★★ GRAND HYATT SAN FRANCISCO. *345 Stockton St (94108). 415/398-1234 or 415/398-1234; fax 415/392-2536; res 800/233-1234.* 685 rms, 36 story, 30 suites. S, D $199-$300; each addl $25; suites $450-$1,550; under 18 free; package plans. Crib free. Valet parking, garage in/out $25. TV; cable (premium), VCR avail. Restaurant 6:30 am-10 pm. Bar 11-2 am; entertainment. Ck-out noon, ck-in 3 pm. Convention facilities. Business center. In-rm modem link. Concierge. Shopping arcade. Barber, beauty shop. Exercise equipt. Health club privileges. Massage. Refrigerators, minibars, bathrm phones; some wet bars; microwaves avail. Luxury level. Cr cds: A, C, D, DS, ER, JCB, MC, V.

★ GRANT PLAZA HOTEL. *465 Grant Ave (94108). 415/434-3883; fax 415/434-3886; toll-free 800/472-6899. www.grantplaza.com.* 72 rms, 6 story. S $65-$75; D $65-$109; each addl $10; under 10 free. Crib $10. Garage $14.50. TV; cable (premium), VCR avail. Restaurant adj open 24 hrs. No rm serv. Ck-out noon. Business servs avail. Microwaves avail. Cr cds: A, C, D, JCB, MC, V.

★★ HANDLERY UNION SQUARE HOTEL. *351 Geary St (94102). 415/781-7800; fax 415/781-0216; toll-free 800/843-4343. www.handlery.com.* 377 rms, 8 story. S, D $145-$195; each addl $10; suites $185-$370; under 16 free. Crib free. Garage in/out $20. TV; cable, VCR avail. Heated pool. Sauna. Coffee in rms. Restaurant 7 am-11 pm. Rm serv 7-10:30 am, 5-10 pm. Bar 10 am-11:30 pm. Ck-out noon. Meeting rms. Business servs avail. In-rm modem link. Concierge. Gift shop. Barber, beauty shop. Luxury level. Cr cds: A, C, D, DS, ER, JCB, MC, V.

Coit Tower, San Francisco

★★ THE HARBOR COURT MOTEL. *165 Stuart St (94105). 415/882-1300; fax 415/882-1313; toll-free 800/346-0555.* 131 rms, 5 story. Apr-mid-Nov: S, D $135-$245. Crib free. Parking in/out $24. TV; cable (premium). Indoor pool; whirlpool, lifeguard. Complimentary coffee, evening refreshments. Restaurant 11:30 am-10 pm. Bar to 2 am; entertainment. Ck-out noon. Meeting rm. Business center. In-rm modem link. Concierge. Exercise rm; sauna. Refrigerators, minibars. On waterfront. Cr cds: A, C, D, DS, ER, JCB, MC, V.

★★★ **HILTON AND TOWERS.** *333 O'Farrell St (94102). 415/771-1400; fax 415/771-6807; toll-free 800/445-8667. www.sanfrancisco.hilton.com.* 1,896 rms, 19, 23 and 46 story. S $185-$265; D $205-$275; each addl $20; suites $300-$2,500; wkend rates. Garage, in/out $28. TV; cable (premium), VCR avail. Pool on 16th floor in garden court. Restaurants 6-1 am. Bars 10:30-1:30 am. Ck-out noon. Convention facilities. Business center. In-rm modem link. Shopping arcade. Barber, beauty shop. Exercise equipt; sauna. Health club privileges. Massage. Balconies. Some penthouse suites with solarium. 16th floor lanai rms. 46-story tower with distinctive rms and rooftop dining. Luxury level. Cr cds: A, MC, V.

★ **HOTEL BIJOU.** *111 Mason St (94102). 415/771-1200; fax 415/346-3196; res 800/738-7477. www.sftrips.com.* 65 rms, 6 story. No A/C. S $129-$149; D $149-$169; each addl $10; under 14 free; hol rates. Crib free. Garage in/out parking $14. TV. Complimentary coffee in lobby. Restaurant opp open 24 hrs. No rm serv. Ck-out noon. Concierge. Cr cds: A, D, DS, ER, JCB, MC, V.

D

★★ **HOTEL BOHEME.** *444 Columbus Ave (94133). 415/433-9111; fax 415/362-6292. www.hotelboheme.com.* 15 rms, 2-3 story. S, D $164-$184; each addl $10; under 2 free. TV; cable. Restaurant adj 7-1 am. Ck-out noon, ck-in 2 pm. Concierge serv. Business servs avail. In-rm modem link. Cr cds: A, C, D, DS, ER, JCB, MC, V.

★ **HOTEL BRITTON.** *112 7th St (94103). 415/621-7001; fax 415/626-3974; res 800/444-5819. www.renesonhotels.com.* 79 rms, 5 story. Apr-Oct: S, D $105-$145; each addl $10; suites $145-$175; lower rates rest of yr. Crib free. TV; cable (premium). Coffee in rms. Restaurant 6 am-10 pm. Ck-out noon. Coin lndry. Business servs avail. In-rm modem link. Microwaves avail. Convention Center 3 blks. Cr cds: A, C, D, DS, ER, JCB, MC, V.

D

★★ **HOTEL DIVA.** *440 Geary St (94102). 415/885-0200; fax 415/346-6613; toll-free 800/553-1900. www.personalityhotels.com.* 111 rms, 7 story. S, D $149; each addl $10; suites $169-$450; under 12 free. Crib free. Valet parking, in/out $17. TV; cable (premium), VCR (movies). Complimentary continental bkfst. Restaurant 11:30 am-10 pm; Fri, Sat to 11 pm; Sun 1-9 pm. Rm serv 7 am-10 pm. Ck-out noon. Meeting rm. Business center. Concierge. Exercise equipt. Bathrm phones, refrigerators, minibars. Cr cds: A, C, D, DS, JCB, MC, V.

D

★★ **HOTEL GRIFFON.** *155 Steuart St (94105). 425/495-2100; fax 415/495-3522; res 800/321-2201. www.hotelgriffon.com.* 62 rms, 5 story. S, D $220-$285; suites $395-$495; under 18 free. Crib free. Garage parking $15. TV; cable. Complimentary continental bkfst. Restaurant 11:30 am-10:30 pm; Sat, Sun from 5:30 pm. Ck-out noon. Meeting rms. Business servs avail. Concierge. Cr cds: A, C, D, DS, JCB, MC, V.

D

★★★ **THE HOTEL MAJESTIC.** *1500 Sutter St (94109). 415/441-1100; fax 415/673-7331; toll-free 800/869-8966. www.hotelmajestic.net.* 57 rms, 5 story. S $159; D $269; each addl $15; suites $215-$350. Covered parking $18; valet parking. TV; VCR avail. Restaurant 7-10:30 am, 5:30-10:30 pm; Sun brunch 7 am-2 pm. Rm serv 24 hrs. Bar 11 am-midnight; pianist. Ck-out noon. Lndry serv. Meeting rms. Business servs avail. Concierge. Health club privileges. Many fireplaces, refrigerators. Each rm individually decorated with antiques, custom furnishings. Restored Edwardian hotel (1902); antique tapestries. Cr cds: A, C, D, DS, JCB, MC, V.

D

★★ **HOTEL MILANO.** *55 5th St (94103). 415/543-8555; fax 415/543-5843; toll-free 800/398-7555. www.citysearch.com.* 108 rms, 8 story. S, D $179-$199; each addl $20; under 12 free; wkend, hol rates. Crib free. Parking $19. TV; cable (premium). Restaurant (see also M POINT). Bar 5-11 pm. Ck-out noon. Meeting rms. Business servs avail. Concierge. Exercise equipt. Minibars. Cr cds: A, D, DS, MC, V.

★★★ **HOTEL MONACO.** *501 Geary St (94102). 415/292-0100; fax 415/292-0111; res 800/214-4220. www.monaco-sf.com.* 201 rms, 7 story, 34 suites. S, D $269; suites $299-$439; under 16 free; hol rates. Crib free. Pet accepted. Valet parking; in/out $24. TV; cable (premium), VCR avail. Complimentary coffee in rms. Restaurant (see also GRAND CAFE). Bar 11:30-1:30 am. Ck-out noon. Meeting rms. Business servs avail. In-rm modem link. Concierge. Exercise rm. Massage. Minibars. Cr cds: A, C, D, DS, ER, JCB, MC, V.

★ **HOTEL MONARCH.** *1015 Geary St (94109). 415/673-5232; fax 415/885-2802; res 800/777-3210. www.themonarchhotel.com.* 101 rms, 6 story. No A/C. S, D $89-$119; each addl $10; under 12 free. Crib free. Valet parking in/out $15/day. TV; cable (premium). Complimentary coffee. Restaurant 7-11 am. Ck-out noon. Meeting rm. Business servs avail. Game rm. Some refrigerators. Cr cds: A, C, D, DS, ER, JCB, MC, V.

★★★ **HOTEL NIKKO SAN FRANCISCO.** *222 Mason St (94102). 415/394-1106; fax 415/394-1106; res 800/645-5687.* 523 rms, 25 story, 33 suites. S $250-$340; D $280-$370; each addl $30; suites $525-$2,000; under 18 free; wkend rates. Crib free. Covered parking, in/out $27; valet. TV; cable, VCR avail. Indoor pool; whirlpool, poolside serv. Complimentary bkfst, refreshments. Restaurant 6:30 am-10 pm. Rm serv 24 hrs. Bar 11-2 am. Ck-out noon. Convention facilities. Business center. Concierge. Sundries. Barber, beauty shop. Exercise rm; sauna, steam rm. Minibars. 2-story marble staircase in lobby frames cascading waterfall. Luxury level. Cr cds: A, C, D, DS, JCB, MC, V.

★★★★ **HOTEL PALOMAR.** *12 Fourth St (94103). 415/348-1111; fax 415/348-0302; toll-free 877/294-9711. www.hotelpalomar.com.* Located on floors 5-9 of a refurbished 1908 building in downtown San Francisco, this hotel offers exceptional in-room technology like faxes, printers, and photocopiers. The guest room decor is contemporary and sophisticated. Be sure to book your table at Fifth Floor restaurant upon check-in since reservations are in demand. 198 rms, 4 story, 12 suites. Apr-Oct: S $325; D $475; suites $930; each addl $15; lower rates rest of yr. Crib avail. Pet accepted, some restrictions, fee. Valet parking. TV; cable (premium), VCR avail, CD avail. Complimentary coffee in rms, newspaper, toll-free calls. Restaurant. Bar. Ck-out noon, ck-in 3 pm. Meeting rms. Business servs avail. Luggage handling. Concierge serv. Dry cleaning. Exercise equipt. Supervised children's activities. Cr cds: A, C, D, DS, ER, JCB, MC, V.

★★★ **HOTEL REX.** *562 Sutter St (94102). 415/433-4434; fax 415/433-3695; res 800/738-7477. www.thehotelrex.com.* 94 rms, some A/C, 7 story. S, D $175-$255; each addl $20; suites $575. Crib free. Valet $25 in/out. TV; cable. Complimentary coffee in lobby. Restaurant 7-10 am; Sat, Sun to 11 am. Bar 5 pm-midnight. Ck-out noon. Business servs avail. In-rm modem link. Concierge. Health club privileges. Minibars. Microwaves avail. Renovated hotel with 1920s atmosphere. Cr cds: A, C, D, DS, V.

★★★ **HOTEL TRITON.** *342 Grant Ave (94108). 415/433-6611; fax 415/433-6611; res 800/433-6611. www.hotel-tritonsf.com.* 140 rms, 7 story. S, D $239; suites $245-$299; under 16 free. Crib free. Valet, in/out parking $24. Pet accepted; $15. TV; cable, VCR avail. Complimentary afternoon refreshments. Restaurants 6:30 am-10 pm. Bar from 11 am. Ck-out noon. Meeting rm. Business servs avail. Concierge. Exercise equipt. Health club privileges. Minibars. Cr cds: A, D, DS, JCB, MC, V.

★★ **HOTEL UNION SQUARE.** *114 Powell St (94102). 415/397-3000; fax 415/399-1874; toll-free 800/553-1900. www.hotelunionsquare.com.* 131 rms, 6 story. S, D $115-$169; each addl $10; suites $159-$350; under 12 free. Garage in/out $18. TV. Complimentary continental bkfst. Restaurant adj

11 am-11 pm. Bar 11 am-9 pm. Ck-out noon. Business servs avail. Health club privileges. Refrigerators avail. Penthouse suites with deck. Cr cds: A, C, D, DS, JCB, MC, V.

★★ **HOTEL VINTAGE COURT.** *650 Bush St (94108). 415/392-4666; fax 415/433-4065; toll-free 800/853-1750. www.vintagecourt.com.* 106 rms, 65 A/C, 8 story. S, D $175; each addl $10; under 12 free. Crib free. Valet parking in/out $21. TV; cable (premium), VCR avail. Complimentary coffee in lobby. Restaurant (see also MASA'S). Ck-out noon. Meeting rm. Business servs avail. In-rm modem link. Health club privileges. Refrigerators. Built 1912. Cr cds: A, C, D, DS, MC, V.

★★★ **HUNTINGTON HOTEL.** *1075 California St (94108). 415/474-5400; fax 415/474-6227; res 800/525-4800. www.huntingtonhotel.com.* 100 rms, 12 story, 40 suites. S $275-$420; D $300-$445; suites $475-$1,125; under 6 free. Crib free. Garage, in/out $19.50. TV; cable, VCR avail. Restaurant (see also THE BIG FOUR). Rm serv 6 am-11:30 pm. Bar 11:30-12:30 am; pianist. Ck-out noon. Meeting rms. Business servs avail. Concierge. Health club privileges. Minibars; many wet bars; microwaves avail. Cr cds: A, D, DS, MC, V.

★★★ **HYATT AT FISHERMAN'S WHARF.** *555 N Point St (94133). 415/563-1234; fax 415/749-6122; res 800/233-1234. www.hyatt.com.* 313 rms, 5 story. S $175-$265; D $190-$290; suites $375-$800; under 18 free. Crib free. Garage $23 in/out. TV; cable (premium), VCR avail. Heated pool; whirlpool. Restaurant 6:30 am-11 pm; Fri, Sat to 2 am. Bar noon-11 pm, Fri, Sat to 2 am. Ck-out noon. Coin lndry. Meeting rms. Business center. In-rm modem link. Concierge. Gift shop. Exercise equipt; sauna. Some bathrm phones. Cable car line opp. Cr cds: A, D, DS, ER, JCB, MC, V.

★★★ **HYATT REGENCY.** *5 Embarcadero Ctr (94111). 415/788-1234; fax 415/398-2567; res 415/788-1234. www.hyatt.com.* 803 rms, 15 story. S, D $199; each addl $25; suites $425-$1,400; under 18 free. Crib free. Covered parking, valet $27. TV; cable (premium), VCR avail. Coffee in rms. Restaurant 6-10 pm. Rm serv 6 am-midnight. Bars; entertainment; revolving rooftop restaurant/bar. Ck-out noon. Convention facilities. Business center. In-rm modem link. Concierge. Shopping arcade. Exercise equipt. Health club privileges. Refrigerators; microwaves avail. Balconies. Spacious 17-story atrium in lobby. Luxury level. Cr cds: A, D, DS, JCB, MC, V.

★★★ **INN AT THE OPERA.** *333 Fulton St (94102). 415/863-8400; fax 415/861-0821.* 30 rms, 7 story, 18 suites. A/C in suites only. S $140-$215; D $165-$230; suites $240-$315. Crib $15. Parking $22. TV; cable (premium), VCR avail. Complimentary bkfst. Restaurant 5-10 pm. Bar; Fri, Sat to 1 am; entertainment exc Mon. Ck-out noon. Business servs avail. In-rm modem link. Concierge. Health club privileges. Refrigerators, microwaves, minibars. Elegant European decor. In Performing Arts district. Cr cds: A, D, DS, JCB, MC, V.

★★ **JULIANA HOTEL.** *590 Bush St (94108). 415/392-2540; fax 415/391-8447; res 800/328-3880. www.julianahotel.com.* 107 rms, 9 story. S, D $135-$185; suites $165-$245; monthly rates. Crib free. TV; cable (premium). Complimentary coffee in lobby; afternoon refreshments. Ck-out noon. Business servs avail. In-rm modem link. Health club privileges. Refrigerators, honor bars. Cr cds: A, D , DS, JCB, MC, V.

★★ **KENSINGTON PARK HOTEL.** *450 Post St (94102). 415/788-6400; fax 415/399-9484; res 800/553-1900. www.kensingtonparkhotel.com.* 87 rms, 12 story. S, D $159-$189; each addl $10; suites $255-$550; under 13 free. Crib free. Valet parking $17. TV; VCR avail. Complimentary continental bkfst; afternoon refreshments. Ck-out noon. Meeting rms. Business servs avail. In-rm modem link. Exercise equipt. Bathrm phones; some

WATERFRONT WALK

While most visitors to San Francisco make their way to the city's waterfront, many confine their walking to the few blocks along Jefferson Street comprising Fisherman's Wharf, culminating at Pier 39. This tour will also take you to that area; however, the focus is on often-missed attractions along the way. Start just to the east of Presidio National Park at the corner of Baker Street and Marina Boulevard. The neoclassical domed and pillared structure here is the Palace of Fine Arts; it was built for an exposition in 1915 and now houses the Exploratorium, one of the country's top science museums. An adjacent tree-shaded lagoon harbors ducks and swans. Cross Marina Boulevard and go north to the end of Baker Street, turning right on Yacht Road. As you follow the path past the Saint Francis Yacht Club, you'll have prime views of the Marina Small Craft Harbor, where dozens of yachts bob in the water. Continue out to the end of the breakwater, where there are exceptional views of the Golden Gate Bridge to the west and Alcatraz Island ahead. You'll also find one of San Francisco's lesser-known delights: the Wave Organ. The tides make "natural music" as they filter through stone pipes here. You can relax on the steps while you enjoy the "concert" and the bay views. To continue on, retrace your steps back to Marina Boulevard and turn left (east) along the pedestrian walkway that leads past the southern edge of the yacht harbor and the Marina Green. One of San Francisco's prettiest parks, the Marina Green is a favorite of kite-flyers. Note the well-kept houses of the Marina District on the opposite side of Marina Boulevard, then try to picture the rubble that marked this area following the devastating 1989 earthquake. It is amazing that no evidence of this disaster remains. Follow the walkway past another yacht harbor to Fort Mason Center. This former military outpost is now a cultural center and includes several small museums, as well as the excellent Greens Restaurant (at the end of Building A), the city's longtime favorite for vegetarian food. Greens has a take-out stand where you can pick up a delicious sandwich for a picnic lunch. Climb the steps that lead up the hillside (across from Building E) to the park, where you'll find rolling hills of green grass, paved pathways, and benches to relax on. From here, follow the concrete walkway that leads up the hill (northeast) at the rear of the park; as you come over the crest of the hill, you'll be treated to one of the best views of the western edges of Fisherman's Wharf. Ahead lies Aquatic Park, with a small beach and a fishing pier. The surf here is usually calm enough for swimming, though the water is too chilly for most. The Ghirardelli Square shopping complex hovers on a hillside above it. The cable car turnaround boards passengers for the Powell-Hyde line, which climbs up steep Hyde Street. At the foot of Hyde Street stands the Hyde Street Pier, home to the world's largest fleet of historic ships. You can tour the ships, including the *Balclutha*, a magnificent 1886 square-rigged sailing ship. Then, if you wish, you can continue walking into the always-crowded Fisherman's Wharf area along Jefferson Street.

refrigerators. Renovated 1924 hotel, guest rms on floors 5-12. Grand piano in lobby. Traditional English decor. Theater in building. Cr cds: A, C, D, DS, ER, JCB, MC, V.

D

★★ **KING GEORGE HOTEL.** *334 Mason St (94102). 415/781-5050; fax 415/391-6976; toll-free 800/288-6005. www.kinggeorge.com.* 141 rms, 9 story. No A/C. S $99-$150; D $99-$165; each addl $10; suites $225; package plans. Crib free. Garage, in/out $16.50. TV; cable. Restaurant 7-10 am, 3-6:30 pm. Rm serv 24 hrs. Bar; entertainment. Ck-out noon. Meeting rms. Business servs avail. In-rm modem link. Concierge. Health club privileges. Union Square one blk. Cr cds: A, C, D, DS, JCB, MC, V.

SC

★★★★★ **MANDARIN ORIENTAL, SAN FRANCISCO.** *222 Sansome St (94104). 415/276-9888; fax 415/433-0289; toll-free 800/622-0404. www.mandarinoriental.com.* Each and every luxurious guest room at the Mandarin Oriental boasts a stunning view of San Francisco as they are all located on the 38th-48th floors of a high-rise building. Bathrooms are all marble and the room boasts every amenity one can think of, though should they think of anything lacking the attentive staff will fetch it promptly. Silks restaurant is an excellent spot for intricate Asian inspired food. 158 rms, 11 story; on floors 38-48 of the twin towers in the California Center. S $475-$700; D $500-$725; suites $1,400-$3,000; under 12 free; wkend rates. Crib free. Covered parking $30. TV; cable (premium), VCR avail. Restaurant (see SILKS). Rm serv 24 hrs. Bar 11 am-11 pm; entertainment Mon-Sat. Ck-out noon. Meeting rms. Business center. In-rm modem link. Concierge. Exercise equipt. Health club privileges. Bathrm phones, refrigerators, minibars. Cr cds: A, C, D, DS, JCB, MC, V.

★★ MARINA INN. *3110 Octavia St (94123). 415/928-1000; fax 415/928-5909; toll-free 800/274-1420. www.marinainn.com.* 40 rms, 4 story. S, D $65-$135; each addl $10. TV; cable. Complimentary continental bkfst; afternoon refreshments. Ck-out noon, ck-in 2 pm. Business servs avail. Luggage handling. Barber, beauty shop. Restored 1928 building; English country ambiance. Cr cds: A, D, MC, V.

★★★★ MARK HOPKINS INTER-CONTINENTAL SAN FRANCISCO. *1 Nob Hill (94108). 415/392-3434; fax 415/421-3302; res 800/327-0200. www.markhopkins.net.* This grand dame of a hotel has been restored to its proper place in San Francisco's hotel hierarchy due to a stunning $50 million restoration. Though the hotel's amenities are more limited than others in the same price range, most guests are charmed by the Mark Hopkins' aura of stately elegance and history. The lounge, Top of the Mark, boasts unparalleled views of the city. 390 rms, 19 story. S, D $240-$340; each addl $30; suites $425-$1,600; under 17 free; wkend rates. Crib free. Garage parking $26/day. TV; cable, VCR avail. Restaurant 6:30 am-11 pm (see also NOB HILL). Bars noon-1:30 am. Ck-out noon. Conference facilities. Business center. Concierge. Exercise equipt. Health club privileges. Minibars. Some balconies. Luxury level. Cr cds: A, C, D, DS, JCB, MC, V.

★★ MAXWELL HOTEL. *386 Geary St (94102). 415/986-2000; fax 415/397-2447; toll-free 888/734-6299. www.maxwellhotel.com.* 153 rms, 12 story. Apr-mid-Nov: S, D $155-$165; each addl $10; under 18 free; some wkends, hols (2-day min); lower rates rest of yr. Crib free. Garage, in/out parking $18. TV; cable. Restaurant 7-1 am. Bar. Entertainment Fri, Sat. Ck-out noon. Meeting rms. Business servs avail. In-rm modem link. Concierge. Health club privileges. Bathrm phones; refrigerators avail. Cr cds: A, C, D, DS, JCB, MC, V.

★★★ MONTICELLO INN. *127 Ellis St (94102). 415/392-8800; fax 415/398-2650; toll-free 800/669-7777. www.monticelloinn.com.* 91 rms, 5 story, 28 suites. S, D $115-$195; suites $165-$255. Crib free. Valet parking $20. TV; cable (premium). Complimentary continental bkfst. Restaurant 11:30 am-10 pm. Ck-out noon. Business servs avail. In-rm modem link. Concierge. Health club privileges. Minibars. 18th-century decor. Renovated hotel built 1906. Cr cds: A, C, D, DS, ER, JCB, MC, V.

SC

★★★ NOB HILL LAMBOURNE HOTEL. *725 Pine St (94108). 415/433-2287; fax 415/433-0975; toll-free 800/274-8466. www.nobhilllambourne.com.* 20 kit. units, 3 story, 6 suites. No A/C. S, D $230; suites $295; family, monthly rates. Crib avail. Garage; valet, in/out $24. TV; cable, VCR (free movies). Complimentary continental bkfst, coffee in rms. Restaurant nearby. Ck-out noon. Business center. In-rm modem link. Concierge. Exercise equipt. Health club privileges. Microwaves, wet bars. Balconies. Totally nonsmoking. Cr cds: A, D, DS, MC, V.

★★★ PALACE HOTEL. *2 New Montgomery St (94105). 415/512-1111; fax 415/543-0671; toll-free 800/325-3535. www.luxurycollection.com.* 550 rms, 8 story. S $350; D $370; each addl $20; suites $475-$2,900; family, wkend rates. Crib free. Valet parking $22. TV; cable (premium), VCR avail (movies). Indoor pool; whirlpool, poolside serv. Restaurant (see also GARDEN COURT). Rm serv 24 hrs. Bar from 11 am; entertainment. Ck-out noon.

Convention facilities. Business center. In-rm modem link. Concierge. Shopping arcade. Exercise rm; sauna. Health club privileges. Bathrm phones, refrigerators. Cr cds: A, C, D, DS, ER, JCB, MC, V.

D

★★★★ **THE PAN PACIFIC.** *500 Post St (94102). 415/771-8600; fax 415/398-0267; toll-free 800/533-6465. www.panpac.com.* Located on fashionable Post Street in Union Square, this hotel is one of only two US outposts of its luxury Pacific Rim chain. The architecture and design of the public spaces and 329 rooms and suites are Asian-inspired. The penthouse-level terrace is the highlight of the 14,000 square feet of meeting space with its panoramic views of the Bay. 330 units, 21 story. S, D $325; suites $460-$1,800; under 18 free; wkend rates. Crib free. Garage, in/out $27; valet parking. Pet accepted, some restrictions. TV; cable (premium), VCR avail. Restaurant 6:30 am-10:30 pm (see also PACIFIC). Rm serv 24 hrs. Bar 11 am-11:30 pm; pianist. Ck-out noon. Meeting rms. Business center. In-rm modem link. Concierge. Exercise equipt. Health club privileges. Minibars, bathrm phones. Cr cds: A, C, D, DS, MC, V.

D

★★★★ **PARK HYATT.** *333 Battery St (94111). 415/392-1234; fax 415/421-2433; res 800/223-1234. www.hyatt.com.* A chic Asian aesthetic characterizes this businessperson's haven in the heart of San Francisco's financial district. Travelers will find everthing they need to relax after a taxing day, from the excellent fitness center to luxurious bathrooms to genuinely hospitable staff members who will cater to every need. Park Grill is one of the premier power lunch spots in the city. 360 rms, 24 story, 37 suites. S, D $215; each addl $25; suites $415-$3,350; under 18 free; wkend rates. Crib free. Pet accepted, some restrictions. Covered valet parking; in/out $26. TV; cable (premium), VCR avail (movies). Afternoon refreshments. Restaurant (see PARK GRILL). Rm serv 24 hrs. Bar 11-1 am; entertainment. Ck-out noon. Meeting rms. Business center. Concierge. Exercise equipt for in-rm use. Health club privileges. Bathrm phones, minibars; microwaves avail. Some balconies. Cr cds: A, C, D, DS, JCB, MC, V.

D

★★★ **PRESCOTT HOTEL.** *545 Post St (94102). 415/563-0303; fax 415/563-6831; res 800/283-7322. www.prescotthotel.com.* 166 rms, 7 story. S, D $215-$295; each addl $10; suites $250-$1,200; hol rates. Crib free. Covered valet parking, in/out $24. TV; cable, VCR avail. Pool privileges. Dining rm (see also POSTRIO). Complimentary coffee; afternoon refreshments. Rm serv 6 am-midnight. Bar 11-2 am. Ck-out noon, ck-in 3 pm. Business servs avail. In-rm modem link. Concierge serv. Health club privileges. Minibars; some wet bars. Union Square shopping one blk. Luxury level. Cr cds: A, C, D, DS, ER, JCB, MC, V.

D SC

★★ **THE QUEEN ANNE HOTEL.** *1590 Sutter St (94109). 415/441-2828; fax 415/775-5212; toll-free 800/227-3970. www.queenanne.com.* 48 rms, 4 story. No A/C. S, D $139-$199; each addl $10; suites $199-$315; under 12 free. Parking in/out $12. TV; cable (premium). Crib free. Complimentary continental bkfst; afternoon refreshments. Ck-out noon, ck-in 3 pm. Meeting rm. Business servs avail. In-rm modem link. Luggage handling. Health club privileges. Bathrm phones; some wet bars, fireplaces. Restored boarding school for young girls (1890); stained glass, many antiques, carved staircase. Cr cds: A, D, DS, MC, V.

D

★★★ **RADISSON MIYAKO.** *1625 Post St (94115). 415/922-3200; fax 415/921-0417; toll-free 800/533-4567.* 218 rms, 5 and 16 story. S $139-$179; D $159-$199; each addl $20; suites $179-$299; under 18 free. Crib free. Garage in/out $10. Valet $15. TV; cable, VCR avail. Restaurant (see also YOYO). Bar 10-1 am. Ck-out 1 pm. Meeting rms. Business center. In-rm modem link. Concierge. Exercise equipt. Health club privileges. Massage. Refrigerator, sauna in suites. Balconies. Japanese decor; authentic Japanese furnishings in some rms. Cr cds: A, C, DS, MC, V.

D

★★★ **RENAISSANCE PARC 55 HOTEL.** *55 Cyril Magnin St (94102). 415/392-8000; fax 415/403-6602; toll-free 800/468-3571. www.renaissance hotels.com.* 1,009 rms, 32 story. S, D $169-$375; each addl $15; suites $340-$1,200; under 19 free. Crib free. Garage $25. TV; cable (premium), VCR avail. Restaurants 6:30 am-10 pm. Bar 11-1 am; pianist. Ck-out noon. Convention facilities. Business center. In-rm modem link. Concierge. Drugstore. Exercise equipt; sauna. Health club privileges. Massage. Bathrm phones. Luxury level. Cr cds: A, D, DS, JCB, MC, V.

Japanese Tea Garden, Golden Gate Park

★★★ **RENAISSANCE STANFORD COURT.** *905 California St (94108). 415/989-3500; fax 415/391-0513; toll-free 800/227-4736.* 393 rms, 8 story. S $255-$400; D $275-$420; each addl $30; 1-bedrm suites $675-$750; 2-bedrm suites $875-$4,500; under 18 free. Crib free. Valet parking, in/out $27/day. TV; cable (premium), VCR avail. Restaurant (see also FOURNOU'S OVENS). Afternoon tea in lobby. Rm serv 24 hrs. Bars 11-1 am. Ck-out noon. Meeting rms. Business center. In-rm modem link. Concierge. Shopping arcade. Exercise equipt. Health club privileges. Marble bathrms with phone. Microwaves avail. Cr cds: A, D, DS, JCB, MC, V.

★★★★ **THE RITZ-CARLTON, SAN FRANCISCO.** *600 Stockton St (94108). 415/296-7465; fax 415/291-0288; res 415/364-3450. www. ritz-carlton.com.* This decidedly cosmopolitan hotel located on Nob Hill provides genteel service and plush surroundings. Guests can relax in nicely appointed guest rooms before and after exploring San Francisco sites, and gourmets will appreciate cuisine served in The Dining Room. The lovely marble indoor pool area feels as though it was brought to San Francisco from a chateau in Europe. 336 rms, 9 story, 44 suites. S, D $400-$440; suites $525-$3,800; under 18 free; package plans. Crib avail. Garage; valet, in/out $30. TV; cable (premium), VCR avail. Indoor pool; whirlpool. Restaurants 6:30 am-11 pm (see also THE DINING ROOM). Rm serv 24 hrs. Bar; entertainment. Ck-out noon. Convention facilities. Business servs avail. In-rm modem link. Concierge. Gift shop. Exercise rm; sauna. Spa. Bathrm phones, minibars; some wet bars. Luxury level. Cr cds: A, C, D, DS, ER, JCB, MC, V.

★★★ **SAN FRANCISCO MARRIOTT.** *55 Fourth St (94103). 415/896-1600; fax 415/777-2799; toll-free 800/228-9290.* 1,500 rms, 39 story, 141 suites. S, D $195-$249; each addl $20; suites $280-$2,400; under 18 free. Crib free. Garage $27, in/out 24 hrs. TV; cable (premium), VCR avail. Indoor pool; poolside serv. Restaurant 6:30 am-11 pm; Fri, Sat to midnight. Bar 10:30-2 am. Ck-out noon. Convention facilities. Business center. In-rm modem link. Concierge. Gift shop. Sundries. Exercise equipt; sauna, steam rm. Minibars; some bathrm phones. Refrigerator, wet bar in suites. Some balconies. Six-story atrium lobby. Luxury level. Cr cds: A, C, D, DS, JCB, MC, V.

★★★ **SAN FRANCISCO MARRIOTT FISHERMANS WHARF.** *1250 Columbus Ave (94133). 415/775-7555; fax 415/474-2099; res 800/228-9290.*

www.marriotthotels.com/sfofw. 285 rms, 5 story. S, D $209-$269; suites $300-$800; under 18 free; wkend rates. Crib free. Valet parking in/out $19. TV; cable (premium), VCR avail. Restaurant 6 am-10 pm. Bar 11-1 am. Ck-out noon. Meeting rms. Business center. In-rm modem link. Gift shop. Exercise equipt; sauna. Bathrm phones. Marble floor in lobby. Cr cds: A, C, D, DS, ER, JCB, MC, V.

★★★ **SAN RAMON MARRIOTT.** *2600 Bishop Dr, San Ramon (94583). 925/867-9200. www.marriott.com*. 368 rms, 6 story. S, D $145-$275; each addl $15; under 17 free. Crib avail. Pet accepted. TV; cable (premium), VCR avail. Complimentary coffee in rms, newspaper. Restaurant 6 am-10:30 pm. Bar. Ck-out noon. Meeting rms. Business center. Valet serv. Gift shop. Exercise rm. Some refrigerators, minibars. Cr cds: A, C, D, DS, MC, V.

★ **SAN REMO HOTEL.** *2237 Mason St (94133). 415/776-8688; fax 415/776-2811; toll-free 800/352-7366. www.sanremohotel.com*. 62 rms, shared baths, 2 story. No rm phones. Apr-Oct: S $75; D $85; lower rates rest of yr. Bar 5-11 pm. Parking $10. Ck-out 11 am, ck-in 2 pm. Business servs avail. Lndry facilities. Health club privileges. Italianate Victorian building; antiques, art. Cr cds: A, C, D, ER, JCB, MC, V.

★ **SAVOY HOTEL.** *580 Geary St (94102). 415/441-2700; fax 415/441-0124; toll-free 800/227-4223*. 83 rms, 7 story, 13 suites. Apr-Oct: S, D $125-$145; each addl $15; suites $195-$245; under 12 free; wkends, hols (2-day min); higher rates special events; lower rates rest of yr. Crib free. Valet, in/out parking $18. TV; cable (premium). Complimentary coffee in rms; afternoon refreshments. Restaurant (see also BRASSERIE SAVOY). Bar; piano wkends. Ck-out noon. Meeting rms. Business servs avail. Concierge. Health club privileges. Minibars. Cr cds: A, C, D, DS, MC, V.

★★★ **SERRANO HOTEL.** *405 Taylor St (94102). 415/885-2500; fax 415/474-4879; res 877/294-9709*. 236 rms. S $199; D $269. Pet accepted. TV; cable (premium). Ck-out noon. Business center. Cr cds: A, C, D, DS, ER, JCB, MC, V.

★ **SHEEHAN.** *620 Sutter St (94102). 415/775-6500; fax 415/775-3271; toll-free 800/848-1529. www.sheehanhotel.com*. 64 rms, 60 with bath, 6 story. No A/C. S $89-$119; D $99-$169; each addl $10; under 12 free. Crib free. Garage $16. TV; cable. Indoor pool; lifeguard. Complimentary continental bkfst. No rm serv. Ck-out 11 am. Meeting rms. Business servs avail. Beauty shop. Exercise equipt. Cr cds: A, C, D, DS, JCB, MC, V.

★★★ **SHERATON FISHERMAN'S WHARF.** *2500 Mason St (94133). 415/362-5500; fax 415/956-5275; res 800/325-3535. www.sheratonatthewharf.com*. 524 rms, 4 story. S, D $230-$275; each addl $20; suites from $400-$600; under 17 free; package plans. Crib free. Garage $14. TV; cable (premium), VCR avail. Heated pool. Restaurant 6:30 am-10 pm. Rm serv to midnight. Bar to 11:30 pm, Fri, Sat to midnight; entertainment Sat. Ck-out noon. Convention facilities. Business center. In-rm modem link. Valet serv. Concierge. Gift shop. Barber, beauty shop. Health club privileges. Luxury level. Cr cds: A, D, DS, MC, V.

★★★ **SIR FRANCIS DRAKE.** *450 Powell St (94102). 415/392-7755; fax 415/677-9341; toll-free 800/227-5480. www.sirfrancisdrake.com*. 417 rms, 21 story. S, D $175-$259; each addl $20; suites $350-$650; under 18 free; package plans. Crib free. Valet parking in/out $24. TV; cable (premium), VCR avail. Restaurant (see also SCALA'S BISTRO). Bar 11:30-1 am. Ck-out noon. Meeting rms. Business servs avail. In-rm modem link. Concierge. Shopping arcade. Exercise equipt. Cr cds: A, D, DS, JCB, MC, V.

★★ **VILLA FLORENCE.** *225 Powell St (94102). 415/397-7700; fax 415/397-1006; toll-free 800/553-4411. www.citysearch.com/sfo/villaflorence*. 183 rms, 7 story, 36 suites. S, D $135-$199; suites $165-$199; under 16 free. Crib free. Valet parking, $23.

TV; cable, VCR avail. Coffee in rms. Restaurant 7 am-11 pm. Bar. Ck-out noon. Meeting rms. Business servs avail. In-rm modem link. Concierge. Health club privileges. Refrigerators, minibars. Cr cds: A, C, D, DS, ER, JCB, MC, V.

D SC

★★★ **WARWICK REGIS.** *490 Geary St (94102). 415/928-7900; fax 415/441-8788; res 800/827-3447. www.warwickhotels.com.* 80 rms, 8 story. S $139-$149; D $159-$169; each addl $15; suites $150-$239; under 15 free. Crib free. Valet parking in/out $25. TV; cable (premium), VCR avail. Restaurants 7-10 am, 6-10 pm. Bar 11-2 am. Ck-out 1 pm. Meeting rms. Business center. In-rm modem link. Health club privileges. Refrigerators; some fireplaces. Balconies. Louis XVI decor. Built 1911. Cr cds: A, C, D, DS, JCB, MC, V.

D

★★★★ **THE WESTIN ST. FRANCIS.** *335 Powell St (94102). 415/397-7000; fax 415/774-0124. www.westin.com.* This magnificent hotel, built in 1904, combines old-world charm with modern amenities and luxurious guest rooms. The excellent service and attention to detail are just two reasons why the legendary St. Francis remains an unforgettable experience. 1,019 rms, 31 story, 84 suites. S, D $209; suites $450. Crib avail. Pet accepted, some restrictions, fee. Valet parking. TV; cable (premium), VCR avail. Complimentary coffee in rms, newspaper. Rm serv 24-hr. Ck-out noon, ck-in 3 pm. Conference center, meeting rms. Business center. Luggage handling. Concierge serv. Dry cleaning. Gift shop. Exercise equipt, steam rm. Cr cds: A, C, D, DS, JCB, MC, V.

D

★★★★ **W HOTEL SAN FRANCISCO.** *181 Third St (94103). 415/777-5300; fax 415/817-7823; res 877/946-8357. www.whotels.com.* Another chic spot in this national chain's list of hotels geared to meet the ever-increasing demands of tech-savvy business clientele. In the South of Market district and adjacent to the Museum of Modern Art, the 423 stylishly modern rooms all contain a signature "heavenly bed." The eclectic and aptly-named restaurant, XYZ, finishes off the dramatic three-story lobby. 423 rms, 31 story. S, D $289-$319; each addl $20; under 17 free. Crib $20. Pet accepted. TV; cable (premium), VCR avail. Indoor pool. Restaurant 6:30 am-10 pm. Meeting rms. Business center. Bellhops. Concierge. Exercise rm. Cr cds: A, C, D, DS, JCB, MC, V.

D

★★ **YORK HOTEL.** *940 Sutter St (94109). 415/885-6800; fax 415/885-6990; toll-free 800/808-9675. www.yorkhotel.com.* 96 rms, 7 story. S, D $95-$137; each addl $10; suites $210; under 12 free; lower rates Nov-mid-Apr. Crib $10. Parking $14-$25. TV; cable. Complimentary continental bkfst, coffee in rms. Ck-out noon. Meeting rm. Business servs avail. In-rm modem link. Exercise equipt. Health club privileges. Minibars; some refrigerators. Renovated 1922 hotel; marble floors, ceiling fans. Hitchcock's *Vertigo* filmed here. Cr cds: A, C, D, DS, ER, JCB, MC, V.

SC

B&Bs/Small Inns

★★ **ALAMO SQUARE INN.** *719 Scott St (94117). 415/922-2055; fax 415/931-1304; toll-free 800/345-9888. www.alamoinn.com.* 14 rms in 2 buildings, 10 with shower only, 3 story. No A/C. S, D $85-$125; each addl $25; suites $195-$295; wkly rates; wkends (2-day min). Crib free. TV in some rms; VCR avail. Complimentary full bkfst; afternoon refreshments. Restaurant nearby. Ck-out noon, ck-in 2-9 pm. Business servs avail. Concierge. Some balconies. Picnic tables. Inn complex includes two restored Victorian mansions, 1895 Queen Anne and 1896 Tudor Revival, located in historic district. Antique furnishings, some wood-burning fireplaces; stained-glass skylight. Garden. Overlooks Alamo Square; panoramic view of city skyline. Totally nonsmoking. Cr cds: A, MC, V.

★ **ALBION HOUSE INN BED AND BREAKFAST.** *135 Gough St (94102). 415/621-0896; fax 415/621-3811; res 800/625-2466.* 8 rms, 2 story. S, D $95-$155; suite $195-$235. TV. Complimentary full bkfst; afternoon refreshments. Ck-out noon, ck-in 4 pm. Business servs avail. Built 1906; individually decorated rms, antiques; piano in parlor. Cr cds: A, D, DS, MC, V.

★★ THE ANDREWS HOTEL. *624 Post St (94109). 415/563-6877; fax 415/928-6919; res 800/738-7477. www.andrewshotel.com.* 48 rms, 7 story. No A/C. S, D $99-$119; each addl $10; suites $132. Parking adj, $15 in/out. TV. Complimentary continental bkfst. Dining rm 5:30-10 pm. Ck-out noon, ck-in 3 pm. Business servs avail. European decor; impressionist prints. Former Turkish bathhouse built 1905. Totally nonsmoking. Cr cds: A, D, JCB, MC, V.

★★★ ARCHBISHOP'S MANSION. *1000 Fulton St (94117). 415/563-7872; fax 415/885-3193; toll-free 800/543-5820. www.archbishopsmansion.com.* 15 rms, 3 story. S $129-$199; D $159-$259; each addl $20; suites $215-$385; under 12 free. TV; cable, VCR (free movies). Complimentary continental bkfst; afternoon refreshments. Restaurant nearby. Ck-out 11:30 am, ck-in 3 pm. Business servs avail. Concierge serv. Health club privileges. Stained-glass skylight over stairwell. Built 1904; antiques. Individually decorated rms. Cr cds: A, D, DS, MC, V.

★★★ INN AT UNION SQUARE. *440 Post St (94102). 415/397-3510; fax 415/989-0529; toll-free 800/288-4346.* 30 rms, 6 story. No A/C. S, D $175-$220; each addl $15; suites $220-$350. Crib free. Valet parking in/out $22. TV; cable, VCR avail. Pool privileges. Complimentary afternoon refreshments. Rm serv 5am-10 pm. Bar. Ck-out noon, ck-in 2 pm. Business servs avail. In-rm modem link. Luggage handling. Concierge serv. Health club privileges. Sitting area, fireplace most floors; antiques. Robes in all rms. Penthouse suite. Totally nonsmoking. Cr cds: A, C, D, DS, ER, MC, V.

D

★★★ INN SAN FRANCISCO. *943 S Van Ness Ave (94110). 415/641-0188; fax 415/641-1701; toll-free 800/359-0913. www.innsf.com.* 21 rms, 18 baths, 3 story. No A/C. S $155; D $175; each addl $20; suites $175-$235. Limited parking avail; $10. TV. Complimentary full bkfst. Restaurant nearby. Ck-out noon, ck-in 2 pm. Business servs avail. Whirlpools. Refrigerators. Balconies. Library. Italianate mansion (1872) near Mission Dolores; ornate woodwork, fireplaces; antique furnishings; garden with redwood hot tub, gazebo; view of city, bay from rooftop sun deck. Cr cds: A, C, D, DS, MC, V.

★★ JACKSON COURT. *2198 Jackson St (94115). 415/929-7670; fax 415/929-1405.* 10 rms, shower only, 3 story. No A/C. S, D $139-$195; each addl $25; under 12 free; wkends (2-day min). TV; cable (premium). Complimentary continental bkfst; afternoon refreshments. Restaurant nearby. Ck-out 11 am, ck-in 2 pm. Concierge serv. Street parking. Some fireplaces; microwaves avail. Brownstone mansion built in 1900. Totally nonsmoking. Cr cds: A, MC, V.

★★★★ THE SHERMAN HOUSE. *2160 Green St (94123). 415/563-3600; fax 415/563-1882; toll-free 800/424-5777. www.theshermanhouse.com.* Built by Leander Sherman during the turn of the last century, this Italianate Victorian house has been painstakingly restored to its original splendor. The music room pays homage to Sherman's love of music, the rest of the house is full of Victorian antiques, and the grounds have been manicured in the English style. Many of the 14 individually designed guest rooms have views of the Golden Gate Bridge. The romantic, tiny dining room is open to hotel guests only, and features a different menu each night. 14 rms, 4 story. No elvtr. S, D $435; suites $675-$850; under 12 free. TV; cable (premium), VCR (movies). Dining rm (by res) 5:30-9 pm. Rm serv 24 hrs. Ck-out noon, ck-in 4 pm. Business servs avail. In-rm modem link. Concierge serv. Butler serv. Health club privileges. Bathrm phones; many wet bars. Private patios, balconies. Totally nonsmoking. Cr cds: A, C, D, DS, MC, V.

★★ **STANYAN PARK HOTEL.** *750 Stanyan St (94117). 415/751-1000; fax 415/668-5454. www.stanyanpark.com.* 36 rms, 3 story, 6 kits. No A/C. S, D $150; suites $185-$225. Municipal parking $5. TV, cable. Complimentary continental bkfst; afternoon refreshments. Ck-out noon, ck-in 3 pm. Business servs avail. In-rm modem link. Luggage handling. Refrigerator in suites. Restored Victorian hotel. Cr cds: A, C, D, DS, MC, V.

D

★★ **VICTORIAN INN ON THE PARK.** *301 Lyon St (94117). 415/931-1830; fax 415/931-1830; toll-free 800/435-1967.* 12 rms, 4 story. No A/C. No elvtr. S, D $124-$174; each addl $20; suites $174-$345. Parking $13. TV in lounge, rm TV avail. Complimentary continental bkfst; afternoon refreshments. Ck-out 11:30 am, ck-in 2 pm. Business servs avail. In-rm modem link. Health club privileges. Some fireplaces; microwaves avail. Historic building (1897); Victorian decor. Cr cds: A, C, D, DS, MC, V.

★★ **WASHINGTON SQUARE INN.** *1660 Stockton St (94133). 415/981-4220; fax 415/397-7242; toll-free 800/388-0220.* 15 rms, 2 story. No A/C. S, D $150; each addl $15. Valet parking $20. TV; cable, VCR avail. Complimentary continental bkfst; afternoon refreshments. Ck-out noon, ck-in 3 pm. Business servs avail. In-rm modem link. Luggage handling. Concierge serv. Health club privileges. Individually decorated rms with English and French country antiques. Opp historic Washington Square. Totally nonsmoking. Cr cds: A, C, D, DS, JCB, MC, V.

D

Restaurants

★★ **42 DEGREES.** *235 16th St (94118). 415/777-5558.* Hrs: 11:30 am-3 pm, 6:30-11:30 pm; Mon, Tues to 3 pm. Closed Sun; hols. Res accepted. Mediterranean menu. Bar. Lunch $5-$11, dinner $5-$20. Specialties: pan-seared sea bass, Iberian sausage, slow-roasted lamb shank. Entertainment Wed-Sat. Outdoor dining. Casual decor. Totally nonsmoking. Cr cds: A, DS, MC, V.

D

★★ **ACE WASABI'S ROCK AND ROLL SUSHI.** *3339 Steiner St (94123). 415/567-4903. www.citysearch.com/sfo/acewasabis.* Hrs: 5:30-10:30 pm; Fri, Sat to 11 pm; Sun 5-10 pm. Closed Jan 1, July 4, Dec 25. Japanese menu. Bar. Dinner $4.95-$9.50. Specialties: ahi and Hamachi pot stickers, flying kamikaze roll. Modern Japanese decor. Totally nonsmoking. Cr cds: A, MC, V.

D

★★★ **ACQUERELLO.** *1722 Sacramento St (94109). 415/567-5432. www.acquerello.com.* Hrs: 5:30-10:30 pm. Closed Sun, Mon; hols. Res accepted. Northern Italian menu. Wine, beer. A la carte entrees: dinner $22-$28. Prix fixe dinner: $55/person. Menu changes seasonally. Totally nonsmoking. Cr cds: A, D, DS, MC, V.

★ **ALAMO SQUARE SEAFOOD GRILL.** *803 Fillmore St (94117). 415/440-2828. www.citysearch.com/sfo/alamosquare.* Hrs: 10 am-2 pm, 5:30-10 pm; Sun (brunch) 10 am-2 pm. Seafood menu. Wine, beer. A la carte entrees: dinner $8.50-$13.50. Sun brunch $5.50-$6.95. Specialties: crab cake, blackened swordfish with beurre blanc sauce, grilled tuna with beurre rouge sauce. Cr cds: MC, V.

D

★★ **ALBONA RISTORANTE ITALIANO.** *545 Francisco St (94133). 415/441-1040.* Hrs: 5-10 pm. Closed Sun, Mon; Thanksgiving, Dec 25. Res accepted. Northern Italian menu. Wine, beer. A la carte entrees: dinner $12.50-$16.75. Specializes in Italian cuisine with Austrian-Hungarian influence. Free valet parking. Intimate dining. Chef-owned. Totally nonsmoking. Cr cds: A, D, DS, MC, V.

★ **ALEGRIA'S FOODS FROM SPAIN.** *2018 Lombard St (94123). 415/929-8888.* Hrs: 5:30-11 pm. Res accepted. Spanish menu. Bar. A la carte entrees: dinner $12.50-$14.95. Specialties: zarzuela de mariscos, tapas, paella. Entertainment Thurs-

Sun. Spanish decor. Totally non-smoking. Cr cds: A, D, MC, V.

D

★★ **ANJOU.** *44 Campton Pl (94108). 415/392-5373. www.anjou-sf.com.* Hrs: 11:30 am-2:30 pm, 5:30-10 pm. Closed Sun, Mon. Res accepted. French menu. Bar. A la carte entrees: lunch $8-$17, dinner $12-$18. Prix fixe: lunch $12.50. Specialties: Chilean sea bass, confit of duck leg, honey-roasted chicken. Bi-level dining area, high ceiling. Cr cds: D, DS, MC, V.

D

★ **ANNABELLE'S BAR AND BISTRO.** *68 4th St (94103). 415/777-1200. www.victorianhotelcom.* Hrs: 7 am-10:30 pm. Closed Dec 25. Res accepted. No A/C. Bar. Bkfst $5.95-$10.50, lunch, dinner $6-$14.95. Specializes in rotisserie cooking. Streetfront cafe was once a bank; teller cages from 1900s. Totally non-smoking. Cr cds: A, D, MC, V.

D

★ **ANTICA TRATTORIA.** *2400 Polk St (94109). 415/928-5797.* Hrs: 5:30-10 pm; Fri, Sat to 10:30 pm. Closed Mon; hols. Res accepted. No A/C. Italian menu. Wine, beer. A la carte entrees: dinner $8-$15. Children's menu. Specializes in pasta. Casual corner cafe. Totally nonsmoking. Cr cds: A, C, D, MC, V.

D

★★★ **ANZU.** *222 Mason St (94102). 415/394-1100. www.anzunikko.com.* Japanese cuisine menu. Specializes in sushi, steak. Hrs: 6:30-10:30 am, 11:30 am-2 pm, 5:30-10 pm; Sun brunch 10 am-2 pm. Res accepted. Wine, beer. Lunch $12-$25; dinner $8-$35. Children's menu. Entertainment. Cr cds: A, D, DS, JCB, MC, V.

D SC

★★★★ **AQUA.** *252 California St (94111). 415/956-9662.* Seafood lovers will rejoice in this sleek eatery where fish receives the royal treatment. Tuna can be mixed tableside in a delicious tartar or it can receive richness by being paired with foie gras for a decadent combination. The stark industrial decor is softened by pretty flower arrangements, and service is professional. Specialties: medallions of ahi tuna (rare) with foie gras in wine sauce. Hrs: 11:30 am-2:15 pm, 5:30-10:30 pm; Fri, Sat to 11 pm. Closed Sun; most hols. Bar. Res accepted. A la carte entrees: lunch $14-$19, dinner $27-$45. Complete meals: lunch $35, dinner $65. Cr cds: A, D, MC, V.

D

★★★ **A. SABELLA'S.** *2766 Taylor St (94133). 415/771-6775. www.asabella.com.* Hrs: 11 am-10:30 pm; Sat to 11 pm. Closed Dec 25. Res accepted. Bar. Wine list. A la carte entrees: lunch $7.50-$15, dinner $11.75-$46.75. Children's menu. Specialty: fresh local seafood. Own desserts. Dinner theater Fri-Sat (7:30 pm). 1,000 gallon crab, abalone, and lobster tanks. Overlooks wharf, bay. Family-owned. Cr cds: A, D, DS, MC, V.

D

★★ **ASIA SF.** *201 9th St (94103). 415/255-2742. www.asiasf.com.* Specializes in Pan Asian entrees. Hrs: 5-10 pm. Res accepted. Wine, beer. Dinner $8-$21. Entertainment. Cr cds: A, D, DS, MC, V.

D

★★ **AVENUE 9.** *1243 9th Ave (94122). 415/664-6999.* Hrs: 11:30 am-10 pm; Fri, Sat to 11 pm; Sun from 10 am; Sun brunch 10 am-3 pm; early-bird dinner 5:30-7 pm (seasonal). Closed July 4, Thanksgiving, Dec 25. Res accepted. Contemporary American menu. Bar. A la carte entrees: lunch $7-$15, dinner $10-$18. Sun brunch $5-$10. Children's menu. Specializes in hand-crafted

Lombard Street, San Francisco

cuisine. Street parking. American bistro decor. Totally nonsmoking. Cr cds: A, MC, V.

D

★★★ **AZIE.** *826 Folsom St (94107). 415/538-0918*. French, Asian cuisine. Specializes in seared Maine cod with manilla clams, black beans, and white wine sauce. Hrs: 11:30 am-10:30 pm; Fri, Sat to 11:30 pm. Lunch, dinner $17-$35. Wine list. Res accepted. Valet parking. Entertainment. Cr cds: A, D, MC, V.

★ **BAKER STREET BISTRO.** *2953 Baker St (94123). 415/931-1475*. Hrs: 10 am-2 pm, 5:30-10:30 pm; Sun 5-9:30 pm; Sat, Sun brunch 10 am-2:30 pm. Closed Mon. Res accepted. No A/C. Country French menu. Wine. Lunch $4.75-$7.50, dinner $8.75-$13.50. Prix fixe: dinner $14.50. Sat, Sun brunch $4.75-$7.50. Specializes in rabbit, duck, escargot. Street parking. Outdoor dining. Bistro atmosphere; trompe l'oeil painting on front of building. Cr cds: A, MC, V.

D

★★ **BALBOA CAFE.** *3199 Fillmore St (94123). 415/921-3944*. Hrs: 11 am-10 pm; Sun brunch 10:30 am-4 pm. Bar to 2 am. A la carte entrees: lunch, dinner $8-$16. Sun brunch $7-$14. Specializes in beef. Built 1897. Cr cds: A, MC, V.

D

★★ **BASIL.** *1175 Folsom St (94103). 415/552-8999. www.citysearch7.com/sfo/basilthai*. Hrs: 11:45 am-3 pm, 5-10 pm; Fri to 10:30 pm; Sat 5-10:30 pm; Sun 5-10 pm. Thai menu. Bar. A la carte entrees: lunch, dinner $7.50-$14. Specializes in curries. Street parking. Totally nonsmoking. Cr cds: A, MC, V.

D

★★ **BASTA PASTA.** *1268 Grant St (94133). 415/434-2248. www.basta pasta.citysearch.com*. Hrs: 11:30-1:45 am. Closed hols. Res accepted. Italian menu. Bar. Lunch, dinner $7.95-$16.50. Specializes in pizza baked in wood-burning oven, pasta, veal. Valet parking. Outdoor (rooftop) dining. Main dining rm on 2nd floor. Cr cds: A, D, DS, MC, V.

D

★★ **BETELNUT PEJIU WU.** *2030 Union St (94123). 415/929-8855. www.citysearch.com*. Hrs: 11:30 am-11 pm; Fri, Sat to midnight. Closed Thanksgiving, Dec 25. Res accepted. Southeast Asian menu. Bar. A la carte entrees: lunch $8-$13, dinner $14-$20. Specializes in multi-regional Pacific Rim cuisine. Outdoor dining. Asian decor. Totally nonsmoking. Cr cds: D, DS, MC, V.

D

★★★ **BIG FOUR.** *1075 California St (94109). 415/771-1140. www.bigfour.com*. Hrs: 7-10 am, 11:30 am-3 pm, 5:30-10:30 pm; Sat, Sun 7-11 am, 5:30-10:30 pm. Res accepted. Bar 11:30 am-midnight. Contemporary American cuisine. A la carte entrees: bkfst $5-$12.95, lunch $9.50-$18.50, dinner $18-$28.50. Complete meal: bkfst $15. Specialties: seasonal wild game dishes, lamb sausage with black pepper papardelle noodles. Pianist eves. Valet parking. Traditional San Francisco club atmosphere. Cr cds: A, D, MC, V.

D

★ **BISCUITS AND BLUES.** *401 Mason St (94102). 415/292-2583. www.sanfrancisco/citysearch.com*. Hrs: 5 pm-1 am. Southern, New Orleans cuisine. Bar. A la carte entrees: dinner $9.95. Specializes in biscuits, catfish, jambalaya. Entertainment. Casual decor. Cr cds: A, C, D, MC, V.

D

★★ **BISTRO AIX.** *3340 Steiner St (94123). 415/202-0100*. Specializes in crispy roasted half-chicken, house-cured salmon. Hrs: 6-10 pm. Res accepted. Wine, beer. Dinner $8.95-$15.95. Entertainment. Cr cds: A, D, MC, V.

D

★★ **BIX.** *56 Gold St (94133). 415/433-6300*. Hrs: 11:30 am-11 pm; Fri to midnight; Sat 5:30 pm-midnight; Sun 6-10 pm. Closed hols. Res accepted. Bar to 1:30 am. A la carte entrees: lunch $10-$15, dinner $18-$28. Specializes in classic American dishes with California influence. Jazz nightly. Valet parking (dinner). Modernized 40's supper club with grand piano. Cr cds: A, D, DS, MC, V.

★★ **BIZOU.** *598 Fourth St (94107). 415/543-2222.* Hrs: 11:30 am-2:30 pm, 5:30-10 pm; Fri to 10:30 pm; Sat 5:30-10:30 pm. Closed Sun, most hols. Res accepted. No A/C. French, Italian menu. Bar. Lunch $5.50-$14.50, dinner $11.50-$19. Specialties: batter-fried green beans, beef cheek, bittersweet chocolate, and coffee vacherin. Street parking. Totally nonsmoking. Cr cds: A, D, DS, MC, V.

D

★ **BOBBY RUBINO'S.** *245 Jefferson St (94133). 415/673-2266.* Hrs: 11:30 am-11 pm. Res accepted. No A/C. Bar. A la carte entrees: lunch $4.95-$12.95, dinner $6.95-$17.95. Children's menu. Specializes in steak, baby back ribs, fresh seafood. Casual, family dining, on two levels. View of fishing fleet. Cr cds: A, D, DS, MC, V.

SC

★★ **BOCCA ROTIS.** *1 W Portal Ave (94127). 415/665-9900.* Hrs: 7 am-10 pm; Sat from 11 am; Sun from 9 am. Closed Thanksgiving, Dec 25. Italian, French menu. Bar. A la carte entrees: bkfst $7-$12, lunch $7-$14, dinner $7-$16. Children's menu. Specialties: rotisserie chicken, pork chops. Own desserts. Street parking. Totally nonsmoking. Cr cds: MC, V.

D

★★ **BONTA RISTORANTE.** *2223 Union St (94123). 415/929-0407. www.bontaristorante.com.* Hrs: 5:30-10:30 pm; Fri, Sat to 11 pm; Sun 5-10 pm. Closed Mon; hols. Res accepted. No A/C. Italian menu. Wine, beer. A la carte entrees: dinner $10.50-$18.75. Children's menu. Large vegetarian selection. Storefront dining rm. Totally nonsmoking. Cr cds: MC, V.

D

★★★★ **BOULEVARD.** *1 Mission St (94105). 415/543-6084. www.boulevardrestaurant.com.* Earthy, slow-cooked flavors are the signature of chef Nancy Oakes, who continues to keep Boulevard on the top of most San Francisco lists with her work. Boulevard is housed in an historic space in the SoMa area and has been designed by Pat Kuleto to incorporate three distinct art nouveau dining rooms. Servers are genuinely pleasant, and are clearly proud to serve Oakes's excellent cuisine. Contemporary American menu. Specializes in roasted chicken breast, pork loin, pan-roasted halibut. Hrs: 11:30 am-2:15 pm, 5:30-10 pm; Thurs-Sat to 10:30 pm. Closed hols. Bar. Res accepted. Lunch $20-$30, dinner $45-$60. Valet parking. Totally nonsmoking. Cr cds: A, C, D, MC, V.

D

★★ **BRASSERIE SAVOY.** *580 Geary St (94102). 415/441-8080. www.savoyhotel.net.* Hrs: 7 am-noon, 5-10 pm; Wed, Thurs to 10:30 pm; Fri, Sat to 11 pm. Closed July 4, Labor Day. Res accepted. French menu. Bar. A la carte entrees: bkfst $4-$13, dinner $16-$20. Complete meal: dinner $28. Specialties: coulibiac of salmon, beef cheeks, oysters in champagne sauce. Pianist wkends. Valet parking. Elegant decor. Totally nonsmoking. Cr cds: A, D, MC, V.

D

★ **CAFE BASTILLE.** *22 Belden Pl (94104). 415/986-5673. www.cafebastille.com.* Hrs: 11 am-11 pm. Closed Sun; also hols. Res accepted. French menu. Bar. Lunch, dinner $8-$13. Children's menu. Specializes in crÎpes, mussels. Entertainment Thurs-Sat. Outdoor dining. French bistro decor. Totally nonsmoking. Cr cds: A, D, MC, V.

D

★★ **CAFE DE LA PRESSE.** *352 Grant Ave (94108). 415/398-2680. www.hotel-tritonsf.com.* Specializes in veal morengo, lamb shank. Hrs: 11 am-11 pm. Res accepted. Wine, beer. Lunch, dinner $8-$17. Entertainment. Cr cds: A, D, DS, MC, V.

D

★ **CAFE KATI.** *1963 Sutter St (94115). 415/775-7313.* Eclectic menu. Wine, beer. Hrs: 5:30-10 pm. Closed Mon; hols. Res accepted. Dinner $15-$19. Specialties: vegetarian risotto, miso-marinated chicken sea bass, cider-marinated tenderloin of pork. Valet parking Fri, Sat. Contemporary Asian decor. Totally nonsmoking. Cr cds: A, MC, V.

D

★ **CAFE MARIMBA.** *2317 Chestnut St (94123). 415/776-1506.* Mexican menu. Specialties: chicken breast with mole sauce, Veracruz-style fresh fish, margaritas. Hrs: 11:30 am-10 pm; Mon from 5:30 pm; Fri, Sat to 11 pm; Sat, Sun brunch 11:30 am-2 pm. Closed Thanksgiving, Dec 25. Res accepted. Bar. A la carte entrees: lunch, dinner $6.25-$11.95. Sun brunch $6.75-$8.25. Children's menu. Brightly colored restaurant with papier mache figures and Mexican folk art. Cr cds: A, MC, V.

D

★★ **CAFE PESCATORE.** *2455 Mason St (94133). 415/561-1111.* Italian, American menu. Specializes in fresh seafood, oak-burning oven pizza. Hrs: 7 am-10 pm; Fri, Sat to 11 pm. Closed Dec 25. Bar. Res accepted. A la carte entrees: bkfst $5.95-$9.95, lunch $6.95-$16.95, dinner $8.75-$16.95. Children's menu. Outdoor dining. Trattoria-style dining with maritime memorabilia. Cr cds: A, DS, MC, V.

D

★★ **CAFE TIRAMISU.** *28 Belden Pl (94104). 415/421-7044.* Hrs: 11:30 am-3 pm, 5-10 pm; Sat 5-11 pm. Closed Sun; hols. Res accepted. Italian menu. Wine, beer. Lunch $8.50-$16.50, dinner $11-$25. Specialties: rack of lamb, risotto. Outdoor dining. Italian decor. Totally nonsmoking. Cr cds: A, D, MC, V.

★★★★ **CAMPTON PLACE DINING ROOM.** *340 Stockton St (94108). 415/955-5555.* Gascon native Laurent Manrique took over the kitchen of this sophisticated restaurant last year and has transformed the menu to include a French sensibility amidst the California flavors. Dishes are divided into two categories: "Tradition" may include delectable foie gras, simply prepared in a tureen with brioche toast; "Evolution" could include a delicious concoction of John Dory sprinkled with fresh almonds, bay leaves, calamari, and raisins. The wine list does a fine job of matching French and American wines with the food. French cuisine. Hrs: 7-10:30 am, 11:30 am-2 pm, 6-10 pm; Fri to 10:30 pm; Sat 8-11 am, noon-2 pm, 5:30-10:30 pm; Sun 8 am-2 pm, 6-9:30 pm. Bar 10 am-11 pm; Fri, Sat to midnight. Wine list. Res accepted. A la carte entrees: bkfst $9-$16, lunch $9.50-$16.50, dinner $23-$36. Prix fixe: lunch $21.50, dinner $48-$69. Sun brunch $9-$14.50. Children's menu. Own baking. Valet parking. Cr cds: A, D, DS, MC, V.

D

★★ **CARNELIAN ROOM.** *555 California St (94104). 415/433-7500. www.carnelianroom.com.* Hrs: 6-10 pm; Sun brunch 10 am-2 pm. Closed hols. Res accepted. Bar from 3 pm; Sun from 10 am. Wine cellar. A la carte entrees: dinner $21-$39. Prix fixe: dinner $35. Sun brunch $27. Children's menu. Vintage 18th-century decor; antiques. 11 dining rms. Panoramic view of city. Jacket. Cr cds: A, D, DS, MC, V.

D

★★ **CARTA.** *1760 Market St (94102). 415/863-3516. www.cartasf.com.* Hrs: noon-3 pm, 5:30-10:30 pm; Fri to 11 pm; Sat 5:30-11 pm; Sun brunch 10 am-3 pm. Closed Mon; Thanksgiving, Dec 25; also 1st wk Jan and 1st wk Aug. Res accepted. Continental menu. Bar. A la carte entrees: lunch $5-$12, dinner $6-$20. Sun brunch $2-$10. Menu changes monthly. Street parking. Outdoor dining. Totally nonsmoking. Cr cds: A, C, D, DS, MC, V.

D

★ **CHA CHA CHA.** *1801 Haight St (94117). 415/386-7670.* Hrs: 11:30 am-4 pm, 5-11 pm; wkends to 11:30 pm. Closed Dec 25. Caribbean, Cuban menu. Wine, beer. A la carte entrees: lunch $4.75-$7, dinner $5.25-$13.50. Specializes in tapas. Casual dining in colorful atmosphere. Totally nonsmoking. Cr cds: A, MC, V.

D

★★★ **CHARLES NOB HILL.** *1250 Jones St (94111). 415/771-5400. www.aquarestaurant.com.* Hrs: 5:30-10 pm; Fri, Sat to 10:30 pm. Closed Mon. Res accepted. French menu. Bar. Dinner $19-$32. Complete meals: dinner $65. Specialties: lobster, squab, loin of lamb. Formal decor. Cr cds: A, D, MC, V.

D

★★★ **CHAYA.** *132 The Embarcadero (94105). 415/777-8688.* Specializes in sauteed bluenose sea bass, grilled rib-eye steak with peppercorn sauce. Hrs: 11:30 am-2:30 pm, 5:30-10:30 pm;

Sun to 9:30 pm. Res accepted. Wine, beer. Lunch $11-$17; dinner $20-$27. Entertainment. Cr cds: A, D, MC, V.
D

★★ **CHIC'S SEAFOOD.** *Pier 39 (94133). 415/421-2442.* Hrs: 9 am-11 pm. Res accepted. Bar. Bkfst $5.95-$7.50, lunch $5.95-$10.95. A la carte entrees: dinner $9.95-$19.95. Specializes in seafood. Own desserts. Parking. View of bay, Alcatraz, Golden Gate Bridge. Cr cds: A, C, D, DS, MC, V.
D SC

★★ **CHOW.** *215 Church St (94114). 415/552-2469.* Specializes in smiling noodles, spaghetti meatballs, pot roast. Hrs: 11 am-11 pm; Fri, Sat to midnight. Wine, beer. Lunch, dinner $5.50-$10.95. Entertainment. Cr cds: MC, V.
D

★★ **CITYSCAPE.** *333 O'Farrell St (94102). 415/923-5002.* Specializes in prime rib, salmon. Hrs: 5:30-10 pm; Fri, Sat to 10:30 pm; Sun brunch 10 am-2 pm. Res accepted. Wine, beer. Dinner $19-$29. Entertainment. Cr cds: A, DS, MC, V.
D

★ **CLIFF HOUSE.** *1090 Point Lobos Ave (94121). 415/386-3330. www.cliffhouse.com.* Specializes in stuffed petrale sole. Hrs: 9 am-3:30 pm, 11 am-10:30 pm; Sun brunch 9 am-2 pm. Res accepted. Wine, beer. Lunch $11-$25; dinner $16-$25. Entertainment. Historic district. Cr cds: A, D, MC, V.

★★★ **CYPRESS CLUB.** *500 Jackson St (94133). 415/296-8555. www.cypressclub.citysearch.com.* Hrs: 5:30-10 pm; Fri, Sat to 11 pm. Closed hols. Res accepted. Contemporary American menu. Bar 4:30 pm-2 am. Wine list. A la carte entrees: dinner $20-$29. Menu changes daily. Jazz nightly. Whimsical, 1940s-style design. Cr cds: A, D, DS, MC, V.
D

★★★ **DELFINA.** *3621 18th St (94110). 415/552-4055.* Specializes in Neman ranch flatiron steak, Fulton Valley chicken. Hrs: 5:30-10 pm; Fri, Sat to 11 pm. Closed Sun. Res accepted. Wine, beer. Dinner $10-$15. Entertainment. Cr cds: MC, V.
D

★★★★ **THE DINING ROOM.** *600 Stockton St (94108). 415/296-7465. www.ritz-carlton.com.* The Dining Room's jewelbox setting with floral accents, widely spaced tables, polished silver accoutrements, and a harpist who weaves romantic tunes, is everything a formal dining experience should be. Service is unobtrusively attentive and Sylvain Portay's contemporary French menu will delight with subtlety and precision. Contemporary French cuisine. Hrs: 6-10 pm. Closed Sun. Bar. Extensive wine list. Res accepted. Prix fixe: $61-$75. Entertainment. Valet parking. Totally nonsmoking. Cr cds: A, C, D, DS, MC, V.
D

★★★ **E AND O TRADING CO.** *314 Sutter St (94108). 415/693-0303. www.eotrading.com.* Specializes in Japanese salmon, grilled ahi tuna with sweet chili soy. Hrs: 11:30 am-midnight; Sun 5-10 pm. Res accepted. Wine, beer. Lunch $7.95-$14.95; dinner $9.95-$19.95. Jazz entertainment. Cr cds: A, D, DS, MC, V.
D

★★★★ **ELISABETH DANIEL.** *550 Washington St (94111). 415/397-6129.* Elisabeth and Daniel Ramsey's restaurant in the financial district is a recent addition to San Francisco's top restaurants. They offer a six-course prix fixe dinner of refined quality each night and the service is close to perfect. However, valet service is missing, so good luck finding parking. Contemporary menu. Menu changes seasonally. Hrs: 11:30 am-2 pm, 6-10 pm. Closed Sun. Res accepted. Wine list. Lunch $15-$20; dinner $20-$30. Entertainment. Cr cds: A, C, D, MC, V.
D

★ **ELIZA.** *1457 18th St (94107). 415/648-9999.* Hrs: 11 am-3 pm, 5-10 pm; Sat 11 am-10 pm; Sun noon-10 pm. Closed Thanksgiving, Dec 25. Res accepted. Chinese menu. Bar. Dinner $5.25-$10.15. Specialties: lotus root with prawns, Mongolian beef, Hunan salmon. Modern Chinese decor. Cr cds: MC, V.
D

★ **EL TOREADOR.** *50 W Portal (94127). 415/566-2673.* Hrs: 11 am-9 pm; Fri, Sat to 10 pm. Closed Mon;

Easter, Dec 25. No A/C. Mexican menu. Wine, beer. Lunch, dinner $7.25-$12.95. Children's menu. Specialties: mole poblano, mole de cacahuate, el pipian de pollo. Eclectic, brightly colored decor. Totally nonsmoking. Cr cds: A, MC, V.

SC

★★ **EMPRESS OF CHINA.** *838 Grant Ave (94108). 415/434-1345.* Hrs: 11:30 am-3 pm, 5-11 pm. Chinese menu. Res accepted. Bar. A la carte entrees: lunch $7.50-$10.50, dinner $12.50-$29. Complete meals (2 or more persons): lunch $9.50-$16.95, dinner $16.95-$33.95. Specialties: regional delicacies of China. Oriental decor; ancient art objects. View of city, Telegraph Hill. Jacket (dinner). Cr cds: A, D, MC, V.

D

★ **ENRICO'S SIDEWALK CAFE.** *504 Broadway (94133). 415/982-6223.* Hrs: 11:30 am-11 pm; Fri, Sat to midnight. Closed Jan 1, Dec 25. Res accepted. No A/C. Mediterranean menu. Bar. A la carte entrees: lunch $8-$10, dinner $8-$19. Live jazz. Outdoor dining. Bistro with glass wall, large terrace. Local artwork. Cr cds: A, MC, V.

D

★★ **EOS.** *901 Cole St (94117). 415/566-3063.* Hrs: 5:30-close; Sun from 5 pm. Closed hols. Res accepted. No A/C. Eclectic Asian menu. Bar. Dinner $18-$30. Specialties: shiitake mushroom dumplings, Peking duck breast. Street parking. Corner café. Cr cds: DS, MC, V.

D

★★★ **FARALLON.** *450 Post St (94102). 415/956-6969. www.farallonrestaurant.com.* Seafood menu. Specialties: Housemade caviar, seafood indulgence, fresh fish, fresh sorbet. Hrs: Sun-Wed 11:30 am-2:30 pm, 5:30-10:30 pm; Thurs-Sat 5:30-11 pm. Closed hols. Res accepted. Bar. Wine list. A la carte entrees: lunch $11-$15, dinner $22-$32. Prix fixe lunch $22. Valet parking. Underwater theme; unique decor with painted mosiac, jellyfish lamps. Totally nonsmoking. Cr cds: A, D, DS, MC, V.

D

★ **FATTOUSH.** *1361 Church St (94114). 415/641-0678.* Hrs: 11:30 am-2:30 pm, 5:30-9:30 pm; Fri to 10 pm; Sat 9 am-3 pm, 5:30-10 pm; Sun 9 am-3 pm, 5:30-9 pm. Closed Mon. Res accepted. Middle Eastern menu. Wine, beer. Lunch $4.50-$9.95, dinner $9.95-$14.95. Sat, Sun brunch $4.50-$8.95. Specialty: sesame chicken. Patio dining. Built 1903. Totally nonsmoking. Cr cds: A, C, D, DS, MC, V.

D SC

★★ **FAZ.** *161 Sutter St (94104). 415/362-0404.* Hrs: 11:30 am-3 pm, 5-10 pm. Closed Sat, Sun; hols. Res accepted. Italian, Mediterranean menu. Bar. A la carte entrees: lunch, dinner $8.95-$19.95. Specializes in fresh pasta. Jazz Mon-Fri 5-9 pm. Outdoor dining. Elegant fine dining. Cr cds: A, D, MC, V.

D

★★★★ **FIFTH FLOOR.** *12 Fourth St (94103). 415/348-1555. www.kimptongroup.com.* Chef George Morrone's classic dishes contribute to the buzz surrounding this restaurant. Tucked among the guest rooms on the fifth floor of new Palomar Hotel, the clubby atmosphere and tasting menu can turn a regular dinner into an epic experience. Contemporary French menu. Specializes in French cuisine. Hrs: 5:30-11 pm. Closed Sun. Res accepted. Wine, beer. Dinner $24-$37. Entertainment. Jacket. Cr cds: A, C, D, DS, MC, V.

D

★ **FIGARO.** *414 Columbus Ave (94133). 415/398-1300.* Hrs: 10 am-midnight. Closed Dec 25. Res accepted. Italian menu. Bar. A la carte entrees: bkfst $4.50-$8.25, lunch, dinner $7.50-$16.95. Specializes in pizza, pasta, oversize salads. Outdoor dining. Murals on ceiling. Cr cds: A, C, D, DS, ER, MC, V.

D

★★ **FINO.** *624 Post St (94109). 415/928-2080.* Hrs: 5:30-10 pm. Closed hols. Res accepted. Italian menu. Bar. Dinner $8.95-$16.95. Specializes in fresh seafood, fresh pasta. Descending staircase leads to dining area; marble fireplace. Totally nonsmoking. Cr cds: A, MC, V.

★★ **FIOR D'ITALIA.** *601 Union St (94133). 415/986-1886. www.fior.com.* Hrs: 11:30 am-10:30 pm. Res accepted. Northern Italian menu. Bar. A la carte entrees: lunch, dinner $11-$22. Specializes in veal, risotto. Own pasta. Valet parking. On Washington Square Park; Tony Bennett memorabilia. Family-owned. Totally nonsmoking. Cr cds: A, C, D, DS, ER, MC, V.

D

★ **FIREFLY.** *4288 24th St (94114). 415/821-7652.* Hrs: 5:30-9:30 pm; Fri, Sat to 10 pm. Res accepted. Contemporary menu. Bar. Dinner $11.50-$16. Specializes in seafood, organic produce, and meats. Contemporary decor. Totally nonsmoking. Cr cds: A, MC, V.

D

★★ **FIRST CRUSH.** *101 Cyril Magnin (94102). 415/982-7874. www.firstcrush.com.* Specializes in fresh seafood, game, pastas. Hrs: 5 pm-midnight; Fri, Sat 5 pm-1 am; Sun 5-11 pm. Res accepted. Wine list. Dinner $11-$17. Children's menu. Entertainment. Cr cds: A, C, D, MC, V.

D SC

★★★★ **FLEUR DE LYS.** *777 Sutter St (94109). 415/673-7779. www.citysearch.com.* The dramatic dining room of this beloved French restaurant is draped in more than 800 yards of rich fabric, creating a romantic tent-like atmosphere. It's a suitable setting in which to enjoy Hubert Keller's contemporary French cooking. Keller eschews heavy cream and butter sauces for lighter reductions. He turns vegetarian cooking into an art with his special all-vegetable menu. The formal, attentive service and elegant accoutrements suitably complete the world-class dining experience. French menu. Specialties: Maine lobster tail and salsify en tartelete, boneless quail, Grand Finale dessert. Hrs: 6-9:15 pm; Fri, Sat 5:30-10:30 pm. Closed Sun, New Year's Eve. Res required. Bar. Extensive wine list. A la carte entrees: dinner $28-$36. Prix fixe: dinner $70, vegetarian $58. Valet parking. Jacket required. Totally nonsmoking. Cr cds: A, MC, V.

D

★★★ **FLY TRAP.** *606 Folsom (94107). 415/243-0580.* Hrs: 11:30 am-10 pm; Fri to 10:30 pm; Sat, Sun 5:30-10:30 pm. Closed hols. Res accepted. No A/C. Continental menu. Bar. A la carte entrees: lunch, dinner $8-$18. Specialties: coq au vin, oysters Rockefeller, celery Victor. Own pasta, desserts. Jazz Sun. Valet parking. Courtyard entrance; named after 1898 restaurant. Totally nonsmoking. Cr cds: A, C, D, ER, MC, V.

D

★★ **FOG CITY DINER.** *1300 Battery St (94111). 415/982-2000.* Hrs: 11:30 am-11 pm; Fri, Sat to midnight. Closed Thanksgiving, Dec 25. Res accepted. Bar. A la carte entrees: lunch, dinner $10-$24. Specializes in cocktails, seafood. Oyster bar. Railroad dining car atmosphere. Cr cds: C, D, DS, ER, MC, V.

D

★ **FOREIGN CINEMA.** *2534 Mission St (94110). 415/648-7600. www.foreigncinema.com.* Specializes in lobster bouillabaisse, duck leg confit, and fois gras. Hrs: 6-11 pm. Res accepted. Wine, beer. Dinner $13-$19. Entertainment. Cr cds: A, D, MC, V.

D

★ **FOUNTAIN COURT.** *354 Clement St (94118). 415/668-1100.* Hrs: 11 am-3 pm, 5 pm-midnight; Fri, Sat to 2 am. Closed Thanksgiving. Res accepted. Chinese menu. Wine, beer. A la carte entrees: lunch $4-$4.50, dinner $6-$10. Specializes in Shanghai cuisine, catfish, chicken. Modern decor. Cr cds: A, MC, V.

D

★★★ **FOURNOU'S OVENS.** *905 California St (94108). 415/989-1910. www.renaissancehotels.com.* Hrs: 6:30 am-2:30 pm, 5:30-10 pm; Fri, Sat to 10:30 pm; Sat and Sun brunch 11 am-2:30 pm. Res accepted; required hols. Mediterranean setting with continental cuisine. Bar. Wine cellar. A la carte entrees: bkfst, lunch $9.75-$17.95, dinner $9-$28. Table d'hote: dinner $25-$45. Sun brunch $12-$18.50. Children's menu. Specializes in rack of lamb, farm-raised meats, fish selections. Own pasta. Valet parking. Cr cds: A, C, D, DS, ER, MC, V.

D

★★★ **FRANCISCAN.** *Pier 43 1/2 Embarcadero (94133). 415/362-7733. www.franciscanrestaurant.com.* Hrs: 11 am-10 pm; Fri-Sat to 10:30 pm. Closed Thanksgiving, Dec 25. Res accepted. Bar. A la carte entrees: lunch, dinner $6.95-$39. Children's menu. Specializes in California contemporary cuisine. Own desserts. View of bay, city, Alcatraz, Golden Gate Bridge. Cr cds: A, D, MC, V.

D

★★★ **FRASCATI.** *1901 Hyde St (94109). 415/928-1406.* Hrs: 5:30-10 pm; Fri, Sat to 10:30 pm. Closed Mon; Dec 25. Res accepted. No A/C. Contemporary American menu. Wine list. A la carte entrees: dinner $13-$17. Monthly menus of new American cuisine. Valet parking. Outdoor dining. Storefront location; bistro atmosphere. Cr cds: A, MC, V.

D

★★ **FRINGALE.** *570 Fourth St (94107). 415/543-0573.* Hrs: 11:30 am-3 pm, 5:30-10:30 pm; Sat from 5:30 pm. Closed Sun; hols. Res accepted. No A/C. French menu. Bar. A la carte entrees: lunch $7.50-$14, dinner $11-$17. Upscale bistro fare. Atmosphere of European country café. Totally nonsmoking. Cr cds: A, MC, V.

D

★★ **GABBIANO'S.** *1 Ferry Plaza (94111). 415/391-8403.* Hrs: 11 am-10 pm; Sun brunch 10:30 am-2 pm. Res accepted. Italian, American menu. Bar. A la carte entrees: lunch $7.50-$15.25, dinner $9.75-$19.50. Sun brunch $24.95. Specializes in fresh seafood, pasta. Valet parking. Patio dining. Waterfront with views of Alcatraz, Oakland, and Mt Tamalpais. Cr cds: A, DS, MC, V.

D

★★★★★ **GARY DANKO.** *800 N Point (94109). 415/749-2060. www.garydanko.com.* The former Ritz-Carlton superstar chef is cooking his heart out with superb results. Gary Danko uses the freshest ingredients along with his trademark enthusiasm to create a superb menu. If not for the great food, come for the exceptional wine and cheese selection, including a fantastic tableside cheese cart. Californian, French cuisine. Specialties: Horseradish crusted salmon medallion with dilled cucumbers, vegetarian artichoke, tomato, chickpea stew, Moroccan spiced squab with chermoula, orange-cumin carrot. Hrs: 5:30-9:30 pm. Prix fixe: 3-course $48, 4-course $57, 5-course $66, 6-course $75. Closed hols. Valet. Res required. Jacket, tie preferred. Cr cds: A, C, D, DS, ER, MC, V.

D

★★ **GAYLORD INDIA.** *900 N Point St (94109). 415/771-8822. www.gaylords.com.* Hrs: 11:45 am-1:45 pm, 5-10:45 pm; Sun brunch noon-2:45 pm. Closed Thanksgiving, Dec 25. Res accepted. Indian menu. Bar. Lunch $9.75-$13.25, dinner $9.95-$21. Complete meals: dinner $22.70-$28.75. Specializes in tandoori dishes, Indian desserts. Parking. View of bay. Totally nonsmoking. Cr cds: A, DS, MC, V.

SC

★★ **GLOBE.** *290 Pacific (94111). 415/391-4132.* Hrs: 11:30-1 am; Sat 6 pm-1 am. Closed Sun, Thanksgiving, Dec 25. Res accepted. Contemporary American menu. Bar. A la carte entrees: lunch $8-$13, dinner $14-$20. Specialties: double cut t-bone for 2 with potatoes au gratin, grilled salmon on baccacino pasta, baked mussels with scallops, rock shrimp with Thai basil and garlic butter. Street parking. Outdoor dining. Totally nonsmoking. Cr cds: A, MC, V.

D

★★★ **GORDON'S HOUSE OF FINE EATS.** *500 Florida St (94110). 415/861-8900.* Specializes in corn flake fried chicken, seared dayboat scallops, lamb T-bone. Hrs: 11:30 am-4:30 pm, 5:30-10 pm; Tues, Wed to 11 pm; Thurs-Sat to midnight. Res accepted. Lunch $7-$15; dinner $13-$28. Entertainment: Jazz Tues-Sat. Cr cds: C, D, DS, JCB, MC, V.

D

★★★ **GRAND CAFE.** *501 Geary St (94102). 415/292-0101.* Hrs: 7 am-10:30 pm; wkends to 11:30 pm; Sat, Sun brunch 9 am-2 pm. Closed July 4, Thanksgiving, Dec 25. Res accepted. Continental menu. Bar 11:30-1:30 am. A la carte entrees: bkfst $7.95-$9.95, lunch $8.95-$16.50, dinner $11.95-$22.95. Sat,

Sun brunch $7.95-$12.95. Specialties: polenta souffle, roasted rack of lamb, veal sweetbread fricassee. Valet parking. Chandeliers and bronze sculpture add elegance to this hotel dining rm. Totally nonsmoking. Cr cds: A, DS, MC, V.

D

★ **GRANDEHO'S MAMEKYO.** *2721 High St (94109). 415/673-6828.* Specializes in sushi. Hrs: 11:30 am-3 pm, 5-10 pm; Sat, Sun 5-10:30 pm. Res accepted. Wine, beer. Lunch $9-$15; dinner $10-$30. Entertainment. Cr cds: A, MC, V.

D

★★ **GREENS.** *Building A at Fort Mason (94123). 415/771-6222.* Hrs: 11:30 am-2 pm, 5:30-9:30 pm; Sat 11:30 am-2:30 pm, 5:30-9:30 pm; Sun brunch 10 am-2 pm; Mon-Sat 9:30-11 pm (dessert only). Closed most hols. Res accepted. Vegetarian menu. Wine, beer. A la carte entrees: lunch $7-$12, dinner $11-$15. Prix fixe: dinner (Sat) $40. Sun brunch $7-$11. Parking. View of bay. Totally nonsmoking. Cr cds: DS, MC, V.

D

★★ **HARRIS'.** *2100 Van Ness Ave (94109). 415/673-1888. www.harrisrestaurant.com.* Hrs: from 5:30 pm; Sat, Sun from 5 pm. Closed Jan 1, Dec 25. Res accepted. A la carte entrees: dinner $24-$34. Specializes in beef, fresh seafood, Maine lobster. Jazz Thurs-Sun. Valet parking. Cr cds: A, DS, MC, V.

D

★★★★ **HAWTHORNE LANE.** *22 Hawthorne St (94105). 415/777-9779. www.hawthornelane.com.* Sophisticated yet informal, this charming restaurant offers brilliant food, wine, and service. You'll be sure the California spot shrimp are as fresh as can be when you see them being fished out of the tank in the dining room especially for your dinner. Continental menu. Specialties: miso-glazed black cod, fresh spot prawns, glazed quail. Hrs: 11:30 am-2 pm, 5:30-10 pm; Fri, Sat to 10:30 pm. Closed hols. Bar to midnight. Res accepted. A la carte entrees: lunch $8.50-$14, dinner $18-$26. Children's menu. Valet parking. Modern decor. Cr cds: DS, MC, V.

D

★★ **HAYES STREET GRILL.** *324 Hayes St (94102). 415/863-5545.* Hrs: 11:30 am-2 pm, 5-9:30 pm; Fri to 10:30 pm; Sat 5:30-10:30 pm; Sun 5-8:30 pm. Closed hols. Res accepted. Seafood menu. Bar. A la carte entrees: lunch $9.50-$17, dinner $13-$25. Specializes in fresh seafood, salads, charcoal-grilled fish. Cr cds: A, DS, MC, V.

D

★★ **HELMAND.** *430 Broadway (94133). 415/362-0641.* Hrs: 5:30-10 pm; Fri, Sat to 11 pm. Res accepted. Afghanistan menu. Wine, beer. Dinner $9.95-$15.95. Specialties: shish kebab, mantwo, rack of lamb. Paintings and photos of Afghani scenes. Cr cds: A, MC, V.

D

★★★ **HOUSE.** *1230 Grant Ave (94133). 415/986-8612.* Hrs: 11:30 am-3 pm, 5:30-10 pm; Fri to 11 pm; Sat 5-11 pm. Closed Sun. Continental menu. Wine, beer. Lunch $5.95-$15.95, dinner $8.95-$16.95. Specializes in fish, rack of lamb, noodles. Contemporary decor. Totally nonsmoking. Cr cds: A, D, MC, V.

D

★★★ **HOUSE.** *1269 9th Ave (94122). 415/682-3898. www.thehse.com.* Asian menu. Specializes in Chilean sea bass, deep fried salmon roll, wasabi noodles. Hrs: 5-10 pm. Res accepted. Wine, beer. Dinner $12-$17. Entertainment. Cr cds: A, D, MC, V.

D

★★★ **HOUSE OF PRIME RIB.** *1906 Van Ness Ave (94109). 415/885-4605.* Hrs: 5:30-10 pm; Fri, Sat from 4:30 pm; Sun from 4 pm; hols vary. Res accepted. Bar. Wine list. A la carte entrees: dinner $18.75-$23.95. Children's menu. Specializes in corn-fed, 21-day aged prime rib of beef. Prime rib carved at table. Valet parking. English decor. Cr cds: A, MC, V.

D

★ **HUNAN.** *924 Sansome St (94111). 415/956-7727.* Hrs: 11:30 am-9:30 pm. Closed July 4, Thanksgiving, Dec 25. Res accepted. No A/C. Chinese menu. Bar. A la carte entrees: lunch, dinner $5-$9.95. Specializes in smoked Hunan dishes. Chinese decor. Cr cds: A, C, D, ER, MC, V.

D

★★ **I FRATELLI.** *1896 Hyde St (94109). 415/474-8240. www.citysearch.com/sfo/ifratelli.* Hrs: 5:30-10 pm. Closed hols. Italian menu. Bar. A la carte entrees: dinner $11-$18. Children's menu. Specializes in homemade pasta. Piano bar Tues, Thurs. Cafe atmosphere; photos of Italian street scenes. Cr cds: A, MC, V.

D

★★ **INDIGO.** *687 McAllister St (94102). 415/673-9353. www.indigorestaurant.com.* Specializes in grilled pork tenderloin, pan roasted Pacific salmon. Hrs: 5-11 pm. Closed Mon. Res accepted. Wine, beer. Dinner $12-$18. Children's menu. Entertainment. Cr cds: A, MC, V.

D

★ **INFUSION.** *555 Second St (94107). 415/543-2282. www.citysearch.com/sfo/infusion.* Hrs: 11:30-2 am; Sat, Sun from 5 pm. Closed most hols. Res accepted. No A/C. Bar. Lunch $5-$13, dinner $12-$20. Specialties: peppered filet mignon, fresh fruit-infused vodkas. Musicians Thurs-Sat. Street parking. Modern lighting, artwork. Totally nonsmoking. Cr cds: A, C, D, ER, MC, V.

D

★★★★ **JARDINIERE.** *300 Grove St (94102). 415/861-5555. www.opentable.com.* Chef Traci Des Jardin (formerly from Rubicon) has hit her stride, turning out delectable modern French fare in her snazzy Civic Center digs. Jardin makes full use of earthy ingredients, turning out dishes like a duo of foie gras with vanilla verjus and crispy chicken with chanterelles. The dimly-lit round bar, with interesting stained-glass detailing, is the focal point of the room, and the balcony overlooking it is home to Jardiniere's prime seating. French California menu. Menu changes seasonally. Hrs: 5:30-10:30 pm. Closed hols. Res accepted. Bar. Wine list. A la carte entrees: dinner $19-$27. Complete meal (6-course): $75. Jazz duo. Valet parking. Cr cds: A, D, DS, MC, V.

D

★★ **JULIUS CASTLE.** *1541 Montgomery St (94133). 415/392-2222. www.JuliusCastleRestaurant.com.* Hrs: 5-10 pm. Res accepted. No A/C. Italian menu. Bar. A la carte entrees: dinner $19-$39. Specializes in veal, rack of lamb, seafood. Own pastries, pasta, ice cream. Valet parking. Turreted castle overlooking San Francisco Bay. Historic landmark (1922). Totally nonsmoking. Cr cds: A, DS, ER, MC, V.

★ **KABOTO SUSHI.** *5116 Geary Blvd (94118). 415/752-5652.* Hrs: 5:30-11 pm. Closed Mon; hols. Res accepted. Japanese menu. Dinner $9-$18. Specializes in sushi. Street parking. Fish tanks. Cr cds: MC, V.

D

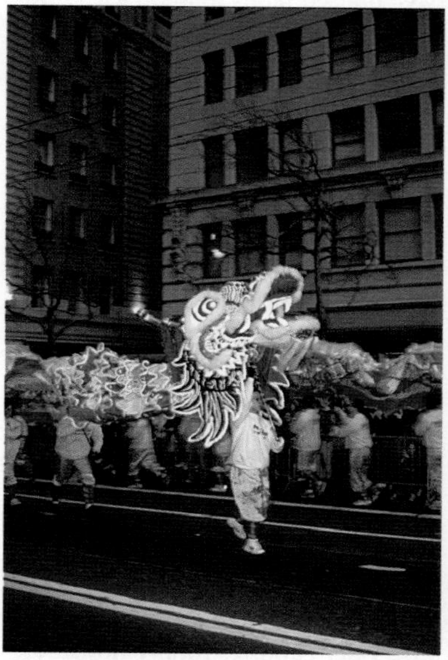

Chinese New Year's Parade

★ **KATIA'S RUSSIAN TEA ROOM.** *600 5th Ave (94118). 415/668-9292. www.citysearch.com/sfo/katias.* Hrs: 11:30 am-2:30 pm, 5-9 pm; Fri, Sat to 10 pm; Sun from 5 pm. Closed Mon; hols. Res accepted. No A/C. Russian menu. Wine, beer. Lunch, dinner $9-$14.50. Children's menu. Specializes in Russian pastries. Accordianist, guitarist nightly. Intimate corner cafe. Totally nonsmoking. Cr cds: A, C, D, DS, ER, MC, V.

D

★★ **KHAN TOKE THAI HOUSE.** *5937 Geary Blvd (94121). 415/668-6654.* Hrs: 5-11 pm. Closed Labor Day, Thanksgiving, Dec 25. Res accepted. Thai menu. Wine, beer. A la carte entrees: dinner $4.95-$10.95. Complete meal: dinner $16.95. Specialties: pong pang (seafood), choo chee goong (prawn in coconut milk curry). Thai classical dance performance Sun (8:30 pm). Thai decor and furnishings. Family-owned. Street parking. Totally nonsmoking. Cr cds: A, MC, V.

D

★★ **KOKKARI.** *200 Jackson St (94111). 415/981-0983. www.kokkari.com.* Greek menu. Specializes in roasted wild boar, seared Chilean sea bass, braised lamb shank. Hrs: 11:30 am-2 pm, 5:30-10 pm; Fri, Sat to 11 pm. Closed Sun. Lunch $13.95-$20.95; dinner $19.95-$32.95. Valet parking.

★★ **KULETO'S.** *221 Powell St (94102). 415/397-7720.* Hrs: 7-10:30 am, 11:30 am-11 pm; Sat, Sun from 8 am. Closed Labor Day, Thanksgiving, Dec 25. Res accepted. Northern Italian menu. Bar 11 am-midnight. Complete meals: bkfst $4.50-$8.95. A la carte entrees: lunch, dinner $8.25-$17.50. Specializes in grilled fish, chicken, pasta. Italian decor. Cr cds: A, DS, MC, V.

D

★★★ **KYO YA.** *2 New Montgomery St (94105). 415/512-1111.* Japanese Menu. Specialties: sukiyaki, shabu shabu, yosinabi, Hrs: 11:30 am-2 pm, 6-10 pm; Sat 6-10 pm. Closed Sun, Mon. Lunch $15-$24, dinner $27-$37. Valet Parking. Totally nonsmoking. Cr cds: A, DS, MC, V.

D

★★★★ **LA FOLIE.** *2316 Polk St (94109). 415/776-5577. www.lafolie.com.* Billowy clouds are painted on the pale blue walls of this charming restaurant that truly reflects chef Roland Passot's joie de vivre. Those who sample the nightly "discovery menu" will sample the greatest range of Passot's contemporary French cuisine. Vegetarians will appreciate the all-vegetarian menu. The wine list runs toward expensive Bordeaux wines, but also does an admirable job of finding some unusual lower priced options from the New World. French cusine. Hrs: 5:30-10:00 pm. Closed Sun and hols. Res required. A la carte entrees: $30-$40. Extensive wine list. Valet parking. Cr cds: A, DS, MC, V.

D

★★★ **LAPIS.** *Pier 33, The Embarcadero (94111). 415/982-0203.* Specializes in Mediterranean cuisine. Hrs: 11:30 am-2:30 pm, 5:30-10 pm; Fri, Sat 5:30-11 pm. Closed Sun. Res accepted. Wine, beer. Lunch $9-$16; dinner $16-$36. Children's menu. On the water, great views, open kitchen. Cr cds: A, D, DS, ER, JCB, MC, V.

D

★ **LA VIE.** *5830 Geary Blvd (94121). 415/668-8080.* Hrs: 11 am-10 pm; Fri, Sat to 10:30 pm. Res accepted. Vietnamese menu. Wine, beer. A la carte entrees: lunch $4.65-$5.25, dinner $6.95-$10.95. Street parking. Family-style dining. Totally nonsmoking. Cr cds: D, DS, MC, V.

D

★★ **LE CHARM.** *315 5th St (94107). 415/546-6128.* Hrs: 11:30 am-2:30 pm, 5:30-9:30 pm; Sat 5:30-10 pm. Closed Sun; hols; also 3 wks in August. Res accepted. No A/C. French menu. Wine, beer. A la carte entrees: lunch $6.50-$9, dinner $11-$14. 3-course prix fixe: dinner $20-$33. Specialties: onion soup, escargot, roasted salmon. Street parking. Outdoor dining. French bistro atmosphere. Totally nonsmoking. Cr cds: A, MC, V.

D

★★ **LIVE FIRE RESTAURANT.** *100 Brannan St (94107). 415/227-0777. www.livefiresf.com.* Specializes in grilled dishes. Hrs: 11:30 am-3 pm, 5-10 pm; Fri, Sat 5-11 pm; Sun brunch 11 am-3 pm. Res accepted. Wine, beer. Lunch $6.95-$15.95; dinner $8.95-$24.95. Brunch $7.95-$14.95. Children's menu. Entertainment. Fruitswood grill and woodfired oven. Cr cds: A, C, D, DS, JCB, MC, V.

D

★★ **LOLLI'S CASTAGNOLA.** *286 Jefferson St (94133). 415/776-5015.* Hrs: 9 am-11 pm. Closed Dec 25. Bar. Bkfst $3.95-$9.95, lunch, dinner $7-$30. Children's menu. Specializes in seafood. Outdoor dining. View of fishing fleet. Cr cds: A, DS, MC, V.

D

★★ **LULU.** *816 Folsom St (94107). 415/495-5775. www.citysearch.com/sfo/lulu.* Hrs: 11:30 am-2:30 pm, 5:30-10:30 pm; Fri, Sat to 11:30 pm. Res accepted. French, Italian menu. Bar. Lunch $6.50-$14, dinner $9-$18.50. Cr cds: A, D, MC, V.

D

★★ **MACARTHUR PARK.** *607 Front St (94111). 415/398-5700. www.citysearch.com/ffo/macarthur.com.* Hrs: 11:30 am-3:30 pm, 5-10 pm; Fri to 11 pm; Sat 5-11 pm; Sun 4:30-10 pm. Closed Thanksgiving, Dec 25. Res accepted. Bar. A la carte entrees: lunch, dinner $7.95-$24.95. Specializes in barbecued ribs, mesquite-grilled fish. Complimentary valet parking (dinner). Cr cds: A, DS, MC, V.

D

★★ **MANDARIN.** *900 N Point St (94109). 415/673-8812. www.themandarin.com.* Hrs: 11:30 am-11 pm. Res accepted. Northern Chinese, Mandarin menu. Bar. Lunch $8.95-$13, dinner $13-$35. Complete meals: dinner $16-$38. Mandarin banquet for 8 or more, $25-$58 each. Specialties: minced squab, beggar's chicken (1-day notice), Peking duck (1-day notice). Chinese decor; artifacts. 19th-century structure. View of bay. Cr cds: A, D, MC, V.

D **SC**

★ **MANGIAFUCCO.** *1001 Guerrero St (94110). 415/206-9881.* Hrs: 5:30-10:30 pm; Fri, Sat to 11 pm. Closed hols. Res accepted. No A/C. Italian menu. Wine, beer. A la carte entrees: dinner $7.50-$16. Specializes in regional Italian grilled meats. Own pasta. Valet parking. Rustic Italian decor; countryside atmosphere. Totally nonsmoking. Cr cds: A, DS, MC, V.

D

★★ **MARRAKECH MOROCCAN.** *419 O'Farrell St (94102). 415/776-6717.* Hrs: 6-10 pm. Res accepted. Moroccan menu. Bar. Prix fixe: dinner $24.95. Specialties: chicken with lemon, lamb with honey, couscous fassi. Belly dancing. Seating on floor pillows or low couches. Moroccan decor. Cr cds: A, DS, MC, V.

★★★★ **MASA'S.** *648 Bush St (94108). 415/989-7154.* Despite the defection of Masa's longtime chef, Julian Serrano, to a new home in Las Vegas, Masa's continues to deliver excellent food in lovely surroundings. The new chef, Chad Callanhan, is clearly inspired by the opulent, yet understated, dining room and prepares his own brand of impeccable French cuisine that truly lives up to its surroundings. The wine list is also exceptional. French menu. Specialties: foie gras sauté with Madeira truffle sauce, lobster salad with crispy leeks and truffle vinaigrette, sauteed medallions of New Zealand fallow deer. Hrs: 6-9:30 pm. Closed Sun, Mon; closed 2 wks in Jan and week of July 4. Bar. Wine cellar. Res accepted. Prix fixe: 4- or 5-course dinner $75-$80. Valet parking $9. Cr cds: A, DS, MC, V.

D

★★★ **MAYA.** *303 Second St (94107). 415/543-2928.* Gourmet menu. Specializes in langosta y camarones, huachinango a la talla. Hrs: 11:30 am-2 pm, 5-10 pm; Fri, Sat to 11 pm; Sun to 9 pm. Res accepted. Wine, beer. Lunch $13-$20; dinner $17-$25. Entertainment. Cr cds: A, C, D, DS, MC, V.

D

★★★ **MC2.** *470 Pacific Ave (94133). 415/956-0666.* French Californian cuisine. Specialties: seared tuna, tart flambeé. Hrs: Mon-Fri 11:30 am-2 pm; Mon-Wed 5:30-9:30 pm; Thurs-Sat 5:30-10:30 pm. Lunch $12-$16, dinner $23-$28. Bar. Valet for dinner. Res reqd. Cr cds: A, DS, MC, V.

D

★★ **MCCORMICK AND KULETO'S.** *900 N Point St (94109). 415/929-1730. www.mccormickandschmick.com.* Hrs: 11:30 am-11 pm; Sun from 10:30 am. Res accepted. Bar. A la carte entrees: lunch, dinner $5-$50. Children's menu. Specializes in fresh seafood. Parking. Crab Cake Lounge has open kitchen. View of bay. Cr cds: A, C, D, DS, MC, V.

D

★★★ **MECCA.** *2029 Market St (94114). 415/621-7000. www.sfmecca.com.* Hrs: 6-11 pm; Thurs-Sat to midnight. Closed Thanksgiving, Dec 25. Res accepted; required Fri, Sat. Mediterranean, American menu. Bar. A la carte entrees: dinner $14-$24. Own baking. Valet parking. Ultra-modern ambience. Totally nonsmoking. Cr cds: A, D, MC, V.
D

★★ **MEETING HOUSE.** *1701 Octavia St (94109). 415/922-6733. www.citysearch.com.* Hrs: 5:30-9:30 pm. Closed Sun, Mon; July 4, Dec 25. Res accepted. Wine, beer. A la carte entree: dinner $13-$20. Specialties: hominy-crusted catfish, rock shrimp, and scallion johnnycakes. Totally nonsmoking. Cr cds: A, D, MC, V.
D

★★★ **MOOSE'S.** *1652 Stockton St (94133). 415/989-7800. www.mooses.com.* Hrs: Mon-Wed 5:30-10pm; Thurs-Fri 11:30 am-2:30 pm, 5:30-10 pm, 10-11pm with lighter menu; Sat 10 am-2:30 pm, 5:30-11 pm; Sun brunch 9:30 am-2:30 pm, 5-10 pm. Closed hols. Res accepted. Bar. Wine cellar. A la carte entrees: lunch $4.95-$14.50, dinner $7.50-$28. Sun brunch $2.95-$12.95. Children's menu. Jazz evenings start at 8 pm. Valet parking. Cr cds: A, D, MC, V.
D

★★ **MORTON'S OF CHICAGO.** *400 Post St (94102). 415/986-5830. www.mortons.com.* Hrs: 5-11 pm; Sun to 10 pm. Closed most hols. Res accepted. Bar. A la carte entrees: dinner $20.95-$30.95. Specializes in steak. Club atmosphere. Totally nonsmoking. Cr cds: A, C, D, MC, V.
D

★★ **M POINT SUSHI BAR AND GRILL.** *55 5th St Fl 4 (94103). 415/543-7600.* Hrs: 7-10:30 am, 11:30 am-2:30 pm, 5-10 pm. Res accepted. Bar. A la carte entrees: bkfst $5.50-$7.50, lunch $11.25-$13.50, dinner $18-$26. Specializes in sushi. Valet parking. Mural stretching full length of restaurant. Totally nonsmoking. Cr cds: A, C, D, DS, ER, MC, V.
D

★★ **MURRAY'S.** *740 Sutter St (94109). 415/474-6478.* Hrs: 6:30-11 am, 5-10:30 pm. Res accepted. Bar. Buffet: bkfst $11.95. Dinner $13.95-$29.95. Children's menu. Specializes in organic cuisine. Valet parking. Tropical decor. Totally nonsmoking. Family-owned. Cr cds: A, C, D, DS, MC, V.
D

★★ **NEW GOLDEN TURTLE.** *2211 Van Ness Ave (94109). 415/441-4419.* Hrs: 5-10:30 pm. Closed Mon. Res accepted. Vietnamese menu. Wine, beer. A la carte entrees: dinner $8.95-$18.95. Specialties: spicy calamari saute, chili chicken, pan-fried Dungeness crab. Carved wooden panels depict scenes of Vietnamese culture. Cr cds: A, D, MC, V.
D

★★★ **NOB HILL.** *1 Nob Hill (94108). 415/616-6944. www.interconti.com.* Hrs: 11:30 am-11 pm. Res accepted. Bar. A la carte entrees: lunch $9-$21, dinner $18-$26.50. Children's menu. Specialties: steamed or grilled salmon, sauteed duck foie gras, grilled lamb. Pianist. Jazz trio Fri, Sat. Valet parking. Cr cds: A, D, DS, MC, V.
D

★★★ **NORTH BEACH.** *1512 Stockton St (94133). 415/392-1700.* Hrs: 11:30-1 am. Closed hols. Res accepted. Northern Italian menu. Wine cellar. A la carte entrees: lunch $8.50-$24, dinner $11.75-$19.75. Specializes in fresh fish, veal, pasta. Valet parking. Cr cds: A, C, D, DS, ER, MC, V.
D

★★★ **ONE MARKET.** *1 Market St (94105). 415/777-5577. www.opentable.com/reservations/onemarket.* Hrs: 11:30 am-2 pm, 5:30-9:30 pm; Fri to 10 pm; Sat 5-10 pm. Closed Sun; hols. Res accepted. Contemporary American menu. Bar. A la carte entrees: lunch $12-$18, dinner $20-$30. Children's menu. Specialties: ahi tuna Rossini, Hudson Valley foie gras two ways. Own desserts. Pianist. Totally nonsmoking. Cr cds: A, D, DS, MC, V.
D

★ **O'REILLY'S.** *622 Green St (94133). 415/989-6222.* Hrs: 11-2 am; Sat, Sun from 8 am. Res accepted. Irish menu.

Bar. Lunch, dinner $5.95-$16. Specializes in corned beef and cabbage, cottage pie. Outdoor dining. Photos and memorabilia from Ireland. Cr cds: MC, V.

D

★★ **ORITALIA.** *586 Bush St (94108). 415/782-8122.* Specializes in Mediterranean entrees. Hrs: 5:30-9:30 pm; Fri, Sat 5:15-10 pm. Res accepted. Wine, beer. Dinner $26-$37. Entertainment. 7 curtained booths, fortuny chandeliers, safron covered walls. Cr cds: A, D, DS, MC, V.

D

★★ **OSAKA GRILL.** *1217 Sutter St (94109). 415/440-8838.* Hrs: 11:30 am-2 pm, 5:30-10 pm. Closed hols. Res accepted. Hibachi cuisine. Wine, beer. Complete meal: lunch $6.50-$10, dinner $14-$30. Specialties: Chilean sea bass, grilled king prawns, center-cut filet mignon. Street parking. Dinner prepared at table. Totally nonsmoking. Cr cds: A, C, D, DS, ER, MC, V.

D

★★★ **PACIFIC.** *500 Post St (94102). 415/929-2087. www.panpac.com.* Hrs: 6:30 am-11 pm; Sun brunch 10 am-2 pm. Res accepted. Bar 3 pm-11:30 pm. Wine list. A la carte entrees: bkfst $5-$14, lunch $9.50-$16, dinner $18.50-$26. Sun brunch $9-$16. Specializes in Pacific Rim cuisine with French accent. Pianist. Valet parking. Modern decor; atrium setting in lobby of hotel. Cr cds: A, DS, MC, V.

D

★★ **PALIO D'ASTI.** *640 Sacramento St (94111). 415/395-9800. www.paliodasti.com.* Hrs: 11:30 am-2:30 pm, 5:30-10 pm. Closed Sat, Sun; hols. Res accepted. Italian menu. Bar. A la carte entrees: lunch $15-$20, dinner $19-$25. Specialties: risotto, mezzelune alla monferrina. Exhibition pasta-making and pizza-making kitchens; wood-burning ovens. Cr cds: A, C, D, DS, MC, V.

D

★★ **PANE E VINO.** *3011 Steiner St (94123). 415/346-2111.* Hrs: 11:30 am-2:30 pm, 5-10 pm; Fri, Sat 11:30 am-10:30 pm. Closed hols. Res accepted. Italian menu. A la carte entrees: lunch, dinner $8.25-$19.95. Specialties: osso buco, branzino. Italian decor. Totally nonsmoking. Cr cds: A, D, MC, V.

D

★★ **PARAGON.** *701 2nd St (94107). 415/537-9020.* Specializes in grilled New York steak. Menu changes seasonally. Hrs: 11:30 am-2:30 pm, 5:30-10 pm. Res accepted. Wine, beer. Lunch $8-$14; dinner $10-$23. Entertainment. Open Kitchen. Cr cds: A, D, MC, V.

D

★ **PARC HONG KONG.** *5322 Geary Blvd (94121). 415/668-8998.* Hrs: 11 am-2:30 pm, 5-9:30 pm; Sat, Sun from 10 am. Res accepted. Chinese menu. Bar. A la carte entrees: lunch $8-$10, dinner $15-$25. Complete meals: dinner (for 4) $88. Street parking. Oriental decor. Cr cds: A, D, DS, MC, V.

D

★★ **PARK GRILL.** *333 Battery St (94111). 415/296-2933. www.hyatt.com.* Hrs: 6:30 am-9:30 pm; Sun brunch 10 am-2:30 pm. Res accepted. Bar 11 am-9:30 pm. Wine list. A la carte entrees: bkfst $9.75-$17.50, lunch $9.75-$19, dinner $17-$23. Sun brunch $22.50. Children's menu. Specializes in mixed grills. Own baking. Pianist. Valet parking. Outdoor dining. Club rm atmosphere; original art. Cr cds: A, D, DS, MC, V.

D

★★★ **PASTIS.** *1015 Battery St (94111). 415/391-2555.* Hrs: 11:30 am-3 pm, 5:30-10:30 pm. Closed Sun; most hols. Res accepted. French menu. Bar. A la carte entrees: lunch $7-$12, dinner $8-$19. Specialties: oxtail rouelle with gribiche, roast magret of duck, warm banana and chocolate pannequet. Street parking. Outdoor dining. Original artwork. Cr cds: A, MC, V.

D

★★ **PATPONG.** *2415 Clement St (94121). 415/379-9726.* Hrs: 5-10 pm. Closed Tues; Dec 25. Res accepted. Wine, beer. A la carte entrees: dinner $7.95-$11.75. Specializes in cioppino, salmon cakes. Contemporary decor. Totally nonsmoking. Cr cds: MC, V.

D

★ **PERRY'S.** *1944 Union St (94123). 415/922-9022.* Hrs: 9 am-10 pm; Wed, Thurs to 11 pm; Fri, Sat to midnight. Closed Thanksgiving, Dec 25. Res accepted. Bar. A la carte entrees: bkfst $5.95-$13.95, lunch, dinner $8.50-$19.95. Children's menu. Specializes in steaks, chops, salads. Street parking. Outdoor dining. Family-owned since 1969. Totally nonsmoking. Cr cds: A, DS, MC, V.

D

★ **PERRY'S DOWNTOWN.** *185 Sutter St (94104). 415/989-6895.* Hrs: 7 am-9:30 pm. Closed Sun; hols. Res accepted. Bar to midnight. A la carte entrees: lunch, dinner $5.50-$17.95. Specializes in lobster, pasta. Casual decor. Cr cds: A, D, MC, V.

D

★★ **PLOUF.** *40 Belden Pl (94104). 415/986-6491.* Hrs: 11:30 am-3 pm, 5:30-10 pm; Sat from 5:30 pm. Closed Sun; hols. Res accepted. No A/C. French, seafood menu. Bar. Lunch $12-$15, dinner $12-$17. Specializes in seafood. Outdoor dining. Totally nonsmoking. Cr cds: A, D, MC, V.

D

★★★ **PLUMPJACK CAFE.** *3127 Fillmore St (94123). 415/563-4755. www.plumpjack.com.* Hrs: 11:30 am-2 pm, 5:30-10 pm; Sat from 5:30 pm. Closed Sun; most hols. Res accepted; required dinner. Extensive wine list. Lunch $8-$15, dinner $15-$20. Specializes in duck, risotto, seasonal dishes. Street parking. Henry VIII decor; intimate dining. Totally nonsmoking. Cr cds: A, D, DS, MC, V.

D

★★★★ **POSTRIO.** *545 Post St (94102). 415/776-7825. www.postrio.com.* Only Wolfgang Puck could make a restaurant feel so modern Californian and so timeless at the same time. This San Francisco standby is still an excellent choice for lunch or dinner. Aromas waft from the open kitchen, making it difficult to choose from the many menu selections that reflect California's cultural diversity and agricultural bounty. Signature dishes include grilled quail with spinach and egg ravioli and Chinese style duck. American contemporary menu. Specialties: Chinese duck, roasted salmon. Own baking. Hrs: 7-10 am, 11:30 am-2 pm, 5:30-10 pm; Sat from 11:30 am; Sun from 5:30 pm. Sun brunch 9 am-2 pm. Closed July 4, Thanksgiving, Dec 25. Bar 11:30 am-midnight. Wine list. Res required. A la carte entrees: bkfst $5-$12, lunch $25-$30, dinner $55. Sun brunch $12-$22. Valet parking. Totally nonsmoking. Cr cds: A, D, MC, V.

D

★ **POT STICKER.** *150 Waverly Pl (94108). 415/397-9985.* Hrs: 11 am-10 pm. Res accepted. No A/C. Hunan/Mandarin/Sechuan menu. A la carte entrees: lunch, dinner $5.25-$18. Complete meals: lunch $4.50-$5, dinner $6.50-$9.95. Specialties: pot stickers, Szechwan crispy fish, orange spareribs. Cr cds: A, DS, MC, V.

D

★★ **PREGO.** *2000 Union St (94123). 415/563-3305.* Hrs: 11:30 am-midnight. Closed Thanksgiving, Dec 25. Res accepted. Northern Italian menu. Bar to midnight. A la carte entrees: lunch, dinner $8.95-$17.95. Specialties: carpaccio, agnolotti d'aragosta, pizza baked in wood-burning oven. Outside dining. Cr cds: A, D, DS, MC, V.

D

★★ **PUCCINI AND PINETTI.** *129 Ellis St (94102). 415/392-5500.* Hrs: 11:30 am-10 pm; Fri, Sat to 11 pm; Sun 5-10 pm. Closed July 4, Thanksgiving, Dec 25. Res accepted. Italian menu. Bar. A la carte entrees: lunch $5.25-$12.95, dinner $6.95-$14.95. Specializes in spaghetti putanesca, wood-fired pizza. Open kitchen with wood burning oven. Totally nonsmoking. Cr cds: A, DS, MC, V.

D

★★★ **RISTORANTE ECCO.** *101 S Park (94107). 415/495-3291.* Specialty: pasta. Hrs: 11:30 am-2:30 pm, 5:30-10 pm. Closed Sun. Res accepted. Wine, beer. Lunch $8.50-$15; dinner $17-$22. Entertainment. Cr cds: A, D, MC, V.

D

★ **RISTORANTE IDEALE.** *1309 Grant Ave (94133). 415/391-4129.* Hrs: 11:30 am-2 pm, 5:30-10:30 pm; Fri, Sat to 11 pm; Sun to 10 pm. Closed Mon; Dec 25. Res accepted. Italian menu. Bar. Lunch $4.50-$9, dinner $9-$17.50. Children's menu. Specialties: fettuccine alla Norcina, saltimbocca alla Romana. Contemporary decor. Cr cds: A, DS, MC, V.
D

★★ **ROCCO'S SEAFOOD GRILL.** *2080 Van Ness Ave (94109). 415/567-7600.* Hrs: 5-10 pm; Fri, Sat to 11 pm. Closed Jan 1, Dec 25. Res accepted. Bar to midnight. A la carte entrees: dinner $13-$19.50. Children's menu. Specializes in seafood, oyster bar. Valet parking. Contemporary decor. Cr cds: A, DS, MC, V.
D

★★★ **ROSE PISTOLA.** *532 Columbus Ave (94133). 415/399-0499.* Hrs: 11:30 am-10:30 pm; Fri, Sat to 1 am. Closed hols. Res accepted. Northern Italian menu. Bar. A la carte entrees: lunch, dinner $9-$23. Children's menu. Specialties: cioppino, zucchini chips, gnocci. Entertainment. Outdoor dining. Contemporary decor. Totally nonsmoking. Cr cds: A, D, MC, V.
D

★★ **ROSE'S CAFE.** *2298 Union St (94123). 415/775-2200.* Hrs: 7 am-10 pm; Fri to 11 pm; Sat 8 am-11 pm; Sun from 8 am. Closed July 4, Thanksgiving, Dec 25. Res accepted (dinner). Italian menu. Bar. Bkfst $5-$9, lunch $5-$10, dinner $7-$13. Specialties: iron skillet-roast mussels, salmon sandwich, Italian-style pizzas. Street parking. Outdoor dining. Totally nonsmoking. Cr cds: A, D, MC, V.
D

★★★ **RUBICON.** *558 Sacramento (94111). 415/434-4100. www.myriadrestaurantgroup.com.* Hrs: 11:30 am-2:30 pm, 5:30-10 pm; Sat from 5:30 pm. Closed Sun. Res accepted. French Californian menu. Bar. Wine cellar. Lunch $12.50-$15, dinner $19-$25. Prix fixe: $31-$45. Menu changes seasonally. Totally nonsmoking. Cr cds: A, D, MC, V.
D

★ **RUE LEPIC.** *900 Pine St (94108). 415/474-6070.* Hrs: 11:30 am-2:30 pm, 5:30-10 pm; Sat, Sun from 5:30 pm. Closed hols. Res accepted; required wkends. French menu. A la carte entrees: lunch $6-$17, dinner $17-$21. Complete meals: dinner $35-$38. Specialties: roast medallion of veal with mushroom sauce, lobster tail, roasted rack of lamb with garlic. Totally nonsmoking. Cr cds: A, MC, V.
D

★★★ **RUTH'S CHRIS STEAK HOUSE.** *1601 Van Ness Ave (94109). 415/673-0557. www.ruthschris.com.* Hrs: 5-10:30 pm; Sun to 10 pm. Closed Thanksgiving, Dec 25. Res accepted. Bar. A la carte entrees: dinner $18.95-$29.95. Specializes in steak. Club atmosphere. Totally nonsmoking. Cr cds: A, DS, MC, V.
D

★ **SAM'S GRILL & SEAFOOD.** *374 Bush St (94104). 415/421-0594. www.citysearch.com/sfo/samsgrill.* Hrs: 11 am-9 pm. Closed Sat, Sun; hols. Res accepted. Seafood menu. Bar. A la carte entrees: lunch, dinner $7-$25. Specializes in fresh fish. Outdoor dining (lunch). 1867 building with original wooden booths. Family-owned. Cr cds: A, D, MC, V.
D

★★ **SCALA'S BISTRO.** *432 Powell St (94102). 415/395-8555.* Hrs: 7-10:30 am, 11:30 am-midnight; Fri, Sat from 8 am. Closed hols. Res accepted. Italian menu. Bar. A la carte entrees: bkfst $7-$12; lunch, dinner $8.75-$24. Specialties: persillade tagliatelle, seared salmon. Own baking. Contemporary decor. Cr cds: A, DS, MC, V.
D

★ **SCHROEDER'S.** *240 Front St (94111). 415/421-4778. www.schroederssf.com.* Hrs: 11 am-9 pm; Fri, Sat to 9:30 pm. Closed Sun; hols. Res accepted. German, American menu. Bar. Lunch $5.95-$14, dinner $9.50-$16.50. Children's menu. Specializes in baked chicken and noodles, sauerbraten, Wiener schnitzel. German decor, murals. Established 1893. Family-owned. Cr cds: A, D, DS, MC, V.
D

★★ **SCOMA'S.** *Pier 47 (94133). 415/771-4383. www.scomas.com.* Hrs: 11:30 am-10:30 pm; Fri, Sat to 11:30 pm. Closed Thanksgiving, Dec 24, 25. Italian, seafood menu. Bars. A la carte entrees: lunch, dinner $14.95-$54.95. Children's menu. Specialties: calamari, cioppino, sauteed shellfish. Complimentary valet parking. View of fishing fleet. Originally a fishing shack. Family-owned. Cr cds: A, D, DS, MC, V.

D

Aerial view of Alcatraz Island

★★★ **SILKS.** *222 Sansome (94104). 415/986-2020. www.mandarinoriental.com.* Hrs: Mon-Fri 6:30-10 am, 11:30 am-2 pm, 6-9:30 pm; Sat-Sun 7-11 am, 6-9:30 pm. Res accepted. California cuisine. Bar 11 am-11 pm. Wine list. A la carte entrees: bkfst $10.95-$16, lunch $18-$23, dinner $19-$32. Prix fixe: dinner $75, $95. Specializes in contemporary American cuisine with Asian accents. Own pastries. Valet parking. Cr cds: A, D, DS, MC, V.

D

★★ **SLANTED DOOR.** *584 Valencia (94110). 415/861-8032. www.slanteddoor.com.* Hrs: 11:30 am-3 pm, 5:30-10 pm; Fri, Sat to 10:30 pm. Closed Mon; most hols. Res accepted. No A/C. Vietnamese menu. Bar. A la carte entrees: lunch $5.50-$7, dinner $8.50-$18.50. Specialties: Shaking beef, steamed sea bass, spring rolls. Street parking. Modern Asian decor. Totally nonsmoking. Cr cds: MC, V.

D

★★★ **SPLENDIDO.** *4 Embarcadero Center (94111). 415/986-3222. www.citysearch.com.sfo.* Hrs: 11:30 am-2:30 pm, 5:30-10 pm. Closed hols. Res accepted. Contemporary Italian menu. A la carte entrees: lunch $11-$18, dinner $11-$28. Specializes in fresh seafood, game, baked goods. Own baking, ice cream. Outdoor dining. Cr cds: A, D, DS, MC, V.

D

★★ **STARS.** *555 Golden Gate (94102). 415/861-7827. www.citysearch.com.* Hrs: 11:30 am-2 pm, 6-10 pm; Fri, Sat from 5:30 pm. Closed Dec 25. Res accepted. Bar from 11 am, wkends from 4 pm. A la carte entrees: lunch $8-$15, dinner $19-$30. Pianist. Changing menu. Bistro decor. Cr cds: A, D, MC, V.

D

★★ **SWISS LOUIS.** *Pier 39 (94133). 415/421-2913.* Hrs 11:30 am-10 pm; Sat-Sun brunch 10:30 am-4 pm. Closed Thanksgiving, Dec 25. Res accepted. No A/C. Italian menu. Bar. Lunch $9.50-$15, dinner $11.50-$25. Sat, Sun brunch $10.50. Children's menu. Specializes in veal dishes, seafood. Own desserts. View of bay, Golden Gate Bridge. Cr cds: A, D, DS, MC, V.

D

★ **TADICH GRILL.** *240 California St (94111). 415/391-1849.* Hrs: 11 am-9:30 pm; Sat from 11:30 am. Closed Sun; hols. Bar. A la carte entrees: lunch, dinner $12-$25. Children's menu. Specializes in fresh seafood. Also counter serv. Turn-of-the-century decor. Established in 1849. Family-owned since 1928. Cr cds: MC, V.

D

★★★ **TOMMY TOY'S.** *655 Montgomery St (94111). 415/397-4888.* Hrs: 11:30 am-2:30 pm, 5:30-9:30 pm; Sat and Sun open from 5:30-9:30 pm. Closed Jan 1, Dec 25. Res required. Chinese menu. Bar. A la carte entrees: lunch $11.95-$15.95, dinner $14-$18.95. Table d'hôte: lunch $18.50-$32.50. Prix fixe: 6-course dinner $55/person. Specializes in seafood, Peking duck. Valet parking (dinner). Jacket and tie required. Cr cds: A, DS, MC, V.

D

★ **UNIVERSAL CAFE.** *2814 19th St (94110). 415/821-4608.* Hrs: 7:30 am-10 pm; Sat from 9 am; Sun 9 am-9:30 pm. Closed Mon; most hols. Res accepted (dinner). Wine, beer. Bkfst $5-$8.50, lunch $5-$12, dinner $5-$20. Outdoor dining. Contemporary decor. Totally nonsmoking. Cr cds: A, MC, V.

★★ **WATERFRONT.** *Pier 7 (94111). 415/391-2696. www.waterfrontsf.com.* Hrs: 11:30 am-10 pm; Sun from 5:30 pm. Res accepted. Bar. A la carte entrees: lunch $9-$22, dinner $9-$32. Specializes in seafood with Asian influences. Valet parking. View of bay. Cr cds: A, D, DS, MC, V.

D

★ **WATERGATE.** *1152 Valencia St (94110). 415/648-6000. www.watergaterestaurant.com.* Specializes in Asian/French entrees. Hrs: 5:30-10 pm; Fri, Sat to 11 pm. Res accepted. Dinner $14-$20. Entertainment. Cr cds: A, D, JCB, MC, V.

D

★★★ **WOODWARD'S GARDEN.** *1700 Mission (94103). 415/621-7122. www.citysearch.com.* Specializes in salmon, grilled foie gras and truffle oil. Hrs: 6-8:30 pm. Closed Sun-Tues. Dinner $14-$23. Entertainment. Built in 1866 by Robert Woodward, who opened the amusement park. Cr cds: MC, V.

★★★ **XYZ.** *181 3rd St (94103). 415/817-7836. www.whotels.com.* French influence menu. Menu changes seasonally. Hrs: 6:30-10:30 am, 11:30 am-2:30 pm, 5:30-10 pm. Res accepted. Wine list. Lunch $12-$16; dinner $20-$27. Entertainment. Cr cds: A, C, D, DS, JCB, MC, V.

D

★★ **YABBIE'S COASTAL KITCHEN.** *2237 Polk St (94109). 415/474-4088. www.citysearch.com.* Hrs: 6-10 pm; Fri, Sat to 10:30 pm. Closed hols. Res accepted. No A/C. Seafood menu. Bar. Complete meals: dinner $14-$21 Specialties: tuna pokee, oyster bar feast. Contemporary decor. Totally nonsmoking. Cr cds: MC, V.

D

★★ **YANK SING.** *101 Spear St (94111). 415/957-9300. www.yanksing.com.* Hrs: 11 am-3 pm; Sat-Sun 10 am-4 pm. Res accepted. Bar. Lunch $14-$16. Specialty: dim sum. Tableside carts in addition to menu. Cr cds: A, MC, V.

D

★★ **YOSHIDA-YA.** *2909 Webster St (94123). 415/346-3431. www.citysearch.com.* Hrs: 11:30 am-2 pm, 5-10:30 pm; Fri to 11 pm; Sat 5-11 pm; Sun 5-10:30 pm. Closed hols. Japanese menu. Bar. Complete meals: dinner $20-$25. Specialties: sushi, yakitori. Oriental decor; traditional dining upstairs. Totally nonsmoking. Cr cds: A, C, D, DS, ER, MC, V.

D

★★ **YOYO BISTRO.** *1625 Post St (94115). 415/922-7788. www.mim.com/miyako.* Hrs: 6:30 am-10 pm. Res accepted. Asian bistro. Bar. A la carte entrees: lunch $7-$10, dinner $12-$20; buffet: bkfst $12.50. Mix of modern American and Asian decor. Cr cds: A, MC, V.

D

★ **ZARZUELA.** *2000 Hyde St (94109). 415/346-0800.* Hrs: 5:30-10:30 pm; Fri, Sat to 11 pm. Closed Sun, Mon; hols. Spanish menu. Wine, beer. Dinner $8.95-$13.95. Specialties: zarzuela, tapas, paella. Spanish decor. Totally nonsmoking. Cr cds: A, MC, V.

D

★★ **ZAX.** *2330 Taylor St (94133). 415/563-6266.* Hrs: 5:30-10 pm. Closed Sun, Mon; wk of July 4, Thanksgiving, Dec 25. Res accepted. Mediterranean menu. Wine, beer. Dinner $14-$19.50. Specialties: goat cheese souffle. Contemporary decor. Totally nonsmoking. Cr cds: MC, V.

★★ **ZINGARI.** *501 Post St (94102). 415/885-8850.* Hrs: 6:30 am-10:30 pm; Fri, Sat to 11 pm. Res accepted. Italian menu. Wine, beer. Bkfst $8-$13.95, lunch $7-$12.95, dinner $11.50-$22.50. Specializes in filet mignon, pork chop, veal. Italian decor. Totally nonsmoking. Cr cds: A, DS, MC, V.

D

★★ **ZUNI CAFE.** *1658 Market St (94102). 415/552-2522.* Hrs: 11:30 am-midnight; Sun to 11 pm; Sun brunch 11 am-3 pm. Closed Mon;

hols. Res accepted. Italian, French menu. Bar. A la carte entrees: lunch $8-$14, dinner $10-$18. Sun brunch $5.50-$14.50. Own desserts. Pianist Fri, Sat. Outdoor dining. Changing art displays. Cr cds: A, MC, V.

D

Unrated Dining Spots

DAVID'S. *474 Geary St (94102). 415/276-5950.* Open 24 hrs. Closed Jewish high hols. Jewish deli menu. Beer, wine. Bkfst $3.35-$9.75, lunch $4.95-$9.95, dinner from $6.95. Complete meal: dinner $16.95. Specializes in chopped chicken liver, stuffed cabbage, cheese blintzes. Cr cds: A, DS, MC, V.

D SC

DOTTIE'S TRUE BLUE CAFE. *522 Jones St (94102). 415/885-2767.* Hrs: 7:30 am-2 pm. No A/C. Wine, beer. Bkfst $4-$7.95, lunch $4-$8.50. Specializes in all-American bkfst. Own breads. Cr cds: DS, MC, V.

D

ISOBUNE. *1737 Post St (94115). 415/563-1030.* Hrs: 11:30 am-10 pm. Closed Jan 1-3, Thanksgiving, Dec 25. Japanese sushi menu. Wine, beer. A la carte entrees: lunch $5-$8, dinner $10-$12. Specializes in sashimi. Dining at counter; selections pass in front of diners on small boats. Cr cds: MC, V.

JUST DESSERTS. *3 Embarcadero Ctr (94111). 415/421-1609. www.justdesserts.com.* Hrs: 6:30 am-7 pm; Sat 11 am-5 pm; Sun noon-5 pm. Closed hols. A la carte entrees: pastries, cakes, muffins $2.50-$4. Specializes in cheesecake. Own baking. Outdoor dining. Modern café atmosphere. Cr cds: MC, V.

LA BODEGA. *1337 Grant Ave (94133). 415/433-0439.* Hrs: 5 pm-midnight. Res accepted. Spanish menu. Bar. Dinner $4-$9. Specialties: tapas, paella. Entertainment. Spanish decor. Totally nonsmoking. Cr cds: A, MC, V.

D

MARIO'S CAFE. *401 Van Ness (94102). 415/989-2233.* Hrs: 8 am-2:30 pm. Closed Sat, Sun; hols. No A/C. Nouvelle California/northern Italian menu. Wine, beer. Bkfst avg $3.50, lunch avg $7. Specializes in fresh fish, fresh pasta, salads. Stylish cafeteria in landmark Art Deco skyscraper; mirrored Deco interior with marble counters, tray ledges, floors.

D SC

MIFUNE. *1737 Post St (94115). 415/922-0337.* Hrs: 11 am-10 pm. Closed Jan 1-3, Thanksgiving, Dec 25. Japanese menu. A la carte entrees: lunch, dinner $3.50-$13. Specializes in noodle dishes. Own noodles. Validated parking. Cr cds: A, D, DS, MC, V.

D

MO'S GOURMET HAMBURGERS. *1322 Grant Ave (94133). 415/788-3779.* Hrs: 11:30 am-10:30 pm; Fri, Sat to 11:30 pm. Closed Dec 25. Wine, beer. Lunch, dinner $4.75-$7.75. Specializes in grilled or charbroiled hamburgers. Casual dining with Art Deco design. Kitchen with rotating grill over lava rocks at front window. Cr cds: MC, V.

D

SEARS FINE FOODS. *439 Powell St (94102). 415/986-1160.* Hrs: 6:30 am-2:30 pm. Closed Jan 1, Thanksgiving, Dec 25. Bkfst, lunch $7-$15. Children's menu. Specialties: 18 Swedish pancakes, sourdough French toast. Casual decor. Totally nonsmoking.

SWAN OYSTER DEPOT. *1517 Polk St (94109). 415/673-1101.* Hrs: 8 am-5:30 pm. Closed Sun; hols. No A/C. Seafood menu. Wine, beer. A la carte entrees: dinner $6.50-$13.95. Children's menu. Specializes in seafood salads, fresh fish, oysters. Street parking. Family-owned since 1912. Totally nonsmoking.

D

TITANIC CAFE. *817 Sutter St (94109). 415/928-8870.* Hrs: 7 am-2 pm. Bkfst, lunch $3.50-$6. Specializes in omelets, applewood smoked bacon. Casual decor. Cr cds: MC, V.

D

TRIO CAFE. *1870 Fillmore St (94115). 415/563-2248.* Hrs: 8 am-6 pm; Sun 10 am-4 pm. Closed Mon; Easter, Thanksgiving; also Dec 24-Jan 2. Eclectic menu. Bar. A la carte entrees: bkfst, lunch $4-$6. Outdoor dining in café setting. Storefront entrance. Totally nonsmoking.

D

San Francisco Airport Area

See also Hayward, Oakland, Redwood City, San Francisco, San Mateo

Web www.flysfo.com

Services and Information

Information. 650/761-0800.

Lost and Found. 650/876-2261.

Weather. 831/656-1725.

Cash Machines. South Terminal, business center.

Airlines. Aeroflot, Air Canada, Air China, Air France, Air Jamaica, Alaska Arlns, American West, American, American Trans Air, Asiana Arlns, Austrian, British Airways, Canadian Arlns International, China Arlns, Continental, Delta, EVA Airways, Frontier, Hawaiian Arlns, Japan Arlns, KLM, Korean Air, LACSA, Lufthansa, Mexicana, Northwest, Philippine Arlns, Qantas, Reno Air, Singapore Arlns, Southwest, Swissair, TACA, Tri Star, TWA, United, USAir, Vanguard, Virgin Atlantic, Western Pacific Arlns.

Motels/Motor Lodges

★★ **BEST WESTERN EL RANCHO INN.** *1100 El Camino Real, Millbrae (94030). 650/588-8500; fax 650/871-7150; toll-free 800/826-5500. www.elranchoinn.com.* A/C, 1-3 story. S $135; D $145; each addl $10; kit. units, suites $135-$160; under 18 free. Crib free. TV; cable (premium). Heated pool; whirlpool. Coffee in rms. Restaurant 6:30 am-10 pm. Bar. Ck-out 1 pm. Coin lndry. Meeting rms. Business servs avail. In-rm modem link. Bellhops. Valet serv. Free airport transportation. Exercise equipt. Some refrigerators. Cr cds: A, C, D, DS, MC, V.

D

★★ **BEST WESTERN GROSVENOR HOTEL.** *380 S Airport Blvd, South San Francisco (94080). 650/873-3200; fax 415/589-3495; toll-free 800/528-1234. www.bestwestern.com.* 207 rms, 9 story. June-mid-Oct: S, D $99-$169; each addl $15; suites $175; under 12 free; lower rates rest of yr. Crib free. TV; cable (premium). Heated pool. Complimentary continental bkfst, coffee in rms. Restaurant 6 am-2 pm, 5-10 pm. Bar 4 pm-midnight. Ck-out noon. Meeting rms. Business servs avail. Bellhops. Valet serv. Sundries. Free airport transportation. Health club privileges. Some refrigerators. Cr cds: A, D, DS, JCB, MC, V.

D SC

★★ **COURTYARD BY MARRIOTT.** *1050 Bayhill Dr, San Bruno (94066). 650/952-3333; fax 415/952-4707; toll-free 800/321-2211.* 147 rms, 3 story. S, D $159; each addl $10; suites $179; under 13 free. Crib free. TV; cable (premium). Indoor pool; whirlpool. Complimentary coffee in rms. Restaurant 6-11 am, 5-10:30 pm. Ck-out 1 pm. Coin lndry. Meeting rms. Business servs avail. Free airport transportation. Exercise equipt. Refrigerators, microwaves avail. Some balconies. Cr cds: A, C, D, DS, MC, V.

D SC

★ **LA QUINTA INN.** *20 Airport Blvd, South San Francisco (94080). 650/583-2223; fax 650/589-6770; res 800/531-5900.* 172 rms. S $119; D $159. Pet accepted. Pool. TV; cable (premium). Ck-out noon. Coin lndry. Cr cds: A, C, D, DS, JCB, MC, V.

D

★★ **MILLWOOD INN.** *1375 El Camino Real, Millbrae (94030). 650/583-3935; fax 415/875-4354; toll-free 800/345-1375. www.millwoodinn.com.* 34 rms, 2 story. S $65-$100; D $75-$110; suites $85-$160. Crib $4. TV; cable (premium), VCR. Complimentary continental bkfst, coffee in rms. Restaurant nearby. Ck-out 11 am. Coin lndry. Business servs avail. In-rm modem link. Exercise equipt. Bathrm phones, refrigerators, microwaves. Cr cds: A, DS, MC, V.

D

★★ **RAMADA INN - SAN FRANCISCO AIRPORT NORTH.** *245 S Airport Blvd, South San Francisco (94080). 650/589-7200; fax 650/588-5007; toll-free 800/272-6232.* 172 rms, 2 story. S $139; D $169; each addl $10; under 18 free; wkend rates. Crib free. Pet accepted, some restrictions. TV; cable (premium). Pool; whirlpool. Coffee in rms. Restaurant 6:30 am-1:30 pm, 5-10 pm. Bar 4 pm-midnight; Sat,

Sun from 11 am. Ck-out noon. Coin lndry. Meeting rms. Business servs avail. Bellhops. Gift shop. Barber shop. Free airport transportation. Exercise equipt. Health club privileges. Cr cds: A, C, D, DS, ER, JCB, MC, V.

D SC

★ **TRAVELODGE.** *326 S Airport Blvd, South San Francisco (94080). 650/583-9600; fax 650/873-0282; toll-free 800/578-7878. www.travelodge.com.* 197 rms, 100 with shower only, 2 story. S $79; D $115; each addl $7; under 17 free. Crib free. TV; cable (premium). Heated pool. Complimentary coffee in rms. Restaurant open 24 hrs. Ck-out noon. Meeting rms. Business servs avail. Valet serv. Sundries. Free airport transportation. Picnic tables. Cr cds: A, C, D, DS, MC, V.

D SC

Hotels

★★ **DOUBLETREE HOTEL SF AIRPORT.** *835 Airport Blvd, Burlingame (94010). 650/344-5500; fax 650/340-8851; toll-free 800/222-8733.* 292 rms, 8 story. S, D $179-$239; each addl $10; suites $229-$300; under 18 free. Crib free. TV; cable (premium), VCR avail. Coffee in rms. Restaurant 6:30 am-10 pm. Bar 2:30 pm-1:30 am. Ck-out noon. Meeting rms. Business center. In-rm modem link. Gift shop. Free airport transportation. Exercise equipt. Refrigerator, wet bar in suites. Cr cds: A, C, D, DS, JCB, MC, V.

D SC

★★★ **HYATT REGENCY SAN FRANCISCO AIRPORT.** *1333 Bayshore Hwy, Burlingame (94010). 650/347-1234; fax 650/696-2669; toll-free 800/233-1234. www.hyatt.com.* 793 rms, 9 story. S, D $255-$270; each addl $25; suites $249-$750; under 18 free; wkend rates. Crib free. Valet parking $15. TV; cable (premium). Heated pool; whirlpool. Restaurant 6:30 am-11 pm. Rm serv 24 hrs. Bar 11-1 am. Ck-out noon. Convention facilities. Business center. Concierge. Gift shop. Free airport transportation. Exercise equipt; sauna. Some bathrm phones, wet bars; refrigerators avail. Atrium. Luxury level. Cr cds: A, C, D, DS, ER, JCB, MC, V.

D SC

★★ **PARK PLAZA HOTEL SAN FRANCISCO.** *1177 Airport Blvd, Burlingame (94010). 650/342-9200; fax 415/342-1655; toll-free 800/411-7275. www.parkplaza.com.* 302 rms, 10 story. S, D $180; each addl $10; suites $250-$395; wkend rates. Crib avail. TV; cable (premium), VCR avail. Indoor/outdoor pool; whirlpool. Restaurant 6 am-11 pm. Bar; entertainment. Ck-out noon. Coin lndry. Convention facilities. Gift shop. Barber, beauty shop. Free airport transportation. Exercise equipt. Cr cds: A, DS, MC, V.

D

★★★ **SAN FRANCISCO AIRPORT MARRIOTT.** *1800 Old Bayshore Hwy, Burlingame (94010). 650/692-9100; fax 650/692-8016; toll-free 800/228-9290. www.marriott.com/sfobg.* 684 rms, 11 story. S, D $249; suites $450-$600; under 18 free; wkend, wkly rates. Crib free. Pet accepted, some restrictions. Valet parking $13. TV; cable (premium), VCR avail. Indoor pool; whirlpool, poolside serv. Restautant 6 am-11 pm. Rm serv to 1 am. Piano bar. Ck-out noon. Coin lndry. Convention facilities. Business center. In-rm modem link. Concierge. Gift shop. Free airport transportation. Exercise equipt; sauna. Health club privileges. Some bathrm phones, refrigerators. Luxury level. Cr cds: A, C, D, DS, ER, JCB, MC, V.

D

★★★ **SHERATON GATEWAY HOTEL SAN FRANCISCO AIRPORT.** *600 Airport Blvd, Burlingame (94010). 650/340-8500; fax 650/343-1546; res 800/325-3535. www.sheratonsfo.com.* 404 rms, 15 story. S $239-$279; D $259-$289; each addl $10; suites $450-$650; under 18 free; wkend rates. Crib free. TV; cable (premium). Indoor pool; whirlpool. Restaurant 6 am-midnight. Bar 11-1:30 am; entertainment. Ck-out noon. Meeting rms. Business servs avail. Gift shop. Free covered parking. Free airport transportation. Exercise equipt; sauna. Refrigerators avail. Luxury level. Cr cds: A, C, D, DS, JCB, MC, V.

D

★★★ **WESTIN.** *1 Old Bayshore Hwy, Millbrae (94030). 650/692-3500; fax 650/872-8111; res 800/301-1111. www.westin.com.* 393 rms, 7 story. S, D $219-$254; each addl $20; suites $400-$600; under 18 free; wkend rates. Crib free. Pet accepted, some restrictions. Valet parking $14; self-park $10. TV; cable (premium), VCR avail. Indoor pool; whirlpool, poolside serv. Restaurant 6 am-10 pm. Rm serv 24 hrs. Bar noon-1 am; entertainment. Ck-out 1 pm. Convention facilities. Business center. Concierge. Gift shop. Free airport transportation. Exercise equipt. Refrigerators, minibars. Cr cds: A, C, D, DS, JCB, MC, V.

D

All Suite

★★★ **EMBASSY SUITES SAN FRANCISCO.** *250 Gateway Blvd, South San Francisco (94080). 650/589-3400; fax 650/876-0305; toll-free 800/362-2779. www.embassy-suites.com.* 312 suites, 10 story. S, D $165; each addl $10; under 18 free; wkend rates. Crib free. TV; cable (premium), VCR avail. Indoor pool; whirlpool. Sauna. Complimentary full bkfst, coffee in rms. Restaurant 11 am-11 pm. Bar 11-1 am; entertainment. Ck-out 1 pm. Coin lndry. Meeting rms. Business servs avail. Gift shop. Free airport transportation. Health club privileges. Refrigerators. Balconies. Atrium courtyard. Cr cds: A, C, D, DS, JCB, MC, V.

D

Restaurants

★★ **KULETO'S.** *1095 Rollins Rd, Burlingame (94010). 650/342-4922.* California influence menu. Specializes in linguini, fresh fish, pork chops. Hrs: 11:30 am-3 pm, 5-10 pm. Res accepted. Wine, beer. Lunch, dinner $8-$20. Children's menu. Entertainment. Cr cds: A, C, D, DS, JCB, MC, V.

D

★★★★ **PISCES.** *1190 California Dr, Burlingame (94010). 650/401-7500. www.nextcenturyrestaurants.com.* Michael Mina and Charles Condy (of San Franciscoís Aqua) have done it again—this time on the Peninsula in the heart of Silicon Valley. Pisces is every bit as sophisticated and "big city" as Aqua. The seafood-focused menu is as exciting and includes some of the Aqua classics like tuna tartare and root beer float. The seafood hors d'oeurve (lightly fried oysters, calamari, and other finger foods) are a must before the meal. If Pisces can sustain its current level of service and culinary execution, it will quickly become one of the Valley's best. Specializes in Chilean sea bass, dayboat sea scallops, pasta. Hrs: 11:30 am-2:30 pm, 5:30-10 pm; Fri, Sat 5:30-11 pm; Sun 5-10 pm. Res required. Wine, beer. Lunch, dinner $16-$27. Entertainment. Cr cds: A, D, MC, V.

D

★★ **YAKINIKU HOUSE JUBAN.** *1204 Broadway, Burlingame (94010). 650/347-2300.* Hrs: 11:30 am-2 pm, 5-10 pm; Sat 11:30 am-10 pm; Sun 4:30-10 pm. Closed Jan 1, Thanksgiving, Dec 25. Res accepted. Japanese menu. Wine, beer. Lunch, dinner $5-$38. Specialties: wagyu loin, short ribs. Street parking. Tableside preparation of dinner. Totally nonsmoking. Cr cds: A, C, ER, MC, V.

D

San Gabriel

(see Arcadia, Los Angeles, Pasadenda)

San Jose

(A-1, G-3) *See also Fremont, Livermore, Santa Clara, Santa Cruz, Saratoga*

Founded 1777 **Pop** 782,248 **Elev** 87 ft **Area code** 408

Information Convention & Visitors Bureau, 333 W San Carlos St, Suite 1000, 95110; 408/295-2265 (24-hr recording)

Web www.sanjose.org

At the south end of San Francisco Bay, 50 miles from San Francisco, San Jose is known as the "Capital of

Silicon Valley." San Jose was founded as Pueblo de San Jose de Guadalupe in the name of Charles III of Spain; the first American flag was raised above the town hall in 1846. The city was one of the first to be incorporated in California. Before California was even a state, San Jose became the first state capital; the first state legislature assembled here on December 15, 1849. In recent years it has become an important electronic and aerospace center. It is also the home of San Jose State University.

What to See and Do

Alum Rock Park. These 720 acres are known as "Little Yosemite" because of the natural formations. Hiking, bicycle, bridle trails. Picnic grounds, playground. (Daily) 16240 Alum Rock Ave, 6 mi E. Phone 408/259-5477. ¢¢ Also in park is

Youth Science Institute. Natural science classes, exhibits, and nature trips. (Tues-Sun) 16260 Alum Rock Ave. Phone 408/258-4322. ¢

The Children's Discovery Museum. Provides children and their families with hands-on exhibits that explore the relationships between the natural and created worlds, and among people of different cultures and times. Exhibits incl the Streets, a 5⁄8 scale replica of an actual city, with street lights, parking meters, fire hydrants; Waterworks allows operation of pumps and valves to move water through a reservoir system. (Tues-Sun) 180 Woz Way, in Guadalupe River Park. Phone 408/298-5437. ¢¢¢

J. Lohr Winery. Producer of J. Lohr varietal wines. Tasting rm (daily; closed hols). Tours (wkends, two departures: late morning and early afternoon). 1000 Lenzen Ave. Phone 408/288-5057. **FREE**

Kelley Park. Keyes St at Senter Rd. Phone 408/277-4191. Incl

Happy Hollow Park and Zoo. On 12 acres. Themed children's rides; creative play areas; zoo and contact area; special events. (Daily; no admittance during last hr open; closed Dec 25) 1300 Senter Rd. Phone 408/277-3000. ¢¢

History San Jose. Original and replica structures have been placed on the grounds to re-create most elements of early San Jose. Outdoor exhibits incl original pioneer houses, doctor's office, print shop, fruit barn, 1927 gas station; replicas of early landmarks, incl hotel, stables, trolley barn, firehouse, bank, 117-ft electric light tower, operating ice cream store, and 1880 Chinese Temple with original altar. Indoor hotel exhibits trace history of area's Native American, Spanish, Mexican, and Chinese background. Museum (Sat-Sun; closed Jan 1, Thanksgiving, Dec 25). At South Kelley Park, 1650 Senter Rd. Phone 408/287-2290. ¢¢¢

Japanese Friendship Garden. A 6½-acre Japanese Stroll Garden patterned after Korakuen Park in Okayama, Japan; on two levels with a waterfall dropping from lake on upper level into one of two lakes on lower level; 22 symbolic features incl bridges and lanterns; teahouse; ¾-mi paved walkway trail. (Daily) 1300 Senter Rd. **FREE**

Lick Observatory. Main building has astronomical exhibits, guide lectures, and 36-inch refracting telescope. At a 120-inch reflecting telescope there is a Visitors Gallery with a self-guided tour. Maintained by the University of California at Santa Cruz. (Daily; closed hols) 25 mi SE on CA 130 at Mt Hamilton. Phone 408/274-5061. **FREE**

Mirassou Winery. Produces vintage wines and champagnes. Wine tasting and tours. (Mon-Sun afternoons; closed hols) 3000 Aborn Rd. Phone 408/274-4000. **FREE**

Municipal Rose Garden. Approx 5,000 rose plants on six acres, peak blooming in late Apr-May. Picnicking. (Daily) Naglee and Dana aves. Phone 408/277-5422. **FREE**

Overfelt Gardens. This 33-acre botanical preserve incl extensive natural areas, a formal botanic garden, and a wildlife sanctuary. Migratory waterfowl and other wildlife inhabit three lakes; wooded areas with wildflowers; Chinese Cultural Garden has a bronze and marble statue of Confucius overlooking a reflecting pond, an ornate Chinese gate, and three Chinese pavilions—all a gift from the Chinese community. (Daily) No pets, skates, skateboards, or bicycles. McKee Rd, at Educational Park Dr. W of Jackson Ave, via US 101 and I-680. Phone 408/251-3323. **FREE**

Paramount's Raging Waters. Water theme amusement park with more than 35 water park attractions, incl the Shark, a double tube ride; river rides; Wacky Water Works, a children's activity area; water slides; lagoon and a beach. (Mid-June-late Aug, daily; mid-May-mid-June and late Aug-Sept, Sat and Sun) 2333 S White Rd, in Lake Cunningham Regional Park. Phone 408/238-9900. **¢¢¢¢¢**

Peralta Adobe and Fallon House. Built in 1797, the Peralta adobe is the last remaining home of the first pueblo (city) in California. The Fallon house is a Victorian home built for a wealthy resident. Both homes are furnished in the period. (Tues-Sun) 175 W St John St. Phone 408/993-8182. **¢¢¢**

Professional sports.

San Jose Earthquakes (MLS). Spartan Stadium, Phone 408/985-4625.

San Jose Sharks (NHL). San Jose Arena. 525 W Santa Clara St. Phone 408/287-7070.

Rosicrucian Park. Headquarters of the English Grand Lodge of the Rosicrucian Order, AMORC; worldwide philosophical fraternity. Park and Naglee aves. Phone 408/947-3636. **¢¢¢** On grounds are

Egyptian Museum. One of largest collections of Egyptian antiquities west of the Mississippi; mummy collection incl those of children, adults, and animals; replica of a nobleman's tomb. Also art gallery with contemporary works on display. (Tues-Sun; closed hols) Phone 408/947-3636. **¢¢¢**

Planetarium & Science Center. The feature exhibit "Geological Gems" looks at mineral properties, crystals, quartz, gemstones, and rock types. (Tues-Sun; closed hols) Children under age five not admitted to planetarium shows. Phone 408/947-3636. **FREE** Planetarium shows **¢¢**

San Jose Museum of Art. International exhibits featuring contemporary art; multimedia resource center. Book and gift shop. Cafe. (Tues-Sun; closed hols) Web www.sjmusart.org. 110 S Market St. Phone 408/294-2787. **¢¢¢**

San Jose Museum of Quilts & Textiles. Regularly changing exhibits feature quilts and other textiles from around the world. Museum's collection incl quilts and coverlets from the 19th century. Explores the role of quilts in cultural traditions, the lives of their makers, and their significance as historical documents. (Tues-Sun; closed hols) Web www.sjquiltmuseum.org. 110 Paseo de San Antonio. Phone 408/971-0323. **¢¢**

The Tech Museum of Innovation. This 132,000-square-ft facility offers visitors four themed galleries: Innovation, Exploration, Communication, and Life Tech. See how a microchip is made, design a roller coaster, or make a movie in the Digital Studio. Also IMAX Dome Theater (fee). (Daily; closed Jan 1, Thanksgiving, Dec 25) 201 S Market St. Phone 408/294-TECH. **¢¢¢**

Winchester Mystery House. Started in 1884 by widow of the firearms manufacturer. Told by a medium that she would never die as long as she kept building, Sarah Winchester kept a crew of carpenters busy 24 hrs a day until her death in 1922, 38 yrs later. The expenditures cost more than $5 million. The mansion incl 160 rms, thousands of doors and windows, 40 stairways (most with 13 steps, many that go nowhere), blank walls, blind chimneys, trapdoors, and secret passageways. Sixty-five-min guided mansion tour; behind-the-scenes-tour; self-guided gardens and outlying buildings tour. Guided tours (daily; closed Dec 25); admission to Historic Museum of Winchester Rifles incl in tour. 525 S Winchester Blvd, at I-280 and CA 17. **¢¢¢¢¢**

Special Events

Obon Festival. Japanese-American outdoor celebration with hundreds of costumed dancers and Taiko drummers; games, food, crafts. Phone 408/293-9292. Early or mid-July.

San Jose America Festival. Food booths, arts and crafts; rides, games, entertainment. Early July. Phone 408/294-2100.

Santa Clara County Fair. Santa Clara County Fairgrounds, 344 Tully Rd, 3 mi S off US 101. Phone 408/494-FAIR. Late July-early Aug. Phone 408/494-3257.

Tapestry in Talent's Festival of the Arts. Downtown. Multicultural arts festival celebrates the arts and ethnic diversity of Santa Clara County. Labor Day wkend. Phone 408/293-9728.

Motels/Motor Lodges

★★ **BEST WESTERN GATEWAY INN.** *2585 Seaboard Ave (95131). 408/435-8800; fax 408/435-8879; toll-free 800/437-8855.* 146 rms, 2 story. S, D $149; each addl $5; under 18 free; wkend rates. Crib free. TV; cable (premium), VCR avail (movies). Pool; whirlpool. Complimentary continental bkfst. Ck-out noon. Meeting rms. Business servs avail. Valet serv. Sundries. Free airport transportation. Health club privileges. Refrigerators; microwaves avail. Totally nonsmoking. Cr cds: A, C, D, DS, MC, V.

D

★★ **COMFORT INN AIRPORT SOUTH.** *2118 The Alameda (95126). 408/243-2400; fax 408/243-5478; res 800/423-6184.* 40 rms, 2 story. S, D $115-$125; suites $135; under 18 free. Crib avail. TV; cable (premium), VCR (free movies). Heated pool; whirlpool. Complimentary continental bkfst, coffee in rms. Restaurant nearby. Ck-out 11 am. Business servs avail. In-rm modem link. Some bathrm phones, in-rm whirlpools; refrigerators, minibars in suites. Cr cds: A, C, D, DS, MC, V.

D SC

★★ **COURTYARD BY MARRIOTT.** *10605 N Wolfe Rd, Cupertino (95014). 408/252-9100; fax 408/252-0632; toll-free 800/321-2211. www.marriott.com.* 149 rms, 3 story, 12 suites. S, D $184; suites $204; under 18 free. Crib free. TV; cable (premium). Heated pool; whirlpool. Continental bkfst, coffee in rms. Ck-out noon. Coin lndry. Meeting rms. Business servs avail. Exercise equipt. Some refrigerators. Balconies. Cr cds: A, C, D, DS, MC, V.

D SC

★★ **HOLIDAY INN.** *399 Silicon Valley Blvd (95138). 408/972-7800; fax 408/972-0157; res 800/465-4329. www.holiday-inn.com.* 210 rms, 3 story, 24 suites. S, D $209-$249; each addl $10; suites $229-$309; under 18 free. Crib free. TV; cable (premium). Pool. Complimentary coffee in lobby. Restaurant adj 6 am-10 pm. Bar. Ck-out noon. Meeting rms. Business servs avail. In-rm modem link. Valet serv. Free airport, RR station, bus depot transportation. Exercise equipt. Refrigerator in suites. Cr cds: A, D, DS, MC, V.

D

★★★ **PRUNEYARD INN.** *1995 S Bascom Ave, Campbell (95008). 831/559-4300; fax 408/559-9919; toll-free 800/559-4344.* 118 rms, 3 story, 11 kits. S $179; D $189; each addl $10; suites $265; kits. $189; under 12 free; wkend rates. Crib free. TV; cable (premium), VCR (free movies). Heated pool; whirlpool. Complimentary continental bkfst. Ck-out noon. Meeting rms. Business servs avail. In-rm modem link. Bellhops. Valet serv. Free airport, RR station, bus depot transportation. Some in-rm whirlpools. Bathrm phones, refrigerators, minibars; some fireplaces. Cr cds: A, D, DS, MC, V.

D SC

Hotels

★★★ **BEVERLY HERITAGE HOTEL.** *1820 Barber Ln, Milpitas (95035). 408/943-9080; fax 408/432-8617; toll-free 800/443-4455. www.beverlyheritage.com.* 196 rms, 3 story, 67 suites. S $229; D $239; each addl $10; suites $199-$500; under 18 free; wkend package plans. Crib free. TV, cable (premium). Heated pool; whirlpool, wading pool, poolside serv. Complimentary continental bkfst (wkdays). Restaurant 6:30 am-10 pm. Bar from 11 am. Ck-out noon. Meeting rms. Business servs avail. Free airport transportation. Exercise equipt. Health club privileges. Bathrm phones. Mountain bikes avail. Cr cds: A, C, D, DS, MC, V.

D

★★★ **CROWNE PLAZA.** *282 Almaden Blvd (95113). 408/998-0400; fax 408/289-9081; toll-free 800/227-6963.* 231 rms, 9 story. S, D $219; each addl $10; suites $239-$249; under 18 free. Crib free. TV; cable (premium), VCR avail. Restaurant 6 am-midnight. Bar 11:30-1:30 am;

entertainment. Garage. Ck-out noon. Meeting rms. Business servs avail. In-rm modem link. Gift shop. Airport, RR station, bus depot transportation. Exercise equipt. Cr cds: A, C, D, DS, JCB, MC, V.

D SC

★★★ **CROWNE PLAZA HOTEL.** *777 Bellew Dr, Milpitas (95035). 408/321-9500; fax 408/321-7443; res 800/838-5827. www.crowneplaza.com.* 305 rms, 12 story. S $209; D $259; each addl $10; suites $280-$325; under 18 free; wkend, hol rates. Crib free. TV; cable (premium). Heated pool; whirlpool, poolside serv. Restaurant 6 am-2 pm, 5-10 pm. Bar 11-1 am; entertainment Mon-Thurs. Ck-out noon. Coin lndry. Convention facilities. Business servs avail. In-rm modem link. Bellhops. Valet serv. Sundries. Gift shop. Free airport transportation. Exercise equipt; sauna. Refrigerator avail. Cr cds: A, C, D, DS, JCB, MC, V.

D SC

★★★ **DOUBLETREE.** *2050 Gateway Pl (95110). 408/453-4000; fax 408/437-2899; res 800/227-8733.* 505 rms, 10 story. S, D $265-$285; each addl $20; suites $495-$695; under 17 free; wkend rates. Crib free. Pet accepted, some restrictions; $15 refundable. TV; cable (premium), VCR avail. Heated pool; poolside serv. Restaurants 6 am-midnight. Bar to 1:30 am; entertainment. Ck-out noon. Convention facilities. Business center. In-rm modem link. Concierge. Gift shop. Barber, beauty shop. Free airport, RR station transportation. Exercise equipt; sauna. Refrigerator in suites. Balconies. Luxury level. Cr cds: A, D, DS, JCB, MC, V.

D

★★★★ **THE FAIRMONT SAN JOSE.** *170 S Market St (95113). 408/998-1900; fax 408/995-5037; res 800/866-5577. www.fairmont.com.* Located in the heart of Silicon Valley, the Fairmont provides a glittering reminder of the area's historic past. Guest rooms are comfortable and many have pretty views. There is a spa and salon where guests can indulge in facials and body treatments, as well as a pool and a health club. Due to the location, plenty of attention is devoted to business services. 541 rms, 20 story. S $129-$329; D $159-$359; each addl $25; suites $329-$1,000; hol plans. Covered parking $15/day. TV; cable (premium). Heated pool; poolside serv. Restaurants 6:30 am-10:30 pm; Fri, Sat to 11 pm (see also GRILL ON THE ALLEY). Rm serv 24 hrs. Bar 11-1:30 am; entertainment. Ck-out 1 pm. Convention facilities. Business center. In-rm modem link. Concierge serv. Shopping arcade. Barber, beauty shop. Exercise equipt; sauna, steam rm. Massage. Bathrm phones, minibars. Some private patios. Cr cds: A, C, D, DS, MC, V.

D

★★★ **HAYES CONFERENCE CENTER.** *200 Edenvale Ave (95136). 408/226-3200; fax 408/362-2388; res 800/420-3200. www.hayesconferencecenter.com.* 135 rms, 2-3 story. S $245; D $260; suites $325; wkend rates. Crib free. TV; cable (premium), VCR avail (movies). Complimentary coffee in rms. Restaurant 11:30 am-2 pm, 5:30-9:30 pm. Meeting rms. Business center. In-rm modem link. Concierge. Gift shop. Airport, RR station transportation. Tennis privileges. Exercise equipt; sauna. Massage. Heated pool; poolside serv. Playground adj. Rec rm. Lawn games. Bathrm phones, refrigerators; microwaves, wet bars avail. Balconies avail. Cr cds: A, D, DS, JCB, MC, V.

D

★★★ **HILTON AND TOWERS.** *300 Almaden Blvd (95110). 408/287-2100; fax 408/947-4489; res 800/345-6565.* 355 rms, 16 story. S $119-$259; D $134-$274; each addl $15; suites $395; under 18 free; wkend rates. Crib free. Pet accepted, some restrictions. Valet parking $11; garage parking $7. TV; cable (premium). Complimentary coffee in rms. Restaurant 6 am-10 pm. Bar 10-2 am. Ck-out noon. Convention facilities. Business center. In-rm modem link. Concierge. Gift shop. Coin lndry. Exercise equipt. Massage. Heated pool; whirlpool, poolside serv. Many minibars; refrigerator, wet bar in suites; microwaves avail. Luxury level. Cr cds: A, D, DS, JCB, MC, V.

D

★★★ **HOTEL DE ANZA.** *233 W Santa Clara St (95113). 408/286-1000; fax 408/286-0500; toll-free 800/843-*

3700. www.hoteldeanza.com. 101 units, 10 story. S $329; D $344; each addl $15; suites $195-$1,300; under 16 free; wkend rates. Valet parking $11.50. TV; cable (premium), VCR (movies). Restaurant 7 am-2 pm, 5-10 pm. Bar 11-2 am; entertainment Wed-Sat. Ck-out noon. Meeting rms. Business servs avail. In-rm modem link. Exercise equipt. Health club privileges. Bathrm phones, refrigerators, minibars; some wet bars. Some balconies. Cr cds: A, D, DS, MC, V.

★★★ **HYATT.** *1740 N 1st St (95112). 408/993-1234; fax 408/453-0259; res 800/233-1234.* 508 rms, 2-3 story. S, D $180-$250; each addl $25; suites $199-$599; under 18 free; wkend rates. Pet accepted. TV; cable (premium), VCR avail. Heated pool, whirlpool; poolside serv. Coffee in rms. Restaurant 5:30 am-midnight. Bar 11-2 am. Ck-out noon. Meeting rms. Business servs avail. In-rm modem link. Gift shop. Free airport transportation. Exercise equipt. Some refrigerators; wet bar in suites. Many private patios, balconies. Cr cds: A, C, D, DS, MC, V.

★★★ **HYATT SAINTE CLAIRE.** *302 S Market St (95113). 408/885-1234; fax 408/977-0403; res 800/233-1234.* 170 rms, 6 story, 18 suites. Feb-Oct: S, D $235-$265; each addl $20; suites $300-$900; under 12 free. Crib free. Valet, garage parking $11. TV; cable (premium). Restaurants 6:30 am-11 pm. Bar 11:30 am-11 pm. Ck-out noon. Meeting rms. Business servs avail. In-rm modem link. Bellhops. Exercise equipt. Bathrm phones, refrigerators. Renovation of 1926 hotel. Cr cds: A, C, D, DS, JCB, MC, V.

★★★ **RADISSON PLAZA HOTEL SAN JOSE AIRPORT.** *1471 N 4th St (95112). 408/452-0200; fax 408/437-8819; res 800/333-3333. www.radisson.com.* 185 rms, 5 story. S, D $234. each addl $10; suites $250-$325; under 17 free. Crib free. TV; cable (premium). Heated pool; whirlpool, poolside serv. Complimentary coffee in rms. Restaurant 6:30 am-11 pm. Bar 10:30-1 am. Ck-out noon. Meeting rms. Business servs avail. In-rm modem link. Covered parking. Free airport transportation. Exercise equipt. Refrigerators; in-rm whirlpool in suites. Luxury level. Cr cds: A, C, D, DS, JCB, MC, V.

★★★ **SHERATON SAN JOSE.** *1801 Barber Ln, Milpitas (95035). 408/943-0600; fax 408/943-0484; res 800/325-3535.* 229 rms, 9 story, 60 suites. S $220; D $229; each addl $10; suites $260; under 18 free; wkend rates, packages. Crib free. TV; cable (premium). Heated pool; whirlpool, poolside serv. Complimentary coffee in rms. Restaurant 6 am-10 pm. Bar 11-2 am; entertainment. Ck-out 1 pm. Meeting rms. Business center. Concierge. Gift shop. Free airport transportation. Exercise equipt. Health club privileges. Bathrm phones. Refrigerator, wet bar in suites. Balconies. Luxury level. Cr cds: A, C, D, DS, JCB, MC, V.

★★ **WYNDHAM HOTEL.** *1350 N 1st St (95112). 408/453-6200; fax 408/437-9693; toll-free 800/538-6818.* 355 rms, 9 story. S, D $229-$249; each addl $20; suites $249-$350; under 12 free; wkend rates. Crib free. TV; cable (premium). Pool; poolside serv. Restaurant 6 am-11 pm. Bar. Ck-out 3 pm. Convention facilities. Business servs avail. Gift shop. Free airport transportation. Exercise equipt. Refrigerator in suites. Cr cds: A, C, D, DS, JCB, MC, V.

B&Bs/Small Inns

★★ **BRIAR ROSE BED & BREAKFAST.** *897 E Jackson St (95112). 408/279-5999; fax 408/279-4534.* 6 rms, 4 baths, 2 story. S, D $85-$140; each addl $20; under 5 free. TV. Complimentary full bkfst. Restaurant nearby. Ck-out 11 am, ck-in 4-6 pm. Street parking. Restored Victorian farm house (1875); antique furnishings; garden with pond, fountain. Totally nonsmoking. Cr cds: A, D, DS, MC, V.

★★★ **CAMPBELL INN.** *675 E Campbell Ave, Campbell (95008). 408/374-4300; fax 408/379-0695; toll-free 800/582-4449. www.campbell-inn.com.* 95 rms, 2 story, 8 suites. S, D $150-$185; suites $275-$325; under 12 free; wkend rates. Pet accepted, some restrictions; $10 per night. TV; VCR (free movies). Heated pool; whirlpool. Complimentary full buffet bkfst. Ck-out noon. Business servs avail. Valet serv. Free airport, RR station, bus depot transportation. Lighted tennis. Health club privileges. Bathrm phones, refrigerators; steam bath, fireplace in suites. Private patios, balconies. Cr cds: A, C, D, DS, MC, V.

D SC

Winchester Mystery House, San Jose

All Suites

★★★ **EMBASSY SUITES MILPITAS/SILICON VALLEY.** *901 E Calaveras Blvd, Milpitas (95035). 408/942-0400; fax 408/262-8604. www.embassysuites.com.* 266 suites, 9 story. S, D $199-$249; each addl $10; under 18 free; wkend rates. TV; cable (premium). Indoor pool; whirlpool. Complimentary full bkfst. Coffee in rms. Restaurant 11 am-10 pm. Bar. Ck-out 1 pm. Convention facilities. Business servs avail. In-rm modem link. Gift shop. Sauna. Health club privileges. Refrigerators. Some private patios, balconies. Atrium. Cr cds: A, C, D, DS, JCB, MC, V.

D SC

★★★ **SUMMERFIELD SUITES BY WYNDHAM.** *1602 Crane Court (95112). 408/436-1600; fax 408/436-1075; res 800/833-4353. www.wyndham.com.* 98 kit. units, 2-3 story. S, D $209-$259. Pet accepted, some restrictions; $75 plus $10/day. TV; cable (premium), VCR (movies). Heated pool; whirlpool. Complimentary continental bkfst, coffee in rms. Restaurant nearby. Ck-out noon. Coin lndry. Meeting rms. Business servs avail. Valet serv. Sundries. Free airport transportation. Exercise equipt. Health club privileges. Some fireplaces. Picnic tables, grills. Cr cds: A, D, DS, JCB, MC, V.

Extended Stay

★★ **RESIDENCE INN BY MARRIOTT.** *2761 S Bascom Ave, Campbell (95008). 408/559-1551; fax 408/371-9808; toll-free 800/331-3131. www.residenceinn.com/sjcba.* 80 kit. suites, 2 story. Kit. suites $169-$189. Crib free. Pet accepted, some restrictions; $75 plus $10/day. TV; cable (premium). Heated pool; whirlpool. Complimentary continental bkfst. Ck-out noon. Coin lndry. Meeting rm. Business servs avail. Free airport transportation. Health club privileges. Refrigerators, fireplaces. Balconies. Grills. Cr cds: A, C, D, DS, MC, V.

D SC

Restaurants

★★ **840 NORTH FIRST.** *840 N 1st St (95112). 408/282-0840. www.840.com.* Hrs: 11:30 am-10 pm. Closed Sun; also hols. Res accepted. Contemporary American menu. Bar. Wine list. A la carte entrees: lunch $8.95-$15.95, dinner $9.95-$24.95. Specializes in game, seafood, pasta. Valet parking. Jacket. Totally nonsmoking. Cr cds: A, D, DS, MC, V.

D

★★★ **EMILE'S.** *545 S 2nd St (95112). 408/289-1960. www.emiles.com.* Hrs: 6-10 pm; Fri 11:30 am-2 pm, 6-10 pm. Closed Sun, Mon; hols. Res accepted. Contemporary French menu. Bar. Wine cellar. A la carte entrees: lunch $14.95-$18.95, dinner $25-$35. Specialties: salmon filet in potato crust, rack of lamb, cappuccino souffle. Valet parking. Cr cds: A, C, D, DS, ER, MC, V.

D

★★ **EULIPA.** *374 S 1st St (95112). 408/280-6161.* Hrs: 11 am-2:30 pm, 5:30-10 pm. Closed Mon; hols. Res accepted. Bar. A la carte entrees: lunch $8.95-$13.50, dinner $7.95-$22. Specializes in pasta, steaks, fish. Cr cds: A, DS, MC, V.

D

★★ **FUNG LUM.** *1815 S Bascom Ave, Campbell (95008). 408/377-6956.* Hrs: 11:30 am-2 pm, 5-9:30 pm; Fri, Sat to 10 pm; Sun 11 am-3 pm (brunch), 4:30-9 pm. Closed Thanksgiving. Chinese menu. Bar. A la carte entrees: lunch $5-$8.25, dinner $5.25-$30. Complete meals: lunch $10.50-$20.50, dinner $14.50-$32.50. Sun buffet, brunch $10.95. Specialties: lemon chicken, Fung Lum spareribs. Chinese decor. Totally nonsmoking. Cr cds: A, D, MC, V.

D

★★ **THE GRILL ON THE ALLEY.** *172 S Market St (95113). 408/294-2244.* Hrs: Mon-Fri 11:30 am-11 pm; Sat-Sun 4:30-11pm. Res accepted. Bar. Wine cellar. A la carte entrees: lunch $7.75-$18.75, dinner $14.50-$32.50. American cuisine specializing in crab Louis, USDA prime beef, lamb chops. Valet parking. Cr cds: A, D, MC, V.

D

★★★ **LA PASTAIA.** *233 W Santa Clara (95113). 408/286-8686. www.lapastaia.com.* Hrs: 11 am-10 pm; Fri to 10:30 pm; Sat noon-2 pm, 5-10 pm; Sun noon-2 pm, 5-9 pm. Closed hols. Res accepted. Italian menu. Wine list. A la carte entrees: lunch $9.95-$24.95, dinner $10.25-$24.95. Specialties: carpaccio, osso buco, linguine vongole. Valet parking. Outdoor dining. Cr cds: A, DS, MC, V.

D

★★★ **LOU'S VILLAGE.** *1465 W San Carlos St (95126). 408/293-4570. www.lousvillage.com.* Hrs: 11:30 am-10 pm; Sat 5-11 pm; Sun 4:30-9 pm. Closed Jan 1, Dec 25. Res accepted. Lunch $9.95-$19.95, dinner $13.95-$32.95. Children's menu. Specializes in seafood, pasta. Own desserts. Nautical decor. Family-owned. Cr cds: A, MC, V.

D

★★ **ORIGINAL JOE'S.** *301 S 1st St (95113). 408/292-7030. www.originaljoes.com.* Hrs: 11-1:30 am. Closed hols. Italian, American menu. Bar. A la carte entrees: bkfst $4.95-$16.95, lunch $6.95-$12.95, dinner $8.95-$26.95. Children's menu. Family-owned. Cr cds: A, C, D, DS, ER, MC, V.

D

San Juan Bautista

(A-1) *See also Gilroy, Salinas*

Pop 1,570 **Elev** 150 ft **Area code** 831 **Zip** 95045

Information Chamber of Commerce, 1 Polk St, PO Box 1037, 95045-1037; 831/623-2454

Web www.sanjuanbautista.com

The San Andreas Fault intersects this little town, providing residents with a few minor tremors and a topic of speculation, but little worry; most of the buildings have been standing more than 150 years. San Juan Bautista began in 1797 with the Spanish mission. The town that spread around the mission prospered as a center of cattle ranching and commerce from a nearby lode of quicksilver. However, in 1870 the Southern Pacific Railroad ran the region's first tracks through a nearby town and San Juan Bautista began to decline. Today, tourists and artists contribute to the economy of the town.

What to See and Do

Pinnacles National Monument. (see) 8 mi E on CA 156, then 35 mi S on CA 25.

San Juan Bautista State Historic Park. 2nd St, 3 mi E of US 101. Phone 831/623-4881. Here are

Mission San Juan Bautista. (1797) Fifteenth and largest mission church built by the Franciscans. Church, finished in 1812 and still in use, contains many original items. The museum has old vestments, music books, barrel organ, relics, and original kitchen and dining rm. Cemetery has graves of 4,300 Native Americans. (Daily; closed hols) 2nd and Mariposa sts. Phone 831/623-2127. **Donation**

Plaza Stable. (1861) Houses collection of restored horse-drawn carriages, blacksmith and wagonwright equipment, and tools; **Castro-Breen House** (1841) (self-guided tours); **Plaza Hall** (1868), used as a residence, assembly place, and dance hall; **Plaza Hotel**, restored. Picnicking. (Daily; closed Jan 1, Thanksgiving, Dec 25) All buildings ¢

Special Events

Early Days Celebration. Commemorates founding of mission; food, entertainment, history demonstrations. Mid-June.

San Benito County Saddle Horse Show, Parade & Rodeo. 8 mi W on CA 156 to Hollister, then 8 mi S on CA 25. Phone 831/628-3421. Late June.

Motel/Motor Lodge

★ **SAN JUAN INN.** *410 Alameda St and Hwy 156 (95045). 831/623-4380; fax 408/623-0689.* 42 rms, 2 story. S $45-$65; D $55-$85; each addl $6. Crib $5. TV; cable. Pool; whirlpool. Restaurant nearby. Ck-out noon. Microwaves avail. Cr cds: A, D, MC, V.

SC

Restaurants

★ **DONA ESTER.** *25 Franklin St (95045). 831/623-2518.* Hrs: 9 am-10 pm. Closed Easter, Thanksgiving, Dec 25. Res accepted. Mexican menu. Bar. Bkfst $3-$7.45, lunch $3.95-$6.95, dinner $4.50-$9.95. Buffet: Sun lunch $7.75. Specializes in fish, authentic Mexican dishes. Guitarist, vocalist Thurs-Sun. Outdoor dining. Cr cds: A, DS, MC, V.

D SC

★ **JARDINES DE SAN JUAN.** *115 3rd St (95045). 831/623-4466. www.jardinesrestaurant.com.* Hrs: 11:30 am-9 pm; Fri, Sat to 10 pm. Closed Thanksgiving, Dec 25. Res accepted. No A/C. Mexican menu. Bar. A la carte entrees: lunch, dinner $2.95-$9.75. Complete meal (dinner Fri-Sun): $13. Children's menu. Specialties: carne asada, crab and shrimp tostada, red snapper Veracruz. Outdoor dining. Extensive garden area; Mexican decor. Family-owned. Totally nonsmoking. Cr cds: MC, V.

D

San Juan Capistrano

(F-5) *See also Anaheim, Laguna Beach, San Clemente*

Founded 1776 **Pop** 26,183 **Elev** 104 ft **Area code** 949 **Zip** 92675

Information Chamber of Commerce, 31781 Camino Capistrano, Suite 306; 949/493-4700

Web www.sanjuanchamber.com

Because of its colorful mission and its euphonious name, this town has been romanticized in song, legend, short stories, and movies. Perched between mountains and ocean, San Juan Capistrano developed around the mission and today is occupied, in part, by descendants of early Mexican settlers. At one time the village declared war on Mexico.

What to See and Do

Mission San Juan Capistrano. Famous for its swallows, which depart each yr on St. John's Day, Oct 23, and return on St. Joseph's Day, Mar 19. Founded by Fray Juneípero Serra in 1776 and named for St. John of Capistrano, the Crusader, the church was built in the form of a cross and was one of the most beautiful of all California missions. The arched roof, five domes, nave, cloister, and belfry collapsed during the 1812 earthquake. Pillars, arches, the garden, and quadrangle remain. Self-guided tour incl the Serra Chapel (still in use), oldest building in California, ruin of the Great Stone Church, padres' living quarters, soldiers' barracks, and three museum rms exhibiting artifacts from Native American and early Spanish culture.

Also the site of a major archaeological dig. (Daily; closed Easter, Thanksgiving, Dec 25) 2 blks W of I-5, Ortega Hwy exit. Phone 949/248-2048. ¢¢

O'Neil Museum. Housed in a restored Victorian house, museum features collections of historical photographs, rare books, period furniture and clothing, Native Americans artifacts; also genealogical information. (Tues-Fri, Sun; closed hols) 31831 Los Rios St. Phone 949/493-8444. ¢

Regional Library and Cultural Center. Architecturally noteworthy post-modern building, designed by Michael Graves, combines Spanish, Egyptian, Greek, and pre-Columbian American influences in its design. (Mon-Thurs, Sat, Sun; tours by appt) 31495 El Camino Real. Phone 949/493-1752. **FREE**

Ronald W. Caspers Wilderness Park. Wilderness on 8,060 acres. Riding and hiking trails, nature center. Camping (fee). Inquire in advance for camping and trail use information and restrictions. (Daily) No pets. 33401 Ortega Hwy, I-5 Ortega exit, approx 8 mi E on Ortega Hwy. Phone 949/728-0235. Day use per vehicle ¢

Tour of old adobes. Sponsored by the San Juan Capistrano Historical Society. (Sun) Contact the Historical Society, 31831 Los Rios St. Phone 949/493-8444. ¢

Special Events

Festival of Whales. Dana Point Harbor, in Dana Point. Educational and entertainment events saluting visit of California gray whales. Phone 949/496-1094. Late Feb-mid-Mar, wkends.

Fiesta de las Golondrinas. Mission San Juan Capistrano. Celebrates the return of the swallows to the mission; dance pageant, art exhibits. Mid-Mar. Phone 949/493-4700.

Motel/Motor Lodge

★★ BEST WESTERN CAPISTRANO INN. *27174 Ortega Hwy (92675). 949/493-5661; fax 949/661-8293; res 800/528-1234.* 108 rms, 2 story. Mar-Sept: S, D $74-$89; each addl $6; kit. units $79-$84; under 18 free; lower rates rest of yr. Crib $5. Pet accepted; $250 deposit. TV; cable (premium), VCR avail. Heated pool; whirlpool. Complimentary full bkfst (Mon-Fri). Complimentary coffee in rms. Restaurant adj open 24 hrs. Ck-out noon. Meeting rm. Business servs avail. In-rm modem link. Health club privileges. Microwaves avail. Some balconies. Cr cds: A, D, DS, MC, V.

D

Restaurants

★★ EL ADOBE DE CAPISTRANO. *31891 Camino Capistrano (92675). 949/493-1163.* Hrs: 11 am-9 pm; Sat to 10 pm; Sun from 10 am. Res accepted. Mexican, American menu. Bar. Lunch $5.75-$15.50, dinner $9.50-$18.50. Sun brunch $6.25-$12.95. Children's menu. Specialty: President's choice. Entertainment Fri-Sun. Patio dining. Spanish adobe courthouse (1776). Cr cds: A, D, DS, MC, V.

D

★★ L'HIRONDELLE. *31631 Camino Capistrano (92675). 949/661-0425.* Hrs: 11:30 am-2 pm, 5-9 pm; Fri, Sat to 10 pm; Tues 5-9 pm; early-bird dinner Tues-Thurs, Sun 5-6:30 pm; Sun brunch 11 am-2 pm. Closed Mon; Jan 1, Dec 25. Res accepted. French, Belgian menu. Wine, beer. Lunch $6.75-$8.95, dinner $11.95-$18.95. Sun brunch $12.50. Specializes in braised duckling, rabbit, sweetbreads. Own baking. Patio dining. Many antiques. Cr cds: A, MC, V.

D

★ WALNUT GROVE. *26871 Ortega Hwy (92675). 949/493-1661.* Hrs: 6:30 am-9 pm; Fri, Sat to 9:45 pm; early-bird dinner 3-6 pm. Closed Dec 25. Wine, beer. Bkfst $2.45-$10.50, lunch $3.95-$7.95, dinner $7.75-$10.95. Children's menu. Specializes in home-style cooking. Patio dining. Family-owned. Cr cds: A, C, D, DS, ER, MC, V.

D SC

San Luis Obispo

(C-2) *See also Morro Bay, Pismo Beach*

Founded 1772 **Pop** 41,958 **Elev** 315 ft **Area code** 805

Information Chamber of Commerce, 1039 Chorro St, 93401; 805/781-2777

Web www.slochamber.org

Father Juneípero Serra, who established the mission in 1772, saw a resemblance to a bishop's mitre in two nearby volcanic peaks and named the mission San Luis Obispo de Tolosa (St. Louis, Bishop of Toulouse). After the thatched mission roofs burned several times, a tilemaking technique was developed that soon set the style for all California missions. Located in a bowl-shaped valley, the town depends on government employment, tourism, agriculture, retail trade, and its university population.

What to See and Do

Ah Louis Store. (1874) Leader of the Chinese community, Ah Louis was an extraordinary man who achieved prominence at a time when Asians were given few opportunities. The two-story building, which served as the Chinese bank, post office, and general merchandise store, was the cornerstone of the Chinese community. (Mon-Sat; closed hols) 800 Palm St. Phone 805/543-4332.

California Polytechnic State University. (1901) 17,000 students. On campus are three art galleries, working livestock and farm units, horticultural, architectural, and experimental displays. Campus tours (Mon, Wed, Fri; res required). N edge of town. Phone 805/756-5734. **FREE** Also here are

Performing Arts Center of San Louis Obispo. 91,500-sq-ft center offers professional dance, theater, music, and other performances all year. The 1,350-seat Herman Concert Hall is JBL Professional's exclusive North American test and demonstration site. Grand Ave. Phone 805/756-2787.

Shakespeare Press Printing Museum. Collection of 19th-century printing presses, type and related equipment; demonstrations for prearranged tours. (Mon, Wed; closed hols) Graphic Communication Building. Phone 805/756-1108. **FREE**

Children's Museum. A hands-on museum for children preschool through elementary school (must be accompanied by an adult); houses many interactive exhibits; themes change monthly. (Tues-Sun; closed hols) 1010 Nipomo St, jct Monterey St. Phone 805/544-KIDS. **¢¢**

Mission San Luis Obispo de Tolosa. Fifth of the California missions, founded in 1772, still serves as the parish church. Eight-rm museum contains extensive Chumash collection and artifacts from early settlers. First olive orchard in California planted here; two original trees still stand. (Daily; closed hols) Chorro and Palm sts. Phone 805/543-6850. **Donation**

San Luis Obispo County Historical Museum. (1905) Local history exhibits; decorative arts; turn-of-the-century parlor re-creation. (Wed-Sun; closed hols) 696 Monterey St, near mission. Phone 805/543-0638. **FREE**

Special Events

Madonnari Italian Street Painting Festival. Mission San Luis Obispo de Tolosa. Local artists decorate the streets around the mission with chalk drawings. Also music, Italian cuisine, and open-air market. Apr. Phone 805/781-2777.

Renaissance Festival. Celebration of the Renaissance; period costumes, food booths, entertainment, arts and crafts. July. Phone 707/864-5706.

Mozart Festival. Recitals, chamber music, orchestra concerts, and choral music. Held at various locations throughout the county, incl Mission San Luis Obispo de Tolosa and Cal Poly State University campus. Contact PO Box 311. Late July-early Aug. Phone 805/781-3008.

SLO International Film Festival. Downtown. Showcases history and art of filmmaking. Screenings of new releases and classics. Four days Nov. Phone 805/546-3456.

Motels/Motor Lodges

★★★ **APPLE FARM TRELLIS COURT.** *2015 Monterey St (93401). 805/544-2040; fax 805/546-9495; res 800/255-2040. www.applefarm.com.* 34 rms, 1-2 story. July-mid-Sept: S, D $89-$129; each addl $20; under 18 free; higher rates: wkends, hols; lower rates rest of yr. Crib free. TV; cable (premium). Restaurant (see also APPLE FARM). Ck-out noon. Business servs avail. Bellhops. Valet serv. Gift shop. Free airport, RR station, bus depot transportation. Pool; whirlpool. Fireplaces. Cr cds: A, DS, MC, V.

SC

★★ **BEST WESTERN ROYAL OAK.** *214 Madonna Rd (93405). 805/544-4410; fax 805/544-3026; toll-free 800/545-4410. www.pacificplaza hotels.com.* 99 rms, 2 story. May-mid-Nov: S, D $69-$99; each addl $7; under 12 free; higher rates: special events, hols; lower rates rest of yr. Crib free. Pet accepted, some restrictions. TV; cable (premium). Heated pool; whirlpool. Complimentary continental bkfst, coffee in rms. Restaurant 6 am-10 pm. Ck-out noon. Coin lndry. Meeting rms. Business servs avail. In-rm modem link. Valet serv. Some refrigerators; many microwaves. Balconies. Cr cds: A, C, D, DS, ER, JCB, MC, V.

D SC

★ **ECONO LODGE.** *950 Olive St (93405). 805/544-8886; fax 805/543-1611; res 800/553-2555.* 32 rms, 2 story. Mid-June-late Sept: S $55-$125; D $65-$130; each addl $8; suites $80-$165; under 12 free; higher rates: hols (2-day min), graduation, county fair; lower rates rest of yr. Crib free. TV; cable (premium). Complimentary coffee in rms. Restaurant adj 6:30 am-9 pm. Ck-out 11 am. Business servs avail. Whirlpool. Refrigerators avail. Cr cds: A, DS, MC, V.

D

★★ **LAMPLIGHTER INN AND SUITES.** *1604 Monterey St (93401). 805/547-7777; fax 805/547-7787; toll-free 800/214-8378.* 40 rms, 2-3 story, 2 cottages. No elvtr. S $42-109; D $45-$139; each addl $10; suites $75-$225; higher rates special events. TV; cable (premium), VCR avail. Heated pool; whirlpool. Complimentary bkfst, coffee in rms. Restaurant nearby. Ck-out 11 am. Coin lndry. Business servs avail. In-rm modem link. Refrigerators. Cr cds: A, C, D, DS, MC, V.

★★ **HOLIDAY INN EXPRESS.** *1800 Monterey St (93401). 805/544-8600; fax 805/541-4698; toll-free 800/544-0800. www.holiday-inn.com/hotels/sbpex.* 100 rms, 3 story. June-Sept, wkends: S $110-$120; D $120-$130; each addl $10; suites $130-$150; under 18 free; higher rates: special events, hols (2-day min); lower rates rest of yr. Crib free. TV; cable (premium), VCR avail (movies). Heated pool; whirlpool. Complimentary continental bkfst, coffee in rms. Restaurant (see also IZZY ORTEGA'S). Bar 11:30 am-9 pm. Ck-out noon. Meeting rm. Business servs avail. In-rm modem link. Valet serv. Refrigerators avail. Cr cds: A, C, D, DS, JCB, MC, V.

D SC

★★ **OLIVE TREE INN.** *1000 Olive St, San Luis Obispo (93405). 805/544-2800; fax 805/787-0814; toll-free 800/777-5847.* 38 rms, 2 story, 6 kits. S $55-$58; D $62-$95; each addl $6; suites $85-$125; kits. $85-$95; higher rates: wkends, special events. Crib free. Pet accepted. TV; cable (premium). Heated pool. Complimentary continental bkfst. Restaurant 7 am-9 pm; Mon, Tues to 2 pm. Ck-out 11 am. Coin lndry. Business servs avail. In-rm modem link. Sundries. Sauna. Many refrigerators; microwaves avail. Balconies. Cr cds: A, C, D, DS, JCB, MC, V.

★★ **QUALITY SUITES.** *1631 Monterey St (93401). 805/541-5001; fax 805/546-9475; res 800/228-5151.* 138 suites, 3 story. May-Labor Day: S $115-$155; D $119-$155; each addl $10; under 18 free; higher rates special events; lower rates rest of yr. Crib free. TV; cable (premium), VCR (movies $6). Heated pool; wading pool, whirlpool. Complimentary full bkfst. Coffee in rms. Restaurant 6:30-9:30 am; wkends 7-10 am. Ck-out noon. Coin lndry. Meeting rm. Business servs avail. In-rm modem link.

Valet serv. Sundries. Gift shop. Free airport, RR station, bus depot transportation. Health club privileges. Refrigerators, microwaves. Private patios, balconies. Library. Grill. Cr cds: A, D, DS, MC, V.

★★★ **SANDS SUITES & MOTEL.** *1930 Monterey (93401). 805/544-0500; fax 805/544-3529; toll-free 800/441-4657.* 56 rms, 1-2 story, 14 suites. May-Sept: S $59-$79; D $69-$89; each addl $7; suites $69-$139; under 12 free; higher rates: special events, hols; lower rates rest of yr. Crib $5. Pet accepted, some restrictions; $5. TV; cable, VCR (free movies). Heated pool; whirlpool. Complimentary continental bkfst. Restaurant adj 6-1 am. Ck-out 11 am. Coin lndry. Meeting rms. Business servs avail. In-rm modem link. Sundries. Some covered parking. Free airport, RR station, bus depot transportation. Refrigerators. Some private patios, balconies. Picnic tables, grill. Delicatessen. Cr cds: A, C, D, DS, MC, V.

★★ **VILLA.** *1670 Monterey St (93401). 805/543-8071; fax 805/549-9389; toll-free 800/554-0059.* 14 rms, 1-2 story. S $39-$79; D $45-$89; each addl $4; higher rates: university events, hols. Crib free. TV; cable (premium), VCR avail. Heated pool in season. Complimentary continental bkfst. Coffee in rms. Restaurant nearby. Ck-out 11 am. Refrigerators; some microwaves. Cr cds: A, D, DS, JCB, MC, V.

B&Bs/Small Inns

★ **ADOBE INN.** *1473 Monterey St (93401). 805/549-0321; fax 805/549-0383; toll-free 800/676-1588. www.adobeinns.com.* 15 rms, 2 story, 7 kit. units. Some A/C. May-Sept: S $59-$99; D $65-$120; each addl $6; lower rates rest of yr. TV; cable. Complimentary full bkfst. Restaurant nearby. Ck-out 11 am, ck-in 2 pm. Meeting rm. Business servs avail. In-rm modem link. Southwestern decor. Totally nonsmoking. Cr cds: A, DS, MC, V.

★★★ **APPLE FARM.** *2015 Monterey St (93401). 805/544-2040; fax 805/546-9495; toll-free 800/374-3705. www.applefarm.com.* 69 rms, 3 story. July-mid-Sept, wkends, hols: S, D $119-$239; each addl $20; under 18 free; lower rates rest of yr. Crib free. TV; cable. Pool; whirlpool. Restaurant (see also APPLE FARM). Ck-out noon. Business servs avail. In-rm modem link. Gift shop. Free airport, bus depot, RR transportation. Fireplaces. Sitting rm. Antiques. Bakery, millhouse. Cr cds: A, DS, MC, V.

★★★ **GARDEN STREET INN.** *1212 Garden Street Inn (93401). 805/545-9802; fax 805/545-9403; toll-free 800/488-2045.* 13 rms, 2 story, 4 suites. S, D $90-$130; suites $150-$175; hols (2-day min). Children over 16 yrs only. Complimentary full bkfst; afternoon refreshments. Restaurant nearby. Ck-out 11 am, ck-in 3-7 pm. Business servs avail. Free airport, RR, bus depot transportation. Some in-rm whirlpools, fireplaces. Restored Victorian house (1887) furnished with antiques. Totally nonsmoking. Cr cds: A, MC, V.

★★ **MADONNA INN.** *100 Madonna Rd (93405). 805/543-3000; fax 805/543-1800; toll-free 800/543-9666. www.madonnainn.com.* 109 rms, 1-4 story. Some A/C. No elvtr. S $117; D $127; suites $160-$240. Crib free. TV; cable (premium). Complimentary coffee in rms. Restaurant 7 am-10 pm, dining rm from 5:30 pm. Bar noon-midnight; entertainment Tues-Sat. Ck-out noon. Meeting rms. Business servs avail. Sundries. Gift shops. Free airport transportation. Some refrigerators; fireplace in suites. Some balconies. Individually decorated rms, each in motif of different nation or period. On hill with mountain view. Totally nonsmoking. Cr cds: A, C, JCB, MC, V.

All Suite

★★★ **EMBASSY SUITES.** *333 Madonna Rd (93405). 805/549-0800; fax 805/543-5233; toll-free 800/864-6000. www.embassysuitesslo.com.* 196 suites, 4 story. S $114-$169; D $124-

$169; each addl $10; under 18 free. Crib free. TV; cable (premium). Indoor pool; whirlpool. Complimentary full bkfst. Coffee in rms. Restaurant 11:30 am-2 pm, 5-10 pm. Bar 11 am-11 pm. Ck-out noon. Coin lndry. Meeting rms. Business servs avail. In-rm modem link. Shopping arcade. Free airport, RR station, bus depot transportation. Exercise equipt. Refrigerators, microwaves. Balconies. Atrium lobby; glass elevators. Cr cds: A, C, D, DS, ER, JCB, MC, V.

D

Restaurants

★ **APPLE FARM.** *2015 Monterey St (93401). 805/544-6100. www.applefarm.com.* Hrs: 7 am-9:30 pm; Fri, Sat to 10 pm; early-bird dinner Mon-Fri 2:30-5 pm. Wine, beer. Bkfst $3.25-$8.95, lunch $3.95-$8.95, dinner $6.95-$16.95. Specialties: prime rib, apple dumplings, homemade ice cream. Salad bar. Patio dining. Gift shop, bakery; water-powered grist mill. Totally nonsmoking. Cr cds: A, DS, MC, V.

D

★★ **CAFE ROMA.** *1020 Railroad Ave (93401). 805/541-6800. www.fix.net/~caferoma.* Hrs: 11:30 am-2:30 pm, 5:30-9:30 pm. Closed Mon, hols. Res accepted. Italian menu. Bar. Lunch $6-$11.75, dinner $6.75-$19. Specialties: canelloni Maria Rosa, scampi alla diavolo, ravioli della casa. Outdoor dining. Italian murals. Romantic dining. Totally nonsmoking. Cr cds: A, DS, MC, V.

D

★ **IZZY ORTEGA'S.** *1850 Monterey St (93401). 805/543-3333.* Hrs: 11:30 am-9 pm; Fri, Sat to 9:30 pm. Closed hols. Res accepted (lunch). Mexican menu. Bar. Lunch $4.50-$10.95, dinner $5.95-$10.95. Children's meals. Specialties: fajitas, chile relleños, nachos. Parking. Outdoor dining. Authentic Mexican decor; cantina atmosphere. Totally nonsmoking. Cr cds: A, DS, MC, V.

D

San Marino

See also Arcadia, Los Angeles

Pop 12,959 **Elev** 566 ft **Area code** 626 **Zip** 91108

Information Chamber of Commerce, 2304 Huntington Dr, Suite 202; 626/286-1022

Web www.smnet.org

What to See and Do

El Molino Viejo. (ca 1816). First gristmill to be operated by water in southern California. Changing exhibits of paintings and prints of California and the West. (Tues-Sun afternoons; closed hols) 1120 Old Mill Rd. Phone 626/449-5458. **FREE**

Huntington Library, Art Collections, and Botanical Gardens. Comprehensive collection of British and French 18th- and 19th-century art and American art. Home of Gainsborough's *Blue Boy,* a Shakespeare First Folio, Ellesmere manuscript of Chaucer's *Canterbury Tales,* and manuscript of Franklin's autobiography; 150-acre botanical gardens. (Tues-Sun; closed hols) Free admission first Thurs of month. 1151 Oxford Rd. Phone 626/405-2141. **¢¢¢**

San Mateo

(G-3) *See also Redwood City, San Francisco Airport Area*

Settled 1851 **Pop** 85,486 **Elev** 28 ft **Area code** 650

Information Redwood City San Mateo County Chamber of Commerce, 1675 Broadway, Redwood City, 94063; 650/364-1722

Web www.sanmateoca.org

Once a stop between the chain of missions established by Fray Juneípero Serra, San Mateo is now a busy suburban area within easy access to both the coast and the bay.

What to See and Do

Coyote Point Museum. Museum features four-level exhibition incl ecological concepts, dioramas, computer games, live insect colonies, aquarium displays. Two-acre Wildlife Center features native bay-area animals, walk-through aviaries, and native plants. (Tues-Sun; closed hols) Free admission first Wed of month. 1651 Coyote Point Dr, 1 mi E via US 101; northbound exit Dore Ave; southbound exit Poplar Ave. Phone 650/342-7755. **¢¢**

Horse racing. Bay Meadows Racecourse. Turf club, clubhouse, grandstand, and infield park. Thoroughbred racing (late Aug-mid-Nov, Wed-Sun). Parking fee. Bayshore Fwy (US 101), CA 92 and Hillsdale Blvd. Phone 650/574-7223. **¢¢**

Japanese Tea Garden. Collection of *koi* (carp), bonsai specimens; pagoda from Toyonaka, Japan; teahouse. (Daily; closed Dec 25) In Central Park, 5th and Laurel aves. Phone 650/377-4640. **FREE**

Woodside Store. (1854). First store between San Jose and San Francisco. The building, once used as a post office and general store, still contains original equipment and furnishings. (Tues, Thurs, Sat, Sun afternoons) Tours by appt. 10 mi SW via I-280 then E on CA 84 (Woodside Rd) to Kings Mt and Tripp rds in Woodside. Phone 650/851-7615. **FREE** Also in Woodside is

Filoli Gardens. This was a filming location for *Dynasty* TV program. Georgian-style mansion and 16 acres of gardens. Guided tours of mansion (Feb-Oct, Tues-Sat; res required). Cañada Rd. Phone 650/364-8300. **¢¢¢¢**

Special Event

San Mateo County Fair & Floral Fiesta. Expo Center. Phone 650/574-FAIR. Aug.

Motels/Motor Lodges

★★ **HOLIDAY INN EXPRESS.** *350 N Bayshore Blvd (94401). 650/344-6376; fax 650/343-7108; toll-free 800/465-4329.* 110 rms, 4 story. S $89; D $99; suites $109-$135; under 18 free. Crib free. TV; cable (premium). Complimentary continental bkfst. Restaurant adj 6:30 am-9:30 pm. Ck-out 11 am. Coin lndry. Meeting rm. Business servs avail. In-rm modem link. Valet serv. Sundries. Free airport, RR station transportation. Health club privileges. Refrigerator in suites. Cr cds: A, D, DS, JCB, MC, V.

★★ **VILLA HOTEL.** *4000 S El Camino Real (94403). 650/341-0966; fax 650/573-0164; toll-free 800/341-2345.* 285 rms, 2-5 story. S $89-$109; D $99-$119; each addl $10; suites $139-$269; under 18 free. Crib free. Pet accepted, some restrictions; $50 refundable. TV; cable (premium). Pool; poolside serv. Complimentary coffee in rms. Restaurant open 24 hrs. Bar 10-2 am. Ck-out 1 pm. Convention facilities. Business servs avail. Bellhops. Gift shop. Barber, beauty shop. Massage. Free airport transportation. Exercise equipt. Some refrigerators. Some balconies. Cr cds: A, C, D, DS, ER, JCB, MC, V.

Hotels

★★ **HILTON GARDEN INN.** *2000 Bridgepoint Cir (94404). 650/522-9000; fax 650/522-9099; res 800/445-8667.* 156 rms. S $109; D $199. Pool. TV; cable (premium). Ck-out noon. Business center. Coin lndry. Cr cds: A, C, D, DS, MC, V.

★★★ **SAN MATEO MARRIOTT.** *1770 S Amphlett Blvd (94402). 650/653-6000. www.marriott.com.* 476 rms, 6 story; 80 suites. S, D $155-$295; each addl $15; under 17 free. Crib avail. Pool. TV; cable (premium), VCR avail. Complimentary coffee in rms, newspaper. Restaurant 6 am-10:30 pm. Bar. Ck-out noon. Meeting rms. Business center. Valet serv. Gift shop. Exercise rm. Some refrigerators, minibars. Cr cds: A, C, D, DS, MC, V.

B&B/Small Inn

★★★ **COXHEAD HOUSE B&B.** *37 E Santa Inez Ave (94401). 650/685-1600; fax 650/685-1684. www.*

coxhead.com. 4 rms, 2 story, 3 suites. S $129; D $145; suites $165; each addl $30. Parking lot. TV; cable. Complimentary full bkfst, newspaper. Restaurant nearby. Ck-in 4 pm. Meeting rms. Business center. Concierge serv. Dry cleaning. Gift shop. Free airport transportation. Exercise privileges. Golf, 18 holes. Tennis, 4 courts. Beach access. Bike rentals. Hiking trail. Picnic facilities. Cr cds: A, D, MC, V.

Surfers enjoying the waves

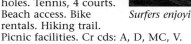

Restaurants

★★★ **LARK CREEK.** *50 E Third Ave (94401). 650/344-9444.* Contemporary American cuisine. Specializes in BBQ short ribs, chicken and dumplings, meatloaf. Hrs: 11 am-9 pm; Fri, Sat to 10 pm; Sun to 6 pm. Lunch $7.95-$17.95; dinner $15.95-$32.95. Early American arts and crafts decor. Cr cds: A, MC, V.

★★★ **VIOGNIER.** *222 E 4th St (94401). 650/685-3727. www.viognier restaurant.com.* Specializes in seafood and steak. Hrs: 11:30 am-2:30 pm, 5:30-10 pm; Sat, Sun brunch 11:30 am-2:30 pm. Res accepted. Wine list. Lunch $10-$18; dinner $12-$30. brunch prix fixe: 3-course $24. Entertainment. Cr cds: A, D, DS, MC, V.

D

San Pedro (L.A.)

See also Los Angeles

Elev 20 ft **Area code** 310

Information Chamber of Commerce, 390 W 7th St, 90731; 310/832-7272

Web www.sanpedrochamber.com

Nestled in the Palos Verdes hills, this community is a neighborhood of Los Angeles, but is regarded by many as a separate entity.

What to See and Do

Cabrillo Marine Aquarium. Extensive marine life displayed in 34 seawater aquariums; interpretive displays, environmental conservation, multimedia shows, "Touch Tank." (Tues-Sun; closed Thanksgiving, Dec 25) Seasonal grunion programs, whale-watching, tidepool tours. Access to beaches, picnic areas, fishing pier, launching ramp (beach parking fee). 3720 Stephen White Dr. Phone 310/548-7562. **Donation**

Los Angeles Maritime Museum. Features scale models of ships, numerous displays and artifacts from sailing vessels of all types. Models incl the *Titanic* and movie studio models from the films *The Poseidon Adventure* and *Mutiny on the Bounty.* (Tues-Sun; closed hols) Berth 84, foot of 6th St at Los Angeles Harbor. Phone 310/548-7618. **Donation**

Ports o'Call Village. Area with many specialty shops and a number of restaurants, all with waterfront dining. E at Berth 77.

Motel/Motor Lodge

★★ **BEST WESTERN SUNRISE HOTEL.** *525 S Harbor Blvd (90731). 310/548-1080; fax 310/519-0380; res 800/528-1234.* 112 rms, 3 story. S, D $65-$78; each addl $4; suites $99; under 12 free. Crib free. TV; cable (premium). Pool; whirlpool. Complimentary continental bkfst. Ck-out noon. Meeting rms. Bellhops. Valet serv. Some bathrm phones, refrigerators, wet bars. Shuttle to nearby cruise terminal; harbor view. Cr cds: A, C, D, DS, MC, V.

D

Hotels

★★★ **HILTON PORT OF LOS ANGELES/SAN PEDRO.** *2800 Via Cabrillo Marina (90731). 310/514-3344; fax 310/514-8945. www.portoflosangelessanpedro.hilton.com.* 226 rms, 3 story. S, D $179; each addl $10; suites $180-$325; under 18 free; wkend rates. Crib free. Pet accepted. TV; cable (premium). Pool; whirlpool. Restaurant 6:30 am-11 pm. Bar. Ck-out noon. Meeting rms. Business center. Gift shop. Barber, beauty shop. Free parking. Lighted tennis. Exercise equipt; sauna. Refrigerators avail. On marina. Cr cds: A, C, D, DS, ER, JCB, MC, V.

D

★★★ **SHERATON LOS ANGELES HARBOR.** *601 S Palos Verdes St (90731). 310/519-8200; fax 310/519-8421; res 800/325-3535. www.sheratonlaharbor.com.* 244 rms, 10 story, 54 suites. S, D $148-$158; each addl $20; suites $225-$500; under 18 free. Crib free. TV; cable (premium). Heated pool; whirlpool. Restaurant 6:30 am-2:30 pm, 5-10 pm. Rm serv 24 hrs. Bar; entertainment. Ck-out noon. Coin lndry. Meeting rms. Business servs avail. Gift shop. Exercise equipt; sauna. Luxury level. Cr cds: A, DS, MC, V.

Restaurant

★★ **22ND STREET LANDING SEAFOOD.** *141 W 22nd St #A, (90731). 310/548-4400.* Hrs: 11 am-10 pm. Closed Dec 25. Res accepted. Bar. Lunch $9.95-$14, dinner $14.95-$39.95. Specializes in grilled seafood. Outdoor dining. Waterfront fish house overlooking harbor. Cr cds: A, C, D, DS, ER, MC, V.

D

San Rafael

(F-3) *See also San Francisco*

Founded 1817 **Pop** 48,404 **Elev** 34 ft **Area code** 415

Information Chamber of Commerce, 817 Mission Ave, 94901; 415/454-4163

Web www.sanrafael.org

Built around an early Spanish mission, San Rafael is a busy residential community across the Golden Gate Bridge, north of San Francisco. It is the commercial, cultural, and governmental hub of scenic Marin County.

What to See and Do

Marin County Civic Center. Complex designed by Frank Lloyd Wright; one of his last major projects. Tours (res required). (Mon-Fri; closed hols) 2 mi N on N San Pedro Rd off US 101. Phone 415/499-7407. **FREE**

Mission San Rafael Arcángel. The 20th in a chain of California missions; built in 1817 and rebuilt in 1949. Gift shop. Chapel (daily). 1104 5th Ave at A St, 3 blks W of US 101. Phone 415/454-8141.

Motels/Motor Lodges

★★ **BEST WESTERN NOVATO OAKS INN.** *215 Alameda Del Prado, Novato (94949). 415/883-4400; fax 415/883-4128; toll-free 800/625-7466. www.renesonhotels.com.* 106 rms, 3 story. S $89-$114; D $94-$119; each addl $8; family rates. Crib free. TV; cable, VCR avail. Pool; whirlpool. Complimentary bkfst. Coffee in rms. Restaurant nearby. Ck-out noon. Meeting rms. Business servs avail. In-rm modem link. Valet serv. Exercise equipt. Some refrigerators; microwaves avail. Balconies. Cr cds: A, C, D, DS, ER, JCB, MC, V.

D SC

★ **VILLA INN.** *1600 Lincoln Ave (94901). 415/456-4975; fax 415/456-1520; res 415/456-4975.* 60 rms, 2 story, 9 kits. S $69-$75; D $71-$83; kit. units $10 addl (3-day min); suite $112; under 12 free. Crib free. Pet accepted. TV; cable. Pool; whirlpool. Complimentary continental bkfst. Restaurant 11:30 am-2 pm, 5:30-9:30 pm; closed Sun. Bar 11:30 am-11 pm. Ck-out noon. Coin lndry. Business servs avail. Refrigerators; microwaves avail. Cr cds: A, DS, MC, V.

D

Hotel

★★ FOUR POINTS BY SHERATON BARCELO SAN RAFAEL. *1010 Northgate Dr (94903). 415/479-8800 or 415/479-8800; fax 415/479-2342; res 800/325-3535. www.fourpoints.com.* 235 rms, 4 story. S $218; D $226; each addl $10; suites $238-$248; under 18 free; wkend rates. Crib free. TV; cable (premium). Heated pool; whirlpool, poolside serv. Restaurant 6:30 am-10 pm; wkends from 7 am. Rm serv 4-10 pm. Bar 4 pm-midnight. Ck-out noon. Meeting rms. Business servs avail. In-rm modem link. Valet serv. Exercise equipt. Some refrigerators. Cr cds: A, D, DS, MC, V.

B&B/Small Inn

★★★ GERSTLE PARK INN. *34 Grove St (94901). 415/721-7611; fax 415/721-7600; res 800/726-7611. www.gerstleparkinn.com.* 12 rms, 2 with shower only, 4 kit. units. No A/C. S, D $159; each addl $15; kit. units $169-$189; wkly rates; wkends, hols (2-day min). TV; VCR (free movies). Complimentary full bkfst. Restaurant nearby. Ck-out noon, ck-in 3 pm. Business servs avail. In-rm modem link. Concierge serv. Free bus, ferry transportation. Tennis privileges. Some in-rm whirlpools. Balconies. Picnic tables. Built in 1895. Elegant decor with garden, antiques. Totally nonsmoking. Cr cds: A, D, DS, MC, V.

Restaurants

★★ CACTI. *1200 Grant Ave, Novato (94945). 415/898-2234.* Hrs: 11:30 am-2 pm, 5-9 pm; Fri, Sat 5-10 pm. Closed Jan 1, Thanksgiving, Dec 25. Res accepted. Southwestern menu. Bar. A la carte entrees: lunch $9.95-$14.95, dinner $10.95-$18.95. Specialties: steaks, crab cakes, grilled mahi mahi with tropical salsa. Formerly a Mission-style church; white stucco walls, open kitchen. Cr cds: A, D, DS, MC, V.

D

★ GIOVANNI'S. *999 Andersen Dr #190 (94901). 415/454-8000.* Hrs: 11:30 am-2:30 pm, 5-9:45 pm. Closed Jan 1, Memorial Day, Dec 25. Res accepted. Italian menu. Wine, beer. A la carte entrees: lunch $8.50-$14.50, dinner $9.50-$15. Children's menu. Specialties: linguine tutto mare, caciucco (bouillabaise), grilled seafood. Own pasta. Parking. Outdoor dining. Totally nonsmoking. Cr cds: A, MC, V.

D

★★ KASBAH. *200 Merrydale Rd (94903). 415/472-6666.* Hrs: 5:30-10 pm. Closed Mon. Res accepted Fri, Sat. Moroccan menu. Wine, beer. A la carte entrees: dinner $10-$13. Complete meal: dinner $25.75. Specialty: couscous. Belly dancing Thurs-Sun. Moroccan decor; Persian-carpeted walls, inlaid patterned wood tables, tented ceiling. Totally nonsmoking. Cr cds: A, MC, V.

D

San Simeon

(C-1) *See also Cambria, Morro Bay, Paso Robles*

Pop 250 **Elev** 20 ft **Area code** 805 **Zip** 93452

Information Chamber of Commerce, 9255 Hearst Dr; 805/927-3500

Web www.sansimeon-online.com

San Simeon is an historical old whaling village. About 100 years ago, death-defying forays took place off these rocky shores when whales were spotted. Sea lion, sea otter, and whale watching are popular during northward migration in March, April, and May, and also during December and January, when southward migration occurs. Deep-sea fishing is especially popular all year.

What to See and Do

Hearst-San Simeon State Historical Monument. (see)

Motel/Motor Lodge

★★ SAN SIMEON PINES RESORT. *7200 Moonstone Beach Dr (93428). 805/927-4648.* 60 rms, 1-2 story. No A/C. S, D $74-$98. TV; cable. Pool. Complimentary continental bkfst, coffee in rms. Restaurant nearby. Ck-out 11 am. Meeting rm. 9-hole par 3 golf course. Hiking. Lawn games. Many fireplaces. Some patios. 8 wooded acres on ocean. Cr cds: A, MC, V.

D

Resort

★★ CAVALIER OCEANFRONT RESORT. *9415 Hearst Dr (93452). 805/927-4688; fax 805/927-6472; res 800/528-1234. www.cavalierresort.com.* 90 rms, 2 story. No A/C. May-Oct: S, D $69-$199; each addl $6; lower rates rest of yr. Crib free. Pet accepted, some restrictions. TV; cable (premium), VCR (movies avail). 2 heated pools; whirlpool. Restaurant 7 am-10 pm; summer to 11 pm. Serv bar. Ck-out noon. Coin lndry. Meeting rms. Business servs avail. In-rm modem link. Shopping arcade. Exercise equipt. Refrigerators, minibars; many wet bars, fireplaces. Many private patios, balconies. On ocean. Cr cds: A, C, D, DS, ER, JCB, MC, V.

D

Santa Ana

(E-5) *See also Anaheim, Irvine, Long Beach, Newport Beach, Orange*

Pop 293,742 **Elev** 110 ft
Area code 714

Information Chamber of Commerce, 2020 N Broadway, 2nd Floor, 92706; 714/541-5353

Web www.santaanacc.com

What to See and Do

The Bowers Kidseum. For children ages 6-12. Focuses on art and culture of the Americas, Pacific Rim, and Africa. (Sat-Sun; closed hols) 1802 Main St. Phone 714/480-1520. ¢¢¢

The Bowers Museum of Cultural Art. Over 80,000 objects in its collection, which focuses on the artworks of pre-Columbian, Oceanic, Native American, African, and Pacific Rim cultures. (Tues-Sun; closed Jan 1, Thanksgiving, Dec 25) 2002 N Main St. Phone 714/567-3600. ¢¢¢

Discovery Museum of Orange County. A hands-on museum, geared to families, that helps make the history of Orange County come alive. Visitors can talk through a hand-cranked telephone, play a pump organ, try on Victorian clothing, wash clothes on a scrub board, and more. (Wed-Fri, Sun) 3101 W Harvard St. Phone 714/540-0404. ¢¢

Discovery Science Center. Spin-off of the Discovery Museum of Orange County; features more than 100 hands-on, interactive exhibits with emphasis on math, science, and technology for kids and their parents. (Daily) 2500 N Main St. Phone 714/542-2823. ¢¢¢

Santa Ana Zoo at Prentice Park. Playgrounds, picnic area; zoo. (Daily; closed Jan 1, Dec 25) 1801 E Chestnut, I-5 to 1st St exit. Phone 714/836-4000.

Motel/Motor Lodge

★★ HOLIDAY INN ORANGE COUNTY AIRPORT. *2726 S Grand Ave (92705). 714/481-6300; fax 714/966-1889; toll-free 800/522-6478. www.holidayinn-oca.com.* 175 rms, 3 story. S, D $98; under 18 free. Crib free. TV; cable. Heated pool; whirlpool, poolside serv. Coffee in rms. Restaurant 6:30 am-1:30 pm, 5-9:30 pm. Bar 5-10 pm. Ck-out noon. Coin lndry. Meeting rms. Business center. In-rm modem link. Valet serv. Free airport, Disneyland transportation. Exercise equipt. Many refrigerators. Microwaves avail. Some private patios. Cr cds: A, C, D, DS, MC, V.

D

Hotel

★★ DOUBLETREE CLUB HOTEL ORANGE COUNTY AIRPORT. *7 Hutton Centre Dr (92707). 714/751-2400; fax 714/662-7935; res 800/222-8733. www.doubletree.com.* 167 rms, 6 story. S $129; each addl $10; suites $150-$200; under 12 free; wkend rates. Crib free. TV; cable (premium). Heated pool; whirlpool. Coffee in rms. Restaurant 6-9 am, 11 am-2 pm, 5-10 pm; Sat, Sun 7-10 am, 5-10 pm. Bar 5-11 pm. Ck-out noon. Meeting rms. Business servs avail. In-rm modem link. Free airport transportation. Exercise equipt. Refrigerators.

Microwaves avail. Cr cds: A, C, D, DS, JCB, MC, V.
D SC

All Suites

★★ **COMFORT SUITES.** *2620 Hotel Terrace Dr (92705). 714/966-5200; fax 714/979-9650; res 800/228-5150. www.thegrid.net/comfortsuites.* 130 suites, 3 story. S $65; D $85; each addl $10; under 18 free. Crib free. TV; cable (premium). Heated pool; whirlpool. Continental bkfst. Ck-out noon. Coin lndry. Business servs avail. In-rm modem link. Free airport transportation. Health club privileges. Refrigerators; microwaves avail.
D

★★★ **EMBASSY SUITES ORANGE COUNTY AIRPORT.** *1325 E Dyer Rd (92705). 714/241-3800; fax 714/662-1651; res 800/362-2779.* 301 suites, 10 story. S, D $119-159; each addl $10; under 16 free; wkend rates. Crib free. TV; cable (premium). Pool; whirlpool. Coffee in rms. Restaurant 11 am-11 pm. Bar to 1 am; entertainment. Ck-out noon. Meeting rms. Business servs avail. In-rm modem link. Gift shop. Free airport transportation. Exercise equipt; sauna. Refrigerators, microwaves. Balconies. Cr cds: A, C, D, DS, ER, JCB, MC, V.
D

★★ **QUALITY SUITES.** *2701 Hotel Terrace Dr (92705). 714/957-9200; fax 714/641-8936; res 800/228-5151. www.meristar.com.* 177 suites, 3 story. S $79-$129; D $89-$139; each addl $10; under 18 free; wkend rates. Crib free. TV; cable (premium), VCR (movies). Heated pool; whirlpool. Complimentary full bkfst; evening refreshments. Coffee in rms. Ck-out noon. Coin lndry. Business servs avail. In-rm modem link. Gift shop. Free airport, RR station, bus depot, Disneyland transportation. Health club privileges. Minibars, microwaves. Private patios, balconies. Cr cds: A, C, D, DS, ER, JCB, MC, V.
D SC

Restaurants

★★★ **ANTONELLO.** *1611 Sunflower (92704). 714/751-7153.* Hrs: 11:30 am-2 pm, 5:45-10 pm; Fri to 11 pm; Sat 5:30-11 pm. Closed Sun; hols. Res accepted. Northern Italian menu. Bar. Wine list. A la carte entrees: lunch $6.75-$16.50, dinner $12-$32. Specializes in seafood, veal, pasta. Own breads, pasta. Valet parking. Jacket. Cr cds: A, C, D, ER, MC, V.
D

★★★★ **GUSTAF ANDERS.** *3851 Bear St #B21 (92704). 714/668-1737. www.imenu.com.* The sleek Nordic decor and icy cold Aquavits will transport you strait to the Baltic Sea before you even taste the inspired Scandinavian cuisine. There are classic Swedish delights like house-cured gravlax, a variety of pickled herring, Swedish meatballs, and beef Lindstrom, as well as as other continental dishes. Continental menu. Specialties: gravlax, parsley salad with sun-dried tomatoes, fillet of beef with Stilton and red wine sauce. Hrs: 11:30 am-2 pm, 5:30-10 pm; Sun from 5:30 pm. Closed Mon; also Memorial Day, July 4, Labor Day. Bar. Extensive wine list. Res accepted. A la carte entrees: lunch $10-$20, dinner $20-$45. Outdoor dining. Totally nonsmoking. Cr cds: A, D, MC, V.
D

Santa Barbara

(D-3) *See also Ojai, Solvang, Ventura*

Founded 1769 **Pop** 85,571 **Elev** 37-850 ft **Area code** 805

Information Conference & Visitors Bureau & Film Commission, 12 E Carrillo St, 93101; 805/966-9222 or 800/676-1266

Web www.santabarbaraca.com

Spanish charm hangs over this city, with its colorful street names, Spanish and Moorish-style architecture, adobe buildings, and beautiful houses and gardens on the slopes of the Santa Ynez Mountains. It faces east and west on the Pacific Ocean along the calmest stretch of the California coast. Although the Spanish explorer Vizcaino entered the channel on Saint Barbara's Day, December 4, 1602, and named the region after the saint, a Portuguese navigator, Juan Rodriguez Cabrillo, is credited with the discovery of the channel in 1542. Its large harbor and breakwater can accommodate many boats and offers boat rentals and excursions. A Ranger District office of the Los Padres National Forest is located in Santa Barbara.

What to See and Do

Beach areas. East Beach (E Cabrillo Blvd, next to Stearns Wharf), West Beach (W Cabrillo Blvd, between Stearns Wharf and Harbor), and Ledbetter Beach (Shoreline Dr and Loma Alta Dr) are some of the outstanding beaches in Santa Barbara, known for great sand and surf, plus bike paths, picknicking, and play areas. (Daily)

Carpinteria State Beach. Swimming, lifeguard (summer), fishing. Picnicking. Camping (some hookups, dump station; fee). (Daily) 12 mi SE on US 101. Phone 805/684-2811.

El Paseo. Courtyards and passageways similiar to old Spain. Shops, art galleries, restaurants. Opp City Hall, de la Guerra St.

El Presidio de Santa Barbara State Historic Park. Original and reconstructed buildings of the last presidio (military and government outpost) built by Spain in the New World. Museum displays, slide show. (Daily; closed hols) 123 E Cañon Perdido. Phone 805/965-0093. **FREE**

Island & Coastal Fishing Trips. Scuba diving trips, fishing, dinner cruises; whale-watching in season. Phone 805/963-3564. **¢¢¢¢¢**

Los Padres National Forest. Forest of 1,724,000 acres encompassing the La Panza, Santa Ynez, San Rafael, Santa Lucia, and Sierra Madre Mtns. The vegetation ranges from chaparral to oak woodlands to coniferous forests, which incl the Santa Lucia fir, the rarest and one of the most unusual firs in North America. Also contains the mountainous 149,000-acre San Rafael Wilderness, the 64,700-acre Dick Smith Wilderness, and the 21,250-acre Santa Lucia Wilderness. There is also the Sespe Condor Refuge. Fishing for trout in 485 mi of streams; hunting. Hiking and riding on 1,750 mi of trails. Camping. Contact the District Ranger Office, 3505 Paradise Rd, 93105. N of town. Phone 805/967-3481.

Mission Santa Barbara. Founded in 1786, the present church was completed in 1820. Known as "Queen of the Missions" because of its architectural beauty, the tenth California mission stands on a slight elevation and at one time served as a beacon for sailing ships. Its twin-towered church and monastery represent the earliest phase of Spanish Renaissance architecture. Self-guided tours. Display rms exhibit mission building arts, mission crafts, and examples of Native American and Mexican art. (Daily; closed hols) E Los Olivos and Upper Laguna Sts, 2 mi N. Phone 805/682-4149. **¢¢**

Moreton Bay fig tree. Believed to be largest of its kind in the US. Planted in 1877, it is considered possible for the tree to attain a branch spread of 160 ft. A Santa Barbara city engineer estimated that 10,450 persons could stand in its shade at noon. Chapala and US 101.

Santa Barbara Botanic Garden. Native trees, shrubs, and wildflowers of California on 65 acres; Old Mission Dam (1806). Guided tours. (Daily) 1212 Mission Canyon Rd, 1¼ mi N of Mission. Phone 805/682-4726. **¢¢**

Santa Barbara County Courthouse. Resembles a Spanish-Moorish palace. Considered one of the most beautiful buildings in the West. (Daily; closed Dec 25) Guided tours (Mon, Tues, Fri at 10:30 am; Mon-Sat at 2:00 pm). 1100 Anacapa St. Phone 805/962-6464. **FREE**

Santa Barbara Historical Museum. Documents, paintings, costumes, and artifacts from three cultures: Spanish, Mexican, and American. Large, gilded Chinese *Tong* shrine. Library (Tues-Fri). Museum (Tues-Sun; closed hols). 136 E de la Guerra St. Phone 805/966-1601. **FREE**

Santa Barbara Maritime Museum. Museum at the harbor with interactive maritime-related exhibits, incl historic vessels, whales, shipwrecks, and a virtual-reality submarine ride. Call for pricing. (Wed-Sun) 113 Harbor Way. Phone 805/962-8404.

Santa Barbara Museum of Art. Collections of ancient and Asian art; 19th-century French art; American and European paintings and sculpture; 20th-century art; photography

DOWNTOWN SANTA BARBARA

Providing ample evidence that Santa Barbara is more than a series of beautiful beaches, this easy walk offers samplings of history, art, and distinctive architecture, as well as chances to shop and eat. If you stop to see some of the museums along the way, you could spend the better part of a day finishing the tour; if you stick mainly to walking, it can be completed in an hour or two. Starting in the 1100 block of Anacapa Street, you'll come upon what looks like a Spanish-Moorish "palace." This is actually the Santa Barbara County Courthouse, a wonderland of Moorish tiles, arched doorways, and tropical gardens that was built in 1929. You can ride the elevator to the deck of its clock tower for a panoramic view of the city. Across the street is the Spanish-style Public Library. Now walk about two blocks southeast down Anacapa Street (toward the harbor) to Canon Perdido Street; go left a short distance to find El Presidio de Santa Barbara State Historic Park, located at 210 East Canon Perdido Street. Dating from 1782, the reconstructed Presidio was a Spanish fort and Santa Barbara's birthplace. At Santa Barbara Street, take a right and then another right at De la Guerra Street. At the Santa Barbara Historical Museum (136 East De la Guerra), you can view artifacts—ranging from Spanish fans to silver saddles and a Chinese temple—that reflect the city's surprisingly varied history. (To view two historic adobes dating from 1817 and 1836, go around the corner from the museum to 715 Santa Barbara Street.) Continue down De la Guerra until you reach State Street; across State is the Paseo Nuevo, an attractive open-air mall where you can browse among specialty shops or stop at a cafe for lunch or a snack. On the other side of State, midblock, is El Paseo ("A Street in Spain"), a shopping arcade constructed around the 1827 adobe of the prominent De la Guerra family. Walk northwest along State Street (away from the harbor) for about three blocks until you reach the Santa Barbara Museum of Art (1130 State Street), which has a nice collection of European paintings and exceptional displays of Asian art and artifacts. To extend your tour, walk back down State Street toward the harbor. Turn right at Montecito Street, and walk to the intersection of Chapala Street (near Highway 101) to behold the 1877-vintage Moreton Bay fig tree. The largest of its kind in the United States, its 160-foot breadth may leave you breathless. But save your remaining breath for the walk back to State Street, where you'll turn right to find Stearn's Wharf, the West Coast's oldest operating wharf. It's lined with shops, marine exhibits, and restaurants with harbor views.

collection; changing exhibits; lectures; guided tours. (Tues-Sun; closed hols) 1130 State St. Phone 805/963-4364. **¢¢**

Santa Barbara Museum of Natural History. Exhibits of fauna, flora, geology, and prehistoric life of the Pacific coast; lectures, shows, planetarium. (Daily; closed Jan 1, Thanksgiving, Dec 25) 2559 Puesta del Sol Rd, beyond Mission. Phone 805/682-4711. **¢¢¢**

Santa Barbara Zoo. Zoo with walk-through aviary, monkeys, big cats, elephants, and other exhibits; miniature railroad (fee); snack bar; picnic, barbecue sites. (Daily; closed Thanksgiving, Dec 25). 500 Niños Dr, just off US 101. Phone 805/962-6310. **¢¢¢**

Stearn's Wharf. Oldest operating wharf on the West Coast. Restaurants, shops, sportfishing pier, beautiful view of harbor and city. Wharf open 24 hrs. Three blk extension of State St.

Truth Aquatics. Direct boat service to Channel Islands National Park (see). (One departure daily) For fee information and res, Phone 805/962-1127.

University of California, Santa Barbara. (1944) 18,500 students. An 815-acre seaside campus. Tours (Mon-Fri). Approx 10 mi N on US 101, in Goleta. Phone 805/893-2485. On campus is

Art Museum. Sedgwick collection of Old Master and Baroque period paintings; Morgenroth collection of Renaissance medals and plaques; Dreyfus collection of Mid-Eastern and pre-Columbian artifacts; changing exhibits. (Tues-Sun) Arts Building. Phone 805/893-2951. **FREE**

Special Events

Santa Barbara International Orchid Show. Earl Warren Showgrounds, US 101 and Las Positas Rd. Mar. Phone 805/683-3788.

Summer Sports Festival. (Semana Nautica). More than 50 land and water sports. Late June or early July.

Santa Barbara National Horse Show. Earl Warren Showgrounds. Mid-July.

Old Spanish Days Fiesta. City-wide. Re-creates city's history from Native American days to arrival of American troops. Early Aug. Phone 805/962-8101.

Motels/Motor Lodges

★ **BEACHCOMBER INN.** *202 W Cabrillo Blvd (93101). 805/965-4577; fax 805/965-9937; toll-free 800/965-9776. www.beachcomberinn.com.* 32 rms, 2 story. S, D $55-$300. Pet accepted. TV; cable. Heated pool. Complimentary continental bkfst. Restaurant nearby. Ck-out 11 am. Business servs avail. In-rm modem link. Sun decks. Large fountain patio. Beach opp. Cr cds: A, D, DS, MC, V.

★★ **BEST WESTERN CARPINTERIA INN.** *4558 Carpinteria Ave, Carpinteria (93013). 805/684-0473; fax 805/684-4015; res 800/528-1234. www.bestwestern.com/carpinteriainn.* 145 rms, 3 story. S $89-$105; D $109-$135; each addl $10; suites $200; under 18 free; hols (2-day min). Crib free. Pet accepted, some restrictions. TV; cable (premium). Complimentary coffee in rms. Restaurant 7-11 am, 5:30-10:30 pm. Bar 4:30 pm-midnight. Ck-out noon. Business servs avail. In-rm modem link. Health club privileges. Heated pool; whirlpool. Many balconies. Cr cds: A, C, D, DS, MC, V.

D

★★ **BEST WESTERN ENCINA LODGE AND SUITES.** *2220 Bath St (93105). 805/682-7277; fax 805/563-9319; res 800/526-2282. www.sbhotels.com.* 121 rms, 2 story, 33 kit. units. S $116-$126; D $126-$136; each addl $10; kit. units $134-$154; under 12 free; wkly rates. Crib free. TV; cable (premium). Heated pool; poolside serv, whirlpool. Sauna. Complimentary coffee in rms. Restaurant 6:30 am-10:30 pm. Bar. Ck-out noon. Coin lndry. Business servs avail. Bellhops. Gift shop. Barber, beauty shop. Valet serv. Free airport, RR station transportation. Health club privileges. Refrigerators; microwaves avail. Balconies. Cr cds: A, C, D, DS, ER, JCB, MC, V.

D SC

★★ **BEST WESTERN PEPPER TREE INN.** *3850 State St (93105). 805/687-5511; fax 805/682-2410; toll-free 800/338-0030. www.sbhotels.com.* 150 rms, 1-2 story. S $138-$154; D $148-$164; each addl $10; under 12 free. Crib free. TV; cable (premium). 2 heated pools. Complimentary coffee in rms. Restaurant 6 am-9:30 pm. Bar 10-2 am. Ck-out noon. Coin lndry. Meeting rms. Business servs avail. In-rm modem link. Concierge. Sundries. Gift shop. Barber, beauty shop. Valet serv. Free airport, RR station transportation. Exercise equipt; sauna. Health club privileges. Refrigerators. Private patios, balconies. Cr cds: A, C, D, DS, ER, JCB, MC, V.

D SC

★★ **COAST VILLAGE INN.** *1188 Coast Village Rd (93108). 805/969-3266; fax 805/969-7117; toll-free 800/257-5131.* 27 rms, 1-2 story, 2 kits. No A/C. Mid-May-Sept: S, D $115-$145; suites, kit. units $155-$165; higher rates hols, wkends; lower rates rest of yr. TV; cable. Heated pool. Complimentary continental bkfst. Ck-out noon. Business servs avail. Totally nonsmoking. Cr cds: A, C, D, DS, MC, V.

★★ **EL PRADO INN.** *1601 State St (93101). 805/966-0807; fax 805/966-6502; res 805/966-0807. www.elprado.com.* 68 rms, 1-2 story, 6 suites. Mid-May-Sept: S, D $75-$160; each addl $10; suites $120-$160; 2-day min stay wkends, hols in season; lower rates rest of yr. Crib free. TV; cable (premium). Heated pool. Complimentary continental bkfst. Restaurant nearby. Ck-out noon. Meeting rm. Business servs avail. In-rm modem link. Valet serv. Beauty shop. Garage parking. Some refrigerators; microwaves avail. Cr cds: A, D, DS, MC, V.

D

★★ **HOLIDAY INN.** *5650 Calle Real, Goleta (93117). 805/964-6241; fax 805/964-8467; res 800/465-4329. www.holidayinn.com.* 160 rms, 2 story. S, D $109-$149; each addl $10; under 18 free; higher rates special events; lower rates rest of yr. Crib free. Pet accepted; $25. TV; cable. Complimentary coffee in lobby. Restaurant 6:30 am-9 pm. Ck-out noon. Meeting rms. Business servs avail. In-rm modem link. Free airport transportation. Pool. Cr cds: A, D, DS, MC, V.

D SC

★★ **MARINA BEACH MOTEL.** *21 Bath St (93101). 805/963-9311; fax 805/564-4102; toll-free 877/627-4621. www.marinabeachmotel.com.* 32 rms, 18 kits. Some A/C. Mid-May-mid-Sept: S, D $81-$172; lower rates rest of yr. TV; cable. Complimentary continental bkfst. Coffee in rms. Restaurant nearby. Ck-out noon. Business servs avail. Bicycles. Beach ½ blk. Cr cds: A, D, DS, MC, V.

D

★★★ **PACIFICA SUITES.** *5490 Hollister Ave (93111). 805/683-6722; fax 805/683-4121; toll-free 800/338-6722. www.pacificasuites.com.* 87 suites, 2 story. Memorial Day-Labor Day: S, D $160-$200; each addl $10; under 11 free; lower rates rest of yr. Crib free. TV; cable, VCR (movies $6). Heated pool; whirlpool. Complimentary full bkfst, coffee in rms. Ck-out noon. Meeting rms. Business servs avail. In-rm modem link. Valet serv. Sundries. Gift shop. Free airport transportation. Health club privileges. Refrigerators; microwaves avail. Balconies. Cr cds: A, C, D, DS, ER, JCB, MC, V.

D SC

★★ **RAMADA LIMITED.** *4770 Calle Real (93110). 805/964-3511; fax 805/964-0075; res 800/272-6232. www.sbramada.com.* 126 rms, 2 story. S $75-$120; D $100-$135; each addl $10; suites $120-$160; under 12 free. Crib free. TV; cable (premium). Heated pool; whirlpool. Complimentary continental bkfst. Coffee in rms. Ck-out noon. Coin lndry. Meeting rms. Business servs avail. Valet serv. Airport, RR station transportation. Refrigerators avail. Private patios, balconies. Cr cds: A, C, D, DS, JCB, MC, V.

D

★ **TRAVELODGE.** *22 Castillo St (93101). 805/965-8527; fax 805/965-6125; res 800/578-7878.* 19 rms, 1-2 story. May-mid-Sept: S, D $95-$150; each addl $10; under 17 free; higher rates: special events, wkends; lower rates rest of yr. Crib free. TV; cable (premium). Complimentary coffee in rms. Restaurant nearby. Ck-out 11 am. Business servs avail. Some refrigerators. Some private patios. Park opp; beach ½ blk. Cr cds: A, C, D, DS, ER, JCB, MC, V.

D

★★ **TROPICANA INN AND SUITES.** *223 Castillo St (93101). 805/966-2219; fax 805/962-9428; toll-free 800/468-1988.* 31 rms, 2 story, 16 suites. No A/C. S, D $102-$132; each addl $5; suites $122-$218; under 3 free; wkly rates; wkends, hols (2-day min). Crib free. TV; cable. Heated pool; whirlpool. Complimentary continental bkfst. Restaurant nearby. Ck-out noon. Coin lndry. Business servs avail. Valet serv. Garage parking. Refrigerators, microwaves. Bicycles (rentals). Totally nonsmoking. Cr cds: A, D, DS, MC, V.

D

Hotels

★★★ **EL ENCANTO HOTEL & GARDEN.** *1900 Lasuen Rd (93103). Fax 805/687-3903; res 800/223-5652.* 84 cottages. Some A/C. S, D $179-$199; cottage suites $239-$999. Crib avail. TV; cable, VCR avail (movies). Heated pool. Coffee in rms. Restaurant (see also EL ENCANTO DINING ROOM). Bar 11 am-midnight; entertainment. Ck-out noon. Coin lndry. Meeting rm. Business servs avail. Bellhops. Concierge. Free valet parking. Tennis, pro. Golf privileges. Health club privileges. Minibars; some fireplaces; microwaves avail. Private patios, balconies. Formal gardens. Ocean view. Cr cds: A, D, MC, V.

D

★★★ **HARBOR VIEW INN.** *28 W Cabrillo Blvd (93101). 805/963-0780; fax 805/963-7967; toll-free 800/755-0222. www.santabarbaraca.com.* 80 rms, 3 story. S, D $180-$350; each addl $10; under 16 free; 2-day min stay wkends. Crib free. TV; cable (premium). Heated pool; wading pool, whirlpool. Coffee in rms. Restaurant 7 am-9 pm. Bar. Ck-out noon. Meeting rms. Business servs avail. In-rm modem link. Valet serv. Concierge. Health club privileges. Refrigerators. Balconies. Opp beach. Cr cds: A, C, D, MC, V.

D

★★ HOTEL SANTA BARBARA. *533 State St (93101). 805/957-9300; fax 805/962-2412; toll-free 888/259-7700. www.hotelsantabarbara.com.* 75 rms, 4 story. June-Sept: S $99-$189; D $109-$199; hols (2-day min); higher rates special events; lower rates rest of yr. Crib free. Valet parking $5. TV; cable (premium). Complimentary continental bkfst, coffee in rms. Restaurant nearby. Meeting rms. Business servs avail. Valet serv. Refrigerators, microwaves. Cr cds: A, C, D, DS, JCB, MC, V.

D

★★ MONTECITO INN. *1295 Coast Village Rd (93108). 805/969-7854; fax 805/969-0623; toll-free 800/843-2017. www.montecitoinn.com.* 60 rms. Some A/C. May-Sept: S $185, D $195; suites from $265; 2-night min wkends, 3-night min hols; lower rates rest of yr. Crib $10. TV; cable (premium), VCR (free movies). Heated pool. Complimentary continental bkfst. Restaurant 11:30 am-2:30 pm, 5:30-10 pm. Ck-out noon. Guest lndry. Meeting rm. Business servs avail. Free valet parking. Exercise equipt; sauna. Bicycles. Refrigerators avail. Established in 1928 by Charlie Chaplin and Fatty Arbuckle; inspiration for Richard Rodgers's "There's a Small Hotel." Beach 3 blks. Cr cds: A, D, DS, MC, V.

★★ RADISSON. *1111 E Cabrillo Blvd (93103). 805/963-0744; fax 805/962-0985; res 800/333-3333. www.radisson.com/santabarbaraca.* 174 rms, 3 story. July-early Oct: S, D $149-$319; each addl $20; suites $275-$775; under 17 free; lower rates rest of yr. Crib free. TV; cable (premium). Heated pool; poolside serv. Coffee in rms. Restaurant 6:30 am-10:30 pm. Bar 11-1 am; entertainment Thurs-Sat. Ck-out noon. Meeting rms. Business servs avail. In-rm modem link. Concierge. Gift shop. Beauty shop. Free covered parking. Exercise equipt. Massage. Minibars. Balconies. Ocean opp. Cr cds: A, C, D, DS, ER, JCB, MC, V.

D

★★★ UPHAM HOTEL & GARDEN COTTAGES. *1404 de la Vina St (93101). 805/962-0058; fax 805/963-2825; res 800/727-0876. www.upham hotel.com.* 50 rms, 1-2 story. No A/C. S, D $145-$195; each addl $10; suites $205-$370; under 12 free. Crib $10. TV; cable, VCR avail. Complimentary continental bkfst. Dining rm 11:30 am-2 pm, 6-10 pm. Ck-out noon, ck-in 3 pm. Meeting rms. Business servs avail. Valet serv Mon-Fri. Health club privileges. Whirlpool in master suite. Fireplace in cottages. Some private patios. Historic Victorian hotel established 1871. Period furnishings incl antique armoires, beds. Garden with roses, camellias. Cr cds: C, D, DS, ER, JCB, MC, V.

Resorts

★★★★ BACARA RESORT & SPA. *8301 Hollister Ave (93117). 805/968-0100; fax 806/688-2510. www.bacara resort.com.* You'll find this Mediterranean resort nestled between the Pacific Ocean and the Santa Ynez mountains. The natural beauty of its location offers views from each room. Each of the luxuriously appointed rooms offer a patio or balcony and are furnished with all the comforts of home. 311 rms, 4 story; 49 suites. S, D $395-$650; suites $750-$1,250. Crib avail. TV; cable (premium), VCR avail. Pool; whirlpool. Restaurants 6:30 am-10:30 pm. Rm serv 24 hrs. Ck-out noon. Meetings rms. Business center. In-rm modem link. Bellhops. Valet serv. Concierge. Exercise center. Massage. Bathrm phones, minibars, fireplaces. Balconies.Cr cds: A, D, DS, MC, V.

D

★★★ FESS PARKER'S DOUBLETREE RESORT. *633 E Cabrillo Blvd (93103). 805/564-4333; fax 805/564-4964; res 877/398-5182. www.fpdtr.com.* 360 rms, 3 story. S, D $179-$309; each addl $15; suites $429-$849; under 18 free; package plans. Pet accepted, some restrictions. TV; cable (premium), VCR avail (free movies). Heated pool; poolside serv. Coffee in rms. Restaurants 6:30 am-11 pm. Rm serv 24 hrs. Bar 11-1 am; entertainment. Ck-out noon. Coin lndry. Convention facilities. Business servs avail. In-rm modem link. Valet serv. Concierge. Barber, beauty shop. Valet parking. Free airport transportation. Lighted tennis, pro. Exercise equipt. Massage. Game rm. Lawn games. Minibars; microwaves avail. Private patios, balconies. Atrium lobby. On 24 acres; ocean opp. Cr cds: A, C, D, DS, MC, V.

D

★★★★ **FOUR SEASONS RESORT SANTA BARBARA.** *1260 Channel Dr (93108). 805/969-2261; fax 805/565-8323; res 800/332-3442. www.fourseasons.com.* This Spanish Colonial jewel located at the base of the Santa Ynez mountains is a resort with something for everyone. Guests can relax by the beachfront pool, take in nearby winery tours, or indulge in a relaxing massage. There are two restaurants that boast water views, and the attentive staff can easily arrange boating excursions or golf outings. 217 rms, 2 story. S, D $435; suites from $795; under 18 free. Crib free. Pet accepted. Valet parking $16. TV; cable (premium), VCR. 2 heated pools; wading pool, whirlpool, poolside serv. Supervised children's activities (June-Aug, rest of yr wkends); ages 5-12. Restaurants 7 am-10 pm (see also LA MARINA). Rm serv 24 hrs. Bar 11:30 am-midnight; Fri, Sat to 2 am; entertainment. Ck-out noon. Meeting rms. Business center. In-rm modem link. Concierge serv. Gift shop. Beauty salon. Lighted tennis, pro. Golf privileges, putting green. Exercise rm; sauna. Massage. Bicycles. Lawn games. Bathrm phones, minibars; many fireplaces. Many private patios, balconies. Cr cds: A, C, D, DS, JCB, MC, V.

D

★★ **SANTA BARBARA INN.** *901 E Cabrillo Blvd (93103). 805/966-2285; fax 805/966-6584; toll-free 800/231-0431. www.santabarbarainn.com.* 71 rms, 4 story. Some A/C. July-Aug: S $189-$234; D $199-$239; each addl $15; kit. units $15 addl; suites $225-$375; lower rates rest of yr. Crib free. TV; cable. Heated pool; whirlpool, poolside serv. Coffee in rms. Restaurant (see also CITRONELLE). Bar 11 am-9 pm. Ck-out noon. Meeting rms. Business servs avail. Valet parking. Health club privileges. Massage. Bathrm phones, refrigerators. Balconies. Adj to beach, ocean. Cr cds: A, C, D, DS, ER, JCB, MC, V.

D SC

B&Bs/Small Inns

★★ **CASA DEL MAR.** *18 Bath St (93101). 805/963-4418; fax 805/966-4240; toll-free 800/433-3097. www.casadelmar.com.* 21 rms, 2 story, some kits. June-Sept: S, D $74-$204; each addl $10; suites $114-$199; under 13 free; lower rates rest of yr. Pet accepted, some restrictions; $10/day. TV; cable. Complimentary continental bkfst; evening refreshments. Ck-out noon. Business servs avail. In-rm modem link. Whirlpool. Many fireplaces. Near ocean. Cr cds: A, D, DS, MC, V.

D

★★★ **CHESHIRE CAT INN.** *36 W Valerio St (93101). 805/569-1610; fax 805/682-1876. www.cheshirecat.com.* 17 rms, 2 story, 5 suites, 3 cottages. S, D; $180; suites $190-$270; cottages $300; wknds 2-day min. TV, VCR (free movies) in 5 rms. Complimentary full bkfst; afternoon refreshments. Restaurants nearby. Ck-out noon, ck-in 3-6 pm. Business servs avail. Some in-rm whirlpools, microwaves. Lawn games. Balconies. Sitting rm; antiques. Built 1880s. Alice in Wonderland theme. Totally nonsmoking. Cr cds: A, DS, MC, V.

★★ **FRANCISCAN INN.** *109 Bath St (93101). 805/963-8845; fax 805/564-3295. www.fransicaninn.com.* 53 rms, 2 story, 25 kit. suites. S, D $80-$109; each addl $8; kit. suites $99-$140; monthly, wkly rates; lower rates rest of yr. Crib free. TV; cable (premium), VCR avail (free movies). Heated pool; whirlpool. Complimentary continental bkfst; afternoon refreshments. Restaurant nearby. Ck-out noon. Coin lndry. Business servs avail. Valet serv. Many refrigerators. Balconies. Beach, marina 1 blk. Cr cds: A, D, MC, V.

D

★★ **GLENBOROUGH INN.** *1327 Bath St (93101). 805/966-0589; fax 805/564-8610; toll-free 800/962-0589. www.glenboroughinn.com.* 12 rms in 4 houses, 2 story. Some A/C. Mid-May-mid-Sept: S, D $100; each addl $30; suites $170-$250; lower mid-wk rates rest of yr; wkends, hols (2-day min). Complimentary full bkfst. Ck-out 11 am, ck-in 3-6 pm. Business servs avail. Whirlpool. Some fireplaces. Turn-of-the-century home; antiques; garden. Totally nonsmoking. Cr cds: A, C, D, DS, JCB, MC, V.

★ INN BY THE HARBOR. *433 W Montecito St (93101). 805/963-7851; fax 805/962-9428; toll-free 800/626-1986. www.sbhotels.com.* 43 rms, 2 story, 23 kit. suites. No A/C. S, D $92-$128; each addl $5; kit. suites $99-$160; under 3 free; wkly rates; wkends, hols (2-day min). Crib free. TV; cable. Heated pool; whirlpool. Complimentary continenal bkfst. Restaurant nearby. Ck-out noon. Coin lndry. Business servs avail. Valet serv. Microwaves; refrigerator in suites. Totally nonsmoking. Cr cds: A, D, DS, JCB, MC, V.

★★★ INN ON SUMMER HILL. *2520 Lillie Ave, Summerland (93067). 805/969-9998; fax 805/565-9946; toll-free 800/845-5566. www.innonsummerhill.com.* 16 rms, 2 story. S, D $245-$215; each addl $25; suite $295; package plans. TV; cable, VCR (free movies). Complimentary full bkfst; afternoon refreshments. Complimentary coffee in rms. Restaurant nearby. Ck-out 11 am, ck-in 3 pm. Business servs avail. Whirlpool. Bathrm phones, refrigerators, fireplaces. Balconies. New England-style inn with view of ocean or landscaped grounds. Totally nonsmoking. Cr cds: A, DS, MC, V.

★★ OLD YACHT CLUB INN. *431 Corona Del Mar Dr (93103). 805/962-1277; fax 805/962-3989; toll-free 800/676-1676. www.oldyachtclubinn.com.* 12 rms, 2 story. No A/C. S, D $90-$110; mid-wk rates in winter. Complimentary full bkfst; evening refreshments. Ck-out 11 am, ck-in 2-6 pm. Business servs avail. Some in-rm whirlpools. Bicycles. Former headquarters of Santa Barbara Yacht Club (1912); antiques, Oriental rugs. Totally nonsmoking. Cr cds: A, DS, MC, V.

SC

★★ OLIVE HOUSE. *1604 Olive St (93101). 805/962-4902; fax 805/962-9983; toll-free 800/786-6422. www.sbinns.com/oliveinn.* 6 rms, 2 story. No A/C. S $75-$110; D $125-$195. TV in sitting rm; cable. Complimentary full bkfst; afternoon refreshments. Restaurant nearby. Ck-out 11 am, ck-in 3-7 pm. Built in 1904; antiques. Totally nonsmoking. Cr cds: A, DS, V.

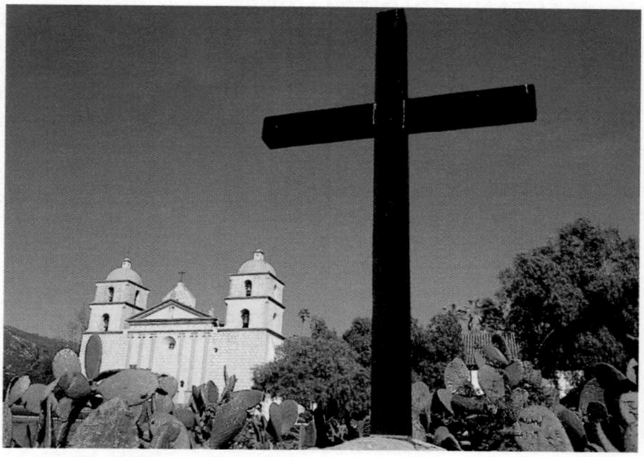

Mission Santa Barbara

★★ PRUFROCK'S GARDEN INN BY THE BEACH. *600 Linden Ave, Santa Barbara (93013). 805/566-9696; fax 805/566-9404. www.prufrocks.com.* 7 rms, 2 air-cooled rms, 2 share bath, 2 suites. No A/C. S, D $100-$150; each addl $25; suites $150-$229; higher rates special events. Complimentary full bkfst, coffee in rms. Restaurant nearby. Street parking. In-rm whirlpool in suites. Picnic tables. Built in 1904; seaside village. Totally nonsmoking. Cr cds: DS, MC, V.

D

★★★★ SIMPSON HOUSE INN. *121 E Arrellaga St (93101). 805/963-7067; fax 805/564-4811; toll-free 800/676-1280. www.simpsonhouseinn.com.* This beautifully restored Victorian home, built in 1874, provides a romantic bed-and-breakfast retreat. Guests can choose among three types of rooms, all decorated with period furnishings. There are rooms in the main house overlooking the manicured gardens, four unique rooms in a converted barn, and three English-style cottages that have separate sitting rooms and working fireplaces. S, D $175-$295; suites $400; cottages $425. TV. Complimentary full bkfst; afternoon refreshments. Ck-out 11 am, ck-in 3 pm. Business servs avail. In-rm modem link. Massage. Heath club privileges. Lawn games. Sitting rm with fireplace. Microwave avail. Balconies. Picnic tables. Totally nonsmoking. Cr cds: A, DS, MC, V.

D

★★★ TIFFANY COUNTRY HOUSE. *1323 de la Vina St (93101). 805/963-2283; fax 805/962-0994; res 800/999-5672. www.tiffanycountryhouse.com.* 6 rms, 3 story, 1 suite. S, D $135-$215; suite $225; mid-wk rates off-season. TV and VCR in suite. Complimentary full bkfst; afternoon refreshments. Ck-out 11 am, ck-in 3:30-7 pm. Business servs avail. Whirlpool in suites. Restored Victorian house (1898); antique furnishings; many fireplaces. Garden. Totally nonsmoking. Cr cds: A, C, D, DS, MC, V.

★★★ VILLA ROSA INN. *15 Chapala St (93101). 805/966-0851; fax 805/962-7159.* 18 rms, 2 story, 3 kits. July-Sept, wkends (2-day min): S, D $100-$210; suite, kit. units $85-$185; mid-wk, winter rates; lower rates rest of yr. Children over 14 yrs only. TV avail; cable. Heated pool; whirlpool. Complimentary continental bkfst. Ck-out noon, ck-in 3 pm. Business servs avail. Health club privileges. Some refrigerators, fireplaces. Balconies. Spanish architecture; Southwestern decor. Near beach. Totally nonsmoking. Cr cds: A, MC, V.

Guest Ranch

★★★ SAN YSIDRO RANCH. *900 San Ysidro Ln (93108). 805/969-5046; fax 805/565-1995; toll-free 800/368-6788. www.sanysidroranch.com.* 38 cottages units. S $355-$399; D $399-$625; suites $750-$3,500. Crib free. Pet accepted; $75. TV; cable (premium), VCR (movies). Heated pool; wading pool, poolside serv. Playground. Coffee in rms. Dining rm (see also STONEHOUSE). Rm serv 24 hrs. Box lunches. Bar 5 pm-midnight, wkends to 1 am; entertainment Thurs, Fri. Ck-out noon, ck-in 3 pm. Grocery 1 mi. Meeting rms. Business servs avail. In-rm modem link. Bellhop. Gift shop. Tennis. Driving range. Summer activities. Exercise rm. Massage. Lawn games. Refrigerators, fireplaces; some in-rm whirlpools; microwaves avail. 550 acres in mountains. Cr cds: A, D, JCB, MC, V.

D

Restaurants

★★ ANDRIA'S HARBORSIDE. *336 W Cabrillo Blvd (93101). 805/966-3000. www.1andriasharborside.com.* Hrs: 8 am-11 pm. Res accepted. Bar. Wine list. Bkfst $3.95-$7.95, lunch $5.95-$8.95, dinner $10.95-$19.95. Specializes in mesquite charbroiled fresh seafood, steak, chicken. Own desserts. Entertainment. Parking. Oyster bar. Cr cds: A, DS, MC, V.

D

★★ BIG YELLOW HOUSE. *108 Pierpont Ave, Summerland (93067). 805/969-4140. www.bigyellowhouse.com.* Hrs: 8 am-9 pm; Fri, Sat to 10 pm; Sun brunch 8 am-2:30 pm. Closed Dec 24, 25. Res accepted. Bar. Bkfst $4.95-$11, lunch $5.95-$12, dinner $8.95-$16.95. Sun brunch $4.95-$12. Children's menu. Specializes in fried chicken, pot roast. Parking. In Victorian house. Totally nonsmoking. Cr cds: A, DS, MC, V.

D

★★★ BLUE SHARK BISTRO. *21 W Victoria St (93101). 805/564-7100.* Hrs: 5-9:30 pm; Fri, Sat to 10 pm; Sun to 9 pm. Closed Mon; Jan 1, Dec 25. Res accepted. Bar. Wine list. A la carte entrees: dinner $8.95-$19.95. Children's menu. Specializes in seafood, steak, soups. Outdoor dining. In turn-of-the-century Victorian house. Cr cds: A, DS, MC, V.

D

★★★ BOUCHON. *9 W Victoria St (93101). 805/730-1160. www.bouchon.net.* California wine country menu. Specializes in sage and prosciutto crispy chicken breast, onion dusted

Santa Ynez venison. Hrs: 5:30-10 pm. Res accepted. Wine, beer. Dinner $18-$29. Entertainment. Cr cds: A, D, MC, V.

D

★★ **BRIGITTE'S.** *1325 State St (93101). 805/966-9676.* Hrs: 11:30 am-2:30 pm, 5-10 pm; Fri, Sat to 11 pm; Sun 5-10 pm. Closed hols. Bar. A la carte entrees: lunch, dinner $8.75-$18.95. Specialties: smoked salmon with caviar, fresh fish. California-style bistro. Totally nonsmoking. Cr cds: A, C, D, DS, ER, MC, V.

D

★★★ **CITRONELLE.** *901 E Cabrillo Blvd (93103). 805/963-0111. www.sbinn.com.* Hrs: 7 am-10 pm; Sun brunch 10:30 am-2:30 pm. Res accepted. Bar. Award of excellence wine list. Bkfst $10.50-$12.00, lunch $12-$18, dinner $21-$31. Sun brunch $17-$25. Specialties: roast duck with cider sauce, grilled swordfish. Valet parking. 3rd flr of Santa Barbara Inn; view of ocean. Totally nonsmoking. Cr cds: A, DS, MC, V.

D

★★★★ **DOWNEY'S.** *1305 State St (93101). 805/966-5006. www.downeyssb.com.* This unpretentious restaurant is housed in a converted storefront, providing a relaxing backdrop to the seasonal fare. John Downey changes the menu each day to reflect the best of what the market has to offer. Expect simple dishes that let the ingredients speak for themselves, like porcini soup and grilled local swordfish. Well-selected California wines round out the meal. Specialties: grilled lamb loin, fresh Dungeness crab, local swordfish with fresh papaya vinaigrette. Hrs: 5:30-9 pm; Fri, Sat to 9:30 pm. Closed Mon; hols. Wine, beer. Res accepted. A la carte entrees: dinner $21.95-$26.95. Cr cds: DS, MC, V.

D

★★★ **EL ENCANTO DINING ROOM.** *1900 La Suen Rd (93103). 805/687-5000.* Hrs: 7 am-10 pm. Res accepted. French, American menu. Bar 11 am-midnight. Wine cellar. A la carte entrees: bkfst $8.75-$12.50, lunch $8.75-$14.50, dinner $16-$28. Children's menu. Specialties: El Encanto pagella, cioppino, roasted sea bass. Piano Thurs-Sun. Valet parking. Outdoor dining. Ocean view; romantic decor. Cr cds: A, V.

D

★★ **EL PASEO.** *10 El Paseo Pl (93101). 805/962-6050.* Hrs: 11:30 am-10 pm; Fri to midnight; Sat to 2 am; Sun from 10:30 am; Sun brunch 10:30 am. Closed Dec 25. Res accepted. Mexican menu. Bar. A la carte entrees: lunch $5.95-$10.95, dinner $7.95-$24.95. Sun brunch $16.95, $21.95. Specialties: Mexican-stuffed porkchop, shrimp espanoles, filet al chipotle. Latino music Sat. Valet parking. Outdoor dining. In historic courtyard. Opened over 70 yrs ago. Cr cds: A, C, D, ER, MC, V.

D

★★ **HARBOR AND LONGBOARD'S GRILL.** *210 Stearns Wharf (93101). 805/963-3311.* Hrs: 11 am-midnight; Fri to 1 am; Sat 8-1 am; Sun 8 am-11 pm; Sun brunch 10:30 am. Res accepted. Bar. Bkfst $7.50-$11.95, lunch $7.95-$19.95, dinner $12.95-$39.95. Sun brunch $19.95. Children's menu. Specializes in fresh seafood. Valet parking. Outdoor dining. Mountains and islands views. On ocean. Cr cds: A, MC, V.

D

★★★ **LA MARINA.** *1260 Channel Dr (93108). 805/969-2261. www.fshr.com.* California contemporary menu. Specialties: roasted Maine lobster, angel hair pasta with prawns, chocolate Grand Marnier souffle. Hrs: 6-10 pm; Sun brunch 10 am-2 pm. Res suggested. No A/C. Bar 11:30 am-midnight; Fri, Sat to 2 am. Extensive wine list.. A la carte entrees: dinner $17-$35. Sun brunch with outside dining avail $49.95. Complimentary valet parking. Ocean view. Cr cds: A, C, D, DS, ER, MC, V.

D

★★ **LEFT AT ALBUQUERQUE.** *803 State St (93101). 805/564-5040. www.1spot.com/left.* Hrs: 11:30 am-10 pm; Fri, Sat to 11 pm. Closed Thanksgiving, Dec 25. Res accepted. Southwestern menu. Bar. Lunch $6-$10, dinner $8-$13. Children's menu. Specializes in enchiladas, burritos, fajitas. Outdoor dining. Southwestern motif;

large tequila collection. Totally nonsmoking. Cr cds: A, MC, V.
D SC

★★★ **PALACE GRILL.** *8 E Cota St (93101). 805/963-5000. www.palacegrill.com.* Hrs: 5:30-11 pm; Fri, Sat to midnight. Res accepted. Cajun, Creole menu. Bar. Dinner $9-$24. Children's menu. Specialties: crawfish etouffee, blackened redfish, Louisiana bread pudding souffle. New Orleans Mardi Gras atmosphere. Totally nonsmoking. Cr cds: A, C, D, ER, MC, V.
D

★★★ **PALAZZIO.** *1151 Coast Village Rd (93108). 805/969-8565. www.palazzios.com.* Hrs: 5:30-11 pm; Fri, Sat to midnight; Sun from 5:30 pm. Closed Thanksgiving, Dec 25. Res accepted. Italian menu. Bar. A la carte entrees: dinner $7-$16. Specialties: capellini shrimp, tiramisu, fusilli roasted eggplant. Parking. Outdoor dining. Murals. Totally nonsmoking. Cr cds: A, MC, V.
D

★★ **PALAZZIO DOWNTOWN.** *1026 State St (93101). 805/564-1985. www.palazzios.com.* Hrs: 11:30 am-3 pm, 5:30-11 pm; Fri to midnight. Closed Thanksgiving, Dec 25. Res accepted. Italian menu. Bar. A la carte entrees: lunch, dinner $8.95-$15.95. Children's menu. Specialties: penne al fumo, capellini shrimp, capellini grilled chicken. Parking. Outdoor dining. Family-style. Cr cds: A, MC, V.
D

★★★ **SAGE & ONION.** *34 E Ortega St (93101). 805/963-1012. www.sageandonion.com.* Specializes in pan-roasted halibut, sage wrap chicken breast, rack of Colorado lamb. Hrs: 5:30-10 pm; Fri, Sat to 10:30 pm. Res accepted. Wine, beer. Dinner $19-$29. Entertainment. Cr cds: A, MC, V.
D

★ **STATE.** *1201 State St (93101). 805/966-1010.* Hrs: 11 am-midnight. No A/C. Bar. Lunch, dinner $4.25-$10.95. Specializes in steak, international salads, seafood. Salad bar. Entertainment Thurs-Sat. Outdoor dining. Cr cds: A, C, DS, ER, MC, V.
D

★★ **STONEHOUSE.** *900 San Ysidro Ln (93108). 805/969-5046.* Specialties: lobster, caviar, veal chop. Hrs: 8 am-9:30 pm; Fri, Sat to 10:30 pm; Sun brunch 11:30 am-2:30 pm. Res accepted. Bar to midnight. Wine cellar. Bkfst $9.95-$14.95, lunch $10.45-$17.95, dinner from $23. Prix fixe: lunch $22.95. Sun brunch $29.95. Children's menu. Entertainment Thurs, Fri. Valet parking. Adobe walls, Spanish tile floors and antiques create a contemporary rustic atmosphere. Totally nonsmoking. Cr cds: A, C, D, DS, ER, MC, V.
D

★★ **TEE OFF.** *3627 State St (93105). 805/687-1616.* Hrs: 4-11 pm; Fri, Sat to midnight; Sun to 10 pm. Res accepted. Bar. Dinner $8.95-$29.95. Specialty: prime rib. Parking. Cr cds: A, MC, V.

★★★ **WINE CASK.** *813 Anacapa St (93101). 805/966-9463. www.winecask.com.* Hrs: 11:30 am-3 pm, 5:30-10 pm; Fri to 11 pm; Sat, Sun 5:30-10 pm; Sat, Sun brunch 10 am-3 pm. Closed hols. Res accepted. Bar. Wine cellar. A la carte entrees: lunch $7-$14, dinner $19-$27. Sat, Sun brunch $7-$13. Children's menu. Specializes in seafood, chicken, pasta, grilled meat. Seasonal menu. Valet parking. Patio dining. Fine dining. Totally nonsmoking. Cr cds: A, D, MC, V.
D

Santa Clara

(see San Francisco map) *See also Fremont, Livermore, San Jose, Saratoga*

Founded 1777 **Pop** 93,613 **Elev** 88 ft **Area code** 408

Information Convention & Visitors Bureau, 1850 Warburton Ave, 95050; 408/244-9660 or 800/272-6822

Web www.santaclara.org

Santa Clara, the "Mission City," is in the heart of Silicon Valley, just 50 minutes south of San Francisco.

What to See and Do

Intel Museum. A 3,500-sq-ft museum that explores the computer chip industry. Hands-on exhibits describe the differences between various types of chips, how they are used, and how they are constructed. (Mon-Sat; closed hols) 2200 Mission College Blvd, at the headquarters of Intel Corporation. Phone 408/765-0503. **FREE**

Paramount's Great America. In this 100-acre park is a blend of movie magic and theme park thrills. Features an array of thrilling rides, live stage shows, and entertainment; among Paramount's Great America's premier attractions are "Top Gun," a mind boggling inverted roller coaster and "Invertigo," a face-to-face roller coaster. Also featured are *Star Trek*, Nickelodeon, and Hanna Barbera characters. Also spectacular are the IMAX theater and the world's tallest double-decker carousel, Carousel Columbia, which is near the park's entrance. There is a Nickelodeon area for children called "Splat City." (Apr-Oct; inquire for schedule) Admission incl rides and attractions. Great America Pkwy, off I-101. Phone 408/988-1776. ¢¢¢¢¢

Santa Clara University. (1851) 7,900 students. Oldest institution of higher learning in California, founded in 1851. Self-guided tour of the Mission Gardens, which incl the Adobe Lodge and Wall (restored) from the 1822-1825 mission. Olive trees and grinding stones in the gardens also date to the early mission period. On both sides of The Alameda between Bellomy and Franklin sts. Phone 408/554-4700. On campus are

De Saisset Museum. Rotating exhibits (all yr); California Historical Collection focuses on precontact Native American period, Mission period, and early yrs of the university. (Tues-Sun) 500 El Camino Real. Phone 408/554-4528. **FREE**

Mission Santa Clara de Asís. (1777) The modern mission, dedicated in 1928, is an enlarged and adapted replica of the original mission. The present roof contains 12,000 cover tiles salvaged from earlier missions. Of the four mission bells in the tower, one was a gift from Carlos IV of Spain in 1798 and survived the 1926 fire; another was a gift from Alfonso XIII of Spain in 1929. Surrounded by beautiful gardens and restored Adobe Lodge and Wall; part of the 1822 mission quadrangle. (Mon-Fri) Phone 408/554-4023.

Triton Museum of Art. Permanent and changing exhibits of 19th- and 20th-century American and contemporary works; sculpture garden; landscaped grounds on seven acres. (Tues-Sun; closed hols) 1505 Warburton Ave, opp Civic Center. Phone 408/247-3754. **FREE**

Special Event

Santa Clara Art & Wine Festival. Sept.

Motels/Motor Lodges

★★ **BEST WESTERN INN SANTA CLARA.** *4341 El Camino Real (95051). 408/244-3366; fax 408/246-1387; res 800/528-1234.* 52 rms, 1-2 story. S $70-$135; D $75-$135; each addl $6. Crib $4. TV; cable (premium), VCR. Pool. Continental bkfst. Coffee in rms. Restaurant nearby. Ck-out 11 am. Coin lndry. Business servs avail. In-rm modem link. Refrigerators; microwaves. Cr cds: A, C, D, DS, MC, V.

D

★ **GUESTHOUSE INN & SUITES.** *2930 El Camino Real (95051). 408/241-3010; fax 408/247-0623; res 800/214-8378.* 69 units, 2 story, 16 kits. S $89-$200; D $99-$200; each addl $10; kit. units $149-$250; under 17 free. Crib $10. Pet accepted; $10. TV; cable, VCR (movies). Heated pool. Complimentary continental bkfst, coffee in rms. Restaurant nearby. Ck-out 11:30 am. Business servs avail. In-rm modem link. Valet serv. Health club privileges. Refrigerators. Some balconies. Cr cds: A, D, DS, JCB, MC, V.

D

★ **HOWARD JOHNSON.** *5405 Stevens Creek Blvd (95051). 408/257-8600; fax 408/446-2936; toll-free 800/446-4656.* 96 rms, 2 story. S, D $145-$185; under 18 free. Crib free. TV; cable (premium). Pool; wading pool. Restaurant adj 6 am-10 pm. Ck-out noon. Meeting rms. Business servs avail. Coin lndry. Health club privileges. Some refrigerators. Some balconies. Cr cds: A, D, DS, MC, V.

D SC

★★ **MARIANI'S INN.** *2500 El Camino Real (95051). 408/243-1431; fax 408/243-5745.* 143 units, 1-2 story, 53 kits. S $99; D $120; each addl $8; kit. suites $109-$125; under 12 free. Crib free. TV; cable (premium), VCR avail. Heated pool; whirlpool. Complimentary continental bkfst. Restaurant 6:30 am-11 pm. Bar 11-12:30 am; entertainment. Ck-out 11 am. Coin lndry. Meeting rms. Business servs avail. In-rm modem link. Valet serv. Free airport transportation. Health club privileges. Cr cds: A, D, DS, JCB, MC, V.

D

★ **VAGABOND INN.** *3580 El Camino Real (95051). 408/241-0771; fax 408/247-3386; toll-free 800/522-1555.* 70 rms, 2 story. S, D $89; each addl $5; under 18 free. Crib $5. Pet accepted; $5. TV; cable (premium). Heated pool. Complimentary continental bkfst. Coffee in rms. Restaurant nearby. Ck-out noon. Coin lndry. Business servs avail. In-rm modem link. Valet serv. Some refrigerators, microwaves. Cr cds: A, D, DS, MC, V.

Hotels

★★★ **SANTA CLARA MARRIOTT.** *2700 Mission College Blvd (95054). 408/988-1500; fax 408/727-4353; toll-free 800/228-9290.* 754 rms, 2-14 story. S, D $239; suites $400; under 18 free; wkend plans. Crib free. Pet accepted, some restrictions. TV; cable (premium), VCR avail. Indoor/outdoor pool; whirlpool, poolside serv. Restaurants 6 am-11 pm. Rm serv to midnight. Bar 11:30-2 am. Ck-out 11 am. Convention facilities. Business center. Gift shop. Airport transportation. Lighted tennis. Exercise equipt. Some refrigerators; bathrm phone in suites. Some private patios, balconies. Luxury level. Cr cds: A, C, D, DS, ER, JCB, MC, V.

D SC

★★★ **WESTIN HOTEL.** *5101 Great America Pkwy (95054). 408/986-0700; fax 408/980-3990; toll-free 800/937-8461.* 505 rms, 14 story. S $265; D $285; each addl $20; suites $450-$650; under 18 free; wkend, hol rates. Crib free. Pet accepted, some restrictions. Valet parking $11. TV; cable (premium). Heated pool; whirlpool, poolside serv. Restaurant 6 am-10 pm. Rm serv 24 hrs. Bar 11 am-midnight. Ck-out noon. Convention facilities. Business center. In-rm modem link. Concierge. Gift shop. Exercise equipt; sauna. Health club privileges. Tennis privileges. Golf privileges. Minibars; refrigerators avail. Balconies. Picnic tables. Near airport. Cr cds: A, C, D, DS, ER, JCB, MC, V.

D SC

★★★ **WOODCREST HOTEL.** *5415 Stevens Creek Blvd (95051). 408/446-9636; fax 408/446-9739; toll-free 800/862-8282.* 60 rms, 4 story. S, D $145-$165; each addl $15; suites $165-$300; under 12 free; wkend rates. Crib free. TV; cable (premium), VCR (free movies). Complimentary bkfst buffet. Coffee in rms. Bar 5:30-10:30 pm; closed Fri-Sun. Ck-out noon. Meeting rms. Business servs avail. Covered parking. Health club privileges. Bathrm phones; some fireplaces; refrigerator, wet bar in suites. Resembles French country estate with courtyard. Cr cds: A, C, D, MC, V.

D

B&B/Small Inn

★★ **MADISON STREET INN.** *1390 Madison St (95050). 408/249-5541; fax 408/249-6676; res 408/249-5541. www.madisonstreetinn.com.* 6 rms, 4 baths. S, D $75-$115. TV avail. Pool. Complimentary full bkfst. Ck-out noon, ck-in 4 pm. Health club privileges. Picnic tables, grills. Victorian furnishings (1895); library, antiques, bearclaw tubs. Garden. Totally nonsmoking. Cr cds: A, D, DS, MC, V.

All Suite

★★ **QUALITY SUITES SILICON VALLEY.** *3100 Lakeside Dr (95054). 408/748-9800; fax 408/748-1476; toll-free 800/345-1554. www.qualitysuites-sv.com.* 220 suites, 7 story. S, D $250-$270; each addl $10; under 18 free; lower rates wkends. Crib free. TV; cable (premium), VCR avail (movies). Heated pool. Complimentary full bkfst, coffee in rms. Restaurant nearby. Ck-out noon. Coin lndry. Meeting rms. Business center. Bellhops. Sundries. Gift shop. Free garage parking. Free airport, RR station, bus depot transportation. Exercise equipt. Minibars. Cr cds: A, C, D, DS, JCB, MC, V.

D

Restaurants

★★ **LA GALLERIA.** *2798 El Camino Real (95051). 408/296-6800.* Hrs: 11:30 am-9 pm; Fri to 9:30 pm; Sat 5-9:30 pm. Closed Sun; Thanksgiving, Dec 25. Res accepted. Northern Italian menu. Wine, beer. Lunch $7.95-$16.95, dinner $8.50-$17.95. Specialties: osso buco Milanese, fettucine alla Galleria. Parking. Cr cds: A, DS, MC, V.

D

★ **LA PALOMA.** *2280 El Camino Real (95050). 408/247-0990.* Hrs: 11 am-9:30 pm; Fri, Sat to 10 pm; Sun 4-9 pm. Closed July 4, Thanksgiving, Dec 25. Res accepted. Mexican menu. Bar. Lunch, dinner $6.50-$11.95. Children's menu. Specialties: pollo al cilantro, burrito ranchero. Parking. Mexican village decor. Cr cds: A, D, DS, MC, V.

D

Santa Cruz

(A-1) *See also Los Gatos, Santa Clara*

Founded 1840 **Pop** 49,040 **Elev** 20 ft **Area code** 831

Information Santa Cruz County Conference & Visitors Council, 1211 Ocean St, 95060; 831/425-1234 or 800/833-3494

Web www.scccvc.org

Santa Cruz is a bustling seaside resort and arts and crafts center with 29 miles of public beaches. The county is home to a wide variety of agricultural products such as strawberries, apples, and begonias. The present town is predated by the village of Branciforte, which it has now assimilated. Branciforte was founded in 1797 as a colonial venture of the Spanish government. Lacking financial support, the village failed to develop, and its shiftless colonists made much trouble for the nearby mission. The Santa Cruz Valley was given its name, which means Holy Cross, by Don Gaspar de Portola and Father Crespi, who discovered it in 1769.

What to See and Do

Año Nuevo State Reserve. Wild, windswept coastal reserve where thousands of massive elephant seals come to mate and give birth each winter. (Daily; park accessible by guided walks only, mid-Dec-Mar) New Year's Creek in Pescadero; take Hwy 1 about 22 mi N. Phone 650/879-0227.

Bargetto Winery. Family winery with tours and tasting (daily; closed hols). 3535 N Main St, E on CA 1, exit Capitola/Soquel exit, right on Main St in Soquel. Tasting rm, 700 Cannery Row, Suite L, Monterey 93940; Phone 831/475-2258. **FREE**

Felton covered bridge. Built in 1892; spans San Lorenzo River 80 ft above the water.

Municipal Wharf. Extends ½ mi into Monterey Bay. One of few piers of this type to permit auto traffic. Restaurants, gift shops, fish markets, charter boats; free fishing area. Phone 831/420-5250.

The Mystery Spot. Area 150 ft in diameter that "defies" conventional laws of gravity, perspective; balls roll uphill, trees grow sideways. Discovered in 1939. Guided tours. (Daily) 465 Mystery Spot Rd. Phone 831/423-8897. ¢¢

Roaring Camp & Big Trees Narrow-Gauge Railroad. Authentic 19th-century narrow-gauge steam locomotives carry passengers up North America's steepest railroad grades through groves of giant redwoods. Stopover at Bear Mtn for picnicking, hiking; round trip six mi, 1¼ hrs. Historic townsite with 1880s depot, old-time general store, covered bridge. Trains leave Roaring Camp depot, ½ mi SE of Felton at jct Graham Hill and Roaring Camp rds. (Schedule varies; additional trains wkends, hols, and in summer) Chuckwagon barbecue (May-Oct, wkends). 6 mi N on Graham Hill Rd in Felton. Phone 831/335-4484. ¢¢¢¢¢ Also here is

Santa Cruz, Big Trees & Pacific Railway. 1920s-era railroad operating vintage passenger coaches over spectacular rail route between redwoods at Roaring Camp and beach and boardwalk at Santa Cruz. A 2½-hr round-trip excursion through tunnel, over trestles, and along rugged San Lorenzo River Canyon on its way to the beach at Santa Cruz. Historic railroad dates back to 1875. (June-Sept, daily; rest of yr, wkends and hols) Phone 831/335-4484. ¢¢¢¢¢

Santa Cruz Beach Boardwalk. Only remaining beachside amusement park on the West Coast. Incl famous Cocoanut Grove ballroom, Neptune's Kingdom with entertainment and attractions, restaurants, shops, outdoor shows at beach bandstand, miniature golf, arcades, games, rides, the Giant Dipper roller coaster, and 1911 Looff carousel. Boardwalk (Memorial Day-Labor Day, daily; rest of yr, wkends and hols; closed Dec 25, 26). Neptune's Kingdome (daily; closed Dec 24, 25). Phone 831/423-5590. All-day unlimited ride pass ¢¢¢¢¢

Santa Cruz City Museum of Natural History. Natural and cultural history of the northern Monterey Bay region. California Native American exhibits; tidepool aquarium. (Tues-Sun; closed hols) 1305 E Cliff Dr. Phone 831/420-6115. **Donation**

Santa Cruz Mission State Historical Park. Casa Adobe (Neary-Rodriguez Adobe) is the only remaining building of the old Santa Cruz Mission; the date of construction is 1822-1824; displays. (Thurs-Sun) 144 School St. Phone 831/425-5849. ¢

State parks.

Big Basin Redwoods State Park. (see) 23 mi N via CA 9, 236.

Forest of Nisene Marks. Seismologists identified the epicenter of the Oct 1989 earthquake (7.1 magnitude) in this 10,000-acre state park. Diagonal fault ridges are evident although the earthquake epicenter can barely be distinguished. Hiking, bicycling. Picnicking. Primitive camping (fee; six-mi hike to campsite). 6 mi SE on CA 1 to Aptos, then N on Aptos Creek Rd. Phone 831/763-7063.

Henry Cowell Redwoods. These 1,737 acres contain some of the finest specimens of coastal redwood in the world, incl one tree that has a base large enough to shelter several people. Self-guided nature trail, hiking, bridle trails, picnicking, camping. Some campfire programs and guided walks conducted by rangers. 5 mi N on CA 9. Phone 831/335-4598. ¢¢

Natural Bridges Beach. Ocean-formed sandstone arch; winter site for monarch butterflies. Fishing; nature trail, picnicking. Displays of local tidepool life. Day use only. W of city limits on W Cliff Dr. Phone 831/423-4609. ¢¢

Seacliff Beach. Fishing pier leads to *"The Cement Ship,"* sunk here in 1929 to serve as an amusement center. Swimming beach, seasonal lifeguards, fishing; picnicking, campsites (full hookups, no tents). 5 mi S on CA 1. Phone 831/685-6500. ¢¢¢

Wilder Ranch. Coastal terraces, pocket beaches, and historic farm on 3,000 acres. Nature, hiking, biking, bridle trails. Interpretive displays. Farm and blacksmith demonstrations. Day use only. 3 mi NW on CA 1. Phone 831/426-0505. ¢¢¢

University of California, Santa Cruz. (1965) 10,000 students. Made up of eight colleges on a 2,000-acre campus overlooking Monterey Bay. The Institute of Marine Sciences offers guided tours of the Long Marine Laboratory. Art galleries, astronomical exhibits, agroecology farm, and arboretum. NW section of town. Phone 831/459-0111.

West Cliff Drive. One of the most renowned ocean drives in the state. On N shoreline of Santa Cruz Beach.

Special Events

Shakespeare/Santa Cruz Festival. UCSC Campus. Presentation of Shakespearean and contemporary plays by professional actors; indoor and outdoor performances. Phone 831/459-2121. Mid-July-late Aug.

Capitola Begonia Festival. 5 mi E, in Capitola. Height of blooming season. Fishing derbies, parade. Sept. Phone 831/476-3566.

Santa Cruz County Fair. Santa Cruz County Fairgrounds. Phone 831/724-5671. Early-mid-Sept.

Mountain Man Rendezvous. Reenactment of an early-days rendezvous with participants authentically costumed as trappers and traders as they gather to exchange products, swap tales, and engage in old-time games. Thanksgiving wkend. Phone 831/335-4484.

Motels/Motor Lodges

★★ **BEST INN AND SUITES, SANTA CRUZ.** *600 Riverside Ave (95060). 831/458-9660; fax 831/426-8775; res 877/877-8886. www.bestinnssantacruz.com.* 79 rms, 3 story, 9 suites. Mid-June-Sept: S, D $79-$129; each addl $10; suites $127-$250; under 19 free; higher rates wkends; lower rates rest of yr. Crib free. TV; cable. Pool; whirlpools. Complimentary continental bkfst. Ck-out 11 am. Meeting rm. Business servs avail. Private patios, balconies. Beach, boardwalk 4 blks. Cr cds: A, C, D, DS, MC, V.
D SC

★★ **BEST WESTERN SEACLIFF INN.** *7500 Old Dominion Ct, Aptos (95003). 831/688-7300; fax 831/685-3603; toll-free 800/367-2003. www.seacliffinn.com.* 140 rms, 2 story. Mid-Mar-mid-Oct: S, D $99-$149; each addl $10; suites $179-$239; under 18 free; higher rates: hols, special events; lower rates rest of yr. Crib free. TV; cable (premium). Heated pool; whirlpool, poolside serv. Complimentary continental bkfst (Mon-Fri), coffee in rms. Restaurant 6:30 am-9 pm. Bar 11 am-midnight; entertainment. Ck-out noon. Meeting rms. Business servs avail. Bellhops. Refrigerator in suites. Balconies. Beach ¼ mi. Cr cds: A, C, D, DS, MC, V.
D SC

★ **CAROUSEL MOTEL.** *110 Riverside Ave (95060). 831/425-7090; fax 831/423-4801; toll-free 800/214-7400.* 34 rms, 3 story. No A/C. Late Mar-early Sept: S, D $59-$159; under 16 free; vacation packages; higher rates: spring break, Easter, hols; lower rates rest of yr. Crib $10. TV; cable. Complimentary continental bkfst. Restaurant nearby. Ck-out 11 am. Many refrigerators, microwaves. Balconies. Ocean nearby. Boardwalk view. Cr cds: A, C, D, DS, MC, V.
D

★★ **SEA AND SAND INN.** *201 W Cliff Dr (95060). 831/427-3400; fax 831/427-3400. www.beachboardwalk.com.* 18 rms, 2 story, 2 kit. cottages. Memorial Day-Labor Day: S, D $119-$239; each addl $10; kit. cottages $229-$299; under 12 free; Sat (2-day min); lower rates rest of yr. Crib $10. TV; cable, VCR (movies $3). Complimentary continental bkfst; afternoon refreshments. Ck-out 11 am. Some in-rm whirlpools. On cliffs overlooking Monterey Bay. Ocean swimming, beach. Cr cds: A, D, DS, MC, V.
SC

★★ **WESTCOAST SANTA CRUZ HOTEL.** *175 W Cliff Dr (95060). 831/426-4330; fax 831/427-2025; toll-free 800/426-0670.* 163 rms, 1-10 story. Mid-June-mid-Sept: S, D $179-$199; suites $249-$329; under 18 free; lower rates rest of yr. Crib free. TV; cable (premium). Heated pool; whirlpools, poolside serv. Coffee in rms. Restaurants 7 am-10 pm. Bar to midnight. Ck-out noon. Meeting rms. Business servs avail. Bellhops. Refrigerators. Private balconies. Overlooks beach. Cr cds: A, C, D, DS, MC, V.
D SC

B&Bs/Small Inns

★★★ **BABBLING BROOK INN.** *1025 Laurel St (95060). 831/427-2437; fax 831/427-2457; res 800/866-1131. www.babblingbrookinn.com.* 14 rms. S, D $165; each addl $20. Adults preferred. TV; cable. Complimentary full bkfst buffet; afternoon refreshments. Ck-out 11:30 am, ck-in 3 pm. Many wood-burning stoves. Some in-rm whirlpools. Many balconies. Former gristmill and tannery. Country French decor. Garden walkways, waterfalls, avail for weddings. Boardwalk 7 blks. Totally nonsmoking. Cr cds: A, MC, V.
D

★★ **BAYVIEW HOTEL.** *8041 Soquel Dr, Aptos (95003). 831/688-8656; fax 408/688-5128; toll-free 800/422-9843. www.bayviewhotel.com.* 11 rms, 7 with shower only, 3 story, 1 suite. No A/C. S, D $90-$160; each addl $20; suite $150; wkends, hols (2-day min). TV; cable. Complimentary contintental bkfst. Restaurant 11 am-10 pm. Ck-out 11:30, ck-in 3 pm. Bellhops. Concierge serv. Built in 1878; antiques. Totally nonsmoking. Cr cds: A, MC, V.

SC

★★ **CHATEAU VICTORIAN.** *118 1St St (95060). 831/458-9458. www.travelguides.com/bb/chateauvictorian.* 7 rms, 2 story. No A/C. No rm phones. D $120-$150. Adults only. Complimentary bkfst, evening refreshments. Restaurant nearby. Ck-out noon, ck-in 3:30-6:30 pm. Victorian house; fireplaces. 1 blk to beach. Totally nonsmoking. Cr cds: MC, V.

★★★★ **INN AT DEPOT HILL.** *250 Monterey Ave, Capitola (95010). 831/462-3376; fax 831/462-3697; res 800/572-2632. www.innatdepothill.com.* This turn-of-the-century railroad depot has been transformed into a romantic, sophisticated inn. Each of the beautiful rooms is uniquely decorated. All have large two-person marble showers, fireplaces, built-in stereo systems, color televisions, and VCRs to complement the inn's large video library. The casually elegant public rooms and brick patio (with lush landscaping) offer the perfect setting to relax and reflect. 12 rms, 2 story, 5 suites. Some A/C. S, D $195-$275; each addl $20; suites $210-$275. TV; cable, VCR (movies). Complimentary full bkfst; afternoon refreshments, complimentary evening wine and hors d'oeuvres, complimentary coffee in rms. Restaurants nearby. Limited rm serv. Ck-out 11:30 am, ck-in 3 pm. Meeting rm. Business servs avail. In-rm modem link. Concierge serv. Health club privileges. Fireplaces; some in-rm whirlpools. Ocean 2 blks; swimming beach. Most rms w/private patios and hot tubs. Cr cds: A, DS, MC, V.

D

Restaurants

★★ **BITTERSWEET BISTRO.** *787 Rio del Mar Blvd, Rio del Mar (95003). 831/662-9799. www.bittersweetbistro.com.* Hrs: 5:30-10 pm. Closed Mon; also Jan 1, Dec 25. Res accepted. Contemporary American menu. Bar. A la carte entrees: bkfst, lunch $6-$14, dinner $12-$21. Sun brunch $6-$14. Children's menu. Specialties: halibut en papillote, goat cheese salad, chocolate trio. Parking. Outdoor dining. Bistro atmosphere. Totally nonsmoking. Cr cds: A, MC, V.

D

★★ **CAFE SPARROW.** *8042 Soquel Dr, Aptos (95003). 831/688-6238. www.cafesparrow.com.* Hrs: 11 am-2 pm, 5:30-9 pm; Sun brunch 9 am-2 pm. Closed hols; also Halloween. Res accepted. French menu. Wine, beer. Lunch $7.95-$12.95, dinner $17-$22. Sun brunch $8-$15. Specializes in country French cooking. Country French theme. Totally nonsmoking. Cr cds: A, MC, V.

D

★★ **CROW'S NEST.** *2218 E Cliff Dr (95062). 831/476-4560. www.crowsnest-santacruz.com.* Hrs: 11:30 am-2:30 pm, 5:30-9 pm; Sat 11 am-3 pm, 5-10 pm; Sun 11 am-3 pm, 5-9 pm. Closed Dec 25. Res accepted. Bar. A la carte entrees: lunch $6.95-$14.95, dinner $8.95-$17.95. Children's menu. Specializes in fresh seafood, steak. Salad bar. Entertainment. Outdoor dining. On beach, at yacht harbor; view of bay. Cr cds: A, DS, MC, V.

D

★★ **GILBERT'S SEAFOOD GRILL.** *Municipal Wharf #25 (95060). 831/423-5200.* Hrs: 11:30 am-10 pm; Fri-Sat to 11 pm. Res accepted. Bar. Lunch $7.95-$14.95, dinner $7.95-$29.95. Children's menu. Specializes in fresh local fish, seafood, pasta. View of Monterey Bay and beach from wharf. Totally nonsmoking. Cr cds: A, C, DS, ER, MC, V.

D

★★ **SANDERLINGS RESTAURANT.** *1900 Seascape Village Rd, Aptos (95003). 831/688-6800. www.seascaperesort.com.* Specializes in halibut, swordfish, salmon, pasta, steaks. Hrs: 7-11 am, 5:30-10 pm; Sun brunch 8 am-2 pm. Res accepted. Wine, beer. Lunch $7.95-$15.95; dinner $16.95-$26.95. Brunch $12.95-$21.95. Children's menu. Entertainment: guitarist Fri, Sat. Crown jewel of Monterey Bay, on the ocean. Cr cds: A, D, DS, MC, V.

D

★★★ **SHADOWBROOK.** *1750 Wharf Rd, Capitola (95010). 831/475-1511.* Hrs: 5:30-9 pm; Sat 4-10 pm; Sun 4-9 pm; Sun brunch 10 am-2:30 pm. Res accepted. Bar from 5 pm. Complete meals: dinner $13.95-$24.95. Sun brunch $7.95-$16.95. Children's menu. Specializes in seafood, prime rib. Own baking. Free parking. Small dining rm on rooftop. Garden stairway to restaurant; garden decor. Overlooks river. "Cable car" from parking lot to restaurant. Totally nonsmoking. Cr cds: A, C, D, DS, MC, V.
D

★★★ **THEO'S.** *3101 N Main St, Soquel (95073). 831/462-3657. www.theosrestaurant.net.* Hrs: 5:30-9:30 pm, closed Sun, Mon. Res accepted. California-French menu. Wine cellar. Dinner $14-$24. Specializes in duck, lamb, fresh seafood. Own baking. Outdoor dining, garden patio for receptions. French country decor. Organic garden. Uses locally grown produce. Cr cds: A, D, MC, V.
D

Santa Maria

(D-2) *See also Lompoc, San Luis Obispo, Solvang*

Pop 61,284 **Elev** 216 ft **Area code** 805

Information Chamber of Commerce, 614 S Broadway, 93454; 805/925-2403 or 800/331-3779

Web www.santamaria.com

A Ranger District office of the Los Padres National Forest (see KING CITY, SANTA BARBARA) is located in Santa Maria.

What to See and Do

Santa Maria Historical Museum. Early settler and Chumash artifacts. (Tues-Sat; closed hols) 614 S Broadway. Phone 805/922-3130. **FREE**

Special Events

Santa Barbara County Fair. Santa Maria Fairgrounds. July. Phone 805/925-8824.

Elks Rodeo & Parade. Elks Event Center. First wkend June.

Motel/Motor Lodge

★★ **BEST WESTERN BIG AMERICA.** *1725 N Broadway (93454). 805/922-5200; fax 805/922-9865; toll-free 800/528-1234. www.bigamerica.com.* 106 units, 2 story, 16 suites. S $77-$89; D $77-$89; suites $75-$130; under 18 free; wkly rates. Crib free. TV; cable (premium), VCR avail (movies). Heated pool; whirlpool. Complimentary continental bkfst. Restaurant 6 am-9 pm. Bar. Ck-out noon. Meeting rms. Business servs avail. Valet serv. Free airport, bus depot transportation. Refrigerators, wet bars. Cr cds: A, C, D, DS, MC, V.
D SC

Hotel

★★★ **SANTA MARIA INN.** *801 S Broadway (93454). 805/928-7777; fax 805/928-5690; toll-free 800/462-4276. www.santamariainn.com.* 166 rms, 2-6 story. S, D $79-$99; each addl $15; suites $150-$340; under 12 free; golf plan. Crib free. TV; cable, VCR avail (movies $4). Pool; whirlpool, poolside serv in season. Coffee in rms. Restaurant (see also SANTA MARIA INN). Bar 10:30-2 am; entertainment. Ck-out noon. Business servs avail. Bellhops. Valet serv. Shopping arcade. Barber, beauty shop. Airport transportation. Pitch and putt course. Exercise equipt; sauna. Refrigerators; some bathrm phones, fireplaces. Private patios, balconies. 1917 inn; antique fountain, English antiques, stained glass. Cr cds: A, C, D, DS, JCB, MC, V.
D SC

Restaurant

★★★ **SANTA MARIA INN.** *801 S Broadway (93454). 805/928-7777. www.santamariainn.com.* Hrs: 6:30 am-10 pm; early-bird dinner 5-6:30 pm; Sun brunch 10:30 am-2 pm. Res accepted. Bar. Bkfst $5.95-$9.25, lunch $6.95-$9.95, dinner $10.95-

$20.95. Sun brunch $16.95. Children's menu. Specializes in prime rib, fresh seafood, Santa Maria barbecue. Parking. Outdoor dining. Totally nonsmoking. Cr cds: A, C, D, DS, ER, MC, V.
D SC

Santa Monica

(E-4) *See also Beverly Hills, Buena Park, Fullerton, Los Angeles, Malibu, Marina del Rey*

Founded 1875 **Pop** 86,905 **Elev** 101 ft **Area code** 310

Information Visitor Center, 1400 Ocean Ave, 90401; 310/393-7593

Web www.santamonica.com

With its wide, white beaches, continual sunshine, and casual ambience, Santa Monica is one of southern California's undiscovered beachside resorts. Located at the end of famed Wilshire Boulevard, Santa Monica is perhaps best known for its popular bay. Here the scenery of palm trees, beach, and mountains has been popular for years in snapshots, movies, and postcards.

What to See and Do

California Heritage Museum. Built along palisades in 1894. Moved to present site and restored. Houses changing history exhibits; contemporary art and photo gallery. (Wed-Sat; closed hols) 2612 Main St. Phone 310/392-8537. ¢¢

Museum of Flying. Historical and current aviation exhibits, models, and memorabilia; Donald Douglas Library and Archives. Most aircraft on display are in fully operational condition. Special events, exhibitions. (Wed-Sun; closed hols) At Santa Monica Airport. Phone 310/392-8822. ¢¢¢

★ **Palisades Park.** Parks, paths, and gardens on 26 acres overlooking the ocean. Senior recreation center (all yr). Ocean Ave from Colorado Ave to Adelaide Dr. Phone 310/458-8310. **FREE**

Santa Monica Mountains National Recreation Area. A huge park incorporating both federal lands (with a number of old ranch sites) and four state parks ranging from Will Rogers State Historic Park to Point Mugu (also Topanga and Malibu Creek state parks) and state beaches (Leo Carillo, Topanga, and Will Rogers among them). Surfing; hiking, horseback riding, and mountain biking trails. (Daily) Headquarters at 30401 Agoura Rd, Suite 100, Agoura 91301. Phone 818/597-9192.

Santa Monica Pier. Restaurants, shops; also antique carousel with 46 hand-carved horses housed in restored building (1916). On Ocean Ave at the foot of Colorado Ave. Phone 310/458-8900. **FREE** Also here are

Pacific Park. Two-acre amusement park with 11 rides, incl a nine-story Ferris wheel and roller coaster. (Summer, daily; winter, schedule varies) Phone 310/260-8744.

UCLA Ocean Discovery Center. Innovative, interactive aquarium, Wet Lab, Pier Tank. (July-Memorial Day, daily; rest of yr, wkends) Phone 310/393-6149. ¢¢

Santa Monica State Beach. Considered one of the best in Los Angeles area; three mi long; lifeguards, surfing, volleyball, bike path, play equipt, snack bars. Parking ¢¢¢

Third Street Promenade. Popular pedestrian-only street lined with cafes, restaurants, shops, and theaters, and featuring an array of street performers. (Daily) Third St.

Venice Beach and Boardwalk. Oceanfront beach and walkway known for its muscle-builders, skaters, joggers, street entertainers, and merchants. Food stands and cafes, picnicking, beach. Ocean Front Walk in Venice. Phone 310/396-7016. **FREE**

Motels/Motor Lodges

★★ **BEST WESTERN GATEWAY HOTEL.** *1920 Santa Monica Blvd (90404). 310/829-9100; fax 310/829-9211; res 800/528-1234. www.gatewayhotel.com.* 122 rms, 4 story. Mid-June-mid-Sept: S, D $89-$159; each addl $5; under 18 free; higher rates special events; lower rates rest of yr. Crib free. TV; cable. Restaurant 6:30 am-10 pm. Rm serv 7 am-9 pm. Ck-out noon. Meeting rms. Business servs avail. In-rm modem link. Bellhops. Valet serv. Exercise equipt. Cr cds: A, C, D, DS, ER, JCB, MC, V.

D 🚶 🚭 🔥 SC

★★ **BEST WESTERN OCEAN VIEW.** *1447 Ocean Ave (90401). 310/458-4888; fax 310/458-0848; res 800/528-1234.* 66 rms, 4 story. Mid-June-mid-Sept: S, D $149-$199; each addl $10; under 18 free; 2-day min wkends; lower rates rest of yr. Crib free. Garage parking $7, in/out $7. TV; cable (premium), VCR avail. Complimentary coffee in lobby. Restaurant adj 10 am-11 pm. Ck-out noon. Business servs avail. In-rm modem link. Bellhops. Valet serv. Concierge. Some refrigerators. Microwaves avail. Cr cds: A, C, D, DS, JCB, MC, V.

D

★★ **COMFORT INN.** *2815 Santa Monica Blvd (90404). 310/828-5517; fax 310/829-6084; res 800/228-5150.* 108 rms, 3 story. June-Sept: S $69-$79; D $79-$89; each addl $10; under 18 free; lower rates rest of yr. Crib $10. TV, cable (premium). Heated pool. Complimentary coffee. Ck-out noon. Health club privileges. Refrigerators. Cr cds: A, C, D, DS, JCB, MC, V.

D 🏊 🚭 🔥

★★ **HOLIDAY INN SANTA MONICA BEACH.** *120 Colorado Ave (90401). 310/451-0676; fax 310/393-7145; res 800/465-7039. www.basshotels.com/holiday-inn.* 132 rms, 7 story. Apr-Oct: S $159-$189; D $174-$204; each addl $15; under 18 free; higher rates Rose Bowl, other special events; lower rates rest of yr. Crib free. Pet accepted; $50 deposit. Valet parking $6.60, in/out $6.60. TV; cable (premium), VCR avail (movies). Pool. Restaurant 6:30-11 am, 5-10 pm. Ck-out noon. Coin lndry. In-rm modem link. Concierge. Gift shop. Health club privileges. Some refrigerators. Cr cds: A, C, D, DS, ER, JCB, MC, V.

D 🐕 🏊 🚶 🚭 🔥

★ **TRAVELODGE.** *3102 Pico Blvd (90405). 310/450-5766; fax 310/450-8843; res 800/231-7679.* 85 rms, 6 with shower only, 2 story. Mid-May-Sept: S $79; D $89; each addl $6; under 12 free; wkly rates; lower rates rest of yr. Crib free. TV; cable (premium). Complimentary continental bkfst, coffee in rms. Restaurant nearby. Ck-out 11 am. Business servs avail. Airport, RR station transportation. Many refrigerators; some microwaves. Picnic tables, grills. Cr cds: A, C, D, DS, JCB, MC, V.

D ✈ 🚶 🚭 🔥

Hotels

★★★ **THE FAIRMONT MIRAMAR HOTEL SANTA MONICA.** *101 Wilshire Blvd (90401). 310/576-7777; fax 310/319-3144; res 800/866-5577. www.fairmont.com.* 302 rms, 10 story. S, D $219-$299; each addl $20; suites $365-$900; under 17 free; wkend rates. Crib free. TV; cable (premium), VCR avail (movies). Pool; whirlpool; poolside serv. Coffee in rms. Restaurants 6:30 am-11 pm. Rm serv 24 hrs. Bar; pianist. Ck-out noon. Meeting rms. Business servs avail. In-rm modem link. Concierge. Gift shop. Barber, beauty shop. Exercise rm; sauna. Massage. Bathrm phones, minibars. Beach opp. Cr cds: A, C, D, DS, JCB, MC, V.

D 🏊 🚶 🚭 🔥 SC

★★ **FOUR POINTS BY SHERATON.** *530 W Pico Blvd (90405). 310/399-9344; fax 310/399-2504; res 800/495-7776.* 309 rms, 9 with shower only, 9 story. S $145-$185; D $165-$205; each addl $10; suites $350; under 12 free. Crib free. TV; cable (premium). 2 pools; whirlpools, poolside serv. Complimentary coffee in rms. Restaurant 6:30 am-11 pm. Ck-out noon. Coin lndry. Convention facilities. Business servs avail. In-rm modem link. Gift shop. Exercise equipt. Cr cds: A, C, D, DS, JCB, MC, V.

D 🏊 🚶 🚭 🔥 SC

★★★★ **LE MERIGOT BEACH HOTEL & SPA SANTA MONICA.** *1740 Ocean Ave (90401). 310/395-9700; fax 310/395-9200; res 888/539-7899. www.lemerigotbeachhotel.com.* Business travelers will appreciate the room desk and two-line telephones in each room, and all guests will enjoy the personalized service—including a butler available at a moment's notice. An excellent health spa and lavish pool area provide a retreat from the city, though the sleek decor gives an urban sophistication to the property. 173 rms, 6 story, 2 suites. S, D $199. Pool. TV; cable (premium). Ck-out 11 am. Meeting rms. Cr cds: A, DS, JCB, MC, V.

★★★ LOEWS SANTA MONICA HOTEL. *1700 Ocean Ave (90401). 310/458-6700; fax 310/458-6761. www.loewshotels.com.* 345 rms, 8 story, 35 suites. S $290-$305, D $330-$340; each addl $20; suites $575-$2,500; under 18 free. Valet parking $18; self-park $15.40. TV; cable (premium), VCR avail (movies). Indoor/outdoor pool; whirlpool, poolside serv. Supervised children's activities; ages 5-12. Crib free. Restaurants 6 am-10 pm (see also LAVANDE). Rm serv 24 hrs. Bar 10-1 am; entertainment. Ck-out noon. Convention facilities. Business center. In-rm modem link. Concierge. Gift shop. Barber, beauty shop. Tennis privileges. Golf privileges. Exercise rm; sauna, steam rm. Massage. Bicycle and roller skate rentals. Bathrm phones, minibars; some wet bars. Balconies. Atrium. Beach approx 50 yds. Cr cds: A, C, D, DS, ER, JCB, MC, V.

★★★ RADISSON HUNTLEY HOTEL. *1111 Second St (90403). 310/394-5454; fax 310/458-9776; res 800/333-3333.* 213 rms, 18 story. June-Oct: S, D $189; each addl $20; suite $450; under 17 free; lower rates rest of yr. Crib free. Valet parking $8.50, in/out $8.50. TV; cable, VCR avail (movies). Restaurant 6-2 am. Ck-out noon. Meeting rms. Business servs avail. In-rm modem link. Concierge. Gift shop. Barber, beauty shop. Exercise equipt. Minibars; some refrigerators, microwaves. Cr cds: A, C, D, DS, ER, JCB, MC, V.

★★★ RENAISSANCE AGOURA HILLS. *30100 Agoura Rd, Agoura Hills (91301). 818/707-1220. www.renaissancehotels.com.* 280 rms, 5 story. S, D $150-$295; each addl $20; under 17 free. Crib avail. Pool. TV; cable (premium), VCR avail. Complimentary coffee in rms, newspaper. Restaurant 6 am-10:30 pm. Bar. Ck-out 11 am. Meeting rms. Business center. Valet serv. Gift shop. Exercise rm. Some refrigerators, minibars. Cr cds: A, C, D, DS, MC, V.

Santa Monica Pier

★★ SHANGRI-LA. *1301 Ocean Ave (90401). 310/394-2791; fax 310/451-3351; toll-free 800/345-7829. www.shangrila-hotel.com.* 55 units, 7 story, 47 kits. S, D $160; each addl $15; suites $205-$470. Crib $15. TV; cable (premium). Complimentary continental bkfst; afternoon refreshments. Ck-out noon. Balconies. Large terrace, tropical grounds. Beach opp. Cr cds: A, C, D, DS, JCB, MC, V.

★★★ SHUTTERS ON THE BEACH. *One Pico Blvd (90405). 310/458-0030; fax 310/458-4589; toll-free 800/334-9000. www.shuttersonthebeach.com.* 196 rms in 2 buildings, 7 story. S, D $355; each addl $50; suites $750-$2,500; under 5 free; wkend plans. Valet parking $18. TV; cable (premium), VCR (movies). Pool; whirlpool, poolside serv. Restaurants 6:30 am-11 pm (see also I PICO). Rm serv 24 hrs. Bar 11-2 am. Ck-out noon. Meeting rms. Business center. In-rm modem link. Concierge. Gift shop. Exercise equipt; sauna, steam rm. Massage. Minibars; microwaves avail. Balconies. Oceanfront boardwalk.

Named for distinctive sliding shutter doors of each guest rm. Cr cds: A, C, D, DS, ER, JCB, MC, V.

Resorts

★★★★ CASA DEL MAR. *1910 Ocean Way (90405). 310/581-5533; fax 310/581-5503; toll-free 800/898-6999. www.hotelcasadelmar.com.* This Italian Renaissance-style hotel has been restored to its former 1920s glory, with warm Art Deco detailing and elegant public spaces. Overlooking Santa Monica beach, the lobby is a magnet for outside visitors. Service is attentive and personable. 109 rms, 7 story, 20 suites. May-Sept: S, D $335; each addl $50; under 12 free; lower rates rest of yr. Crib avail. Valet parking. Pool; lap pool, whirlpool. TV; cable (DSS), VCR avail. Complimentary newspaper. Restaurant 6:30 am-10 pm. Rm serv 24 hrs. Meeting rms. Business center. Luggage handling. Concierge serv. Gift shop. Exercise privileges, sauna. Golf, 18 holes. Tennis, 4 courts. Beach access. Bike rentals. Supervised children's activities. Hiking trail. Picnic facilities. Cr cds: A, C, D, DS, ER, JCB, MC, V.

★ THE GEORGIA HOTEL. *1415 Ocean Ave (90401). 310/395-9945; fax 310/656-0904; res 800/538-8147. www.georgianhotel.com.* 84 rms, 8 story, 28 suites. July-Aug: S, D $210-$235; each addl $25; suites $295-$350; family, wkly rates; package plans; lower rates rest of yr. Crib free. Pet accepted; $250. Valet parking $12. TV; cable (premium), VCR avail. Complimentary coffee in rms. Restaurant 6:30-10:30 am. Ck-out noon. Meeting rms. Business servs avail. In-rm modem link. Concierge. Health club privileges. Minibars. Opp ocean. Cr cds: A, D, DS, JCB, MC, V.

B&Bs/Small Inns

★★★ CHANNEL ROAD INN. *219 W Channel Rd (90402). 310/459-1920; fax 310/454-9920. www.channelroadinn.com.* 14 rms, 3 story, 2 suites. S, D $225; suites $245-$275. Crib free. TV; cable (premium), VCR avail (free movies). Complimentary full bkfst. Restaurants opp 7 am-11 pm. Ck-out noon, ck-in 3 pm. Business servs avail. In-rm modem link. Whirlpool. Bicycles. Colonial Revival house built in 1910; library, fireplace, antiques. 1 blk from beach, bike path. Cr cds: A, MC, V.

★ VENICE BEACH HOUSE. *15 30th Ave, Venice (90291). 310/823-1966; fax 310/823-1842.* 9 units, 5 baths, 4 share bath, 2 story. Shared bath $85-$95; private bath $120-$165. TV; cable. Complimentary continental bkfst; afternoon refreshments. Ck-out 11 am, ck-in 2-8 pm. Some private patios, balconies. 1911 California Craftsman house. Venice Beach ¼ blk. Totally nonsmoking. Cr cds: A, MC, V.

All Suite

★★ DOUBLETREE GUEST SUITES - SANTA MONICA. *1707 4th St (90401). 310/395-3332; fax 310/452-7399; toll-free 800/222-8733. www.doubletree.com.* 253 suites, 8 story. July-Sept: S, D $225-$245; each addl $20; under 18 free; wkly rates; package plans; lower rates rest of yr. Crib free. Garage parking $12, valet $15. TV; cable (premium), VCR avail. Pool; whirlpool; poolside serv. Complimentary coffee in rms. Restaurant 6:30 am-10 pm. Bar 5 pm-12:30 am. Ck-out noon. Coin lndry. Convention facilities. Business center. In-rm modem link. Gift shop. Airport transportation. Exercise equipt; sauna. Refrigerators, minibars; microwaves avail. Some rms with ocean view. Cr cds: A, C, D, DS, ER, JCB, MC, V.

Restaurants

★★ I PICO. *1 Pico Blvd (90405). 310/458-0030. www.shuttersonthebeach.com.* Specializes in pasta, seafood. Hrs: 11:30 am-2:30 pm, 6-10:30 pm; Sun brunch 11 am-2:30 pm. Res accepted. Bar 12:30 pm-1:30 am. Wine list. A la carte entrees: lunch $11.75-$17.75, dinner $14.50-$29. Sun brunch $10.25-$17.50. Valet parking. Floor-to-ceiling windows give view of ocean. Totally nonsmoking. Cr cds: A, D, MC, V.

D

★★★ **THE BEACH HOUSE.** *100 W Channel Rd (90402). 310/454-8299.* Specializes in BBQ baby back ribs, sea bass. Hrs: 6-10:30 pm; Sun to 9 pm. Closed Mon. Res accepted. Wine, beer. Dinner $28-$32. Entertainment. Cr cds: A, D, DS, MC, V.

D

★★ **BOB BURNS.** *202 Wilshire Blvd (90401). 310/393-6777.* Continental menu. Specializes in fresh fish, lamb chops, roast duckling. Hrs: 11:30 am-11 pm; Fri, Sat to midnight; Sun brunch to 3 pm. Closed Dec 25. Res accepted. Bar to midnight, Fri, Sat to 2 am. Lunch $8-$16, dinner $13-$29. Sun brunch $9.50-$15.95. Children's menu. Jazz pianist. Valet parking. Fireplace. Cr cds: A, C, D, DS, ER, MC, V.

D

★★ **BORDER GRILL.** *1445 4th St (90401). 310/451-1655. www.bordergrill.com.* Mexican menu. Own desserts. Hrs: 11:30 am-3 pm, 5:30-10 pm; Mon from 5:30 pm. Closed Jan 1, Thanksgiving, Dec 25. Res accepted. Bar. A la carte entrees: lunch $8-$12, dinner $10-$22. 2-story murals. Cr cds: A, C, D, DS, ER, MC, V.

D

★ **BROADWAY BAR AND GRILL.** *1460 3rd St Promenade (90401). 310/393-4211.* Hrs: 11:30 am-10:30 pm; wkends to midnight; Sun brunch 11:30 am-3 pm. Res accepted. Bar Fri, Sat to 2 am. A la carte entrees: lunch $7.95-$12.95, dinner $8.95-$18.95. Sun brunch $7.95-$13.95. Specializes in pork chops, steak, fresh fish. Entertainment Tues eves. Outdoor dining. Antique oak bar. Cr cds: A, DS, MC, V.

D

★ **BROADWAY DELI.** *1457 3rd St Promenade (90401). 310/451-0616.* Hrs: 7 am-midnight; Fri to 1 am; Sat 8-1 am; Sun 8 am-midnight. Bar. A la carte entrees: bkfst $5-$8, lunch $6-$12, dinner $12-$16. Specialties: rotisserie-cooked herb chicken, creme brulee, fruit cobbler. Valet parking. Contemporary decor. Gourmet market on premises. Cr cds: A, DS, MC, V.

D

★★★ **CEZANNE.** *1740 Ocean Ave (90430). 310/395-9700. www.lemerigotbeachhotel.com.* Specializes in seafood, lamb. Hrs: 6 am-6 pm, 5:30-10:30 pm; Sat, Sun 7 am-3:30 pm, 5:30-10:30 pm; Sun brunch 11 am-3 pm. Res accepted. Wine, beer. Lunch $8-$19; dinner $22-$38. Children's menu. Entertainment. Cr cds: A, D, DS, JCB, MC, V.

D

★★ **CHAYA VENICE.** *110 Navy St, Venice (90291). 310/396-1179.* Specializes in sushi, filet mignon, Chilean sea bass. Hrs: 11:30 am-2:30 pm, 6 pm-midnight; Sun to 10 pm; Mon to 10:30 pm; Fri, Sat to 11 pm. Res accepted. Wine, beer. Lunch $9-$16; dinner $13-$30. Entertainment. Cr cds: A, C, D, MC, V.

D

★★★ **CHINOIS ON MAIN.** *2709 Main St (90405). 310/392-3038. www.wolfgangpuck.com.* Hrs: 6-10:30 pm; Wed-Fri also 11:30 am-2 pm; Sun 5:30-10 pm. Closed hols. Res required. Chinese, French menu. Bar. A la carte entrees: lunch $9.50-$18.50, dinner $19.50-$29.50. Specialties: sizzling catfish, curried oysters. Valet parking. Cr cds: A, DS, MC, V.

D

★★ **DRAGO.** *2628 Wilshire Blvd (90403). 310/828-1585.* Hrs: 11:30 am-3 pm, 5:30-11 pm. Closed hols. Res accepted; required Thurs-Sat (dinner). Italian menu. Bar. A la carte entrees: lunch, dinner $9-$24. Specialties: loin of venison with red wine and cherries, Sicilian swordfish with caponata. Valet parking. Cr cds: A, DS, MC, V.

D

★★ **FISH COMPANY.** *174 Kinney St (90405). 310/392-8366.* Hrs: 11:30 am-10 pm; Fri, Sat to 11 pm. Closed Thanksgiving, Dec 25. Res accepted. Bar. Lunch $7-$10, dinner $10-$17. Children's menu. Specializes in fresh fish, Alaskan king crab legs, oyster bar. Sushi bar. Patio dining. In restored railroad warehouse (ca 1910). Nautical decor; large saltwater aquarium. Cr cds: A, C, D, ER, MC, V.

D

★ **THE HUMP.** *3221 Donald Douglas Loop S (90405). 310/313-0977. www.thehump-sushi.com.* Specializes in sauteed abalone, stuffed eggplant. Hrs: noon-2 pm, 6-10:30 pm; Fri, Sat 6-11 pm; Sun 6-10 pm. Res accepted. Wine, beer. Lunch $7-$15; dinner $8-$50. Entertainment. Cr cds: A, D, MC, V.

D

★★★ **JIRAFFE.** *502 Santa Monica Blvd (90401). 310/917-6671. www.jirafferestaurant.com.* French, American menu. Specializes in chicken, fish, seasonal game. Valet parking. Hrs: noon-2 pm, 6-10 pm; Fri, Sat 6-11 pm; Sun 5:30-9 pm. Closed Mon; hols. Res required. Wine cellar. A la carte entrees: lunch $7-$14, dinner $17-$26. Totally nonsmoking. Cr cds: A, MC, V.

D

★★ **JOE'S.** *1023 Abbot Kinney Blvd, Venice (90291). 310/399-5811.* Hrs: 11 am-3 pm, 6-11 pm. Closed Mon; Jan 1, Dec 25. Res accepted. Wine, beer. A la carte entrees: lunch $9-$11, dinner $15-$18. Specialties: grilled salmon, chicken ravioli with tomato coulis. Own pastas, pastries. Patio dining. Contemporary artwork. Cr cds: A, MC, V.

D

★★ **KNOLL'S BLACK FOREST INN.** *2454 Wilshire Blvd (90403). 310/395-2212. www.calendarlive.com/knollsblackforest.* Hrs: 11:30 am-2:30 pm, 5-10:30 pm; Sat, Sun from 5 pm. Closed Mon; Dec 25. Res accepted. German, continental menu. Bar. Wine cellar. Lunch $8.50-$15, dinner $11.50-$23.50. Prix fixe $26.50. Specializes in venison, fresh fish, Wiener schnitzel. Valet parking. Patio dining. Casual atmosphere in elegant surroundings. Family-owned. Cr cds: A, DS, MC, V.

D

★ **LA SERENATA DE GARBALDI.** *1416 4th St (90401). 310/656-7017.* Hrs: 11 am-10 pm; Fri, Sat to 11 pm. Res accepted. Wine, beer. Lunch $7-$11; dinner $9-$21. Entertainment. Cr cds: A, MC, V.

D

★★★ **LAVANDE.** *1700 Ocean Ave (90401). 310/576-3181. www.loewshotels.com.* Hrs: 11 am-2:30 pm, 5:30-10 pm; Sun (brunch) 10:30 am-2:30 pm. Res accepted. French menu. Bar 11-1 am. A la carte entrees: lunch $12-$16, dinner $19-$27. Prix fixe: lunch $19, dinner $55. Sun brunch $41. Children's menu. Specialties: veal daube, fish soup, vacherin glace with lavender ice cream. Jazz. Valet parking. Outdoor dining. View of ocean. Totally nonsmoking. Cr cds: A, C, D, DS, ER, MC, V.

D

★★★ **THE LOBSTER.** *1602 Ocean Ave (90401). 310/458-9294. www.thelobster.com.* Specializes in lobster, crab cakes, swordfish. Hrs: 11:30 am-10 pm; Fri, Sat to 11 pm. Res accepted. Wine, beer. Lunch $9-$23; dinner $13-$29. Entertainment. Cr cds: A, D, DS, JCB, MC, V.

D

★★★★ **MELISSE.** *1104 Wilshire Blvd (90401). 310/395-0881. www.melisse.com.* Josiah Citrin, who made his name at the popular Santa Monica spot JiRaffe, is creating delicious French/Californian fare at this refined eatery. The young service staff has clearly absorbed Citrin's enthusiasm for his food, seeming truly eager to serve his exciting dishes to guests. Look for deceptively simple preparations, like yellowfin tuna with roasted shiitakes, that explode with flavor. Specializes in sauteed line-caught black bass, pan-roasted veal chop. Hrs: noon-2 pm, 6-10:30 pm; Mon-Thurs 6-10 pm; Sun 6-9 pm. Res accepted. Wine, beer. Lunch $16-$22; dinner $27-$38. Entertainment. Jacket. Cr cds: A, D, MC, V.

D

★★★ **MICHAEL'S.** *1147 3rd St (90403). 310/451-0843.* Hrs: 11:30 am-2:30 pm; 5:30-10:30 pm. Closed Sun, Mon; hols. Res accepted. French, American menu. Bar. Wine cellar. A la carte entrees: lunch $16.50-$19.75, dinner $19.50-$29.95. Prix fixe: lunch $16.50, dinner $26.50. Serv charge 15%. Specializes in fresh fish, seafood, fine meats. Own pastries. Valet parking. Outdoor, private dining with fireplace. Contemporary decor; modern art collection. Garden. Cr cds: A, D, DS, MC, V.

D

★★ **OCEAN AVENUE SEAFOOD.** *1401 Ocean Ave (90401). 310/394-5669. www.kingsseafood.com.* Regional

American menu. Specializes in sake kasu, lobster taquitos. Hrs: 10:30 am-11:30 pm; Fri, Sat 11:30 am-11 pm. Res accepted. Wine, beer. Lunch $9.95-$18.95; dinner $9.95-$36.95. Children's menu. Entertainment. Cr cds: A, C, D, DS, JCB, MC, V.

D

★★★★ **OCEAN FRONT.** *1910 Ocean Front Way (90405). 310/581-7714. www.hotelcasadelmar.com.* Guests sit in deep wicker chairs amidst potted palms while taking in the glorious sunset views at this new eatery—located within the restored Casa Del Mar hotel—overlooking the Santa Monica Pier. Despite occasional overcooking, chef Andrew DeGroot does wonderful things with seafood, from his signature lobster pot-au-feu to Chilean sea bass wrapped in applewood smoked bacon. All of the elements are in place for Ocean Front to become a premier L.A. destination. Specializes in fettuccine, crispy river salmon, applewood bacon-wrapped Chilean sea bass. Hrs: 7 am-2:30 pm, 6-10:30 pm. Res accepted. Wine, beer. Bkfst, lunch $12-$18; dinner $15-$28. Children's menu. Entertainment. Cr cds: A, C, D, DS, MC, V.

D

★★ **P.F. CHANG'S CHINA BISTRO.** *326 Wilshire Blvd (90401). 310/395-1912. www.pfchangs.com.* Specializes in Chang chicken in soothing lettuce wraps, lemon pepper shrimp, Mongolian beef. Hrs: 11 am-11 pm; Fri, Sat to midnight. Wine, beer. Lunch, dinner $2.95-$12.95. Entertainment. Handpainted murals, life-size, terracotta replicas of warriors. Cr cds: A, D, MC, V.

D

★★★ **ROCKENWAGNER.** *2435 Main St (90405). 310/399-6504. www.rockenwagner.com.* Specialties: crab souffle; napoleon of salmon, potatoes, tomatoes and spinach. Hrs: 11:30 am-2:30 pm, 6-9:45 pm; Mon from 6 pm; Sat 5:30-10:30 pm; Sun 5:30-9:30 pm; Sat, Sun brunch 9 am-2:30 pm. Closed Dec 25. Res accepted. Serv bar. A la carte entrees: lunch $8.50-$12.50, dinner $17.50-$23. Sat, Sun brunch $7.50-$12.50. Valet parking. Outdoor dining. Modern decor. Totally nonsmoking. Cr cds: A, D, MC, V.

D

★ **TEASERS.** *1351 3rd St Promenade (90401). 310/394-8728.* Hrs: 11:30 am-midnight; Fri-Sun to 1 am; early-bird dinner 4:30-6 pm. Closed Thanksgiving, Dec 25. Res accepted. Bar. Lunch $6.50-$9, dinner $6.50-$14.95. Children's menu. Specialties: Southwest chicken platter, Alfredo pasta, Sunday pot roast. Own breads. Entertainment Tues, Wed, Fri-Sun. Sports bar. Casual atmosphere. Cr cds: A, D, DS, MC, V.

D

★★★ **VALENTINO.** *3115 Pico Blvd (90405). 310/829-4313. www.welovewine.com.* Contemporary Italian menu. Own baking, pasta. Hrs: 5:30-11:30 pm; Fri also noon-3 pm. Closed Sun; hols. Bar. Wine list. Res accepted. A la carte entrees: dinner $20-$29.50. Prix fixe: dinner $65. Valet parking. Cr cds: A, D, MC, V.

D

★ **WOLFGANG PUCK CAFE.** *1323 Montana Ave (90403). 310/393-0290. www.wolfgangpuck.com.* Hrs: 11:30 am-10 pm; Fri, Sat to 11 pm; Sun to 9:30 pm. Closed Nov 26, Dec 25. Res accepted. Bar. A la carte entrees: lunch, dinner $8.50-$18.95. Children's menu. Specialties: Chinois chicken salad, smoked salmon, wild mushroom tortellini. Modern decor. Totally nonsmoking. Cr cds: A, D, MC, V.

D

Santa Nella (A-2)

Pop 500 **Area code** 209 **Zip** 95322

Motels/Motor Lodges

★★ **BEST WESTERN ANDERSEN'S INN.** *12367 S Hwy 33 (95322). 209/826-5534; fax 209/829-1448; res 800/528-1234.* 94 rms, 2 story. S $61; D $72; each addl $7; under 18 free. Crib free. Pet accepted, some restrictions. TV; cable (premium). Heated pool. Complimentary continental bkfst. Restaurant adj 7 am-10 pm.

Ck-out 11 am. Private patios, balconies. Cr cds: A, C, D, DS, MC, V.

D

★★ **RAMADA INN MISSION DE ORO.** *13070 South Hwy 33, at I-5 (95322). 209/826-4444; fax 209/826-8071; res 888/298-2054.* 159 rms, 2 story. S $49-$59; D $59-$69; each addl $10; under 13 free. Pet accepted; $10. TV; cable (premium). Heated pool; whirlpool. Playground. Restaurant 6:30 am-10 pm. Bar 2 pm-2 am. Ck-out noon. Coin Indry. Meeting rms. Sundries. Some private patios, balconies. Spanish-style mission structure. Cr cds: A, C, D, DS, MC, V.

D

Restaurant

★ **PEA SOUP ANDERSEN'S.** *12411 S Hwy 33 (95322). 209/826-1685.* Hrs: 7 am-10 pm; Fri-Sun to 11 pm; Sun brunch 10 am-2 pm. Res accepted. Bar. Bkfst $3.45-$9.50, lunch, dinner $7-$16. Sun brunch $9.95. Children's menu. Specializes in pea soup, salads, sandwiches. Gift and wine shop. Danish decor, windmill, heraldic flags. Cr cds: A, DS, MC, V.

D SC

Santa Rosa

(F-2) *See also Calistoga, Healdsburg, Petaluma, Sonoma*

Settled 1829 **Pop** 113,313 **Elev** 167 ft **Area code** 707

Information Sonoma Valley Visitors Bureau, 453 First St, 95476; 707/996-1090

Web www.sonoma.com

Surrounded by vineyards and mountains, the county seat of Sonoma County is within minutes of more than 150 wineries. The rich soil and even climate of the Sonoma Valley lured famed horticulturist Luther Burbank here to develop innumerable new and better plants. Many farm and ranch products originate from the area today.

What to See and Do

Luther Burbank Home & Gardens. Features work of the famous horticulturist who lived and worked in Santa Rosa. Site incl greenhouse, gardens, carriage house exhibits. Gift shop. Home tours (Apr-Oct, Tues-Sun). Gardens (daily, all yr; free). Santa Rosa and Sonoma aves. Phone 707/524-5445. ¢¢

Snoopy's Gallery. Houses a museum of Charles Schulz's original drawings of the *Peanuts* characters; awards and trophies. Gift shop. (Daily; closed hols) 1665 W Steele Ln. Phone 707/546-3385. **FREE**

Sonoma County Museum. Regional history and art museum of Sonoma County and northern California. Changing exhibits. Guided tours (by appt). Special events throughout the yr. (Wed-Sun; closed hols) 425 7th St. Phone 707/579-1500. ¢

Special Events

Luther Burbank Rose Festival. Three days of art and flower shows, parade. Mid-May.

Sonoma County Fair. Horse racing Mon-Sat, exhibits, stock shows, rodeos, entertainment. Phone 707/528-3247. Late July-early Aug.

Motels/Motor Lodges

★★ **BEST WESTERN GARDEN INN.** *1500 Santa Rosa Ave (95404). 707/546-4031; fax 707/526-4903; toll-free 800/929-2771.* 78 rms. June-Oct: S, D $69-$89; suites $140-$150; each addl $6; under 12 free; lower rates rest of yr. Crib free. Pet accepted, some restrictions; $10. TV; cable (premium). 2 pools. Coffee in rms. Restaurant 6:30-11 am. Coin Indry. Business servs avail. Health club privileges. Some refrigerators. Some patios. Cr cds: A, C, D, DS, MC, V.

D SC

★★ **FLAMINGO RESORT HOTEL.** *2777 4th St (95405). 707/545-8530; fax 707/528-1404; toll-free 800/848-8300. www.flamingoresort.com.* 170 rms, 2 story. Apr-Oct: S, D $199-$249; each addl $10; suites $149-$199; under 12 free (up to 2); monthly rates; lower rates rest of yr. Crib free. TV; cable (premium), VCR avail. Pool; wading pool, whirlpool, poolside serv. Restaurant 6:30 am-10 pm. Bar. Ck-out 11 am. Meeting rms. Business center. In-rm modem link. Beauty shop. 5 tennis courts. Golf privileges. Exercise rm; steam rm, sauna. Lawn games. Refrigerators. Microwaves avail. Balconies. Gardens. Totally nonsmoking. Cr cds: A, D, MC, V.

★ **LOS ROBLES LODGE.** *1985 Cleveland Ave (95401). 707/545-6330; fax 707/575-5826; toll-free 800/255-6330.* 104 units, 2 story. May-Oct: S $75-$90; D $85-$105; each addl $10; under 16 free; lower rates rest of yr. Crib free. Pet accepted, some restrictions. TV; cable, VCR avail. Heated pool; wading pool, whirlpool, poolside serv. Complimentary coffee in rms. Restaurant 6 am-10 pm. Bar 11 am-midnight; entertainment. Ck-out noon. Coin lndry. Meeting rms. Business servs avail. In-rm modem link. Valet serv. Exercise equipt. Refrigerators; microwaves avail. Private patios, balconies; many overlook pool. Cr cds: A, C, D, DS, JCB, MC, V.

★ **SUPER 8.** *2632 N Cleveland Ave (95403). 707/542-5544; fax 707/542-9738; res 800/800-8000.* 100 rms, 3 story. Apr-Oct: S $50-$60; D $54-$65; suites $85-$90; under 12 free; lower rates rest of yr. Crib free. TV; cable. Pool. Restaurant 6 am-10 pm. Ck-out 11 am. Business servs avail. Health club privileges. Microwaves avail. Cr cds: A, D, DS, MC, V.

Hotels

★★★ **FOUNTAINGROVE INN.** *101 Fountain Grove Pkwy (95403). 707/578-6101; fax 707/544-3126; toll-free 800/222-6101. www.fountaingroveinn.com.* 126 units, 2 story. S, D $109-$159; each addl $10; suites $165-$275; under 13 free. Crib free. TV; cable, VCR avail. Heated pool; whirlpool, poolside serv. Complimentary bkfst buffet. Restaurant (see also EQUUS). Rm serv from 6 am. Entertainment. Ck-out noon. Meeting rms. Business center. In-rm modem link. Valet serv. Sundries. Free local airport, bus depot transportation. Tennis privileges. 18-hole golf privileges, greens fee $75-$110. Health club privileges. Refrigerators. Redwood sculpture, waterfall in lobby. Equestrian theme. Cr cds: A, D, DS, JCB, MC, V.

★★★ **HILTON SONOMA COUNTY/SANTA ROSA.** *3555 Round Barn Blvd (95403). 707/523-7555; fax 707/569-5550; toll-free 800/445-8667. www.sonomacounty.hilton.com.* 246 rms, 3 story. S $119-$139; D $129-$149; each addl $15; suites $250-$300; under 18 free. Crib free. TV; cable (premium). Pool; whirlpool. Coffee in rms. Restaurant 6:30 am-10 pm. Bar 2:30 pm-1:30 am. Ck-out noon. Valet serv. Tennis privileges. 18-hole golf privileges, pro, greens fee $45-$70. Exercise equipt. Health club privileges. Bathrm phones; some refrigerators; microwaves avail. Cr cds: A, C, D, DS, MC, V.

★★ **HOTEL LA ROSE.** *308 Wilson St (95401). 707/579-3200; fax 707/579-3247; toll-free 800/527-6738. www.hotellarose.com.* 49 rms, 4 story, 11 suites. May-Oct: S $119-$179; D $134-$194; each addl $15; suites $219; lower rates rest of yr. Crib $10. TV; cable, VCR avail. Complimentary bkfst. Restaurant (see also JOSEF'S). Rm serv 24 hrs. Bar. Ck-out noon. Lndry facilities. Meeting rms. Business center. In-rm modem link. Health club privileges. Microwaves avail. In historic Railroad Square. Cr cds: A, C, D, DS, MC, V.

★★★ **VINTNERS INN.** *4350 Barnes Rd (95403). 707/575-7350; fax 707/575-1426; toll-free 800/421-2584. www.vintnersinn.com.* 44 rms, 2 story. S, D $168-$208; each addl $20; under 6 free. Crib $6. TV; VCR avail (movies). Complimentary continental bkfst. Restaurant (see also JOHN ASH AND CO). Bar. Ck-out noon. Meeting rms. Business servs avail. In-rm modem link. Valet serv. Bellhops. Concierge. Tennis privileges. Golf privileges, greens fee $32-$55 (incl cart), pro. Whirlpool. Health club privileges. Refrigerators; many fireplaces. Private patios, balconies. Views of vineyards, courtyard with fountain. Cr cds: A, D, MC, V.

B&Bs/Small Inns

★★★ **THE GABLES.** *4257 Petaluma Hill Rd (95404). 707/585-7777; fax 707/584-5634.* 3 rms, 4 suites, 1 cottage. No rm phones. S, D $135; each addl $25; suites $135-$225. Complimentary full bkfst. Ck-out 11 am, ck-in 3-6 pm. Picnic tables. House of 15 gables in Gothic Revival style (1877) with unusual keyhole window in each gable. Interior boasts 12-ft ceilings, Italian marble fireplaces, and mahogany spiral staircase. Antique furnishings and fixtures. Whirlpool in cottage. Totally nonsmoking. Cr cds: A, D, DS, MC, V.

D

★★★ **KENWOOD INN & SPA.** *10400 Sonoma Hwy, Kenwood (95452). 707/833-1293; fax 707/833-1247; toll-free 800/353-6966.* 12 rms, 2 story. No rm phones. Apr-Oct: S, D $325-$350; each addl $35; suite $425; spa plans; 2-day min wkends; lower rates rest of yr. Adults only. Pool; whirlpool. Sauna. Complimentary full bkfst. Restaurant nearby. Ck-out 11 am, ck-in 3 pm. Luggage handling. Concierge serv. Business servs avail. Spa. Balconies. Totally nonsmoking. Cr cds: A, MC, V.

D

Restaurants

★★ **CA BIANCA ITALIAN RESTAURANT.** *835 2nd St (95404). 707/542-5800.* Italian menu. Specializes in homemade bread and pasta. Hrs: 11 am-2:30 pm, 5-10 pm. Wine, beer. A la carte entrees: lunch $7-$15, dinner $9-$15. Outdoor dining. In Victorian house built 1876. Cr cds: A, DS, MC, V.

D

★ **CAFE CITTI.** *9049 Sonoma Hwy, Kenwood (95452). 707/833-2690.* Italian menu. Specialties: rotisserie chicken, homemade pasta, dessert. Hrs: 11 am-3:30 pm, 5-9 pm ; Fri, Sat to 9:30 pm. Closed hols. Wine, beer. A la carte entrees: lunch $5-$12, dinner $9-$16. Parking. Outdoor dining. Totally nonsmoking. Cr cds: MC, V.

D

★★ **CRICKLEWOOD.** *4618 Old Redwood Hwy (95403). 707/527-7768.* Specializes in prime rib, steak, seafood. Salad bar. Hrs: 11:30 am-2:30 pm, 5-9:30 pm; Fri to 10 pm; Sat, Sun 5-10 pm. Closed Easter, Thanksgiving, Dec 25. Bar to 10 pm. Lunch $4.95-$7.95, dinner $8.95-$20. Parking. Outdoor dining. Cr cds: A, MC, V.

D

★★ **EQUUS.** *101 Fountaingrove Pkwy (95403). 707/578-0149. www.FountaingroveInn.com.* Wine country cuisine. Specializes in dishes made from local meats and produce. Hrs: 11:30 am-2:30 pm, 5:30-9:30 pm; Fri to 10 pm; Sat 5:30-10 pm; Sun brunch 10 am-2 pm. Res accepted. Bar. Wine list. Lunch $7.95-$11.95, dinner $15.95-$25. Pianist wkends. Parking. Elegant dining; equine mural and original oils. Totally nonsmoking. Cr cds: A, C, D, DS, ER, MC, V.

D

★★ **FABIANI.** *75 Montgomery Dr (95404). 707/579-2682.* Italian menu. Specializes in pasta, seafood. Hrs: 11 am-2 pm, 5-10 pm; Sat from 5 pm. Closed Sun; Jan 1, Thanksgiving, Dec 25. Res accepted. Wine, beer. A la carte entrees: lunch $6.50-$13, dinner $7.50-$14.50. Parking. Patio dining. Totally nonsmoking. Cr cds: MC, V.

★★ **GARY CHU'S.** *611 5th St (95404). 707/526-5840. www.sterba.com/sro/garychu.* Chinese menu. Specialties: orange-peel beef, walnut prawns, sweet basil chicken. Hrs: 11:30 am-9:30 pm. Closed Mon; July 4, Thanksgiving, Dec 25. Wine, beer. A la carte entrees: lunch $6.75-$7.25, dinner $7.50-$10.95. Chinese decor. Totally nonsmoking. Cr cds: A, D, MC, V.

★★★ **JOHN ASH & CO.** *4330 Barnes Rd (95403). 707/527-7687. www.johnashco.com.* Wine country cuisine. Hrs: 11:30 am-2 pm, 5:30-9:30 pm; Mon from 5:30 pm; Fri, Sat to 10 pm; Sun from 10:30 am. Res accepted. Bar. Wine cellar. A la carte entrees: lunch $9.95-$15.95, dinner $15.95-$26.95. Sun brunch $9.95-$15.95. Parking. Outdoor dining. View of vineyards. Totally nonsmoking. Cr cds: A, D, MC, V.

D

★★ **JOSEF'S.** *308 Wilson St (95401). 707/571-8664. www.josefs.com.* Continental menu. Specializes in fresh fish, veal, spaetzle. Hrs: 11:30 am-2 pm, 5:30-9 pm; Mon from 5:30 pm; Fri, Sat to 9:30 pm. Closed Sun; hols. Res accepted. Bar. Lunch $8.50-$12.50, dinner $14.50-$22. Patio dining. Intimate, European-style restaurant with mahogany bar. Totally nonsmoking. Cr cds: A, MC, V.

D

★★ **KENWOOD.** *9900 Sonoma Hwy, Kenwood (95452). 707/833-6326.* Continental menu. Specializes in California cuisine with French influence. Hrs: 11:30 am-9 pm. Closed Mon, Tues; Jan 1, Thanksgiving, Dec 25. Res accepted. Bar. Extensive Sonoma Valley wine selection. A la carte entrees: lunch, dinner $4.75-$25. Parking. Outdoor dining. Totally nonsmoking. Cr cds: MC, V.

D

★★ **LA GARE.** *208 Wilson St (95401). 707/528-4355.* French, Continental menu. Specialties: baked salmon, beef Wellington. Hrs: 5:30-10 pm; Fri, Sat from 5 pm; Sun 5-9 pm. Closed Mon, Tues; Jan 1, Thanksgiving, Dec 25. Res accepted. Dinner $11.25-$18.95. Children's menu. Totally nonsmoking. Cr cds: A, MC, V.

D

★★ **LISA HEMENWAY'S BISTRO.** *1612 Terrace Way (95404). 707/526-5111. www.lisahemenway.com.* Sonoma County cuisine. Specializes in seafood, pasta. Hrs: 11:30 am-2:30 pm, 5:30-9:30 pm; Sun brunch 11 am-2:30 pm. Closed Jan 1, Dec 25. Res accepted. Lunch $7.95-$13.95, dinner $15.95-$23. Sun brunch $6.95-$16.95. Outdoor dining. Totally nonsmoking. Cr cds: A, D, MC, V.

D

★★ **MISTRAL.** *1229 N Dutton Ave (95401). 707/578-4511. www.mistral restaurant.com.* Mediterranean menu. Specializes in grilled seafood, homemade pasta, fresh local produce. Hrs: 11:30 am-9:30 pm; Sat 5:30-10 pm; Sun 5-9 pm. Closed hols. Res accepted. Beer. Wine list. A la carte entrees: lunch $7.75-$11.75, dinner $8.75-$15.75. Children's menu. Outdoor dining on brick terrace with stone fountain. Totally nonsmoking. Cr cds: A, D, DS, MC, V.

D

★★ **MIXX-AN AMERICAN BISTRO.** *135 4th St (95401). 707/573-1344. www.sterba.com/sro/mixx.* Specializes in fresh fish, local lamb, pasta. Own desserts. Hrs: 11:30 am-2 pm, 5:30-9:30 pm; Fri to 10:30 pm; Sat from 5:30 pm. Closed Sun, Dec 25. Res accepted. Bar from 5 pm. Wine list. Lunch $4-$19, dinner $3.95-$25. Children's menu. Art deco decor. Totally nonsmoking. Cr cds: A, D, MC, V.

D

★ **OLD MEXICO EAST.** *4501 Montgomery Dr (95409). 707/539-2599.* Mexican, American menu. Specialties: prawns rancheros, chimichangas, quesadillas. Hrs: 11 am-10 pm; Fri, Sat to 11 pm; Sun to 9 pm. Res accepted. Bar to 2 am. Lunch $5, dinner $6.50-$14. Children's menu. Parking. Outdoor dining. Family-owned. Cr cds: A, DS, MC, V.

D

★★ **TOPOLOS RUSSIAN RIVER VINEYARDS.** *5700 Gravenstein Hwy, Forestville (95436). 707/887-1562.* California, Greek menu. Specializes in Greek dishes, seafood. Hrs: 11:30 am-2:30 pm, 5:30-9:30 pm; Sun brunch 10:30 am-2:30 pm; off-season days vary. Res accepted. Complete meals: lunch $7.50-$10.50, dinner $10-$20. Sun brunch $8-$10.50. Children's menu. Entertainment. Parking. Outdoor dining. Own herb garden. Garden area with many native plants. Family-operated winery and restaurant. No A/C. Totally nonsmoking. Cr cds: A, D, DS, MC, V.

D

★★ **WILLOWSIDE CAFE.** *3535 Guerneville Rd (95401). 707/523-4814.* Hrs: 5:30-9 pm. Closed Mon, Tues; also 3 wks Jan. Res accepted. Wine, beer. A la carte entrees: dinner $11.95-$17.95. Parking. Eclectic decor. Totally nonsmoking. Cr cds: MC, V.

D

San Ysidro (San Diego) (F-6)

Area code 619

Information Chamber of Commerce, 663 E San Ysidro Blvd, 92173; 619/428-1281

Just across the border from Tijuana, San Ysidro reflects the combined influences of the United States and Mexico.

This community is an integral part of San Diego, but is regarded by many as a separate entity.

Motels/Motor Lodges

★★ **AMERICANA INN AND SUITES.** *815 W San Ysidro Blvd, San Ysidro (92173). 619/428-5521; fax 619/428-0693; toll-free 800/553-3933.* 125 units, 2 story, 15 suites. July-Sept: S, D $35-$42; each addl $5; suites $59-$89; under 16 free; lower rates rest of yr. Crib free. TV; cable (premium). Heated pool; whirlpool. Complimentary continental bkfst. Restaurant adj open 24 hrs. Ck-out noon. Coin lndry. Refrigerators, wet bars; microwaves avail. Cr cds: A, C, D, DS, MC, V.

★ **ECONOMY INN.** *230 Via de San Ysidro, San Ysidro (92173). 619/428-6191; fax 619/428-0068; toll-free 888/884-7440.* 121 rms, 2 story. S, D $28-$50; family rates; higher rates: wkends, special events. Pet accepted; $10/day. TV; cable (premium). Heated pool. Complimentary coffee in lobby. Restaurant adj open 24 hrs. Ck-out 11 am. Coin lndry. Cr cds: A, DS, MC, V.

D

★★ **INTERNATIONAL MOTOR INN.** *190 E Calle Primera, San Ysidro (92173). 619/428-4486; fax 619/428-3618.* 92 rms, 2 story, 35 kit. units. S, D $52; each addl $3; kit. units $50-$56; under 18 free. Crib free. Pet accepted. TV; cable (premium), VCR avail. Complimentary coffee in rms. Restaurant adj open 24 hrs. Ck-out 11 am. Business servs avail. Sundries. Coin lndry. Pool; whirlpool. Refrigerators. Cr cds: A, C, D, DS, MC, V.

D SC

Saratoga

(see San Francisco map) *See also Palo Alto, Redwood City, San Jose, Santa Clara, Sunnyvale*

Pop 28,061 **Elev** 455 ft **Area code** 408 **Zip** 95070

Information Chamber of Commerce, 20460 Saratoga-Los Gatos Rd; 408/867-0753

Web www.saratogachamber.org

An early California lumber town nestled in the lush, redwood-covered foothills of the Santa Cruz Mountains, Saratoga was named after Saratoga, New York, when mineral springs were found nearby. Located just 26 miles east of the Pacific Coast, this quaint town offers many restaurants and cultural activities in the tranquillity of the romantic Santa Clara Valley. Visitors enjoy strolling through the village Main Street with its historic homes and intriguing shops.

What to See and Do

Big Bear State Park. (see) 18 mi W on CA 9.

Hakone Gardens. Japanese gardens, pond, bridge, Japanese-style houses, waterfall, picnic area. (Daily; closed hols) 21000 Big Basin Way. Phone 408/741-4994. **¢¢**

Villa Montalvo. (1912) Mediterranean-style summer house of Senator James D. Phelan. Now a cultural center with art galleries, concerts, plays, lectures, poetry readings, artists in residence. Formal gardens with hiking trails, arboretum, outdoor amphitheater, and Carriage House Theatre. Grounds (daily; free). Galleries (Wed-Sun afternoons; closed Jan 1, Thanksgiving, Dec 25). 15400 Montalvo Rd, ½ mi S, just off CA 9. Phone 408/961-5800. **FREE**

Special Event

Villa Montalvo Performing Arts. Winter and summer series. Phone 408/961-5858. Jan-Oct.

B&B/Small Inn

★★★ THE INN AT SARATOGA. *20645 Fourth St (95070). 408/867-5020; fax 408/741-0981; toll-free 800/543-5020.* 45 rms, 5 story, 4 suites. S, D $175-$195; suites $435-$475; under 18 free. Crib free. TV; cable (premium), VCR (free movies). Complimentary continental bkfst; afternoon refreshments. Restaurants nearby. Ck-out noon, ck-in 3 pm. Meeting rms. Business servs avail. In-rm modem link. Valet serv. Concierge. Bathrm phones, refrigerators. Balconies. Patio. All rms are oversized, each overlooking Saratoga Creek and a wooded park. Totally nonsmoking. Cr cds: A, C, D, MC, V.

D

Restaurants

★★★ LA MERE MICHELLE. *14467 Big Basin Way (95070). 408/867-5272. www.lameremichelle.com.* French, Continental menu. Specializes in veal, beef, seafood. Own pastries. Hrs: 11:30 am-2 pm, 6-9:30 pm; Fri, Sat 6-10 pm; Sun 11 am-2 pm (brunch), 5:30-9 pm. Closed Mon; hols. Res accepted. Bar. Wine list. A la carte entrees: lunch $7.50-$13.50, dinner $17.50-$24.50. Sun brunch $8.50-$13.50. Entertainment Fri, Sat. Elegant French decor. Family-owned. Patio dining. Cr cds: A, D, DS, MC, V.

D

★★★ LE MOUTON NOIR. *14560 Big Basin Way (95070). 408/867-7017. www.lemoutonnoir.com.* French menu. Specialties: duck confit, Grand Marnier souffle. Hrs: 6-9 pm; Sat 11:30 am-2 pm, 5-9 pm. Closed Jan 1, Thanksgiving, Dec 25. Res accepted. Wine list. A la carte entrees: lunch $10.95-$18.95, dinner $20.95-$28.95. Complete meal: dinner $69.95. Valet parking. Outdoor dining. French country atmosphere. Fireplace. Totally nonsmoking. Cr cds: A, D, DS, MC, V.

D

★★★ PLUMED HORSE. *14555 Big Basin Way (95070). 408/867-4711. www.plumedhorse.com.* Country French menu. Specializes in fresh game birds, venison, rack of lamb. Own pastries. Hrs: 6-10 pm. Closed Sun; hols. Res accepted. Bar 4 pm-2 am. Wine cellar. A la carte entrees: dinner $17-$34. Prix fixe: dinner $25-$42. Jazz trio. Elegant country decor; originally a stable (1883). Cr cds: A, D, MC, V.

D

★★★ SENT SOVI. *14583 Big Basin Way (95070). 408/867-3110. www.sentsovi.com.* Contemporary French menu. Specialties: braised lamb shank, wild mushroom and black truffle soup. Hrs: 5:30-9:30 pm; Sun 5-9 pm. Closed Mon; hols; also 1st 2 wks Jan. Res accepted. Wine list. A la carte entrees: dinner $24-$30. Street parking. Outdoor dining. Totally nonsmoking. Cr cds: A, MC, V.

D

Sausalito

(see San Francisco map) *See also San Francisco, Tiburon*

Settled 1800 **Pop** 7,152 **Elev** 14 ft **Area code** 415 **Zip** 94965

Information Chamber of Commerce, 29 Caledonia St, 94965; 415/332-0505 or 415/331-7262

Web www.sausalito.org

Sausalito, a picturesque town above San Francisco Bay, is an art colony and residential suburb in the shadow of the Golden Gate Bridge. Whalers first used the cove here. The town's name is a corruption of the Spanish for willows, which flourished here at one time. Sausalito's springs were San Francisco's major source of water for many years.

What to See and Do

Bay Area Discovery Museum. Museum filled with interactive exhibits for kids age one-ten; special focus is on science and discovery. Incl special areas for toddlers and a play area with views of bay and bridge. (Tues-Sun) Fort Baker, 557 E

McReynolds Rd. Phone 415/487-4398. ¢¢¢

San Francisco Bay & Delta Hydraulic Model. Hydraulic model reproduces tidal action, currents, and mixing of salt and fresh water and indicates trends in sediment deposition; the 850-square-mi bay-delta area is duplicated in a three-acre building. Interactive exhibits, nine-min orientation video, and 45-min general information audio tour. Self-guided tour; audio tours avail in six languages: English, French, German, Japanese, Spanish, and Russian. (Tues-Sat) 2100 Bridgeway. Model in operation only during testing. **FREE**

Village Fair. Fascinating and colorful three-story complex of specialty shops selling unusual crafts, artifacts, and imports. The building was once a Chinese gambling hall, opium den, and distillery for bootleg whiskey. Cafeteria. (Daily; closed Thanksgiving, Dec 25) 777 Bridgeway, opp Yacht Harbor.

Special Event

Sausalito Art Festival. Labor Day wkend. Phone 415/332-3555.

Motel/Motor Lodge

★★ ALTA MIRA HOTEL. *125 Bulkley Ave (94966). 415/332-1350; fax 415/331-3862.* 35 rms, 2 story, 14 cottages. No A/C. S, D, cottages $90-$200; each addl $10. TV; cable. Restaurant 7 am-11 pm. Bar. Ck-out noon. Meeting rm. Business servs avail. Bellhops. Valet parking. Fireplace in cottages. Some balconies. On hillside above city; view of bay from many rms. Cr cds: A, D, MC, V.

B&Bs/Small Inns

★★★ CASA MADRONA HOTEL. *801 Bridgeway (94965). 415/332-0502; fax 415/332-2537. www.casamadrona.com.* 29 rms, 5 cottages, 2 with kit. S, D $188; cottages $188-$205. TV; VCR avail (free movies). Parking $7. Complimentary bkfst. Restaurant (see MIKAYLA). Ck-out noon, ck-in 3 pm. Meeting rm. Business servs avail. Luggage handling. Valet serv. Concierge serv. Whirlpool. Refrigerators, fireplaces. Many balconies, decks. Victorian house (1885); antiques. Cr cds: A, D, DS, ER, MC, V.

D

★★★ THE INN ABOVE TIDE. *30 El Portal (94965). 415/332-9535; fax 415/332-6714; toll-free 800/893-8433. www.innabovetide.com.* 30 rms, 3 story. S, D $215; suites $325-$445; 2-day min wkends. Crib free. TV; cable (premium), VCR avail. Complimentary continental bkfst; afternoon refreshments. Restaurant adj 7 am-9 pm. Ck-out noon, ck-in 3 pm. Luggage handling. Concierge serv. Massage. Business servs avail. In-rm modem link. Parking $8. Minibars. Balconies. Picnic table. Built over water, rooms provide view of bay and San Francisco. Totally nonsmoking. Cr cds: A, D, MC, V.

D

Restaurants

★★ HORIZONS. *558 Bridgeway (94965). 415/331-3232.* Specializes in fresh seafood. Hrs: 11 am-10 pm; Fri to 11 pm; Sat, Sun 10 am-10 pm. Closed Thanksgiving, Dec 25. Bar. Lunch, dinner $6.50-$25. Daily brunch $7.25-$14. Entertainment Fri, Sat eves. Valet parking. Outdoor dining. View of San Francisco, East Bay. Family-owned. No A/C. Cr cds: A, D, MC, V.

D

★★★ MIKAYLA. *801 Bridgeway (94965). 415/331-5888.* American cuisine with west coast influence. Own baking. Hrs: 6-10 pm; Sun brunch 10 am-2:30 pm. Res accepted. Wine list. A la carte entrees: dinner $14.95-$21.50. Sun brunch $24.50. Valet parking $3. Outdoor dining. View of bay. Cr cds: A, D, DS, MC, V.

★★★ ONDINE. *558 Bridgeway Dr (94965). 415/331-1133. www.ondinerestaurant.com.* Specializes in fusion cooking. Hrs: 5:30 pm-1 am, Sat, Sun 5-10 pm, Sun brunch 10 am-2 pm. Res required. Wine, beer. Dinner $28-$45. Brunch prix fixe $28. Entertainment. Original yachthouse. Cr cds: A, D, DS, MC, V.

D

★★ SCOMA'S. *588 Bridgeway (94965). 415/332-9551.* Specializes in seafood, pasta. Hrs: 11:30 am-9:30

pm; Tues, Wed from 5:30 pm. Closed Thanksgiving, Dec 25-Jan 1. Bar. Lunch $7-$15, dinner $15-$32. Children's menu. Landmark Victorian building at end of wharf; view of bay. Family-owned. Cr cds: A, D, DS, MC, V.

D

★★ **SPINNAKER.** *100 Spinnaker Dr (94965). 415/332-1500. www.thespinnaker.com.* Specializes in fresh seafood, fresh pasta. Hrs: 11 am-11 pm; Sun brunch to 3 pm. Closed Thanksgiving, Dec 24-25. Res accepted. Bar. A la carte entrees: lunch $7.95-$16.95, dinner $9.95-$18.95. Sun brunch $6.75-$12. Children's menu. Valet parking. View of bridges and bay. Family-owned. Cr cds: A, D, DS, MC, V.

D

★★ **SUSHI RAN.** *107 Caledonia St (94965). 415/331-3620. www.sushiran.com.* California cuisine. Specializes in seafood, sake. Hrs: 11:45 am-2:30 pm, 5:30-11 pm; Sun 5:30-10:30 pm. Res accepted. Wine, beer. Lunch $15-$20; dinner $25-$30. Entertainment. Cr cds: A, DS, MC, V.

D

★ **WINSHIPS.** *670 Bridgeway (94965). 415/332-1454. www.winships.com.* Specializes in soups, fresh seafood, pasta. Hrs: 8 am-3 pm; Sun brunch to 1 pm. Closed Thanksgiving, Dec 25. Res accepted. Bar. Bkfst $5.95-$11.95, lunch $5.95-$15.95. Sun brunch $3.50-$12.95. Children's menu. Nautical decor; ship models, marine artifacts. Family-owned. Totally nonsmoking. Cr cds: A, D, DS, MC, V.

D

Sequoia & Kings Canyon National Parks

(B-4) *See also Porterville, Three Rivers*

(55 mi E of Fresno on CA 180; 35 mi E of Visalia on CA 198)

Although independently established, Sequoia and Kings Canyon National Parks are geographically and administratively one. Lying across the heart of the Sierra Nevada in eastern central California, they comprise more than 1,300 square miles and include more than 25 isolated groves of spectacular giant sequoias, towering granite peaks, deep canyons, and hundreds of alpine lakes. Giant sequoias reach their greatest size and are found in the largest numbers here. Mount Whitney, 14,495 feet, is the highest point in the lower 48 states. Some rocks of the foothill and summit area indicate that this whole region once lay under the ocean.

Allow plenty of driving time due to the gradient into and out of the mountains. Limited groceries are available all year in both parks. Gasoline may not be available; inquire before entering. Camping (no trailer hookups) is restricted to designated areas. Many of the campgrounds are closed by snow, Oct-late May. Winter visitors should carry tire chains. Entry fee valid for seven days. For information contact Sequoia and Kings Canyon National Parks, Three Rivers 93271; 559/565-3134.

What to See and Do

Boyden Cavern. A 45-min tour on lighted, handrail-equipped trail through ornate chambers with massive stalagmites, stalactites, and columns. (Daily) Located in King's River Canyon, in Sequoia National Forest between Grant Grove and Cedar Grove. Phone 209/736-2708. ¢¢¢

Cedar Grove. Towering peaks rise a mile high above the stream. Horses, pack animals. Hiking trails. Road closed Nov-Apr. In canyon of South Fork of Kings River.

Fishing. Trout are abundant in a few lakes and streams; the most popular spots are along Kings River and the forks of the Kaweah River. Some stores in the park sell state fishing licenses.

Foothills, Lodgepole, and Grant Grove visitor centers. Exhibits, photos, data about the parks; expert advice on how to organize sightseeing. Schedules of campfire talks and guided trips are posted here. (Daily) Phone 559/565-3134.

General Grant Grove. Incl the General Grant Tree, 267 ft tall with a cir-

Avenue of the Giants

cumference of 108 ft. Saddle rides. Hiking trails.

Giant Forest. One of the finest groves of giant sequoias. The General Sherman Tree is the largest living thing on earth. At 275 ft high and 103 ft in circumference, it is estimated to be 2,300-2,700 yrs old. Moro Rock, Crescent Meadow, Crystal Cave, and Tokopah Valley are in this section of the park. Horses, pack animals avail at Wolverton Pack Station. Hiking trails.

The high country. Vast region of wilderness, mountains, canyons, rivers, lakes, and meadows, accessible by trail. The Sierra Crest forms the eastern boundary.

Redwood Mountain Grove. Incl the Hart Tree, a large sequoia; accessible by trail.

Motels/Motor Lodges

★ **CEDAR GROVE LODGE.** *Hwy 180 (93633). 559/561-3311; fax 559/565-0101; res 559/335-5500.* 21 rms, 2 story. No rm phones. Late Apr-Oct: S, D $93.25; each addl $6; under 12 free. Closed rest of yr. Crib free. Restaurant 7 am-8 pm. Ck-out 11 am. Coin lndry. Gift shop. Picnic tables, grills. Cr cds: DS, MC, V.

D

★ **GRANT GROVE VILLAGE.** *5755 E Kings Canyon (93633). 559/561-3311; fax 559/452-1353; toll-free 888/252-5757.* 63 rms, 24 cottages. No A/C. No elvtrs. No rm phones. S, D $80-$85; each addl $8; cottages without kit. unit $35-$55; under 12 free. Crib free. Restaurant 7 am-9 pm. Ck-out 11 am. Sundries. Gift shop. X-country ski on-site. Fireplace in cottages. Picnic tables. Totally nonsmoking. Cr cds: MC, V.

Solvang

(D-3) *See also Lompoc, Santa Barbara*

Founded 1911 **Pop** 4,741 **Elev** 495 ft **Area code** 805 **Zip** 93463

Information Information Center, 1511-A Mission Dr, PO Box 70, 93464; 800/468-6765

Web www.solvangusa.com

Founded by Danes from the Midwest in 1911, a corner of Denmark has been re-created here. Solvang is a community of picturesque Danish-style buildings, which include four windmills. Rich Danish pastries and Danish imports are featured in its shops.

What to See and Do

Lake Cachuma Recreation Area. Swimming pool (summer), fishing, boating (rentals). General store. Camping (hookups). Fees for some activities. (Daily) 6 mi E on CA 246, then 6 mi S on CA 154. Per vehicle day use ¢¢

Old Mission Santa Inés. (1804) Established by Fray Estevan Tapis as the 19th mission. A gold adobe building with red-tiled roof, garden, and arched colonnade in front. Used as a church; many artifacts, manuscripts, and vestments on exhibit; recorded tour. (Daily; closed hols) 1760 Mission Dr. Phone 805/688-4815.

Special Events

Solvang Theaterfest. 420 Second St. The Pacific Conservatory of the Performing Arts (PCPA) presents musicals, dramas, new works, and classics in an outdoor theater. Phone 805/922-8313. Early June-early Oct.

Danish Days Festival. Danish folk dancing, singing, band concerts; parade on Sat. Third wkend Sept. Phone 805/688-6144.

Motels/Motor Lodges

★★ **BEST WESTERN PEA SOUP ANDERSEN.** *51 E Hwy 246, Buellton (93427). 805/688-3216; fax 805/688-9767; res 800/528-1234. www.bestwestern.com.* 97 rms, 2 story. May-Sept: S, D $59-$89; each addl $10; under 12 free; lower rates rest of yr. Crib $5. TV; cable (premium). Heated pool; whirlpool. Complimentary continental bkfst. Coffee in rms. Restaurant 7 am-10 pm. Bar from 11 am. Ck-out noon. Business servs avail. Sundries. Putting green. Some refrigerators; microwaves avail. Private patios. Grill, picnic area, gazebo. Cr cds: A, C, D, DS, ER, MC, V.

D

★★ **CHIMNEY SWEEP INN.** *1564 Copenhagen Dr (95476). 805/688-2111; fax 805/688-8824; toll-free 800/824-6444.* 56 units, 1-2 story, 6 kit. cottages. S, D $85-$145; each addl $10; suites $115-$165; kit. cottages $155-$275; wkends (2-day min). Crib $5. TV; cable (premium). Whirlpool. Complimentary continental bkfst. Coffee in rms. Ck-out 11 am-noon. Business servs avail. Health club privileges. Swimming privileges. Microwaves; many in-rm whirlpools in kit. cottages. Cr cds: A, DS, MC, V.

D SC

★★★ **COUNTRY INN & SUITES.** *1455 Mission Dr (93463). 805/688-2018; fax 805/688-1156; res 800/456-4000. www.rimcorp.com.* 82 rms, 3 story, 9 suites. S, D $148-$158; each addl $10; suites $185; under 12 free; golf plans. Crib free. Pet accepted; $25. TV; cable, VCR (movies $4). Heated pool; whirlpool. Complimentary full bkfst. Restaurant 6:30-9:30 am. Ck-out noon. Meeting rms. Business servs avail. In-rm modem link. Garage parking. Refrigerators. Balconies. Country inn elegance. Sitting rm. Antiques. Cr cds: A, C, D, DS, MC, V.

D

★★ **DAYS INN WINDMILL.** *114 East Hwy 246, Buellton (93427). 805/688-8448; fax 805/686-1338; res 800/329-7466.* 108 rms, 2 story. Mar-Aug: S $42-$86; D $48-$92; each addl $8; suites $98-$156; under 12 free; lower rates rest of yr. Crib free. TV; cable. Heated pool; whirlpool. Complimentary continental bkfst wkends. Bar 4 pm-2 am. Ck-out noon. Coin lndry. Meeting rms. Business servs avail. Sundries. Microwaves avail. Patios, balconies. Danish-style architecture. Cr cds: A, C, D, DS, MC, V.

D

★★ **ROYAL COPENHAGEN.** *1579 Mission Dr (93463). 805/688-5561; fax 805/688-7029; toll-free 800/624-6604.* 48 units, 1-2 story. S, D $80-$90; each addl $5; suites $110. TV; cable. Heated pool. Complimentary continental bkfst. Restaurant nearby. Ck-out 11 am. Business servs avail. Danish motif. Large rose garden. Cr cds: A, DS, MC, V.

D

Hotel

★★★ **MARRIOTT RANCHO SANTA BARBARA .** *555 McMurray Rd, Buellton (93427). 805/688-1000. www.marriott.com.* 149 rms, 4 story; 27 suites. S, D $150-$275; each addl $15; suites $295; under 17 free. Crib avail. Pool. TV; cable (premium), VCR avail. Complimentary coffee in rms, newspaper. Restaurant 6 am-10:30 pm. Bar. Ck-out 11 am. Meeting rms. Business center. Valet serv. Gift shop. Exercise rm. Golf. Some refrigerators, minibars. Cr cds: A, C, D, DS, MC, V.

★★★ **ROYAL SCANDINAVIAN INN.** *400 Alisal Rd (93464). 805/688-8000; fax 805/688-0761; toll-free 800/624-5572. www.solvangrsi.com.* 133 rms, 3 story. June-Sept: S, D $84-$179; each addl $10; suites $135-$245; under 18 free; golf plan; lower rates rest of yr. Crib free. TV; cable (premium), VCR avail. Heated pool; whirlpool. Restaurant (see ROYAL SCANDIA). Bar 11-1:30 am; entertainment. Ck-out 11 am. Meeting rms. Business servs avail. Valet serv. Refrigerator, wet bar in suites. Many patios, balconies. Custom-made Danish furniture. Cr cds: A, C, D, DS, MC, V.

D SC

B&Bs/Small Inns

★★★ **THE BALLARD INN.** *2436 Baseline Ave, Ballard (93463). 805/688-7770; fax 805/688-9560; toll-free 800/638-2466. www.ballardinn.com.* 15 rms, 1-2 story. Rm phones avail. S $170; D $250; each addl $50; golf plan; wkends, hols (2-day min). TV and VCR in sitting rm. Complimentary full bkfst; afternoon refreshments. Dining rm 6-9 pm; closed Mon, Tues. Ck-out noon, ck-in 3 pm. Luggage handling. Business servs avail. 18-hole golf privileges. Mountain bikes avail. Games in parlor. Individually decorated rms, each with theme of local history. Totally nonsmoking. Cr cds: A, MC, V.

D

★★ **FESS PARKER'S WINE COUNTRY INN.** *2860 Grand Ave, Los Olivos (93441). 805/688-7788; fax 805/688-1942; toll-free 800/446-2455. www.fessparker.com.* 21 rms, 2 story. S $175-$275, D $175-$295; suite $340; package plans. Crib free. TV; cable, VCR avail. Heated pool; whirlpool, poolside serv. Complimentary full bkfst; afternoon refreshments. Dining rm 8 am-2:30 pm, 5:30-9 pm; Sat, Sun 8 am-3 pm, 5:30-10 pm. Ck-out noon, ck-in 2 pm. Meeting rms. Business servs avail. Luggage handling. Golf privileges. Health club privileges. Bicycles avail. Fireplaces. Library. Elegant decor with many antiques; extensive landscaping. Totally nonsmoking. Cr cds: A, MC, V.

★★★ **PETERSEN VILLAGE INN.** *1576 Mission Dr (93463). 805/688-3121; fax 805/688-5732; toll-free 800/321-8985.* 42 rms, 3 story. S, D $125-$195; suites $195-$235. Children over 7 yrs only. TV; cable (premium), VCR avail. Complimentary bkfst buffet. Complimentary coffee in rms. Restaurants nearby. Ck-out 1 pm, ck-in 3 pm. Business servs avail. In-rm modem link. Luggage handling. Health club privileges. Whirlpool, fireplace in suites. Some private patios, balconies. Replica of old Danish village; 28 shops on premises; garden area. Cr cds: A, MC, V.

D

★★ **SVENDSGAARD'S DANISH LODGE.** *1711 Mission Dr (93436). 805/688-3277; fax 805/686-5616; res 800/341-8000.* 48 rms, 3 story, 4 kits. S, D $58-$103; each addl $6; suites, kit. units $66-$107; golf plan. Crib free. TV; cable. Heated pool; whirlpool. Complimentary continental bkfst. Coffee in rms. Restaurant nearby. Ck-out 11 am. Business servs avail. Refrigerators; some microwaves, fireplaces. Private balconies. Sun deck. Mission opp.

Guest Ranch

★★★ **ALISAL GUEST RANCH & RESORT.** *1054 Alisal Rd (93463). 805/688-6411; fax 805/688-2510; res 805/688-6411. www.alisal.com.* 73 units. No A/C. No rm phones. MAP (2-day min): S $285, D $375; each addl: 3-6 yrs $40, over 6 yrs $65; under 3 free; package plans. Crib free. TV in lounge; cable, VCR avail. Heated pool; whirlpool, poolside serv in season, lifeguard in summer. Supervised children's activities (June-Labor Day, hols). Coffee in rms. Restaurant 7:30-10 am, 6:30-9 pm (jacket dinner); closed to public. Cookouts in season, picnic lunches, bkfst rides. Snack bar at golf course. Bars 11 am-midnight. Ck-out 1 pm, ck-in 4 pm. Guest lndry. Meeting rm. Business servs avail. Bellhops. Tennis, pro. 36-hole golf, greens fee $75, cart $26, pro, putting green. Fly-fishing, canoes, kayaks, sailboats, rowboats, windsurfing. Indoor, outdoor games. Hayrides. Horseback trail rides. Bicycle rentals. Health club privileges. Adult, child rec rms. Entertainment nightly. Winery tours. Fireplaces, refrigerators. Library. 10,000-acre working ranch, up to 2,000 head of cattle, petting zoo. Large private lake. Cr cds: A, C, D, MC, V.

D

Restaurants

★★ **ANDERSEN'S.** *376 Ave of the Flags, Buellton (93427). 805/688-5581. www.silcom.com/~splitpea.* Danish, American menu. Specialties: split pea soup, Danish sausage sandwich, pot roast. Hrs: 7 am-10 pm; early-bird dinner (Mon-Thurs) 4-7 pm. Bar. A la carte entrees: $3.95-$6.95, lunch $5.95-$7.95, dinner $7.95-$16.95. Children's menu. Parking. Outdoor dining. Totally nonsmoking. Cr cds: A, DS, MC, V.

D SC

★★ **CABERNET BISTRO.** *478 Fourth Pl (93463). 805/693-1152.* Specializes in French dishes. Hrs: 5:30 pm-1 am; Sun-Tues, Thurs to 9 pm. Closed Wed. Res accepted. Wine, beer. Dinner $13.95-$24.95. Children's menu. Entertainment. In historical abode house. Cr cds: A, DS, MC, V.

D SC

★ **LINTON'S RESTAURANT & LOUNGE.** *1547 Mission Dr (93463). 805/688-4311.* Danish menu. Specializes in Wiener schnitzel, pasta Valerie, steak Diane. Hrs: 11 am-9 pm. Res accepted. Wine, beer. Lunch $5.95-$12.95; dinner $12.95-$22.95. Children's menu. Cr cds: A, D, DS, MC, V.

D

★★ **MASSIMI'S RISTORANTE.** *2375 Alamo Pintado Ave, Los Olivos (93441). 805/693-1941.* Specializes in osso bucco, pasta, cioppino. Hrs: 11:30 am-3 pm, 5:30-9:30 pm; Sun from 5:30 pm. Res accepted. Wine, beer. Lunch $6.50-$11; dinner $13-$21. Entertainment. Cr cds: A, MC, V.

D

★★ **MOLLERKROEN.** *435 Alisal Rd (93463). 805/688-4555.* Danish, American menu. Specializes in open-face Danish sandwiches, smorgasbord. Hrs: 11:30 am-9 pm. Closed Dec 25. Res accepted. Bar to midnight. Lunch $3.95-$9.95. Complete meals: dinner $9.50-$18.95. Children's menu. Family-owned since 1973. Cr cds: A, D, DS, MC, V.

D

★ **MUSTARD SEED.** *1655 Mission Dr (93463). 805/688-1318.* Specializes in omelets, soup, salad. Hrs: 7 am-2:30 pm, 4:30-9 pm. Closed Thanksgiving, Dec 25. Res accepted. Wine, beer. Bkfst $3.25-$6.25, lunch $3.95-$6.95, dinner $6.95-$10.95. Children's menu. Parking. Outdoor dining. Casual dining. Cr cds: MC, V.

D

★ **ROYAL SCANDIA.** *400 Alisal Rd (93464). 805/688-8000. www.solvangrsi.com.* Hrs: 7 am-9 pm; Sun brunch 11 am-2 pm. Res accepted, required hols. Danish, American menu. Bar 11 am-midnight. Bkfst $4.95-$7.25, lunch $5.25-$9.25, dinner $10.95-$19.95. Sun brunch $12.95. Children's menu. Specializes in fresh salmon, prime rib, smorgasbord. Salad bar. Entertainment. Outdoor dining. Scandinavian decor. Totally nonsmoking. Cr cds: A, D, DS, MC, V.

D SC

★★★ **THE VINTAGE ROOM.** *2860 Grand Ave, Los Olivos (93441). 805/688-7788. www.fessparker.com.* Specializes in eclectic dishes. Hrs: 8-10:30 am, 11:30 am-2:30 pm, 5-9 pm; Fri, Sat to 1 am; Sun brunch 10:30 am-2:30 pm. Res accepted. Wine list. Lunch $8-$15; dinner $24-$36. Brunch $10.50-$13.50. Children's menu. Entertainment. Cr cds: A, MC, V.

D

Sonoma

(F-3) *See also Calistoga, Napa, Petaluma, St. Helena, Santa Rosa*

Founded 1823 **Pop** 8,121 **Elev** 84 ft **Area code** 707 **Zip** 95476

Information Sonoma Valley Visitors Bureau, 453 First St E; 707/996-1090

Web www.sonomavalley.com

Mission San Francisco Solano (1823) was secularized under Mariano Guadalupe Vallejo in 1834. Vallejo had been sent by Governor Figueroa to investigate Russian activities at Fort Ross (see FORT ROSS STATE HISTORIC PARK). This mission was the last and most northerly of the 21 Franciscan missions in California and the only one established under Mexican rule. On June 14, 1846, Sonoma was the scene of the Bear Flag Revolt—establishing the California Republic, which lasted until July 9.

Sonoma Valley is the birthplace of the California wine industry. More than 40 premium wineries can be found here amongst 18,000 acres of vineyards.

What to See and Do

Haraszthy Villa. Villa built in 1861 by Count Agoston Haraszthy has been re-created; also vineyard and gazebo. Picnicking. (Wed, Sat, Sun) E via Napa St, then N on Old Winery Rd, in Bartholomew Memorial Park. **FREE**

Jack London State Historic Park. Memorial, "House of Happy Walls," and grave of author. Wolf House ruins, Jack London cottage; farm building; winery structure ruins located in beautiful Valley of the Moon. Hiking trails. Park (daily). Museum (daily; closed Jan 1, Thanksgiving, Dec 25). 2400 London Ranch Rd. 8½ mi W on CA 12, then 1½ mi W of Glen Ellen on London Ranch Rd. Phone 707/938-5216. **¢¢¢**

Sears Point Raceway. Motor sports entertainment, incl NASCAR Cup, NHRA drag racing, SCCA pro and amateur road races, AMA and AFM motorcycle events, vintage car races, amateur drag racing, car clubs. Under 12 yrs with adult only. (Daily; closed Dec 25) CA 37 and CA 121. **¢¢¢¢¢**

Sonoma State Historic Park. General Vallejo's house (1851-1880), W Spain St and 3rd St W; Mission San Francisco Solano (1823-1846), barracks (1840-1846), E Spain St and 1st St E; other buildings on and near Sonoma Plaza. Picnicking. (Daily; closed Jan 1, Thanksgiving, Dec 25) Phone 707/938-1519. **¢**

Train Town. Steam- or diesel-powered miniature railroad makes 20-min run through landscaped park with animals, waterfalls, and historic replica structures. (June-Sept, daily; rest of yr, Fri-Sun) 20264 Broadway. Phone 707/938-3912. **¢¢**

Wineries.

Buena Vista Winery. Cellars built in 1857. Historical panels, tasting rm, art gallery, picnic area. Concerts in summer; special events. Tours (daily; closed Jan 1, Thanksgiving, Dec 25). 18000 Old Winery Rd, 1½ mi E. Phone 707/938-1266. **FREE**

Gloria Ferrer Champagne Caves. Guided tours through "champagne caves" (inquire for schedule); wine tasting. (Daily; closed Thanksgiving, Dec 25, also early Jan) 23555 CA 121, 6 mi S. Phone 707/996-7256. **FREE**

Sebastiani Sonoma Cask Cellars. Large collection of carved casks. Guided tours; tasting rm and aging cellars may be visited. Free tram ride to winery from Sonoma Plaza. (Daily; closed hols) 389 4th St E. Phone 707/938-5532. **FREE**

Special Event

Valley of the Moon Vintage Festival. Sonoma Plaza. California's oldest wine festival. Parades, wine tasting, folk dancing. Sept. Phone 707/996-2109.

Motels/Motor Lodges

★★ BEST WESTERN SONOMA VALLEY INN. *550 2nd St W (95476). 707/938-9200; fax 707/938-0935; toll-free 800/334-5784.* 75 rms, 2 story. Apr-Dec: S, D $119-$249; each addl $10; under 12 free; lower rates rest of yr. Crib free. Pet accepted; $15/day. TV; cable (premium). Pool; whirlpool. Complimentary continental bkfst in rms. Restaurant nearby. Ck-out noon. Free guest lndry facilities. Business servs avail. Valet serv. Exercise equipt. Refrigerators; many fireplaces; some in-rm whirlpools; microwaves avail. Private patios, balconies. Totally nonsmoking. Cr cds: A, C, D, DS, MC, V.

D

★ EL PUEBLO. *896 W Napa St (95476). 707/996-3651; fax 707/935-5988; toll-free 800/900-8844.* 38 units, 2 story. Apr-Oct: S $75-$90; D $80-$110; each addl $10; lower rates rest of yr. Crib $5. TV; cable. Heated pool. Complimentary coffee in rms. Restaurant nearby. Ck-out noon. Business servs avail. Microwaves avail. Cr cds: A, D, DS, MC, V.

D

Resorts

★★★ THE LODGE AT SONOMA RENAISSANCE HOTEL & SPA. *1325 Broadway (95476). 707/935-6600. www.renaissancehotels.com.* 180 rms, 2 story. S, D $195-$350; each addl $25; under 17 free. Crib avail. Pool. TV; cable (premium), VCR avail. Complimentary coffee in rms, newspaper.

Restaurant 6 am-10:30 pm. Bar. Ck-out noon. Meeting rms. Business center. Valet serv. Gift shop. Exercise rm. Some refrigerators, minibars. Cr cds: A, C, D, DS, MC, V.

★★★★ SONOMA MISSION INN & SPA. *18140 Sonoma Hwy (95476). 707/938-9000; fax 707/938-4250; toll-free 800/862-4945. www.sonomamissioninn.com.* 165 rms, 3 story, 63 suites. Apr-Oct: D $449; suites $1200; each addl $30; under 12 free; lower rates rest of yr. Crib avail. Valet parking avail. Pool, whirlpool. TV; cable (premium), VCR avail. Complimentary newspaper. Restaurant 6-9:30 pm. Bar. Ck-out noon, ck-in 4 pm. Meeting rms. Business center. Bellhops. Concierge serv. Dry cleaning. Gift shop. Salon/barber avail. Exercise rm, sauna, steam rm. Golf, 18 holes. Bike rentals. Cr cds: A, C, D, JCB, MC, V.

D

B&Bs/Small Inns

★★★★ GAIGE HOUSE INN. *13540 Arnold Dr, Glen Ellen (95442). 707/935-0237; fax 707/935-6411; res 800/935-0237. www.gaige.com.* Located in the beautiful Sonoma Valley, this tranquil oasis with its well-manicured grounds is a relaxing getaway. It offers a beautiful pool and whirlpool, hammocks, a large deck with lounge chairs, and a 24-hour cook. 13 rms, 2 with shower only, 3 story. Apr-Oct: S, D $170-$250; each addl $25; lower rates rest of yr. Children over 12 yrs only. TV in parlor. Pool; whirlpool. Complimentary full bkfst; afternoon refreshments. Restaurant nearby. Ck-out 11 am, ck-in 3-7 pm. Concierge serv. Twin parlors. Built in the late 1890s; antiques. Totally nonsmoking. Cr cds: A, D, DS, MC, V.

★★ THISTLE DEW. *171 W Spain St (95476). 707/938-2909; fax 707/996-8413; toll-free 800/382-7895. www.thistledew.com.* 6 rms, 3 with shower only, 1 suite. Mar-Nov: S, D $125-$135; each addl $30; suite $180; lower rates rest of yr. Complimentary full bkfst. Restaurant nearby. Ck-out noon, ck-in 3 pm. Luggage handling. Concierge serv. Bicycle. Many fireplaces. Many balconies. Picnic tables, grills. Built in 1869. Antique furniture. Totally nonsmoking. Cr cds: A, MC, V.

D

★★ TROJAN HORSE. *19455 Sonoma Hwy (95476). 707/996-2430; fax 707/996-9185; toll-free 800/899-1925. www.trojanhorseinn.com.* 6 rms. No rm phones. Apr-mid-Nov: S, D $148-$175; each addl $20; lower rates rest of yr. Crib $20. Complimentary full bkfst, evening refreshments. Restaurant nearby. Ck-out 11 am, ck-in 3 pm. Business servs avail. Whirlpool. Picnic tables. Restored pioneer family home (1887); period antiques. Totally nonsmoking. Cr cds: A, D, DS, MC, V.

SC

★★ VICTORIAN GARDEN INN. *316 E Napa St (95476). 707/996-5339; fax 707/496-1689; res 800/543-5339. www.victoriangardeninn.com.* 4 rms, 2 story. No rm phones. S $109; D $199. Complimentary full bkfst. Ck-out noon, ck-in 2-5 pm. Business servs avail. Exercise equipt. Whirlpool. Private patios. Picnic tables. Former farmhouse (1870); gardens. Totally nonsmoking. Cr cds: A, D, JCB, MC, V.

Restaurants

★★ CAFE AT SONOMA MISSION INN. *18140 Sonoma Hwy (95476). 707/938-9000. www.sonomamissioninn.com.* Hrs: 7 am-9:30 pm; Sun brunch to 3 pm. Res accepted. Bar. A la carte entrees: bkfst $6.50-$12.50, lunch $8-$14, dinner $9-$21. Sun brunch $7-$14. Children's menu. Specialties: apple oatcakes, pizza from wood-burning oven. Casual atmosphere. Totally nonsmoking. Cr cds: A, D, MC, V.

D

★ CAFE LAHAYE. *140 E Napa St (95476). 707/935-5994. www.cafelahaye.com.* Hrs: 5:30-9:30 pm; Sat 11:30 am-2:30 pm, 5:30-9:30 pm; Sun 10 am-2 pm. Closed Mon; hols. Res accepted (dinner only). Eclectic menu. Wine, beer. Lunch $5.95-$8.95, dinner $11.95-$16.95. Specialty: seared black pepper-lavender filet of beef with gorgonzola potato gratin. Street parking. Original art. Totally nonsmoking. Cr cds: MC, V.

D

SONOMA PLAZA

A walk around Sonoma Plaza—California's largest and prettiest town square—combines local history with opportunities to sample foods of the Wine Country and relax in a shady park. Begin at the corner of Spain Street and First Street East, where you'll find the Sonoma Mission (its formal name is Mission San Francisco de Solano). The mission, which is open daily for tours, dates back to 1823. It is the last and farthest north of the 21 Franciscan missions that dot the state from San Diego to the northern San Francisco Bay Area. The Sonoma Cheese Factory is on Spain Street, just west of the mission. Stop in to watch the production of Sonoma Jack Cheese and perhaps pick up some picnic supplies. Continuing west on Spain Street, you'll pass the Sonoma Barracks, which were built in 1836 (when California was still a Mexican outpost) to quarter Mexican army troops. Walk another 1/2 mile west on Spain Street (a 10- to 15-minute walk beyond the plaza) to reach Lachryma Montis. This splendidly furnished 1852 Gothic-Victorian home belonged to General Mariano Vallejo, the charismatic figure who commanded the aforementioned Mexican troops. California's last Mexican governor, General Vallejo laid out the original Sonoma Plaza in 1834. Guided tours of the house are available, and there are picnic facilities in the gardens where you can enjoy the supplies you picked up at Sonoma Jack Cheese. Continuing on, retrace your steps back to the northwest corner of the plaza (Spain Street and First Street West) to the Sonoma Hotel, a three-story 19th-century adobe whose furnishings reflect the era (step into the lobby for a look around). Across the intersection (heading south on First Street West) is the El Dorado Hotel, an 1843 white-trimmed adobe built by Don Salvador Vallejo, brother of the general. Unlike the Sonoma Hotel, this hotel's interior has been modernized. Continue walking around the plaza counterclockwise until you return to the Sonoma Mission. Your stroll will take you past a variety of restaurants and shops, many located in restored adobes. Besides the Sonoma Cheese Factory, there are several places to buy picnic food and ice cream. If you like, you can carry your snacks to the park that occupies the center of the plaza, where you'll find plenty of green grass, shade trees, two children's playgrounds, and a duck pond. The Sonoma Valley Visitors Bureau has an office at 453 First Street East, on the eastern side of the plaza.

★★ **DELLA SANTINA'S.** *133 E Napa St (95476). 707/935-0576.* Hrs: 11 am-9:30 pm. Closed hols. Res accepted. Italian menu. Wine, beer. A la carte entrees: lunch $4.75-$13.25, dinner $4.75-$16.25. Children's menu. Specializes in Tuscan cuisine, rotisserie. Own pasta, desserts. Street parking. Outdoor dining. Fountain on patio. Totally nonsmoking. Cr cds: D, MC, V.

D

★★ **THE DEPOT HOTEL CUCINA RUSTICA.** *241 1st St W (95476). 707/938-2980. www.depothotel.com.* Hrs: 11:30 am-2 pm, 5-9:30 pm; Sat, Sun from 5 pm. Closed Mon, Tues; Jan 1, Dec 25. Res accepted. Northern Italian menu. Beer, wine. A la carte entrees: lunch $6.75-$14.50, dinner $7.75-$18.50. Children's menu. Parking. Outdoor dining around pool. Historic stone building (1870); originally a hotel, later a saloon and private residence. Restored in 1962. Herb and vegetable garden. Chef-owned. Cr cds: A, MC, V.

D

★★ **DEUCE.** *691 Broadway (95476). 707/933-3823.* Hrs: 11:30 am-9 pm. Closed Dec 25. Res accepted. Contemporary American menu. Bar. A la carte entrees: lunch $4.95-$11.95, dinner $4.95-$19.95. Children's menu. Specialties: beet salad, onion-crusted chicken breast, club steak. Outdoor dining. Unique woodwork. Totally nonsmoking. Cr cds: A, MC, V.

D

★★★ **GENERAL'S DAUGHTER.** *400 W Spain St (95476). 707/938-4004.* Hrs: 11:30 am-9:30 pm; Fri, Sat to 10:30 pm; Sun brunch 11 am-2:30 pm. Closed Dec 25. Res accepted. Bar. Wine list. Lunch, dinner $8-$22.50. Sun brunch $8-$15. Specializes in lamb chops, flatbread, local produce. Parking. Casual elegance in 1874 building; patio dining with views of landscaped grounds. Totally nonsmoking. Cr cds: MC, V.

D

★★ **THE GIRL & THE FIG.** *110 W Spain St (95476). 707/938-3634. www.thegirlandthefig.com.* Hrs: 5:30-9 pm; Sat, Sun brunch 10 am-2:30 pm. Closed Thanksgiving, Dec 25. Res accepted. Country French bistro menu. Wine, beer. A la carte entrees: dinner $12.95-$19.95. Sat, Sun brunch $6.50-$15.95. Children's menu. Specializes in fresh local meats, seafood, cheese. Parking. Outdoor dining. Art changes every 6 wks. Totally nonsmoking. Cr cds: A, MC, V.

D

★★ **GLEN ELLEN INN.** *13670 Arnold Dr, Glen Ellen (95442). 707/996-6409. www.glenelleninn.com.* Hrs: 5:30-9:30 pm. Closed Wed in winter. Res accepted. Wine, beer. A la carte entrees: dinner $11.95-$23.95. Specialties: smokin' chicken Napoleon, wild mushroom and sausage purse, grilled filet mignon. Outdoor dining. Intimate cottage. Totally nonsmoking. Cr cds: A, MC, V.

D

★ **LA CASA.** *121 E Spain St (95476). 707/996-3406. www.lacasarestaurant.com.* Hrs: 11:30 am-10 pm. Closed Thanksgiving, Dec 25. Res accepted. Mexican menu. Bar. Lunch, dinner $4-$13. Children's menu. Specialties: fresh snapper Veracruz, tamales, chimichangas. Mexican decor. Outdoor dining. Cr cds: A, D, DS, MC, V.

D

California vineyard

★ **MES TROIS FILLES.** *13648 Arnold Dr, Glen Ellen (95442). 707/938-4844.* Hrs: 5-9:30 pm. Closed Mon, Tues. Res accepted. Country French, Continental menu. Wine, beer. A la carte entrees: dinner $14.50-$20.50. Children's menu. Specialties: smoked salmon terrine and cilantro cream in wasabi-dill, wild mushroom ravioli. Street parking. Intimate dining. Totally nonsmoking. Cr cds: MC, V.

D

★★ **PIATTI.** *405 First St W (95476). 707/996-2351. www.piatti.com.* Hrs: 11:30 am-10 pm; Fri, Sat to 11 pm. Res accepted. Italian menu. Bar. A la carte entrees: lunch $9.95-$16.95, dinner $11.95-$22.95. Children's menu. Specialties: ravioli with lemon cream, lasagne al pesto. Outdoor dining. Italian country atmosphere. Totally nonsmoking. Cr cds: A, D, MC, V.

D

★★★ **THE RESTAURANT.** *18140 Sonoma Hwy, Boyes Hot Springs (95416). 707/938-9000. www.sonomamissioninn.com.* Hrs: 6-9:30 pm; Sun brunch 10 am-2 pm. Res accepted. Bar 11 am-11 pm. Wine cellar. A la carte entrees: dinner $22-$29. Sun brunch $7-$20. Complete meals: dinner $40. Specializes in wine country cuisine featuring local seafood, game, produce. Own baking. Pianist. Valet parking. Totally nonsmoking. Cr cds: A, MC, V.

D

★★ **SAFFRON.** *13648 Arnold Dr, Glen Ellen (95442). 707/938-4844.* California cuisine menu. Specializes in Spanish dishes. Hrs: 5-9 pm. Closed Sun, Mon. Res accepted. Dinner $14-$20. Entertainment. Small, intimate. Cr cds: MC, V.

D

★★ **SONOMA MERITAGE.** *522 Broadway (95476). 707/938-9430.* Specializes in Northern Italian, Southern French entrees. Oyster bar. Res accepted. Wine list. Hrs: 11:30 am-3 pm, 5:30-9 pm. Closed Tues. Lunch $7-$19; dinner $9-$45. Brunch

$5-$19. Children's menu. Entertainment: Jazz. Cr cds: A, MC, V.
D

★ **ZINOS RESTAURANT ON THE PLAZA.** *420 1st St E (95476). 707/996-4466.* Hrs: 11 am-10 pm. Res accepted; required wkends. Italian menu. Lunch $7.50-$12.50, dinner $9.50-$16. Specializes in pasta, seafood. Bistro-style dining in converted storefront. Patio dining. Totally nonsmoking. Cr cds: A, D, DS, MC, V.
D SC

Sonora

(F-5) *See also Modesto, Oakdale*

Settled 1848 **Pop** 4,153 **Elev** 1,825 ft **Area code** 209 **Zip** 95370

Information Tuolumne County Visitors Bureau, 542 W Stockton Rd, PO Box 4020; 209/533-4420 or 800/446-1333

Mexican miners named this the Sonoran Camp for their home state. Mexicans, Chileans, and Americans did not mix well and the camp became peaceful only after the varied groups dispersed. At the Big Bonanza, richest pocket mine in the Mother Lode, $160,000 in nearly pure gold was harvested in a single day. Stretching across seven hills, this colorful town, the seat of Tuolumne County, was the setting for several tales by Mark Twain and Bret Harte.

What to See and Do

Calaveras Big Trees State Park. State park featuring groves of giant sequoias; hiking, x-country skiing, camping. Contact Box 120, Arnold 95223. Along Hwy 4, 4 mi NE of Arnold. Phone 209/795-2334. ¢¢¢¢

Columbia State Historic Park. The 1850 gold town of Columbia is restored to its early glory. The gold boom brought stages, freight wagons, brick stores, all the facilities of civilization,and thousands of gold-hungry miners. Operating gold mine tour; gold panning; stagecoach ride; concessions (fees). Free slide show in museum. Guided tours (summer, wkends). Most of the buildings are open (daily; closed Thanksgiving, Dec 25; some shops closed wkdays in winter). 4 mi N via CA 49 and Parrotts Ferry Rd. Phone 209/532-4301. **FREE** Among the 40 buildings on the self-guided tour are

City Hotel. Refitted as period restaurant and hotel. Phone 209/532-1479.

Eagle Cotage. *[sic]* Reconstructed boardinghouse. Outside viewing only. Phone 209/532-4301.

Firehouse. Tuolumne Engine Co #1 and pumper "Papeete." **FREE**

Schoolhouse. (1860). One of the oldest of its kind in the state; in use until 1937; authentically refurnished. Phone 209/532-4301. **FREE**

Don Pedro Lake Recreation Area. A 26-mi-long lake impounded by 580-ft dam. Swimming (fee), fishing, boat launching (marinas); picnicking, camping (fee; hookups). No pets. (Daily) Fee for activities. 13 mi S off CA 120. Phone 209/852-2396. ¢¢

Mercer Caverns. Stalagmites, stalactites, aragonite, other formations in caves discovered in 1885. Ten rms; lighted walkways; 55°F; 45-min guided tours. Picnic area. (June-Sept, daily; rest of yr, wkends and school hols; closed Thanksgiving, Dec 25) 10 mi N on CA 49, then 5 mi NE on CA 4. Phone 209/728-2101. ¢¢¢

Moaning Cavern. Discovered in 1849. View formations from 100-ft spiral staircase. Walking tour (45 min). Visitors may also descend into the cavern via 180-ft rope rappel; or take a three-hr tour into the undeveloped cavern depths (by appt). Display of Native American and mining artifacts. (Daily) 5350 Moaning Cave Rd, 12 mi N near Vallecito. Phone 209/736-2708. ¢¢¢

New Melones Lake Recreation Area. When full, the lake offers more than 100 mi of shoreline for water and fishing sports, as well as seven-lane launch ramps, fish-cleaning facilities, and a marina. During low lake levels, river rafting is popular on the Stanislaus River. Improved camping and day-use facilities avail in the Glory Hole and Tuttletown recreation areas. (All yr, daily; some sections of day-use areas and campgrounds may be closed during winter) 10 N via CA 49, situated between Angels Camp, Sonora, and Columbia. Phone 209/536-9094. ¢¢¢

Railtown 1897 State Historic Park. Steam passenger train rides (daytime, one hr; evening, two hrs) over the Sierra foothills. Roundhouse tour. Park (daily). Rides (Mar-Nov, Sat, Sun, hols). Res necessary for eve rides. Combination tickets avail. 3 mi S in Jamestown at 5th Ave and Reservoir Rd. Phone 250/953-2720. ¢¢¢

Skiing.

Bear Valley. Two triple, seven double chairlifts, two surface lifts; patrol, school, rentals; restaurant, cafeteria, concession area, bar; lodging. Longest run three mi; vertical drop 1,900 ft. (Nov-Apr, daily) 17 mi NW on CA 49, then 50 mi E on CA 4. x-country skiing also avail in area. Phone 209/753-2301. ¢¢¢¢¢

Dodge Ridge. Two triple, five double chairlifts, four rope tows; patrol, school, rentals; cafeteria, bar, day-lodge, nursery. Twenty-eight runs; longest run 2¼ mi; vertical drop 1,600 ft. Snowboarding. (Mid-Nov-mid-Apr, daily) 30 mi E on CA 108. Phone 209/965-3474. ¢¢¢¢¢

Stanislaus National Forest. More than 890,000 acres; contains Emigrant Wilderness, Carson-Iceberg Wilderness, and a portion (22,917 acres) of the Mokelumne Wilderness. The forest has many developed recreation sites with swimming, fishing, boating, rafting; hiking, bridle trails, picnicking, winter sports. More than 40 developed campgrounds (fee). NE and SE of town. For further information contact the Forest Supervisor's Office, 19777 Greenley Rd. Phone 209/532-3671.

Special Events

Fireman's Muster. Antique fire engines, parade, pumping contests. Early May. Columbia State Historic Park. Phone 209/536-1672.

Mother Lode Roundup Parade and Rodeo. Mother's Day wkend. Mother Lode Fairgrounds on CA 108. Phone 800/446-1333.

Mother Lode Fair. Four days mid-July. Fairgrounds.

Calaveras County Fair and Jumping Frog Jubilee. In Angels Camp, 18 mi NW. Fair highlighted by frog-jumping contest, inspired by Mark Twain short story. Contact Box 489, Angels Camp 95222; Phone 209/736-2561 or 800/225-3764. Third wkend May.

Motel/Motor Lodge

★ **DAYS INN.** *160 S Washington St (95370). 209/532-2400; fax 209/532-4542; res 800/329-7466.* 64 rms, 3 story. S, D $49-$79; each addl $5; suites $99-$169; under 18 free; ski plans. Crib avail. Pet accepted; $10. TV; cable (premium). Pool. Complimentary coffee in rms. Restaurant 6 am-10 pm. Bar 4 pm-2 am. Ck-out 11 am. Meeting rms. Some refrigerators. Cr cds: A, D, DS, MC, V.

Hotel

★★ **MURPHYS HISTORIC HOTEL.** *457 Main St, Murphys (95247). 209/728-3444; fax 209/728-1590; toll-free 800/532-7684.* www.*murphyshotel.com.* 29 rms, 20 with A/C, 20 with bath, 20 with rm phones, 1-2 story, 2 suites. S, D $80; each addl $6; suites $75-$90; under 12 free; ski, golf plans. Crib $6. Cable TV in many rms. Complimentary continental bkfst. Restaurant 7 am-9 pm. Bar; entertainment Fri, Sat. Ck-out 11 am. Meeting rms. Business servs avail. Downhill/x-country ski 20 mi. Some balconies. Cr cds: A, C, D, DS, MC, V.

B&Bs/Small Inns

★★ **BARRETTA GARDENS.** *700 S Barretta St (95370). 209/532-6039; fax 209/532-8257; toll-free 800/206-3333. www.barrettagardens.com.* 5 rms, 2 story. S, D $95-$105. Crib free. TV. Complimentary full bkfst; refreshments. Ck-out 11 am, ck-in 3-5 pm. Antiques. 3 parlors, one with fireplace. Solarium, porches looking out on acre of lawns and gardens. Victorian house (1903). Totally nonsmoking. Cr cds: A, MC, V.

★★★ **CITY HOTEL.** *22678 Main St, Columbia (95310). 209/532-1479; fax 209/532-7027; toll-free 800/532-1479. www.cityhotel.com.* 10 rms, 2 story.

No rm phones. S $90-$110; D $95-$115; each addl $10. Crib free. Complimentary continental bkfst; afternoon refreshments. Restaurant (see CITY HOTEL). Bar. Ck-out noon, ck-in 2 pm. Meeting rm. Business servs avail. Luggage handling. Balconies. Restored Gold Rush-era hotel (1856). Many antiques. Totally nonsmoking. Cr cds: A, DS, MC, V.

★★ **FALLON HOTEL.** *11175 Washington St, Columbia (95310). 209/532-1470; fax 209/532-7027; toll-free 800/532-1479. www.cityhotel.com.* 14 rms, 2 story. No rm phones. S, D $90-$95; suite $155; package plans. Crib free. Continental bkfst. Ck-out noon, ck-in 2 pm. Meeting rms. Business servs avail. Concierge serv. Balconies. Established 1857; in Columbia State Historic Park. Totally nonsmoking. Cr cds: A, DS, MC, V.

★★ **HISTORIC NATIONAL HOTEL BED AND BREAKFAST.** *18183 Main St, Jamestown (95327). 209/984-3446; fax 209/984-5620; res 800/894-3446. www.national-hotel.com.* 9 rms, 2 story. No rm phones. S, D $90-$130; each addl $10. Children over 10 yrs only. Pet accepted, some restrictions; $50 deposit. TV avail. Complimentary bkfst. Dining rm 11 am-10 pm; Sun to 9 pm. Bar 9 am-10 pm. Ck-out noon, ck-in 2 pm. Balconies. Continuously operated since 1859. Totally nonsmoking. Cr cds: A, C, D, DS, MC, V.

★★ **JAMESTOWN HOTEL.** *18153 Main St, Jamestown (95370). 209/984-3902; fax 209/984-4149; toll-free 800/205-4901. www.jamestownhotel.com.* 11 rms, 2 story. S, D $110-$140; lower rates Oct-Apr (Sun-Thurs). TV; cable. Complimentary full bkfst. Restaurant. Bar 10 am-10 pm. Ck-out noon, ck-in 2 pm. Balconies. Antique furnishings, lace curtains. Some in-rm whirlpools. Totally nonsmoking. Cr cds: A, D, DS, MC, V.

★ **LAVENDER HILL BED AND BREAKFAST.** *683 Barretta St (95370). 209/532-9024; toll-free 800/446-1333.* 4 rms, 2 story. No rm phones. S $65-$85; D $75-$85; each addl $15; package plans; hols (2-day min). Cable TV in common rm. Complimentary full bkfst; refreshments. Restaurant nearby. Ck-out 11 am, ck-in 2 pm. Luggage handling. Concierge serv. Built in 1900. Totally nonsmoking. Cr cds: A, DS, MC, V.

★★★ **MCCAFFREY HOUSE BED & BREAKFAST INN.** *23251 Highway 108, Twain Harte (95383). 209/586-0757; fax 209/586-3689; toll-free 888/586-0757. www.mccaffreyhouse.com.* 7 rms, 3 story. No elvtr. S $110; D $125; each addl $10; package plans; hols, wkends 2-day min. Crib free. TV; cable, VCR (movies). Complimentary afternoon refreshments. Restaurant nearby. Ck-out 11 am, ck-in 2 pm. Business servs avail. In-rm modem link. Luggage handling. Concierge serv. Downhill ski 19 mi; x-country ski 15 mi. Lawn games. Fireplaces. Many balconies. Picnic tables, grills. Adj to forest. Original art. Totally nonsmoking. Cr cds: A, MC, V.

★★ **PALM HOTEL BED & BREAKFAST.** *10382 Willow St, Jamestown (95327). 209/984-3429; fax 209/984-4929; res 888/551-1851. www.palmhotel.com.* 9 rms, 2 story. No rm phones. S, D $95-$155. TV; cable. Complimentary full bkfst; refreshments. Restaurant nearby. Ck-out 11 am, ck-in 3-6 pm. Business servs avail. Concierge serv. Lawn games. Picnic tables. Built in 1890, remodeled in 1982. Totally nonsmoking. Cr cds: MC, V.

★★ **REDBUD INN.** *402 Main St, Murphys (95247). 209/728-8533; fax 209/728-8132; res 209/728-8533. www.redbudinn.com.* 13 rms, 2 story, 3 suites. No rm phones. Apr-Nov: S, D $90-$160; each addl $15; suites $175-$245; ski, golf plans; hols (2-day min). Crib free. Complimentary full bkfst; afternoon refreshments. Restaurant 11:30 am-10 pm. Ck-out 11 am, ck-in 2-3 pm. Business servs avail. Luggage handling. Street parking. Downhill/x-country ski 20 mi. Massage. Many fireplaces; some in-rm whirlpools, refrigerators, wet bars.

Many balconies. Totally nonsmoking. Cr cds: MC.

Restaurants

★★★ **CITY HOTEL.** *22768 Main St, Columbia (95310). 209/532-1479. www.cityhotel.com.* Hrs: 5-9 pm; Sun brunch 11 am-2 pm. Closed Mon; Dec 24-25. Res accepted. Contemporary French menu. Bar to 11 pm. A la carte entrees: dinner $15-$23. Complete meals: dinner $30-$38. Sun brunch $6-$15. Specializes in California French cuisine. Own baking. Restored Gold Rush-era hotel (1856). Totally nonsmoking. Cr cds: A, DS, MC, V.

D

South Lake Tahoe (Lake Tahoe Area) (E-5)

Pop 21,586 **Elev** 6,260 ft
Area code 530

Motels/Motor Lodges

★★ **BEST WESTERN STATION HOUSE INN.** *901 Park Ave, South Lake Tahoe (96150). 530/542-1101; fax 530/542-1714; res 800/822-5953. www.stationhouseinn.com.* 102 rms, 2 story. June-Oct, hols: S, D $88-$108; each addl $10; suites $125-$200; under 12 free; ski plan; lower rates rest of yr. TV; cable. Heated pool; whirlpool, poolside serv. Complimentary full bkfst. Restaurant 7:30-10:30 am, 5:30-10 pm; Wed to 10:30 am. Bar from 5 pm. Ck-out noon. Meeting rms. Business servs avail. Valet serv. Downhill ski 1 mi; x-country ski 14 mi. Microwaves avail. Private beach 1½ blks. Cr cds: A, C, D, DS, MC, V.

D

★★ **BEST WESTERN TIMBER COVE.** *3411 Lake Tahoe Blvd, South Lake Tahoe (96150). 530/541-6722; fax 530/541-7959; res 800/528-1234. www.timbercovetahoe.com.* 262 rms, 192 with shower only, 3 story. Mid-June-Sept: S, D $100-$160; each addl $10; under 17 free; family rates; ski plans; wkends, hols (2-day min); higher rates special events; lower rates rest of yr. Crib free. TV; cable. Complimentary coffee in rms. Restaurant 6:30 am-2 pm, 5:30-10 pm. Bar 4 pm-midnight. Ck-out noon. Meeting rms. Business servs avail. Bellhops. Concierge. Sundries. Gift shop. Coin lndry. Downhill ski 1 mi; x-country ski 5 mi. Pool; whirlpool, poolside serv. Some fireplaces. Some balconies. On lake. Cr cds: A, DS, MC, V.

D

★ **CEDAR LODGE.** *4069 Cedar Ave, South Lake Tahoe (96150). 530/544-6453; fax 530/542-1290; res 800/222-1177.* 34 rms, 2 story. No A/C. Mid-June-mid-Sept, wkends, hols: S, D $58-$98; each addl $10; ski plans; lower rates rest of yr. TV; cable. Pool; whirlpool (winter). Complimentary coffee in rms. Restaurant nearby. Ck-out noon. Downhill ski 1 mi; x-country ski 15 mi. Some fireplaces. Beach privileges 4 blks. Cr cds: A, DS, MC, V.

★ **DAYS INN.** *3530 Lake Tahoe Blvd, South Lake Tahoe (96150). 530/544-3445; fax 530/544-3466. www.visitlaketahoe.com.* 42 rms. S, D $49-$160; under 12 free; higher rates wkends, hols. Crib $10. TV; cable. Pool. Complimentary continental bkfst. Restaurant nearby. Ck-out 11 am. Downhill ski 2 mi; x-country 14 mi. Microwaves avail. 4 blks to lake. Cr cds: A, D, DS, MC, V.

★★ **FOREST INN SUITES.** *1 Lake Pkwy, South Lake Tahoe (96150). 530/541-6655; fax 530/544-3135; toll-free 800/822-5950.* 118 rms, 3 story, 101 suites. Jan-mid-Apr, mid-June-mid-Sept: S, D $140-$175; suites $130-$225; under 17 free; lower rates rest of yr. Crib free. TV; cable. 2 pools; whirlpool. Complimentary continental bkfst. Coffee in rms. Restaurant nearby. Bar 4-10 pm. Ck-out noon. Meeting rms. Business servs avail. Coin lndry. Downhill ski 2 mi; x-country 5 mi. Exercise equipt; sauna. Game rm. Microwaves; refrigerators in suites. Cr cds: A, C, D, DS, MC, V.

SC

★★ **HOLIDAY INN EXPRESS.** *3961 Lake Tahoe Blvd, South Lake Tahoe (96150). 530/544-5900; fax 530/544-5333. www.basshotels.com/holiday-inn.* 89 rms, 2 story. Mid-June-Aug: S, D $89-$99; kit. suites $129-$179; under 19 free; ski plan; higher rates: wkends, hols; lower rates rest of yr. Crib free. TV; cable (premium). Heated pool in season; whirlpools. Sauna. Complimentary continental bkfst. Coffee in rms. Restaurant adj 6:30 am-midnight. Ck-out noon. Coin lndry. Business servs avail. Downhill ski 1 mi; x-country ski 5 mi. Refrigerators; microwaves avail; some wet bars. Cr cds: A, C, D, DS, JCB, MC, V.

D

★ **MATTERHORN MOTEL.** *2187 Lake Tahoe Blvd, South Lake Tahoe (96150). 530/541-0367; fax 530/541-0367.* 18 rms, 2 story. No A/C. Mid-June-mid-Sept, wkends, hols: S $30-$99; D $39-$99; kit. units $10 addl; lower rates rest of yr. Pet accepted; $10 per day. TV; cable. Pool; whirlpool. Complimentary coffee in lobby. Ck-out 11 am. Business servs avail. Downhill ski 3 mi; x-country ski 10 mi. Microwaves avail. Near marina. Cr cds: A, DS, MC, V.

★★ **QUALITY INN & SUITES.** *3838 Lake Tahoe Blvd, South Lake Tahoe (96150). 530/541-5400 or 530/547-5400; fax 530/541-7170; res 530/541-5400. www.visitlaketahoe.com.* 121 rms, 2 story. S, D $58-$88; kit. units $110-$130; under 12 free; higher rates: wkends, hols. Crib free. TV; cable. Pool. Complimentary coffee in rms. Restaurant. Bar. Ck-out 11 am. Coin lndry. Meeting rms. Business servs avail. Downhill ski 1 mi; x-country ski 13 mi. Lake 4 blks. Cr cds: A, D, DS, JCB, MC, V.

★ **ROYAL VALHALLA MOTOR LODGE.** *4104 Lakeshore Blvd, South Lake Tahoe (96150). 530/544-2233; fax 530/544-1436; toll-free 800/999-4104.* 80 rms, 3 story, 30 kits. (some equipt). No A/C. June-Sept: S, D $82-$108; each addl $10; suites $112-$212; kit. units $5 addl; under 12 free; higher rates hols; lower rates rest of yr. TV; cable. Heated pool; whirlpool. Complimentary continental bkfst, coffee in rms. Restaurant nearby. Ck-out 11 am. Coin lndry. Business servs avail. Sundries. Downhill ski 1½ mi; x-country ski 14 mi. Many private patios, balconies. Private beach. Cr cds: A, C, D, MC, V.

D

★ **TAHOE CHALET INN.** *3860 Lake Tahoe Blvd, South Lake Tahoe (96156). 530/544-3311; fax 530/544-4069; toll-free 800/821-2656.* 66 units, 2 story, 14 suites, 6 kits. Some A/C. Mid-June-Sept and mid-Dec-Mar: S $58-$82; D $82-$88; suites $98-$220; higher rates hols; lower rates rest of yr. TV; cable (premium), VCR avail (movies). Heated pool; whirlpool. Sauna. Complimentary continental bkfst. Restaurant nearby. Ck-out 11 am. Coin lndry. Meeting rms. Business servs avail. Downhill ski 2½ mi. Many refrigerators. Some bathrm phones, wet bars. Some rms with in-rm whirlpool, fireplace. ½ mi to lake. Cr cds: A, C, D, DS, MC, V.

SC

★ **TRAVELODGE.** *3489 Lake Tahoe Blvd, South Lake Tahoe (96156). 530/544-5266; fax 530/544-6985; toll-free 800/578-7878.* 59 rms, 2 story. S, D $49-$110; each addl $5; under 18 free; higher rates: wkends, hols. TV; cable (premium). Heated pool. Complimentary coffee in rms. Restaurant adj 7 am-2 pm. Ck-out noon. Business servs avail. Downhill ski 1 mi; x-country ski 11 mi. Cr cds: A, C, D, DS, ER, JCB, MC, V.

SC

★ **TRAVELODGE.** *4003 US 50 Stateline, South Lake Tahoe (96150). 530/541-5000; fax 530/544-6910; toll-free 800/578-7878.* 66 rms, all with shower only, 2 story. S, D $49-$110; each addl $5; under 18 free; higher rates: wkends, hols. TV; cable (premium). Complimentary coffee in rms. Restaurant nearby. Ck-out noon. Pool. Refrigerators. Lake 3 blks. Cr cds: A, C, D, DS, MC, V.

SC

★ **TRAVELODGE STATELINE.** *4011 Lake Tahoe Blvd, South Lake Tahoe (96150). 530/544-6000; fax 530/544-6869; toll-free 800/982-3466.* 50 rms, 49 with shower only, 2 story. S, D $49-$110; each addl $5; under 18 free; higher rates: hols, special events. TV; cable (premium). Complimentary coffee in rms. Restaurant nearby. Ck-out noon. Pool. Refrigerators. Cr cds: A, C, D, DS, MC, V.

Hotels

★★★ **INN BY THE LAKE.** *3300 Lake Tahoe Blvd, South Lake Tahoe (96150). 530/542-0330; fax 530/541-6596; toll-free 800/877-1466. www.innbythelake.com.* 100 rms, 3 story. June-Sept: S $98-$198, D $128-$198; suites $175-$395; ski, golf plans; lower rates rest of yr. TV; cable (premium). Heated pool; whirlpool. Sauna. Complimentary continental bkfst. Coffee in rms. Restaurant adj 24 hrs. Ck-out noon. Coin lndry. Meeting rm. Business servs avail. In-rm modem link. Valet serv. Sundries. Downhill ski 1½ mi; x-country ski 10 mi. Some refrigerators, wet bars, bathrm phones. Balconies. Picnic area. Lake opp. Cr cds: A, C, D, DS, JCB, MC, V.

★★ **LAKELAND VILLAGE BEACH AND SKI RESORT.** *3535 Lake Tahoe Blvd, South Lake Tahoe (96150). 530/544-1685; fax 530/544-0193; toll-free 800/822-5969. www.lakeland-village.com.* 212 kit. units, 1-3 story. July-Aug, mid-Dec-Mar, hols (2-day min): S, D $135-$875; town houses $170-$530; ski plans; lower rates rest of yr. Crib free. TV; cable (premium). 2 pools, heated; wading pool, 2 whirlpools, sauna. Playground. Coffee in rms. Restaurant adj 7 am-10 pm. Ck-out 11 am. Coin lndry. Meeting rms. Business servs avail. Some garage parking. Tennis, pro. Downhill ski 1½ mi; x-country ski 15 mi. 1½-2 baths in most units. Refrigerators, microwaves, fireplaces. Private patios, balconies. Pier; dock. Private sand beach. Spacious grounds, 19 acres. Cr cds: A, MC, V.

★ **TAHOE COLONY INN.** *3794 Montreal Rd, South Lake Tahoe (96150). 530/544-6481; fax 530/544-2775; toll-free 800/338-5552. www.americana-inns.com.* 104 rms, 2 story. No A/C. Mid-June-Sept: S, D $60-$110; wkend rates; hols (2-day min); lower rates rest of yr. Crib free. Pet accepted, some restrictions. TV; cable. Complimentary continental bkfst. Restaurant opp open 24 hrs. Ck-out noon. Meeting rms. Business servs avail. Pool; whirlpool. Some balconies. Grills. Cr cds: A, DS, MC, V.

Resort

★★★ **EMBASSY SUITES RESORT.** *4130 Lake Tahoe Blvd, South Lake Tahoe (96150). 530/544-5400; fax 530/544-4900; toll-free 800/362-2779. www.embassytahoe.com.* 400 suites, 9 story. Jan-Mar and July-Aug: S, D $149-$359; under 12 free; ski, golf plans; higher rates hols; lower rates rest of yr. Crib free. Valet parking $2. TV; cable (premium), VCR (movies). Indoor pool; whirlpool, poolside serv. Complimentary full bkfst, coffee in rms. Restaurant 11 am-11 pm. Bar to 2 am; entertainment. Ck-out noon. Coin lndry. Convention facilities. Business servs avail. Concierge. Gift shop. Downhill ski 1 mi; x-country ski 5 mi. Exercise equipt; sauna. Refrigerators, microwaves, minibars, wet bars; some bathrm phones. Some balconies. Cr cds: A, DS, MC, V.

B&B/Small Inn

★★ **FANTASY INN AND WEDDING CHAPEL.** *3696 Lake Tahoe Blvd, South Lake Tahoe (96150). 530/541-4200; fax 530/541-6798; res 800/367-7736. www.fantasy-inn.com.* 53 rms, 2 story, 15 suites. Mid-Mar-mid-Oct: S, D $159-$359; suites $98-$299; ski, golf plans; wkends, hols (2-day min); higher rates special events; lower rates rest of yr. TV. Complimentary coffee in rms. Restaurant nearby. Ck-out 11 am. Business servs avail. Downhill ski 2 mi; x-country ski 10 mi. In-rm whirlpool; some refrigerators, fireplaces. Opp lake. Open courtyard wedding chapel. Cr cds: A, C, D, DS, JCB, MC, V.

Restaurants

★★★ **EVANS AMERICAN GOURMET CAFE.** *536 Emerald Bay Rd, South Lake Tahoe (96150). 530/542-1990. www.evanstahoe.com.* Hrs: 6-10 pm. Closed Sun; Easter, Thanksgiving, Dec 25. Res accepted. Wine list. A la carte entrees: dinner $15.95-

$22.95. Specializes in veal, venison, seafood. Small clapboard house with French country atmosphere. Totally nonsmoking. Cr cds: D, DS, MC, V.
D

★★ **FRESH KETCH.** *2433 Venice Dr E, South Lake Tahoe (96150). 530/541-5683.* Hrs: 11:30-10:30 pm. Closed Thanksgiving, Dec 25. Res accepted. Bar 11:30-1:30 am. A la carte entrees: dinner $13.95-$30. Children's menu. Specializes in seafood, rack of lamb. Valet parking (summer). Outdoor dining. View of marina. Cr cds: A, C, D, DS, MC, V.
D

★★ **NEPHELE'S.** *1169 Ski Run Blvd, South Lake Tahoe (96150). 530/544-8130. www.nepheles.com.* Hrs: 5-10 pm. Res accepted. Bar 2 pm-2 am. Dinner $15-$25. Children's menu. Specializes in fresh fish and game. Own pasta. Mountain house and cabins converted into restaurant and boutique shops. Casual dining. Totally nonsmoking. Cr cds: A, D, DS, MC, V.
SC

★★★ **SWISS CHALET.** *2544 Lake Tahoe Blvd, South Lake Tahoe (96150). 530/544-3304.* Hrs: 5-10 pm. Closed Mon; Easter, Thanksgiving, Dec 25; also 3 wks in Nov. Res accepted. Continental menu. Bar from 4 pm. Dinner $13.50-$21. Children's menu. Specializes in veal dishes, fondues, fresh seafood. Own baking. Swiss decor. Family-owned. Cr cds: A, MC, V.
D

South San Francisco

(see San Francisco Airport Area)

Squaw Valley

(see Lake Tahoe Area)

Stockton

(F-4) *See also Lodi, Modesto*

Founded 1849 **Pop** 210,943 **Elev** 13 ft **Area code** 209

Information Stockton/San Joaquin Convention and Visitors Bureau, 46 W Fremont St, 95202; 209/943-1987 or 800/350-1987

Web www.ssjcvb.org

Connected to San Francisco Bay by a 78-mile deepwater channel, Stockton is an important inland port with giant ore-loading facilities and grain terminals accessible to large ships. In its early days as the gateway to the Mother Lode country, it became a "city of a thousand tents." Many of the 49ers settled here and became rich when irrigation systems turned the surrounding countryside into fertile grain fields.

What to See and Do

Children's Museum. Interactive displays covering 24,000 sq ft; special events. (Tues-Sat, also Sun afternoon; closed hols) 402 W Weber Ave. Phone 209/465-4386. ¢¢

Haggin Museum. State and local historical exhibits; 19th-century European and American paintings and decorative arts; Native American arts. Guided tours (Sat or by appt); changing exhibits. (Tues-Sun afternoons; closed hols) 1201 N Pershing Ave, at Rose St in Victory Park. Phone 209/462-4116 or 209/462-1566. ¢¢

Municipal recreation facilities. The city maintains 50 parks, tennis courts, playgrounds, swimming pools, picnic areas; two golf courses; boat launching facilities and berths; ice arena; community and senior citizen centers. Fee for activities. Phone 209/937-8206.

Pixie Woods. Mother Goose and Fairyland characters; puppet shows in Toadstool Theatre; train, boat, and merry-go-round rides. (June-Labor Day, Wed-Sun; late Feb-May and after Labor Day-late Oct, Sat, Sun, hols, incl Easter wk) In Louis Park, W end of Monte Diablo Blvd. Phone 209/937-8206. ¢

World Wildlife Museum. Over 2,000 mounted zoological specimens represent wildlife from every continent. Incl deer, elk, African animals, wolves, antelope, bears, crocodiles and alligators, birds, Arctic animals. (Wed-Sun) 1245 W Weber Ave. Phone 209/465-2834. ¢¢

Special Events

Asparagus Festival. Musical entertainment, asparagus dishes, car show, wagon rides. Late Apr. Phone 800/350-1987.

San Joaquin County Fair. Horse racing, agricultural and livestock displays, entertainment. June. Phone 209/466-5041.

Greek Festival. Food, music, dancing. Phone 209/951-7272. Wkend after Labor Day.

Obon Festival and Bazaar. Street dance, food, exhibits, authentic Japanese costumes, colorful decorations at the Buddhist Temple. Phone 209/466-6701. July.

Motels/Motor Lodges

★ HOWARD JOHNSON EXPRESS INN. *1672 Herndon Rd, Ceres (95307). 209/537-4821; fax 209/537-1040; toll-free 800/446-4656. www.hojo.com.* 50 rms, 25 with shower only, 1-2 story. Apr-Sept: S $58; D $75; each addl $10; under 18 free. Crib free. Pet accepted, some restrictions. TV; cable (premium), VCR avail (movies). Complimentary continental bkfst, coffee in rms. Restaurant nearby. Ck-out 11 am. Meeting rms. Business servs avail. In-rm modem link. Valet serv. Pool. Some refrigerators, microwaves. Cr cds: A, C, D, DS, JCB, MC, V.

D

★ RED ROOF INN. *2654 W March Ln (95207). 209/478-4300; fax 209/478-1872. www.redroof.com.* 123 rms, 3 story. S $52; D $59; each addl $4; suites $80-$100; under 11 free. Crib free. TV; cable (premium). Pool; whirlpool. Complimentary coffee in lobby. Restaurant adj open 24 hrs. Ck-out 11 am. Meeting rms. Business servs avail. In-rm modem link. Refrigerator, wet bar in suites. Cr cds: A, D, DS, MC, V.

D

Hotel

★★★ RADISSON HOTEL STOCKTON. *2323 Grand Canal Blvd (95207). 209/957-9090; fax 209/473-0739; res 800/333-3333.* www. *radisson.com.* 198 rms, 5 story. S, D $99; each addl $21; suites $250-$350; under 21 free; wkend rates. Crib free. TV; cable (premium), VCR avail. Pool. Restaurant 6:30 am-11 pm. Bar noon-midnight. Ck-out 11 am. Meeting rms. Business servs avail. In-rm modem link. Health club privileges. Some balconies. Cr cds: A, D, DS, MC, V.

D

Restaurant

★★ LE BISTRO. *3121 W Benjamin Holt Dr (95219). 209/951-0885.* Hrs: 11:30 am-3 pm, 5-9 pm; Fri, Sat to 10 pm. Closed hols. Res accepted. Continental menu. Bar. Lunch $10.50-$13.95, dinner $19.95-$25. Specializes in fresh fish, souffles, European-style cuisine. Own desserts. Totally nonsmoking. Cr cds: A, D, DS, MC, V.

D

Studio City (L.A.)

Area code 818 **Zip** 91604

This community, located in the San Fernando Valley, is a neighborhood of Los Angeles, but is regarded by many as a separate entity.

Motel/Motor Lodge

★★ SPORTSMEN'S LODGE HOTEL. *12825 Ventura Blvd, Studio City (91604). 818/769-4700; fax 818/769-4798; toll-free 800/821-8511.* 198 rms, 2-5 story. S, D $105-$138; each addl $10; suites $180-$290; under 18 free. Crib free. TV; cable (premium). Heated pool; whirlpool, poolside serv. Restaurants 6:30 am-10 pm. Bars 11 am-midnight. Ck-out noon. Coin lndry. Meeting rms. Business servs avail. Bellhops. Valet serv. Gift shop. Beauty salon. Free airport

transportation. Exercise equipt. Private patios, balconies. Gardens; ponds. Cr cds: A, C, D, DS, MC, V.
D

Hotel

★★★ **RADISSON VALLEY CENTER HOTEL.** *15433 Ventura Blvd, Sherman Oaks (91403). 818/981-5400; fax 818/981-3175; res 800/333-3333. www.radisson.com/shermanoaksca.* 198 rms, 13 story. S, D $140-$170; suites $165-$495; under 18 free. Crib free. Garage parking $5.50. TV; cable (premium), VCR avail. Heated pool; whirlpool, poolside serv. Complimentary continental bkfst. Restaurant 6:30 am-10 pm. Rm serv 24 hrs. Bar 11-2 am. Ck-out noon. Meeting rms. Business servs avail. Gift shop. Barber, beauty shop. Valet serv. Health club privileges. Cr cds: A, D, DS, JCB, MC, V.
D

Restaurants

★★ **CAFE BIZOU.** *14016 Ventura Blvd, Sherman Oaks (91423). 818/784-3536. www.cafebizou.com.* Hrs: 11:30 am-2:30 pm, 5:30-10 pm; Fri to 11 pm; Sat, Sun 11 am-2:30 pm, 5-11 pm. Closed Jan 1, Dec 25. Res required (dinner). California, French menu. Bar. A la carte entrees: lunch $5.50-$9.95, dinner $5.95-$15.95. Sat, Sun brunch $6.50-$8.95. Specialties: sauteed sesame-seed-coated salmon in a red wine sauce, steak au poivre in a peppered veal sauce. Valet parking. Outdoor dining. Casual French cafe. Totally nonsmoking. Cr cds: A, D, DS, MC, V.
D

★★ **THE GREAT GREEK.** *13362 Ventura Blvd, Sherman Oaks (91423). 818/905-5250.* Hrs: 11:30 am-11 pm; Fri, Sat to midnight. Res accepted. Greek menu. Bar. Lunch $6.45-$14.95, dinner $9.95-$20.95. Specialties: oven-roasted spring lamb, stuffed grape leaves, moussaka. Own desserts. Greek music, dancing. Greek decor. Totally nonsmoking. Cr cds: A, D, DS, MC, V.

★★ **LA LOGGIA.** *11814 Ventura Blvd, Studio City L.A. (91604). 818/985-9222.* Hrs: 11:30 am-2:30 pm, 5:30-10:30 pm; Fri to 11 pm; Sat 5:30-11 pm; Sun 5-10 pm. Closed hols. Res accepted. Italian menu. Bar. A la carte entrees: lunch, dinner $8.25-$17.95. Specializes in fresh pasta, Northern Italian dishes. Valet parking. Menu changes quarterly. Trattoria setting. Totally nonsmoking. Cr cds: A, D, MC, V.
D

★★ **PERROCHE.** *11929 Ventura Blvd, Studio City L.A. (91604). 818/971-3800.* Hrs: noon-2 pm, 6-10 pm. Closed Sun; also hols. Res required (dinner). Continental menu. Bar. A la carte entrees: lunch $12-$18, dinner $13-$22. Specialties: Perroche smoked trout with horseradish; roasted Kendor farm young chicken, asparagus and morels; creme caramel. Valet parking. Outdoor dining. Provincial country decor; casual dining. Cr cds: A, D, DS, MC, V.
D

★★ **SUSHI NOZAWA.** *11288 Ventura Blvd, Studio City L.A. (91604). 818/508-7071.* Japanese menu. Specializes in sushi. Hrs: 11 am-10 pm. Closed Sun. Lunch, dinner $20-$40. Wine list. Japanese decor. Cr cds: MC, V.

★★ **WINE BISTRO.** *11915 Ventura Blvd, Studio City L.A. (91604). 818/766-6233.* Hrs: 11:30 am-10:30 pm; Sat from 5:30 pm. Closed Sun; hols. Res accepted. French, Continental menu. Bar. Lunch $9.95-$13.95, dinner $10.95-$19.95. Prix fixe: dinner $28.95. Specializes in bouillabaisse, duck. Valet parking. Outdoor dining. Cr cds: A, C, D, DS, MC, V.
D

Sunnyvale

(G-3) *See also Santa Clara*

Pop 117,229 **Elev** 130 ft
Area code 408
Information Chamber of Commerce, 101 W Olive Ave, 94086; 408/736-4971

What to See and Do

Sunnyvale Historical Museum. Houses historical artifacts and pictures of area as well as information on pioneering families. (Tues, Thurs, Sun; closed hols) 235 E California Ave, in Martin Murphy Jr. Park. Phone 408/749-0220. **FREE**

Motels/Motor Lodges

★★ RAMADA INN SILICON VALLEY. *1217 Wildwood Ave (94089). 408/245-5330; fax 408/732-2628; res 800/272-6232. www.ramadasv.com.* 176 rms, 2 story. S $155; D $165; each addl $10; under 18 free; wkend rates; special package plans. Crib free. TV; cable (premium), VCR avail. Pool; whirlpool, poolside serv. Coffee in rms. Restaurants 6 am-10 pm; Sat, Sun from 7 am. Bars. Ck-out noon. Coin lndry. Meeting rms. Business center. Bellhops. Valet serv. Concierge. Free airport transportation. Health club privileges. Cr cds: A, D, DS, JCB, MC, V.

D

★★★ SUNDOWNER INN. *504 Ross Dr (94089). 408/734-9900; fax 408/747-0580; toll-free 800/223-9901.* 105 units, 2 story. S, D $176-$196; each addl $10; suites $200-$260; wkend rates. Crib free. TV; cable (premium), VCR avail (free movies). Heated pool. Complimentary continental bkfst. Restaurant 6 am-10:45 pm; Sat, Sun from 9 am. Bar to 2 am; entertainment Tues-Sat. Ck-out noon. Meeting rms. Business servs avail. Valet serv. Exercise equipt; sauna. Health club privileges. Library. Refrigerators. Cr cds: A, C, D, DS, JCB, MC, V.

SC

Hotels

★★ FOUR POINTS BY SHERATON. *1250 Lakeside Dr (94086). 408/738-4888; fax 408/737-7147; toll-free 800/543-3322. www.sheraton.com.* 372 rms, 2-3 story. S, D $189-$269; each addl $15; suites $350; family, wkend rates. Crib free. TV; cable (premium). Heated pool; poolside serv, whirlpool. Coffee in rms. Restaurants 6 am-10 pm. Bar 10-2 am. Ck-out noon. Bellhops. Convention facilities. Business servs avail. Gift shop. Free airport transportation. Health club privileges. Bathrm phones. Park, duck pond, small beach. Cr cds: A, D, DS, JCB, MC, V.

D

★★ MAPLE TREE INN. *711 E El Camino Real (94087). 408/720-9700; toll-free 800/423-0243. www.mapletreeinn.com.* 181 rms, 2-3 story. S $150; D $160; each addl $10; suites, kit. unit $150-$175; under 12 free; wkend, hol rates; higher rates Stanford graduation. Crib free. Pet accepted, some restrictions. TV; cable (premium). Pool. Complimentary continental bkfst. Restaurant nearby. Ck-out noon. Coin lndry. Meeting rm. Business servs avail. In-rm modem link. Valet serv. Health club privileges. Some refrigerators. Cr cds: A, C, D, DS, ER, JCB, MC, V.

D

★★★ RADISSON INN SUNNYVALE. *1085 E El Camino Real (94087). 408/247-0800; fax 408/984-7120; toll-free 800/333-3333. www.radisson.com.* 136 rms, 3 story. S, D $180-190; each addl $10; suites $200-$210; under 13 free; wkend rates. Crib free. TV; cable (premium). Pool. Complimentary bkfst buffet. Restaurant 6 am-10 pm; Sat, Sun from 7 am. Rm serv 6-10 pm. Bar from 4 pm. Ck-out noon. Meeting rms. Business servs avail. Bellhops. Valet serv. Free garage parking. Free airport transportation. Exercise equipt. Health club privileges. Minibars. Atrium. Cr cds: A, D, DS, JCB, MC, V.

D

★★★ SHERATON SUNNYVALE HOTEL. *1100 N Mathilda Ave (94089). 408/745-6000; fax 408/734-8276; res 800/325-3535. www.sheraton.com.* 174 units, 2 story. S, D $189-$219; each addl $15; under 18 free; wkend rates. Crib free. TV; cable (premium). Heated pool; whirlpool, poolside serv. Complimentary coffee in rms. Restaurant 6:30 am-10 pm; Sat and Sun from 7:30 am. Bar noon-10 pm. Ck-out 1 pm. Meeting rms. Business servs avail. Bellhops. Valet serv. Free airport transportation. Exercise equipt. Bathrm phones. Refrigerators avail. Garden with gazebo for special events. Cr cds: A, D, DS, JCB, MC, V.

★★★ **WYNDHAM SUNNYVALE.** *1300 Chesapeake Terrace (94089). 408/747-0999. www.wyndham.com.* 180 rms, 5 story. S, D $175-$275; each addl $15; under 17 free. Crib avail. Heated pool. TV; cable (premium), VCR avail. Complimentary coffee in rms, newspaper. Restaurant 6 am-10:30 pm. Bar. Ck-out noon. Meeting rms. Business center. Valet serv. Gift shop. Exercise rm. Some refrigerators, minibars. Cr cds: A, C, D, DS, MC, V.

All Suite

★★★ **SUMMERFIELD SUITES BY WYNDHAM.** *900 Hamlin Ct (94089). 408/745-1515; fax 408/745-0540; res 800/833-4353. www.wyndham.com.* 138 kit. suites, 2-3 story. S $209; D $259; wkend rates. Crib free. Pet accepted, some restrictions; $10/day. TV; cable (premium), VCR (movies $3). Pool; whirlpool. Complimentary bkfst buffet, coffee in rms. Restaurant nearby. Ck-out noon. Coin lndry. Meeting rms. Business servs avail. In-rm modem link. Valet serv. Sundries. Free airport transportation. Exercise equipt. Health club privileges. Some fireplaces. Grills. Cr cds: A, C, D, DS, JCB, MC, V.

D

Extended Stay

★★ **RESIDENCE INN BY MARRIOTT.** *750 Lakeway (94086). 408/720-1000; fax 408/737-9722; res 809/234-6022. www.residenceinn.com.* 231 kit. units, 2 story. S $179; D $199. Pet accepted; $10/day. TV; cable (premium). Pool; 2 whirlpools. Complimentary continental bkfst. Restaurant nearby. Ck-out noon. Coin lndry. Meeting rm. Business servs avail. Valet serv. Free airport transportation. Tennis. Exercise equipt. Lawn games. Picnic tables, grills. Small lake. Cr cds: A, C, D, DS, JCB, MC, V.

Susanville (C-4)

Settled 1853 **Pop** 7,279 **Elev** 4,258 ft **Area code** 530 **Zip** 96130

Information Lassen County Chamber of Commerce, 84 N Lassen St, PO Box 338; 530/257-4323

Susanville is currently a trading center for an area producing livestock, lumber, alfalfa, garlic, and strawberries. There is fine hunting for deer, bear, antelope, pheasant, grouse, quail, ducks, and geese, and fishing in many lakes and rivers in the surrounding hills and mountains. Lassen National Forest headquarters and a Ranger District office are located here. In 1856, Susanville was the capital of the Republic of Nataqua, an area of 50,000 square miles. Isaac Roop, the town's first settler, helped establish the republic, which later joined the Nevada Territory. Roop was first Provisional Governor of Nevada and later senator. California surveys showed the area was part of Plumas County. The locals refused to join and holed up in Roop's house in 1864. After a day of gunfighting, California won back what is now Lassen County. Susanville was named by Roop in honor of his only daughter.

What to See and Do

Bizz Johnson Trail. Multipurpose trail winding 25 mi from Susanville to Mason Station, four mi N of Westwood. Transverses rugged Susan River canyon on former railroad route. Fishing on river; hiking, bicycling, horseback riding, camping, x-country skiing. Begins ½ mi S via S Weatherlow St, left on Richmond Rd to Susanville Depot Trailhead; parking avail. Phone 530/257-0456. **FREE**

Eagle Lake. Called by scientists "the lake that time forgot," this 26,000-acre lake was formed by the receding waters of a primeval lake larger than Lake Erie. It is the second-largest natural lake in California and home to Eagle Lake trout, a species averaging three to five lbs that has adapted to living in the lake's alkaline water. Gallatin Beach, at S end of lake, provides swimming, waterskiing, Five campgrounds avail. (fee). Marina has boat rentals. 2 mi W on CA 36, then 15 mi N on County A1, in Lassen National Forest. For additional information contact Eagle Lake Resource Area, Phone 530/257-0456.

Gallatin Marina. Adj to Lassen National Forest Campgrounds. Fishing, boating (ramps, rentals); groceries. (Late May-mid-Oct) Phone 530/257-2151.

Lassen National Forest. More than one million acres. Swimming, excellent trout fishing in lakes and streams; hunting, x-country and downhill skiing, snowmobiling. 7 mi W on CA 36. Phone 530/257-2151. Incl

Wilderness Areas. All offer backpacking, primitive camping. (Daily) **Caribou Peak.** Gentle rolling forested terrain with many small crystal lakes. Many small cinder cones. **Thousand Lakes.** Contrasting topography; hiking trails. 25 mi E & S of Burney via CA 299, 89, Forest Rd 26. **Ishi Wilderness.** Dotted with rock outcroppings and bizarre pillar lava formations. 35 mi W via CA 36 & County A21. Phone 530/257-2151.

Roop's Fort & Lassen Historical Museum. Fort (1854), built by Isaac Roop, was the capitol of the Nataqua Republic. (May-Oct, Mon-Fri) N Weatherlow St. Phone 530/257-3292. **FREE**

Special Event

Lassen County Fair. Fairgrounds, off Russell Ave and Main St. Livestock and horse shows, rodeos, parade, livestock auction; entertainment. Phone 530/257-4104. Third wkend July.

Motel/Motor Lodge

★★ BEST WESTERN TRAILSIDE INN. *2785 Main St (96130). 530/257-4123; fax 530/257-2665. www.bestwestern.com.* 108 rms, 2 story. Apr-Oct: S, D $49-$85; each addl $5; suites $90; lower rates rest of yr. TV; cable (premium). Heated pool. Restaurant open 24 hrs. Rm serv 6 am-10 pm. Ck-out 11 am. Meeting rm. Business servs avail. Health club privileges. X-country ski 2 mi. Some refrigerators. Microwaves avail. Cr cds: A, C, D, DS, MC, V.

D

Tahoe City (Lake Tahoe Area) (E-5)

Pop 2,500 **Elev** 6,240 ft
Area code 530 **Zip** 95730

At north end of Lake Tahoe.

Motel/Motor Lodge

★ TRAVELODGE. *455 N Lake Blvd, Tahoe City (96145). 530/583-3766; fax 530/583-8045; toll-free 800/578-7878. www.travelodge.com.* 47 rms, 2 story. No A/C. July-Labor Day: S $69-$101; D $81-$106; each addl $5; under 17 free; higher rates: wkends, hols; lower rates rest of yr. Crib free. TV; cable. Pool; whirlpool. Sauna. Complimentary coffee, tea in rms. Restaurant nearby. Ck-out 11 am. Business servs avail. Tennis privileges. Golf privileges. Downhill ski 5 mi; x-country ski 2 mi. Sun deck. Microwaves; some balconies. Lake opp. Cr cds: A, C, D, DS, ER, JCB, MC, V.

SC

Resorts

★★ GRANLIBAKKEN RESORT & CONFERENCE CENTER. *725 Granlibakken Rd, Tahoe City (96145). 530/583-4242; fax 530/583-7641; toll-free 800/543-3221. www.granlibakken.com.* 76 kit. units, 3 story. No elvtr. Late Dec-early Jan: S, D $100-$125; each addl $25; 2-5-bedrm units $230-$727. Crib $5. TV; cable. Heated pool (seasonal); wading pool, whirlpool. Sauna. Complimentary full bkfst. Snack bar (winter). Ck-out 11 am, ck-in 4 pm. Grocery, package store 1 mi. Coin lndry. Convention facilities. Business servs avail. Airport, RR station, bus depot transportation. Tennis. Downhill/x-country ski on site. Rental equipt. Sledding. Hiking. Many fireplaces; microwaves avail. Many balconies. Cr cds: A, C, D, DS, JCB, MC, V.

D

★★★ RESORT AT SQUAW CREEK. *400 Squaw Creek Rd, Olympic Valley (96146). 530/583-6300; fax 530/581-5407; toll-free 800/403-4434. www.squawcreek.com.* 405 units, 9 story,

205 suites. Mid-Dec-Jan: S, D $375; suites $425-$1,800; under 17 free; lower rates rest of yr. Crib free. TV; cable, VCR avail. 3 heated pools; wading pool, whirlpool, poolside serv, lifeguard. Supervised children's activities; ages 3-13. Coffee in rms. Dining rms 6:30 am-11 pm (see also GLISSANDI). Bar 11-1 am. Ck-out 11 am, ck-in 4 pm. Package store. Grocery 2 mi. Coin lndry 6 mi. Convention facilities. Business center. Bellhops. Valet serv. Concierge. Gift shop. Beauty shop. Valet parking. Airport transportation. Sports dir. Lighted tennis, pro golf, greens fee (incl cart) $110. Aquatic center; 250-ft waterfall, waterslide, stream. Downhill/x-country ski on site. Rental equipt. Ice-skating. 7 mi of landscaped hiking and bicycle paths; bicycle rentals. Exercise rm; saunas. Massage. Microwaves avail. Cr cds: A, D, DS, MC, V.

SC

B&Bs/Small Inns

★★★ **CHANEY HOUSE.** *4725 W Lake Blvd, Tahoe City (96145). 530/525-7333; fax 530/525-4413. www.chaneyhouse.com.* 4 rms, 2 story, 3 suites. No A/C. S $110-$180; D $130-$210; each addl $20; suites $120-$195; ski plans; wkends, hols (2-3 day min); lower rates rest of yr. Complimentary full bkfst; afternoon refreshments. Restaurant nearby. Ck-out 11 am, ck-in 2 pm. Concierge serv. Downhill ski 1 mi; x-country ski on site. Picnic tables, grills. Built in 1928; original stone construction. Totally nonsmoking. Cr cds: DS, MC, V.

★★★ **THE COTTAGE INN.** *1690 W Lake Blvd, Tahoe City (96145). 530/581-4073; fax 530/581-0226; toll-free 800/581-4073. www.thecottageinn.com.* 15 units. No A/C. No rm phones. S, D $140-$210. Children over 12 yrs only. TV; cable, VCR (free movies). Complimentary full bkfst; afternoon refreshments. Restaurant nearby. Ck-out 11 am, ck-in 3 pm. Business servs avail. Downhill/x-country ski 3 mi. Sauna. Lawn games. Microwaves avail. Picnic tables. Library. Rustic cabins in the woods. Totally nonsmoking. Cr cds: MC, V.

Restaurants

★★★ **GLISSANDI.** *400 Squaw Creek Rd, Olympic Valley (96146). 530/581-6621. www.squawcreek.com.* Hrs: 6-10 pm. Closed Sun. Res required. Continental menu. Serv bar. Wine cellar. Dinner $22-$32. Prix fixe: dinner $49. Specializes in wild game, filet mignon, rack of lamb. Valet parking. Elegant dining with view of mountains. Totally nonsmoking. Cr cds: A, C, D, DS, MC, V.

D

★★★ **SWISS LAKEWOOD.** *5055 W Lake Blvd, Homewood (96141). 530/525-5211.* Hrs: 5:30-10 pm. Closed Mon exc hols. Res required. French, Continental menu. Bar. Dinner $18.50-$26.50. Swiss, European decor; many antiques; wagon wheel chandeliers. Totally nonsmoking. Cr cds: A, MC, V.

D

★ **WOLFDALE'S.** *640 N Lake Blvd, Tahoe City (96145). 530/583-5700. www.wolfdales.com.* Hrs: 5:30-10 pm; wkends from 6 pm. Closed Tues Sept-June. Res accepted. Bar to midnight. A la carte entrees: dinner $16-$21. Specializes in seafood. Outdoor dining. Local artwork. Cr cds: C, MC, V.

D SC

Tahoe Vista (Lake Tahoe Area) (E-5)

Pop 1,144 **Elev** 6,232 ft
Area code 530

At north end of Lake Tahoe.

Motels/Motor Lodges

★★ **CAL NEVA INN.** *9937 N Lake Blvd, Brockway (96143). 530/546-3341; fax 530/546-9054; toll-free 800/648-2324.* 94 rms, 70 with shower only, 2 story. Mid-May-Sept:

S, D $69-$89; each addl $10; under 10 free; ski plans; wkend rates; 2-day min hols; lower rates rest of yr. Crib $10. TV; cable. Pool; whirlpool. Complimentary coffee in lobby. Restaurant opp open 24 hrs. Ck-out 11 am. Meeting rm. Downhill/x-country ski 5 mi. Microwaves avail. Cr cds: A, C, D, DS, MC, V.

D

★ **CEDAR GLEN LODGE.** *6589 N Lake Blvd , Tahoe Vista (96148). 530/546-4281; fax 530/546-2250; res 888/315-2378. www.cedarglenlodge.com.* 31 rms in 2-story motel, cottages, 14 kits. No A/C. Mid-June-mid-Sept, Dec-Apr: S, D $45-$65; each addl $5; kit. units, cottages $80-$129; wkly rates; lower rates rest of yr. Crib free. TV; cable, VCR avail (movies). Pool; whirlpools. Sauna. Playground. Complimentary continental bkfst, coffee in rms. Restaurant nearby. Ck-out 11 am. Business servs avail. Downhill ski 8 mi; x-country ski 4 mi. Some refrigerators; microwaves avail. Private patios. Picnic tables, grills. Beach opp. Cr cds: A, DS, MC, V.

Resort

★ **VISTA VILLA RESORT.** *6750 N Lake Blvd, Tahoe Vista (96148). 530/546-1550; fax 530/546-4100.* 13 rms, 10 kits. No A/C. S, D $75; each addl $10; studio rms $85-$165; kit. units for 1-4, $85-$165; wkly rates in summer. TV; cable, VCR avail (movies). Pool. Coffee in rms. Ck-out 11 am. Coin lndry. Business servs avail. Downhill ski 15 mi; x-country ski 10 mi. Refrigerators, microwaves. Private patios. Picnic tables, grill. Sun deck. On private sand beach; moorage. Cr cds: A, DS, MC, V.

B&Bs/Small Inns

★★★ **SHORE HOUSE AT LAKE TAHOE.** *7170 N Lake Blvd, Tahoe Vista (96148). 530/546-7270; fax 530/546-7130; toll-free 800/207-5160. www.tahoeinn.com.* 9 rms, 4 with shower only, 2 story. No A/C. No rm phones. S, D $175-$200; each addl $20; wkends, hols (2-day min); higher rates special events. Complimentary full bkfst. Restaurant adj 11 am-10 pm. Ck-out 11 am, ck-in 4 pm. Concierge serv. Business servs avail. Whirlpool. Downhill ski 8 mi, x-country ski 1 mi. Refrigerators, fireplaces. Picnic tables. On lake. Totally nonsmoking. Cr cds: DS, MC, V.

★★★ **TAHOE VISTA INN AND MARINA.** *7220 N Lake Blvd, Tahoe Vista (96148). 530/546-7662; fax 530/546-0667; toll-free 800/521-6656.* 6 suites, 5 A/C. Jan-Mar and mid-June-Sept: S, D $160-$240; lower rates rest of yr. TV; cable. Complimentary coffee in rms. Restaurant (see also CAPTAIN JON'S). Ck-out noon, ck-in 3 pm. Business servs avail. Downhill/x-country ski 15 mi. Microwaves, whirlpools, fireplaces. Balconies. On Lake Tahoe. Cr cds: MC, V.

Restaurants

★★ **CAPTAIN JON'S.** *7220 N Lake Blvd, Tahoe Vista (96148). 530/546-4819.* Hrs: 10:30 am-10 pm (summer), 5:30-10:30 pm (winter). Res accepted. Country French seafood menu. Bar 3 pm-2 am, summer from 11 am. Lunch $8-$12, dinner $16-$23. Specializes in seafood. Pianist Thurs-Sat 5:30-11 pm. Valet parking. Nautical decor. Outdoor dining. On lakefront. Cr cds: A, MC, V.

D

★★ **GAR WOODS GRILL & PIER.** *5000 N Lake Blvd, Carnellian Bay (96140). 530/546-3366. www.garwoods.com.* Hrs: 10:30 am-10 pm; winter from 4 pm; wkends from 11:30 am; Sun brunch 9:30 am-2 pm. Res accepted. No A/C. Bar. A la carte entrees: bkfst $7-$10, lunch $8-$13.95, dinner $12-$22. Sun brunch $18.95-$22.95. Children's menu. Specializes in fresh seafood, steak. Acoustic duo Fri, Sat. Outdoor dining. View of lake and sunsets. Cr cds: A, MC, V.

D

★★★ **LE PETIT PIER.** *7238 N Lake Blvd, Tahoe Vista (96148). 530/546-4464. www.lepetitpier.com.* Hrs: 6-10 pm. Closed Tues. Res accepted. French menu. Bar. Wine cellar. A la carte entrees: dinner $19-$26. Complete meal: dinner $50. Children's menu. Specialties: asparagus shiitake feuilletage, baked oysters, noisette of lamb en croute. Valet parking. Fam-

ily-owned since 1972. Many separate dining areas with lake views. Intimate dining. Totally nonsmoking. Cr cds: A, C, D, DS, MC, V.
D

Tehachapi

See also Bakersfield

Pop 5,791 **Elev** 3,973 ft
Area code 661 **Zip** 93581
Information Greater Tehachapi Chamber of Commerce, PO Box 401; 661/822-4180
Web www.tehachapi.com/chamber

Tehachapi was founded when the railroad made its way through the pass between the San Joaquin Valley and the desert to the east. The Tehachapi Pass, east of town, is one of the windiest areas in the world; of the approximately 15,000 wind turbines in the state, 5,000 are located here. The best time to see the turbines spinning is late afternoon, when heat on the nearby Mojave Desert is greatest. Historians believe the name Tehachapi is derived from a Native American word meaning "sweet water and many acorns," but others believe it means "windy place." Both are true of the area.

What to See and Do

Tehachapi Loop. Visitors and railroad buffs enjoy watching trains (with 85 or more boxcars) pass over themselves when rounding the "Tehachapi Loop." Built in 1875-1876, the loop makes it possible for trains to gain the needed elevation in a short distance. It can be seen by taking Woodford-Tehachapi Rd to a viewpoint just above the loop. NW of town.

Special Events

Indian Pow Wow. Native American cultural and religious gathering of various tribes. Open to public viewing: dance competition, arts and crafts, museum display of artifacts. Usually last wkend June. Phone 805/822-1118.

Wind Fair. Windmill demonstrations, arts and crafts, entertainment, food, electric car races. July. Phone 805/831-1038.

Mountain Festival and PRCA Rodeo. Incl arts and crafts, food booths, parade, events. Third wkend Aug. Phone 805/822-4180.

Motels/Motor Lodges

★★ **BEST WESTERN.** *416 W Tehachapi Blvd (93561). 661/822-5591; fax 661/822-6197; toll-free 800/780-7234. www.bestwestern.com.* 74 rms, 2 story. S $55-$65; D $65-$75; each addl $3; under 18 free. Crib free. Pet accepted. TV; cable (premium). Pool. Restaurant 5:30 am-midnight. Ck-out noon. Coin lndry. Refrigerators; microwaves avail. Cr cds: A, C, D, DS, MC, V.
D SC

★★★ **STALLION SPRINGS.** *18100 Lucaya Way (93561). 661/822-5581; fax 661/822-4055; toll-free 800/244-0864. www.stallionsprings.com.* 63 rms in main building, 2 story, 21 kit. cottages (1-2 bedrms). S, D, suites $72-$195; each addl $10; kit. cottages $150-$185; golf plans. Crib free. Pet accepted; $20 deposit. TV; cable (premium). Heated pool; whirlpool. Playground. Dining rm 7:30 am-1:30 pm, 6-8:30 pm. Bar 5-9 pm, wkend hrs vary; entertainment. Ck-out noon, ck-in 3 pm. Meeting rms. Sports dir. Lighted tennis, pro. 18-hole golf, greens fee $22-$32, pro, 2 putting greens, driving range. Hiking. Lawn games. Exercise equipt; sauna. Balconies. Situated atop hill; overlooks golf course, lakes, forests. Cr cds: A, C, D, DS, MC, V.
D SC

★ **SUMMIT TRAVELODGE.** *500 Steuber Rd (93561). 661/823-8000; fax 661/823-8006. www.travelodge.com.* 76 units, 2 story. S $49-$52; D $56-$59; each addl $7; suites $61-$64; kit. unit $90; under 18 free. Crib free. Pet accepted. TV; cable (premium). Heated pool; whirlpool. Complimentary coffee in rms. Restaurant. Bar 2-10 pm. Ck-out 11 am. Meeting rms. Business servs avail. In-rm modem link. Gift shop. Some refrigerators. Balconies. Cr cds: A, C, D, DS, JCB, MC, V.
D SC

Temecula

(F-5) *See also Fallbrook*

Pop 27,099 **Elev** 1,006 ft
Area code 909
Information Temecula Valley Chamber of Commerce, 27450 Ynez Rd, Suite 124, 92590; 909/676-5090
Web www.temecula.org

The Temecula Valley, bordered on the west by Camp Pendleton Marine Corps Base and the Cleveland National Forest, is approximately mid-way between Los Angeles and San Diego. This area offers activities for everyone, from tours of 12 local wineries to golfing on any of five championship courses.

Special Event

Balloon and Wine Festival. Wine tasting, hot-air balloon race, musical entertainment, children's activities. Phone 909/676-6713. June.

Motel/Motor Lodge

★★ RAMADA INN. *28980 Front St (92590). 909/676-8770; fax 909/699-3400; toll-free 888/298-2054. www.ramada.com/ramada.html.* 70 rms, 2 story. S, D $54-$64; each addl $5; under 17 free. Crib free. TV; cable (premium). Pool; whirlpool. Complimentary continental bkfst, coffee in rms. Restaurant adj 6 am-10 pm. Ck-out noon. Meeting rm. Business servs avail. Refrigerators; some wet bars, microwaves. Cr cds: A, C, D, DS, MC, V.
D SC

Hotel

★★★ EMBASSY SUITES TEMECULA. *29345 Rancho California Rd (92591). 909/676-5656; fax 909/699-3928; res 800/362-2779. www.embassysuites.com.* 136 suites, 4 story. S, D $109-$149; each addl $10; under 18 free. Crib free. TV; cable (premium), VCR. Heated pool; whirlpool, poolside serv. Complimentary full bkfst. Coffee in rms. Restaurant 6:30-9:30 am, 11 am-2 pm, 5-10 pm. Bar noon-10 pm. Ck-out noon. Coin lndry. Meeting rms. Business servs avail. Valet serv. Gift shop. Exercise equipt. Refrigerators, microwaves, wet bars. Many balconies. Cr cds: A, C, D, DS, MC, V.
D

Resort

★★★ TEMECULA CREEK INN. *44501 Rainbow Canyon Rd (92592). 909/694-1000; fax 909/676-8961; toll-free 877/517-1823. www.temeculacreekinn.com.* 80 rms in 5 buildings, 2 story. S, D $130-$205; each addl $20; package plans; under 12 free. Crib free. TV; cable. Heated pool; whirlpool, poolside serv. Complimentary coffee in rms. Dining rm 6:30 am-10 pm. Bar 9:30 am-11 pm; entertainment Fri, Sat. Ck-out noon, ck-in 4 pm. Meeting rms. Business servs avail. Tennis. 27-hole golf, greens fee $55-$90, pro, putting green, driving range. Lawn games. Bicycle rental. Refrigerators, minibars. Balconies. Picnic tables. Cr cds: A, C, D, DS, MC, V.
D SC

B&B/Small Inn

★★ LOMA VISTA BED AND BREAKFAST. *33350 La Serena Way (92591). 909/676-7047; fax 909/676-0077.* 6 rms, 2 story. No rm phones. S, D $100-$150; each addl $25; some 2-day min wkends. TV in sitting rm. Complimentary full bkfst; evening refreshments. Restaurant opp 11 am-9 pm. Ck-out 11 am, ck-in 3-8 pm. Whirlpool. Some balconies. Mission-style house surrounded by citrus groves and vineyards. Totally nonsmoking. Cr cds: MC, V.

Restaurants

★★ BAILY WINE COUNTRY CAFE. *27644 Ynez Rd M-11 (92591). 909/676-9567. www.baily.com.* Hrs: 11 am-2:30 pm, 5-9 pm; Fri to 9:30 pm; Sat 11 am-9:30 pm; Sun 11 am-9 pm; Sun brunch 11 am-2 pm. Closed Tues, Wed, hols. Res accepted. Continental menu. Wine, beer. Lunch $7.95-$10.95, dinner $12.95-$21.95. Sun brunch $7.95-$8.95. Specialties: sauteed crab cakes, salmon Wellington, southwestern pork tenderloin.

Parking. Outdoor dining. Casual decor; modern artwork, silk trees. Cr cds: A, D, DS, MC, V.

D

★ **BANK OF MEXICAN FOOD.** *28645 Front St (92590). 909/676-6160.* Hrs: 11 am-9 pm. Closed Easter, Thanksgiving, Dec 25. Res accepted. Mexican menu. Wine, beer. Complete meals: lunch $4.50-$8.95, dinner $5.95-$8.95. Specialties: homemade chile relleno, crab enchiladas. Children's menu. Patio dining. In refurbished bank building (1913). Family-owned since 1978. Cr cds: A, MC, V.

★★ **CAFE CHAMPAGNE.** *32575 Rancho California Rd (92591). 909/699-0088. www.temelink.com/thornton.* Hrs: 11 am-9 pm; Mon to 4 pm; Sun brunch to 4 pm. California eclectic menu. Bar. A la carte entrees: lunch $12.95-$23.95, dinner $18.95-$27.95. Sun brunch $12.95-$23.95. Specializes in mesquite-grilled foods, award-winning sparkling wines. Own baking. Parking. Outdoor dining. View of vineyard. Herb garden. Cr cds: A, C, D, DS, MC, V.

D

Thousand Oaks

(E-4) *See also Los Angeles*

Pop 104,352 **Elev** 800 ft
Area code 805

Information Thousand Oaks/Westlake Village Regional Chamber of Commerce, 600 Hampshire Rd, Suite 200, Westlake Village, 91361; 805/370-0035

What to See and Do

Stagecoach Inn Museum Complex. Reproduction of 1876 building with Victorian furnishings; contains Chumash display; pioneer artifacts; changing exhibits; carriage house with antique vehicles; gift shop. Tri-Village consists of Chumash hut, Spanish adobe, and pioneer house representing three early cultures in Conejo Valley. One-rm schoolhouse. Nature trail. (Wed-Sun afternoons; closed Easter, Thanksgiving, Dec 25) 51 S Ventu Park Rd, ½ mi S of US 101 in Newbury Park. Phone 805/498-9441. ¢¢

Motel/Motor Lodge

★★ **CLARION HOTEL.** *1775 Madera Rd, Simi Valley (93065). 805/584-6300; fax 805/527-9969; toll-free 800/228-5050. www.hotelchoice.com.* 120 rms, 2 story. S, D $84-$104; each addl $10; suites $150-$400; under 18 free; wkly, monthly rates. TV; cable (premium). Heated pool; whirlpool. Complimentary full bkfst, coffee in rms. Restaurant 6:30-9 am. Bar 5-10 pm. Ck-out noon. Coin lndry. Meeting rms. Business servs avail. In-rm modem link. Bellhops. Valet serv. Airport transportation. Health club privileges. Some refrigerators. Private patios, balconies. Garden courtyard with waterfall. Cr cds: A, C, D, DS, ER, JCB, MC, V.

D SC

Hotel

★★★ **HYATT WESTLAKE PLAZA.** *880 S Westlake Blvd, Westlake Village (91361). 805/557-1234; fax 805/379-9392; res 800/233-1234. www.hyattwestlake.com.* 262 rms, 5 story. S $199; D $224; each addl $25; suites $200-$500; under 18 free; wkend rates; package plans. Crib free. TV; cable (premium), VCR avail (movies). Heated pool; whirlpool, poolside serv. Restaurant 6:30 am-10:30 pm. Bar 11-1 am; entertainment. Ck-out noon. Meeting rms. Business center. In-rm modem link. Concierge. Gift shop. Valet parking. Tennis privileges. Golf privileges. Exercise equipt. Bicycle rentals. Refrigerators avail. Private patios, balconies. Garden atrium. Spanish mission-style architecture. Cr cds: A, C, D, DS, ER, JCB, MC, V.

D

B&B/Small Inn

★★★ **WESTLAKE VILLAGE INN.** *31943 Agoura Rd, Westlake Village (91361). 818/889-0230; fax 818/879-0812; toll-free 800/535-9978. www.westlakevillageinn.com.* 141 units, 2 story. S $190; D $200; each addl $10;

suites $165-$350; under 12 free; golf plan. Crib free. TV; cable (premium), VCR (movies $6). Heated pool; whirlpool. Complimentary continental bkfst. Coffee in rms. Restaurant 7 am-10 pm; Sun 10 am-2:30 pm, 5-9 pm. Bar 11:30-2 am; entertainment. Ck-out noon. Meeting rms. Business servs avail. In-rm modem link. Concierge. Gift shop. Valet serv. Lighted tennis. 18-hole golf, greens fee $25, cart $17, pro. Exercise equipt. Minibars. Fireplace in suites. Private patios, courtyards. Balconies overlook lake. Spacious grounds incl waterfalls and a rose garden. Cr cds: A, C, D, DS, ER, JCB, MC, V.

Restaurant

★ CORRIGAN'S STEAK HOUSE. *556 E Thousand Oaks Blvd (91360). 805/495-5234. www.corriganssteak house.com.* Hrs: 11 am-10:30 pm; Sat, Sun from 9 am. Closed Thanksgiving, Dec 25. Res accepted. Bar to midnight. Bkfst $3.75-$10.50, lunch $5.75-$10.95, dinner $8.95-$20.95. Specializes in steak, seafood, chili. Old-time Western decor; Western movies memorabilia. Totally nonsmoking. Cr cds: A, DS, MC, V.

Three Rivers

(B-4) *See also Sequoia & Kings Canyon Naional Parks*

Pop 2,000 **Elev** 1,200 ft
Area code 559 **Zip** 93271

Motels/Motor Lodges

★★ BEST WESTERN HOLIDAY LODGE. *40105 Sierra Dr (93271). 559/561-4119; fax 559/561-3427; toll-free 888/523-9909. www.bestwestern.com.* 54 rms, 1-2 story. May-Oct: S $61-$105; D $71-$105; each addl $4; suites $77-$91; lower rates rest of yr. Crib $4. Pet accepted. TV; cable. Pool; whirlpool. Playground. Continental bkfst, coffee in rms. Ck-out 11 am. Refrigerators; some microwaves, fireplaces. Balconies. Grills. Cr cds: A, C, D, DS, JCB, MC, V.

★★ HOLIDAY INN EXPRESS. *40820 Sierra Dr; Hwy 198 (93271). 559/561-9000; fax 559/561-9010; toll-free 800/331-2140. www.3rivers holidayinn.com.* 62 rms, 2 story, 16 suites. Apr-Oct: S $99; D $99-$129; each addl $10; suites $109-$149; under 18 free; family rates; higher rates Jazzfest; lower rates rest of yr. Crib free. TV; cable (premium), VCR avail. Complimentary continental bkfst, coffee in rms. Restaurant adj 6 am-11 pm. Ck-out 11 am. Meeting rms. Business servs avail. In-rm modem link. Sundries. Coin lndry. X-country ski 15 mi. Exercise equipt; sauna. Heated pool; whirlpool. Refrigerators, microwaves; some in-rm whirlpools, fireplaces. Cr cds: A, C, D, DS, ER, JCB, MC, V.

★★ LAZY J RANCH MOTEL. *39625 Sierra Dr (93271). 559/561-4449; fax 559/561-4889; toll-free 800/341-8000.* 20 rms, 12 with shower only. S $45-$60; D $46-$70; suites $150-$170; kit. units $88-$98; wkly rates; hols (3-day min). Crib free. Pet accepted, some restrictions. TV; cable. Pool. Playground. Complimentary coffee in rms. Ck-out 11 am. Coin lndry. X-country ski 20 mi. Refrigerators; some fireplaces. Picnic tables. On river. Cr cds: A, C, D, DS, MC, V.

★ SIERRA LODGE. *43175 Sierra Dr (93271). 559/561-3681; fax 559/561-3264; toll-free 800/367-8879. www.sierra-lodge.com.* 22 units, 1-3 story, 5 kit. suites. No elvtr. May-Sept: S, D $49-$72; each addl $3; suites $85-$165; lower rates rest of yr. Pet accepted, some restrictions. TV; cable (premium). Pool. Complimentary continental bkfst, coffee in rms. Restaurant nearby. Ck-out 11 am. Meeting rm. Business servs avail. Sundries. Refrigerators; some fireplaces. Balconies. Cr cds: A, C, D, DS, MC, V.

Tiburon

(see San Francisco map) *See also Mill Valley, San Francisco, San Rafael, Sausalito*

Pop 7,532 **Elev** 90 ft **Area code** 415 **Zip** 94920

What to See and Do

China Cabin. Elegant social saloon of the 19th-century transpacific steamship SS *China.* The 20-by-40-ft cabin was removed in 1886 and used as a waterfront cottage until 1978. Completely restored; intricate woodwork, gold leaf, cut glass windows, brass and crystal chandeliers; period furnishings. Tours (Apr-Oct, Wed, Sun afternoons or by appt) 54 Beach Rd, Belvedere Cove, near jct Tiburon Blvd. Phone 415/435-1853. **Donation**

Hotel

★★ **TIBURON LODGE.** *1651 Tiburon Blvd, Belvedere Tiburon (94920). 415/435-3133; fax 415/435-2451; toll-free 800/762-7770. www.tiburonlodge.com.* 101 rms, 3 story. May-Oct: S $139-$159; D $154-$174; each addl $15; kit. suites $260-$290; under 12 free; lower rates rest of yr. Crib free. TV; cable, VCR avail (free movies). Heated pool. Restaurant 7-10 am. Ck-out noon. Meeting rms. Business servs avail. In-rm modem link. Bellhops. Valet serv. Some in-rm whirlpools. Some private patios, balconies. San Francisco ferry 1 blk. Cr cds: A, C, D, DS, ER, MC, V.

D

Restaurant

★★ **GUAYMAS.** *5 Main St (94920). 415/435-6300.* Hrs: 11:30 am-10 pm; Fri, Sat to 11 pm; Sun 10:30 am-10 pm. Closed Thanksgiving, Dec 25. Res accepted. Mexican menu. Bar. Lunch, dinner $8.95-$18.95. Specializes in authentic Mexican cuisine. Mariachi Sun. Outdoor dining. On bay. Totally nonsmoking. Cr cds: A, D, DS, MC, V.

D

Torrance (E-4)

Pop 133,107 **Elev** 84 ft **Area code** 310
Information Chamber of Commerce, 3400 Torrance Blvd, Suite 100, 90503; 310/540-5858
Web www.torrancechamber.com

Motels/Motor Lodges

★★ **COURTYARD BY MARRIOTT TORRANCE PLAZA DEL AMO.** *2633 W Sepulveda Blvd (90505). 310/533-8000; fax 310/533-0564; res 800/321-2211. www.marriot.com.* 149 rms, 3 story. S, D $104; suites $119; under 18 free; wkend rates. Crib free. TV; cable (premium), VCR avail. Heated pool; whirlpool. Complimentary coffee in rms. Ck-out 1 pm. Coin lndry. Meeting rms. Business servs avail. In-rm modem link. Valet serv. Free parking. Exercise equipt. Balconies. Cr cds: A, C, D, DS, JCB, MC, V.

D

★★ **QUALITY INN SOUTH BAY.** *888 E Dominguez St, Carson (90746). 310/715-6688; fax 310/715-2957; res 800/228-5151. www.qualityinn.com.* 167 rms, 2 story. S $59-$69; D $69-$79; each addl $10; suites $125-$275; under 18 free. Crib free. TV; cable (premium). Pool. Restaurant 7 am-10 pm. Bar 11-2 am. Ck-

Golden poppies

out 1 pm. Coin lndry. Meeting rms. Valet serv. Beauty shop. Exercise equipt. Microwaves avail. Cr cds: A, C, D, DS, ER, JCB, MC, V.

D SC

Hotels

★★★ **HILTON TORRANCE.** *21333 Hawthorne Blvd (90503). 310/540-0500; fax 310/540-2065; toll-free 800/932-3322. www.hiltontorrance.com.* 371 rms, 12 story. S $129-$189; D $139-$199; each addl $10; suites $295-$650; under 18 free; wkend rates. Crib free. TV; cable (premium), VCR avail. Pool; whirlpool. Complimentary coffee in rms. Restaurant 6 am-10 pm. Bar 11-1 am; entertainment Tues-Sat. Ck-out noon. Convention facilities. Business servs avail. In-rm modem link. Concierge. Gift shop. Coin lndry. Exercise equipt; sauna. Many refrigerators. Some balconies. Luxury level. Cr cds: A, C, D, DS, JCB, MC, V.

D SC

★★★ **MARRIOTT TORRANCE .** *3635 Fashion Way (90503). 310/316-3636; fax 310/543-6076; toll-free 800/228-9290. www.marriott.com.* 487 rms, 17 story. S, D $134-$169; suites from $275; under 18 free; wkend rates. Crib free. Valet parking $8/day; self-park free. TV; cable (premium), VCR avail. Indoor/outdoor pool; whirlpool, poolside serv. Restaurant 6:30 am-10 pm; Fri, Sat to 11 pm. Bars 11-2 am. Ck-out 1 pm. Coin lndry. Meeting rms. Business center. In-rm modem link. Concierge. Gift shop. Barber, beauty shop. Tennis privileges. Golf privileges. Exercise equipt; sauna. Some bathrm phones. Balconies. Opp shopping center. Luxury level. Cr cds: A, C, D, DS, ER, JCB, MC, V.

D SC

All Suite

★★★ **SUMMERFIELD SUITES - TORRENCE/REDONDO BEACH.** *19901 Prairie Ave (90503). 310/371-8525; fax 310/542-9628; res 800/996-3426. www.summerfieldsuites.com.* 144 kit. suites, 3 story. S $190; D $220. Kit. suites $184-$230; under 12 free. Crib avail. Pet accepted. TV; cable. Heated pool; whirlpool. Complimentary continental bkfst, coffee in rms. Restaurant nearby. Ck-out noon. Coin lndry. Meeting rm. Airport transportation. Exercise equipt. Microwaves. Lawn games. Picnic tables, grills. Cr cds: A, C, D, DS, ER, JCB, MC, V.

D

Restaurants

★★ **CHRISTINE.** *24530 Hawthorne Blvd (90505). 310/373-1952.* Hrs: 11 am-2 pm, 5:30-9 pm; Sat 5-10 pm; Sun 5-9 pm. Closed hols. Res accepted. Eclectic menu. Bar. A la carte entrees: lunch $7.95-$12.95, dinner $8.95-$19.95. Children's menu. Specialties: portabella mushroom, peppered-crusted filet mignon, Asian grazing sampler. Parking. Outdoor dining. Tuscan villa atmosphere. Totally nonsmoking. Cr cds: A, D, MC, V.

D

★★★ **DEPOT.** *1250 Cabrillo Ave (90501). 310/787-7501.* Hrs: 11 am-2 pm, 5:30-10 pm; Fri to 10:30 pm; Sat 5-10:30 pm. Closed Sun; hols. Res accepted. Continental menu. Bar. Wine list. Lunch $7.95-$12.95, dinner $8.95-$20. Children's menu. Specialties: Thai barbecue chicken over stir-fry orzo, rock shrimp sausage with garlic, mushroom-crusted lamb chops. Valet parking. Outdoor dining. Elegant dining in casual atmosphere; original art displayed. Cr cds: A, D, MC, V.

D

Trinidad

(B-1) *See also Eureka*

Pop 362 **Elev** 40 ft **Area code** 707 **Zip** 95570

Information Chamber of Commerce, PO Box 356; 707/677-1610

Web www.trinidadcalifchamber.org

When leaders of a Spanish expedition landed here on June 18, 1775, it was Trinity Sunday, so the leaders named the area Trinidad. The city was founded in 1850 and was a port of entry for supplies packed into the upriver gold country. Offshore is Prisoner Rock; in the old days, constables took drunks here and gave them two options: swim the sobering length ashore or dry out here.

What to See and Do

Patrick's Point State Park. On 650 acres. Ocean fishing, beachcombing, tidepooling; hiking trails, picnicking, camping facilities in unusual rain-forest type of growth (res suggested). Museum exhibits, naturalist programs, Yorok Village. Standard fees. 5 mi N on US 101. Phone 707/677-3570.

Telonicher Marine Laboratory. Marine teaching and research facility of Humboldt State University. Touch-tank with local tidepool marine life; display aquariums. Self-guided tours of hallway exhibits. (Sept-May, daily; rest of yr, Mon-Fri; schedule may vary; closed school hols) 570 Ewing St, at Edwards St. Phone 707/826-3671. **FREE**

B&B/Small Inn

★★ LOST WHALE BED & BREAKFAST. *3452 Patricks Point Dr (95570). 707/677-3425; fax 707/677-0284; toll-free 800/677-7859. www.lostwhaleinn.com.* 8 rms. No A/C. No rm phones. May-Oct: S $114-$174; D $124-$184; each addl $20-$25; mid-June-mid-Sept (2-day min); lower rates rest of yr. Crib free. Playground. Complimentary full bkfst; afternoon refreshments. Ck-out 11 am, ck-in 3-6 pm. Business servs avail. Whirlpool. Balconies. Ocean view. Private beach. Greenhouse. On four acres. Totally nonsmoking. Cr cds: A, DS, MC, V.

Cottage Colony

★★ BISHOP PINE LODGE. *1481 Patricks Point Dr (95570). 707/677-3314; fax 707/677-3444; res 707/677-3314.* 12 cottage units (1-2-rm), 10 kits. No A/C. Apr-mid-Oct, hols: S, D $80; each addl $8; kit. units $8 addl; wkly rates mid-Oct-Mar; lower rates rest of yr. Crib $8. TV; cable (premium). Playground. Complimentary coffee. Ck-out 11 am. Business servs avail. In-rm modem link. Free airport transportation. Exercise equipt. Picnic tables, grills. Fish storage. Gazebo. Rustic cottages surrounded by wild azaleas, wooded grounds. Totally nonsmoking. Cr cds: A, DS, MC, V.

Truckee

(E-5) *See also Tahoe City (Lake Tahoe Area), Tahoe Vista (Lake Tahoe Area)*

Pop 3,484 **Elev** 5,820 ft
Area code 530 **Zip** 96161

Information Truckee-Donner Chamber of Commerce, 10065 Donner Pass Rd; 530/587-2757

Web www.truckee.com

Once a lumbering camp, now a railroad and recreation center, Truckee becomes important in winter as the gateway to one of California's best winter sports areas. In 1913 the first California ski club was organized; today more than 20 ski clubs make their headquarters here. Truckee is surrounded by Tahoe National Forest; a Ranger District office of the forest is located here.

What to See and Do

Donner Lake. Sparkling blue lake surrounded by mountain slopes of Sierras. Fishing, water sports. Nearby is Donner Pass, main route into California for more than a century. 3 mi W on US 40.

Donner Memorial State Park. A 353-acre area that serves as monument to Donner Party, stranded here in Oct 1846 by early blizzards. Of a party of 81 who pitched camp, only 48 survived. Emigrant Trail Museum has exhibits on Donner Party, construction of first transcontinental railroad, geology of the Sierra Nevada, wildlife, and Native Americans (daily; closed Jan 1, Thanksgiving, Dec 25; fee). Swimming, fishing; nature trail, x-country ski trail, picnicking, camping (Memorial Day-Labor Day). Ranger, naturalist programs (seasonal). Park (daily). Standard fees. 2 mi W on Donner Pass Rd. Phone 530/582-7892.

Skiing.

Boreal. Two quad, two triple, six double chairlifts; patrol, school, rentals, snowmaking; cafeteria, bar,

HISTORIC TRUCKEE

An Old West-style town tucked high in the Sierra Nevada near the northern shores of Lake Tahoe, Truckee offers not only atmosphere, but also a good aerobic workout—if you want to tackle a hill along the way. Park your car at one of the spaces or lots along Commercial Row, which is lined with Western-front 19th-century stores and buildings. Head first for the town's visitor center, which is housed in the old railway depot built in 1896. A plaque marks the 1868 date when the first transcontinental railroad reached Truckee. Walking west along Commercial Row, you'll find an old loading dock once used by the Southern Pacific Railroad, the town's oldest railway structure. Lumber was shipped from here to San Francisco, Sacramento, and other cities. Walk north up Spring Street to Jibboom Street, site of the town's aptly named Old Jail; one of the oldest in the West, it was in use from 1875 to 1964. If you're feeling energetic, you can make the rather strenuous climb farther up Spring Street to High Street, then go west (left) along High Street to see the 17-ton rocking stone, which Native Americans once used for drying food. The stone no longer rocks—it has been stabilized to ward off vandals and protect sightseers from accidents. Walking back down the hill to Commercial Row, stay on the north side of the street (opposite the visitor center). Historic buildings here include the 601, where Truckee's "Vigilance Committee" once met to combat crime, and the Capitol, an 1870 building that is the oldest on the street and has served as a saloon, county courthouse, and theater. Charlie Chaplin is said to have hung out at the Capitol while filming his classic *The Gold Rush* in Truckee. Just across the Bridge Street intersection is the old Truckee Hotel, which dates from 1868—though it was rebuilt in the early 20th century following a fire and renovated again in 1977. Walking north up Bridge Street, turn right on Church Street to find Gray's Log Waystation, Truckee's oldest building (1863). Return to Bridge Street and walk south. Across the railroad tracks, at East River Street, you'll find the gabled Swedish House, a rustic one-time boarding house that accommodated area lumbermen, ice cutters, railroad workers, and *Gold Rush* film crews. Go another block south, and cross the river via the walkway adjacent to the bridge. On Southeast River Street you'll see an old brick building that was once a Chinese herb shop. Returning north and recrossing the river, follow Bridge Street to West River Street where, to your left, you'll find the Victorian-style house of the man who owned the town's first lumber mill. From there, return up Bridge Street to Commercial Row, where several restaurants and cafes offer hearty cooking.

lodge. Forty-one runs, longest run one mi; vertical drop 600 ft. (Nov-May, daily) Night skiing. 10 mi W on I-80, Castle Peak exit. ¢¢¢¢¢

Donner Ski Ranch. Triple, five double chairlifts; patrol, school, rentals; bar, restaurant, cafeteria. Longest run one mi; vertical drop 750 ft. (Nov-May, daily) 10 mi W, 3½ mi off I-80 at Soda Springs exit. Phone 530/426-3635. ¢¢¢¢¢

Northstar. Two quad, three triple, three double chairlifts, gondola; patrol, school, rentals, snowmaking; cafeteria, restaurants, bars, lodging. Longest run three mi; vertical drop 2,280 ft. X-country skiing; rentals. (Nov-Apr, daily) Half-day rates. Summer activities incl tennis, 18-hole golf, mountain biking, horseback riding, and swimming. 6 mi S on CA 267 via I-80. Phone 530/562-1010.

Royal Gorge Cross-Country Ski Resort. Approx 80 x-country trails over 200 mi of rolling terrain. Patrol, school, rentals; restaurants, two lodges. Longest trail 14 mi. (Mid-Nov-mid-May) 12 mi W on I-80. Phone 800/500-3871. ¢¢¢¢¢

Sugar Bowl. Quad, six double chairlifts, gondola; patrol, school, rentals; restaurant, cafeterias, bar, nursery, lodging. Forty-seven runs, longest run 1½ mi; vertical drop 1,500 ft. (Nov-Apr, daily) 11 mi W on I-80. Phone 530/426-9000. ¢¢¢¢¢

Tahoe Donner. One double chairlift, surface tow; patrol, school, rentals; cafeteria, restaurant, bar. (Dec-Apr, daily; closed Easter) X-country trails (fee). 6 mi NW off I-80. Phone 530/587-9444. ¢¢¢¢¢

Special Events

Truckee-Tahoe Airshow. Mid-June. Phone 530/587-4540.

Truckee Rodeo. Second wkend Aug. Phone 530/582-9852.

Donner Party Hike. First wkend Oct.

Motels/Motor Lodges

★★ BEST WESTERN TAHOE INN. *11331 Hwy 267 (96161). 530/587-4525; fax 530/587-8173; res 800/528-1234. www.bestwesterntahoe.com.* 100 rms, 2 story. S $95-$119; D $102-$126; each addl $7; under 12 free; golf, fishing, ski packages; higher rates hol wkends. Crib free. TV; VCR avail (free movies). Pool; whirlpool. Complimentary continental bkfst. Restaurant nearby. Ck-out 11 am. Meeting rms. Business servs avail. Downhill ski 5 mi. Exercise equipt; sauna. Microwaves avail. Cr cds: A, C, D, DS, ER, MC, V.

D

★★ DONNER LAKE VILLAGE RESORT. *15695 Donner Pass Rd (96161). 530/587-6081; fax 530/587-8782; toll-free 800/621-6664.* 66 rms, 2 story. No A/C. July-Sept, mid-Dec-Apr: S, D $100-$135; each addl $10; suites $135-$180; under 12 free; higher rates hols; lower rates rest of yr. Crib free. TV; cable. Complimentary coffee in rms. Ck-out 11 am. Meeting rms. Business servs avail. Downhill ski 4 mi; x-country ski 7 mi. Sauna. Balconies, grills. On lake; marina. Cr cds: A, C, D, DS, MC, V.

SC

Resort

★★ NORTHSTAR-AT-TAHOE. *Hwy 267 and Northstar Dr (96161). 530/562-1010; fax 530/562-2215; toll-free 800/466-6784. www.skinorthstar.com.* 30 rms in 3-story lodge, 205 condos, 27 houses (3-5-bedrm). No A/C. Mid-Nov-mid-Apr: S, D $149-$454; condos $149-$454; houses $366-$599; ski, golf plans; higher rates: Dec 25, hols; lower rates rest of yr. TV; cable. 2 heated pools; whirlpool, wading pool. Playground. Coffee in rms. Bar. Ck-out 11 am, ck-in 5 pm. Grocery, delicatessen. Coin lndry. Meeting rms. Business center. Free railroad station, bus depot transportation. Tennis, pro. 18-hole golf, pro, greens fee $67 (incl cart), putting green, driving range. Downhill/x-country ski on site. Game rm. Exercise equipt; sauna. Many fireplaces. Private decks, balconies. Picnic tables. Cr cds: A, DS, MC, V.

D

B&B/Small Inn

★ TRUCKEE HOTEL. *10007 Bridge St (96161). 530/587-4444; fax 530/587-1599; toll-free 800/659-6921. www.thetruckeehotel.com.* 36 rms, 4 story, 5 suites. No A/C. No elvtr. No rm phones. Thanksgiving-Mar: S, D $85-$125; each addl $15; suites $110-$125; under 5 free; hols (2-day min); lower rates rest of yr. Crib free. Street parking. Complimentary continental bkfst, coffee in rms. Bar. Ck-out 11 am, ck-in 3 pm. Meeting rms. Business servs avail. Gift shop. Sundries. Airport, railroad station transportation. Game rm. Opp river. Totally nonsmoking. Cr cds: A, MC, V.

Restaurant

★ OB'S PUB & RESTAURANT. *10046 Donner Pass Rd (96160). 530/587-4164.* Hrs: 11:30 am-10:30 pm. Bar. Lunch $3.95-$7.95. A la carte entrees: dinner $10.95-$16. Specializes in seafood, beef. Built in early 1900s; many antiques, woodburning stove. Cr cds: D, DS, MC, V.

D

Ukiah

(E-2) *See also Clear Lake Area*

Settled 1855 **Pop** 14,599 **Elev** 639 ft **Area code** 707 **Zip** 95482

Information Greater Ukiah Chamber of Commerce, 200 S School St; 707/462-4705

Web www.ukiah.com

In the center of a valley that Native Americans called Ukiah, or Deep Valley, this is the seat of Mendocino County. It is the trading place of an agricultural area that produces a $75-million annual crop of pears, grapes, and other products. Recreational activities incl golf, tennis, and fishing.

What to See and Do

Grace Hudson Museum. Permanent exhibits on Pomo people; regional artists and photographers; early 20th-century paintings by Mendocino County artist Grace Hudson. Changing exhibits. **The Sun House** (1911) is the six-rm craftsman house of Grace and John Hudson. Tours. (July 4-Labor Day, Tues-Sun; rest of yr, Wed-Sun) 431 S Main St. Phone 707/467-2836. **FREE**

Lake Mendocino. Artificial lake produced by Coyote Dam, which controls Russian River. Dedicated in 1959, the lake provides swimming, waterskiing, fishing, boating (ramps, docks); hiking, picnicking, camping (fee). Interpretive programs. (Apr-Sept, daily) Pets on leash only. 3 mi NE, off US 101. Phone 707/462-7651. **FREE**

Wineries.

Dunnewood Vineyards. Winery tours (by appt). Tasting rm (daily; closed hols). Picnic area. 2399 N State St. Phone 707/462-2987. **FREE**

Parducci Wine Cellars. Guided tours; wine tasting (daily; closed hols). 501 Parducci Rd. Phone 707/462-9463. **FREE**

Special Event

Mendocino County Fair & Apple Show. Boonville. Three days mid- or late Sept. Phone 707/895-3011.

Motels/Motor Lodges

★★★ **DISCOVERY INN.** *1340 N. State St (95482). 707/462-8873; fax 707/462-1249.* 177 rms, 2 story. May-Sept: S $68-$71; D $75-$81; each addl $5; suites $65-$80; kit. units $85; lower rates rest of yr. Crib free. TV; cable (premium). Complimentary continental bkfst. 2 heated pools; whirlpools. Restaurant 6 am-11 pm. Ck-out noon. Coin lndry. Meeting rms. Business servs avail. In-rm modem link. Refrigerators. Redwood theme park on grounds. Cr cds: A, C, D, DS, ER, JCB, MC, V.

★ **ECONOMY INN.** *406 S State St (95482). 707/462-8611; fax 707/468-9476; toll-free 800/578-7878.* 40 rms, 2 story. May-Sept: S, D $55-$65; each addl $5; higher rates: hols, special events; lower rates rest of yr. TV; cable (premium). Pool. Complimentary coffee in rms. Restaurant opp 9 am-10 pm. Ck-out 11 am. Business servs avail. Some refrigerators. Cr cds: A, C, D, DS, MC, V.

SC

★★ **RAMADA LIMITED.** *601 Talmage Rd (95482). 707/462-8868; fax 707/468-9043; res 800/272-6232.* 40 rms, 2 story. May-Sept: S, D $55-$75; each addl $5; lower rates rest of yr. TV; cable (premium). Pool. Complimentary continental bkfst, coffee in rms. Restaurant nearby. Ck-out 11 am. Business servs avail. In-rm modem link. Refrigerators. Cr cds: A, C, D, DS, MC, V.

Resort

★★★ **VICHY HOT SPRINGS RESORT AND INN.** *2605 Vichy Springs Rd (95482). 707/462-9515; fax 707/462-9516. www.vichysprings.com.* 20 rms, 3 cottages. S $110; D $145; each addl $35; cottages $195; hols (2-day min). TV avail; VCR avail. Complimentary full bkfst. Restaurant nearby. Ck-out noon, ck-in 3 pm. Business servs avail. Luggage handling. Free railroad station, bus depot transportation. Lighted tennis privileges. 18-hole golf privileges. Pool; whirlpool. Refrigerator, microwave, fireplace in cottage. Balconies. Picnic tables, grills. Built between 1854-1870; country decor. Totally nonsmoking. Cr cds: A, C, D, DS, ER, JCB, MC, V.

B&B/Small Inn

★★★ **THATCHER INN & RESTAURANT.** *13401 S Hwy 101, Hopland (95449). 707/744-1890; fax 707/744-1219; toll-free 800/266-1891. www.thatcherinn.com.* 20 rms, 3 story, 2 suites. 3 A/C. S $95-$115; D $115-

$130; each addl $25; suites $150-$165; under 10 free. TV in game rm. Pool. Complimentary full bkfst. Dining rm 11:30 am-2 pm, 5:30-9:30 pm. Bar 11 am-10 pm. Ck-out noon, ck-in 3 pm. Business servs avail. In-rm modem link. Victorian inn (1890) with period furnishings. Totally nonsmoking. Cr cds: A, MC, V.

Vacaville

(F-3) *See also Fairfield*

Pop 71,479 **Elev** 179 ft **Area code** 707 **Zip** 95688

What to See and Do

Factory Stores at Vacaville. Approx 120 outlet stores. (Daily) I-80, Orange Dr exit, 321-2 Nut Tree Rd. Phone 707/447-5755.

Motels/Motor Lodges

★★ BEST WESTERN HERITAGE INN. *1420 E Monte Vista Ave (95688). 707/448-8453; fax 707/447-8649; res 800/528-1234. www.bestwestern.com.* 41 rms, 2 story. S $63; D $70; each addl $5; suites $90; under 12 free. Crib $5. TV; cable. Pool. Complimentary continental bkfst. Restaurant adj open 24 hrs. Ck-out 11 am. Business servs avail. Refrigerators, microwaves avail. Cr cds: A, C, D, DS, MC, V.
D

★★ COURTYARD BY MARRIOTT. *120 Nut Tree Pkwy (95687). 707/451-9000; fax 707/449-3952; res 800/321-2211.* 107 rms, 10 suites, 2 story. S, D $84-$94; each addl $10; suites $120-$150; under 18 free; wkend rates. Crib free. TV; cable. Complimentary coffee in rms. Restaurant 6:30-10 am; Sat, Sun 7-11 am. Rm serv 5-10 pm. Bar 5-10 pm. Ck-out noon. Meeting rms. Business servs avail. In-rm modem link. Coin lndry. Exercise equipt. Health club privileges. Pool; whirlpool. Refrigerators, microwaves avail. Cr cds: A, D, DS, MC, V.
D SC

★★ QUALITY INN. *950 Leisure Town Rd (95687). 707/446-8888; fax 707/449-0109; toll-free 800/638-7949.* 120 rms, 2 story. S $50-$55; D $60-$65; each addl $5; under 18 free. Crib free. TV; cable. Pool; whirlpool. Complimentary continental bkfst. Restaurant opp 7 am-9 pm. Ck-out 11 am. Business servs avail. In-rm modem link. Cr cds: A, D, DS, MC, V.
D SC

Restaurant

★ COFFEE TREE. *100 Nut Tree Pkwy (95687). 707/448-8435.* Hrs: 6 am-9 pm. Closed Dec 25. Bkfst $3.95-$8.55, lunch, dinner $3.95-$14.95. Children's menu. Own desserts. Colorful decor; art display. Family-owned. Totally nonsmoking. Cr cds: A, D, DS, MC, V.
D SC

Valencia

(E-4) *See also Los Angeles*

Pop 30,000 **Area code** 661 **Zip** 91355

Information Santa Clarita Valley Chamber of Commerce, 23920 Valencia Blvd, Suite 100, Santa Clarita; 661/259-4787 or 800/718-TOUR, ext 123

Web www.scvchamber.org

What to See and Do

Pyramid Lake Recreation Area. Lake with swimming, waterskiing, windsurfing, fishing, boating (rentals, ramp); picnicking, concession, camping (fee). (Daily; closed hols) 20 mi N on I-5. ¢¢¢

Six Flags California. Incl Magic Mountain theme park and Hurricane Harbor water park. Theme park features over 100 rides, shows, and attractions, incl Superman The Escape—the first ride ever to break the 100-mph speed barrier; Batman & Robin Live Action Show; eight major roller coasters; children's play area with scaled-down rides, animal farm, petting zoo. Theme park Apr-Oct, daily; rest of yr, wkends). Water park features 75-ft-tall enclosed speed slides; adult activities pool and body slides; 7,000-sq-ft lagoon with water sports; children's Castaway Cove.

Water park (June-Labor Day, daily; mid-late May and mid-late Sept, wkends). 26101 Magic Mtn Pkwy, off I-5. Phone 661/255-4100. ¢¢¢¢¢

Motels/Motor Lodges

★★ **BEST WESTERN INN.** *27413 Championship Way (91355). 661/255-0555; fax 661/255-2216; toll-free 800/528-1234. www.bestwestern.com.* 182 rms, 2 suites in 4 buildings, 2 story. S, D $80-$110; each addl $10; suites $175; under 18 free. Crib free. TV; cable (premium). 2 heated pools; wading pool, whirlpool. Complimentary coffee in rms. Restaurant 7 am-10 pm. Bar 4-10 pm. Ck-out noon. Coin lndry. Meeting rms. Business servs avail. Refrigerators avail. Some patios. Cr cds: A, C, D, DS, MC, V.
D SC

★★ **HAMPTON INN.** *25259 The Old Rd, Santa Clarita (91381). 661/253-2400; fax 661/253-1683; res 800/426-7866. www.hamptoninn.com.* 130 rms, 4 story. S, D $99-$109. Crib free. TV; cable (premium). Heated pool; whirlpool. Complimentary continental bkfst. Coffee in rms. Restaurant opp open 24 hrs. Ck-out noon. Coin lndry. Meeting rm. Business center. Valet serv. Sundries. Health club privileges. Some refrigerators; microwaves avail. Some balconies. Cr cds: A, C, D, DS, V.
D

Hotels

★★★ **HILTON.** *27710 The Old Rd (91355). 661/254-8800; fax 661/254-9399; toll-free 800/445-8667. www.hilton.com.* 152 rms, 2 story. S $89-$129; D $99-$139; each addl $10; suites $198-$250; under 18 free; family rates. Crib free. TV; cable (premium). Heated pool; whirlpool, poolside serv. Complimentary coffee in rms. Restaurant 6:30 am-10 pm. Rm serv 5:30-10:30 pm. Bar 5-10:30 pm. Ck-out noon. Sundries. Coin lndry. Meeting rms. Business center. In-rm modem link. Exercise equipt. Refrigerators, microwaves; some bathrm phones. Some balconies. Cr cds: A, C, D, DS, ER, JCB, MC, V.
D SC

★★★ **HYATT VALENCIA AND SANTA CLARITA CONFERENCE CENTER.** *24500 Town Center Dr (91355). 661/799-1234. www.hyatt.com.* 244 rms, 6 story. S, D $175-$295; each addl $20; under 17 free. Crib avail. Valet parking. Heated pool. TV; cable (premium), VCR avail. Complimentary coffee in rms, newspaper. Restaurant 6 am-10:30 pm. Bar. Ck-out noon. Meeting rms. Business center. Valet serv. Gift shop. Exercise rm. Some refrigerators, minibars. Cr cds: A, C, D, DS, MC, V.

Vallejo

(F-3) *See also Berkeley, Fairfield, Martinez, Oakland*

Founded 1851 **Pop** 109,199 **Elev** 50 ft **Area code** 707

Information Convention & Visitors Bureau, 495 Mare Island Way, 94590; 800/4-VALLEJO

Web www.visitvallejo.com

This was California's capital in 1852 for about a week; and again, a year later, for just over one month. Despite the departure of the legislature in 1853 for Benicia, the town prospered because the United States purchased Mare Island for a Navy yard in 1854. The former Mare Island Naval Shipyard is a 2,300-acre spread of land between the Mare Island Strait and San Pablo Bay.

What to See and Do

Benicia Capitol State Historic Park. Building has been restored and furnished in style of 1853-1854, when it served as state capitol. (Daily; closed Jan 1, Thanksgiving, Dec 25) 1st and G sts, 6 mi SE, in Benicia. Phone 707/745-3385. ¢

Six Flags Marine World. Wildlife theme park. Major shows featuring killer whales, dolphins, sea lions, tigers, exotic and predatory birds, and waterski/boat show. Rides and attractions incl two roller coasters. Participatory exhibits incl Elephant Encounter, Butterfly World, giraffe feedings, and lorikeet feedings. (Memorial Day-Labor Day, daily; Mar-Memorial Day and Labor Day-Oct, wkends) Jct I-80 and CA 37, Marine World Pkwy. ¢¢¢¢¢

Vallejo Ferry. One-hr direct ferry service between Vallejo and San Francisco. Also to Angel Island State Park. Ferry packages incl Marine World Package, Napa Valley Wine Tour, and Napa Valley Wine Train (schedules vary; fee). (Daily; closed Jan 1, Thanksgiving, Dec 25) 495 Mare Island Way. One-way **¢¢¢**

Vallejo Naval and Historical Museum. Two galleries house changing exhibits on local history. Two additional galleries house permanent exhibits on Navy and Mare Island Naval Shipyard history. Naval exhibits incl models, murals, and a functioning submarine periscope. Also here is a local history research library (by appt) and a book/gift shop. (Tues-Sat; closed hols) 734 Marin St, located in the old City Hall building. Phone 707/643-0077. **¢**

Special Events

Solano County Fair. Fairgrounds, Fairgrounds Dr, N off I-80. Phone 707/644-4401. July.

Jazz, Art, and Wine Festival. Waterfront at Mare Island Way. Late Aug. Phone 707/642-3653.

Whaleboat Regatta. Marina Vista Park. Early Oct. Phone 707/648-4217.

Motels/Motor Lodges

★★ BEST WESTERN HERITAGE INN. *1955 E 2nd St, Benicia (94510). 707/746-0401; fax 707/745-0842; toll-free 800/528-1234. www.bestwestern.com.* 99 rms, 3 story. S, D $65-$85; each addl $5; suites $85-$100; kit. units $75-$85; under 12 free; wkly, monthly rates. Crib free. Pet accepted, some restrictions; $25 refundable. TV; cable (premium). Pool; whirlpool. Complimentary continental bkfst. Coffee in rms. Restaurant nearby. Ck-out 11 am. Meeting rms. Business servs avail. Valet serv. In-rm whirlpools; some refrigerators, wet bars; microwaves avail. Cr cds: A, C, D, DS, MC, V.

D SC

★★ RAMADA INN. *1000 Admiral Callaghan Ln (94591). 707/643-2700; fax 707/642-1148; toll-free 800/677-4466.* 130 rms, 3 story, 36 suites. May-Sept: S $95-$100; D $110; each addl $15; suites $105-$130; under 18 free. Crib free. TV; cable (premium). Pool; whirlpool. Complimentary continental bkfst, coffee in rms. Restaurant nearby. Ck-out noon. Coin lndry. Meeting rms. Business servs avail. In-rm modem link. Valet serv. Health club privileges. Refrigerators, microwaves. Picnic tables, grill. Cr cds: A, C, D, DS, ER, JCB, V.

D SC

Van Nuys (L.A.)

Area code 818

This community in the San Fernando Valley is an integral part of Los Angeles, but is regarded by many as a separate entity.

Motel/Motor Lodge

★ TRAVELODGE AT VAN NUYS. *6909 Sepulveda Blvd, Van Nuys (91405). 818/787-5400; fax 818/782-0239; toll-free 800/578-7878. www.travelodge.com.* 74 rms, 3 story. S, D $49-$79; each addl $6; under 12 free. TV; cable (premium). Pool. Complimentary continental bkfst, coffee in rms. Restaurant nearby. Ck-out 11 am. Meeting rm. Refrigerators. Cr cds: A, C, D, DS, MC, V.

D SC

Hotel

★★★ AIRTEL PLAZA HOTEL. *7277 Valjean Ave, Van Nuys (91406). 818/997-7676; fax 818/785-8864; toll-free 800/224-7835. www.airtelplaza.com.* 268 rms, 3-5 story. S, $129; D $139; each addl $10; suites $165-$600; under 18 free. Crib free. TV; cable (premium). Heated pool; whirlpools, poolside serv. Restaurants 6 am-10 pm. Bar 10-2 am. Ck-out noon. Convention facilities. Business servs avail. In-rm modem link. Bellhops. Gift shop. Exercise equipt. Some refrigerators. Some private patios, balconies. Cr cds: A, C, D, DS, ER, JCB, MC, V.

D

Ventura

(E-3) *See also Ojai, Oxnard, Santa Barbara, Thousand Oaks*

Founded 1782 **Pop** 93,483 **Elev** 50 ft **Area code** 805

Information Visitor & Convention Bureau Information Center, 89 S California St, Suite C, 93001; 805/648-2075 or 800/333-2989

Web www.ventura-usa.com

What was once a little mission surrounded by huge stretches of sagebrush and mustard plants is now the busy city of Ventura. The sagebrush and mustard have been replaced by citrus, avocado, and other agriculture, but the mission still stands. With the Pacific shore at its feet and rolling foothills at its back, Ventura attracts a steady stream of vacationers. It is in the center of the largest lemon-producing county in the United States.

What to See and Do

Albinger Archaeological Museum. Preserved archaeological exploration site and visitor center in downtown area. Evidence of Native American culture 3,500 yrs old; Chumash village site, settled approx A.D. 1500; foundation of original mission; Chinese and Mexican artifacts; audiovisual programs. (Wed-Sun; closed hols) 113 E Main St. Phone 805/648-5823. **FREE**

Camping. Emma Wood State Beach. North Beach. Swimming, surfing, fishing; two RV group camping sites, 61 primitive camp sites. Standard fees. Access from W Pacific Coast Hwy, state beaches exit northbound US 101. Phone 805/968-1033.

Channel Islands National Park. (see)

Channel Islands National Park Visitor's Center. Displays, exhibits and scale models of the five islands; marine life exhibit; observation tower; film of the islands (25 min). (Daily; closed Thanksgiving, Dec 25) 1901 Spinnaker Dr. Phone 805/658-5730. **FREE**

Island Packer Cruises. Boat leaves Ventura Harbor for picnic, sightseeing, and recreational trips to Channel Islands National Park. Res required. (Memorial Day-Sept, five islands; rest of yr, two islands) For details contact 1867 Spinnaker Dr, 93001. Phone 805/642-7688. **¢¢¢¢¢**

Mission San Buenaventura. (1782) Ninth California mission and the last founded by Fray Juneípero Serra. Massive, with a striped rib dome on the bell tower; restored. Garden with fountain. Museum (enter through gift shop at 225 E Main St) features original wooden bell. Museum (daily; closed hols). Church and gardens (daily). 211 E Main St, off US 101. **¢**

Olivas Adobe. (1847). Restored with antique furnishings; displays; gardens; visitor center, video. Tours (by appt). House open for viewing (Sat, Sun). Grounds (daily; closed hols). Special programs monthly. 4200 Olivas Park Dr, off US 101 Victoria Ave exit. Phone 805/644-4346. **FREE**

Ortega Adobe. (1857) Restored and furnished adobe built on the Camino Real. Furnished with rustic handmade furniture from the 1850s. Tours (by appt). Grounds (daily). 215 W Main St. Phone 805/658-4726. **FREE**

Ronald Reagan Presidential Library and Museum. Museum and library dedicated to the 40th President of the US, with exhibits, documents, and more. (Daily; closed Jan 1, Thanksgiving, Dec 25) 40 Presidential Dr in Simi Valley, 30 mi E. Phone 805/522-8444. Adults **¢¢** Children 15 and under **FREE**

San Buenaventura State Beach. Approx 115 acres on a sheltered sweep of coast. Offers swimming, lifeguard (summer), surf fishing; coastal bicycle trail access point, picnicking, concession. Standard fees. (Daily) Phone 805/968-1711. **¢¢**

Ventura County Museum of History and Art. Collection of Native American, Spanish, and pioneer artifacts; George Stuart Collection of Historical Figures; changing exhibits of local history and art; outdoor areas depicting the county's agricultural history; educational programs, research library, gift shop. (Tues-Sun; closed Jan 1, Thanksgiving, Dec 25) 100 E Main St. Phone 805/653-0323. **¢¢**

Ventura Harbor. Accommodates more than 1,500 boats; three marinas, launch ramp, mast up dry storage boat yard, drydock and repair facilities, fuel docks, guest slips. Sportfishing and island boats; sailboat rentals; cruises. Swimming, fishing; hotel, shops, restaurants; Channel Islands National Park headquarters. 1603 Anchors Way Dr. Phone 805/644-0169.

Special Events

Whale watching. Gray whales, Dec-Mar; blue whales, July-Sept. Phone 805/642-1393.

Ventura County Fair. Seaside Park. Parade, rodeo, carnival, entertainment, livestock auction. Aug. Phone 805/648-3376.

Motels/Motor Lodges

★★ CLARION HOTEL VENTURA BEACH. *2055 Harbor Blvd (93001). 805/643-6000; fax 805/643-7137; toll-free 877/983-6887. www.venturabeachhotel.com.* 284 rms, 4 story. July-Labor Day: S, D $79-$120; each addl $10; suites $139; under 18 free; package plans; lower rates rest of yr. TV; cable (premium), VCR avail. Heated pool; whirlpool. Coffee in rms. Restaurant 6:30 am-10 pm; Sat, Sun 7 am-10:30 pm. Bar 3-11 pm. Ck-out noon. Convention facilities. Business servs avail. In-rm modem link. Valet serv. Gift shop. Exercise equipt; sauna. Balconies. Beach 1 blk. Cr cds: A, C, D, DS, ER, JCB, MC, V.

D SC

★★★ COUNTRY INN & SUITES - VENTURA. *298 Chestnut St (93001). 805/653-1434; fax 805/648-7126; res 800/456-4000. www.countryinns.com.* 120 kit. units, 3 story. S, D $79-$99; each addl $10; suites $209; under 12 free. Garage parking. Pet accepted. TV; cable, VCR (movies $4). Heated pool; whirlpool. Complimentary full bkfst. Ck-out noon. Coin lndry. Meeting rm. Business servs avail. In-rm modem link. Valet serv. Bathrm phones; some fireplaces. Private patios, balconies. Country decor. Opp ocean. Cr cds: A, DS, MC, V.

D

★ VAGABOND INN. *756 E Thompson Blvd (93001). 805/648-5371; fax 805/648-5613; res 800/522-1555.* 82 rms, 2 story. S $45-$68; D $50-$80; each addl $5; higher rates special events. Crib free. Pet accepted; $5. TV; cable (premium). Heated pool; whirlpool. Complimentary continental bkfst, coffee in rms. Restaurant open 5 am-10 pm. Ck-out noon. Business servs avail. Cr cds: A, C, D, DS, MC, V.

SC

B&Bs/Small Inns

★★ CLOCKTOWER INN. *181 E Santa Clara St (93001). 805/652-0141; fax 805/643-1432; toll-free 800/727-1027. www.clocktowerinn.com.* 49 rms, 2 story. S $79-$129; D $89-$139; each addl $10; under 12 free. TV; cable (premium), VCR avail. Complimentary continental bkfst. Restaurant 11 am-2:30 pm, 5-9:30 pm; Fri-Sun to 10 pm. Ck-out noon. Meeting rms. Business servs avail. In-rm modem link. Some fireplaces. Private patios, balconies. Near beach, downtown. Southwestern decor. Renovated firehouse in park setting; atrium. Cr cds: A, C, D, DS, ER, JCB, MC, V.

D SC

★★ LA MER EUROPEAN BED & BREAKFAST. *411 Poli St (93001). 805/643-3600; fax 805/653-7329. www.lamerbnb.com.* 5 rms, 2 story, 1 suite. No A/C. No rm phones. S $110; D $115; suite $150-$155; midwk rates, packages avail. Children over 13 yrs only. Complimentary buffet bkfst; afternoon refreshments. Ck-out noon, ck-in 4 pm. Business servs avail. Massage. Antique horse-drawn carriage rides. 1890 building, library. Antiques. Each rm individually decorated to represent a European country. Private patios. Overlooks ocean. Totally nonsmoking. Cr cds: A, MC, V.

★★ PIERPONT INN. *550 Sanjon Rd (93001). 805/643-6144; fax 805/641-1501; toll-free 800/285-4667. www.pierpontinn.com.* 72 rms, 2-3 story. No A/C. No elvtr. S, D $115-$125; each addl $10; suites $169; cottages $189-$289; under 12 free. Crib free. TV; cable (premium), VCR avail (movies). Pool. Complimentary continental bkfst. Coffee in rms. Restaurant 6:30-9 am, 11:30 am-closing. Bar 11 am-midnight. Ck-out noon. Meeting rms. Business servs avail. Valet serv.

Tennis privileges. Health club privileges. Some fireplaces. Many private verandas, balconies. Established in 1908. Overlooks Pierpont Bay. Cr cds: A, C, D, DS, MC, V.

SC

Victorville

(D-5) *See also Barstow, Big Bear Lake, Lake Arrowhead*

Founded 1878 **Pop** 40,674 **Elev** 2,715 ft **Area code** 760

Information Chamber of Commerce, 14174 Green Tree Blvd, 92392; 760/245-6506

Web www.vvchamber.com

You may never have been in Victorville, but you've probably seen the town before—it has been the setting for hundreds of cowboy movies. This aspect of the town's economy has waned, replaced by light industry. On the edge of the Mojave Desert, the town serves as a base for desert exploration. The presence of lime has attracted four major cement plants to the vicinity.

What to See and Do

California Route 66 Museum. A tribute to the first national highway to connect Chicago with Los Angeles. Exhibits on different artists' views of Route 66 and its history. (Thurs-Mon) 16825 Route 66 "D" St. Phone 760/951-0436. **FREE**

Mojave Narrows Regional Park. Fishing, boating; hiking, bridle trails, picnicking, snack bar, camping (fee). Park (daily; closed Dec 25). 2 mi S on I-15, then 4 mi E on Bear Valley Rd, 3 mi N on Ridgecrest. Phone 760/245-2226. Per vehicle **¢¢**

Roy Rogers-Dale Evans Museum. Western-style fort depicting the personal and professional lives of the Rogers. (Daily; closed Easter, Thanksgiving, Dec 25) 15650 Seneca Rd. Phone 760/243-4547. **¢¢¢**

Special Events

San Bernardino County Fair. 14800 7th St. Rodeo, livestock and agricultural exhibits, carnival. Phone 760/951-2200. May.

Huck Finn Jubilee. At Mojave Narrows Regional Park. River-raft building, fence painting, bluegrass and clogging activities; food. Father's Day wkend. Phone 760/245-2226.

Motels/Motor Lodges

★★ BEST WESTERN GREEN TREE INN. *14173 Green Tree Inn (92392). 760/245-3461; fax 760/245-7745; res 800/528-1234.* 168 rms, 2-3 story. S $60-$64; D $64-$68; each addl $4; suites $70-$80; kit. units, studio rms $64-$70; under 12 free. Crib free. TV; cable. Heated pool; wading pool, whirlpool, poolside serv. Complimentary coffee in rms. Restaurant open 24 hrs. Rm serv 7 am-10 pm. Bar 10-2 am; entertainment. Ck-out 1 pm. Meeting rms. Business center. Shopping arcade. Beauty shop. Health club privileges. Refrigerators. View of desert, mountains. Cr cds: A, C, D, DS, MC, V.

★ HOWARD JOHNSON. *16868 Stoddard Wells Rd (92392). 760/243-7700; fax 760/243-4432. www.hojo.com.* 101 rms, 2 story. S $27-$36; D $36-$58; each addl $5; suites $65-$85; under 17 free. Crib free. TV; cable (premium). Pool. Complimentary coffee in lobby. Restaurant opp open 24 hrs. Ck-out noon. Coin lndry. Business servs avail. Some in-rm whirlpools. Cr cds: A, D, DS, MC, V.

D

Restaurant

★★ CHATEAU CHANG. *15425 Anacapa Rd (92392). 760/241-3040.* Hrs: 11:30 am-2:30 pm, 5-9:30 pm; Fri, Sat to 10:30 pm. Closed Sun; hols. Res accepted. French, continental menu. Bar. Lunch $6-$6.50. Complete meals: dinner $9.95-$33.95. Specialties: flaming filet mignon, roast duck with orange sauce, whole lobster Thermidor. Contemporary decor; gray marble floors; saltwater aquarium. Cr cds: A, D, DS, MC, V.

D

Visalia

(B-3) *See also Hanford, Porterville, Three Rivers*

Pop 75,636 **Elev** 331 ft **Area code** 559

Information Convention & Visitors Bureau, 301 E Acequia St; 559/730-7000

Web www.cvbvisalia.com

What to See and Do

Chinese Cultural Center. Chinese artifacts, paintings, rare archaeological findings. Chinese garden. Confucius Temple. (Wed-Sun; closed hols) 500 S Akers Rd. Phone 559/625-4545. **FREE**

Sequoia & Kings Canyon National Parks. (see) Approx 50 mi E on CA 198.

Tulare County Museum. Ten buildings set in a 140-acre park house historical exhibits. Park features *End of the Trail* statue by James Earl Fraser. Museum has Native American artifacts, early farm equipment, antique guns, clocks, dolls; log cabin. (Mon, Thurs-Sun; closed hols) Mooney Grove, 27000 S Mooney Blvd. Phone 559/733-6616. **¢¢**

Motel/Motor Lodge

★ **ECONO LODGE.** *1400 S Mooney Blvd (93277). 559/732-6641; fax 559/739-7520; res 800/242-4261.* 49 rms, 2 story. S $55; D $61; each addl $5. Crib $4. TV; cable (premium). Pool. Complimentary continental bkfst, coffee in rms. Restaurant 5:30-10 pm. Ck-out 11 am. Some refrigerators, microwaves. Cr cds: A, C, D, DS, ER, JCB, MC, V.

SC

Hotel

★★★ **RADISSON HOTEL VISALIA.** *300 S Court (93291). 559/636-1111; fax 559/636-8224; res 800/333-3333. www.radisson.com.* 201 rms, 8 story. S, D $138-$148; each addl $10; suites $200-$450; family rates. Crib free. TV; cable. Pool; whirlpool; poolside serv. Complimentary coffee in rms. Restaurant 6 am-10 pm. Bar 11-2 am. Ck-out noon. Meeting rms. Business servs avail. In-rm modem link. Concierge. Valet parking. Free airport, RR station transportation. Exercise equipt. Minibars. Wet bar in suites. Cr cds: A, C, D, DS, ER, JCB, MC, V.

D

B&B/Small Inn

★★ **THE SPALDING HOUSE.** *631 N Encina (93291). 559/739-7877; fax 559/625-0902.* 3 suites, 2 story. No rm phones. S $75; D $85. TV in living rm; VCR avail. Complimentary full bkfst. Restaurant nearby. Ck-out noon, ck-in 3 pm. Colonial Revival house built 1901; fully restored. Elegant furnishings; some fireplaces, antiques. Library; piano in music rm; sitting rm. Totally nonsmoking. Cr cds: A, MC, V.

Restaurant

★★★ **THE VINTAGE PRESS.** *216 N Willis (93291). 559/733-3033.* Hrs: 11:30 am-2 pm, 6-10:30 pm; Fri, Sat to 11 pm; Sun 10 am-2 pm, 5-9 pm. Closed Dec 25. Res accepted. California menu. Bar 11-2 am. Lunch $6.95-$12.95, dinner $15.95-$37. Children's menu. Outdoor dining. Antiques. Family-owned. Cr cds: A, C, D, MC, V.

D

Walnut Creek

(see San Francisco map) *See also Berkeley, Concord, Oakland*

Pop 60,569 **Elev** 135 ft **Area code** 925

Motel/Motor Lodge

★★★ **LAFAYETTE PARK HOTEL.** *3287 Mt Diablo Blvd, Lafayette (94549). 925/283-3700; fax 925/284-1621; toll-free 800/368-2468. www.woodsidehotels.com.* A soaring rotunda, polished marble floors, rich woods, and a handsome roaring fireplace greet guests as they enter this boutique French chateau hotel. The spacious, nonsmoking rooms in the four-story property are enhanced with surprise gifts, attentive service, and luxurious appointments. Immaculate landscaped grounds, a secluded pool and spa, a fitness room, a sauna, and two restaurants round out the indulgent experience. 139 rms, 4 story. S, D $180-$260; suites $250-$450. TV; cable (premium), VCR avail. Heated pool; whirlpool, poolside serv. Restaurant (see also DUCK CLUB). Rm serv 24 hrs. Bar 11 am-midnight. Ck-out noon. Meeting rms. Business servs avail. In-rm modem link. Valet serv. Concierge. Covered parking. Exercise equipt; sauna. Health club privileges. Bathrm phones, refrigerators, minibars; microwaves avail. Some private patios. Cr cds: A, C, D, DS, MC, V.

D

Hotels

★★★ **EMBASSY SUITES HOTEL.** *1345 Treat Blvd (94596). 925/934-2500; fax 925/256-7233; toll-free 800/362-2779. www.embassy-suites.com.* 249 suites, 8 story. S $129-$179; D $144-$194; each addl $15; under 18 free. Crib free. Pet accepted; $100. In/out parking $7. TV; cable (premium), VCR avail. Complimentary full bkfst, coffee in rms. Restaurant 11:30 am-2:30 pm, 5-10 pm. Rm serv 11 am-11 pm. Bar 11 am-midnight. Ck-out 1 pm. Meeting rms. Business servs avail. In-rm modem link. Gift shop. Coin lndry. Exercise equipt. Heated indoor pool; whirlpool. Refrigerators, microwaves, wet bars. Cr cds: A, C, D, DS, JCB, MC, V.

D SC

★★★ **MARRIOTT.** *2600 Bishop Dr, San Ramon (94596). 925/867-9200; res 800/228-9290.* 368 rms, 6 story. S, D $159; suites $300-$600; under 18 free; wkend rates. Crib free. Pet accepted. TV; cable (premium), VCR avail. Pool; whirlpool. Restaurant 6:30 am-10 pm. Bar 11:30 am-midnight. Ck-out noon. Coin lndry. Convention facilities. Business servs avail. In-rm modem link. Concierge. Sundries. Exercise equipt; sauna. Health club privileges. Microwaves avail; wet bar in suites. View of Mt Diablo. Luxury level. Cr cds: A, C, DS, JCB, MC, V.

D

★★★ **WALNUT CREEK MARRIOTT.** *2355 N Main (95338). 925/934-2000; fax 925/934-6374; toll-free 800/228-9290. www.marriott.com.* 338 rms, 6 story. S $149; D $159; suites $184-$450; under 18 free; wkend rates. Crib free. TV; cable, VCR avail. Pool; whirlpool. Coffee in rms. Restaurant 6:30 am-10 pm; Fri, Sat to 11 pm. Bar 11 am-midnight. Ck-out noon. Meeting rms. Business servs avail. In-rm modem link. Concierge. Gift shop. Exercise equipt. Bathrm phones; some refrigerators. Balconies. Luxury level. Cr cds: A, C, D, DS, ER, JCB, MC, V.

D SC

Restaurants

★★★ **DUCK CLUB.** *3287 Mt Diablo Blvd, Lafayette (94549). 925/283-7108. www.woodsidehotels.com.* Hrs: 6:30 am-2 pm, 6-9:30 pm; wkend hrs vary. Closed Jan 1 (eve). Res accepted. French bistro cuisine. Bar 11:30 am-midnight. Wine cellar. Bkfst $6-$12, lunch $8.95-$14.95, dinner $11.95-$26. Children's menu. Specialties: roast duck, five-onion soup, crab cakes. Valet parking. Outdoor dining. Overlooks courtyard and fountain. Rotisserie oven. Totally nonsmoking. Cr cds: A, C, D, DS, ER, MC, V.

D

★★ **LARK CREEK.** *1360 Locust St (94596). 925/256-1234. www.larkcreek.com.* Hrs: 11:30 am-9 pm; Fri, Sat to 10 pm; Sun 4:30-9 pm; Sat, Sun brunch 10 am-3 pm. Closed Jan 1, Dec 25. Res accepted. Bar. Lunch $7.95-$14.50, dinner $8.95-$23.95. Children's menu. Specialties: pot roast, tamale pancake, meatloaf. Street, garage parking. Outdoor dining. Casual decor. Totally nonsmoking. Cr cds: A, MC, V.

D

★★ **MUDD'S.** *10 Boardwalk, San Ramon (94583). 925/837-9387. www.mudds.com.* Hrs: 11:30 am-2:30 pm, 5:30-9 pm; Sat 5-10 pm; Sun 5-9 pm; Sun brunch 10 am-2 pm. Res accepted; required wkends, hols. Bar 11:30 am-10:30 pm. Lunch $9.50-$15, dinner $14.50-$27.95. Sun brunch $8-$14. Specializes in fresh salads, homemade pasta, loin chops. Outdoor dining. Cedarwood ceilings.

2-acre garden. Totally nonsmoking. Cr cds: A, C, D, DS, ER, MC, V.

D

★★★ **POSTINO.** *3565 Mt Diablo Blvd, Lafayette (94549). 925/299-8700. www.postinorestaurant.com.* Hrs: 5:30-10 pm; Fri, Sat 5-10:30 pm; Sun from 5 pm. Closed hols. Res accepted. Italian menu. Bar. A la carte entrees: dinner $10.95-$22.50. Children's menu. Outdoor dining. Cr cds: A, D, MC, V.

D

★★ **PRIMA TRATTORIA E NEGOZIO-VINI.** *1522 N Main St (94596). 925/935-7780. www.primawine.com.* Hrs: 11:30 am-3 pm, 5-9 pm; Fri, Sat 11:30 am-11 pm; Sun from 5 pm. Closed hols. Res accepted. Italian menu. Bar. Lunch $8-$16, dinner $12-$25. Pianist Wed-Sat. Valet parking. Outdoor dining. Mediterranean atmosphere. Wine shop on premises. Family-owned. Cr cds: A, D, MC, V.

D

★★ **SPIEDINI.** *101 Ygnacio Valley Rd (94596). 925/939-2100. www.spiedinirestaurant.com.* Hrs: 11:30 am-10 pm; Fri to 11 pm; Sat 5-11 pm; Sun 5-9:30 pm. Closed Jan 1, Thanksgiving, Dec 25. Res accepted. Italian menu. Bar. A la carte entrees: lunch $8.50-$17.75, dinner $9.95-$18.95. Specializes in rotisserie grilled meats. Own pasta. Parking. Outdoor dining. Upscale dining. Totally nonsmoking. Cr cds: A, D, DS, MC, V.

D

★★ **WALNUT CREEK HOFBRAU HOUSE.** *1401 Mt Diablo Blvd (94596). 925/947-2928.* Hrs: 11:30 am-10 pm; Sun 5-10 pm. Closed Jan 1, Thanksgiving, Dec 25. Res accepted. Seafood menu. Bar. Lunch, dinner $10.50-$19.50. Children's menu. Specializes in raw bar, fresh grilled fish. Parking. Outdoor dining. Totally nonsmoking. Cr cds: A, MC, V.

D

Weaverville

(C-2) *See also Redding*

Founded 1849 **Pop** 3,370 **Elev** 2,011 ft **Area code** 530 **Zip** 96093

Information Trinity County Chamber of Commerce, 210 N Main St, PO Box 517; 530/623-6101 or 800/487-4648

Web www.trinitycounty.com

Weaverville's birth was linked with the discovery of gold. Within a few years the town's population had jumped to 3,000—half of it composed of Chinese miners. A Ranger District office of the Shasta-Trinity National Forest (see REDDING) is located here.

What to See and Do

Highland Art Center. Exhibits by local and other artists incl paintings, photography, sculpture, textiles, and pottery. (Tues-Sat) 530 Main St. Phone 530/623-5211. **FREE**

J.J. Jackson Memorial Museum. Local historical exhibits. (Apr-Nov, daily; rest of yr, Tues and Sat) 508 Main St, on CA 299. Phone 530/623-5211. **Donation**

Trinity Alps Wilderness Area. Reached from Canyon Creek, Stuart Fork, Swift Creek, North Fork, New River, or Coffee Creek. Unsurpassed alpine scenery, called US counterpart of Swiss Alps. Backpacking, fishing, pack trips. 15 mi N in Shasta-Trinity National Forest (see REDDING). Resort areas on fringes. Wilderness permit necessary (free); obtain at Ranger District Office, PO Box 1190; Phone 530/623-2121. **FREE**

Weaverville Joss House State Historic Park. Temple, built in 1874 by Chinese during gold rush, contains priceless tapestries and gilded wooden scrollwork. Hrly guided tours (Wed-Sun; closed Jan 1, Thanksgiving, Dec 25). Main and Oregon sts, on CA 299. Phone 530/623-5284. ¢

West Covina

See also Pomona

Pop 96,086 **Elev** 381 ft **Area code** 626

Motels/Motor Lodges

★★ **COMFORT INN.** *2804 E Garvey Ave (91791). 626/915-6077; fax 626/339-4587. www.comfortinn.com.* 58 rms, 3 story. S $49-$79; D $54-$84; each addl $5; under 18 free. Crib $5. TV; cable, (premium). Heated pool; whirlpool. Complimentary continental bkfst. Restaurant nearby. Ck-out 11 am. Meeting rm. Refrigerators; some in-rm whirlpools. Cr cds: A, C, D, DS, MC, V.

★ **EL DORADO MOTOR INN.** *140 N Azusa Ave (91791). 626/331-6371.* 82 rms, 2 story. S, D $39; suites $45-$90; wkly rates. Crib free. TV; cable (premium). Pool. Restaurant nearby. Ck-out 11 am. Private patios, balconies. Cr cds: A, D, DS, MC, V.

D

★★ **HOLIDAY INN.** *3223 E Garvey Ave N (91791). 626/966-8311; fax 626/339-2850. www.holiday-inn.com.* 134 rms, 5 story. S, D $79-$120; each addl $10; under 18 free. Crib free. Pet accepted. TV; cable (premium). Heated pool. Complimentary full bkfst, coffee in rms. Restaurant 6 am-2 pm, 5-10 pm. Bar from 5 pm. Ck-out noon. Coin lndry. Meeting rms. Business servs avail. Valet serv. Refrigerators. Cr cds: A, C, D, DS, JCB, MC, V.

D

Resort

★★★ **SHERATON RESORT & CONFERENCE CENTER.** *1 Industry Hills Pkwy, Industry (91744). 626/810-4455; fax 626/964-9535; res 800/325-3535. www.sheraton.com.* 294 rms, 11 story. S $150-$165; D $165-$175; each addl $15; suites $295-$375; under 17 free; wkend rates; package plans. Crib free. TV; cable (premium), VCR avail. 2 heated pools; whirlpools. Coffee in rms. Restaurants 6 am-11 pm. Bars 11-2 am; entertainment. Ck-out noon. Convention facilities. Business servs avail. Concierge. Gift shop. Lighted tennis, 17 courts, pro. Two 18-hole golf courses, pro, driving range. Exercise equipt; sauna. Some refrigerators, wet bars. Many balconies. Cr cds: A, C, D, DS, JCB, MC, V.

D

Restaurant

★★ **MONTEREY BAY CANNERS.** *3057 E Garvey Ave (91791). 626/915-3474.* Hrs: 11 am-10 pm; Fri, Sat to 11 pm. Closed Thanksgiving, Dec 25. Res accepted. Bar. Lunch $6.50-$12.95, dinner $7.95-$18.95. Children's menu. Specializes in mesquite-grilled seafood, chowders. Oyster bar. Rustic, nautical decor. Totally nonsmoking. Cr cds: A, D, DS, MC, V.

D SC

Westwood Village (L.A.)

Area code 310

This community is an integral part of Los Angeles, but is regarded by many as a separate entity.

What to See and Do

Westwood Memorial Cemetery. Graves of movie stars Marilyn Monroe, Peter Lorre, and Natalie Wood. (Daily) Glendon Ave, 1 blk E of Westwood Blvd.

Hotels

★★★ **DOUBLETREE HOTEL LOS ANGELES-WESTWOOD.** *10740 Wilshire Blvd (90024). 310/475-8711; fax 310/475-1862; res 800/222-8733. www.hilton.com/doubletree.* 295 rms, 19 story. S $149; each addl $10; suites $200-$230; under 18 free. Crib free. TV; cable (premium). Pool; whirlpool, poolside serv. Restaurant 6:30 am-11 pm. Bar 4 pm-midnight. Ck-out noon. Meeting rms. Business center. In-rm modem link. Concierge. Gift shop. Valet parking.

Exercise equipt; sauna. Refrigerators avail. Cr cds: A, C, D, DS, MC, V.

D

★★ **HILGARD HOUSE HOTEL.** *927 Hilgard Ave (90024). 310/208-3945; fax 310/208-1972; toll-free 800/826-3934. www.hilgardhouse.com.* 47 rms, 4 story. S $124; D $134; each addl $10; under 18 free. Crib free. TV; cable (premium). Complimentary continental bkfst. Ck-out noon. Guest lndry. Free covered parking. Refrigerators avail. Cr cds: A, C, D, DS, JCB, MC, V.

D

★★ **HOTEL DEL CAPRI.** *10587 Wilshire Blvd (90024). 310/474-3511; fax 310/470-9999. www.hoteldelcapri.com.* 80 units, 2-4 story, 46 kit. suites. S $95; D $105-$115; each addl $10; kit. suites $120-$150. Crib $10. Pet accepted, some restrictions; fee. TV; cable (premium), VCR avail. Heated pool. Complimentary continental bkfst. Restaurants nearby. Ck-out noon. Guest lndry. Business servs avail. Bellhops. Valet serv. Health club privileges. Bathrm phones, refrigerators; many in-rm whirlpools. Cr cds: A, D, MC, V.

Restaurants

★ **CAPRICCIO RISTORANTE ITALIANO.** *16925 Ventura Blvd, Encino (91364). 818/905-6595.* Hrs: 11:30 am-10 pm; Sat, Sun 5:30-10:30 pm. Res accepted. Italian menu. A la carte entrees: lunch $5.95-$9.95, dinner $7-$18. Specializes in traditional Italian pizza. Outdoor dining. Cr cds: A, MC, V.

D

★★ **TANINO RISTORANTE BAR.** *1043 Westwood Blvd (90024). 310/208-0444. www.tanino.com.* Specializes in spaghetti with squid ink, risotto with porcini mushrooms. Hrs: 10:30 am-3 pm, 5-10 pm; Sat, Sun 5-11 pm. Res accepted. Wine, beer. Lunch $13-$25; dinner $15-$32. Entertainment. Jacket. Cr cds: A, D, MC, V.

D

★★ **TENGU.** *10853 Linbrook Dr, Westwood Village (90024). 310/209-0071.* Specializes in wasabi butter filet mignon, Chilean sea bass. Hrs: 11:30 am-2:30 pm, 5:30 pm-midnight. Res accepted. Wine, beer. Lunch, dinner $3-$24. Cr cds: A, D, DS, MC, V.

D

Whittier

See also Anaheim, Buena Park, West Covina

Founded 1887 **Pop** 77,671 **Elev** 365 ft **Area code** 562

Information Chamber of Commerce, 8158 Painter Ave, 90602; 562/698-9554

This Quaker-founded community was named for John Greenleaf Whittier, the Quaker poet. At the foot of the rolling Puente Hills, this residential city was once a citrus empire. It is the home of Whittier College.

What to See and Do

Richard Nixon Library & Birthplace. Archives, original home, and burial place of the 37th president of the US. Nine-acre grounds incl the library's main hall with display of gifts from world leaders, life-size statues; video forum allows guests to ask questions via "touchscreen"; 75-seat amphitheater; reflecting pool; First Lady's garden. Only privately funded presidential library in the country. Nixon grew up in Yorba Linda before moving to Whittier and graduating from Whittier College. (Daily; closed Thanksgiving, Dec 25) 18001 Yorba Linda Blvd, in Yorba Linda. Phone 714/993-3393. ¢¢¢

Rose Hills Memorial Park. Gardens and cemetery covering 2,500 acres. Pageant of Roses Garden has more than 7,000 rose bushes of over 600 varieties in bloom most of the yr; Japanese gardens with a lake, arched bridge, and meditation house. (Daily) 3888 S Workman Mill Rd. Phone 562/692-1212. **FREE**

Motel/Motor Lodge

★ **VAGABOND INN.** *14125 E Whittier Blvd (90605). 562/698-9701; fax 562/698-8716; toll-free 800/522-1555. www.vagabondinn.com.* 48 rms, 3 story. S, D $60-$70; each addl $5; under 18 free. Crib free. Pet accepted, some restrictions; $5/day. TV; cable. Heated pool. Complimentary continental bkfst. Coffee in rms. Restaurant opp 7 am-11 pm. Ck-out noon. Refrigerators avail. Cr cds: A, C, D, DS, MC, V.

SC

Hotel

★★★ **HILTON.** *7320 Greenleaf Ave (90602). 562/945-8511; fax 562/945-6018; res 800/345-6565. www.whittierhilton.com.* 202 units, 8 story, 9 suites. S $109-$135; D $119-$145; each addl $10; suites $195-$475; under 18 free; family, wkly, wkend rates. Crib free. TV; cable (premium). Heated pool; whirlpool, poolside serv. Coffee in rms. Restaurant 6 am-10 pm. Bar 11-1 am; entertainment Fri, Sat. Ck-out noon. Meeting rms. Business servs avail. Gift shop. Exercise equipt. Health club privileges. Some refrigerators, microwaves. Some private patios. Cr cds: A, D, DS, MC, V.

D

Restaurant

★ **SEAFARE INN.** *16363 E Whittier Blvd (90603). 562/947-6645.* Hrs: 11:30 am-9 pm; Fri 11 am-10 pm. Closed Mon; hols. Wine, beer. Lunch $3.25-$5.95, dinner $5.95-$12.75. Children's menu. Specializes in seafood. Own desserts. Nautical decor. Family-owned since 1961. Totally nonsmoking. Cr cds: MC, V.

D

Willits

(D-2) *See also Fort Bragg, Mendocino, Ukiah*

Pop 5,027 **Elev** 1,364 ft **Area code** 707 **Zip** 95490

Information Chamber of Commerce, 239 S Main St; 707/459-7910

Nestled in the Little Lake Valley, Willits is the hub of three railroads: the California Western "Skunk Train" (see FORT BRAGG), the North Coast Railroad, and the Northwestern Pacific.

What to See and Do

Mendocino County Museum. History of area depicted by artifacts, incl unique collection of Pomo baskets; stagecoaches, redwood logging tools, antique steam engines; contemporary art shows. Special programs. (Wed-Sun; closed hols) 400 E Commercial St. Phone 707/459-2736. **FREE**

Willits Community Theatre. 37 W Van Ln. Phone 707/459-2281.

Motels/Motor Lodges

★★ **BAECHTEL CREEK INN.** *101 Gregory Ln (95490). 707/459-9063; fax 707/459-0226; res 800/459-9911. www.baechtelcreekinn.com.* 46 rms, 2 story. June-Oct: S, D $65-$105; each addl $3; under 12 free; lower rates rest of yr. Crib free. Pet accepted; $10. TV; cable. Pool; whirlpool. Complimentary continental bkfst. Restaurant adj 6 am-11 pm. Ck-out 11 am. Meeting rms. Some refrigerators. Cr cds: A, DS, MC, V.

SC

★ **HOLIDAY LODGE.** *1540 S Main St (95490). 707/459-5361; fax 707/459-2334; toll-free 800/835-3972.* 16 rms. Mid-May-mid-Oct: S $42-$52; D $48-$62; each addl $5; lower rates rest of yr. Crib free. Pet accepted, some restrictions. TV; cable (premium). Pool. Complimentary continental bkfst, coffee in rms. Restaurant opp 8 am-11 pm. Ck-out 11 am. Business servs avail. Refrigerators. Cr cds: A, DS, MC, V.

Willows (D-3)

Pop 5,988 **Elev** 135 ft **Area code** 530 **Zip** 95988

Information Willows Area Chamber of Commerce, 130 N Butte St; 530/934-8150

What to See and Do

Mendocino National Forest. More than one million acres. Swimming, fishing for steelhead and trout, boating at 2,000-acre Pillsbury Lake; hiking, bridle and off-road vehicle trails, camping (fee at more developed sites; some water; high elevation sites closed in winter). Hang gliding. Approx 25 mi W via CA 162. Contact the Forest Supervisor, 824 N Humboldt Ave. Phone 530/934-3316.

Sacramento National Wildlife Refuge Complex. Two-refuge complex attracts millions of migrating waterfowl, incl ducks, geese, swans, pelicans, egrets, and herons; auto routes, hiking trails. (Daily) Sacramento Refuge: County Rd 99W (take Norman-Princeton Rd exit off I-5, about 6 mi S of Willows). Colusa Refuge: E of Williams off I-5. Phone 530/934-2801. Per vehicle ¢¢

Motels/Motor Lodges

★★ **BEST WESTERN GOLDEN PHEASANT INN.** *249 N Humboldt Ave (95988). 530/934-4603; fax 530/934-4275; res 800/528-1234.* 104 rms. S $55-$69; D $69-$89; each addl $10; suites $90. Crib $6. Pet accepted; $10. TV; cable, VCR avail (movies $3.50). 2 heated pools. Complimentary continental bkfst. Coffee in rms. Restaurant 6-10 am, 11:30 am-9 pm. Bar from 10 am. Ck-out 11 am. Coin lndry. Meeting rms. Business servs avail. Free airport, bus depot transportation. 7 acres of gardens and park. Cr cds: A, C, D, DS, JCB, MC, V.

D

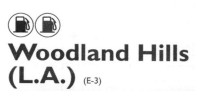

★ **CROSS ROADS WEST INN.** *452 N Humboldt Ave (95988). 530/934-7026; fax 530/934-7028; toll-free 800/814-6301.* 41 rms, 2 story. S $37.33; D $41.96-$46.59; each addl $6; under 6 free. Pet accepted. TV; cable (premium). Pool. Restaurant adj 7 am-9 pm. Ck-out 11 am. Cr cds: A, DS, MC, V.

SC

★★ **WOODCREST INN.** *400 C St, Williams (95987). 530/473-2381; fax 530/473-2418.* 60 rms, 2 story. S $50; D $55; each addl $5. Crib free. Pet accepted; $5. TV; cable. Pool; whirlpool. Complimentary continental bkfst. Restaurant nearby. Ck-out noon. Business servs avail. Refrigerators avail. Cr cds: A, C, D, DS, ER, MC, V.

D SC

Woodland Hills (L.A.) (E-3)

Elev 460 ft **Area code** 818

This community, located in the San Fernando Valley, is a neighborhood of Los Angeles, but is regarded by many as a separate entity.

Motels/Motor Lodges

★★ **CLARION SUITES HOTEL.** *20200 Sherman Way, Canoga Park (91306). 818/883-8250; fax 818/883-8268; toll-free 800/252-7466. www.clarioninn.com.* 99 rms, 3 story, 88 kit. suites. S, D $99-$119; each addl $10; kit. suites $119-$149; under 18 free; monthly rates. Crib free. Pet accepted. TV; cable (premium). Heated pool. Complimentary continental bkfst, coffee in rms. Restaurant nearby. Ck-out noon. Coin lndry. Meeting rm. Valet serv. Lighted tennis. Health club privileges. Refrigerators, microwaves. Some balconies. Cr cds: A, C, D, DS, ER, JCB, MC, V.

SC

★ **VAGABOND INN.** *20157 Ventura Blvd, Woodland Hills (91364). 818/347-8080; fax 818/716-5333; toll-free 800/522-1555. www.vagabondinns.com.* 99 rms, 3 story. S $60-$75; D $65-$85; each addl $5; under 19 free. Crib free. Pet accepted, some restrictions; $5. TV; cable (premium). Heated pool; whirlpool. Complimentary continental bkfst. Restaurant adj open 24 hrs. Ck-out noon. Meeting rm. Business servs avail. Cr cds: A, C, D, DS, MC, V.

D SC

★ **WARNER GARDENS MOTEL.** *21706 Ventura Blvd, Woodland Hills (91364). 818/992-4426; fax 818/704-1062; toll-free 800/824-9292.* 42 rms, 2 story. S, D $46-$54; suites $58-$65;

under 17 free; wkly rates. Crib free. TV; cable (premium). Pool; whirlpool. Complimentary continental bkfst. Restaurant adj 8 am-8 pm. Ck-out 11 am. Valet serv. Cr cds: A, C, D, DS, MC, V.

D SC

Hotels

★★★ WARNER CENTER MARRIOTT HOTEL. *21850 Oxnard St, Woodland Hills (91367). 818/887-4800; fax 818/340-5893; toll-free 800/228-9290. www.marriott.com.* 463 rms, 16 story. S, D $150-$165; suites $250-$500; under 18 free; wkend rates. Crib free. Garage $5; valet parking $9. TV; cable (premium). Heated indoor/outdoor pools; whirlpool, poolside serv. Restaurant 6:30 am-11 pm. Bar 11-1 am. Ck-out noon. Convention facilities. Business servs avail. Gift shop. Airport transportation. Exercise equipt; sauna. Balconies. Luxury level. Cr cds: A, C, D, DS, JCB, MC, V.

D SC

★★★ WOODLAND HILLS HILTON. *6360 Canoga Ave, Woodland Hills (91367). 818/591-1000; fax 818/596-4578; toll-free 800/922-2400. www.hilton.com.* 330 rms, 14 story. S, D $159; each addl $10; suites $195-$550; family; wkend rates. Crib free. Garage $5; valet parking $8. TV; cable (premium). Heated pool; whirlpool. Coffee in rms. Restaurant 6 am-10:30 pm. Bar 3 pm-1 am. Ck-out noon. Convention facilities. Business servs avail. Concierge. Airport transportation. Lighted tennis. Health club privileges. Some balconies. Luxury level. Cr cds: A, C, D, DS, ER, JCB, MC, V.

D

All Suite

★★ COUNTRY INNS & SUITES - CALABASAS. *23627 Calabasas Rd, Calabasas (91302). 818/222-5300; fax 818/591-0870; res 800/456-4000. www.countryinns.com.* 122 rms, 3 story. S, D $148; each addl $10; kit. suites $275-$300; under 12 free. Crib free. Pet accepted; $25. TV; VCR (movies $4). Heated pool; whirlpool. Complimentary full bkfst. Restaurant nearby. Ck-out noon. Coin lndry. Meeting rm. Business servs avail. In-rm modem link. Valet serv. Health club privileges. Refrigerators, microwaves, wet bars. Cr cds: A, C, D, DS, MC, V.

D

Restaurants

★★ BACIO TRATTORIA. *23663 Calabasas Rd, Calabasas (91302). 818/591-1355.* Hrs: 11:30 am-10 pm; Fri to 11 pm; Sat 5-11 pm; Sun 5-10 pm. Closed Jan 1, Thanksgiving, Dec 25. Northern Italian menu. Wine, beer. A la carte entrees: lunch, dinner $3.95-$15.95. Children's menu. Specialties: fettuccine bacio, cioppino, tortini risotto. Parking. Outdoor dining. Italian cafe; casual dining. Cr cds: A, C, D, ER, MC, V.

D

★★ COSMOS GRILL & ROTISSERIE. *23631 Calabasas Rd, Calabasas (91302). 818/591-2211.* Hrs: 11:30 am-10 pm; Fri, Sat to 11 pm; Sun from 4:30 pm. Closed July 4, Thanksgiving, Dec 25. Res accepted. Beer, wine. A la carte entrees: lunch, dinner $4.50-$17.95. Children's menu. Specialties: marinated skirt steak, penne country chicken. Outdoor dining. Modern artwork. Cr cds: A, D, MC, V.

D

★★ LE SANGLIER FRENCH RESTAURANT. *5522 Crebs, Tarzana (91356). 818/345-0470.* Hrs: 5:30-9:30 pm; Fri, Sat to 10:30 pm. Closed Mon; hols. Res accepted. French menu. Bar. Dinner $18.95-$24.95. Prix fixe: dinner $35. Specializes in French country cuisine. French hunting lodge interior. Totally nonsmoking. Cr cds: A, C, D, DS, MC, V.

Yosemite National Park

(F-5, G-5, F-6, G-6) *See also Lee Vining (67 mi NE of Merced on CA 140; 62 mi N of Fresno on CA 41; 13 mi W of Lee Vining on CA 120)*

Area code 209, 559 **Zip** 95389

John Muir, the naturalist instrumental in the founding of this national park, wrote that here are "the most songful streams in the world...the noblest forests, the loftiest granite domes, the deepest ice sculptured canyons." More than four million people visit Yosemite year-round, and most agree with Muir. An area of 1,169 square miles, it is a park of lofty waterfalls, sheer cliffs, high wilderness country, alpine meadows, lakes, snowfields, trails, streams, and river beaches. There are magnificent waterfalls during spring and early summer. Yosemite's granite domes are unsurpassed in number and diversity. Entrance fee is $20 per car. Routes to Yosemite National Park involve some travel over steep grades, which may extend driving times. Tioga Rd (CA 120) is closed in winter.

Half Dome at sunset, Yosemite National Park

For general park information contact Public Information Office, PO Box 577, Yosemite National Park; phone 209/372-0200. For lodging information contact Yosemite Concession Services, Yosemite National Park; phone 559/252-4848. For recorded camping information phone 209/372-0200. Camping reservations taken by NPRS, the National Park Reservation System for Yosemite Valley (800/436-7275) and other campgrounds.

What to See and Do

Boating. No motors permitted.

Campfire programs. At several campgrounds; in summer, naturalists present nightly programs on park-related topics and provide tips on how to enjoy the park. Evening programs all yr in the Valley only.

Camping. Limited to 30 days in a calendar yr; May-mid-Sept, camping is limited to 7 days in Yosemite Valley, in the rest of the park to 14 days. Campsites in the Valley campgrounds, Hodgdon Meadow, Crane Flat, Wawona, and half of Tuolumne Meadows campgrounds may be reserved through NPRS. Other park campgrounds are on a first-come, first-served basis. Winter camping in the Valley, Hodgdon Meadow, and Wawona only.

Fishing. California fishing regulations pertain to all waters. State license, inland waters stamp, and trout stamp are required. Special regulations for Yosemite Valley also apply.

The Giant Sequoias. Located principally in three groves. Mariposa Grove is near the south entrance to the park; toured on foot or by 50-passenger trams (May-early Oct; fee). Merced and Tuolumne groves are near Crane Flat, northwest of Yosemite Valley. The Grizzly Giant in Mariposa Grove is estimated to be 2,700 yrs old and is 209 ft high and 34.7 ft in diameter at its base.

Glacier Point. Offers one of the best panoramic views in Yosemite. From here the crest of the Sierra Nevada can be viewed, as well as Yosemite Valley 3,214 ft below. Across the valley are Yosemite Falls, Royal Arches, North Dome, Basket Dome, Mt Watkins and Washington Column; up the Merced Canyon are Vernal and Nevada Falls; Half Dome, Grizzly Peak, Liberty Cap, and the towering peaks along the Sierran crest and the Clark Range mark the skyline. (Road closed in winter)

The High Country. The Tioga Rd (closed in winter) crosses the park and provides the threshold to a vast wilderness accessible via horseback or on foot to mountain peaks, passes, and lakes. Tuolumne Meadows is the major trailhead for this activity; one of the most beautiful and largest of the subalpine meadows in the High Sierra, 55 mi from Yosemite Valley by way of Big Oak Flat and Tioga rds. Organized group horse and hiking trips start from Tuolumne Meadows (exc winter), follow the High Sierra Loop, and fan out to mountain lakes and peaks. Each night's stop is at a High Sierra Camp; the pace allows plenty of time to explore at each camp. Phone 559/253-5674.

Hiking and backpacking. On 840 mi of maintained trails. Wilderness permits are required for all overnight backcountry trips. Advance res for permits may be made up to 24 wks in advance; phone 209/372-0740.

The Nature Center at Happy Isles. Exhibits on ecology and natural history. (Summer, daily) E end of Yosemite Valley.

Pioneer Yosemite History Center. A few mi from Mariposa Grove in Wawona. Has a covered bridge, historic buildings, wagons, and other exhibits. Living history program in summer.

Swimming. Prohibited at Hetch Hetchy Reservoir and in some areas of the Tuolumne River watershed. Swimming pools are maintained at Camp Curry, Yosemite Lodge, and Wawona.

Visitor Center. Orientation slide program on Yosemite (daily). Exhibits on geology and ecology; naturalist-conducted walks and evening programs offered throughout the yr on varying seasonal schedules. Native American cultural demonstrators (summer, daily). At Park Headquarters in Yosemite Valley. Phone 209/372-0265.

The Indian Cultural Museum. Located in the building west of the Valley visitor center, the museum portrays the cultural history of the Yosemite Native Americans. Consult *Yosemite Guide* for hrs. Adj is

Indian Village (Ahwahnee). Reconstructed Miwok-Paiute Village behind Visitor Center has self-guided trail.

Yosemite Fine Arts Museum. Gallery featuring contemporary art exhibits and the Yosemite Centennial. Consult *Yosemite Guide* for hrs.

Walks and hikes. Conducted all yr in the Valley and, during summer, at Glacier Point, Mariposa Grove, Tuolumne Meadows, Wawona, White Wolf, and Crane Flat.

★ **Waterfalls.** Reaching their greatest proportions in mid-May, they may, in dry years, dwindle to trickles or disappear completely by late summer. The Upper Yosemite Fall drops 1,430 ft; the lower fall drops 320 ft. With the middle Cascade they have a combined height of 2,425 ft and are the fifth-highest waterfall in the world. Others are Ribbon Fall, 1,612 ft; Vernal Fall, 317 ft; Bridalveil Fall, 620 ft; Nevada Fall, 594 ft; and Illilouette Fall, 370 ft.

Winter sports. Centered around the **Badger Pass Ski Area**, 23 mi from Yosemite Valley on Glacier Point Rd. One triple, three double chairlifts, cable tow; patrol, rentals; snack stand, sun deck, nursery (min age three yrs); instruction (over four yrs). (Mid-Dec-mid-Apr, daily, weather permitting) X-country skiing. Ice-skating (fee) in Yosemite Valley; scheduled competitions. Naturalists conduct snowshoe tours (fee) in the Badger Pass area. Phone 209/372-1000. ¢¢¢¢¢

Yosemite Mountain-Sugar Pine Railroad. Four-mi historic narrow-gauge steam train excursion through scenic Sierra National Forest. Picnic area. Museum; gift shops. Logger steam train (mid-May-Sept, daily; early May and Oct, wkends). Jenny Railcars (Mar-Oct, daily). Evening steam train, outdoor barbecue, live entertainment (late May-early Oct, Sat eves; res advised). 4 mi S of south park entrance on CA 41. Phone 559/683-7273. ¢¢¢¢¢

Yosemite Valley. Surrounded by sheer walls, waterfalls, towering domes, and peaks. One of the most spectacular views is from Tunnel View, looking up the Valley to Clouds Rest. El Capitan (7,569 ft) on the left, Bridalveil Falls on the right. The east end of the Valley, beyond Camp Curry, is closed to automobiles, but is accessible by foot, bicycle and, in summer, shuttle bus (free); special placards permit the disabled to drive in restricted area when the route is drivable. The placards are avail at visitor centers and entrance stations.

Motels/Motor Lodges

★★ COMFORT INN. *4994 Bullion St, Mariposa (95338). 209/966-4344; fax 209/966-4655; res 800/228-5150.* 61 rms, 2-3 story. Apr-Oct: S $75-$80; D $85-$90; each addl $6; suite $96-$185; kit. units $140-$185; under 18 free; lower rates rest of yr. Crib free. TV; cable (premium). Complimentary continental bkfst. Restaurant nearby. Ck-out 11 am. Meeting rms. Business servs avail. In-rm modem link. Pool; whirlpool. Cr cds: A, C, D, DS, MC, V.

D

★ MINERS INN MOTEL. *5181 Hwy 49 N Mariposa (95338). 209/742-7777; fax 209/966-2343; toll-free 888/646-2244. www.yosemite-rooms.com.* 78 rms, 2 story. Apr-Oct: S $49-$59; D $59-$75; each addl $6; suites $149; kit. units $125; under 6 free; lower rates rest of yr. Crib free. Pet accepted; $6. TV; cable (premium). Complimentary coffee in rms. Restaurant 6:30 am-10 pm. Bar; entertainment Fri, Sat. Ck-out 11 am. Business servs avail. Sundries. Gift shop. Pool; whirlpool. Some bathrm phones, in-rm whirlpools, refrigerators, microwaves, fireplaces. Many balconies. Cr cds: A, DS, MC, V.

★★ PINES RESORT. *54449 Rd 432, Bass Lake (93604). 559/642-3121; fax 559/642-3902; toll-free 800/350-7463.* 104 units, 2 story. Apr-Oct: S, D $159-$279; family rates; wkends, hols (2-3 day min); higher rates special events; lower rates rest of yr. Crib free. TV; cable (premium), VCR (movies avail). Heated pool; whirlpool, poolside serv. Complimentary continental bkfst, coffee in rms. Restaurant 11 am-midnight. Bar; entertainment Fri, Sat. Ck-out noon. Coin lndry. Meeting rms. Business servs avail. Tennis. X-country ski 5 mi. Refrigerators. Balconies. Split-level units on lake. Cr cds: A, D, DS, MC, V.

D

★★ YOSEMITE LODGE. *CA 41/140 (95389). 209/372-1275; fax 209/372-1444. www.yosemitepark.com.* 226 rms, 2 story. No A/C. Apr-Oct: S, D $76-$90; each addl $6-$12; lower rates rest of yr. Crib $5. Pool; lifeguard. Supervised children's activities (June-Aug); ages over 3. Restaurant 6:30 am-7 pm. Bar noon-10 pm. Ck-out 11 am. Meeting rms. Sundries. Gift shop. Valley tours. Cr cds: C, D, DS, JCB, MC, V.

D

★ YOSEMITE RIVERSIDE INN. *11399 Cherry Lake Rd, Groveland (95321). 209/962-7408; fax 209/962-7400; toll-free 800/626-7408. www.yosemiteriversideinn.com.* 18 rms, 2 kit units. No rm phones. May-Sept: S, D $99-$129; each addl $10; kit. units $79-$89; under 5 free; wkly rates; lower rates rest of yr. Crib free. TV. Pool privileges. Complimentary continental bkfst. Ck-out 11 am. Refrigerators avail. Balconies. Picnic tables. On stream. Cr cds: A, C, D, DS, JCB, MC, V.

★★ YOSEMITE VIEW LODGE. *11156 Hwy 140, El Portal (95318). 209/379-2681; fax 209/379-2704; res 800/321-5261. www.yosemite-motels.com.* 280 kit. units, 2-3 story. Apr-Oct: S $99-$129; D $99-$139; each addl $10; ski plans; hols (2-day min); lower rates rest of yr. Crib $5. Pet accepted; $5. TV; cable (premium). Complimentary coffee in rms. Restaurant 7 am-10 pm. Bar. Ck-out 11 pm. Meeting rms. Business servs avail. Sundries. Gift shop. Grocery store. Coin lndry. Downhill/x-country ski 20 mi. 2 pools, 1 indoor; whirlpool. Many in-rm whirlpools, fireplaces. Many balconies. On river. Cr cds: MC, V.

D

Hotels

★★ CEDAR LODGE. *9966 Hwy 140, El Portal (95318). 209/379-2612; fax 209/379-2712; res 800/321-5261.* 224 rms, 1-2 story. Mar-Nov: S $85; D $99; suites $120-$400; kit. units $104; hols (2-day min); lower rates rest of yr. Crib $5. TV; cable (premium), VCR avail (movies). Complimentary coffee in lobby. Restaurant adj 7 am-10 pm. Bar. Ck-out 11 am. Meeting rms. Business servs avail. In-rm modem link. Sundries. Gift shop. 2 pools, 1 indoor; whirlpool. Many refrigerators, microwaves; some in-rm whirlpools. Some balconies. Picnic tables, grills. On river. Cr cds: A, MC, V.

★★ **GROVELAND HOTEL.** *18767 Main St, Groveland (95321). 209/962-4000; fax 209/962-6674; toll-free 800/273-3314. www.groveland.com.* 17 rms, 2 separate 2-story buildings (one is CA Resource Adobe), 3 suites. Open year-round. May-Sept: S,D $135; each addl $15 for 12 under and $25 for over 12 years; suites $200. Crib free. Pet accepted. TV in common rm/bar; cable, VCR avail (movies). Complimentary innkeeper bkfst, coffee in rms. Restaurant (see also THE VICTORIAN ROOM). Ck-out noon, ck-in 2 pm. Conference/Business servs avail. In-rm modem link. Concierge serv. Downhill/x-country ski 20 mi. In-rm whirlpool, fireplace in suites. Picnic tables. Built in 1849; European antiques. Totally nonsmoking. Cr cds: A, C, D, DS, JCB, MC, V.

★ **MARIPOSA LODGE.** *5052 Highway 140, Mariposa (95338). 209/966-3607; fax 209/742-7038; res 800/341-8000. www.mariposalodge.com.* 44 rms, 13 rms with shower only. Apr-Oct: S, D $65-$76; each addl $6; lower rates rest of yr. Crib $6. Pet accepted, some restrictions; $6. TV; cable (premium), VCR avail. Heated pool; whirlpool. Complimentary coffee in rms. Restaurant adj 7 am-9 pm. Ck-out 11 am. Free airport transportation. Gazebo. Cr cds: A, D, DS, MC, V.

★ **WAWONA HOTEL.** *Yosemite National Park, Wawona (95389). 209/375-6556; fax 209/375-6601.* 104 rms, 50 with bath, 1-2 story. No A/C. No rm phones. Mid-Apr-late Dec: S, D $80-$110.55; each addl $13.75. Crib avail. TV in lounge; VCR. Heated pool. Dining rm 7:30-10:30 am, noon-1:30 pm, 5:30-9 pm. Ck-out 11 am. Meeting rm. Tennis. 9-hole golf, greens fee $13.75-$22, putting green. Saddle trips, stagecoach rides. Historic summer hotel. Cr cds: A, D, DS, JCB, MC, V.

Resorts

★★★ **THE AHWAHNEE.** *Yosemite Valley (95389). 559/372-1407 559/456-0542; res 559/252-4848. www.yosemitepark.com.* 99 rms, 4 suites, 6 story, 24 cottages. S, D $247-$275; each addl $20; suites $286-$510; 3-12 yrs free. TV; VCR avail. Heated pool. Restaurant (res required). Rm serv 6 am-11 pm. Bar noon-10:30 pm; entertainment. Ck-out noon. Meeting rms. Concierge. Gift shops. Free valet parking. Tennis. Some fireplaces. Some balconies. Stone building with natural wood interior, Native American decor. Tire chains may be required by Park Service Nov-Mar to reach lodge. Cr cds: A, C, D, DS, JCB, MC, V.

★★★ **TENAYA LODGE AT YOSEMITE.** *1122 Highway 41, Fish Camp (93623). 559/683-6555; fax 559/683-8684; res 888/574-2167. www.tenayalodge.com.* 244 rms, 3-4 story, 20 suites. Mid-May-mid-Sept: S, D $149-$279; under 18 free; package plans; lower rates rest of yr. Crib free. Pet accepted, some restrictions. TV; cable (premium), VCR avail. 2 pools, 1 indoor; whirlpool. Supervised children's activities; ages 3-12. Complimentary coffee in rms. Dining rm 6:30-11 am, 5:30-10 pm. Ck-out noon, ck-in 3 pm. Coin lndry. Convention facilities. Business center. In-rm modem link. Bellhops. Valet serv. Concierge. Gift shop. X-country ski on site. Exercise equipt; saunas, steam rm. Massage. Game rm. Guided hikes and tours. Bicycle rentals. Bathrm phones, minibars; wet bar in suites. On river; water sports. Southwest, Native American decor; rustic with an elegant touch. June-Sept Western jamboree cookouts, wagon rides. Totally nonsmoking. Cr cds: A, C, D, DS, ER, JCB, MC, V.

B&B/Small Inn

★ **LITTLE VALLEY.** *3483 Brooks Rd, Mariposa (95338). 209/742-6204; fax 209/742-5099; toll-free 800/889-5444. www.littlevalley.com.* 3 rms. No rm phones. S, D $95; kit. units $115; each addl $15. TV; VCR (movies). Complimentary full bkfst, coffee in rms. Ck-out noon, ck-in 4 pm.

Concierge serv. Luggage handling. Picnic tables. Smoking on deck only. Cr cds: A, JCB, MC, V.

D

Cottage Colony

★★ **THE HOMESTEAD.** *41110 Rd 600, Ahwahnee (93601). 559/683-0495; fax 559/683-8165. www.homesteadcottages.com.* 5 kit. cottages, shower only. No rm phones. S $145; D $170; wkly rates. TV; cable (premium). Complimentary continental bkfst. Ck-out 11 am, ck-in 3-6 pm. On 160 acres bordering Fresno River. Totally nonsmoking. Cr cds: A, DS, MC, V.

D

Restaurants

★★ **CHARLES STREET DINNER HOUSE.** *5043 Charles St, Mariposa (95338). 209/966-2366. www.charlesstreetdinnerhouse.com.* Hrs: from 5 pm. Closed Mon, Tues; Thanksgiving, Dec 24, 25; also Jan. Res accepted. Beer. Dinner $10-$30. Specializes in steak, fresh seafood. Own desserts. 19th-century house. Cr cds: A, DS, MC, V.

D SC

★★ **THE VICTORIAN ROOM.** *18767 Main St, Groveland (95321). 209/962-4000. www.groveland.com.* Hrs: 6-11 pm. Res accepted. Contemporary American menu. Bar from noon. Dinner $13.50-$27. Specialties: baby back ribs, rack of lamb. Parking. Outdoor dining. Victorian decor. Totally nonsmoking. Cr cds: A, C, D, DS, MC, V.

D

Yountville

(F-3) *See also Napa, St. Helena*

Settled 1831 **Pop** 3,259 **Elev** 97 ft **Area code** 707 **Zip** 94599

Information Chamber of Commerce, 6516 Yount St, PO Box 2064; 707/944-0904

Web www.yountville.com

In the heart of the Napa Valley, Yountville has retained the turn-of-the-century charm of a quiet farming community. The town dates from 1831 with the settlement of George Yount, a North Carolina trapper. Although now a major tourist destination, surrounded by world-famous wineries, the town has successfully protected its rural atmosphere and historic character, reflected in its quaint hotels, restaurants, and shops.

What to See and Do

Hot-air ballooning. One-hr trips above Napa Valley vineyards. Contact Adventures Aloft. (Daily, usually at sunrise) Phone 707/944-4408. ¢¢¢¢¢

Vintage 1870. Restored brick winery complex houses five restaurants, a bakery, and more than 40 specialty shops. Wine-tasting cellar. Entertainment and holiday demonstrations in Dec. Picnic areas. (Daily; closed hols) 6525 Washington St. Phone 707/944-2451. **FREE**

Wineries.

Domaine Chandon. Subsidiary of French producers of champagne and cognac. Visitors observe all phases of the *méthode champenoise,* the classic French method of producing champagnes. Guided tours, salon, retail sales, restaurant. Tasting (fee). (May-Oct, daily; rest of yr, Wed-Sun) W of CA 29, California Dr. Phone 707/944-2280. **FREE**

Robert Mondavi. Graceful, mission-style building. Guided tours, wine tasting. Res recommended. (Daily; closed hols) 7801 St. Helena Hwy, N in Oakville. Phone 707/226-1335. **FREE**

Hotels

★★★ **NAPA VALLEY LODGE.** *2230 Madison St (94599). 707/944-2468; fax 707/944-9362; toll-free 800/368-2468. www.woodsidehotels.com.* 55 rms, 2 story. S, D $282; each addl $25; suites $212-$325. Crib free. TV; cable. Heated pool; whirlpool. Complimentary continental bkfst, coffee in rms. Restaurant nearby. Ck-out noon. Meeting rms. Business servs avail. In-rm modem link. Bellhops. Valet serv. Exercise equipt; sauna. Refrigerators, minibars, fireplaces.

Private patios, balconies. Park opp. Cr cds: A, C, D, DS, MC, V.

D

★★★ VILLAGIO INN AND SPA. *6481 Washington St (94599). 707/944-8877; fax 707/944-8855; toll-free 800/351-1133.* 80 rms in 9 buildings, 1-2 story. S, D $200-$275; each addl $25; suites, villas $225-$275; under 12 free TV; cable, VCR avail (movies). Heated pool; whirlpool. Complimentary continental breakfast, afternoon refreshments. Coffee in rms. Restaurant adj 11:30 am-10 pm. Bar 10 am-10 pm. Ck-out noon. Meeting rms. Business servs avail. Concierge. Bellhops. Valet serv exc Sun. Tennis. Health club privileges. Refrigerators, fireplaces. Verandas. Vineyard, mountain views. Cr cds: A, D, DS, JCB, MC, V.

D

B&Bs/Small Inns

★★★ MAISON FLEURIE FOUR SISTERS INN. *6529 Yount St (94599). 707/944-2056; fax 707/944-9342; res 800/788-0369. www.foursisters.com.* 13 rms, 6 with shower only, 2 story. Apr-Oct: S, D $110-$230; each addl $15; lower rates rest of yr. Crib free. TV; cable. Complimentary full bkfst; afternoon refreshments. Restaurant adj 11:30 am-10 pm. Ck-out noon, ck-in 2 pm. Luggage handling. Concierge serv. Bicycles. Pool; whirlpool. Some in-rm whirlpools, fireplaces. Some balconies. Picnic tables. Built in 1876. French country ambience. Totally nonsmoking. Cr cds: A, D, MC, V.

D

★ NAPA VALLEY RAILWAY. *6503 Washington St (94599). 707/944-2000; fax 707/944-8710; toll-free 800/275-8777.* 9 rms. No rm phones. Apr-Oct: S, D $95-$130; each addl $10; under 5 free; lower rates rest of yr. TV. Complimentary coffee. Restaurant nearby. Ck-out 11 am, ck-in 2 pm. Health club privileges. Unique lodging in restored turn-of-the-century railroad cars; bay windows, skylights; private entrance. Vineyards nearby. Cr cds: MC, V.

D

★★ OLEANDER HOUSE. *7433 St. Helena Hwy (CA 29) (94599). 707/944-8315; fax 707/944-0980; toll-free 800/788-0357. www.oleander.com.* 5 rms, 2 story. No rm phones. S $145; D $160; each addl $25; wkends, hols (2-day min). Complimentary full bkfst; afternoon refreshments. Restaurant adj 11 am-10 pm. Ck-out 11 am, ck-in 1 pm. Business servs avail. Whirlpool. Balconies. Individually decorated rms; wood-burning fireplaces. Rose garden. Totally nonsmoking. Cr cds: A, MC, V.

Restaurants

★★★ BISTRO JEANTY. *6510 Washington St (94599). 707/944-0103. www.bistropeople.com.* Hrs: 11:30 am-10:30 pm. Res accepted. French menu. Bar. A la carte entrees: dinner $9.50-$16.50. Specialties: rabbit and sweetbread ragout, mussels steamed in red wine. Parking. Outdoor dining. French bistro atmosphere. Totally nonsmoking. Cr cds: MC, V.

D

★★★ BOUCHON. *6629 Washington St (94599). 707/944-8037.* Specializes in French bistro dishes. Hrs: 11:30 am-2:30 pm, 5:30-10:30 pm. Res accepted. Wine, beer. Lunch, dinner $12.50-$18.50. Entertainment. Cr cds: A, MC, V.

D

★★★ BRIX. *7377 St. Helena Hwy (94558). 707/944-2749. www.brix.com.* Hrs: 11:30 am-9:30 pm; Fri, Sat to 10 pm. Res accepted. Contemporary American menu. Bar to midnight. A la carte entrees: lunch $7-$12.95, dinner $14-$24. Children's menu. Specialties: Thai pesto smoked rack of lamb, black and blue seared ahi tuna. Own baking. Totally nonsmoking. Cr cds: A, D, DS, MC, V.

D

★ CAFE KINYON. *6525 Washington St (94599). 707/944-2788.* Hrs: 11:30 am-2 pm. Closed Jan 1, Easter, Dec 25. Res accepted. Bar. Lunch $3.50-$9.75. Specialty: peanut chicken salad. Original art. Totally nonsmoking. Cr cds: A.

D

★ COMPADRES. *6539 Washington St (94599). 707/944-2406.* Hrs: Sun-Thurs 8 am-10 pm; Fri, Sat to 11 pm. Closed Thanksgiving, Dec 25. Mexican grill menu. Bar. Lunch, dinner

$6.99-$16.99. Specializes in grilled meat and seafood. Parking. Outdoor dining. Atrium; fireplace. Cr cds: A, MC, V.

D SC

★ **THE DINER.** *6476 Washington St (94599). 707/944-2626.* Hrs: 8 am-3 pm, 5:30-9 pm. Closed Mon; Thanksgiving, Dec 25. Mexican, American menu. Wine, beer. Complete meals: bkfst, lunch $4-$9.95, dinner $6-$13.25. Children's menu. Specialties: cornmeal pancakes, huevos rancheros. Organic bakery on premises. Cr cds: MC, V.

D

★★★ **DOMAINE CHANDON.** *1 California Dr (94599). 707/944-2892. www.chandon.com.* Specialties: carmelized scallops with sweet pea sauce, pan-seared yellowfin tuna, Monterey Bay sardines on basil potatoes. Menu changes wkly. Hrs: 11:30 am-2:30 pm, Wed-Sun dinner only 6-9:00 pm. May-Oct open for lunch, also 2 wks Jan. Res accepted. French, California menu. Wine list. A la carte entrees: lunch $15-$21, dinner $24-$38. Own desserts. Outdoor dining at lunch (May-Nov). Totally nonsmoking. Cr cds: A, C, D, DS, MC, V.

D

★★★★★ **THE FRENCH LAUNDRY.** *6640 Washington Ave (94599). 707/944-2380.* The unassuming country-house setting belies the fact that The French Laundry is currently one of the most celebrated restaurants in the entire world. If you manage to achieve the astonishing feat of getting a reservation, you will be treated to an unparalleled culinary odyssey that spans the breadth of chef Thomas Keller's genius. Dinner may incl the lightest pike quenelles, a fanciful dish of "oysters and pearls" that mixes fresh Pacific oysters with tapioca, or the tiniest baby lamb chops. While the food and exquisite desserts challenge the senses, the service remains refreshingly casual. Lunch in the bucolic garden is a singular treat. American, French cuisine. Specialties: lamb chops, pike quenelles, oysters with tapioca. Hrs: 5:30-10:30 pm; Fri-Sun also 11 am-1 pm. Closed Mon (Nov-May); Dec 25; also 1st 3 wks Jan. Extensive wine list. Res accepted. Complete meals: 5-course $80, 9-course $95. Parking. Totally nonsmoking. Cr cds: A, C, MC, V.

D

★★ **LIVE FIRE RESTAURANT.** *6518 Washington St (94599). 707/944-1500. www.livefireyountville.com.* Specializes in grilled steaks, seafood. Hrs: 11:30 am-4 pm, 4:30-9 pm; Fri, Sat 4:30 pm-1 am. Res accepted. Wine, beer. Lunch $7.95-$15.95; dinner $11.95-$25.95. Children's menu. Entertainment. Fireplace. Cr cds: A, D, DS, JCB, MC, V.

D

★★★ **MUSTARD'S GRILL.** *7399 St. Helena Hwy (CA 29) (94599). 707/944-2424.* Hrs: 11:30 am-10 pm; Nov-Apr to 9 pm. Closed Thanksgiving, Dec 25. Res accepted. Bar. A la carte entrees: lunch, dinner $7.95-$17.95. Specializes in smoked and grilled fish, fowl, beef. Parking. Totally nonsmoking. Cr cds: C, D, DS, MC, V.

D

★★ **NAPA VALLEY GRILLE.** *6795 Washington St (94599). 707/944-8686. www.calcafe.com/napavalleygrille/yountville.* Hrs: 11:30 am-9:30 pm; Fri, Sat to 10:30 pm; Sun from 10:30 am; Sun brunch to 2:30 pm. Closed Dec 25. Res accepted. Contemporary American menu. Bar. Lunch $7.95-$15.95, dinner $9.95-$25. Sun brunch $8.95-$16.95. Children's menu. Specialty: homemade focaccia. Jazz Fri (summer). Outdoor dining. Contemporary decor; over 600 wines avail. Totally nonsmoking. Cr cds: A, D, DS, MC, V.

D

Yreka

(A-3) *See also Mount Shasta*

Founded 1851 **Pop** 6,948 **Elev** 2,625 ft **Area code** 530 **Zip** 96097

Information Chamber of Commerce, 117 W Miner St; 530/842-1649 or 800/ON-YREKA (recording)

Web www.yrekachamer.com

Yreka (Why-RE-ka) was known in gold rush days as Thompson's Dry

Diggings, later as Shasta Butte City, and finally, since 1852, as Yreka. Yreka today is the seat of Siskiyou County and a trade center for ranchers, loggers, and miners. Many historic buildings may be seen in the Historic Preservation District, in the vicinity of Miner and Third streets. Hunting and fishing are popular in the area.

What to See and Do

County Gold Exhibit. Extensive display of gold nuggets taken from mines in Siskiyou County. (Mon-Fri; closed hols) County Courthouse, 311 4th St. Phone 530/842-8340. **FREE**

Iron Gate Dam and Lake. Water sports, fishing, boating (ramps, launching facilities); picnicking, camping. 13 mi NE on I-5, then 6 mi E on Klamath River Rd.

Klamath National Forest. Approx 1.72 million acres, of which 1.69 million acres are in California and the remainder in Oregon. Within the forest are the Klamath, Scott, Salmon, Siskiyou, and Marble mountain ranges and the Klamath, Scott, and Salmon rivers. Fishing, whitewater boating on the three rivers; camping; hunting, hiking, x-country skiing. E and W of town via CA 263, turn left onto CA 96. The western section of the forest also incl the

Marble Mountain Wilderness. On 241,000 acres. Once part of the flat bottom of a shallow ocean, volcanic upheaval and the erosive action of rivers and glaciers have since combined to form what is now one of the most attractive wilderness areas in California. Marble Mountain itself is composed primarily of prehistoric marine invertebrate fossils. Camping, hiking; fishing in many streams and 79 trout-stocked lakes. Fire permit for this wilderness area is required and may be obtained at the Supervisor's office or any Ranger District Office. Access off CA 96. Contact the Forest Supervisor, 1312 Fairlane Rd; Phone 530/842-6131. Also at the Supervisor's office is the

Northwest Interpretive Museum. Lookout model; displays of wildlife, mining, timber production, fire management. (Mon-Fri; closed hols) **FREE**

Siskiyou County Museum. Exhibits of Siskiyou County from prehistoric era, Native Americans, trappers, gold rush, transportation, logging, agriculture. First and second floors incl period rms and environments. Research library on premises. (Tues-Sat) 910 S Main St. Phone 530/842-3836. ¢ Also on grounds is

Outdoor Museum. On 2½ acres with pioneer cabin, schoolhouse, blacksmith shop, logging skid shack, miner's cabin, church, operating general store. (Tues-Sat) Phone 916/842-3836. **FREE**

Yreka Western Railroad. Steam engine-powered 1915 historic train takes visitors on a three-hr tour of the Shasta Valley. (Memorial Day-Labor Day, Wed-Sun; one departure mid-morning) 300 E Miner St. Phone 530/842-4146. ¢¢¢

Motel/Motor Lodge

★★ KLAMATH MOTOR LODGE. *1111 S Main St (96097). 503/842-2751; fax 530/842-4703.* 28 rms, 1-2 story. S $41-$44; D $45-$52; each addl $4; suites $74-$84. TV; cable (premium). Heated pool. Coffee in rms. Restaurant nearby. Ck-out 11 am. Business servs avail. In-rm modem link. Refrigerators. Picnic table. Gardens. Cr cds: A, C, D, DS, JCB, MC, V.

SC

ATTRACTION LIST

Attraction names are listed in alphabetical order followed by a symbol identifying their classification and then city. The symbols for classification are: [S] for Special Events and [W] for What to See and Do

Acres of Orchids (Rod McLellan Co) [W] *San Francisco*
Adobe de Palomares [W] *Pomona*
Adventureland [W] *Disneyland*
Afton Canyon [W] *Barstow*
Ah Louis Store [W] *San Luis Obispo*
Alabama Hills Recreation Area [W] *Lone Pine*
Alameda County Fair [S] *Pleasanton*
Alameda County Fairgrounds [W] *Pleasanton*
Alamitos Bay [W] *Long Beach*
Alamitos Bay Marina [W] *Long Beach*
Albinger Archaeological Museum [W] *Ventura*
Alcatraz Island [W] *San Francisco*
All-American Canal [W] *Indio*
Allied Arts Guild [W] *Menlo Park*
Alpine Meadows [W] *Lake Tahoe Area*
Alpine Slide at Magic Mountain [W] *Big Bear Lake*
Alum Rock Park [W] *San Jose*
Amador County Museum [W] *Jackson*
Amateur Athletic Foundation [W] *Los Angeles*
American Century Investments Celebrity Golf championship [S] *Lake Tahoe Area*
Anaheim Angels (MLB) [W] *Anaheim*
Ancient Bristlecone Pine Forest [W] *Bishop*
Angeles National Forest [W] *Pasadena*
Angel Island State Park [W] *San Francisco*
Angels Flight Railway [W] *Los Angeles*
Antelope Valley Fair and Alfalfa Festival [S] *Lancaster*
Anthony Chabot Regional Park & Lake Chabot [W] *Oakland*
Antique and Art Galleries [W] *Carmel*
Antique Gas & Steam Engine Museum [W] *Oceanside*
Año Nuevo State Reserve [W] *Santa Cruz*
Aquatic Park [W] *San Francisco*
Arboretum of Los Angeles County, The [W] *Arcadia*
Arcata Architectural Tour [W] *Eureka*
Archival Center [W] *San Fernando*
ARCO Olympic Training Center [W] *Chula Vista*
ARCO Plaza [W] *Los Angeles*
Ardenwood Regional Preserve and Historic Farm [W] *Fremont*
Armstrong Redwoods State Reserve [W] *Guerneville*
Arrowhead Queen [W] *Lake Arrowhead*
Artesa Winery [W] *Napa*
Artist's Palette [W] *Death Valley National Park*
Art Museum [W] *Berkeley*
Art Museum [W] *Santa Barbara*
Asian Art Museum [W] *San Francisco*
Asilomar State Beach and Conference Center [W] *Pacific Grove*
Asistencia Mission de San Gabriel [W] *Redlands*
Asparagus Festival [S] *Stockton*
AT&T-Pebble Beach National Pro-Amateur Golf Championship [S] *Monterey*
Atascadero Historical Society Museum [W] *Atascadero*
Atascadero Lake Park [W] *Atascadero*
Autry Museum of Western Heritage [W] *Los Angeles*
Avenue of the Giants [W] *Garberville*
Avila Adobe [W] *Los Angeles*

Bade Institute of Biblical Archaeology [W] *Berkeley*
Badwater [W] *Death Valley National Park*
Baker Beach [W] *San Francisco*
Balboa Fun Zone [W] *Newport Beach*
Balboa Park [W] *San Diego*
Balboa Park-Off Park Blvd are [W] *San Diego*
Balboa Park—On Laurel St (El Prado) are [W] *San Diego*
Balboa Park recreational facilities include [W] *San Diego*
Balloon and Wine Festival [S] *Temecula*
Bargetto Winery [W] *Santa Cruz*
Barnsdall Art Park [W] *Hollywood (L.A.)*
Barnyard, The [W] *Carmel*
Battery Point Lighthouse [W] *Crescent City*
Bay Area Discovery Museum [W] *Sausalito*
Bay to Breakers Footrace [S] *San Francisco*
Beach areas [W] *Carmel*
Beach areas [W] *Los Angeles*
Beach areas [W] *Malibu*
Beach areas [W] *San Diego*
Beach areas [W] *Santa Barbara*
Beaches [W] *Los Angeles*
Beach recreation [W] *Cambria*
Bear Mountain Riding Stables [W] *Big Bear Lake*
Bear Valley [W] *Sonora*
Beaulieu Vineyard [W] *St. Helena*
Beckwourth Frontier Days [S] *Marysville*
Belmont Park [W] *San Diego*
Benicia Capitol State Historic Park [W] *Vallejo*
Beringer Vineyards [W] *St. Helena*
Berkeley Marina [W] *Berkeley*
Berkeley Museum of Art, Science, and Culture [W] *Pleasanton*
Berkeley Rose Garden [W] *Berkeley*
Bernhard Museum Complex [W] *Auburn*
Biblical Garden [W] *Carmel*
Bidwell Bar Days [S] *Oroville*
Bidwell Classic Marathon [S] *Chico*
Bidwell Mansion State Historic Park [W] *Chico*
Bidwell Park [W] *Chico*
Big Basin Redwoods State Park [W] *Santa Cruz*
Big Bear Mountain Resort [W] *Big Bear Lake*
Big Bear Mountain Ski Resort [W] *Big Bear Lake*
Big Bear Queen Tour Boat [W] *Big Bear Lake*
Big Fresno Fair, The [S] *Fresno*
Bill Graham Civic Auditorium [W] *San Francisco*
Birch Aquarium at Scripps [W] *La Jolla (San Diego)*
Bizz Johnson Trail [W] *Susanville*
Black Diamond Mines Regional Preserve [W] *Antioch*
Blackhawk Auto Museum [W] *Pleasanton*
Blue Diamond Growers Visitors Center & Retail Store [W] *Sacramento*
Blue Grass Festival [S] *Grass Valley*
Boating [W] *Yosemite National Park*
Boat Parades [S] *Long Beach*
Boat rides [W] *Lake Tahoe Area*
Bob Hope Chrysler Classic [S] *Palm Desert*
Bodie State Historic Park [W] *Bridgeport*
Bok Kai Festival [S] *Marysville*
Bok Kai Temple [W] *Marysville*
Boreal [W] *Truckee*
Boston Store [W] *Monterey*
Botanical Garden [W] *Berkeley*
Bouchaine Vineyards [W] *Napa*
Bowers Kidseum, The [W] *Santa Ana*
Bowers Museum of Cultural Art, The [W] *Santa Ana*
Boyden Cavern [W] *Sequoia & Kings Canyon National Parks*
Briones Regional Park [W] *Martinez*
Broadway Plaza [W] *Los Angeles*
Brooks Hall [W] *San Francisco*
Buena Vista Winery [W] *Sonoma*
Buffalo paddock [W] *San Francisco*
Butterfly Parade [S] *Pacific Grove*
Cable Car Museum [W] *San Francisco*
Cabrillo Festival [S] *San Diego*
Cabrillo Marine Aquarium [W] *Los Angeles*
Cabrillo Marine Aquarium [W] *San Pedro (L.A.)*

Cabrillo National Monument [W] *San Diego*
Calaveras Big Trees State Park [W] *Sonora*
Calaveras County Fair and Jumping Frog Jubilee [S] *Sonora*
Cal Expo [W] *Sacramento*
Calico Days [S] *Barstow*
Calico Early Man Site [W] *Barstow*
Calico Fine Arts Festival [S] *Barstow*
Calico Ghost Town Regional Park [W] *Barstow*
Calico Hullabaloo [S] *Barstow*
Calico Spring Festival [S] *Barstow*
California Academy of Sciences, Natural History Museum & Aquarium [W] *San Francisco*
California Dally Team Roping Championships [S] *Oakdale*
California Heritage Museum [W] *Santa Monica*
California International Airshow [S] *Salinas*
California Living Museum [W] *Bakersfield*
California Mid-State Fair [S] *Paso Robles*
California Museum of Photography [W] *Riverside*
California Palace of the Legion of Honor [W] *San Francisco*
California Polytechnic State University [W] *San Luis Obispo*
California Prune Festival [S] *Marysville*
California Rodeo [S] *Salinas*
California Route 66 Museum [W] *Victorville*
California Scenario [W] *Costa Mesa*
California Science Center [W] *Los Angeles*
California Speedway [W] *Ontario*
California State Fair [S] *Sacramento*
California State Polytechnic University, Pomona [W] *Pomona*
California State Railroad Museum and Railtown State Historic Park [W] *Sacramento*
California State University, Chico [W] *Chico*
California State University, Fresno [W] *Fresno*
California State University, Long Beach [W] *Long Beach*
California State University, Sacramento [W] *Sacramento*
California Strawberry Festival [S] *Oxnard*
California Surf Museum [W] *Oceanside*
Camanche Recreation Area, South Shore [W] *Lodi*
Camarillo Factory Stores [W] *Camarillo*
Campfire programs [W] *Yosemite National Park*
Campgrounds [W] *Mount Shasta*
Camping [W] *Death Valley National Park*
Camping [W] *Joshua Tree National Park*
Camping [W] *Yosemite National Park*
Camping. Emma Wood State Beach [W] *Ventura*
Camron-Stanford House [W] *Oakland*
Cannery, The [W] *San Francisco*
Cannery Row [W] *Monterey*
Canoe trips [W] *Blythe*
Canoe trips [W] *Healdsburg*
Capitola Begonia Festival [S] *Santa Cruz*
Carlsbad Village Street Faire [S] *Carlsbad*
Carmel Art Festival [S] *Carmel*
Carmel Bach Festival [S] *Carmel*
Carmel Sand Castle Contest [S] *Carmel*
Carnaval [S] *San Francisco*
Carnegie Art Museum [W] *Oxnard*
Carneros Creek Winery [W] *Napa*
Carpinteria State Beach [W] *Santa Barbara*
Carter House Natural Science Museum [W] *Redding*
Cartoon Art Museum [W] *San Francisco*
Casa de Estudillo [W] *San Diego*
Casa de Rancho Cucamonga (Rains House) [W] *Rancho Cucamonga*
Casa Soberanes [W] *Monterey*
Castle Air Museum [W] *Merced*
Castle Amusement Park [W] *Riverside*
Castle Crags State Park [W] *Dunsmuir*
Castle Lake [W] *Mount Shasta*
Caswell Memorial State Park [W] *Modesto*

Catalina Express [W] *Long Beach*
Catalina Island Museum [W] *Avalon (Catalina Island)*
Catalina tours and trips [W] *Avalon (Catalina Island)*
CBS Television City [W] *Los Angeles*
CCInc Auto Tape Tours [W] *San Francisco*
CEC/Seabee Museum [W] *Oxnard*
Cedar Grove [W] *Sequoia & Kings Canyon National Parks*
Central Library [W] *Los Angeles*
Central Pacific Passenger Depot [W] *Sacramento*
Central Valley Band Review [S] *Merced*
Chabot Observatory and Science Center [W] *Oakland*
Chaffee Zoological Gardens [W] *Fresno*
Channel Islands Aviation [W] *Camarillo*
Channel Islands Harbor [W] *Oxnard*
Channel Islands National Park [W] *Oxnard*
Channel Islands National Park [W] *Ventura*
Channel Islands National Park Visitor's Center [W] *Ventura*
Charcoal kilns [W] *Death Valley National Park*
Charles Krug Winery [W] *St. Helena*
Charles Paddock Zoo [W] *Atascadero*
Chateau Souverain [W] *Healdsburg*
Cherry Blossom Festival [S] *San Francisco*
Cherry Festival [S] *Beaumont*
Chico Chamber Expo [S] *Chico*
Chico Museum [W] *Chico*
Children's Discovery Museum, The [W] *San Jose*
Children's Fairyland [W] *Oakland*
Children's Lawn Festival [S] *Redding*
Children's Museum [W] *San Luis Obispo*
Children's Museum [W] *Stockton*
China Beach [W] *San Francisco*
China Cabin [W] *Tiburon*
Chinatown [W] *Los Angeles*
Chinatown [W] *San Francisco*
Chinese Cultural Center [W] *Visalia*
Chinese Memorial Pavilion [W] *Riverside*
Chinese New Year [S] *Los Angeles*
Chinese New Year [S] *San Francisco*
Chinese Temple [W] *Oroville*
Chocolate Festival [S] *Oakdale*
Christmas at the Inns [S] *Pacific Grove*
Christmas Boat Parade [S] *Newport Beach*
Christmas-Light Boat Parade [S] *San Diego*
Christmas on the Prado [S] *San Diego*
Chronicle Pavilion at Concord [W] *Concord*
Cibola National Wildlife Refuge [W] *Blythe*
Cinco de Mayo Celebration [S] *Los Angeles*
City Hall [W] *Los Angeles*
City Hall [W] *San Francisco*
City Hotel [W] *Sonora*
City River Park [W] *Red Bluff*
Civic Center [W] *San Francisco*
Claremont Colleges, The [W] *Claremont*
Clarke Memorial Museum [W] *Eureka*
Clear Lake State Park [W] *Clear Lake Area*
Cleveland National Forest [W] *Pine Valley*
Clovis Rodeo [S] *Fresno*
Coleman National Fish Hatchery [W] *Redding*
Colonel Allensworth State Historic Park [W] *Bakersfield*
Colony Days [S] *Atascadero*
Colorado River Country Music Festival [S] *Blythe*
Colorado River Country Fair [S] *Blythe*
Colton Hall Museum [W] *Monterey*
Columbia State Historic Park [W] *Sonora*
Commander's House, The [W] *Lone Pine*
Concannon Vineyard [W] *Livermore*
Constitution Day Parade [S] *Nevada City*
Contra Costa County Fair [S] *Antioch*
Contra Loma Regional Park [W] *Antioch*

Cooper-Molera House [W] *Monterey*
Cornish Christmas [S] *Grass Valley*
Corporate Helicopters of San Diego [W] *San Diego*
Corpus Christi Fiesta [S] *San Diego*
County Gold Exhibit [W] *Yreka*
Cow Hollow [W] *San Francisco*
Cow Palace [W] *San Francisco*
Coyote Hills [W] *Fremont*
Coyote Point Museum [W] *San Mateo*
Crab and Wine Days Festival [S] *Mendocino*
Critter Country [W] *Disneyland*
Crocker Art Museum [W] *Sacramento*
Cross-Country Kinetic Sculpture Race [S] *Eureka*
Crystal Cathedral [W] *Garden Grove*
Crystal Lake Recreation Area [W] *Pasadena*
Custom House [W] *Monterey*
Danish Days Festival [S] *Solvang*
Dante's View [W] *Death Valley National Park*
Davis Campus of the University of California [W] *Davis*
Death Valley National Park [W] *Lone Pine*
Deer Park [W] *Escondido*
Del Mar Fair [S] *Del Mar*
Del Mar Thoroughbred Club [S] *Del Mar*
Del Norte Coast Redwoods State Park [W] *Crescent City*
Del Norte County Historical Society Main Museum [W] *Crescent City*
Del Valle Regional Park [W] *Livermore*
De Saisset Museum [W] *Santa Clara*
Descanso Gardens [W] *Los Angeles*
Devil's Golf Course [W] *Death Valley National Park*
Discovery Center, The [W] *Fresno*
Discovery Museum [W] *Sacramento*
Discovery Museum of Orange County [W] *Santa Ana*
Discovery Science Center [W] *Santa Ana*
Disneyland [W] *Anaheim*
Disneyland [W] *Los Angeles*
Disney's California Adventure [W] *Anaheim*
Dodge Ridge [W] *Sonora*
Domaine Carneros by Taittinger [W] *Napa*
Domaine Chandon [W] *Yountville*
Donner Lake [W] *Truckee*
Donner Memorial State Park [W] *Truckee*
Donner Party Hike [S] *Truckee*
Donner Ski Ranch [W] *Truckee*
Don Pedro Lake Recreation Area [W] *Modesto*
Don Pedro Lake Recreation Area [W] *Sonora*
Downtown [W] *Los Angeles*
Dry Creek Pioneer Regional Park [W] *Hayward*
Dunnewood Vineyards [W] *Ukiah*
Dunsmuir House and Gardens [W] *Oakland*
Eagle Cotage [W] *Sonora*
Eagle Lake [W] *Susanville*
Early Days Celebration [S] *San Juan Bautista*
East Bay Regional Park District [W] *Oakland*
Eastern California Museum [W] *Lone Pine*
Easter Sunrise Pilgrimage [S] *Riverside*
Easter Sunrise Services [S] *Hollywood (L.A.)*
Edward-Dean Museum of Decorative Arts [W] *Beaumont*
Edwards Air Force Base [W] *Lancaster*
Egyptian Museum [W] *San Jose*
El Dorado County Fair [S] *Placerville*
El Dorado County Historical Museum [W] *Placerville*
El Dorado East Regional Park and Nature Center [W] *Long Beach*
El Dorado National Forest [W] *Placerville*
Elks Rodeo & Parade [S] *Santa Maria*
El Molino Viejo [W] *San Marino*
El Paseo [W] *Santa Barbara*
El Presidio de Santa Barbara State Historic Park [W] *Santa Barbara*
El Pueblo de Los Angeles Historic Monument [W] *Los Angeles*
Elysian Park [W] *Los Angeles*
Embarcadero, The [W] *San Francisco*

Empire Mine State Historic Park [W] *Grass Valley*
Escondido Heritage Walk [W] *Escondido*
Eugene O'Neill National Historic Site [W] *Pleasanton*
Exploratorium [W] *San Francisco*
Exposition Park [W] *Los Angeles*
Factory Merchants Outlet Mall [W] *Barstow*
Factory Stores at Vacaville [W] *Vacaville*
Fall Color Spectacular [S] *Nevada City*
Fandango Days [S] *Alturas*
Fantasyland [W] *Disneyland*
Fantasy Springs Casino [W] *Indio*
Farmers Fair [S] *Hemet*
Farmers Market [W] *Los Angeles*
Feast of Lanterns [S] *Pacific Grove*
Feather Falls [W] *Oroville*
Feather Fiesta [S] *Oroville*
Feather River Fish Hatchery [W] *Oroville*
Federal and State Buildings, The [W] *San Francisco*
Felton covered bridge [W] *Santa Cruz*
Ferndale Architectural Tour [W] *Eureka*
Ferndale Museum [W] *Eureka*
Ferrara [W] *Escondido*
Ferry Building [W] *San Francisco*
Festival de la Familia [S] *Sacramento*
Festival of Arts & Pageant of the Masters [S] *Laguna Beach*
Festival of Bells [S] *San Diego*
Festival of Whales [S] *San Juan Capistrano*
Fiesta Broadway [S] *Los Angeles*
Fiesta de las Golondrinas [S] *San Juan Capistrano*
Filoli Gardens [W] *San Mateo*
Filoli House and Gardens [W] *Menlo Park*
Firehouse [W] *Sonora*
Firehouse No. 1 [W] *Nevada City*
Fireman's Muster [S] *Sonora*
Fisherman's Village [W] *Marina del Rey*
Fisherman's Wharf [W] *Monterey*
Fisherman's Wharf [W] *Oxnard*
Fisherman's Wharf [W] *San Francisco*
Fishing [W] *Red Bluff*
Fishing [W] *Sequoia & Kings Canyon National Parks*
Fishing [W] *Yosemite National Park*
Fishing, boating, rentals [W] *Mammoth Lakes*
Flower Festival [S] *Lompoc*
Flower Fields at Carlsbad Ranch [S] *Carlsbad*
Folsom Lake State Recreation Area [W] *Auburn*
Folsom Premium Outlets [W] *Roseville*
Foothills, Lodgepole, and Grant Grove Visitor Centers [W] *Sequoia & Kings Canyon National Parks*
Forbes Mill Museum of Regional History [W] *Los Gatos*
Forestiere Underground Gardens [W] *Fresno*
Forest of Nisene Marks [W] *Santa Cruz*
Forest Tree Nursery [W] *Fort Bragg*
Fort Humboldt State Historic Park [W] *Eureka*
Fortino Winery [W] *Gilroy*
Fort Mason [W] *San Francisco*
Fort Mason Center [W] *San Francisco*
Fort Point National Historic Site [W] *San Francisco*
Fortuna Depot Museum [W] *Eureka*
Fowler Museum of Cultural History, UCLA [W] *Los Angeles*
Franciscan Vineyards [W] *St. Helena*
Fremont Festival of the Arts [S] *Fremont*
Fresno County Blossom Trail [S] *Fresno*
Fresno Metropolitan Museum [W] *Fresno*
Frontierland [W] *Disneyland*
Gallatin Marina [W] *Susanville*
Gamble House, The [W] *Pasadena*
Garin Regional Park [W] *Hayward*
Gaslamp Quarter [W] *San Diego*
General George S. Patton Memorial Museum [W] *Indio*
General Grant Grove [W] *Sequoia & Kings Canyon National Parks*
General Phineas Banning Residence Museum [W] *Long Beach*
Getty Center, The [W] *Los Angeles*

Ghirardelli Square [W] *San Francisco*
Giant Forest [W] *Sequoia & Kings Canyon National Parks*
Giant Sequoias, The [W] *Yosemite National Park*
Gilroy Garlic Festival [S] *Gilroy*
Glacier Point [W] *Yosemite National Park*
Glen Helen Regional Park [W] *San Bernardino*
Glen Ivy Hot Springs [W] *Corona*
Gloria Ferrer Champagne Caves [W] *Sonoma*
Gold Bug Mine [W] *Placerville*
Gold Country Fair [S] *Auburn*
Gold Country Museum [W] *Auburn*
Golden Canyon [W] *Death Valley National Park*
Golden Gate Bridge, The [W] *San Francisco*
Golden Gate National Recreation Area [W] *San Francisco*
Golden Gate Park [W] *San Francisco*
Golden Gate Promenade [W] *San Francisco*
Golden State Museum [W] *Sacramento*
Golden State Warriors (NBA) [W] *Oakland*
Gold Rush District State Parks [W] *Sacramento*
Golf [W] *San Diego*
Good Old Days [S] *Pacific Grove*
Governor's Mansion [W] *Sacramento*
Grace Hudson Museum [W] *Ukiah*
Graduate School Art Building [W] *Claremont*
Grand Central Market [W] *Los Angeles*
Grand National Rodeo, Horse & Stock Show [S] *San Francisco*
Grape Harvest Festival [S] *Rancho Cucamonga*
Gray Line bus tours [W] *Monterey*
Gray Line bus tours [W] *San Diego*
Gray Line bus tours [W] *San Francisco*
Great Gatsby Festival [S] *Lake Tahoe Area*
Great Petaluma Mill, The [W] *Petaluma*
Great Valley Museum of Natural History [W] *Modesto*
Greek Festival [S] *Stockton*
Greek Theatre [W] *Los Angeles*
Greek Theatre in Griffith Park [S] *Los Angeles*
Greenhorn Mountain Park [W] *Kernville*
Greenhouse Tour [S] *Lompoc*
Griffith Observatory and Planetarium [W] *Los Angeles*
Griffith Park [W] *Los Angeles*
Grizzly Peak Blvd [W] *Berkeley*
Grover Hot Springs State Park [W] *Lake Tahoe Area*
Guided walking tours [W] *Los Angeles*
Gull Wings Children's Museum [W] *Oxnard*
Haas-Lilienthal House [W] *San Francisco*
Haggin Museum [W] *Stockton*
Haight-Ashbury [W] *San Francisco*
Hakone Gardens [W] *Saratoga*
Hall of Justice [W] *Los Angeles*
Happy Hollow Park and Zoo [W] *San Jose*
Haraszthy Villa [W] *Sonoma*
Harbor cruises [W] *Morro Bay*
Hastings Building [W] *Sacramento*
Hat Creek Recreation Area [W] *Burney*
Hat in Three Stages of Landing [W] *Salinas*
Hayward Area Historical Society Museum [W] *Hayward*
Healdsburg area wineries [W] *Healdsburg*
Healdsburg Harvest Century Bicycle Tour [S] *Healdsburg*
Hearst Greek Theatre [W] *Berkeley*
Hearst-San Simeon State Historical Monument [W] *Cambria*
Hearst-San Simeon State Historical Monument [W] *San Simeon*
Heavenly Ski Resort [W] *Lake Tahoe Area*
Henry Cowell Redwoods [W] *Santa Cruz*
Henry W. Coe State Park [W] *Gilroy*
Heritage House [W] *Riverside*
Hershey Chocolate USA [W] *Oakdale*
Hess Collection Winery [W] *Napa*
Hidden Valley Nature Trail [W] *Joshua Tree National Park*
high country, The [W] *Sequoia & Kings Canyon National Parks*

High Country, The [W] *Yosemite National Park*
Highland Art Center [W] *Weaverville*
Highland Gathering and Games [S] *Costa Mesa*
Highland Gathering and Games [S] *Fresno*
Hiking and backpacking [W] *Yosemite National Park*
Historical Society of Pomona Valley [W] *Pomona*
Historic Judge C. F. Lott House [W] *Oroville*
Historic Miners Foundry [W] *Nevada City*
History San Jose [W] *San Jose*
Hollyhock House [W] *Hollywood (L.A.)*
Hollywood [W] *Los Angeles*
Hollywood Blvd [W] *Hollywood (L.A.)*
Hollywood Bowl [W] *Hollywood (L.A.)*
Hollywood Christmas Parade [S] *Hollywood (L.A.)*
Hollywood Entertainment Museum [W] *Hollywood (L.A.)*
Hollywood Forever Cemetery [W] *Hollywood (L.A.)*
Hollywood Heritage Museum [W] *Hollywood (L.A.)*
Hollywood Park [W]
Hollywood Wax Museum [W] *Hollywood (L.A.)*
Hoover Tower [W] *Palo Alto*
Hornblower Cruises [W] *Lake Tahoe Area*
Horseback riding [W] *Big Bear Lake*
Horse racing [S] *Los Angeles*
Horse racing. Bay Meadows Racecourse [W] *San Mateo*
Horton Plaza [W] *San Diego*
Hot-air ballooning [W] *Napa*
Hot-air ballooning [W] *Yountville*
Hot Creek Fish Hatchery [W] *Mammoth Lakes*
Hot Creek Geological Site [W] *Mammoth Lakes*
Hotel del Coronado [W] *San Diego*
House of Pacific Relations [W] *San Diego*
Huck Finn Jubilee [S] *Victorville*
Humboldt Bay Harbor Cruise [W] *Eureka*
Humboldt Bay Maritime Museum [W] *Eureka*
Huntington Library, Art Collections, and Botanical Gardens [W] *San Marino*
Hurkey Creek [W] *Idyllwild*
Hyde Street Pier Historic Ships [W] *San Francisco*
Idyllwild [W] *Idyllwild*
Indian Canyons [W] *Palm Springs*
Indian Cultural Museum, The [W] *Yosemite National Park*
Indian Grinding Rock State Historic Park [W] *Jackson*
Indian Lore Monument [W] *Blythe*
Indian Pow Wow [S] *Tehachapi*
Indian Village (Ahwahnee) [W] *Yosemite National Park*
Indio Desert Circuit Horse Show [S] *Indio*
Indio International Tamale Festival [S] *Indio*
Industrial tour. Graber Olive House [W] *Ontario*
Intel Museum [W] *Santa Clara*
International Festival [S] *Modesto*
International House [W] *Berkeley*
International Teddybear Convention [S] *Nevada City*
In the area are [W] *Los Angeles*
Iron Gate Dam and Lake [W] *Yreka*
Isabella Lake [W] *Kernville*
Island & Coastal Fishing Trips [W] *Santa Barbara*
Island Packer Cruises [W] *Ventura*
Jack London Square [W] *Oakland*
Jack London State Historic Park [W] *Sonoma*
Jackson Square [W] *San Francisco*
Japan Center [W] *San Francisco*
Japanese American National Museum [W] *Los Angeles*
Japanese Friendship Garden [W] *San Jose*
Japanese Tea Garden [W] *San Francisco*
Japanese Tea Garden [W] *San Mateo*
Jazz, Art, and Wine Festival [S] *Vallejo*
Jazz Festival [S] *Eureka*
Jazz Festival [S] *Long Beach*
Jedediah Smith Redwoods State Park [W] *Crescent City*

J.J. Jackson Memorial Museum [W] *Weaverville*
J. Lohr Winery [W] *San Jose*
Joaquin Miller Park [W] *Oakland*
John Muir National Historic Site [W] *Martinez*
Judah L. Magnes Museum [W] *Berkeley*
Jughandle Ecological Staircase [W] *Fort Bragg*
June Mountain Ski Area [W] *June Lake*
Junior Museum & Zoo [W] *Palo Alto*
Kaiser Center [W] *Oakland*
Kearney Mansion Museum [W] *Fresno*
Kelley House Museum & Library [W] *Mendocino*
Kelley Park [W] *San Jose*
Kellogg Arabian Horse Center [W] *Pomona*
Kellogg Park [W] *La Jolla (San Diego)*
Kelly-Griggs House Museum [W] *Red Bluff*
Kern County Fair [S] *Bakersfield*
Kern County Museum [W] *Bakersfield*
Kernville Rod Run [S] *Kernville*
Keys View [W] *Joshua Tree National Park*
Kidspace [W] *Pasadena*
Kimberly Crest House and Gardens [W] *Redlands*
King Range National Conservation Area [W] *Garberville*
Kingsburg [W] *Fresno*
Kirkwood [W] *Lake Tahoe Area*
Klamath National Forest [W] *Yreka*
Knott's Berry Farm [W] *Buena Park*
Knott's Berry Farm [W] *Los Angeles*
Korbel Champagne Cellars [W] *Guerneville*
Kruse Rhododendron State Reserve [W] *Fort Ross State Historic Park*
La Casa Primera [W] *Pomona*
Laguna Playhouse [W] *Laguna Beach*
Lake Arrowhead Children's Museum [W] *Lake Arrowhead*
Lake Berryessa [W] *St. Helena*
Lake Cachuma Recreation Area [W] *Solvang*
Lake Casitas Recreation Area [W] *Ojai*
Lake County Fair and Horse Show [S] *Clear Lake Area*
Lake County Rodeo [S] *Clear Lake Area*
Lake Gregory Regional Park [W] *Crestline*
Lake Mendocino [W] *Ukiah*
Lake Merritt [W] *Oakland*
Lake Nacimiento Resort [W] *Paso Robles*
Lake Oroville State Recreation Area [W] *Oroville*
Lake Recreation [W] *June Lake*
Lake Redding-Caldwell Park [W] *Redding*
Lake San Antonio Recreation Area [W] *Paso Robles*
Lake Shasta Caverns [W] *Redding*
Lakeside Park [W] *Oakland*
Lake Siskiyou [W] *Mount Shasta*
Lake Siskiyou Camp-Resort [W] *Mount Shasta*
Lake Tahoe Historical Society Museum [W] *Lake Tahoe Area*
Lake Yosemite Park [W] *Merced*
La Mirada [W] *Monterey*
La Purisima Mission State Historic Park [W] *Lompoc*
Larkin House [W] *Monterey*
Lassen County Fair [S] *Susanville*
Lassen National Forest [W] *Burney*
Lassen National Forest [W] *Susanville*
Lassen Volcanic National Park [W] *Red Bluff*
Lassen Volcanic National Park [W] *Redding*
Lathrop House [W] *Redwood City*
Lawrence Hall of Science [W] *Berkeley*
Lawrence Livermore National Laboratory's Visitor Center [W] *Livermore*
Laws Railroad Museum & Historical Site [W] *Bishop*
Legoland [W] *Carlsbad*
Lewiston Dam and Lake [W] *Redding*
Lick Observatory [W] *San Jose*
Lincoln Memorial Shrine [W] *Redlands*
Lindsay Museum [W] *Berkeley*
Little Tokyo [W] *Los Angeles*

Living Desert, The [W] *Palm Desert*
Lodi Grape Festival and Harvest Fair [S] *Lodi*
Lodi Lake Park [W] *Lodi*
Lodi Spring Wine Show [S] *Lodi*
Lola Montez House [W] *Grass Valley*
Lombard Street [W] *San Francisco*
Lone Pine Film Festival [S] *Lone Pine*
Long Beach Aquarium of the Pacific [W] *Long Beach*
Long Beach Blues Festival [S] *Long Beach*
Long Beach Convention & Entertainment Center [W] *Long Beach*
Long Beach Museum of Art [W] *Long Beach*
Long Beach Sport Fishing [W] *Long Beach*
Lopez Recreational Area [W] *Pismo Beach*
Los Angeles Clippers (NBA) [W] *Los Angeles*
Los Angeles County Fair [S] *Los Angeles*
Los Angeles County Fair [S] *Pomona*
Los Angeles County Museum of Art [W] *Los Angeles*
Los Angeles Dodgers (MLB) [W] *Los Angeles*
Los Angeles Galaxy (MLS) [W] *Los Angeles*
Los Angeles Kings (NHL) [W] *Los Angeles*
Los Angeles Lakers (NBA) [W] *Los Angeles*
Los Angeles Mall [W] *Los Angeles*
Los Angeles Maritime Museum [W] *Los Angeles*
Los Angeles Maritime Museum [W] *San Pedro (L.A.)*
Los Angeles Memorial Coliseum and Sports Arena [W] *Los Angeles*
Los Angeles Music Center Opera [S] *Los Angeles*
Los Angeles Sparks (WNBA) [W] *Los Angeles*
Los Angeles State and County Arboretum [W] *Los Angeles*
Los Angeles Zoo [W] *Los Angeles*
Los Encinos [W] *Los Angeles*
Los Gatos Museum of Art & Natural History [W] *Los Gatos*
Los Padres National Forest [W] *King City*
Los Padres National Forest [W] *Santa Barbara*
Lost Palms Canyon [W] *Joshua Tree National Park*
Lotus Festival [S] *Los Angeles*
Louise M. Davies Symphony Hall [W] *San Francisco*
Louis M. Martini Winery [W] *St. Helena*
Lucy Evans Baylands Nature Interpretive Center [W] *Palo Alto*
Lummis Home and Garden State Historical Monument [W] *Los Angeles*
Luna Vineyards [W] *Napa*
Luther Burbank Home & Gardens [W] *Santa Rosa*
Luther Burbank Rose Festival [S] *Santa Rosa*
MacKerricher State Park [W] *Fort Bragg*
Madonnari Italian Street Painting Festival [S] *San Luis Obispo*
Main St, U.S.A [W] *Disneyland*
Malakoff Diggins State Historic Park [W] *Nevada City*
Mammoth Adventure Connection [W] *Mammoth Lakes*
Mammoth Lakes Pack Outfit [W] *Mammoth Lakes*
Mammoth Mountain Ski Area [W] *Mammoth Lakes*
Mammoth Visitor Center Ranger Station [W] *Mammoth Lakes*
Mann's Chinese Theatre [W] *Hollywood (L.A.)*
Marble Mountain Wilderness [W] *Yreka*
Marching Band Festival [S] *Pacific Grove*
Marina [W] *Monterey*
Marina Green [W] *San Francisco*
Marinas [W] *Long Beach*
Marinas. Port of Redwood City Yacht Harbor [W] *Redwood City*
Marin County Civic Center [W] *San Rafael*
Marin French Cheese Company [W] *Petaluma*
Maritime Museum of Monterey [W] *Monterey*

Market Street [W] *San Francisco*
Marshall Gold Discovery State Historic Park [W] *Placerville*
Martin Luther King, Jr Regional Shoreline [W] *Oakland*
Mary Connolly Children's Playground [W] *San Francisco*
McArthur-Burney Falls Memorial State Park [W] *Burney*
McConaghy Estate [W] *Hayward*
McGee Creek Pack Station [W] *Mammoth Lakes*
McHenry Mansion [W] *Modesto*
McHenry Museum [W] *Modesto*
Mendocino Art Center [W] *Mendocino*
Mendocino Christmas Festival [S] *Mendocino*
Mendocino Coast Botanical Gardens [W] *Fort Bragg*
Mendocino County Fair & Apple Show [S] *Ukiah*
Mendocino County Museum [W] *Willits*
Mendocino Headlands [W] *Mendocino*
Mendocino Music Festival [S] *Mendocino*
Mendocino National Forest [W] *Willows*
Merced County Courthouse Museum [W] *Merced*
Merced County Fair [S] *Merced*
Merced Multicultural Arts Center [W] *Merced*
Merced River Development Project [W] *Merced*
Mercer Caverns [W] *Sonora*
Merryvale Vineyards [W] *St. Helena*
Methuselah Redwood [W] *Redwood City*
Metreon [W] *San Francisco*
Mexican Museum, The [W] *San Francisco*
Micke Grove Park & Zoo [W] *Lodi*
Mickey's Toontown [W] *Disneyland*
Mighty Ducks of Anaheim (NHL) [W] *Anaheim*
Millerton Lake State Recreation Area [W] *Fresno*
Mingei International Museum of World Folk Art [W] *San Diego*
Mining Museum-North Star Powerhouse [W] *Grass Valley*
Mirassou Winery [W] *San Jose*
Mission Basilica San Diego de Alcala [W] *San Diego*
Mission Bay Park [W] *San Diego*
Mission District Murals [W] *San Francisco*
Mission Dolores [W] *San Francisco*
Mission San Antonio de Padua [W] *King City*
Mission San Antonio de Padua Fiesta [S] *King City*
Mission San Buenaventura [W] *Ventura*
Mission San Carlos Borromeo del Rio Carmelo [W] *Carmel*
Mission San Fernando Rey de España [W] *Los Angeles*
Mission San Fernando Rey de España [W] *San Fernando*
Mission San Jose [W] *Fremont*
Mission San Juan Bautista [W] *San Juan Bautista*
Mission San Juan Capistrano [W] *San Juan Capistrano*
Mission San Luis Obispo de Tolosa [W] *San Luis Obispo*
Mission San Luis Rey de Francia [W] *Oceanside*
Mission San Miguel Arc Angel [W] *Paso Robles*
Mission San Rafael ArcÂngel [W] *San Rafael*
Mission Santa Barbara [W] *Santa Barbara*
Mission Santa Clara de AsíÌs [W] *Santa Clara*
Moabi Regional Park [W] *Needles*
Moaning Cavern [W] *Sonora*
Modoc County Historical Museum [W] *Alturas*
Modoc National Forest [W] *Alturas*
Modoc National Wildlife Refuge [W] *Alturas*
Modoc-The Last Frontier Fair [S] *Alturas*
Mojave Narrows Regional Park [W] *Victorville*
Mojave River Valley Museum [W] *Barstow*
Monarch Butterfly Grove [W] *Pismo Beach*
Monarch Grove Sanctuary [W] *Pacific Grove*
Mono Lake [W] *Lee Vining*
Montana de Oro State Park [W] *Morro Bay*

Monterey Bay Aquarium [W] *Monterey*
Monterey County Fair [S] *Monterey*
Monterey Jazz Festival [S] *Monterey*
Monterey Museum of Art [W] *Monterey*
Monterey State Historic Park [W] *Monterey*
Monterey Wine Festival [S] *Carmel*
Montgomery Art Gallery [W] *Claremont*
Montgomery Street [W] *San Francisco*
Moorten's Botanical Garden [W] *Palm Springs*
Moreton Bay fig tree [W] *Santa Barbara*
Morro Bay Aquarium [W] *Morro Bay*
Morro Bay State Park [W] *Morro Bay*
Morro Rock [W] *Morro Bay*
Mother Goose Parade [S] *San Diego*
Mother Lode Fair [S] *Sonora*
Mother Lode Roundup Parade and Rodeo [S] *Sonora*
Mountain Festival and PRCA Rodeo [S] *Tehachapi*
Mountain High Ski Area [W] *San Bernardino*
Mountain Man Rendezvous [S] *Santa Cruz*
M.H. deYoung Memorial Museum [W] *San Francisco*
Mount Rubidoux Memorial Park [W] *Riverside*
Mount San Jacinto State Park [W] *Idyllwild*
Mount Shasta [W] *Mount Shasta*
Mount Shasta Ski and Board Park [W] *Mount Shasta*
Mount St. Helena [W] *Calistoga*
Mount Tamalpais State Park [W] *Mill Valley*
Mount Tamalpais State Park [W] *San Francisco*
Movieland Wax Museum [W] *Buena Park*
Mozart Festival [S] *San Luis Obispo*
MS *Dixie II* Cruises [W] *Lake Tahoe Area*
Muir Beach [W] *San Francisco*
Muir Woods National Monument [W] *San Francisco*
Mule Canyon and Fiery Gulch [W] *Barstow*
Mule Days [S] *Bishop*
Mulholland Drive [W] *Los Angeles*
Municipal Art Gallery [W] *Hollywood (L.A.)*
Municipal Beach [W] *Long Beach*
Municipal recreation facilities [W] *Stockton*
Municipal Rose Garden [W] *San Jose*
Municipal Wharf [W] *Santa Cruz*
Mural Walk [W] *Lompoc*
Museo ItaloAmericano [W] *San Francisco*
Museum of Contemporary Art [W] *La Jolla (San Diego)*
Museum of Contemporary Art (MOCA) [W] *Los Angeles*
Museum of Contemporary Art, San Diego [W] *San Diego*
Museum of Craft & Folk Art [W] *San Francisco*
Museum of Flying [W] *Santa Monica*
Museum of History and Art, Ontario [W] *Ontario*
Museum of Natural History [W] *Morro Bay*
Museum of Photographic Arts [W] *San Diego*
Museum of Tolerance [W] *Los Angeles*
Music Center of Los Angeles County [W] *Los Angeles*
Music Circus [S] *Sacramento*
Mystery Spot, The [W] *Santa Cruz*
Napa County Fair [S] *Calistoga*
Napa Valley Wine Train [W] *Napa*
National Hotel [W] *Nevada City*
National Maritime Museum [W] *San Francisco*
National Orange Show [S] *San Bernardino*
National Steinbeck Center Museum [W] *Salinas*
Natural Bridge [W] *Death Valley National Park*
Natural Bridges Beach [W] *Santa Cruz*
Natural History Museum of Los Angeles County [W] *Los Angeles*
Nature Center at Happy Isles, The [W] *Yosemite National Park*
Naval ship tour [W] *San Diego*
NBC Studios Tour [W] *Los Angeles*

Nevada City Classic Bicycle Tour [S] *Nevada City*
Nevada County Fair [S] *Grass Valley*
Nevada Theatre [W] *Nevada City*
New Melones Lake Recreation Area [W] *Sonora*
New Orleans Square [W] *Disneyland*
Nisei Week [S] *Los Angeles*
Nob Hill [W] *San Francisco*
Northstar [W] *Truckee*
Norton Simon Museum of Art [W] *Pasadena*
Noyo [W] *Fort Bragg*
Nuestra Señora La Reina de Los Angeles [W] *Los Angeles*
Oakdale Cowboy Museum [W] *Oakdale*
Oakland Athletics (MLB) [W] *Oakland*
Oakland Museum of California [W] *Oakland*
Oakland Raiders (NFL) [W] *Oakland*
Oakland Zoo in Knowland Park [W] *Oakland*
Oasis Visitor Center [W] *Joshua Tree National Park*
Oasis Waterpark [W] *Palm Springs*
Obon Festival [S] *San Jose*
Obon Festival and Bazaar [S] *Stockton*
Ocean Beach [W] *San Francisco*
Oceano Dunes State Vehicular Recreation Area [W] *Pismo Beach*
Oceanside Harbor and Marina [W] *Oceanside*
Ocean View Blvd [W] *Pacific Grove*
Ocean World [W] *Crescent City*
Odessa Canyon [W] *Barstow*
Ojai Center for the Arts [W] *Ojai*
Ojai Festivals [S] *Ojai*
Ojai Shakespeare Festival [S] *Ojai*
Ojai Studio Artists Tour [S] *Ojai*
Ojai Valley Museum [W] *Ojai*
Old Eagle Theatre [W] *Sacramento*
Old Faithful Geyser of California [W] *Calistoga*
Old Globe Theatre [W] *San Diego*
Old Miner's Days [S] *Big Bear Lake*
Old Mission Santa Inés [W] *Solvang*
Old Plaza Firehouse [W] *Los Angeles*
Old Spanish Days Fiesta [S] *Santa Barbara*
Old Time Fiddlers' Contest [S] *Oroville*
Old Town [W] *Auburn*
Old Town [W] *Eureka*
Old Town [W] *Los Gatos*
Old Town [W] *San Diego*
Old Town San Diego State Historic Park [W] *San Diego*
Olivas Adobe [W] *Ventura*
Olvera Street [W] *Los Angeles*
O'Neil Museum [W] *San Juan Capistrano*
Ontario Mills [W] *Ontario*
Orange County Fair [S] *Costa Mesa*
Orange County Museum of Arts [W] *Newport Beach*
Orange Empire Railway Museum [W] *Riverside*
Orfila [W] *Escondido*
Oroville Dam & Reservoir [W] *Oroville*
Ortega Adobe [W] *Ventura*
Outdoor Museum [W] *Yreka*
Outlets at Gilroy [W] *Gilroy*
Overfelt Gardens [W] *San Jose*
Pacific Asia Museum [W] *Pasadena*
Pacific Coast Sightseeing (Gray Line Anaheim, A Coach U.S.A. Company) [W] *Anaheim*
Pacific Grove Museum of Natural History [W] *Pacific Grove*
Pacific House [W] *Monterey*
Pacific Park [W] *Santa Monica*
Pacific Repertory Theatre [W] *Carmel*
Pack trips [W] *Mammoth Lakes*
Page Museum at the La Brea Discoveries [W] *Los Angeles*
Palace of Fine Arts [W] *San Francisco*
Palisades Park [W] *Santa Monica*
Palm Canyon [W] *Palm Springs*
Palm Springs Aerial Tramway [W] *Palm Springs*
Palm Springs Air Museum [W] *Palm Springs*
Palm Springs Desert Museum [W] *Palm Springs*
Palms to Pines Highway [W] *Palm Desert*
Palomar Observatory [W] *Escondido*
Palo Verde Lagoon [W] *Blythe*

Paramount Film and Television Studios [W] *Los Angeles*
Paramount's Great America [W] *Santa Clara*
Paramount's Raging Waters [W] *San Jose*
Paramount Theatre [W] *Oakland*
Parducci Wine Cellars [W] *Ukiah*
Parent Washington Navel Orange Tree [W] *Riverside*
Pasadena Historical Society [W] *Pasadena*
"Path of History" tour [W] *Monterey*
Patrick's Point State Park [W] *Trinidad*
Paul Bunyan Days [S] *Fort Bragg*
Paul Bunyan's Forest Camp [W] *Redding*
Pepperdine University [W] *Malibu*
Peralta Adobe and Fallon House [W] *San Jose*
Performing Arts Center [W] *San Francisco*
Performing Arts Center of San Louis Obispo [W] *San Luis Obispo*
Petaluma Adobe State Historic Park [W] *Petaluma*
Petaluma Historical Museum and Library [W] *Petaluma*
Petaluma Village Factory Outlets [W] *Petaluma*
Petersen Automotive Museum [W] *Los Angeles*
Petrified Forest [W] *Calistoga*
Pharaoh's Lost Kingdom [W] *Redlands*
Phoebe Apperson Hearst Museum of Anthropology [W] *Berkeley*
Picnic Day [S] *Davis*
Pier 39 [W] *San Francisco*
Pine Ridge Winery [W] *Napa*
Pinnacles National Monument [W] *King City*
Pinnacles National Monument [W] *Salinas*
Pinnacles National Monument [W] *San Juan Bautista*
Pioneer Yosemite History Center [W] *Yosemite National Park*
Pismo Beach Clam Festival [S] *Pismo Beach*
Pixie Woods [W] *Stockton*
Placer County Fair [S] *Auburn*
Planes of Fame Air Museum [W] *Ontario*
Planetarium & Science Center [W] *San Jose*
Plaza Stable [W] *San Juan Bautista*
Plumas County Fair [S] *Quincy*
Plumas County Museum [W] *Quincy*
Plumas National Forest [W] *Quincy*
Point Arena Lighthouse and Museum [W] *Gualala*
Point Lobos State Reserve [W] *Carmel*
Point Mugu Airshow [S] *Oxnard*
Point PiÒos Lighthouse [W] *Pacific Grove*
Point Reyes National Seashore [W] *Inverness*
Point St. George [W] *Crescent City*
Pomona School of Fine Arts [W] *Pomona*
Ponderosa Ranch and Western Theme Park [W] *Lake Tahoe Area*
Pop concerts [S] *San Francisco*
Ports o'Call Village [W] *Los Angeles*
Ports o'Call Village [W] *San Pedro (L.A.)*
Prado Regional Park [W] *Ontario*
Prairie Creek Redwoods State Park [W] *Crescent City*
Prayerbook Cross [W] *San Francisco*
PRCA Rodeo [S] *Oakdale*
Presidio, The [W] *San Francisco*
Presidio of Monterey [W] *Monterey*
Presidio Park [W] *San Diego*
Professional sports [W] *Anaheim*
Professional sports [W] *Los Angeles*
Professional Sports [W] *Oakland*
Professional sports [W] *Sacramento*
Professional sports [W] *San Diego*
Professional sports [W] *San Francisco*
Professional sports [W] *San Jose*
Prosellis Bowl [W] *Redlands*
Providence Mountains State Recreation Area [W] *Needles*
Pyramid Lake Recreation Area [W] *Valencia*
Queen Mary Seaport [W] *Long Beach*
Raging Waters [W] *Ontario*
Railtown 1897 State Historic Park [W] *Sonora*
Rainbow Basin [W] *Barstow*
Ramona Pageant [S] *Hemet*

Rancho Cañada Golf Club [W] *Carmel*
Rancho Los Alamitos [W] *Long Beach*
Rancho Los Cerritos [W] *Long Beach*
Rancho Santa Ana Botanic Garden [W] *Claremont*
Randall Museum [W] *San Francisco*
Red Bluff Roundup [S] *Red Bluff*
Redding Museum of Art & History [W] *Redding*
Redondo Beach Pier [W] *Redondo Beach*
Red's Meadow Pack Station and Resort [W] *Mammoth Lakes*
Redwood Mountain Grove [W] *Sequoia & Kings Canyon National Parks*
Redwood National and State Parks [W] *Crescent City*
Redwood Regional Park [W] *Oakland*
Regional Library and Cultural Center [W] *San Juan Capistrano*
Regional parks [W] *Fremont*
Renaissance Faire [S] *San Bernardino*
Renaissance Festival [S] *San Luis Obispo*
Renaissance Festival & Jousting Tournament [S] *Redding*
Reuben H. Fleet Science Center and Space Theater [W] *San Diego*
Rhododendron Festival [S] *Eureka*
Rhododendron Show [S] *Fort Bragg*
Rhyolite Ghost Town [W] *Death Valley National Park*
Richard Nixon Library & Birthplace [W] *Whittier*
Riding. Camp Richardson Corral [W] *Lake Tahoe Area*
Rim of the World Highway [W] *San Bernardino*
Ripley's Believe It or Not Museum [W] *Buena Park*
Ripley's Believe It or Not Museum [W] *San Francisco*
Riverbank Cheese & Wine Exposition [S] *Modesto*
River Festival [S] *Dunsmuir*
Riverfront camping [W] *Blythe*
River rafting. Kern River Tours [W] *Kernville*
Riverside Art Museum [W] *Riverside*
Riverside County Fair and National Date Festival [S] *Indio*
Riverside County parks [W] *Idyllwild*
Riverside Municipal Museum [W] *Riverside*
Roaring Camp & Big Trees Narrow-Gauge Railroad [W] *Santa Cruz*
Robert Louis Stevenson House [W] *Monterey*
Robert Mondavi [W] *Yountville*
Rockin' K Riding Stables [W] *Big Bear Lake*
Rodeo [S] *Livermore*
Rodeo Drive [W] *Los Angeles*
Rodeo Week [S] *Redding*
Roeding Park [W] *Fresno*
Romano Gabriel Wooden Sculpture Garden [W] *Eureka*
Ronald Reagan Presidential Library and Museum [W] *Ventura*
Ronald W. Caspers Wilderness Park [W] *San Juan Capistrano*
Roop's Fort & Lassen Historical Museum [W] *Susanville*
Rose Bowl [W] *Pasadena*
Rose Hills Memorial Park [W] *Whittier*
Rosicrucian Park [W] *San Jose*
Rotary Nature Center [W] *Oakland*
"Rough and Ready" Town [W] *Grass Valley*
Royal Gorge Cross-Country Ski Resort [W] *Truckee*
Royal Presidio Chapel [W] *Monterey*
Roy Rogers-Dale Evans Museum [W] *Victorville*
Russian Gulch [W] *Mendocino*
Russian River Blues Festival [S] *Guerneville*
Russian River Jazz Festival [S] *Guerneville*
Sacramento Jazz Jubilee [S] *Sacramento*
Sacramento Kings (NBA) [W] *Sacramento*
Sacramento Monarchs (WNBA) [W] *Sacramento*
Sacramento National Wildlife Refuge Complex [W] *Willows*
Salmon Barbecue [S] *Fort Bragg*
Salt Point State Park [W] *Fort Ross State Historic Park*
Samuel P. Taylor State Park [W] *Inverness*

San Antonio Winery [W] *Los Angeles*
San Benito County Saddle Horse Show, Parade & Rodeo [S] *San Juan Bautista*
San Bernardino County Fair [S] *Victorville*
San Bernardino County Museum [W] *Redlands*
San Bernardino National Forest [W] *San Bernardino*
San Buenaventura State Beach [W] *Ventura*
San Clemente Fiesta [S] *San Clemente*
San Clemente State Beach [W] *San Clemente*
Sand dunes [W] *Death Valley National Park*
San Diego Aerospace Museum [W] *San Diego*
San Diego Bay and the Embarcadero [W] *San Diego*
San Diego Chargers (NFL) [W] *San Diego*
San Diego Children's Museum, The [W] *San Diego*
San Diego-Coronado Ferry [W] *San Diego*
San Diego Hall of Champions Sports Museum [W] *San Diego*
San Diego Harbor Excursion [W] *San Diego*
San Diego Maritime Museum and Star of India [W] *San Diego*
San Diego Museum of Art [W] *San Diego*
San Diego Museum of Man [W] *San Diego*
San Diego Natural History Museum [W] *San Diego*
San Diego Padres (MLB) [W] *San Diego*
San Diego Scenic Tours [W] *San Diego*
San Diego Trolley [W] *San Diego*
San Diego *Union* Historical Restoration [W] *San Diego*
San Diego Wild Animal Park [W] *Escondido*
San Diego Wild Animal Park [W] *San Diego*
San Diego Zoo [W] *San Diego*
San Francisco 49ers (NFL) [W] *San Francisco*
San Francisco African American Historical & Cultural Society [W] *San Francisco*
San Francisco Ballet [S] *San Francisco*
San Francisco Bay & Delta Hydraulic Model [W] *Sausalito*
San Francisco Bay cruises [W] *San Francisco*
San Francisco Bay National Wildlife Refuge [W] *Fremont*
San Francisco Giants (MLB) [W] *San Francisco*
San Francisco Maritime National Historical Park [W] *San Francisco*
San Francisco Museum of Modern Art [W] *San Francisco*
San Francisco Musuem of Modern Art Rental Gallery [W] *San Francisco*
San Francisco-Oakland Bay Bridge [W] *San Francisco*
San Francisco Opera [S] *San Francisco*
San Francisco Public Library [W] *San Francisco*
San Francisco Symphony Orchestra [S] *San Francisco*
San Francisco Zoo [W] *San Francisco*
San Jacinto Valley Museum [W] *Hemet*
San Joaquin County Fair [S] *Stockton*
San Jose America Festival [S] *San Jose*
San Jose Earthquakes (MLS) [W] *San Jose*
San Jose Museum of Art [W] *San Jose*
San Jose Museum of Quilts & Textiles [W] *San Jose*
San Jose Sharks (NHL) [W] *San Jose*
San Juan Bautista State Historic Park [W] *San Juan Bautista*
San Luis Obispo County Historical Museum [W] *San Luis Obispo*
San Mateo County Fair & Floral Fiesta [S] *Redwood City*
San Mateo County Fair & Floral Fiesta [S] *San Mateo*
San Pasqual Battlefield State Historic Park and Museum [W] *Escondido*

Santa Ana Zoo at Prentice Park [W] *Santa Ana*
Santa Anita Park [W]
Santa Anita Park [W] *Arcadia*
Santa Barbara Botanic Garden [W] *Santa Barbara*
Santa Barbara County Courthouse [W] *Santa Barbara*
Santa Barbara County Fair [S] *Santa Maria*
Santa Barbara Historical Museum [W] *Santa Barbara*
Santa Barbara International Orchid Show [S] *Santa Barbara*
Santa Barbara Maritime Museum [W] *Santa Barbara*
Santa Barbara Museum of Art [W] *Santa Barbara*
Santa Barbara Museum of Natural History [W] *Santa Barbara*
Santa Barbara National Horse Show [S] *Santa Barbara*
Santa Barbara Zoo [W] *Santa Barbara*
Santa Clara Art & Wine Festival [S] *Santa Clara*
Santa Clara County Fair [S] *San Jose*
Santa Clara University [W] *Santa Clara*
Santa Cruz Beach Boardwalk [W] *Santa Cruz*
Santa Cruz, Big Trees & Pacific Railway [W] *Santa Cruz*
Santa Cruz City Museum of Natural History [W] *Santa Cruz*
Santa Cruz County Fair [S] *Santa Cruz*
Santa Cruz Mission State Historical Park [W] *Santa Cruz*
Santa Maria Historical Museum [W] *Santa Maria*
Santa Monica Mountains National Recreation Area [W] *Malibu*
Santa Monica Mountains National Recreation Area [W] *Santa Monica*
Santa Monica Pier [W] *Santa Monica*
Santa Monica State Beach [W] *Santa Monica*
Sausalito Art Festival [S] *Sausalito*
Sawdust Fine Arts and Crafts Festival [S] *Laguna Beach*
Scenic drive [W] *Bakersfield*
Scenic drive [W] *San Diego*
Schoolhouse [W] *Sonora*
Scotty's Castle [W] *Death Valley National Park*
Scripps Park at La Jolla Cove [W] *La Jolla (San Diego)*
Seacliff Beach [W] *Santa Cruz*
Seal Rocks & Cliff House [W] *San Francisco*
Seaport Village [W] *San Diego*
Sears Point Raceway [W] *Sonoma*
Sea World [W] *San Diego*
Sebastiani Sonoma Cask Cellars [W] *Sonoma*
Seeley Stable [W] *San Diego*
Self-guided nature tours [W] *Chico*
Sepulveda House [W] *Los Angeles*
Sequoia & Kings Canyon National Parks [W] *Fresno*
Sequoia & Kings Canyon National Parks [W] *Visalia*
Sequoia National Forest [W] *Porterville*
Sequoia Park Zoo [W] *Eureka*
Serra Museum [W] *San Diego*
Seventeen-Mile Drive [W] *Carmel*
Seventeen-Mile Drive [W] *Monterey*
Shadow Cliffs Regional Recreation Area [W] *Livermore*
Shakespeare Press Printing Museum [W] *San Luis Obispo*
Shakespeare/Santa Cruz Festival [S] *Santa Cruz*
Sharpsteen Museum and Sam Brannan Cottage [W] *Calistoga*
Shasta Dam and Power Plant [W] *Redding*
Shasta District Fair [S] *Redding*
Shasta State Historic Park [W] *Redding*
Shasta-Trinity National Forest [W] *Redding*
Sherman Library & Gardens [W] *Newport Beach*
Shoreline Village [W] *Long Beach*
Sierra at Tahoe [W] *Lake Tahoe Area*
Sierra National Forest [W] *Fresno*
Sierra Summit Ski Area [W] *Fresno*
Sightseeing [W] *San Diego*
Sightseeing cruises [W] *Long Beach*
Sightseeing tours [W] *Monterey*
Sightseeing tours [W] *San Francisco*
Sigmund Stern Memorial Grove [W] *San Francisco*
Silverado Museum [W] *St. Helena*
Silver Dollar Fair [S] *Chico*

Silverwood Lake State Recreation Area [W] *Crestline*
Simi Winery [W] *Healdsburg*
Siskiyou County Museum [W] *Yreka*
Sisson Museum [W] *Mount Shasta*
Six Flags California [W] *Los Angeles*
Six Flags California [W] *Los Angeles*
Six Flags Marine World [W] *Vallejo*
Six Rivers National Forest [W] *Eureka*
Skiing [W] *Big Bear Lake*
Skiing [W] *Lake Tahoe Area*
Skiing [W] *Sonora*
Skiing [W] *Truckee*
"Skunk Train", The [W] *Fort Bragg*
Skyline Blvd [W] *Oakland*
SLO International Film Festival [S] *San Luis Obispo*
Smith River National Recreation Area [W] *Eureka*
Snoopy's Gallery [W] *Santa Rosa*
Snow Summit [W] *Big Bear Lake*
Snow Valley Ski Resort [W] *Lake Arrowhead*
Solano County Fair [S] *Vallejo*
Solvang Theaterfest [S] *Solvang*
Sonoma Coast State Beach [W] *Fort Ross State Historic Park*
Sonoma County Fair [S] *Santa Rosa*
Sonoma County Museum [W] *Santa Rosa*
Sonoma-Marin Fair [S] *Petaluma*
Sonoma State Historic Park [W] *Sonoma*
Sony Pictures Studio Tour [W] *Los Angeles*
South Carlsbad State Beach [W] *Carlsbad*
South Coast Botanic Garden [W] *Los Angeles*
Southwest Museum [W] *Los Angeles*
Spanish Village Arts and Crafts Center [W] *San Diego*
Special areas [W] *San Francisco*
Sports [W] *San Francisco*
Spreckels Lake [W] *San Francisco*
Spreckels Outdoor Organ Pavilion [W] *San Diego*
Spring Blossom Tour [W] *Chico*
Squaw Valley USA [W] *Lake Tahoe Area*
S.S. *Jeremiah O'Brien* [W] *San Francisco*
"The Stack" [W] *Los Angeles*
Stagecoach Inn Museum Complex [W] *Thousand Oaks*
Stampede Days [S] *Marysville*
Stands of Joshua trees [W] *Joshua Tree National Park*
Stanford Guide Service [W] *Palo Alto*
Stanford Linear Accelerator Center (SLAC) [W] *Menlo Park*
Stanford Medical Center [W] *Palo Alto*
Stanford Stadium [W] *Palo Alto*
Stanford University [W] *Palo Alto*
Stanislaus National Forest [W] *Sonora*
Starlight Bowl [W] *San Diego*
State Capitol [W] *Sacramento*
State Fish Hatchery [W] *Mount Shasta*
State historic parks [W] *Los Angeles*
State Indian Museum [W] *Sacramento*
State parks [W] *Mendocino*
State parks [W] *Santa Cruz*
Stearn's Wharf [W] *Santa Barbara*
Steinbeck Festival [S] *Salinas*
Steinbeck House [W] *Salinas*
Sterling Vineyards [W] *Calistoga*
Stern Grove Midsummer Music Festival [S] *San Francisco*
Stinson Beach [W] *San Francisco*
Stow Lake [W] *San Francisco*
Sugar Bowl [W] *Truckee*
Summer Sports Festival [S] *Santa Barbara*
Sunnyvale Historical Museum [W] *Sunnyvale*
Sunol Regional Wilderness [W] *Fremont*
Sunset Publishing Corporation and Gardens [W] *Menlo Park*
Sutter's Fort State Historic Park [W] *Sacramento*
Swedish Festival [S] *Fresno*
Swimming [W] *Yosemite National Park*
Swimming. Municipal Pier & Beach [W] *San Clemente*
Tahoe Donner [W] *Truckee*
Tahoe State Recreation Area [W] *Lake Tahoe Area*
Tahquitz Creek Palm Springs Golf Resort [W] *Palm Springs*
Tapestry in Talent's Festival of the Arts [S] *San Jose*

Taste of Newport [S] *Newport Beach*
Tech Museum of Innovation, The [W] *San Jose*
Tehachapi Loop [W] *Tehachapi*
Tehama District Fair [S] *Red Bluff*
Telegraph Hill [W] *San Francisco*
Telescope Peak [W] *Death Valley National Park*
Telonicher Marine Laboratory [W] *Trinidad*
Tennessee Valley and Beach and Bonita Cove [W] *San Francisco*
Tennis Tournament [S] *Ojai*
Third Street Promenade [W] *Santa Monica*
Thomas Welton Stanford Art Gallery [W] *Palo Alto*
Tilden Regional Park [W] *Berkeley*
Timken Museum of Art [W] *San Diego*
Tomales Bay State Park [W] *Inverness*
Tomorrowland [W] *Disneyland*
Torrey Pines State Reserve [W] *La Jolla (San Diego)*
Tournament of Roses [S] *Pasadena*
Tour of old adobes [W] *San Juan Capistrano*
Towe Ford Museum [W] *Sacramento*
Toyota Grand Prix [S] *Long Beach*
Train Town [W] *Sonoma*
Travel Town [W] *Los Angeles*
Trees [W] *Palo Alto*
Trees of Mystery [W] *Crescent City*
Trial and Show Gardens [W] *Oakland*
Tri-County Fair, Wild West Rodeo [S] *Bishop*
Trinity Alps Wilderness Area [W] *Weaverville*
Trinity Dam and Lake [W] *Redding*
Trips to Catalina Island [W] *Los Angeles*
Triton Museum of Art [W] *Santa Clara*
Truckee Rodeo [S] *Truckee*
Truckee-Tahoe Airshow [S] *Truckee*
Truth Aquatics [W] *Santa Barbara*
Tucker Wildlife Sanctuary [W] *Orange*
Tulare County Museum [W] *Visalia*
Tule Elk State Reserve [W] *Bakersfield*
Turlock Lake State Recreation Area [W] *Modesto*
Turtle Bay [W] *Redding*
TV production studios [W] *Los Angeles*
20-Mule-Team Canyon [W] *Death Valley National Park*
Twin Peaks [W] *San Francisco*
Ubehebe Crater [W] *Death Valley National Park*
UCLA Mildred Mathias Botanical Garden [W] *Los Angeles*
UCLA Ocean Discovery Center [W] *Santa Monica*
Union Square [W] *San Francisco*
Universal Studios Hollywood [W] *Hollywood (L.A.)*
Universal Studios Hollywood [W] *Los Angeles*
Universities [W] *Los Angeles*
University of California [W] *Berkeley*
University of California, Irvine [W] *Irvine*
University of California, San Diego [W] *La Jolla (San Diego)*
University of California, Los Angeles (UCLA) [W] *Los Angeles*
University of California at Riverside [W] *Riverside*
University of California, Santa Barbara [W] *Santa Barbara*
University of California, Santa Cruz [W] *Santa Cruz*
University of Southern California [W] *Los Angeles*
Uprising Rock Climbing Center [W] *Palm Springs*
US Forest Service Visitor Center [W] *Lake Tahoe Area*
USS *Potomac* [W] *Oakland*
Vallejo Ferry [W] *Vallejo*
Vallejo Naval and Historical Museum [W] *Vallejo*
Valley of the Moon Vintage Festival [S] *Sonoma*
Van Damme [W] *Mendocino*
Venice Beach and Boardwalk [W] *Santa Monica*
Ventura County Fair [S] *Ventura*
Ventura County Maritime Museum [W] *Oxnard*
Ventura County Museum of History and Art [W] *Ventura*
Ventura Harbor [W] *Ventura*
Victorian Christmas [S] *Nevada City*

Vikingsholm [W] *Lake Tahoe Area*
Village Fair [W] *Sausalito*
Village Green Heritage Center [W] *Palm Springs*
Villa Montalvo [W] *Saratoga*
Villa Montalvo Performing Arts [S] *Saratoga*
Villa Montezuma/Jesse Shepard House [W] *San Diego*
Vintage 1870 [W] *Yountville*
Visitor Center [W] *Death Valley National Park*
Visitor Center [W] *Yosemite National Park*
Visitor Center & Overlook [W] *Oroville*
Wagon Train Week [S] *Placerville*
Walking tours [W] *Nevada City*
Walk of Fame [W] *Hollywood (L.A.)*
Walks and hikes [W] *Yosemite National Park*
War Memorial/Opera House [W] *San Francisco*
Warm Springs Dam/Lake Sonoma [W] *Healdsburg*
Washington Square [W] *San Francisco*
Waterfalls [W] *Yosemite National Park*
Waterworks Park [W] *Redding*
Waterworld USA [W] *Concord*
Watts Towers [W] *Los Angeles*
Wax Museum at Fisherman's Wharf [W] *San Francisco*
Weaverville Joss House State Historic Park [W] *Weaverville*
Welk Resort Center Theatre-Museum [W] *Escondido*
Wells Fargo Bank History Museum [W] *San Francisco*
Wells Fargo History Museum [W] *Los Angeles*
Wente Bros Winery [W] *Livermore*
West Cliff Drive [W] *Santa Cruz*
West Coast Antique Fly-in [S] *Merced*
Western Railway Museum [W] *Fairfield*
Westwood Memorial Cemetery [W] *Hollywood (L.A.)*
Westwood Memorial Cemetery [W] *Westwood Village (L.A.)*
Whaleboat Regatta [S] *Vallejo*
Whale Festival [S] *Fort Bragg*
Whale Festival [S] *Mendocino*
Whale Watch [S] *Fort Bragg*
Whale watching [S] *Ventura*
Whale-watching trips [W] *San Diego*
Whaley House [W] *San Diego*
Whiskey Flat Days [S] *Kernville*
Whiskeytown Dam and Lake [W] *Redding*
Whiskeytown-Shasta-Trinity National Recreation Area, Whiskeytown Unit [W] *Redding*
White Water Canyon [W] *San Diego*
Wildcat Canyon Regional Park [W] *Berkeley*
Wilderness Areas [W] *Susanville*
Wilder Ranch [W] *Santa Cruz*
Wildflower Season [S] *Lancaster*
Wildflower Show [S] *Pacific Grove*
Wild Rivers [W] *Irvine*
Wild Water Adventures [W] *Fresno*
Wild West Stampede [S] *Auburn*
William B. Ide Adobe State Historic Park [W] *Red Bluff*
William HIll Winery [W] *Napa*
William Land Park [W] *Sacramento*
Willits Community Theatre [W] *Willits*
Will Rogers [W] *Los Angeles*
Winchester Mystery House [W] *San Jose*
Wind Fair [S] *Tehachapi*
Wind'n'sea Beach [W] *La Jolla (San Diego)*
Wine and Honey Festival [S] *Livermore*
Wine Festival [S] *Paso Robles*
Wineries [W] *Escondido*
Wineries [W] *Livermore*
Wineries [W] *Napa*
Wineries [W] *Paso Robles*
Wineries [W] *Sonoma*
Wineries [W] *St. Helena*
Wineries [W] *Ukiah*
Wineries [W] *Yountville*
Wineries of the Edna Valley & Arroyo Grande Valley [W] *Pismo Beach*
Winesong [S] *Fort Bragg*
Winter Bird Festival [S] *Morro Bay*
Winter Lodge [W] *Palo Alto*
Winter Migratory Waterfowl Tour [W] *Chico*

Winter sports [W] *Yosemite National Park*
Woodley Island Marina [W] *Eureka*
Woodminster Summer Musicals [S] *Oakland*
Woodside Store [W] *San Mateo*
Woodward Park [W] *Fresno*
Woodward Reservoir [W] *Oakdale*
World Championship Crab Races & Crustacean Festival [S] *Crescent City*
World Trade Center [W] *Los Angeles*
World Wildlife Museum [W] *Stockton*
World Wrist Wrestling Championships [S] *Petaluma*
Wrigley Memorial and Botanical Garden [W] *Avalon (Catalina Island)*
Yerba Buena Gardens [W] *San Francisco*
Yosemite Fine Arts Museum [W] *Yosemite National Park*
Yosemite Mountain-Sugar Pine Railroad [W] *Yosemite National Park*
Yosemite National Park [W] *Bridgeport*
Yosemite National Park [W] *Fresno*
Yosemite National Park [W] *Lee Vining*
Yosemite Valley [W] *Yosemite National Park*
Youth Science Institute [W] *Los Gatos*
Youth Science Institute [W] *San Jose*
Yreka Western Railroad [W] *Yreka*
Zabriskie Point [W] *Death Valley National Park*

LODGING LIST

Establishment names are listed in alphabetical order followed by a symbol identifying their classification and then city and state. The symbols for classification are: [AS] for All Suites, [BB] for B&Bs/Small Inns, [CAS] for Casinos, [CC] for Cottage Colonies, [CON] for Villas/Condos, [CONF] for Conference Centers, [EX] for Extended Stays, [HOT] for Hotels, [MOT] for Motels/Motor Lodges, [RAN] for Guest Ranches, and [RST] for Resorts

ABIGAIL'S ELEGANT VICTORIAN MANSION [BB] *Eureka*

ADAGIO INN [BB] *St. Helena*

ADELAIDE INN [MOT] *Paso Robles*

ADOBE INN [BB] *Carmel*

ADOBE INN [BB] *San Luis Obispo*

AHWAHNEE, THE [RST] *Yosemite National Park*

AIRTEL PLAZA HOTEL [HOT] *Van Nuys (L.A.)*

ALAMO SQUARE INN [BB] *San Francisco*

ALBION HOUSE INN BED AND BREAKFAST [BB] *San Francisco*

ALBION RIVER INN [BB] *Mendocino*

ALISAL GUEST RANCH & RESORT [RAN] *Solvang*

ALISO CREEK INN [MOT] *Laguna Beach*

ALPINE LODGE [MOT] *Mammoth Lakes*

ALTA MIRA HOTEL [MOT] *Sausalito*

AMBER HOUSE BED AND BREAKFAST INN [BB] *Sacramento*

AMERICANA INN AND SUITES [MOT] *San Ysidro (San Diego)*

AMSTERDAM HOTEL [HOT] *San Francisco*

ANAHEIM BEST INN [MOT] *Anaheim*

ANCHORAGE INN [MOT] *Clear Lake Area*

ANDREA VILLA INN [MOT] *La Jolla (San Diego)*

ANDREWS HOTEL, THE [BB] *San Francisco*

ANDRUSS MOTEL [MOT] *Coleville*

APPLE FARM [BB] *San Luis Obispo*

APPLE FARM TRELLIS COURT [MOT] *San Luis Obispo*

APPLEWOOD INN & RESTAURANT [RST] *Guerneville*

ARCHBISHOP'S MANSION [BB] *San Francisco*

ARGENT HOTEL [HOT] *San Francisco*

ARGYLE HOTEL, THE [HOT] *Hollywood (L.A.)*

ARTIST'S INN [BB] *Pasadena*

ASCOT SUITES [HOT] *Morro Bay*

ATHERTON HOTEL [HOT] *San Francisco*

ATRIUM HOTEL [HOT] *Irvine*

AUBERGE DU SOLEIL [RST] *St. Helena*

AUBURN BEST INN AND SUITES [MOT] *Auburn*

AVALON HOTEL [HOT] *Beverly Hills*

BABBLING BROOK INN [BB] *Santa Cruz*

BACARA RESORT & SPA [RST] *Santa Barbara*

BAECHTEL CREEK INN [MOT] *Willits*

BAKERSFIELD DAYS INN [MOT] *Bakersfield*

BALBOA PARK INN [BB] *San Diego*

BALLANTINES HOTEL [BB] *Palm Springs*

BALLARD INN, THE [BB] *Solvang*

BANCROFT HOTEL [CONF] *Berkeley*

BARBARA WORTH GOLF RESORT AND CONVENTION CENTER [RST] *El Centro*

BARNABEY'S HOTEL [HOT] *Los Angeles Intl Airport Area*

BARRETTA GARDENS [BB] *Sonora*

BAY CLUB HOTEL AND MARINA [HOT] *San Diego*

BAY PARK HOTEL [MOT] *Monterey*

BAYVIEW HOTEL [BB] *Santa Cruz*

BAYVIEW INN [MOT] *Crescent City*

BAY VIEW LODGE [MOT] *Morro Bay*

BEACHCOMBER INN [MOT] *Santa Barbara*
BEACHWALKER INN [BB] *Morro Bay*
BEAZLEY HOUSE [BB] *Napa*
BED AND BREAKFAST INN AT LA JOLLA [BB] *La Jolla (San Diego)*
BELLE DE JOUR INN [BB] *Healdsburg*
BENBOW INN [RST] *Garberville*
BERESFORD ARMS HOTEL [HOT] *San Francisco*
BERESFORD HOTEL [HOT] *San Francisco*
BERNARDUS LODGE [RST] *Carmel Valley*
BEST INN AND SUITES [MOT] *Red Bluff*
BEST INN AND SUITES, SANTA CRUZ [MOT] *Santa Cruz*
BEST VALUE INN [MOT] *Blythe*
BEST VALUE INN [MOT] *Crescent City*
BEST WESTERN [MOT] *Bakersfield*
BEST WESTERN [MOT] *Del Mar*
BEST WESTERN [MOT] *La Jolla (San Diego)*
BEST WESTERN [MOT] *Mount Shasta*
BEST WESTERN [MOT] *Pacific Grove*
BEST WESTERN [MOT] *Placerville*
BEST WESTERN [MOT] *San Francisco*
BEST WESTERN [MOT] *Tehachapi*
BEST WESTERN AIRPORT [MOT] *Ontario*
BEST WESTERN AMADOR INN [MOT] *Jackson*
BEST WESTERN AMERICANIA [MOT] *San Francisco*
BEST WESTERN ANDERSEN'S INN [MOT] *Santa Nella*
BEST WESTERN ANTELOPE VALLEY INN [MOT] *Lancaster*
BEST WESTERN BAY SHORES INN [MOT] *Newport Beach*
BEST WESTERN BAYSIDE INN [MOT] *San Diego*
BEST WESTERN BAY VIEW INN [MOT] *Carmel*
BEST WESTERN BIG AMERICA [MOT] *Santa Maria*
BEST WESTERN BLACK OAK MOTOR LODGE [MOT] *Paso Robles*
BEST WESTERN BUENA PARK INN [MOT] *Buena Park*
BEST WESTERN CANTERBURY HOTEL [MOT] *San Francisco*
BEST WESTERN CAPISTRANO INN [MOT] *San Juan Capistrano*
BEST WESTERN CARPINTERIA INN [MOT] *Santa Barbara*
BEST WESTERN CASA [MOT] *Ojai*
BEST WESTERN CASA GRANDE INN [MOT] *Pismo Beach*
BEST WESTERN COLORADO INN [MOT] *Pasadena*
BEST WESTERN CONTINENTAL INN [MOT] *El Cajon*
BEST WESTERN CORDELIA INN [MOT] *Fairfield*
BEST WESTERN CORTE MADERA INN [MOT] *Corte Madera*
BEST WESTERN DATE TREE HOTEL [MOT] *Indio*
BEST WESTERN DESERT VILLA INN [MOT] *Barstow*
BEST WESTERN DIAMOND BAR [MOT] *Pomona*
BEST WESTERN DRY CREEK INN [MOT] *Healdsburg*
BEST WESTERN EAGLE ROCK INN [MOT] *Los Angeles*
BEST WESTERN, EL GRANDE INN [MOT] *Clear Lake Area*
BEST WESTERN EL RANCHO [MOT] *Morro Bay*
BEST WESTERN EL RANCHO INN [MOT] *San Francisco Airport Area*
BEST WESTERN EL RANCHO MOTOR INN [MOT] *Beaumont*
BEST WESTERN ENCINA LODGE AND SUITES [MOT] *Santa Barbara*
BEST WESTERN EXECUTIVE SUITE [MOT] *Redwood City*
BEST WESTERN FIRESIDE INN [MOT] *Cambria*
BEST WESTERN FRANCISCAN INN [MOT] *Fallbrook*
BEST WESTERN GADEN INN AND SUITES [MOT] *Desert Hot Springs*
BEST WESTERN GARDEN COURT INN [MOT] *Fremont*
BEST WESTERN GARDEN INN [MOT] *Santa Rosa*
BEST WESTERN GATEWAY HOTEL [MOT] *Santa Monica*
BEST WESTERN GATEWAY INN [MOT] *San Jose*

BEST WESTERN GOLDEN KEY [MOT] *Glendale*

BEST WESTERN GOLDEN PHEASANT INN [MOT] *Willows*

BEST WESTERN GOLDEN SAILS HOTEL [MOT] *Long Beach*

BEST WESTERN GRAND MANOR INN [MOT] *Oroville*

BEST WESTERN GREEN TREE INN [MOT] *Victorville*

BEST WESTERN GROSVENOR HOTEL [MOT] *San Francisco Airport Area*

BEST WESTERN HACIENDA HOTEL [AS] *San Diego*

BEST WESTERN HARBOR INN AND SUITES [MOT] *Sacramento*

BEST WESTERN HEMET [MOT] *Hemet*

BEST WESTERN HERITAGE INN [MOT] *Antioch*

BEST WESTERN HERITAGE INN [MOT] *Chico*

BEST WESTERN HERITAGE INN [MOT] *Concord*

BEST WESTERN HERITAGE INN [MOT] *Rancho Cordova*

BEST WESTERN HERITAGE INN [MOT] *Rancho Cucamonga*

BEST WESTERN HERITAGE INN [MOT] *Vacaville*

BEST WESTERN HERITAGE INN [MOT] *Vallejo*

BEST WESTERN HILLTOP INN [MOT] *Redding*

BEST WESTERN HOLIDAY LODGE [MOT] *Three Rivers*

BEST WESTERN HOLIDAY SPA LODGE [MOT] *Bishop*

BEST WESTERN HOSPITALITY [MOT] *Redding*

BEST WESTERN HUMBOLDT BAY INN [MOT] *Eureka*

BEST WESTERN INN [MOT] *Camarillo*

BEST WESTERN INN [MOT] *Los Angeles*

BEST WESTERN INN [MOT] *Marysville*

BEST WESTERN INN [MOT] *Merced*

BEST WESTERN INN [MOT] *Palm Springs*

BEST WESTERN INN [MOT] *Petaluma*

BEST WESTERN INN [MOT] *Placerville*

BEST WESTERN INN [MOT] *Valencia*

BEST WESTERN INN AT THE SQUARE [MOT] *Oakland*

BEST WESTERN INN AT THE VINES [MOT] *Napa*

BEST WESTERN INN SANTA CLARA [MOT] *Santa Clara*

BEST WESTERN ISLAND PALMS [MOT] *San Diego*

BEST WESTERN KINGS INN [MOT] *Corona*

BEST WESTERN LAGUNA BRISAS SPA HOTEL [MOT] *Laguna Beach*

BEST WESTERN LAGUNA REEF INN [MOT] *Laguna Beach*

BEST WESTERN LAS BRISAS [MOT] *Palm Springs*

BEST WESTERN MADERA VALLEY INN [MOT] *Madera*

BEST WESTERN MARTY'S VALLEY INN [MOT] *Oceanside*

BEST WESTERN MIKADO HOTEL [MOT] *North Hollywood (L.A.)*

BEST WESTERN MISSION INN [MOT] *Carmel*

BEST WESTERN MIYAKO INN [MOT] *San Francisco*

BEST WESTERN MONTEREY BEACH HOTEL [MOT] *Monterey*

BEST WESTERN NEWPORT MESA INN [MOT] *Costa Mesa*

BEST WESTERN NORTHWOODS INN [MOT] *Crescent City*

BEST WESTERN NOVATO OAKS INN [MOT] *San Rafael*

BEST WESTERN OCEANSIDE INN [MOT] *Oceanside*

BEST WESTERN OCEAN VIEW [MOT] *Santa Monica*

BEST WESTERN PEA SOUP ANDERSEN [MOT] *Solvang*

BEST WESTERN PEPPER TREE INN [MOT] *Santa Barbara*

BEST WESTERN PLAZA INTERNATIONAL INN [MOT] *Garden Grove*

BEST WESTERN ROYAL HOST INN [MOT] *Lodi*

BEST WESTERN ROYAL OAK [MOT] *San Luis Obispo*

BEST WESTERN SAHARA [MOT] *Blythe*

BEST WESTERN SANDMAN MOTEL [MOT] *Redlands*

BEST WESTERN SEACLIFF INN [MOT] *Santa Cruz*

BEST WESTERN SEVEN SEAS LODGE [MOT] *San Diego*

BEST WESTERN SONOMA VALLEY INN [MOT] *Sonoma*
BEST WESTERN STATION HOUSE INN [MOT] *South Lake Tahoe (Lake Tahoe Area)*
BEST WESTERN STOVALL'S INN [MOT] *Anaheim*
BEST WESTERN SUNRISE AT REDONDO BEACH MARINA [MOT] *Redondo Beach*
BEST WESTERN SUNRISE HOTEL [MOT] *San Pedro (L.A.)*
BEST WESTERN TAHOE INN [MOT] *Truckee*
BEST WESTERN TIMBER COVE [MOT] *South Lake Tahoe (Lake Tahoe Area)*
BEST WESTERN TOWN HOUSE LODGE [MOT] *Carmel*
BEST WESTERN TRAILSIDE INN [MOT] *Alturas*
BEST WESTERN TRAILSIDE INN [MOT] *Susanville*
BEST WESTERN TUSCAN INN [MOT] *San Francisco*
BEST WESTERN UNIVERSITY LODGE [MOT] *Davis*
BEST WESTERN VICTORIAN INN [MOT] *Monterey*
BEST WESTERN VILLAGE INN [MOT] *Fresno*
BEST WESTERN YOSEMITE GATEWAY INN [MOT] *Oakhurst*
BEVERLY GARLAND'S HOLIDAY INN [MOT] *North Hollywood (L.A.)*
BEVERLY HERITAGE HOTEL [HOT] *San Jose*
BEVERLY HILLS HOTEL, THE [HOT] *Beverly Hills*
BEVERLY HILLS PLAZA HOTEL [AS] *Los Angeles*
BEVERLY PLAZA HOTEL [HOT] *Los Angeles*
BIDWELL HOUSE BED AND BREAKFAST [BB] *Chester*
BIG BEAR LAKE INN [MOT] *Big Bear Lake*
BISHOP PINE LODGE [CC] *Trinidad*
BISHOP THUNDERBIRD MOTEL [MOT] *Bishop*
BLACKBERRY INN [BB] *Mendocino*
BLACKTHORNE INN [BB] *Inverness*
BLUE LANTERN INN [BB] *Laguna Beach*
BLUE SAIL INN [MOT] *Morro Bay*
BODEGA BAY LODGE & SPA [RST] *Bodega Bay*
BODEGA COAST INN [RST] *Bodega Bay*
BORREGO SPRING RESORT [MOT] *Borrego Springs*
BORREGO VALLEY INN [BB] *Borrego Springs*
BOULDER LODGE MOTEL [MOT] *June Lake*
BRANNAN COTTAGE INN [BB] *Calistoga*
BREAKERS INN [BB] *Gualala*
BREAKERS MOTEL [MOT] *Morro Bay*
BRIAR ROSE BED & BREAKFAST [BB] *San Jose*
BRIARWOOD INN [BB] *Carmel*
BRIDGE BAY RESORT [MOT] *Redding*
BUENA VISTA MOTOR INN [MOT] *San Francisco*
BURTON DRIVE INN [BB] *Cambria*
CAIN HOUSE [BB] *Bridgeport*
CALIFORNIA INN [MOT] *Bakersfield*
CALIPATRIA INN AND SUITES [MOT] *El Centro*
CALISTOGA INN [BB] *Calistoga*
CALISTOGA SPA HOT SPRINGS [RST] *Calistoga*
CAL NEVA INN [MOT] *Tahoe Vista (Lake Tahoe Area)*
CAMBRIA SHORES INN [MOT] *Cambria*
CAMELLIA INN [BB] *Healdsburg*
CAMPBELL INN [BB] *San Jose*
CAMPTON PLACE HOTEL [HOT] *San Francisco*
CAMPUS MOTEL [MOT] *Berkeley*
CANDLE LIGHT INN [MOT] *Carmel*
CANDLEWOOD SUITES [AS] *Pleasanton*
CANNERY ROW INN [MOT] *Monterey*
CARLSBAD INN BEACH RESORT [RST] *Carlsbad*
CARLTON HOTEL [HOT] *San Francisco*
CARLYLE INN [BB] *Los Angeles*
CARMEL GARDEN COURT INN [BB] *Carmel*
CARMEL RESORT INN [MOT] *Carmel*
CARMEL VALLEY LODGE [BB] *Carmel Valley*
CARMEL VALLEY RANCH [RST] *Carmel Valley*

CAROUSEL INN AND SUITES [HOT] *Anaheim*
CAROUSEL MOTEL [MOT] *Santa Cruz*
CARRIAGE HOUSE INN [BB] *Carmel*
CARTER INN AND CARTER HOUSE [BB] *Eureka*
CARTER INN AND CARTER HOUSE BED AND BREAKFAST [BB] *Eureka*
CARTWRIGHT HOTEL [HOT] *San Francisco*
CASA CODY BED AND BREAKFAST INN [BB] *Palm Springs*
CASA DEL MAR [BB] *Mill Valley*
CASA DEL MAR [BB] *Santa Barbara*
CASA DEL MAR [RST] *Santa Monica*
CASA LAGUNA INN [BB] *Laguna Beach*
CASA MADRONA HOTEL [BB] *Sausalito*
CASA MALIBU INN ON THE BEACH [HOT] *Malibu*
CASA PALMERO PEBBLE BEACH [HOT] *Pebble Beach*
CASA SIRENA HOTEL AND MARINA [MOT] *Oxnard*
CASTLE CREEK INN RESORT AND SPA [RST] *Escondido*
CASTLE INN AND SUITES [MOT] *Anaheim*
CASTLE INN BY THE SEA [MOT] *Cambria*
CATAMARAN RESORT HOTEL [HOT] *San Diego*
CATHEDRAL HILL HOTEL [HOT] *San Francisco*
CAVALIER OCEANFRONT RESORT [RST] *San Simeon*
CEDAR GLEN LODGE [MOT] *Tahoe Vista (Lake Tahoe Area)*
CEDAR GROVE LODGE [MOT] *Kings Canyon National Park*
CEDAR LODGE [MOT] *South Lake Tahoe (Lake Tahoe Area)*
CEDAR LODGE [HOT] *Yosemite National Park*
CEDAR LODGE MOTEL [MOT] *Dunsmuir*
CENTRELLA INN [BB] *Pacific Grove*
CENTURY PLAZA HOTEL AND SPA, THE [HOT] *Los Angeles*
CHABLIS INN [MOT] *Napa*
CHALFANT HOUSE BED&BREAKFAST [BB] *Bishop*
CHANCELLOR HOTEL ON UNION SQUARE [HOT] *San Francisco*
CHANDLER INN [MOT] *Palm Springs*
CHANEY HOUSE [BB] *Tahoe City (Lake Tahoe Area)*
CHANNEL ROAD INN [BB] *Santa Monica*
CHASE HOTEL AT PALM SPRINGS, THE [MOT] *Palm Springs*
CHASE SUITE HOTEL [AS] *Fullerton*
CHATEAU DU LAC [BB] *Lake Arrowhead*
CHATEAU DU SUREAU [BB] *Oakhurst*
CHATEAU HOTEL [HOT] *Napa*
CHATEAU INN BY PICCADILLY INNS [MOT] *Fresno*
CHATEAU MARMONT [HOT] *Hollywood (L.A.)*
CHATEAU VICTORIAN [BB] *Santa Cruz*
CHELSEA MOTOR INN [MOT] *San Francisco*
CHESHIRE CAT INN [BB] *Santa Barbara*
CHIMNEY SWEEP INN [MOT] *Solvang*
CHRISTOPHER'S INN [BB] *Calistoga*
CINNAMON BEAR INN [BB] *Mammoth Lakes*
CIRCLE C LODGE [MOT] *Desert Hot Springs*
CLARION BAYVIEW HOTEL [HOT] *San Diego*
CLARION CARRIAGE HOUSE DEL MAR INN [MOT] *Del Mar*
CLARION HOTEL [MOT] *Sacramento*
CLARION HOTEL [MOT] *San Francisco*
CLARION HOTEL [MOT] *Thousand Oaks*
CLARION HOTEL VENTURA BEACH [MOT] *Ventura*
CLARION SUITES HOTEL [MOT] *Woodland Hills (L.A.)*
CLARION SUITES, LAKE MERRITT HOTEL [MOT] *Oakland*
CLEONE GARDENS INN [BB] *Fort Bragg*
CLIFFS RESORT, THE [HOT] *Pismo Beach*
CLIFT, THE [HOT] *San Francisco*
CLOCKTOWER INN [BB] *Ventura*
COAST VILLAGE INN [MOT] *Santa Barbara*
COBBLESTONE INN [BB] *Carmel*
COLOMA COUNTRY INN [BB] *Placerville*
COLONY INN [MOT] *Buena Park*

COLUMBIA CITY HOTEL [BB] *Sonora*
COLUMBUS MOTOR INN [MOT] *San Francisco*
COMFORT INN [MOT] *Bishop*
COMFORT INN [MOT] *Calistoga*
COMFORT INN [MOT] *Concord*
COMFORT INN [MOT] *Escondido*
COMFORT INN [MOT] *Hayward*
COMFORT INN [MOT] *Oakhurst*
COMFORT INN [MOT] *Pasadena*
COMFORT INN [MOT] *Rancho Cordova*
COMFORT INN [MOT] *Salinas*
COMFORT INN [MOT] *San Francisco*
COMFORT INN [MOT] *Santa Monica*
COMFORT INN [MOT] *West Covina*
COMFORT INN [MOT] *Yosemite National Park*
COMFORT INN AIRPORT SOUTH [MOT] *San Jose*
COMFORT INN & SUITES [MOT] *Anaheim*
COMFORT INN AND SUITES [MOT] *San Diego*
COMFORT INN AND SUITES [MOT] *San Francisco*
COMFORT INN MAINGATE [MOT] *Anaheim*
COMFORT INN- REDWOOD CITY [MOT] *Redwood City*
COMFORT INN RIVERSIDE [MOT] *Riverside*
COMFORT SUITE [MOT] *Palm Springs*
COMFORT SUITES [MOT] *Huntington Beach*
COMFORT SUITES [AS] *Santa Ana*
COMMODORE HOTEL SAN FRANCISCO [HOT] *San Francisco*
CONESTOGA HOTEL AT THE PARK [HOT] *Anaheim*
CORAL REEF MOTEL & SUITES [MOT] *Oakland*
COTTAGE GROVE INN CALISTOGA [BB] *Calistoga*
COTTAGE INN, THE [BB] *Tahoe City (Lake Tahoe Area)*
COUNTRY GARDEN INN [BB] *Napa*
COUNTRY INN, THE [MOT] *Corona*
COUNTRY INN AND SUITES [MOT] *Oxnard*
COUNTRY INN & SUITES [MOT] *Solvang*
COUNTRY INN AND SUITES BY AYRES [MOT] *Costa Mesa*
COUNTRY INN & SUITES - VENTURA [MOT] *Ventura*
COUNTRY INN AT CAMARILLO, THE [MOT] *Camarillo*
COUNTRY INN BY AYERS [MOT] *Del Mar*
COUNTRY INN BY AYRES [BB] *Orange*
COUNTRY INN MOTEL [MOT] *Palo Alto*
COUNTRY INNS & SUITES - CALABASAS [AS] *Woodland Hills (L.A.)*
COUNTRY SIDE SUITES [MOT] *Ontario*
COUNTRY SUITES [AS] *Anaheim*
COUNTRY SUITES [MOT] *Ontario*
COUNTY INN [MOT] *Mountain View*
COURTESY INN [MOT] *King City*
COURTYARD BY MARRIOTT [MOT] *Bakersfield*
COURTYARD BY MARRIOTT [MOT] *Buena Park*
COURTYARD BY MARRIOTT [MOT] *Fremont*
COURTYARD BY MARRIOTT [MOT] *Long Beach*
COURTYARD BY MARRIOTT [MOT] *Los Angeles*
COURTYARD BY MARRIOTT [MOT] *Marina del Rey*
COURTYARD BY MARRIOTT [MOT] *Modesto*
COURTYARD BY MARRIOTT [MOT] *Palm Springs*
COURTYARD BY MARRIOTT [MOT] *Pleasanton*
COURTYARD BY MARRIOTT [MOT] *Rancho Cordova*
COURTYARD BY MARRIOTT [MOT] *Riverside*
COURTYARD BY MARRIOTT [MOT] *San Francisco Airport Area*
COURTYARD BY MARRIOTT [MOT] *San Jose*
COURTYARD BY MARRIOTT [MOT] *Vacaville*
COURTYARD BY MARRIOTT AT LAX [MOT] *Los Angeles*
COURTYARD BY MARRIOTT LAGUNA HILLS [MOT] *Laguna Beach*

COURTYARD BY MARRIOTT TORRANCE PLAZA DEL AMO [MOT] *Torrance*
COVENTRY MOTOR INN [MOT] *San Francisco*
COW HOLLOW MOTOR INN AND SUITES [MOT] *San Francisco*
COWPER INN [BB] *Palo Alto*
COXHEAD HOUSE B&B [BB] *San Mateo*
COZY INN [MOT] *Costa Mesa*
CREEKSIDE INN [MOT] *Palo Alto*
CROSS ROADS WEST INN [MOT] *Willows*
CROWN CITY INN [MOT] *Coronado*
CROWNE PLAZA [HOT] *Irvine*
CROWNE PLAZA [HOT] *Los Angeles*
CROWNE PLAZA [HOT] *Pleasanton*
CROWNE PLAZA [HOT] *San Jose*
CROWNE PLAZA HOTEL [HOT] *San Jose*
CROWNE PLAZA REDONDO BEACH [RST] *Redondo Beach*
CROWNE PLAZA UNION SQUARE [HOT] *San Francisco*
CRYSTAL TERRACE INN [BB] *Carmel*
CULVER MANSION [BB] *Calistoga*
CURLY REDWOOD LODGE [MOT] *Crescent City*
CYPRESS GARDENS INN [MOT] *Monterey*
CYPRESS INN [BB] *Carmel*
CYPRESS INN [BB] *Half Moon Bay*
CYPRESS TREE INN [MOT] *Monterey*
DALY INN [BB] *Eureka*
DANA INN AND MARINA [RST] *San Diego*
DANA POINT INN AND SUITES [MOT] *Laguna Beach*
DAYS INN [MOT] *Anaheim*
DAYS INN [MOT] *Barstow*
DAYS INN [MOT] *Morro Bay*
DAYS INN [MOT] *Redwood City*
DAYS INN [MOT] *San Diego*
DAYS INN [MOT] *San Francisco*
DAYS INN [MOT] *Sonora*
DAYS INN [MOT] *South Lake Tahoe (Lake Tahoe Area)*
DAYS INN AND SUITES [MOT] *Pacific Grove*
DAYS INN DISCOVERY PARK [MOT] *Sacramento*
DAYS INN WINDMILL [MOT] *Solvang*
DEER HAVEN INN [MOT] *Pacific Grove*
DESERT HOT SPRINGS SPA HOTEL [RST] *Desert Hot Springs*
DESERT VIEW MOTEL [MOT] *Desert Hot Springs*
DINAH'S GARDEN HOTEL [HOT] *Palo Alto*
DISCOVERY INN [MOT] *Ukiah*
DISNEYLAND HOTEL [RST] *Anaheim*
DISNEYLAND PARADISE PIER HOTEL [RST] *Anaheim*
DOLPHIN INN [BB] *Carmel*
DOLPHIN'S COVE RESORT [RST] *Anaheim*
DONATELLO, THE [HOT] *San Francisco*
DONNER LAKE VILLAGE RESORT [MOT] *Truckee*
DORAL PALM SPRINGS RESORT [RST] *Palm Springs*
DORYMAN'S OCEANFRONT INN [BB] *Newport Beach*
DOUBLETREE [HOT] *Fresno*
DOUBLETREE [HOT] *Ontario*
DOUBLETREE [HOT] *San Jose*
DOUBLETREE CLUB HOTEL LAX [HOT] *Los Angeles Intl Airport Area*
DOUBLETREE CLUB HOTEL ORANGE COUNTY AIRPORT [HOT] *Santa Ana*
DOUBLETREE GOLF RESORT [RST] *San Diego*
DOUBLETREE GUEST SUITES [AS] *Laguna Beach*
DOUBLETREE GUEST SUITES - SANTA MONICA [AS] *Santa Monica*
DOUBLETREE HOTEL [HOT] *Orange*
DOUBLETREE HOTEL [HOT] *Pasadena*
DOUBLETREE HOTEL [HOT] *Sacramento*
DOUBLETREE HOTEL LOS ANGELES-WESTWOOD [HOT] *Los Angeles*
DOUBLETREE HOTEL MODESTO [HOT] *Modesto*
DOUBLETREE HOTEL MONTEREY [HOT] *Monterey*
DOUBLETREE HOTEL SAN DIEGO MISSION VALLEY [HOT] *San Diego*

DOUBLETREE HOTEL SF AIRPORT [HOT] *San Francisco Airport Area*
DOWNTOWN MOTEL [MOT] *Hanford*
DOW VILLA MOTEL [MOT] *Lone Pine*
DR WILKINSON'S HOT SPRINGS RESORT [RST] *Calistoga*
DYNASTY SUITES [MOT] *Buena Park*
DYNASTY SUITES [MOT] *Corona*
DYNASTY SUITES [HOT] *Riverside*
EAGLES NEST BED AND BREAKFAST [BB] *Big Bear Lake*
ECONO LODGE [MOT] *San Luis Obispo*
ECONO LODGE [MOT] *Visalia*
ECONO LODGE WILDWOOD INN [MOT] *Mammoth Lakes*
ECONOMY INN [MOT] *San Ysidro (San Diego)*
ECONOMY INN [MOT] *Ukiah*
EILER'S INN [BB] *Laguna Beach*
EL ADOBE INN [MOT] *Monterey*
EL BONITA [MOT] *St. Helena*
EL CAJON TRAVELODGE [MOT] *El Cajon*
EL CORDOVA [MOT] *Coronado*
EL DORADO MOTEL [MOT] *El Centro*
EL DORADO MOTOR INN [MOT] *West Covina*
EL DRISCO HOTEL [HOT] *San Francisco*
EL ENCANTO HOTEL & GARDEN [HOT] *Santa Barbara*
ELK COVE INN [BB] *Mendocino*
ELMS BED & BREAKFAST INN, THE [BB] *Calistoga*
EL PRADO INN [MOT] *Santa Barbara*
EL PUEBLO [MOT] *Sonoma*
EL RANCHO LODGE [MOT] *Palm Springs*
ELSBREE HOUSE BED AND BREAKFAST [BB] *San Diego*
EL TERADO TERRACE [MOT] *Avalon (Catalina Island)*
EMBASSY SUITES [HOT] *Arcadia*
EMBASSY SUITES [AS] *Buena Park*
EMBASSY SUITES [HOT] *Irvine*
EMBASSY SUITES [HOT] *Lompoc*
EMBASSY SUITES [HOT] *Los Angeles Intl Airport Area*
EMBASSY SUITES [HOT] *Oxnard*
EMBASSY SUITES [AS] *Palm Desert*
EMBASSY SUITES [AS] *San Diego*
EMBASSY SUITES [AS] *San Luis Obispo*
EMBASSY SUITES ANAHEIM [AS] *Anaheim*
EMBASSY SUITES HOTEL [HOT] *Walnut Creek*
EMBASSY SUITES HOTEL ON MONTEREY BAY [AS] *Monterey*
EMBASSY SUITES LA JOLLA [HOT] *San Diego*
EMBASSY SUITES MILPITAS/SILICON VALLEY [AS] *San Jose*
EMBASSY SUITES NAPA VALLEY [HOT] *Napa*
EMBASSY SUITES ORANGE COUNTY AIRPORT [AS] *Santa Ana*
EMBASSY SUITES RESORT [RST] *South Lake Tahoe (Lake Tahoe Area)*
EMBASSY SUITES SAN FRANCISCO [AS] *San Francisco Airport Area*
EMBASSY SUITES TEMECULA [HOT] *Temecula*
EMMA NEVADA HOUSE [BB] *Nevada City*
EMPRESS HOTEL [HOT] *La Jolla (San Diego)*
ESCAPE FOR ALL SEASONS [CON] *Big Bear Lake*
ESSEX HOTEL [HOT] *San Francisco*
ESTRELLA INN [BB] *Palm Springs*
EUREKA INN [HOT] *Eureka*
EUREKA TRAVELODGE [MOT] *Eureka*
EVERGREEN BED AND BREAKFAST [BB] *Pleasanton*
EXECUTIVE INN [MOT] *El Centro*
EXECUTIVE INN [MOT] *Hayward*
FAIRFIELD INN [MOT] *Anaheim*
FAIRFIELD INN [MOT] *Buena Park*
FAIRFIELD INN [MOT] *Ontario*
FAIRFIELD INN [MOT] *Palm Desert*
FAIRFIELD INN BY MARRIOTT [MOT] *Anaheim*
FAIRMONT MIRAMAR HOTEL SANTA MONICA, THE [HOT] *Santa Monica*
FAIRMONT SAN FRANCISCO, THE [HOT] *San Francisco*
FAIRMONT SAN JOSE, THE [HOT] *San Jose*
FALLBROOK LODGE [MOT] *Fallbrook*
FALLON HOTEL [BB] *Sonora*
FALLON HOTEL [BB] *Sonora*

FANTASY INN AND WEDDING CHAPEL [BB] *South Lake Tahoe (Lake Tahoe Area)*
FERN VALLEY INN [BB] *Idyllwild*
FESS PARKER'S DOUBLETREE RESORT [RST] *Santa Barbara*
FESS PARKER'S WINE COUNTRY INN [BB] *Solvang*
FINLANDIA MOTEL [MOT] *Mount Shasta*
FIRESIDE INN [BB] *Idyllwild*
FIRST CHOICE INN [MOT] *Roseville*
FLAMINGO RESORT HOTEL [MOT] *Santa Rosa*
FLUME'S END BED AND BREAKFAST [BB] *Nevada City*
FOGHORN HARBOR INN [MOT] *Marina del Rey*
FOOTHILL HOUSE BED AND BREAKFAST [BB] *Calistoga*
FOREST INN SUITES [MOT] *South Lake Tahoe (Lake Tahoe Area)*
FOUNTAINGROVE INN [HOT] *Santa Rosa*
FOUR POINTS BY SHERATON HOTEL [MOT] *Bakersfield*
FOUR POINTS BY SHERATON HOTEL [MOT] *Fresno*
FOUR POINTS BY SHERATON FULLERTON [MOT] *Fullerton*
FOUR POINTS BY SHERATON RANCHO BERNARDO [HOT] *San Diego*
FOUR POINTS BY SHERATON BARCELO SAN RAFAEL [MOT] *San Rafael*
FOUR POINTS BY SHERATON [MOT] *Santa Monica*
FOUR POINTS BY SHERATON [MOT] *Sunnyvale*
FOUR SEASON [HOT] *San Francisco*
FOUR SEASONS HOTEL LOS ANGELES [HOT] *Los Angeles*
FOUR SEASONS HOTEL NEWPORT BEACH [HOT] *Newport Beach*
FOUR SEASONS RESORT AVIARA [RST] *Carlsbad*
FOUR SEASONS RESORT SANTA BARBARA [RST] *Santa Barbara*
FOXES IN SUTTER CREEK [BB] *Jackson*
FRANCISCAN INN [BB] *Santa Barbara*
FRANCISCO BAY MOTEL [MOT] *San Francisco*
FURAMA HOTEL LOS ANGELES [HOT] *Los Angeles*
FURNACE CREEK INN [RST] *Death Valley National Park*
FURNACE CREEK RANCH [RAN] *Death Valley National Park*
GABLES, THE [BB] *Santa Rosa*
GAIGE HOUSE INN [BB] *Sonoma*
GALLERIA PARK, THE [HOT] *San Francisco*
GARDEN COURT HOTEL [HOT] *Palo Alto*
GARDEN STREET INN [BB] *San Luis Obispo*
GARRATT MANSION [BB] *Oakland*
GATE HOUSE INN [BB] *Jackson*
GATEHOUSE INN, THE [BB] *Pacific Grove*
GEORGIA HOTEL, THE [RST] *Santa Monica*
GERSTLE PARK INN [BB] *San Rafael*
GEYSERVILLE INN [MOT] *Healdsburg*
GINGERBREAD MANSION [BB] *Eureka*
GLENBOROUGH INN [BB] *Santa Barbara*
GLENMORE PLAZA HOTEL [HOT] *Avalon (Catalina Island)*
GLORIETTA BAY INN [HOT] *Coronado*
GOLDMINE LODGE AND DOC'S GET AWAY [RST] *Big Bear Lake*
GOOD NITE INN [MOT] *San Diego*
GOOD NITE INN [MOT] *San Diego*
GOOSE AND TURRETS BED AND BREAKFAST INN [BB] *Half Moon Bay*
GOSBY HOUSE INN [BB] *Pacific Grove*
GOVERNORS INN [MOT] *Sacramento*
GRAND COLONIAL, THE [HOT] *La Jolla (San Diego)*
GRAND HYATT SAN FRANCISCO [HOT] *San Francisco*
GRANDMERE'S BED & BREAKFAST INN [BB] *Nevada City*
GRANLIBAKKEN RESORT & CONFERENCE CENTER [RST] *Tahoe City (Lake Tahoe Area)*
GRANT GROVE VILLAGE [MOT] *Kings Canyon National Park*
GRANT PLAZA HOTEL [HOT] *San Francisco*
GRAPE LEAF INN [BB] *Healdsburg*
GREEN GABLES INN [BB] *Pacific Grove*
GREEN LANTERN INN [BB] *Carmel*

GREY GABLES BED AND BREAKFAST INN [BB] *Jackson*
GREY WHALE INN BED AND BREAKFAST [BB] *Fort Bragg*
GROVELAND HOTEL [HOT] *Yosemite National Park*
GUEST HOUSE [MOT] *Long Beach*
GUESTHOUSE INN AND SUITES [MOT] *San Luis Obispo*
GUESTHOUSE INN & SUITES [MOT] *Santa Clara*
HACIENDA MOTEL [MOT] *Alturas*
HALF MOON BAY LODGE AND CONFERENCE CENTER [RST] *Half Moon Bay*
HALLMARK INN [HOT] *Davis*
HALLMARK SUITES [AS] *Rancho Cordova*
HAMPTON INN [MOT] *Arcadia*
HAMPTON INN [MOT] *Blythe*
HAMPTON INN [MOT] *Fairfield*
HAMPTON INN [MOT] *Oakland*
HAMPTON INN [MOT] *Palm Springs*
HAMPTON INN [MOT] *Valencia*
HAMPTON INN KEARNY MESA [MOT] *San Diego*
HAMPTON INN LAX [MOT] *Los Angeles Intl Airport Area*
HANALEI HOTEL [RST] *San Diego*
HANDLERY HOTEL RESORT [RST] *San Diego*
HANDLERY UNION SQUARE HOTEL [HOT] *San Francisco*
HANFORD HOUSE B&B INN [BB] *Jackson*
HAPPY LANDING INN [BB] *Carmel*
HARBOR COURT MOTEL, THE [HOT] *San Francisco*
HARBOR HOUSE INN [BB] *Mendocino*
HARBOR LITE LODGE [MOT] *Fort Bragg*
HARBOR VIEW INN [HOT] *Santa Barbara*
HARVEST INN [BB] *St. Helena*
HAWTHORN SUITES [AS] *Orange*
HAWTHORN SUITES [AS] *Sacramento*
HAYDON STREET INN [BB] *Healdsburg*
HAYES CONFERENCE CENTER [HOT] *San Jose*
HEADLANDS INN [BB] *Mendocino*
HEALDSBURG INN ON THE PLAZA [BB] *Healdsburg*
HEMET SUPER 8 [MOT] *Hemet*
HERITAGE HOUSE INN [BB] *Mendocino*
HERITAGE PARK INN [BB] *San Diego*
HIGHLANDS INN [RST] *Carmel*
HIGHLANDS INN [MOT] *Clear Lake Area*
HILGARD HOUSE HOTEL [HOT] *Los Angeles*
HILL HOUSE INN OF MENDOCINO [BB] *Mendocino*
HILTON [HOT] *Concord*
HILTON [HOT] *Pasadena*
HILTON [HOT] *Valencia*
HILTON [HOT] *Whittier*
HILTON AIRPORT [HOT] *Ontario*
HILTON ANAHEIM [HOT] *Anaheim*
HILTON AND TOWERS [HOT] *San Francisco*
HILTON AND TOWERS [HOT] *San Jose*
HILTON BURBANK AIRPORT & CONVENTION CENTER [HOT] *Burbank*
HILTON COSTA MESA / ORANGE COUNTY [HOT] *Costa Mesa*
HILTON DEL MAR NORTH SAN DIEGO [HOT] *Del Mar*
HILTON GARDEN INN [HOT] *San Mateo*
HILTON HOTEL [HOT] *Beverly Hills*
HILTON HOTEL [HOT] *Fremont*
HILTON HOTEL [HOT] *Oakland*
HILTON LA JOLLA TORREY PINES [RST] *La Jolla (San Diego)*
HILTON LONG BEACH [HOT] *Long Beach*
HILTON LOS ANGELES AIRPORT [HOT] *Los Angeles*
HILTON MISSION VALLEY [HOT] *San Diego*
HILTON MONTEREY [HOT] *Monterey*
HILTON PALM SPRINGS RESORT [RST] *Palm Springs*
HILTON PLESANTON AT THE CLUB [HOT] *Pleasanton*
HILTON PORT OF LOS ANGELES/SAN PEDRO [HOT] *San Pedro (L.A.)*
HILTON SACRAMENTO ARDEN WEST [HOT] *Sacramento*
HILTON SAN BERNARDINO [HOT] *San Bernardino*
HILTON SAN DIEGO AIRPORT [HOT] *San Diego*

HILTON SAN DIEGO RESORT [HOT] *San Diego*
HILTON SONOMA COUNTY/SANTA ROSA [HOT] *Santa Rosa*
HILTON SUITES [HOT] *Orange*
HILTON TORRANCE [HOT] *Torrance*
HILTON UNIVERSAL CITY &TOWERS [HOT] *North Hollywood (L.A.)*
HILTON WATERFRONT BEACH RESORT [RST] *Huntington Beach*
HILTON WOODLAND HILLS [HOT] *Woodland Hills (L.A.)*
HISTORIC NATIONAL HOTEL BED AND BREAKFAST [BB] *Sonora*
HOFSAS HOUSE [BB] *Carmel*
HOLIDAY INN [MOT] *Anaheim*
HOLIDAY INN [MOT] *Arcadia*
HOLIDAY INN [MOT] *Bakersfield*
HOLIDAY INN [MOT] *Camarillo*
HOLIDAY INN [MOT] *Chico*
HOLIDAY INN [MOT] *Costa Mesa*
HOLIDAY INN [MOT] *Laguna Beach*
HOLIDAY INN [MOT] *Lodi*
HOLIDAY INN [MOT] *Modesto*
HOLIDAY INN [MOT] *Oakland*
HOLIDAY INN [MOT] *Ontario*
HOLIDAY INN [MOT] *Riverside*
HOLIDAY INN [MOT] *Sacramento*
HOLIDAY INN [MOT] *San Diego*
HOLIDAY INN [MOT] *San Francisco*
HOLIDAY INN [MOT] *San Jose*
HOLIDAY INN [MOT] *Santa Barbara*
HOLIDAY INN [MOT] *West Covina*
HOLIDAY INN BAYSIDE [MOT] *San Diego*
HOLIDAY INN BIG BEAR CHATEAU [MOT] *Big Bear Lake*
HOLIDAY INN BRENTWOOD BEL AIR [MOT] *Los Angeles*
HOLIDAY INN BUENA PARK [MOT] *Buena Park*
HOLIDAY INN CARLSBAD-BY-THE-SEA [MOT] *Carlsbad*
HOLIDAY INN CIVIC CENTER [MOT] *San Francisco*
HOLIDAY INN EXPRESS [MOT] *Chula Vista*
HOLIDAY INN EXPRESS [MOT] *Crescent City*
HOLIDAY INN EXPRESS [MOT] *Half Moon Bay*
HOLIDAY INN EXPRESS [MOT] *Laguna Beach*
HOLIDAY INN EXPRESS [MOT] *Los Angeles*
HOLIDAY INN EXPRESS [MOT] *Mill Valley*
HOLIDAY INN EXPRESS [BB] *Monterey*
HOLIDAY INN EXPRESS [MOT] *Palm Desert*
HOLIDAY INN EXPRESS [MOT] *San Luis Obispo*
HOLIDAY INN EXPRESS [MOT] *San Mateo*
HOLIDAY INN EXPRESS [MOT] *South Lake Tahoe (Lake Tahoe Area)*
HOLIDAY INN EXPRESS [MOT] *Three Rivers*
HOLIDAY INN EXPRESS HOTEL & SUITES - TOWNCENTER [MOT] *Mountain View*
HOLIDAY INN GOLDEN GATEWAY [MOT] *San Francisco*
HOLIDAY INN HARBORVIEW [MOT] *San Diego*
HOLIDAY INN LA DOWNTOWN [MOT] *Los Angeles*
HOLIDAY INN LOS ANGELES CITY CENTER [MOT] *Los Angeles*
HOLIDAY INN MISSION VALLEY STADIUM NORTH [MOT] *San Diego*
HOLIDAY INN ON THE BAY [MOT] *San Diego*
HOLIDAY INN ORANGE COUNTY AIRPORT [MOT] *Santa Ana*
HOLIDAY INN RANCHO [MOT] *San Diego*
HOLIDAY INN SAN CLEMENTE [MOT] *San Clemente*
HOLIDAY INN SANTA MONICA BEACH [MOT] *Santa Monica*
HOLIDAY INN SELECT [MOT] *Fairfield*
HOLIDAY INN SELECT [MOT] *Pomona*
HOLIDAY LODGE [MOT] *Grass Valley*
HOLIDAY LODGE [MOT] *Willits*
HOLLYWOOD ROOSEVELT HOTEL [HOT] *Hollywood (L.A.)*
HOMESTEAD, THE [CC] *Yosemite National Park*
HONOR MANSION [BB] *Healdsburg*
HORIZON INN [MOT] *Carmel*
HORTON GRAND HOTEL [HOT] *San Diego*
HOTEL BEL AIR [HOT] *Los Angeles*
HOTEL BIJOU [HOT] *San Francisco*

HOTEL BOHEME [HOT] *San Francisco*
HOTEL BRITTON [HOT] *San Francisco*
HOTEL DE ANZA [HOT] *San Jose*
HOTEL DEL CAPRI [HOT] *Los Angeles*
HOTEL DEL CORONADO [RST] *Coronado*
HOTEL DIVA [HOT] *San Francisco*
HOTEL DURANT [HOT] *Berkeley*
HOTEL GRIFFON [HOT] *San Francisco*
HOTEL HERMOSA [MOT] *Redondo Beach*
HOTEL HUNTINGTON BEACH [HOT] *Huntington Beach*
HOTEL LAGUNA [HOT] *Laguna Beach*
HOTEL LA JOLLA [HOT] *La Jolla (San Diego)*
HOTEL LA ROSE [HOT] *Santa Rosa*
HOTEL MAJESTIC, THE [HOT] *San Francisco*
HOTEL METROPOLE [HOT] *Avalon (Catalina Island)*
HOTEL MILANO [HOT] *San Francisco*
HOTEL MONACO [HOT] *San Francisco*
HOTEL MONARCH [HOT] *San Francisco*
HOTEL NIKKO SAN FRANCISCO [HOT] *San Francisco*
HOTEL PACIFIC [HOT] *Monterey*
HOTEL PALOMAR [HOT] *San Francisco*
HOTEL PARISI [HOT] *La Jolla (San Diego)*
HOTEL REX [HOT] *San Francisco*
HOTEL SAINT HELENA [BB] *St. Helena*
HOTEL SANTA BARBARA [HOT] *Santa Barbara*
HOTEL SHATTUCK PLAZA [HOT] *Berkeley*
HOTEL SOFITEL [HOT] *Los Angeles*
HOTEL SOFITEL [HOT] *Redwood City*
HOTEL ST LAUREN [BB] *Avalon (Catalina Island)*
HOTEL TRITON [HOT] *San Francisco*
HOTEL UNION SQUARE [HOT] *San Francisco*
HOTEL VILLA PORTOFINO [RST] *Avalon (Catalina Island)*
HOTEL VINTAGE COURT [HOT] *San Francisco*
HOTEL VISTA DEL MAR [HOT] *Avalon (Catalina Island)*
HOUNDS TOOTH INN [BB] *Oakhurst*
HOWARD JOHNSON [MOT] *Santa Clara*
HOWARD JOHNSON [MOT] *Victorville*
HOWARD JOHNSON EXPRESS INN [MOT] *Fullerton*
HOWARD JOHNSON EXPRESS INN [MOT] *Stockton*
HOWARD JOHNSON HOTEL - ANAHEIM RESORT [MOT] *Anaheim*
HOWARD JOHNSON RESORT [MOT] *Palm Springs*
HUMBOLDT REDWOODS INN [MOT] *Garberville*
HUMMINGBIRD INN [MOT] *Ojai*
HUMPHREY'S HALF MOON INN [RST] *San Diego*
HUNTINGTON HOTEL [HOT] *San Francisco*
HYATT [HOT] *San Jose*
HYATT AT FISHERMAN'S WHARF [HOT] *San Francisco*
HYATT GRAND CHAMPIONS RESORT [RST] *Palm Desert*
HYATT NEWPORTER [HOT] *Newport Beach*
HYATT REGENCY [HOT] *Irvine*
HYATT REGENCY [HOT] *Long Beach*
HYATT REGENCY [HOT] *Los Angeles*
HYATT REGENCY [HOT] *Sacramento*
HYATT REGENCY [HOT] *San Diego*
HYATT REGENCY [HOT] *San Francisco*
HYATT REGENCY ISLANDIA [HOT] *San Diego*
HYATT REGENCY LA JOLLA AT AVENTINE [HOT] *San Diego*
HYATT REGENCY MONTEREY [HOT] *Monterey*
HYATT REGENCY ORANGE COUNTY [HOT] *Anaheim*
HYATT REGENCY SAN FRANCISCO AIRPORT [HOT] *San Francisco Airport Area*
HYATT REGENCY SUITES PALM SPRINGS [HOT] *Palm Springs*
HYATT RICKEYS [HOT] *Palo Alto*
HYATT SAINTE CLAIRE [HOT] *San Jose*
HYATT VALENCIA AND SANTA CLARITA CONFERENCE CENTER [HOT] *Valencia*
HYATT WEST HOLLYWOOD [HOT] *Hollywood (L.A.)*

HYATT WESTLAKE PLAZA [HOT] *Thousand Oaks*
IMPERIAL HOTEL [BB] *Jackson*
INDIAN WELLS RESORT HOTEL [RST] *Palm Desert*
INGLESIDE INN [BB] *Palm Springs*
INN ABOVE TIDE, THE [BB] *Sausalito*
INN AT 213 SEVENTEEN MILE DRIVE, THE [HOT] *Pacific Grove*
INN AT DEEP CANYON, THE [HOT] *Palm Desert*
INN AT DEPOT HILL [BB] *Santa Cruz*
INN AT HARRIS RANCH [MOT] *Hanford*
INN AT LAGUNA BEACH [MOT] *Laguna Beach*
INN AT LA JOLLA [MOT] *La Jolla (San Diego)*
INN AT MORRO BAY [RST] *Morro Bay*
INN AT OCCIDENTAL OF SONOMA WINE COUNTRY [BB] *Bodega Bay*
INN AT PARKSIDE [BB] *Sacramento*
INN AT PLAYA DEL REY [BB] *Marina del Rey*
INN AT RANCHO SANTA FE, THE [BB] *Rancho Santa Fe*
INN AT SARATOGA, THE [BB] *Saratoga*
INN AT SCHOOLHOUSE CREEK [BB] *Mendocino*
INN AT SOUTHBRIDGE [BB] *St. Helena*
INN AT SPANISH BAY, THE [RST] *Pebble Beach*
INN AT THE OPERA [HOT] *San Francisco*
INN AT THE TIDES [RST] *Bodega Bay*
INN AT UNION SQUARE [BB] *San Francisco*
INN BY THE HARBOR [BB] *Santa Barbara*
INN BY THE LAKE [HOT] *South Lake Tahoe (Lake Tahoe Area)*
INN OF LONG BEACH [MOT] *Long Beach*
INN ON MOUNT ADA [BB] *Avalon (Catalina Island)*
INN ON SUMMER HILL [BB] *Santa Barbara*
INN SAN FRANCISCO [BB] *San Francisco*
INNS OF AMERICA [MOT] *Carlsbad*
INNS OF AMERICA [MOT] *Fresno*
INNS OF AMERICA [MOT] *Rancho Cordova*
INN SUITES HOTEL [HOT] *Buena Park*
INTERNATIONAL LODGE [MOT] *Palm Desert*
INTERNATIONAL MOTOR INN [MOT] *San Ysidro (San Diego)*
IRWIN STREET INN [BB] *Hanford*
JABBERWOCK BED AND BREAKFAST [BB] *Monterey*
JACKSON COURT [BB] *San Francisco*
JACKSON GOLD LODGE [MOT] *Jackson*
JAMESTOWN HOTEL [BB] *Sonora*
JETER VICTORIAN INN [BB] *Red Bluff*
JOHN MUIR INN [HOT] *Napa*
JOLLY ROGER'S INN [MOT] *Anaheim*
JOSHUA GRINDLE INN [BB] *Mendocino*
JOSHUA TREE INN [BB] *Desert Hot Springs*
J PATRICK HOUSE BED AND BREAKFAST [BB] *Cambria*
J STREET INN [HOT] *San Diego*
JULIANA HOTEL [HOT] *San Francisco*
JULIAN GOLDRUSH HOTEL [BB] *San Diego*
JULIAN WHITE HOUSE BED AND BREAKFAST [BB] *San Diego*
KEEFER'S INN [MOT] *King City*
KENSINGTON PARK HOTEL [HOT] *San Francisco*
KENWOOD INN & SPA [BB] *Santa Rosa*
KERN RIVER INN BED AND BREAKFAST [BB] *Kernville*
KERNVILLE INN [MOT] *Kernville*
KING GEORGE HOTEL [HOT] *San Francisco*
KLAMATH MOTOR LODGE [MOT] *Yreka*
KON TIKI INN [MOT] *Pismo Beach*
KORAKIA PENSIONE [BB] *Palm Springs*
LA AVENIDA INN [MOT] *Coronado*
LA CASA DEL ZORRO [RST] *Borrego Springs*
LA COSTA RESORT AND SPA [RST] *Carlsbad*
LAFAYETTE PARK HOTEL [MOT] *Walnut Creek*
LAGUNA HOUSE [BB] *Laguna Beach*
LAGUNA RIVIERA HOTEL [RST] *Laguna Beach*
LA HACIENDA INN [BB] *Los Gatos*

LA JOLLA BEACH & TENNIS CLUB [RST] *La Jolla (San Diego)*
LA JOLLA BEACH TRAVELODGE [MOT] *La Jolla (San Diego)*
LA JOLLA COVE SUITES [MOT] *La Jolla (San Diego)*
LA JOLLA SHORES INN [MOT] *La Jolla (San Diego)*
LAKE ARROWHEAD RESORT [RST] *Lake Arrowhead*
LAKE ARROWHEAD TREE TOP LODGE [MOT] *Lake Arrowhead*
LAKELAND VILLAGE BEACH AND SKI RESORT [HOT] *South Lake Tahoe (Lake Tahoe Area)*
LAKE OROVILLE BED AND BREAKFAST [BB] *Oroville*
LA MANCHA PRIVATE RESORT AND VILLAS [RST] *Palm Springs*
LA MER EUROPEAN BED & BREAKFAST [BB] *Ventura*
LAMPLIGHTER LODGE [MOT] *Red Bluff*
LA PLAYA HOTEL [HOT] *Carmel*
LA QUINTA INN [MOT] *Bakersfield*
LA QUINTA INN [MOT] *Redding*
LA QUINTA INN [MOT] *Sacramento*
LA QUINTA INN [MOT] *Sacramento*
LA QUINTA INN [MOT] *San Bernardino*
LA QUINTA INN [MOT] *San Diego*
LA QUINTA INN [MOT] *San Francisco Airport Area*
LA QUINTA RESORT CLUB [RST] *Palm Springs*
LARCHWOOD-DEER HAVEN INN, THE [MOT] *Pacific Grove*
LA RESIDENCE [BB] *Napa*
LARIAT LODGE [MOT] *Quincy*
LA SERENA INN [HOT] *Morro Bay*
LA SIESTA VILLAS [MOT] *Palm Springs*
L'AUBERGE DEL MAR RESORT AND SPA [RST] *Del Mar*
LAUREL INN MOTEL [MOT] *Salinas*
LA VALENCIA [HOT] *La Jolla (San Diego)*
LAVENDER HILL BED AND BREAKFAST [BB] *Sonora*
LAZY J RANCH MOTEL [MOT] *Three Rivers*
LEGACY INN [MOT] *Blythe*
LEISURE INN AND SUITES [MOT] *San Bernardino*
LE MERIDIEN AT BEVERLY HILLS [HOT] *Los Angeles*
LE MERIGOT BEACH HOTEL & SPA SANTA MONICA [HOT] *Santa Monica*
LE MONTROSE SUITE HOTEL [HOT] *Hollywood (L.A.)*
L'HORIZON GARDEN HOTEL [MOT] *Palm Springs*
LITTLE VALLEY [BB] *Yosemite National Park*
LOBOS LODGE [MOT] *Carmel*
LODGE AT NOYO RIVER [BB] *Fort Bragg*
LODGE AT PEBBLE BEACH, THE [RST] *Pebble Beach*
LODGE AT SKYLONDA, THE [MOT] *Redwood City*
LODGE AT SONOMA RENAISSANCE HOTEL & SPA, THE [RST] *Sonoma*
LODGE AT VILLA FELICE [MOT] *Los Gatos*
LOEWS CORONADO BAY RESORT [RST] *Coronado*
LOEWS SANTA MONICA HOTEL [HOT] *Santa Monica*
LOMA VISTA BED AND BREAKFAST [BB] *Temecula*
LOMBARD MOTOR INN [MOT] *San Francisco*
LORD BRADLEY'S INN [BB] *Fremont*
LOS GATOS LODGE [MOT] *Los Gatos*
LOS LAURELES LODGE [BB] *Carmel Valley*
LOS ROBLES LODGE [MOT] *Santa Rosa*
LOST WHALE BED & BREAKFAST [BB] *Trinidad*
LUXE HOTEL RODEO DRIVE [HOT] *Beverly Hills*
LUXE SUMMIT HOTEL BEL-AIR [HOT] *Los Angeles*
MADISON STREET INN [BB] *Santa Clara*
MADONNA INN [BB] *San Luis Obispo*
MADRONA MANOR [BB] *Healdsburg*
MAISON FLEURIE FOUR SISTERS INN [BB] *Yountville*
MALIBU BEACH INN [HOT] *Malibu*
MALIBU COUNTRY INN [MOT] *Malibu*
MAMMOTH MOUNTAIN INN [HOT] *Mammoth Lakes*

MANDARIN ORIENTAL, SAN FRANCISCO [HOT] *San Francisco*

MANKA'S INVERNESS LODGE [BB] *Inverness*

MAPLE TREE INN [HOT] *Sunnyvale*

MARIANI'S INN [MOT] *Santa Clara*

MARINA BEACH MARRIOTT [HOT] *Marina del Rey*

MARINA BEACH MOTEL [MOT] *Santa Barbara*

MARINA DEL REY HOTEL [MOT] *Marina del Rey*

MARINA INN [HOT] *San Francisco*

MARINA RESORT [RST] *Big Bear Lake*

MARINA VILLAGE INN [MOT] *Oakland*

MARIN SUITES HOTEL [HOT] *Corte Madera*

MARIPOSA INN [MOT] *Monterey*

MARIPOSA LODGE [HOT] *Yosemite National Park*

MARK HOPKINS INTER-CONTINENTAL SAN FRANCISCO [HOT] *San Francisco*

MARRIOT HOTEL & MARINA SAN DIEGO [HOT] *San Diego*

MARRIOTT [HOT] *Fullerton*

MARRIOTT [HOT] *Fullerton*

MARRIOTT [HOT] *Irvine*

MARRIOTT [HOT] *Los Angeles*

MARRIOTT [HOT] *Walnut Creek*

MARRIOTT ANAHEIM [HOT] *Anaheim*

MARRIOTT CITY CENTER OAKLAND [HOT] *Oakland*

MARRIOTT DOWNTOWN LOS ANGELES [HOT] *Los Angeles*

MARRIOTT FISHERMANS WHARF SAN FRANCISCO [HOT] *San Francisco*

MARRIOTT FREEMONT [HOT] *Fremont*

MARRIOTT HOTEL [HOT] *Rancho Cordova*

MARRIOTT HOTEL AND TENNIS CLUB NEWPORT BEACH [HOT] *Newport Beach*

MARRIOTT HOTEL WARNER CENTER [HOT] *Woodland Hills (L.A.)*

MARRIOTT LA JOLLA SAN DIEGO [HOT] *La Jolla (San Diego)*

MARRIOTT LONG BEACH [HOT] *Long Beach*

MARRIOTT MANHATTAN BEACH [HOT] *Los Angeles*

MARRIOTT MISSION VALLEY SAN DIEGO [HOT] *San Diego*

MARRIOTT MONTEREY [HOT] *Monterey*

MARRIOTT NAPA VALLEY [HOT] *Napa*

MARRIOTT NORWALK [HOT] *Buena Park*

MARRIOTT NORWALK [HOT] *Los Angeles*

MARRIOTT ONTARIO AIRPORT [HOT] *Ontario*

MARRIOTT RANCHO SANTA BARBARA [HOT] *Santa Barbara*

MARRIOTT RESORT & SPA DESERT SPRINGS [RST] *Palm Desert*

MARRIOTT RESORT CORONADO ISLAND [RST] *Coronado*

MARRIOTT RESORT LAGUNA CLIFFS [RST] *Laguna Beach*

MARRIOTT SAN FRANCISCO [HOT] *San Francisco*

MARRIOTT SAN FRANCISCO AIRPORT [HOT] *San Francisco Airport Area*

MARRIOTT SAN MATEO [HOT] *San Mateo*

MARRIOTT SAN RAMON [HOT] *San Francisco*

MARRIOTT SANTA CLARA [HOT] *Santa Clara*

MARRIOTT'S RANCHO LAS PALMAS RESORT & SPA [RST] *Palm Springs*

MARRIOTT SUITES COSTA MESA [HOT] *Costa Mesa*

MARRIOTT SUITES DOWNTOWN AT SYMPHONY TOWERS SAN DIEGO [AS] *San Diego*

MARRIOTT SUITES NEWPORT BEACH [AS] *Newport Beach*

MARRIOTT TORRANCE [HOT] *Torrance*

MARRIOTT WALNUT CREEK [HOT] *Walnut Creek*

MARTINE INN, THE [BB] *Pacific Grove*

MATLICK HOUSE BED AND BREAKFAST, THE [BB] *Bishop*

MATTERHORN MOTEL [MOT] *South Lake Tahoe (Lake Tahoe Area)*

MAXWELL HOTEL [HOT] *San Francisco*

MCCAFFREY HOUSE BED & BREAKFAST INN [BB] *Sonora*

MCCLOUD HOTEL BED AND BREAKFAST [BB] *Mount Shasta*
MEADOWLARK COUNTRY HOUSE AND INN [BB] *Calistoga*
MEADOWOOD RESORT HOTEL [RST] *St. Helena*
MELODY RANCH MOTEL [MOT] *Paso Robles*
MENDOCINO HOTEL [BB] *Mendocino*
MENLO PARK INN [MOT] *Menlo Park*
MERRITT HOUSE INN [BB] *Monterey*
MERV GRIFFIN'S RESORT & GIVENCHY SPA [RST] *Palm Springs*
MILL ROSE INN [BB] *Half Moon Bay*
MILL VALLEY INN [BB] *Mill Valley*
MILLWOOD INN [MOT] *San Francisco Airport Area*
MINERS INN MOTEL [MOT] *Yosemite National Park*
MIRAMONTE RESORT [RST] *Palm Springs*
MISSION INN [HOT] *Riverside*
MISSION RANCH [BB] *Carmel*
MONDRIAN [HOT] *Hollywood (L.A.)*
MONTECITO INN [HOT] *Santa Barbara*
MONTEREY BAY INN [MOT] *Monterey*
MONTEREY HOTEL, THE [BB] *Monterey*
MONTEREY PLAZA HOTEL [HOT] *Monterey*
MONTICELLO INN [HOT] *San Francisco*
MOONSTONE INN [CON] *Cambria*
MORGAN RUN RESORT & CLUB [RST] *Rancho Santa Fe*
MOTEL 6 [MOT] *Bishop*
MOTEL 6 [MOT] *Palm Springs*
MOUNTAIN HOME INN [BB] *Mill Valley*
MOUNTAIN VIEW INN [MOT] *Mountain View*
MOUNT SHASTA RESORT [RST] *Mount Shasta*
MOUNT VIEW HOTEL AND SPA [HOT] *Calistoga*
MURPHYS HISTORIC HOTEL [HOT] *Sonora*
NAPA VALLEY LODGE [HOT] *Yountville*
NAPA VALLEY RAILWAY [BB] *Yountville*
NEW OTANI HOTEL AND GARDEN [HOT] *Los Angeles*
NOB HILL LAMBOURNE HOTEL [HOT] *San Francisco*
NOB HILL MOTOR INN [MOT] *San Francisco*
NORMANDY INN [BB] *Carmel*
NORTH COAST COUNTRY INN [BB] *Gualala*
NORTHSTAR-AT-TAHOE [RST] *Truckee*
NORTHWOODS RESORT & CONFERENCE CENTER [RST] *Big Bear Lake*
OASIS OF EDEN INN AND SUITES [HOT] *Desert Hot Springs*
O'BRIEN MOUNTAIN INN [BB] *Redding*
OCEAN PALMS BEACH RESORT [MOT] *Carlsbad*
OCEAN PARK INN [MOT] *San Diego*
OCEANSIDE DAYS INN [MOT] *Oceanside*
OJAI VALLEY INN AND SPA [RST] *Ojai*
OLD MONTEREY INN [BB] *Monterey*
OLD THYME INN [BB] *Half Moon Bay*
OLD TOWN BED AND BREAKFAST INN [BB] *Eureka*
OLD TOWN INN [MOT] *San Diego*
OLD WORLD INN, THE [BB] *Napa*
OLD YACHT CLUB INN [BB] *Santa Barbara*
OLEANDER HOUSE [BB] *Yountville*
OLEMA INN [BB] *Inverness*
OLIVE HOUSE [BB] *Santa Barbara*
OLIVER HOUSE [BB] *St. Helena*
OLIVE TREE INN [MOT] *San Luis Obispo*
OMNI LOS ANGELES HOTEL [HOT] *Los Angeles*
ONTARIO AIRPORT COMFORT INN [MOT] *Ontario*
ORCHARD HILL COUNTRY INN [BB] *San Diego*
ORCHID TREE INN [BB] *Palm Springs*
OTTER INN [MOT] *Monterey*
OXFORD PALACE [HOT] *Los Angeles*
OXFORD SUITES RESORT [AS] *Pismo Beach*
PACIFICA SUITES [MOT] *Santa Barbara*
PACIFIC GROVE INN [BB] *Pacific Grove*

PACIFIC HEIGHTS INN [MOT] *San Francisco*
PACIFIC TERRACE INN [MOT] *San Diego*
PALACE HOTEL [HOT] *San Francisco*
PALA MESA RESORT [RST] *Fallbrook*
PALM CANYON RESORT [MOT] *Borrego Springs*
PALM HOTEL BED & BREAKFAST [BB] *Sonora*
PALMS AT INDIAN HEAD, THE [BB] *Borrego Springs*
PALM SPRINGS MARQUIS RESORT [RST] *Palm Springs*
PALM SPRINGS RIVIERA RESORT & RACQUET CLUB [RST] *Palm Springs*
PALOS VERDES INN [HOT] *Redondo Beach*
PAN PACIFIC, THE [HOT] *San Francisco*
PARK HYATT [HOT] *San Francisco*
PARK HYATT LOS ANGELES [HOT] *Los Angeles*
PARK PLAZA HOTEL SAN FRANCISCO [HOT] *San Francisco Airport Area*
PARK VUE INN [MOT] *Anaheim*
PEACOCK SUITES HOTEL [MOT] *Anaheim*
PENINSULA BEVERLY HILLS, THE [HOT] *Beverly Hills*
PENNY SLEEPER INN [MOT] *Anaheim*
PETERSEN VILLAGE INN [BB] *Solvang*
PHOENIX INN, THE [MOT] *San Francisco*
PICCADILLY INN AIRPORT [HOT] *Fresno*
PICCADILLY INN UNIVERSITY [HOT] *Fresno*
PIERPONT INN [BB] *Ventura*
PINE BEACH INN & SUITES [MOT] *Fort Bragg*
PINE COVE INN [BB] *Idyllwild*
PINE INN [HOT] *Carmel*
PINES RESORT [MOT] *Yosemite National Park*
PINK MANSION [BB] *Calistoga*
PLACE IN THE SUN [MOT] *Palm Springs*
PLAZA INTERNATIONAL INN [HOT] *El Cajon*
POINT REYES SEASHORE LODGE [BB] *Inverness*
PORTOFINO BEACH HOTEL [HOT] *Newport Beach*
PORTOFINO HOTEL AND YACHT CLUB, THE [RST] *Redondo Beach*
POST RANCH INN [RST] *Big Sur*
PRESCOTT HOTEL [HOT] *San Francisco*
PROSPECT PARK INN [BB] *La Jolla (San Diego)*
PRUFROCK'S GARDEN INN BY THE BEACH [BB] *Santa Barbara*
PRUNEYARD INN [MOT] *San Jose*
QUAIL LODGE AND RESORT AND GOLF CLUB [RST] *Carmel*
QUAIL'S INN HOTEL [RST] *Escondido*
QUALITY HOTEL MAIN GATE [MOT] *Anaheim*
QUALITY INN [MOT] *Bakersfield*
QUALITY INN [MOT] *Calexico*
QUALITY INN [MOT] *Eureka*
QUALITY INN [MOT] *Indio*
QUALITY INN [MOT] *Lompoc*
QUALITY INN [MOT] *Los Angeles*
QUALITY INN [MOT] *Mammoth Lakes*
QUALITY INN [MOT] *Palm Springs*
QUALITY INN [MOT] *Petaluma*
QUALITY INN [MOT] *Vacaville*
QUALITY INN & SUITES [MOT] *South Lake Tahoe (Lake Tahoe Area)*
QUALITY INN SOUTH BAY [MOT] *Torrance*
QUALITY RESORT MISSION VALLEY-SAN DIEGO [RST] *San Diego*
QUALITY SUITES [AS] *San Diego*
QUALITY SUITES [MOT] *San Luis Obispo*
QUALITY SUITES [AS] *Santa Ana*
QUALITY SUITES SILICON VALLEY [AS] *Santa Clara*
QUEEN ANNE HOTEL, THE [HOT] *San Francisco*
QUIET CREEK INN [BB] *Idyllwild*
RADISSON [HOT] *Fresno*
RADISSON [HOT] *La Jolla (San Diego)*
RADISSON [RST] *Sacramento*
RADISSON [HOT] *Santa Barbara*
RADISSON HOTEL [HOT] *Fullerton*
RADISSON HOTEL AT LOS ANGELES AIRPORT [HOT] *Los Angeles*
RADISSON HOTEL BERKELEY MARINA [HOT] *Berkeley*
RADISSON HOTEL CONVENTION CENTER [HOT] *San Bernardino*

RADISSON HOTEL NEWPORT BEACH [HOT] *Newport Beach*
RADISSON HOTEL OXNARD [HOT] *Oxnard*
RADISSON HOTEL SAN DIEGO [HOT] *San Diego*
RADISSON HOTEL STOCKTON [HOT] *Stockton*
RADISSON HOTEL VISALIA [HOT] *Visalia*
RADISSON HUNTLEY HOTEL [HOT] *Santa Monica*
RADISSON INN SUNNYVALE [HOT] *Sunnyvale*
RADISSON MAIN GATE HOTEL [HOT] *Anaheim*
RADISSON MIYAKO [HOT] *San Francisco*
RADISSON PLAZA HOTEL SAN JOSE AIRPORT [HOT] *San Jose*
RADISSON RESORT KNOTTS BERRY FARM [HOT] *Buena Park*
RADISSON SUITES HOTEL RANCHO BERNARDO [AS] *San Diego*
RADISSON VALLEY CENTER HOTEL [HOT] *Studio City (L.A.)*
RADISSON WILSHIRE PLAZA [HOT] *Los Angeles*
RAFFLES L'ERMITAGE BEVERLY HILLS [HOT] *Beverly Hills*
RAILROAD PARK RESORT [RST] *Dunsmuir*
RAMADA - HOLLYWOOD / UNIVERSAL STUDIOS [MOT] *Hollywood (L.A.)*
RAMADA INN [MOT] *Anaheim*
RAMADA INN [MOT] *Antioch*
RAMADA INN [MOT] *El Centro*
RAMADA INN [MOT] *Hollywood (L.A.)*
RAMADA INN [MOT] *Oakdale*
RAMADA INN [MOT] *Palmdale*
RAMADA INN [MOT] *San Diego*
RAMADA INN [MOT] *Temecula*
RAMADA INN [MOT] *Vallejo*
RAMADA INN AND SUITES [MOT] *San Diego*
RAMADA INN & SUITES CARLSBAD [MOT] *Carlsbad*
RAMADA INN & TENNIS CLUB [MOT] *Claremont*
RAMADA INN MAIN GATE/SAGA [MOT] *Anaheim*
RAMADA INN MISSION DE ORO [MOT] *Santa Nella*
RAMADA INN - SAN FRANCISCO AIRPORT NORTH [MOT] *San Francisco Airport Area*
RAMADA INN SILICON VALLEY [MOT] *Sunnyvale*
RAMADA INN SOUTH CHULA VISTA [MOT] *Chula Vista*
RAMADA LIMITED [MOT] *Anaheim*
RAMADA LIMITED [MOT] *Costa Mesa*
RAMADA LIMITED [MOT] *Huntington Beach*
RAMADA LIMITED [MOT] *San Diego*
RAMADA LIMITED [MOT] *Santa Barbara*
RAMADA LIMITED [MOT] *Ukiah*
RAMADA LIMITED SUITES [MOT] *Anaheim*
RAMADA LTD OLD TOWN [MOT] *San Diego*
RAMADA PLAZA HOTEL [MOT] *San Diego*
RAMADA PLAZA HOTEL [MOT] *San Francisco*
RAMADA PLAZA HOTEL-LAX [MOT] *Culver City*
RAMADA RESORT INN [MOT] *Palm Springs*
RANCHITO MOTEL [MOT] *Quincy*
RANCHO BERNARDO INN [RST] *San Diego*
RANCHO CAYMUS [BB] *St. Helena*
RANCHO SAN GREGORIO [BB] *Half Moon Bay*
RANCHO VALENCIA RESORT [RST] *Rancho Santa Fe*
RANKIN RANCH [RAN] *Bakersfield*
REDBUD INN [BB] *Sonora*
RED CASTLE [BB] *Nevada City*
RED LION HOTEL [MOT] *Eureka*
RED LION HOTEL [MOT] *Redding*
RED LION HOTEL SACRAMENTO [MOT] *Sacramento*
REDONDO PIER LODGE [MOT] *Redondo Beach*
RED ROOF INN [MOT] *Buena Park*
RED ROOF INN [MOT] *Stockton*
REGAL BILTMORE HOTEL [HOT] *Los Angeles*
REGENCY PLAZA HOTEL [HOT] *San Diego*
REGENT BEVERLY WILSHIRE [HOT] *Beverly Hills*

RENAISSANCE [HOT] *Los Angeles*
RENAISSANCE AGOURA HILLS [HOT] *Santa Monica*
RENAISSANCE BEVERLY HILLS [HOT] *Los Angeles*
RENAISSANCE ESMERALDA RESORT [RST] *Palm Desert*
RENAISSANCE LONG BEACH HOTEL [HOT] *Long Beach*
RENAISSANCE PARC 55 HOTEL [HOT] *San Francisco*
RENAISSANCE STANFORD COURT [HOT] *San Francisco*
RESIDENCE INN BY MARRIOTT - ARCADIA [EX] *Arcadia*
RESIDENCE INN BY MARRIOTT [EX] *Fremont*
RESIDENCE INN BY MARRIOTT [EX] *La Jolla (San Diego)*
RESIDENCE INN BY MARRIOTT MANHATTAN BEACH [EX] *Los Angeles*
RESIDENCE INN BY MARRIOTT [EX] *Mountain View*
RESIDENCE INN BY MARRIOTT ONTARIO AIRPORT [EX] *Ontario*
RESIDENCE INN BY MARRIOTT [EX] *Orange*
RESIDENCE INN BY MARRIOTT RIVERSIDE [EX] *Oxnard*
RESIDENCE INN BY MARRIOTT [EX] *Pleasanton*
RESIDENCE INN BY MARRIOTT - CAL EXPO [EX] *Sacramento*
RESIDENCE INN BY MARRIOTT [EX] *San Jose*
RESIDENCE INN BY MARRIOTT [EX] *Sunnyvale*
RESORT AT SQUAW CREEK [RST] *Tahoe City (Lake Tahoe Area)*
RIDENHOUR RANCH HOUSE INN [BB] *Guerneville*
RITZ-CARLTON, HALF MOON BAY, THE [RST] *Half Moon Bay*
RITZ-CARLTON, HUNTINGTON HOTEL & SPA, THE [RST] *Pasadena*
RITZ-CARLTON, LAGUNA NIGUEL, THE [RST] *Laguna Beach*
RITZ-CARLTON, MARINA DEL REY, THE [HOT] *Marina del Rey*
RITZ-CARLTON, PALM SPRINGS, THE [RST] *Palm Springs*
RITZ-CARLTON, SAN FRANCISCO, THE [HOT] *San Francisco*
RIVER INN MOTOR HOTEL [MOT] *Redding*
ROBIN HOOD INN [MOT] *Big Bear Lake*
ROCKLIN PARK HOTEL [HOT] *Roseville*
RODEWAY INN [MOT] *Chula Vista*
RODEWAY INN [MOT] *San Diego*
ROMANTIQUE LAKEVIEW LODGE [BB] *Lake Arrowhead*
ROSEDALE INN [BB] *Pacific Grove*
ROSE GARDEN INN [BB] *Berkeley*
ROYAL COPENHAGEN [MOT] *Solvang*
ROYAL PACIFIC MOTOR INN [MOT] *San Francisco*
ROYAL SCANDINAVIAN INN [HOT] *Solvang*
ROYAL VALHALLA MOTOR LODGE [MOT] *South Lake Tahoe (Lake Tahoe Area)*
RYAN HOUSE BED & BREAKFAST [BB] *Sonora*
SAFARI INN [MOT] *Burbank*
SAGA MOTOR HOTEL [MOT] *Pasadena*
SAINT ORRES [BB] *Gualala*
ST. REGIS, LOS ANGELES, THE [HOT] *Los Angeles*
ST. REGIS MONARCH BEACH, THE [RST] *Laguna Beach*
SALT POINT LODGE [MOT] *Fort Ross State Historic Park*
SAN CLEMENTE BEACH TRAVELODGE [RST] *San Clemente*
SANDCASTLE INN [HOT] *Pismo Beach*
SAND DOLLAR INN [MOT] *Monterey*
SAN DIEGO PARADISE POINT RESORT [RST] *San Diego*
SANDPIPER INN AT THE BEACH CARMEL [BB] *Carmel*
SANDS SUITES & MOTEL [MOT] *San Luis Obispo*
SANDY COVE INN [BB] *Inverness*
SAN FRANCISCO BAYSIDE TRAVELODGE [MOT] *San Francisco*
SAN JOAQUIN SUITE HOTEL, THE [MOT] *Fresno*
SAN JUAN INN [MOT] *San Juan Bautista*
SAN REMO HOTEL [HOT] *San Francisco*
SAN SIMEON PINES RESORT [MOT] *Cambria*

SANTA BARBARA INN [RST] *Santa Barbara*

SANTA MARIA INN [HOT] *Santa Maria*

SAN YSIDRO RANCH [RAN] *Santa Barbara*

SAVOY HOTEL [HOT] *San Francisco*

SCOTT COURTYARD [BB] *Calistoga*

SEA AND SAND INN [MOT] *Santa Cruz*

SEA CREST RESORT MOTEL [MOT] *Pismo Beach*

SEA GYPSY MOTEL [MOT] *Pismo Beach*

SEAL BEACH INN AND GARDENS, THE [BB] *Long Beach*

SEAL COVE INN [BB] *Half Moon Bay*

SEA LODGE OCEANFRONT HOTEL [MOT] *La Jolla (San Diego)*

SEA RANCH LODGE [HOT] *Gualala*

SEA VENTURE RESORT [MOT] *Pismo Beach*

SERRANO HOTEL [HOT] *San Francisco*

SEVEN GABLES INN [BB] *Pacific Grove*

SHADOW MOUNTAIN RESORT [RST] *Palm Desert*

SHANGRI-LA [HOT] *Santa Monica*

SHEEHAN [HOT] *San Francisco*

SHELTER POINTE HOTEL AND MARINA [RST] *San Diego*

SHERATON ANAHEIM HOTEL [HOT] *Anaheim*

SHERATON CONCORD HOTEL AND CONFERENCE CENTER [HOT] *Concord*

SHERATON FISHERMAN'S WHARF [HOT] *San Francisco*

SHERATON GATEWAY HOTEL LAX [HOT] *Los Angeles*

SHERATON GATEWAY HOTEL SAN FRANCISCO AIRPORT [HOT] *San Francisco Airport Area*

SHERATON HOTEL [HOT] *Buena Park*

SHERATON LOS ANGELES HARBOR [HOT] *San Pedro (L.A.)*

SHERATON ONTARIO AIRPORT HOTEL [HOT] *Ontario*

SHERATON PALO ALTO [HOT] *Palo Alto*

SHERATON PASADENA HOTEL [HOT] *Pasadena*

SHERATON RESORT & CONFERENCE CENTER [RST] *West Covina*

SHERATON SAN DIEGO HOTEL & MARINA [HOT] *San Diego*

SHERATON SAN JOSE [HOT] *San Jose*

SHERATON SUNNYVALE HOTEL [HOT] *Sunnyvale*

SHERATON UNIVERSAL HOTEL [HOT] *North Hollywood (L.A.)*

SHERIDAN INN [MOT] *Escondido*

SHERMAN HOUSE, THE [BB] *San Francisco*

SHERWOOD FOREST MOTEL [MOT] *Garberville*

SHILO HILLTOP SUITES [MOT] *Pomona*

SHILO INN [MOT] *Mammoth Lakes*

SHILO INN [MOT] *Palm Springs*

SHILO INN YOSEMITE [MOT] *Oakhurst*

SHORE HOUSE AT LAKE TAHOE [BB] *Tahoe Vista (Lake Tahoe Area)*

SHUTTERS ON THE BEACH [HOT] *Santa Monica*

SIERRA LODGE [MOT] *Three Rivers*

SILVERADO COUNTRY CLUB & RESORT [RST] *Napa*

SILVER MAPLE INN [MOT] *Bridgeport*

SILVER ROSE INN AND SPA [BB] *Calistoga*

SIMPSON HOUSE INN [BB] *Santa Barbara*

SINGING HILLS RESORT [RST] *El Cajon*

SIR FRANCIS DRAKE [HOT] *San Francisco*

SNOWGOOSE INN B&B [BB] *Mammoth Lakes*

SONOMA COAST VILLA INN & SPA [BB] *Bodega Bay*

SONOMA MISSION INN & SPA [RST] *Sonoma*

SPA HOTEL AND CASINO [RST] *Palm Springs*

SPALDING HOUSE, THE [BB] *Visalia*

SPENCER HOUSE [BB] *San Francisco*

SPINDRIFT INN [BB] *Monterey*

SPORTSMEN'S LODGE HOTEL [MOT] *Studio City (L.A.)*

SPYGLASS INN SHELL BEACH [MOT] *Pismo Beach*

SQUIBB HOUSE [BB] *Cambria*

STALLION SPRINGS [MOT] *Tehachapi*

STANFORD INN BY THE SEA, THE [BB] *Mendocino*

STANFORD PARK [MOT] *Menlo Park*

STANFORD TERRACE INN [MOT] *Palo Alto*
STANYAN PARK HOTEL [BB] *San Francisco*
STERLING HOTEL, THE [HOT] *Sacramento*
STONEHOUSE INN [BB] *Carmel*
STONEPINE ESTATE RESORT [BB] *Carmel Valley*
STOVEPIPE WELLS VILLAGE [MOT] *Death Valley National Park*
STRAWBERRY CREEK INN [BB] *Idyllwild*
STRAWBERRY VALLEY INN [MOT] *Mount Shasta*
SUITES AT FISHERMAN'S WHARF, THE [MOT] *San Francisco*
SUMMERFIELD SUITES BY WYNDHAM [AS] *Los Angeles*
SUMMERFIELD SUITES BY WYNDHAM [AS] *Los Angeles Intl Airport Area*
SUMMERFIELD SUITES BY WYNDHAM [AS] *San Jose*
SUMMERFIELD SUITES BY WYNDHAM [AS] *Sunnyvale*
SUMMERFIELD SUITES - TORRENCE/REDONDO BEACH [AS] *Torrance*
SUMMIT TRAVELODGE [MOT] *Tehachapi*
SUNDANCE VILLAS [CON] *Palm Springs*
SUNDOWNER INN [MOT] *Sunnyvale*
SUNSET HOUSE BED & BREAKFAST [BB] *Carmel*
SUNSET MARQUIS HOTEL & VILLAS [HOT] *Hollywood (L.A.)*
SUNSET TRAVELODGE [MOT] *Morro Bay*
SUPER 8 [MOT] *Bakersfield*
SUPER 8 [MOT] *Buena Park*
SUPER 8 [MOT] *Crescent City*
SUPER 8 [MOT] *Redlands*
SUPER 8 [MOT] *Santa Rosa*
SUPER 8 - HOLLYWOOD [MOT] *Los Angeles*
SUPER 8 LODGE [MOT] *Palm Springs*
SUPER 8 MOTEL [MOT] *Anaheim*
SUPER 8 MOTEL [MOT] *Sacramento*
SURF AND SAND HOTEL [HOT] *Laguna Beach*
SURF MOTEL [MOT] *Fort Bragg*
SUTTER CREEK INN [BB] *Jackson*
SUTTON PLACE HOTEL, THE [HOT] *Newport Beach*
SVENDSGAARD'S DANISH LODGE [BB] *Solvang*
SVENDSGAARDS INN [MOT] *Carmel*
SWISS HOLIDAY LODGE [MOT] *Mount Shasta*
SWITZERLAND HAUS BED AND BREAKFAST [BB] *Big Bear Lake*
TAHOE CHALET INN [MOT] *South Lake Tahoe (Lake Tahoe Area)*
TAHOE COLONY INN [HOT] *South Lake Tahoe (Lake Tahoe Area)*
TAHOE VISTA INN AND MARINA [BB] *Tahoe Vista (Lake Tahoe Area)*
TALLY HO INN [MOT] *Carmel*
TEMECULA CREEK INN [RST] *Temecula*
TENAYA LODGE AT YOSEMITE [RST] *Yosemite National Park*
TEN INVERNESS WAY [BB] *Inverness*
THATCHER INN & RESTAURANT [BB] *Ukiah*
THISTLE DEW [BB] *Sonoma*
THRIFTLODGE [MOT] *El Cajon*
TIBURON LODGE [HOT] *Tiburon*
TICKLE PINK COUNTRY INN CARMEL [MOT] *Carmel*
TIFFANY COUNTRY HOUSE [BB] *Santa Barbara*
TIMBER COVE INN [MOT] *Fort Ross State Historic Park*
TOLL HOUSE HOTEL [HOT] *Los Gatos*
TOWN AND COUNTRY RESORT & CONVENTION CENTER [CONF] *San Diego*
TOWN HOUSE INN [MOT] *Palo Alto*
TRADEWINDS LODGE [MOT] *Sacramento*
TRAVELODGE [MOT] *Anaheim*
TRAVELODGE [MOT] *Buena Park*
TRAVELODGE [MOT] *Hemet*
TRAVELODGE [MOT] *La Jolla (San Diego)*
TRAVELODGE [MOT] *Palm Springs*
TRAVELODGE [MOT] *San Diego*
TRAVELODGE [MOT] *San Diego*
TRAVELODGE [MOT] *San Francisco Airport Area*
TRAVELODGE [MOT] *Santa Barbara*
TRAVELODGE [MOT] *Santa Monica*
TRAVELODGE [MOT] *South Lake Tahoe (Lake Tahoe Area)*

TRAVELODGE [MOT] *South Lake Tahoe (Lake Tahoe Area)*
TRAVELODGE [MOT] *Tahoe City (Lake Tahoe Area)*
TRAVELODGE AT VAN NUYS [MOT] *Van Nuys (L.A.)*
TRAVELODGE HOTEL AT LAX AIRPORT [MOT] *Los Angeles*
TRAVELODGE SOUTH [MOT] *Bakersfield*
TRAVELODGE STATELINE [MOT] *South Lake Tahoe (Lake Tahoe Area)*
TRES PALMAS BED AND BREAKFAST [BB] *Palm Desert*
TROJAN HORSE [BB] *Sonoma*
TROPICANA INN AND SUITES [MOT] *Santa Barbara*
TRUCKEE HOTEL [BB] *Truckee*
TURRET HOUSE VICTORIAN BED AND BREAKFAST, THE [BB] *Long Beach*
TWIN DOLPHIN [MOT] *Morro Bay*
TWO BUNCH PALMS RESORT AND SPA [RST] *Desert Hot Springs*
UPHAM HOTEL & GARDEN COTTAGES [HOT] *Santa Barbara*
U.S. GRANT HOTEL [HOT] *San Diego*
VACATION INN [MOT] *El Centro*
VACATION INN HOTEL AND SUITE [MOT] *Palm Desert*
VACATION VILLAGE HOTEL [MOT] *Laguna Beach*
VAGABOND HOUSE INN [BB] *Carmel*
VAGABOND INN [MOT] *Chico*
VAGABOND INN [MOT] *Costa Mesa*
VAGABOND INN [MOT] *Glendale*
VAGABOND INN [MOT] *Modesto*
VAGABOND INN [MOT] *Palm Springs*
VAGABOND INN [MOT] *Sacramento*
VAGABOND INN [MOT] *Sacramento*
VAGABOND INN [MOT] *Salinas*
VAGABOND INN [MOT] *San Diego*
VAGABOND INN [MOT] *San Francisco*
VAGABOND INN [MOT] *Santa Clara*
VAGABOND INN [MOT] *Ventura*
VAGABOND INN [MOT] *Whittier*
VAGABOND INN [MOT] *Woodland Hills (L.A.)*
VENICE BEACH HOUSE [BB] *Santa Monica*
VENTANA INN & SPA [RST] *Big Sur*
VICHY HOT SPRINGS RESORT AND INN [RST] *Ukiah*
VICTORIAN GARDEN INN [BB] *Sonoma*
VICTORIAN INN ON THE PARK [BB] *San Francisco*
VILLA [MOT] *San Luis Obispo*
VILLA FLORENCE [HOT] *San Francisco*
VILLAGE INN, THE [MOT] *Carmel*
VILLAGIO INN & SPA [HOT] *Yountville*
VILLAGIO INN AND SPA [HOT] *Yountville*
VILLA HOTEL [MOT] *San Mateo*
VILLA INN [MOT] *San Rafael*
VILLA MOTEL [MOT] *Oroville*
VILLA ROSA INN [BB] *Santa Barbara*
VILLA ROYALE INN [BB] *Palm Springs*
VINEYARD COUNTRY INN [BB] *St. Helena*
VINTNERS INN [HOT] *Santa Rosa*
VISTA VILLA RESORT [RST] *Tahoe Vista (Lake Tahoe Area)*
VIZCAYA [BB] *Sacramento*
WALKER RIVER LODGE [MOT] *Bridgeport*
WARNER GARDENS MOTEL [MOT] *Woodland Hills (L.A.)*
WARWICK REGIS [HOT] *San Francisco*
WASHINGTON INN [HOT] *Oakland*
WASHINGTON SQUARE INN [BB] *San Francisco*
WATERFRONT PLAZA HOTEL [HOT] *Oakland*
WAWONA HOTEL [HOT] *Yosemite National Park*
WAYSIDE INN [BB] *Carmel*
WAY STATION INN [MOT] *Monterey*
WEDGEWOOD INN [BB] *Jackson*
WELK RESORT - SAN DIEGO [RST] *Escondido*
WESTCOAST HOTELS LONG BEACH [HOT] *Long Beach*
WESTCOAST SANTA CRUZ HOTEL [MOT] *Santa Cruz*
WESTGATE HOTEL, THE [HOT] *San Diego*
WESTIN [HOT] *Los Angeles*
WESTIN [HOT] *Palo Alto*
WESTIN [HOT] *San Francisco Airport Area*
WESTIN BONAVENTURE HOTEL, THE [HOT] *Los Angeles*

WESTIN HOTEL [HOT] *Santa Clara*
WESTIN HOTEL AT HORTON PLAZA [HOT] *San Diego*
WESTIN LONG BEACH [HOT] *Long Beach*
WESTIN MISSION HILLS [RST] *Palm Springs*
WESTIN SOUTH COAST PLAZA [HOT] *Costa Mesa*
WESTIN ST. FRANCIS, THE [HOT] *San Francisco*
WESTLAKE VILLAGE INN [BB] *Thousand Oaks*
WHALE WATCH INN BY THE SEA [BB] *Gualala*
WHARF INN [MOT] *San Francisco*
WHISPERING PINES LODGE [MOT] *Kernville*
WHITEGATE INN [BB] *Mendocino*
WHITE SULPHUR SPRINGS RETREAT AND SPA [RST] *St. Helena*
W HOTEL SAN FRANCISCO [HOT] *San Francisco*
WILDWOOD [CC] *Big Bear Lake*
WILLOWS HISTORIC PALM SPRINGS INN, THE [BB] *Palm Springs*
WILSHIRE HOTEL AND CENTRE [HOT] *Los Angeles*
WINE AND ROSES COUNTRY INN [BB] *Lodi*
WINE COUNTRY INN, THE [BB] *St. Helena*
WINE WAY INN [BB] *Calistoga*
WINNEDUMAH COUNTRY INN [BB] *Lone Pine*
W LOS ANGELES [HOT] *Los Angeles*
WOODCREST HOTEL [HOT] *Santa Clara*
WOODCREST INN [MOT] *Willows*
WOODLAND PARK MANOR [MOT] *Idyllwild*
W SUITES NEWARK [AS] *Fremont*
WYNDHAM BEL AGE HOTEL [AS] *Hollywood (L.A.)*
WYNDHAM CHECKERS [HOT] *Los Angeles*
WYNDHAM COMMERCE [HOT] *Los Angeles*
WYNDHAM EMERALD PLAZA [HOT] *San Diego*
WYNDHAM GARDEN HOTEL [HOT] *Pleasanton*
WYNDHAM GARDEN HOTEL - ORANGE COUNTY [HOT] *Costa Mesa*
WYNDHAM HOTEL [HOT] *San Jose*
WYNDHAM PALM SPRINGS [HOT] *Palm Springs*
WYNDHAM SAN DIEGO [HOT] *San Diego*
WYNDHAM SUNNYVALE [HOT] *Sunnyvale*
YORK HOTEL [HOT] *San Francisco*
YOSEMITE GATEWAY MOTEL [MOT] *Lee Vining*
YOSEMITE LODGE [MOT] *Yosemite National Park*
YOSEMITE RIVERSIDE INN [MOT] *Yosemite National Park*
YOSEMITE VIEW LODGE [MOT] *Yosemite National Park*
ZABALLA HOUSE [BB] *Half Moon Bay*
ZOSA GARDENS BED AND BREAKFAST [BB] *Escondido*

RESTAURANT LIST

Establishment names are listed in alphabetical order followed by a symbol identifying their classification and then city and state. The symbols for classification are: [RES] for Restaurants and [URD] for Unrated Dining Spots.

150 GRAND CAFE [RES] *Escondido*
1 PICO [RES] *Santa Monica*
21 OCEANFRONT [RES] *Newport Beach*
22ND STREET LANDING SEAFOOD [RES] *San Pedro (L.A.)*
42 DEGREES [RES] *San Francisco*
72 MARKET STREET OYSTER BAR AND GRILL [RES] *Los Angeles*
840 NORTH FIRST [RES] *San Jose*
ABALONETTI SEAFOOD TRATTORIA [RES] *Monterey*
ACCENTS [RES] *Newport Beach*
ACE WASABI'S ROCK AND ROLL SUSHI [RES] *San Francisco*
ACQUERELLO [RES] *San Francisco*
AESOP'S TABLES [URD] *San Diego*
AFGHANISTAN KHYBER PASS [RES] *San Diego*
AGO [RES] *Hollywood (L.A.)*
AJANTA [RES] *Berkeley*
A LA CARTE [URD] *Laguna Beach*
ALAMO SQUARE SEAFOOD GRILL [RES] *San Francisco*
ALBION RIVER INN [RES] *Mendocino*
ALBONA RISTORANTE ITALIANO [RES] *San Francisco*
ALEGRIA'S FOODS FROM SPAIN [RES] *San Francisco*
ALL SEASONS CAFE [RES] *Calistoga*
ALTO PALATO TRATTORIA [RES] *Los Angeles*
AMARIN [RES] *Monterey*
AMBER INDIA [RES] *Mountain View*
AMELIA'S [RES] *Newport Beach*
ANAHEIM WHITE HOUSE [RES] *Anaheim*
ANDERSEN'S [RES] *Solvang*
ANDRIA'S HARBORSIDE [RES] *Santa Barbara*
ANJOU [RES] *San Francisco*
ANNABELLE'S BAR AND BISTRO [RES] *San Francisco*
ANNA'S [RES] *Los Angeles*
ANNELIESE'S BAVARIAN INN [RES] *Long Beach*
ANTHONY'S FISH GROTTO [RES] *San Diego*
ANTICA TRATTORIA [RES] *San Francisco*
ANTON AND MICHEL [RES] *Carmel*
ANTONELLO [RES] *Santa Ana*
ANTONIO'S [RES] *Hollywood (L.A.)*
ANTONIO'S PIZZERIA & CABARET [RES] *Avalon (Catalina Island)*
ANZU [RES] *San Francisco*
APPLE FARM [RES] *San Luis Obispo*
APPLEWOOD [RES] *Guerneville*
AQUA [RES] *San Francisco*
ARMSTRONG'S FISH MARKET AND SEAFOOD [RES] *Avalon (Catalina Island)*
ARNIE MORTON'S OF CHICAGO [RES] *Los Angeles*
A. SABELLA'S [RES] *San Francisco*
ASHOKA [RES] *La Jolla (San Diego)*
ASIA DE CUBA [RES] *Hollywood (L.A.)*
ASIA SF [RES] *San Francisco*
ATHENS MARKET TAVERNA [RES] *San Diego*
A THOUSAND CRANES [RES] *Los Angeles*
AUBERGE DU SOLEIL [RES] *St. Helena*
AVENUE 9 [RES] *San Francisco*
AZIE [RES] *San Francisco*
AZUL [RES] *La Jolla (San Diego)*
AZZURA POINT [RES] *Coronado*
BACI [RES] *San Diego*
BACIO TRATTORIA [RES] *Woodland Hills (L.A.)*
BAILY WINE COUNTRY CAFE [RES] *Temecula*
BAKER STREET BISTRO [RES] *San Francisco*
BALBOA CAFE [RES] *San Francisco*

BANK OF MEXICAN FOOD [RES] *Temecula*
BARBARA'S AT THE BREWERY [RES] *Los Angeles*
BARBARA WORTH GOLF RESORT AND CONVENTION CENTER [RES] *El Centro*
BASIL [RES] *San Francisco*
BASTA PASTA [RES] *San Francisco*
BAYOU BAR AND GRILL [RES] *San Diego*
BAY VIEW [RES] *Bodega Bay*
BAY WOLF [RES] *Oakland*
BEACH HOUSE, THE [RES] *Santa Monica*
BEACH HOUSE INN [RES] *Laguna Beach*
BECKHAM GRILL [RES] *Pasadena*
BELGIAN LION [RES] *San Diego*
BELLA LUNA [RES] *San Diego*
BELLEFLEUR [RES] *Carlsbad*
BELVEDERE, THE [RES] *Beverly Hills*
BENBOW INN [RES] *Garberville*
BENIHANA [RES] *San Diego*
BERNARD'S [RES] *Borrego Springs*
BERNARD'S [RES] *Los Angeles*
BETELNUT PEJIU WU [RES] *San Francisco*
BIBA [RES] *Sacramento*
BIG FOUR [RES] *San Francisco*
BIG YELLOW HOUSE [RES] *Santa Barbara*
BIRD ROCK CAFE [RES] *La Jolla (San Diego)*
BISCUITS AND BLUES [RES] *San Francisco*
BISTRO 201 [RES] *Newport Beach*
BISTRO 45 [RES] *Pasadena*
BISTRO AIX [RES] *San Francisco*
BISTRO DON GIOVANNI [RES] *Napa*
BISTRO JEANTY [RES] *Yountville*
BISTRO RALPH [RES] *Healdsburg*
BITTERSWEET BISTRO [RES] *Santa Cruz*
BIX [RES] *San Francisco*
BIZOU [RES] *San Francisco*
BLUE CHALK CAFE [RES] *Palo Alto*
BLUE COYOTE [RES] *Palm Springs*
BLUE PARROT [RES] *Avalon (Catalina Island)*
BLUE POINT [RES] *San Diego*
BLUE SHARK BISTRO [RES] *Santa Barbara*
BLUE WHALE LAKESIDE RESTAURANT [RES] *Big Bear Lake*
BOB BURNS [RES] *Santa Monica*
BOBBY RUBINO'S [RES] *San Francisco*
BOCCA ROTIS [RES] *San Francisco*
BONTA RISTORANTE [RES] *San Francisco*
BORDER GRILL [RES] *Santa Monica*
BOUCHON [RES] *Santa Barbara*
BOUCHON [RES] *Yountville*
BOULEVARD [RES] *San Francisco*
BRAMBLES DINNER HOUSE, THE [RES] *Cambria*
BRANNAN'S GRILL [RES] *Calistoga*
BRASSERIE SAVOY [RES] *San Francisco*
BRAVA TERRACE [RES] *St. Helena*
BRIDGES [RES] *Walnut Creek*
BRIGANTINE [RES] *Coronado*
BRIGANTINE, THE [RES] *San Diego*
BRIGITTE'S [RES] *Santa Barbara*
BRITANNIA ARMS PUB & RESTAURANT [RES] *Carmel*
BRIX [RES] *Yountville*
BROADWAY BAR AND GRILL [RES] *Santa Monica*
BROADWAY DELI [RES] *Santa Monica*
BROCKTON VILLA [RES] *La Jolla (San Diego)*
BUCCI'S [RES] *Oakland*
BUCKEYE ROADHOUSE [RES] *Mill Valley*
BUNGALOW, THE [RES] *Corona del Mar*
BUONA SERA [RES] *Petaluma*
BUON GIORNO [RES] *Chula Vista*
BUSALACCHI'S [RES] *San Diego*
BUTCHER SHOP [RES] *Chula Vista*
CABERNET BISTRO [RES] *Solvang*
CA BIANCA ITALIAN RESTAURANT [RES] *Santa Rosa*
CA'BREA [RES] *Los Angeles*
CACTI [RES] *San Rafael*
CAFE ABREGO [RES] *Monterey*
CAFE AT SONOMA MISSION INN [RES] *Sonoma*
CAFE BASTILLE [RES] *San Francisco*
CAFE BEAUJOLAIS [RES] *Mendocino*
CAFE BERNARDO [RES] *Davis*
CAFE BIZOU [RES] *Studio City (L.A.)*
CAFE CHAMPAGNE [RES] *Temecula*
CAFE CITTI [RES] *Santa Rosa*
CAFE COYOTE [RES] *San Diego*

CAFE DE LA PRESSE [RES] *San Francisco*
CAFE DES ARTISTES [RES] *Los Angeles*
CAFE FINA [RES] *Monterey*
CAFE JAPENGO [RES] *La Jolla (San Diego)*
CAFE KATI [RES] *San Francisco*
CAFE KINYON [RES] *Yountville*
CAFE LAHAYE [RES] *Sonoma*
CAFE LUCY - LE PETITE BISTRO [URD] *Napa*
CAFE MARIMBA [RES] *San Francisco*
CAFE PACIFICA [RES] *San Diego*
CAFE PESCATORE [RES] *San Francisco*
CAFE PINOT [RES] *Los Angeles*
CAFE ROMA [RES] *San Luis Obispo*
CAFE ROUGE [RES] *Berkeley*
CAFE SANTORINI [RES] *Pasadena*
CAFE SPARROW [RES] *Santa Cruz*
CAFE TIRAMISU [RES] *San Francisco*
CAFFE NAPOLI [RES] *Carmel*
CALIFORNIA CAFE [RES] *Corte Madera*
CALIFORNIA CUISINE [RES] *San Diego*
CALISTOGA INN [RES] *Calistoga*
CAMPANILE [RES] *Los Angeles*
CAMPTON PLACE DINING ROOM [RES] *San Francisco*
CAPRICCIO RISTORANTE ITALIANO [RES] *Los Angeles*
CAPTAIN JON'S [RES] *Tahoe Vista (Lake Tahoe Area)*
CARNELIAN ROOM [RES] *San Francisco*
CARTA [RES] *San Francisco*
CASA DE BANDINI [RES] *San Diego*
CASANOVA [RES] *Carmel*
CASK 'N CLEAVER [RES] *Fallbrook*
CASSELL'S [URD] *Los Angeles*
CATAHOULA [RES] *Calistoga*
CAT AND THE CUSTARD CUP [RES] *La Habra*
CATCH, THE [RES] *Anaheim*
CATELLI'S THE REX [RES] *Healdsburg*
CAVA [RES] *Los Angeles*
CEDAR CREEK INN [RES] *Laguna Beach*
CEDAR CREEK INN [RES] *Palm Desert*
CEDAR CREEK INN [RES] *Palm Springs*
CELADON [RES] *Napa*
CELLAR, THE [RES] *Fullerton*
CEZANNE [RES] *Santa Monica*
CHA CHA CHA [RES] *San Francisco*
CHAMELEON CAFE [RES] *Coronado*
CHANNEL HOUSE [RES] *Avalon (Catalina Island)*
CHANTECLAIR [RES] *Irvine*
CHANTERELLE [RES] *Napa*
CHANTERELLE [RES] *Sacramento*
CHARISMA CAFE [RES] *Los Angeles*
CHARLES NOB HILL [RES] *San Francisco*
CHARLES STREET DINNER HOUSE [RES] *Yosemite National Park*
CHART HOUSE [RES] *Monterey*
CHATEAU CHANG [RES] *Victorville*
CHATEAU ORLEANS [RES] *Pacific Beach (San Diego)*
CHATEAU SOUVERAIN [RES] *Healdsburg*
CHATTER BOX CAFE [URD] *Jackson*
CHAYA [RES] *San Francisco*
CHAYA BRASSERIE [RES] *Hollywood (L.A.)*
CHAYA VENICE [RES] *Santa Monica*
CHECKERS [RES] *Los Angeles*
CHEF PAUL'S [RES] *Oakland*
CHEZ LOMA [RES] *Coronado*
CHEZ MICHEL [RES] *San Francisco*
CHEZ PANISSE RESTAURANT AND CAFE [RES] *Berkeley*
CHEZ SATEAU [RES] *Arcadia*
CHEZ T.J. [RES] *Mountain View*
CHIANTI CUCINA [RES] *Los Angeles*
CHIANTI RISTORANTE AND CUCINA [RES] *Los Angeles*
CHICAGO JOE'S [RES] *Irvine*
CHIC'S SEAFOOD [RES] *San Francisco*
CHIEU-ANH [RES] *San Diego*
CHIMAYO GRILL [RES] *Newport Beach*
CHINOIS ON MAIN [RES] *Santa Monica*
CHOW [RES] *San Francisco*
CHRISTINE [RES] *Torrance*
CIAO BELLA [RES] *Riverside*
CIAO TRATTORIA [RES] *Los Angeles*
CIBO RISTORANTE ITALIANO [RES] *Monterey*
CICADA [RES] *Los Angeles*
CIELO BIG SUR [RES] *Big Sur*
CIN CIN [RES] *Calistoga*
CITRONELLE [RES] *Santa Barbara*

CITRUS [RES] *Hollywood (L.A.)*
CITY DELICATESSEN [URD] *San Diego*
CITY HOTEL [RES] *Sonora*
CITYSCAPE [RES] *San Francisco*
CIUDAD [RES] *Los Angeles*
CLIFF HOUSE [RES] *San Francisco*
CLUB XIX [RES] *Pebble Beach*
COFFEE TREE [RES] *Vacaville*
COMPADRES [RES] *Yountville*
CORRIGAN'S STEAK HOUSE [RES] *Thousand Oaks*
CORVETTE DINER [URD] *San Diego*
COSMOS GRILL & ROTISSERIE [RES] *Woodland Hills (L.A.)*
COTTAGE, THE [RES] *La Jolla (San Diego)*
COTTAGE, THE [RES] *Laguna Beach*
COTTAGE RESTAURANT [RES] *Carmel*
CRAB CATCHER [RES] *La Jolla (San Diego)*
CRESCENT SHORES GRILL [RES] *La Jolla (San Diego)*
CRICKLEWOOD [RES] *Santa Rosa*
CROCE'S [RES] *San Diego*
CROCODILE CAFE [RES] *Pasadena*
CROWN ROOM [RES] *Coronado*
CROW'S NEST [RES] *Santa Cruz*
CRUSTACEAN [RES] *Beverly Hills*
CUISTOT [RES] *Palm Desert*
CYPRESS CLUB [RES] *San Francisco*
CYPRESS GROVE [RES] *Pacific Grove*
DAILY'S FIT AND FRESH [URD] *La Jolla (San Diego)*
DAKOTA GRILL AND SPIRITS [RES] *San Diego*
D AND E'S [RES] *Borrego Springs*
DAN TANA'S [RES] *Hollywood (L.A.)*
D'ANTONIO'S RISTORANTE [RES] *Pomona*
DA PASQUALE CAFE [RES] *Beverly Hills*
DATTILO [RES] *Hemet*
DAVID'S [URD] *San Francisco*
DA VINCI [RES] *Beverly Hills*
DELFINA [RES] *San Francisco*
DELICIAS [RES] *Rancho Santa Fe*
DELLA SANTINA'S [RES] *Sonoma*
DELMONICO'S SEAFOOD GRILLE [RES] *Los Angeles*
DEPOT [RES] *Oroville*
DEPOT [RES] *Torrance*
DEPOT HOTEL CUCINA RUSTICA, THE [RES] *Sonoma*
DERBY, THE [RES] *Arcadia*
DE SCHMIRE [RES] *Petaluma*
DEUCE [RES] *Sonoma*
DIAGHILEV [RES] *Los Angeles*
DICK'S LAST RESORT [URD] *San Diego*
DINER, THE [RES] *Yountville*
DINING ROOM, THE [RES] *Beverly Hills*
DINING ROOM, THE [RES] *Laguna Beach*
DINING ROOM, THE [RES] *Marina del Rey*
DINING ROOM, THE [RES] *Palm Springs*
DINING ROOM, THE [RES] *San Francisco*
DIVA [RES] *Costa Mesa*
DOBSON'S [RES] *San Diego*
DOMAINE CHANDON [RES] *Yountville*
DOMENICO'S [RES] *Monterey*
DONA ESTER [RES] *San Juan Bautista*
DOTTIE'S TRUE BLUE CAFE [URD] *San Francisco*
DOWNEY'S [RES] *Santa Barbara*
DRAGO [RES] *Santa Monica*
DRAGON FLY [RES] *Corte Madera*
DUCK CLUB [RES] *Bodega Bay*
DUCK CLUB [RES] *Menlo Park*
DUCK CLUB, THE [RES] *Monterey*
DUCK CLUB [RES] *Walnut Creek*
D.Z. AKIN'S [URD] *San Diego*
EAGLES NEST [RES] *Merced*
E AND O TRADING CO. [RES] *San Francisco*
ED DEBEVIC'S [URD] *Beverly Hills*
EDGEWATER GRILL [RES] *San Diego*
EL ADOBE DE CAPISTRANO [RES] *San Juan Capistrano*
EL BIZCOCHO [RES] *San Diego*
EL CHOLO [RES] *Los Angeles*
EL EMBARCADERO [RES] *San Diego*
EL ENCANTO DINING ROOM [RES] *Santa Barbara*
EL FAROLITO [RES] *Healdsburg*
EL INDIO MEXICAN [URD] *San Diego*
ELISABETH DANIEL [RES] *San Francisco*
ELIZA [RES] *San Francisco*
EL PASEO [RES] *Santa Barbara*

EL TAPATIO [RES] *Lancaster*
EL TOREADOR [RES] *San Francisco*
EL TORITO [RES] *Monterey*
EL TORITO [RES] *Oakland*
EL TORITO GRILL [RES] *Costa Mesa*
EL TORITO GRILL [RES] *Newport Beach*
EMILE'S [RES] *San Jose*
EMPRESS OF CHINA [RES] *San Francisco*
ENGINE CO. NO. 28 [RES] *Los Angeles*
ENRICO'S SIDEWALK CAFE [RES] *San Francisco*
EOS [RES] *San Francisco*
EPAZOTE [RES] *Del Mar*
EQUUS [RES] *Santa Rosa*
ERNA'S ELDERBERRY HOUSE [RES] *Oakhurst*
EULIPA [RES] *San Jose*
EUROCHOW [RES] *Los Angeles*
EUROPA [RES] *Palm Springs*
EVANS AMERICAN GOURMET CAFE [RES] *South Lake Tahoe (Lake Tahoe Area)*
EVVIA [RES] *Palo Alto*
FABIANI [RES] *Santa Rosa*
FAIROUZ CAFE AND GALLERY [RES] *San Diego*
FANDANGO [RES] *Pacific Grove*
FARALLON [RES] *San Francisco*
FAR NIENTE [RES] *Glendale*
FATTOUSH [RES] *San Francisco*
FAZ [RES] *San Francisco*
FELIX AND LOUIE'S [RES] *Healdsburg*
FENIX [RES] *Hollywood (L.A.)*
FIFTH FLOOR [RES] *San Francisco*
FIGARO [RES] *San Francisco*
FINO [RES] *San Francisco*
FIOR D'ITALIA [RES] *San Francisco*
FIO'S [RES] *San Diego*
FIREFLY [RES] *San Francisco*
FIREHOUSE [RES] *Sacramento*
FIREHOUSE GRILL [RES] *Bishop*
FIRST CRUSH [RES] *San Francisco*
FISH COMPANY [RES] *Santa Monica*
FISH MARKET [RES] *Del Mar*
FISHWIFE [RES] *Pacific Grove*
FIVE CROWNS [RES] *Corona del Mar*
FIVE FEET RESTAURANT [RES] *Laguna Beach*
FLEMING'S PRIME STEAKHOUSE & WINE BAR [RES] *San Diego*
FLEMING'S STEAKHOUSE [RES] *Newport Beach*
FLEUR DE LYS [RES] *San Francisco*
FLOWER DRUM [RES] *Palm Springs*
FLYING FISH GRILL - KENNY'S [RES] *Carmel*
FLY TRAP [RES] *San Francisco*
F. MCCLINTOCK'S [RES] *Pismo Beach*
F. MCCLINTOCK'S SALOON [RES] *Paso Robles*
FOG CITY DINER [RES] *San Francisco*
FOREIGN CINEMA [RES] *San Francisco*
FORGE IN THE FOREST AND GENERAL STORE, THE [RES] *Carmel*
FORTUNE COOKIE [RES] *San Diego*
FOUNTAIN COURT [RES] *San Francisco*
FOURNOU'S OVENS [RES] *San Francisco*
FOUR OAKS [RES] *Los Angeles*
FOXFIRE [RES] *Anaheim*
FRANCISCAN [RES] *San Francisco*
FRANK FAT'S [RES] *Sacramento*
FRANTOIO [RES] *Mill Valley*
FRASCATI [RES] *San Francisco*
FRED 62 [URD] *Los Angeles*
FRENCH LAUNDRY, THE [RES] *Yountville*
FRENCH MARKET GRILLE [RES] *San Diego*
FRENCH PASTRY SHOP [URD] *La Jolla (San Diego)*
FRENCH POODLE [RES] *Carmel*
FRESH CREAM [RES] *Monterey*
FRESH KETCH [RES] *South Lake Tahoe (Lake Tahoe Area)*
FRIAR TUCK'S [RES] *Nevada City*
FRINGALE [RES] *San Francisco*
FUNG LUM [RES] *San Jose*
FUSILLI RISTORANTE [RES] *Fairfield*
GABBIANO'S [RES] *San Francisco*
GALLEY [RES] *Morro Bay*
GARDENS [RES] *Los Angeles*
GAR WOODS GRILL & PIER [RES] *Tahoe Vista (Lake Tahoe Area)*
GARY CHU'S [RES] *Santa Rosa*
GARY DANKO [RES] *San Francisco*
GASTROGNOME [RES] *Idyllwild*
GAYLORD INDIA [RES] *San Francisco*
GENERAL'S DAUGHTER [RES] *Sonoma*

GEOFFREY'S [RES] *Malibu*
GEORGE'S [RES] *Fresno*
GEORGE'S AT THE COVE [RES] *La Jolla (San Diego)*
GERARD'S [RES] *Riverside*
GERNOT'S VICTORIA HOUSE [RES] *Pacific Grove*
GILBERT'S SEAFOOD GRILL [RES] *Santa Cruz*
GINGER ISLAND [RES] *Berkeley*
GINZA SUSHIKO [RES] *Beverly Hills*
GIOVANNI'S [RES] *San Rafael*
GIRASOLE [RES] *Pleasanton*
GIRL & THE FIG, THE [RES] *Sonoma*
GLEN ELLEN INN [RES] *Sonoma*
GLISSANDI [RES] *Tahoe City (Lake Tahoe Area)*
GLOBE [RES] *San Francisco*
GOLDEN TRUFFLE [RES] *Costa Mesa*
GOLDEN TURTLE [RES] *San Francisco*
GORDON'S HOUSE OF FINE EATS [RES] *San Francisco*
GRAND CAFE [RES] *Los Angeles*
GRAND CAFE [RES] *San Francisco*
GRANDEHO'S MAMEKYO [RES] *San Francisco*
GRANITA [RES] *Malibu*
GRANT GRILL [RES] *San Diego*
GRAY WHALE PUB AND PIZZERIA [RES] *Inverness*
GRAZIANO'S [RES] *Petaluma*
GREAT GREEK, THE [RES] *Studio City (L.A.)*
GREAT WALL [RES] *Palm Springs*
GREEK CORNER [URD] *San Diego*
GREEN FLASH [RES] *Pacific Beach (San Diego)*
GREENS [RES] *San Francisco*
GREYSTONE [RES] *St. Helena*
GREYSTONE - THE STEAKHOUSE [RES] *San Diego*
GRILL, THE [RES] *Pasadena*
GRILL ON OCEAN AVENUE [RES] *Carmel*
GRILL ON THE ALLEY [RES] *Beverly Hills*
GRILL ON THE ALLEY, THE [RES] *San Jose*
GUAYMAS [RES] *Tiburon*
GUSTAF ANDERS [RES] *Santa Ana*
GUSTAV'S JAGERHAUS [RES] *Anaheim*
HABANA [RES] *Costa Mesa*
HAMILTON'S [RES] *Palm Desert*
HANSA HOUSE SMORGASBORD [RES] *Anaheim*
HARBOR AND LONGBOARD'S GRILL [RES] *Santa Barbara*
HARBOR HOUSE [RES] *San Diego*
HARBOR VIEW GROTTO [RES] *Crescent City*
HARD ROCK CAFE [URD] *Los Angeles*
HARRIS' [RES] *San Francisco*
HAWTHORNE LANE [RES] *San Francisco*
HAYES STREET GRILL [RES] *San Francisco*
HEADQUARTER HOUSE [RES] *Auburn*
HELMAND [RES] *San Francisco*
HEMINGWAY'S [RES] *Sonora*
HOBBIT [RES] *Orange*
HOB NOB HILL [RES] *San Diego*
HOG'S BREATH INN [RES] *Carmel*
HOLLYWOOD HILLS COFFEE SHOP [URD] *Hollywood (L.A.)*
HORIZONS [RES] *Sausalito*
HOUSE [RES] *San Francisco*
HOUSE [RES] *San Francisco*
HOUSE OF PRIME RIB [RES] *San Francisco*
HUGO MOLINA [RES] *Pasadena*
HUMP, THE [RES] *Santa Monica*
HUMPHREY'S BY THE BAY [RES] *San Diego*
HUNAN [RES] *San Francisco*
HUNGRY BEAR [RES] *Needles*
HYDRO BAR AND GRILL [RES] *Calistoga*
IDLE SPURS STEAK HOUSE [RES] *Barstow*
I FRATELLI [RES] *San Francisco*
IL CIELO [RES] *Beverly Hills*
IL FORNAIO [RES] *Corte Madera*
IL FORNAIO [RES] *Del Mar*
IL FORNAIO [RES] *Los Angeles*
IL FORNAIO CUCINA ITALIANO [RES] *Carmel*
IL PASTAIO [RES] *Beverly Hills*
IL PESCATORE [RES] *Oakland*
IMPERIAL DYNASTY [RES] *Hanford*
IMPERIAL HOUSE [RES] *San Diego*
INDIAN SUMMER [RES] *Monterey*
INDIGO [RES] *San Francisco*
INDOCHINE [RES] *Hollywood (L.A.)*
INFUSION [RES] *San Francisco*
INN DINING ROOM [RES] *Death Valley National Park*

INYO COUNTRY STORE AND RESTAURANT [RES] *Bishop*
ISOBUNE [URD] *San Francisco*
ITRI [RES] *San Diego*
IVY, THE [RES] *Los Angeles*
IZZY ORTEGA'S [RES] *San Luis Obispo*
JACK AND GIULIO'S [RES] *San Diego*
JACK'S BISTRO [RES] *Oakland*
JAKE'S DEL MAR [RES] *Del Mar*
JARDINES DE SAN JUAN [RES] *San Juan Bautista*
JARDINIERE [RES] *San Francisco*
JASMINE [RES] *San Diego*
JILLIAN'S [RES] *Palm Desert*
JIRAFFE [RES] *Santa Monica*
JOE GREENSLEEVES [RES] *Redlands*
JOE'S [RES] *Santa Monica*
JOHN ASH & CO [RES] *Santa Rosa*
JOHNNY MCNALL'S FAIRVIEW LODGE [RES] *Kernville*
JOHN PISTO'S WHALING STATION [RES] *Monterey*
JONESY'S FAMOUS STEAK HOUSE [RES] *Napa*
JOSEF'S [RES] *Santa Rosa*
JOVANNA'S BISTRO GRILL [RES] *Palm Desert*
JOZU [RES] *Hollywood (L.A.)*
J. TAYLOR'S [RES] *Del Mar*
JULIUS CASTLE [RES] *San Francisco*
JUST DESSERTS [URD] *San Francisco*
KABOTO SUSHI [RES] *San Francisco*
KAISER GRILLE [RES] *Palm Desert*
KARL STRAUSS' BREWERY AND GRILL [RES] *San Diego*
KASBAH [RES] *San Rafael*
KASS BAH [RES] *Los Angeles*
KATIA'S RUSSIAN TEA ROOM [RES] *San Francisco*
KELLY'S STEAKHOUSE [RES] *San Diego*
KENWOOD [RES] *Santa Rosa*
KHAN TOKE THAI HOUSE [RES] *San Francisco*
KING'S FISH HOUSE [RES] *Laguna Beach*
KING'S FISH HOUSE [RES] *Long Beach*
KIRBY'S CREEKSIDE [RES] *Nevada City*
KNOLL'S BLACK FOREST INN [RES] *Santa Monica*
KOKKARI [RES] *San Francisco*
KOTO [RES] *Newport Beach*
KULETO'S [RES] *San Francisco*
KULETO'S [RES] *San Francisco Airport Area*
KYO YA [RES] *San Francisco*
LA BODEGA [URD] *San Francisco*
LA BOHEME [RES] *Carmel*
LA BOHEME [RES] *Hollywood (L.A.)*
LA BOUCANE [RES] *Napa*
LA BRASSERIE [RES] *Orange*
LA BRUSCHETTA [RES] *La Jolla (San Diego)*
LA CACHETTE [RES] *Los Angeles*
LA CASA [RES] *Sonoma*
LA FAYETTE [RES] *Garden Grove*
LA FOLIE [RES] *San Francisco*
LA GALLERIA [RES] *Santa Clara*
LA GARE [RES] *Santa Rosa*
LA GOLONDRINA MEXICAN CAFE [RES] *Los Angeles*
LALIME'S CAFE [RES] *Berkeley*
LA LOGGIA [RES] *Studio City (L.A.)*
LA MARINA [RES] *Santa Barbara*
LA MERE MICHELLE [RES] *Saratoga*
L'AMIE DONIA [RES] *Palo Alto*
LAMONT ST GRILL [RES] *Pacific Beach (San Diego)*
L'ANGOLO [RES] *Hollywood (L.A.)*
LA PALOMA [RES] *Oceanside*
LA PALOMA [RES] *Santa Clara*
LA PARISIENNE [RES] *Arcadia*
LA PASTAIA [RES] *San Jose*
LA PAVILION AT RAMS HILL [RES] *Borrego Springs*
LAPIS [RES] *San Francisco*
LA QUINTA CLIFFHOUSE [RES] *Palm Desert*
LARK CREEK [RES] *San Mateo*
LARK CREEK [RES] *Walnut Creek*
LARK CREEK INN [RES] *Corte Madera*
LAS BRISAS DE LAGUNA [RES] *Laguna Beach*
LA SCALA [RES] *Beverly Hills*
LAS CASUELAS NUEVAS [RES] *Palm Springs*
LAS CASUELAS TERRAZA [RES] *Palm Springs*
LA SERENATA DE GARBALDI [RES] *Santa Monica*
LA SERENATA DE GARIBALDI [RES] *Los Angeles*
L'AUBERGE [RES] *Ojai*

LAUREL [RES] *San Diego*
LA VACHE AND COMPANY [RES] *San Diego*
LAVANDE [RES] *Santa Monica*
LA VIE [RES] *San Francisco*
LA VIE EN ROSE [RES] *Fullerton*
LAWRY'S THE PRIME RIB [RES] *Beverly Hills*
LE BEAUJOLAIS [RES] *Redondo Beach*
LE BISTRO [RES] *Stockton*
LE CHARM [RES] *San Francisco*
LE COLONIAL [RES] *Hollywood (L.A.)*
LE COQ D'OR [RES] *Carmel*
LE DOME [RES] *Los Angeles*
LE DONNE CUCINA ITALIANA [RES] *Palm Desert*
LE FOUNTAINEBLEAU [RES] *San Diego*
LEFT AT ALBUQUERQUE [RES] *Santa Barbara*
LEFT BANK [RES] *Menlo Park*
LEMON GRASS [RES] *Sacramento*
LE MOUTON NOIR [RES] *Saratoga*
LE PAON [RES] *Palm Desert*
LE PETIT FOUR [RES] *Hollywood (L.A.)*
LE PETIT PIER [RES] *Tahoe Vista (Lake Tahoe Area)*
LE POT AU FEU [RES] *Menlo Park*
LE SAINT GERMAIN [RES] *Palm Desert*
LE SANGLIER FRENCH RESTAURANT [RES] *Woodland Hills (L.A.)*
LES DEUX CAFES [RES] *Hollywood (L.A.)*
LES FRERESTAIX [RES] *Los Angeles*
LE VALLAURIS [RES] *Palm Springs*
LG'S PRIME STEAKHOUSE [RES] *Palm Desert*
L'HIRONDELLE [RES] *San Juan Capistrano*
LIDO DI [RES] *Los Angeles*
LINO'S [RES] *San Diego*
LINQ [RES] *Los Angeles*
LINTON'S RESTAURANT & LOUNGE [RES] *Solvang*
LISA HEMENWAY'S BISTRO [RES] *Santa Rosa*
LITTLE NAPOLI [RES] *Carmel*
LIVE FIRE RESTAURANT [RES] *San Francisco*
LIVE FIRE RESTAURANT [RES] *Yountville*
LOBSTER, THE [RES] *Santa Monica*
LOCANDA VENETA [RES] *Los Angeles*
LOLA'S [RES] *Hollywood (L.A.)*
LOLLI'S CASTAGNOLA [RES] *San Francisco*
L'OPERA RISTORANTE [RES] *Long Beach*
L'ORANGERIE [RES] *Hollywood (L.A.)*
LORNA'S ITALIAN KITCHEN [URD] *San Diego*
LOS GATOS BREWING COMPANY [RES] *Los Gatos*
LOTUS [RES] *Healdsburg*
LOTUS GARDEN [RES] *San Bernardino*
LOU LA BONTE'S [RES] *Auburn*
LOU'S VILLAGE [RES] *San Jose*
LUCA'S WHARF [RES] *Bodega Bay*
LUCQUES [RES] *Los Angeles*
LUGANO SWISS BISTRO [RES] *Carmel*
LULU [RES] *San Francisco*
LYON'S [RES] *Placerville*
LYONS ENGLISH GRILLE [RES] *Palm Springs*
MACARTHUR PARK [RES] *San Francisco*
MADEO [RES] *Los Angeles*
MADRONA MANOR [RES] *Healdsburg*
MAGIC LAMP INN [RES] *Rancho Cucamonga*
MAISON AKIRA [URD] *Pasadena*
MAMA TOSCA'S [RES] *Bakersfield*
MANDARIN, THE [RES] *Beverly Hills*
MANDARIN [RES] *San Francisco*
MANGIAFUCCO [RES] *San Francisco*
MANGIAMO [RES] *Los Angeles*
MANHATTAN [RES] *La Jolla (San Diego)*
MANHATTAN BAR AND GRILL [RES] *Los Angeles*
MANKA'S INVERNESS LODGE [RES] *Inverness*
MANZELLA'S SEAFOOD LOFT [RES] *Hayward*
MAPLE DRIVE [RES] *Beverly Hills*
MARINE ROOM [RES] *La Jolla (San Diego)*
MARINUS [RES] *Carmel Valley*
MARIO'S CAFE [URD] *San Francisco*
MARKET BROILER [RES] *Riverside*
MARK'S [RES] *Laguna Beach*
MARRAKECH MOROCCAN [RES] *San Francisco*
MASA'S [RES] *San Francisco*
MASSIMI'S RISTORANTE [RES] *Solvang*
MATSUHISA [RES] *Beverly Hills*

MAYA [RES] *San Francisco*
MAZZINI TARTTORIA [RES] *Berkeley*
MC2 [RES] *San Francisco*
MCCORMICK AND KULETO'S [RES] *San Francisco*
MCCORMICK & SCHMICK'S - BEVERLY HILLS [RES] *Beverly Hills*
MCCORMICK AND SCHMICK'S [RES] *Irvine*
MCCORMICK & SCHMICK SEAFOOD [RES] *Los Angeles*
MCCORMICK AND SCHMICK'S [RES] *Los Angeles Intl Airport Area*
MCCORMICK & SCHMICK SEAFOOD [RES] *Pasadena*
MECCA [RES] *San Francisco*
MEDIEVAL TIMES DINNER AND TOURNAMENT [URD] *Buena Park*
MEETING HOUSE [RES] *San Francisco*
MELISSE [RES] *Santa Monica*
MELVYN'S [RES] *Palm Springs*
MEMPHIS SOUL CAFE [RES] *Costa Mesa*
MES TROIS FILLES [RES] *Sonoma*
MEXICAN VILLAGE [RES] *Coronado*
MICHAEL'S [RES] *Santa Monica*
MIFUNE [URD] *San Francisco*
MIKAYLA [RES] *Sausalito*
MILLE FLEURS [RES] *Rancho Santa Fe*
MI PIACE [RES] *Burbank*
MI PIACE [RES] *Pasadena*
MISSION RANCH [RES] *Carmel*
MISTRAL [RES] *Santa Rosa*
MIXX [RES] *San Diego*
MIXX-AN AMERICAN BISTRO [RES] *Santa Rosa*
MIYAKO [RES] *Pasadena*
MOJO [RES] *Los Angeles*
MOJO [RES] *Westwood Village (L.A.)*
MOLLERKROEN [RES] *Solvang*
MONEY PANCHO [RES] *Camarillo*
MONEY PANCHO [RES] *Oxnard*
MONTANA'S AMERICAN GRILL [RES] *San Diego*
MONTEREY BAY CANNERS [RES] *West Covina*
MONTRIO [RES] *Monterey*
MOON'S [RES] *Quincy*
MOONSHADOWS [RES] *Malibu*
MOOSE'S [RES] *San Francisco*
MORTON'S [RES] *Los Angeles*
MORTON'S [RES] *Los Angeles*
MORTON'S OF CHICAGO [RES] *Sacramento*
MORTON'S OF CHICAGO [RES] *San Francisco*
MO'S GOURMET HAMBURGERS [URD] *San Francisco*
MOSS BEACH DISTILLERY [RES] *Half Moon Bay*
MOUNTAIN HOME INN [RES] *Mill Valley*
M POINT SUSHI BAR AND GRILL [RES] *San Francisco*
MR. CHOW [RES] *Beverly Hills*
MR STOX [RES] *Anaheim*
MUDD'S [RES] *Walnut Creek*
MULBERRY STREET [RES] *Fullerton*
MUM'S [RES] *Long Beach*
MUM'S VEGETARIAN [RES] *Sacramento*
MURRAY'S [RES] *San Francisco*
MUSSO & FRANK GRILL [RES] *Hollywood (L.A.)*
MUSTARD SEED [RES] *Solvang*
MUSTARD'S GRILL [RES] *Yountville*
NAPA VALLEY GRILLE [RES] *Yountville*
NAPA VALLEY WINE TRAIN [RES] *Napa*
NATIONAL HOTEL VICTORIAN DINING ROOM [RES] *Nevada City*
NATI'S [RES] *San Diego*
NEO [RES] *San Francisco*
NEPENTHE [RES] *Big Sur*
NEPHELE'S [RES] *South Lake Tahoe (Lake Tahoe Area)*
NEST [RES] *Palm Desert*
NEW GOLDEN TURTLE [RES] *San Francisco*
NEWPORT BEACH BREWING COMPANY [RES] *Newport Beach*
NICK & STEF'S [RES] *Los Angeles*
NICK'S AT THE BEACH [RES] *San Diego*
NOB HILL [RES] *San Francisco*
NOB HILL [RES] *San Francisco*
NOBU [RES] *Malibu*
NORTH BEACH [RES] *San Francisco*
NORTH INDIA [RES] *San Francisco*
OB'S PUB & RESTAURANT [RES] *Truckee*

OCEAN AVENUE SEAFOOD [RES] *Santa Monica*
OCEAN FRONT [RES] *Santa Monica*
O CHAME [RES] *Berkeley*
OFF VINE [URD] *Los Angeles*
OLD BATH HOUSE [RES] *Pacific Grove*
OLD MEXICO EAST [RES] *Santa Rosa*
OLD SAN FRANCISCO EXPRESS [RES] *Fairfield*
OLD TOWN MEXICAN CAFE AND CANTINA [RES] *San Diego*
OLEMA INN [RES] *Inverness*
OLIVETO [RES] *Oakland*
OLIVETO [RES] *Oakland*
OLSEN'S CABIN [RES] *Quincy*
OLYMPIA GREEK RESTAURANT [RES] *Palm Springs*
ONDINE [RES] *Sausalito*
ONE [RES] *Los Angeles*
ONE MARKET [RES] *San Francisco*
O'REILLY'S [RES] *San Francisco*
ORIGINAL JOE'S [RES] *San Jose*
ORITALIA [RES] *San Francisco*
OSAKA GRILL [RES] *San Francisco*
OTTAVIO'S [RES] *Camarillo*
OYE [RES] *Pasadena*
PACIFIC [RES] *San Francisco*
PACIFICA DEL MAR [RES] *Del Mar*
PACIFIC COAST GRILL [RES] *Del Mar*
PACIFIC DINING CAR [RES] *Los Angeles*
PACIFICO [RES] *Calistoga*
PACIFIC'S EDGE [RES] *Carmel*
PALACE GRILL [RES] *Santa Barbara*
PALAZZIO [RES] *Santa Barbara*
PALAZZIO DOWNTOWN [RES] *Santa Barbara*
PALIO D'ASTI [RES] *San Francisco*
PALM [RES] *Los Angeles*
PALMIE [RES] *Palm Springs*
PALOMINO [RES] *Palm Desert*
PANDA INN [RES] *San Diego*
PANE E VINO [RES] *San Francisco*
PARADISO TRATTORIA [RES] *Monterey*
PARAGON [RES] *San Francisco*
PARC HONG KONG [RES] *San Francisco*
PARIS RESTAURANT [RES] *Anaheim*
PARKER'S LIGHTHOUSE [RES] *Long Beach*
PARK GRILL [RES] *Los Angeles*
PARK GRILL [RES] *San Francisco*
PARKWAY GRILL [RES] *Pasadena*
PARTNERS BISTRO [RES] *Laguna Beach*
PASCAL [RES] *Newport Beach*
PASSION FISH [RES] *Pacific Grove*
PASTA ITALIA [RES] *Palm Desert*
PASTA MOON [RES] *Half Moon Bay*
PASTIS [RES] *San Francisco*
PATINA [RES] *Hollywood (L.A.)*
PATINETTE AT MOCA [RES] *Los Angeles*
PATISSERIE BOISSIERE [RES] *Carmel*
PATPONG [RES] *San Francisco*
PAVILION [RES] *Newport Beach*
PEA SOUP ANDERSEN'S [RES] *Santa Nella*
PEKING CHINESE RESTAURANT [RES] *Red Bluff*
PEOHE'S [RES] *Coronado*
PEPPER MILL [RES] *Pasadena*
PEPPERS MEXICALI CAFE [RES] *Pacific Grove*
PERROCHE [RES] *Studio City (L.A.)*
PERRY'S [RES] *San Francisco*
PERRY'S DOWNTOWN [RES] *San Francisco*
P.F. CHANG'S [RES] *Irvine*
P.F. CHANG'S [RES] *Los Angeles*
P. F. CHANGS [RES] *San Diego*
P.F. CHANG'S CHINA BISTRO [RES] *Los Angeles*
P.F. CHANG'S CHINA BISTRO [RES] *Newport Beach*
P.F. CHANG'S CHINA BISTRO [RES] *Santa Monica*
PHILIPPE THE ORIGINAL [URD] *Los Angeles*
PIATTI [RES] *Sonoma*
PIATTI RISTORANTE [RES] *La Jolla (San Diego)*
PIEMONT [RES] *Mount Shasta*
PILOTHOUSE [RES] *Sacramento*
PINOT BISTRO [RES] *Studio City (L.A.)*
PINOT BLANC [RES] *St. Helena*
PINOT HOLLYWOOD [RES] *Los Angeles*
PINOT PROVENCE [RES] *Costa Mesa*
PISCES [RES] *San Francisco Airport Area*
PLOUF [RES] *San Francisco*
PLUMED HORSE [RES] *Saratoga*
PLUMPJACK CAFE [RES] *San Francisco*
POLO LOUNGE [RES] *Beverly Hills*

POSTINO [RES] *Walnut Creek*
POSTO [RES] *Los Angeles*
POSTRIO [RES] *San Francisco*
POT STICKER [RES] *San Francisco*
PRADO AT BALBOA PARK, THE [RES] *San Diego*
PREGO [RES] *Beverly Hills*
PREGO [RES] *San Diego*
PREGO [RES] *San Francisco*
PRESIDIO [RES] *Borrego Springs*
PRIMA TRATTORIA E NEGOZIO-VINI [RES] *Walnut Creek*
PRIMAVERA [RES] *Coronado*
PRINCE OF WALES [RES] *Coronado*
PUB'S PRIME RIB [RES] *Salinas*
PUCCINI AND PINETTI [RES] *San Francisco*
QUIET WOMAN [RES] *Corona del Mar*
QUINN'S LIGHTHOUSE [RES] *Oakland*
R23 [RES] *Los Angeles*
RAFFAELLO CARMEL [RES] *Carmel*
RAFFLES L'ERMITAGE BEVERLY HILLS [RES] *Beverly Hills*
RAINWATER'S [RES] *San Diego*
RAJDOOT [RES] *Buena Park*
RANCH HOUSE [RES] *Ojai*
RAPPA'S SEAFOOD [RES] *Monterey*
RAVENOUS [RES] *Healdsburg*
RAYMOND [RES] *Pasadena*
RED SAILS INN [RES] *San Diego*
REEDS [RES] *Los Angeles*
REIGN [RES] *Beverly Hills*
RENDEZVOUS [RES] *Fort Bragg*
RESTAURANT [RES] *Fort Bragg*
RESTAURANT, THE [RES] *Los Angeles*
RESTAURANT, THE [RES] *Sonoma*
RESTAURANT 301 [RES] *Eureka*
RESTAURANT AT MEADOWOOD, THE [RES] *St. Helena*
RESTAURANT GETTY CENTER, THE [RES] *Los Angeles*
RICK'S DESSERT DINER [URD] *Sacramento*
RIO GRILL [RES] *Carmel*
RIPE TOMATO [RES] *Fresno*
RISTORANTE ECCO [RES] *San Francisco*
RISTORANTE IDEALE [RES] *San Francisco*
RISTORANTE MAMMA GINA [RES] *Palm Desert*
RISTORANTE PIATTI [RES] *Sacramento*
RITZ, THE [RES] *Newport Beach*
R J'S THE RIB JOINT [RES] *Beverly Hills*
ROAST TO GO [URD] *Los Angeles*
ROBATA GRILL AND SAKE BAR [RES] *Carmel*
ROBATA GRILL AND SUSHI [RES] *Mill Valley*
ROBERT'S BOULEVARD BISTRO [RES] *Carmel*
ROBIN'S [RES] *Cambria*
ROCCO'S SEAFOOD GRILL [RES] *San Francisco*
ROCK [RES] *Marina del Rey*
ROCKENWAGNER [RES] *Santa Monica*
ROCK GARDEN CAFE [RES] *Palm Springs*
ROCKY POINT [RES] *Carmel*
ROPPONGI [RES] *La Jolla (San Diego)*
ROSA'S [RES] *Bakersfield*
ROSA'S [RES] *Ontario*
ROSA'S [RES] *Pismo Beach*
ROSEBUD'S CLASSIC CAFE [URD] *Jackson*
ROSE PISTOLA [RES] *San Francisco*
ROSE'S CAFE [RES] *San Francisco*
ROSE'S LANDING [RES] *Morro Bay*
ROSY'S [RES] *Roseville*
ROYAL OAK [RES] *Lake Arrowhead*
ROYAL SCANDIA [RES] *Solvang*
ROY'S AT PEBBLE BEACH [RES] *Pebble Beach*
RUBICON [RES] *San Francisco*
RUE DE MAIN [RES] *Hayward*
RUE LEPIC [RES] *San Francisco*
RUFFINO'S [RES] *Napa*
RUMARI [RES] *Laguna Beach*
RUSTY DUCK [RES] *Sacramento*
RUTH'S CHRIS STEAKHOUSE [RES] *Beverly Hills*
RUTH'S CHRIS STEAKHOUSE [RES] *Irvine*
RUTH'S CHRIS STEAK HOUSE [RES] *Palm Desert*
RUTH'S CHRIS STEAK HOUSE [RES] *San Diego*
RUTH'S CHRIS STEAK HOUSE [RES] *San Francisco*
SADDLE PEAK LODGE [RES] *Los Angeles*
SAFFRON [URD] *San Diego*
SAFFRON [RES] *Sonoma*

SAGE & ONION [RES] *Santa Barbara*
ST. JAMES AT THE VINEYARD [RES] *Palm Springs*
ST. JAMES BAR [RES] *La Jolla (San Diego)*
ST ORRES [RES] *Gualala*
SALADANG [RES] *Pasadena*
SALLY'S [RES] *San Diego*
SALVATORE'S [RES] *San Diego*
SAMMY'S CALIFORNIA WOOD-FIRED PIZZA [RES] *La Jolla (San Diego)*
SAM'S GRILL & SEAFOOD [RES] *San Francisco*
SANDBAR AND GRILL [RES] *Monterey*
SANDCRAB CAFE [RES] *Escondido*
SANDERLINGS RESTAURANT [RES] *Santa Cruz*
SAN DIEGO PIER CAFE [RES] *San Diego*
SAN SHI GO [RES] *Laguna Beach*
SANS SOUCI [RES] *Carmel*
SANTA FE BAR AND GRILL [RES] *Berkeley*
SANTA MARIA INN [RES] *Santa Maria*
SANTE [RES] *La Jolla (San Diego)*
SAPORI [RES] *Newport Beach*
SARDINE FACTORY [RES] *Monterey*
SAVANNA GRILL [RES] *Corte Madera*
SAVANNAH CHOP HOUSE [RES] *Laguna Beach*
SCALA'S BISTRO [RES] *San Francisco*
SCHEIDEL'S [RES] *Grass Valley*
SCHROEDER'S [RES] *San Francisco*
SCOMA'S [RES] *San Francisco*
SCOMA'S [RES] *Sausalito*
SCOTT'S SEAFOOD [RES] *Oakland*
SCOTT'S SEAFOOD [RES] *Palo Alto*
SCOTT'S SEAFOOD GRILL & BAR [RES] *Costa Mesa*
SCRIBBLES [RES] *El Centro*
SEAFARE INN [RES] *Whittier*
SEA GRILL [RES] *Eureka*
SEARS FINE FOODS [URD] *San Francisco*
SENT SOVI [RES] *Saratoga*
SEOUL JUNG [RES] *Los Angeles*
SHADOWBROOK [RES] *Santa Cruz*
SHIRO [RES] *Pasadena*
SIERRA INN [RES] *June Lake*
SIERRA MAR RESTAURANT [RES] *Big Sur*
SILKS [RES] *San Francisco*
SILVA'S SHELDON INN [RES] *Sacramento*
SILVER DRAGON [RES] *Oakland*
SIRINO'S [RES] *Escondido*
SIROCCO [RES] *Palm Desert*
SISLEY ITALIAN KITCHEN [RES] *Los Angeles*
SKATES ON THE BAY [RES] *Berkeley*
SKY ROOM RESTAURANT [RES] *La Jolla (San Diego)*
SLANTED DOOR [RES] *San Francisco*
SLOCUM HOUSE [RES] *Rancho Cordova*
SMALLEY'S ROUNDUP [RES] *Salinas*
SMOKE HOUSE CAFE [RES] *Calistoga*
SOGA'S [RES] *Davis*
SOIZIC [RES] *Oakland*
SONOMA MERITAGE [RES] *Sonoma*
SONORA CAFE [RES] *Los Angeles*
SORRENTINO'S SEAFOOD HOUSE [RES] *Palm Springs*
SPADO'S [RES] *Salinas*
SPAGO [RES] *Los Angeles*
SPAGO [RES] *Palo Alto*
SPAGO BEVERLY HILLS [RES] *Beverly Hills*
SPIEDINI [RES] *Walnut Creek*
SPINNAKER [RES] *Sausalito*
SPIRITO'S [RES] *Carlsbad*
SPLENDIDO [RES] *San Francisco*
STARS [RES] *San Francisco*
STATE [RES] *Santa Barbara*
STATION HOUSE CAFE [RES] *Inverness*
STILLWATER BAR AND GRILL [RES] *Pebble Beach*
STINKING ROSE [RES] *Beverly Hills*
STOKES ADOBE [RES] *Monterey*
STONEHOUSE [RES] *Santa Barbara*
SUMMIT HOUSE [RES] *Fullerton*
SUSHI BAR AT AYSIA [RES] *Newport Beach*
SUSHI NOZAWA [RES] *Studio City (L.A.)*
SUSHI RAN [RES] *Sausalito*
SWAN OYSTER DEPOT [URD] *San Francisco*
SWISS CHALET [RES] *South Lake Tahoe (Lake Tahoe Area)*
SWISS LAKEWOOD [RES] *Tahoe City (Lake Tahoe Area)*
SWISS LOUIS [RES] *San Francisco*
TADICH GRILL [RES] *San Francisco*

TAKA [RES] *San Diego*
TALE OF THE WHALE [RES] *Newport Beach*
TALIA'S [RES] *Los Angeles*
TAM-O-SHANTER INN [RES] *Los Angeles*
TANINO RISTORANTE BAR [RES] *Los Angeles*
TAPENADE [RES] *La Jolla (San Diego)*
TARPY'S ROADHOUSE [RES] *Monterey*
TASTE CAFE AND BISTRO [RES] *Pacific Grove*
TEA AND SYMPATHY [URD] *Costa Mesa*
TEASERS [RES] *Santa Monica*
TEE OFF [RES] *Santa Barbara*
TENGU [RES] *Westwood Village (L.A.)*
TERRA [RES] *St. Helena*
TERRACE GRILL AT LAPLAYA [RES] *Carmel*
THAI ISSAN [RES] *Petaluma*
THEE BUNGALOW [RES] *San Diego*
THEO'S [RES] *Santa Cruz*
THUNDERBIRD BOOKSHOP CAFE [URD] *Carmel*
TINNERY AT THE BEACH [RES] *Pacific Grove*
TITANIC CAFE [URD] *San Francisco*
TOMATINA [RES] *St. Helena*
TOM HAM'S LIGHTHOUSE [RES] *San Diego*
TOMMY TOY'S [RES] *San Francisco*
TOPAZ CAFE [RES] *Santa Ana*
TOP OF THE MARKET [RES] *San Diego*
TOPOLOS RUSSIAN RIVER VINEYARDS [RES] *Santa Rosa*
TOP O' THE COVE [RES] *La Jolla (San Diego)*
TORREYANA GRILLE [RES] *La Jolla (San Diego)*
TORREY PINES CAFE [RES] *Del Mar*
TRADER VIC'S [RES] *Oakland*
TRATTORIA ACQUA [RES] *La Jolla (San Diego)*
TRATTORIA LA STRADA [RES] *San Diego*
TRATTORIA SPIGA [RES] *Costa Mesa*
TRA VIGNE [RES] *St. Helena*
TRAXX [RES] *Los Angeles*
TRIO CAFE [URD] *San Francisco*
TROQUET [RES] *Costa Mesa*
TUSCANY [RES] *Carlsbad*
TUSCANY [RES] *Palm Desert*
TUTTO MARE [RES] *La Jolla (San Diego)*
TUTTO MARE [RES] *Newport Beach*
TWIN PALMS [RES] *Pasadena*
UNCLE BILL'S PANCAKE HOUSE [URD] *Los Angeles*
UNIVERSAL CAFE [RES] *San Francisco*
VALENCIA [RES] *Rancho Santa Fe*
VALENTINO [RES] *Santa Monica*
VERCOLLINI'S [RES] *Idyllwild*
VICTORIAN ROOM, THE [RES] *Yosemite National Park*
VIGILUCCI'S TRATTORIA ITALIANA [RES] *Carlsbad*
VILLA NOVA [RES] *Newport Beach*
VINCINO MARE [RES] *San Diego*
VINTAGE PRESS, THE [RES] *Visalia*
VINTAGE ROOM, THE [RES] *Solvang*
VINTNERS COURT [RES] *Napa*
VIOGNIER [RES] *San Mateo*
VIVACE [RES] *Carlsbad*
VIVO'S [RES] *Pacific Grove*
WALLY'S DESERT TURTLE [RES] *Palm Springs*
WALNUT CREEK HOFBRAU HOUSE [RES] *Walnut Creek*
WALNUT GROVE [RES] *San Juan Capistrano*
WAPPO BAR AND BISTRO [RES] *Calistoga*
WATERFRONT [RES] *San Francisco*
WATERGATE [RES] *San Francisco*
WATER GRILL [RES] *Los Angeles*
WENTE VINEYARDS [RES] *Livermore*
WESTERN BOOT STEAK HOUSE [RES] *Healdsburg*
WHARF, THE [RES] *Fort Bragg*
WHISKEY CREEK [RES] *Bishop*
WILDE GOOSE [RES] *Palm Springs*
WILD HARE [RES] *Menlo Park*
WILLOWSIDE CAFE [RES] *Santa Rosa*
WILL'S FARGO [RES] *Carmel*
WINE AND ROSES [RES] *Lodi*
WINE BISTRO [RES] *Studio City (L.A.)*
WINE CASK [RES] *Santa Barbara*
WINESELLAR AND BRASSERIE [RES] *San Diego*
WINSHIPS [RES] *Sausalito*
WOLFDALE'S [RES] *Tahoe City (Lake Tahoe Area)*
WOLFGANG PUCK CAFE [RES] *Santa Monica*

WOLFGANG PUCK'S CAFE [RES] *Los Angeles Intl Airport Area*
WOLFGANG PUCK'S CAFE [RES] *North Hollywood (L.A.)*
WOODWARD'S GARDEN [RES] *San Francisco*
WOOL GROWERS [RES] *Bakersfield*
WYNSOR'S [RES] *Los Angeles*
XIOMARA [RES] *Pasadena*
XYZ [RES] *San Francisco*
YABBIE'S COASTAL KITCHEN [RES] *San Francisco*
YAKINIKU HOUSE JUBAN [RES] *San Francisco Airport Area*
YAMABUKI [RES] *Anaheim*
YANK SING [RES] *San Francisco*
YARD HOUSE, THE [RES] *Long Beach*
YEN CHING [RES] *Orange*
YIANNIS [RES] *Claremont*
YOSHIDA-YA [RES] *San Francisco*
YOYO BISTRO [RES] *San Francisco*
YUJEAN KANG'S [RES] *Hollywood (L.A.)*
YUJEAN KANG'S [RES] *Pasadena*
ZARZUELA [RES] *San Francisco*
ZAX [RES] *San Francisco*
ZIBIBBO [RES] *Palo Alto*
ZINGARI [RES] *San Francisco*
ZINOS RESTAURANT ON THE PLAZA [RES] *Sonoma*
ZUNI CAFE [RES] *San Francisco*

City Index

Alturas, 15
Anaheim, 15
Antioch, 22
Anza-Borrego Desert State Park, 23
Arcadia, 23
Atascadero, 24
Auburn, 25
Avalon, 26
Bakersfield, 28
Barstow, 30
Beaumont, 32
Berkeley, 32
Beverly Hills, 35
Big Basin Redwoods State Park, 40
Big Bear Lake, 40
Big Sur, 43
Bishop, 44
Blythe, 46
Bodega Bay, 47
Borrego Springs, 48
Bridgeport, 50
Buena Park, 50
Burbank, 53
Burlingame, 54
Burney, 54
Calexico, 54
Calistoga, 54
Camarillo, 58
Cambria, 59
Carlsbad, 60
Carmel, 63
Carmel Valley, 70
Catalina Island, 72
Channel Islands National Park, 72
Chester, 73
Chico, 73
Chula Vista, 74
Claremont, 75
Clear Lake Area, 76
Coleville, 76
Coloma, 77
Concord, 77
Corona, 77
Corona del Mar, 78
Coronado, 79
Corte Madera, 81
Costa Mesa, 82
Crescent City, 85
Crestline, 87
Cucamonga, 87
Culver City, 87
Dana Point, 87
Davis, 87
Death Valley National Park, 88
Del Mar, 90
Desert Hot Springs, 92
Devils Postpile National Monument, 93
Disneyland, 93
Dunsmuir, 95
El Cajon, 95
El Centro, 96
Encino, 97
Escondido, 98
Eureka, 00
Fairfield, 103
Fallbrook, 104
Felton, 104
Fort Bragg, 104
Fort Ross State Historic Park, 107
Fremont, 107
Fresno, 109
Fullerton, 113
Garberville, 114
Garden Grove, 115
Gilroy, 116
Glendale, 116
Grass Valley, 117
Gualala, 118
Guerneville, 119
Half Moon Bay, 120
Hanford, 121
Hayward, 122
Healdsburg, 123
Hearst-San Simeon State Historical Monument (Hearst Castle), 126
Hemet, 127
Hollywood, 128
Humboldt Redwoods State Park, 134
Huntington Beach, 134
Idyllwild, 135
Indio, 136
Inverness, 137
Inyo National Forest, 139
Irvine, 139
Jackson, 141
Joshua Tree National Park, 143
June Lake, 144
Kernville, 145
King City, 146
Kings Canyon National Park, 146
Laguna Beach, 147
La Habra, 152

La Jolla, 152
Lake Arrowhead, 159
Lake County, 160
Lake Tahoe Area, 160
Lancaster, 163
Lassen Volcanic National Park, 163
Lava Beds National Monument, 164
Lee Vining, 165
Livermore, 166
Lodi, 166
Lompoc, 167
Lone Pine, 168
Long Beach, 169
Los Angeles, 174
Los Angeles Area,
Los Angeles Intl Airport Area, 193
Los Gatos, 197
Madera, 198
Malibu, 198
Mammoth Lakes, 199
Manhattan Beach, 201
Marina del Rey, 201
Martinez, 203
Marysville, 203
Mendocino, 204
Menlo Park, 207
Merced, 208
Millbrae, 209
Mill Valley, 209
Modesto, 210
Monterey, 212
Morro Bay, 220
Mother Lode Country, 223
Mountain View, 223
Mt Diablo State Park, 224
Mount Shasta, 224
Muir Woods National Monument, 226
Napa, 227
Needles, 230
Nevada City, 231
Newport Beach, 233
North Hollywood, 237
Oakdale, 238
Oakhurst, 238
Oakland, 240
Oceanside, 245
Ojai, 246
Ontario, 247
Orange, 249
Oroville, 251
Oxnard, 252
Pacific Beach, 254
Pacific Grove, 255
Palmdale, 258
Palm Desert, 258
Palm Springs, 263
Palm Springs Area, 273
Palo Alto, 274
Pasadena, 277
Paso Robles, 281
Pebble Beach, 282
Petaluma, 284
Pine Valley, 285
Pinnacles National Monument, 285
Pismo Beach, 286
Placerville, 288
Pleasanton, 289
Pomona, 291
Porterville, 292
Quincy, 293
Rancho Bernardo, 294
Rancho Cordova, 294
Rancho Cucamonga, 295
Rancho Santa Fe, 295
Red Bluff, 296
Redding, 298
Redlands, 300
Redondo Beach, 301
Redwood City, 303
Redwood Highway, 304
Richardson Grove State Park, 304
Riverside, 304
Roseville, 306
Sacramento, 307
St. Helena, 314
Salinas, 318
Salton Sea State Recreation Area, 319
San Bernardino, 319
San Clemente, 321
San Diego, 321
San Fernando, 347
San Fernando Valley Area, 347
San Francisco, 348
San Francisco Airport Area, 397
San Gabriel, 399
San Jose, 399
San Juan Bautista, 406
San Juan Capistrano, 407
San Luis Obispo, 409
San Marino, 412
San Mateo, 412
San Pedro, 414
San Rafael, 415
San Simeon, 416
Santa Ana, 417
Santa Barbara, 418
Santa Clara, 428
Santa Cruz, 431
Santa Maria, 435
Santa Monica, 436
Santa Nella, 442
Santa Rosa, 443
San Ysidro, 447
Saratoga, 447
Sausalito, 448
Sequoia & Kings Canyon National Parks, 450
Solvang, 451
Sonoma, 454

Sonora, 459
South Lake Tahoe, 462
South San Francisco, 465
Squaw Valley, 465
Stockton, 465
Studio City, 466
Sunnyvale, 467
Susanville, 469
Tahoe City, 470
Tahoe Vista, 471
Tehachapi, 473
Temecula, 474
Thousand Oaks, 475
Three Rivers, 476
Tiburon, 477
Torrance, 477
Trinidad, 478
Truckee, 479
Ukiah, 481
Vacaville, 483
Valencia, 483
Vallejo, 484
Van Nuys, 485
Ventura, 486
Victorville, 488
Visalia, 489
Walnut Creek, 489
Weaverville, 491
West Covina, 492
Westwood Village, 492
Whittier, 493
Willits, 494
Willows, 494
Woodland Hills, 495
Yosemite National Park, 496
Yountville, 501
Yreka, 503

Mobil Travel Guide®

Northwest
Idaho
Montana
Oregon
Washington
Wyoming
Alberta
British Columbia
Manitoba

Great Plains
Iowa
Kansas
Minnesota
Missouri
Nebraska
North Dakota
Oklahoma
South Dakota

Great Lakes
Illinois
Indiana
Michigan
Ohio
Wisconsin

New England Eastern Canada
Connecticut
Maine
Massachusetts
New Hampshire
Rhode Island
Vermont
New Brunswick
Nova Scotia
Ontario
Prince Edward Island
Quebec

California

New York New Jersey

Southwest
Arizona
Colorado
Nevada
New Mexico
Texas
Utah

Southeast
Alabama
Arkansas
Georgia
Kentucky
Louisiana
Mississippi
North Carolina
South Carolina
Tennessee

Florida

Mid-Atlantic
Delaware
Maryland
Pennsylvania
Virginia
Washington, D.C.
West Virginia

Mobil Travel Guides

Please check the 2002 guides you would like to order:

☐ 0-7853-5811-0
California
$16.95

☐ 0-7853-5810-2
Florida
$16.95

☐ 0-7853-5817-X
Great Lakes
Illinois, Indiana, Michigan,
Ohio, Wisconsin
$16.95

☐ 0-7853-5818-8
Great Plains
Iowa, Kansas, Minnesota,
Missouri, Nebraska, North
Dakota, Oklahoma, South
Dakota
$16.95

☐ 0-7853-5815-3
Mid-Atlantic
Delaware, Maryland,
Pennsylvania, Virginia,
Washington D.C., West
Virginia
$16.95

☐ 0-7853-5814-5
**New England and Eastern
Canada**
Connecticut, Maine, Massachu-
setts, New Hampshire, Rhode
Island, Vermont, Canada
$16.95

☐ 0-7853-5812-9
New York/New Jersey
$16.95

☐ 0-7853-5819-6
Northwest
Idaho, Montana, Oregon, Wash-
ington, Wyoming, Canada
$16.95

☐ 0-7853-5816-1
Southeast
Alabama, Arkansas, Georgia, Ken-
tucky, Louisiana, Mississippi,
North Carolina, South Carolina,
Tennessee
$16.95

☐ 0-7853-5813-7
Southwest
Arizona, Colorado, Nevada, New
Mexico, Texas, Utah
$16.95

Please ship the books above to:

Name: _____

Address: _____

City: _____ State _____ Zip _____

Total Cost of Book(s) $_____ ☐ Please charge my credit card.

Shipping & Handling $_____ ☐ Discover ☐ Visa
(Please add $2.00 for
first book $1.00 for each ☐ MasterCard ☐ American Express
additional book)

Add 8.75% sales tax $_____ Card #_____

Total Amount $_____ Expiration _____

☐ My Check is enclosed. Signature _____

Please mail this form to: **Mobil Travel Guides
7373 N. Cicero Avenue
Lincolnwood, IL 60712**

Notes

Add your opinion!

Help make the Guides even more useful. Tell us about your experiences with the hotels and restaurants listed in the Guides (or ones that should be added).

Find us on the Internet at www.exxonmobiltravel.com/feedback

Or copy the form below and mail to Mobil Travel Guides, 7373 N Cicero Ave, Lincolnwood, IL 60712. All information will be kept confidential.

Your name ______________________ Were children with you on trip? ☐ Yes ☐ No

Street ______________________ Number of people in your party ________

City/State/Zip ______________________ Your occupation ______________

Establishment name ______________________ ☐ Hotel ☐ Resort ☐ Restaurant ☐ Motel ☐ Inn ☐ Other

Street ______________________ City ______________ State ______

Do you agree with our description? ☐ Yes ☐ No If not, give reason ______________________

____

Please give us your opinion of the following:

Decor	Cleanliness	Service	Food
☐ Excellent	☐ Spotless	☐ Excellent	☐ Excellent
☐ Good	☐ Clean	☐ Good	☐ Good
☐ Fair	☐ Unclean	☐ Fair	☐ Fair
☐ Poor	☐ Dirty	☐ Poor	☐ Poor

2002 Guide rating ______ ★

Check your suggested rating

☐ ★good, satisfactory
☐ ★★very good
☐ ★★★excellent
☐ ★★★★outstanding
☐ ★★★★★ one of best in country
☐ ✓unusually good value

Date of visit ____________ First visit? ☐ Yes ☐ No

Comments ____

____

Establishment name ______________________ ☐ Hotel ☐ Resort ☐ Restaurant ☐ Motel ☐ Inn ☐ Other

Street ______________________ City ______________ State ______

Do you agree with our description? ☐ Yes ☐ No If not, give reason ______________________

____

Please give us your opinion of the following:

Decor	Cleanliness	Service	Food
☐ Excellent	☐ Spotless	☐ Excellent	☐ Excellent
☐ Good	☐ Clean	☐ Good	☐ Good
☐ Fair	☐ Unclean	☐ Fair	☐ Fair
☐ Poor	☐ Dirty	☐ Poor	☐ Poor

2002 Guide rating ______ ★

Check your suggested rating

☐ ★good, satisfactory
☐ ★★very good
☐ ★★★excellent
☐ ★★★★outstanding
☐ ★★★★★ one of best in country
☐ ✓unusually good value

Date of visit ____________ First visit? ☐ Yes ☐ No

Comments ____

____